Max Weber

Max Weber

A Biography

Joachim Radkau

translated by
Patrick Camiller

polity

First published in German as *Max Weber* © Carl Hanser Verlag München Wien, 2005

This English edition published 2011

Polity Press
65 Bridge Street
Cambridge CB2 1UR, UK

Polity Press
350 Main Street
Malden, MA 02148, USA

ISBN-13: 978-0-7456-4147-8
ISBN-13: 978-0-7456-4148-5 (pb)

A catalogue record for this book is available from the British Library.

Typeset in 10 on 11 pt Times NR
by Servis Filmsetting Ltd, Stockport, Cheshire
Printed and bound in Great Britain by the MPG Books Group

The publisher has used its best endeavours to ensure that the URLs for external websites referred to in this book are correct and active at the time of going to press. However, the publisher has no responsibility for the websites and can make no guarantee that a site will remain live or that the content is or will remain appropriate.

Every effort has been made to trace all copyright holders, but if any have been inadvertently overlooked the publisher will be pleased to include any necessary credits in any subsequent reprint or edition.

For further information on Polity, visit our website: www.politybooks.com

The translation of this work was supported by a grant from the Goethe-Institut that is funded by the Ministry of Foreign Affairs.

Contents

Part I The Violation of Nature

Part II Nature's Revenge

Acknowledgements

The publishers would like to acknowledge permission to reproduce the following copyright material:

Page 15, 73, 202, 273 and 331, BPK; 21, 26, 32, 44, 50, 54, 200, 214, 453, 485, 501, 521, 546, Haus der Geschichte Baden-Wurttemberg, Sammlung Leif Geiges; 121, Staatliche Graphische Sammlung, Munchen; 236, Russian Academy of Science, Moscow; 289, Eva Kretzschmar/Private Collection; 304, Professor Karen Hagemann/Private Collection; 361, Tilman Evers/Private Collection; 374, Georg Lukács Archives/Edith Hajós; 484, Dr Ernst Ludwig Heuss; 552, Professor Guenther Roth/Private Collection; 554, Marion Herzo-Hoinkis.

Preface to the English Edition

A first suspicion that there was a tale to be told about Max Weber came to me, not untypically for my generation, from the United States forty years ago. At the time I was working on my dissertation concerning the post-1933 German emigration to the USA, and I became friendly with one member of this group, the historian George W. F. Hallgarten, who finally ended up in Washington. We subsequently wrote a book together, *Deutsche Industrie und Politik*, in which several passages had to be blacked out under pressure from the Deutsche Bank: this made us comrades-in-arms (for Weber, the strongest bond after an erotic relationship), despite our 42-year age difference. As a student, in the summer of 1920, Hallgarten had attended Weber's final lecture and wept at the news of his death, and for the rest of his life he felt under his spell. Shortly before his own death (1975) he was even planning to write a book on 'Max Weber's Sociology – a Tool in the Hands of the Historian'. Nor was he alone in being so enchanted by the great enchanter: a cult of 'Saint Max' was actually typical among German emigrés; Franz L. Neumann once famously said, '*It is here, in the United States, that Max Weber really came to life.*' I later also came in contact with Karl August Wittfogel – formerly, in his communist period, an opponent of Weber's – who tried in his way to complete Weber's fragments on the natural basis of society. I feel myself to be his successor in this respect.

Through Hallgarten I developed a kind of psycho-physical contact with Weber. But again and again the cult associated with the 'myth of Heidelberg' aroused feelings of aversion in me. For a long time I had a sense that Werner Sombart and Georg Simmel – both on familiar terms with Weber, though later in his shadow – offered greater inspiration, or at least greater challenges. Thus, in the 1980s I attacked Sombart's thesis that a shortage of wood had threatened capitalism with collapse in the eighteenth century, and I thereby triggered endless controversy among historians of the forest. From Simmel's essay 'The Metropolis and Mental Life' (1903) I drew important stimuli for my history of *Nervosität* in Germany.

Unexpectedly, this very subject opened me up to the correspondence of Max and Marianne Weber, a real treasure trove for the semantics of 'the nerves' at the turn of the twentieth century. The decoding of old reports on neurasthenic patients also proved valuable training for my Weber researches; you don't get far with hard-to-read handwriting unless you have a certain kind of sporting ambition. Forty years ago I read with pleasure the collective volume *The Historian as Detective*, edited by Robert W. Winks. And the young Talcott Parsons read Weber's *The Protestant Ethic* 'as if it were a detective story'. Similarly, a biographer of Weber needs a detective's instinct for clues. There is an ocean of literature about Max Weber, but it should not be thought that all the facts about him have long been clear and that only a theory is required to distil them. In my study of the sources, I would have one amazing experience after another.

With hindsight I can see how Weber had already been long at work in my unconscious. In his footsteps I devoted myself for a time to the history of Pietism, and again to the history of music, but in each case I eventually got stuck. When I tried to prove, through a comparison with Asian civilizations, that Europe's centuries-long complaint about wood shortages had paradoxically reflected its relative abundance of forest, I followed Weber's strategy of a vast circling movement in the East to gain victory for the thesis (in his case, the historical function of Protestantism as a catalyst for capitalism). And after I had finished my biography of Weber, when I was preparing my 'world history of the environment' for an American translation (*Nature and Power*, New York, 2008), it dawned on me that I had unconsciously taken Weber's *Economy and Society* as my model. Much as Weber there went into the social history of 'original types' of 'socialization', so did I set out the environmental history of 'original symbioses between man and nature'. In the end my new study of Weber became a way into my own subconscious. Indeed, why not? The point of working *on* Weber is ultimately to work *with* Weber and thereby to develop one's own intellectual resources.

I received quite a boost from Lawrence A. Scaff's book about Weber, *Fleeing the Iron Cage*, which I took with me on a three-week cycling tour. In particular there was the sentence: 'What is needed, above all, is to encounter Weber once again from the beginning and with a sense of judgment alert to the potentials of what he actually wrote and said.' Yes, that was precisely what I wanted to do. Fortune then came to my aid when a chain of coincidences gave me access to correspondence of Max and Marianne Weber which had previously been hidden from the public eye, and in which a new Weber began to emerge. Weber first became famous through *The Protestant Ethic*, but that 'worldly asceticism' was not his own religion; this is something that has often been misunderstood. Stanislav Andreski (*Max Weber's Insights and Errors*, 1984) thought he had found in Weber a case 'which fits Freud's idea that creativity stems from repression and sublimation of sexual desire'. But, oh no, Max Weber is not at all a good example of that.

This is not to say that the exact opposite is true. The German media have sometimes given the impression that I see Weber as illustrating Wilhelm Reich's theory of the orgasm as man's only salvation. I am not one of the eternal sixty-eighters, however, and I am far from denying that the spirit has its own life and its own pleasures. Sexuality is not a *prima causa*; on the contrary, Weber's life-story shows how intellectual developments open the individual to erotic experiences. Weber's life ended under the sign of Venus, not of Mars. Lawrence Scaff, in his review of the German edition of my book, recalled that 'the relationship between intellect and eros, Athena and Aphrodite, is an old theme, from Plato onward'. In Weber's case the story of this relationship was an exciting drama.

In my view, a high point in this drama was the formation of the concept of charisma. There have been heated discussions of this in Germany. Gangolf Hübinger reproached me for underestimating the extent to which Gladstone served as Weber's model of the charismatic leader. But Thomas Karlauf, in his major biography of Stefan George (*Stefan George – Die Entdeckung des Charisma*), brilliantly reconstructed the erotic aura that surrounded the concept of charisma. As our two biographies developed, they had a mutually stimulating influence on each other. Ralf Dahrendorf has said that the 'rediscovery of Max Weber' is bringing the social sciences back down to earth, from the clouds of 'systems' and 'domination-free communication'. 'Personal networks', with their anthropological side and their connectedness through lifestyles and life-crises, are shaping up as the new 'Weber paradigm'. In this respect, Weber's encounter with George seems to have been a pointer to things to come. I do not believe, however, that Weber would have thought much of a 'Weber paradigm'. In an admittedly rather high-spirited essay 'The Heroic Ecstasy of Drunken Elephants: The Substrate of Nature in Max Weber – a Missing Link between his Life and Work' (in Volker Berghahn and Simone Lässig, eds, *Biography between Structure and Agency: Central European Lives in International Historiography*, New York: Berghahn Books, 2008), I have argued matters out with a number of critics.

'A Struggle over Weber' is the title of a piece by Wilhelm Hennis on the current state of Weber research. The struggle among different branches of science over the dead Weber – each one would like to have him for itself – sometimes reminds one of the wrangling between Hellenes and Trojans over the dead body of Patroclus. I prefer to keep out of this myself (which does not mean that I prefer to avoid any fight). Historians take delight in quoting Weber's outburst against 'this damned science of sociology' (MWG II/6, 641), at the Frankfurt Sociologists' Conference in 1910 of all places; or the heartfelt groan in 1918, in his farewell speech at Heidelberg, that 'most of what goes by the name of sociology is a fraud'. But, in what he said about Georg Simmel, the same Weber mocked 'the ridiculous self-crucifixion before the name of sociology', as if it were the devil incarnate. He cannot be pinned down in this or that single quote. The dispute among university faculties obstructs our view of the *whole* Weber. For this reason, I removed a chapter about Weber and sociology from the manuscript of this book.

Stanislav Andreski (*Social Sciences as Sorcery*, 1972) counts Weber among the chief sorcerers of the social sciences. But he becomes confused about this, for he thinks that a good social scientist must have a sense of humour and he can find no trace of one in Weber. It is the old cliché of Weber the sombre ascetic. In 2007 a song at the Cologne carnival, 'I'm so happy not to be a Protestant', was still repeating it: 'Max Weber hat gesagt, daß nur die Arbeit wichtig ist / daß der Herrgott den begnadigt, der die Pflichten nicht vergißt . . . Dagegen sind die Katholiken richtig supercool / bei denen sind die Pfaffen Polen, Inder oder schwul.'[1] I am pretty sure that Weber would have roared with laughter at these words. Theodor Heuss, the first president of the Federal Republic of Germany, who knew Weber well and made some of the most intelligent observations about him, had relished his 'earthy laughter' (WzG 72). Even the philosopher Heinrich Rickert, who already knew Weber in his school days and later tried to torpedo the Weber cult, had to admit: 'Weber's enchanting geniality and his delightful, wide-ranging sense of humour were irresistible' (WzG 111). In 1932 Eduard Baumgarten thought he could hear the dead Weber laugh when Marianne Weber said in public that she 'couldn't care less' about Goethe.

From what we know today, Weber laughed most often and most heartily in the company of Americans: during his trip to the USA in 1904, after his years of deep depression. By no means did he see America through the spectacles of *The Protestant Ethic*. There is also a lot of disguised humour to be discovered in his work. A term such as 'trained professional ecstatics' [*schulmäßigen Berufsekstatikern*] (AJ 96) is full of comedy, though perhaps this is not so evident in translation. With regard to the difficulties that translators have had with Weber – ever since Parsons rendered 'stahlharte Gehäuse' as 'iron cage' in 1928 – he sometimes reminds us of Lao-tse, whose *Tao Te Ching* is read differently in every translation. (I once joked to Sam Whimster, the editor of *Weber Studies*, that nowadays perhaps 'Geist des Kapitalismus' would be better translated as 'ghost' rather than 'spirit' of capitalism – how loudly Weber would have denounced the lack of professional honour in today's bankers!)

All the more grateful am I to Patrick Camiller, who translated my often very German style into smoothly flowing English and, in quite a number of places, found English equivalents for the melody of the German language or German wordplay; 'Schnauzel' and 'Spatz' – the nicknames for Marianne Weber and Else Jaffé – became 'Snouty' and 'Sparrow'. He also took the trouble, whenever possible, to find and insert the English source material or bibliographical references corresponding to the German original. I have cut the thousand and more pages of the German by just under a third for the English edition, sacrificing, for example, detailed accounts of Weber's ancestors and the reception history of Weber's work, as well as sections of chapters dealing with his writings on the stock exchange, his

---

[1] 'Max Weber said that only work is important / that the Lord pardons those who remember their duties. . . . Catholics, on the other hand, are really supercool; / their priests are Poles, Indians or gays.'

debate with Karl Marx, his relations with Rickert, Simmel and the neurologist Willy Hellpach, and his quarrels with Arnold Ruge and Adolf Koch. But I have also worked into the text a large number of new discoveries and new ideas. The German edition had the subtitle *Die Leidenschaft des Denkens*, but Lord Ralf Dahrendorf assured me that 'The Passion of Thinking' sounds alien to English ears. I would like to thank John Thompson of Polity Press for his friendly collaboration, and Inter Nationes for the financial support it gave to the translation.

Edward A. Shils, one of the American discoverers of Weber, recalls that 'reading Max Weber was literally breathtaking' – so much so that he sometimes had to stand up and catch his breath. My own experience was similar. And, precisely when I read Weber again after finishing my book, I became anxious that I had overlooked something because of my lack of distance. Be that as it may, I never cherished the absurd ambition to write the 'ultimate Weber biography', as one critic accused me of doing. Weber is a neverending subject. The best that my book could achieve was, as Lawrence A. Scaff might have put it, to make it easier 'to encounter Weber once again', unencumbered by prejudices and with the explorer's fresh curiosity. The point is not to erect a monument to Weber but to bring him back to life.

Joachim Radkau
Bielefeld,
February 2008

Abbreviations

All letters mentioned in the text without further reference have been quoted from copies in the possession of Prof. Dr Richard Grathoff (Oerlinghausen): this collection, which also contains much other written material, is referred to throughout by the abbreviation SG (Sammlung Grathoff). According to information provided by Edith Hanke, these are copies of transcriptions prepared for the Heidelberg research office, the Max-Weber-Forschungsstelle, and their wording may therefore be considered reliable. All sources beginning with 'Ana 446' refer to the Weber papers in the Bavarian State Library in Munich.

AJ   Max Weber, *Ancient Judaism*, trans. and ed. Hans H. Gerth and Don Martindale, New York, 1967.

AS   Max Weber, *Agrarian Sociology of Ancient Civilizations*, trans. R. I. Frank, London, 1988.

AWG   Alfred Weber, *Gesamtausgabe*, Marburg, 1997–.

B   Eduard Baumgarten, *Max Weber: Werk und Person*, Tübingen, 1964.

BA   Bundesarchiv

CS   Max Weber, *Critique of Stammler*, trans. Guy Oakes, New York, 1977.

EG   Melchior Palyi (ed.), *Erinnerungsgabe für Max Weber* (2 vols), Munich, 1923.

EM   Marianne Weber, *Ehefrau und Mutter in der Rechtsentwicklung*, Tübingen, 1907.

E&S   Max Weber, *Economy and Society: An Outline of Interpretive Sociology*, ed. Guenter Roth and Claus Wittich (2 vols), Berkeley and London, 1979.

FMW   *From Max Weber: Essays in Sociology*, trans. and ed. H. H. Gerth and C. Wright Mills, London, 1970.

GASS   Max Weber, *Gesammelte Aufsätze zur Soziologie und Sozialpolitik*, ed. Marianne Weber, Tübingen, 1924.

GLA   General-Landesarchiv

GStA   Geheimes Staatsarchiv

JB   Max Weber, *Jugendbriefe*, ed. Marianne Weber, Tübingen, 1936.

K   Max Weber, *Schriften 1894–1922*, ed. Dirk Kaesler, Stuttgart, 2002.

L   Marianne Weber, *Max Weber: Ein Lebensbild* (1926), Munich, 1989.

LE   Marianne Weber, *Lebenserinnerungen*, Bremen, 1948.

M   Max Weber, *Die rationalen und soziologischen Grundlage der Musik*, Tübingen, 1972.

MWG   *Max Weber-Gesamtausgabe*, ed. Horst Baier, M. Rainer Lepsius, Wolfgang J. Mommsen, Wolfgang Schluchter and Johannes Winckelmann, Tübingen, 1984–.

PE   Max Weber, *The Protestant Ethic and the Spirit of Capitalism* (1930), trans. Talcott Parsons, London, 1992.

PW   Max Weber, *Political Writings*, ed. Peter Lassman and Ronald Speirs, Cambridge, 1994.

R   Guenther Roth, *Max Webers deutsch-englische Familiengeschichte 1800–1950*, Tübingen, 2001.

RC   Max Weber, *The Religion of China*, trans. and ed. Hans H. Gerth, New York, 1964.

RI   Max Weber, *The Religion of India*, trans. and ed. Hans H. Gerth and Don Martindale, New York, 1958.

RR   Max Weber, *The Russian Revolutions*, trans. and ed. Gordon C. Wells and Peter Baehr, Cambridge, 1995.

S   Max Weber, *Gesammelte Aufsätze zur Soziologie und Sozialpolitik* (1924), ed. Marianne Weber, 2nd edn, Tübingen, 1988.

SWG   Max Weber, *Gesammelte Aufsätze zur Sozial- und Wirtschaftsgeschichte* (1924), ed. Marianne Weber, 2nd edn, Tübingen, 1988.

WB   Marianne Weber, *Max Weber: A Biography*, trans. Harry Zohn, New York, 1975.

WG   Max Weber, *Wirtschaftsgeschichte: Abriß der universalen Sozial- und Wirtschaftsgeschichte* (1923) [posthumously published lectures], ed. Sigmund Hellmann and Melchior Palyi, 5th edn, Berlin, 1991.

WL   Max Weber, *Gesammelte Aufsätze zur Wissenschaftslehre* (1922), ed. Johannes Winckelmann, 7th edn, Tübingen, 1988.

WuZ   Wolfgang J. Mommsen and Wolfgang Schwentker (eds), *Max Weber und seine Zeitgenossen*, Göttingen, 1988 (= publications of the German Historical Institute, London, vol. 21).

WzG   René König and Johannes Winckelmann (eds), *Max Weber zum Gedächtnis*, Cologne, 1963 (= *Kölner Zeitschrift für Soziologie und Sozialpsychologie* 1963, special issue 7).

At the Den of the Sick Lion

In one of Aesop's fables a fox comes to the den of a sick lion. The lion calls out for him to enter, but the cunning fox remains outside. 'Why won't you come in?' the lion asks. And the fox answers: 'I'd come straight away if I didn't see a lot of tracks going in but none coming out.' In Horace's version: '*Vestigia terrent*', 'The footprints are scary'; it has become a familiar quotation. Weber gave the impression of a sick lion to those who saw him during his illness[1] – though certainly not a lion without danger. This '*vestigia terrent*' kept going through my head as I ventured deeper into the field of Weber studies. Was it wise of me? Doubts rose up again and again. Here too there were many tracks going in but so few coming out. I had been used to conducting research in open ground, on the outer edges of the social sciences fraternity. But now Weber had landed me right at the centre, where space is tight and you can feel the elbows pushing.

My consolation was that Weber too had operated in frontier zones, and had actually specialized in crossing the boundaries between disciplines. Someone who is mainly interested in enlisting Weber for his own special subject does not know how to appreciate this characteristic. The more specialized the discipline, the more the *whole* Weber drops out of sight and gives way to a half or even a quarter of the man. Even *Science as a Vocation* can be invoked in support of one's own narrowness. Yet that text is a perfect example of how we should be wary of tying Weber to particular quotations, instead of seeing the whole person all the way from *The Protestant Ethic* to the love letters. Weber's impact was due not only to certain concepts and theories but even more to what he *was*.

In this biography we shall be especially concerned with Weber's boundary-crossing between anthropology and natural science; it has been the least remarked upon in Weber studies but, as we shall try to show, is of the greatest significance. Until now Weber has been thought of as an enemy of nature, as a writer who widened the gulf between Snow's 'two cultures': literary and sociological culture on the one hand, natural science and technology on the other. I would like to show that this is based on a fundamental misunderstanding of Weber.

During decades of moving in a triangle formed by the history of technology, environment and medicine, I have come to realize that despite the ocean of literature there are still many unnoticed ways of approaching Weber which partly overlap with one another and allow new discoveries to be made. It became one of my favourite games to surf the CD-ROM of Weber's collected works and to keep hitting on passages that I had previously overlooked; it would scarcely have occurred to me from the secondary literature that the words 'technology' and 'technological' [*Technik* and *technisch*] appear there no fewer than 1145 times, often in a far from trivial sense. My research on the history of nervousness had already shown me what a treasure trove were Weber's letters – and especially those of Marianne – for the 'nervous' semantics of the period. In the eyes of 'immanentist' interpreters, all this may appear to be what Weber's editor Johannes Winckelmann once called 'women's stories' [*Tantengeschichten*]. Yet even experts in Weber's biography can be heard to say that it regularly runs into the sand, because no one really knows what was involved in the 'nervous' complaint that cast its shadow on most of Weber's creative activity.

Finally, *nature* and its composites appear no fewer than 3583 times on the CD-ROM of Weber's work. Many instances tell us nothing in particular, but others, though seemingly trivial in themselves, become much less so when they are seen in context. In fact, nature may well constitute the missing link that has often been sought between Weber's life and work – not least when he is railing against nature, both outside and inside himself. Nor should we limit ourselves to 'nature', since nature is present even without the word. Weber's declared belief in *passion* is belief in a part of nature within human beings: not only in their autonomous reactions but also in their thinking. At the end of his inaugural lecture at Freiburg in 1895 he evoked 'the great passions that nature has implanted in us' (PW 28). In 1893, in his letter of courtship to Marianne, he sighed that he had been trying 'with difficulty' 'to tame the elemental passions with which nature has endowed me' (WB 177). And one of the key sentences in *Science as a Vocation* reads: 'For nothing is worthy of man as man unless he can pursue it with passionate devotion' (FMW 135).

'Nature, so long violated, was beginning to take revenge', is how Marianne Weber commented on her husband's breakdown (WB 235), believing not without reason that her own knowledge of nature, not least human nature, was a little more advanced than his. Although a modern Weberian must try to shake off the viewpoint of Weber's widow – that gatekeeper it is so difficult to get past – her comment may here be thought rather pertinent, perhaps in a broader and more enigmatic sense than she intended. Weber's hitherto unknown love letters to Else Jaffé from the last period of his life suggest that he himself interpreted his destiny in a similar way. Accordingly, my aim is to present Weber's life as a three-act play, with nature as the generator of dramatic tension: a project in the style of a myth or, better, in that of an ideal type. Why indeed should Weber's method not be applied to himself? We learn from him that ideal types are necessary in order to grasp reality, although it should never be imagined that reality can be *derived* from them. Certainly we shall not find it too embarrassing that life contains something over and above the schematic drama of ideal types.

Work on a biography inevitably sets up identification processes, however much various biographers, most notably of Hitler, may deny this. For months I experienced a kind of depression, many of whose symptoms were devilishly similar to Weber's, and I thought that I was coming to see many things about him in a new light. From time to time my wife would say that my identification with Weber was giving her the creeps. I protested: 'I am not Weber!' As I engaged in this work, I felt more than ever how distant I was from him. But this man parks himself in your subconscious and stares at you with his dark challenging eyes; I was not the first to have this experience. I could sense how many admirers of Weber might sometimes be seized with fury at this incubus weighing upon them.

But who was Weber really? And who were those significant others to whom he related most deeply: Marianne, Helene, Else, Alfred? The more stories I heard – and there is no end of them – the more I noticed the contradictions, and the more Weber became for me the Sphinx. He himself once described the comprehension of the individual as the atomic physics of sociology,[2] and it is true that in the social sciences biography does play a role similar to that of atomic theory in physics: it leads to discovery of the uncertainty principle. It is precisely in individuals, the smallest units of history, that shape and form vary according to the position of the observer. Sometimes there are not just one but several possible histories.

A lot of things in Weber become apparent only when you pay closer attention to figures in his milieu. In general, you have to train your eyes on Weber's significant others in order to understand his own development; the I takes shape through the Thou. Weber thought he was living in an age of epigones and disenchantment, and yet both he and his interlocutors open before us a truly enchanting and intellectually dazzling world. In the end we no longer know whether Weber was a 'great man' among his contemporaries – assuming we know what a 'great man' is anyway. The good sense of Weber's postulate of value-freedom is particularly striking when we take it seriously in his own biography.

But, great or not, Weber is certainly one of the thinkers through whom the social sciences have acquired a distinctive complexion and against whom one can often sharpen one's own thinking; he seems to grow and grow as you keep reading his texts. In a way just a poor sod,[3] he nevertheless offers the comfort that, even when you are up against it and have already wasted a lot of energy, you may find your way in the end. Above all, he encourages you to withstand tensions, to think more boldly, to sharpen your analytical faculties, to advance 'what if?' hypotheses, to give full expression to intellectual passion, but at the same time to curb flights of the intellect by raising objections along the way. Weber is a vivid reminder that there can be something better than Thomas S. Kuhn's 'normal science', which finds its satisfaction in the confirmation of existing paradigms. By contrast, Weberian science is an ever tense wrestling match between the superabundance of life and cold intellectual dissection.

The unity of a biography is formed by the body of a human individual – an unsatisfactory circumstance for historians who shy away from 'naturalism'. Body and soul cannot be separated from each other, and a biographer should declare his or her faith in their unity. Emotions are not a contamination of thought but the basis that underlies thought processes; anyone who reflects on human thought must also consider this foundation. That ideas and emotions are inseparable, that many decisions 'come from the gut', is something which lay people have always intuited, and through the science of neurophysiology it has permeated the ranks of the most up-to-date science. Brain scientists have never found a realm of pure reason separate from the emotions, even if philosophers of science act as if there were one. Lichtenberg already knew better when he demanded of scholars: 'Learn to know your body, and what you are able to know of your soul.'[4] Marianne Weber also knew the importance of somatic history in the life of her husband. I think that most Weber scholars are basically aware of this, although many keep it to themselves as an occult science.

Weber's creativity, we shall argue, was rooted not least in an ever more developed capacity to make his own experience of life a key to the world, not only through generalization but also through the raising of self-critical objections. We can 'learn from Weber' by following these tracks, and also by following them in our own unexhausted opportunities for knowledge and experience. This for me is the ultimate purpose of a biography of Max Weber. Science and life, science and love, science and happiness: after four decades of academic existence I see no more important or more stirring subject. Weber's life and loves, his illness and his thought are an endless source of inspiration, whether for the peculiarities of academic or erotic life – or, more important, for the Eros of science with its pain so full of relish. This is probably not the least reason why the old lion holds people in his den.

Part I

The Violation of Nature

Max Weber was born on 21 April 1864 in Erfurt, the first of eight children. His brother Alfred, with whom he repeatedly argued throughout his life, was four years younger. In 1869 the Weber family moved to Charlottenburg, when the Berlin city council appointed the father, Max Weber, senior, as a paid councillor. At the age of two Max Weber, junior, fell ill with meningitis; it took several painful years for him to be cured of it. His father pursued a dual career, as head of the Berlin building department and as a National Liberal representative in the Reichstag and the Prussian parliament, while his mother Helene did voluntary work for relief of the poor. At that time a number of leading academics and National Liberals used to meet in the Weber home. In 1882 Max Weber passed his Abitur and went to study in Heidelberg, then in 1884 switched to law and economics in Berlin. In between he performed his military service in Alsace. In 1889 he gained his doctorate with a thesis in the history of law, concerning North Italian trading companies in the Middle Ages. In 1891 he qualified as a university lecturer with a work on Roman agrarian history. Having joined the influential Verein für Sozialpolitik in 1888, he was commissioned by it in 1890 to evaluate the material on the German territories east of the Elbe contained in a country-wide survey of farm-workers; this resulted in 1892 in his first major work, which immediately made a name for him. On 20 September 1893 he married his second cousin Marianne Schnitger (b. 1870). In 1894 he accepted the offer of a chair in economics at Freiburg, where his inaugural address, 'The Nation State and Economic Policy' (13 May 1895), attracted attention because of its combination of brusque nationalism and attacks on the big landlords east of the Elbe. In 1897 he accepted an offer in Heidelberg. On 14 June 1897 he provoked a violent quarrel with his father by accusing him of making demands on the mother for his own selfish reasons. When the father died on 10 August 1897, there had been no reconciliation. In the summer of 1898 'nervous' disorders made Max Weber increasingly incapable of work, and in 1899 he was excused from further teaching duties. In 1903, at his own request, he was released from academic service.

1

Great Mother and Harsh Nature: A Precocious Youth on the Margins of Berlin

'Family communism': the primal form of society

The family, which in traditional conceptions is part of the natural order but for modern social science only appears to be so, remained Weber's most stable lifeworld, although shortly before his own breakdown he wrecked his parents' marriage in a violent rage. All other communities – academic faculties, political parties, civil associations – detained him only for a time. This fundamental experience marked his thinking. The historian Friedrich Meinecke, who knew Weber well, already pointed out that he 'could be thoroughly understood only on the ground of his family' (WzG 143f.). The microcosm of the family was all the more significant for him precisely because the wider macrocosm was brimming with irreconcilable struggle and coldly rational calculation; it remained a source of great warmth and trust, whatever the tensions and quarrels, and offered many gifts in which there was no thought of anything in return.

For Weber, then, 'domestic' or 'family' communism had something primeval and homely that distinguished it from political communism. 'Society', in the sense of a specific gathering of people crystallized in the family (independent of state institutions), was a primary experience – although, to be sure, it was not only natural instincts but also capital that held the family together. 'A domestic community binds only if it is geared to indisputably common *tasks*', Weber taught the young Arthur Salz in 1912 (MWG II/7–1, 428). Yet for Weber the family never had the mere function of an economic system; it always preserved a vitality of its own. Which was not at all to say that it was a harmonious idyll, as it showed its strength precisely in the midst of a quarrel.

With an eye to the slave barracks of ancient Rome, the 32-year-old Weber let slip a phrase that could have come from an instructor in Catholic social thinking: 'Man can develop only in the bosom of the family' (K 57). This sounds like a wise aphorism or a well-known and generally applicable law of nature. But Weber's own parental home was not exactly a bed of roses: his mother did not think twice about interfering in the affairs of her grown-up children, nor they in hers, and letters were routinely passed around – even the 'thoroughly intimate correspondence' that Max exchanged with Marianne and Helene when he was staying in a sanatorium (MWG II/6, 575). In any event, whereas the young Werner Sombart complained that his parents did not understand him, and that even their goodness made him feel unhappy ('I felt at ease only with others of my age'),[1] Weber's experience of life as a young man sharply differed from that of his nearest contemporaries in the world of social science, and this difference affected his whole intellectual-spiritual bearing. The 'crisis of the family' – a favourite theme of the early sociologists, especially the French[2] – was for Weber neither a major sociological issue nor a personal experience.

'Family' and its various compounds appear 786 times on the German CD-ROM edition of Weber's works, and 'kinship group' [*Sippe*] 736 times. Sometimes in his writings he explicitly refers to his own family experiences. Lujo Brentano, who knew from his own merchant family of Italian origin that Catholicism and capitalism can at best only tolerate each other, once remarked with a touch of derision: 'If Max Weber, to prove the correctness of his views, can adduce observations from the business circle close to him, then perhaps I may be allowed to do the same' (R 65). Weber's notes to the later edition of *The Protestant Ethic* reveal how much this criticism wounded him, although the brilliant Brentano was one of the colleagues with whom he restrained his quarrelsome proclivities.

In the web of an extended family

In a popular romantic view of society, the old extended family including grandparents and relations has shrunk in modern times to the nuclear family consisting only of parents and children. On closer inspection, we can see that the nuclear family was also a normal phenomenon in earlier times. Max Weber, however, experienced the intense (and often tense) cohesion of an extended family, of that whole web of kinship relations which is so confusing for anyone outside it.

Even his loves remained within the family circle. The first love of his youth was 'Klärchen', his sister Klara, whom he sometimes tenderly called 'Kätzchen' (kitten) and used to kiss on the mouth; their mother, feeling unmoved at Max's wedding, poked fun at Klara's weakness for her eldest brother by performing a sketch in which she despairingly sang: 'Abandoned, abandoned, oh abandoned am I – such must be my grief as the "first woman" I once was . . .'[3] A certain brutal candour was part of the Weber family style. Max's first semi-fiancée, Emmy ('Emmerling') Baumgarten, was his cousin; Marianne was his second cousin. Indeed, when he fell in love with Else Jaffé, she was already family in the wider sense, as Marianne's close friend for many years and Alfred Weber's companion in life – which did not exactly make the situation easier. And Mina Tobler had for a long time been in and out of the house when she and Max became physically close: she figures in Marianne's letters as 'Tobelchen'. Family intimacy was part of love for Max Weber, and in his writings the erotic appeal of the exotic is at most reflected through the Eastern religions. He is the best illustration of Freud's idea that the libido is originally incestuous.

Intellectual and economic bourgeois combined

Marianne Weber the idealist was fond of presenting her husband as a scion of the German *Bildungsbürgertum*. In reality, however, Max Weber was at least as much an offspring of the economic bourgeoisie, and this origin also left its mark on his consciousness. He developed a positive revulsion from the world of officialdom and was always aware that the material foundation for most of his adult life was not a state income but an annual yield on capital. The professorships he held were all in economics, and he liked to make use of his family's insider knowledge on economic issues. As Marianne emphasizes, he left no doubt 'that he valued the qualities of the successful businessman and merchant at least as highly as those of the academic and littérateur'.[4] He liked to demonstrate that he had not developed any prejudices towards business people.

It was actually a characteristic feature of the Weber family that it combined elements of the *Bildungsbürgertum* and the economic bourgeoisie. The Fallenstein grandfather, son of a headmaster who fell on hard times, had already improved his finances by marrying the wealthy heiress Emilie Souchay and built that spacious villa on the Neckar, with its magnificent views over the ruins of Heidelberg Castle, which became Max's and Marianne's home in 1910, replete with memories of the family history. Max knew that 'nine-tenths' of his parents' fortune came from 'Mother's side' (B 629); her power was based on that fact. Helene Weber was one of the inheritors of the Huguenot Souchay dynasty, which had grown rich through commerce, a global family network stretching as far as Canada, South Africa and Indonesia.[5] In Max Weber's time, Carl David Weber – the elder brother of Max Weber, senior and head of the Oerlinghausen textile company – was the richest man in the family, but his wealth was mostly self-acquired and did not derive from the family legacy to which Max's father also had an entitlement. Only through Marianne, the granddaughter of the company head, did Max gain a share of the assets after the latter's death.

A cerebral childhood

When he was two Weber fell ill with meningitis, and it was several years before his health was reasonably well restored. At the age of thirty, he wrote to his mother recalling 'the long years in which I was part physically, part mentally your problem child'.[6] In those days, the brain infection was especially dangerous for children, with a death rate between 70 and 100 per cent; the aetiology was unknown and medicine could offer no help. Even when the cause was discovered in 1887, it took another fifty years for a successful treatment to be developed. Attitudes influenced by bacteriology identified meningitis as the 'classical secondary illness', supposedly resulting from a tubercular lung infection or parental syphilis. And, as the second of these factors was long regarded as the main culprit, Max's illness was a reason for suspicion about his father's widely reputed 'lust for life'. As late as 1923 a standard medical textbook offered a 'grave' prognosis for chronic meningitis and suggested that most children succumb to hydrocephalus: water on the brain.[7] Still today one reads that, 'even with immediate treatment . . . it is difficult to avoid residual symptoms such as reduced emotional-intellectual agility and affectivity, behavioural phenomena or impulsive disorders.'[8] In the early stages, often before the disease is diagnosed, considerable damage to the central nervous system may become apparent.[9]

In the late nineteenth century, it was feared that a child would be left feeble-minded if he or she survived meningitis. Moreover, Weber already had an 'over-large' head at birth, and during the illness it grew 'noticeably, while the limbs remained girlishly small'. Later, he thought he could remember his head wobbling like an old man's, 'too heavy for the child's delicate stem'.[10] 'The doctor predicted either hydrocephalus or room for a great many things under the arching cranium' (WB 33). Such contrary prognoses from the boy's physical proportions! One way or another, anxiously or hopefully, all the attention was focused on Weber's head.

The child must have sensed the mother's fear that he would be left mentally deficient. This gave him a strong impetus to demonstrate his normality, and it must have been a huge relief when he began to feel that he was mentally superior to many others of his age and was able, without much effort, to excel at the demands made of him at school. On the other hand, there is no mention in Weber of the typical boyish pranks that men recall in later life with a broad grin on their face.[11] As a twenty-year-old, he assured his mother that he had done 'some very light-minded things' – like many students, he lived beyond his means – 'but no wicked pranks', for the reason that 'I was thinking of you' (JB 115). But in 1919 he wrote to Else that he had been living a 'second youth' with her – 'and where did I ever have a "first" one?'[12] So, we have to doubt whether the adult Weber still felt his virtuous youth to have been such a merit. Later he wanted so much to be a fighter, but he recognized that not too many upright men prove to be war heroes. 'In cases of war, for example, boys who were once punished for fighting or locked up for alcohol abuse or striking a non-commissioned officer are usually considerably more astute and, when the enemy is breathing down their neck, more useful and intrepid than moral cowards who . . . have behaved respectably for a couple of years' (JB 105).

One typical long-term consequence of childhood meningitis is a weak capacity to remember the period of illness. Presumably this was also the case with Weber. Whereas many other self-aware people like to recall their earliest years, one is struck by the paucity of such memories in Weber; the popular practice of returning in the imagination to a childhood paradise was blocked for him. His recollections appear to take clear shape only with the beginning of his school years. Weber's lifelong difficulties with his psyche may have something to do with an inability to hold early childhood experiences at a conscious level. Not infrequently, the ancient world in which he lived so intensely functioned as a substitute for the lost memory of childhood.

From the beginning Weber occupied a contradictory position in his family: the problem child, but also the 'big boy', the first in a series of eight children (six of whom reached adulthood). This status contained an opportunity for early self-confidence that the young Weber gladly seized. He particularly liked to shower his younger siblings with instructions and admonitions, and to extend an avuncular tenderness toward his sisters. For many years the illness left behind a susceptibility to headaches and cramps, but this was also an invitation to motherly love – especially when conjugal love faded away. 'The young mother now tended her child constantly and never left the house without leaving word as to where she might be found' (WB 32). It was thus one of Weber's primal experiences that illness compels loving attention – most especially, attention to his poor head. The father and mother set examples of two different senses of self: the one, a hedonist's absorption in himself; the other, a woman's increasing preparedness to endure suffering. The young Weber would have liked to be as happy as any other child. But the other, maternal opportunity for self-confidence was presented to him at an early age, and for a long time it was the only one he had.

Weber's angst

A child's experiences of fear and pleasure leave their mark on the psyche. In many areas, it is not easy to separate fear and pleasure from each other. How did Weber cope with fear? 'I'm no hypochondriac!' he assured the ailing Emmy Baumgarten in 1887 (JB 279), but others did not always agree. Later, for all his complaints about his nerves, he cultivated a bearing of personal fearlessness. This led Ernst Nolte to the view that Weber had been immune from any kind of fascism, since the source of fascism is fear – fear of socialism and, more generally, of anything beyond the bounds of tradition.[13] It is certainly true that Weber was free of the Wilhelmine-bourgeois fear of social democracy, but all the more was he haunted over the years by fear of the 'demons' within himself. His often pointless displays of aggression show that he must have experienced dread without any clear object, even less capable of controlling it because he did not acknowledge it. In 1943, when Eduard Baumgarten once had occasion to glimpse Hitler at close quarters and saw 'the eyes of a startled animal in flight', he thought he could remember that Weber's eyes had been like that when he was in the grip of a blind rage.[14] In *The Protestant Ethic* Weber describes how the original nature of human beings is subdued by another natural power, that is, the power of the fear of eternal damnation. In *Ancient Judaism* it is 'crazed fear' of cruel and superior enemies which enables the prophets to gain victory over the orgiastic cult of Baal.

For normal children, their initial shyness overcome, it is pure fun to splash around in water. But when Max's mother Helene, in keeping with her ideology of toughening through cold water, again and again dragged her barely recovered five-year-old into the sea at Borkum, 'every day there was so much screaming that the bathers demanded a stop to the treatment', with the result that, 'even as a grown man, Max Weber did not forget the terrors of this procedure' (WB 33). In later years Weber often went to the sea, but there was never any question of his entering it, even after Marianne became a keen swimmer. Bathing in the surf, that libidinal foundation of overseas naval imperialism, was not one of Weber's pleasures in life.

One of the very few memories that Weber reported from childhood was of a railway accident in Belgium whose effects he witnessed at the age of four. The image came back to him in 1903 when he was making another trip through Belgium: 'Near Verviers I remembered the first "shattering" event of my life: the train derailment 35 years ago. What was shattering for me about it was not everything that happened but the sight of a locomotive, such an awe-inspiring thing for a child, lying like a drunkard in a ditch – my first experience of the transitoriness of the great and beautiful on this earth.'[15] The locomotive as the epitome of force! At home Max played a lot with railway toys, 'chattering almost incessantly', and used to let himself be shrouded in the smoke of locomotives as he looked down on them from an overpass near his home by Erfurt station (WB 32).

Now that the railway has long been outdone by racing cars, aircraft and rockets, it is scarcely possible to imagine the spell that locomotives used to cast on a child's imagination. They were the great miracles of technology, the embodiment of power and the future, but they also had a frightening side in that any railway accident, unlike the car crashes that have become part of our everyday lives, was a public event capable of producing a collective shock. For Weber the railway became paradigmatic of danger. On New Year's Eve in 1889, following all the hopes he had placed in the new young emperor, he wrote to Hermann Baumgarten about Wilhelm II's 'new course': 'You feel as though you are seated in a high-speed railway train, but with doubts about whether the next points will be set correctly.' The image pleased him, since a year later he used it again in a letter to his uncle. And this time he added: 'If only the Kaiser is not ruining, or has not already ruined, his mental powers!' (JB 324, 330) He was beginning to transfer the worries he had about himself to the Kaiser, who from early on was considered the leading neurasthenic in the Reich.

In the beginning: harsh nature

Weber's relationship to nature began with his relationship to his own nature – or to that unfeeling goddess *Natura* who bestowed his natural disposition. He had reason to feel that she had treated him cruelly, already as a child, though not equally badly in all periods of his life. In his appalling handwriting the word 'nature' is often especially difficult to decipher, and it never offered itself to him as a keyword for rhetorical flourishes. Instead, his attitude to life held the door open for a realistic relationship to nature, far removed from any kind of idyll.

On the other hand, as he grew more aware that he could never be completely healthy or capable of work, Darwinian nature must have tormented him with its perpetual struggle and 'survival of the fittest'. According to the yardstick of pure Darwinism, he would have had to think of himself as one of those condemned to go under in a bare-knuckle process of natural selection. After his breakdown, Weber had an inner block against the kind of pure and brutal naturalism that does not recognize any cultural qualities worth preserving. Earlier, however, his political thinking had contained a Darwinian element; he had put into the nature of politics more force than his own not exactly powerful disposition could endure.

At the age of fourteen, Max Weber made an oft-quoted admission to his cousin Fritz Baumgarten that, if he had not previously communicated his feelings about his upcoming confirmation, this was not because he had not had any. 'I think there is something in my nature', he wrote, 'which means that I rarely tell others of my feelings; it often costs me too much of an effort to do it. I usually enjoy any pleasure by myself, but my feelings are none the lesser as a result' (JB 21). Of course, a young person is not necessarily emotionally impoverished if an approaching confirmation does not elicit an outpouring of his heart. But Helene often worried that her 'big boy' was so aloof towards her and did not give her the satisfaction of being able to shape him psychologically with her tireless care. But it was precisely through such reproaches that she forced him into brooding confessions. At the age of twenty, for example, Max guiltily admitted his 'inability, precisely with those closest to me, to communicate orally and to express myself about all manner of things'. Assuming that people acquire their identity not from themselves but through others, it would seem to follow that the young Max Weber's perception of himself came mainly from his mother; it was through her that he came to see himself throughout life as someone aloof by nature. Much later he wrote that 'Nature did not make me an open person', to the regret of those who loved him (WB 533).

His own nature as an open question

For Max Weber, his own nature became more and more an open question. There were periods when he was bubbling over with a sense of his own strength. Marianne even asserted: 'All his life Weber vehemently rejected the notion that nature pre-shapes us in accordance with inevitable laws; he was convinced that in him either of two polar tendencies could have prevailed. For example, he might have become a confirmed egotist, an essentially amoral hedonist who by virtue of his intellectual superiority would have appropriated for himself the right to force others to serve his purposes' (WB 84–5). Weber's conception of nature, then, was not determinist but 'possibilist'; he thought not in terms of structures but in terms of opportunities for action.

During his time in the army, Weber once described church attendance to his mother as 'the most awful military service there is' (JB 333). He knew that this would not hurt his pious mother, as she too kept her distance from the usual ecclesiastical Christianity. One of the young Weber's rare mentions of a sermon – normally a favourite topic in middle-class letters and journals of the time – referred to one given in Strasbourg in 1882 by a pastor named Riff, whose book of sermons he had already read in excerpts to his mother (WB 57). In fact, he had some reason to hold a grudge against the Alsatian priest, since Weber knew him to be 'completely French-oriented' and was deeply vexed by the anti-German sentiment that had developed in Alsace since its annexation by Germany. On the other hand, Riff evidently impressed him in a way that no other clergyman had done before: he celebrated Whitsun in a spirit of natural religion which, Weber thought, would have provoked a 'scandal' in orthodox Protestant northern Germany.

> His Whitsun service actually consisted in painting and explaining a single great picture: the awakening of nature, which was supposed to illustrate the awakening of the Holy Spirit in the hearts of the young. What was so special, however, was not only that he explained it in such a way that it stood as a pure picture alongside the idea, but that the picture was supposed to elucidate what really happened in the minds of the Apostles. He presented a psychological account to the congregation, as if he were delivering a theological treatise on something like 'A natural-psychological explanation of the events on Whit Sunday'. Yet it cannot be said that he overtaxed the heads of his Alsatian farmers, since he explained the events really naturally and intelligibly while dwelling as far as possible on the picture itself. (JB 53f.)

As we see, this Whitsun sermon gave Weber a fascinating lesson in the visual thinking that most bookish people find so difficult, and initiated him into a natural religion that corresponded to the farmers' practical experience of nature and was not simply a middle-class intellectual construction. On these matters, he could count on his mother's understanding when he wrote to her about the sermon.

Weber's religious starting point: William Channing's pantheism

Max Weber's internationally famous turn to Anglo-American popular theology was prepared in advance by his mother, who, prompted in her youth

Figure 1.1 The young Max Weber, photographed in Berlin. 1878

by her sister Ida, had gone deeply into the 'non-dogmatic' (and, for theologians in her Erfurt milieu, excessively 'radical') writings of Theodore Parker and William Channing (WB 28). Channing (1780–1842), a Unitarian clergyman in Boston, was opposed to the doctrine of the Trinity, and his belief in the unity of God's carnal and spiritual nature and in the divine potential within both human and extra-human nature conflicted with the official Calvinism.[16] (In 1572, at the instigation of the Calvinists, the anti-Trinitarian Johannes Sylvanus had been publicly beheaded in Heidelberg.) His was not the strict and sombre Calvinism of the Huguenot tradition to which Helene adhered, but rather a heterodox natural religion with pantheist undertones that had a liberatory effect on the narrow Puritanical world of New England.[17] For Channing, nature was a revelation of divine wisdom.

Helene felt worried that, in the preparations for confirmation, her son Alfred wanted to be instructed in an overly authoritarian religiosity (JB, 113). She agreed with Marianne in her revulsion from the doctrine of original sin.[18] As to the Puritans in Weber's *The Protestant Ethic*, the main significance of theology for her was in relation to practical living, though as an invitation not to strictly disciplined acquisitiveness but to charitable activity within the limits of her strength. She saw this as her 'vocation' after her husband's death (WB 507). In 1904, at the age of sixty, it even developed into a formal vocation, when she became the first woman in Prussia

to be appointed to an honorary position on the Charlottenburg Welfare
Board (WB 509).

An overpowering mother

The telephone rang constantly in Helene's house in the Charlottenburg
district of Berlin – a still novel disturbance of the peace which, with that
frequency, used to drive Max and Marianne mad. Once in 1912 Marianne,
otherwise so unruffled by her mother-in-law, burst out: 'The telephone is
running your life – that is barbarism.'[19] Helene offered her jittery children
the model of someone with a seemingly unlimited ability to cope with
stress. Indeed, Marianne sighed that Helene's capacity to keep going from
morning till night was 'so *shaming*' that it was unbearable to live with her,
'because a person would lose all his self-respect' (WB 510). Helene's
perpetual 'haste' meant that Max felt no security in their Charlottenburg
home, but rather a 'lack of confidence'.[20] But in 1910, under pressure
from her children finally to enjoy some peace and quiet, the 66-year-old
Helene wrote them a veritable 'self-defence' that laid out her convictions, her view of the meaning of her life (MWG II/6, 677). 'Helene', we
read in Marianne Weber's biography, 'always applied absolute standards
and in every situation demanded the utmost from herself. Therefore, she
was never satisfied with herself and always felt inadequate before God'
(WB 29).

Between the lines we see the picture of an extremely demanding mother
and mother-in-law, who instilled guilt feelings in herself and others. She
was the kind of lady of the house who, however considerate towards her
domestics, is constantly angry with them because (to quote Max Weber) she
does not know how 'to teach them to take responsibility' and does not even
see this as a shortcoming on her part.[21] Her son probably more than once
felt towards her what he wrote in 1915 about an acquaintance of Helene's
who was equally filled with a sense of her charitable mission: 'It's odd that
the assuredly splendid and good-natured woman so often gets on my
nerves, that her trivial goodness and excellence are actually wearing. One
is . . . so defenceless against that kind of thing. . . . I find her positively
numbing.'[22] Weber's 'nervousness' is also palpable in his marked allergy to
social-political concepts that involve a mothering of the lower classes by the
state. When he compares the German urge for state provision to a 'devilish
scrubbing mania' [*Scheuerteufel*], the metaphor tells us that he thought a
state matriarchy even worse than patriarchal rule.

In Meinecke's view, Helene was the epitome of the Great Mother: 'a
wonderful, pure, selfless and strong woman' (WzG 144). She embodied
'Great Motherhood', in the words of Theodor Heuss, or of her protégé
Friedrich Naumann.[23] Despite her delicate exterior, she was for Troeltsch
a 'monumental figure of a woman' and for Gertrud Bäumer a 'magnificent figure' (WzG 43, 117). The question of 'Helene and Max Weber' is

the most remarkable gap in the extensive 'Weber and . . .' literature, for there can be no doubt that his mother, who passed away only a year before his own death, was of the utmost significance to him. One is reminded of Sigmund Freud's mother, who also unobtrusively accompanied him for the greatest part of his life, and who is similarly overlooked in the secondary literature; the Oedipus complex directs attention to the drama of the child's relationship with the father, only scantily documented in Freud's own work. Erich Fromm quotes one of the few places where Freud reveals something of the significance of the attachment to his mother: 'A man who has been the indisputable favourite of his mother keeps for life the feeling of a conqueror, that confidence of success that often induces real success.'[24]

Madonna and messiah

Weber could probably have said something similar of himself. One of his very few recollections of the Erfurt period that shed some light on his inner being is contained in the letter he wrote to his mother in 1914 on her seventieth birthday. Here he reminds her of the engraving of the Sistine Madonna that used to hang in their Erfurt home: he always took the Madonna to be Helene, and himself 'with characteristic immodesty' to be the child Jesus (MWG II/8, 614).

Helene's reading of Parker and Channing filled her with revivalist hopes: 'First a towering man must come for this period too, to awaken those who are dreaming' – and Parker might well be the John the Baptist preparing the way for the Saviour.[25] Here the original form of Weber's idea of the charismatic leader is still a dream bound up with religious salvation rather than politics, but 'to his mother's sorrow' the young Weber 'never felt any need to attach himself to a leader' (WB 92). For a time, Helene appears to have seen in Friedrich Neumann this religious leader moved by the spirit, and her son allowed himself, with some reservations, to be carried along by her enthusiasm.

Those who are remote from religion often have an undiscriminating image of 'pious people'. Weber, however, with his mother in mind, learned from an early age to distinguish among various forms of piety or religiosity, and this feeling for subtle distinctions would later be one of his strengths as a sociologist of religion. In contrast to ordinary church-going Christians, he must have soon become aware that members of sects and free churches were not necessarily ridiculous oddities. Nevertheless, after reading Channing for a while, he began to feel angry that he had declared himself a pacifist on strict religious grounds. If Channing characterized killing in wartime as 'far beneath the hangman's trade' – since the hangman only kills convicted criminals – this was 'simply reprehensible' for the Weber who had just completed his military service. Besides, as Weber realistically perceived, to place the army 'on the same level as a band of murderers' does not help to make war 'a whit more humane'; the jurist is here thinking of the tradition in which rules of war serve to protect prisoners and the civilian population.

Weber's ultimately irreconcilable conflict between ethic of conviction and ethic of responsibility was already beginning to emerge. But a reader who expects Helene to have been hostile to any military service will be disappointed. Just as she repeatedly dragged her screaming five-year-old into the sea, so did she later believe that the army would prove good in the end for the beer-bloated student, hard though it might be for him at first (JB 92). He did protest at this maternal assurance, however, and complained about his 'painfully swollen ankles' resulting from the daily seven hours of drill (JB 76). His mother, believing as she did in the benefits of salutary hardening, was unimpressed by such complaints and reproached him for his grousing – which only provoked him to voice even more dramatic laments (JB 89).

The mother and sexuality

'That saintly woman' is how Helene appears in Marianne's biography (WB 176). But, like so many passages in the book, this too is double-edged. In the same sentence Marianne notes that she herself is 'made of entirely different material' (WB 176), a mere 'child of the earth', as the German original adds (L 186). This is preceded by an obscure allusion to the 'not yet fully absorbed misfortune of her (Helene's) youth' and to the mother's incapacity for 'natural enjoyment of the moment'. An attentive reader is thus given to understand that the conjugal sexual relations of her mother-in-law – whether because of her temperament or because of a traumatic experience in her youth – were 'not a source of joy but a heavy sacrifice and also a *sin*' (WB 30), and that she implanted in her eldest son 'indestructible inhibitions against a surrender to his drives' (WB 91). Marianne presents this here as a mercy for which the mother had reason to be 'thankful'. But anyone familiar with Marianne's letters knows that her biography of Max Weber is nowhere more insincere than at this point. For she was perfectly aware that the sexual block was the main cause of her husband's despair. The 'saintly woman' was thus in reality Weber's misfortune.

We may assume that Marianne's biography here reflects part of Weber's own view of things. In 1911, at a time when he was rather more favourably disposed to his own sexuality, he wrote in ironical vein to Marianne about his mother, who, because of her compulsion to be constantly active, was brooding over a three-month health cure that had been prescribed for her. It would, Max suggested, be necessary to 'console her a little' by pointing out that she could afterwards be even more active, 'and that the "bodily frame" she hated so much was after all only a "means" to something else' (MWG II/7, 201). At a hidden level, without ever daring to give vent to it, Max Weber must have harboured a deep resentment towards his mother; this would account for his emotional block towards Helene, which she experienced as obduracy on his part. It would also explain, as an expression of personal injury, the utter rage he felt over Bachofen's theory of a primal matriarchal paradise of free love – an increasingly fashionable theory that was one of the attractions of early sociology and ethnology. Already in 1893, in a letter to Lujo Brentano, he loudly denounced the 'mischief' that people are getting up to with the spectre of "matriarchy"' (JB 363), although during the same period he was also taking his mother's side against his father. And, in his inaugural speech at Freiburg, he fulminated against the 'demon of matriarchy', even though this had nothing to do with his chosen topic.

Marianne's relationship to Helene is especially hard to fathom. Often she experienced her mother-in-law as a substitute for her own mother, whom she had scarcely known. For many years she wrote Helene a long letter every week, beginning it with 'Dearest Mother' or 'Darling Mother', but from time to time a slightly cadging tone developed as she expressed a need for financial support. In 1894, shortly before New Year's Eve, the prospect of a trip to Charlottenburg elicited from her a 'cry of joy' with five exclamation marks: 'I could sing and rejoice all day long . . .'[26] In 1916 Max Weber spoke in brutal and vulgar terms of his mother as the 'little ducat man' who achieves 'digestion' in response to the clamorous demands of her children.[27]

When Weber's father was dead and could no longer read Marianne's letters to his wife, Marianne had no inhibitions about keeping Helene up to date concerning the sexual misery of her eldest. In her biography she sometimes describes Weber's family in accordance with the feminist image of oppressive patriarchy, but her correspondence and diaries leave no doubt that his mother was totally dominant and that his father was a rather awkward, if affable, marginal figure. Occasional outbursts of Marianne's against parental matriarchy reveal that, in the outpourings of her heart to her 'Dearest Mother', she choked back quite a lot of bitterness.

Marianne's biography has led to exaggerated ideas about Helene's horror of sexuality. With her allusions, Marianne probably wanted to ward off suspicions that she herself was the main reason for Max Weber's inhibitions, which had already given rise to some speculation. There are clear signs that Helene's attitude to sex was more divided than the biography suggests. Many aspects of Weber's inner tension may be explained by the fact that, during his sexual development, he received highly ambiguous rather than clear-cut signals from the parental home. Helene's religiosity was not of the monastic type: she unquestionably thought it natural that married couples should have sexual intercourse with each other. When Marianne, shortly after her marriage, read to Helene extracts from Tolstoy's *Kreutzer Sonata*, the mother made it clear that she did not like that kind of anti-sexual literature.[28] She repeatedly felt uneasy and irritated that the young Weber took no pleasure in dancing and was disturbed by the low necklines of ladies at the ball. This even struck her as negligence on his part, since she thought it the natural duty of a young man to make young women happy. Her maternal insistence made Max truly stubborn and awkward. The 'most trivial lunchtime drink' among 'sensible people' – that is to say, 'men' – was far more welcome to him than 'a so-called ball', where you 'work hard to earn your piece of meat by engaging in kangaroo-type leaps' and have to 'squeeze stealthily out on to the staircase to enjoy a cigar and a glass of beer' (JB 202f.). He annoyed his mother by demonstratively stating that, even at balls, what appealed to him was not the girls but only the meat dishes, the beer and the cigars. For her part, Helene was not prudish in principle and firmly believed that every real woman – and, of course, every real man – should experience a 'great passion' once in their life.[29] Her kind of asceticism did not rule out all passion.

Especially revealing is a passage in the biography that does not seem to have been noticed before. In the spring of 1903 the sickly Weber once more sought relief in Rome, but by then Rome no longer had the same effect. 'If only we could go to a different world – to Constantinople, for example! But there are not the funds for that.' Really? Once more Helene was prepared to help out; she even wanted to tempt Max further south, 'to Africa and the Biskra oasis, where he would certainly find some sun'! 'Dearest darling Mama', Marianne answered (31 March 1903), 'so, you would like to send us among the heathens and Turks or into the desert, oh dear!' But Weber held back from this exotic idea and went instead to the Historians' Congress in Heidelberg (WB 262). The Biskra oasis in Algeria is now the kind of place where scarcely anyone could possibly go for pleasure, but things were very different in those days. The oasis had become famous as a result of André Gide's novella *The Immoralist* (1902), in which he describes how his latent homosexuality was aroused by brown-skinned Arab boys. Already in 1880 Nietzsche knew that 'every girl from the nearby peoples lives for a time from prostitution', and years later in Nice he was preoccupied with the question 'whether the Biskra oasis in the Sahara would not be suitable as a ten-year retreat for a Zarathustra'.[30] Helene had long been aware of her eldest son's sexual misery and must have supposed that that was the kernel of his illness. So, in her practical and direct manner, she was offering what seemed to her a straightforward piece of advice.

The Gervinus trauma and the 1848 generation

Max and Marianne Weber saw the origin of their mother's troubled relationship to sexuality in a youthful encounter with the literary and political historian Georg Gottfried Gervinus (1805–1871), who had been thirty-nine years older than her. In 1910 Max wrote to his younger brother Arthur about a hidden factor in their parents' estrangement from each other – a factor which he must earlier have considered in mitigation when he had been raging against his father: 'Gervinus was Mama's rapturously admired teacher, the famous historian. Mama had the terrible experience that he tried to *force* himself on her in a sudden wave of lust. This became decisive

Figure 1.2 View from the Fallenstein–Weber villa over Heidelberg Castle (painting): Georg Gottfried Gervinus stands between Weber's grandparents Emilie and Georg Friedrich Fallenstein

for everything she later felt about *sensual* life' (MWG II/6, 763). How far Gervinus actually took his violent advances is not clear from the surviving sources; he subsequently appears to have kept a clear conscience and to have thought of himself as a man of honour. But he stemmed from that sentimental era in which even solid *Bildungsbürger* thought that love was a law unto itself, so long as it was felt with sufficient urgency. And the 55-year-old scholar writing the letter evidently also believed in this higher law of love.

At the beginning of 1861, Helene wrote to Ida about Gervinus that sometimes she no longer knew whether she 'should *loathe* or *love* Uncle'. 'He was not loving to me as someone would be to a child, but rather as to a beloved. But he made demands on me that a lover *should* not make on his beloved, and anyway I was and am not his *woman*. . . . How often he said: Ah, if only I were just thirty years younger – I'd know what to do. He didn't stop when I reproached him for the wrong he was doing Auntie. Nor did he stop when I was sitting on his knee and asked him to be loving to me as his child, but not *like that*.' She 'had been on the edge of a terrible precipice' and would often have liked nothing more than to jump in the Neckar (R 667f.).

She does not, however, seem to have had a physical aversion to him; it was mainly a guilty conscience towards his wife that tormented her. The Weber family kept a fondness for him in later years. They were not so prudish and unworldly as to consider a man totally depraved because he had abnormal erotic tendencies. The playful, high-spirited love letters that the young Helene wrote to her fiancé ('My dearest, one and only good-for-nothing!') do not give the slightest indication of an earlier trauma. And later Max wrote to his mother that she 'had Gervinus and the old Heidelberg atmosphere to thank' for the 'historical imagination' which enabled her to enjoy Italy to the full (WB 257).

Yet Weber must have suspected that Gervinus's lack of restraint was indirectly to blame for his own sexual block, and this was probably one reason why he developed an emotional as well as intellectual unease towards the old 1848 liberalism exemplified by Gervinus. Unlike most of the Göttingen Seven[31] and many 1848ers who finally managed to make a career for themselves, Gervinus won a martyr's glory when he again lost his professorship in 1853 (this time for ever) after a sensational treason trial.[32] For Max Weber, however, the Gervinus affair in the family was a lesson that people who appear publicly as high-minded victims may privately be far from honourable wrongdoers. The grandiloquence of literary people always aroused in Weber a suspicion of hypocrisy.

The young Weber and Berlin: a subterranean theme

Weber's ambivalent relationship to liberalism, both intellectually and emotionally, was associated with an ambivalent relationship to Berlin, the North German stronghold of liberalism and city of his childhood and youth. It is true that, if one so wished, it was still possible in refined Charlottenburg to remain separate from the explosively growing metropolis, but a young person's imagination was captivated by it all the more. Helene's charitable work brought her into permanent contact with the big-city poverty.

In the letter he wrote on his mother's seventieth birthday, Weber remarked that 'very many of the problems and difficulties' encountered after their move from Erfurt were 'the result of being transplanted to the atmosphere of Berlin'. The 'alienating city atmosphere', which disturbs the relationship of children (especially sons) to their parents, displays its effects 'when the children are – as nearly all of us were – nervous, easily influenced and with a tendency to be blasé' (MWG II/8, 614f.).[33] The big city holds many more attractions for pubescent boys than for middle-class girls, who are well protected from them at home. When Max Weber tried in 1910 to calm Helene's agitation over the liaison between Alfred and Else, he recognized that self-denial testified to strength of character, but asked her to bear in mind that 'those of us *today* who have grown up in the *big city* feel *innumerable* "sins of thought" come over us' and 'have to agree that we too might do that once passion is taken beyond a certain point' (MWG II/6, 677). He knew what he was talking about.

In 1884 in Strasbourg, when he was barely twenty years old, Weber obtained from Hermann Baumgarten a copy of *La Société de Berlin*, a 'brand-new but already notorious' French book published under a pseudonym.[34] He liked it and spent weeks immersed in it, finding more and more confirmation of his own impressions of Berlin. It seemed highly unjust that the German press had labelled it as 'nothing less than defamatory' and that it had apparently been 'already impounded'. In fact, it was 'in many respects first-rate' and actually quite 'restrained' for a French person; it contained, 'in a very calm and objective manner, a wealth of interesting judgements on all the public figures in Berlin', 'some of which are strikingly accurate' (JB 93f., 102f.). We therefore need to look at this French exposé to get a sense of how the young Weber saw Berlin.

The picture is anything but flattering. The social elites of Berlin, 'as united as any camorra', appear to form a veritable snake-pit of intrigues, but unfortunately without Parisian charm and wit; everyone spies on everyone else. Almost the only bright spot is the salon of Countess Marie von Schleinitz, 'the best-informed and most intelligent woman in Berlin', who spreads the Wagner cult right up to the imperial court. Everything is under the spell of Bismarck, whose cold, refined power games and surprising chess moves offer new daily material for conversation. Bismarck does not allow other talented leaders to make their way in politics – this is the complaint of Hermann Baumgarten and Max Weber too. The typical upperclass woman in Berlin spends the whole day chattering, even while she is dressing and undressing. 'She does not have two serious ideas in her head, nor two respectable thoughts in her heart.' Even a hardened Parisian observer of Berlin is shaken by the uninhibited directness with which such ladies take and change lovers whenever they feel like it. There is no trace of Puritanism, and not much of German efficiency either; the German elites are rather lacking in a modern business sense. This must have been similar to Weber's own view of the trend-setting Germany of his time, and anyone who is familiar only with today's cliché of a Puritanical and disciplined empire will find many of Weber's remarks incomprehensible. It is particularly astonishing to read in *La Société de Berlin* that the Reichstag lacked all patriotism.[35] In retrospect imperial Germany seems hypernationalist, but for the young Weber nationalism – or anyway an intelligent, politically consequential nationalism – was a courageous, clear-sighted novelty.

Throughout his life Max Weber found Berlin, and especially the showy new cathedral and Reichstag, 'thoroughly ugly';[36] he never 'felt in the least at home' in the city of his youth (B 492). Yet his relationship to Berlin was not only negative. Although today he has become part of the myth of Old Heidelberg, it would never have entered his head to play off Heidelberg romanticism against the grim metropolis with its million-plus inhabitants; Berlin stood too much for that modern reality which he sought to penetrate and grasp intellectually. In March 1896, when he again spent some time in

Berlin after a year and a half in Freiburg, he was surprised at how good he felt there in spite of the noise all around: 'The Berlin air agrees with me remarkably well. Nervously, one feels more productive, for the "stress and strain" of the last few days has been great and yet I am completely fresh' (WB 203, translation modified). He was still using the word 'nervous' [*nervös*] to mean simply 'with regard to the nerves', and not 'nervously over-wrought'. In fact, the current opinion that the big city makes one 'nervous' (in the sense of overwrought) cannot be found in Weber around that time, even though he had grown up in Berlin and experienced himself as a highly nervous individual.

Weber spoke in greatest detail about the modern metropolis in 1910 in Frankfurt, at the first German congress of sociologists, during his second contribution to the discussion on Sombart's lecture on technology and culture.[37] The agile Sombart, who a decade earlier had professed to be 'a Berliner in heart and soul', now wallowed in nostalgic Viennese romanticism and raged against the 'desert of modern technological culture'.[38] That was going too far for Weber. He found it completely unrealistic to offer nothing but a negative-destructive account of the relationship between modern tech-nology and culture; and his main argument stressed that 'very definite formal values in our modern artistic culture could only be born through the existence of the modern metropolis, with its railways, subways, electric and other lights, shop windows, concert and catering halls, cafés, smokestacks, and piles of stone, the whole wild dance of sound and colour impressions that affect sexual fantasy, and the experiences of variations in the soul's con-stitution that lead to a hungry brooding over all kinds of seemingly inex-haustible possibilities for the conduct of life and happiness.'[39]

Weber's words sound like a reflection of the expressionist art that was developing around that time. We can see how he was carried away by his own images. He could not get the thought out of his mind (S 453f.), but he considered his special gift to be a feel for the relationship among different cultural spheres. As never before, technology was becoming a special kind of cultural factor. And Weber was fascinated above all by the metropolis at night, when he began to come to terms with sexuality. On other occa-sions, too, he gladly fought against anti-modernist attitudes of the *Bildungsbürgertum*: against its horror of stockbrokers, journalists and party politicians. This modernism is not the least of the reasons why he sounds like an anachronistic contemporary of ours among the scholars of his own time.

2

Max and Minimax: Blood Brothers and Drinking Companions – Surly Fraternity as a Primary Social Experience

Max and Alfred Weber: a lifelong brotherly dialectic

If we assume that the ego develops not out of one's own self but through a Thou figure, through the reciprocal relationship with an Other, then the question arises of what this meant in the case of Max Weber. Many who got to know him only later in life thought of him as a great loner. But he repeatedly made use of others to hone his ego, thereby developing that characteristic touchiness which is not the least attraction of his writings.

The principal Thou figure for Max Weber was his mother, and later his wife. Such women as Marianne and Helene were not, however, sufficiently rough for a man of his qualities to sharpen himself against. His brother Alfred (1868–1958), four years younger than himself, was an ideal interlocutor. It was a high-tension relationship, at an intellectual as well as an erotic and even a religious level, which recalls the one between Thomas and Heinrich Mann, and sometimes almost the one between Cain and Abel. But, for all the estrangement, rivalry and hatred, their brotherhood remained until the end astonishingly stable: the blood kinship was a bond that endured much stress and strain that would have destroyed any other relationship. In an age when boys and men still cultivated sensitive friendships, indeed when the youth movement had revived them one last time,[1] Max Weber proved not to be cut out for them. After his death, Marianne remarked that 'his relations with men of his own age were mostly limited to practical matters';[2] only within the circle of family and relatives, or of young men with whom he could play the role of teacher, did he sometimes become warmer. His later theory of socialization was based on a transfer of brotherly feelings to wider communities. As far as his own person was concerned, however, the mature Weber appears to have shied away from using the fraternal *du* pronoun with men to whom he was not related.

In his youth, Max Weber played the role of elder brother in an overbearingly didactic manner. But for many years Alfred was actually more successful, both academically, politically and erotically, and it was only

Figure 2.1 The Weber family in 1887 in Berlin (from left to right): Arthur (1877–1952), Klara (1875–1953), Alfred, Lili (1880–1920), Helene, Karl, Max Weber senior, Max

after Max's death that Alfred was completely overshadowed by his posthumous fame and acquired the nickname 'Minimax' among students in Heidelberg.[3] In later life he again slipped into the hated role he had played in their childhood and youth; the increasingly international discipline of Max Weber studies treated him as an insignificant younger brother, even though the great importance of their brotherhood had been evident to both Alfred and Max, and many of Max's distinctive characteristics had stood out more sharply through the comparison with Alfred. For it should not be forgotten that their paths crossed again and again in areas of interest to them both.

The school report for the sixteen-year-old Alfred states that he was 'not sharp in his thinking'.[4] This judgement, which placed him as an antitype of his brother Max, continued to apply more or less throughout his life. Admirers of his elder brother tended to consider Alfred's writings rather woolly, and in a letter to his parents in 1889 – when both brothers were trying to cure themselves of nervous disorders – he said of himself that 'the field of activity assigned to him by Nature' was more in the theoretical than the hard-empirical branch of research.[5] Later he thought that the 'damned computation of statistical surveys on domestic industry' had damaged his nerves.[6] Theory as a refreshing mountain cure for empiricism: a truly scandalous attitude for Max Weber, the champion of large surveys. Yet Alfred

Weber already had a chair by the age of thirty-six, and so even did Karl, the third-born, whom Max ultimately considered a 'windbag' (WB 150). One cannot help thinking that – to use the language of Max Weber – a 'genteel charisma' played its part in the careers of the three Webers.

Max Weber's youthful correspondence with Alfred testifies to an intense exchange of ideas about most of the themes that were later of importance to them: religion, politics, history, bouts of depression. We can see Max developing here a number of the positions that would later become associated with him. In these younger years, Alfred felt himself to be much more unstable than Max, both mentally and nervously. In 1899 he wrote to his desperate elder brother, whom he would eventually survive by thirty-eight years, that his (Max's) 'neurasthenia' was 'of course only a passing phenomenon' in the context of his 'whole constitution', whereas his own was 'constitutional';[7] a doctor had diagnosed in him an incurable 'weakness of the cortex'.[8] Even in 1902 Alfred thought that 'he and Max were equally placed in terms of health'.[9] The two brothers would play the role of nerve specialist with each other, and Marianne believed that the tensions between them were not least a problem of nerves.[10] For many years Alfred was incensed by their mother's preference for her eldest. In 1916 he could still write to Else Jaffé: 'But you know – Mother can be *unjust* – she really only sees Max.'[11] All through his life he preserved 'a veritable phobia for everything going by the name of family',[12] and the idea never came to him to start one of his own.

It is clear from an argument between the brothers in 1887 that Max Weber was then already moving towards a critique of knowledge but also orienting towards practical reality, and that both of them were thinking of how to stave off depression. The nineteen-year-old Alfred was suffering from severe attacks, sometimes so intense that they affected his speech.[13] He had gone up a 'terribly wrong path' and 'lost everything unconscious', he complained to his elder brother, expressing a vision of the unconscious as the source of *joie de vivre*; 'and, in trying to get to know myself and finding only weakness and incompetence, I have come to feel a positive revulsion for myself.'[14] Max suggested that his gloomy pictures of the world were no more than arbitrary projections, and that he would do better to ask himself how he had arrived at them. As to Emmy, he assured her that he had previously been 'most intimately acquainted' with the 'spectres' with which his 'undoubtedly troubled brother' was now grappling (JB 227) – a revelation concerning Weber's youthful bouts of depression about which other sources are silent. He was trying to bring it home to Alfred that he was taking theory much too seriously, if he thought he had to despair of the world because of certain theoretical views. But anyone who appreciated even a little 'the slight value and general shakiness of our cognitive tools' would never for that reason give up the 'striving for knowledge'. Only practice helps us to extricate ourselves from 'theoretical difficulties', 'but it does so easily enough' (JB 263, 265). Max Weber himself remained a theorist – but in his thinking he was oriented to action.

Alfred Weber: the naturalistic challenge

In later years this brotherly relationship developed into a field of tension such as no novelist could have better imagined, in which rivalry over the same woman and confrontation at an intellectual and moral level combined with mutual learning processes and temporary convergence in the political struggle. In Alfred, Max Weber found himself facing the naturalism that he detested so much at that time. This took three forms: the introduction of organological categories into the social sciences; sympathy for the kind of love of nature associated with the Wandervogel youth movement; and, last but not least, affirmation of one's own physical-psychological nature, especially in the sexual sphere. Alfred repelled Marianne and Helene with his remark that he needed 'people free of priggishness', and they drew a connection between his personal morals and his scientific 'naturalism' and Darwinism.[15] On one occasion Max exploded in front of his then assistant, Hans Staudinger, and abused Alfred as a 'corrupter of the youth who puts his personal judgement and fantasies in the place of objective knowledge'. Max thought it fashionable prattle when Alfred, following a new trend in Germany, counterposed 'culture' and 'civilization' to each other, but he shared his brother's horror at the ever increasing bureaucratization.[16]

For some time Alfred Weber, whose first professorial appointment was in Prague, kept his distance from German imperialism. In October 1900 Marianne reported to her husband that Alfred (for whose charm she otherwise had a weakness) had again 'expressed quite comical visions of national expansion – though for the time being he wants nothing to do with them'. In 1914, however, he was swept along even more strongly than Max by the pro-war mood and displayed the whims of a naturalism untouched by any critique of knowledge. 'By some standards of civilization we really are barbarian', he wrote in 1915 to his beloved Else, before putting it in print, 'but at bottom this is only because our nature is so strong, and so directly perceives and does what is essential, that it repeatedly breaks through the limits of convention.' Nor was that enough. 'In general', he added, 'the most fruitful way of looking at the state is to see it as primordially biological – that is, as born out of the pressure to struggle and expand.'[17] One would not contradict the view expressed by Max in 1916, when he wrote of his brother that he was 'impulsive, suggestible and liable to go to extremes', theatrical and sometimes 'lacking a sense of proportion'.[18]

For some years he no longer cared to see Alfred. Towards the end of the war, however, the two brothers drew closer to a left liberalism, where each in his way experienced political failure. After Max's death, when Alfred had no initial success in resuming his love affair with Else, Max's other lover, Mina Tobler, tried to seduce him – in vain, it would seem.[19] Already before the affair with Else, Alfred had had a reputation for a lively sex life, but apparently the gossips had overdone it.[20] According to what we know today, Else was *the* great love of his life, and he fell into despair whenever a separation was threatened. He was more serious in love than he often appeared to be externally – which is probably one reason why Max Weber always preserved a certain respect for him as well as a feeling of attachment. In 1958, after Karl Jaspers had spoken at a memorial meeting following Alfred's death, the 84-year-old Else wrote to him: 'It especially moved me that you spoke of his ascetic nature; this was left to you to discover and it is an accurate description. He was quite remote from any self-indulgence, even of the permissible kind.'[21] When Else wrote those lines – knowing how highly Jaspers valued asceticism – she probably had on her lips that slightly amused smile which so drew men to her, but they may well contain more than half the truth.

Phratry and fraternitas: brotherhood as the key to social history and ultimately to mysticism

'Brotherhood' and 'confraternity': these terms acquired remarkable salience in Weber's writings after, but not before, 1910. It was in that year, at the sociological conference in Frankfurt, that he first introduced the confusing concept of 'acosmic love of humanity' – a boundless love beyond legal systems and responsibilities – and added that such love was 'community' on the 'purely human foundation of "brotherhood"'. However different were the forces driving early Christian communism and its later descendants, they were always connected with the 'old tradition of naturally evolved brotherhood relations', in which 'the community of eating and drinking grounded a family-style community'. This also explains the ancient Christian prohibition of interest on loans, since 'brothers do not haggle with one another or employ *droit de seigneur* (and interest is *droit de seigneur*); among brothers one does not seek one's own advantage but practises brotherhood' (GASS 470). Brothers may hate each other, but they do not bargain with each other.

Weber spoke of this association with 'naturally evolved' brotherhood as a law of nature, and from that time on he liked to dwell on the theme. It should be noted that consanguinity is not necessarily decisive for such brotherhood, but the bonding factor always involves something intensely physical: a shared feast of eating and drinking (the primal pleasure for the young Weber); the swearing of oaths ('all those primitive contracts' in which blood or saliva is mingled and drunk (E&S 672)); or, not least, the common struggle in which even more blood flows. For Weber, such fraternity became the model of socialization *tout court*. His feeling for the elemental and the passionate, even to the point of offensiveness, is not the least attraction of his work and raises it above the level of a sociological seminar paper.

First of all Weber discovered the phratries, those 'brotherhoods' which were originally the forms of socialization in ancient Greece (AS 149f.). He could not have derived this special significance of the phratry from the wording of ancient sources, but must have reconstructed it mainly from a study of ethnological findings, especially among the Iroquois peoples.[22] He thought that phratries did not necessarily originate in blood relationships but were based more on 'shared food'; they originally had a duty to exact blood revenge, however, and therefore offered the only legal guarantee in early times. He did not doubt that they were 'very old'. Weber also discovered phratries in ancient India; the *raja* was originally the head of the phratry, which was an 'association of militarily (at first, magically) trained soldiers' (MWG I/20, 115). An almost natural law was discernible through all the vicissitudes of Indian history: 'the social process always resumed its firm course of charismatic clan organization of tribes, phratries and sibs' (RI 54). They were not simply a starting-point for the development of larger social units, but a form of socialization that could be found over and over again.[23]

The productive power of confraternity reached its peak in the 'old Christian spirit of brotherhood'[24] and the autonomous city republic of the medieval West. In the case of the early Christians, Weber needed only to follow their own appellation. The theologian Adolf von Harnack, whom Weber knew personally, noted in a study of early Christian 'We-consciousness' that they did not use the obvious reference to one another as 'friends', because they preferred 'a term which was still more warm and close, viz. "brethren" '.[25] The terminology of brotherhood has persisted into modern times among monks, priests and 'revivalist' Christians, and Weber must have been familiar with it from that milieu. 'Brotherhood as a force of selfless sacrificial community and of human solidarity generally' is for the later Weber – though not yet for the Weber of *The Protestant Ethic* – the heart of any religion of salvation (WB 323). It enters into a tense relationship with the other great redemptive power, eroticism, which 'inevitably leads to unbrotherly behaviour, secret lovelessness' (WB 323); in other words, sexual love endangers spiritual love. Sexual asceticism is therefore not a value in itself but a prerequisite for boundless fraternal love. Max Weber himself experienced over many years the capacity of Eros to disturb brotherhood. Yet brotherly love does stand somewhere close to erotic love: the two are equally remote from cold purposive rationality; the original confraternity means that those participating in it, beyond any mere attachment for a purpose, 'allow another "soul" to enter into themselves'.[26]

Weber's ideas concerning 'brotherliness' are at their most intense in the characteristic *Zwischenbetrachtung*, where highly personal reflections on erotic life insinuate themselves into his scholarly writing. Whereas ethnologists usually place the phratry within the context of a system, ranging it under a tribe or a clan or kinship group – much as already for Aristotle it was an intermediate level between *phyle* and *genos* – brotherhood for Weber is a union of people's own natural vitality, not a function of a social system. And if, towards the end of the famous *Zwischenbetrachtung*, the 'intermediate reflection' in his essays on the sociology of religion, he discerns the 'rising world dominion of unbrotherliness' (FMW 357), we can hear a definite undertone of mourning. In *Science as a Vocation*, he interjects quite in passing that 'every act of genuine brotherliness may be linked with the awareness that it contributes something imperishable to the superpersonal realm' (FMW 155), only to add at once that this point does not belong there. For one moment a spiritualist idea flashes across the page: belief in a spiritual realm where nobility of mind accedes to eternity.

In fraternity strengthened by an oath, Weber thought he could detect the kernel of the medieval municipality's striving for 'freedom', and hence the origin of the West's special path in world history. Here, unlike in the case of Christian communities, he moved away from the historical sources:[27] for these use the term *fraternitas* mainly for religious communities *within* the commune, and only rarely for its burghers as a collective. Most typically, as Klaus Schreiner points out, it was thirteenth-century urban theologians who evoked the *vinculum fraternitatis*, which was supposed to 'bind burghers to a *naturalis societas* on the basis of their common human nature (*naturaliter*)', against the widening gap between rich and poor.[28] In reality, there was not only brotherly love but also a lot of deadly hatred within the communes. In Max Weber's own experience, however, hate and brotherliness were not contradictory. He did not love all his brothers, but he did feel attached to them all through his life. And he found everywhere in history elements of such a tense brotherliness.

The student fraternity of song and drink: one of Weber's elemental experiences of socialization

In Germany in those days people became drinking brothers, and alcohol was also fundamental to the life of student fraternities. Here too we encounter one of the love–hate relationships so typical of Weber. In April 1882, on the train taking him to his first summer semester at Heidelberg, he already merrily joined other students in their high-spirited drinking and smoking, to the annoyance of other passengers. Ideally he would have liked to have been jostled by a member of a student duelling society, so that he could have challenged him there and then (JB 38). But undoubtedly he had a thirst not only for beer but also for knowledge, and he was careful not to fritter away his course of studies. At least he attached great value to them in the letters he sent home, especially as, like so many 'merry' students, he did not always get by on his monthly allowance.

In the medical records of students and ex-students who were admitted to a sanatorium with suspected neurasthenia or syphilis, one quite often finds the formulation that the patient had indulged in alcoholic and sexual excesses, '*in Baccho et venere excediret*'.[29] Students commonly followed a booze-up with a visit to a brothel together. The *Burschenschaften* fraternities were traditionally more decorous in sexual matters than the *Korporationen* (regular student societies), but since 1877–8 – Weber was able to date it that precisely – 'libertinism' had been raging among them too (MWG II/5, 639, 617). When he was asked 'how he was able to save himself from being

Figure 2.2 Max Weber as a member of the Alemannia student fraternity in Heidelberg

dragged along to a brothel, the answer came in a deep voice: "I outfought them all and drank them all under the table" ' (B 619). As we see, it was the style of students in Weber's circle to speak very openly about sex, and he himself, in his bear's growl, made no secret of the fact that, precisely because he did not show off his manhood sexually – a wise decision in view of the risk of syphilis – he paraded it all the more proudly in fighting and drinking.

In Heidelberg he experienced a little of the old gulf between the *Burschenschaften*, with their roots in liberalism and progressive national- ism, and the old student duelling societies or *Korps*, with their high pecu- niary demands and their elitist arrogance that led them to set dogs on anyone they considered *non grata*. (Weber's uncle Adolf Hausrath had once been on the receiving end, when he crossed them in his role as vice- chancellor during a riotous confrontation with the police (JB 58).) In 1895, at a celebration to mark eighty years of the German *Burschenschaften*, Max Weber, by then a professor, praised them as a 'bulwark of liberty' against 'the poisonous reptile of overambition' (MWG I/4-2, 731). After some hes- itation, he had joined the *Burschenschaft der Alemannen*, the one to which his father already belonged. It set his mind at ease that the fraternity did not monopolize his time, since 'most of the medical students were in upper grades and close to their exams' (JB 60f.). We sense his respect for the work discipline of practical scientists: then, unlike today, a humanities student did not inhabit a milieu purely given over to the humanities. When Weber continued his studies in Berlin and Göttingen (in 1884–5), his letters no longer made any mention of life in the student fraternities.

In his early period of concentrated work as a professor, after seven long and often dull years (1886–93) in the Charlottenburg parental home, Max Weber turned again to *Burschenschaft*-style drinking bouts that lasted well into the night. But, when his health collapsed, so too did this male company based on beer and wine. Some years later, once he became capable of writing again, he displayed reservations verging on contempt for the life of the student societies, together with revulsion for the 'parvenu', the 'big shot' and the 'characterless' type of the civil servant. Weber always remained an advocate of elite education, and so for him the starting point was that student societies, despite the empty phrases churned out by 'old boys', actually encouraged negative selection and cultivated inferior 'plebeians'. He even resorted to the concept of 'degeneracy', which he otherwise considered rather suspect. 'For many, the main point of these student associations is not at all to cultivate honour and morals but simply to secure advancement in life. As things are nowadays, the puniest offspring of German privy councillors or councillors of commerce' – Weber here uses the feminine form of the noun 'councillor', evidently assuming that paternity is never certain – 'have to show truly modest "pluck" in getting themselves marked by a few scars, because ... it is indispensable for "connections"' (MWG I/8, 183f.). He revealed that he was speaking from painful personal experience and had retained from it what is nowadays called 'body memory': 'I have no hesitation in saying this quite openly ... I have myself experienced the difficulty of getting out of my system the gestures that are instinctively practised at the university when one is immature. The same thing may be said – and again I speak from my own rather serious experience – about the significant effect of a fraternity student's drinking habits on his productive power' (WB 427).

Weber's love–hate relationship to duelling

Already in 1897, with Saar coal baron Freiherr von Stumm in mind, Weber railed against 'the repugnant phenomenon of a new industrial nobility, with its public reputation for duelling that the very supporters of the duel find so disgusting' (MWG I/4-2, 634). (Stumm had recently challenged to a duel Adolph Wagner, a leading *Kathedersozialist*, who had refused to accept the challenge and taken the opportunity to heap public scorn on the whole practice of the duel,[30] nevertheless receiving loud acclaim from the student population; even in the imperial period it was sometimes possible to boost one's popularity by *rejecting* a challenge to a duel.)[31] At the same time, however, Weber hinted that he fully defended duelling in principle, and a prickly notion of honour was always part of his personal bearing and even his style of sociology. In 1920 the obituary of Weber in the *Frankfurter*

Zeitung said that this was in evidence 'at all times, whether at the speaker's rostrum, before a stormy mass meeting or in a students' duel' (WzG 35) – and there were certainly many such situations in the latter period of his life.

For all his political aversion to the corporations, Weber retained a weakness for the student duel. Later he recalled: 'There were no *problems* for us – we were convinced that anything which came up could somehow be settled by a duel.' Needing some kind of abreaction, the sensitive Weber experienced duelling as an opportunity to resolve atmospheric tensions, to clear the air and to overcome his youthful uncertainty about how he should behave; the 'snappiness' inculcated through the student fraternity and then in the army 'removed the pronounced inner shyness and insecurity of my boyhood years' (WB 70). Until the end of his life he thought of duelling not as a feudal relic but as a custom with a future. In 1918, in a speech to Austrian officers, he said that in 1904 American students had asked him 'about nothing' more often than the German practice of duelling; for they considered it 'chivalrous' and 'a sport they had to have too' (PW 278). The duel was a kind of fighting which at the same time consolidated common feeling, precisely with the opponent; this pleased Weber and had a beneficial effect on him. The *Burschenschaft* cultivated a distinctly unsentimental kind of fraternity: 'The brothers did not associate with friendly warmth, but were cold as ice toward one another. . . . The only poetic element was the choral singing of those magnificent student and patriotic songs' (WB 70). 'Right up to his death he used to hum the songs he had sung in those days' (B 619).

At the sociologists' conference in 1910, however, he spoke with biting irony of the German male choirs that were then experiencing their golden age. 'Someone who is daily accustomed to letting powerful emotions stream from his breast through his larynx, with no relationship to his behaviour and therefore no adequate abreaction of the mighty feeling in correspondingly mighty actions – such is the essence of choral society art – is someone who will very easily be a "good citizen", in the passive sense of the word' (GASS 445). Here we see Weber, who reacted so angrily to the theory that people should discharge their libido for the sake of their health, present an abreaction theory of his own. Treitschke had once celebrated male singing during the Wars of Liberation as the most wonderful expression of a new German strength and joy in battle;[32] but then song and struggle had gone together, and it was a hundred years in the past. In Weber's time the fencing room was often played off in universities against sentimental male choirs.[33] For Weber, willingness to fight was part of the primal male society; without clear-cut sources he even detected a warrior society behind the ancient Greek polis.[34] Patriotic male choirs were genuine only where this fighting spirit was present – otherwise they were painful imitations. It was the guarantee of their sonorous quality.

Weber's attitude to duelling has many personal elements and is not just a reflection of his age. The constitutional historian Georg von Below, whom Weber valued highly as an academic ally, had been maimed in his left arm through duelling and later conducted a historically based campaign against it as an un-Germanic custom imported from France. His polemics found an echo in public opinion and appear to have done no harm to his reputation; a professor in imperial Germany did not need to engage in duelling, especially if he lived far from Prussia in the south of the country. In fact, despite repeated threats of a duel, Weber did not really take the practice seriously outside the student fraternities. We should consider what it meant to 'demand and give satisfaction' through duelling in imperial German society, where certain unwritten limits applied. Paradoxically, of all the leading figures in Germany, only the labour leader Ferdinand Lassalle – who had no feel for the limits – actually died in a duel. Prince Philipp of Eulenburg, on the other hand, the influential confidant of Wilhelm II, loathed the division of the population into those 'capable' and 'incapable' of 'giving and demanding satisfaction', and described it as an instance of Prussian narrow-mindedness.[35]

The army: a high point of physical experience

Military service for Weber proved to be an emotional roller coaster. At no other time are his early letters so detailed and so dramatic. In the first few months there is no end to the complaints; Alfred moaned much less when his turn came a few years later. At the beginning of 1884, Max snorted to his father about the 'perfidy of this beautiful military service' and constantly denounced 'army life' as 'too revolting and soul-destroying' (JB 86, 115). The tone is maintained, but the worst comes when he complains of the wasted time, the 'terrible killing of time' or *Zeittotschlag* (the standard term for the kind of playing at soldiers in which nothing else is killed) (JB 91, 90, 102), and when he rages about all the knowledge he could have been acquiring. He feels the resentment of lower-class recruits and NCOs against the 'one-yearer' with higher education, who does not even have to sleep in the murk of the barracks. And again and again he notes the humiliation at the hands of coarse NCOs, who have a whole arsenal of colourful insults and mockery at their disposal when they make the conscripts crawl through the mud. 'That one-yearer over there, you nasty piece of work, stick your nose right in the muck!' 'You lump of rat meat, you one-yearer there, your bayonet is hanging down behind you like a white elephant's tail!' (JB 95) Weber had to put up with 'endless cheek from the most wretched of scoundrels' (JB 90), without being able to hit back by challenging them to a duel. Among the 'ingenious instruments of torture', in which, 'as Papa put it', he might 'learn to recognize Jesus Christ' (JB 77), a particularly bad one was the horizontal bar on which he could feel all the flab he had acquired from his student drinking. 'Man, it's like a couple of thousand gallons o' Schlitz swingin' from the bars', ranted the NCO in Berlin dialect (WB 72). The officers thought it funny that Weber sweated so profusely; the captain even presented him as a perspiration 'monster' (JB 130).

When we read such things today, we might think that Weber had every reason to become an anti-militarist. Already in the war games he gained an idea of the brutal and odiously primitive nature of war, and of the fact that in the harsh real world it is by no means a rational form of conduct. In a letter to his mother, who thought military service healthy, he tried to shock her by drawing the most dramatic picture of what happens in an attack:

> Finally, the whole line rushes at the enemy with fixed bayonets, howling like beasts (they are supposed to be shouts of 'Hurrah!'). In the process, of course, one is regularly knocked down or gets one's hands stepped on or is hit over the head with a gun barrel or is stabbed in the hollow of the knee by the bayonet of the man behind. The officers involved ride in the rear and give a thousand fast and furious commands which, of course, are not understood, and this finally degenerates into a horrible, elephantine roar. (WB 75).

We do not need to take all this quite literally: complaining is part of the soldier's style, as much today as it was then. Besides, Weber had to be sure of making the greatest possible impression on his parents, since he had never spent as much money as he did in the army (on the constant washing of sweat-stained shirts, among other things).

Exciting torments

Between the lines, however, one senses that Weber also enjoyed these descriptions; scarcely anywhere else did he draw such masterful strokes of burlesque or express physical experiences so earthily. In March 1894 during manoeuvres in Poland, as he sat on the mattress into which a bony-bottomed predecessor had pressed an acute angle, he wrote in detail about his own bulging posterior (WB 194); the main focus in the army is rightly on the body, the whole body, rather than the head. For many hitherto sheltered sons of the bourgeoisie, and certainly for Max Weber, military service meant a physical experience that got deep under their skin: a loss of privacy and a previously unknown lack of detachment from their own body. Quite a few seem to have had then their first education in sexual matters.

In Weber's graphic accounts of army life there is an increasing undertone of contentment. Especially when the exercises in the mud were over and he was preparing to become a reserve officer, he actually began 'to enjoy the business' (JB 156). He also quite liked the fact that in the army there was always an excuse for high alcohol consumption: he repeatedly wrote home about the 'patriotic soldiers' songs', in which 'brandy (*Branntewein*) always rhymed with German Rhine, and fatherland with schnapps in the hand' (JB 83, 96). In this context he described 'beer honesty' as the 'fundamental tenet of my life' (WB 193).

All in all, Weber's letters from the army are much jollier than those from his honeymoon. Besides, the military exercises near Posen (today's Poznań) in 1888 gave him the first impetus for his major work on east German farm-workers, which was decisive for his start in academic life. To a Max Weber such exercises imparted a sense for the flat landscape and the dependence of social conditions on the soil. 'The manoeuvres will be in a poor region, so I shall get a bit of cultural history out of them', he wrote to Alfred from Posen in 1888 (JB 305).

In the spring of 1887, when the popularity of France's revanchist war minister General Boulanger was undergoing a meteoric rise, the pro-Bismarck press in Germany kept fuelling expectations of war in order to pressure the Reichstag to pass the military budget. For a time Weber held the 'firm belief' that hostilities 'would start within a few days'; he made himself 'almost completely ready for war' as a reserve officer and, as he wrote to his mother, even sprinkled his quarters with 'all manner of mur-derous instruments'. He brushed aside as despicable the really unfounded 'claim of the liberal press that the war cries had been staged for electoral purposes' (JB 217f.). One gets the impression that there was something thrilling about the prospect of war, especially as he was bored stiff at the time with his legal studies.

Male society as the primal pleasure and the prototype of socialization

For the newly qualified Professor Max Weber, alcohol-tinged male company, even without deeper friendships, seems to have been what excited him *par excellence*: it was the only society in which the sense of being eter-nally harried left him. Marriage was not able to offer him that. In Eduard Baumgarten's view, there was clearly 'a quite elemental kind of sociability in Weber: he was a buddy with all his soul, a buddy for the moment thought capable of creating happiness; a drinking pal, a song mate, an accomplice in furious story-telling and boasting' (B 618). Weber felt the delight of this male company as a primal social experience and a key to the earliest processes of human socialization. 'We're happy as cannibals, happy as swine, hundreds of swine', sing the boozers in Auerbach's tavern whom Mephisto has made drunk.[36] The students of Weber's time felt in their drinking bouts like the old Germans in Wilhelm Ruer's song: 'They lay upon bear skins / And drink ever just one more.' Intoxicated by alcohol, growling and laughing, one feels indeed like primeval man.

Weber read with pleasure[37] the great work of Heinrich Schurtz pub-lished in 1902, *Altersklassen und Männerbünde – Eine Darstellung von Grundformen der Gesellschaft*, a novel and knowledgeable account of early socialization based upon critical analysis of recent discoveries in ethnology. The book, which gave an impression of meticulous research, had a 'breath-taking' effect on the academic world.[38] It was a shot across the bows of the fashionable theory of primitive matriarchy, which had already met with robust opposition on the part of Max and Marianne Weber. According to Schurtz, the 'pure sociability drive' leading beyond the relationship between the sexes was originally male, not female. 'The male pleasure in fighting is by no means inconsistent with the presence of this sociability drive, but is its necessary complement in so far as combat is regularly the prelude to lasting unity based upon mutual discovery of the other's value and prowess.' An understanding of this allows us 'in the main to settle the dispute that has been raging for years over the primal forms of society, without having recourse to artificial theories of reality'. We must not project back into the earliest times contemporary idealist images of humanity or fantasies about free love, but must recognize 'that man emerged from animal and lower beginnings and still plainly carries the traces of this origin'.[39]

Schurtz was just the right reading to strengthen the conclusions that Weber drew from his own experience of male company for the history of human society. Even from today's point of view, we can say that this heuristic use of his own experience was not entirely misguided. But it was Weber's style to keep applying a cold shower to his own emotions. 'Sober' (*nüchtern*) became one of his favourite words: 'sobriety', in both the literal and the metaphorical sense, characterizes the Puritans as well as 'conscientious scholars'. The path from the pleasant companionship of fellow drinkers to the scholarship typical of the later Weber is not direct and unmediated but has to pass through a cold shock.

3

From Father's Boy to Mother's Boy: A Comradely Marriage and the Day of Judgement for the Father

Max Weber as 'old bear' and as bridegroom

The love story between Max and his distant cousin Marianne Weber began on 11 January 1893, with a shattering declaration to Marianne by the young theologian Paul Göhre. It was the most terrible day of her youth, for she already secretly loved Max and felt a certain apprehension towards Göhre. But Helene, the mistress of the house, most energetically supported his courtship of Marianne, and so she feared that she would waste away in the little town of Lemgo, with no more invitations to Charlottenburg, if she were to reject him. She therefore decided to tell Helene of her love for Max. Helene was extremely upset, but she was clever enough to see that she was dealing with a stronger will than her own and that she would do best to join forces with it.

But Max? How did he stand in relation to the drama unfolding before his eyes? At that time he was working with Göhre every day on the farmworkers' survey, and the theologian enjoyed a certain reputation in socially conscious Protestant circles because of his first-hand report *Drei Monate Fabrikarbeiter und Handwerksbursche*. The truth is that Weber's feelings at that point are somewhat of a mystery. Marianne wanted to believe in a tacit understanding that she and Max belonged to each other, but they had not yet made things open between them and, rather oddly, found no opportunity to do so in the period immediately following 11 January. Helene decided that Max would be too agitated by meetings with Marianne, and the two seem to have accepted her maternal command.[1]

Weber's relationship with his first cousin Emmy Baumgarten had something strangely imaginary about it: he had not seen her for five years, and even in autumn 1892, when she became a long-term patient in a health resort, he visited her only briefly (WB 177). Yet he still felt a sense of duty towards her. And he also entertained doubts about whether he was cut out for marriage or for a bachelor's existence. 'An old bear like me is better off trudging alone in his cage', he wrote to Klara shortly before his engagement (JB 361), perhaps also to give his beloved sister the illusion that he would not betray her with a fiancée. 'What an old bachelor you have taken for yourself, my child', he wrote to Marianne when they were already engaged, referring to her as if she too were now above all his niece. 'Sometimes I am still quite depressed, as though I were the object of an enormous aberration of taste on your part' (WB 181).[2] Again and again we find this (actually well-founded) concern that Marianne did not really know him and was placing in him hopes that he could not fulfil. Before he became Marianne's fiancé, as again towards the end of his life when he was wavering between Marianne and Else, he would much rather have left the decision up to the women. Sometimes he shocked women close to him with the crude view 'that to create and maintain human happiness is of little importance'.[3] In private life he was already taking the position that he would apply in 1895 to politics and political science, in his inaugural address at Freiburg.

A puzzling letter of courtship

What are we to make of the long and mysterious letter that Marianne received from Max Weber twelve days after the unpleasant surprise of 11 January 1893? Was it even a letter of courtship? Essentially Max played the part of the one being wooed.[4] But what was his response to Marianne's wooing? She heard from him only the YES that she so eagerly awaited, although she knew that it was a conditional 'yes' which assumed that he would be able to save face towards Emmy. Later, Marianne wrote that his letter had sent her into 'ecstasy' – but only for a while (WB 180), because its ambiguity was soon brought home to her.

In her diary Marianne describes her reading of the letter as if it were a religious revelation: 'When I had read it, having truly experienced "the miraculous", I felt that my life had not been lived in vain and that this hour made everything worthwhile – even if the future were to bring nothing other than privation. It was like a miracle from God.' Then she called Helene, who was already familiar with the contents of the letter and could only sigh mysteriously: 'Child, you don't know yet how hard it will be!' The sharp-sighted mother clearly suspected that her eldest faced a block in the realm of the senses.[5]

So, what was in the letter to his bride-to-be that Marianne reproduces over four pages of the German edition of her biography (WB 177ff.)?[6] Even today everyone reads something else from the cryptic formulations contained in it, and women interpret it differently from men. Female readers are struck by the author's colossal egocentricity as he keeps circling around his own emotional depths. He also sets out his conditions for marriage – so that at times we feel the presence of the legal expert, for whom marriage is first and foremost a contract. We should bear in mind that the letter was also intended for the eyes of his mother, and it becomes clear that

Paul Göhre – towards whom Max Weber had a guilty conscience – would be informed of its contents.

Max Weber begins with a solemn and animated assurance: 'I shall *never* dare to offer a girl my hand like a free gift. Only if I myself am under the divine compulsion of complete, unconditional devotion do I have the right to demand and accept it for myself.' He can demand 'unconditional devotion', but a woman cannot demand it of him. A bond of love is based not on free choice but on 'divine compulsion'. Did he at that time feel such a compulsion from on high towards Marianne? The woman would have liked to believe so. For Weber, however, what he felt in his inner being was evidently still hazy and ambiguous.

Only one thing was clear to him: that he was not spontaneously capable of devotion. Whereas a 'normal' man can to some extent steer his libido, Weber felt that it was completely beyond his power – and it was a realistic assessment of himself. In these matters he was at the mercy of the gods. In the letter he is remarkably shy to use the word 'love': 'The word must not pass my lips, for I have a double debt to pay to the past and do not know whether I am able to do so.' It is doubtful whether we should take literally the pathos of this self-tormenting attempt to come to terms with his past. When he later fell in love with Else the thought of her husband did not cause him any scruples, even though he was then funding Weber's journal. So, it seems clear that he himself doubted whether what he felt for Marianne was sexual love.

Then come the two key parts of the mysterious letter in which Max Weber speaks of his 'passions'. 'But you do not know me, you cannot possibly know me. You do not see how I try, with difficulty and varying success, to tame the elemental passions with which nature has endowed me' (WB 178). Marianne can ask his mother, who knows all about it. And further on:

> The tidal wave of passion runs high, and it is dark around us – come with me, my high-minded comrade, out of the quiet harbour of resignation, out onto the high seas, where men grow in the struggle of souls and the transitory is sloughed off. But *bear in mind*: in the head and heart of the mariner there must be clarity when all is surging underneath him. We must not tolerate any fanciful surrender to unclear and mystical moods in our souls. For when feeling rises high, you must control it to be able to steer yourself with sobriety'. (WB 178, 179)

Countless admirers of Weber have read these passages, but has anyone ever been able to interpret them? What did Marianne detect in the letter, and what did she understand by 'elemental passions'? Probably she thought of a seething erotic desire, which Max resolutely wished to contain within marriage but would be able to do so only with difficulty. How is her 'ecstasy' to be explained? And what did Max Weber himself wish to convey through the nautical metaphor? Probably he meant that he experienced his own sexuality as a wild force of nature, a violent and unsettling power that was both uncontrollable and ultimately unfathomable; we sense the degree to which marriage was for him an alarming leap into the unknown. At the same time, he turned himself and Marianne into mythical heroes, into comrades of Odysseus and the Argonauts, or even demigods from whom 'the transitory is sloughed off'.[7] Twenty years later, among the 'enchantresses' on Monte Verità, he wrote to Marianne that he, a new Odysseus, was being courted by 'the nymph Calypso' (WB 491f.).

In the same breath, however, a sharp rebuff of 'unclear and mystical moods'! A belief in sober realism combined with renunciation of the German Romantic tradition: these future character traits of Weber the academic are already emphatically found here – this too one of the first shafts of light illuminating the intimate relationship between science and life's troubles. But why this fear of fantasy even in love? One suspects here that Weber's own erotic fantasies were of such a kind that he could not stand by them – not yet anyway. He could not ground a bourgeois marriage on such fantasies. But did he seriously believe in such a marriage anyway? He calls his bride-to-be *Kamerad*, and Marianne herself liked the term.[8] In her biography she often speaks of Max and herself as '*Kameraden*'.[9] At that time the 'comradely marriage' [*Kameradschaftsehe*] had acquired a definite meaning from the eponymous bestseller by Ben B. Lindsen and Wainwright Evans: that is, a marriage with legally recognized birth control. By using this vocabulary, Marianne therefore gave the impression that her childlessness had been intentional.

Of course, we should read the letter not with today's eyes but against the cultural background of the feelings expressed in middle-class correspondence at that time, when love letters served as a kind of high school. Marianne later read a lot into such letters: for example, the correspondence between Wilhelm and Karoline von Humboldt, whose seven published volumes provide the most extensive documentation about a German marriage. At the age of fifty-six, Marianne brooded over them to Karl Jaspers: 'Sometimes I have the feeling: Are these people not *deceiving* each other? Are their amorous relations not in essence a kind of sentimental "literature"? Are they not secretly leading a double life, which originates in a divided consciousness?'[10] When she wrote those lines Siegfried A. Kaehler had just revealed, to the horror of Humboldt's idealistic admirers, that his ostensibly perfect marriage had concealed an abyss of alienation, infidelity and sado-masochism.[11] It may be that this gave Marianne some consolation and assisted her in the literary stylization of her own marriage.

The Webers' marriage contract

Although Weber addressed his bride-to-be as '*Kamerad*', he did not in 1893 conceive of their marriage as one of comradeship or companionship in the sense used by women's rights activists. As the legal expert Stephan Buchholz discovered, the marriage contract between the Webers was even by the standards of the time 'a model of lordly omnipotence among the living', while making generous provision for the eventuality of Marianne's widowhood (R 550). Since Marianne, in addition to a dowry of 16,619 marks that she brought to the marriage,[12] had the prospect of a handsome legacy from Oerlinghausen – a greater sum than what Max Weber could expect from his own parents – the critical issue was power of disposal over her future inheritance. It would mean not having to depend on a career in the civil service or business. And so, in the marriage contract Max Weber ensured that he would be assigned full powers of disposal, even though it was already quite common for wives to have at least limited rights themselves. (None other than Baron von Stumm, whom Weber furiously attacked as the worst kind of reactionary, had fought for women of means to have such rights.) Max Weber later spoke of Marianne's dowry as if it formed part of his own assets (MWG II/7-1, 328), but at the time she seems to have been too wrapped up in her love to bother about the details of the contract. In her history of the rights of married women, however, one can detect a certain bitterness about the imposition of his will in financial matters.

Marriage as 'an animal institution'

Already in 1892, during Weber's time as a student in Heidelberg, his cousin Otto Baumgarten reported the danger to the family from Max's description of marriage as 'an animal institution' and other naturalist trimmings with which he sprinkled his conversation (B 627). The highly moral Otto's attempts to re-educate his cousin were in vain. He sensed in the newly qualified student fraternity member an inclination to satisfy his sexual needs with loose-living girls rather than along the path of Christian marriage. But in reality it was precisely the sexual demands of marriage that frightened Weber; he saw the core of marriage as 'naturalistic' (or, more precisely, 'sexual'), and that is what nauseated him.

On a hot summer's day in 1892 Max and Marianne Weber were sitting 'quite alone for hours in the garden'. Max was working flat out on his report about farm-workers east of the Elbe. Marianne noted: 'It struck me as very sad when he said that man exists primarily to fulfil the purposes of nature, and that to do this he needs to have a feeling of happiness from time to time. He said this in his quiet, resigned way, which went straight through my heart.'[13] Again: Weber's picture of the world and man was thoroughly naturalistic, but he felt in himself no urge to fulfil the 'purposes of nature'. It is clear that reproduction was the specific issue here; and it saddened Marianne to feel that the thought of it was a mere burden to Max. Many years earlier he had written to Emmy that, 'as is well known', nature is 'nowhere as inventive and creative' as in the creation of 'difficulties' for man (JB 285).

In her biography, Marianne writes that in Max she could feel 'the crusts which feelings of guilt, renunciation, and repressions of all kinds had deposited on his nature' (WB 180). By then she had long since read Freud.

Figure 3.1 Max and Marianne Weber after their wedding, 1893

But in 1893 Weber had not yet committed the act of psychological patricide, and neither the student society nor the army was a milieu conducive
to the repression of sexual desires. In any event, Marianne had little success
in her efforts to loosen up her future spouse. Even the thirteen-year-old Lili
noticed that her eldest brother did not behave as men were wont to do with
their fiancée; engaged couples were usually 'much more tender and kissed
each other much more' (R 544).

   Of all occasions it was the family's celebration of Max Weber senior's
birthday which became for Marianne one of her 'days of grieving'. We can
deduce that it was not the only day of grieving during her engagement. She
felt that Max treated her badly; he never spoke to her at table, and it
seemed to her that he was deliberately ignoring her. In the end she burst
into tears. A few days later Helene made her explain what had happened,
going straight up to her – evidently in Max Weber's presence – and adding
these words to her eldest: 'So, Max, now you have a word with her.' And
Max does it, and Marianne puts up with it like a good girl. As her fiancé
instructs her, 'one has to control one's mood precisely at the critical
moment, otherwise the reaction is inevitable and there's nothing more to
be done.'[14] Mother and son think they can detect a serious lack of restraint
in Marianne's expression of her feelings; and she promises to do better in
future. After the wedding, however, she confesses to her husband – who
immediately passes it on to his mother – that she had 'been looking

ahead to marriage with a secret horror' but now found herself 'agreeably disabused'.[15]

The elderly Jaspers, though an ascetic admirer of Max Weber, put forward as a psychiatrist the succinct diagnosis that the marriage had made Marianne a 'sexual cripple'.[16] Did she also, in her innermost being, experience the fate of her marriage in the same way? We shall never know for sure. The old woman summed up in her memoirs: 'My life was so full in the personal and professional domain that little space remained for unrealizable desires in the conjugal sphere' (LE 56). The 'conjugal sphere': that was the sphere of sexuality and child-bearing. Marianne certainly felt such desires, and she had to recognize that they were 'unrealizable'. She developed a view of life that gave a meaning to this renunciation. She never complained about her childlessness, even though she could write that for many women the longing for love was fulfilled in motherhood. Was this a taboo subject? But there were scarcely any taboos in the Weber household.

In reality, the responsibility of children would have restricted her development 'personally and professionally'; she seems to have already thought that during her engagement. She never became an enthusiastic housewife and spoke rather disparagingly about women who were totally absorbed in the 'dreadful machinery of housekeeping';[17] the fiancée already preferred to help her future husband with his survey evaluation rather than prepare herself for the running of a household. She learned to 'cook properly' only in the hard times of autumn 1918.[18] 'Would the connubial duties not be a heavy sacrifice for her? Marianne thought: "Everything in due time"' (WB 189). But that time never came. And until the end of her life Marianne would brood over whether her childlessness was not contrary to her female nature.

Love–hate: stronger than harmonious love

Although Max Weber was by nature so aggressive and irritable, and although Marianne was anything but an embodiment of peace and quiet, there never seem to have been any major quarrels between the married couple; as a rule, the beginnings of one were soon cut short as both sides swallowed their annoyance. As in relations with his mother, Max evidently did not dare with Marianne to give free rein to his anger – in part probably because he knew that his mother got to hear of everything – and this may also have contributed to the fact that with Marianne, as with Helene, he had inhibitions about declaring his love. For raging came naturally to him. Perhaps he was able to love Else so uninhibitedly because over the years he had made her the object of an intense love–hate – a love–hate in which his whole relationship to nature culminated.

The memoirs of the philosopher Hermann Glockner contain a chapter that energetically seeks to dispel the 'myth of Heidelberg' side of Max Weber, although Weber himself never encountered the author in real life but only as a myth. Glockner allows the philosopher Heinrich Rickert – who knew Weber from their school days in Berlin and was again with him a lot during their time in Freiburg – to tell us what he has to say about the Weber couple in Freiburg:

> They lived in a rented house above a petty-bourgeois family who kept a close eye on when Max came home and what happened next. When he bought a leather cushion and dog whip and began to flog the cushion during the night, Marianne screamed on top of the noise. Of course, it was soon being said everywhere that Professor Weber beat his wife while drunk; they both thought this very funny. They wanted to attract attention, and that was not hard to do in the solidly Catholic town of Freiburg. Weber also said that he suffered from obsessional thoughts and, especially after nights of drinking, sometimes imagined for the whole of the next day that he was Jumbo the elephant and lived in a zoo. But those were his happiest hours, because he was not living alone. Smiling to himself with little twinkling eyes, he appeared each time to sink into sweet reveries. And when someone asked: 'What's the matter, Professor?' he whispered absent-mindedly: 'Those wicked, wicked women! You've no idea how nice it is when you have such a trunk!'[19]

This story is usually passed over by Weber's biographers: it is supposed to be untrustworthy, because it clashes too violently with the traditional image of Weber. However, the argument most commonly heard reminds one of the sentiment expressed by Palmström in Christian Morgenstern's poem 'Die unmögliche Tatsache': 'Such is his razor-sharp conclusion, / What must not be cannot be.' Glockner's memoirs are a mine of information about the scholarly Heidelberg milieu in the old days. An experienced historian will savour with caution some of the spiciest anecdotes, but is it conceivable that a man of Rickert's calibre would invent *such* stories?[20] To be sure, both he and Glockner would have derived a mischievous pleasure from presenting a Weber quite different from the myth: a man who had nothing, nothing whatsoever in common with the Knight of the Swan, that noble ascetic figure of medieval legend.[21] But that has no bearing on the reliability of these stories.

We must rid ourselves of the idea that Weber was at heart always the same as the man who later became world-famous. During his early years as a professor, there were evidently periods of high spirits when, with his inhibitions loosened by alcohol, he tried to break free from all constraints after the rigid limits imposed by his daily work routine; the night-time drinking bouts were for him the height of bliss. In Rickert's portrait we can detect the same pleasure in shocking others with his brutality that made itself felt in his inaugural address of 1895 in Freiburg. As a young professor, he still engaged in the kind of student pranks liable to annoy the petty bourgeoisie. He thought he could allow himself this luxury, since professors and students shared a world of their own in the university towns of the age; they simply laughed at what the petty bourgeois said about them.

In 1886 Krafft-Ebing's *Psychopathia sexualis* was published in the first of seventeen editions, and soon sadism and masochism became favourite topics of private conversation. Max Weber, one of whose strengths was that he never had too many illusions about himself, would have sensed that such feelings of pleasure were also part of his make-up. It is not psychologically absurd to imagine that, in a tipsy state, he might have pursued such pleasures as a joke – out of a probably correct instinct that it was best for him to gain a ludic relationship to his sexual abnormality. That elephants were present in his fantasies is apparent even in his scientific work. As we know, Weber attributed sexuality to the animal side of man; so, in his wishful dreams, it would have sometimes suggested itself to indulge in being an animal. And he could have known, even without reading Freud, that the elephant's trunk was a phallic symbol.

Marianne and sensual nature

But what of Marianne? As we have seen, she repeatedly declared her faith in a marital ideal in which the nobility of culture transcended nature. But not even Jaspers, who usually had a high opinion of the human capacity for sublimation, bought that kind of idealism from her. The truth is that 'nature' always remained a thorn in Marianne's side, both intellectually and emotionally. In 1909, when for the first time she noticed with despair Max Weber's love for Else, she did not feel able to condemn it; she was honest enough to admit that, caught between conjugal frustration and erotic feelings, she too had felt a longing for a new love. 'And had I not myself, in the times of upheaval caused by all the intake of erotic air around us, . . . played with the desire for new passion?'[22]

Again in 1911, after a boisterous summer festival, she noted: 'What a solid dose of "earthly desires" lies deep within my soul!' – although, at forty-one years of age, one 'no longer [has] any right to that kind of Dionysian existence, or at least one should never go looking for it.'[23] But that does not mean one has to resist if Dionysus appears all by himself! 'Ah, everyone needs a man's love', she sighed on 19 January 1912 in a letter to Helene, who had already been a widow for fifteen years. She did not believe the unmarried feminists when they said that they found in their profession an emotional substitute for a relationship with a partner.[24] As a fiancée she had felt 'very sorry' for the 'unsatisfied old maids'.[25] The fact that Bertha Schandau, her faithful and headstrong housekeeper for twenty-four years (1893–1917), was 'without any sexuality' seemed to Marianne a sign that there was something wrong with her.[26] She expected that maidservants in particular, being culturally incapable of sublimating their drives, permanently needed a sexual partner – which did not stop her from becoming indignant if any of her maids had an extra-marital relationship that was not a prelude to marriage.

In order to achieve a degree of peace, Max and Marianne Weber had to agree on a decidedly 'non-naturalistic', asexual conception of marriage. To be sure, this did not come quickly or unproblematically, especially as they both felt a deep need for their conduct in life to be consistent with their world-view. No realist can fail to recognize that sexuality is part of human nature and one of the elemental processes of socialization. And so it followed that, if conjugal relations failed, extra-marital sexual contacts had a law of nature on their side. This conclusion remained unspoken, but Max Weber drew it in practice during the last decade of his life. Marianne, on the other hand, wrestled with the problem all her life and was unable to solve it.

In their letters, the Webers cultivated an eternal honeymoon style brimming with a thousand embraces, without ever having experienced a real honeymoon. Today's reader should not be deceived by this style: much of it came out of a long tradition of sentimentality. The psychiatrist Hans W. Gruhle, a close acquaintance of the Webers, wrote in his contribution to the Weber memorial volume that letters were an especially dangerous source: 'I once knew a goldsmith who later murdered his lover to save on maintenance money, and shortly before the crime he was still writing her warm love letters – not because he felt so warmly about her but because "that's how people write"' (EG I 173). At least we may assume greater credibility in the case of Max Weber's letters, for he went along with the sentimental style less than other *Bildungsbürger* of his generation were inclined to do.

In her biography, Marianne attaches a higher meaning to the difficult years of their marriage. But it took a long time for this to become clear to her, and again and again she railed against her fate. She is silent about much of this in the biography, yet honest enough to hint to the attentive reader that her married life was for a long time far removed from the desirable ideal and that already 'the wedding trip, with its nervous haste', was a disappointment (WB 213). The wedding had to be timed to fit in with completion of the farm-worker project;[27] but if she thought a period of quiet would ensue she was thoroughly let down. The trip took place in the same mad rush as the work project before it. Weber had the same experience as countless workaholics after him: if you don't take active countermeasures, all the stress of your work conditions is transferred to your leisure time.

In those days, the honeymoon trip was still quite a new custom, typical more of the railway than the mail-coach age; it had only recently become possible to count on finding a clean hotel room for each overnight stay. Of course, honeymooners had the classical trips to Italy in mind, and they hoped, like Goethe, to find refreshment and a loss of sexual inhibitions in 'the land where lemons blossom'. But the railway and the growing tourist business helped to ensure that the economics of time continued to make itself felt on holiday. Marianne, who in later years often worried about her husband's overeating, was still able in Paris to enjoy the long French menus, which at least meant that Max calmed down for a while. 'We get along almost sadly well – Max talks a lot!!!!', Marianne wrote to Helene from the Seine, the four exclamation marks being her own.[28] In the biography the remark is slightly retouched: 'We get along almost too well' (WB 191). 'Sadly well' presumably alludes to their consensus about children: Max feels no desire to produce any, and Marianne no desire to bear any. When she talks a lot, however, she gets on her husband's nerves; at Whitsun 1895 he asks her to keep quiet during their evening stroll.

The misery of professorial marriages

Of course, we should be wary of using an ideal image of a 'normal' relationship to read too much abnormality into the Webers' marriage. If we look more closely at the stories of many relationships, we will see that the normal is the abnormal. At least by the standards of modern psychotherapists, quite a number of the Heidelberg professors of the time, who were thought of as comparatively relaxed and full of a zest for life, actually led a neurotic existence. This explains why the academic milieu there reacted with great understanding rather than attitudes of exclusion in the wake of Weber's breakdown. As Eberhard Demm wrote of colleagues and acquaintances of Weber's: 'The philosopher Heinrich Rickert suffers from agoraphobia and must therefore be accompanied and supported when he goes for a walk; Karl Jaspers had tics on his face which he has learned to control, but only at the price of a rigidly strained expression; the art historian Carl Neumann suffers from bouts of depression, repeatedly tries to take his life and has to be treated in psychiatric hospitals.'[29] For Marianne, Rickert in particular was 'a chronic Lazarus – now a problem here, now a problem there . . .'[30]

Marianne Weber spent a lot of time with Frau Rickert and was exposed to all her marital frustrations. Her husband was an interminable speaker: he could neither listen to his wife nor simply leave her in peace. 'And sometimes it is as if she chokes on the many things unsaid and all that is never abreacted. . . . She always has a pent-up store of irritability.' And Marianne waxes philosophical about professorial marriages: 'The drawback of marriage is that it becomes boring for the husband to listen to his wife, and generally in such academic marriages the wife is condemned to passivity as the one untrained in dialectic.'[31] Marianne knew such situations from her own marriage, and Max too got on her nerves with his penchant for monologue. But then he left her alone with their friends, and unlike other, poorly educated professors' wives she had something to say on many topics.

Above all, however, Marianne later had constantly before her eyes the cautionary example of the marriage of theologian Ernst Troeltsch, which at the same time gave her comfort that in her own marriage she had come off quite reasonably after all. Probably she tended for this reason to exaggerate 'old Troeltschie's' disagreeable character traits,[32] although sometimes she would have liked most to 'take him on (her) lap and stroke him'.[33]

Figure 3.2 Max Weber as professor in Heidelberg

Max Weber had a lot in common with Troeltsch, both as an academic and as a man. His *The Protestant Ethic* already owed so much to Troeltsch's stimulating suggestions that a number of reviewers gave him the main credit for the work, and from 1910 the two couples shared the same household in the Fallenstein villa. But long before that it continually irritated Marianne that Troeltsch was decidedly liberal as a theologian but incorrigibly patriarchal as a man. He probably reminded her of the loathed Adolf Hausrath, his fellow theologian at Heidelberg, with whom he shared not only liberal views but also the pleasure of running down every colleague.[34]

For some ten years 'Troeltschie's' glum stories about women were a constant theme in Marianne's letters to Helene. Again and again the theologian would whine for a wife,[35] but when he had one he did not know what to do with her and punished her with his disregard. Or, at least, that was how things appeared to Marianne, who doubtless also wanted to show Helene that her own marriage was quite reasonable in comparison with such misery. Troeltsch's first betrothal, to the daughter of a colleague, ended in an embarrassing altercation when his constant burial in work left her feeling too neglected.[36] Like Max Weber, Troeltsch cut a very masculine figure with his booming laughter.[37] But Marianne considered that he was also sexually impotent: she followed him with a smirk as he finally met the love-hungry captain's daughter Marta Fick, married her in 1901 and turned her into a total hysteric through his lack of sexual interest, with the result that she ran him down in company and he reacted with 'all kinds of moral contortions'.[38] Whereas the theologian wanted his marriage to be seen as 'actually very happy',[39] Marianne wrote to Helene that 'everyone had the impression of a very unhappy marriage';[40] she saw a striking lack of worldly wisdom in the fact that, unlike Max Weber, he was so blinkered in his male way that, when he was unable to satisfy his wife's 'conjugal needs', he did absolutely nothing to promote her 'practical' interests, either through education or in the women's movement. Moreover, she wrote to Helene in 1903, he suffered 'terribly from her completely uncontrolled temper': 'the poor creature evidently has neither a moral nor an intellectual counterweight that would allow her to bear the renunciation that fate demands of her.' And a year later: 'Oh, men are so stupid! They even train their wives to be intellectual nonentities!'[41] Seven years further on, she added in her diary some philosophical reflections on the tragedy of Troeltsch's marriage:

> How strong his nerves must be to endure the tension of life on a volcano, in the proximity of someone whom, for all the love, he is destroying psychologically. She is sullen about her fate, as it withholds the happiness to which she thinks herself entitled and which she needs more than almost anyone else for her moral development. Only 'nature', the fulfilment of her female destiny, could bring her peace. All other sources of help, all of life's other treasures, do not exist for her. It is a tragedy, for everything evil in her – and there is no little of it – . . . is growing – the good is being smothered.[42]

The sexually unsatisfied woman as a 'volcano', as a walking natural disaster! Marianne, already haunted by Else Jaffé's carefree attitude to sex, came to believe that the sensual woman who was 'all nature' – not therefore, as moralists thought, a deformation of female nature – needed sexual fulfilment to be capable of moral development. She felt womanly nature within herself too, and it was not easy for her to renounce it; her diary entry shows that, if only indirectly. We should not trust in oral history to deepen our knowledge of Marianne, for people alive today were acquainted with her only in the resignation of old age.

As other cases of academic marriage show, the Webers were not alone in their frustrations. It is true that, after the invitation to sail on the 'tidal wave of passion', Marianne must have expected something very different from what followed. But much in their marriage was then more normal than it sounds today: for example, imposition of the woman's will on the man in household matters, and of the man's will on the woman in the political and intellectual sphere. No special psychological explanation is required for the role-playing in which Max Weber verbally treated his wife as a child and she went along with it like a good girl – although it should be said that in reality she controlled everyday life in the home and even deleted from her manuscript such offensive references to her husband as a 'cowardly creature' or 'the dirty old devil' (meaning Aristophanes).[43] Other men like to have a map with them on their travels, but Marianne was expected to plan the route. More, he wanted her to decide whether he should accept or refuse the offer of a post, and he grew annoyed if she did not think herself capable of it (WB 191). A lot of today's clichés about the 'patriarchal' society of the nineteenth century – for example, that women asked their husband's permission to read the political pages of a newspaper – are quite remote from the reality. They greatly underestimate the independence of mind exhibited by many women.

For a time after their marriage, Marianne complained of the constant stream of evening visitors who talked and talked and never left, so that she was almost never alone. 'Max said comfortingly that we have fifty years to go till our golden wedding!!!'[44] Marianne thought this a grotesque remark, since her husband always worked in such a rush as if there were no time left at all. Such an extreme attitude to the use of time was not yet the rule in academic life, especially for professors with life tenure who were no longer under pressure to qualify. At some point in the autumn of 1894 it came to one of the rare marital flare-ups that Marianne has reported. To her complaints at being constantly neglected, Max countered that things were nevertheless relatively good, 'since he worked at home for part of the day', and that recently she had seen 'particularly much of him, more than 90 per cent of married people do'. In future it could easily happen that he 'would have to go out six evenings a week' – 'if he had some political activity, for example'.

> This rather shook me, as I imagined he would be fairly willing to give me quite a lot of time in this first year of marriage, and I cannot think of a marriage as ideal if we have little time for each other – in the end he was pale and so was I – I could no longer control myself and had to leave and cry my eyes out.[45]

It obviously did not occur to her to weep in his presence or to talk frankly about how such different ideas of life could be made consistent with each other; she presumably could not imagine how such a conversation would proceed. Max Weber revealed ever more clearly that for him there could be no reconciliation between such radically different attitudes to life. Where the differences could not be resolved through struggle, there was basically nothing more to be done. Helene, drawing on experience, did not need much imagination to realize that there was something wrong in the marriage, but she saw her daughter-in-law as the one who had to do something about it. Marianne afterwards called 'darling mother' the 'voice of the priest in the wilderness'![46]

Sexual polarity in Weber's thought

For many years Weber would define his own masculinity in a non-sexual way, and yet, perhaps for that very reason, masculinity was a high value for him.

In his writings – despite all the raging polemics against value-judgements in science and, precisely, the opposition to misogynistic prejudices – an identification of 'male' with 'fearless' and of 'female' with 'faint-hearted' and 'irrational' keeps creeping in. Towards the end of his life this actually becomes more pronounced: the most striking quotation on masculinity and science is to be found in *Science as a Vocation*, from 1919.

In 1905, when Weber supported the right to strike at the Mannheim congress of the Verein für Sozialpolitik, he branded the law that defended strike-breakers against any threat from strikers as a 'law for old women'. 'It protects cowardice', he said (MWG I/8, 256f.). Under German conditions, 'a strengthening of the trade unions' meant 'a guarantee of political, masculine, free independence within the Party' (MWG I/8, 279). 'Political', 'masculine' and 'free'! From the unions he expected a strengthening of the spirit of self-help, whereas from the Social Democratic Party he feared greater bureaucratic impositions on citizens. Later, in his treatise on the Indian religions, he stresses that the uninhibited way in which the Buddha's followers associated with women did not at all imply a 'feminine' character of the Buddha's message; on the contrary, the message distinguished itself by its 'manly clarity' (RI 213). Weber recognizes 'manly beauty' in a brave memorandum written in 1901, in which a Confucian blamed the Chinese empress for certain errors; on the opposite side he sees eunuchs and magic (RC 140).

These are more than just occasional slips of the tongue; they suggest a closed world-view in which male and female are naturally determined rather than a product of society. This difference gives rise to the values that Weber ranks most highly: heroic courage and fearless commitment to truth. 'Polytheism of values' has a natural origin in the polarity of the sexes. Thus, with an eye on the ancient Germans, Weber noted in 1905 in a questionable interpretation of Tacitus: 'The sexual division of labour is primeval and lies "in the nature of things"; it is the archetype of social "differentiation"; men regularly shun doing specifically women's work' (SWG 536) – it never occurred to him either to perform such work. When Marianne praised her husband for seeing women 'primarily as human beings and only secondarily as members of the opposite sex', the evidence that she herself gives is not exactly convincing (WB 110). The elderly Jaspers, who had once glorified Weber as the 'only' and the 'last great man',[47] detected with his psychiatrist's eye 'a violent, intensified masculinity'. And he noted that, precisely when a man's sexuality is not 'normal', his 'dependence on it' is experienced in a more 'intense' way as dependence on women.[48]

Paternal and maternal world

If both the domestic family unit and the battle-ready male association are primal forms of society, then the question arises as to how the two can fit

Figure 3.3 Max Weber's parents

together. Should both be seen as subsystems of a social system in which the individual – especially the male individual – has to play diverse roles? But Max Weber did not think within the logic of social systems: the basic unit for him was not 'society' but the individual; and from the beginning the socialization process led in different directions, which could come into a tense relationship with each other. Weber constantly experienced among his family and relatives a tension between the then totally male world of politics and science and the female world of the home.

Weber's parents offered him an ideal type of this contrast: the father was a man of politics and administration, while the mother devoted herself with growing passion to a very personal religion and poor relief. Until recently we knew the father only through Marianne's spectacles, which meant that the Weber literature unquestioningly took over the image of a jovial but, in conflicts, tyrannical patriarch – an image that fitted the usual clichés about the society of the time. Only Guenther Roth has made intensive efforts to gain genuine access to the father.

Max Weber senior: politics as a vocation

Unlike Max Weber junior, the father was the youngest of six children – and, while his eldest brother Carl David, Marianne's grandfather, inherited the family firm, he had to make his own way in life. At first he toyed with the idea of an academic career,[49] but it was not long before he decided to go into politics. His son later gave a famous address entitled *Politics as a Vocation*. But in 1872 the father was already saying that he had 'so to speak' had 'politics in mind as a vocation' during his student years – and unlike his son he took the intention seriously (R 374).

> He combined a parliamentary career with professional activity at municipal level. In 1862, at the age of twenty-six, he became a paid adviser to Erfurt city council, and in 1869, at the age of thirty-three, he shot up into a leading position in the administration of the budding capital of the Reich. At the time of his move to Berlin, he also entered the Prussian House of Representatives and, three years later, the Reichstag. He remained for nearly ten years in the Reichstag and nearly twenty in the House of Representatives. . . . In both parliaments he sat on the most important committee, the one dealing with the budget, for which he often acted as rapporteur! (R 372)

As an expert on financial and fiscal matters, he had chosen the toughest area of politics. Whereas the son later told his students that politics meant 'long and heavy drilling through hard wood', the father was capable of singing its praises. Besides, as a law student, Max Weber senior had already realized that politics was not an applied science and that the 'professors' parliament' – the name given to the Frankfurt assembly of 1848 – was a thing of the past. Let us quote again from his election speech of 1872, one of the very few confessions he ever gave about himself: 'For a moment I was in two minds whether to start up again in academic teaching; but it seemed to me that nowadays, when we are faced with the solution of very real and sober tasks, professors are not the main ones called to political activity, as they used to be in an age when it was still chiefly a question of working up and disseminating political ideas' (R 381). His son would certainly have agreed with that – yet he chose the path not of politics but of academic work.

It is doubtful, however, whether Max Weber junior thought of his father as a full-blooded politician. For, if the public limelight is seen as the real element of politics, his father did not at all cut an impressive figure. His main work was performed behind closed doors: in the administration and on parliamentary committees (R 444). He was at the same time a National Liberal parliamentarian *and* a paid official, and it is likely that his son experienced him mainly as the latter. In 1884 Max junior even reported to his uncle Hermann Baumgarten that generally his father 'rather kept away from political life' (R 418).

In his younger years the father could feel called to something higher. In 1860–61 he edited the *Preußische Wochenblatt*, mouthpiece of the 'Wochenblattpartei', whose influence extended to the highest circles;

its sympathizers included the crown prince, Wilhelm I. It was no more averse than Bismarck to a unification of Germany through 'blood and iron', but unlike its opponent, the ultraconservative 'Kreuzzeitungspartei', it adhered to a pro-British and anti-Russian line. The grouping was Bismarck's most dangerous rival in his rise to power, as he himself confirms by the spiteful thoroughness with which he treats it in his memoirs. Had the 'Wochenblattpartei' been victorious, the road would have been open for Weber senior to rise to the heights of power. But Bismarck's fairy-tale ascent meant that Weber's father got stuck in a position well below such bold expectations.

The father did not share the bourgeois prejudice against 'the Reds'. In everyday politics he even learned to value the Berlin Social Democrats, especially when it came to the imposition of planning and building regulations, and the defence of public interests more generally, against the powerful coalition of house-owners and property speculators. In 1907, in a discussion at the Verein für Sozialpolitik on the condition and administration of cities, Max Weber junior recalled that it had once 'made a deep impression' when his father, 'who was certainly no lover of social democracy', had 'repeatedly told me that his *most solid* support in the Berlin planning deputation against the invasion of speculative interests was the representative Paul Singer' (GASS 408), a highly professional Social Democrat who was head of the Berlin refuge for homeless people as well as a flourishing producer of women's coats.[50] Max Weber already knew from his father that the enemy image of 'the Reds', which united conservatives and liberals, was based on ignorance, and that the SPD type of politician was more useful for constructive work than many a party leader from the bourgeoisie or the nobility.

Was the bourgeoisie politically impotent in imperial Germany?

Under the influence of Weber and other liberal critics of the Empire, it has often been claimed that the Bismarckian neofeudal structures prevented conscious representatives of the bourgeoisie such as Weber from achieving the political positions to which they should have been entitled. But this is true only with reservations. After all, two of Weber's own relatives were ministers: Theodor Adolf von Möller, Prussian trade minister from 1901 to 1905, and Julius Jolly, Baden interior minister from 1866 to 1868 and then prime minister until 1876. Weber also witnessed the career of the ennobled Johannes von Miquel, a party colleague and rival of his father, who, after successful service in the office of mayor, rose to become Prussian finance minister (1891–1901) and strategist of the ruling conservative–liberal cartel. As minister, Miquel once invited the young Weber to his home and seated him next to his daughter (JB 358). And it was from him that Max learned that the traditional feudal estates in the east were 'no longer a solid base for rule' – an insight which for him became the key to the political economy of Prussia-Germany. But when Miquel (who had meanwhile become a loyal supporter of the agrarians) spoke disparagingly in 1899 about Weber's study of farm-workers, Weber abused him in a letter to Schmoller as a 'scaramouch', a cowardly buffoon (MWG I/4, 680) – a view he later repeated in characterizing him as a paragon of spinelessness (I/10, 411). In 1917 Weber remarked that parliamentarians 'such as Miquel and Möller' who made it to ministerial office must first have become 'politically unprincipled' (I/15, 480). Miquel, who started off far on the left, did indeed acquire the reputation of a political chameleon, and although his progressive income tax became a model far beyond the borders of Prussia he eventually bowed to the pressure of the agrarians, who were more used to obtaining privileges than to paying taxes.

The Reichstag was not simply a sham institution without real powers, even if it did not decide who should form the government of the day. Precisely because central governments were not chosen by parliament, they could not automatically rely on a parliamentary majority but had to work each time to line one up behind them. The great historical ages of parliamentarianism often occurred in such a period, when parliament stood facing government from a position of its own and the division of powers between the legislative and the executive was much sharper than it is today. When Weber looked back on the 1870s, the high point of the Bismarck era, from the vantage point of 1917, it appeared to him as the 'heyday of the Reichstag'. He raged that it was 'a most impertinent distortion of the truth for political littérateurs [in this case, of the new Right] . . . to try to persuade the nation that "Parliament here in Germany has failed so far to produce great political talents" ' (PW 138). In fact, Weber himself had often doubted whether, under the conditions of the Bismarckian empire, the Reichstag was capable of producing an elite of political leaders; the negative image of his father must have nourished such doubts.

Local government in the German Reich: a model of bourgeois autonomy

When Max Weber spoke of the 'spurious parliamentary system' in tsarist Russia during the time of the Duma, he also had in mind the political situation in Germany. In comparison with later democratic parliaments, however, the German imperial Reichstag carried out respectable legislative work and often held discussions of a high level concerning political issues. In the course of time it inconspicuously weakened Prussian hegemony within the Reich.[51] Debates in the Reichstag attracted greater public attention than do today's debates in the Bundestag.

Those who speak of imperial Germany's fake parliamentarianism and emphasize its civil deficit in comparison with the West usually overlook the fact that the German middle classes had a local field of political activity that was better developed than that in Britain or France. Anyway, for most citizens the opportunity to exercise influence in local politics was far more real than the hypothetical possibility of being elected head of government. Claims regarding Germany's supposed civic deficit do not stand up to scrutiny,[52] especially as they are usually based on idealized images of Western parliamentarianism and fail to take into account the de facto rule by exclusive elites in London and Paris.

In theory the municipalities had a much wider circle of activity than the Reich authorities, whose powers in internal affairs were actually very limited. Precisely in reaction to the major new challenges of 'hygiene' and 'technology' that had appeared in the wake of industrialization and urbanization – supply and disposal systems for gas, water and electricity, as well as city transport, hospitals, slaughterhouses, baths and parks – local politics was experiencing its last great age, although only a pale glimmer remained of the municipal autonomy of the Middle Ages.

The history of Germany's large cities in the late nineteenth and early twentieth centuries contains a long and impressive gallery of reform-minded mayors. But it should not be forgotten that, unlike the central parliamentary system, local administrations operated on the basis of a highly undemocratic suffrage. As in premodern times, local citizenship embraced only a fraction of people living in the area – and that fraction had shrunk with the growth of the proletariat. In Hamburg, for example, the electorate fell from 8.74 per cent of local residents in 1875 to just 4 per cent in 1892.[53] In the eyes of the young Weber, however, the elite suffrage was not a disadvantage. When his father failed to be re-elected to the Reichstag in 1884, Max vented his indignation in a letter to his uncle Hermann Baumgarten: 'The basic mistake is the Greek gift of Bismarckian Caesarism: the universal suffrage that is pure murder of equal rights *in the truest sense of the term*' (JB 143). It had led to the rise of parties such as Social Democracy and the Centre, which then had to be kept in check through police methods.

The father: prototype of a local politician

As a Berlin city councillor, Max Weber senior was at the centre of events. In 1873, the year in which he became head of the Berlin building department, the municipal council decided after heated debates to build a sewerage system covering the whole city.[54] At the time it was one of Europe's largest construction projects and a model for other world metropolises. The works manager, James Hobrecht, became famous for his radial system intended for expansion, especially as the disposal of waste water posed considerable problems for a city of millions located on the plain, with a high groundwater level yet far from the sea.[55] Hobrecht's brother Arthur, who for a time was mayor of Berlin, shared many of Weber's political views (JB 170) and was a regular guest at the house in Charlottenburg. But, although civil engineering was Weber's responsibility, his name does not figure in the history of sewerage systems – a clear indication of the extent to which the new technological feats had become a matter for experts. Besides, as a national and regional parliamentarian, Max Weber senior had too much on his plate to keep abreast of this complex technical field; he appeared in the election propaganda of his conservative opponent as a busybody keen on accumulating offices (R 428). This could not have made a good impression on his son, who certainly wanted to be an expert in the style of the new times.

Max Weber junior disappointed his father by showing little interest in the 'major building works in which we are now engaged here' (JB 162). It is true that experts were conducting a Europe-wide discussion of the various sewerage systems and the best ways of dealing with urban excreta, but these were not topics to be raised in the Webers' living room – unlike the perennial theme of Bismarck. The son later regarded the technology of large cities as a distinctive element in modern art and culture, but not as an opportunity for local politics in the grand style. Anyway, Berlin's planning autonomy was already quite limited: the building inspectorate was answerable to the chief of police, not to the *Magistrat* (R 391). Nor did the city council always play a praiseworthy role in high-cost projects involving urban hygiene; many were pushed through only after pressure from central government or the medical archpriests Rudolf Virchow and Robert Koch.

Max Weber and local politics

Be this as it may, the local administration that was a source of pride for many other liberal theorists of the state never became a major theme for Max Weber.[56] In his dramatic vision of politics as a great contest over ultimate value decisions, local politics with its fluid transitions was marginal to the bureaucracy that he came to despise so much. The autonomous city republic of the Middle Ages, whose freedom he saw as deriving essentially from rights usurped for itself rather than being conferred by the sovereign prince, became in his eyes the origin of the special Western path in world history. By contrast, what struck him in the modern local authority was mainly its dependence on the state and administration.

In one of the very few cases when Weber explicitly talked of 'local administration', he displayed a dismissive lack of interest. He conceded that there was reason to be proud of it in Germany too, but his main point was that 'it is an enormous error on the part of the littérateurs to imagine that the *politics* of a major state are basically no different from the self-government of any middle-sized town. Politics is *struggle*' (PW 154). In 1909, at the Vienna congress of the Verein für Sozialpolitik, he mocked the 'absurdity of saying that local government should be cheaper because it is conducted on a voluntary basis'. On this occasion he first introduced his key formulation, with its underlying tone of resignation: 'The technological superiority of the bureaucratic mechanism is firm and unshakable, like the technical superiority of mechanized labour over handicraft' (GASS 413).

From his father's insider knowledge he must have gained the conviction that the bureaucracy was the true nerve centre of the much-acclaimed local self-government.[57] At the time, there was a dispute among German theorists of the state about whether local government was essentially part of the state administration or its opposite. In the view of Hugo Preuss, an expert in constitutional law, Prussia was deliberately muddying the waters by declaring local state authorities to be 'organs of self-government', since urban notables were still part of them in an honorary capacity[58] – as Helene Weber would be later. Max Weber, with his father in mind, probably also regarded this kind of 'self-government' as conceptual humbug.

It was well known to him from the history of the Roman empire that municipal self-government could be a mere façade covering something quite different. The despotic state of late antiquity made the municipal *decurio* legally responsible for the tax levy; if he tried to run away from this unpopular task, 'towns pursued their errant councillors the way a village pursued a runaway bull from the common herd' (AS 402). This is one of the funniest passages in Weber's work; he used the comparison of a councillor to a bull at a time when, as we shall see, he was working himself up into a rage against his father, the former city councillor.

Patriarchy in the Weber household?

In Marianne's biography, her father-in-law is depicted in an ambiguous way. At one level he appears as quite an attractive figure, presumably reflecting Max's and Marianne's original perception of him. Evidence of this are the sketches she made of him during the time of her engagement, when he kept pleasantly in the background while Helene, the real terror, wanted to hook her up to Paul Göhre. At certain points, then, the biography presents Max's father as he appeared at the time, raised higher by Marianne's tendency to idealize 'good people'. He was 'totally honourable, utterly unselfish in politics and in his job, intelligent, good-natured, warmhearted and amiable' – though with the qualification 'so long as things went his way' (WB 63).

In the days when he was still a man of position and authority, Max Weber *père* was certainly a model and superego for his eldest child and namesake: an embodiment of political power, professional competence, *joie de vivre* and colourful living – all in sharp contrast to the mother. To her sorrow, Helene could not for many years get through to the son for whom she had shown such care. One reason for this was what he later saw as his 'secret intellectual arrogance' during those years: 'His mother really had nothing to offer to his precocious, superior mind, and his heart remained a tightly closed bud' (WB 60); she did not seem very intelligent beside his father. There was nothing more natural than that the young Max should have wanted to become a lively and successful man well versed in the ways of the world. And there is talk of long hikes together: of a way of experiencing nature more typical of a growing boy than is religious rapture over the springtime blossoms.

The father's connections may well have been instrumental in getting Weber's career off to a good start. If, without a suitable work record, he was considered by the Verein für Sozialpolitik for its survey of farm-workers, it seems likely that one factor was the father's role in the Prussian parliamentary commission that worked on the so-called Polish law of 1886 promoting the settlement of Germans in Posen and West Prussia.[59] Similarly, the father's links with the powerful ministerial head Friedrich Althoff (who was responsible for decisions about academic careers in Prussia)[60] were probably not without importance when the little-known Max Weber, at the mere age of thirty, joined the circle of those discussed for a professorial appointment. Weber's later fury over Althoff's interference in the universities – which indeed was often better for science than faculty autonomy was – contained some old anger over the dependence on his father. Nevertheless, Althoff had had good reasons for his patronage of the young Weber, who had already cut a brilliant figure as a lecturer;[61] in those days he made a stronger impression orally than in writing.

A liberal-anticlerical father given to earthly pleasures and a pious mother who worked off in charitable activity her unsatisfied yearning for love: this constellation, not untypical of the time, was familiar to Weber not only from the parental home but also from his close relatives; it was a constant source of marital tensions that could escalate into a battle of the sexes.[62] Adolf and Henriette Hausrath in Heidelberg, Hermann and Ida Baumgarten in Strasbourg: always the same role-playing. The sisterly trio of Ida, Helene and Henriette strengthened one another against their husbands, who for their part did not stick together (R 335ff.). Adolf Hausrath, a lifelong admirer of Heinrich von Treitschke, was full of contempt when Hermann Baumgarten picked an argument with the famous historian; he wrote mockingly to the nineteen-year-old Weber 'how many dozens of Baumgartens could be made out of one Treitschke' (JB 74).

Weber encountered more female than male solidarity in his circle of relatives. The self-confidence of the three sisters supported itself on a feeling of religious superiority and on the inherited Fallenstein–Souchay fortune. Ida and Helene, in particular, tried to gain firmer control of their legacy in order to underpin their commitment to Christian social work. Later, a passionate plea for wives to have complete disposal over their inherited wealth would be the most fully elaborated idea in Marianne's major work on the legal position of women (EM 458–95). Anyone who recalls Max Weber's snorts of rage against the industrial patriarchalism of 'King Stumm'[63] – who made cowards of the men turned over to him (B 520ff.) – will read with incredulity how Marianne presents him over four pages as an exemplary champion of women's rights, whose 'demands in relation to marriage law' coincide 'almost entirely with those of the extreme Left', and who publicly formulated such key statements as: 'Marriage will be all the more normal, the more women are the equals of men', or: 'The law must protect women not so much through men as *from* men' (EM 479ff.). But there is a simple solution to the puzzle: Stumm had lost his only son, and he was incensed at the idea that the officers who married his daughters might rob them of the power to dispose of their fortunes.[64] As a woman, Marianne's attitude on the heated issue of Stumm was thus contrary to that of her husband.

The original revolt against domestic matriarchy

When the adolescent Weber observed the growing tension between his parents, he apparently sided for a long time with the father, though without any open affront to the mother. The box on the ears that she administered to her eldest when he returned from his first semester was probably a reaction to the fact that the newly enrolled member of the student fraternity, already marked by drinking bouts and duelling, gave a more striking impression than ever of being his father's son. In the years ahead Weber would still occasionally show anger at the way in which she interfered in the relationships of her grown children.

When Weber visited the Baumgartens in Strasbourg – which in itself was always a ray of light in the darkness of his military service in Alsace – he felt repelled by the 'attitude to life' prevailing in their home. But his criticism was directed only at Aunt Ida, since the historical-political discussions with Hermann Baumgarten were an intellectual high point for the young man. In fact, Weber's letters to Helene reveal how his disparaging remarks about Ida were indirectly, never directly, aimed at his own mother. Since childhood she had been strongly under the influence of Ida, her elder sister, and of her pronounced religiosity. Weber saw the 'danger' that such views would 'lead to certain eccentricities', and that these 'can – nay, *must* – easily spoil the zest for life of those affected by them'. He did not think she would 'deny' that this was already the case with her son Otto, the theologian (JB 80), who in one of their family's not uncommon alliances between cousins had married the ailing Emily Fallenstein, seven years older than himself – an act which, especially for the men in the family, would have meant giving up a normal sexual life.[65]

For Max Weber, Otto's development was a sign that that there was something unhealthy in the Baumgarten home, a reckless 'turning away from reality'. *Reality*: a central concept for Weber, not only in life but also in scholarly work. Lack of a sense of reality had led to a situation where the Baumgartens 'treat and regard other people not as they *are* but as they *ought* to be from a very exacting point of view' or as they 'apparently have to be *conceived* through logical deductions'. Here we already see the cardinal sin identified in Weber's later theory of science: the confusion of 'is' and 'ought' and the deducing of actuality from abstractions. The violence of his later polemics had its roots in early experiences. Weber's outburst against the Baumgartens went so far that he also 'protested' at the way in which Helene, in her previous letter, had placed 'the Baumgartens' attitude to life so unconditionally above the one prevailing in our home' (JB 81); the word 'prevailing' refers here specifically, of course, to the father's attitude to life. The issue, then, was one of defending his father against his mother.[66]

In this situation, the young Weber championed nature and a healthy sense of reality against any kind of supersensory spiritualism. Yet he felt at home at the Baumgartens. In her biography, probably basing herself on Weber's own analysis, Marianne thought that, 'without his being quite aware of it', he had fallen in Strasbourg under the influence of Ida and her self-assured religiosity, and that she had even taught him to understand his mother better (WB 84). Weber's later fascination with the Puritan ethic appears to bear this out. Ida was an integrated personality, whereas Hermann was at odds with himself – both in his fractured liberalism and in his fractured admiration for Bismarck. For all that Weber learned from him, he did not offer a model to follow.

Still less of a model was the other uncle, Adolf Hausrath, who was a presence for Weber during his studies. This theologian was a living warning that insensitive patriarchy damages not only the wife but also the husband. Adolf Hausrath (1837–1909), from 1871 to 1907 full professor in theology at Heidelberg, was living in the Fallenstein villa when Max Weber was a student there. As a free-thinking historian of religion, but also as a man with a passion for politics who cut an eccentric figure in the eyes of students, he was by no means lacking in interest to Weber, although particularly for women he had disgraced himself in the family through tyrannical behaviour towards his wife Henriette (1840–95), Helene's elder sister. For his part he felt that he had been treated badly, and in *romans à clef* that he wrote under a pseudonym, some of which were even translated into English, he took his revenge by drawing not exactly flattering portraits of other members of the family. When Marianne visited the Hausraths early in 1895, her subsequent letter to Helene was like a cry of terror: 'Ah, if you have once breathed that stifling air, in which any free expression of opinions, any slight contradiction, any trivial practical activity . . . is practically impossible, you will completely understand Aunt Henriette, including her present inner turmoil and despair.' Henriette had an 'indescribable' longing to see Helene, but her husband would forbid her to make the trip.[67] Here already is the contentious issue that would break out two years later in the Weber household: the wife's freedom to travel!

Six weeks after Marianne's despairing letter, Henriette suffered a fatal stroke. The thought arose that her husband should be assigned some moral blame for her death, and in addition that there was reason to be concerned about Helene, who increasingly felt her marriage to be oppressively restrictive. Indeed, there were times when she gave her children the impression of being seriously distraught: in early 1897, not only Max[68] but also Alfred registered their concern about her 'very poor nervous capacity', not least because of the 'constant fights with Papa'.[69] The warning contained in Henriette's death probably helped to exacerbate the crisis in the Weber family.

Turning against the father

Nevertheless, the young Weber's radical change of mind about his father is in need of some explanation, leading as it did to a deadly hatred of the man he had previously looked up to. Normally the anti-paternal rebellion happens some years earlier, in the child's 'difficult age' and in puberty; it does not first appear in a situation where the son has long been a regular professor and no longer needs to assert himself against his father. But there is no record of such a revolt on the part of Max as a child or adolescent. The estrangement came later, in the seven long years (1886–93) that he again spent in the parental home in Charlottenburg following the merriment of student life.

During that time he must have thought and read a great deal. Yet, as he wrote to Emmy Baumgarten in 1893, they were years 'whose cheerless desolation I now look back at with horror'. The 'bookshop existence' did not go hand in hand with a gladdening creativity but plunged him into 'complete resignation, not free from a certain bitterness'. He felt prematurely aged and thought wistfully of the happy time gone by (JB 367). When he wrote in 1893, with the downtrodden farm-workers of eastern Germany in mind, that 'the most terrible thing of all' was a state of miserable dependence at home, even worse than poverty in foreign parts (MWG I/4-1, 189 and 461), one feels the influence of his own still fresh experience. In part it was his activity as a law student that he looked back at 'with horror'; he had felt as if he were being 'pulled down by lead weights on to the unassuming couch of intellectual idleness' (JB 338f.). He must often have cursed his decision to follow his father into the law.

At the same time, he felt 'with infinite bitterness' the financial dependence on his father (WB 185), who stood there as a living reproach. At an age when the son was still sitting around at home, the father had long been a success in life – and he evidently thought his son was old enough to look after himself. The image of his mother – Weber wrote in 1893 – had given him strength in those 'often desolate and nearly always hopeless years' (JB 374). She did not push him out, but rather gave him an opportunity to regress into the child's pleasant state of being looked after. He could permit himself more as his mother's son than as his father's. Besides, she was a stronger personality than the father, and Max Weber was the kind of man who liked most to submit to a strong woman.

Many years later Marianne remarked in her observations on love: 'The first-born child often wants to have the mother to himself and suffers jealousy if he has to share with later children the importance he has had for her. Jealousy may even arise towards the father, as the main person in the home whose demands on the mother take precedence over his own,'[70] It is scarcely conceivable that she had not been thinking of Max. In 1901 she wrote to Helene from Rome that Max was expecting her to come there also for six weeks. 'Otherwise Max will be furious. He says that *we* are *also* your children and now have a cumulative claim to you.'[71] In his childhood he had had no cause for jealousy, since his illness had meant that the mother was there above all for himself. Now things were different. In the only surviving statement of Max Weber senior about the conflict with his son, he laconically remarks with little display of agitation: 'Max and Marianne would like best of all to have Helene entirely to themselves, if possible with no relative here.' And Max, for his part, insinuated to the father that 'his jealousy alone was the reason for the strife' between them (R 528f.).

Much earlier there had been another period of estrangement between father and son, during a trip to Venice of all times. There, in the city of carnival and honeymooning, the seventeen-year-old Max had 'suddenly wanted to go home by himself', because 'he could not bear the way his father expected him to express his enthusiasm' (WB 63). A strange episode! In contrast to what has repeatedly been claimed, Max Weber was no victim of the supposedly pleasure-hating and repressive bourgeois society of imperial Germany. Rather, it was the new society of fun, with its demonstrative displays of hedonism, which caused him so much nervous irritation. Only twenty-eight years later did he discover Venice as the city of love.

When Max's younger sister Helene died in 1877 at the age of four, his mother sank into a lengthy depression. She felt that her husband had left her alone in her mourning. 'He did not go with me.' 'He did not want to suffer' (WB 37f.). In those days many children died in the first few years of life. It is often said that, as there were many other children and no antibiotics, parents were more prepared for such losses than they are today – that they *must* have been inured against them. That was true of Max Weber's father, but in this case not of his mother. At first sporadically, then more consistently, Weber came to feel that his own path was more that of his mother's than his father's: not to cling to beautiful illusions, not to want to be happy all the time, but to look clear-sightedly at the darker side of the world, especially the darker side. The conviction that religion was deeply rooted in man – which was so fundamental in his later work – also alienated him from his father and brought him closer to his mother. As we have seen, he thought that his father had basically conceived of religion as 'hypocrisy'.

The day of judgement and the father's death

The experience of sexual impotence in marriage must have ultimately strengthened Max Weber in his belief that he could gain a sense of himself only by taking a path radically different from that of his father. Perhaps he also suspected that Helene's sexual inhibition, which she passed on to her son, stemmed in part from her husband's importunate manner. In one way or another, then, Max must have blamed him rather than her for his own misery. He became increasingly angry that his father would not let her travel alone to see the children, and he finally exploded when he again accompanied Helene to Heidelberg in June 1897. Max rebuked his father before the assembled family and said that he wanted nothing more to do with him until he left his wife free to visit her children for four to five weeks a year. The son staged the scene as a day of judgement on paternal insincerity and mendacity – as a struggle for truth![72] There was to be no agreement and no reconciliation.

In his letters to Alfred from that time, Max Weber repeatedly fumed against his father's 'need for pleasure' and 'need for amusement'; he saw that as the reason why he would not allow Helene to travel alone.[73] In plain language: a demand for regular sexual intercourse. Later, in a footnote to *The Protestant Ethic*, Weber loudly denounced the 'patriarchal sentimentality' typical of Germany even in the circles of the 'intellectual aristocracy' (Weber's own quotation marks), in contrast to the 'blossoming of matrimonial chivalry' among peoples influenced by Puritanism (PE 264). In earlier editions Weber had added 'boorish' to 'patriarchal sentimentality' – an epithet probably meant to imply 'with a claim to daily sexual intercourse as a self-evident right'.

A kinder interpretation of the father's behaviour might have been that he was demonstrating his marital fidelity: men who have a lover are happy when their wife goes away on a trip. Moreover, the parents' wedding anniversary fell during the time of the planned journey to Heidelberg.[74] But Max Weber, as a male feminist, saw only the patriarchal side of it all. In his letters he bellows with rage: he has often broken into a 'cold sweat' out of 'disgust and revulsion'; it should be constantly brought home to Father that he must treat Mother 'as something other than a bootjack or a bottle of wine'.[75] Of course, the father would never have expected Helene to put on his boots or otherwise bossed her around in the home. His son can only have meant that he was using her for sexual gratification when she felt no wish for it.

When his sister Klara, his beloved Klärchen, made a move to defend her father, Max threatened to stop being her child's godfather. His brother Karl, who at that time was closest to the mother, wanted to intercede, but Max abused the 27-year-old as a 'stupid boy' who should kindly keep his mouth shut. Max seems to have suppressed any thought that in the end it was not he but his mother who had to go on living with the father, that she would have to carry the can for his outburst. In vain did she try to prevent him from brutally flinging what he had to say into his father's face.[76] To Alfred, Max even mooted giving up his professorship and returning to Berlin, in order to protect his mother from his father (R 530)! On the day following the explosion, he assured him that he felt 'better' after the hour of truth. But it is doubtful whether the satisfaction lasted for long. As Marianne wrote in her biography, Max's inner change under Ida's influence, which in the end led to the great family explosion, 'conflicted with certain aspects of his personality' (WB 86). In his later years, he himself recognized that he had scorned and condemned the natural side of his father, and done violence to his own nature.

In 1906 Marianne paid Helene an ambiguous compliment: 'You see, the children all become as you *would like* them to be, only later than you would have wished.'[77] Already in 1897, relying on Alfred's understanding, she had written to him with amazing candour that the forthcoming visit of Helene, for whose travel autonomy Max had fought so furiously, actually got on her nerves. This outburst – incidentally, a striking declaration of belief in the pleasure principle and testimony to the contemporary preoccupation with the nerves – suggests that we should treat with caution her piles of letters to 'Darling Mother'. It also shows that, even while her husband was alive, Helene was not seriously prevented from giving expression to her social commitment:

> Sometimes, though, I get the feeling that Mama can no longer really 'rest' at all or concentrate, for example, on serious reading; or that it takes a much longer period of rest to completely relax her nerves and, as it were, to bring her from constant inner vibration into a state of calm. . . . Such long meetings for the sake of personal interchanges are a strain for me, and, since I *hate* any nervous fatigue that results in feelings of listlessness or irritability, I too prefer to limit myself a little in some areas – from Mama's point of view such 'sparing of oneself' is actually a lack of interest in other people and a kind of mollycoddling to be extirpated by all means possible. As I have often teasingly said to Mama, if there are two paths to something she will surely consider the more difficult one to be right, on the Christian principle of 'crucifying the flesh'.[78]

So, for Marianne a maternal visit meant a lost 'week of rest'!

In a passage from the autobiographical novel *Mister Noon*, in which he works through experiences from the Weber family, D. H. Lawrence reproduces a significant dialogue where the wife complains about modern mothers:

> 'Mothers are awful things nowadays, don't you think?'
> . . . 'Why?'
> 'Don't you think they all want to swallow their children again, like the Greek myth? There isn't a man worth having, nowadays, who can get away from his mother. Their mothers are all in love with them, and they're all in love with their mothers. . . . One wants a man to oneself, and one gets a mother's darling.'[79]

To be sure, Marianne learned to handle this situation: she slipped into the maternal role herself, at least sometimes, though perhaps not enough for Max.

On 10 August 1897, less than two months after the 'day of judgement' in Heidelberg, the father died unexpectedly a long way from the family in Riga – a 'heart seizure', it was said – without ever having seen his son again (R 533).

Did Max Weber junior from then on feel himself to be his father's murderer? Was this the reason for the onset of his illness the following year? Love of the mother, jealousy of the father, patricide and self-punishment: everything perfectly fits Freud's theory of the Oedipus complex, and Marianne, who came to know Freud's theory well, suggests this interpretation in her biography. In Weber's correspondence from that time, however, we find no indication that his father's death seriously weighed on the mind of anyone involved. Marianne's biography speaks of a 'gastric haemmorhage' as the cause of death and refers to 'pathogenic organisms' that had been present for a long time (WB 232) – which would mean that acute mental stress may not have had lethal implications. In 1969 the 95-year-old Else Jaffé replied to a question on the subject by saying that she did not think Weber 'carried a sense of guilt around with him for the rest of his life'.[80] We should bear in mind that Weber had a pronounced talent for feeling himself to be in the right, and there is no doubt that in 1897 he felt himself to be absolutely in the right towards his father.

Already in 1894 Max Weber was lecturing his mother, probably to urge her to remain intransigent towards the father and to make a formal philosophical duty out of 'anti-harmonism'. The son was no more timid towards the mother than she towards him:

> Fundamentally opposed starting points for a philosophy of life produce opposites that one should make no attempt to bridge, since that would threaten one's life-tasks. . . . Any attempt to regain the joyful sense of unity by surrendering one's inner autonomy is certainly, from a long-term point of view, built on sand. . . . As I see it, the correctness of my view on this matter is beyond all doubt.[81]

The meaning of one's life as the ultimate basis of conduct, the irreconcilability of different attitudes to life: here we already find in Weber the eternal quarrel among the gods or, more specifically, a quarrel between the sexes. But, in that case, would it not have been spineless on his father's part to surrender? In a sense, his standpoint contains a deeper insight into the limited character of the human sphere of activity: an understanding that, when people work well within the limits of their profession, they rightly enjoy their lives and are burdened neither by thoughts of death nor by the sufferings of the world. The contrary position, with its sense of unlimited responsibility for suffering in the world, contains an element of megalomania, and precisely that is its secret attraction. The later Max Weber, like his father before him, got annoyed at Helene's high expenditure on charitable causes, which seemed to him dubious.[82]

In the end – at least as Marianne reports it – he 'regarded his hostile outburst against his own father as guilt never to be expiated' (WB 389). In the wake of his own reconciliation with nature, he excused his father's behaviour by referring to his nature, as Helene had done before, and to the times in which he had lived. In 1914, on the occasion of Helene's seventieth birthday, a changed Weber who was lingering at Lake Maggiore eager to live life to the full devoted an almost festive obituary to his father: 'We all certainly have a just view of him today; now that all the difficult tensions are forgotten we can take pleasure in his uncommonly solid and pure civic sense; we know that the fractures in his life were the tragedy of his whole generation, which has never been given due attention for its political and other ideals . . ., which had lost the old faith in authorities yet still thought in an authoritarian way in matters where we were no longer able to do so' (MWG II/8, 616f.). Once, after the death of the great hope of the liberals, Kaiser Friedrich III, Max's father had identified himself in one of his few surviving letters as a member of the old liberal 'generation' and of a 'race' 'irretrievably cheated of *its* emperor'. He had not dwelled tearfully on the painful memory, however, but rather delighted in 'drinking a proper strawberry punch in the moonlit garden' to celebrate his silver wedding anniversary.[83] That too was a good civic tradition.

4

Antaeus, Antiquity and Agrarians: The Unshackling of Creativity through the Earthing of Culture

The earthing of antiquity

In Greek mythology Heracles does battle with the giant Antaeus, the son of Gaia. Antaeus was invincible as long as he maintained contact with his mother, the earth, who gave him new strength whenever all appeared to be lost. In 1896 Weber used this as a metaphor in his account of the decline of ancient civilization: urban culture in the classical age was always but a fragile structure on the ground of a natural economy that lost its regenerative capacity when the supply of slaves dried up. 'Thus the framework of ancient civilization weakened and then collapsed, and the intellectual life of Western Europe sank into a long darkness. Yet its fall was like that of Antaeus, who drew new strength from Mother Earth each time he rested on her bosom' (AS 410).[1] So, the much-lamented decline of antiquity was in truth an act of regeneration. Mere contact with the earth becomes in Weber 'resting on the bosom of Mother Earth'. He passes over the final act, however, in which Heracles lifts the giant off the ground and strangles him.

For years Weber felt 'fettered to the rather desolate sphere of law', as he wrote in a letter to his mother.[2] He was comparing himself to Prometheus bound – except that this modern Prometheus always remained quite fond of his particular rock. From early on, Weber's imagination was filled with images from antiquity; others who had a passion for the latest modernity often left school deeply resentful at the years wasted on old languages, but not Weber. Whereas a scientific pioneer such as Wilhelm Ostwald branded the philology-dominated *Abitur* a 'crime against our intellectual youth', Weber dismissed the long-sounding alarms over 'scholastic overburdening' as mere 'hogwash' peddled by 'a load of people without talent'; and in 1919, when the educational reformers thought their time had come, he emphatically declared his belief in the humanities-based Gymnasium.[3] Throughout his life he felt at home in classical antiquity and the world of the Old Testament; 'he might refer to it at any time in metaphorical phrases and "quotations".'[4] Of course, that was much less uncommon than it is nowadays. When the historian Meinecke visited Reich Chancellor Bethmann-Hollweg during the First World War, the chancellor said gloomily that the conflict 'should not be compared to the war between Rome and Carthage but rather to the Peloponnesian War', in which Hellas tore itself apart.[5] It was not rare for antiquity to find its way back into the present.

Ancient culture and human nature

For Weber, as for many people educated in the humanities, it seems to go without saying that ancient thinkers present in classical form many of the basic ideas of our intellectual world. Not only did Machiavelli develop his political theory in commentaries on Livy; Foucault too concentrated on the authors of classical antiquity in his history of the discourse of sexuality. Like the Renaissance humanists, Weber believed that classical antiquity held not only the origin but also the essence of our culture: the nature of culture, so to speak. At the age of fourteen he wrote to Fritz Baumgarten that he liked Homer most of all writers, especially because of the 'great naturalness with which each action is narrated' (JB 9).

From today's point of view, the most pioneering aspects of Weber's understanding of antiquity were his keen eye for the mainly local resource base of ancient civilization and the misleading analogies between ancient and modern capitalism, ancient and modern technological innovation.[6] Since Weber had a quite distinctive idea of the medieval city of trade and commerce, he saw more clearly than many other historians that it was not covered markets and guildhalls but temples and baths which were the core of the ancient city. All the more, however, did he emphasize natural restraints as the *fundamental* characteristic of the ancient economy. Weber's penchant for antiquity conceals a longing for natural culture. When he speaks at the end of *The Protestant Ethic* of the 'iron cage' of modern capitalism, the famous metaphor also betrays the ancient myth of a golden, silver and iron age – the decline of the world of beauty.

Inhabiting antiquity in his inner life, Weber found alien the modern belief in progress – or, at best, could detect progress only up to the 'Renaissance', the revival of antiquity. Universal pessimism was for him the sign of a noble cast of mind. In his worst year, 1900, he sought fortification in Jacob Burckhardt's *History of Greek Culture*: he wrote to Burckhardt's disciple Carl Neumann – another melancholic with a nervous complaint – that he found the great historian's account of a 'distinctively Greek pessimism' especially 'wonderful'. This letter, which he dictated to Marianne in a year when he mostly felt incapable of correspondence, contains one of his strongest expressions of faith in the spirit of antiquity. He thinks above all of the 'atmosphere' of 'constant threats to one's whole existence' produced by the 'war of all against all' among the Greek city-states; and he then moves in a curve to a Christian sense of the proximity of death: 'In the

midst of life we are in death.'[7] That struggle and death mark the whole consciousness of the citizen of the Greek polis: this idea, so irritating to philo-
Hellenes and so far from the minds of tourists strolling among peaceful
ruins, is always central to Weber's thinking. Willingness to fight to the death
is for him a key natural element in human existence, even if until 1914 this
irresistible urge is disguised by various illusions.

Having grown corpulent from student boozing, Weber thought he had
acquired an 'army commander's physiognomy somewhat reminiscent of
Nero and Domitian' (JB 163). He seems to have held imperial Rome, the
'manliest' state in history, in even higher regard than the Greek polis, and
he had a special fondness for the Stoa, the philosophy of Rome's senatorial
aristocracy. He associated the Stoic view of life with basic attitudes that he
held dear: with pride or heroism, with illusion-free clarity of mind, and
with a sense of what cannot be changed. When Weber later described the
Confucian ethic of ancient China, there was something left over from his
own philosophy of life; noble humanity included a 'faith in providence' and
that 'Stoic heroism' which meant 'accepting the unalterable with equanimity and in so doing the attitude of the cultivated and educated cavalier' (RC
207). Also originating in the Stoa, as Weber knew, was the idea of 'natural
law': a thoroughly 'rational' idea of law (E&S 866f.). At the Frankfurt
congress of sociologists in 1910 he commented at length on his friend
Troeltsch's lecture concerning 'Stoic–Christian natural law'. What the
modern ecological movement has forgotten was well known to Weber: the
ideal of 'a life in harmony with nature' originated in the ancient Stoa, and
the nature in question was not only 'blossoming nature' but also 'the nature
of things' and nature in man, including his own death.

'The Agrarian History of Rome' (1891)

Weber's dissertation on the medieval trading companies of northern Italy
was a weak start to an academic career. Real success came only in 1891,
with his postdoctoral *Habilitationsschrift* on the connection between land
measurement and agrarian law in ancient Rome. This initiated a lifelong
interest in the soil basis of human civilization; the kind of Weber studies
which regard his naturalism as un-Weberian have paid little attention to this
constant element in his work. Whereas in his writings on the stock market
he rediscovered the old value of honour in the most modern reality, we find
the opposite pattern in his *Habilitationsschrift* on Roman agrarian history:
namely, an attempt to grasp classical antiquity with the plainest and most
modern instrument, an analysis of agrarian measurement techniques. His
childhood images of the ancient world are dissected with the sharp tools of
the adult. At the same time, antiquity – the idol of the idealists – is brought
back down to earth.

Weber's work on the subject had been prepared by a new edition of land
surveying material from ancient Rome: the *Schriften der römischen*

Figure 4.1 The Mommsen family at Marchstrasse, Charlottenburg, Berlin, at the wedding-eve party for the son Karl, May 1891 (on the steps, left to right): sons Ernst and Hans, Klara (née Weber, wife of Ernst), Frau Wilamowitz-Möllendorf (née Mommsen) and her husband Ulrich, an unknown guest; (seated, left to right): daughters Hildegard, Luise and Anna, wife and husband Marie and Theodor, daughter Adelheid; standing behind Mommsen are sons Konrad and Karl, with Karl's bride-to-be between them

Feldmesser, edited by Karl Lachmann et al.[8] With this support, he tried to astound the reader with legal and agronomic shop-talk, to such a degree that today even a well-versed historian does not find it easy to understand what was the real point of the exercise.[9] Later statements by Weber give the impression that he had been searching for the agrarian basis of Roman statecraft, the Roman method of creating 'colonies' (in the sense of farm settlements) on conquered land (SWG 219). At the time, however, around 1890, it seemed to him to be a question not so much of particular theses as of an approach to Roman history via land measurement and land distribution.

Already in the *Habilitationsschrift* Weber was honest enough to admit the essentially hypothetical character of his theses. When Theodor Mommsen reproached the young scholar in a footnote with 'confusing gromatic and legal concepts', Weber understood that the criticism went to the very core of his method: the imbrication of surveying techniques with the legal order. He even detected a regular Mommsen-led 'campaign' against himself, although Mommsen thought the 'legal and economic' approach to antiquity was promising[10] and, like Weber, saw the unprecedented character of Roman expansion in the fact that Rome conquered new land with the plough as well as the sword.[11]

Mommsen also had a background in law, and on legal issues in ancient Rome he scarcely found a more competent and quick-witted interlocutor than the young Max Weber. He already knew him from the family, and in 1896 his son Ernst would marry Max's beloved Klärchen. Already in 1889, at the oral examination for his doctor's degree, Weber defended positions that would become part of his *Habilitationsschrift* and caused Mommsen to contradict him. But, after the two had had a good argument, the 72-year-old ancient historian ended with a dramatic gesture. The younger generation, he said, often had new ideas with which the older generation could not agree, and this might be a case in point. 'But when I have to go to my grave someday, there is no one to whom I would rather say, "Son, here is my spear; it is getting too heavy for my arm"' (WB 114). The young Weber would happily have reached for Mommsen's spear, but he did not accept the older man's offer to become his scholarly father and to open up for him a career as an ancient historian.[12] Mommsen was an academic pope, who demanded subordination from his disciples. At the latest after his *Habilitation*, Weber must have recognized that that was not the thing for him.

Concerning his method, Weber explained that he could not always keep strictly to the sources but had to construct the agrarian context partly by drawing 'conclusions from "the nature of things"'. He started from the fact that the agrarian sector had laws of its own, the laws of land use,[13] which allowed for only a limited range of agrarian forms; nature introduced a certain law-like regularity into human affairs. Following his teacher August Meitzen, Weber made use of the 'method of inference', which tried to reconstruct earlier times from well-documented modern agrarian conditions, on the assumption that land use had an element of inertia and that later forms often contained relics from earlier ones (MWG I/2, 97, 101).[14] He was one of the first to use intensively as historical sources the ancient Roman writers such as Cato, Varro and Columella, who had previously been deployed mainly as classical models by advocates of agrarian reform. Weber had respect for these reformers, who approached antiquity with a practical interest.

Unlike those agrarian reformers, however, who based themselves on individual quotations to present the Romans as a model, Weber analysed a mass of evidence and was able to see also the weaknesses of agrarian practices in ancient Italy. Thus, he correctly pointed out that, according to the sources, crop rotation was fairly uncommon in ancient agriculture (MWG I/2, 297f.). And he referred without comment to the cynicism of Roman agrarian theory, for which only the capitalist interests of latifundium-owners existed: 'Varro advises . . . the use of free labourers in unhealthy places, so that, if they fall ill and die, this will not be a burden on the landlord. . . . Columella recommends . . . in principle working slaves to the point of total exhaustion, so that they think only of sleep and not of other things' (MWG I/2, 312f., 315). Only then slaves were as little capable of reproduction as Max Weber, who in the evening, much to Marianne's concern, always sank late and exhausted into bed. According to Weber, the Roman empire fell because of this lack of sustainability – an insight which, two generations later, came as a sudden flash for Santo Mazzarino (the founder of an Italian school of ancient historians) and inspired all his subsequent research.[15] Later, however, Weber seems to have believed, without any confirmation in the sources, that it was 'general promiscuity' in sexual matters which impeded the reproduction of slaves (AS 324); so the slave's existence acquires a pleasurable side.

In his 1896 lecture on the decline of ancient civilization, Weber recalled Pliny's phrase '*Latifundia perdidere Italiam*', 'The large estates ruined Italy'. As for the idea of the German agrarians that large landholdings provided the empire with a solid foundation, he mocked it as tantamount to claiming that, 'had agriculture been protected by high tariffs, the empire would exist to this day' (AS 390). In his *Habilitationsschrift* Weber naturally abstained from contemporary political polemics, but even there we can sometimes see between the lines that he had the Prussian agrarians in his sights when he discussed the Roman latifundia. Again and again he notes that the latifundia, like the estates east of the Elbe, destroyed the natural organism of agriculture. 'Whereas Cato still treated livestock-breeding in an organic association with agriculture, the *res pecuaria* acquires an independent position in Varro' (MWG I/2, 306). Like the agrarian reformers of his day, Weber had an eye for the combination of agriculture and stockbreeding which maintains the fertility of the soil.

Germanic long strip fields and the plough

Fifteen years later, Weber returned to the old field system in his treatise on 'the dispute regarding the character of the old German social order' (1905). The question in dispute was whether the ancient Germanic order had been based on relations of domination or cooperation – hence whether feudal relations of dependence stretched back into ancient times, or whether there had been a primeval period marked, as it were, by 'liberty, equality and fraternity'. It was an argument between a conservative and a liberal interpretation of history; people were looking for the German essence in ancient times. Furthermore, many representatives of the domination hypothesis assumed that the ancient Germans had been seminomadic and that feudal armies had emerged out of the great herd owners, whereas the liberals tended to think of the ancient Germans as farmers tied to the land.

The domination hypothesis was the more modern of the two; it had the attractiveness of a sceptical neoconservatism, which dispelled the old liberal raptures about the Teutonic world of the past. Weber was on the side of his old teacher Meitzen, for whom the idea of 'equality among freely cooperating farmers' remained more plausible and had actually gained fresh support from his own analysis of field maps (SWG 512). With good arguments, Weber maintained that the much-disputed sentence in Tacitus's *Germania*: *'arva per annos mutant'* (which Weber translates as: 'They change their plots of land every year') does not indicate Teutonic semi-nomadism but rather the practice of migratory agriculture, such as we may observe today among 'indigenous peoples', which therefore did not even necessarily involve more primitive agricultural techniques (SWG 543, 530n).

Yet Weber rejected the popular romanticization of the ancient Germans when he tried to show, with more legal subtlety than historical plausibility, that such typically 'agrarian capitalist' institutions as the mortgaging of land had their origins in Germanic rather than Roman law. He was later glad to revisit the subject: both to spike the cult of folk cooperation associated with the historian Otto von Gierke, and to pull to pieces the Romantic notion that a 'return to German law' would bring a 'solution to the social question'.[16] As far as Weber was concerned, equality among agricultural cooperators did not spring from some primeval Teutonic sense of justice but only from a situation in which land was scarce and fought over (SWG 548ff.). Logically, he concluded, land could become a basis for domination only when it was scarce.

Land is the basis of history – but so is technology. In this treatise we come across the word 'plough' more often than in all the other writings of Weber; in this too he was following in Meitzen's footsteps. One of Meitzen's 'most splendid services' was to have seen the connection between the plough and the ancient German land strip field, and the fact that the scratch plough, which compelled the development of cross ploughing, led to a different division of land among the Romans and Slavs (SWG 520). Here, as at many other places in Weber's work, technology makes its appearance as an explanatory factor: sometimes as material artefact, but more often as labour technique, as know-how. This too is an aspect that Weber studies, marked as it is by Snow's gulf between 'two cultures', has largely ignored. Marc Bloch, on the other hand, one of the founders of the French *Annales* school geared to *'l'histoire totale'*, took up Meitzen's idea of a connection between plough and land distribution, while for the American medievalist Lynn White knowledge of this was an initiation experience that led to his becoming a founding father of modern technological and ecological history.[17] Meanwhile the dispute between the domination and cooperation hypotheses has not advanced much, owing to the lack of precise sources about the ancient Germans. For a Max Weber, who loved large-scale investigations and the copious use of sources, the earliest times were not in the long run suitable terrain.

Military service as experience of the land

For Weber as for Meitzen, study of the land contained an element of sensory experience. His surviving letters suggest that military service, in which the conscript had to crawl through the mud, was solid experience indeed of the 'reality' with which the young Weber was striving to grapple; and it also provided constant experience of the earth and its farmers. Weber was stationed first in Alsace, then in Posen. There he witnessed as clearly as possible the extreme contrast between farmers in the far west and the far east of Germany, the one half-French and the other half or three-quarters Polish. Later he often lamented the fact that Germany had been divided in two by its agrarian relations. During the period of his investigation into farm-workers, Weber got to know eastern German agriculture not only through questionnaires but also, on three occasions, through military exercises.

Lujo Brentano, who had been a professor in Strasbourg since 1882, was mainly concerned to use German social policy to win the local workers to the Reich and to expose as Potemkin villages the model dwellings presented by Alsace industrialists at international exhibitions in Paris.[18] At the same time, Weber the conscript was developing a strong dislike for the Alsatian lower classes, whom he depicted as a 'revolting' and 'dreadfully filthy' bunch (JB 129); the 'splendid farming people' (JB 135), however, were the 'quaintest human group of people' he had ever come across, with whom it was 'most interesting' to have dealings (JB 139), unlike with the often Germanophobic town-dwellers. When he was stationed in the Posen region he found almost no farmers of this kind. Posen was for him a 'stinking hole',[19] a thoroughly negative culture shock; his ideal solution would have been to transplant to the east an old German farming culture of the Rhineland type.

Science versus a 'policy of reconciliation'

This all suited Prussia's resettlement policy in the eastern provinces, which first took shape in 1886 with a view to establishing German medium-sized farmers as a barrier to Slav encroachment. Of course, it would be possible to see things quite differently, since until then Prussia's Polish citizens had given scarcely any reason to doubt their loyalty to the Prussian state. Historically speaking, Poland might even be regarded as a human barrier against the Russians and steppe peoples, and the influx of Polish migrants to the large estates during the sugar-beet harvest as a normal result of economic laws. The many surnames of Slav origin in Germany, including Treitschke, the idol of all German chauvinists, left no doubt that Slavs too could become good Germans. But the new German nationalism had a different view of things, and at least in the eastern provinces it increasingly came up against a Polish nationalism that reinforced it and provided it with raw material for political conflict.

For most of Weber's admirers, his sharp polemic over the years against Polish immigration in the east, together with a contempt for the Poles that came to the surface from time to time, is the most embarrassing aspect of his career. But little attention has been paid to an underlying premise: namely, that the farming community is the foundation of a healthy nation. In Weber's eyes the nation, like the giant Antaeus, lives off its contact with the soil.

In those days, traces of such a *Blut und Boden* ideology were by no means to be found only among Romantic nationalists. Even Eduard Bernstein, the theoretician of social democratic revisionism, held the view that industrial workers needed 'contact with Mother Earth', and that life in the 'grim' working-class districts of the big cities was 'infinitely less attractive' than that of farm-workers, 'who are not exactly on the bottom rung of their class'.[20] Of course, both Weber and Bernstein knew that for Germany there could be no way back to an agrarian country. In his speech to the Evangelical Social Congress in 1897, Weber attacked people with such nostalgic hopes – and this became the prelude to a long dispute over whether Germany should be an agricultural or an industrial country, which sometimes proceeded as if the question had not already been irrevocably decided in practice.[21] After Weber fell ill, Lujo Brentano picked up the baton and in his tone of mocking superiority made his opponents appear ridiculous; the title of his little book *Die Schrecken des überwiegenden Industriestaats* (Horrors of the Overpowering Industrial State)[22] is purely ironical. But Weber himself did not ridicule the opposing position; he even continued to call Brentano's opponent Karl Oldenberg his 'friend' (MWG I/4-2, 640). What he objected to among the agrarians and company was not their disaffection with the industrial state but their dishonesty in setting themselves up as trustees for national and farming interests while at the same time blocking the rise of a German farming community in the east.

Unlike agrarian party leaders and later *Blut und Boden* ideologists, Weber followed his teacher Meitzen in rejecting the advocacy of entailed or ancestral estates: he did not believe that the quality of the farming community hinged on the indivisibility or inalienability of large landholdings. He knew from the Rhineland that not only *Anerbenrecht* (which gave the eldest or youngest son right of succession to undivided farm estate) but also *Realteilung* (the division of real estate among the children of a family) were old German traditions stemming from a sense of natural justice within the family or 'family communism'.[23] He found there, in the Rhineland, an industrious farming community geared to nearby urban markets, which had made smallholdings profitable and continually broken up larger holdings through marriage and sound business. It was not only attachment to the soil but also energy generated through the market and competition which produced good farmers. Weber believed that agriculture should not enjoy special rights vis-à-vis other sectors of the economy; he wanted to banish the *idée fixe* of politicians that landowners should always be given certain privileges.

And yet, as Weber saw it, the farming economy had a special quality because of its closeness to nature. In 1892, in an educational document of the Evangelical Social Congress for country clergymen, he wrote that it looked as if 'we are at the beginning of an upward trend for farmers', and that one had to recognize the city-induced 'atrophy of certain aspects of normal intellectual and spiritual life' (B 372, 371). The widespread sense of living in a 'nervous age' – Weber too would soon feel a victim of this *mal de siècle* – was generally associated with a sympathy for country people and scepticism towards the big city, although by no means all the signs indicated that the city had a pathogenic effect.

The study of farm-workers

On 13 March 1893, the committee of the Verein für Sozialpolitik appointed Weber to handle the most important and politically most delicate part of its study of farm-workers, the one dealing with the east Prussian provinces, even though he had no previous experience of the subject. The report on the survey was supposed to be printed in time for the Verein's general assembly in Posen at the end of September, which in the end was postponed for half a year because of an outbreak of cholera (MWG I/3-1, 22);[24] it was thus probably meant to be more a bare presentation of the facts than a detailed scientific analysis.

Weber eventually produced at 'lightning speed' (WB 136) a thick two-volume work with well-rounded conclusions, which must have astounded those who had commissioned it. It was a real outburst of creativity, the first of its kind in Weber's career. He must have felt like Antaeus himself, having drawn on unsuspected strength through this new contact with the land. For nearly two more decades, until his long contribution to a manual in 1909 on 'agrarian relations in antiquity', the issues of farmers and the land inspired him in a way that commercial law and the stock market (to which he turned his attention after the study of farm-workers) were never able to do. Agriculture and religion would remain the greatest elements of continuity in his life's work. Eduard Baumgarten thought he could detect feelings with 'the warmth of blood' hidden beneath the surface of Weber's first major study (B 419).

Whether in scholarly work or politics, Weber always valued highly the large-scale investigations that were the core activity of the Verein für Sozialpolitik. This style of work corresponded to Weber's idea of a 'science of reality' [*Wirklichkeitswissenschaft*], although he was not the ideal team-worker and, despite all his plans, never himself managed such a major project. He would have dearly loved to make macro-surveys a regular feature of German political life; he was thinking of the parliamentary committees that gave a new impulse to British economic studies, and also of the London School of Economics, recently founded in 1895 in the space between economic theory and practice.[25] The Verein für Sozialpolitik saw its investigations as a substitute for Germany's missing parliamentary reports.[26] Precisely today, when economics has become more abstract than ever before, we are again learning the value of such reports.

Weber had a strong sense for the richness of reality, which the individual could not grasp in a single commanding view or construct in his study by means of ideas. Had Weber thought his object to be essentially intellectual, he might have believed in the possibility of grasping it with his mind alone. But that was not how he saw the world. In 1895, when Marianne put a list of questions to her husband about the position of women in society, he said that 'a survey was necessary, because up to now no one really knew about it'.[27] And later he liked to compile long lists of subjects for a major survey, which he never managed to get off the ground.

It was not so easy for Weber to contribute something independent to the 1892 study of farm-workers, since everything had to be done quickly and he had not been involved in formulating the questionnaire. Moreover, the sheets of paper were sent out mainly to landowners, not to the farm-workers who were the object of the study – a scandalous methodology by today's standards, and one which was already being criticized by people on the left. Heinrich Herkner, for example, who made his name in the Verein as a leading expert on the 'labour question', was successfully using 'secret private surveys' to approach workers for his investigation of factory conditions in Alsace – but such methods were unthinkable for an official survey by the Verein.

Of course, Weber knew that the landowners were an interested party: their complaints about the 'scarcity of manpower' concerned a scarcity for themselves, in a situation where the 'manpower' was free to choose among different employers; and for them 'really terrible conditions' were ones in which the 'men' found 'work everywhere' (MWG I/3-2, 739). Weber's ingenuity was, as it were, to read between the lines of the answers and to extract some things that were not to the respondents' liking. In the end he pulled off the trick of filing a report that won great respect in all quarters, from the conservatives on the right to Karl Kautsky, the leading ideologue of social democracy, on the left. Weber showed much understanding for the tragedy of the noble landowners, who in their prime had been the mainstay of the Prussian state and whose traditional way of life was being undermined by capitalist competition. Yet the investigation led to biting criticism of the old system that had become harmful to the nation, and in lectures and popular articles that followed his report Weber formulated the criticism still more trenchantly. In his view, the greatest scandal was the introduction of Polish farm-workers to displace the German rural lower classes.

It is doubtful whether Weber's empirical findings were really sufficient to sustain his concluding diagnosis. Often his material is presented in a more or less raw state; one senses the haste in which the work was written. For long sections the pure facts do not exactly make a dramatic impact – assuming that the answers to the questionnaires can be believed. If we make a comparison with the problems that Germany faces today, with its millions of immigrants from foreign cultures, the problems associated with Polish workers in those days appear quite bland – indeed, the responses to the questionnaire scarcely ever speak of tensions among the different nationalities. At most one can infer that Polish and Russian immigration meant that wretched work conditions could be maintained in the eastern provinces, thereby fuelling the westward movement of Germans (or *Sachsengängerei*, as it was called at the time).

From a distance, many objections can be made to the analytical quality of Weber's survey evaluation. But Georg Friedrich Knapp, the leading agrarian historian of east Prussia and the best authority on the subject,[28] not only felt overwhelmed by the record time in which the report was produced but admitted 'our expertise no longer exists and we must begin our study again'.[29] He saw the study as the crowning glory of the Verein; none of its previous general meetings had been so well prepared (B 362).

Today it is not so easy to comprehend that enthusiasm. To be sure, Knapp was deeply impressed by Weber's bold leap from the driest empirical material into the realm of idealism, which, philosophically and psychologically speaking, was similar to the acrobatics that he subsequently performed by jumping into questions of honour in his writings on the stock exchange. No doubt the agricultural economist was fascinated by the connection that Weber had drawn between soil quality and spiritual values – a connection which promised to raise agrarian studies to the level of a cultural science. On 21 March 1893, at the mere age of twenty-nine, Max Weber joined the leading circle of the Verein für Sozialpolitik when he was co-opted on to its committee (MWG I/4-1, 160). In those days the Verein was the key network for careers in political and economic science, and in the following months it became clear that the young scholar was now also thought of as professorial material.

Not only did Weber's report address a political issue of the greatest significance; it also appeared in a delicate political situation. Whereas the relations of the Prussian state with its Polish citizens had for a long time been undramatic, a new policy since 1885 sought to stem the influx of Polish and other Slav farm-workers from the east, even though this shift conflicted with the material interests of the big landowners in the east, of whom Bismarck was one. From a national point of view, then – at least as far as Bismarck was concerned – it was an instance of 'idealism'. Caprivi, however, as part of his 'new course' after 1891, felt impelled to withdraw the restrictions as a quid pro quo for the agrarians' lowering of grain tariffs. This was the situation in which the Verein für Sozialpolitik decided on its investigation. Weber's study of farm-workers came right in the middle of Caprivi's policy of 'reconciliation' towards the Poles and provided ammunition for the 'Pan-German League' (AGU) to campaign against the Slav advance in the east (the main topic at the League's first congress in 1894). It was during this period that Weber joined the Pan-Germans, and when he left them in 1899 he did so on the grounds that they had shown a lack of courage vis-à-vis the agrarians by failing to campaign consistently against the influx of Polish and Russian farm-workers.

Weber's main point was to recommend an urgent return to the restrictive policy of the late Bismarck period. This did happen in 1895, so that by 1907 Ludwig Bernhard, in his extensive study of the 'Polish question', could claim that 'since 1896' the Germans had been aware that the Poles were proving 'superior in the struggle for land'.[30] This would mean that in 1893 Max Weber discovered something which most people had not yet noticed. In Bernhard's view, however, the Polish superiority was due not to a primitive lack of material needs but to a highly effective community life – that is, to the very sense of community which Gierke and his supporters considered to be characteristically German. Most of Bernhard's long book is taken up with this theme. But unlike Weber, who spoke no Polish, Bernhard made full use of Polish sources and got to know the shrewder side of Poles; he did not lag behind Weber in his enthusiasm for Germanization, however, and after the latter's death proclaimed a sentimental attachment to him as the great mind behind the policy of Germanization,[31] even though Weber in his lifetime had treated him badly and loudly denounced his appointment.

A paradoxical ecological determinism

In fact, Weber's approach to the 'eastern' problem was quite different from Bernhard's. It is by comparing the two that we can see the degree to which he based himself on the land and agrarian relations – virtually absent themes in Bernhard – and reconstructed the course of things as a kind of natural process rather than one intentionally steered by communities. In this respect, he may be said to have developed a paradoxical kind of ecological determinism, as the leitmotif in his evaluation of the survey results was that *good* land does not keep its people on it. Those on the good land were Germans who would no longer tolerate their old subservience, whereas poor Poles settled on the worse land, happy to have at last a little plot of their own. But the new agrarian capitalism had a much stronger impact on the good land than the bad, with the result that the 'advantage of especially favourable soil . . . accrues to the owners in relatively greater measure than to the workers' (MWG I/3-1, 359). A general correlation does exist between the land and human social behaviour, but it is not a relationship of simple or direct causality.

Cows and freedom

A constant theme in the responses to the questionnaire is that ownership of a cow of their own is mainly what keeps German small farmers in their cottage;[32] the next thing tying a man to his native region is a capable wife

(MWG I/3-1, 98). But neither cow nor wife receives a mention in Weber's final balance-sheet, where it is the basic human desire for *freedom* which drives Germans westward. This certainly does not follow directly from the empirical findings,[33] but is an expression of Weber's core belief that only strong and deep passions can cause people to change their whole way of life and drive them from their native land. Hunger and material greed are not enough: there must also be a higher passion counteracting the human law of inertia. This will also be the fundamental axiom of his *The Protestant Ethic*. It is a tragedy that the freedom so longed for in the West is ultimately an illusion. The emphasis of the old liberal attitude to freedom remains alien to Weber.

How did Weber's balance-sheet tally with the responses to the questionnaire? The landowners were understandably concerned to avoid giving the impression that low wages and wretched working conditions had been forcing their 'people' to emigrate. This reluctance of theirs certainly matched Weber's aim of not lingering on a simplistic material causality. In the Reichstag, Bismarck himself had more than once mentioned some of his 'people' who, when asked what had driven them to move to Berlin from a home where they would have lived and eaten better, could 'with a slight blush' name only one 'decisive reason': 'Okay, but in Varzin you don't have a place with open-air music where you can sit outdoors and drink beer.'[34] One could, if one so desired, make out of this a longing for freedom. But perhaps it did only represent a wish for music and beer.

In 1893 Weber and Paul Göhre from the Evangelical Social Congress were entrusted with another survey of farm-workers, in which the questionnaires were this time to be sent to country parsons as comparatively objective witnesses. Göhre's connections with socially committed clergymen were useful for this purpose. In 1894 he and Weber delivered an interim report to the Evangelical Social Congress in Frankfurt, but this brought to light an estrangement between the two men. Weber took a clear distance from Göhre's radical proposal to divide up the large estates into smaller farms (MWG I/4-1, 335ff.).

Weber had wanted to handle the study professionally and with the use of statistics, but over time he lost his enthusiasm (MWG I/4-2, 688). Besides, he did not feel disposed to do the calculations himself: he saw that as women's work, in opposition to the usual cliché that rationality corresponds to men's nature and emotion to women's. Marianne was only too pleased to lend a hand. In 1896 she wrote to Helene Weber: 'Everything feminine in us is calculating pigs, cattle, Jews, Poles, children, meadows, land areas, prices, etc. etc. and saving us a tidy sum.'[35] From time to time, she was even the driving force behind the project for which Max had lost his enthusiasm: 'I'm always trying to gear Max up', so that the 'hard-working pastors' who filled in the long questionnaires 'don't lose patience'.[36] But for Max Weber the subject was obviously exhausted: nothing very new occurred to him. One notes, not without a smile, how even such a dogged pioneer of 'drilling through thick board' in the social sciences treated the 'numbers stuff' as a tiresome menial job to be hived off to assistants for the sake of keeping possible critics at bay. Marianne even thought that calculations put too much of a strain on him, until the point came when his brain would no longer be able to take it.[37]

Rationalization or regression?

Did Weber see the development of agriculture as progress? The reformers on whom he drew for many observations in his agrarian studies had been as sanguine as only reformers can be. But Weber could see for himself many of the long-term effects of the agrarian reforms propagated in the years around 1800 – for example, the division and privatization of common land, which deprived many lower-class people of the possibility of owning a cow of their own, or the reformers' pet project of potato cultivation. The experience of Ireland had shown how potatoes heaped more troubles on small farmers, and the ratio of potato to meat consumption was for Weber always an indicator of poverty or relative prosperity. The potato harvest, during which farmers slid around on their knees in the mud together with their wives and children, had none of the charm of 'modernization'. At the Evangelical Social Congress in 1894, Weber referred to the fact that in south-west Germany 'the strongest local patriotism among workers' was found where the division of common land had 'made the least progress' (MWG I/4-1, 320f.) and the lower classes had preserved their customary rights to the land. In 1916, on a trip through eastern Germany, he noted 'how all these villages [had] been scattered around and robbed of any formal unity through the resettlement that took place in the process of privatization and concentration'.[38]

Some of what Weber described in his study of farm-workers would later reappear as 'rationalization', but at the time he saw it mainly as the advance of a lower culture. 'Capitalism' here meant specifically the advance of sugar beet instead of grain crops, and consequently an increase in migrant labour and social regression. 'Is the rationally managed and financially strong *large enterprise* also an economic and social step forward for *agrarian* conditions?' Weber asked in 1893 in a letter to Lujo Brentano. And he immediately answered: 'At the present time I think it is in no case a social step forward, and an economic step forward (only) in our *German* conditions' (JB 364). On this issue he found himself in agreement with quite a few agricultural economists of the time. It was possible to argue that modern agrarian technique required large-scale enterprise, but there were advantages then, and right down to the early 1950s, on the side of an intensive horticulture in which farmers had an interest in keeping an eye on everything. Large-scale enterprise did embody progress in terms of the steam plough and the threshing-machine, but that was not the perspective in which Weber saw things. In 1918 he still detected a tendency for the farming population to *increase* (GASS 507).

In 1896, in a lecture to socially committed lawyers and economists, Weber spoke of the 'good, medium-sized farming community resting on scientific foundations' (MWG I/4-2, 808), in pointed contrast to the large landowners who speculated on the grain market. Nor were such remarks simply tailored to the situation. 'For Weber the peasant was the last free human being', wrote Hennis[39] – or, at any rate, the farmer whose self-provision gave him a certain independence of market conjunctures. In 1912, in a report for the statement on social policy that Lujo Brentano had proposed mainly in the interests of the workers, Weber wrote under point 1 that 'an increase in the numbers of settled independent farmers with a stake in land ownership' was 'absolutely desirable' (MWG II/7-2, 749). In comparison, the 'unstoppable rise in the numbers' of office employees concerned a lesser class of people who, 'because of their occupational conditions, were often more severely threatened in their personal development than many of the upper layers of workers, and in particular ran the risk . . . of becoming, in their innermost being, an uncultured layer of dependent individuals bred in a mixture of dejection and unfulfilled ambitions' (GASS 750). In this concentration of disparaging remarks, the author seems to forget that the rising generation of academics also displayed quite a few of the features attributed to this unhappy section of the population.

Was it economic autonomy, 'freedom', which in Weber's eyes constituted the special value of farmers capable of self-provision? But he must have known, as a matter of historical fact, that such freedom had frequently not amounted to much; that, when farmers had been legally free, they had often suffered all the more from the pressure of debts and taxes. Rather, it was a certain closeness to nature which Weber saw as the distinctive quality of the farmer's life: the fact that he grew into life, did his work, produced children and died as if all these things were a matter of course. 'At the level of the peasant, the sexual act is an everyday occurrence', Weber later remarked; 'primitive people do not regard this act as containing anything unusual, and they may indeed enact it before the eyes of onlooking travellers without the slightest feeling of shame' (E&S 607) – an exaggerated view of the 'naturalness' of 'primitive people' [*Naturmenschen*], as we know today. And a little further on he describes the 'emergence' of man 'from the organic cycle of simple peasant existence' as a process of rationalization and refinement that generates agonizing tensions. The 'organic cycle' is for Weber not only a metaphor but a reality; he is repeatedly gratified by the idea that self-sufficient farmers fertilize the soil with their own excreta.[40]

What was the practical import of all this for Weber? Later, none at all: pure knowledge would be enough for him. But things were different in the 1890s: he was actively involved in the Verein für Sozialpolitik, which, to use a modern expression, saw itself as a think tank for social policy. It is still unclear to what extent that was true, as the answer depends largely on the political weight one attaches to a dominant position in public discourse.[41] Weber's own evolution tells us something of the difficulty of drawing practical consequences from academic reflections. After years of suffering, he disposed of this dangerous problem by drawing a sharp distinction between science and practice.

Already in the 1890s Weber did not have much to offer in the way of actual policy conceptions – a shortcoming which, given his great desire to be consistent, must have depressed him over the years. Wolfgang Mommsen detects in the Weber of that time an underlying tone of 'resignation' as soon as he turned his mind to practical perspectives for the future.[42] His ideal was the small or medium-sized farmer working intensively for nearby urban markets. But what was to be done when, as in the eastern territories, there were no such markets? Unlike Göhre, Weber would not have dreamt of calling for the large estates to be broken up; that was anyway excluded in the conditions of imperial Germany. Nor was he inclined like Goerke to preach the cooperative gospel, as he had too lively a picture of the elemental individualism of the peasantry. Only Leo Wegener, Weber's most emotional admirer among his early students (WB 244),[43] gained 'almost fairy-tale popularity' in the east as the brains behind the German Cooperative Movement.[44] Sometimes Weber struck a radical tone by advocating the settlement of tenant farmers on expanded state domains,[45] but he did not go much further than that. He called for state intervention, but also recognized that it was 'the rule in the life of society that state intervention in the economy comes, like remorse, as a limping messenger – too late' (MWG I/4-1, 197).

On 13 March 1897, Weber spoke to the Freiburg branch of the Pan-German League (of which he was still a member) about 'the Polish population in the eastern territories'. The press report makes it clear that Weber saw the problem of establishing a local German community there as essentially insoluble (MWG I/4-2, 822ff.); to settle German farmers in the east, without creating the conditions for them to remain there, would be a waste of effort. On 21 March 1893, in his report to the general meeting of the Verein für Sozialpolitik, Weber concluded that, given the fall in grain prices, 'small-scale enterprises are today more able to survive than large estates producing for the market'. And he continued: 'A landowner who delivers his produce mainly to a place where the world-market price is least important – that is, to his own stomach – is presently the one most able to survive in the east' (MWG I/4-1, 191). Here is the germ of an idea which is becoming topical again at today's level of 'globalization': namely, that growing worldwide competition, together with the superior strength of big capital, forces everyone whose position in this struggle is hopelessly inferior to resort on an increasing scale to self-provision.[46]

Antaeus as a dwarf: the down-to-earth Poles

The subsistence farmer was comparable to the mythical figure of Antaeus, who derived his strength from the earth. In the modern economy, however, that meant being a dwarf rather than a giant. The Polish migrant workers who settled as small farmers on poor land left to them by big landowners in the east were actually people who suited that land; their advance was in keeping with the natural environment. As they irresistibly undermined the culture of the old aristocratic estates, whose material foundations were crumbling away, Weber must have been reminded of the decline of ancient civilization, whose path to barbarism, from his point of view, was at the same time a recovery leading it back to 'the bosom of Mother Earth'. Was not something similar happening in the eastern territories?

The terrible vision of a young and vigorous Polish nation with unfettered reproductive energy was haunting the dreams of Germany's educated middle classes. Melitta Maschmann, former leader of Hitler's BDM (League of German Girls), spoke in her memoirs of her path to National Socialism. As a child, she saw a map on which various pictures represented the relative position of Europe's children: for Germans, a 'frightened little girl'; for Poles, a 'sturdy little boy crawling on all fours aggressively in the direction of the German frontier'. 'Look at the boy', her father said to her. 'He is bursting with health and strength. One day he will overrun the little girl.'[47] Similar worries must have haunted the childless Max Weber, who over the years experienced for himself the agonizing connection between high culture and instinctual inhibitions. It was a common belief that Slavs were ruled more by their physical impulses than were Germans. Thus, in Fontane's novel *The Stechlin*, when Czako makes one of his characteristically lewd innuendoes, his German fellow officers jokingly taunt him: 'Czako, you're getting frivolous again. . . . It's that Slavic blood that bubbles up in you, latent sensuality.'[48]

Now and again Weber quite seriously creates the impression that Germans and Poles have different bodies, or at least different stomachs – and that therefore, on the barren soil in the east, the Germans stand no chance of competing against the Poles. 'It is not possible to allow two nationalities with different physical constitutions – differently constructed stomachs, to be quite specific – to compete entirely freely as workers on one and the same territory. . . . We want to get along with our Polish compatriots; we hope to raise the Polish proletariat inside the country to the level of German culture. But this will be impossible if the continual swarm of eastern nomads regularly undoes this cultural work and turns it into its opposite' (MWG I/4-1, 182). The 'influx of Poles' was indeed 'far more dangerous from a cultural viewpoint' than even the introduction of Chinese coolies, for 'our German workers do not integrate with coolies but, in the case of the Poles, they do integrate with the half-Germanized Slavs in the east of the country.' This was Weber in 1893, addressing the general meeting of the Verein für Sozialpolitik.

For rhetorical effect he dropped a few clangers that would have been more in place at an officer's mess in Posen than in a scientific investigation. The military exercises in Posen had instilled in him a horror of that region: the city itself was filled with dirt and stench; 'the potato country outside it was bad and sandy'; and everywhere there was an atmosphere of tedium and lethargy (JB 302f.). One cannot help thinking that it was at least as much this experience in Posen as his evaluation of the questionnaires which shaped his major study of farm-workers. Guenther Roth is of the view that 'Weber's fast-acquired reputation as an agrarian expert had more to do with his nationalist sentiment than with his analytic astuteness' (R 50). At the founding meeting of Friedrich Naumann's National-Social Association in Erfurt in November 1896, where Weber tried to steer the evangelical philanthropists away from a preoccupation with the sordid aspects of life towards an imperial power politics, he heatedly engaged with the idea that Poles were being turned into 'second-class citizens': 'The opposite is true', he argued; 'we have turned the Poles from animals into human beings' (MWG I/4-2, 622).[49] And he concluded: 'Landgrave, harden yourself!'[50]

In the long term, however, a man of Weber's intellectual calibre could not fail to see that he was getting carried away on the Polish question and becoming entangled in contradictions. If a bodily gulf really separated Germans from Poles, why did they so easily integrate with each other? Was it not the case that, as soon as Poles had enough money, they were just as likely to shop at the delicatessen? Weber's later anti-naturalism may contain an element of shame that, out of sheer emotionalism, he had once landed himself in a patently unscientific (and moreover apolitical) kind of naturalism.

Love–hate towards the Junkers

Weber also vacillated in his attitude to the landowners who brought the Poles into the country. The Junkers, along with the Jews, were one of the great emotive issues for Weber and many of his contemporaries – especially as it aroused contradictory feelings. Weber could fume like a typical liberal against the lords and masters east of the Elbe: against the agrarian noblemen who set themselves up as the mainstay of the German nation but in practice ruthlessly pursued their own self-interest, far more narrow-mindedly than the 'materialistic' labour movement; who invoked higher values and often displayed a singular lack of education; who claimed high officer's ranks for themselves, without having the competence and iron discipline needed in modern warfare; who had recently adopted a nationalist and anti-Semitic register yet imported Slavs into the country and were the best customers of Jewish moneylenders; and who often retained of their 'patriarchal' care only a penchant for seducing their female farmhands (MWG I/3-2, 738f.).

And yet Weber had a dislike for the usual liberal clichés about the Junkers. His attacks on the landowners of eastern Prussia are often lumped together with the usual liberal polemics in the name of the progressive character of industrial society,[51] but on closer inspection it is clear that something else was at stake. A lack of technical innovation was the last thing for which many large landowners could be reproached, as they were often at the top of the table of European agriculture. But the 'sugar-beet barons' were the lowest of all in Weber's estimation; the capitalist magnates in question, who had learned well how to calculate, were no longer noble landowners of the old school. 'On their brow the flush of passion is mixed with the paleness of thought', Weber wrote mockingly (MWG I/4-1, 326). Was that not true also of himself? He sounds as torn as Theodor Fontane in his feelings towards the landowners.

In Weber's time, liberals and conservatives were at odds over whether to promote free trade or tariff protection. Weber repeatedly pinned his flag to the mast of high tariffs, on the grounds that free international competition on the grain market would turn large parts of eastern Germany into 'desert' (MWG I/4-1, 334, 338, 343). When Theodor Mommsen, thinking of the pro-tariff propaganda of the League of Landowners (Bund der Landwirte), described them to the like-minded Lujo Brentano as 'gangs of crooks' in search of 'plunder',[52] the tone probably nauseated Weber, for whom the economic 'life-and-death struggle' of the nobility had the makings of tragedy.

In 1890, when Weber cast a ballot for the first time in national elections, he voted for the Conservatives. Marianne Weber turns this into 'Free Conservatives' (WB 125), although in his constituency at that time there was only one conservative candidate.[53] At the general meeting of the Verein für Sozialpolitik in March 1893, which discussed the study of farmworkers, Weber robustly countered a left-wing critic, the social democrat journalist Max Quarck, by saying that he was unable 'to share the whole inane hatred of everything called landownership, especially landownership in the east'. 'On the contrary', he continued, 'the labour situation that used to exist in eastern Germany partly gives me pleasure, albeit only a historical-aesthetic pleasure, from the point of view of an effective organization of work' (MWG I/4-1, 199).

There may have been a tactical element in this remark, but it did partly reflect the feelings that Weber had towards the Junkers. Those old warhorses, 'cabbage Junkers' for urban liberals but men who had known how to fight when the chips were down, embodied for Weber 'the eastern marches on which nature has showered so few gifts' (MWG I/3-2, 927) and the historical roots of Prussia's greatness. Early in 1895 he wrote to Karl Oldenberg from Freiburg – certainly also as a friendly gesture – that he had 'often been forced to speak up for our Junkers' vis-à-vis the 'petty bourgeois of southern Germany'.[54] The 'rule of the narrow-minded petty bourgeoisie' was the main danger for Germany (MWG I/4-1, 341), which in plain language referred to southern German liberals who were not filled with enthusiasm for Prussia's glory and service of the Mark Brandenburg nobility. Anyone like Weber, who had such a sense of honour, gentlemanly instinct and warrior-like ruggedness, could not be free of any weakness for such human types. In late 1897, he confessed in one of his lectures in Mannheim that, if the only choice was between 'rule by north German Junkerdom' and 'rule by the south German petty bourgeoisie', he would prefer the former

(MWG I/4-2, 852). And in *Economy and Society* he portrays feudalism not as mere rule by force but, in an idealistic touch, as a relationship of mutual allegiance between lord and vassal (E&S 1070ff.). At most he blamed the Junkers of his time for the fact that they were no longer loyal lords and masters but banal lobbyists who held the interests of the nation in contempt.

Towards the end of 1917, in the midst of his general assault on outmoded conditions in Prussia-Germany, Weber paid the feudal landowners a compliment that drew on his own experience: 'Anyone who knows the much (and often unjustly) maligned and (equally unjustly) idolized Junkers of the eastern provinces is bound to take delight in them on a purely personal level – when out hunting, drinking a drop of something decent, at the card-table, amidst the hospitality of the estate farm – in these areas everything about them is genuine' (PW 114). He then continues in quite a different vein, yet at this point a deep contentment breaks through in what he writes. The 'Junker' clearly speaks to his instinctual side, precisely because of a rustic vitality that neither the asceticism of work nor over-refinement of the intellect has caused to decline into ill health. He had once before associated the 'feudalization' of the German bourgeoisie with a loosening of sexual morality (MWG I/4-2, 634).[55] To put it succinctly, Weber's love–hate relationship to nature is reflected in his 'love–hate towards the Prussian Junkers' (Helmuth Plessner).

The ubiquitous Bismarck

Weber's feelings towards the estate owners – how could it have been otherwise? – were bound up not least with his feelings towards Bismarck. He had been a major figure in Weber's life ever since childhood, as he had in the lives of most politically aware Germans. Bismarck was a constant presence in the political discussions in Weber's parental home – even when no one was actually speaking about him. The German American Friedrich Kapp, who made a strong impression on the young Weber, knew the chancellor very closely; he felt utter contempt for the Reichstag's 'eunuch majority', which had let itself be politically emasculated by Bismarck yet remained under the powerful man's spell: 'The man is not broken by the routine of office, the rigidity of bureaucratism.' Kapp described those in his entourage who went around 'with a dog-collar' as masochists addicted to the pleasure of submission.[56] Max Weber too knew that pleasure.

For Weber, however, Bismarck was evidently *not* the model of a charismatic leader. Most of the qualities that Weber ascribed to such a figure do not apply at all to the chancellor: he was not possessed in the manner of a prophet, nor did he have any inclination for revolutionary demagogy. Some evidence of Bismarck's magic may be seen in Weber's cousin Otto Baumgarten, born in 1858, whose political life falls into a first part, when he was under the spell of the 'Iron Chancellor', and a second part when he energetically broke free of it. Otto was at the beginning of adolescence in 1870 when he was bowled over by Prussia's victory at the battle of Sedan, a day on which the bells rang all over Germany and the German Michel grew overnight into the Archangel Michael.[57] It was a 'glorious' time which, like the first erotic experiences, left its mark on the whole personality. 'Militarism and monarchism' were from then on 'deeply rooted in my young heart', Otto confessed in 1929 in a self-critical retrospect.[58] He wrote a book about 'Bismarck's faith', thereby clashing with the views of his sceptical cousin.[59]

For Max Weber thought otherwise about the 'Iron Chancellor'. He was born in 1864 and lived through Bismarck's wars without being conscious of them: a period of six years – from 1864 to 1870 – which in those days marked a difference of generations.[60] It was especially popular to reflect about generations, and the experience of victories was thought to have been constitutive of one. Ricarda Huch, born like Weber in 1864 and in her way thoroughly 'national' in her thinking, felt only 'boredom' at the war of 1870 that had been flogged to death in the imperial culture of reminiscence, and Bismarck himself was a 'nightmare' for her.[61] During the battle of Königgrätz, in the Austro-Prussian war of 1866, the two-year-old Max lay sick with meningitis; at the time of Sedan he had only barely recovered from it. He belonged to the same age group as Otto Hintze (b. 1861), Friedrich Meinecke (b. 1862), Werner Sombart (b. 1863) and Ernst Troeltsch (b. 1865) – and, for all their differences, a generational affinity is visible among these well-known scholars. All were deeply, though not compulsively, marked by Bismarck's founding of the Reich, and over time they developed a capacity for sober detachment. They became politically conscious during the great disillusionment following the 'Imperial Spring', in the hangover brought on by the 'Great Crash', when it was clear that the victorious war and the new empire had created more social problems than they had solved. This came as no surprise for those familiar with the history of ancient Rome.

News of Bismarck's death on 30 July 1898 reached Weber at the Konstanzerhof psychiatric clinic. Whereas many Germans broke into tears, the report left him cold: 'However great my admiration, it will always be impossible for me to think with truly unalloyed pleasure of the great statesman, who was not a great man.'[62] Many of his contemporaries, feeling deeply disappointed in Wilhelm II, bought into the new Bismarck cult promoted by Maximilian Harden's journal *Die Zukunft*. But Max Weber did not go along with this and, to Marianne's regret, did not even take out a subscription to *Die Zukunft*,[63] which was as popular then as *Der Spiegel* has become in recent decades.

From his childhood Weber knew inside out the whole list of liberal complaints about Bismarck. In 1937 Alfred Weber recalled: 'When Bismarck "drove the National Liberals to the wall" in 1878-79, those affected would very often discuss things at our house. My father let me listen, as if this were the most natural thing in the world for a ten-year-old.'[64] And, of course, the fourteen-year-old Max would have pricked up his ears even more. If

Bismarck was a man who crushed the big grown-ups, this did not necessarily make him unattractive for a teenage boy. And in Max's student years,
when his uncle Hermann Baumgarten used to have fits of rage in his presence about Berlin politicians, Weber became 'a silent and therefore faulty
lightning conductor for them' (JB 117), especially as the uncle, in a moment
of weakness, said with a deep sigh that '*we* are the only ones to blame if he
wreaks so much havoc, because we are complete nonentities'. We can
imagine how this must have sounded to Weber! 'Yet there is a great strength
in what Bismarck says' (JB 153).

What infuriated the twenty-year-old Weber about Bismarck was not so
much his militarism and autocratic bearing: 'The basic mistake . . . is the
Greek gift of Bismarckian Caesarism: universal suffrage, sheer murder for
the equal rights of all *in the true sense of the term*' (JB 143). His own father
became a victim of this when he failed to be re-elected to the Reichstag.
Weber's reasoning at the time was that universal suffrage encouraged the
growth of social democracy, which in turn led to anti-SPD legislation and
the curbing of liberal acquisitions.

For Weber in 1885, the 'sorest point' of Bismarck's policy was 'naturally'
the now long-forgotten 'Schweninger affair' (JB 151). At the time Bismarck
had ignored the protests of the Berlin medical faculty and imposed as professor his personal physician Ernst Schweninger, who, he thought, had
saved him from death; he must have derived special pleasure from the fact
that this angered his old liberal foe, Virchow. In fact, Schweninger was a
prophet of natural healing who always said that the point was to cure not
illnesses but ill people, and who ridiculed the '*Ubi est morbus?*' principle
behind Virchow's localization approach. Rather as Marianne interpreted
Weber's later breakdown, Schweninger regarded Bismarck's major health
problems of 1883 as nature's punishment for a lifestyle that had been constantly against nature. Bismarck adopted this way of looking at things[65]
and, in accordance with the model of Antaeus, used to seek regeneration
in the rural solitude of his estate at Varzin. In a terrible turn of events,
which came as a free gift to his medical opponents, the stocky black-
bearded Schweninger was caught *in flagrante* with a society lady at a lonely
Munich cemetery and sentenced to a term of imprisonment.[66] But this evidently did not damage his reputation in Bismarck's eyes.

One element of Weber's love–hate for nature may also be found in the
way he related to Bismarck. Soaring above cows and sugar beets, his major
study of farm-workers concludes with a glance at Bismarck and the discovery of his link to the soil. 'Essential features of his nature cannot be
understood without the soil on which he grew up.' Here the earth becomes
a vast organism extending deep into society. And Bismarck's 'profound
contempt for human beings' is attributed to 'the soil of the patriarchal
system' and considered 'peculiar to the grandest and most energetic natures
of his social group' (MWG I/3-2, 928). Nature here is not an idyll, but it is
certainly powerful. Now, however, that soil is exhausted; the age requires a
new kind of leader.

From earth to water

Agrarian conditions became a theme that often triggered Weber's thundering rhetoric and occupied him academically. The last dissertation that he supervised before he gave up university duties dealt with economic conditions in the marshes and heathland of Hanover province.[67] Nor was it only in social science and politics that the roots of human culture in the soil interested him; many travel letters show that his agrarian reflections were based upon observation of the landscape, although it is also noticeable that he saw mainly what he *wanted* to see. Whereas a normal tourist in rural Britain delights in the 'Arcadian' park vistas, Weber focused on the traces of depopulation and the resulting emptiness of the countryside (WB 208, 495). No doubt he had in mind the old (but actually not everywhere well-founded) complaint that the enclosures had replaced people with sheep.

Whereas in *The Protestant Ethic* one finds between the lines much admiration for Puritanism and the British spirit of work, a different perception is evident in the travel letters: namely, Britain as a country which drove the farmers from the land and thereby severed its own links to nature. For Weber, the powerful impression made by the Norman village churches came from the fact that they had become far too big for their pathetically shrunken villages.[68] He transferred to the British Isles some of the main themes of his criticism of conditions in eastern Germany. In 1895 he wrote from Ireland that the home rule movement rightly saw the British 'landlord' as the 'root of all evil'. 'My heart tightened when I saw the people in their rags . . . and then thought of the incredible wealth to be seen in the parks.'[69]

In the Limousin region in 1897, he observed with pleasure the well-balanced and harmonious subsistence farmers. There, 'the country frees itself from the city: the farmer still eats what he grows.'[70] He examined the devastating effects of phylloxera in the vineyards of southern France, and in northern Spain, where his incipient illness became ever more noticeable (WB 233f.), he nevertheless found 'opportunity enough to discover the huge contrast between the industriousness of the rural population in these beautiful parts and the vileness of the Spanish state administration'. The officials were lazy and corrupt. 'On the other hand, the peasantry is surely one of the most splendid in the world. . . . The whole constitution of society, its customs and institutions, are thoroughly democratic.'[71] Those familiar with Spanish history will find this a surprising assertion. Was not Spain, of all European countries, the one with the most arrogant aristocracy and an especially primitive peasantry? But what counted for Weber were not only the legal conditions but the ability of people to run their own daily lives – and this he found more among the Spanish peasantry than among German office workers. Not without reason was a peasant anarchism then taking shape precisely in Spain.

Weber's last lecture in Heidelberg, in the winter semester of 1899-1900, dealt with agrarian policy. And the liveliest of the writings following his return to health – the long treatise on 'The Entailment Question in Prussia'

(1904) – also took up the polemics on agrarian policy. He was furious at the intention visible in a new draft law: namely, to make it more attractive for moneyed people to acquire indivisible noble estates. Usually most attention is directed at Weber's attacks on the feudalization of the bourgeoisie; but his concluding point here, as in the study of land workers, is that the advantage given to large estates hinders the rise of a 'strong and numerous farming population' (GASS 393). Besides, he is not absolutely opposed to entailment and even regards it as useful for the preservation of forests, nearly half of entailed estates consisting of forest land. Weber knows how to appreciate the 'joy in forest . . . that has always been characteristic of the feudal sensibility' (GASS 329). Much later, in his farewell address in Heidelberg in 1919, he celebrated the German forests as a lasting treasure, when, as Jaspers put it, he 'could find nothing' else 'that could truly create courage as a visible substance of German essence'.[72]

After the years of illness religion became Weber's main theme, which for the most part came out of himself. Even in his writings on the sociology of religion, however, we continually encounter peasants and landlords – especially among the Israelites of the Old Testament. At the St Louis world exhibition of 1904, he spoke not about the Puritan ethic but about agrarian conditions in Germany. When he turned to the Russian Revolution in 1905, he saw far more clearly than others that its kernel was the peasant 'hunger for land'.[73] And, when someone called him 'a disciple of Schmoller', leader of the 'Historical School of economics', he replied: 'Meitzen was my teacher' (WzG 212).

In 1909, when Weber, according to today's sociologists, should have been concentrating on *Economy and Society*, he turned his manual entry on 'agrarian conditions in antiquity' into a book-length study that worked out from agriculture to take in a large part of ancient social history. Soon after he had begun work on it, he complained that the 'wretched article' would again make him dependent on sleeping potions (MWG II/5, 478), but the actual text, with its many passages of several pages without a paragraph break, strikes the reader as bubbling over with ideas. Although not exactly an easy read, it is described by Alfred Heuss as 'the most original, audacious and forceful account ever given of the economic and social development of the ancient world'.[74] This work, to which little attention has been given in Weber studies, leaves no doubt that, in the twenty years since publication of *Die römische Agrargeschichte* and his study of farm-workers, Weber had continued to read extensively in the field of both ancient and agrarian history.

This time, along with the soil, a more prominent place is occupied by the other great leitmotif of agrarian history: *water*. Weber points out that the culture of antiquity was a coastal culture; he now attaches greater value to trade and often tones down the emphasis on natural economy that he had taken over from Rodbertus.[75] Whereas he previously had a touchy relationship with geography (WzG 191f.), he now regards not the Protestant ethic but 'geographical nature' as the decisive condition for Europe's special path of development (PE I 359). Above all, he keeps returning to the significance of irrigated agriculture for the bureaucratic system of rule in the ancient Near East (AS 38, 46, 84, 91) and in China. It inspired Karl August Wittfogel's famous, or notorious, theory of 'hydraulic society'.[76] When Weber claims that in ancient Egypt it was 'the technical necessity of a public regulation of the water economy' which created 'the apparatus of scribes and officials' (E&S 971f.), he exaggerates even the economic determinism; for the Nile manages to water parts of its valley even in the complete absence of a hydraulic bureaucracy.[77] According to Weber, the charisma of the Chinese emperor rested essentially upon magical powers over water and broke down when there was a breach in the dikes (MWG I/19, 176f.). But, since China continued to need hydraulic charisma, imperial power kept being reproduced.

Towards the end of his life, Weber no longer analysed the great change in world history mainly in terms of the triumphal march of the Puritan work ethic, but attributed it more to the subsequent liberation of 'production from the organic limits in which nature held it trapped'. 'In this way, however, crises also became an immanent part of the economic order' (WG 251). Detachment from nature makes crisis intrinsic to the economy – and also to man. From now on, Weber's experience of the world and of himself would revolve around this process.

5

Eruptions from the Ice: Creativity as Natural Catastrophe

The puzzle of Weber's fame

It is not easy to say, and still harder to theorize, why Weber became as famous as he did. Those who have done research on him for many years are all too familiar with his weaknesses and may sometimes feel downright anger that they are devoting so much valuable time to him.[1] As to why they do this, the answers centre on certain of his concepts, theses, theories and methods: the types of legitimate rule, the supposed elective affinity between Puritan ethic and 'spirit' of capitalism, the theory of ideal types and the value-freedom of science. That is all very well. But it was already questionable in Weber's day whether *The Protestant Ethic* stood up to empirical scrutiny, and as to 'value-freedom' it has long been a virtual truism among social scientists that it is more sensible to face up to one's own cognitive interests and the value-judgements contained in them, instead of imagining that one can write in value-free terms about (at least the major) historical-sociological questions.

What of the concepts? 'Charisma' – which, though not originating with Weber, did become famous through him – has probably had the greatest success. But the social sciences have not been able to do much with the 'a-cosmic love' that is supposed to break social orders into pieces. In general, Weber showed no great skill in finding a succinct conceptualization of his thoughts.[2] In his haste he continually placed words in quotation marks,[3] probably because he thought that he did not yet have the most precise term: this is one indication of the fact that, unlike so many Weberians, he thought on the basis of phenomena rather than a precise terminology. He was not the kind of academic whose reputation rests mainly on artful coining of his own trademark concepts. He was drawn to the concrete not least because 'the test of concrete historical situations' reveals 'seemingly unambiguous concepts in their ambiguity'.[4]

Especially in the years from 1903 to 1907, often in debate with other thinkers, Weber published a series of lengthy essays on the theory and methodology of science, from which his executors assembled his ostensible 'theory of science'. These writings, some of the least enjoyable in his whole body of work, were composed in troubled times when his health was teetering from one relapse to another. In 1913, when he was feeling well, he detested the 'methodological pestilence' with which he thought sociology had been struck (B 139).[5] Certainly it would be hard to find the enduring essence of his work in the supposed 'theory of science'. But his endlessly quoted lecture of 7 November 1917, 'Science a Vocation', is itself only a very partial reflection of his way of conducting scientific investigation. He was the polar opposite of the modern type of blinkered specialist whom he describes there. It is impossible to grasp what is special about him by assembling a handful of quotes from these texts.

Scholars would dearly love to have an understanding of Weber's creative process and work technique, how ideas came to him and how he developed them in his thinking, for it is on these factors, not so much on textbook theories and methods, that intellectual productivity mainly depends. The process of creation in Weber is not easy to reconstruct, however. Marianne Weber, for whom his style of work was not exactly exemplary, probably covered up many traces of it. Scarcely any manuscripts or corrected drafts of his writings have been preserved (and, even if they had, it is doubtful whether anyone would be able to make head or tail of them). He did not write out his lectures in advance but merely jotted down some keywords on a piece of paper.[6] 'Yesterday I packed your lecture notebooks, but they were an absolute mess, you untidy little boy', Marianne wrote to Max in 1910 when they were moving home in Heidelberg.[7] Later, in his Munich work room, he made notes on sheets of paper and spread them out on a couple of tables. Marianne developed an aesthetic repulsion for this kind of 'chaos':

Yes, the desk was taboo! A chaotic jumble of papers, (where) he often got into a frenzy looking for a note or letter and experienced the cussedness of inanimate objects. It was a long time before my appetite for beauty would tolerate such an island of disorder in his room, and the few angry outbursts I caused in him were nearly always provoked by what he called my quadratic drive for order, which, he claimed, had to work itself out in quadratic rearrangement of books and sheets of paper. . . . He claimed that he would be less annoyed at having to search for things if he knew for sure that he and he alone had mislaid them. On countless occasions I rushed with secret female pride to assist him in his male helplessness.[8]

Actually she almost never speaks of an angry outburst by her husband against herself. Anyone who works with such a chaos of papers around him will understand Weber's rage, but there can be no doubt that, although he found rationalization processes everywhere in world history, his own work methods show no sign of them. As Theodor Heuss remarked, Weber's 'style of work' gave an impression of 'irrationality or restlessness in the series of questions that he addressed' (WzG 157). We are struck by the incapacity for any economy of work. At the same time, we note how well Marianne knew her way around his study room.

Weber's hasty and fluttery handwriting is a nightmare for biographers, as it already was for those who received his letters or for typesetters who had to puzzle over his manuscripts; it testifies to an astonishing disregard for others and an inability to control his own motor functions. His illness made matters still worse.[9] When Marianne tried in late 1902 to copy out one of his manuscripts, she was beside herself: 'It's like having to guess some cuneiform script or word puzzle, and I sometimes have a good snarl as I do it . . .'[10] Again and again the illegibility of his handwriting delayed publication and meant that he had to put up money of his own, or borrow it from his mother (MWG I/5, 52f.). However good his intentions, he found it extremely hard to discipline his hand. At times he even thought that, because of his 'calligraphic incompetence', he would have to give up writing altogether! (I/5, 123).

If his hand flew over the paper, so that letters tilted now one way, now the other, this was probably due not only to his nervous disposition but also to the fact that he could not express simultaneously 'several correlative lines of thought' (WB 309); he later envied Richard Wagner for his ability to have many instruments playing at once in a massive orchestra,[11] and he was annoyed by 'a current trend to attach undue importance to formal values and to waste time in an endeavour to bestow upon scholarly creations the character of a work of art' (WB 309). It was an attitude which limited his impact on contemporaries but contributed to the fact that his writings long outlived the Wilhelmine era.

The stream of ideas and the stream of history

On 30 April 1919 Max Weber described to Else the 'boundless *torture* of work', which he nevertheless could not give up 'without going to waste'; he spoke not only of the effort of forcing himself to sit at the desk, through a 'technique of constantly voting down (his) own incredible states of mind', but also of the desperate struggle to give a linguistic form to the flow of his thoughts. It caused such tension:

> that you put on paper only a *tiny* fraction of everything that shapes up inside you. . . . For, when I 'receive' ideas or contemplatively allow them to form *inside* me, everything flows – no matter whether it is a lot or a little, valuable or valueless – it flows in abundance – and then the struggle begins to capture it for the *paper* . . . and for me that is the true, almost unbearable 'torture', which may well be noticeable in my 'style'.

This deep sigh, with its undertone of relish, sheds more light on Weber's innermost creative process than almost anything else he said about himself. Certainly for the late Weber, ideas come at best in a state of *con-templation*, sometimes about imagined situations or at least in relation to polemics or practical decisions.[12] Weber was an irritable person, who easily became abusive and experienced states of rage that might last a long time. But unlike for Marx, nearly all of whose major writings have a polemical character, Weber's aggressive phases were not periods of great creativity. In oral debate with contrary positions, cogent points would repeatedly occur to him; but, in writing, his creativity blossomed best in a process of contemplation. Often he is remarkably unconcerned about the effect on the public, especially in the years after his breakdown when he still felt weak. Late in 1905 Marianne regretted that Max 'writes one essay after another that is then buried in the archive and read by only a few! But this profligacy with oneself is the mark of all really fertile minds.'[13] The more that research became for Weber an act of contemplation, the more it became a value in itself and the less important it was to publish books.

Weber, who as a child had panicked at the Baltic Sea, loved the metaphorical power of water, currents and the surging sea. He experienced both history and his own thoughts as a flow. Were they ultimately just part of the great stream – the natural process so utterly different from Hegel's self-unfolding of the world spirit? Did the possibility of knowing the world ultimately rest upon a basic identity of the self and the world? Theodor Lessing once mocked in verse the stream metaphors employed by historians: *'Da steht er und sagt: "alles schwimmt" | Bis der Strom ihn selber nimmt'* ('There he stands and says: All is afloat / Until the stream carries him away too').[14] Max Weber, on the other hand, appears to have been convinced both rationally and emotionally that he had no Archimedean point outside the flow of history. This may well account also for the puzzling lack of ambition to work up his books into a perfect final shape, with the result that what he left behind consisted mainly of fragments, and his successors felt driven to complete the uncompleted. In Weber's bad years, when he was incapable of finishing any major work, he must have found actual consolation in thinking about the transience of all scientific repute.

It seems paradoxical that such an inwardly driven man as Max Weber was impelled by external impulses to write many of his works (apart from those on religion) – even if he created those impulses for himself. Evidently he had no need to feel that he was initiating a whole new direction in research, but saw his role as one of critically inserting himself into an intellectual process already under way. When he once, obeying one of Marianne's dearest wishes, set out to write on Leo Tolstoy, he asked Rickert for one of his son's studies of the novelist, 'because, without an initial impetus, I probably won't make up my mind to say anything myself. I always require a "cause" for something like that' (MWG II/7-1, 250). In the case of Tolstoy, he waited in vain for the external impetus.

Precocious and inquisitive scholarship

Since Weber looked for an external 'impetus', curiosity often led him to put this or that aside instead of being strictly economical in the use of time. Someone like Georg Simmel was quite different: when Lukács sent him a manuscript in 1909, he bluntly gave him to understand that he read only what he might use for his next publications. 'I have forgotten how to ask objective questions about whether or not a book is good or bad. I am only interested in whether or not the book serves my purpose.'[15] Many scholars are similarly obsessed with their own publication prospects – but Weber was not like that. Indeed, the halting style of his own works reflects the fact that he took in not only what smoothly fitted his own thought processes but also things that appeared more cumbersome. He is often almost exaggerated in his penchant for open questions.

If, following Weber's own method, we were to construct ideal types of scholars, we might distinguish between a precocious and an inquisitive type. The former already has quite definite ideas in his head when he approaches the object of investigation, whereas the latter finds his object exciting precisely because he does not yet know what it will present to him. They are different kinds of scientific libido, which are usually associated with different human types. Ideally every scholar will have something of both, but in most cases one inclination is more strongly developed than the other. Which type did Weber belong to? Some evidence suggests that it was mainly the first type. There is already a lot in his youthful correspondence which sounds awesomely precocious. Weber could be hugely self-opinionated, and he had a highly developed capacity to construct reality in his own head. Yet he must also have been extremely curious, at least in his better times. How else can we explain that, during the Russian Revolution of 1905, he learned Russian in great haste to inform himself as accurately as possible about events, or that he intensively studied the 'psychophysics' of modern industrial labour without ever arriving at a conclusive position? The constant jumps to new issues, which a biographer such as Gregor Schöllgen sees as a symptom of mental illness,[16] point to an excessive curiosity on his part, whose results are all the stranger because it is often intermingled with an equally striking precocity.[17]

Wild scholarship

People who knew Weber sometimes spoke of the eruptive side of his creativity, and this kind of perception became a familiar trope. While Robert Michels detected traces of a difficult birth in Weber's writings – 'You can clearly see that it was painful for the author to push them on their way'[18] – Weber's mother used to describe how Max 'walked up and down in the room and how everything burst out of him as from a volcano'.[19] For Karl Loewenstein, who was part of the Weber circle from 1912 on, Weber was a 'daemonic personality': 'There was something incalculable, explosive about him. You never knew when the inner volcano would erupt.'[20] Immanuel Birnbaum, who helped persuade Weber to give his famous addresses on 'Science as a Vocation' and 'Politics as a Vocation', later recalled that the first of these burst 'like spasmodic explosions from the speaker's breast' (WzG 20). No wonder that Weber had trouble seeing through a whole semester of lectures! As to Helmuth Plessner, Weber struck him as a man who had 'become master of his chthonic eruptivity' (WzG 32). The classical formulations of this kind come from the historian Friedrich Meinecke, a sensitive man with a liking for harmony who was in many respects the antitype of Weber. It is with a mixture of admiration and distance that he speaks of Weber:

> When he began, he aroused the greatest interest in Mommsen, but soon also his concern. 'He bubbles over', he said of him (Weber), 'but he bubbles over for too long; first he should bubble, then he should flow.' Nor has there been any peaceful flowing since then. The classical striving for a harmonious life of scholarly work, which marked the preceding generation, lay far behind him. His disharmonious style – which often massed ideas together with dazzling force but then overloaded them with justifications and digressions wriggling shapelessly out of the first abstract conception – betrayed the increased restlessness and energy of his time, but also a quite singular, titanic temperament. He addressed all his topics in mighty bounds and claw-strokes, but with strong intellectual self-discipline and a rational method, which he saw as the indispensable counterweight to his natural passions, and which he had therefore striven to cultivate for himself as a sacred duty.[21]

A wildness tamed with great effort: the scholar Weber as a beast of prey who forces himself behind bars! Meinecke was certainly no volcano and had no need to control passions, but he developed an art of allowing emotions and value-judgements to flow half-concealed into his account.[22] Subliminally, as it were, his text expresses an aversion for Weber's style, which was the complete opposite of his own. In 1927, for all his admiration of Marianne's biography and its hero, he wrote in even plainer language that Weber's 'neglect of form' had made his content less persuasive and done harm to academic culture in general. 'Were the neglect of form to become widespread in scholarly work, we would face the prospect of its barbarization' (WzG 145). For the economist Moritz Julius Bonn, who venerated the classical Latin clarity of a Lujo Brentano, Weber's manner contained 'a large element of primitive German barbarism, which sometimes frenetically burst all its casing'. And again the metaphor of a natural catastrophe: 'He reminded one of a vast expanse of rubble, which a volcanic eruption has covered with lumps of lava and which has not yet grown sufficiently hard.'[23]

Mommsen's 'He bubbles but he does not flow' became a familiar quotation among insiders who found the Weber cult rather dubious. When the philosopher Hermann Glockner complained to Rickert of all the 'chaff' in Weber's style, Rickert nodded in agreement and said that the historian Alfred Dove, a close friend of Meinecke's,[24] had said exactly the same thing: 'He claimed that nothing at all would remain of Weber, except for the many ideas he had come up with. Yes, I can still hear him saying it: Max Weber is not of the first rank; he bubbles and bubbles but he does not flow; he should first bubble and then flow.'

The philosopher Paul Hensel, who declared that he had felt the 'rustling wings of genius' in few others as strongly as in Weber, admitted the 'sloppiness and shapelessness' of his writings and added that, 'in personal conversation, the fleeting and torrent-like side of his productive powers manifested itself with overwhelming force'. 'But for that he needs the room to be full of people', Hensel added. 'In a small circle he behaves more as a listener: he adapts to his conversation partner and participates in a cordial spirit.'[25] Weber's academic work reflected different communicative styles: inconsiderate monologue as well as sensitive understanding. When the worst of depression was over and he slowly regained his capacity for work, he found himself, in Marianne's absence, 'relying on monologues . . ., such as are spoken by characters in Chinese and Indian plays', because *any company* spoils my pleasure' (WB 269).[26] At least intellectual pleasure is back again.

Weber himself was reported as saying: 'I couldn't care less about style; I just cough up my thoughts.'[27] In his attitude to work, periods of depressive aversion evidently alternated with ones of euphoria when he would be overwhelmed by the rush of ideas and 'intellectual voraciousness' (WB 499), but when, at the same time, he would feel he had to make the greatest possible use of the mental state as he did not know how long it would last. If we think of all the time he lost in the long years of illness or reduced capacity for work, or in the quarrels that cost him so much without advancing his scholarly work by one inch, we have to wonder how on earth he was able to read all those books and to conceive and write down all the ideas that have come down to us. His letters do not tell us much about this, as he was little inclined to make confessions there and dried up completely when the frenzy of creativity was upon him. At such times, with the ideas flowing freely, he must have worked at the same furious pace as in 1892, the year of the study of farm-workers. The 'footnote inflation' (WB 336) that Marianne complained about in many of his essays[28] shows that his texts first bubbled out of him before he concerned himself – if he ever did – with supporting evidence.

Often he wrote several pages without a paragraph break.[29] No little subunits took shape in the flow of his thoughts. Unlike many scholars, he did not inch his way forward from one index card to the next, from one quotation to the next; he just blazed away when everything was 'ready in his head' (MWG I/19, 44). The lawyer of Paul Siebeck, Weber's publisher, found 'simply dreadful' his preface to the great collective project of the *Grundriß der Sozialökonomik*; he had not often come across 'such a mass of foreign words and convoluted sentences nesting on top of each other' (MWG II/8, 625n.). One has only to copy out such monster sentences word by word to realize how overloaded they are with extraneous insertions and terminological duplications, and it is only after several readings that one is able to grasp everything.

Even in lectures Weber often presented his ideas in such an unstructured manner that Marianne really lost her temper. In 1919 Else Jaffé reported to Alfred Weber that Max 'poured out a sea of knowledge' and let 'his audience gradually drown in it', 'to the anger of Marianne, who accompanied the lecture with softly whispered "bad marks" '.[30] This meant that the attraction of Weber's lectures tended to wane once people's curiosity about the legendary figure was satisfied (WzG 34). But, after a torrent of words that overwhelmed most listeners and readers, a formulation might strike them like a flash of lightning, as if to say that, if Weber wanted to, he could also strike a different, even demagogic tone.

Leaping across boundaries

Max Weber certainly knew about surprise effects. Especially characteristic of him was the sudden leap across spatial, temporal and disciplinary boundaries, and not least across the distance between lower and higher, material and ideal realms. Some of this is already apparent in his early writings: toing and froing between antiquity and modernity, use of land measurement in analysing the material base of the Roman empire, identification of a certain sense of honour as integral to a well-functioning stock market, and so on. In his later writings, the leaps across boundaries are more and more audacious; they become one of the main attractions in both his oral and written statements.

In comparison with the narrowness of the corporate academic world, these leaps convey a sense of freedom and transcendence. Particularly as Weber familiarized himself with ancient Israel and the cultures of the East, he enjoyed bringing to bear the superiority he thus acquired over mere specialists in the field; he seasoned his observations on Western culture with side glances at Hindu yogis, Confucian mandarins and ancient Jewish prophets and priests of Baal, not least in order to dismantle misconceptions about the specificity of the West. He drew an analogy between modern socialists and ancient Egyptian bureaucrats, while Kurt Eisner, leader of the Bavarian revolutionary government, reminded him of a shaman; Georg Lukács later considered this an appalling example of Weber's 'formalism'.[31] Again and again he liked to draw analogies across broad expanses of time and space, which logically presupposed – even if he scarcely ever said so in as many words – that the nature of man and his social forms were always essentially the same. One particular appeal of

Weber's work, ever since his early years,[32] is his constant ability to throw new and surprising light on phenomena from the viewpoint of different academic disciplines – first law and economics, then the study of religion, and finally even musicology.[33]

Strangely enough, although Weber tortured himself for a time with the theory of science, he does not seem to have thought much at all about his preference for the large-scale. When he started lecturing again in 1918, after a pause of nearly twenty years, Marianne noted: 'He was asked about the reasons for his passionate emotion, e.g. in presenting such distant problems as the Indian caste system – admittedly his account ended at a point where light was unexpectedly cast on problems close to us today – all he could say was: "Oh, well, those things are so fabulously interesting".'[34] Curiosity was for him a drive that did not need to be justified by a theory or some practical benefit.

In Weber's time, his manner of boundary-crossing was by no means as uncommon as it is today, when academic specialization has advanced much further and the breadth of general education has decreased. Not only such authorities of his day as Simmel or Sombart, but also near-forgotten colleagues such as Brentano and Schmoller or even Roscher and Schulze-Gävernitz, surprise today's readers by such a range of scholarship that one sometimes wonders whether Weber was really so out of the ordinary. Yet in terms of knowledge he stood head and shoulders above the greater part of his colleagues,[35] most of all in the way in which he combined a broad horizon with sharpness of vision. As a rule, a universal perspective comes with a certain wooliness and arbitrariness of vision – for example, in Alfred Weber or Oswald Spengler (whose 'Pergamon and Bayreuth' image yoked together the great Hellenistic city and Richard Wagner's famous centre). Weber's analogic leaps did not sound like the cultural pages of a daily newspaper. Hermann Kantorowicz – the legal expert who in private was much more unfavourable than Weber to the German position on war guilt[36] – wrote of him in 1922, after the publication of Weber's collected writings: 'Never in modern times has so much and such diverse knowledge been gathered in one head, or presented in such language with the hardness of steel.' 'But', he continued, 'in the end doubts appear about "Where does all this lead?" and reach the point of despair' (WzG 95).

Weber's 'naturalness'

Weber often expressed himself more clearly and pointedly in speech than in writing. During his lifetime, moreover, he made an impact not only because of the content of what he said and wrote but also by virtue of his own appearance – his 'charisma', to use one of his own words. Given that for many years he only sporadically showed himself in public, it is astonishing how he radiated in the presence of others. When he came out in support of value-freedom in science, there was still a strong sense that he embodied certain values in his own person: truthfulness, courage, a kind of nobility and generosity of mind. And, although he had no institutional power after being released from faculty duties, he was still highly regarded as an incorruptible figure standing outside academic cliques and was more than once asked to give his advice on a professorial appointment. Jaspers tells us that, when Weber started teaching again after a long interval, it was above all his 'naturalness' which people found captivating:

> In appearance and gesture he was true to his original self, never cloaking himself in style and pretence. Protection via conventions and masks was not for him. He was not self-important. The way he was by nature revealed his magic directly and left him vulnerable to all kinds of attack. In him we see a man who was truly human, a man who devoted his thought to everything in the reach of human experience.

According to Jaspers, Weber's cognitive grasp transformed 'original experience' into 'interlocking knowledge'.[37] Other contemporary witnesses also report having a strong sense that Weber's thoughts were not just creatures of his head but came from deep personal experience, and that his whole human personality stood behind what he said and wrote. The *Neue Wiener Tagblatt* wrote of Weber's appearance in the summer of 1918: 'His gaze comes from deep inside, from hidden galleries, and wanders into the far distance. His mode of expression is in keeping with this external manifestation. It has something infinitely plastic about it.' Weber wielded this powerful effect not so much through the content of his argument as through his 'capacity to arouse feelings that lay slumbering in the souls of others'[38] – through media skills, as it were. There are scarcely any reports of this kind from his early years as a professor: it seems to have been only the later Weber, marked by his illness, who became the medium of a shaken and despairing academic world at the end of the world war, not least because he steered onto the paths of strict science a set of emotions which at that time were often directed *against* scientific thinking. Of course, those who were in no mood to go along with this interplay between speaker and listener were less enthusiastic and failed to notice the structure at work. As we have seen, this was true even of Marianne.

A boundary that Weber routinely crossed was the one between theory and empirical knowledge, between abstraction and living reality (not least his own experience). Perhaps it is precisely in this respect that he is today most appropriate as a model. Franz Neumann – who after 1933, inspired by Weber's concept of charisma, wrote the most famous analysis of Nazi rule – had special praise for the unique way in which Weber combined 'a theoretical frame' with 'mastery of a tremendous number of data, and a full awareness of the political responsibility of the scholar'.[39] Similarly, for Jaspers, Weber combined 'the most concrete historical research with systematic thought', in a way that had previously seemed impossible.[40]

Such coupling of theory and exemplary cases is certainly an art that any good university teacher should more or less master, but the talent for it does vary greatly from one type of individual to another. Detail drawn from precise observation was not, for example, the forte of Alfred Weber, who sometimes thought that he should abstain on health grounds from the exertions of empirical research. Else Jaffé, probably with her smile of amusement on her lips, wrote to him after a conversation with Max in April 1920: 'Your task is to provide the "heuristic principle" . . .; others can create the material. I spoke along the same lines with Max, who talked very nicely about it. *Of course* you must read a lot, to develop a view of your own, but you should never descend from the bird's-eye view to the level of detail. You stay there up above, far from individual things.'[41]

Alfred Weber probably sensed the mocking undertone in the reference to his 'bird's-eye view'; he knew that Else then loved Max more than himself. For those well versed in classical German philosophy, this question of scholarly style contains some erotic symbolism; Hegel, after all, said that it was the 'laziness of abstract thought to shrink monastically from the presence of the senses'.[42] And for Max Weber, who had managed to find his way out of asceticism, scholarship that remained at high altitude had something dull and insipid. In his programmatic article of 1904 for the *Archiv*, he attached special value to the close association of ideas and facts and presented it as a question of scientific gourmandise: 'There are . . . "material specialists" and "interpretive specialists". The hunger of the first can be satisfied only with legal documents, statistical tables and surveys; he is insensitive to the quality of a new idea. The latter on the other hand dulls his taste for facts by ever newer conceptual distillations.'[43] One is reminded of Mehring's scornful remark that Lamprecht, in switching from materialist to spiritualist, gave the impression of having eaten whipped cream for weeks on end.[44] Weber would have agreed with that. But his side-swipes at fact-gatherers are also evidence of disgust and self-disgust; he too knew periods of truly self-destructive voracity. To an ever increasing extent, collectors of historical facts in the style of Schmoller had something gross and shallow about them.

Max Weber understood better and better how to combine the two intellectual pleasures; he developed, at least in his best periods, a rare virtuosity both in the art of illustration and in the ability to let concepts take on the varied hues of reality. 'The more *examples* there are, the better and more convincing it is', he impressed upon Robert Michels (MWG II/5, 99). A scholarly ethos of sharp thinking as well as sharp-eyed examination pervades the whole of his work. One of those who attended his last lectures praised the 'wealth of images' and 'the keen knowledge of the human soul' with which 'he evoked the Puritan farmer or American businessman as vividly as the old Prussian noble landowner or the Florentine patrician from the time of Dante' (WzG 38).

Much of the ground for this was laid through the study of law, with its sharp (sometimes bordering on pedantic) distinctions between related concepts and its fondness for piquant, even slightly cynical examples. But for Weber reality was much more than an arsenal of case material for normative conceptualization. Gertrud Bäumer, who for many years was in close touch with the Webers, underlined the 'quite distinctive agitation in his speech', 'whose strange, logical sharpness and representational qualities together reflected the intellectual process: the inflow of ideas from all four corners of the earth, and the way in which they were then tightly grasped and skilfully brought into logical relationship with one another. His hands repeatedly stretch out as he labours to draw all the new material together' (WzG 124). An intellectual Eros, then, to whom this woman – herself a similar combination – was especially well attuned. After Weber's death, a competition developed among kindred virtuosos over which one best appreciated his virtuosity.

Weber's art of observation

In his appropriation of Max Weber, who until then had been cornered by the conservative Raymond Aron in the field of French sociology, Pierre Bourdieu says that 'it was his wonderful observations which so captivated me', 'the rare wealth of powerful descriptions'.[45] Weber developed the art of intelligent observation in his early travel accounts. To be sure, he was not alone in this: it was the age of great travel writing, and in merchants' families the keen observation of foreign parts was a particularly strong tradition.[46] But Weber's travel correspondence has a special fascination, since, although Marianne was more inclined than he to become emotional about nature, she found her own reports actually prosaic in comparison with those of her husband.[47] 'Almost all the things that he absorbed in this way left traces in his work', noted Marianne (WB 268).

Did Max Weber's travel impressions really inspire him, or does the motto of the DuMont publishing house also apply to him: 'One sees only what one knows'? In 1903 he complained from the North Sea coast that he was 'a bookworm turned pedant', who has 'forgotten how to enjoy things intuitively' and can 'lay hold of impressions only discursively' (WB 269). But this very complaint makes it clear that it is not his proud aim always to intercept reality with concepts and 'ideal types'; that he would dearly like to surrender, if only once, to the teeming abundance of reality, without immediately grasping everything in words. 'How I envy those who are better off in this respect' (WB 269), he sighs at the end of this reflection on himself.[48] Over the years he evidently made progress – which explains how later admirers of Weber could experience a meeting with the scholar as a natural event.

Weber's depiction of the pilgrimage site in Lourdes is a particularly exciting item in his early travel correspondence; it is also highly informative about the way in which prior conceptions and fresh discoveries interacted with each other. In Weber's sociology of religion, Catholicism is the greatest and strangest blank. Whether in Freiburg or Munich or on his many trips in southern Europe, he had Catholic culture constantly before his eyes – and yet it was obviously hard for him to process his impressions intellectually, especially as for a long time his attitude was full of *Kulturkampf* clichés. Still, he did not block out those impressions, nor did he have any liberal-Protestant illusions that Catholic piety was just a matter of priestly tricks. He knew that he was dealing with powerful passions.

It is true that Weber's portrait of 'priestly physiognomies' in Lourdes partly recalls Wilhelm Busch's satirical picture story *Pater Filuzius*, first published in 1872, but he also shows an understanding that Catholicism has many very different faces.[49] Above all, in this pilgrimage site in the south of France, Weber for the first time had a sensory impression of the element of collective ecstasy in religion, when, after long and monotonous chanting of '*Mère de Dieu, priez pour nous!*' that reached a trance-like climax, mass hysteria suddenly broke out at the sight of real or supposed cures. All genuine religion is not about details but about salvation from profound distress: that may never have been clearer to the Protestant Weber than it was in Lourdes, although only much later did he build his sociology of religion on that idea. At first this religious ecstasy gave him an eerie feeling: he witnessed it without having a theory for it. 'I'll never forget that poor little twelve-year-old girl, who lay on a stretcher looking timidly around her, her teeth chattering, yellow and beside herself with excitement.'

Behind all the commotion, however, he saw a Catholic art of mass control that he described with a musical metaphor: to 'a superficial observer', 'the whole business gave the impression of a crowd milling around with all kinds of junk'. 'But anyone who knows the psychology of the Catholic church will watch the individuals in the milling crowd, and only then track down the mighty chord that it strikes in the nervous system of the masses. . . . As an instrument of power . . . the whole set-up is almost without parallel.'[50] As we see, the key to power lay then more in psychology than sociology. For Eduard Meyer, the German historian of the time closest to Weber in his universal horizon, the ecstasies associated with the Madonna cult before the mountain grotto in Lourdes showed that Catholicism had been infiltrated by the old natural religion of the Great Mother: a religion that had nothing in common with Christian theology.[51] Weber, still full of the battle with his father, did not yet have eyes for the matriarchal element in religion.

Understanding as a semantic, experiential act and as an act of love–hate

Marianne praises Max Weber's 'precocious ability to sympathize and empathize even with qualities that were far removed from his own nature' (WB 152). By no means did he display this ability in every situation, but he certainly did have it in personal as well as academic life. Honigsheim even portrays him as a virtuoso of understanding: 'Weber's capacity for empathetic interpretation of human behaviour was indeed . . . unlimited' (WzG 187).

Weber's 'empathetic understanding' (*Verstehen*), social science based on understanding in this Weberian sense: there is another theme for endless discussion. For understanding is a multivalent term, in the interpretation of which different philosophies of science collide with one another. It can be meant in the sense of our understanding of a text: as reconstruction of the intended meaning. But it can also refer to that which is unspoken, indeed unconscious, between the lines of the text. It may be a rational act of interpretation, but also an intuitive act of moving into something or even a *unio mystica* with that which is to be understood, an emotional after-experience of the experience of others. The young Ranke spoke of the Venetian emissaries' reports in which he delightedly immersed himself as his 'beautiful Italian mistress', with whom he daily kept 'sweet and wonderful lovers' trysts' until he 'rose to his feet completely exhausted'.[52]

In the nineteenth century, Droysen made understanding the kernel of his theory of history – indeed, the foundation of a doctrine justifying historiography in general: 'It is not "objectivity" that is the greatest glory of a historian. The justice of his conduct is that he tries to understand.' As soon as he speaks of understanding, he oscillates between simple naming of an acoustic process and a code for a pan-erotic centre of history. The 'act of understanding', he says in rapturous language, is 'like a direct intuition, like a creative act, like a flash of light between two electrophorous bodies, like an act of conception. In understanding, the whole mental-sensuous nature of man is completely implicated, at once giving and taking, at once producing and receiving.'[53] The full-blooded historian as a kind of androgynous eroticist! In Weber's time, Wilhelm Dilthey advanced this understanding-based philosophy of science; he too sometimes spoke in the language of enthusiasm, but he was more aware than Droysen that understanding required not only a reliving of innermost feelings but also the reconstruction of a world-view. The philosophy of *Verstehen* was not necessarily a programme of irrationalism.[54]

Was Droysen's and Dilthey's understanding the same as what Weber understood by scientific understanding? Did understanding for Weber also have something to do with lived or relived experience (*Erlebnis*)? To answer this question, we must not stick to what he wrote about '*Erlebnis*' (often between ironical quotation marks) in his tortured methodological writings[55] – where one does sense, however, that the whole question intrigued him[56] – but should look at how he actually handled reality: whether it concerned farm-workers east of the Elbe, the Protestant ethic or Oriental religions.

Weber more than once expressed annoyance at the fashion for 'hunting down lived experience', not least in his address 'Science as a Vocation'. But Manfred Hettling has shown that we should not take too literally Weber's inquisitorial attitude to the 'idol' called *Erlebnis*.[57] The displaying of one's own experiences [*Erlebnisse*] often has a narcissistic element: the original experience of satisfaction was erotic experience, so it is no wonder that for Weber 'experiences' of such a kind belonged more in the world of pleasant illusion than in scholarly investigation. On the other hand, the deep experiences [*Erfahrungen*] that mark and change people are not necessarily suited to be shown off to others; Weber knew that only too well. And, whether or not they correspond to the model of *Erlebnis*, traces of personal experience [*Erfahrung*], including emotional experience, are present throughout his work – and account for the special attraction of many of his writings. Without doubt, understanding was for Weber not only an intellectual but also an emotional act; his work is positively teeming with passages that testify to his attempts to feel himself into deep layers of emotion. Helmuth Plessner is of the view that Weber, with his method of *Verstehen*, broke through the 'strict separation between nature and culture';[58] the act of empathetic understanding took place not only through the intellect but also through the natural side of man, the premise being that there is a nature common to all human beings.

Weber's career clearly demonstrates that he achieved the breakthrough to creativity at moments when he was able to combine his research with strong emotional experiences of his own. The mutual responsibility of family members – the main theme of his dissertation on North Italian trading companies – certainly resonated with his own family experiences, but not with those of pleasure and passion. This changed with his major study of farm-workers, where he could create space for his own drive for *freedom*: freedom from the parental home, which after his studies had held on to him for seven 'barren' years. Now he was able to bring to bear his army experience of farmers, the land and the physical side of life, and not least the militant nationalism that he felt as a kind of masculine emancipation from his mother's compassionate world of charity work and the socially committed priests around Naumann and Göhre. Even in his literary style we can follow how Weber came to terms with himself through the study of farm-workers.[59]

Especially in his later years, he seems to have been most attracted intellectually to the divided passion of love–hate: whether towards asceticism, ecstatic emotions or the nation. Contradictory feelings bathe the object in a suspicious half-light. 'The deeper Max Weber engages in research', wrote Karl Jaspers, 'the more intense this twilight becomes, so that upon thorough examination, we do not know whether Max Weber affirmed or denied while valuing.'[60] Rather like modernists in the field of music, Weber discovered the attraction of dissonance in scholarship. The special tone of many of his writings comes from the fact that they maintain tensions for a long time and do not even resolve them at the end.

Weber must have recognized the partly rational, partly instinctual sources of his creativity; he often looked for tangible insights and experience, whether directly or through other people's reports. His trip to the United States in 1904, with its surfeit of new impressions, was evidently his first great emotional peak after the bad years: a self-confirmation that gave him a new feeling of strength and creativity, all the more as experiences of America were still rare in Germany and therefore a source of superiority for much-travelled people. Marianne was sometimes incapable of handling the flood of new things: so much was alien to her, and she did not know where to begin. 'Weber, on the other hand, remained intensely receptive; after all, he had the ability to make something of everything by recasting it intellectually' (WB 300). 'By recasting it intellectually': it is not always easy to tell how far the later reports of his travels in America are really genuine.

Weber's impressions of America do not feature at all prominently in *The Protestant Ethic*, parts of which had already been conceived and written before the trip, but they are even more striking in later writings: for example, when he ridicules the racist theory that whites instinctively recoil from the odour of black bodies, or when he invokes the interest of American students in duelling to argue that this German tradition has a future. It is generally in his more enthralling passages that Weber likes to spice things up with details from his own life, or with the kind of inside information that is the privilege of people 'in the know'. Weber was fond of the connoisseur's gesture ('as every expert knows'):[61] the person who disposes of special skills as well as wide experience. He knew 'very well the Saar coalfields and the stale air which that system [the system of informers used by Saar industrialist Stumm] spreads around there', he told the Mannheim congress of the Verein für Sozialpolitik in 1905, in answer to economists who did not wish to see that, for the sake of the workers' dignity as human beings, the excessive power of big industry had to be countered with the weight of the trade unions (GASS 395). In Weber's view, 'countless experiences' left no doubt that, in the bureaucracy, it is usually not the most capable but the most pliant who make a career for themselves, and that subordinates therefore only exceptionally believe that their superiors 'deserve' to be in their post (E&S 1449). Or: 'As every cavalry officer knows . . . the maxim of *caveat emptor* [let the buyer beware] obtains mostly . . . in horse trading among comrades' (E&S 638).

Karl Loewenstein, the expert in constitutional law who knew Weber well in the last eight years of his life, thought it 'demonic how this man, who remained in moral awe of any genuine religious faith – while pillorying a certain kind of tortured mysticism – knew how to grasp through the power of reason both the orgiastic ecstasy of an Indian holy man and the mechanization of Chinese religious feeling' (WzG 51). Really only 'through the power of reason'? Is not the assuredness of Weber's distinction between genuine and non-genuine mysticism, ecstatic and orgiastic religiosity, the best indication that he must have had religious experiences himself – or anyway a feeling of having them – and that he thought he found them again as primal human experiences in other periods and cultures? In 1909 he wrote to Tönnies that, in order to understand the historical significance of mysticism, it was necessary to have the 'ability to *experience* such psychological states': 'there – only there' (MWG II/6, 70).

Really only there? At the beginning of *Economy and Society*, Weber remarks that 'all scientific observations strive for clarity and verifiable accuracy of insight and comprehension', for *Evidenz*. 'Recapturing an experience' may not be 'an absolute precondition for its understanding', but it is 'important for accurate understanding' (*die Evidenz des Verstehens*) (E&S 5). Weber's 'understanding' is more than mere understanding of the meaning of a text. For the later Weber, scientific *method* does not consist mainly of conceptual and procedural tools but is in many respects akin to the 'method' of religious exercises: a path whose changing stages – enthusiasm as well as self-chastisement – take one mentally and spiritually closer to a truth.

The element of personal experience in Weber's 'science of man'

Weber's cognitive interest developed in a direction in which headway could sometimes be made only through personal experience, on the supposition that one could thereby arrive at elemental human experiences. This applies to his early interest in people that Wilhelm Hennis has placed at the centre of attention: an interest in the human types associated with various cultures, religions and economic forms. In his inaugural lecture in Freiburg, Weber explained that political economy, as a 'science of people', was 'concerned above all else with the *quality* of the human beings reared under those economic and social conditions of existence' (PW 15) – an enquiry in which progress could not be made with the usual tools of economics.

In the spring of 1898, when he evidently felt at a scientific dead end, he complained in a letter to the art historian Carl Neumann: 'My specialism condemns me to bury myself first in the *conditions* of antiquity and only then, by this stubborn material detour, to arrive at the *human beings* of antiquity.'[62] Analysis of structures was simply a means to knowledge of human beings – not the other way round, as it is for many of today's social scientists. In his considerations on future social policy, Weber also mainly asked – in this case, like his brother Alfred –'what type of personality it promoted' (WB 415).

As a rule, of course, information about the human type that will develop under certain conditions is not explicitly found in any empirical findings, for human types mostly belong to the category of phenomena that a culture takes for granted. Nor does one get very far along a purely theoretical route. Only through comparisons with other cultures and an imaginative capacity supported by wide experience does one draw nearer to this cognitive goal – and become able to draw analogies for the future on the assumption that there is a constant bedrock in everything human. To understand how Weber's work took shape, we must, like Hennis, mainly try to imagine the way in which he 'developed his "antennae", his sensitivity to the problems which then became the material for his scientific work'.[63]

Everywhere in Weber's work we come across passages which, on close examination, gain their clarity and accuracy neither from pure logic nor from the sources he quotes, but only from an element of emotional sensitivity; this is true not least of his most famous hypothesis, the connection between a Puritan-ascetic ethic and the spirit of capitalism. Whether writing on landed property and labour migration, Protestantism and capitalism, or eroticism and intellectual life, Weber continually demonstrates a special gift for the construction of tense connections that derive not from pure logic but from a passionate recapturing of experience.

Characteristic of Weber is not only his own scientific passion but also his special feeling for the element of passion in all things human; this is not the least of the reasons why his work always has something exciting about it. His major writings point to the premise that everything great in the world springs from passion (MWG I/4-2, 573f.). Towards the end of his inaugural lecture in Freiburg, he declares that a man is 'young as long as he is able to feel the great passions that nature has implanted in us' – passion as a natural element, the best element, in man! (PW 28).[64] And twenty-four years later, in 'Science as a Vocation', it is again his credo: 'For nothing is worthy of man as man unless he can pursue it with passionate devotion' (FMW 135). Since he felt himself to be a passionate man, this suggests that Weber saw himself as having a special natural feeling for the driving forces of existence.

Outlines of a theory of knowledge

From what we know of Weber, we may perhaps construct the following epistemological stance. Reality in its bewildering abundance – Weber liked to speak of the 'infinite abundance of phenomena' – has something resistant to the human mind. It is not easy for the mind to take hold of nature completely; rather, to avoid being taken in by its own fancies, it must in its exploration of reality always take into account what it does and how it proceeds. 'The most radical doubt is the father of knowledge', Weber taught in 1913. So, even an anarchist can be a 'very good "legal mind" ' so long as he seriously familiarizes himself with the legal order of the hated state.[65]

The quality of a research project is apparent in this self-critical endeavour and the labour of 'drilling through thick board', in a feeling for the resistance of reality. The provocative contours of reality come precisely from the resistance that it opposes to the human mind. If the researcher faces up to this resistance and does not just verbally jump over the hurdle, intellectual labour is inwardly assigned to practical action. Reality *exists*, of course, and up to a point is knowable; our knowledge is not merely a reflex of our own categories. Our thought does not simply refer back to itself, but also – precisely if it is self-critical – refers to the object of thought.

As Jaspers rightly pointed out, we sense beneath the surface in Weber a prevailing 'existentialist' mood which implies that an existence drawing on every capacity of the intellect and senses contains a reality check and a road to many-sided knowledge of the real world. Many passages in Weber's work presuppose that intuitive knowledge is possible. How else could he have known that Sappho was 'unequalled by man in the capacity for erotic feeling' (FMW 345)? That comes from the famous *Zwischenbetrachtung*, which some may see as a special case. For Weber the scientist, of course, intuition is admissible only if one has grappled discursively with the matter in question and fully probed its resistance. Weber's 'ideal types', unlike the Kantian categories, stem not only from the nature of thought but also from the external world. 'Puritanism', 'bureaucracy' and 'autonomous commune' are not concepts at which thought can arrive merely by reflecting on itself. Helmuth Plessner has pointed out that, in contrast to neo-Kantianism with its strict separation between concepts and reality, Weber's ideal types opened 'the way to phenomenology' (WzG 33).

An anti-Wilhelmine figure

In 1961 Ernst Bloch wrote of Weber that 'something Wilhelmine has long kept company with aesthetes' (WzG 28). Now, even in the heyday of the empire, Weber clearly did not belong at all in the ranks of these Wilhelmine aesthetes – which is one reason why he outlived the Wilhelmine era. Let us compare him with the economist Gerhart von Schulze-Gaevernitz, a colleague of his at Freiburg; he was a highly educated man with broad horizons, very knowledgeable about the Anglo-American world and politically far more active than Weber, yet in a speech in 1908 he could declare that nations were 'the rays in which the divine light most magnificently spread on earth'.[66] After 1918 no one even on the far right could have stomached that kind of apotheosis, and Max Weber, even in his chauvinist period, would never have been capable of speaking so pompously of the nation. His style lacked that pliable Wilhelmine sleekness, with its smooth regularity of rhythm. He did not want harmony but liked to torture himself with the tension between irreconcilable opposites, without dissolving it through a sudden accord. It was an aesthetic of dissonance, in keeping with the general style of those times. Weber did not have in his repertoire that smug smile of the established great professor which so irritated up-and-coming academics.

Leopold von Ranke, who still today counts as the founding father of the science of history, was not a good public speaker, yet many who listened to him could never forget 'the impression of his sparkling eyes and the lively hand movements with which he seemed to pluck his ideas from the air'.[67] Weber's audience, rather, felt they were witnessing the difficult birth of ideas or an eruption from the depths – in any event, a process that came not just from the head but from the whole person. It was not the nimble performance beloved of a Georg Simmel or Werner Sombart, the stars of the newly developing discipline of sociology. Weber always gave the impression that it was not easy for the mind to get to grips with reality. So much greater was the sense of triumph when he finally achieved it.

The pleasurable torment of knowledge

Heinrich Rickert, who had known Weber since schooldays and watched not without irony the rise of the Weber myth, said after his death: 'The fascinating effect that he had at the lectern may have been partly due to a sense that the man up there was violently suppressing something in himself and was basically very much more than what he said' (WzG 114f.). From the mouth of a philosopher, who thought it the scholar's business to make an impact through clear speaking, this was an ambiguous appreciation. But there was a degree of truth in it. Many obviously sensed something wild and unrestrained in Weber, which then brought itself back under control: a kind of self-tormenting, which had something exciting for both himself and his listeners and corresponded to Weber's erotic disposition.

Weber's scholarly work, during his creative periods, had its origin in love and pleasure (albeit a special kind of pleasure), not in rage and even less in cynicism. On the one hand, he was inclined by temperament to be aggressively (and quite dreadfully) self-opinionated, whether in relation to his father or to certain critics of *The Protestant Ethic*; on the other hand, he was overcome at some point by the pleasure of scourging his spontaneous passions and insisting in an equally overbearing way on the relativity of all theoretical positions. He loved the nation and then coolly dissected nationalism; he loved ancient Rome and approached it with the stone-cold sobriety of a surveyor; he could feel the passion in religion and music, but discovered the element of rationalization in both.

Such is Weber's style: to expose ardent emotion to the shock of cold water,[68] to destroy splendid illusions, and sometimes to dismiss an attractive new idea in favour of a conventional viewpoint, as at the end of his essay on the 'the social constitution of ancient Germany'. 'It may appear trivial', he wrote. 'But trivial conclusions, precisely because of this characteristic of theirs, are unfortunately very often the correct ones' (SWG 556). That is certainly true – even if many academics like to show off their competence by making their subject as complicated as possible.

Paul Feyerabend, the enthusiast for an 'anarchist' science free of methodological compulsion, claimed to be transforming science from a strict and demanding mistress into an attractive lover who anticipated each of her partner's wishes. It was up to us 'to choose either a dragon or a pussy cat for our company', and Feyerabend's preference was clear enough.[69] So too was Max Weber's: science for him was not a pussy cat but a strict mistress, who often tormented her lovers, although this did not mean that the torments were without their own kind of pleasure. It would appear, however, that Weber learned this kind of pleasure only gradually. As long as he tried to place science in the service of politics, he needed to have clear signals rather than brief glimpses. Only when he drew a clear demarcation between science and practice, conceiving the former as a mistress who would brook no one else beside her, did the pleasurable torment of critical thought make itself felt in sufficient, indeed excessive, measure.

Ice on the brain

Illness and recovery brought the tension between torment and pleasure, dream and disillusionment, to ever new heights of intensity. Half a century after Weber's death, Else Jaffé thought: 'One never knew which was stronger in him: the keen-eyed realist without illusions or the great dreamer.'[70] She had come to know a Weber who remained hidden to most people. He complained to her that his brain was a 'power hostile to love', an 'ice box' or 'ice saint', but often the 'last salvation' against 'the Devil, who played around with me when I was sick'. It will seem incredible that he was seriously disowning his whole life and everything he created. For a man who periodically suffered because of an inner heat, there was something pleasant about a cooling system, at least for a while.

We should not imagine that Weber's style of work was at all times taut and concentrated. As a young man, he hit upon his ideas in a state of tension, *con amore*, and the same applies at least as much to the Weber of the *Zwischenbetrachtung*. If he did not go in for 'joyful science' à la Nietzsche, he did offer, in his better periods, the model of a developed joy in knowledge that many in today's academia can scarcely imagine. If he really felt his brain to be an 'ice box', the process of knowledge was for him not rooted in reason alone; his audience, fascinated by his wild, eruptive element, perhaps saw this more clearly than he did himself.

6

A 'Gospel of Struggle' and Old German Corpulence: From Lifestyle Crisis through Creativity Crisis to Existential Crisis

The period of high spirits and heavy eating

Most accounts of Weber's appearance and manner – especially those which depict him as a grim ascetic – come from the period after his death and refer to his later years. Rickert, on the other hand, stresses that he 'also knew the young, healthy and jolly Max Weber' (WzG 110) – there was that one too. Friedrich Meinecke, who went to Freiburg ten years after Weber's departure and heard only other people's stories about him, even thought that Weber was 'originally' – Marianne's biography only hints at this – a 'passionate hedonist' who, 'with an energy that let all his instincts flow more than abundantly at one and the same time', threw himself equally 'into life and science' (WzG 144) – from which the reader can infer amorous adventures. It is true that Carl Neumann, a fellow sufferer from bouts of depression, did not take this act very seriously: 'He considered it a weakness that Max Weber liked to play the he-man and generally tended to excess in every respect.' Rickert also described Weber to others as a 'fitness show-off', who gave the appearance of being 'much more robust' than he was in reality.[1]

Nevertheless, in his years as a student and young professor, Weber would undoubtedly have liked to think of himself as a paragon of energy. In part this was a reaction against a childhood marked by illness: 'Little Max was a rather weak, small boy, shy and clumsy in all physical exercise. His neck seemed too thin to support his large, pear-shaped head' (WB 40), which for a time was thought to be a sign of incipient hydrocephalus. As a schoolboy, he had been 'lanky and skinny, a "candidate for consumption" with his delicate limbs and sagging shoulders' (WB 64). This was a reason for fresh worries, as tuberculosis, marked by a gradual wasting away, was still the main cause of death in early life. Health concerns shape the collective mentality, and fear of tuberculosis certainly contributed to the fact that, unlike today, a corpulent person was thought of as being in good physical shape. 'My health . . . is really looking up, and I'm getting fatter every day', the newly matriculated student wrote to his mother, together with a request for money to ensure that he did not become thin again (JB 51). His brother Alfred had a similar attitude as an undergraduate and informed his father: 'According to the latest theory, thinking uses up brain mass that has to be continually replaced through hearty eating – from which it follows that the cleverest people are always the ones with the greatest hunger.'[2]

Even in those days, however, there was also a slimmer ideal physique. Max's mother impulsively gave him a box on the ears when, at the end of the first semester, he returned home bloated from over-indulgence. Helene was worried that her eldest son disliked 'all other kinds of physical training, such as swimming, gymnastics and skating' (WB 36); the health benefits of exercise are not a discovery of the twentieth century. During his military service, Weber's new corpulence caused him trouble, as he found himself being treated as one of the 'fatsoes'. 'First with horror, then with pleasure, I noticed how quickly I was getting slim again; men of the same age as myself now consider me "well-proportioned" and no longer a "fatso"' (JB 88). But the weight loss ended when he returned to student life; indeed, now that swotting for exams had replaced fencing practice, he no longer had 'exercise of any kind' but instead would consume in the evening a whole pound of chopped raw beef and four fried eggs (WB 105). Marianne records with critical accuracy each phase in the history of his body.

Years later, the special attraction of military exercises was still the accompanying booze-ups: when Weber returned to Posen in March 1894, he was received in the mess 'with a loud hurrah'; the men 'still think of my capacity for alcoholic drinks as my only significant quality', and it was a point of pride for him to live up to this reputation.[3] At the time he liked to think that he had a particularly robust constitution, whether for the purposes of work or for drinking, and in 1894 his appointment as a full professor in Freiburg boosted this sense of vitality. In his late twenties, still living in the parental home without money of his own, he had already felt old; the full professor in his thirties was young again, and financially independent. He was also a long way from home, in south-western Germany; Weber knew how to appreciate the lighter air and milder climate, although there too he could sometimes play the gruff northern German. Had he had strong political ambitions, it would have been better for him to remain in Berlin; the move to Freiburg and then Heidelberg was also an option for the world of the free intellect. He had reason to feel lucky; he was a well-paid professor in political economy, without yet having a great deal to show for himself in that field.[4]

Social gatherings where food and drink were consumed in abundance used to play an important role in the lives of professors in south-western Germany; they absorbed some of their time and energy. Marianne was not so appreciative of this and spoke of the 'self-contented, pleasure-mad Freiburgers'.[5] Social life in Heidelberg was at a smarter level, but that did not mean a lower consumption of wine. For the Jellineks, friends of the Webers who did not exactly come from a humble background, the 'truly lavish lifestyle' of the Heidelberg professors was a novel experience: 'Food as the reason for the gathering, as an end in itself, was something new and surprising. . . . Above all else, the time must not be abridged because of the wine.' Seven to ten wines were served with every large meal. 'With what expertise was each drop greeted, as many guessed at once its precise place and time of birth.'[6] When Weber later withdrew from most such occasions, the change in lifestyle – and not only his freedom from teaching duties – released some of his capacity for intellectual work. But previously he had sometimes given himself up to gluttony out of a sense of boredom. Early in 1895 the Webers attended a court ball in Freiburg which, according to Marianne, was 'highly tedious', especially as her husband did not dance. 'Of course Max felt much more bored than I – and claims to have demolished at least forty sandwiches in revenge plus something like twenty beers, so that he afterwards felt like a boa constrictor' – and then, on top of all that, six Berlin pancakes.[7]

In those days, he sought in eating and drinking the orgiastic element that would later become an important theme in his sociology of religion. He was even proud of his huge capacity for consumption and obviously thought that such a way of life was part of his nature. As Marianne notes in an ambiguous passage in her biography, Weber's 'drinking ability created as much astonishment' in Freiburg as his academic achievements. 'At an advanced hour Weber wagered that he weighed a hundred kilograms and committed himself to emptying his glass for every pound he weighed less. Amidst loud shouting he was weighed on the house scales, lost the bet, and had to pay the penalty.' At a fraternity banquet he won a drinking contest with a student and again caused amazement: 'Was that a hero from the Teutonic woods who had come to life again?' they wondered (WB 205–6). This is the image of the ancient Germans in the book of students' drinking songs – people who, when not actually fighting, lay down on their bearskins and always drank 'just one more', but never, at least in the legends, lost any of their strength for battle. Shortly before the turn of the century, however, a slimmer, more youthful ideal of physical fitness began to get a grip. In 1896 Marianne told her mother-in-law: Max 'often runs in twenty minutes to the Kanonenplatz and back, because everyone teases us so because of his "corpulence." Something does seem to be having an effect on him.'[8] No doubt, Marianne joined the slimmers' party.

In the summer of 1895, during the trip to England and Scotland, Weber was not yet an admirer of the Puritan tradition but, together with Gierke, a eulogist of the ancient Teutonic community, noisily wallowed in a feast of merriment and gluttony, happy to stand out among the 'whispering' Britons, one of whom remarked: 'merry Germany'. Gierke 'began to eat as though we were in the Teutoburg Forest, and I joined in' (WB 209). But he did not take well to the bacon and eggs breakfast followed by 'a couple of fish': he apparently polished off a whole pound of bacon and was 'very ill for a whole day'.[9] Later he would bitterly regret the Germans' lack of a tough, ascetic tradition and saw this as the reason for their inferiority to the British.

Secretly, with her woman's eye, Marianne did not see her husband's eating and drinking habits as an expression of Teutonic prowess, but rather felt worried, and bitter, that he had so little time for her yet was so extraordinarily generous with his time when it came to another male drinking bout. Alcoholism was then becoming a major topic in psychiatry: Emil Kraepelin, for example, the budding pope of German psychiatry who was teaching in Heidelberg and became Weber's most important source of information on the subject, declared that alcohol was the worst threat to mental health.[10] Women were usually more receptive than men to this new gospel. Certainly Marianne's reproaches drew an ill-natured response from Weber: 'Good heavens, I'll never become a soda-water man; the old student fraternity people would find that strange and unnatural' – and besides, in comparison with his 'heroic feats' of the past, he was no longer drinking much at all. 'I'm afraid that I've fouled up as a model husband.'[11]

In a letter that Marianne wrote to Helene in 1896, which for once she could be sure would not reach the eyes of Weber *père*, she gave vent to what was troubling her:

> Since you'll read this letter alone, may I tell you that it sometimes gives me the shudders that he has so many opportunities here to go drinking; right now, for example, invitations are pouring in for various student society evenings, etc. etc. I know it doesn't do him any harm and will never hold him in its sway – but I find it so disagreeable, I can't help it. I certainly don't begrudge him the relaxation, but when it often happens three or four times a week, even before a meal when he leaves a message that he'll be having a lunchtime drink with someone or other, then it makes me feel sad inside.

If she mentioned it to him, he scolded her 'in a pedantic and schoolmasterly manner'.[12] But was she really sure that this kind of life did her husband no harm? In any event, she was worried that he might be getting his pleasure from drinking bouts instead of in their marriage. As time went by, Max also became less sure that a high alcohol intake was good for him. In May 1897 he still assured his favourite sister, Klara, that it was really 'pretty much the same' 'what people let run through them', but at the same time he reported that, after weeks spent in alcohol like an 'anatomical specimen', he had for several days been drinking three or four bottles of mineral water a day and blowing himself up into a 'carbon dioxide balloon'.[13] Following the worst years of his illness, he must have put some of the blame for his breakdown on his earlier alcoholism; this seems to be lurking not least behind the absolute hatred with which he writes of Germany's lack of an ascetic tradition. The lifestyle of the ancient Germans supposedly contained an enticement to alcohol.

In Weber's high-spirited years – if we are to believe the stories reported by Rickert – he apparently made fun of his abnormal sexual tendencies. He

Figure 6.1 *Eve and the Future*, by Max Klinger: a reproduction of this etching hung beside the Webers' wedding photo

probably thought his sexual difficulties were only temporary, as otherwise he would not have been able to think of himself as a muscleman. After the move to Freiburg, he gave his wife a set of six etchings by Max Klinger, *Eve and the Future*, which had a mysteriously arousing erotic effect and caused offence to their visitors:[14] they were sign of a loose attitude to sex. Sooner or later, however, Max's he-man act must have seemed suspicious to his wife. Was it not all too clear in Nietzsche (whose weak points Marianne knew extremely well from the philosopher Alois Riehl) that a superman cult could actually involve compensation for one's own weaknesses? Was this not also true of the deaf Treitschke, idol of German chauvinists, whose strong nationalist language stirred up the student masses but who spoke in a way that sounded like howling and screeching?[15]

Body history and politics

Later, Marianne established a connection between Weber's early chauvinism
and his experience of his body, implying that she found that kind of nationalism irrational: 'Weber's passion for the national power state evidently
sprang from an innate instinct that could not be affected by any reflection.
The powerful nation is the extension of the body of a greatly gifted person,
and to endorse it is to endorse oneself' (WB 125). In Marianne's biography
this passage sounds superficially admiring, but she knew better than anyone
that his feeling of strength – as well as the conceptual world springing from
it – rested upon illusions. She, like Helene, sensed that the way in which
people relate to their body also reveals something about their mind.

Marianne did experience her husband as gluttonous, but also as
harassed. Later, she made every effort to think mainly of his better periods:

> Eating, which always so delighted him, was over in the shortest time;
> one could never stop him eating too quickly, and if there were guests
> comfortably chatting at table he suffered secret torments of impa-
> tience, so that I too was on tenterhooks, or else he ate and ate – always
> another helping. . . . But all these disagreeable feelings communicated
> themselves to me until they became a torment for me too.[16]

But there is not only the history of a Weber filled with contentment in a
circle of colleagues and students, gobbling and boozing late into the night.
There is also the very different story of the constantly harassed professional
academic, whose compulsive haste is apparent in his impossible handwriting. The contrast between the two could scarcely be greater. To her regret,
Marianne experienced mainly the darker side of her husband, until his
breakdown.

Time pressure

Weber's youthful letters already swarm with tales of woe about time pressure. To some extent, such complaints were part of the dawning 'age of
nervousness'. Whereas the old European aristocratic culture, with its
Roman ideal of *otium cum dignitate*, had valued displays of imperturbability and a relaxed attitude to time, a complete turnaround took place in the
nineteenth century and had effects that are still with us today. People now
tried to demonstrate their importance by always being in a hurry and never
having enough time, even when they did not really have such a terrible
amount to do. The extreme shift in the emperor's bearing, from the tran-
quility of Wilhelm I to the restlessness of Wilhelm II, embodies this change
in ideal-typical form.

But, although time pressure was a new habit of mind, this does not mean
that many people were not overwhelmed by its tormenting and compulsive

presence. This was evidently the case with Weber, perhaps all the more because his childhood illness had left him with a sense that he was mentally too slow and had 'lost too much time before' (JB 251). 'Time passes through your hands like butter', he wrote at the age of fifteen (JB 27), and in his first semester as a student he reported 'that here in Heidelberg time runs away like a bicycle' (JB 46), which, in 1882, seemed excitingly fast. During his military service, the thing that tortured him most was the 'eerily conducted killing of time' (JB 91). When he was swotting for an exam, he saw the time flow with 'raging speed' (JB 162) – and so, to keep the time loss to a rational minimum, he drew up each day a precise plan from morning to night (JB 188). Dancing, he snootily wrote to his mother, was not worth a tenth of the time he had to squander on it (JB 199). Time spent dallying with girls was time wasted.

As we have seen, Weber worked 'at lightning speed' to make his concluding report on farm-workers a major contribution that would astound its readership and establish his reputation in the academic world. The sense of time pressure then became a permanent condition, however, which was not due only to external conditions and did not ease up even when he had lifelong tenure and material independence of his father. On his return from the Evangelical Social Congress in Erfurt in 1896, where he had given an irritable address exposing the pointlessness of the Naumann movement – why did he go there at all, in fact? – he indulged in 'forceful expressions about the loss of time', even though it pleased him that he had been able to give vent to his feelings in Erfurt.[17] And that Easter, when he wanted to go to Oerlinghausen, Marianne could already see it coming that he would afterwards 'slave' all the harder to make up for the lost time.[18] This background makes it clearer how much Weber needed 'Teutonic' overindulgence as a way of combating his inner unrest, especially as he found no rest in his married life.

It was painful to Marianne that her husband was always rushing around, but impulses to save time also came from her side. During their engagement she already noted that 'being in control of my time has always had a great attraction for me';[19] she obviously wanted to make sure of keeping as much temporal autonomy as possible in their marriage. When illness forced Max to be more generous with his time, it was Marianne who complained of time pressure. From the sanatorium in Urach, where she was visiting her husband, she wrote to Helene: 'But I hope to get down to studying very soon – the greatest danger for "Israel in the diaspora" is to fritter away one's time.'[20] She was not really able to look forward even to the America trip of 1904; more than half a year before they were due to leave, she complained that worries about finishing all her tasks by then weighed on her 'like an incubus'.[21] After their return from the United States, she wrote to Helene: 'As you know, I need to exert myself to the limits of my strength.'[22] Beneath the surface, the couple probably worked each other up into states of full exertion.

Now, a fast pace of life can be exciting. People gripped by the quest for speed are the ones most likely to drive themselves to the point where it becomes painful. Traditionally, many Germans who looked to Paris or London complained that, during the Biedermeier period from 1815 to 1848, everything worked so slowly in their land of ponderous phlegmatics. When the first railways arrived, the acceleration kindled a feeling of elation; the superstitious opponent of the iron horse was largely an invention of its enthusiastic supporters. Max Weber, however, belonged to a later generation for which speed meant no longer just a new freedom but partly also an inherited burden. Some of the early Weber's hectic lifestyle was a phenomenon affecting his generation. Nevertheless, such a fixation on the use of time was not so common, at least for well-established members of the educated middle classes. Not by chance did Weber focus his attention for a time on the stock exchange, as the seat of the new 'hecticism'. For, given that his origins combined *Bildungsbürgertum* and economic bourgeoisie, he was one of those who early on subjected this kind of modernity to scientific investigation.

Although Weber, like so many others, happily used time pressure as an excuse, there is plenty of evidence that mad rushes became a compulsive and agonizingly painful part of his life. Even in July 1895, on the point of leaving for a month-long trip to England, Scotland and Ireland, he felt himself to be a 'hunted wild animal',[23] and as with so many workaholics the worst stress came amid the freedom of leisure time, as in 1897–8, when the first acute signs of his illness appeared during holiday trips. As was often the case with 'neurasthenics' in those days, it was not the hectic pace of life as such that produced the sense of being a wreck and made therapy an urgent necessity; rather, sexual failure, or fear of sexual failure, often went together with a hectic syndrome that manifested itself throughout the body. In Weber's case, another likely factor was that his particular kind of libido did not match his he-man acts and could not be integrated into his self-image.

Having from an early age firmly intended to harbour no illusions either about external reality or about himself, Weber recognized in 1894 that his work mania was a flight from depression and confessed as much to Marianne:

> After years of dreadful torment I feared a profound depression would set in. It did not happen, and I believe it was because I worked constantly and did not let my brain or nervous system get any rest. Quite apart from my natural need to work, this is one reason why I am so very reluctant to make a really perceptible pause in my work. . . . I believe I could not take the risk of letting the incipient relaxation of my nerves – which I am enjoying with the feeling of a truly new happiness – turn into enervation.[24]

So, in 1894 Weber is already brooding over his 'nervous system' and its peculiar laws, but he still believes, like the neurologists of the Biedermeier period, that the greatest danger is not excessive agitation but nervous enervation.[25] Then comes a strange addendum: he explains his behaviour by 'a certain timidity and a fear of acting too soon as if I were normal'; in himself he does not feel 'normal', despite all the macho performances. In the early years of his professorship he is afraid that words will desert him at the lectern.[26]

A clash of lifestyles

All in all, we can see how in those days two incompatible lifestyles collided with each other in Weber: an 'ancient German' *Gemütlichkeit* best expressed in the relaxed informality of a drinking session; and a modern orientation to productivity, with one eye constantly on the clock. This clash was typical of the age and can be seen in many a case history of its 'neurasthenics'.[27] It seems to have been more pronounced in Germany than elsewhere,[28] because an especially rapid industrialization collided there with a luxuriant culture of *Gemütlichkeit* centred on clubs, student societies and groups of regulars. At the same time, the German cultural area became the centre of lifestyle movements that proclaimed a new ideal of youthfulness and clear vision, which aroused a sense of inferiority among those who could not keep up with it.

In the course of his life Max Weber played a full part in all of this, and he exemplifies the way in which tensions between the two lifestyles could develop into a major existential crisis. Another factor was probably a pathological individual disposition; the attention of Weber himself, as of most of his fellow sufferers, certainly focused on personal aetiology. But lifestyle and ways of living then became leitmotifs in Weber's sociological work, where eating and drinking sometimes occupied a significant place, as they already had in his study of farm-workers east of the Elbe. For Weber, the long-term economic effects of various religions depended not on their fundamental ideas as such but, rather, on the 'methodical pattern of life' [*Lebensmethodik*] accompanying them: this was the key idea that would now run through Weber's work. Neither education nor possession or non-possession of means of production was decisive for his social group, but rather – all-importantly after his own lifestyle crisis[29] – everything that goes to make up a group's lifestyle. Benjamin Franklin's 'time is money' marked for Weber a momentous lifestyle revolution: he interpreted it in the sense of his own compulsively hectic life, without taking into account the background appreciation of pleasure that was still there in Franklin. None other than Eduard Baumgarten, Weber's nephew and executor, later wrote a whole book that drew attention to this.[30]

Freiburg 1895: youth verified through expansion

The famous, and ill-famed, inaugural lecture at Freiburg, delivered on 13 May 1895, falls into the period of he-manship when Weber's lifestyle crisis was already shaping up beneath the surface. It reflects Weber's divided posture: on the one hand, a concentration of nationalist strong language such as one does not often find in a university lecture; on the other hand, undertones of deep pessimism and fears of national degeneration. In a way it is an anti-Wilhelmine manifesto, a slap in the face for the eternal Sunday of which the young emperor was so fond and for sayings of his such as 'I shall lead you towards glorious times!' or 'I won't stand for people who always look on the dark side of things' – after all, Weber's public image was that of someone who persistently looked on the dark side. At the same time, however, Weber's lecture is uncommonly Wilhelmine in its rising sequence of power gestures, without ever making it clear what the speaker actually *wants*. The next year at the Evangelical Social Congress in Erfurt, when he shouted out to Naumann and his followers, 'What do you actually *want?*', they could well have flung the question back at him. His lecture challenged the basis of Junker rule and the bureaucracy and 'personal regiment' of Wilhelm II, but he did not consider the bourgeoisie or the workers sufficiently 'mature' (an organological metaphor he would later remove) to rule in their stead.

Weber prefaces the published text of the lecture, 'The Nation State and Economic Policy', with a distillation of his study of farm-workers that provides its empirical backbone. We again find talk of closing the eastern frontier to the 'tide of Slavs' (PW 12). It is not a new idea: Bismarck had already decreed as much, and had also ranted against the 'cancerous Polonization that eats up everything around it' (R 445). But that alone had not done much to strengthen the German nation, which is Weber's main concern here. In essence, what he urges is the very thing he later detested so much in Wilhelm II: in the area of German settlement east of the Elbe, which required painstaking yet unobtrusive work with close attention to detail, he arrives with little precise to offer and launches hollow fanfares and insulting attacks on the Poles – 'the small Polish peasant . . . prepared even to eat grass' (PW 10) – which provoke a Polish spirit of resistance more than they encourage German settlers.

The 'inner unification of the nation', Weber continues in this city of Catholic Baden, has, 'as every one of us knows, not been achieved' (PW 22). Then he suggests a fact and a consensus, both in need of demonstration, without presenting any arguments for either. Are socialist workers and Catholic Centre voters, in the year 1895, really still 'enemies of the Reich'? Was it not Bismarck's persecution which first turned them into that? Did they not fight valiantly in 1870 and prove to be loyal citizens in many later situations? Was that not apparent especially outside Prussia, in Baden? Critical minds could detect that, unlike in previous centuries, the greatest woe was not a lack of German unity but the excess of government-controlled conformism – that foolhardy '*Bismarck sans phrase*', in fact an a-political posture, which Weber already loathed in the student fraternities of the new Germany.

Then comes the oft-quoted kernel: '*We have to understand the fact that the unification of Germany was a youthful prank carried out by the nation in its old age, and that it would have been better, on grounds of expense, to leave it undone if it was to have been the end rather than the beginning of Germany's involvement in world politics'* (PW 26). Naturally it would be anachronistic to measure this by the standards of today's 'political correctness', condemning it from the viewpoint of peace movements and the European Union. In those days, German imperialism was by no means as irrational as it sounds today; the time had not yet come when Germans would be happy for the United States to accept them as a junior partner. Only a few people allowed for a future collapse of the colonial empires, and the art of diplomacy had by then accumulated some experience of colonial conflicts; the wars expected to result from colonial imperialism would not necessarily be major ones. From a later vantage point, the period around 1900 appears as a relatively free and peaceful heyday of world trade, but in the light of previous history one might have argued that trade and naval power were closely conjoined and that powerful trends to protectionism were present even in that golden age. It was not illogical to conclude that in the long term a 'German world' had to be built 'for German goods'.

Weber, however, did not argue very rationally for a German *Weltmacht* policy, nor did he have the slightest clue as to what he actually envisaged by a world power. Instead, he came up with an organological image: a nation had to assert its youthful vigour by growing; youth ended when growth stopped, soon to be followed by the first signs of age. This from a Weber who, in the preceding years, had been unsure whether he was himself still young or prematurely old.

But is youth not a gift of nature? Did Weber seriously believe that people or nations could be *made* young? The National-Romantics based themselves on the pseudo-historical idea that the German nation was not a nineteenth-century innovation but had its days of glory in the time of Otto the Great and the medieval Hohenstaufen dynasty. But, in that case, one could not but think of the Germans as an *old* nation and consider the rapidly multiplying Poles, who lived under the harshest conditions, as the new barbarians. Weber's Freiburg address, then, has an undertone of dark pessimism. '*Lasciate ogni speranza!*', 'Abandon all hope!', stands placed 'over the portal into the unknown future of human history' (PW 15). They are the words above the gate to Hell in Dante's *Inferno*.

Even after 1945 Weber's admirers kept trying to find a far-sighted political vision in his Freiburg address, as if he had been prophesying the demise of Wilhelmine Germany. Yet it was precisely his obsession with 'growth or decline', in which 'growth' was equated with territorial expansion, which ultimately led the empire to catastrophe. Weberians are fond of the idea that everything would have turned out better if a man such as Weber had stood at the helm of the Reich. But this is to turn things on their head: the minutes of the German Foreign Office evince a generally much cooler and more thoughtful approach than do Weber's national speeches of the 1890s. The way in which the imperial government manoeuvred the Reich into the Great War in the crisis of July 1914 is to be explained at least as much by the pressure of nationalist public opinion for an expansionist course as by any traditions of Prussian-German foreign policy.

In the beginning there was the *Zeitgeist* – or was it Max Weber?

Was expansionism already the 'spirit of the age' in the Germany of 1895? Was Max Weber, with his *Weltmacht* fanfares, just one among many? This is a popular idea in Weber studies. Those who have their eyes fixed on Weber, often only dimly perceiving the surrounding milieu, tend unquestioningly to ascribe to him ideas that seem brilliant to us today, while crediting his chauvinist blindness to the account of the 'Zeitgeist'. But Gerd Fesser, the most thorough authority on Bülow's 'world policy', is quite right to say that in 1895 none other than Max Weber gave the 'initial push' in German public opinion for the turn to an impatient imperialism.[31] To be sure, he did not stand completely alone; colonial propagandists had been beating the drum since the 1880s, but he was one of the very first prominent liberal intellectuals to adopt the new tone. Fritz Fischer and his followers, who have combed through the history of the empire looking for evidence of the striving for world power, have repeatedly come across Weber's Freiburg address as one of the earliest high-profile signals of this kind. And even Fischer's adversary in debate, Gerhard Ritter, named Max Weber and Hans Delbrück as the ones whom 'educated youth' followed down the path of imperialism.[32]

Even Delbrück, Treitschke's successor as editor of the *Preußische Jahrbücher*, only followed behind Weber with his *Weltmacht* fanfares, although his sunny disposition meant that the latter's bleak pessimism was quite alien to him. With good reason he did not see his age as one of epigones, and in 1893, in an extensive anthology of quotations on which he must have worked for a long time, he actually made fun of the common trope that the old times had been much better and that the present age was irredeemably corrupt.[33] Six years after Weber's address, in the *Preußische Jahrbücher*, he described the Polish peasantry in the eastern territories quite differently: the old-style 'Polish economy' with its 'traces of barbarism' was all over; the Pole had become 'a modern, educated, financially strong owner of land who rejoiced at his successes'.[34] The contrast with Max Weber could not have been greater.

The later Chancellor Bülow, who nicknamed Delbrück 'Hans Taps' or 'Hans the Fool',[35] steered well away from Weberian *Weltmacht* ideas until he became foreign minister in 1897; this ever jovial, operetta-like charmer also found Weber's bleak fatalism quite alien. The mood in the broad mass of the population was not yet marked by pan-German chauvinism, and even a year after his appointment Bülow himself noted: 'The German masses are clerical, social-democratic or particularist, not nationally minded.'[36] Not the least attraction for Weber of this hard-line expansionism was that it had not yet become a banal refrain in every German bar but was a new and original position allowing him to present himself as a bold trailblazer. Later, under the impact of the world wars, openness to the wider world became a basic attitude of new elites, but in Weber's early years a certain kind of cosmopolitanism sounded like a jaded and conventional legacy of the old Enlightenment. Two days after the Freiburg address, Weber wrote with undisguised satisfaction to his brother Alfred that he had 'aroused general consternation about the brutality of (his) opinions'.[37] What reaction must Polish readers have had to Weber's outburst? A quarter of a year later, he received a letter from one Zdinski in Lemberg (today's Lviv), in which the author addressed him with the contemptuously familiar *du* and turned 'Weber', 'W.Eber', into 'Wilder Eber' ['wild boar' or 'raving lunatic']:

> This name suits you! Shame and disgrace on the mother who gave birth to one of the meanest predators. Even such mean and fierce predators as the wolf do not devour their fellow wolves, but you recognize as your highest ideal the devouring of your fellow men who have done nothing bad to you, the Poles, who for centuries protected your ancestors from the invasion of the Tartars and Turks. A pity that a Tartar pig did not eat up your seed centuries ago.[38]

Today, after two world wars and the crimes of National Socialism, it is long since forgotten that until the Bismarck period Germans were considered a highly peaceful and good-natured people, in the eyes of others as well as their own. The best evidence of this is Germaine de Staël's book *De l'Allemagne*, written in the period of Napoleonic rule, whose long-enduring picture of the 'German Michel' explains Weber's and Naumann's calls for toughness that sound so horrific after Auschwitz. Weber continued to believe for a long time that Germans reared in the casual ways of Lutheranism, if not in southern German Catholicism, were too weak and flabby; they needed a training in greater toughness and strictness if they were to stand up to the great Puritan 'work nations', the English and the Americans.

A week after the inaugural lecture in Freiburg, Marianne reported to Helene:

> The thought process was very complex and, for most people there, raised new and uncomfortable ways of looking at things. It presented today's political and economic conditions as a problem in which only an optimist could think he saw any way out. All economic issues are first of all issues of national power, and the cultivation of power instincts is for him much more important than all theories of the people's happiness. . . . This speech worked Max up so much that he made many slips of the tongue and looked white as a sheet; afterwards he had to face all possible objections, and Fritz (Baumgarten) argued with him for a whole evening.[39]

It is strange that Marianne found the thought process so 'complex'. Part of the speech consisted of nothing other than the conclusions from the study of farm-workers, which Marianne must by then have known inside out. But the ensuing crescendo, with its whole *Weltmacht* fanfare, had evidently not featured in their domestic conversations: it must have been one of those partly spontaneous eruptions with which Weber gave vent to things deep inside him. A further indication of this is the fact that he turned pale with excitement.

Did he feel that he was scandalously departing from the solid ground of scientific research? Even after reading the printed version of the speech over and over again, one is still alarmed by the degree of impulsiveness in such a high-ranking scholar. Right at the beginning Weber announces that his theme will be 'the role played by physical and psychological racial differences', although in reality he knows absolutely nothing about any racial determinant in the differences between German and Polish farm-workers in the eastern territories. Even more unpleasant than the chauvinism is the permanent sense of academic bluff: he repeatedly suggests a superior insight where there is actually no talk of one. He rages against 'the political philistinism of the lower middle classes', which lack any feeling for colonial policy or even 'the most rudimentary economic understanding' of 'what it would mean for Germany's trade in far-off oceans' (PW 25). But did economics in those days so much as hint at a higher insight into the advantages of colonial possessions? Were they not considered questionable precisely from an economic point of view? Did not Weber himself refer to the opportunity presented by the fact that Britain was Germany's largest trading partner (MWG I/4-2, 628f.)?[40]

Above all in the last part of the lecture, Weber constantly practises what he would later decry in the cultural historian Lamprecht: suggestive effects without precision and without clear argument. What he claims about the contemporary writing of history – that the 'monstrous notion of "matriarchy"' relegates major battles to a subordinate clause – is sheer nonsense; speculative feminism and anti-militarism were certainly not one of its main evils. Lamprecht, probably the unnamed object of Weber's attack, was an exception where matriarchy was concerned.

Towards the end, Weber rages against the 'hackneyed yelping of the ever-growing chorus of amateur social politicians' (PW 27), deliberately leaving them unnamed. Was this defamatory language directed at the highly competent Heinrich Herkner, the later follower of Schmoller, who four years previously had given his inaugural lecture in Freiburg on 'social reform as a requirement of economic progress'?[41] What remains of Weber's political instinct if his diatribes against social politicians are even more insulting than those of the Saar industrialist 'King Stumm' (with whom he was picking a violent quarrel at the very same time) and provide him with the best ammunition to use against his opponents? Did he completely forget that he had made his own the cause of social policy and the struggle against the rising tide of reaction? If, as Wolfgang Mommsen and Wilhelm Hennis assert, the Freiburg lecture was 'the most significant document for Max Weber the man of politics until the war years',[42] then it is compelling evidence that Weber was *not* a born politician. We have to wonder why the secondary literature so often shies away from stating this obvious fact.

Struggle: nature in politics

The leitmotif of the Freiburg address is that *life is struggle* – economic struggle, political struggle, but at bottom also physical violence. Even Hans-Ulrich Wehler, who values Weber more in spite of than because of his naturalist elements, thinks it obvious that violence was for him a 'natural anthropological constant'.[43] This conviction represents the peak of Weberian naturalism. For Arnold Bergstraesser, too, the address documents 'the effects of contemporary natural science on the whole of his thinking',[44] especially the effects of Darwinism. Most Weber scholars prefer to dismiss this natural element as a foreign body in his work, but their position is demonstrably wrong. Discussion of man's relationship to nature runs all through his work, as does the social-Darwinist belief that violence is a natural basic element of human life. The later Weber, however, discovered a still deeper passion in man: a longing for redemption.

Two years after the Freiburg address, a declaration of faith in struggle again provided a resounding finale when Weber, speaking on 10 June 1897 to the Evangelical Social Congress in Leipzig, countered Oldenberg's warning of the approach of an industrial state with an attack that his listeners greeted 'with lively applause and hissing':

> If my colleague Herr Oldenberg warned that the earth and its bread will one day become scarce, it is our view that . . . *population increase* . . . is what will again make harsher the struggle for existence, the struggle of men against men, and we deduce that the gospel of *struggle* is a duty of the nation, an economically unavoidable task for both the individual and the collective, and we are not 'ashamed' of this struggle, of the only road to greatness. (MWG I/4–2, 638)

This concluding passage contains not only a reference to Oldenberg, as the MWG commentator notes, but also an allusion to the words of Saint Paul (Romans 1:16): 'For I am not ashamed of the gospel of Christ: for it is the power of God.' Struggle as Weber's religion! He fully agrees with Oldenberg that a growing export orientation by German industry contains a 'huge risk', but he argues that 'we are not pursuing a policy of national *contentment* but one of national *greatness* and therefore must also shoulder this risk if we want our national existence to be different from that of Switzerland, for example' (MWG I/4–2, 630) – the all too neutral Switzerland which Weber's opposite, the pacifist Friedrich-Wilhelm

Foerster, later held up to Germans as an ideal.[45] Oldenberg had – to put it in modern terms – operated with a 'limits to growth' concept; Weber trumped this by arguing that struggle was the inevitable outcome of growth bottlenecks. In Freiburg his secret weapon, as it were, had been the 'sombre gravity of the population problem' (PW 14); in Leipzig he revealed that this gravity filled him with a sombre sense of triumph over happiness-seeking contemporaries, and that he liked to think of them as weak even though they might be psychologically stronger than himself.

The word 'struggle' [*Kampf*] occurs no fewer than 785 times in the electronic edition of Weber's works. When Weber proclaims the necessity of struggle, he plays his favourite role of tenacious truth-seeker destroying the illusions of wishful thinking, but in reality the omnipotence of struggle is a case of wishful thinking on Weber's part: struggle is more pleasurable than the routine work on committees that occupied his father's life, and which may be seen as an element of modern politics at least as fundamental as major battles. In his plea for parliamentary rule in wartime Germany, Weber again and again hammered out the message to his readers: *Politics is struggle!*

In the middle of the war, however, it was no longer an original idea to stress the necessity of *physical* struggle. Although Weber declares: 'The essence of all politics – as we will have to emphasize time and again – is *struggle*, the recruitment of *allies* and a *voluntary following*' (E&S 1414; PW 173), he now also appreciates that the rhetorical parliamentary struggle between parties is a means of cultivating leadership elites. Unlike nationalists who glorify conflict between nations but loathe party politics and wish to preserve harmony within the nation, Weber has come round to affirming the value of inter-party struggle. He even speaks of 'market struggle' and of money as a 'weapon in this struggle' (E&S 108). The later Weber had a more diverse notion of the natural basis of human affairs than did the Weber of 1895; after an anti-naturalist phase, we can see both in him and in Marianne an idea of nature that includes the life of the mind. He also maintained – and this is undoubtedly realistic – that the recruitment of reliable allies is a part of successful struggle; if that had not been the case, Weber would today be forgotten as a political thinker. But violence never disappears from his gospel of struggle.

In the 1890s Weber embraced the Darwinian concept of nature, including its violent side. In Freiburg he spoke of an ever-present 'struggle for existence' (PW 2), but paradoxically he also maintained that, if this natural struggle was allowed to run its course, it would lead not to the higher development of man but to the suppression of inferior, or barbarian, culture in the shape of the Polish small farmers. Even then Weber was sensitive to the teleology of progress that had been smuggled into Darwinism: he perceived, again quite realistically, that Darwinian assumptions did not logically imply that anything pleasant for human beings would come out of the 'struggle for existence'. Darwin might believe that out of pride in British world domination, but things looked different from the viewpoint of eastern Germany. If higher culture was to survive there, it would have to call a forcible halt to the natural process. And that was possible only if it mobilized its own natural element, its survival instinct, those 'natural political instincts' which, according to Weber, were at risk of being 'corroded' by modern economic development (PW 27). This nature of high culture had an aggressive element, in contrast to the naturalness of the Polish small farmers, which was rooted in sluggish self-sufficiency.

The refusal of happiness

Is not the need for pleasure and happiness a natural instinct *par excellence*? But that was what Weber least wanted to hear about. At every opportunity he rejected any such striving, all the more because, like so many of his contemporaries, he saw Germany at that time as a fun-loving society. Immediately after his reference to 'natural political instincts', he disgustedly associates 'the illusion of independent "socio-political" ideals' with a 'soft eudaemonistic outlook' (PW 27). And, earlier in the same lecture, he rounds on the goal of 'adding to the "balance of pleasure" in human existence' as a typically 'vulgar conception of political economy' (PW 14).

In his diatribe against hedonism, Weber repeatedly warns of the 'terrible gravity of the demographic problem' and concludes that the 'expansion of Germany's power' to the point where it becomes an 'economic and political *Weltmacht*' is a 'vital question for us' (MWG I/4–2, 610f.). In Weber, as in so many nationalists of the following period, two opposing demographic concerns are actually muddled with each other: that Germany may not be able to feed its growing population, and that a declining German population in the eastern territories will encourage the advance of the cheerfully multiplying Slavs. According to Weber, the Roman empire went under because the slave class that sustained its agriculture lacked a will to reproduce.

All in all, it seems undeniable that Weber's 'gospel of struggle' and his rejection of 'eudaemonism' did not spring from a soberly rational logic but were eruptions from his inner depths. This was the period in which he lambasted his father's 'need for pleasure', working himself up to a fury that bordered on mental patricide. The inaugural lecture in Freiburg, like other speeches, is also permeated with an aggressive he-manship that suggests an incapacity for peaceful enjoyment of life, if not actual fear of belonging to a degenerate race of epigones. Dismissing any idea that true vitality is expressed in a calm *joie de vivre*, Weber fulminates against the 'petty-bourgeois philistines' of southern Germany who would rather have an early evening drink in their garden house or among the family than march off to war. The very person who is trying to fight off depression can get a grim pleasure from showing others the darker side of the world. And the Weber of that time reminds one of the sinister figure of Alberich in Wagner's *Rheingold*, who cursed love in order to gain power over the world. Already in 1894, having heard in Naumann's speech an 'infinite longing for human happiness', Weber declared his contempt for the same at the Evangelical Social Congress. He even came up with a pseudo-quantification:

> The subjective feeling of happiness is greater in layers of the popula-
> tion that are at a low intellectual level and tend towards impassive
> resignation than it is in any of you present here, greater in an agricul-
> tural labourer than in a farmer, greater in an impassively resigned
> worker from the eastern territories than in an urban proletarian,
> greater in an animal than in a man. (MWG I/4–1, 339)

So, for him there was no doubt that Poles were happier than Germans and the agricultural labourers of eastern Germany happier than himself, Max Weber. But why did they nevertheless move westward? Was Weber no longer sure of the key conclusions from his study of farm-workers?

Friedrich Naumann: from St Francis to Machiavelli

One direct political effect of the Freiburg lecture can be demonstrated: the impact on Friedrich Naumann – according to his colleague Theodor Heuss – was 'of the greatest significance'.[46] Naumann's friend Gertrud Bäumer later remarked: 'If Naumann's first step outside Franciscan Christianity was to realize the importance of a scientific organization of life for the achievement of social ideals, the speech by his friend Max Weber was the impetus for a second stage in this re-education: namely, the knowl-edge that the extent and power of national existence is a second condition for broad layers of the population to live a life fit for human beings' (WzG 120). Naumann had already been toying with *Weltmacht* policies based on a strong navy, but only with a guilty conscience. Then Weber said the magic word that gave free rein to Naumann's imperial enthusiasm.[47]

There is little sign of a social-political ethos in Weber's speech, however. What one senses, rather, is weariness of the 'social policy' (his quotation marks) with which German political economy had been concerned for the previous two decades. Theodor Heuss's picture of Naumann's development is not as harmonious as the one that Gertrud Bäumer liked to paint. Thus, in a letter to Alfred Weber from 1937, he emphasized the 'broken-down aspect of his figure', which he somewhat exaggeratedly reduced to the 'Francis and Machiavelli formula'.[48] No doubt Weber deepened this split in Naumann's human and political make-up and helped the Machiavelli in him to break through. Naumann's political patron Adolf Stoecker had tried to use anti-Semitism to win the workers to the cause of the nation. But, as Jew-baiting was repugnant to Naumann, his stirring rhetoric drew all the more on imperialist themes to spread enthusiasm for Germany among the lower classes. And for this Max Weber, already his expert on eco-nomic issues, provided a supposedly scientific legitimacy.

Months before Weber's Freiburg speech, Naumann had called in *Hilfe* (his house periodical) for new battleships and even roped in Jesus to bridge the gap between naval rearmament and the Evangelical message of peace.

> Jesus stands in spirit before us and asks how peace is better served, with or without weapons? We answer: Oh, Lord, weapons are a heavy load to carry, and we will be glad when we can shed it, but today disarmament means calling death into the country! Lord, do you wish that? It is as if I can hear Jesus saying: I do not wish that; go forth and build ships and pray God that you will not need to use them![49]

Did anyone in Germany with any political savvy really believe that a renunciation of the naval programme would cause the enemy to attack? Naumann's pastoral rhetoric did not allow critical questions to be raised about what a large navy would actually mean. And then came Weber's speech, which led even Naumann to deal rather dismissively with social policy. 'Is he not right? What use is the best social policy if the Cossacks come here?'[50] But what use was the navy against Cossacks? In fact, the naval programme considerably weakened Germany's arms drive on land, to an extent that may have proved the Reich's undoing in the world war. It is staggering that no trace of such ideas may be found in either Weber or Naumann, so overpowering was their need for muscular gestures.

For the liberals, the navy had the further attraction of representing a more modern form of armament than the land army and its officer corps dominated by the aristocracy. As the Kaiser knew, professors were particularly receptive to the naval craze. At that time, with the agrarians opposed to naval armament, it was a suitable issue on which to question the national feeling of the Junkers and to make them unpopular with Wilhelm II. Weber, however, unlike Naumann, did not have the slightest ambition to be promoted to the Kaiser's paladin, and he soon became aware that Wilhelm II was drawing on a similar imperialist register to the one he had used in Freiburg, albeit without any of his darker undertones. His attempt to project in this way a defiant image of himself was a thorough failure.

A political dead end

For Naumann, too, the new hard line did not prove to be a successful political formula. Like Wilhelm II he always won respect for his rhetoric, but without achieving anything at all definite; it is therefore questionable that Weber served him well as a political adviser. In November 1896, at the founding meeting of the National-Social Association in Erfurt, Weber suspected his audience of excessive softness and spoke as curtly as possible: 'But politics is a tough business, and anyone who wishes to take responsibility for interfering with the spokes of political development in his fatherland must have solid nerves and not be too sentimental to conduct a worldly policy' (MWG I/4–2, 622). 'Tough' in this context meant tough towards the Poles. But was Weber himself a model of 'solid nerves'? Although he may not have been clearly aware of it at that moment, he was disqualifying himself for politics by the words he chose.

Theodor Heuss thought that in those years Weber was 'at the beginning of a wonderful development'.[51] That may be true of 1893–4, the years of the study of farm-workers and his appointment in Freiburg, but the 'wonderful development' was soon over, both politically and theoretically – and that cannot have been lost on a man such as Weber, who, in between his periods of self-opinionatedness, was capable of sharp self-criticism. As Eduard Baumgarten put it, in the second half of the 1890s Weber 'withdrew from the arena with his hopes dashed' (B 339). From 1895 on he increasingly doubted whether he could achieve anything politically, and in 1899 he sank into a 'state of despair and wrathfulness' (B 349). Johannes Winckelmann, a long-standing executor of the Weber estate, suggested in 1963 that Weber's collapse had been due to '*massive disappointment*':

> His colossal effort since the beginning of the farm-workers study to give a new direction to social, agrarian and ecclesiastical policy – an effort which linked him to Göhre and Naumann – had abruptly been condemned to failure with the advent of the age of reaction. This sudden frustration of all his non-academic endeavours must have crippled his political initiative and led to a very strong sense of resignation.

In Winckelmann's view, the preface that Weber wrote early in his illness to the abandoned second study of farm-workers (the one commissioned by the Evangelical Social Congress) expressed 'huge bitterness' or even 'sheer despair and hopelessness'.[52] In the preface we read:

> In our German conditions, the 'changing majorities' of parliamentary states . . . are replaced by changing *fashions* in politics and social policy among the leading strata. . . . It has been sufficiently shown that the incipient social policy of 1890 . . . was one such unstable fashion, resulting in part, moreover, from politically naive and morally not very elevated speculation on the *gratitude* of the masses so to be favoured. . . . Thus, when the expected 'gratitude' failed to materialize, the natural sequel was disappointment and aimless inward rage. The top political positions were then all the more apt . . . to become playthings of those agile businessmen who promoted the victorious belief that, in social policy too, the only *ultima ratio* is powder and lead. (MWG I/4-2, 709f.)

Strong words, to be sure. But Weber was forgetting that none other than himself had set the tone for the change in fashion: 'world politics' instead of 'social politics'. 'Powder and lead'? Had he not proclaimed not so long ago a 'gospel of struggle', whereas the imperial government had never in peacetime used military force against the workers' movement? The text demonstrates not only a lack of political clarity but, worse, a lack of sincerity.

A theoretical dead end

But the dead end in which Weber found himself was not only political but theoretical. The Freiburg inaugural lecture testifies to this, and for a man of such insight it could not remain hidden for long once he had lost his euphoric feeling of strength. Actually, if the address had been seriously intended as a theoretical programme, it would have had to be followed by an analysis of race as a factor in the development of agriculture. But that there was absolutely no solid evidence of this, and that it was even uncertain how any could be acquired, later became as clear as daylight to Weber. He demanded of political economy that it should become a *national* science. But why did it have to be that, and anyway what would it have meant? Most important, what *programme of work* would it have entailed? Weber argued that, as soon as political economy became practical and made value-judgements, it was 'tied to the particular strain of humankind we find within our own nature' (PW 15). But this very Wilhelmine national metaphysic, with its rhetorical invocation of a 'German essence', is utterly un-Weberian. In his writings on the stock market, the idea never occurred to him that there was an exemplary stock market corresponding to some 'German essence'; on the contrary, he thought that Germans could and should learn from the City of London. To associate the German economy with a German essence: that was soap-box oratory rather than a research programme.

Of course, there might have been ways of developing the conception of a national political economy. The Schmoller school, in particular, had set itself the task of investigating German institutional traditions – the craft guild, the business fraternity, the trade cartel, the mercantilist state-run enterprise – and their possible usefulness for the contemporary economic system. By the 1890s, however, business associations and cartels had so shaped the German economy that an economist who regarded competitive struggle as an indispensable stimulus would have had a hard time making a further case for it on the basis of scientific evidence. The German social state, which began to be constructed in the 1880s, would have been a better argument for a special German path in political economy – but Weber defamed those who concentrated on social policy.

In 1894 Weber took up the Freiburg professorship in political economy, and his later appointments in Heidelberg and Munich were also essentially in that field. This fact is too easily forgotten, as Weber's later reputation was not built on his work in economics. Nor did he, as a professor, have any illusions that he was anything but a dilettante in the subject. According to Marianne, his Freiburg colleague Schulze-Gaevernitz initially thought of him as 'a blockhead and, moreover, a scoundrel who had been appointed over his head'.[53] In 1891 Weber wrote to Hermann Baumgarten that he had 'over time become roughly one-third of a political economist' (JB 327): not a lot for a man who two years later would take up a chair in the subject. It is also doubtful whether he went on to feel more of one. In 1895 he openly admitted to Adolf Wagner, one of the leading figures in German political economy: 'I look on myself as a beginner in nine-tenths of the field I am supposed to cover.'[54] He never felt really at home in economics. Originally, economic theory had extended into history and philosophy, but the more specialized it became in the field of economics alone, the more difficult it was for academics with wide intellectual interests to feel comfortable in the discipline.

Up to a point, the increased stress was normal for a newly qualified professor who, having become a narrow specialist through the path of examination and promotion, was now expected to cover the whole breadth of his subject. The preparation of his first lectures proved more difficult than he had anticipated (WB 201), one reason for this probably being that he had no passion for the subject and initially had little original to contribute. In fact, he was not very fond of *homo oeconomicus*, yet one had to be that ideal type to arrive at any kind of theory in economics. In his inaugural lecture, Weber declared his contempt for 'eudaemonism', but it is an essential part of economic theory that it considers people only in so far as they wish to make money – as much as possible – and to satisfy consumption needs stretching as far as possible beyond the bare necessities of life.

It is true that, in contrast to the *homo oeconomicus* of the Manchester School, the German Historical School of political economy theorized whole people living in historically constituted communities, not just individuals pursuing isolated material needs. But the kind of theory that they developed in this way gave a central place to historical stages of development, which Weber found a dubious concept in itself. Without such theoretical models, however, the Historical School was at risk of degenerating into the trivial collection of facts. At the turn of the century, it was becoming ever clearer that there were rosy prospects for economics as an autonomous discipline, but that the future lay with the Viennese marginal utility school founded by Schmoller's opponent, Carl Menger. It was inevitable that in the long run this new direction would make more of an impression on Weber, who liked rigorous thinking, than on Schmoller, towards whom he anyway developed a psychological and physical revulsion.

The marginal utility theorists were, however, eudaemonists of the kind to which Weber had thrown down the gauntlet in Freiburg. For they presupposed a human nature governed by the pleasure principle – one respect in which they had an affinity with the up-and-coming Freudian school in

Vienna – and assessed economic conduct in accordance with the strength or weakness of the pleasure gain; hence the name 'hedonist school', which was also used for them at that time.[55] The price of a commodity was given by the 'marginal utility' whereby, in the purchaser's mind, the increment of pleasure outweighed the foregoing of other pleasure that he might have gained by using his money in a different way. In 1891 Menger's comrade-in-arms, Böhm-Bawerk, rapturously described 'the idea of marginal utility as 'the "open sesame", the key to the most complicated phenomena of economic life, affording a solution of its most difficult problems'.[56] Whatever the truth of the matter, it became clear in Weber's time that this approach made it possible to do excellent *work* and offered huge scope for fascinating intellectual games. Economic science has lived off it down to the present day.

Weber's Freiburg lecture, with its stark rejection of happiness, was spiritually miles away from the Viennese world of the marginalist school, which conceived people as calculating sexpots; indeed, it blocked any path to that vision of humanity. Weber's pet ideas gave him material for a few effective speeches, but not for whole semesters of lectures, and still less for the kind of painstaking work with which a rising generation of academics wins its spurs. Not much testimony has come down to us concerning Weber's early lectures. Robert Liefmann, one of his first doctoral students, recalled: 'Weber was then still a pure historian and, as always, completely unsystematic.'[57] We are still a long way from the Weber of *Economy and Society*. A printed 'outline' of Weber's 1898 lectures on 'general (theoretical) economics' follows the doctrine of marginal utility for long sections, but clearly indicates that nothing original occurred to him in connection with it.[58]

Weber's socialist students appear to have been the most disappointed in him. A report in *Der Sozialistische Akademiker* attacked the 'Social-Economic Association' founded by Weber after his appointment in Heidelberg, describing it as 'spreading the leaden boredom of the most barren compartmentalized nonsense, under the protectorate of the time-serving professor'. Then a surprising observation: 'After some fine-sounding verbiage', Weber soon exposed himself as a 'champion of the Austrian school'.[59] If Weber at first had novelty appeal for his students, he evidently became less attractive after a few years: his Heidelberg lecture in the summer of 1898 still had an audience of eighty-three – not such a large figure even then – but the winter figure was down to thirty-six, and his last lecture in the 1899–1900 winter semester also drew no more than thirty-six. Whereas Marianne, Else and Leo Wegener were among those who attended in summer 1898, they had all abandoned him by the winter of 1899–1900.[60]

All told, we can glimpse a deep theoretical disorientation in Weber at that time, matched by a wavering strategy in faculty politics. In 1895, on his initiative, the University of Freiburg decided to transfer the political economy department from the philosophy faculty to the newly created faculty of legal and constitutional studies;[61] one would have expected the opposite from a professor who liked to include economics among the cultural sciences. After his appointment in Heidelberg, on the other hand, he explicitly argued that political science was not one of his teaching responsibilities.[62] What was left of the 'national mission' that he had assigned to political economy in Freiburg?

The violation of both German nature and his own

When Marianne Weber in her biography interprets Max's breakdown as the 'revenge of nature', the metaphor superficially evokes a mental and physical reaction to years of overwork. At that time it was common, at least publicly, to give this as the explanation of 'neurasthenia' in worthy individuals, although among themselves both doctors and laymen ascribed it mainly to dissipation and onanism. In the case of Max Weber, nothing suggested itself as more plausible than the diagnosis of overwork. Knut Borchardt has rightly pointed out, however, that in the years 1897 and 1898, when Weber's illness was becoming acute, there are no indications at all of a heavier workload:[63] he repeated a lecture on general and theoretical economics that he had already given several times in Freiburg; his research projects on farm-workers and the stock exchange were discontinued; and the Webers went on holiday for months during the university vacations.

It would seem that what led to Weber's breakdown was not overwork but the exact opposite: the flight from creeping depression into work no longer succeeded. It must have become dismally clear to him that neither scholarship nor politics offered bright prospects for the future, and this very loss of a purpose in life must have made the lack of sexual fulfilment more of a torture than ever.[64] About this, too, Weber could no longer kid himself: his marital impotence was a permanent condition, not a passing phenomenon explicable by work stress or the spouses' unfamiliarity with each other. For a man such as Weber, who defined himself in terms of male vitality, this knowledge was enough to drive him to despair, especially on brooding nights without sleep. The period of constant insomnia and agonizing strain was beginning. It is likely that Weber's crisis was all the more intense because of a long-present predisposition: we can only speculate about that today. From the indications given by Karl Jaspers late in life, we know that there was something distinctly 'masochistic' about Weber's erotic inclinations. But his image of himself at that time as a 'valiant hero' made it impossible for him to acknowledge and live out those inclinations. This inner mismatch may have been a deeper reason for his sexual block, and it may have increasingly blocked him in his scientific work too. Only when he looked more positively on the contemplative side of his creativity was he able to enter the productive period that made him internationally famous.

The truth is that, although he would not yet admit it, he was not at all a born warrior or ruler. In this sense we may say that he 'did violence' to his own nature, by developing a forced and mistaken interpretation of it. This went together with a no less forced interpretation of the 'German essence', as his introductory lecture in Freiburg eloquently testifies. Like so many German chauvinists, he revered an ideal image of the German while dismissing actually existing Germans as 'petty-bourgeois philistines', with an ineradicable penchant for the smug companionability of '*Gemütlichkeit*'. In his study of farm-workers, he moved from affection for the peaceful cow that held the farmer to the soil, all the way to a concluding burst of martial fanfares. Both ways of violating nature landed him in the worst crisis of his life. When external objects of aggression ran out, his unconscious aggressiveness was turned on himself. That too is a possible interpretation of what happened to him.

Part II

Nature's Revenge

From the summer of 1898 Weber became increasingly incapable of work, and in 1899 he obtained dispensation from teaching duties. Only in 1918, almost twenty years later, did he feel to some extent in a condition to resume regular lecturing. The doctors diagnosed neurasthenia. In 1898 and 1900 he spent several months in sanatoria: first at the Konstanzer Hof on Lake Constance, then at Dr Klüpfel's establishment in Urach at the foot of the Swabian Alb. The courses of treatment were unsuccessful. Instead, between 1899 and 1903, Weber sought relief in travels to Corsica and then Italy. In 1902 he gradually regained his capacity for scholarly work, although until 1909 creative periods were continually interrupted by relapses. He began by settling accounts with the Historical School of German political economy (in Roscher and Knies*) and followed this with essays on the theory of science. In 1903, when to his relief he was definitively released from his teaching post, he began work on the two parts of* The Protestant Ethic and the Spirit of Capitalism *(published in 1904–5), which established his international reputation. In 1904 he travelled with his wife to the United States, having been invited to attend an international scholarly congress on the occasion of the St Louis world exhibition in Missouri. He took the opportunity to make a month-long trip through the country and later drew repeatedly on his impressions. Upon his return, he took over the editorship of the* Archiv für Sozialwissenschaft und Sozialpolitik, *which would become the most important outlet for his writings. Under the impact of the 1905 Revolution he learned the Russian language and made himself familiar with conditions in Russia; in 1906 he published two extensive articles on the crisis there. He now began to make occasional public appearances again and to take positions on various political issues. In 1907 Marianne Weber published* Ehefrau und Mutter in der Rechtsgeschichte [Wife and Mother in the History of Law], *a major work written with her husband's help in which some of the themes of his later work were already discernible. In 1908 the couple achieved a degree of financial independence thanks to Marianne's inheritance of 350,000 marks; they could now afford to gather together a circle of mainly young scholars, who met at their home on a regular basis. From April 1910 they lived in a villa on the Neckar built by Max Weber's grandfather, Fallenstein.*

7

The Demons: The Wildness of Nature and the Riddle of Sexuality

Inability to work and neurasthenia: Max Weber's need for therapy

In people who like to be thought of as well and have no special inclination to consult doctors, a sense of being ill and needing to seek medical attention usually manifests itself through an inability to work; this was the case with Max Weber. He had experienced periods of irritability and depression long before 1898,[1] but they do not seem to have reduced his mania for work – on the contrary. In 1894 he confessed to Marianne that uninterrupted work was a means for him to ward off 'serious depression'; it was a 'natural need', whereas a 'relaxing' of the nerves spelled danger.

Already in those years, however, there were increasing signs that the main danger was not 'relaxation' but nervous strain.[2] Max was often tense and agitated during his trip to Spain with Marianne in the autumn of 1897, shortly after the 'day of judgement' and his father's death; he wanted to keep moving and constantly complained at 'the lackadaisical transport system' (WB 233). In Saragossa they had a row that brought Marianne to tears[3] – a rare occurrence between them. In response to his mother, who urged him to take things easier, he justified himself by talking of the abnormal state of his nerves: 'It's true what you write: that under normal conditions it would not do us good to let so many impressions pass us by. But, so long as there was no talk of my working, I would not have been able to stand it in one place; now my nerves are gradually calming down.'[4] He felt at the mercy of his nerves and apparently did not think that over time they could also become calmer in conditions of outer peace.

In the spring of 1898 Weber was overcome by an acute attack of what Kraepelin diagnosed as 'neurasthenia due to years of overwork'.[5] But good periods were still mixed in with the bad. After a stay on Lake Geneva, Weber wrote that, 'apart from the strain on particular nerves in the head', he felt 'especially well mentally . . . now more than ever'; he even thought that Marianne was more ill and spoke of her 'terrible state' that was probably 'again caused by chlorosis'. Chlorosis? It was already an old-fashioned popular term for what the textbooks called anaemia, which, especially among women with heavy periods, was supposedly connected with hysteria and neurasthenia.[6] Taking both Marianne's troubles and his own on his light shoulders, Max continued: 'Of course we all remain oddballs when it comes to the nerves; there's nothing to be done about that. But now that we've gradually got over everything that was weighing on us, we can laugh and pay it no attention.'[7] He felt all this 'nervousness' to be something that ran in the family, not an individual destiny. Indeed, he had reason to believe that both he and Marianne had inherited a certain predisposition to nervous strain.

When Weber resumed his duties in the summer semester, however, he began to feel really ill. Until then sleep had not been an issue, but now he was suffering from the insomnia that would torment him for years and persecute him for the rest of his life. As the semester wore on, words came to him with ever greater difficulty; he apparently later confided to Eugen Rosenstock-Huessy that, in the middle of a lecture, he was tortured by the obsessional idea that an ape's mask was pressed on his face.[8] This would suggest that his illness was not 'just a case of nerves' but had psychotic elements. Things went so far that he could not complete the semester but had to apply for immediate leave a few weeks before it was over so that he could begin a course of treatment – a clear sign of panic on his part.[9] The ministry granted the request without delay. In those days the German bureaucracy treated nervous professors more gently.

Weber was also readily granted leave in the following years, without loss of pay, until his time off for convalescence totalled more than four years – as long as the whole of the time he had spent teaching. In the end, out of shame that he was doing nothing to earn his professorial income, he himself energetically sought the termination of his academic employment and finally achieved this on 1 October 1903. It caused raging pain to Marianne, who did not want to accept that he was permanently incapable of exercising his profession, or to lose the social and material status that went with being a professor's wife. She resorted to a kind of autogenic training to rid herself of this *idée fixe*: 'I shall tell myself every day that I am being a silly goose when I hanker after the professorship.'[10] Weber did not think he was alone capable of convincing his wife,[11] although in such cases even a doctor cannot do much more than follow the patient's assessment of himself.

Weber as a sanatorium patient

Weber spent several months of 1898, from the end of the summer semester until shortly before the beginning of the winter semester, at the Konstanzer Hof 'sanatorium for nervous disorders' on Lake Constance. He still thought of his illness as temporary. The sanatorium, which had been founded in 1890, was then regarded as one of the most up to date in Germany: a publicity brochure emphasized[12] that, unlike in the older hydropathic establishments (many of which were then mutating into 'clinics for nervous complaints'),[13] its 'main special feature (was) not the *method of treatment* but the kind of illnesses treated', that is, nervous illnesses. As in science in general, there was a problem of individualization, and cases would be handled with the most effective combination of methods for each particular condition. If, when he regained his capacity for work, Weber first turned his attention to problems of scientific theory, we should not forget that years of personal experience of illness and therapies were an important background.

At the Konstanzer Hof, as at similar establishments springing up on all sides, the 'effects of the material apparatus of diet, air, hydrotherapy, massage and electricity' were combined with the encouragement of lifestyle changes, essentially 'a simple patriarchal life supported by high morals'. On the other hand, the director was sceptical about the 'flood of new drugs that modern chemistry has poured over ailing humanity', and also distanced himself from the 'so-called natural cures that have desperately little to do with *natural science* and natural living'. We see how the disputes over 'nature' had been penetrating the health establishment. The disputes over culture too. Music was admitted there only selectively, with a ban on anything that 'makes people nervous': certainly Wagner, but also the 'piano pest', that dilettante plunking which was often held to have a fatal effect on the nerves. The *personae gratae* were the 'old masters': Bach, Mozart, Schubert. Later, however, Weber's healing process would unfold to the strains of Wagner.

'Any cure for the nerves is a matter of trial and error'

At first Weber was quite happy with the Konstanzer Hof. 'We lunatics have it good here', he wrote home; 'the electricity treatment and massage' was doing him good. His depression made itself felt only briefly: 'Of course, nothing is too great as far as my mood is concerned.'[14] Only in the sanatorium was he 'really overcome by a sense of being unwell'. He experienced most of his fellow patients as 'pretty dull-witted',[15] and he found no inner peace in the 'noisy and overcrowded establishment'. The doctors experimented with hypnosis, but there was only a 'half dawn' for Weber.[16] The cold-water treatments – typical of sanatoria recently converted from hydropathic establishments – 'only increased his excitement and banished sleep completely' (WB 235). Evidently the doctors were still following a therapeutic philosophy developed in calmer times, according to which 'weakened' nerves had to be tightened again through powerful stimulation. Weber soon recognized the problems with this and tried to persuade his doctors that their stimulation of the metabolism was 'increasing the nervous excitement instead of calming it'.

They simply won't believe me and keep trying to get on top of things by increasing the metabolism. Now I have to explain my opinion and try to persuade them that the main point is to calm my nerves. . . .

> Especially in the realm of the nerves, it is always necessary to test on
> an individual basis what effect a particular method will have.[17]

In relation to individuals, he saw, there can be no *a priori* knowledge in
either the human or the natural sciences. In 1908, when Marianne entered
a sanatorium and had similar experiences to those of her husband, Max
Weber complained as he had done ten years before: 'The nerve doctors *all*
make the mistake of mainly *stimulating* the nerves' (MWG II/5 511). 'Any
medical consultation is poison for Max', she wrote in 1900, 'as well as any
experimentation by the doctors.'[18] And yet he continually sought the advice
of psychiatrists and neurologists. Like other well-informed neurasthenics
who already had experience of many different therapies, he developed 'a
strong mistrust of all medical prescriptions' yet felt the 'deepest need' for
'treatment in general'.[19] Karl Jaspers, himself a former psychiatrist, was
surprised in retrospect at Weber's patience: 'He did not bypass the medical
institutions, although they were a complete failure.'[20]

When Weber returned to Heidelberg in the autumn of 1898, he struggled
through half of the winter semester but then again broke off teaching as he
began to realize that he had a chronic illness linked to his natural disposition.[21] Accustomed as he was to a permanent economy of time, Weber must
at first have constantly wondered how long he would be absent from work
and how he could catch up on the lost time. In July 1899 he still thought
that he would be able to make a damage assessment and work out a new
schedule that took it into account.[22] But the weeks off work turned into
months, then the months into years: his whole way of looking at the future
collapsed. There was no longer any point in thinking about time.[23] From
the 1899 summer semester on, he was excused all teaching duties. The following winter he made a pathetic attempt with a single lecture, and in the
summer of 1900, awkward though it was, he had to give up a last try in mid-
semester. In May the Heidelberg internist Oswald Vierordt certified that he
was suffering from 'severe and persistent neurasthenia'[24] – and 'neurasthenia' accompanied with such intensifiers could be a codeword for something
worse.

On 5 June 1900 Weber wrote to the ministry that his 'recurrent illness
with short intermissions' made him incapable of further exercising his profession.[25] He now formally gave up teaching activity – for a full eighteen
years, or nine-tenths of his remaining life. In June 1904 he urged Rickert,
who was also suffering from a nervous disorder, to break off his lectures
before the end of the semester. 'How can it "depress" you just to postpone
the lecture? In that case I would have to shoot myself.'[26] In the midst of
work on his *The Protestant Ethic*, he tried in vain to cure the philosopher
of his professorial ethic – a warning for those who regard the Puritanical
morality described by Weber as a direct reflection of his own view of life at
that time!

Early in 1900 Marianne complained to her mother-in-law that Weber
often just sat there 'squeaking his nails'; to relieve the mental pressure by

modelling with clay – a method recommended to him – required 'too much concentration'. He even found it too much when Marianne read something to him aloud.[27] The mere thought of his few disciples 'put an enormous strain on him', and he cursed them and suggested that they might like to 'croak'.[28] When Marianne pressed him to write a report for a Jewish student who was finding it difficult to register for the *Habilitation*, he dictated 'four pages in a quarter of an hour' to her. But afterwards his irritability was turned against her for the first time: 'He said that I failed to ensure he was left in peace and that it would take him weeks to overcome this setback; he *had* to have quiet, even if people "croaked" over it' (WB 243). The psychological strain generated a defiant self-centredness – rather as in today's 'how to feel good' workshops, where therapists urge participants to make only themselves important and nothing else in the world.

From July to November 1900 Weber was a patient at the Klüpfel sanatorium in Urach, in the Swabian Alb, while Marianne stopped keeping house in Heidelberg. Max already seems to have been incapable of making decisions, and so it was Marianne who found the establishment for him.[29] After a few days in Urach, Weber felt so weak and lethargic that the thought of having to write to Marianne seemed 'dreadful'. She wrote out little cards for him, 'which he then had to complete – for example, Sleep: "reasonable"; Legs: "weary"; Head: "swimming"'.[30] Urach was the nadir of his whole illness (WB 242). Max Weber must have feared that he was at the last stop before the lunatic asylum, especially as the widespread, though not unchallenged, wisdom of the day held that untreated and aggravated neurasthenia could degenerate into mental illness.

To make matters worse, it turned out that the Urach establishment was not even as peaceful as Weber had hoped. He found his room loud, was again unable to sleep and sent out a veritable 'cry of distress' to the distant Marianne, but he could not himself summon up the energy to ask for a quieter room; he therefore had to endure his wife's accusations of timidity.[31] Otherwise, he was also 'given the electricity treatment' in Urach.[32] In 1908, when Marianne spent some time in Lahmann's 'White Deer' clinic in Dresden, reputedly the largest establishment using a scientifically based 'physical-dietetic method of treatment',[33] her husband was able to play the specialist in therapeutic establishments. If her sleep did not improve, 'the method itself (would have to be) *changed*, since any cure for the nerves is a matter of trial and error!' (MWG II/5, 505). Weber indeed knew this from years of experience. He also instructed his mother: 'Nerve therapy, which initially does without any "theory", is at first geared to purely empirical *experimentation* for each individual case' (MWG II/5, 511). Again and again he brought his own experience of illness and therapy to bear on questions of scientific theory.

But what exactly was his illness? A certain and precise answer to this question is no longer possible. To use modern terminology, we can recognize in the picture of Weber's illness both manic-depressive and schizoid elements, plus a lot that fits into neither category; Max Weber was not a psychiatric ideal type. The neurologist Willy Hellpach, who was in close touch with Weber between 1905 and 1907, depicted him in his memoirs as a split personality;[34] the psychiatrist Karl Jaspers, who got to know Weber later and was outraged at Hellpach's judgement, placed greater emphasis on the manic-depressive side.[35] But what appears decisive today is not which was the most fitting diagnosis but how Weber himself experienced and interpreted his illness, and what consequences he drew from it for his lifestyle and his view of the world. We should focus first of all on the *symptoms*, on the way in which he and his doctors interpreted them, and on the therapeutic conclusions they drew.

Symptoms

The most evident early symptoms of Weber's illness were speech and motor disorders: verbal inhibitions, in particular, were the acute reason for his breaking off lectures; and he once remarked that 'everything makes me unsteady on my feet, like Mama'.[36] He already knew from his mother that psychological tensions could express themselves in motor disturbances. Especially in his worst year, 1900, he felt a crippling constriction in his arms and legs. Whereas, on past trips, he had had hypermotor tendencies and thought it healthy to 'race up' the castle hill in Heidelberg,[37] the shortest walk was now an effort, even if the doctors never found anything physically wrong with him.

He developed an *idée fixe* that brisk walking was harmful to him. In the summer of 1901 in Rome, which always tempted lovers of history to pace the streets, Weber enjoyed 'walking less than ever, and attributed to it any discomfort and any mental fatigue'.[38] Such complaints recur again and again;[39] he never shared the belief that movement was healthy. Certainly this cannot be explained by medical theories of the time. Rather, as in the classical cases of hysteria, motor inhibitions must have been a large part of his psychosomatic crisis. In his own perception of things, however, these physical symptoms and the recurrent day-long attacks of migraine were secondary matters (MWG II/6, 135). Insomnia was the constant issue for him right up to the last years of his life, often appearing as the source of all evil. But nocturnal emissions seemed to the Webers a deeper reason for that tormenting excitability that kept sleep away.

'Sleep, sleep, sleep!' A pattern of life ruled by sleep

In 1898, at the onset of the sleep disturbances that would remain for the rest of his life, Weber also began a habit of painful self-observation and communication with others about his sleep history and the effects of various soporific drugs. Sleepless nights mean suffering from an overactive brain and arouse a huge longing to sink into a 'vegetative' or 'autonomic' existence – which was also a significant concept for the Webers. But Weber also feared the nocturnal emissions and accompanying dreams that sleep brought with it. After his first few weeks in the Konstanzer Hof, he wrote to his wife:

I am sleeping very irregularly. A lot the night before last, but again very badly last night, for no special reason, just like at home. I always take a bromide for it. . . . The whole thing is pretty complicated and not so easy to clear up. [Two days later:] Actually the 'little packets' don't seem very easily digestible. Their purpose is to stimulate the metabolism. You sweat enormously as a result, but at the same time they excite the nerves and therefore disturb your sleep.[40]

If sleep preoccupied Weber to the extent that it did, this was because it had the greatest influence over the shape of his life. At first he could find no reason for his insomnia. But soon he became convinced that any daytime effort – a long period of concentrated reading, an agitated discussion, a tiring walk – had to be paid for by going without a certain amount of sleep: not only if it was performed shortly before he went to bed, but also if it was done much earlier in the day. For a time he thought he might regain his inner balance if he alternated strictly between four weeks of work and four weeks of 'complete inactivity and a change of scene' (WB 260). Although the concept had not yet been introduced, Weber seemed to have made his own the idea of 'body memory'.

Bad sleep was nature's punishment for any overtaxing of one's strength. It was an unavoidable punishment: nature knew no mercy. In 1902 Weber grew very agitated when Marianne asked him to put in an appearance at the wedding of his sister Lili: 'The idea of proposing a toast in front of people who were still strangers to him would cost him three nights' rest' (WB 258). And in June 1909, complaining as so often about the rain and cold, he wrote from the Black Forest: 'It was nice walking quietly for an hour in the rainforest, but it cost three-quarters of the night' (MWG II/6, 151). Was the walk really to blame? For a long time Marianne shared this *idée fixe*. In the spring of 1903 she wrote from Rome that Max had had lively intellectual discussions with the philosopher Lask (of whom she was fond), with a fine view over the Aventine Hill: 'a rare pleasure for me. If only the bill was not always presented at night!'[41]

Weber openly spoke of many ailments even to colleagues with whom he was not particularly close. In 1906, for instance, he wrote to Brentano: 'I can endure well enough even quite difficult intellectual labour, but the physical act of *speaking* makes me sleepless and therefore soon incapable of performing' (MWG I/5, 42). Conversations with Brentano and Sombart during a trip to Heligoland were 'an intellectual excess for which he paid with fresh attacks of insomnia' (WB 266), and days later he cursed that 'damned Heligoland', which was still pestering him and robbing him of sleep.[42] After composing the letter to Else of 13 September 1907, in which

he furiously pulled to pieces Otto Gross's erotic gospel, he complained: 'I
have taken another soporific especially to be able to write this' (WB 380).[43]

Long after the worst days were over, Weber continued to worry about
sleep and the state of his nerves and to believe in strict laws governing the
conservation of nervous energy. He seems to have been convinced that his
illness had given him an insight into general laws of life. If we consider how
violently he combated naturalism in the social sciences, it is all the more surprising how certain he was in later years that not only physical but also
mental-nervous processes were subject to iron laws. This conviction also
runs through his theoretical work.

It remains an open question to what extent Weber had general laws in
mind, and to what extent he thought his weakened constitution made him
subject to especially rigid laws. In the years to come, however, he liked to play
the nerve specialist and to use his bad experience as a warning to others
against overtaxing the brain. In 1908 we find him giving therapeutic advice
to the 32-year-old Robert Michels, whom he evidently found congenial and
thought he was duty-bound to take in hand. Michels's night-time work was
evidence not of intellectual discipline but, on the contrary, of 'an aversion for
a rational discipline of life', which, Weber predicted, he would 'have to atone
for'. 'Exhausted nerve "capital" (and you don't have a lot of that) behaves like
exhausted capital in civil society: when it's gone, it's gone' (MWG II/5, 408).
A year later, on hearing that Michels was unwell, he immediately sounded the
alarm and said with the utter conviction of a nerve prophet:

> *I wish I did not know with such eerie certainty* the fate that your style of
> life and work is storing up for you. . . . You have 'cut down on' your
> *night work*, and that is supposed to help you? You are going to Paris
> 'for relaxation', and that – a cure for over-tiredness through new
> *stimuli* – has (surprise, surprise!) done *nothing* to help? Believe me: I
> know *full well* the bohemian attraction of your 'intensive' lifestyle, but
> anyone who tries to keep it up at *your* age must live alone and be able
> to leave this world at any moment, voluntarily or involuntarily,
> without having to account for it to anyone. Give up for a year *all*
> lecture trips abroad and *all* hurried work, go to bed every (*every*) day
> at 9:30, spend two weeks *at a time* in the summer relaxing without
> books (without *any* books) in the isolated German *forest* (full board:
> 3–4 marks), and you will know after a year how much work capac-
> ity/capital you have left; you will again have the security of feeling
> healthy and, in particular, know precisely *how much* you are able to
> work. But only then . . . Please forgive me if you hear in this the know-
> all attitude of a 'nerve specialist' more than the sympathetic interest of
> a friend, but there are times when one *has to* get the truth off one's
> chest. (MWG II/6, 124f.)

'The truth': Weber thought his own terrible experience had given him
certain knowledge of it in matters of the nerves. At the same time, his illness

had been an impetus for radical changes in his conduct of life, as the once so rushed Weber was now unbelievably generous with his time. Which ambitious academic would allow himself that nowadays in the best years of his life? Michels was thirty-three at the time in question, the same age that Weber had been when the first signs of his breakdown appeared. Scarcely any other testimony left behind by Weber reveals so clearly the essential lesson he drew from his illness. For, as we see, he now subscribed to Marianne's gospel of refreshment for the nerves in the peaceful depths of the forest. Michels seemed to be mirroring his own earlier experience, constantly straining himself in the same way, and so a similar 'collapse' was unavoidable. We should also note that Weber thought it quite normal to take one's own life in such a pitiable situation, so long as one had no responsibility for a wife and children.

With Georg Lukács, the future communist, Weber later developed the same kind of familiarity that he displayed towards Michels, the future fascist. In 1916, when Weber addressed Lukács for the first time as 'Dear friend', instead of 'Dear Herr Doktor', and tried to curb his haste to complete his *Habilitation*, he wrote that he would 'bless the day that you would free yourself of the spectre of the idea that it has to be now, as soon as possible, and absolutely the quickest way'. The period of his illness had taught Weber to see deadline pressure as the greatest evil. Again he played the nerve specialist: 'It would be helpful if you could force yourself to go grazing on a sheep meadow in order to quiet your nerves.'[44] Saving one's nerves through a purely autonomic, animal-like existence: Weber could no longer see any way of being saved through the mind.

Instead, artificial means of inducing sleep became a constant preoccupation for both Max and Marianne. It was known then as it is today that it is not healthy to keep taking soporifics. Not only homeopaths and natural healers regarded them as poison; it was also widely believed in the medical profession that they were a relic of the old 'quackery' – the meteoric rise of the pharmaceuticals industry was only just beginning.[45] For Marianne Weber, too, sleep-inducing drugs were 'poisons'.[46] A man of science such as Max Weber must have felt particularly uncomfortable gulping down sleeping draughts, since the next morning, when the after-effects were much less specific than they are today, a dull feeling in the head must have aroused fears of a loss of intellectual creativity. Weber did not delude himself about the toxicity of such drugs; sometimes he could still feel their effects nearly a week later (MWG II/5, 183). Again and again this man with such a passionate striving for autonomy fell into a humiliating dependence on drugs that threatened to put his mind in chains. His style of work often suggests a revolt against the feeling of dullness in his head, an all the more concentrated effort to achieve energy and clarity of thought.

When the bromides did not help, Weber experimented in the early period of his recovery with trional, one of the most modern and most highly regarded drugs in the sulfone group. Once, when he went on holiday and left it at home, he felt completely at the mercy of what tormented him.[47] But trional eventually repeated an old story in the field of pharmaceuticals: a new drug is at first regarded as more effective and easier to tolerate, but after a time it regularly turns out to have dangers of its own. These were really unpleasant in the case of the sulfone group.[48] In the years after 1900 the latest thing in soporifics, supposedly more effective and even less risky, was the German-developed veronal, which later became notorious through Agatha Christie's novel *The Murder of Roger Ackroyd* and was used by Stefan Zweig in 1942 to commit suicide. The effects of veronal were swifter and disappeared more rapidly the next morning, and it did not adversely affect respiratory or digestive functions.[49] Almost as soon as this wonder drug appeared on the market, Weber turned to it on holiday in Italy,[50] although the justification for his travels in southern Europe was that they were supposed to free him from such artificial 'methods'. In August 1903 Marianne wrote to Helene that Max would 'probably go to the sea again for eight days next week, as we have been working hard with the trional'.[51]

In August 1907, having just missed a train because of oversleeping, Max wrote to the insomniac Marianne: '*And sleep, sleep, sleep – no matter what the means are.*' She could even take the not exactly harmless veronal, with which she had already had some good experiences (MWG II/5, 354, 352).[52] He himself had just started trying 'to exist as far as possible without artificial devices', but three days later he was again taking bromural (II/5, 348, 351). Three days further on, he sighed that it was 'not really possible' to do without such means altogether, and he was using an 'opium ointment' in addition to bromide (II/5, 353). And another week later he wrote to Marianne from Amsterdam: 'My tormenting spirits are never still, of course, and can be calmed only with the help of medicine; it is a less harmful remedy, though, and my head seems to be better' (II/5, 363). Even on holiday by the sea, he was never at peace and his head suffered from the alternating effects of insomnia and sleep-inducing drugs.

In the summer of 1909, when for some time he must have seemed from a distance to be quite stable again, he came upon heroin of all things – a drug which the Bayer company had marketed in 1898 as a soporific, tranquillizer and even cough remedy, free of side-effects and therefore especially suitable for children! (MWG II/6, 156).[53] Apparently, the public only later found out that it was an opiate, like morphine, to which it was very easy to become addicted. 'The greatest disappointment that science had to endure bore the name of heroin', commented Matthias Seefelder, long-serving head of BASF, in a historical review.[54] If, as photos show, the ailing Weber underwent such a physical decline in the space of a few years, even though his life was more peaceful than before, then part of the explanation must be the creeping intoxication due to soporific drugs.

In April 1919, at a time when he was drugged on spring and love, all his sadness and anger at the years of self-intoxication burst out of him, and his fight against insomnia suddenly turned into a fight against the 'torture' of a life 'which has to be beaten down with a thousand drugs and poisons, from opium to cocaine, in the form in which it moves'. Towards the end of his life, then, Weber thought he could see that the ever recurring anxiety and irritability, which robbed him of sleep, was in reality a hunger for life and love. Probably he also realized that, in depressing the libido, soporific drugs intensified his unhappiness with life and completed the vicious circle. Else, for her part, was one of those lucky persons who, even in times of crisis, can simply lie down and go to sleep. 'Sleep comes to my rescue', she wrote to Alfred Weber, in her deep distress following Max's death.[55] It is likely that she managed to pass on a little of her calmness to Max Weber, rather in the manner of Ernst Schweninger, who slept 'like a log' himself and got Bismarck to fall asleep without morphine by holding his hand.[56]

Sleepless nights constantly reminded him of tragedy, of the vicious circle of excessive consciousness which became a subliminal leitmotif in Weber's work. For an overly intense fixation on sleep drives sleep away, and perpetual insomnia cripples thought and fixes it even more on sleep. Weber, a passionate thinker if ever there was one, worked himself into exaggerated ideas about the harmful effects of intellectual work. 'I don't read anything – which means that I sleep passably well', he wrote in spring 1912 from Provence (WB 483). What a tragedy for a man whose fate it was to read all the time, and who devoured literature in greater bulk than nearly all his contemporaries! Even when he had regained his capacity for theoretical work, he remained tragically aware that it condemned him to take the sleeping pills that advanced his self-destruction.

Anyone who has ever suffered from severe insomnia for any length of time can tell a thing or two about how the need for sleep, together with all the nocturnal brooding, marks a person's whole attitude to life. The night – which for Weber in love would later be the realm of Tristan – became the time of fear. People are perceived in a new way and divided into good and bad sleepers; even the circumstances of life are differentiated according to whether they favour or disturb sleep. If you eventually find the longed-for slumber, if 'your weary nerves are not continually pestered and kept alert by all kinds of external stimuli, then you become a different person and look at life with confidence', Marianne wrote in 1901 from Rome, where she and Max always had a noisy hotel room.[57] Insomnia created a new topography, so that in July 1901, when Max had another crisis in Grindelwald (WB 250) and was taking opium, Marianne wrote: 'Everyone here says that many people have *total* insomnia in the Alps.'[58] The need for sleep also produces a new sense of time. Thus, in the spring of 1913 in Ascona, when things were better than ever, Weber thought that good and bad periods for sleep followed one another with law-like regularity – although he was so often sleeping 'brilliantly' that an outsider might wonder why he did not simply trust his own nature and regard the tiresome subject of 'sleep' as no longer important.[59]

Weber early recognized the connection between sleep and religion. The insomniac suddenly realizes the existential meaning that bedtime prayers have for believers. In the plenitude of *unio mystica* with the divine, it is no longer important whether you sleep or not; and you fall asleep precisely when sleep worries disappear. In a long footnote to *The Protestant Ethic*, Weber detects the element of a rational life-order in the 'nocturnal contemplations' of the mystic and recognizes dreams as a path to 'reality'.

> It is by no means accurate to say that the freedom of the mystic consisted entirely in isolation from the world. Especially Tauler has, in passages which from the point of view of the psychology of religion are very interesting, maintained that the order which is thereby brought into thoughts concerning worldly activities is one practical result of the nocturnal contemplation which he recommends, for instance, in case of insomnia. 'Only thereby [the mystical union with God at night before going to sleep] is reason clarified and the brain strengthened, and man is the whole day the more peacefully and divinely guided by virtue of the inner discipline of having truly united himself with God: then all his works shall be set in order; . . . then if he comes into the world [*Wirklichkeit*], his works shall be virtuous and divine.' Thus we see . . . that mystic contemplation and a rational attitude toward the calling are not in themselves mutually contradictory. The opposite is only true when the religion takes on a directly hysterical character, which has not been the case with all mystics or even all Pietists. (PE 230)

Here we see Weber coming upon the mystical origin of the concept of reality [*Wirklichkeit*].[60] The final remark contains a repudiation of anticlerical writers who regarded pious women as hysterics.

'Emissions are always lying in wait'

The theme of 'sleep disturbance' is also significant because, explicitly or implicitly, it points to another issue: the nocturnal emissions that accompany dreams but startle the dreamer out of sleep. This often lies hidden behind Weber's use of such words as 'demons', 'tormenting spirits' or 'catastrophes'. In the Webers' correspondence from summer 1898, it is clearly sexual anxieties associated with sleeplessness and impotence which are producing a sense of acute illness.

In his early days at the Konstanzer Hof, Marianne wrote to him: 'It's wonderful that you are sleeping a little better, my birdie. . . . Are there only "excitations" or also erections?'[61] Emissions without an erection were considered a clear sign of that 'irritable weakness', commonly known as 'neurasthenia', which was *the* epidemic of the age. Hence Marianne always insists on seeing her husband's sexual abnormalities as the expression of a chronic overstimulation: 'Your whole nervous system can recover only *slowly*, and with it will automatically come a recovery of the sexual side of things.' She sees a cure as a lifestyle issue and is very critical of artificial 'devices', much more so than later on when she became increasingly resigned: 'I find these medicines repugnant: they [the doctors – JR] are always trying to force things and believe . . . that this sexual weakness must *à tout prix* be driven away by such "devices". We have seen, however, that any mental effort – for example, a lecture . . . – expressed itself in sexual troubles.'[62]

Marianne seems to sigh with relief as she notes in February 1899: 'True neurasthenia is more pronounced now than it was before, when sexual irritability was so much in the foreground.'[63] The diagnosis of 'neurasthenia' removed the tormenting fixation on sexuality. But Weber seems to have only temporarily adopted this concept; neither Max nor Marianne made much use of abstract terms in their self-diagnoses. For both of them, the nocturnal emissions were a crucial aspect of his illness, which they did not essentially attribute to a depressive disposition on his part. On 18 September 1898, Marianne wrote to Helene from the Konstanzer Hof that Max had been 'quite normally cheerful' in the last few days.

> But the night before last he again had an emission in his sleep (*insertion*: accompanied by those dream images he hates so much and whose repetition he constantly dreads). At present quite normal in itself – and no harm done if another one doesn't follow straight away. But he was very depressed. The local evil, which prevents regular sleep at night because of purely mechanical erections, will take a very slow course . . . and in my view the risk was in the treatment up to now, which set too great store by the earliest possible satisfaction of a normal instinctual life; for Max's condition is not typical . . . – and now there is always a danger that he will be unduly depressed by these irremovable hindrances and give too much thought to them.[64]

In this analysis, it was not the emissions as such but the associated dreams which worried Max Weber so much. Since his libido had a masochistic side to it (as Jaspers later recognized), they were probably dreams in which he was tortured, and the fear that they would be repeated seems to have been enough to prevent him from sleeping. The Webers must have known that nocturnal emissions as such were perfectly harmless. But Weber was completely reassured only when he discussed the matter with Hans Gruhle (1880–1958), who had been known to him since 1908 and belonged to a younger generation of psychiatrists less timid in sexual matters.[65]

Marianne must have started long before to keep a detailed record of her husband's emissions, since by this time she had established what was 'regular' or 'normal'. Earlier in life she had wanted to become a doctor herself; she soon visibly tried to gain medical competence in relation to Max's illness; and she subsequently looked at him with the eye of a doctor as well as a spouse. She also continued to pay special attention to his involuntary emissions of semen. When she learned in July 1901 that Max could not sleep in Grindelwald and was taking opium, she asked: 'Has Meister Iste rebelled more strongly in the mountain air?' 'Meister Iste', the maestro, was a codeword that Goethe used for the penis when it refused to obey its master and stood up only at night when his beloved was asleep: 'Doch Meister Iste hat nun seine Grillen / Und läßt sich nicht befehlen noch erachten, / Auf einmal ist er da, und ganz im Stillen / Erhebt er sich zu allen seinen Prachten.'[66] Surprisingly, both Marianne and Max knew this poem of Goethe's that reached the public only through an indiscretion, and which was certainly not taught at any girls' school. Goethe offered a model for treating the moods of the penis with humour, but the humour often passed the Webers by.

'Emissions are always lying in wait', Marianne wrote to Helene late in 1902; they were 'greatly weakening him' and his 'mood and general feelings (were) much worse than for a *long* time'. The logical conclusion was that he must travel again. 'In short, I'm counting the days until he is able to get away.'[67] The previous summer, Rome had proved a successful remedy for the emissions; Marianne reported from the 'Eternal City' that 'the sexual problems are currently much slighter than at any time since his illness began, and he has not had an emission for twelve weeks'[68] – quite a precise record of these natural 'catastrophes', even at a time when they had become so rare that they no longer merited any attention. But the Webers were used to this kind of observation: it sometimes sounded obsessional in Marianne's case.

What on earth was it about nocturnal emissions that so tormented Weber? The associated dreams and ensuing lack of sleep, to be sure. But probably also a strong sense that his sexual tendencies were not subject to conscious control and that he was therefore constitutionally impotent. Whereas 'normal' men can to some extent bring their sexuality under their will, and may even experience the power of mind over matter in the erections they produce through sexual fantasy,[69] Weber's animality appeared to him as a wild, uncontrollable force. He presumably felt caught in a vicious circle of waking impotence and oneiric ejaculation: the one determined the other. He had learned from his own deeply affecting and painful experience that, although nature can be temporarily suppressed by an oversophisticated intellect, it breaks through all the more powerfully in the end, and in an unnatural way that is felt to be diseased.

Weber must have often pondered what the nocturnal emissions meant for his physical and mental constitution, especially as they were inherently ambiguous and could be a sign either of effervescent youth or of a prematurely ruined nervous system. Weber's own sexual nature set him puzzles that remind us of the open questions about Germany in his Freiburg address: the uncertainty as to whether Germans were a young or an old nation, in which we sense a fear that it had already irreversibly succumbed to the epigones.

Marianne's letters, and sometimes Max's own, keep us well informed about his first few months as a patient at the Konstanzer Hof. There too the doctors' diagnoses tended to focus on his sexuality. Medical theories at that time often display a burning interest in sexual matters, even when they

are unsure whether the main danger lies in too much or too little sexual intercourse.[70] The idea that sex was the best medicine for troubles of the soul
circulated among doctors more by word of mouth than in scientific publications. The doctor who treated Weber at the clinic – a Dr Mühlberger –
soon gained the impression that a lack of sexual satisfaction was the root
cause of Weber's misery. But this irritated Marianne, since it could easily be
seen as a tacit reproach to herself: to her lack of sensuality, feminine charm
and amorous dexterity. Again and again she expressed anger that the
doctors were placing so much emphasis on the sexual side of things. The
'naturalism' seeping into the human sciences from the natural sciences,
deriving mental from physical phenomena, here became for the Webers a
real and distressing challenge that had an impact on all their thinking.
When the couple were later drawn by the women's and sexual emancipation
movement into discussions of marriage reform, Marianne asserted that the
'naturalists' who rejected abstinence before marriage were for the most part
'doctors' (WB 372); the irritating experiences at the Konstanzer Hof came
back to her vividly.

Marianne's 'rage at the doctors' theories'

In August 1898, when Marianne first learned of the doctors' view at the
Konstanzer Hof that it would be better if she remained there another three
weeks and that their priority was to help Weber resume normal sexual
behaviour, she flew into 'something of a rage at the doctors' theories', as
she bluntly wrote to Max. 'In three weeks' time things will probably be not
much different *sexually*, or at least these fluctuations will continue to
appear for much longer, and then they (the doctors – JR) will again discover
that it is necessary to "wait" and for the next eight days promise a complete
change, after which we will be let loose on each other.' 'What an accursed
dilemma! And if you are now completely weaned off me, our seeing each
other again will perhaps revolutionize you good and proper.' The fact that
their living together was not harmful could be seen from all the years of
their marriage, 'when you were not affected sexually, precisely because your
nerves were otherwise healthy. And I am convinced that this sexual neurasthenia is more the *result* of *other* nervous strain and will disappear along
with it, rather than vice versa.' She tried to keep his spirits up:

> Don't despair: we'll get you healthy, I am not in the least worried
> about that, but it can't happen *quickly*. I don't know whether all these
> dreadful manipulations are right, especially the 'packs' that must
> make you very nervous; the doctors shouldn't forget that sexual
> neurasthenia is only a *consequence*, but they do seem to forget it, since
> they assess you so much from that point of view. Alfred again told me
> that he always has problems when his nerves are in a bad way, but *not*
> otherwise.[71]

Marianne – who, as we have seen, once wanted to become a doctor[72] and presumably learned something from books – thought she had a certain medical competence vis-à-vis the doctors, and from today's point of view she was right not to believe in 'all the manipulations' or to think that Weber's illness was rooted in the genital area. She was also more realistic than the doctors in holding that there was no quick cure for her husband's sexual difficulties. Two weeks later, in a letter to Max's mother, Marianne made the revealing remark that Dr Mühlberger 'foregrounded the pathological, "perverse" structure which expressed itself in peculiar fantasies even in his student days, whereas in my view those pathological symptoms were only the result of moral self-control'.[73] So, Marianne assumed that the 'perverse' structure was known to Helene, and the talk of 'moral self-control' might have been partly a dig at the rigid upbringing that the mother had given her eldest son. In any event, the passage refers to the fact that sexual disturbances existed from the beginning of the marriage. She continues:

> There is no way of knowing in advance when he will be truly healthy or 'normal', that is, when he will overcome his state of sexual weakness. Nor did the doctor tell me that one day he will definitely be healthy in *the* relation, but he thought he could say for sure that our happiness will not be in danger as a result. Thank God, I've taught him *that*!

Evidently Marianne wanted to teach the doctor that a marriage without sex could still be happy. But, to her great irritation, the doctor assumed that her husband needed sexual intercourse to become completely healthy. Marianne complained to Mother that she found it so difficult to see eye to eye with him because he was still a bachelor – and, for her, marriageable bachelors were probably on a par with brothel-goers. She thought that the exercises he had prescribed – some of which were apparently designed to reactivate the genital area – actually 'increased the stifling sense of infirmity'.[74] When we read about the advice of other doctors – from hypnosis to the use of 'sedatives against erections' – we can understand Marianne's conclusion 'that the doctors know absolutely nothing about these things'.[75] Yet, with their confidence in the powers of science, the Webers could not give up consulting one doctor after another.

'Descent into hell' or secret wish-fulfilment?

In her biography, Marianne Weber portrays her husband's breakdown as a 'descent into hell' (WB 237), a journey of suffering from the ante-chambers to the depths of hell, albeit punctuated with brief and deceptive phases of recovery. Is her picture over-dramatic? She quotes one letter from her husband that speaks a very different language:

Such an illness really has its very good points – for me, for instance, it has reopened the purely human side of living, which Mama always somewhat missed in me, to an extent that I had not known before. Like John Gabriel Borkmann[76] I could say: 'An icy hand has let go of me', for in past years my sickly disposition [in the original: 'my abnormalities' – JR] expressed itself in a convulsive clinging to scholarly work as to a talisman, without my being able to say what it was supposed to ward off. As I look back upon it this is quite clear to me, and I know that, sick or healthy, I shall never be like that again. The *need* to feel myself succumbing to the load of work is extinguished. I want, above all, to live a full personal life with my *Kindele* [baby] and to see her as happy as it is given to me to make her. (WB 236)[77]

It is a letter modelled on Christian expressions of remorse, with a will to turn back from a mistaken path in life. At the same time, it opens a window into the depths of Weber's soul, such as one seldom finds elsewhere in Marianne's biography. Max would like to make her happy and to confirm what he wrote in a previous letter: that he feels his illness will make their life together more intense. He is certain that the illness is not just a temporary effect of overwork but expresses 'abnormalities' in his nature. With rare candour he allows us to see the irrational side of his relationship to science: the element of 'magic' ('talisman'), the belief in magical powers which science is supposed to dissolve, and the masochistic need to torment himself with science that underlies his work mania.

Weber tried to give his illness a meaning by seeing it as a challenge to a new life: a life with more love, warmth and humanity. Marianne wrote later: 'The years of illness had deflected him from his course and had opened secret chambers of his soul that had previously been closed', such as the feeling for art and poetry (WB 455). And his years of illness were actually not ones of unrelieved gloom but sometimes involved a half-light of contradictory moods, in accordance with the model of neurasthenia, which was typically *not* characterized by depression alone. Montesquieu's aphorism 'As pleasures are often mingled with pains, so too are pains mingled with pleasures'[78] is confirmed in the case of Weber. Even in his worst period in 1901, when it tired him simply to walk, the Mediterranean spring in Corsica afforded him some good hours 'in the fragrance of lavender and thyme', where he rested a lot 'under the olive trees' and 'gratefully absorbed the gentle yet magnificent beauty' (WB 246). Being ill often passes unnoticed into a celebration of being ill, convalescence into holiday. It was a revelation to the Webers that relief from illness comes not from a doctor, a therapy or a medicine but from nature in the South. But it took a long time, much longer than they had initially hoped, until a more than momentary success appeared. Sometimes illness brings a new togetherness to married people, but frequently it creates a sense of separateness. More and more, Max and Marianne got into the habit of taking trips alone.

Marianne also pondered over the meaning of the illness. But, although it heightened their sense of being a couple, she was not able 'for the time being' to recognize what was happening. Sometimes the closeness between two people that accompanies an illness goes too far. When Max gradually became able to work in 1902, his handwriting was even more illegible than before and he had to dictate everything. At first Marianne operated as his secretary, but in the autumn of 1902 she looked around for an assistant, 'since I cannot write for him more than an hour a day if I (*insertion:* with my limited nervous strength) am not to give up my own work altogether'.[79] She too often felt highly nervous, and she used this to stake claims for herself. At the time she was already working on her *magnum opus*.

Like so many sick people, Max Weber knew the comforts of being looked after and freed from all duties. It was a primary experience of his childhood that illness compels attention, and at the age of thirty-four he was becoming a child again. In her letters to Helene, Marianne speaks of him as the 'little boy', 'little Max' or 'our big boy'. For his part, he longs again for the mother from whom he emancipated himself with such effort, and he is repeatedly irritated when he senses that this feeling does not find an echo in her. Marianne energetically tries to dispel such moods, and in a letter to Helene she describes as 'pathological' his idea that 'you are no longer propelled towards us, etc'.[80] When his mother was there, however, he sometimes lapsed into his old 'taciturnity' and made her feel unwanted.[81]

In the following years it becomes a stock expression in Marianne's letters that, when he had too many 'stimuli' and was taking too many drugs, she would have to send him south[82] – as if this was the logical consequence, and as if the decision was hers alone. This kind of matriarchy was agreeable to Weber. The illness had put an end to his perpetual haste, as well as the pressure to perform 'marital duties'. Nowhere in his papers from that period do we find any talk of longing for the time *before* his breakdown.

'Like a starving horse': the wife's pain

Not surprisingly, Marianne often felt more wretched than she confessed to her husband, although sometimes she admitted to herself that her erotic needs were unfulfilled. In January 1902 she wrote from Rome that she needed 'to return to a full life right now, when the dull pressure of everyday worries is abating, since otherwise the unfulfillable desires – I mean, the specifically female ones – take on unpleasant dimensions.'[83] And in February: 'my nerves, despite everything that enthrals me, are like bolting horses.'[84] In the Roman spring of 1902, when Max was slowly regaining his ability to work, when he was surrounded by lists of publications and his illness seemed to be over, she burst out to his mother in raging despair:

Last week we were again pretty low psychologically; Max had three explosions in a week – and he was shattered and depressed as a result, while I felt horribly wild inside. . . . Of course, we often have to live through such disturbances, but I can't claim that the 'oftenness' makes you used to them – in these matters, it is like the horse who got used to starving on the very day it died. I mean, you get more *impatient* the longer it goes on if such stupid obstacles keep getting in the way of the advance you long for so much.[85]

She compares herself to a starving horse: what a metaphor! Ever since the early Fathers of the Church, the horse has counted as symbol of carnal desire, of man's animal nature. Earlier, Marianne had attached considerable importance to relations with the zealous ex-priest and National-Social politician Friedrich Naumann; now she experienced political involvement as pathogenic. She no longer complained about her 'nerves' but about her 'psyche', although in the subsequent period she sometimes emphasized the distinction between nervous and mental strain.[86]

She was not the only person in those days who realized that 'nervous disorders' were connected to the mind at least as much as to the body. Willy Hellpach, later Weber's main source on neurological matters, detected a 'huge psychotherapeutic awakening on the threshold of our century':[87] Freud was by no means the lone figure that Freudians like to believe he was. When Gertrud Bäumer asked Marianne after her husband in 1909, she wished them both a year 'without all the subject-object frills that people carry around on their nerves':[88] people spoke of their nerves as of something different from themselves, and in so doing actually said something true about themselves.

In her biography, Marianne admits that she had 'a much harder time' than her husband adapting to their completely changed circumstances, and that she often experienced 'excruciating pain' (WB 266f.). This was no exaggeration, as her letters show, and in fact the book conceals the full extent of her impatience and raging despair. She wrote there that 'even during the most difficult period' she could feel her husband's 'charisma' (WB 266), but there is no trace of this feeling in her letters from the time. Indeed, her frustration increased during his long, slow recovery punctuated with occasional relapses; perhaps she had expected that a 'normal conjugal life' would begin to develop. Still in 1903, when Weber started work on *The Protestant Ethic* that would make him world-famous, Marianne complained to Mother: 'The thousand disappointments of this year, especially in the last few months, are for the moment still too vivid for me to believe in a new future.' Instead of resignation, she bore a 'rebellious feeling' in her breast. 'But Max mustn't know any of this; it would drive him to despair.'[89] Husband and wife kept up a certain pretence with each other and tried to conceal the intensity of their own pain.

'Our nerves, our lords and masters': the common denominator of marital communication

Weber did not make a once-and-for-all diagnosis of his condition but modified it over time, probably in discussions with Marianne. This was not unusual in nervous cases. Thomas Clifford Albutt, a British authority on neurasthenia who, unlike his German colleagues, added a touch of humour to the subject, noted in 1895 that with the emergence of the 'new woman' both sexes 'began to chant nerves together', to compare symptoms, to speculate about the causes, and to struggle hand in hand through courses of treatment.[90]

The Webers were a model case in this respect. Their correspondence with each other is a veritable treasure trove for the semantics of the nerves at that time, although, as it makes clear, we should not imagine there to have been a single 'turn-of-the-century discourse' on the topic. Different semantics mingled happily with one another. The word *'nervös'* still functioned as a straightforward synonym for 'to do with the nerves', but it also had the modern meaning of 'nervous'. In the 1890s people still sometimes talked of 'the nerves' as of the strings of a bow or violin that might become loose and require tightening. 'Nerves' might refer to a passive condition but also to an aggressive disposition: for example, Marianne wrote to Helene in 1895 that it had 'become an existential need' for Aunt Herta to 'vent' her 'nerves' on her husband; one thought that things would 'explode' at any moment.[91] Marianne also spoke of 'nerves' as a bad excuse used by drunkards and 'weaklings with no sense of responsibility' who were suspected of having a sexually transmitted disease (MWG II/6, 76). And she was familiar with 'nervousness' as an interactive phenomenon and an element in a game of ping-pong: in May 1910 Alfred was 'very nervous' and at the same time 'furious' with his hard-working but demanding student Marie Bernays, 'because of her nervousness' (MWG II/6, 509f.). Although she and Max lived in a highly intellectual milieu, we should not expect to find that the way they spoke of 'the nerves' corresponded to a scientific paradigm. For ailing professors as for everyone else, the starting point was not theory but their own personal experience, which was not silent but expressed itself in everyday language.

The Webers are the best illustration that, although 'nervous people' counted a lot on doctors in those days, the more educated ones in particular tried to develop some medical competence and by no means thought they should meekly submit to a doctor's authority: rightly so, because doctors had no superior knowledge about psychosomatic disorders, however much they liked to give the opposite impression. Marianne started off with a lead over Max in this respect, as she appears to have always been highly-strung and to have worked out medical diagnoses of herself that distinguished between inherited factors and the consequences of a stressful lifestyle. At the time of her husband's 'descent into hell', she often thought that she too was seriously ill and, for that very reason, knew better than any doctor what was wrong with him. In 1900 she felt a 'slave of my body': 'I won't feel hale and hearty for much longer – in fact that has never been the case'; 'I'm training myself now for a natural lifestyle and don't lie on the bed so much during the day.'[92] By 'natural' she therefore meant a regular routine; she would not allow herself to be infected by her husband's irregular way of spending the day.

In 1902 she wrote to Helene: 'Unfortunately my head is still *very* weary, and, as soon as I give it a harder time than it wants, it punishes with a bad night's sleep . . . what a problem the nerves are!'[93] The head is not completely identical with the mind, but it also confronts the ego as an unruly bundle of nerves. So, her ideal is really for the mind to rule over the nerves. By the end of 1901 she thought she could detect that her husband's 'brain is gradually gaining mastery over the tricks of the nerves'.[94] But, unfortunately, the note of triumph was premature. In 1903, at last, she thought she was again reasonably 'in control of her nerves'.[95] But this sense of control never lasted long. In 1909 Max Weber wrote that, 'in the wake of the last major relapse in *my* illness two years ago, which gave her every illusion that I would be healthy again (which I never had)', his wife's '*great* weakness of the nerves has become *very* perceptible, *far* more than even people close to her suspect' (MWG II/6, 90). In 1910 she complained that she would like to have people round regularly in the evening, but 'unfortunately our nerves, our lords and masters, rarely permit that – Max's now more than mine'.[96] Like Max, Marianne knew from experience that, however much one wished it, will power could not achieve much against the dictatorship of the nerves.

Relief through castration?

Early in 1909 Marianne wrote that for the time being Max could do '*many times* as much' as she. All the more horrifying, then, is her letter to Helene of 26 June 1909, in which she says that the internal specialist Ludolf Krehl (1861–1936), who since 1907 had been director of the medical clinic in Heidelberg, had quite seriously discussed with the psychiatrist Nissl (in Max's absence but with Marianne's knowledge) whether Max should be castrated! He himself had previously toyed with the idea.[97] 'The kind Krehl' (Marianne's phrase) was an unusual figure in the medical world; he was working towards an integrated medicine and a theory of man, and was a member of the famous Eranos circle.[98] In 1909 he gave a consultation to Max Weber and came to the view that his 'very unusual and difficult case' belonged more to the sphere of psychiatry than internal medicine; he felt at the end of his scientific tether. For psychiatrists, on the other hand, a simple and brutal operation on the body had no meaning – fortunately for Weber, who that same year became aware of his love for Else. Marianne wrote to Helene as if castration were a therapeutic measure like any other:

In Nissl's view we should not be thinking of castration, since it would probably replace the emissions with a different evil; he says the whole thing must have its seat in the brain. So, to cut a long story short – nothing new!! . . . I can see that there won't be much that can be done; we'll have to keep lugging the chain around.[99]

During the days when Marianne was consulting the doctors, her husband complained from his health resort in the Black Forest: 'The lovely "loins department" people behave as if they're completely crazy, although I don't read a line apart from the newspaper and hardly walked a step yesterday' (MWG II/6, 152). Weber knew about the autonomy of the vegetative nervous system – one of the discoveries of nineteenth-century neurology – whereas the contrary view, that sexuality is partly governed by the brain, could not have been known to him at the time.

It is striking that from this time on there are repeated references in Weber's writings to the Skoptsy, a Russian sect which developed in the eighteenth century and practised self-castration, in the belief that the libido was the main obstacle in the path of salvation. It was always small in numbers, and the obvious approach would be to regard it as a weird and very Russian excrescence on the margins of religious history.[100] Max Weber, however, took it seriously as a rational Pietist sect and an eastern pendant to the Puritans; he even detected behind the self-mutilation a psychologically motivated urge to prevent religious ecstasy from degenerating into sexual orgies that destroyed a sense of fraternity (MWG I/19, 502n.). In psychiatric discussions around the turn of the twentieth century, the Skoptsy were sometimes evoked as evidence of the extent to which male characteristics depended upon full possession of the sexual organs. Weber too, who for a long time defined his masculinity as a-sexual, would have brooded on the matter. Many medical people at the time considered it thoroughly modern to argue that the sexual organs did *not* have the significance for masculinity that popular belief attributed to them.[101]

On the brink of madness? The question of Max Weber's self-diagnosis

The question as to how Weber himself interpreted his illness and came to grips with it intellectually concerns not only his perception and analysis of symptoms, but still more the future prospects that he derived from his analysis. Someone who is ill and does not like it will tirelessly ponder over ways to recovery. Symptoms such as insomnia or nocturnal emissions were ambiguous, as was the diagnosis of neurasthenia, which could either suggest a tone of mollification ('just nerves') or signal the onset of mental illness. The variety of experiences meant that the term was in constant semantic flux, so that the diagnosis as such was not exactly reassuring for Weber in his urge for self-understanding.

Weber's childhood meningitis had once put him in danger of imbecility, and it was unavoidable that this old fear should reappear now, especially as he soon realized that his disorders must have something to do with his constitution and could not just be the passing result of overwork. Exaggerated ideas about a close link between intellectual genius and mental illness were doing the rounds at the time; the book by the Italian psychiatrist Cesare Lombroso, *Genio e follia* (1864),[102] was one of the classics of psychological theory, and the rapid spread of the Nietzsche cult in the 1890s brought with it the iconic image of the sickly philosopher sunk into madness.[103] Through Marianne, who had attended Riehl's lecture on Nietzsche, Weber was up to date about the destiny of that thinker.

For some time now Weber's relationship to Nietzsche has promised to become as popular a topic as 'Weber and Marx' used to be,[104] even though it rests on an even thinner documentary basis. The view that Weber often had Nietzsche in his mind's eye is based mainly on a remark which, according to Eduard Baumgarten, he made to a student shortly before his death: 'The honesty of a scholar today, and especially of a philosopher, may be gauged by how he situates himself in relation to Marx and Nietzsche. Anyone who does not admit that he could not have produced the most important parts of his work without the prior work of those two is hoodwinking both himself and others. The world in which we live intellectually is largely one that bears the stamp of Marx and Nietzsche' (B 554f.). However, we should not attach too much weight to this rather isolated quotation. Weber liked to adopt the air of someone exposing illusions, and in 1920 students could be impressed by such words. Weber's explicit statements about Nietzsche are scanty and mainly derogatory, while his wife was suspicious of the 'superman' philosophy. Someone who feels the constant threat of mental breakdown would inevitably think in this context of the breakdown that Nietzsche himself suffered in Turin in December 1888, from which he never recovered.

Baumgarten reproduces Weber's marginal notes on Simmel's essay on Schopenhauer and Nietzsche, which testify to a thorough rejection of Nietzsche both intellectually and as a person. When Simmel writes that Nietzsche 'must at least have drawn the boundary of his will to power against the *base desire for possessions*', Weber notes: 'But that is precisely *not* Nietzsche's view. Even in this respect he was himself a German petty bourgeois' (B 615). 'Even in this respect' – and in which others? Certainly Weber found his attacks on Christian compassion both narrow-minded and indiscriminate in comparison with the magic of brotherhood and the 'communism of love'. And yet, the fate of Nietzsche reminded him that ebullient intellectual activity can be the final stage before a madness from which there is no return.

If Weber, after his years of depression, tried so desperately to achieve razor-sharp methodological clarity, this may be interpreted as a restless striving to ensure that, whatever the state of his nerves, his mind was still intact. He did not think much of a 'gay science' à la Nietzsche, which, as events showed, did not come from a cheerful heart but was the pioneer of a stern scientific rigour. In his letter of 7 March 1919 to Else Jaffé, in which he cursed his icy brain and its antipathy to love, Weber admitted: 'For years I used this icebox as a last hope, as something that remained "pure" against the devils who had their way with me when I was ill (and probably before).'

A horror of time pressure and the theory of willpower

Throughout his life Max Weber saw science as a vocation, but the day-to-day routine of academic life was increasingly a torture to him. It is striking that his recovery made constant progress precisely from the moment when his professional ties were severed for good. Having in the past had such a hectic attitude to the use of time, he developed a complete horror of fixed deadlines and retained it for many years after his breakdown. Even when he was feeling well, 'any compulsion, pressure or obligation involving a deadline brought the danger of a relapse – as though his body, which had until the outbreak of the illness blindly obeyed his demanding intellect, refused once and for all to bow to any necessity' (WB 258). Weber actually developed a negative obsession with time. In 1908 Marianne was still complaining: 'This working to a deadline is the greatest torture for him; when you are faced with it, you have to fear any interruption by a bad night or any additional burden.'[105] A deadline was like a provocative evil spirit; the time pressure that once had a kind of agreeable charm had become a source of anguish. In this respect, Weber may have experienced his nervous troubles as a typical phenomenon of modernity (the modern nervous condition described by the neurologist Wilhelm Erb), and therefore seen his illness as a key to the understanding of his age.

Marianne, who liked to depict herself as so sensitive to her husband's illness, was honest enough in her biography to admit that she long thought Max should just pull himself together through an effort of will. From his point of view, many doctors had greater understanding than his wife on this matter.[106] Helene's notions of 'willpower' are even more transparent in her austere pedagogy and her suspicion that Marianne was 'mollycoddling'[107] Max, especially as, since the turn of the century, the latest trend in the treatment of nervous disorders (among lay people and natural healers as well as medical specialists) had been to encourage a greater strength of will in relation to deck-chairs and warm baths.[108] This was the early period of excitement about hypnosis and the powers of suggestion and auto-suggestion; the power of mind over matter was another theme that often preoccupied the Webers.

Max Weber knew that his wife and mother expected him to return to his professorship through a strong act of will; he was tortured by this 'most horrible burden on his sense of honour' (WB 261). It forced him, in self-defence, to develop an interpretation of his illness that emphasized the role of fate and reflected his experience that the mind was to some extent capable of emancipating itself from the nerves but never of mastering them. But could the will be free if it was unable to rule? Weber's illness involved an experience of himself that had important implications for the mind, since the question of the freedom of the will is one of the great puzzles in the history of philosophy and, in Weber's day, was a constant bone of contention between legal experts and psychiatrists. Judges assumed that defendants had a free will, whereas in the eyes of many psychiatrists this was an unscientific premise. Precisely because the problem was theoretically insoluble, it was always possible to use one's own experience as the material for new discoveries.[109] For the rest of his life, Weber's frustrations with the theory of the will warned him against asking too much of the mind and underestimating the physical basis of existence. He experienced in himself the indissoluble link between body and mind, and he later introduced this experience along with 'psychophysics' into the realm of science. His aversion for strenuous hikes was for a long time bound up with the fixed idea that overstraining the legs also overstrained the nerves; this even involved exaggerated notions of a 'psychophysics', more in keeping with the premodern image of the body that equated nerves with muscles.

In August 1898, after his first experiences as a patient at the Konstanzer Hof, Weber wrote: 'The whole thing is rather complicated and not so easy to cure. . . . There is no doubt that it is a question of local functional disturbances. . . . It follows that the disturbances appear spasmodically, without any connection to other health issues.'[110] There is no attempt here to conceptualize his illness in medical terms – a constant and remarkable absence in his self-diagnoses. A year later he wrote somewhat irritably to his mother: 'I only wish you'd believe that it is not *mental* apathy if in some stages of exhaustion I shy away from any so-called "excitement", and if I have now taken a holiday. The inability to speak is purely *physical*: my nerves fail me and then my mind simply goes when I look at my lecture notes.'[111]

'Functional' disturbances involved no discernible bodily changes yet were physical rather than mental disturbances. For Weber this term had the advantage of underlining that his mind was still intact, but also of defending him against the two women's demands on his mind; for he could logically conclude that the psyche was powerless against physically grounded disturbances. However, 'local functional disturbances' was presumably a coded expression for sexual disturbances – but did sex have to do only with the body, not with the psyche? During the same period, as Marianne indiscreetly reported to Helene in the winter of 1898, Max Weber was capable of speaking a very different language:

Max is very unhappy with the Lord God and quite scolds the old boy for giving us such a hard time; he also has a terrible cold, which he puts down to his nerves, and he thinks he'll always have something wrong with him and no longer thinks he will be sexually normal. Well, I don't take all that so tragically.[112]

The lines are written in a tone of comic despair, but at the time her husband was certainly no longer in a humorous frame of mind. His constant arguments with God were presumably more than thoughtless curses, as were his complaints about the 'demons' tormenting him. We get the impression that he never felt sexually normal – since he does not say 'normal *again*'. At the same time, he thinks that his sexual problems express a general and incurable mess inside himself. On this point, however, he keeps wavering – even many years later. In April 1906 Marianne reported: 'Max feels more and more strongly that these functional disturbances have absolutely nothing to do with his general state but are purely local and appear completely "at random" . . . but that they still have a considerable effect on his general state.'[113] Yet a year later he is 'depressed and disgruntled': 'He is intellectually sterile and unreceptive, taking no pleasure in work, and his sexually excitable nerves give him no peace . . . it is terrible for him to think that he will have to spend many more sad winters in Germany – he is so fed up with life in the winter.'[114] At first the 'sexually excitable nerves' seem to be the root cause of his misery – again sexuality is a matter of the nerves – but then it is the weather or the German climate, another longstanding complaint of his. At times, however, he experiences the excitability without depression as a purely 'random' business, unrelated to the normal course of the day.[115] Even in his spring of love in 1919, he speaks to Else of 'physiological disasters that keep happening':[116] 'physiological' no longer having anything to do with mental torments. Again and again he experiences his vegetative life as separate from his psyche, and again and again he returns broodingly to the subject.

What was in Weber's analysis of himself?

Neurasthenics in general were known to doctors for the eloquent way in which they described the background to their illness. Dramatic life histories could be constructed around 'the nerves', and this kind of confession evidently gave some relief to many 'nervous' patients.[117] The Webers too tended to weave a major story out of their nervous problems, and today's reader is often struck by the seemingly ruthless candour of their correspondence. It should be borne in mind, however, that Weber remained silent about a lot of aspects. Precisely because sexual problems were at the core of his illness – in his own eyes as well as those of his doctors – he had an understandable reluctance to speak too copiously about them. One part of his illness was that he was scarcely ever able to get the really deep things off his chest.

In June 1907 Weber wrote for the neurologist Johannes Hoffmann a 'report on the pathological disposition, origin, course and nature of his illness' (MWG II/5, 393), which, according to Marianne, was a veritable 'autobiography' that took him several days to compose: a life story as a story of illness! She too, who had to keep 'pestering' him about it, got hold of a copy and later passed it on to Jaspers, who thought it 'quite extraordinary in its self-detachment, objectivity and specific clarity' (B 641). Jaspers later gave the manuscript back to Marianne, and she supposedly destroyed it during the Nazi period for fear that it might fall into the wrong hands and be used to sully her husband's memory. Ever since Baumgarten's mention of this self-diagnosis, everyone who has taken an interest in Weber's character has puzzled over what it might have contained. Martin Green, who learned quite a lot from his contacts with Baumgarten and Else Jaffé, was able to report no more than insomnia due to fear of nocturnal emissions;[118] but that had long been a banality for the Webers and would not have required a special confession. Besides, the discovery of nocturnal emissions would not have harmed a man's reputation more than the 'disclosure' of digestive problems; no one ever doubted that 'great men' had something in addition to an intellect. The self-analysis could not have contained anything about Weber's amorous relations in later life, as these came as a shock even to the aged Jaspers.

Jaspers notes from Weber's 'account of his illness' that 'the first sexual arousals occurred when he was beaten by a servant girl'.[119] Weber evidently attributed his masochistic tendencies to this youthful experience;[120] Jaspers had nothing to add to this, although he generally detested psychoanalysis and its derivation of personality structures from infantile sexual experiences. It looks as if this was the crucial point in Weber's self-diagnosis. It would certainly explain why Marianne was so afraid that it would become public knowledge, as it would have seriously damaged the aura of strength and self-control that he had in the eyes of his admirers.

It is becoming clearer that Weber was more influenced by Freud than he was prepared to admit.[121] His self-analysis was actually super-Freudian, since many disciples of Freud do not assume from the start that a particular experience, especially a non-traumatic one, can mark a strong personality all through life. The other explanation that suggests itself is that masochistic tendencies were already present when the beating by the servant girl first aroused them. The early meningitis, which ensured his mother's tireless attention, would have given him a primal experience of the close connection between pleasure and pain. In 1910 Lukács observed: 'Man has an idea of childhood and all his life will live it, write it and paint it.'[122]

One might further suspect that the person who beat him was not a maidservant but none other than his mother. He would not have confided this even to the anamnesis, as he knew that his mother found out about his most intimate disclosures to other people. We have seen that Helene was capable of spontaneously giving a resounding slap to the young student; and it is hard to imagine that a maid in her service would have dared to beat her eldest son at the age of puberty. If it really was his own mother who did it, this would explain best of all why the memory was so fixed in his consciousness, especially as later experience of maternal power would have continually refreshed it. It would also explain why Weber needed another Great Mother, only this time an erotic one, in order to be saved. But this is speculation.

Weber's most famous letter

All this casts in a new light his famous long letter of 13 September 1907 to Else Jaffé, in which he turned down the manuscript that her former lover, Otto Gross, had submitted to the *Archiv für Sozialwissenschaft*. One does not have to be a fully paid-up Freudian to see the letter as a classical example of *repression*. For the most part, it probably conceals the most important point: that he himself was in love with Else and felt jealous of her lover. He snorts over the 'erotic unsavouriness' of this prophet of free love (MWG II/5, 395) and refuses to see that something in himself ardently yearns for eroticism. He denounces the fact that the 'thoroughly banal swankpot with healthy nerves' should be taken as the ideal (where 'nerves' is synonymous with sex life), but in truth he has for years been desperate to have healthy nerves himself. He complains of the 'medical philistines' who advise him 'to "abreact" and give free rein to *every* abject stirring of my desires and instincts . . . because otherwise my beloved nerves might be damaged' (MWG II/5, 398), but those 'beloved nerves' of which he speaks so disparagingly had for a decade been the source of tormenting worries. He senses 'abject' desires within himself, and probably has a subliminal feeling that he should act some of them out to give his 'nerves' some peace at last. He acts as if his nervous health were a yardstick that did not belong in the realm of science, but the only consideration in medicine is or should be human health. Then comes a revealing passage:

> Freud's cures may have a *hygienic* value for him, but I do not know, for example, what I would gain ethically if some sexual misconduct in which, say, a servant girl might have engaged with me, or a dirty impulse I have 'repressed' or 'forgotten' were brought back. For I make the *en bloc* admission, without having the feeling that I am doing something 'terrible', that nothing 'human' is or was alien to me. Basically, then, I am certainly not learning anything new. (Quoted from WB 379)

He therefore thinks it quite possible that psychoanalysis promotes nervous or mental health – which is good enough reason for him to take the new theory seriously and to subject it to intensive study (MWG II/5, 394ff.).[123] 'Sublimation', one of Freud's key concepts, became part of Weber's own terminology. In the story of the maidservant he inserts the note 'Freudian example!' – but in reality he is speaking of himself. The true motive for this passage may have been that he wanted the enchanting woman, who uninhibitedly pursued her sexual desires, to understand that he too was not simply an 'egghead' and did not have only the kind of feelings that could be expressed in polite company.

The 'demons' – just a metaphor?

In Marianne Weber's biography the word 'demons', or sometimes the singular 'demon', is repeatedly used to refer to the attacks of illness that came over her husband. In July 1901, on her way from the heat of Rome to the Alpine Grindelwald, the mountain air unexpectedly brought no relief: 'The demons that had been kept under control in the south rattled their chains: sleeplessness, excitement, unrest and other torments broke loose' (WB 250). Weber's demons evidently had their home in northern parts. Marianne fairly openly hinted that they were really a matter of repressed sexuality, even though this cast her in an unfavourable light as a wife. The 'indestructible inhibitions against a surrender to his drives', which his mother had implanted in him, appear to have been the ultimate cause; they meant that it was one of Max's precepts 'to struggle more and more painfully against the demonic temptations of the spirit by a robust corporeality than to give nature its due' (WB 92). The 'demons' as a sign that, despite everything, Weber had a robust nature!

In the light of the letters, the 'demons' also operate as a codeword for nocturnal emissions.[124] They therefore give him no peace even when the worst years of illness are over. In May 1905, after Max had had eight bad nights in a row, Marianne wrote to Helene: 'Now the demon seems to want to be placated again; we live in constant fear of him.'[125] At the end of the year, when Weber had finished his first essay on Russia, the demon shrank to a 'little nerve-devil' who, just before Christmas, 'plays a trick that should not be taken amiss, coming as it does after such a long good period'.[126] But things did not remain like that. Even in her lament after Max's death, Marianne wrote: 'He always slept on restless guard duty. He always expected the demons to attack.'

Since the publication of the first volume of letters, we have known that Weber too used the term 'demon' over the years. In spring 1908 he wrote from the French Riviera: 'I'd greatly angered my demon in the last few days, so last night he took his revenge' (MWG II/5, 476). Three days later: 'My demon is now grinding me a little . . .' (480). And, the next day, the demon is again 'rather a nuisance' (484).

The 'demon', whether in the singular or the plural, crops up fairly often in literature. At that time the main associations were Dostoevskyan, but the poem in which Goethe curses his 'Meister Iste' contains the lines: 'Denn zeigt sich auch ein Dämon, uns versuchend, / So waltet was, gerettet ist die Tugend' (For a demon also comes to tempt us, / And something takes charge, virtue is saved). Paintings of the temptations of St Anthony revel in weird images of demons. Were they for the Webers an interchangeable metaphor, a mere codeword for the nocturnal 'disasters'?

Perhaps they were something more, though. Not by accident did Max and Marianne Weber make such constant use of the term. The demons make something significant out of his trivial emissions of seminal fluid, targeting an important man as they generally like to do. When Augustine of Hippo renounced his sexual life and was so seriously disturbed by nocturnal emissions that he began to envy castrati,[127] he thought he was being pursued by demons: he who, as Peter Brown writes, 'had placed sexuality irremovably at the centre of the human person'.[128] According to one 'psychography', Augustine's *Confessions* came out of a struggle with the manifestations of repressed libido.[129] Weber's experience of himself stood in a long tradition. Later, in *Ancient Judaism*, he detected behind the rules of chastity, which applied to warriors as well as priests, 'the conception of the sexual sphere as an area specifically controlled by demons'.[130]

Whereas many of Weber's contemporaries lamented a new kind of '*modern* nervousness', his 'demons' gave his own illness something primeval; they opened the way to an archaic religiosity. He felt in himself how the obsessional idea can spontaneously arise that one is attacked by evil spirits, and what a force for rationalization is contained in a religion whose struggle against magic breaks through such primitive notions. This insight became for him a key to the history of religion; the terms 'demon/demons' and 'demonic' occur no fewer than 110 times in his later scholarly work. The conditions of unintended sexual excitement seemed to come not from inside himself but from outside, and the 'demon' metaphors reveal that he did not care to accept them as part of himself. The demonology changed later, however, when for both him and Marianne there were demons in the sense of Plato's *daimon*: that is, the God-given inner voice pointing out the right path to man.[131]

The riddle of his own illness: a permanent spur to reflection

Weber found neither a convincing medical diagnosis nor a cultural-historical interpretation for his own illness, although it was part of the air people breathed in the 'age of neurasthenia'. He detested no scholar of his time as much as he did the cultural historian Karl Lamprecht, who had identified modernity as the 'age of irritability' and seen this as a mark of cultural progress. From the point of view of his own illness, Weber must have felt that Lamprecht's labelling of epochs was nothing but dilettantism on the part of a man who really did not have a clue. He knew from years of observing himself that the phenomena of human life were worlds apart from speculative general notions, and this was not the least of the reasons why his illness must have become a constant spur for thought and a warning of the provisional character of all knowledge. What was the cause of his illness: hereditary factors, childhood meningitis, a wrong lifestyle, or lack of sexual satisfaction? He must have pondered a lot, but it does not look as if he found an unambiguous answer. All that is clear is that he thought the answer had more to do with laws of nature than with morality. The experience of his illness was paradigmatic for the whole problem of causality that he took up in his theory of science.

In Weber's day, Sigmund Freud was not the only one to believe that, precisely because it was so shrouded in mystery, sexuality was the main key to the riddles of human existence. Similarly, the late Jaspers, an ex-psychiatrist and opponent of Freud, kept pondering over what he knew from Weber's account of his illness and his love letters to Else. Impotence and masochism were for him the basic factors in a 'disposition active since boyhood' – impotence 'associated with sexual desires and . . . nocturnal emissions', but also with a 'powerful urge to free himself, to be no longer a cripple, to be "normal" '. An agonizing situation arose from the fact that, although the outlet for Weber's instincts was blocked, his sexuality was 'powerful' and his 'actual sexual function was abnormally intense'.[132] Weber experienced his sexuality as wild and meaningless nature, not as a function of society – and this left traces in his thought. Only by recognizing this can we understand those phases of his creativity that lay at the basis of his worldwide reputation.

'What would he have been like if he had not fallen ill?' The break in Weber's intellectual development

The chemist Adolf von Baeyer once said that 'only the beginning' of a scholar's biography is 'remarkable',[133] as only the formation of intellectual creativity – a process completed early on – is of interest. Often this does seem to be the case, but it is questionable in relation to Max Weber. When the 83-year-old Jaspers corresponded in 1966 with the 68-year-old Eduard Baumgarten about whether Weber had developed a 'new mental disposition' under the influence of his illness, Baumgarten thought a negative answer was more appropriate, since Weber's early letters showed that the basic themes of his life had already been present when he wrote them. But Jaspers had quite a different opinion. He noted:

> I would say that, before he fell ill, he showed *no sign* of being interested in erotic matters. There was *no sign* that Max Weber turned his attention to the content of religious belief . . . or to its effects. *No sign* previously of a passion for the tension in 'truth'. The quarrelling with God – (his) existence or non-existence – the experience of having no solid foundation.[134]

Already in 1960, before Baumgarten had shocked him with Weber's letters to Else, Jaspers wrote in his sketch for a lecture:

> Can Weber's illness be regarded as a coincidence? His insight into politics was just as clear and true before the onset of his illness as after it.

But his philosophical sense deepened, and the breadth of his vision tended or was led into the immeasurable. What would he have been without the illness? His illness, however, made a full participation in practical politics impossible . . . Does the highest cognition presuppose illness? Kierkegaard, Nietzsche? Hölderlin? Weber's illness was fundamentally different: in comparison with those three he was fully 'a man', with an originally powerful vitality. The illness attacked him not from the outside, but out of his constitution itself. . . . Weber as a person, his spirit, was in no sense sick. No symptoms can be detected in his work.[135]

Jaspers's diagnosis is ambiguous: the illness struck Weber not from outside but from inside (the 'demons' were within), yet it remains separate from Weber's intellect, in the same way that Weber himself kept verifying through his scholarly work that his mind was still sound. This striving for intellectual assurance, probably implanted in Weber since the childhood meningitis, became a leitmotif from 1903 on – a reason for his new interest in scientific theory. And then there was his parting from academia. So long as a professor has secure tenure, the question of scientific credentials is not a problem for him: he has the power to decide what is and what is not science. The Weber of 1903 had lost that foundation, and this sharpened his eye for the question of what constituted the essence of science when it was stripped of its bureaucratic corset.

That suffering can raise our understanding is an age-old belief rooted in Christianity as well as Buddhism, and it is certainly significant that religion became Weber's great theme after his illness. He later saw the 'religious glorification of suffering' as a major turning point in history that gave rise to the religions of salvation.[136] Unlike experiences of love, however, suffering can release only a spiritual potential that is already present – and so it is that anyone who looks hard will find in Weber's early writings many a pointer to things to come. Nor should we imagine that the effects of illness on his scholarly work were just a matter of attraction and reaction; they lasted for the rest of his life, and a two-way process of *interaction* developed between his experience of life and his intellectual labours.

Weber's intellectual development, then, had an impact on his experience of life. And the inner process of coming to terms with his illness took considerable time. In the first few years he must have found it puzzling and oppressive, quite unable to grasp it intellectually, and even afterwards he could achieve only partial insights. It was more than ten years later – perhaps nearly twenty, through his love for Else – that he finally gained the distance necessary for a deeper understanding.

After 1900, a failure in both profession and marriage, lacking financial independence and a secure residence, Max Weber was thrown back into a state of mere existence, at first more physical than mental. Whereas, in the early years of his professorship, he had thought of himself as singularly blessed by fortune, this belief now crumbled along with any faith in a teleology of history. And, just as he had formerly preached a politics free of illusions, now all the illusions he had had about himself broke into pieces. Any vanity or self-complacency went by the board, and with it not only a primary source of professorial glory but also a major factor impairing the creativity of successful scholars. No longer capable of any personal narcissism, he felt all the more disgusted by the narcissism of others: *vanity* became a reproach ever on his lips, whether referring to the 'sexual vanity' of men who unjustly discriminated against women, to the 'compulsive self-importance' (PE 182) of fossilized professorial mandarins, or to the pomposity of those 'literati' drunk with victory who, during the world war, had not wanted to abandon their ambitious war aims even when they had proved to be a phantasm. In those days he praised the 'nobility for not taking itself seriously'.[137] If Walter Rathenau once called vanity the 'progressive taxation of the mind' – an inevitability that makes great minds unbearable to others – Max Weber had the advantage after his illness that he was not subject to that kind of self-deprecation.

From an early age Weber cultivated a sense of himself as an insider and held *parvenus* in contempt – a contempt that still rose in him later in life. He now experienced what it was like to be an outsider. Anyone who knows both situations is aware how different the world looks from each. Many insights are best gained from an external viewpoint. For his part, Weber was best able to ground a new self-awareness on the 'existentialist' conviction that intensive experience of marginal situations was the way to deeper knowledge. Like Dante in the *Divine Comedy*, he could now feel that he was one of those who had 'been through hell'; '*lasciate ogni speranza*' had been one of his favourite quotations since he first used it in 1895 in Freiburg.

At one point in *Economy and Society*, Weber asks the fundamental question how anything new can happen in a world where everything has been 'regularized'. His first answer is, 'through changes in the external conditions of life', but then he realizes that this cannot be conclusive, since a community might react to such changes by going into decline.

> The evidence of ethnology seems rather to show that the most important source of innovation has been the influence of individuals who have experienced certain 'abnormal' states (which are frequently, but not always, regarded by present-day psychiatry as pathological) and hence have been capable of exercising a special influence on others.

Such influences are able to 'overcome the inertia of the customary' (E&S 321), while elsewhere pathological tendencies are seen as one of the attributes of charismatic figures. Now, there can be no doubt that Weber was capable, even exceptionally capable, of 'abnormal states'. Between the lines of such passages, we recognize how he based a new self-awareness – a sense of having a special gift to point out new paths – on such 'abnormality'. Not by accident did religion now become his most characteristic theme, although it is true that he had already inherited some interest in it from his mother. For sick people, religion has a quite different aspect from the one it has for anti-clerical cultural warriors; people in distress think of religion as the best answer to man's longing for redemption.

It would appear that, at least in the early years, Weber's illness also marked his way of acting. During the 1920s – according to Helmut Fogt – his personality and life's fortunes attracted 'quite unusual' attention, 'much wider' than was the case with his scholarly work. The publication of Marianne Weber's biography in 1926 (together with no fewer than fifty-eight known reviews in the press) brought to a peak this interest in the gripping epic of a 'descent into hell' and the rebirth of a genius.[138] It must have found many more readers than Max Weber's writings, and indeed many of these were henceforth read with a sidelong glance at the biography. In comparison with other biographies of deceased spouses, Marianne's book was remarkably indiscreet – at least for people in the know who understood the allusions. Otto Gradenwitz, a colleague of Weber's at Heidelberg, sneered that the 'historical value' of *Lebensbild* came from the better understanding it gave us into the 'too often misunderstood institution of widow-burning' (B 605), but what he found offensive probably added to the appeal of a book that would dominate Weber biography for generations. A new rise after a crashing fall: this was precisely what many Germans dreamed of for themselves and their country; nothing else could have done more to paint Weber's life as an enthralling myth. This was also the view of life held by many of the post-1933 German émigrés who played a key role in the worldwide spread of the Weber cult.[139]

8

'A Sort of Spiritualistic Construction of the Modern Economy': The Protestant Ethic and the Vain Quest for Redemption through the Spirit

The original spiritual impulse behind *The Protestant Ethic*

On 2 April 1905 Weber wrote to Rickert: 'I am working – amid horrible torments, to be sure, but I do manage to work a few hours each day.' In fact, he was writing 'an essay on cultural history that may be of interest to you: Protestant asceticism as the foundation of modern *vocational civilization* [*Berufskultur*] – a sort of "spiritualistic" construction of the modern economy' (WB 356).[1] He spoke as if it were a new essay, but it later appeared as the second part of *The Protestant Ethic and the Spirit of Capitalism*, the first part of which had already been published in 1904 in the *Archiv für Sozialwissenschaft und Sozialpolitik*. Only in this second part does asceticism become a central idea alongside that of a vocation or calling [*Beruf*], a combination that completes the famous 'Weber thesis'. Unfortunately we have very little material relating to the development of the work; the letter to Rickert is the best-known document.

Those who believe that, beyond all particular quotations, there is a set of dogmas containing the *real* Weber will skate over his talk of a 'spiritualistic' construction and insist that he himself later explicitly rejected it; all he had wanted to do in *The Protestant Ethic* was draw out one component of the genesis of modern capitalism, and not at all deny the importance of economic conditions;[2] 'construction' indicated that only one element in the thought process was being referred to, while 'spiritualistic' (with its occult overtones) was in inverted commas. Now, Weber did indeed later stress that *The Protestant Ethic* should not be seen as expressing a world-view in which the mind ruled over sense experience, and he distanced himself from Hans Delbrück, who, like many others after him, made the book a weapon against 'materialism'.[3] 'I must defend myself against that', he explained. 'I am much more materialist than Delbrück thinks' (WzG 202). But Weber was not a supratemporal being identical with himself across time; that is precisely why it is worth writing a biography of him.

Never before had he taken up a field of work so spontaneously, without any recognizable external stimulus, as he did with *The Protestant Ethic*; it was the first major project since his breakdown, and the power of the *mind* was unmistakably the central issue in it for him.[4] At first he placed the 'spirit' of capitalism in inverted commas, but later he omitted them. In his view the 'spirit' was not simply a metaphor but – at least potentially – a real power. 'The Lord is the spirit, and where the Spirit of the Lord is, there is liberty' (2 Corinthians 3:17): this was the quotation once used at his confirmation. And, as Troeltsch pointed out, spiritualism – belief in the redeeming Spirit – was then 'the secret religion of educated people',[5] as it was of Troeltsch himself,[6] and during his illness it became the central question of his life whether the spirit was lord and master within himself.

Rome and the turn to the history of religion

In the years from 1901 to 1903, which preceded the composition of *The Protestant Ethic*, Weber frequently spent time in Rome, where he and Marianne must have felt that the 'eternal city' was doing him good. In *The Protestant Ethic* he even mentions the view that one eats better among Protestants but sleeps better among Catholics (PE 41), a view taken from the dissertation by his disciple Martin Offenbacher, 'Konfession und soziale Schichtung', which gave him an important impetus but whose author remained a nobody in the Weber circle. In 1942 Offenbacher took his own life when he faced imminent deportation, and today he is No. 1530 on the list of Holocaust victims in Nuremberg. The footnotes to *The Protestant Ethic* are the only evidence of his importance for Weber.

The fact that religion became Weber's major new interest and occupied him until the end of his life fits perfectly with his repeated stays in Rome, for scarcely anywhere else in Europe is the power of religion felt so strongly. Nothing would have been more obvious there than to study the history of the Catholic church, the papacy and monasticism; every walk would have offered fresh inspirations, and Weber was receptive to these when they accorded with his inner disposition. How, in Rome of all places, could he have been overcome by a sense of the spiritual power of Anglo-American Puritanism?

However, the intellect – even of a man such as Max Weber – is not simply a mirror of the external world but often develops in a dialectical relationship with external stimuli. Weber was not the first to discover in the South the specificity of the North; many a painter and writer from the North had done this before him. Despite the many references to Catholicism in Weber's sociology of religion, it remained a conspicuous gap in his analysis – even though it was associated with countless optical impressions and he was well read in the history of the Catholic church and orders.[7]

The final volume of Weber's 'Economic Ethic of the World Religions' was intended to cover 'Occidental Christianity' (MWG I/19, 28), but he would never actually take up the task. Evidently the Oriental religions excited him much more in later years, although his study of them had to start at the beginning. It would appear that all his life he had a kind of intellectual and emotional block when it came to Catholicism. In his younger years he regretted that Bismarck had called off the *Kulturkampf* (JB 234, 250), and even later, for all his criticism of Bismarckian methods in relations among the churches, he retained an element of the cultural warrior and regarded the growing political influence of the Centre Party (a counterweight though it was against the self-glorification of Kaiser and Junkers) as a misfortune for the German nation. The mass hysteria at Lourdes, which nauseated him and brought 'a cold sweat to his brow', struck at every notion of the progressive rationalization of modern life. 'It is not easy to behold such a powerful agitation of the nerves.'[8] At the Konstanzer Hof he read Zola's novel *Lourdes* and praised its 'outstandingly successful' picture of the 'infernal hierarchy' of 'black figures' around the grotto.[9] Catholicism did not have the qualities of a Weberian ideal type: it did not embody in pure form the old world of magic, nor had it consistently pressed ahead with the disenchantment of the world.

On 28 February 1902 Marianne reported from Rome: 'Max is at a library reading a great deal about the organization of cloisters and religious orders.'[10] He knew enough Latin to use special library collections in Italy and was able to speak Italian 'without elegance or sparkle'.[11] The orders must have stimulated him far more than the church hierarchy, as it was in them, if anywhere, that he found religious passion, discipline and brotherliness. Much later, Weber even recognized the cloister as the origin of modern rationality in general, including economic rationality, and not least in relation to the discipline of time: 'The monk is the first man to lead a rational life, pursuing a goal methodically and with rational means: the hereafter. Only for him did the clock strike, only for him were the hours of the day organized around prayers. The economy of the cloistered communities was *the* rational economy' (WG 311). Did it not occur to him to tackle *this* theme in Rome in 1902–3?

But asceticism would have been a conventional subject if it had been dealt with in relation to monastic life. What was unusual and surprising was to work on it as an element in the history of Protestantism, and especially as an original source of energy for militant Protestantism in the Anglo-American world; this was quite different from the approach of the theologian Albrecht Ritschl (1822–89), a Lutheran 'Bismarck type of professor' (Otto Baumgarten) from Weber's student days, who had written a thoroughly disparaging three-volume history of Pietism, and for whom all elements of asceticism and mysticism were foreign bodies of Catholic provenance. Weber was drawn precisely to the Protestant asceticism which had never been institutionalized, never screened off from the world behind cloister walls, rules of life and external constraints, and which had sunk roots all the deeper for its worldly form. This was the asceticism that had points of contact with Weber's own experience.

Had Weber's interest in religion been there from the beginning?

In Weber studies there is a tendency for *The Protestant Ethic* to be 'overdetermined', as if the whole of Weber's previous history meant that he could not have written anything else at that time. Those who maintain that everything in Weber was there from the beginning like to detect the origins of this work in the period before his illness; and he too later claimed that he had already tackled the theme in lectures in 1898.[12] As far back as 1875, a man who later became one of his main authorities, the German American Friedrich Kapp, had given Max a copy of Benjamin Franklin's autobiography as a Christmas present ('from his old friend to his dear young friend'); the eleven-year-old would certainly have read it thoroughly, especially as he had a great admiration for Kapp (who nevertheless detested America's Puritan tradition). In any event, Weber had visible evidence of the association between Calvinism and capitalism in the Souchay family of Huguenots from which his mother was descended. And we can see how, in the process of recovery after his breakdown, he tried to find new strength by returning to those roots.

The respect that Weber subsequently accorded to the Protestant sects was anything but a matter of course. From *The Protestant Ethic* onward, he seems convinced that religiosity in its original form was to be found mainly in small communities, since it was there, not in the state churches, that brotherliness and religious passion still had a place. Thus the sects became for him a special object of sociological research. Later he defined the existence of sects as a primary phenomenon in the sociology of religion, which bore the same hallmarks in all times and places; he was even influenced by what he called the 'model sect', the Donatists of late antiquity (GASS 462), who, under the motto 'The true church is that which suffers persecution rather than persecutes others', developed a craving for martyrdom and triggered a wave of suicides – a Satanic aberration for the dominant Christian tradition. Weber drew parallels between the state churches and the entailed estates he detested so much (GASS 462), whose owners enjoyed state guarantees of inviolability and therefore did not need to make any great exertions of their own.

In 1902 Sombart published the first two-volume edition of *Der moderne Kapitalismus*, his *magnum opus* that eventually swelled to six volumes. Like Weber, and unlike Marx, he saw the rise of capitalism as a question not mainly of the accumulation of capital, but rather of the genesis of a capitalist *spirit* (much more secular, though, than for Weber).[13] Weber later thought he had to defend himself from insinuations that *The Protestant Ethic* had been essentially a response to Sombart's challenge. When *Der moderne Kapitalismus* first appeared, Weber's health made him quite incapable of pitching in with a work of similar proportions. Instead, whereas Sombart had often revelled in the abundance of his material, Weber tried to make a reputation for himself by isolating and intensively concentrating on just one aspect. Making a virtue of necessity, he thus created something more permanent than Sombart's work, whose public impact for a long time greatly exceeded that of Weber's.

Another important book that appeared in 1902 was *The Varieties of Religious Experience: A Study in Human Nature*, by William James (1842–1910), one of the founders of American psychology. It is true that James is mentioned only twice in Weber's work, but Hennis rightly attaches much greater significance to Weber's encounter with the American, whom he later got to know personally.[14] The book consists of twenty lectures, the first of which is entitled 'Religion and Neurology'. James, like Weber, felt himself to be an incurable neurasthenic: in *The Gospel of Relaxation* (1899) he had attacked the whole philosophy of rest cures for nervous patients, yet the very next year, while Weber was in Urach, he went for a course of treatment at Bad Nauheim.[15] James discussed religion not as a set of dogmas and beliefs but as a product of human nature and, not least, of certain pathological states; his book was tailor-made to stir Weber deeply in his condition at that time. Weber could read in James: 'Here is the real core of the religious problem: Help! Help!' In James too we sense a love–hate relationship with nature, and he ends the book with an attack on the 'natural theology' of his forefathers: 'Nature has no one distinguishable ultimate tendency with which it is possible to feel a sympathy.'[16] But there can be no doubting the power that nature had for him. Weber's most frequent references to James are in *The Protestant Ethic*, but later too he could not get this American intellectual kinsman out of his mind. In 1910, when *Varieties* appeared in a German translation, Weber worked his way through it so thoroughly that his copy was left 'covered all over with [his] marginal notes' (B 313). Only then did he become open to James's 'salvation by self-surrender'; previously he had had much too Puritanical an image of the American philosopher-psychologist, who in reality had been a philanderer and a man filled with curiosity about spiritualistic experiences.[17]

It is probable, however, that Marianne was even more important than William James for the author of *The Protestant Ethic*,[18] which overlapped in several ways with the history of marital law that she had been writing since 1899. Ascetic Puritanism and its conception of marriage appear in her book, too, in the context of her discussion of natural law. In fact, she was internally divided: she saw the tendency in natural law to recognize equal rights for all, including women; on the other hand, she felt irritated by its tendency towards a predominantly sexual view of marriage and of women's reproductive function. She could therefore appreciate the basic Puritan attitude in relation to sexuality. For, although the Puritans' rigid expulsion of sensuality from marriage appears 'unnatural' to modern eyes, it was 'precisely to this disciplining of male instinctual life that the British and Americans ultimately owe the refinement of spiritual relations between the sexes'. This was not at all detrimental to the emotional bond between married people. On the contrary: 'Only with the fading importance of purely sexual tension . . . could the inwardness of the sociable and spiritual community between the spouses – the growing together of their souls – appear as the central meaning of marriage' (EM 289). Marianne's own experience comes through here.

What was new in the 'Weber thesis'?

The 'Weber thesis' of a connection between Protestantism and capitalism is so often encountered in a truncated or banalized form, and by dint of repetition has become so automatically associated with the name of Weber, that it is no longer easy to reconstruct what was so exciting about it and to understand its worldwide impact. At the time, even a critic could recognize that it was a 'new and interesting way of posing the problem',[19] but what was new about it?

If a German Protestant looked for a religious foundation to the work ethic, the first thing to occur to him would be Luther's concept of a God-given calling or vocation [*Beruf*]; this was already the case with Schleiermacher, the 'church-father of the nineteenth century', and Albert Ritschl[20] (though with a sting in the tail against the sects). Luther's sanctification of the calling seemed to Weber something new in world history, as he tried to show in a footnote stretching over several pages (PE 204ff.), and it was a central focus of the first part of the book that appeared in 1904. So, does the Reformation idea of a calling fully elucidate the connection between Protestantism and the dynamic of the modern economy? Certainly in Luther it still has a conservative element, pointing everyone towards their conventionally assigned station in life. And, from today's viewpoint, 'modern capitalism' involves not so much identification with a particular calling as greater flexibility with regard to possible callings; a tendency in that direction can already be glimpsed in the period in question. 'People are ceaselessly itching after new things', Schmoller observed in 1866 in the United States, in contrast to Europe, where 'thousands go under in failed vocations'.[21] Weber considered that Germans who had been brought up as Lutherans were not especially industrious; the 'great working nations' were the English and the Americans. Consequently the link between Protestantism and capitalism should be looked for in Anglo-American culture, where it must have developed in its most pronounced form.

All this should not make us forget that Weber was not the first to discover that modern industrial capitalism developed overwhelmingly in the Protestant world. This geographical congruence had been an object of debate since the eighteenth century;[22] it used to be much more evident than it is today, when Germany's Catholic regions have far outstripped many traditionally Protestant ones in terms of economic success. Weber's critic Felix

Rachfahl pointed out that, as far back as 1687, the British economist William Petty had shown in his *Political Arithmetic* that the Protestant areas of Europe 'together held three-quarters of world trade'.[23] Weber must have studied Petty in detail, Rachfahl argued, since the quoted passage was enough to identify the basic thesis of *The Protestant Ethic* as a case of 'unconscious plagiarism'.[24] Similarly, the idea that the Huguenots were economically important for the regions of Germany depopulated by the Thirty Years' War was in itself anything but new; it was even a tradition in Prussia to exaggerate the pioneering role of the Huguenots in the development of trade.[25]

What was at issue was not the fact as such but *how* the connection between Protestantism and capitalism should be conceived.[26] The idea suggested itself that the link between the two was not so direct but passed through a shared third element. And for an educated liberal this was likely to be the Enlightenment and modern science, both of which had developed mainly on the ground of Protestantism that was also especially favourable to the advance of secularism. However, it is precisely vis-à-vis Rachfahl's alternative picture of the genesis of capitalism that the distinctiveness of Weber's thesis appears most sharply. For Weber sought the origins of capitalism not in the Enlightenment and the process of secularization, nor in the dissolution of religious attachments, but on the contrary in religious passion. He rightly pointed to something all too familiar from his family tradition: that, in contrast to a widespread notion of his day, Protestantism and especially Calvinism were originally much sterner than Catholicism in the demands they made on believers (PE 37). According to the prevalent view, the Enlightenment had performed the main services in the development of modern rationalism. But Weber identified a process of strict rationalization within the history of religion; he was convinced that the modern vocational ethic must have sprung from a powerful instinctual force, and he located this neither in the Enlightenment nor in philosophical idealism but in the realm of religion.

Weber's focus, however, was not on religious dogma but on popular devotional literature; this marked the difference between the social scientist and the theologian. He was well aware of what recent studies of religion had rediscovered: namely, the pet idea of the Eranos circle that popular religion constituted a separate world from that of the theologians. The crucial point for him was the influence of religion not on people's view of the world but on their everyday lives, on human types and their conduct of life. And this could not be logically deduced from religious dogmas; it had to be extracted from certain devotional texts intended for the everyday use of ordinary men and women. It was above all at this level that Weber thought he could identify the connection between Protestantism and capitalism.

A standard argument against the Weber thesis was that the rise of capitalism could be much better explained by the godless greed for money than by the pursuit of godly favour. Right from the beginning, Weber gave considerable thought to this objection and himself liked to quote Virgil's line about the *auri sacra fames*, the 'accursed greed for money'. But he countered it as follows:

> The greed of the Chinese Mandarin, the old Roman aristocrat, or the modern peasant, can stand up to any comparison. . . . The *auri sacra fames* is as old as the history of man. But we shall see that those who submitted to it without reserve as an uncontrolled impulse, such as the Dutch sea-captain who 'would go through hell for gain, even though he scorched his sails', were by no means the representatives of that attitude of mind from which the specifically modern capitalistic spirit as a mass phenomenon is derived, and this is what matters. (PE 56f.)

It matters for Weber especially because Sombart had emphasized the adventurist side of capitalism. Later, Weber dwelled on this point with a lengthy addendum on adventurers and fortune-hunters, who, though to be found everywhere, would never have been capable by themselves of breaking through the premodern attachment to tradition. The following argument may be reconstructed. So long as the craving for riches was simply a natural urge, it was kept within bounds by the natural need for happiness; the lucky ones enjoyed their fortune in magnificent palaces, complete with opulent banquets and voluptuous mistresses. But, in creating an obstacle to this, Puritanism established a mechanism for the ongoing reinvestment of capital. In today's jargon we might say that Weber, more than Sombart, was interested mainly in the conditions for a *sustainable* capitalism; whereas Sombart's capitalism conflicted with man's natural inertia but also corresponded to elements of human nature such as the striving for happiness, Weber's capitalism painfully cut across human nature and the striving for happiness.

How did work discipline become a permanent feature?

For Weber, 'asceticism' – in the sense of restless labour for the purposes of gain – became a permanent pressure which, though conflicting with human nature, passed down through the generations to the present day. *How is this permanence to be explained?* Curiously, both Weber and his critics gave this relatively little attention, fixated as they were on the question of origins. In the sensational finale to *The Protestant Ethic*, Weber did consider the fact that the asceticism of work had survived to his own times, but he described it as a 'mutation'. According to Richard Baxter (1615–91), the Puritan devotional writer most often quoted by Weber – a chaplain in Cromwell's army and author of *The Saints' Everlasting Rest* – concern for worldly goods should lie on the shoulders of his saints 'like a light cloak, which can be thrown aside at any moment'.

> But fate decreed that the cloak should become an iron cage. Since asceticism undertook to remodel the world and to work out its ideals

in the world, material goods have gained an increasing and finally an inexorable power over the lives of men as at no previous period in history. Today the spirit of religious asceticism – whether finally, who knows? – has escaped from the cage. But victorious capitalism, since it rests on mechanical foundations, needs its support no longer. . . . In the field of its highest development, in the United States, the pursuit of wealth, stripped of its religious and ethical meaning, tends to become associated with purely mundane passions, which often actually give it the character of sport. No one knows who will live in this cage in the future, or whether at the end of this tremendous development entirely new prophets will arise, or there will be a great rebirth of old ideas and ideals, or, if neither, mechanized petrifaction, embellished with a sort of convulsive self-importance. For of the last stage of this cultural development, it might well be truly said: 'Specialists without spirit, sensualists without heart; this nullity imagines that it has attained a level of civilization never before achieved.' (PE 181f.)[27]

Treitschke, in his attacks on socialism, had called the society of complete gratification 'an iron casing of cultural inequality',[28] and in Weber the casing becomes a veritable cage. Now and again a reader might feel that Weber inwardly identifies with the vocational ethic and asceticism of work rooted in Protestantism, but here, right at the end, a deep sadness breaks through – a fierce repugnance that must be highly confusing for all who celebrate Weber as an intellectual force guiding modern processes of rationalization.[29] In the later reworking of *The Protestant Ethic*, this sombre theme is made even stronger.[30]

These few sentences are so overloaded with ideas and allusions that each reading of them uncovers something new. How did Weber conceive of the force driving this new fate of the world? He began by making 'fate' a historical subject, then 'asceticism', and then 'material goods'. Labour and the fruits of labour were supposed to be only means on the road to salvation, but they have gained a menacing autonomy and made it impossible for man to free himself from them; one is reminded of the treacherous 'means' for inducing sleep [*Schlafmittel*] that were one of Weber's constant preoccupations. The religious spirit has undermined itself through the overwhelming success of these means: it has not thereby attained the realm of the eternal, nor is it through the power of religion that the single-minded mania for work has survived and conquered the world. Steely hardness, not religion, remains as the stable subject of history. Earlier in *The Protestant Ethic* the word 'steel-hard' appears once more:

In the place of the humble sinners to whom Luther promises grace if they trust themselves to God in penitent faith are bred those self-confident saints whom we can rediscover in the hard [*stahlhart*] Puritan merchants of the heroic age of capitalism and in isolated instances down to the present. (PE 112)

This passage still contains some ambiguity, as we sense in it Weber's fascination for 'heroic' grandeur. But none of this remains in the conclusion to the book, which reminds us more of the image of history in ancient mythology: that is, a decline from the golden through the silver to the iron age. To be sure, for Weber this iron – the 'mechanical foundations', modern technology – is not the least of the factors which has made capitalist rationalization irreversible. In the first part, Weber had identified 'the capitalistic order of the present day' (so, not yet the early modern order) with the iron cage [*Gehäuse*]:

> The capitalistic order of the present day is an immense cosmos into which the individual is born, and which presents itself to him as an unalterable order of things [*unabänderliches Gehäuse*] in which he must live. It forces the individual, in so far as he is involved in the system of market relationships, to conform to capitalistic rules of action. (PE 54)

This sounds very much like systems theory: the system becomes the subject of events, and the individual becomes a puppet of the system. But Weber developed an allergy to such a way of thinking. In any event, the wording here leaves open the possibility that people might be emancipated *as a group* from the constraints of the 'capitalist economic order'. Sometimes in Weber 'rationalization' operates as the driving force of modern history. But already in the first part of *The Protestant Ethic* – in opposition to Sombart, though without mentioning him by name[31] – he protests at length against any attempt to make 'rationalism' the basic underpinning of modern capitalism. Rationalism did not necessarily mean living for work.

> Finally, if under practical rationalism is understood the type of attitude which sees and judges the world consciously in terms of the worldly interests of the individual ego, then this view of life was and is the special peculiarity of the peoples of the *liberum arbitrium*, such as the Italians and the French are in very flesh and blood. But we have already convinced ourselves that this is by no means the soil in which that relationship of a man to his calling as a task, which is necessary to capitalism, has pre-eminently grown. (PE 77)

If practical rationalism is understood as an art of living that keeps human beings healthy and cheerful, then the *dolce far niente* that an overwrought Weber often envied in the South fits the description at least as well as does an obsessive mania for work. In his eyes, the kind of rationalization that leads to modern capitalism has its roots not in man's natural reason but in pathological structures within human nature. Weber knew this from his own experience of trying to flee depression in work. The Latin peoples are so casual 'in their very flesh and blood' that no capitalist world system could eradicate their lifestyle – at least not in Weber's time. Between the lines of *The Protestant Ethic* it is possible to read the unspoken, but not entirely unconscious, premise that people get a kind of pleasure out of torturing themselves.

The 'iron cage' inside man

The missing link in Weber's argument may therefore be that the asceticism of work grips people not only through the external pressure of competition, but even more through the physical internalization that makes it a second nature. To imagine the 'iron cage' as a social system would not fit Weber's aversion for abstract images of 'society' as a historical agent;[32] Weber's cage had its most durable foundation inside man. For this very reason it was able to survive changes in society and even the process of secularization. Although asceticism originally rested upon a free choice, it became an inner compulsion for later generations who were brought up in it – as Weber knew from himself as the perfect example.

Yet this compulsion had to have a pleasurable side in order to be so powerful and durable. It lay above all in the element of combat, of competitive struggle, which fired ambition, as we may infer from the conclusion of *The Protestant Ethic*, which suggests an affinity between the ascetic compulsion and the passion for sport (then typical of Anglo-Americans, but not of most Germans). In response to Rachfahl's criticisms, Weber still more strongly emphasized the present-day significance of 'competitive drives'.[33] The pleasure of combat was for Weber one of the basic human drives.

The train of thought in *The Protestant Ethic* has the charm of paradox. It conflicts with normal logic that of all things the Calvinist belief in divine predestination, which man can do nothing to influence, should have brought forth the tireless mania for work; one would have thought that the Catholic justification by works was a more appropriate origin, and that a belief in predestination would have promoted passive fatalism. However, the true affinities are explicable not by rational logic but by a psycho-logic. If a man who is presumably hard-working by nature believes that divine election is made manifest in professional success, then this will stimulate his natural tendencies, especially under conditions where greater productivity is rewarded with greater profits. Without this additional assumption, Weber's thesis would have no logical basis.

Yet it is precisely material success, and the goods that it makes available, which tempt people into a worldly mentality that increasingly extinguishes the religious fire. As Jaspers notes, it was 'a concealed connection that could only operate because it was concealed'.[34] Historically, the truth is that effects which take people unawares have sometimes been the most decisive. The Puritan preachers, however, were not so blind in the long term that they did not recognize this danger. The causality described by Weber functioned only at one moment in history, not as a trans-epochal spirit – as he himself recognized. The fame of the 'Weber thesis' rests not least upon the material it offers for a discussion of causality in history.

In keeping with his 'spiritualism' of the time, Weber claimed to be dealing with the spirit of capitalism – but a deep gulf existed between capitalism and the original Puritanism precisely in respect of their distinctive spirits. One line of objection to the 'Weber thesis' has repeatedly pointed to the simple fact that the Puritan preachers were worlds apart from the spirit of capital accumulation.[35] In reality, Weber's argument linking Puritanism and capitalism leaves the path of the spirit and concentrates more on natural elements: on a (spiritually) unintended effect of asceticism and strict rules of life on human nature in successive generations. And yet, Weber knew from his own case that original human nature cannot be completely eradicated.

Two natures

In *The Protestant Ethic* there is a divine nature but also a nature antithetical to the divine. Weber was familiar with the Christian natural-law tradition in Calvinism, which was one of the main research fields of his conversation partner Ernst Troeltsch. The *lex naturae* was God's law, and Calvinists derived from it man's duty to be tirelessly active in work (PE 114, 121). At the same time, however, there was man's sinful, 'creaturely' nature, which had to be combated and repressed (PE 105f.); everything that looked like 'idolatry' was a sin to the Puritans (PE 236n.). The way of the creature led to damnation; the prerequisite for salvation was the repression of creaturely nature. In Weber's view, the modern capitalist discipline of work demanded just such a repression of natural drives, but this was to be explained originally by strong religious impulses, by a panic fear of damnation, not merely by the pursuit of profit.

Weber needed a distinctive picture of human nature so that his argument would be correct even if he placed 'nature' in quotation marks: 'A man does not "by nature" wish to earn more and more money, but simply to live as he is accustomed to live and to earn as much as is necessary for that purpose' (PE 60). This was the mentality of the subsistence economy, which Sombart had described in *Der moderne Kapitalismus* as the archetype of economic life. One might object with Rachfahl that commerce, or any pursuit of gain rising above mere necessity, was an ancient phenomenon in keeping with certain aspects of human nature.[36] Indeed, at times the *Protestant Ethic* debate became an argument about the nature of man. Brentano, too, objected against Weber that capitalism was not fundamentally in contradiction either with human nature or with natural law.[37]

In Weber's view, Lutheranism had stopped halfway in the struggle against sinful nature and been drawn into compromises that treated it as to some extent morally indifferent (PE 84). The consequences had been unfortunate: it was well known that the Lutheran princely courts, unlike the Calvinist ones, were 'often degraded by drunkenness and vulgarity' (PE 127). Weber's great-grandfather Fallenstein had been a boozing companion of the prince of Meiningen, and the Webers seem to have suspected that orgies in Meiningen castle[38] played a part in the degeneration of the family line. With regard to Lutheran alcoholic merriment, Weber made a remark on German 'naturalness' which shows he was thinking not only of the past but also of the present, and not only of religious currents but also of his own nation:

> The typical German quality often called good nature [*Gemütlichkeit*] or naturalness contrasts strongly, even in the facial expressions of people, with the effects of that thorough destruction of the spontaneity of the *status naturalis* in the Anglo-American atmosphere, which Germans are accustomed to judge unfavourably as narrowness, unfreeness, and inner constraint. But the differences of conduct, which are very striking, have clearly originated in the lesser degree of ascetic penetration of life in Lutheranism as distinguished from Calvinism. (PE 127)

Weber seems to have started from the premise that, as soon as man makes the slightest concession to his animal side, he starts to slip into a moral quagmire. However, the German Lutherans, as he depicts them here, might be seen with friendlier eyes. Before his illness, Weber himself had valued the earthy old German zest for life. Did it really conflict with a liberal and industrious cast of mind? Can one be hard-working only in a Puritanical way, not more joyfully?

Rationalization through religion

The Protestant Ethic sees the first, albeit marginal appearance of a theme that would soon become one of Weber's leitmotifs: *rationalization*. Sombart initially spoke of 'rationalism', but it is characteristic of Weber's terminological fluidity that he preferred 'rationalization', much as he referred more to 'socialization' (*Vergesellschaftung*) than to 'society'. At first he placed 'rationalization' in quotation marks, for it was then a new term. In 1912 the Breslau economist Julius Wolf published a book on progressive contraception under the title *Die Rationalisierung des Sexuallebens in unserer Zeit* (The Rationalization of Sexual Life in our Times);[39] evidently Weber was not the only one to recognize how well the concept could be applied in extra-economic realms. In Germany's rationalization era in the 1920s, the term was blown up to become one of the buzzwords of the day. 'Rationalization' sounded like an Americanism, but in reality, as *The Times* noted in 1930, it was a 'clumsy Germanic word'.[40]

'Rationalization' has operated as one of the signal words in the reception history of Weber's work: both those who object to the defective rationality of the real world and those who measure the presence of a higher reason by rationalization processes in the economic or educational sphere have taken up Weber's theme as the material for endless discussion. For, although Weber always championed 'rationalization' in the sense of methodical penetration, he also repeatedly showed that, contrary to the vision of the eighteenth-century Enlightenment, rationalization processes by no means comply with a reason innate in all human beings but may combine with passions of the most diverse kinds. The discovery of such processes in religion became one of Weber's pet themes.

In contrast to the classical Enlightenment thinkers, Weber did not know from his own experience any reason [*Vernunft*] that overcomes the passions once and for all, but only a rational approach [*Ratio*] that enters into symbiotic relations with them. Quite alien to him was any idea that there is a spiritual elite of rational men who, if able to discuss with one another long enough, could reach agreement on all the important questions of human existence. In his later additions to *The Protestant Ethic*, he tried to clear up any misunderstandings: 'If this essay makes any contribution at all, may it be to bring out the complexity of the only superficially simple concept of the rational' (PE 194).[41]

The ideal 'ideal type' of the entrepreneur

Another term that would become one of Weber's trademarks, as it were, also appeared for the first time in *The Protestant Ethic*: *the ideal type*. His ideal type of the capitalist entrepreneur, though meant to be value-free, is in a sense actually an *ideal* type in the sense of German Idealism: that is, a man of moral integrity, completely absorbed in his work, who has nothing in common either with the rapacious adventurer or with the swanky parvenu currying favour with the feudal nobility (PE 71f.). In a footnote Weber concedes that 'in a certain sense . . . to speak in terms of ideal types [does] violence to historical reality' (PE 233).

Many critics have regarded the 'ideal type' method as a trick to evade any empirical verification. On the one hand, with his 'malignant growth of footnotes' (PE 220) (as he cleverly put it in a footnote), he created the impression of uncommonly thorough empirical investigation; on the other hand, as soon as a critic held up a fact that told against him, he defended himself by arguing that – as any intelligent reader should realize – no investigation which sought to draw out typical features could deal with the diversity of historical reality. He could have a clear conscience that his ideal types did not keep him from often grappling with the ambiguities of the real world, but many of those who later invoked his name used the ideal type as a tried and tested means to minimize the efforts of empirical research.[42]

The open question: the generalizability and topicality of *The Protestant Ethic*

Weber did not think of *The Protestant Ethic* simply as a product of empirical history, but nor did he see it as a model that could be generalized at will – or did he? Even today there is a lack of clarity on this point. The worldwide impact of the 'Weber thesis' rests mainly on the perception that it is capable of being generalized, and we sometimes get the impression that Weber himself was interested in these early modern developments not least because they exemplified the dynamic set in train when man, having systematically repressed his own nature, finds that his shackled drives interact with the mechanisms of their repression. Similarly, in the *Zwischenbetrachtung*, Weber would later describe the dialectical interplay between a highly cultivated intellect grown remote from nature and a sexuality highly cultivated for erotic experience.

To some extent, Felix Rachfahl was right to feel that Weber had had in mind not only Anglo-Dutch-American capitalism of the seventeenth and eighteenth centuries but capitalism *tout court*.[43] It is also true that *The Protestant Ethic* would not have had the impact it did if many others had not understood it in the same way. Sometimes Weber emphasized that the 'elective affinity' [*Wahlverwandtschaft*][44] between capitalism and Protestantism had a purely historical significance and was not applicable to his own day. But Friedrich Naumann, the former priest and Weber's main link to the world of politics, embodied more than any other German politician of the time an attempt to bind together the forces of Protestantism and capitalism – and even socialism as well.

In the final crescendo of *The Protestant Ethic* we can hear a hope in 'new prophets'. For Weber it was by no means clear that modernity involved an irreversible trend towards secularism, and that even the loyal state churches of Lutheranism would find themselves emptying; he even feared a new advance of political Catholicism and saw it as one of the main dangers ahead. He wrote to the women's rights campaigner Elisabeth Gnauck-Kühne (1850–1917), deeply uneasy over her recent conversion to Catholicism: 'Were I to weigh up the prospects for the future, there are in my view two powers – bureaucratism in the state and the masterly machinery of the Catholic church – which, when combined with the fragmentation of humanity into economic and other kinds of specialists, are perhaps the best placed to trample all others under foot' – two powers against which he thought it an 'injunction of human dignity' to struggle.[45] Capitalism is not mentioned among the powers of the future: it seems to be merged together with bureaucratic rationalization.

The virtuosity of Weberian empathetic understanding

The main appeal of *The Protestant Ethic*, which even today makes many passages a delight to read, is neither its principal thesis nor its ideal-typical method but its empathetic understanding of religious mentalities, sensitive yet unsentimental in its preservation of rational detachment. In order to appreciate this virtuosity in the context of its time, it is useful to compare it with Ritschl's *History of Pietism*. Weber earnestly ploughed through this great work and quoted it no fewer than thirty times; almost everything he writes about Pietism comes from Ritschl.[46] Rather like Weber, Ritschl was a master of the cold shower; one could learn from him how to read religious sources against the grain, in a sober and critical manner. But it always came with a stern refusal to empathize with anything that showed a trace of mystical contemplation or ecstatic rapture. 'Contemplation is the Catholic form of piety'[47] – full stop, case closed!

For Barth, Ritschl was 'the very epitome of the national-liberal German bourgeois of the age of Bismarck', who stood 'truly with both feet' upon the ground of his 'earthly ideal; a 'sturdy, desiccated, blanched but not at all sentient nodule'.[48] People such as Ritschl failed to see that along with mysticism they banished all Eros from religion and therefore its source of vitality. The ailing Weber, by contrast, who knew the longing for redemption, had had his eyes opened to passion as the original vital element in religion; he therefore took exception to Ritschl's crude and undiscriminating attitude to mystical currents (PE 229f.). Weber was more capable than many a well-appointed theologian of perceiving in religious experience the cry for help in a time of need and the bliss of the state of grace. In reply to a critic who refused to believe in the power of religion in early capitalism, he insisted that people at that time had 'very precise ideas' of death, damnation or redemption, 'however difficult it may be for us modern people to imagine ourselves in the harrowing power of those metaphysical ideas'.[49] Weber's new self-confidence stemmed not least from an ability to empathize with the terrible fear of being among the damned.

How is the worldwide impact of *The Protestant Ethic* to be explained?

The Protestant Ethic is a text which gains from repeated readings in different situations; this is another reason why its impact has been much greater in the long term than in the period immediately after its publication. Nevertheless, its later worldwide resonance cannot be explained only by the book's contents and its power of persuasion. Contrary to the Weber thesis, there is a lot of evidence that the congruence between Protestantism and capitalism over the centuries had its roots not in the depths of religious experience but in common external conditions.

Much of the worldwide impact was due to rather banal factors that would have brought Weber little joy. For all its refinement, the Weber thesis was in keeping with the simple bourgeois axiom of 'no pain, no gain', and superficially at least it appeared as a weapon against Marx's account of the loathsome robber barons at the head of 'primitive accumulation'. The United States came to appreciate Weber as an external corroborator of its own image of itself, in which America's prosperity was based on old-established virtues and not, for example, on robbery of the native Indians, slavery and plunder of natural resources. In the aftermath of two world wars, the new unity of the West found an economic and moral basis in the Weber thesis.

But ideological expediency cannot alone explain why *The Protestant Ethic* has continued to be read so widely. Francis Fukuyama assures us: 'Much of the empirical work on cases that have occurred since Weber wrote have [*sic*] tended to confirm the broad outlines of his hypothesis. . . . This . . . is well understood by development economists who have spent time in the field in preindustrial societies.'[50] The often meagre results of 'development aid' to the third world indicate that successful varieties of industrial capitalism have deeper roots in mental and cultural traditions of the West than the bulk of economists long assumed; even at the height of imperialism, in Weber's lifetime, many thought it just a matter of time until the West was faced with dangerous competitors in other parts of the world. But Weber's dark foreboding of 'specialists without spirit, sensualists without heart' has recently become a standard quotation, and it occurs to many today that an a-moral robber capitalism is destroying its own foundations. *The Protestant Ethic* can also be read like that – not only as a legitimation of capitalism as such.

Zinzendorf's raptures: an embarrassment for *The Protestant Ethic*

The jolly Count Zinzendorf and his Moravian Brethren caused visible difficulties to Weber. On the one hand, they belonged among the currents within German Protestantism most akin to the Anglo-American free churches in their impulse to autonomy; on the other hand, however, they produced the worst forms of pompously erotic and affectedly infantile fanaticism, which were a real gift to Ritschl and provided the climactic material for his history of Pietism. The cult of 'little cross-air birds', 'sacred holes' and 'sweet wounds of Jesu' later sounded awkwardly sexual and necrophiliac in many of the Moravian hymns, so much so that in Weber's time these still circulated only in secret. The basic character of Zinzendorf's doctrine was certainly not ascetic – indeed, Weber found in it that 'free universality of love' which later so fascinated him (PE 250).[51] He even notes that within his community 'Zinzendorf himself continually attempted to counteract the tendency to ascetic sanctification in the Puritan sense' (PE 135). Weber was honest enough to add a remark here and there which did not fit his argument. At that time he did not yet have a feel for the ecstatic element in the history of religion.

Benjamin Franklin: a Puritan ascetic?

Even in one of his star witnesses Weber suppressed certain essential traits that would have cut across his idea that the Puritan-capitalist spirit was inimical to man's natural thirst for happiness; the witness is none other

Figure 8.1 Benjamin Franklin

than Benjamin Franklin. It was not without a sense of triumph that Weber's executor, Eduard Baumgarten, who suffered because of the ascetic model set by Weber, revealed in great detail the extent to which Weber had denied Franklin's basic hedonism. The much-quoted phrase 'time is money' comes from Franklin's *Advice to a Young Tradesman*, written in 1748, and Weber interpreted it in the sense of that self-destructive hecticism to which he had submitted for many long years. What he did not notice was that, in the pre-industrial society of New England in 1748, Franklin's advice had not necessarily been an incentive to thrift in the use of each precious minute.[52] Although Weber had already read Franklin's autobiography in his youth, his interpretation of 'time is money' seems closer to the 'clever and malicious' (PE 51) anti-American novel by Ferdinand Kürnberger, *Der Amerikamüde* (1855),[53] whose author had never been to America, than to Franklin's personal testimony. 'The *summum bonum* of this (Franklin's) ethic', Weber writes, is 'the earning of more and more money, combined with the strict avoidance of all spontaneous enjoyment of life'; it is 'above all completely devoid of any eudaemonistic, not to say hedonistic, admixture'. Life serves money-making, not vice versa. 'This reversal of what we should call the natural relationship, so irrational from a naive point of view, is evidently as definitely a leading principle of capitalism as it is foreign to all peoples not under capitalistic influence' (PE 53).

Weber's judgement may be true for many of those who later quoted Franklin's 'time is money' – but it would certainly not apply to Franklin, who for all his bustle was an expert in the art of living. He sought harmony with nature,[54] and he knew how to enjoy his work as well as sexual pleasures (within the limits of health). He was indeed anything but an orthodox Puritan, more a pantheistic believer in Nature. It is written on his grave: 'Here will I hold – If there is a Pow'r above us / (And that there is, all Nature cries aloud, / Thro' all her Works), He must delight in Virtue / And that which he delights in must be Happy.'[55] According to Baumgarten, Franklin's 'time is money' was said with a wink, for in the same year he gave up his business (at the tender age of forty-two) so that he could spend his life on his hobbies. 'Instead of an ascetic, what appears is a high-spirited Epicurean.'[56] Baumgarten adds with a visible smile that Max Weber, 'a man with a great sense of humour of his own', did not understand Franklin's joke.[57] The ascetic inwardness that Weber considered typically old-American actually came from 'the sphere of German religiosity'.[58] Baumgarten evidently assumed that Weber had obstinately projected a part of himself on to the Americans, so that he failed to notice – or did not wish to see – quite different sides of Franklin.

The Protestant Ethic as Weber's personal testimony – but where and how?

Right from the beginning, it was an accepted fact among those familiar with Weber that *The Protestant Ethic* contained his own personal testimony. To the young Edgar Salin, he appeared as a 'a strictly uncompromising Puritan',[59] and Marianne already mentioned that 'this work is connected with the deepest roots of his personality and in an indefinable way bears his stamp' (WB 335). Really 'in an indefinable way'? A little further on, she writes that 'one also seems to detect some of Weber's own features in the magnificent figures of a heroic Puritanism which he presents' (WB 337). When she remarks that Weber 'strives for a careful causal attribution of intuitively comprehended connections' (WB 336), she reveals that what came first was neither empirical study nor theory but intuition.[60]

Weber's unnecessarily angry and verbose replies to his critics, which could have been much shorter and to the point, reveal the extent to which he always took personal offence if anyone laid hands on his *Protestant Ethic*. One can read these replies several times without really understanding which important issues are in dispute, for, although Weber was such an irritable person, the clarity and creativity of his thought are least in evidence in his polemics. They give a sense of sleepless nights spent fixing his thoughts on various sore points. Why did his anger last a particularly long time in the case of Rachfahl, the expert in the Dutch war of independence with whom he differed neither in world-view nor in the theory of science, and whom he might have valued as an ally against the detested Lamprecht? Eduard Baumgarten had one explanation:

Weber was deeply wounded by him: the robust historian's mockery of the 'asceticism theme' probably touched a deep vulnerability in him. In these grand 'projections', having got over periods of solitude, he was able to see himself in world history and to perceive world history passing through his own history. Rachfahl's scorn for the *objectivity* of this effort made him fall upon him as Ajax on Tersites. (B 620f.) (The reference to the *Iliad* should have Odysseus instead of Ajax, and Thersites instead of Tersites – JR.)

It is a feeble mythological comparison: Rachfahl was by no means a quarrelsome cretin like Thersites;[61] it was rather his self-confident professorial manner that irritated Weber so much.[62] Above all else, however, Weber felt personally wounded by criticism of *The Protestant Ethic*. It is still the prevailing view in Weber studies that this book was his most 'personal' text.[63] The editor of the German edition in Max Weber's collected works, Hartmut Lehmann, has even tried to show passage by passage how it mirrors Weber's own experience. For example, he points to 'a close connection between the personally painful loss of his profession and the radiant vision of a profession as a "calling"' in *The Protestant Ethic*. 'There is not a lot here that needs decoding. Weber's experience and Weber's text form a semantic unity.' 'Weber would seem to have wished for nothing more than to be like the Puritans he described.' 'And "time-wasting" was for devout Calvinists "the first and in principle the deadliest of sins", as it was for him too.' In *The Protestant Ethic*, Weber revealed 'the maxim that helped him to fight and eventually overcome his depression; he was determined to place the highest of all demands on himself'.[64]

In fact, scarcely anyone familiar with Weber's life and *The Protestant Ethic* can resist feeling that there is an intimate connection between the two. But it is worth analysing more closely the type of connection that may be involved. Would Weber really have liked nothing better than to be a Puritan? Did he not in 1903, just as he was getting down to work, feel the final relinquishment of his professorship as a welcome release? And, above all, how does the gloomy conclusion to the book fit this interpretation? Are Puritanical norms not more in keeping with his lifestyle *before* the breakdown: that is, with the hectic routines of a profession that seemed to him in retrospect to have been his undoing, rather like the early modern Puritanism that ended up locking people in an 'iron cage?'

Perhaps Weber, now unable to continue with his profession, experienced himself as an ascetic. The first association with 'asceticism' that comes to mind is the sexual abstinence required of monks. But, instead of this, Weber constructed a type of 'worldly asceticism', which did not include celibacy and did not apply to himself. In *The Protestant Ethic*, he presented a reinterpretation of the concept of asceticism to which Rachfahl took violent objection. His 'worldly asceticism' designated a life lived for the sake of one's profession, with a tightly ordered daily routine and a strict economy of time. This was precisely what Weber was no longer capable of achieving after his breakdown, and what he no longer wished to achieve. For Baxter time-wasting was 'the first and in principle the deadliest of sins', even when it was just a question of 'sociability' and getting 'more sleep than is necessary for health' (PE 157f.). This was the exact opposite of the life-maxims that Weber adopted after his breakdown, and even when his condition improved he felt panic and horror at the thought of any obligation or deadline.

Weber deals with the sexual side of Puritanical asceticism only in a (admittedly lengthy) footnote (PE 262ff.). Here he moves Franklin – who recommended keeping sexual intercourse within healthy limits[65] – into the proximity of religious ascetics: 'For the Puritan the expert was the moral theorist, now he is the medical man; but the principle is the same in both cases: an expert's narrow-mindedness combined with sexual narrow-mindedness' (PE 264 – translation modified). One feels here lingering echoes of Weber's anger with those doctors who urged him to have 'normal' sexual relations. Schulze-Gaevernitz, a former colleague at Freiburg who essentially adopted Weber's thesis in his own major work on British imperialism,[66] brought the sexual side of Puritanism more to the fore, although his reference was to his own day rather than the seventeenth and eighteenth centuries. He even ventured the thesis that 'the ethical shaping of the relationship between the sexes, on the ground of sexual self-discipline', was 'a hidden but powerful pillar of the British view of the world'. Control over one's own sexuality made one capable of controlling the world.[67] The male sexual drive was so strong that 'every demand of the women's movement could be immediately achieved . . . if all women, including street girls, went on strike for just fourteen days.'[68] It is doubtful, however, whether Weber arrived from his own experience at the idea that sexual asceticism was a source of strength.

The Siebeck publishing house urged Weber to do further work on issues of Protestantism, which went down well with the reading public. But he no longer felt in the mood for it. The original edition of *The Protestant Ethic* 'teems with declarations of intent' about future researches, but these are 'tidied away' in the later revised version.[69]

Not a simple mirroring but a dialectic between life and work

Weber defined Puritan asceticism in such a way that he was far removed from it in his own conduct of life. To use Hegelian terms, we might say that the connection between his life and his work consists more in a dialectic than a reflection. Feeling quite unable to exercise a regular profession, or even to submit to any discipline governing his work and time, he came to see the rise of a modern discipline of work as a great puzzle and tried to solve it with an intensity he had never shown before. Anyone who routinely attends to professional duties will scarcely feel the need for explanation of this point, nor ever imagine that such powerful motivating forces as the fear

Figure 8.2 Max Weber in 1903, after his illness

of eternal damnation are required to impose the modern discipline of work. While Weber in *The Protestant Ethic* describes the 'moral justification of worldly activity' as 'one of the most important results of the Reformation' (PE 81), he adds in a later footnote that he cannot understand how 'some investigators' fail to appreciate the import of these changes.

Many themes in the book on Protestantism may be seen as directly mirroring Weber's own situation at the time: his isolation and despair, his feeling of being doomed, his longing for release, his struggle to find a way of living that would save him.[70] Although he detected in the Puritans 'a feeling of unprecedented inner loneliness of the single individual' (PE 104), he imagined, by projecting from his own situation, that many of them were much lonelier than they actually were and wished to be.[71] In reality, Puritan discipline was the product not only of self-control but also of pronounced mutual control within the religious community; it may be thought paradoxical that one of the founders of the sociology of religion paid no heed to this. Weber also ignored Tocqueville's well-known points about the pressure to conform in the New England communities.[72]

Nevertheless, we must not exaggerate the extent to which *The Protestant Ethic* mirrors Weber's situation at the time; that would be neither textually justifiable nor psychologically plausible. A depressive is reluctant to look in the mirror: he does not like what he sees there. He finds most relief in areas which, though including many themes of his illness, divert his thoughts from the torment of certain fixed points. In Weber's case the main such area was sexuality. It is liberating to get away from obsessional brooding about oneself by turning one's thoughts to something else. The special quality of *The Protestant Ethic* comes not least from its blending of self-experience and self-denial. Friedrich Wolters, the disciple of Stephan George, later wrote that Weber was someone who 'always defended the opposite of what suited his nature, and liked best to argue the view that came hardest to him'. That was far from always the case, but his style of work did contain an element of pleasure in torturing himself.[73]

Dubious friends: Troeltsch and Sombart

The Protestant Ethic gives us an advance glimpse of Weber's later relations with Troeltsch and Sombart, without whom the writing of this book would be hard to imagine. Both were viewed by many as eminent scientific authorities, and they were probably more important for Weber's intellectual development than all other scholars in his circle of acquaintances. He sometimes called each of them his 'friend', especially when he thought he was in a common front with them in defence of his work on Protestantism[74] – in certain situations he was very generous with the title 'friend'.[75] In both cases, however, deep respect for the other's scholarly achievement was mixed with undertones of animosity in which differences of character and lifestyle played a role. Marianne, for her part, did not have a high opinion of either Troeltsch or Sombart as human beings. Since there is little documentation about Weber's relations with Sombart, and not even letters in the case of Troeltsch, these central relations for Weber, stretching over nearly twenty years, have not received the attention they deserve in the literature. All three men travelled in 1904 to the congress in St Louis, Missouri, and for all three the trip to the United States was of lasting significance.

Friedrich Wilhelm Graf has shown how much *The Protestant Ethic* owes to Troeltsch – even more than the footnotes reveal. It must have been mainly Troeltsch who introduced Weber to the relevant theological literature.[76] On the other hand, the significance that Troeltsch attached to the *lex naturae* for the development of Christian doctrine was a latent factor disrupting Weber's concept of a Protestant antagonism to nature. The main thrust of Troeltsch's work was to demonstrate a harmonious relationship of Christianity to *lex naturae* since ancient times, and to trace the 'elective affinity' between the Christian gospel and the Stoic law of nature.[77] The Christian 'uniform culture' – not a concept for someone like Weber – owed its unity at least as much to the natural law tradition as to specifically Christian ideas.[78] This corresponded to a general tendency on his part to conceive of religion as a thoroughly worldly phenomenon.

For Karl Barth, writing later in the twentieth century, the 'Troeltsch era' was the last stage in that cultural Protestantism which, unlike the tendency

Figure 8.3 A portrait of Ernst Troeltsch, about 1912

represented by Barth, felt no real longing to rise above the worldly culture of the German bourgeoisie. He saw in Troeltsch 'thorough distraction', a Christianity without a genuinely religious core.[79] Barth would probably have got on a little better with the non-theologian Weber, who in many periods felt far more than Troeltsch a despair at the world and a longing for a quite different life, even if he was as removed as anyone could be from a doctrine of salvation. He spoke as disdainfully as Barth about the cultural Protestantism of his age (MWG I/19, 101). For Troeltsch the vitality of a religion was rooted in the midst of life and in the compromises it struck with 'the world'; for Weber the force of religiosity could spring precisely from a radical rejection of the world, and religion was originally more a phenomenon of passion than a mere element of 'culture'. In 1909 he wrote to Tönnies that 'liberal Protestants' were 'ghastly' when they did 'not inwardly wrestle with themselves' (MWG II/6, 70); he must have had Troeltsch in mind too.

Troeltsch the theologian gave a quite untheological account of the origins of Christian asceticism. He surmised that one of the reasons for the growth of Christian asceticism was 'the neuropathic weakening of vitality, due to a certain weariness and slackness of the sex instinct, caused by ignorance of the laws of sex'; he thought it 'difficult to explain on purely social and ideal grounds why the ideal of chastity should increase to such an extent. . . . It looks rather as though the real reason [was] a nervous disease which sought purification and support in religious ideas.'[80] We see how disinclined he was to take religion seriously as the ultimate ground of asceticism. Similarly, in his later interpretation of the Calvinist observance of work discipline, he tacitly distanced himself from Weber by treating Calvin's doctrine as a reflection of conditions in Geneva, where even then all letters were preoccupied with commercial interests. In a city such as Geneva 'capitalism was able to steal into the Calvinist ethic'.[81] This was more Rachfahl than Weber.

The open break between Weber and Troeltsch came in 1915. During the period when Weber was an officer in a military hospital, it was a matter of honour for him that Germans should be able to visit French prisoners-of-war in his care without supervision; anything else would have been undignified snooping, especially if the visitors were honourable people. In a climate inflamed by fear of spies, however, Alsatians suspected of sympathy for the French were a ticklish subject. Troeltsch therefore allowed an Alsatian teacher to visit the hospital under his command only if he was accompanied by a military man. This led to 'a terrible row' with Weber, he later complained. 'He booted me out of his lodging in the most offensive manner' – the two lived in the same house! – and called Troeltsch's behaviour dishonourable.

Troeltsch was quite right to think that the immediate cause was insufficient to explain Weber's eruption. 'If truth be told, old differences lay behind this outburst. He regarded me as a flabby compromiser and a political numbskull.'[82] Karl Barth's judgement of him would probably have been the same. But it was not altogether fair, since Troeltsch displayed far more political understanding and commitment than most of his colleagues did. Unlike Weber, he left the ivory tower for a while after 1918 and threw himself into politics, even though at the time that was anything but tempting for a scholar.[83] When Marianne asked him to deliver a speech at Weber's graveside in 1920, he said that he was not in a position to do it (WzG 43). No other example is known of a close friend and colleague of Weber who so blatantly offended against common decency.

Sombart's perennial challenge and Weber's bottled-up aggression

While Weber exploded against Troeltsch for seemingly flimsy reasons, he endured repeated provocations from Sombart (1863–1941) without ever making a strongly worded reply. Weber's relationship with Sombart, whom he knew well from the 1890s and with whom he jointly edited the *Archiv für Sozialwissenschaft* from 1904, was in many respects more mysterious than his relations with women.

No other scholar of his time was more similar to Weber in his academic profile. His work too revolved around the genesis and world-historical specificity of modern capitalism; he too extended his economic analysis into a cultural history with ever broader horizons; he too was an insatiable bookworm, who with boundless curiosity accumulated far greater and more varied knowledge than most of his fellow scholars; and he too was always bubbling over with ideas and flashes of inspiration. He was for years greatly superior to Weber in his capacity for work and his impact on public opinion. Whereas, after his breakdown, Weber never managed to produce a finished book, Sombart brought out one title after another; and, however much his colleagues wrinkled their brows, his books sold more copies than Weber could even dream of. Before Christmas 1913 one bookseller reported that Sombart's *Der Bourgeois* was 'doing better than any novel'.[84] Sombart gave his lectures and talks in packed halls and received the top fees.[85]

If our memory of Sombart was not darkened by his later rapprochement with National Socialism and anti-Semitism, he would probably stand today as a scientific authority on a par with Weber.[86] Yet he remained without a regular professorship until the end of the empire. At first he was spurned as a sympathizer with social democracy, and this stigma remained with him even when he developed into a neoconservative with pessimistic ideas about progress. But there was also another factor: whereas Weber understood from the beginning how to give the impression of a thoroughly serious scholar, Sombart acquired the reputation of being unserious. Even for Lujo Brentano, who liked a touch of levity and elegance in academic life, Sombart was 'an utterly frivolous sort, who blew pretty-coloured bubbles in the air'.[87] According to Weber, Sombart had a literally 'blasé attitude' (MWG II/5, 597). Having for a long time been considered an extreme left-winger in the world of science, he trumped his colleagues' enthusiasm for the war in 1915 by publishing an anti-British pamphlet, *Händler und Helden* – the British as 'tradesmen', the Germans as 'heroes' – which laid it on so thick that it became too much even for most of the academic chauvinists, not to speak of Max Weber.

Nevertheless, one has the impression that, even if Weber conducted a running battle against some of Sombart's theses, he always did it with a somewhat benevolent wink. The tone of his letters to Sombart is a mixture of respect and gentle mockery. He never doubted that Sombart was a high-quality scholar and a man of courage, who had been unjustly denied a professorship and often subjected to unfair and narrow-minded criticism, even if he was also to blame for much of his academic misfortune (PE 198; MWG II/5, 638). For these and other reasons, Weber probably felt reluctant to give ammunition to Sombart's opponents. But, when Weber really got worked up, he did not allow university politics to hold him back; there are so many instances of this that the case of Sombart constitutes a revealing counter-example of Weber's 'bite inhibitions'. He who did not happily admit that he was building on others' achievements went out of his way to stress how much the Protestantism book owed to Sombart (PE 198). At the same time, a latent tension was already visible between the two scholars. Otto Hintze referred to this in a well-known formulation: 'For Sombart the spirit of capitalism wears more the colours of the Renaissance, for Weber more those of the Reformation.'[88] This contrast reflected a difference in their personalities.

In the following years, Weber and Sombart had to get along as best they could in their editorial work on the *Archiv für Sozialwissenschaft*, in the Verein für Sozialpolitik and in the German Sociological Society. In the value-judgement controversy, which was the dividing line in the social and economic sciences around the year 1910, Sombart and Weber stood together for a decisive separation between science and value-judgements. They did so for different motives, however: Sombart more out of cynicism and a lack of interest in politics, Weber because the basic values in life were for him beyond all science.

Sombart, evidently feeling challenged by Weber,[89] went on to attack his position on a broad front with three best-sellers in quick succession: *Die Juden und das Wirtschaftsleben* (1911), *Luxus und Kapitalismus* (1912) and *Der Bourgeois: Zur Geistesgeschichte des modernen Wirtschaftsmenschen* (1913).[90] 'On close inspection', wrote Michael Sukale, 'what Sombart did was pull Weber's whole work to pieces.'[91] In comparison with this concentrated offensive, which presented completely alternative accounts of history, the local criticisms of Rachfahl that so enraged Weber were a mere trifle.

Unlike in the past, Sombart now entered Weber's most distinctive field, religion, of which Weber thought he was constitutionally incapable of understanding anything at all. For Sombart in *Der Bourgeois*,[92] the decisive impetus for modern capitalism came from the Jews and their thousands-year-old tradition, or even from Thomas Aquinas's theory of virtue, so that the Puritans were demoted from the role that Weber had assigned to them. If it was true that the most important stimulus came from luxury consumption, then Weber had been barking up the wrong tree with his emphasis on asceticism. This corresponded to Sombart's basic position that the viewpoint of demand rather than production was the appropriate one for an understanding of the economic dynamic; this is the premise later adopted by Keynesian economic theory, although Sombart had intended (and Weber had seen) this and other historical outlines as so many trial balloons rather than fully fledged doctrines. Hartmut Lehmann has shown that the *oeuvres* of Weber and Sombart, in so far as they deal with the rise of capitalism, can be understood as 'almost a kind of dialogue' stretching over more than two decades.[93] From a distance they seem like two magicians who teased and provoked each other for years in friendly rivalry and kept pulling out new tricks from their huge reserve. But only rarely did either launch an open attack on the other.

The theoretical differences must have been all the more provocative to Weber because they were combined with a marked contrast in lifestyles, in a way that he would have found deeply hurtful. For, in his view of life, Sombart belonged among the eroticists: the party of Else Jaffé und Otto Gross. (Weber once advised Else that Gross might publish his article with Sombart (MWG II/5, 396f.).) Sombart developed his theories of capitalism on the basis of his experience that one could perfectly well be a hedonist and a hard worker at the same time. It is likely that he sometimes pretended to be more of a *bon viveur* than he actually was. In 1908 Weber wrote to Michels that Sombart had made himself impossible with his colleagues 'because of his sexual boasting, which I too find repugnant' (MWG II/5, 639). Marianne was happy if for a time Sombart had no need 'to make propaganda for his sexual ethics'.[94] For he fancied himself in the role of 'a Don Juan' (Emil Ludwig),[95] when in truth he must have been a hard-working bookish type whose life was tinged with melancholy.[96] Max Weber must have sensed this – otherwise he would have found it difficult to put up with Sombart's vanity and erotic swanking. Others, though, later put it around that he had had ' as many world-views as women' (WzG 169).

What would Max Weber have said if he had known that early in 1907, after Sombart had given her his book *Der Proletariat* as a Christmas present, Else wrote him an uninhibitedly effusive letter – the book had moved her 'in the heart' – which for a man like Sombart, coming from a woman like Else, could only have been understood as an amorous advance![97] It should almost be a matter for surprise that, as far as we know, the two did *not* have a love affair. On the other hand, Sombart had a close friendship with Lily Braun and her husband Heinrich Braun, Weber's pred-ecessor as editor of the *Archiv*[98] (whom he later denounced as a 'low-down scoundrel' for founding a rival journal) (MWG II/7, 778). One is reminded of Weber's triangle with Edgar and Else Jaffé. Whereas Sombart did not trouble himself too much with the *Archiv*, he kept up relations with its rival: this was another provocation in Weber's eyes.

The collaboration of Weber and Sombart at the *Archiv* began with a 'little row' early in 1904, when Sombart stubbornly insisted that one of his essays should be placed before one of Weber's, as otherwise he would feel 'substantively and personally overshadowed' by him. Weber gave in, but Marianne not without reason felt bitter about it: 'Really Sombart is unbe-lievably vain! – to harbour such feelings towards a man like Max, who is now, as it were, rising again from spiritual death, whereas he has always had opportunities to sparkle!'[99] Marianne was not the only one to think of Sombart in this way; even Hellpach, who had the greatest admiration for Sombart as a scholar and a man, complained that his 'boundless vanity' had put in the shade everything 'one might be used to in German profes-sors'.[100] In 1906 Weber wrote to Michels about Sombart: 'In private he is the most agreeable person I know – but for him three people are already a public' (MWG II/5, 173). And in 1903, after Weber had been on a trip with him to Heligoland that badly affected his 'nerves', he wrote to Marianne: 'Sombart is simply a child, with a child's brutality and bad behaviour, but even more with its underdevelopment, inner insecurity and longing for an honest friend of some kind. You always have to fight back feelings of sympathy, but also of anger and disgust, when he comes out with his confessions like that in the evening.' At the time Weber thought that, for all his philandering and public successes, Sombart was 'in a dreadful state . . . in every respect'.[101] The 'child' was in fact a year older than Weber.

In 1913 Weber learned from Michels of Sombart's complaint to him that 'scholarship was so "Weberianized"', and that he, Sombart, was 'fed up' with it (MWG II/8, 432). This was an opportunity for Weber to have done with the man once and for all, but it was also, whether he liked it or not, confirmation of his own growing academic charisma. It may well be, however, that there was another reason why Weber refused to be provoked by Sombart in the years between 1911 and 1913: namely, that he was then secretly adopting much of the erotic attitude to life. With his two lovers, Mina Tobler and Else Jaffé, he liked to read aloud the 'Requiem' that Rilke wrote for the painter Paula Modersohn after her death. She had been Sombart's lover and painted him in a way that bore no resemblance to the real Sombart, representing him more as a prophet of magical virility.

Later Weber even took over the excessive ecological determinism in Sombart's thesis that the pre-industrial world, resting on organic, renewable resources, had come undone through its destruction of the forests, and that this had forced the transition to coal use and over-exploitation of non-renewable resources (WG 261ff.).[102] It was Sombart, more than Weber, who trusted in the ability of man's creative spirit to triumph over any scarcity of natural resources. Weber's bite inhibition in relation to Sombart brings us to the heart of his later turn.

9

South – North – West – East: Changing Attempts at Spiritual Conquest of the World

A 'desire for universal history': regeneration through expansion, national and individual

Weber's inaugural lecture at Freiburg in 1895 climaxed in the point that the German nation must ensure its youth by rising to become a world power; there was no other choice but expansion or decline. The question is whether Weber was a good prophet for Germany. But in his own mind this point certainly contained a truth. Real and imagined journeys, a global broadening of the mind to the outer limits of human culture, became after the nadir of his illness a strategy for escaping the torments of introverted brooding and gaining a new sense of energy and youth.

It makes sense to consider Weber's trips to southern Europe, the North Sea and North America together with his imagined journey to Russia, and to relate them to his fixed idea that this was the only way of regaining some of his health and breaking some of the hold that soporific drugs had over him. His view of life is documented not only in his letters but also in his behaviour, and this shows best of all how important travelling had become for him. The compass changes appear to reflect his view that 'any cure in matters of the nerves' is a question of 'trial and error'.

In this respect he was going with the trend set by Wilhelm II; a popular joke of the time punned that the 'aged emperor' [*greise Kaiser*], Wilhelm I, had been succeeded by the 'travelling emperor' [*Reise-Kaiser*]. In Wilhelm II as in Weber, an abrupt change of direction sometimes occurred during his travels, in association with a change in wishful dreams. In 1898, during a trip to Constantinople and Jerusalem, the emperor revelled in the magic of the Orient; but then, in a trip to the North, he lost himself in fantasies inspired by Icelandic Eddas and Richard Wagner. The 'zigzag politics' that eventually led to the world war had its pendant in constantly changing travel fantasies, whose varied delights not only reflected the Kaiser's personal inclinations but were also typical of the upper classes in that age of historicism, imperialism and exoticism; they were, as we know today, a portentous characteristic of the surrounding culture.[1] Even the idea that anyone with nerve problems who can afford it should go travelling was common property of the age, although no one could really explain its logical basis; in fact, stimuli unsettling to the nerves were most likely to occur on a trip to foreign parts.[2] As the pleasure of travelling was often associated with erotic wish-dreams, many of the underlying motives were certainly left unsaid. A social psychology of travel would probably get to the heart of the history of German mentalities in the twentieth century, and it would find a treasure house in the testimony of and about Max Weber.

Strangely enough, as a result of the national Romantic movement, song culture and the ramblers' movement, nineteenth-century Germany witnessed the development of a high art in which the mother country became an enchanted land. But German *Gemütlichkeit* – that sense of cosy togetherness on which the *Heimat* cult was based – entered into crisis during what I have called the 'nervous age'; and Weber more than anyone could feel in himself that the 'old German' way of life did not sit well with the modern performance-oriented society. Moreover, it was precisely in his youth that the longing for distant lands became stronger than ever before. The new flood of photographic images meant that the spell of exotic worlds was present on all sides, and within much easier reach thanks to international transport. Around the year 1900 compound nouns including the 'world' were all the rage, as those including the word 'global' are today, and in both cases they were associated with a new kind of libido, a great curiosity and a megalomaniac sense of boundless expansion. One attraction of Christian missions and European colonialism was that they combined wanderlust with nostalgia: the homely sound of ringing bells mingled with African drum rhythms; the black, white and red flag of the German empire fluttered beneath palm trees; and the cannibal isles of the South Seas became the 'Bismarck archipelago'.

Weber's libido was originally directed more towards the familiar than the exotic; his relations with the opposite sex took place within his circle of relatives. He seems to have been surprisingly free from the colonial romanticism that was so popular in his younger years. In 1889, for example, he ridiculed as 'cannibal fodder' six young men who wanted to go and care for the sick in East Africa; he could see in them only 'hair-raising confusion' and a 'terrible awkwardness' (JB 179). Marianne thought that the European intervention in China in 1900 was 'awful': 'I am basically on the side of the Chinese', she wrote to Helene, 'but, you see, we Germans simply *must* take part; we have a duty to assert ourselves.'[3] Friedrich Naumann, however, of whom both Marianne and Helene thought highly, was one of the few to defend the 'Hun speech' in which Wilhelm II shouted to the expeditionary corps: 'No quarter shall be given, no prisoners shall be taken' – an order that clashed not only with the Sermon on the Mount but also with the rules of war and military honour.[4]

Relations with Naumann do not seem to have suffered as a result. For Max, the Chinese were certainly no barbarians but a high culture of ancient pedigree. What we do see in him subsequently, however, is a striving to conquer the world in the mind and to sharpen his understanding of

Germany's specificity by taking the road through other cultures. This already began in 1902–3, when he was torturing himself with the *Roscher and Knies* book: 'In the quiet of his study he was gripped by a desire for universal history – an urge to grasp and present as much as possible of all significant happenings in the world' (WB 3098). Weber's universal curiosity had something manic, as if it were a mental reaction against the onset of depression, although this mania – probably to the detriment of his scholarship – was often mixed up with ill humours that reminded him of his limits.

The art historian Carl Neumann, who was in touch with Weber as a fellow sufferer during the time of his depression, later wrote that in the early years of his acquaintance with Troeltsch Weber had laid out 'the road network for his conquistador expeditions' through which 'the imperialist impulse of his talents was supposed to raise specialist knowledge to an incredible total science'.[5] Eduard Baumgarten remarks that Weber had felt a marked urge to engage in practical activity, and presumably also politics, but that his illness made him aware of his real talent and 'turned his passion for clarity into the paths of a *theoretical* mastery of the world that soon become increasingly universal in scope' (B 425f.). There was often an inner link between this process of intellectual expansion and Weber's physical journeys, and also between both and Weber's search for release.

Therapy through travelling: a new philosophy of the nerves

In 1897 in Spain, in the final period before his breakdown, Weber announced a philosophy that involved strengthening the nerves through travel. When he was working, he never stayed in one place for long: 'We would, of course, not be in the mood for enjoying nature in the usual unconstrained way. One can simply expose oneself to the whole profusion of the powerful impressions, so that one may, first of all, regain one's full nervous strength and then be capable of objectively processing everything that one has experienced' (WB 234). In 1907 he wrote to his sister Klara that travelling was 'the only thing that usually helps' him (MWG II/5, 283). And, during all these years and afterwards, it 'continued to be very necessary' for him (WB 479), so that even in 1910, when Marianne's inheritance had long given the Webers a new prosperity, it was only with mixed feelings that he moved into the Fallenstein villa, since he feared that the high rent might curb the wanderlust for which he repeatedly borrowed money from his mother.

Already in 1900, during his worst period shortly before he went to the clinic in Urach, he would rather have been off travelling: 'He soon feels that he has to leave', Marianne wrote, 'and that he will only find real peace away from home.'[6] This was an *idée fixe* for neurasthenics: that they could not find peace at home, but only in distant lands. To remain at home incapable of work produces a feeling of emptiness, whereas travelling, even if it involves doing nothing, make one think that one is leading a full life. At the same time, however, Weber felt that the irregular life of a traveller was harmful to him. In the summer of 1901 in Rome, 'any deviation from the customary peace and uniformity . . . resulted in a quite disproportionate fatigue'.[7] For a long time, in fact, travelling was not always good for him, especially as he often left for the South too early in the year and was frustrated to find that there too the skies were grey and rainy. In 1909, he once exceptionally admitted that travelling was for the moment making him feel 'maddeningly lousy' (MWG II/6, 143). And in the spring of 1911, when Max complained from Italy of two 'bad nights', Marianne commented with gentle irony: 'I'm glad that at least it is in his beloved South that disaster has overtaken him.'[8]

Marianne had no choice but to swallow any resentment and adopt her husband's therapeutic philosophy. For her, too, it became a strict rule that Max had to get away when things were going badly for him, when nocturnal 'catastrophes' were on the rise and he was taking a 'dreadful' quantity of sleeping pills. On a trip in spring 1901 to Sorrento (not yet a de facto suburb of Naples), when they were living 'in complete rural quiet', Marianne wrote: 'But nothing is better for Max than to be as happy as possible and to see as many beautiful things as possible. I often think that, if we had done a trip like this two years ago and he had taken a semester off, he would have become healthy in a relatively short time. The doctors missed that: not one advised him to do it.'[9] But even on Capri 'one's thoughts keep ambling to home'.[10]

As far as she was concerned – and she too suffered a lot from 'nerves' and poor sleep – Marianne could never really fathom the logic of her husband's therapy. Early on, anger at the constant travelling welled up inside her; she experienced it as a life of 'idling' or 'loafing'.[11] She embodied the Puritan work ethic incomparably better than her husband did. 'To travel as little as possible' was her fond wish in August 1903,[12] at a time when she must already have been working flat out on her history of women and law. She began to let Max travel alone more and more often, and only rarely did she or he talk of regretting that they were not on a trip together. Marianne's resentment at travelling around all the time was inevitably directed against her husband.

Already in December 1902, when Max travelled to the Riviera alone and Helene offered to stand his wife to the journey as well, she expressed 'a thousand thanks' but refused to accept.[13] And in the autumn of 1913, when she was with Max in Rome again, she wrote that he was well but that she was not feeling so good. 'I always have so much difficulty adapting my d . . . nervous system to the changed conditions; one minute this is a problem, the next minute something else – the most awful is the sleep . . .'[14] Marianne too brooded about her 'nervous system', but it was soon clear to her what would do her good: solid work, a regular daily routine and her familiar bed at home. She felt sorry for Max, probably with good reason, since as a typical man and scholar he did not know how to keep busy at home and, without any intellectual work, would sit around in the ugliest of moods.

An obsessional relationship with nature: Weber's sensitivity to the weather

During his illness, Max Weber developed a sensitivity to changes in the weather that is rather astonishing for a desk-bound person who did not even like to go for long walks. For him the German winter was regularly a time of depression, which increased to the point of making him incapable of work. Whereas others found the cold refreshing or bracing, he could not shake off the thought that it was sapping his limited nervous strength and that he would have to rebuild his resources in the warmer months in order to withstand another winter. Naumann's words in the southern sunshine would have been inconceivable on his lips: 'God bless our grey skies! They have in them less joy, but more strength, than these skies south of the Alps!'[15] Weber was quite unable to comprehend this climatic cult of the North that was then coming into fashion. Again and again he complained that his mind froze up in the winter.[16] Still in the autumn of 1912, when things were otherwise going well for him, rainy weather undermined his capacity for work (MWG II/7–2, 667). While he fought against 'naturalism' in science, he fell into an obsessional dependence not only on his own autonomic nature but also on external nature. Later, in a gripping passage in *Economy and Society*, he described how the Egyptian pharaoh Akhenaton's introduction of the cult of the sun, a revolutionary act with 'immeasurable consequences', 'immediately stimulated naturalism': naturalism in art, but also 'the development of mimicry and dance' to conjure away evil spirits (E&S 405). This kind of naturalism was therefore anchored in man.

Following the gloom of winter, spring regularly came as an edgy, agitated time with sharp fluctuations of mood (MWG II/5, 73). 'Spring always considerably raises my nervous tension' (MWG II/5, 83). Willy Hellpach, one of his nerve doctors, subsequently made the link between climate and neurosis one of his hobby horses and wrote about the 'spring crisis' that often led to suicide and sexual crimes,[17] in the hope of teaching patients to see their 'weather sensitivity' as a 'sixth sense' rather than a pathological symptom.[18] But Weber did not experience it as a talent; he felt bound hand and foot by it.

Educated German men used to make fun of the weather as a topic of conversation, but for many years Weber could not stay away from it. Cold rainy weather was capable of arousing in him a serious aversion for the fatherland, causing the emotional basis of his chauvinism to crumble. In the spring of 1903, just after returning home to Heidelberg, Marianne wrote that the 'incredible weather' led her husband 'to curse his "fatherland" every day'.[19] And already in May 1900, before sending him to Urach, she wrote to Helene: 'Max even feels like going off to Italy – in short, I could imagine that he would like it very much there, but the only question is how that kind of climate would affect his sexual condition.'[20] The South was traditionally reputed to stimulate people's sexuality. In 1910, when new surroundings were taking shape around the Webers, she again reported: 'When Max is down-spirited (in English in the original) and the sun is hidden behind clouds, he always talks of our going to Italy in ten years. And I say: yes, then I'll be ready. But I'm afraid that I won't be ready and will have sunk roots here that will scarcely be possible to dig up or chop off.'[21] For some time she had been doing a lot to ensure that her husband too sank roots there.

Only a half-success: the Rome therapy

In the years from 1901 to 1903, however, Rome seems to have become Max Weber's city: *the* place, if there was one, where he felt a hint of recovery after his wretched experiences with the nerve specialists. Rome presented itself to Weber first of all as the Mecca of history and religion. In Eduard Baumgarten's words: 'In no city in the world did Max Weber feel so completely at home with his historical knowledge and attention as he did in Rome. No place in the world could have been better suited to help the slowly convalescing patient to rid himself of "national" economy and turn his gaze to the world religions' (B 666f.). Marianne also made Rome her refuge and salvation.

Earlier, in Ajaccio, Weber was hoping that his impressions of Rome would have a 'big effect';[22] he was already open to Roman revelations. In Richard Wagner's *Tannhäuser*, the eponymous knight who has become enslaved to demonic powers in the Venusberg is at first thrown into despair by the pope's refusal to grant him absolution, but at the end divine intervention finally releases him from his curse; even Protestants did not find it alien to think of Rome as a magical place that could work miracles, especially if, like Weber, they had been inwardly living in antiquity since an early age. The Romans, not the Germans, were for him 'the most virile people on earth'. And, in the academic field of tension, he fiercely defended Roman law with its emphasis on the individual against the constantly deprecatory remarks of experts in Germanic law. The 'dilettante view of the literati' that 'Roman law' promoted capitalism belongs in the 'schools for little children', he wrote. The best example was the joint-stock company, which had its roots precisely in Germanic law (MWG I/15, 454n.).

In her biography, Marianne traces the curative effects of the 'eternal city' to the way in which it blended in with history; there Max could 'expand his being into a vessel of history. Every old stone of the great city spoke to his historical imagination and stimulated him powerfully; this was better than any therapy.' And yet 'all of Rome would fizzle out as a remedy', at least initially, because of the presence of the depressive Otto Benecke (WB 247). The abundance of sights did not tempt Max outdoors, and indeed his walking problems grew worse. He gradually began to feel better only when

Figure 9.1 Max and Marianne Weber on their trip to Italy

the two learned to treat the chaotic city not in terms of sight-seeing quotas but as a place to live quietly by themselves.[23] So, the couple returned to Rome in September 1901 and this time stayed for half a year. In December Marianne wrote that 'we have only now taken the first real step to recovery' – by which she mainly meant a return of the intellectual interests that she had been missing for a long time in her husband: 'His brain is gradually getting under control the trouble caused by his nerves. He is able to read without painful consequences – just think that he could read next to nothing for three years! Now he reads the whole day like a man dying of thirst, and I have to drag him into the fresh air by force.'[24] Shortly afterwards: 'I'm sure Max is now reading five times faster than me.'[25] A new high from reading, after years as an intellectual cripple.

In April 1902 Weber himself wrote from Florence, an aesthetically much more homogeneous city than Rome: 'Here you see what a thoroughly ugly hole Rome really is. Yet I could live my whole life there, but would find it difficult here. Historical imagination is the main thing: if someone doesn't have any, he shouldn't go there.'[26] In February, however, he had been saddened by a visit that Friedrich Naumann made to Rome. The Webers showed him around the city, but they had the impression that 'the past speaks much less to him than to us' – at least that is how Marianne saw it. Naumann 'now feels too "modern", too socially and economically minded'; he lacks 'Max's historical imagination'. Max 'spoke like a waterfall', but then had 'several very bad nights in succession and was completely shattered and depressed, and I was secretly beside myself. I suppose that was the price we paid for Naumann's visit.'[27] Naumann brought Weber's thoughts back to politics and therefore to an area that got him worked up. At the time it was still possible that Naumann's National-Social Association might enter the Reichstag. Its failure to do so in 1903 thus cleared the air and gave Max an element of calm. Now it was finally clear that his path lay only in theoretical work, not in politics.

'Nature and all things did them good'

For the typical lover of Italy, the country's magic lay in its combination of the beauties of culture and nature. It was the nature not only of orange, olive and cypress groves but also of man himself: the naturalness with which people associated with one another in the open air, quite unlike the indoor social gatherings of the frosty North; and the (seemingly) natural way in which they gave full expression to their drives. Goethe – who, as Weber knew, 'changed under the skies of the South' and overcame his sexual inhibitions – was even more enthralled by nature there than by the ancient buildings; he resembled Naumann in the delight he took in Italy.

For Max Weber, too, it was at least as much the nature in Italy as the history which did him good. Marianne had already written from Ajaccio: 'The scenery and climate always do their work on Max and lift him out of depression and anxiety.'[28] Weber's extreme sensitivity to the weather and his truly addictive longing for sun and warmth indicate that it was mainly nature which drew him to the South. When the Webers returned to Rome in the early summer of 1902 'in order to come to terms with the relics of superimposed centuries' – one senses Marianne's irony between the lines – they were especially happy lying on the green grass of the Villa Borghese and watching how 'the young clerics divested themselves of their loose cassocks and played ball like other worldlings. Nature and all inanimate things did them good' (WB 249). When the women's rights campaigner Alice Salomon visited the Webers in Rome in late March 1903 and fell upon them with the latest news from Berlin, Marianne was certainly pleased to see her, but for Max it 'destroyed nature's mood magic'.[29] The Webers had an eye not only for garden settings of nature but also for the semi-wild Campagna landscapes beloved of painters. In 1913 they were saddened to see how the 'grand desolation' of this once Arcadian countryside had been 'gradually chased away by the successful campaign against malaria' and supplanted by agriculture and 'new white houses'. But their melancholy gave them a bad conscience, as any modern person could only welcome this 'reclamation'.[30]

The secret of this enthusiasm for Italian 'nature' was in no small measure sexual, not only for Goethe and all the artists from the North who found graceful nude models in Italy, but also for historians, ranging from Ranke to Meinecke. Friedrich Meinecke, who confessed to having been 'in many respects' a late developer and a very inhibited young man, blithely described how the change came in his mid-thirties when he and his wife did not travel as usual to the Alps but finally wandered south into Italy; ten months later their first child was born.[31] It was almost the normal thing to travel to Italy with erotic expectations, and it would have been a miracle if the Webers had been free of such wish-dreams. But in their case the dream did not come true. At times, however, they were overcome with a feeling of being at one with nature, so that their individual fates were no longer meaningful.

The elective Italian Robert Michels: a Weberian alter ego

Probably more important for Weber's intellectual-erotic development than all his other 'experiences' in Italy was his twelve-year friendship with Robert Michels (1876–1936), who moved to Turin in 1907. Of Weber's acquaintances, he had the best knowledge of Italy and was its most ardent enthusiast; he chose to become Italian during the world war and publicly turned against Germany. This led to a break with Weber, who reproached him for 'stabbing his country in the back in the hour of its gravest mortal danger'.[32] Probably this 'war loss' between friends was even more painful than the break with Troeltsch, for Weber must have felt a deeper attachment to Michels than to any other academic in his milieu.[33]

No fewer than 132 of Weber's letters to Michels have survived, the first dating from New Year's Day 1906. It is between then and 1915 that their friendship is best documented, far better than most of his other relationships about which we would like to know a lot more. On 9 January 1908 Weber addressed him for the first time as 'dear friend'. Wolfgang Mommsen judges the friendship in superlatives: it was an 'extraordinarily close relationship, which had no parallels in Weber's biography for either intimacy or intensity'; 'not by chance do Weber's letters to Michels contain the most spontaneous and direct positions that we have of his on political, scientific and personal problems' (WuZ 197f.).[34] Wilhelm Hennis finds many of the letters 'simply captivating'.[35]

When Weber wrote to Michels – and it evidently gave him a lot of pleasure – he often used a lively and impudent, racy and trenchant tone, such as one would vainly search for in most of his correspondence. He liked to play the older and more experienced man and to reprimand Michels, even though he too was over thirty. Occasionally this occurs to Weber too: 'Again and again I suddenly catch myself in a kind of schoolmaster's pose towards you! I long to give you the opportunity to turn the tables for once' (MWG II/6, 62). He repeatedly pours his heart out to him, apparently seeing a potential fellow sufferer in the highly strung Michels.[36] He sold Michels his piano to get the money for his beloved trips, though not at a price 'between brothers'. He tried to recruit him to work for the *Archiv* and the *Grundriß der Sozialökonomik*. And he took him into his confidence on sexual matters, even on the turmoil caused by Else's affair with Alfred (MWG II/7-1, 172ff.).

When the two first got to know each other, Michels was a supporter of social democracy. But he was sympathetic to radical syndicalism and developed an aversion to the hierarchical discipline of the German Party. Although he had a brilliant mind, he failed in his attempts to qualify as a university lecturer in Germany and, with Weber's support, achieved his ambition only in Turin.[37] Weber was outraged at this politically motivated exclusion of a highly talented scholar by the German university system, especially as he recognized that Michels was thoroughly capable of keeping his political positions (which, as it turned out, were none too stable) separate from his academic work. Weber's fight to demarcate science from value-judgements, and his struggle against the German spirit of subservience, should be understood against the background of his friendship with Michels.

In 1906, when Michels tried without success to gain his *Habilitation* qualification in Jena, it was all too obvious that the decisive criteria for his rejection were political rather than academic. Weber wrote to him that such practices were a mockery of 'scientific freedom' and a 'shame and humiliation for a cultured nation'; even Russia was for the moment ahead of the Germans in academic freedom.[38] Michels's close acquaintance Max Quarck – the social democrat politician and journalist who fourteen years earlier had complained about the one-sided sources used for Weber's study of agricultural labour, and who later again crossed Weber's path in his role as adviser on the Weimar constitution (MWG I/16, 58, 67)[39] – would have liked to publish Weber's letter in his Frankfurt-based *Volksstimme*, but he did not believe that Weber would agree to it. Michels thought differently and made a kind of wager with Quarck – which he lost. In fact, Weber was feeling very ill when he learned of this wager about his own courage, and he exploded at 'Herr Quarck's foolish effrontery' (MWG II/5, 238–46). Seldom had he been faced with behaviour that so offended his sense of honour. The matter gave him no peace; in 1908 he published in the *Frankfurter Zeitung* another polemical article against the German restriction of 'academic freedom' to people considered presentable at court.[40]

From the outside, the Michels affair had some similarity with the case of Sombart, whose university career was also long obstructed by his original proximity to Marxism, and who also had a marked interest in sexual matters. Michels, however, represented something different to Weber: not a philanderer, but a moralist with convictions; and this drew him humanly closer to Weber. 'You are a basically honest fellow', including in your capacity for intellectual self-criticism, he assured him in 1908 (MWG II/5, 616). Mommsen is quite right to suspect that Weber saw in Michels his 'alter ego in the ethics of conviction' (WuZ 198): a kindred spirit who expressed the rigour of conviction that Weber felt in himself, with a thoroughness and consistency that Weber denied himself. At Christmas 1909 he wrote to Frau Michels that he found 'so agreeably much that is similar' in her husband's 'principled way of seeing and approaching things', such as he had come across only rarely in other people (MWG II/6, 349).

Weber participated intensively in the formative stages of Michels's *Political Parties* (MWG II/6, 754–61), which first appeared in 1910, and on reading it today we think we can understand what he meant. It has a powerful analytic grasp, of the same calibre as Weber's own work, a combination of bold astuteness and hard empirical slog. Michels dedicated the first edition to Weber, but was later disappointed that his remarks on political parties in *Economy and Society* were 'only sporadic and disjointed'.[41] Nor does Weber make any mention there of his former friend, who did after all pioneer the sociology of parties. Michels's crossing of lines in the war must have hurt him really deeply.[42]

Weber's main interlocutor on erotic matters

Michels was Weber's best interlocutor not only on questions to do with social democracy and political parties, but also on erotic matters. One of the main reasons for this was probably that Weber, contrary to his usual solicitude, liked to stay up until late at night talking with Michels and his wife without thinking about sleep, and then uncomplainingly used up 'a whole pot of ointment' – presumably opium ointment.[43] The evenings he spent with the couple were indeed highly entertaining. According to Weber, Michels himself was 'nervously fidgety and abrupt, arbitrary in his accusations and intolerant of any contradiction, not to speak of the slightest criticism': little wonder that Weber thought he could apply the lessons of his own nervous problems to Michels without making any cuts.

Michels had a 'graceful' wife, a 'very nervous' son, Mario (whose good nature the father despised as cowardliness), and a daughter, Manon, then six years of age, 'a delightful *nervous* little rascal, naively coquettish, who gesticulates like an actress'. The description of the Michels family already tells us a lot about the spectrum of Weber's nerve semantics. Robert Michels played at 'adultery' with Manon in front of Weber, the six-year-old miming 'the adultery with splendid gestures, facial expressions and conversation'. Frau Michels showed her disapproval of the scene, while Michels bit off 'all his nails . . . in painful embarrassment', and Weber had his fun (MWG II/7-1, 199f.). Then, 'of course, long conversations about eroticism'. Of course: it was not the first time, and it did not bring 'much that was new'. Michels declared: 'The awareness of being able to conquer keeps one young. Therefore: no "marriage", that is, no renunciation of feeling "young".' In reality he was attached to his wife. If Weber could tolerate, even accept, Michels's erotic flights of fancy more than he could those of an Otto Gross, it was probably because Michels recognized that there is also something beautiful in a trusting relationship and that there is not just one patented formula for the expression of all sexual needs. He too shared Weber's basic feeling that it was necessary to live with deep antinomies.

It was with great pleasure that in the spring of 1911, at Vevey on Lake Geneva, Weber read Michels's new book *Die Grenzen der Geschlechtsmoral*,[44] a book dedicated to '*mia piccola prediletta*' Manon. Full of joy, he described how the little one had shamelessly jumped around 'completely naked' during a visit by some painters, but had cried when he had carried her half-undressed to say good night in the drawing-room. When the contradiction in her behaviour was pointed out to her, she protested: '*Nuda, si che mi piace, ma svestita, no, ho vergogna*' ('Naked, yes, I like it, but not undressed – then I feel ashamed').[45] Apparently Michels was disappointed that Weber did not respond as profusely to the erotic book he sent him as to the one on the sociology of parties. But Weber reassured him that he would have liked to write him 'very many' letters on the subject if his health had been better (MWG II/7-1, 178). Evidently Michels was also disappointed that Weber was not indignant at a passage in the book where Michels sang the praises of polygamy:

> Marriage may bring a fine and tranquil felicity, it may be the source of economic well-being, and the basis of a fruitful co-operation between husband and wife . . .; but it is the tomb of lyric love. . . . He therefore who craves for a life full of poetry should renounce marriage. . . . His head will always touch the skies; celestial music will continually assail his ears; . . . he will lead a life socially idle and useless, but individually ecstatic. . . . Besides, for both sexes, a change in love-relationships is equivalent to a sprinkling with the waters of health, physical and psychological. . . . Woe to him, however, when he falls ill. Since he lacks the affectionate love and care of a faithful wife and devoted children . . . age will now advance with rapid strides, and he will be a prey to sadness and tardy penitence.[46]

Weber, who well knew that he would be lost without his 'faithful wife', but that male sexual fantasy did not move along the correct paths of marriage, found it funny that Michels was disappointed at his lack of indignation and took the passages apart as if he was dealing with a scientific work:

> Indignation? At what? My intellect bristles at a way of contrasting things that does not correctly grasp the problems. What should a man avoid if he wishes to live 'poetically'? What *must* he avoid? The registry office? Or the intention to be monogamously 'faithful'? Or the communal household? Or the children's wars? Or all of these together? Or each one individually? For marriage is simply a complex of features, yet people want to know which is here the essential one. (MWG II/7-1, 171f.)

In fact, Weber knew from experience that the reality associated with the word 'marriage' was anything but unambiguous. Moreover, Michels did not suggest that sexual satisfaction was the elixir of life; he even thought that sexual intercourse could be foregone 'without serious physical disadvantages'. And, of course, being married to a charming woman, Michels knew that marriage can also be filled with delights. He thought that German women in particular should be reminded of this, and he even mentioned an anecdote involving the Borgia Pope Alexander VI, otherwise infamous for poisonings and incest. One day he heard of a case of unintentional necrophilia in Germany, where a man performed the sexual act with his wife without noticing that she was dead, since he 'was used to absolute passivity on his wife's part'. The pope grew worried about this and 'issued a Bull recommending the women of Germany to play a more active and lively part in the love-act'. Michels commented, in a loose rendering of Giordano Bruno, that, if the story was not true, it was a happy invention.[47]

For Michels, the god Eros was a 'soul without a fatherland' – as was the socialist in principle[48] – but in his concrete epiphany he appeared in a number of national metamorphoses. This combination of Eros and nation was not the least reason for the intellectual appeal that Michels gave to eroticism, even if, unlike Weber, he did not manage so well to knit together his reflections on erotic and sociological questions; the former remained too pleasure-oriented in his work, too little geared to value-free science. Although Italian pairs of lovers did not smooch in public like German couples, Italians for Michels generally had a natural, uninhibited and unforced relationship to sexuality – and not only sexuality. 'A frank naturalness in all things is a hereditary endowment of the Italian nation.'[49]

It pleased Weber when Michels spoke in erotic metaphors of the 'prudishness' of social democracy 'towards bourgeois lovers' (MWG II/5, 99), probably with the implication that, precisely in the way they bristled at bourgeois embraces, many social democrats revealed to experts that they would secretly like to be loved by the bourgeoisie. Weber too, visibly prompted by Michels's example, gave the appearance of being unprejudiced and worldly wise in sexual matters, and even of having an intimate knowledge of prostitution, which was being investigated at the time by a psychiatrist well known to him, Hans Gruhle. When Michels wrote an article on 'sexual prowling' in German and Roman lanes for a review, *Mutterschutz*, that Weber despised, Weber made fun of his apparent contempt for bourgeois morality and his idealization of the Romans, and referred to memories from Michels's own family to suggest that until recently people had been sexually uninhibited in Germany too:

You are yourself a moralist from head to toe . . . – why don't you confess it? German prostitutes come away from you in too bad a light; they have their firm 'ethic' like everyone else, and Parisians seem to me a little idealized. Otherwise I quite agree! I have the same attitude as Italians to the public 'smooching' of German lovers, although Italians do seem too 'prudish' in this respect. As to intercourse (*sexual* intercourse) between engaged couples, people used to think differently from how they mostly do today: my eldest uncle came into the world a month after the wedding, and the father was Lützower, a 'moralist' and – privy councillor. (MWG II/5, 210f.)

Weber was especially critical of one passage in the first edition of Michels's *Political Parties* where he had equated differences of interest with a 'difference in lifestyles'. This seemed to him 'a relic of *bad* materialism' (MWG II/6, 760) – note that Weber also knew a 'good' materialism. At the time, in 1910, he knew from his own experience how certain lifestyle contradictions ran right through the bourgeoisie, and that quite a few workers corresponded to the current criteria of a 'bourgeois lifestyle' far better than did many a bourgeois citizen. For Weber, lifestyle was something primary and not a mere function of class interests.

Thoughts about natural law on the North Sea

On the early trips to the South with Marianne between 1901 and 1903, Weber at first had only a limited capacity to digest his impressions of Italy. Intellectually more productive horizons opened up with the travels of 1903 to the Dutch and Belgian coasts, which were more in tune with his work on *The Protestant Ethic*. In the nervous topography of the time, the stimulating climate of the North Sea was not held in the highest regard; but Weber was 'less exhausted than usual'. 'He was not only open to new impressions but also felt impelled to preserve in outline form what he had seen and experienced' (WB 268). This marked a new stage in his recovery since Rome. Marianne was therefore even worried in the summer of 1905 when Max showed no inclination to holiday there, which must mean that for a time his travel bug was giving way to the urge to work.[50]

Weber, now travelling alone, was more concerned to find cheap lodgings since he had lost his professorial income, so he stayed at a 'popular hotel' in Ostend along with some itinerant German journeymen and took pleasure in their 'quite uninhibited' and, in its way, 'decent' behaviour.

The discussions about marital *fidelity* are delightful; the wife's right is regarded as the right to her husband's body, that is, its functions. There is a difference of opinion as to whether (in accordance with 'natural right') the wife has an absolute monopoly or whether it is enough that a man does not *weaken* himself (while travelling) and thus does not 'abridge' her rights (very crude jokes at this point); the married men favour the stricter view. (WB 272)

He also discerned 'natural law' outdoors when looking at the sea, in a sense that people in the Low Countries would have found highly offensive: 'behind the dunes the roaring sea demands the land which by rights has been its property for a long time' (WB 274).

One looks in vain for names such as Michelangelo, Titian or Raphael in Weber's letters from Italy, but he was again and again stimulated by Rembrandt in the North. The paintings of the Dutch master drew him into the atmosphere of *The Protestant Ethic*. He knew, of course, that Rembrandt's lifestyle was not exactly Puritanical, but he thought that his artistry was 'very strongly influenced by his religious environment' (PE 169). The art historian Carl Neumann, the foremost Rembrandt scholar of the age, with whom Weber was then in contact, contrasted the animated naturalism of this 'Nordic' painting (which shocked the beholder with extremely ugly female nudes) to the cult of ideal nudity in Italian painting.[51] Rembrandt 'believed in reality', he wrote, but he saw it with the eyes of a mystic and illuminated it with a glow of divine light. Later, Neumann was actually bitter in his polemics against Simmel's book on Rembrandt, which was deaf to any talk of 'holiness' in the Dutchman's art.[52]

Weber's impressions of Rembrandt in The Hague in 1903 are an indication that his eye had been trained by Neumann. He spent a particularly long time in front of *Saul and David* and bought a reproduction to take home; he whose affliction would later be chased away by Mina Tobler's love and piano-playing appears to have identified with the downcast Saul listening to the young harp player, and he was overwhelmed by the way in which Rembrandt could transform gross naturalism into something spiritual. It was 'all but incomprehensible' that 'two obvious Jews (*Knalljuden*) . . . could be painted in such a way that one sees only the human beings and the moving power of the tones' (WB 270).[53] At that time Weber's relationship with nature was expressed more clearly in his aesthetic than in his writings. Much later Marianne stood for a while before *Saul and David* and saw in Saul the 'ominous misery of a man who was chosen as a tool, failed to prove his worth and was rejected by God'; she makes a link between Rembrandt and *The Protestant Ethic*, since Rembrandt 'belonged to a free Protestant sect that rejected dogma and denominationalism in favour of an exclusive orientation to the Bible'.[54]

To America!

The following year, 1904, brought the greatest travel adventure in Max Weber's life: his two-and-a-half-month trip to the United States, from early September through to November, which he undertook together with Marianne. The main destination was the Congress of Arts and Science in St Louis, which the German American psychologist Hugo Münsterberg (known to the Webers from the Freiburg period) had organized side by side with the world exhibition. In this way part of the Webers' travel costs was covered, but they still had to pay out so much that they gave up the idea of buying a 'tiny little house'.[55] Some thirty other German academics, who had agreed to take part when there was an expectation of greater funding, eventually decided to pull out, so that, as Marianne put it, 'German science was pitifully represented in St Louis, much to Münsterberg's sorrow'.[56]

But, although Weber ended the five-year 'spell of silence' in St Louis (WB 291), the congress played a very minor role in their American trip: he does not seem to have left a lasting impression either among the participants or in the wider public.[57] It was precisely around this time that the hold of German scholarship in the United States began to decline, as reactions to European influences made themselves increasingly felt.[58] For the travellers from Germany, however, the extra-curricular impressions of America were the main point of the exercise.

Max and Marianne were both extremely receptive to the new impressions. A few months before the trip, Hugo Münsterberg had sought to improve German–US relations with his voluminous work on the Americans, which countered the cliché of the New World's lack of culture and other prejudices common among Germany's educated middle classes. Münsterberg even found an element of honourable civic culture in the lynch justice against blacks, America's disgrace in the eyes of the world.[59] One critic wrote that his work was 'much too prettified and too narrowly observed from the author's study'.[60] For the Webers, on the other hand, it was the ideal preparatory reading; they therefore landed in New York with a favourable attitude.

Max Weber had already been curious about America as a child: the family's friendship with the German American Friedrich Kapp encouraged him in this, and the boy's curiosity was not diminished in the least when Kapp sometimes angrily described the USA as a dangerously wild 'barbaric country' and the American as the 'most unrestrained child of nature and . . . the most obtuse of all civilized people'[61] – not at all a delicate German idealist's cup of tea. In 1883, Kapp arranged for Weber's father to take part in the inaugural journey of the transcontinental Northern Pacific Railroad (R 483f.). Early in 1893 Weber and Paul Göhre planned to travel together to the world exhibition in Chicago, at the very time when Göhre made his marriage proposal to Marianne, but Max's engagement with her put an end to the project.

The ocean sleep and the new feeling of strength in the New World

Now the youthful dream finally came true and brought with it a sense of rejuvenation. Already Weber had been consoling himself after bad nights by reading Baedeker's guide to America.[62] The first part of *The Protestant Ethic* was influenced by the forthcoming trip, which was presumably a direct impetus for its composition; the last part was completed after his return. Thus, an interrelationship between travel and scientific work was programmed in advance, even if Weber spoke in St Louis not about the Protestant ethic but about his old topic, Prussian-German agrarian relations, now without the nationalist angle of the 1890s.[63]

Weber's New York experience of 1904 was a sharp contrast to his Roman experience of the year before. Whereas the weight of bygone times in Rome had a highly volatile effect in therapeutic terms – Weber had felt at home in antiquity since his early years, and Rome evoked much of his own past – the wild vitality of the New World immediately fascinated him and filled him with a new sense of strength. He already felt better than for a long time during the smooth sea crossing, spared seasickness and blessed with a huge appetite. It was like in the old days of high-spirited eating, and Marianne had to 'resign (herself) to seeing his beauty disappear again' (WB 280); the loss of appetite associated with his illness had made him slimmer and more handsome in his wife's eyes. The 'swell of the green and blue ocean obligingly rocked him to sleep, a sleep for which he ordinarily had to struggle' (WB 280). From now on, the heaving of the sea would be one of the elemental experiences for a man who was anyway fond of ocean metaphors. 'No form of existence is as much designed for vegetating absolutely contentedly and unintellectually as a voyage', Marianne mused. 'One becomes a mere blank, or a jellyfish that consists only of digestive organs' (WB 280).

Weber's trip across the United States often worked on his mood as a continuation of this experience of nature. One has the impression of lasting euphoria after the cheerless years, and of a vitalist enthusiasm that saw life bursting out everywhere and did not stop to ask what was good or bad in it. It did not even seem to bother him that he had to start taking sleeping draughts again after they landed. His reports from America often seem to resonate with the guffaw that strikes Europeans as typically American. In November, on the return voyage, Marianne sometimes felt she was bringing home 'a convalescent who had become aware again of the capital sum of strength that he had ever so slowly accumulated'; all the more was she depressed a month later, when the old insomnia reappeared and Max went off 'at night looking for cheese and other things to eat'.[64]

Experiences of trips to America run like a red thread through German history in the industrial age, from the time of Friedrich List and the early railways down to the present day. People talked of their America trip for the rest of their life and presented it as a kind of initiation into the very latest world, into the future with its frightening as well as its promising side. The history of German technology, economic life and mentalities since the mid-nineteenth century may even be structured according to different stages in the reception of America.[65] The period around 1900 marked a first turning point in this development.

The historian Eduard Meyer, who also travelled to St Louis in 1904, thought he could detect that 'the mad rush of economic life' had made the Americans 'uniformly an overwrought, physically and psychologically unhealthy nation'. 'During my trip to America in 1904 no question was asked me so often as whether I thought the Americans were a race undergoing degeneration and destined to go under.'[66] Weber did not report such questions; presumably the traveller was not without some influence over the questions that were put to him. For the chemist Wilhelm Ostwald –

the proponent of an energy-centred world-view and, in William James's opinion, the most interesting of the German professors assembled in St Louis[67] – the American belief (proclaimed by none other than James) that human energy can be increased through an effort of will was a disastrous error that would cost James his health and his life. As Ostwald's companions tried to impress on him that Americans always expected to be praised by foreign guests, he extended to them a sarcastic compliment in an after-dinner speech: he had been wondering the whole time just where Americans got their highly acclaimed surplus of energy; the solution to the puzzle could only be that they had discovered how to convert noise into energy, since noise was a constant presence in America.[68] At heart he was probably convinced that Americans were well on the way to ruining their nerves in the fashion of William James. Max Weber, however, who was only just recovering from a major nervous breakdown, experienced the United States in quite a different way.

'He watched, listened, transformed himself into his environment'

When Weber landed in New York early in September 1904, his cultured travelling companions took an instant dislike to the turbulence of the traffic and skyscraper architecture; even Troeltsch found 'the external symbols of the American spirit, as they present themselves here in New York, alien and repulsive'. Weber, however, refusing from the outset to play the German *Bildungsbürger* and unworldly idealist, found 'absolutely everything *beautiful* and better than at home' – at least so we are told by Marianne, who herself felt uneasy in the foreign new world.[69] Weber remained in a favourable mood throughout the trip, his constant enthusiasm even leading to episodes of disgruntlement with the much more critical Troeltsch.[70] But he did not idealize the country; his way of observing America was rather an exercise in value-freedom, whereas the others came up with assessment routine as a matter of course and classified impressions according to whether they were ugly or beautiful. One has to read other reports from America at that time to appreciate what was distinctive about Weber's perception.

Weber looked in the USA for traces of the Puritan tradition that he was then analysing in *The Protestant Ethic*, but he by no means saw the country through those spectacles alone. Often we have a sense that the New World fascinated him as a testing-ground where people's conditions of life could be observed in a raw state: a purely cultivated specimen of socialization, with no assistance from the state or bureaucracy.[71] It is true that in retrospect Weber thought that the 'scientific' results of the trip were in no way equal to the outlay (WB 304), but in Marianne's view it brought him advances in his appropriation of the world, as when he stayed once with a half-breed Indian in Oklahoma: 'He watched, listened, transformed himself into his environment, and thus everywhere penetrated to the heart of things.' In all this Weber 'remained intensely receptive; after all, he had the ability to make something of everything by recasting it intellectually' (WB 291, 300).

The star of the group of German professors in St Louis was the theologian Adolf von Harnack. His translated book *What Is Christianity?*[72] was a best-seller, and in American churches a lecture on Harnack's theology would sometimes replace a service (WB 289). Weber, on the other hand, was virtually unknown: few came to listen to him in St Louis, especially as he preferred to speak in German rather than his 'Nigger English'. At least he enjoyed the freedom of anonymity when he mixed with 'good plain people'; they laughed heartily with him, 'often slapped him on the knee and called him a "mighty jolly fellow"' (WB 299f.). It would have been unthinkable for him to come out with the kind of aggrieved professorial remark that one hears in Karl Lamprecht's *Americana*: 'Repeatedly I had to explain to people from good society, sometimes quietly, sometimes with unmistakeable emphasis, that as a German professor I was used to being treated in a certain way'[73] – and Lamprecht, though subject to attack in Germany, was seen abroad as the greatest German historian of his day,[74] far more highly regarded than Weber in the United States.

Seeing the USA through the lens of *The Protestant Ethic*?

To what extent did Weber in America seek and find evidence that his picture of the spirit of Anglo-American capitalism in *The Protestant Ethic* was still valid? Strangely enough, it looks as if the trip was not too productive from that point of view, as it did not strengthen Weber in the 'spiritualist' picture of the world to which he was leaning from time to time. The rough draft for the second part of *The Protestant Ethic* was already basically complete, even if in the United States Weber expanded on it with reference to further Anglo-American literature.[75] He found there less material for his thesis than he could have uncovered through intensive research. His feeling of happiness in America is to be explained not by any confirmation of previous positions, but rather by a presentiment of something new.

An article on Protestant free churches and sects, which Weber published in 1906 and later expanded several times, drew mostly on his experiences in America. His highly debatable general impression started from the premise that the old Puritanical America was 'in fairly rapid decline'[76] and that America was formally repudiating its 'sectarian origins' (PE 218).[77] He made no secret of the fact that he regretted this development: 'In so far as the true Yankee spirit still prevailed, American democracy . . . was never merely a sand-heap of isolated individuals, but to a large extent a maze of *exclusive* associations, whose archetype is the sects.'[78] From the vantage point of 1919, he could write that the once 'very intense church life, which prevailed in all areas not immediately flooded by European immigrants', could not at the time have escaped any visitor to America.[79] But it was no longer the old religiosity of Baxter and Bunyan, which – at least in Weber's imagination – had emerged from a lonely and desperate struggle. The point of several stories that Weber tells of contemporary American sects is that religion has become a mere function of economics and faith identical with credit – and he says as much with brutal directness. When he was staying with relatives in the country in North Carolina, he witnessed a Baptist christening in an icy river, from which the adults who were baptised came out 'snorting' and shivering from the cold.

> A relative,[80] who was standing next to me, and who, in accordance with German traditions, was looking down his nose in an unchurchly manner, became more attentive as one of the young men was dipped in the water: 'Look at him – I told you so!' To the question: 'Why did you, as you say, think you could see it coming?', he replied: 'Because he wants to open a bank in M.' – 'Are there so many Baptists hereabouts, then?' – 'Certainly not. But now that he's baptised, he'll get the customers from the whole area and outcompete everyone else.'[81]

Only in a footnote does Weber correct a little the highly sobering impression. The relative spoke afterwards to the priest: 'Hallo, Bill, wasn't the water pretty cool?' And his 'quite serious answer' was: 'Jeff, I thought of some pretty hot place, and so I didn't care for the cool water.'[82] The 'pretty hot place' was hell. So, after all, Weber found the old Puritanical fear of hell, which he later so effectively depicted in *The Protestant Ethic*.

If Weber had programmed his observations to consolidate the picture he drew in *The Protestant Ethic*, he would certainly have found more by way of confirmation. Other travellers to America around that time were surprised at the continuing strength of the churches there.[83] Naumann believed, on the basis of travel reports, that Chicago was 'a city of churches and chapels, such as only a medieval locality has ever been before'.[84] If Weber had gone further west, he would even have seen the churches gaining ground in quite a few places; it was precisely in the lawless conditions there that a 'business Christianity' was most needed to ensure a minimum of solidity.[85]

'The terrible immigration'

Of the Americans they met in New York, Marianne found the industrial inspector and 'impassioned socialist' Florence Kelley 'by far the most outstanding figure'; she had got the inspectorate accepted in Illinois, headed it for many years and put into it that tenacious energy which Marianne missed in her beloved factory inspector Else Jaffé.[86] In this connection Max Weber remarked that, in spite of everything, the Americans were 'a wonderful people, and only the Negro question and the terrible immigration constitute the big black clouds' (WB 302). The 'terrible immigration'! At the congress of sociologists in 1912, Weber remarked that 'the Yankees' huge capacity for assimilation' was no longer equal to the 'vast' levels of current immigration.[87]

Kapp, himself an expert on immigration, would have preferred to repeal the universal suffrage law, because German Americans were regularly driven into a corner by new immigrants from Ireland.[88] The influx from southern and eastern Europe reached a peak around the year 1900, but Jews also flooded in after the Russian pogroms. Public attitudes, traditionally quite favourable to immigration, began to undergo a marked change.[89] Florence Kelley probably had reason to feel uneasy about immigrants, since strike-breakers typically came from their ranks, and one report claimed that employers were turning a deaf ear to labour protection on the grounds that 'the immigration ships are bringing enough workers'.[90]

Weber must have been reminded of his study of agricultural labourers. Immigration was also repressing the Puritan America whose spirit he had just evoked in *The Protestant Ethic* – although he was scarcely ignorant of the fact that many East European Jews were as close to that spirit as the German Americans with whom the Webers had most contact because of family connections. Cultured German travellers to the United States often felt that fellow countrymen living there were not exactly worthy representatives of German culture.[91] Similarly, Münsterberg complained that, in contrast to the Irish, Germans in the United States were never ready to stick together politically, unless it was against temperance laws or for the 'right to the beer barrel'.[92] Only against the Puritanical tradition did German Americans stick together. The Webers' American relatives had come down in the world and did not make a good impression on them: they had lost their German culture without becoming real Americans; 'they lacked the Yankee spirit', but allowed their children to tyrannize them in the name of a 'democratic' upbringing.[93]

The ecstatic religiosity of the blacks

The Webers could observe the power of religion incomparably better among African Americans than among their German American relatives, and indeed they did not miss the opportunity to attend a 'Negro service'. What they found there was a form of religiosity based on enthusiasm and ecstasy rather than asceticism, which Weber could not yet fit into his thought processes. As the lay preacher reached an ever more passionate crescendo, 'a kind of whispering echo', which at first 'painfully reminded (the Webers) of intestinal rumbling', spread through the congregation. They really began to feel 'uncomfortable and queer' as the shrill voices repeated: 'Yes, Yes!' (WB 300). Nevertheless, the Negro blues in these black churches had greater musical appeal for Weber than the 'intolerable noise' of 'community singing' in the white churches of the United States (PE 272).

It has only recently been rediscovered that Weber attended the annual conference in Atlanta of the black civil rights campaigner William E. B. Du Bois (1868–1963), who in the 1890s had attended his lectures as well as those of Schmoller and Treitschke, and whose recently published book, *The Souls of Black Folk* (1903), in which each chapter began with a song, made him a spiritual leader of the African Americans for the next half-century or more. Weber had a high opinion of the book and in 1905 wanted to arrange a German translation by Else Jaffé;[94] he also published in 1906 in the *Archiv* an impassioned but objective article by Du Bois, 'Die Negerfrage in den Vereinigten Staaten'. He was very enthusiastic about Du Bois at the time, calling him 'the most significant sociological scholar in the southern States', and five letters from Weber are contained in the papers left behind by Du Bois.[95] During the America trip, Weber seems to have toyed with the idea of specializing in ethnic issues.[96] 'I am quite sure to come back to your country as soon as possible and especially to the South', he wrote in English to Du Bois upon his return, 'because I am absolutely convinced that the "colour-line" problem will be the paramount problem of the time to come, here and everywhere in the world.'[97]

'Few men ever worshipped freedom with such unquestioning faith as did the American Negro', Du Bois affirmed;[98] Weber got from him a way of identifying with African Americans and feeling himself above racist prejudices, especially as he made it seem that the urge for freedom was not only a cultural product but contained a natural element which was at least as alive in blacks as in whites. For an intellectual such as Du Bois, too, a 'Negro revival' service had an 'awful frenzy', whose contagious effect was felt even on white services.[99]

Wild America: the ecology of American freedom

'In North America', Hegel taught, 'the wildness of all fantasies is at it most unbridled.' A revolution could not happen, therefore, because the discontented could always go west.[100] Such notions permeated the perception of North America in the Old World well into the twentieth century. When Carl Schurz was a guest with Bismarck, the chancellor listened to his praise of American democracy without contradicting him. 'But', he said, 'will America's democratic institutions not face their real test only when the unusually favourable opportunities provided by our wonderful natural resources (which are in a sense common property) have ceased to exist?' Would not the struggle between poor and rich then begin in America too?

Schurz did not know how to reply.[101] This was indeed the big question. In Weber's day the link between a country's prosperity and its natural resources still seemed much more direct than it does today, when the prevailing view among economists is that the most important resources are capital and know-how. Weber too recognized a link between freedom and 'free land', although the vast expanses of Russia – to which he subsequently turned his attention – offered the best counter-example to such geographical determinism. Neither capitalism nor Protestantism but free spaces were now the guarantee of American freedom. Weber concluded his lecture in St Louis with the 'sibylline words' (Wolfgang Mommsen):

> It was perhaps never before in history made so easy for any nation to become a great civilized power as for the American people. Yet, according to calculation, it is also the last time, as long as the history of mankind shall last, that such conditions for a free and great development will be given; the areas of free soil are now vanishing everywhere in the world.[102]

At the same time, however, the destruction of nature in the United States in that period of heedless plunder of the forests was much more plainly visible than it is today. In 1904 Lamprecht noted during a trip through the burnt-down cedar forests of the Rockies: 'The sins that Americans have committed against the country's nature cry out to heaven. Never has a country – or, to be more precise, a collection of people – more heartlessly treated its country with more powerful means of destruction.'[103] And in San Francisco he reflected: 'The American sense of nature is still that of an animal. The American lives with nature as animals do: he happily lives in it, uses it when he can, and is cruel to it. He lacks the higher feeling for nature, which is usually associated with pantheistic tendencies, and regards nature as a totality and a supreme work of art.'[104]

Weber, by contrast, seems to have deliberately refrained from making apodictic value-judgements during his trip to the United States. He too observed the devastation of virgin forest, but he recorded it without passing judgement: 'Now they [the trees] are dying and stretching their pale, smoky fingers upward in a confused tangle' (WB 292). He sought direct contact with the wilderness and even turned down an invitation to the White House so that he could travel to Oklahoma. In Washington he would have had the opportunity to meet Theodore Roosevelt, a charismatic leader, but he had not yet developed the concept of charisma. The farmers and Indians in the (still nearly) Wild West were more important to him. He was captivated by the 'fabulous bustle' in a city that had sprung up anarchically on the basis of oil: 'I cannot help but find tremendous fascination in it, despite the stench of petroleum and the fumes, the spitting "Yankees" and the racket of the numerous trains' (WB 292f.).

The wildness of American life gave him visible pleasure, although it did not actually fit the argument of *The Protestant Ethic*. From Chicago he reported in the style of sensationalist journalism the civil war conditions on the streets:

> . . . an unsuccessful strike, masses of Italians and Negroes as strikebreakers; daily shootings with dozens of dead on both sides; a streetcar was overturned and a dozen women were squashed because a

'non-union man' had sat in it; dynamite threats [were made] against the 'Elevated Railway', and one of its cars was actually derailed and plunged into the river. (WB 286)

And he continued: 'Except in its exclusive residential districts, the whole violent city – larger in area than London! – resembles a person skinned alive whose innards can be seen working. For you see everything – in the evening, for example, in a side-street in the City, prostitutes displaying themselves with price-tags at the window in the electric light!' By no means did Weber seek in the United States only confirmation for *The Protestant Ethic*.

A year later, at a gathering of the Verein für Sozialpolitik in Mannheim, he waxed indignant over the petty-minded attitude of the German legal system towards workers: 'If a striker today says to someone willing to work that, unless he joins the strike, his daughter Augusta will not dance with him, the striker makes himself liable to prosecution' (MWG I/8, 255f.). In the United States no one seemed to care whether such 'threats' were permitted or not; the labour struggle took much more brutal forms – and one cannot avoid the impression that Weber thought this lack of restraint to be a powerful force, however much it resulted in terrible scenes.

For his part, he made sure that he was not personally affected by American violence. His mother Helene left at home a newspaper report from Guthrie, Oklahoma, which stated that, when Weber had gone to a newspaper editor there with a letter of recommendation, the editor of a rival paper had entered at the same time. 'The two editors immediately started shooting at each other. . . . Professor Weber stood stock still at first; when he had recovered from his surprise, he got his luggage, went to the station and took the first train back to civilization. Neither of the editors was wounded in the shoot-out.'[105] Evidently they had only put on a show for themselves and the guest from Germany. Weber himself seems never to have recounted this not exactly heroic story, which did the rounds in the American press.[106] He even sensed that there was a serious willingness to fight behind the sporting spirit prevalent in American universities. In any event, he claimed to Austrian officers in 1918 that 'it was the American universities and the strata educated by them, not the military contractors who exist in every country, who were the originators of the war' in the United States (PW 278).

The spoils system: the wildness of American politics

For a German official, the most provocative political aspect of America's wildness was the 'spoils system': the distribution of all offices, not just high offices, by the victorious party in elections, without regard to the appointees' qualifications or merit. Carl Schurz, the most prominent German American of his day, who served as secretary of the interior between 1877 and 1881, made a first attempt to replace what seemed in European eyes a thoroughly bad practice with a public career path based on qualifications. Max Weber also thought that a professionalization of the US civil service was in the long run unavoidable. But he developed a growing allergy to the behaviour of Prussian-German bureaucrats, and therefore a certain understanding for the scandalous disorder of American conditions. With a feeling for the piquant detail, he told the Austrian officers of his conversations with American workers about the 'spoils system', which showed that he had some time for the American way of doing things:

> 'How can you let yourselves be governed by these people who are put in office without your consent and who naturally make as much money out of their office as possible, since they owe their post to the party . . ., and then have to leave office after four years without any pension entitlement; how can you let yourselves be governed by these corrupt people who are notorious for robbing you of hundreds of millions?' I would occasionally receive the characteristic reply . . .: 'That doesn't matter, there's enough money there to be stolen. . . . We spit on these "professionals", these officials. We despise them. But if the offices are filled by a trained, qualified class, such as you have in your country, it will be the officials who will spit on us.' (PW 277)

Weber liked the story so much that he repeated it in abridged form in *Economy and Society* (E&S 271). In 1919, when President Friedrich Ebert asked him to report on the American system in the course of consultations about the future German constitution, he asked a question about the spoils system and the resulting quality of officials. At this cue, Weber stood up and delivered an hour-long lecture, despite fruitless attempts by his companion, Kurt Riezler, to cut him short.[107] This was a subject that really got Weber going.

In 1906, however, when the memory of the United States was still fresh, he remarked to Robert Michels that the state of things there was such that the sociology of parties 'always became a pathology of parties' (MWG II/5, 57). In *Economy and Society* he painted it as a criminal underworld, where a 'boss' pulled the strings behind the scenes – an 'absolutely sober man' interested in nothing but power (E&S 1131). It sounded really scandalous – and yet Weber must have been increasingly unsure whether, as he had argued in *The Protestant Ethic*, the strength of the American model rested on the repression of nature or, on the contrary, on an as yet little tamed *wildness* of nature and an undiminished feeling for freedom.

In January 1905 Marianne spoke at a 'National-Social evening on America'. There was a 'large turn-out. Everyone wanted to get in, and the police had to lock the hall, which had room for only six hundred people.' Afterwards she was 'full of enthusiasm'; the evening was 'a dazzling success'. 'The big sensation came at the end, when our "big boy", though suffering from catarrh, spoke until his voice gave out – until 11:30, more than an hour! Dazzling . . . the confounded fellow!'[108] The trip to the

United States broke the spell that had prevented Weber from speaking in public for five years; his impressions there must have given him a sense of inner wealth and superior knowledge. Four years later Marianne was still reporting that, when social conversation turned to the USA, 'our America-traveller Max spoke for half an hour'.[109] In 1916 Weber told Neumann it was an 'unparalleled scandal' that 'no one in Germany knows what an American election campaign is like and what its consequences are'.[110] Thus he felt himself in possession of exclusive knowledge about the United States: he had a clear idea of the demagogy unleashed in its election contests, which in 1916 would use Germany's unlimited submarine warfare as the pretext for a hate campaign against the Reich.

The Russian revolution of 1905 and Weber's sudden turn to the east

Just a few months after his return from the United States, however, having wrapped up the second part of his book on Protestantism, Weber made a 180 degree turn under the impact of the Russian revolution of 1905. The journey in his imagination to Russia became more productive, at least in terms of scholarly output, than the real journey to the United States. For a time, however much the revolutionary events in the east stirred up the 'spirits from the deep' inside him, they spurred him on to work and even quelled his wanderlust. Sometimes the worried Marianne thought it was a 'terrible misfortune',[111] but for once Max felt good in the German spring, and his wife rejoiced that she could 'dance and celebrate with the birds the rejuvenation of life'.[112] Without a doubt, the mental leap into the Russian revolution was at first a wonderful fillip for Weber. Even Michels, who would have liked to attract Weber to Italy, later regretted in his obituary: 'But perhaps it was Russian affairs that attracted him most.'[113] Alluding to Weber's final assertion in *Politics as a Vocation* that 'man would not have attained the possible unless time and again he had reached out for the impossible' (FMW 128), Eduard Baumgarten once wrote in a footnote:

> For Weber, Russia remained stronger than America, . . . the land of fascination – nay, of a quite definite hope that in its length and breadth so much remained of the national origins that *there*, more than anywhere else on earth, people would 'reach out for the impossible', so that (there and elsewhere) the possible too may not be neglected and relinquished by the well-fed and sluggish. (B 662)

In Weber's view, then, there was a sense in which not America but Russia was the 'land of limitless possibilities' for Germany, a country whose open spaces offered a chance of freedom. In the following years, Weber subscribed to Russian newspapers and kept open the possibility of making further studies of Russia. He twice made plans to travel there, but something else always happened in the meantime: Russia remained for him a land of the imagination. Yet he soon felt himself to be an expert in Russian affairs, at least in comparison with most other Germans; hard as it is to believe, he apparently learned enough Russian in a few months in 1905 to understand Russian papers after a fashion; and the Russian reading room in Heidelberg, one of the main places where Russian intellectuals gathered, allowed him to observe with his own eyes the political spectrum of revolutionary Russia. He derived pleasure from being in this milieu and established a number of contacts.

Whereas he went unnoticed in St Louis, he became 'very popular' among Russian émigrés in Heidelberg (MWG I/10, 705). New human surroundings began to take shape. In his writings on Russia he sometimes referred to personal experience: he had seen in July 1904 how news of the assassination of Plehve, the hated Russian minister of the interior, 'caused quiet, otherworldly scholars to fall into a frenzy of wild rejoicing', so he could gauge the extent to which the autocracy had 'made life hell' (PW 38). However, the Russian émigrés tended to exaggerate the incapacity of the tsarist system to reform itself, although Weber later admitted that he himself had not foreseen anything on the scale of the Stolypin era.[114]

An irrational leap into the dark

We should not, however, explain Weber's sudden turn to the east too readily by his intellectual interests, but rather begin by reminding ourselves just how irrational it was from the point of view of his work schedule, health, scholarly strategy and financial situation. He had just half-recovered his capacity for work, but *The Protestant Ethic* and other work had already put a serious strain on him, and now here he was taking on a whole new field where he had to start from scratch. He was venturing with a panoply of heavy theoretical tools into a world where events were coming thick and fast, and he constantly had to reckon with the fact that the knowledge-base on which he was building would be out of date long before he completed work – which is indeed what happened. Although he was editor of the *Archiv*, the printing of his essays on Russia dragged on for so long that they were no longer topical; it is always risky for scholars who write at great length to compete with journalists. In the end Weber said of his Russia essays: 'neither I nor anyone else will consider them scholarly achievements' (MWG II/5, 143). If he had originally hoped that the Russia numbers of the *Archiv für Sozialwissenschaft* would sell well, he was bitterly disappointed when he found himself having to contribute to the costs,[115] at a time when his finances were anyway tight. Marianne found it all 'hair-raising' and 'ghastly',[116] and he too felt on the verge of a nervous breakdown, as he told the publisher Siebeck in a letter from July 1906:

> I don't know what's going to happen with the Russian business at the *Archiv*. If things don't go any faster than now, I can't guarantee that

I'll pull through. . . . I have crammed so much work, health and even *Lebensfreude* into this work, out of which I have got nothing, that I won't see things take that course without extreme bitterness. (MWG II/5, 10)

He became so furious that he was on the point of ending all work for the *Archiv* (MWG II/5, 143) and therefore giving up the only position of academic power that he then held. All in all, the whole episode of the essays on Russia shows how little Weber embodied his much-theorized 'rationalization' in the organization of his own work, and how he sometimes simply allowed curiosity to get the better of him now that he was free of all professional obligations. The highly obscure Russian events could scarcely have served as a paradigmatic case for any preconceived notions of his. Much later, Richard Pipes used Weber's ideal type of 'patrimonial rule' – in which the ruler treats the state as his own property – for his theorization of the tsarist autocracy;[117] but in 1905 Weber did not yet have this concept.[118] Nor was it the case that for him any revolution had something fascinating about it, or that he subscribed to the myth in which the simple dynamic of revolutionary upheavals gave rise to a new quality of life, a new society and a new man. In *Economy and Society*, revolution is not a theme in its own right; it can create something viable only under charismatic leadership. But Weber does not appear to have seen a charismatic leader anywhere in the revolutionary Russia of 1905. His burning interest in Russia cannot be explained on entirely rational grounds.

Peasant land hunger: Weber's key to the Russian enigma

One thing is clear, however: when Weber turned his gaze eastwards, he felt beneath his feet the familiar ground of *agrarian relations*.[119] He must quickly have realized that it was not essentially a question of a 'spirit' – unless one in material guise[120] – or of ideological castles in the air, but rather of a hunger for land. This is quite remarkable, for it was above all revolutionary intellectuals who had attracted the attention of Europe and of Weber himself in Heidelberg. Never had philosophy played such a role in political struggle as it did in Russia in 1905, when neo-Kantian epistemology became such a major spiritual force that even Lenin found he had to grapple with it. Amazingly, Weber of all people – who at the time was himself deeply immersed in epistemology – did not consider that struggle important, even though he knew of it (MWG I/10, 111). With gentle irony he predicted to the philosopher Rickert in 1907: 'Since each party in Russia has its own epistemologist, you will probably be adopted by one of them pretty soon' (MWG II/5, 297). Less than in other publications about Russia at that time does the intelligentsia appear as a political factor in its own right. Weber did not think that the driving forces of revolution came from the intellect. His underestimation of the Russian intelligentsia seems paradoxical,[121] for the

Figure 9.2 Title page of the Russian translation of Max Weber's *On the Situation of Constitutional Democracy in Russia* (Kiev, 1906)

Russian revolutions were essentially its work, and the only Russians that Weber knew belonged to it. Much later, in his lecture on socialism to Austrian officers in June 1918, Weber mentioned it as a well-known fact that the 'Bolshevik government . . . consists of intellectuals' (PW 298–9), but he did not give the impression that the force of the communist revolution came from the intelligentsia. In the electronic edition of his works, Weber uses the term *Intellektuelle* (which at the time in Germany still sounded new and, for many people, disreputable) no fewer than 361 times, but contrary to what one might expect the largest number of instances are in his sociology of religion and the fewest in his writings on contemporary politics. Judging from Weber, intellectuals would seem to have had greater power in ancient China and India than in modern Russia and Germany.

The unusual nature of Weber's essays on Russia will become apparent if we compare them with a quick, sensationalist book by Alexander Ular, a journalist living in Paris, which Fischer Verlag put on the market before the year 1905 was out. This speaks a great deal about intrigues in the tsarist court, which it paints as a hotbed of perverted semi-imbeciles, such as Grand Duke Sergius, 'completely eaten up with tuberculosis' and in the grip of 'delusions of grandeur' and his 'pathological sexual instincts';[122] there is also a lot about the dictatorship of the bureaucracy, but only very little about the peasantry. The revolution appears as the work primarily of the intelligentsia, with Jews at its head. The book gives an idea of the stories about the Russian events that were doing the rounds among Western newspaper readers.

Weber's overlong essays take us into quite another world, one where the unresolved land question underlies all the intrigues, verbal battles and assassination attempts. But what was actually the heart of the problem? Was it the landed property of the nobility and the church, or the tax burden imposed by the state, or the legal position of the peasantry? Weber did not at first have a cut and dried answer, but he did have a starting point in the *obshchina*, the traditional village and its common land, which was a type familiar to him from elsewhere.[123] This had long been a highly controversial subject: for Slavophiles it embodied the old Russian idea of community, while for liberal agrarian reformers it was the essence of Russia's backwardness, which stood in the way of all private initiative on the land. Its champions regarded the *obshchina* as a primeval, natural community rooted in social instincts, its opponents as an institution created by the state in modern times for the purposes of tax extraction.

This kind of controversy was well known to Weber from the dispute over the antiquity of the cooperatives in the German Mark. He left open the question of the origins of communal land (MWG I/10, 228). The Slavophile idealization of the *obshchina* recalled Gierke's idealization of the Mark communities, and in each case there were also analogies in the contrary positions. Among the Russian revolutionaries, however, there was confusion on this central point. Liberal supporters of progress had reason to combat the community of land, and many socialists too believed that the path of progress would pass through the creation of individualist-capitalist relations in rural areas too. But it was also possible for socialists to see the peasant commune as a stage prior to the future collective economy. After 1905 the Russian government itself pursued the dissolution of the *obshchina*. Weber established that the programme of the Russian liberals remained silent about this delicate issue (MWG I/10, 192).

For all the analogies, there were also fundamental differences between the *obshchina* and the German cooperatives in the Mark, since the latter allowed de facto for heritable private land ownership.[124] In Russia the right to the land lay not with individuals but with the family, and from time to time land was redistributed in accordance with family size, though by no means in the proportion that earlier theories of 'primitive communism' imagined.[125] Consequently, there was an incentive to increase the size of the population (since a larger family could demand more land), but not to work the soil more productively. In Weber's view, overpopulation and overexploitation of the land were the logical result, and critical pressures might be released either in a revolution, involving the expropriation of noble and ecclesiastical property, or in expansion abroad. Drawing heavily on reports from the *zemstvo* assemblies (the organs of regional government set up in 1864), Weber found complaints on all sides about 'land hunger'. Sometimes he puts 'land scarcity' in inverted commas, leaving it open

whether it really existed or whether the land hunger resulted from inadequate farming.

Weber mentioned a discussion of this issue at a congress of peasant Old
Believers in Moscow in February 1905. Nearly everyone there agreed that
there was a real scarcity of land; the peasants from the Volokolamsk district reported that they had greatly increased their yield by growing clover,
but they were shouted down with cries of 'That's enough!' (MWG I/10,
338f.). Weber refrained from more detailed discussion of this key issue – it
would have been difficult on the basis of the existing literature. Of course
he started from the assumption that technological improvements could
considerably raise Russian soil yields (MWG II/10, 215).[126] Today it is
argued that soil erosion turned 'Russia's fertile black-earth landscapes into
impoverished areas, and that this ecological crisis created pressure for
expansion into Siberia'.[127] Similar observations were made in Weber's time
by the world traveller Paul Rohrbach, Naumann's expert in international
politics.[128] But even now it is partly an open question, to which it is difficult
to give a blanket answer for every region in Russia.[129]

'The last of the world's natural-law-oriented agrarian revolutions'

It is particularly remarkable that, although Weber thought the *obshchina* to
be so deeply rooted in 'natural law' that it would be difficult to abolish, he
soon found himself overwhelmed by the following events.

> The *obshchina*, where it exists, is indeed not so easy to overcome either
> technologically or psychologically. One reason . . . why the democrats
> are reticent on the matter is that it is undoubtedly impossible to win
> the mass of peasants themselves to an 'individualist' (in the West
> European sense) agrarian programme. First, there can be no doubt
> that, in the preservation of common lands . . ., what is involved are by
> no means only economic class interests, but also ideas deeply rooted in
> 'natural right'. . . . On the other hand, of course, the very redistribu-
> tion of land, which from the outside appears to be the most important
> agrarian-democratic element in the constitution of this society, is often
> not just a matter of words on paper but is thought of as having an
> effect on 'social policy'. Well-off peasants . . . have indebted fellow
> members of the commune at their mercy, and in fact redistribution
> increases their superior strength. (MWG I/10, 223)[130]

As we see, Weber tried to get to the bottom of the mysteries of the *obshchina*
and understood that reality often did not correspond to the vision of an
ideal community. The result is a contradictory picture, which for Weber was
'beyond all doubt'. The hardiness of the rural commune was based on
ancient and deeply rooted ideas of 'natural right', but also on the interests
of rising kulak layers who sought to manipulate the *obshchina* to their

advantage. Weber particularly liked discovering the synergy of heterogeneous forces, as he had already shown in *The Protestant Ethic*. Later he used Russia as an example of the ambiguity of natural right in relation to small peasants, since it could be a right to share land in proportion not only to the input of labour but also to traditional requirements, as well as involving a 'right to the full proceeds of labour'.

> The last of the world's natural-law-oriented agrarian revolutions has been bled to death also by the irresolvable contradictions between its various ideologies. Those first two natural-law positions were incompatible not only with one another, but also with the various peasant programmes, whether they were motivated by historical, realistically political, practically economical, or finally – and in hopeless confusion because of internal contradictions between the inherent basic dogmas – by Marxist-evolutionist considerations. (E&S 872)

Then as now, natural law was usually conceived as a Western tradition and traced to the abstract idea of a human nature everywhere the same. Stefan Breuer, however, has pointed to an older peasant tradition uncovered by Weber in Russia, which led him to the theme of natural law along a path different from that of the Anglo-American world.[131] In that peasant tradition, the reference to nature is clearer than in abstract conceptions of natural law. The peasant can feed himself from his own land, having no need of the state as a source of either food or law. Peasant autarky is the original basis of human autonomy, and the peasant family and neighbourly assistance is the original basis of human community. Within Europe, both survived longest of all in Russia.

In 1905–6 Weber was not yet capable of drawing such a clear balance-sheet, but the lack of congruence between political-ideological struggles and the agrarian basis of the revolution is a basic theme running through his writings on Russia. Between the lines we can discern a critique of most liberal intellectuals: namely, that they have lost touch with the land because of their failure to grasp the value and development potential of the *obshchina*. Weber stressed that the peasant commune, archaic though it may have sounded, was 'absolutely not a "primitive" or crudely communistic institution' and was 'compatible with any intensity of cultivation'. In the case of clover-growing, the *obshchina* actually dragged 'the reluctant ones in its midst on to the path of progress' (MWG I/10, 580ff.). These are only isolated thoughts, however; Weber does not develop a consistent conception in these writings and seems to be struggling far too much with the unfamiliar material.

Weber's feel for 'violent rage'

Weber's encounter with Russia again displays his fascination for the wildness of nature in man, whose reconciliation with rationality seems even more remote than in the case of North America. But it was a period when his terror at this wildness was abating inside himself, and when his curiosity about it was receding. One leitmotif of his essays on Russia is the 'terrible passions' (MWG I/10, 540) unleashed by the revolution: the 'barbaric wildness' (MWG I/10, 320) directed on each side against the other. He evidently felt that he could appreciate better than ordinary Germans the incalculable element in the Russian events: the deadly hatred and the preparedness for death. Weber had an instinct for physical violence.[132] He describes as harshly as possible the 'arbitrariness of the (Russian) police, who encroach upon people's merest existence and human dignity', as an 'insane rule of tyranny' operating 'by the most subtle methods and the most cunning Oriental wiles' (MWG I/10, 606, 674ff.).[133]

Again and again Weber suggests that much of what was happening in Russia came from the belly rather than the head, though in a different sense among intellectuals than among peasants. He thought that horror stories about the 'inconceivably wretched life' of the 'broad masses' of the peasantry corresponded to reality, and that in their case the 'terrible pressure' of 'the most basic survival needs' prevailed over everything else (MWG I/10, 606) – a probably exaggerated, 'naturalistic' vision of things. In the revolutionary intelligentsia too, some of whose members he knew personally in Heidelberg, he sensed a 'violent rage' against the tsarist regime, but also against dissident thinkers in its own ranks (MWG II/5, 102). He repeatedly talked of the 'often decisive' role of the Jews, whose fate 'no words can describe in its terrible gravity' (MWG I/10, 361f.).

From a rational point of view, the prospects for the Russian revolution of 1905 were thoroughly unpromising. Unlike the earlier American or French revolutions, it came up with no impressive ideas, no convincing manifestoes and, as Weber pointed out, no great leader (MWG I/10, 675).[134] The ideological passions vented themselves and passed the 'land hunger' by; the peasant's communal instincts cut across the revolutionary intellectual's obsession with progress. Predictably, the revolutionaries fell out with one another as soon as they scored a victory. So why did Weber invest so much energy in such a desperate enterprise, which, looked at rationally, lacked all sense? The truth is that he who discovered rationalization everywhere was himself far from being only a rationalist. He did not believe either that objective conditions decided everything, but was convinced that new opportunities arise at certain moments[135] and that in 1905 Russia was passing through such a moment.[136] The distinctively 'Weberian' feature of Weber's thinking was not so much its emphasis on structural determinants as its openness to opportunities for action. He believed in a certain power of spontaneity, at least for short periods of time, and in his eyes it was such high points that lent meaning to human existence. He gives a further answer to the question of meaning at the end of his essay on Russia's 'transition to pseudo-constitutionalism', where he again, as he liked to do, raises the often convoluted train of thought to a surprising crescendo. He begins with a gesture of disclosure:

The eye of the spectator, especially that of politically and economically 'sated' nations, is not accustomed, and, from afar, not able, through the veil of all these programmes and collective actions, where such masses are involved, to perceive the stirring spectacle of individual fate, the uncompromising idealism, the relentless energy, the ups and downs of tempestuous hope and agonizing disappointment experienced by those in the thick of the fight. To the outsider, all these individual fates, so dramatic in themselves, become interwoven to form an impenetrable tangle. It is a continuous unrelenting struggle, with wild deeds of murder and merciless acts of tyranny in such numbers that even these horrors finally become accepted as normal. . . . Never has a freedom struggle been waged under such difficult conditions as the Russian struggle, never with such a degree of unconditional readiness for martyrdom; and with such an attitude, it seems to me, any German who has not lost all the idealism of his forefathers should feel deeply in sympathy. (MWG I/10, 675f., 679)[137]

Nowhere did Weber express as clearly as he did here the fascination that the Russian events held for him. It is 'idealism' – not that of a contemporary educated German, but the combative idealism and self-sacrifice of wars of liberation. In the end, although the Russian revolution was fought partly under the aegis of collectivist ideologies, it remained for Weber a 'freedom struggle'. However immature its ideas and however minimal its chances of success, it contained an 'uncompromising idealism' and an 'unconditional readiness for martyrdom' which for Weber were values in themselves. We can sense how he, the man with sick nerves, identified with the 'highly strung' Russian radicals against the Germans resting smugly on their laurels. He, who had turned from a full professor into a desperado, thought he understood the desperate courage of the revolutionaries. 'Weber liked these revolutionaries because of their readiness to die', recalled Paul Honigsheim (WzG 169). Fearlessness in the face of death was for Weber a sign of nobility of character.

Russia as an opportunity and a danger for Germany: Weber's love–hate relationship with Russia

Weber was a man of love–hate attitudes, of deeply divided feelings, and this characteristic grew stronger as a result of his illness. At the end of his writings on Russia, one comes away with a sense of his profound ambivalence towards both Russia and his own nation (MWG I/15, 245). To be sure, he was and remained a German nationalist. But, like so many German nationalists, he preferred Germans from an idealized past to the actually existing Germans of his own time, most of whom struck him as smug petty-bourgeois, all too commonplace in their reasonableness and devoid of any great passion. He found a counter-model in the Russian revolutionaries, far more than he had done in the Americans.

But, as a German, he was pulled this way and that in relation to Russia. For he saw the Russian empire as the greatest danger to Germany: a danger that would be intensified if a revolutionary renewal of Russia gave free rein to the peasants' land hunger (MWG I/10, 273, 679). Otto Hoetzsch, then the leading German expert on Russia, saw things differently: what people had been through in Austria-Hungary would be repeated in Russia; 'every concession to constitutional ideas' would also strengthen the striving of the various nationalities for autonomy.[138] We know today that he was right, but at the time he was 'completely out of line with official German policy'.[139] In the period just before the war, Reich Chancellor Bethmann Hollweg had similar views to Weber's about the Russian danger, and his fatalism determined how he acted in the July crisis of 1914.[140]

During the world war, and particularly in the wake of the Russian revolution of 1917, Weber felt sure that the peasant hunger for land could be satisfied only through dictatorship and external expansion, and hence that a deadly threat to Germany's existence came mainly from the east rather than the west. He detected a deep loathing of Germany among the Russian revolutionaries. Indeed, he could even understand it very well: the typical Germans were their exact opposite, and Baltic Germans held key positions in the Russian repressive apparatus (MWG I/10, 87ff.), their German pedantry carrying to perfection its 'terrible bureaucratic rationalism' (I/10, 404).

Weber's writings on Russia contain many points that apply to conditions in Germany, so many that indirect criticism of his own country sometimes seems like Weber's real interest in turning east (MWG I/15, 245). But then Weber says something that makes him sound completely German again. He sees the 'appalling' lot of the Baltic Germans: they are hated by the revolutionaries, while the ruling layers who seek salvation in pan-Slavism are 'coldly scornful' of their attempts to curry favour. Weber admits that he has deliberately avoided close investigation of Russia's Germans: 'It is impossible to remain "objective" about them' (MWG I/10, 617f.). On 20 December 1912, Weber gave a talk celebrating the fiftieth anniversary of the Russian reading room in Heidelberg; it was the first time he had spoken in the town since his illness, and it was only Marianne's pressure that stopped him pulling out at the last moment. Those who attended the event later wrote curiously dissimilar recollections of it. The Russian-Jewish philosopher Aaron Steinberg (1891–1983) remembered only that Weber had favoured close ties between Germany and Russia:

Max Weber held the view that the future of the Western world . . . depended on harmonious relations between Germany and Russia. *'Wir sind aufeinander angewiesen auf Leben und Tod'* (We have to rely on each other as a matter of life and death). I deliberately quote the German, because that sentence has stayed in my memory ever since. Russia and Germany cannot live without each other, Weber lectured. Russia is the country of limitless possibilities. . . . Tolstoy is too big for Europe; he exceeds the measurements of any one European country.

And the same is true of everything Russian. . . . But if only the Russians could exercise moderation as we Germans do! If this idea of German moderation could be combined with Russian excess, the resulting harmony would save the world.[141]

Here Russia, 'land of limitless possibilities', appears as Germany's potential America, the alter ego which Germans (including Weber), who in the confines of their own country repress too much passion, need in order to become fully human. But Honigsheim's recollection was quite different when he wrote that Weber's speech had been 'of a profundity' that made the others pale by comparison:

> The talk revealed the whole breadth of Weber's vision. For he underlined the world-historic importance and human grandeur of the Russian revolutionaries, but not without adding: 'Should inter-state tensions reach boiling-point and Russia feel it has to stand by Serbia, then the next meeting will be on the field of honour.' (WzG 169)

In 1919, in the wake of Germany's defeat, Weber could still console himself and the German public with the idea that at least the war with Russia had gone well – a war that would have been unavoidable whichever political tendency in Russia had set the tone. At times he legitimated the war by referring to the infamy of tsarist despotism, in the overblown style familiar from revolutionary propaganda: 'Anyone who has ever studied the tsarist administrative system will know that nothing in this wide world can be compared to its refined instruments for popular emasculation.' Today, after the experiences of Stalinism, the police apparatus of the tsarist period still seems almost polite: for example, exiled opponents of the regime were allowed to receive their newspapers, to write books and to go to the hot baths. Weber did not doubt, however, that a revolutionary Russia would be at least as dangerous to the German Reich:

> In the case of this war, there was only one power that wanted it for its own sake, unreservedly and under all circumstances, and had to want it because of its political objectives. That country was *Russia* – i.e., the tsarist system and the social layers . . . dependent on it. The war is coming 'like a natural event', a *Kadet* (Russian Constitutional-Democrat – trans.) said to me shortly before its outbreak. And that belief . . . was held by people much further to the left. The historically rooted distinctiveness of Russian *literati* in every party – which means they are not content to put their domestic Russian affairs in order, but wish to play a world role as well – already appeared in the 1905 revolution and had remained the same until the present day. In the Russia of 1914, no layer with any positive influence did *not* want the war.[142]

With Weber's Russian writings in mind, Eduard Baumgarten joked that 'not only intellectual plebeians but sophisticated minds bewail the existence of *two Max Webers*: a value-free man of science and a passionate politician obsessed with values. . . . Okay, so why should a generous and far-sighted man not love and fear Russia at the same time? – sometimes hate it fearfully?' (B 663). Why not, indeed? Weber really did feel a kind of love–hate towards Russia, and this was inherently associated with his love–hate for nature – his own, above all. In any event, the period in which he felt nature only as an enemy was now over.

Weber and Kistiakovsky: opposing views of the Russian sense of right and wrong

As Weber himself acknowledged by way of introduction, his writings on Russia had 'ruthlessly plundered the factual and personal knowledge' (MWG I/10, 86f.) of Bogdan Kistiakovsky (1868–1920), a philosophically oriented legal theorist from Ukraine, who sometimes wrote under the pseudonym 'Ukrainec' and had been studying in Heidelberg since 1901.[143] He was a member of the 'Emancipation League', an organization built around Peter Struve, who, though originally a Marxist, stood in 1905 on the constitutional-democratic 'right wing' of the revolutionaries and remained trapped in Lenin's mocking term for him, the 'legal Marxist'. Kistiakovsky's first publication in Germany was a Marxist interpretation of the painting of Arnold Böcklin, which he saw as reflecting a need for untouched nature newly awakened by the capitalist exploitation of nature.[144]

Kistiakovsky, however, did not feel any sympathy for the wild element in Russian life. He was the ideal person to make Weber aware, more keenly than at the time of *The Protestant Ethic*, that the rationalization of life which reached a peak in the Anglo-American world was a distinctively Western path;[145] but the Ukrainian's thoughts and feelings were moving in a different direction from Weber's. Kistiakovsky, who, like so many Russian intellectuals, later broke down physically amid the chaos of revolutionary Russia, longed to see a Western-style constitutional order in his own country. His influence is plainly visible in the title Weber gave to his second essay, 'Rußlands Übergang zum Scheinkonstitutionalismus' (Russia's Transition to Pseudo-Constitutionalism); Weber's interest was not limited to the constitution but extended at least as much to other issues. Later, in *Vechi* (Route Markers, 1909), the self-criticism by leading intellectuals active in 1905, Kistiakovsky took biting stock of the defective constitutionalist sense of Russia's revolutionary intelligentsia:

> The Russian intelligentsia consists of people who know no personal or social discipline. This has to do with the fact that the Russian intelligentsia never respects the law and has never seen it as a thing of value. . . . Its blunted sense of right and wrong and its lack of interest in legal matters are the result of an age-old evil – namely, the lack of a legal order in the everyday lives of the Russian people.[146]

Max Weber thought he could see a conception of natural law in the Russian soul, but for Kistiakovsky that kind of sense of right and wrong had no practical value: 'It has recently been argued that there is a revival of natural law in Russia, and a theory of intuitive right has been put forward. . . . Up to now, however, there has been no reason to think that these might acquire greater salience in Russian society.'[147] The 'natural-law-oriented agrarian revolution' was Weber's own discovery.

Religion: an unknown quantity in revolutionary Russia

But what place does religion have in Weber's writings on Russia? He had surprisingly made it the principal factor in the genesis of modern capitalism, so surely he could not ignore it in Russia of all places, where the power of religion had always been a pet subject in travellers' reports. And he did indeed detect religious traits in the passion of Russia's revolutionaries: when he spoke of their 'readiness for martyrdom' or said that the 'somnambulist certainty' of 'Marxist believers' reminded him of the Jesuits, he described these attitudes with a characteristic mixture of admiration and repugnance:

> Resembling the Jesuits in his logical consistency, the Marxist believer gains from his dogma that sense of elation and somnambulist certainty which avoids even a glance at the long-term political results, remains convinced of his own blamelessness, takes calmly and with a mocking smile the collapse of all hopes, including his own, of defeating the mortal enemy. His thoughts always focus exclusively on how to preserve the pure faith and, if possible, augment his own sect by a few souls; how to 'unmask' the 'closet Catholics' there or the 'betrayers of the people' in neighbouring groups here. (MWG I/10, 171f.)

The official Orthodox church was one of the strongest pillars of the old order during the 1905 revolution. There was only one exception: the priest Georgii Gapon, who on 'Bloody Sunday' (9 January 1905) in St Petersburg led the march to hand in a petition by the factory-workers' association he had organized on the instructions of the ministry of the interior; the army's bloody repression of the march – even though people on it were holding icons and images of the tsar – was the spark that triggered the revolutionary explosion. But Gapon was a dubious figure in the eyes of many revolutionaries; he had confessed to being in the service of the Okhrana, the secret police, was thought by many to have remained a police spy, and in 1906, having sought refuge in Finland, was put to death by a revolutionary. Nevertheless, Weber returns to him twelve times in his writings on Russia and takes him seriously as a leading actor in the revolution; although he characterizes him as a 'swindler swindled', the emphasis is still on the 'swindled' (MWG I/10, 492f.). Even Lenin, unlike his fellow revolutionaries, showed a conspicuous interest in Father Gapon, and learned far more about the peasantry from conversations with him than from discussions with Marxists.[148]

It was not easy for Weber to gain access to the Orthodox religion through the literature available to him; there were scarcely any Russian Orthodox theologians who offered Western scholars material for a worthwhile study. The most promising for Weber's purposes were the Old Believers, who broke away from the official church after 1653 when their leader, Patriarch Nikon, ceased to recognize the supremacy of Byzantium. The resulting battle in Russian Orthodoxy outwardly centred on whether the sign of the cross should be made with two or three fingers – some Old Believers went to the stake for insisting that it should be with two. It was an extreme example of the puzzlingly irrational side of Russian religiosity, which seemed quite absurd to those who failed to appreciate the significance of symbols and rituals. But to Weber 'the great schisms in the Russian church – over whether one should cross oneself with two or three fingers and similar issues' – appeared 'readily understandable' (E&S 1174).[149]

The Old Believers continued to exist as a force of millions, and in 1904, during the Russo-Japanese war, many peasants refused at their urging to enlist in the armed forces. Weber devoted the longest footnote in his writings on Russia to these currents that sought the separation of the Orthodox church from the state, and from whose ranks a socialist-oriented 'Christian fraternal struggle' had been taking shape (MWG I/10, 158–61). But religion still remained a matter for the footnotes. Around 1905 Weber found no spirit that he would have found it tempting to engage. Only the modern Russian historian Vsevolod Kerov, following in Weber's footsteps, discovered the Old Believers as a pendant to the Anglo-American Puritans: that is, as bearers of an economic dynamic on a foundation of ascetic discipline. Weber did not know what to make of them – unlike the castration sect of the Skoptsy, who excited him as a counterpoint to the Heidelberg erotic movement.

Tolstoy, the organic cycle of peasant life and the clash between brotherly and sexual love

Things were different in the case of Tolstoy, who had been highly fashionable in Western cultural circles since the turn of the century; his *Resurrection* appeared in Germany in 1899–1900 in no fewer than twelve different translations.[150] For Harnack this new trend had something deeply inauthentic: Tolstoy was a comfortable pretext for 'thousands of our "educated" readers' to steer clear of religion by allowing him to tell them that 'Christianity means denial of the world; for then they know very well that it does not concern them.' Tolstoy's doctrine was 'an offence to all energetic, nay, ultimately, to all true natures'.[151] We should therefore imagine that for Weber he would have been like a red rag to a bull. Yet for a time he was anything but that. Several years *after* his writings on Russia, Weber finally found a way into Russian religiosity when the various kinds of love became a major theme for him, and he set about intensively studying Tolstoy and Solovev. At the German sociologists' congress in 1910, Troeltsch's lecture on Stoic-Christian natural law became the springboard for a long contribution full of densely packed sentences, whose actual reference to Russia is clear only from certain incidental remarks:

> In the Orthodox church there is a specifically mystical belief, living safe in the soil of the East, that brotherly love or love of one's neighbour – those distinctively human relations which, though so colourless to us, have given salvationist religions their radiance – offer a way not to any quite incidental social effects, but to knowledge of the meaning of the world, to a mystical relationship to God; they rest on the simple, thoroughly ancient Christian idea that . . . love of one's neighbour, whoever he or she may be, this amorphous, unformed relationship of love, is the one that gives access to the gates of the eternal, the timeless, the divine. . . . This a-cosmic aspect is the foundation of the whole of Russian religiosity, but also of a special kind of *natural law* that you find strongly present in the Russian sects as well as in Tolstoy, and which, of course, is also sustained by the agrarian communism that still points the peasant to divine law for the regulation of his social interests. (GASS 466f.)

This is one passage where Weber's train of thought, bubbling over with ideas, fixes on and assimilates Russian religiosity – the kind of passage we would look for in vain in his writings on the Russian revolution. It then becomes clear how few bearings he had in dealing with the Russian material. Russia's significance comes not from the context of revolution but from its 'a-cosmic' religiosity (the first time he uses the term)[152] – a theme that also gives Weber a way into Asian religions. The Russian a-cosmism of love stands in curious contrast to the Russian danger.

Weber's concept of brotherliness acquires a dimension of mystical love.[153] It seems to derive with the force of natural law from a certain soil, the 'soil of the East', which should obviously not be understood only in the sense of physical earth. For Weber it is especially important that this kind of love contains the key to knowledge of the world – to insight into the meaninglessness of what happens on earth in accordance with the laws of nature, which undo all the idealist-inspired teleological ideas concerning the higher development of humanity. Later, in *Economy and Society*, Weber returns to this line of thought and, supported by his work on the religions of Asia, places Russia in a broader context:

> Wherever genuine mysticism did give rise to communal action, such action was characterized by the acosmism of the mystical feeling of love. Mysticism may exert this kind of psychological effect, thus

tending – despite the apparent demands of logic – to favour the creation of communities. The core of the mystical concept of the oriental Christian church was a firm conviction that Christian brotherly love, when sufficiently strong and pure, must necessarily lead to unity in all things even in dogmatic beliefs. In other words, men who sufficiently love one another . . . will also think alike and because of the very irrationality of their common feeling, act in a solidary fashion which is pleasing to God. Because of this concept, the Eastern church could dispense with an infallibly rational authority in matters of doctrine. The same view is basic to the Slavophile conception of the community, both within and beyond the church. (E&S 550f.)

One feels in these sentences that Weber is under a spell. The power of mystical love, which actually breaks up any 'cosmic' order, is therefore capable – more by 'psycho-logic' than rational logic – of grounding the solidarity of communal action, without any superordinate 'doctrinal authority'. Love possesses great power for the late Weber. The big issue remains what kind of power it is, and how it relates to the natural power of sexual love.

For Tolstoy the answer was clear: sexual love generates a blind and brutal egoism; it is the worst enemy of brotherly love. For years Tolstoy would not let go of Weber, and he must have been a catalyst for his reflections on love as well as science and nature. Existing science was for Tolstoy inimical to brotherly love: he complained in *What Men Live By* (1884–6) of the 'eunuchs of science'. 'The true science is that of the true welfare of all human beings.'[154]

Weber knew that Tolstoy 'quite simply (found) reprehensible anything other than peasant labour' (MWG I/10, 248). Weber's later ideal of the 'organic cycle of life', which allowed the peasant, unlike the intellectual, to die satisfied that he had lived life to the full, was probably derived from Tolstoy.[155] In his short story 'Three Deaths', Tolstoy compares and contrasts the deaths of a noblewoman, a peasant and a tree. He himself felt a great fear of death when still in the midst of life. He longed for nature yet increasingly experienced the instinctual nature within himself as something alien and loathsome: 'Our animal activity is accomplished without ourselves.'[156] In no other great mind of his age could Weber see a better reflection of his own tormented brooding or raise the misery of his condition to a higher spiritual plane. He thought that 'the whole of Tolstoy's spiritual work' had arisen out of 'his fear of death'.[157] There can be no doubt that his interest in Tolstoy originated in a genuine fascination, and not, for example, in some polemical impetus or other.[158] As Honigsheim reported it, 'one might almost say' that Tolstoy and Dostoevsky were 'present in person' in the discussions at the Weber circle;[159] the encounter with Tolstoy even burned Weber 'on the fingers' (WzG 241).

The previously unarticulated religiosity of the Russian peasant, with which it was so difficult to get to grips, obtained in Tolstoy a prophet of the highest stature, a charismatic *par excellence*, a mind of such dimensions as (Weber believed) could grow only in the expanses of Russia. At the very beginning of his first essay, Weber considers it evident that Tolstoy embodied the soul of the Russian people (MWG I/10, 124).[160] In the period around 1910, when Tolstoy, having left his home and wife, died far away in the waiting-room at Astapovo railway station, Weber even planned to write a book about him. On 1 November 1910 he wrote to Marianne that for the moment he was managing 'without drugs', that is, 'without bromide': 'I now go to sleep if I read (Tolstoy) in bed for two hours!! Such a crazy thing!' (MWG II/6, 675). The eternal insomniac certainly did not mean to say that he found Tolstoy boring; the reading seems rather to have given him a little of that inner peace for which he had so often yearned in vain.

Max and Marianne Weber were both occupied with Tolstoy at the time, as Marianne had been disgusted by reports of how Russian men beat their wives and treated them as sex objects.[161] She knew that Tolstoy shared this disgust. She thought of Max's planned book as 'our' book, which would 'contain the results of his innermost experiences' (WB 466). She had already read *The Kreutzer Sonata* as a young bride, when it was causing an international stir:[162] the life's confessions of a landowner, Pozdnyshev, who stabbed his wife to death in a jealous rage and came to realize that there is a curse on sexual desire, even when it is a question of one's own spouse. *The Kreutzer Sonata* first gave the public a hint of Tolstoy's marital torments. Helene had disapproved of Marianne's reading of the book,[163] but by now Tolstoy's morality was suited to stabilize the Webers' marriage. Marianne kept pestering Max to start work, and in 1913 she complained: ' "our" Tolstoy book's turn has still not come, but I will not let him go – except he write it.'[164] The allusion was to Jacob's struggle with the angel: 'I will not let thee go, except thou bless me.'

Tolstoy was not out of the picture even at the very beginning of Weber's relationship with Mina Tobler. The philosopher Emil Lask, who was then a friend of the pianist, told her that Weber was a follower of Tolstoy (Weber passed this on to Marianne with two exclamation marks), and a subsequent discussion she had with him was 'very nice' (MWG II/7–1, 142). The Tolstoy plan fell through, presumably not by chance; the fascination of asceticism was rapidly subsiding. Instead, Tolstoy would sometimes serve Weber as the butt for a *reductio ad absurdum* of any politics based on the ethics of inner conviction [*Gesinnungsethik*] – although the picture he drew of Tolstoy's fundamentalism was rather distorted.[165] In any event, the Russian probably embodied a secret longing that Weber could not uphold on the basis of scientific or political considerations – or, ultimately, on the basis of his sexual experiences.

10

From the 'Essay of Sighs' to 'Psychophysics': the Seven-Year Fight with Naturalism against Naturalism

Tormented science: the 'essay of sighs'

The history of Weber's illness is an important background to his theory of science. In the autumn of 1902, when he was slowly regaining his capacity for work, one would have thought that he had every reason to start with a simple and pleasant task. He had already decided to give up the professorship, and so he was no longer under anything other than an inner compulsion. But now, in recognizing his incapacity for 'science as a vocation', he seemed to feel more clearly than ever an inner calling to science. The urge for knowledge persisted even without his insertion into the university world – an experience reflected much later in *Science as a Vocation*. The very absence of a profession meant that he had to be even more meticulous in his professionalism, to think things through even more thoroughly than the scholars who had once served as his models. And so, instead of turning again to the riches of reality, he first plunged into fundamental theoretical questions more deeply than ever before. For seven years he kept wrestling with the theory of science, in constant and elaborate arguments with other writers.

It began with a series of essays, *Roscher und Knies und die logischen Probleme der historischen Nationalökonomie* (1903–6), which he wrote for *Schmollers Jahrbuch*, the leading journal of the Historical School of German political economy. At first he seemed to attach himself as before to this school. But, Marianne complained, 'unfortunately this difficult investigation of the modes of thought of his discipline and of history expanded as he worked on it, and yet it had to be ready at a certain date. This soon turned it into a burden and a torment, for his working strength was still unsteady, and only on good days did his brain stand the great strain in the service of logical problems' (WB 260). The essay became much longer than expected; Weber slaved away, slept badly, had to interrupt the 'd..d work',[1] did not meet the deadline and therefore felt even more oppressed by it. The 'essay of sighs' became his stock term for *Roscher and Knies*.

Early in 1903 Weber himself described it as the wretched 'patchwork job' [*Stöpselei*], and Marianne wrote back: 'How terrible that you had to begin with such a devilishly difficult investigation! It is more of a strain than empirical work.'[2] In her biography she still writes about the 'essay of sighs' with more open disparagement than about any other of her husband's works. It was an 'incidental study' with no recognizable purpose;[3] it was 'not really stimulating, for it did not give rise to any new insights into reality' (WB 265). It did not even make him popular at university. He had actually been expected to write an appreciative piece about Roscher for a commemorative volume to be published by Heidelberg University (MWG I/22-1, 12) – and now here he was writing more or less the opposite.

Weberian researchers like to present *Roscher and Knies* as a detour, especially as nowadays the two economists in question are scarcely ever spoken of. At first sight, the essay reads more as a settling of accounts with the Historical School of political economy, which in Weber's view had entered a dead end, even though he owed a great deal to its synthesis of economics, history and sociology, and to the career network associated with it. Even people of the calibre of Tenbruck and Hennis, who have really made an effort with the 'essay of sighs', are unable to extract from it much more than Marianne did.[4] Weber had formerly had direct contact with Knies: he studied under him in Heidelberg, learned from him and took over his chair in 1896. For Hennis, Weber's attack on Knies was 'truly a form of patricide' – the second, after the one of 1897.[5]

But is the torment really so hard to understand? We have only to take Weber at his word and to avoid projecting into his text a contemporary need to find a system. From what we have seen of Weber's life and thought so far, the 'essay of sighs' does not at all appear as pointless and incidental as most students of it have thought. There is a reason why Weber got so bogged down, spending much longer on the essays than his admirers would have wished him to do. In the end, they revolve around his relationship to *nature*, in the broad sense in which the term was then used, and around 'naturalism' in the human sciences. This is also a leitmotif in his subsequent works on scientific theory, where he repeatedly weighs in against naturalistic elements. But it is revealing that this struggle regularly appears such a torturous, and tortuous, exercise. We always have a suspicion that he is also wrestling with part of his self – and indeed his thought processes repeatedly prove awkward, even 'naturalistic'.

'The peculiar drama of an impassioned attack on naturalism from naturalist positions'

What is true of the 'essay of sighs' is true of a large part of Weber's philosophy of science. The question of its internal unity has been the source of endless discussion: whether it has such a unity at all and, if so, what it consists in. The answer to the puzzle seems to be that it consists in Weber's inner *tension* with regard to naturalism. This unity in antinomy fits him well.

'Naturalism' had several meanings in the scientific language of the time: (1) the introduction of 'organological' concepts such as 'organism', 'development' or 'growth', and also 'race' or 'natural selection', into the social sciences; (2) the methodological premise that processes in human history and society can be explained in the same way as natural processes, with general laws, cause and effect relationships or processes of growth and ageing; (3) the epistemological postulate of a unity of man and nature, mind and body, internal and external world. One of the emotional attractions of naturalism lay precisely in this sense of our own unity with nature. In this optic, no problems of principle stood in the way of knowledge of the external world, since there was a continuum between that world and the knowing mind. Intuitive comprehension of the external world was at least not ruled out – a position which, for neo-Kantians, constituted a regression in comparison with the Kantian critique of knowledge.

One leitmotif of Weber's philosophy of science, which first appeared in the 'essay of sighs', was a struggle against naturalism in the first of the above senses: that is, he sought to expose the insecure empirical foundation of organological ideas of state and nation, as well as modes of argument that explained concrete reality as an 'emanation' of such imaginary notions. Weber's naturalist bugbear was essentially a form of idealism. In contrast, his own insistence that the phenomena of the real world should be taken as such and not conceived as an 'emanation' of a great, invisible unity – whether national spirit or national body – involved a robust form of naturalism. Friedrich Tenbruck comments: 'In both question and answer, his works presuppose a naturalist picture of reality and can only be understood on that basis. They offer the peculiar spectacle of an impassioned attack on naturalism from naturalist positions.'[6]

Weber's writings on science did have another side to them, which grew stronger over the years: namely, the rejection of any theory that drew a sharp dividing-line between the natural and social sciences. The standard argument of those who drew such a line was that natural processes ultimately have a causal, and processes in the human world a purposive, explanation; for human behaviour cannot be understood as merely a reflex reaction to natural needs and external stimuli, but is guided by goals and attempts to find meaning. Moreover, the scientist who studies human behaviour needs a different attitude to his object from that which the chemist has when he observes the behaviour of fluids in a test-tube. Those who work in the human sciences are aware of Horace's *tua res agitur* ('it is your concern too') and of the need for evaluatory participation. Being human, we cannot and should not confront human affairs with a sense that they concern us no more than do processes in non-human nature.

This is the point at which things grew complicated for Weber. He knew that he was a passionate person, with a tendency to heated value-judgements and a yearning for a higher meaning beyond the triviality of everyday existence. But he also knew from his own life that the end result can be very different from the original intention – as it was, for example, when world-denying Puritan ascetics set off a chain reaction that led to modern capitalism. The sense that historical actors mean to give to their actions is not unimportant, but it is not identical with the final outcome. The purposive orientation of human behaviour does not conclusively rule out causal explanation in history. The social and natural sciences are different from each other, but it would be wrong to imagine that there is a methodological abyss between them.

We should not forget that Weber had had recent personal encounters with neurology and psychiatry. Where were the sharp boundaries there between the human and natural sciences? The most intelligent people in the two disciplines – represented for Weber by Hellpach and Gruhle – operated in a frontier area between semantic understanding and physiological explanation. Although medical people reached out for general laws, they had to deal in practice with individuals and could never be sure which general laws applied to them.

But was 'individual' synonymous with 'irrational', and did individual freedom entail, as human scientists then liked to claim, that the individual could not be rationally explained? Did human freedom mean human incalculability? For Weber, who over the years had felt himself to be in the power of 'demons', such reasoning rested on one long confusion. The more someone was 'free', he argued, the more he would act in accordance with rational considerations, and the more his behaviour could be explained by a general logic that was not in principle different from that of the natural sciences. While others sought to make freedom of the will a morally superior bastion for the human sciences, Weber knew from his own experience that you do not get very far with freedom of the will when you are in the grip of your own irrational, autonomic powers, and that you do not make irrational use of that freedom when you are in a position freely to decide what to do with yourself. On sober examination, freedom of the will – the eternal issue in dispute between 'materialists' and 'idealists' – is a pseudo-problem without importance for the philosophy of science.

In Weber's works, the term 'freedom of the will' occurs most often by far in *Roscher and Knies*. Will-power was an emotive issue for him throughout the years of his illness; his mother thought that, if he could just energetically activate his will, he would become capable of work again, but he himself could feel the impotence of his will. The will was neither free nor strong enough to overcome the law-governed fatigue of his body and the over-wrought state of his nerves; nothing in his experience of life had made such a deep and brutal impression on him. He therefore thought it preposterous to make freedom of the will the basis for a fundamental dividing-line between the natural and social sciences.

The emotional foundations of human behaviour introduce a natural element that permits statements to be made about the probability of causal effects. In one of the few humorous notes in the 'essay of sighs', Weber refers to Wilhelm Busch:

> This great humorist produces his most droll effects in the following way: the countless trivial experiences of everyday life which we 'interpretively' employ in innumerable connections are clothed in the language of scientific propositions. Consider the charming verse from 'Plisch and Plum': 'Whoever is pleased when he is distressed makes himself, on the whole, unpopular' (*Wer sich freut, wenn wer betrübt / macht sich meistens unbeliebt*). Since he conceives the generic features of this phenomenon quite correctly, not as a necessary truth, but rather as a rule of 'adequate causation', the verse is an altogether irreproachable formulation of a law of history.[7]

This 'undoubtedly' explained much of the anti-German feeling in Britain when the Boers' brave resistance was winning enthusiastic support in Germany (WL 112).

The ethic of responsibility, in which Weber later declared his faith, presupposed that at least probability statements could be made about the consequences of one's action. In this connection, Weber often referred to the work of the philosophically inclined physiologist Johannes von Kries, who was already seeking a basis for responsibility and finding it in the

Figure 10.1 Max Weber as the apostle Luke on the font of the Old Town church in Bielefeld

existence of probabilities.[8] (In 1932 the sculptor son of the philosopher Rickert portrayed Kries and Weber on the font of the Old Town church in Bielefeld as the apostles Matthew and Luke.)[9] There has always been speculation about Weber's theory of causality, and for Richard Swedberg it is 'one of the most difficult parts of his work'.[10] It is best understood if we start from the fact that Weber combines causality in the social and the natural-scientific sense, intentional and non-intentional causality. Precisely when human action is 'irrationally' and emotionally driven, it contains a natural element that permits assertions to be made about general rules.

The 'toad's curse': 'methodological pestilence' as a post-traumatic syndrome

As we can easily see from the chronology of Weber's life and work, his writings on scientific theory largely fall in the period immediately after his worst years of illness, when he did not yet feel capable of undertaking major projects and was still suffering relapses. In these writings we can often feel the torment of his life at that time. The methodological ruminations came compulsively from inside him, not as a result of external stimuli. Such pieces were not popular with readers of the *Archiv*; indeed, in 1906 their 'constant complaints' forced Weber 'into a long pause in [his] methodological work' (MWG II/5, 69).

The beginning of work on *Economy and Society* and the equally large-scale *Wirtschaftsethik der Weltreligionen* brought this phase of his life and production to a close. Later he seemed to look back at it with distaste. In 1913 he raged about the 'methodological pestilence' in sociology,[11] although he himself had previously been one of those most stricken with it. However, once the scientific discoveries were flowing again, the epistemological doubts melted away. As soon as he had things straightened out with his own nature, his relationship with external nature became more trustful again, and his need for polemic against the bogey of 'naturalism' subsided. When the essence of science no longer consisted in method, the gulf between the human and natural sciences closed – a gulf based mainly on differences in method, not in cognitive interest. In 1914 Weber wrote in the preface to the *Grundriß der Sozialökonomik*: 'In respect of method, we shall have to get more used to the idea that in our discipline all roads join up again.'[12]

When Weber wrote in the *Zwischenbetrachtung* that the Greek poetess Sappho was 'unequalled by man in the capacity for erotic feeling' (FMW 345), this bold claim expressed an astonishing confidence in his cognitive powers of intuition. Already in his methodological writings (WL 217, 327; CS 103) we sometimes come across the idea that too much brooding about our capacity for knowledge is not only pointless but can even block the mind from advancing. At the end of all the torture, when he turned against the 'methodological pestilence', he recalled the 'toad's curse': the Buddhist fable recounted by Gustav Meyrink, in which the millipede, when asked by the guileful toad how he manages to coordinate all his feet for walking, ponders and ponders until he is no longer able to move at all. Weber laconically comments: 'You can walk without knowing the anatomy of your legs.'[13] If we follow this through, the argument would be that knowledge – like erotic feeling – has something intuitive or instinctual that is lost if we reflect on it. By nature Weber was not at all inclined to doubt the possibility of knowing the world and, in particular, his own cognitive capacities; he liked to give his assertions additional emphasis by adding phrases such as 'without a doubt' or 'as every well-informed person knows'. And, towards the end of his life, he may have seen in his critique of knowledge one of those 'masks' of which he spoke to Else. Still, even masks have their attraction.

For all the torments, epistemology had a special appeal for a scientist who, having barely recovered his health, was still incapable of undertaking a major work and therefore of returning the favour when colleagues kept sending him their latest title. He had to redefine his role in the pursuit of science, to build a new kind of intellectual self-confidence, and to make some use of his experience of illness. He was faced with men such as Roscher or Knies, Werner Sombart or Eduard Meyer, who had a huge capacity to digest literature and to produce one book after another. Whereas Weber had for years been half-crippled in this respect, others stacked their opus ever higher and gained a lead over him which must have seemed impossible to close, at least quantitatively.

The picture would look quite different if epistemology came first and any certainty about our knowledge was questionable. Then Weber could turn his inability to produce on a massive scale into an actual plus, by critically examining how the great cognitive edifices had come into being. We can imagine how his illness may have brought him to such an attitude of mind. Someone who experiences himself – his own mind and his own nature – as a painful enigma, and whose depressive states prevent him from returning to good times, has reason to be sceptical of the results when he sees scholars intuitively place themselves inside alien persons or communities, especially if the supposed empathy occurs with too much pleasure and enjoyment.

History as a natural process

Weber's essay 'Die 'Objektivität' sozialwissenschaftlicher und sozialpolitischer Erkenntnis' [The 'Objectivity' of Knowledge in Social Science and Social Policy] first appeared in 1904 in the *Archiv für Sozialwissenschaft und Sozialpolitik*, at a time when the editorship was passing from the social democrat Heinrich Braun to Edgar Jaffé, Werner Sombart and Max Weber. The article therefore had a programmatic character, its main tendency being to draw a sharper line than before between social science and social policy; politics is essentially about struggle, commitment and consciously one-sided positions, whereas science can develop its special quality only if it systematically shuns one-sideness.

The climax of Weber's article comes in the well-known passages where he presents history as a dark stream, a natural process with no recognizable meaning or foreseeable end. 'The stream of infinite events flows constantly towards eternity.'[14] One should not fall into the illusion that value-conceptions cherished by the human mind are inherent in this stream: 'The light given off by these highest evaluative ideas falls upon an ever-changing finite part of the monstrously chaotic stream of events that flows through time.'[15] The conception of history as progress towards human perfection, which had been popular ever since the Enlightenment, was therefore erroneous in Weber's eyes.

But the mood of these passages is not uniformly bleak; for historically oriented social scientists, the eternal flow of human affairs offers a great hope, a great opportunity for new questions and answers. Later, at the sociologists' congress in 1910, Weber presented social science as perpetual unrest, which, similarly to the stream of history, uncovers ever new grounds and backgrounds for events. 'Nowhere do we have any point of rest', neither in religion nor in economics and technology (GASS 456). And, for a man who was never finished with anything, this 'never-finished' character of history was undoubtedly agreeable. Already in 1904 he depicted sociology as a probing, self-rejuvenating science that never achieves perfection. Today, as social scientists precociously behave with more overbearing self-confidence, such lines give his theoretical writings a still enduring attraction. 'There are sciences destined to eternal youthfulness' – here we detect Weber's new tone – 'and that includes all *historical* disciplines, all those disciplines to which the eternally advancing flow of culture poses new problems.'[16]

Of course, Weber knew that historians by no means always embodied this eternal youthfulness, but it represented a chance of life in the situation in which he then found himself. He no longer needed to think of his years of incapacity as time he had wasted while other scholars were busily putting together their life's work; the hiatus in his life, the compulsion to begin again, made him capable of tackling new themes brought to him by the stream of time. He could throw a bridge between his old political economy (in which he did not get any further) and the modern, undogmatic study of religion that blossomed in Heidelberg after 1900; he could look around in the United States, to see whether the problems of nationalities and indigenous peoples got him going on a new track; and he could immerse himself in Russian events after the outbreak of revolution in 1905, while his colleagues had to spend their time on lectures and ongoing research. Nowhere did the wild dark stream of history arouse such fascination as in Russia in 1905.

At the end of his article on objectivity, with a sensitivity to the material side of science, Weber described sociological method as not only a problem for epistemology but also a question of intellectual taste, when he distinguished between the hunger for 'facts' of 'material specialists' and the intellectual 'gourmandise' of 'interpretative specialists'. The 'interpretative specialist' was more select, but Weber did not wish be that type only, who 'dulled the taste for facts by ever newer conceptual distillations'.[17] Weber, whose eating and drinking habits oscillated between gluttony and asceticism, alcoholism and teetotalism, knew the two types of specialist and their respective hangovers well enough from his own experience. His new ideal was the many-sided libido: first at the level of the intellect, then in the life of the senses.

Unlike the 'essay of sighs', which simply peters out at the end, the essay on objectivity builds up to a thrilling Weberian finale that offers encouragement to up-and-coming scientists and to Weber himself in his forced new beginning. The dark stream of history gives way to a dawn of delight, when old tracks have disappeared in the darkness and science is finding a new youth:

> But at some point the atmosphere alters: the significance of viewpoints used unreflectively becomes uncertain, the path becomes lost in the twilight. The light cast by the great cultural problems has moved onward. Then even science prepares to shift its ground and change its conceptual apparatus so that it might regard the stream of events from the heights of reflective thought. . . . It follows those stars which are alone able to give meaning and direction to its labour: '. . . *der neue Trieb erwacht, / Ich eile fort, ihr ew'ges Licht zu trinken, / Vor mir den Tag und hinter mir die Nacht, / Den Himmel über mir und unter mir die Wellen*' (A new impulse awakes, / I hurry forth to drink its eternal light, / Before me the day, behind me the night, / Heaven above, beneath me the waves).[18]

The ideal type: a symbolic solution to the problems of knowledge and life

The article on objectivity occupies a prominent position in Weber studies mainly because it was there that Weber introduced his concept of ideal type. Of the 187 appearances of the term in the electronic edition of Weber's works, eighty-two are in this text alone. The ideal type has since been regarded as a distinguishing feature of Weber's method, but it is a subject for inexhaustible discussion since the definition he gave of it was not perfect for the needs of theoreticians. It is possible to construct any number of pedigrees for this concept – from Aristotle through to Simmel[19] – as thinking in types runs through the whole of Western intellectual history; the real task would be to find examples of *not* thinking in types. Marianne Weber refers to the fact that Weber's friend Georg Jellinek, the expert in constitutional law, spoke of 'ideal types' in a book published in 1900 (WB 314), but

Tenbruck has shown that Weber cannot have derived his concept from there. For Jellinek the ideal type was an ideal, a norm, which it certainly was not for Weber. 'There are ideal types of brothels as well as religions', he wrote, and the ideal type of the brothel is not necessarily the 'ideal' brothel from the point of view of a moral police.[20]

Weber himself pointed out that there was nothing new in his reasons for introducing the concept of ideal type: 'The language of the historian contains hundreds of words that are ambiguous constructs created by the unreflecting need for the expression of thought constructs, words whose meaning is only sensed, but not clearly conceived.'[21] It was evident to Weber that man had a spontaneous natural tendency to such 'thought constructs': this idea – that perception in types is prior to the perception of individuals – corresponds to the state of evolutionary research at that time. All Weber did was introduce a concept for the unconscious or half-conscious procedure involved in the articulation of factual data. The argument over who did what first is much ado about nothing.

Weber starts by mentioning 'abstract economic theory' as a rich source of ideal types with which historians, including economic historians, set to work.[22] *Homo oeconomicus* is the best-known ideal type in this field; Weber himself adopted it in his later defences of *The Protestant Ethic*, though not in the original book.[23] Of course, *homo oeconomicus* as such was a construct of classical liberal economics, and the German Historical School repeatedly went out of its way to demonstrate that it was a mere phantom and should by no means be confused with actual people. Weber, too, devoted a large part of his life's work to proving that this human type was characteristic only of modern Western capitalism, and that it had had no place in most of human history. Nevertheless, *homo oeconomicus* did correspond to a *tendency* in modern Western life, and it could be accepted as an ideal type in the Weberian sense, if not as an embodiment of man as such. Plessner rightly detects in Weber the idea that the typical is structurally present within reality and not just projected into it by the human mind (WzG 33).

When discussing Weber's ideal type, we should not forget that he was coming from a background in political economy. The concept was originally, and primarily, suited for a role in the methodological dispute between the Historical School and its theoretically ambitious opponents. On the other hand, it cut across the efforts of the Heidelberg neo-Kantians to ground the autonomy of the human sciences. In 1905, Weber tried to explain his conceptual innovation to the philosopher Rickert and to make it more palatable to him:

> That you have linguistic doubts about the 'ideal type' distresses me in my paternal vanity. But my view is that, if we speak of Bismarck not as the 'ideal' among Germans but as the 'ideal type' of German, we do not mean anything 'exemplary' as such but are saying that he possessed certain German, essentially indifferent and perhaps even

unpleasant qualities – e.g., a great thirst – in a distinctively heightened measure, in their 'conceptual purity'.[24]

The reference to Bismarck's 'thirst' suggests that the letter was not meant to be taken too seriously, but it strengthened Rickert's conviction that Weber did not have the makings of a philosopher. In comparison with the difficult ideal-type debates in later research, the letter is of a staggering platitude. Could Weber really have come up with the idea that Bismarck was a kind of prototype of the Germans of his age, even if it is true that they venerated him as an ideal? For Weber and many others besides, the German dilemma lay precisely in the fact that there was not a second Bismarck! Weber's brash explanation of his ideal type to the critical philosopher makes one suspect that Weber studies people have attached just a little too much importance to his creation of the concept.

Paul Lazarsfeld, the most successful of the sociologists who emigrated to the United States after 1933, thinks we would do best to forget Weber's definition of the ideal type if we wish to learn 'how Weber actually worked'.[25] For logical purists, there has always been something unsatisfactory about the concept of the ideal type, as its purport is derived both from the consistency of an ideal and from the proximity of material reality. But its true meaning is not drawn only from the logic of science; it contains, at least symbolically, a solution to the basic problem of all solitary pondering, in so far as it places the fantasy of the imagination in a relationship with the real world. This had been the problem of many German thinkers since the great age of speculative philosophy. It grew all the more acute as a subjective kind of thinking and feeling became more luxuriant and led to a hypertrophy of the imagination. A deep gulf thus developed between the ego and the external world; thought turned in on itself and became aware that it was certain of nothing other than itself. This was a point of departure for modern philosophy.

The basic problem of philosophy corresponds to the basic problem of sexuality in the age of growing subjectivism and imagination run wild: namely, that a rift may open up between the desired ideal and actually available partners, so that the art of projecting dream-images of the libido on to living people is all too often unsuccessful. This must have been an elementary dilemma for Max Weber too, which caused him even more trouble than it did many other people. There was no connection between the world of nocturnal dreams and the conscious world of the daytime. As he told Marianne in his letter of courtship, his semi-fiancée Emmy Baumgarten had left him with a deeply distressing sense of the gulf between dream-image and reality, and when he saw her again several years later he had felt a sudden incapacity for love: 'I saw her, the appearance and voice of old, and it was as if some invisible hand were extinguishing her image deep in my heart, for the figure that approached me was different from the one that had lived in me, as though it were from another world' (WB 178). Things must have been rather similar with Marianne. The ideal type, an intellectual construct capable of handling reality, was the symbolic solution to the problem of Weber's life, precisely because it was not meant to be a 'desired ideal' but was supposed to help in getting to grips with reality.

What distinguishes the Weberian ideal type from all the other types found in the world of science is that it is comparatively autonomous: it does not stand in a systemic relation to other ideal types, nor is it conceived of as one in a succession of types. 'Domestic economy' does not exist only at the beginning of human history, nor 'bureaucratic rule' only at its end; 'rationalization' may be found in various forms at quite different places in history. The 'charismatic prophet' is not located only in the time from Jeremiah to Muhammad; it is conceivable that he will return in the future.

For someone who thought in terms of the stages of development of the Historical School, Weber's ideal types were left hanging in the air. As Horst Baier showed in his post-doctoral thesis, this kind of ideal type has most in common with biological thinking: 'Goethe was the first to work typologically, in his morphological studies of plants and animals. . . . To be precise, Herder already used a concept of "type" to denote a single basic plan persisting through the diversity of animal forms of life, and this usage had a demonstrable influence on Goethe.'[26] Similarly Helmuth Plessner: 'The ideal type is a way of escaping the straitjacket of a split between nature and culture.'[27] What is so difficult for 'plain sociology' is perfectly straightforward in biology: to imagine an internally harmonious ideal type which, though existing only in variants from the type, is a recurrent tendency in reality.

Against Rudolf Stammler: Weber as an anti-antimaterialist

After the 'essay of sighs', Weber's most substantial (though for researchers also most obscure) treatise on scientific theory is his polemic against the legal philosopher Rudolf Stammler, ironically entitled in German *R. Stammlers 'Überwindung' der materialistischen Geschichtsauffassung* [R. Stammler's 'Supersession' of the Materialist Conception of History].[28] This was not an incidental dispute for Weber, and it continued to occupy him over the years. Even such a good Weber expert as Edith Hanke 'knows of no other book on which Weber worked as meticulously' as on Stammler's *Wirtschaft und Recht nach der materialistischen Geschichtsauffassung* [Economics and Law in the Materialist Conception of History] (orig. 1896).[29] And yet, it has always been difficult even for experts to determine exactly what was at stake for Weber.[30] Stammler himself had the greatest trouble working out just what Weber had against him; he commented mildly yet bitingly that Weber's review of his book was 'no model of a clear refutation'.[31] He was right about that. When discussing Weber's philosophy of science, one should not make it one's whole ambition to fabricate a clear system out of all the unclear elements, but should rather investigate the very ambiguity in the text. That too tells us something. Evidently Weber had problems formulating a clear and consistent position on the issue of naturalism. His *rapprochement* with certain naturalist positions took place without a decisive rejection of his previously robust anti-naturalism.

In the extensive 'Weber and' literature, there is nothing entitled 'Weber and Stammler' – even though Weber repeatedly came back to the legal theorist in *Economy and Society*. At the beginning of the famous section on 'Basic Sociological Terms', he writes that his critique of Stammler already 'contains many of the fundamental ideas of the following exposition' (E&S 4) – which suggests that the dispute had a catalytic effect on his creativity. He still expresses annoyance at the overwhelming role accorded to 'order' in 'the brilliant book of Rudolf Stammler', which is 'nevertheless fundamentally misleading and confuses the issues in a catastrophic fashion' (E&S 32), as if social action were exclusively geared to legal orders established from above. Also directed against Stammler is the remark that 'for the legal theorist . . . the (ideological) validity of a legal norm is conceptually the *prius*', whereas the sociologist attributes 'the beginnings of actual regularity and "usage", shrouded in darkness everywhere, . . . to the instinctive habituation of a pattern of conduct which was "adapted" to given necessities' (E&S 333). In Weber's view, then, what has to be discovered is the natural basis of legal norms. Rules themselves have their origin in the regularity of natural processes: 'Consider the proposition "my digestion is rule-governed". Most obviously, this proposition merely states the following simple "fact of nature": the process of digestion transpires within a certain temporal sequence. The "rule" is an abstraction from the natural process' (CS 105).

In dealing with Stammler, who had done nothing to harm him, Weber adopted a violent and, as he admitted (MWG II/6, 121f.), deliberately offensive tone, which even he later thought had gone too far. He raged against Stammler's 'thicket of apparent truths, half truths and truths incorrectly formulated' and of 'unclear formulations of covert falsities' (CS 60), as if the respected legal theorist were an academic con-man. Rudolf Stammler (1856–1938), from the same generation as Weber, was then one of the leading minds in the German philosophy of law, who belonged to the camp of neo-Kantianism and its front against 'naturalism'. Indeed, the Weber who had joined battle with Roscher and Knies might have been expected to welcome him as an ally – but there was to be nothing like that. Again and again Weber waxed ironical about our 'historical spiritualist' (CS 63, 65), in scare quotes. Later, at the sociologists' congress in Frankfurt, Weber denounced Stammler for grotesquely distorting the 'materialist conception of history' and creating a straw man in which Marx would never have recognized himself (GASS 450).

Weber felt provoked above all by Stammler's thesis that social relationships are constituted only by legal orders. In his own mind, the agents in history were not supra-individual orders but individual human beings, and orders operated only through them by becoming their habits or 'second nature' or inner compulsions, just as worldly asceticism became for the

Puritans. Only in *Economy and Society* did he identify, in condensed form, what he believed to be at stake: acquisition, habituation and tradition 'have a formidable influence in favour of a habituated legal order, even where such an order originally derives from legal enactment. This influence is more powerful than any reflection on impending means of coercion or other consequences considering also the fact that at least some of those who act according to the "norms" are totally unaware of them' (E&S 327). In the last sentence Weber addresses a dilemma for a consistent legal positivism. For, if law becomes law only through state coercion and is not grounded upon a spontaneous human consciousness of right and wrong, how can everyone be expected to obey the law – even people with no knowledge of the latest developments in state legislation?

In the dispute with Stammler, and only there, Weber made some detailed observations about the concept of 'nature'. Their main drift is that a comprehensive struggle against naturalism has as little point as a fundamental separation between the natural and social sciences. 'Nature' is ambiguous and offers no front against which a rational attack can be launched. Weber here takes the opportunity to distinguish among several concepts of nature: 'dead' nature, which is the object of physics and chemistry; 'dead' nature combined with non-human animate nature, which is the object of biology; and the 'vegetative' or 'autonomic' nature that man has in common with animals. In addition, there are nature in the methodological sense of an object of natural science with its own putative general 'laws', and nature as an empirical 'is' as opposed to 'ought', a bare, meaningless suchness contrasted with any meaning (CS 98f., 110f.). He does not speak here of the old Stoic tradition of a spirit of nature that itself becomes the norm. He repeats the objection he had made against Knies: the concrete totality of natural processes can no more be deduced from laws than can human history (CS 149f.). Nowhere else does Weber so clearly retreat from his earlier assault on naturalism as in the critique of Stammler.

Nature and natural law

When it came to nature and the philosophy of law, nothing suggested itself more than the theme of natural law, especially as Stammler had spent some time pulling the whole idea of it to pieces. 'All so-called natural law' was for him a misleading way of packaging what was 'nothing more than an expression of the attempt to draw up legal statutes as they really ought to be, on the basis of generally valid objective knowledge'. It had its roots in past times when nature had been the object of philosophical speculation rather than empirical investigation. The concrete empirical nature of man, being 'subject to constant change and unavoidable alteration', could not be used as the basis for a generally applicable body of laws. Human nature was variously defined in accordance with the result that one wished to achieve: 'Now it is fear or hate that man feels before other men with the force of natural necessity, now it is love and affection and benevolence, as well as a wish for lasting unity.' In reality, then, the 'reference to human nature' affords no legal principles unconditionally valid 'for all times and all nations'.[32] He only fleetingly touches on whether, in certain epochs and cultural spaces, trans-generational habituation could make certain legal principles part of second nature for the great majority of people, even without knowledge of the law, and therefore count in this sense as 'natural law'.

Curiously, in his attacks on Stammler, Weber does not take a bite at the subject of 'natural law'. In his discussion of various concepts of nature he ignores the one that signifies natural law, and indeed the only time he explicitly mentions natural law is when he refers incidentally and ironically to the rules of skat (CS 115f.). For nearly twenty pages he keeps returning with visible pleasure to the example of this card game, to show that people stick to rules even in the absence of a legal system and a police force – simply for the sake of the game, and so as not be a spoil-sport. We can understand why Weber thought an anarchist could be a good legal expert. A game is no fun if the players do not observe certain rules.

Weber does not clearly take the side of natural law against Stammler, with the result that still today he is often thought to have been opposed to natural law, as he was to naturalism in the human sciences. Even such a connoisseur as Leo Strauss, for whom Weber was 'the greatest social scientist of our (i.e., the twentieth) century', spent forty-five pages arguing against Weber's (ultimately diabolical, in Strauss's view) value relativism, and he did so on the premise that Weber had been an opponent of the idea of natural law,[33] totally ignoring Paragraph 7 of Weber's sociology of law.[34]

The triumph of legal positivism, which saw the state as the only source of law, exposed the natural law tradition to ever sharper attacks in Weber's lifetime. Karl Magnus Bergbohm, a pioneering champion of legal positivism, threw down the gauntlet in 1892: 'The weeds of natural law, in whichever form and disguise they appear, must be torn up by the roots, pitilessly and with the utmost thoroughness'; any intellectual labour oriented to natural law was 'foolishly wasted'.[35] But precisely such attacks, which implied that the individual should be completely at the mercy of the respective state, were likely to dampen Weber's eagerness to join battle with natural law.

At the age of twenty-four, in a letter to his brother Alfred, Weber already declared himself unhappy with the position that the state was the only source of law and that the force of customary law depended entirely on endorsement by the state (JB 310f.). Paul Honigsheim, who knew the Catholic natural law tradition and had considerable understanding for it,[36] stressed that Weber conceived of natural law as a historical force and that his own history had 'captivated' him; this 'pronounced interest' linked him to the constitutional theorist Jellinek (WzG 213, 228).[37] Eduard Baumgarten too, who devoted the second chapter of his documentary book on Weber to natural law, pointed out that Weber did not extend his exorcism of naturalistic elements to natural law and felt greater sympathy towards it than he generally displayed (B 428ff.), whereas Marianne, more given than he to nature worship, showed stronger reservations about natural law, especially when it was used to give marriage a sexual foundation (EM 292ff.).

As we have seen, Weber thought of the Russian revolution of 1905 as the 'last of the natural-law-oriented agrarian revolutions'. In this connection, natural law meant that the land belonged to those who worked it, and that within the rural commune held together by brotherliness everyone had an equal right to the fruits of the earth. Here natural law sprang not from a 'natural reason' common to all intelligent people but from the vitality of nature: the basic vital instinct and the interconnected existence of the peasantry and village. Later, when he was working more intensively on the cultures of the East, Weber recognized natural law as the distinctive element of the West's special path. In the *Zwischenbetrachtung*, 'worldly asceticism' takes a 'revolutionary form' 'wherever (it) is capable of opposing an absolute and divine "natural law" to the creaturely, wicked and empirical orders of the world; it then becomes a religious duty to realize this divine natural law, according to the sentence that one must obey God rather than men' (FMW 340). So, divine natural law here gets along with the wickedness of creaturely nature. It is not quite the same as peasant natural law in the Russian revolution, though in both cases there is a heroic consistency that Weber admires.[38] In a curiously little-noted passage of *Economy and Society*, he registers the decline of natural law in modern times, establishes that it does not have only rational grounds, and makes no secret of regretting the trend:

> It would hardly seem possible to eradicate completely from legal practice all the latent influence of unacknowledged axioms of natural law. . . . (However,) all metajuristic axioms in general have been subject to ever continuing disintegration and relativization. In consequence of both juridical rationalism and modern intellectual scepticism in general, the axioms of natural law have lost all capacity to provide the fundamental basis of a legal system. . . . Consequently, legal positivism has, at least for the time being, advanced irresistibly. The disappearance of the old natural law conceptions has destroyed all possibility of providing the law with a metaphysical dignity by virtue of its immanent qualities. . . . But this extinction of the metajuristic implications of the law is one of those ideological developments which . . . have effectively promoted the actual obedience to the power, now viewed solely from an instrumentalist standpoint, of the authorities who claim legitimacy at the moment. Among the practitioners of the law this attitude has been particularly pronounced. (E&S 874f.)

This passage is also revealing for Weber's sociology of rule or domination (*Herrschaft*). His way of differentiating types of rule by their legitimacy makes sense only against the background of natural law conceptions. If law could be manipulated at will by each form of rule, it would mean that any definition of forms of rule by their mode of legitimation was just propaganda. We see how Weber found his way back through jurisprudence from a dully vegetative conception of nature to one replete with spirit and reason. He also showed how it was possible to operate with natural law in concrete cases, potentially even against the state. At a time when the value of the mark was collapsing under the weight of public debt, so that inflation was causing Weber real material worries, he wrote that, in accordance with natural law, the legal order had a duty to allow 'the state to go pieces' rather than that 'the legitimate stability of the law should be sullied by the illegitimacy of "artificially" created paper money' (E&S 870).

An 'infinitely tender, eternally violated sense of justice,' as Theodor Heuss put it, was part of Max Weber's character;[39] it was closely bound up with his highly developed sense of honour. Furthermore, natural law had a deeply personal significance as the feeling grew stronger inside him that the repression of his sexual nature was the main cause of his illness. A natural right to extra-marital sex could be derived from this. The sexual side of natural law was always present in Marianne's women's rights perspective, where the epithet 'natural' referred mainly to man's vegetative nature. In legal history, marriage law was always the 'touchstone for the autonomous validity of *ius naturale*' vis-à-vis state legislation and divine law (Franz Wiesacker).[40]

Large-scale industry and the nature of workers: Weber's 'psychophysics' of industrial labour

Another reason why natural law became an acute issue for Weber was his suspicion that working conditions in modern industrial capitalism were in some degree contrary to human nature, that those affected by them were permanently damaged and suffered a major injury to their human dignity. This is the background to the two long essays that he wrote in 1908–9 on the 'psycho-physical' state of workers in large-scale modern industry. For many researchers, these are isolated pieces in Weber's *oeuvre* and do not have much bearing on his theoretical edifice.[41] Nevertheless, Weber's tense relationship with naturalism in the human sciences here becomes more concrete.

The stimulus for Weber's new field of research came from his brother Alfred, who in 1907 was offered a chair at Heidelberg University and (in a spirit far from brotherly friendship) once more became part of Max's immediate human milieu. Alfred Weber was by then a convinced supporter of naturalism in the social sciences, of social Darwinism and vitalism, and was operating quite uninhibitedly with such concepts as 'development', 'degeneration', 'adaptation' and 'life'. (We should bear in mind that 'degeneration' did not yet evoke any associations with extermination; it was actually the left-liberal Lujo Brentano who argued in vain at the Verein für Sozialpolitik for systematic study of the problem of degeneration, in which Alfred Weber also took a 'burning interest'.)[42]

Soon after his arrival in Heidelberg, Alfred Weber agreed with Max to undertake a joint project on industrial labour, which would mainly consider its physical and psychological demands on workers and its effects on their personality. The Verein für Sozialpolitik gave them its backing, furnished an advance of 10,000 marks and appointed a committee consisting of Herkner, Schmoller and Alfred Weber to oversee the project.[43] Max Weber therefore assumed no personal responsibility, having probably refused to accept any, as he usually did in those years.

Yet, although the idea for the project originally came from Alfred, Max Weber's work behind the scenes far exceeded that of the committee members. First he wrote a 'methodological introduction' to the study, which addressed an endless series of questions and criteria and called up a vision of sociology as Big Science. As if this were not enough, he then wrote another essay, *Zur Psychophysik der industriellen Arbeit*, not directly prompted by the Verein project (MWGI/11, 48), which took on the dimensions of a book and greatly expanded and complicated the range of viewpoints to be addressed in the investigation. Today's experts will be reminded of the intellectual swagger involved in the culture of grandiose research projects, then still in its infancy. The preliminaries got so out of hand that they threatened to swamp the actual research and put off those signed up for it; the results anyway did not remotely live up to the tremendous opening fanfare, although seven volumes did appear by 1915 (MWG I/11, 19). The questionnaire returns were unsatisfactory, as neither employers nor workers took the whole thing to heart.

Why 'psychophysics'?

Why did Max Weber expend all this unnecessary effort on the preliminaries to the Verein für Sozialpolitik project – work that was not even his responsibility? In March 1909 he complained to Friedrich Naumann that his poor brain, 'mistreated' by strong sleeping drugs, was good only for 'calculations to do with work and psychophysics, and so on' (MWG II/6, 85). But why did he expand the 'psychophysics' so much if he thought of it merely as a stopgap? Like his other methodological studies, it had something of the character of systematic self-torture, in which he very rarely reached a climax that released some of the tensions. Towards the end of 1909 he complained to Robert Michels's wife that he was 'completely without a desire to work' since he had 'brought under the roof this dreadful stuff about the "psychophysics of work", deserving only of a *maiden* effort' (MWG II/6, 347).

The very term 'psychophysics' seems scandalous in terms of the usual image of Weber, for it suggests an indissoluble link between the mental and physical make-up of industrial workers and points to a special kind of research programme that includes physiological investigations. It opened a wide gateway for naturalism to enter the social sciences. This physiological version of naturalism was too much even for Ernst Haeckel.[44] The term itself originated with Gustav Theodor Fechner (1801–87), founder of the Leipzig experimental psychology that Weber held in such contempt, whose two-volume work *Elemente der Psychophysik* (1860) had tried to found an 'exact natural theory' of the human soul, while at the same time holding devotedly to a pantheistic faith in the animation of all nature.[45]

Marianne Weber rightly saw the *Psychophysik* as a kind of counterpoint to *The Protestant Ethic*: 'There Weber . . . traced the shaping of those types that are serviceable to modern capitalism by spiritual factors; now their dependency on the technical forms of work was to be investigated' (WB 367). And this was even though Weber had no theory about it, no compelling point in mind. It looks as if he was simply curious and wanted to add to his learning; that too was part of Weber's kind of scholarship. He even used the term 'psychophysics' without his beloved scare-quotes, respectfully referring no fewer than ninety-two times, over many pages of text, to Kraepelin and his school – an uncharacteristic compliment, which the pope of psychiatry, a man well known to Weber who had diagnosed him during his illness, never deigned to return. Kraepelin worked with the methods of the natural sciences, and his psychiatry was based on the indivisibility of body and mind. We may well wonder how much importance Weber really attached to Kraepelin's psychiatry, which had been no more capable than others of curing him. But, in his emphasis on the physical determinants of fatigue and the impossibility of overcoming it by an effort of will, Kraepelin was the best authority to be used against Helene, who tortured her son by suggesting that he could become capable of work again if only he pulled himself together.

Looking for ways to generalize from his experience of illness

Kraepelin, privately a follower of Buddha, took very seriously the widespread complaints about 'excessive burdens of school work', and experimental evidence of fatigue led him to remark that what could stop modern man from becoming a nervous wreck was 'our golden idleness'.[46] Exhaustion affected the whole person and could not be overcome by switching between intellectual and physical activity. Sabine Frommer rightly suspects that 'Max Weber's interest in Kraepelin's studies of fatigue had not only a scientific but also a biographical aspect' (MWG I/11, 26). In particular, this must have been the reason why Weber bit so heavily on the subject; the effort would have been irrational simply as part of a scientific strategy.

To be sure, Weber knew only too well from his own experience that one should not easily accept the diagnosis of 'exhaustion'. The *Psychophysik*, like his own illness, is full of open questions. Was he really a victim of overwork, or did his diagnosis too not have an element of officially prescribed wording? At one point he regretted that 'the far from irrelevant sexual lives of the workers are not investigated at all in connection with their work performance', and in a footnote he even found it 'amazing that no survey has yet been organized among doctors – as international as possible, of course – which might give some idea of what is considered the normal frequency of sexual intercourse in different ethnic, social, cultural and climatic conditions (first of all in marriage, which is the most important thermometer)' (GASS 174). He thought in all seriousness that this could fairly easily provide clear, internationally valid knowledge – of the kind that is still not available to us today. The passage highlights the exaggerated ideas of natural determination that Weber then held, and shows that his battles against naturalism were not much more than rearguard actions in the face of a force often painfully felt to be superior. As we can see, far from believing that everyone shared his own sexual disposition, Weber was aware that sexuality was subject to general rules and that there certainly was such a thing as 'normality'.

Especially in the second part of the *Psychophysik*, where he finally broke free of Kraepelin, Weber had an opportunity to bring to bear his family ties with the Oerlinghausen textile mill, whose internal life initially appeared to him as a hermetic world penetrable only through 'connections'. In the summer of 1908, he spent several weeks at Oerlinghausen to get a more concrete idea of the methodological problems involved in a major project on the 'psychophysics' of industrial labour. He also went into a lot of statistical details, in the hope of becoming as expert as possible in this field (WB 330). He drew fatigue curves,[47] on the assumption that the workers' exhaustion was subject to certain natural laws. In the end the strain on Weber's family connections in Oerlinghausen had its limits, so great was their reluctance to allow the firm's affairs to become known outside. When he returned there in May 1909, this time for a rest, there were 'all kinds of differences with the cousins over what should and should not be published, . . . so dreadfully heated that it was really no good at all for his health'.[48]

In 1911, in his report at the Nuremberg congress of the Verein für Sozialpolitik, Weber emphasized that 'only during his own numerical calculations does the idea come to the researcher that he needs to interpret the figures and to find new questions' (GASS 425): a declaration of faith in the inductive method. But, of course, he was not content with plain figures; the 'real attraction' of the whole thing began only at the point he scarcely reached, where the account turned 'from mere calculation of often ambiguous, always abstract, figures in the accounts to the reality of the workshop and there looked living people and restless machinery in the face' (GASS 232f.). Again the Weberian hunger for reality, for a concrete history of the relationship between man and technology. It was a hunger that would remain unsatisfied.

Alfred Weber was unhappy with the results of his brother's surprising enthusiasm for work on a project that he had suggested in the first place: 'My own interest, altogether centred on the personal fate of the workers, was . . . frustrated and drowned out by the questions that my brother set.

. . . Here it was all about objective analysis of the business as it related to the physiology and psychology of the workforce' (MWG I/11, 54).[49] And indeed, in his 'methodological introduction', Max Weber confirmed that the problem of the workers' performance under various conditions was 'to be addressed entirely from the point of view of *profitability*' (GASS 23). In 1911 Herkner reported to the Nuremberg congress of the Verein that, 'without a doubt', the workers had been 'in their overwhelming majority thoroughly ill-disposed towards the enquiry'; the social democratic newspaper *Die Neue Zeit* 'demanded greater respect for the workers and less academic callousness'.[50]

But Max Weber was no Frederick W. Taylor: his *Psychophysik* was not intended to track down 'soldiering' and hidden reserves in the workforce. In Weber's view, there was a 'brake' in the world of industrial labour whenever workers' solidarity existed without a trade-union organization; it was 'the form in which a workforce consciously and stubbornly, but also speechlessly, haggled and fought with the entrepreneur over the price for their performance' (GASS 156). This is one of the most powerful passages in the otherwise often tiresome essay. Weber knew from experience that slowing down in the nick of time is sometimes necessary for self-preservation; the pressures of work in industry are contrary to natural instincts. The 'methodological introduction' ends with an authentically Weberian crescendo: 'The structure of the peculiar "apparatus" that the large-scale organization of industry has "slapped on the heads" of the population' – a quotation from Alfred Weber – 'has changed and will continue to change the spiritual face of humanity almost beyond recognition' (GASS 59, 60). But until then this process had escaped any exact research. At Nuremberg in 1911 Weber caustically remarked that there was constant talk of the 'great "results"' of these investigations . . ., and of splendid work lying ahead'. But all that was an illusion. 'Up to now, gentlemen, absolutely nothing has come out of it in the way of conclusive results.'[51]

Max versus Alfred Weber: agnosticism versus vitalism

In his epistemological period, Weber tried to create an image of disillusioned agnosticism, in line with the Socratic 'I know that I know nothing'. His brother Alfred did things quite differently: it was no problem for him to present results in Nuremberg. Most attention was paid to his balance-sheet, which had already been drawn a little less abruptly by Heinrich Herkner: 'By and large, the worker ceases at the age of forty to be a really thoroughly useful, highly skilled person standing in a close relationship with fast-working machinery.'[52] Richard Woldt, a social democrat expert on Taylorism, remembered this fifteen years later as the 'terrible insight' that the faster pace of work had led the worker to be 'thrown on the scrap-heap' during his lifetime.[53] In 1911 in Nuremberg, however,

Herkner immediately toned down Alfred Weber's verdict: the 'weeding out' of over-forties was not general but occurred only in 'individual large companies with very short working hours that made especially close calculations'.[54]

Alfred Weber, by contrast, pressed ahead with dramatic theses that blithely mixed facts and value-judgements: specialization was quite unnecessarily leading to a situation where workers performed the same operations all their lives – in his view, 'a paste-and-use fate of the worst kind'. It had been established that workers typically 'stick not only at the same place but in the same firm'; 'a hopeless situation in my eyes'.[55] He had just before been complaining about the fluctuations in the workers' lives, and now he was complaining about the static element, without asking whether it did not give workers a bit of the longed-for feeling of security. He advocated a formal stipulation that large-scale industry should allow employees to 'change between several kinds of task', although he knew that many workers would not be keen on this, and that often 'even a tram conductor would not want to be a tram driver, so used is he to the eternal punching of tickets'.

Sabine Frommer is probably right that Max Weber's epistemological braking actions at crucial points in the 'methodological introduction' and the *Psychophysik* involve a kind of shadow-boxing with his brother (MWG I/11, 52ff.), whose imperturbability had something provocative – not only for Max Weber. Weber himself wrote to Gruhle that, as he well knew, the *Psychophysik* was a 'dilettante piece in the highest sense of the word'; 'between the two of us', one of the reasons why he had made the effort was 'to demonstrate to (his) brother the great (probably insuperable) difficulties of approaching the *heredity* problem in this way' (MWG II/5, 675).

It is scarcely credible, however, that Max Weber would have pursued such an objection only to irritate his brother, especially as, in the Verein für Sozialpolitik at that time, the two appeared so eloquently as pugnacious twins that Schmoller once joked about imposing a joint limit of fifty-nine minutes on their speaking time. Max must also have hoped that his experiences of illness, psychiatry and the Oerlinghausen factory would get him a little further with the big issue of how work in modern industry overtaxes and alters human nature, even if he remained tangled up in methodological difficulties. That there are laws of human nature – if not general, then individual or attributable to certain human types – was something he knew from his own life. 'We repeatedly stumble upon the significance of individual particularity; we may even say that it follows us wherever we go', he wrote in the final résumé on the performance and fatigue curves; these may not be general, but they are typically striking in the individual (GASS 241). In addition there are certain general rules: 'severe strain' is 'nearly always' followed – if not immediately, then after a certain time – by 'breakdown' (GASS 142). This was his personal experience in a nutshell; it seemed to offer him security amid all the questions still open at that point.

Max Weber versus Wilhelm Ostwald: the diversity of living nature versus naturalist reductionism

The trenchant climax and finale of Weber's encounter with naturalism, which, after long stretches of effort and torture, concluded in polemical brilliance with a touch of burlesque, are to be found in Weber's essay of 1909 on Ostwald's 'energetic' theories of culture. The chemist Wilhelm Ostwald (1853–1932), who knew Weber personally from the trip to St Louis in 1904, represented a particular kind of challenge. He too specialized in crossing disciplinary boundaries: first between chemistry and physics, then between the natural and human sciences, with the help of the magic word 'energy'. He too had been led by a psychosomatic breakdown – in 1895, at the age of forty-two – to withdraw from normal academic life and to strike out on unconventional paths. 'Energy' became the basis not only for a physical chemistry but also for a reappraisal of his own trauma.[56] On all sides, whether in technology and politics or in the conduct of life, he found the principle of progress in an economical handling of energy. In 1911, in one of his 'monistic Sunday sermons', he pronounced anathema on all those who 'demand a strict separation . . . between scholarship and life': 'Life itself sweeps by and eliminates these no longer viable forms from a deeper layer of development.' True science was a 'joyful science', which brought people into harmony with themselves through an honest love of truth.[57]

Ostwald was certainly a prominent opponent, but he presented large areas that were not difficult to attack. In the same year, 1909, when Weber was settling accounts with 'energetics', Ostwald received the Nobel prize for chemistry, but he had long been an outsider within his own fraternity. To anyone working in the exact sciences, it was an abomination how Ostwald jumbled up a dozen different concepts of energy.[58] Weber saw clearly that he could mobilize against him the Kantian critique of knowledge and both the social and natural sciences. Although Ostwald might have sounded like a materialist to arts scholars, he had himself openly rejected materialism;[59] and the nature of Ostwald's faith in his 'energy' sometimes put him embarrassingly close to the spiritualist fashion of the day.

Weber's attacks on Ostwald were not at all directed against the presence of natural elements in the human sciences, but were an impressive plea for the living diversity of nature against any abstract and dogmatic attempt to tie it down. Ostwald regarded the dominance of language teaching in higher education as a senseless and detestable waste of intellectual energy and made the promotion of Esperanto one of his life's causes.[60] Weber, however, had a horror of its 'crushing of natural languages' and praised the 'creative significance of the often so troublesome ambiguity of naturally arising linguistic structures' (WL 419). He derided the brutal philistinism that developed when cultural standards of value were eliminated: 'The maximum conversion of energy per square metre of linen is achieved when pictures of explosions or sea battles are painted on it' (WL 416). But this

Figure 10.2 Wilhelm Ostwald, portrait from 1909

was unfair, for Ostwald thought that progress lay precisely in the economical handling of energy, not in its 'maximum conversion', and unlike Weber he disapproved of war and duelling as a sorry waste of energy.

In May 1909 Weber wrote to Herkner that he 'dreaded' Ostwald's 'energetic sociology' (MWG II/6, 116); it was not only the content of Ostwald's writings that he held against him. In his damning criticism of 'energetics' he mockingly suggested that, to be consistent, 'pensioners as well as philologists, historians and other such idlers who cannot improve the quality of their energy' should be strung up without more ado, and not merely castrated, as Ostwald had recommended for 'bearers of murderous instincts' (WL 420f.). Of course, he well knew that such bloodlust was alien to the humane Ostwald; he simply meant that, when Ostwald spoke of 'equal rights', he was operating on the ground of natural law rather than any principles of energy (WL 421).

Weber's polemic shows at several points that he was much better read in the natural sciences than sociologists usually are – yet another sign of the attraction that bridges between the human and natural sciences held for him. He was aware that the conservation of energy principle was partly a construction and not purely a result of physical experiments (WL 117n.). He even countered Ostwald's invocation of the natural sciences by arguing that the exhaustion of non-renewable mineral resources gave more reason for concern than Ostwald admitted in his optimistic vision of the future, where a superabundance of solar energy would be directly converted into electricity (WL 408ff.).

At the end Weber speaks with excessive appreciation of the chemist, implying that he was somehow rather fond of him: 'Notwithstanding our pitiless criticism of his innumerable grotesque slips . . . Ostwald is an intellectual spirit whose refreshing enthusiasm and enduring feel for modern problems, free of any dogmatic rigidity, must make it a pleasure to work with him on the whole problematic of "technology and culture"' (WL 425). It was thus 'quite in order' to keep an eye on 'the physical and chemical energy balances for processes of technological and economic development' (WL 423). No doubt Weber would have liked to have someone with Ostwald's spirit as his interlocutor. But it did not occur to the chemist to get involved in a tussle with Weber.

11

From the Eranos Circle to the 'Erotic Movement': New Roots and New Milieux

'As lonely as the rhinoceros'? Weber's dependence on his surroundings

'To wander as lonely as the rhinoceros' was the way of the enlightened, as later quoted by Weber from a 'famous poem' of the Buddha (MWG I/20, 333f.); also with the rhinoceros's thick hide to ward off sentimentality. One thinks of a solitary Weber trudging along with his thick skin. But were solitude and imperviousness to emotion really *his* path to enlightenment? Eugen Rosenstock-Huessy considered that, although abstract thinkers think of 'conversations with oneself as preferable to conversations with others', this is a great mistake: 'Our thought prepares for speech and analyses it afterwards.'[1] The loneliness of the solitary thinker is only a pretence: thought needs to have other people, real or imaginary, to whom it is addressed.

It would appear that this was true of Max Weber too, and that he liked to have in his mind's eye not only an abstract 'public' but a circle of living people. To understand him, we need to have an idea of these real and imaginary addressees. When Marianne or Eduard Baumgarten listened at his door, they heard him holding a lively discussion with an imaginary other, sometimes seeming to wait for an answer before delivering an even sharper riposte.[2] He may have seen himself as an inwardly driven individualist, but many of his works were written in response to an external stimulus. As Marianne noted (MWG I/16, 92), he expressed himself best in writing when he had formulated his thoughts orally beforehand. A large number of his more striking quotations saw the light of day in a lecture or publication intended for a particular circle of people, whereas he had conspicuously less interest in books for an anonymous public.

In his work on the history of religion, Weber had more dealings with small groups of people personally acquainted to him than with the big anonymous churches. His prophets operated in an arena that offered a clear view and, as Bourdieu pointed out, interacted with this 'religious field'.[3] In the crescendo at the end of *Science as a Vocation*, Weber said it was no accident that 'today only within the smallest and intimate circles, in personal human situations, in *pianissimo*, something is pulsating that corresponds to the prophetic *pneuma*, which in former times swept through the great communities like a firebrand, welding them together' (FMW 155). In politics too, the real players were not the masses but overwhelmingly the small elites and communities bound together by oaths of fraternity. In later years the myth of Weber developed first in limited circles, not in the broad public.

Family and relatives meant more to Weber than they did to many other scholars, even if blood ties were by no means associated only with amicable feelings. His breakdown and withdrawal from university life threw him back on his wife, mother and siblings as his key references, and the family fortune again provided the material basis for his existence. Marianne felt at the time that she and Max were like castaways on a 'desert island': 'For what could friends and even our dearest ones be for us! We had to bear it alone, stand up to it alone, take the wheel alone.'[4] For years the couple regarded contact with strangers as a health risk to Max; in late 1901 Marianne was vetting all visitors 'like a watchdog',[5] and even in 1905 Max still wrote to Hellpach that his volatile state 'ruled out any social intercourse'.[6] This did not mean, however, that social relations were unimportant to him – rather the opposite. Precisely because he found company such a strain and certain people insupportable, the contacts the Webers did cultivate around them became one *definite*, significant element in his life, as they are not for people in whose lives company is an ever-present and therefore indefinite element.

At the nadir of depression, Weber was incapable of building a human milieu around him, or even of sustaining one already in existence. His surroundings appeared alien to him, and his restless travelling may be partly explained by a need to escape this experience of alienation by converting it into tourist experience of the world. However, the process of recovering his health and intellectual productivity went together with a growing capacity to build a new milieu for himself that was not part of the university.

In Heidelberg at that time, the Baltic Baron Jacob von Uexküll was developing his theory that each form of life needed its own environment (*Umwelt*) – something more individual than the sociologist's 'milieu' – and that human beings partly created and built up one for themselves. Again, the story of Weber's life could be thought of in these terms. The theologian Harnack, who knew Uexküll personally, was inspired by him 'to regard the whole of humanity as a kind of coral stock on which males were the original branches and females the further ramifications'.[7] Uexküll also assigned to women a special significance in the fact that all human beings had their own *Umwelt* and needed it to live.[8]

In fact, Marianne and her network of female relations performed a major service in rebuilding a Weberian *Umwelt*. Weber himself was for a long time virtually incapable of taking the social initiative. In 1903 in Scheveningen, without asking him in advance, Marianne 'on behalf of Max Weber' even asked a couple of married colleagues to pay a visit, so that the Webers would not be left completely in the cold. Max proved 'very happy with this arrangement and found it most amusing that I had acted the patriarch on his behalf and would not make it a "matriarchal" dinner'. Marianne sent him a greeting as the 'deputy chairperson of your loving menagerie'. And, at a time when Max was unable to do virtually anything intellectually, she went into such raptures about the power of his intellect that 'everyone' kept teasing her for 'offering her services' to him in that way.[9]

Let us be clear: After Weber gave up his professorship, the university was still part of his *Umwelt*. He did not consistently 'drop out' – unlike Nietzsche he inwardly continued to relate to the university as an institution, and indeed tried to pursue his scholarship even more professionally than before. In the years from 1907 to 1911 the Verein für Sozialpolitik again became an arena for Weber, and from 1910 to 1912 so did the Deutsche Gesellschaft für Soziologie, which he had played a considerable role in helping to found. His reports and contributions at their congresses contain not a few of his most striking passages; as in the past he often made a stronger impression orally than in writing.

But Weber never found an inner home in these two societies, and probably never sought to either. Sometimes he creates a suspicion that he dropped into their congresses mainly to let off steam. When he heard at the Gesellschaft für Soziologie of plans to make him its committee chairman, he resisted with all his might and said he would use the post only to engineer the dissolution of the committee (MWG II/6, 57, 74). The business correspondence he kept up for this society and for the *Grundriß der Sozialökonomik* was a 'torture' (MWG II/6, 608). His various attempts to act as the organizer of major sociological research – whether for the *Psychophysik* or for a study of the modern press – never got past the first post.

The birth of sociology out of self-organized social communities

He also kept in touch with Friedrich Naumann's National-Social network, in which many different strands came together, but until 1914 he never made serious moves to gain a foothold in politics – he felt incapable of it on health grounds alone. Weber's intimate social milieu became and remained the *informal* gathering; this primal experience for him as a person is also a notable element in Weberian sociology. It is constitutive for sociology as an independent science that society should organize itself with its own forces, with a certain autonomy from the state and state-sanctioned institutions. Weber's sociology was to a considerable extent a sociology of domination, but Schmoller-style obedience to the state always set his blood boiling.

Sometimes Max and Marianne Weber had the feeling that they no longer fully belonged to the top circles of Heidelberg academia. In 1905 Marianne indignantly reported that the historian Erich Marcks and his wife had invited her to a party along with 'plain outsiders in our circle who could not be fitted in anywhere else'.[10] Weber sullenly noted that the Gesellschaft für Soziologie had landed him in second-rate company, a *'salon des refusés'*, who had never made it to a chair. As editor of the *Grundriß*, Weber also had problems because he held no academic power: several people who worked with it proved to be thoroughly unreliable or did not respond to Weber's letters (MWG II/6, 442) – whereas they would presumably have behaved differently with a powerful professor such as Schmoller. Weber's opponents sometimes alluded to his pathological sensitivity, implying that his attacks should not be treated as too important;[11] and it has to be admitted that they were not infrequently right. Most of the battles that Weber bitterly launched seem in retrospect to have been thoroughly unnecessary.

Admirers of Weber who cultivate negative clichés about that era like to suggest that he was a victim of Wilhelmine society – of its pressure to conform and perform, of its repressive sexual morality. But there is some reason to reverse the emphasis and to treat Weber's case as an impressive example of the sensitivity with which that society – or at least its higher academic echelons – handled members suffering from a nervous breakdown. For Weber never really felt himself excluded, however uninviting his own behaviour often was. People in his circles did not hold narrow conceptions of 'normality', but were fairly accustomed to neuroses; it was not all that uncommon for important scholars to suffer a temporary breakdown, whether because of an innate predisposition or because of overwork. Wilhelm Ostwald, who had had such an experience himself, even thought: 'This enemy does not seem to have spared anyone who has pushed his work far beyond the norm in the world around him.'[12] Even when Weber's incapacity for work lasted for as many years as the earlier period of his teaching activity, the university tried to keep him on. And, even after his departure, he became a curious mixture of insider and outsider, rather than a non-person whom no one ever mentioned. In the academic society of Heidelberg, 'social capital' could make up for a deficit in institutional position – to speak in the manner of Bourdieu.

Precisely because Weber now stood outside the university in-groups, he was all the more highly valued as an independent adviser known for his honesty and incorruptibility (WB 358); and for his part he knew how to cultivate this image. He sympathized with other outsiders such as Michels, Simmel and Sombart, but he made sure never to quarrel so badly with the academic establishment that he got a reputation for being unserious; on the contrary, his methodological writings gave him such an aura of professionalism that he was sometimes approached as if he were an oracle. When he left academic employment in 1903, he tried all the more to become a reliable centre of information about the qualities of professorial candidates,[13] and he did indeed serve that function on repeated occasions.

Back home in Heidelberg

For Marianne, who was thoroughly sick of travelling and longed to settle down in one place, the long return to Heidelberg in late 1903 initially meant establishing fresh roots beside the Neckar. But at first Max played along only reluctantly: 'My zest for life was far more dependent than his on the beauty of the surroundings', she wrote later. 'For him it was even more important to have some money left over for travelling.'[14] Marianne experienced Heidelberg in spring and summer as a city filled with blossoming nature – a classical experience, described as such by other members of the Weber circle too. Marie Luise Gothein wrote of the first period that her husband, Weber's successor, spent there in 1904: 'What filled him there from the beginning with pure joy and rejoicing was the nature that he enjoyed in deep breaths . . . on his daily walks.'[15] Unlike in the spring of 1919, which he spent there with Else, Weber did not have any idyllic associations with nature; one would look in vain for the usual Heidelberg raptures, and he was anyway not a keen walker. Only in April 1914, to celebrate his fiftieth birthday, did he deign to go with Marianne 'on our first real walk in years through the spring forest' (WB 451).

That Max did not enjoy frequent walks in Heidelberg is one of the mysteries of his life. But for him too a new period was beginning when his everyday surroundings would become more stable. There were several stages in this process, involving roughly parallel changes in residence and in the company they kept. At first, from 1904 on, the Eranos circle of religious scholarship was Weber's most important forum; a kind of interactive relationship developed between *The Protestant Ethic* and this learned company. Weber was only one participant, not the centre of attention; women were not permitted to attend. In the spring of 1906 the Webers moved from the main street in Heidelberg, which Marianne found narrow and ugly, to the south bank of the Neckar, the 'Heidelberg Riviera'. The Webers then had a drawing room again, in which they could receive guests in a manner befitting their station. Marianne was as happy as a child in their new home – 'awfully jolly' – and would dance around with joy. 'I can never see enough of the nature awakening all around us', she wrote to Helene. 'This time I find Max the "blasé" one of the two of us.'[16] But the sun-starved Max also knew how to enjoy the change in his way as he lay naked at midday 'with a long pipe'. 'Sunbathing' on the balcony (WB 360f.): a new element in his lifestyle, inspired by the sun-worshippers of the fashionable cult of nudity in which only the pipe did not fit.

Spring awakening in the ghost house: 'he gradually grows into the garden'

The big qualitative leap in terms of space occurred four years later, however, in the spring of 1910, with which Marianne opens a new chapter in her biography entitled 'The Good Life'. It was then that they moved to the middle floor of the Fallenstein villa on the Neckar, after the death there of Adolf Hausrath. But the Webers had to pay rent, which at 3,000 marks a year was very high for a two-person household. In return, the house was modernized and given all the requisites of an up-to-date home: running water, flush toilet, central heating, gas and electric lighting.

The couple could afford this luxury only because of Marianne's Oerlinghausen legacy following the death of Carl David Weber in 1907, and even so Max was worried that they might be living beyond their means.[17] For Marianne the move to the Fallenstein villa was highly symbolic: it rebuilt her links with the family's past. 'You were always the strongest magnet that drew us here', she flattered Helene, who had always been 'homesick for her parental home' and felt it to be filled with 'the spirits of the departed' (WB 450f.).[18] A ghost house, then – but Marianne planned 'to disenchant the old house and to fill the painfully charged spaces once more with sunshine and the warmth of love'.[19] As we see, 'disenchantment' was not a neologism that Max Weber coined for science.

'For the first time the Webers owned a piece of land', Marianne noted triumphantly in the biography, although they were only tenants paying a rent. 'They became more deeply attached to the earth, experiencing the sweetness of spring more keenly than before. . . . One is worried about all this rash zest for life . . . yet is oneself young and grateful and ready to blossom' (WB 451). For Max too, the German spring gradually ceased to be a time of nervous crisis. Years after their move to the Neckar he still used to say angrily to Marianne that 'he would just have happily lived in the capital'. But in the early summer of 1912, when Mina Tobler appeared in his life, he finally began to identify with the blossoming garden: 'He gradually grows into the garden', Marianne wrote. 'For the past two weeks he has busied himself with the rose arbour for an hour every day'; he poked it around with such zeal that his wife was 'surprised that he has not completely shredded it up by now' (WB 453).[20]

In the new idyll Marianne was sometimes overcome by a southern *dolce far niente*: 'Here in the beautiful sunny house . . . it is so easy to dream and just vegetate like a plant and stretch toward the sun.'[21] Again and again the temptation of a purely vegetative natural existence! But the emblematic house also attracted company: 'Our house is fabulously animated and diverse', she wrote in 1910; 'someone is there every single day, the number of "needy" souls grows of its own accord.' She scarcely went out any more, as people came to her instead.[22] The spatial framework was in place for the new and informal *jours* in which Max Weber was the focus of attention. In late 1911 Marianne had the sense that her whole pace of life was accelerating, that 'life is beating with an ever faster pulse and would like to get you completely out of breath'.[23]

Excursus: Max Weber and the nature of money

The improvement in the Webers' external circumstances had a financial basis in Marianne's Oerlinghausen legacy. 'The cast-off professor, too, was now freed from financial worries', she commented laconically (WB 367). This new turn, which again placed them in the 'upper bourgeoisie', probably did more than a little to stabilize Max's condition. And so this may be a good point at which to glance at Weber's general relationship to money, so important for issues to do with practical everyday 'materialism' or 'idealism'.

In 1894 Max Weber was on a starting salary of 4,000 marks per annum as a professor in Freiburg, and in 1897 he was earning 6,000 marks in Heidelberg, out of which he had to pay 760 marks in rent.[24] Not bad for a young academic. In those years Weber seems to have led a carefree existence, so that by the end of the month, like many other people on a salary, he was 'running a little short', but he had no inhibitions about borrowing from a colleague if he needed to.[25] When he was in high spirits, the newly qualified professor behaved like a student. In 1896 he remarked to Marianne *en passant* that 'the whole shortage of money' meant a summer trip was out of the question.[26] As she was anyway not keen on travelling, she did not think this such a bad thing.

After the onset of his depression, Weber became anxious and niggardly about money. His professor's salary kept coming in for some years, but by 1900 he was longing to be released from academic obligations and felt morally compelled to give up that source of income altogether. His approach to money began to show signs of the hardship to come. Marianne did not yet see why she should scrimp and save; in 1901, for example, when she was staying with Max at the Grand Hotel Victoria in Zurich, she managed to kid him that they were in a 'modest' hotel.[27] The thought that he was doing nothing for his money weighed heavily on Max's conscience, and so in 1902 he paid over to the Heidelberg economics seminar a quarterly sum of 900 marks for the purchase of books, travel grants for outstanding students and help with printing costs.[28] That was more than half his income, and it indicates an unusually scrupulous attitude to money.

When Weber asked for his employment to be terminated in 1903, he stated that he would not claim any pension either then or in the future, since he felt 'embarrassed before the government and his colleagues' to keep taking money for nothing. Ministry officials were amazed at this undemanding attitude and had the 'impression that Professor Dr Weber (was refusing) to accept a pension because of a pathological sensitivity connected to his nervous disorder'.[29] Only illness could explain such qualms about taking the taxpayer's money.

What did the Webers live on between 1904 and 1907? 'If Max gives up his post we shall have to live on credit', Marianne wrote to Helene in January 1903[30] – though with a tacit postscript, 'until Grandfather dies'. Carl David Weber was then nearly eighty and had for years been so ill that – as he once sighed, in 1897 – a dog in his state 'would long since have had a bullet put through its head'; only humans were 'tortured to such an extreme'.[31] It was therefore expected that the Webers' lean times would not last much longer – although they went on for another four years. In 1902 Marianne flew into a panic when she heard that, under the ancient laws of the principality of Lippe, her grandfather's bequest would pass not to

herself but to the father she hated so much; her fears proved to be groundless, however,[32] as the canny grandfather had provided for her in his will,
and the father anyway died in 1903.

In those years Max and Marianne Weber found themselves in a peculiar
financial situation: they lived in such straitened circumstances that, after
moving to better accommodation in 1905, they were overjoyed when Helene
sent them nightclothes from a second-hand clothing depot as a Christmas
present[33] – what a come-down for such a proud professorial couple from
Heidelberg! – and yet they knew at the back of their mind that they could
count on two large fortunes: that of the Oerlinghausen Webers (300,000 to
350,000 marks) and that of the Souchays (more than 100,000 marks).[34] For
the time being, however, they had possession of neither the one nor the
other. When Max and Marianne announced in late 1899 that they were
going to sell some valuable engravings by Max Klinger to raise some money,
Marianne secretly hoped that her grandfather would give them some 'large
sums' to prevent the loss of art; instead, he was unmoved and even hurt his
granddaughter more by remarking that 'we have probably been very extrav-
agant'.[35] In May 1907 Weber noted in a letter to Naumann that he was living
'basically on the proceeds of a successful sale of my Klinger collection'
(MWG II/5, 301). Evidently Weber had been enough of a connoisseur to
know that the price for Klinger's pictures would rise, whereas Else later
thoughtlessly gave away the Picassos left by her husband.

Nothing was to be gained from nice letters to the grandfather, the manufacturer, but the charitably inclined Helene was another matter. True, she
lived until 1919 and often gave her children reason to fear that her constant
hand-outs to the poor would diminish the family legacy; but she was generous with her own children and reacted promptly when, as often happened, Marianne hinted in a letter to 'dearest darling Mother' that she
needed money because of Max. The 'idealist' in her did not find the subject
embarrassing. 'Mama, you terribly hard-worked and exploited dear', she
once wrote to Helene, in a letter in which she sometimes used euphemisms
such as 'golden rain of thalers from heaven' or drew round points inside
little circles to refer to sums of money. Marianne confessed to Helene that
her gifts filled her 'with a sense of powerful well-being more agreeable and
more poetic than other fine ornaments'.[36]

In 1905 Marianne acknowledged that Helene's money had placed Max
and herself 'in secure and solid circumstances'.[37] Max did not like being
financially dependent on his mother.[38] But, in his fear of poverty, he kept
his wife so short of money – being in control of her Oerlinghausen dowry –
that she once blurted out: 'You little beast, again you and your economies
have got me feeling really dejected.'[39] Whereas for Georg Simmel money
was the epitome of infinite possibilities and the source of modern disquiet,
for Max Weber – who did not think much of Simmel's *Philosophy of
Money* – the theme had quite different overtones. In his view, money did not
fit as the dynamic engine of capitalism; asceticism was the opposite of the
greedy disquiet unleashed by large sums of money.[40]

Weber did not gain a full sense of freedom as a result of the large Oerlinghausen legacy in 1908. For the new prosperity entailed a new financial dependence on Marianne, even though, as far as we can tell, she did not make him aware of it. More perceptible was the dependence on the economic conjuncture. In good years the Webers could count on an income of 16,000 or more marks (MWG II/5, 386), two to three times an average professorial salary; in bad years things looked different. Apparently they never thought of living off part of the Oerlinghausen capital. At first, elation at their new-found independence significantly tempered Marianne's joy in writing to Helene;[41] but soon she was sending her flowers to convey the message that some help towards extra expenses would come in handy.[42] When the Webers hired a car in summer 1911, Marianne thought Max suffered from 'obsessional thoughts' that 'we were spending too much money'.[43] Such complaints should not be taken too seriously, however. Often it is those with the money who live with a constant feeling that they have too little.

Max Weber was constantly aware of this material backdrop and anxiously followed the ups and downs of the economy,[44] whereas civil servants on a fixed salary were quite happy with stagnation and the resulting downward pressure on prices. Time and again we see that Weber identified much more with commerce and industry than with the world of officialdom, and that this left its mark on his political and scientific thought. Financial worries were not the least reason why he was only little affected in August 1914 by the euphoria that swept through the ranks of professors; already in 1913, when war fever was spreading, Marianne wrote to the mother: 'We wouldn't expect to receive any income in the case of war.' The fall in share prices induced by the danger of war was enough to cause them losses.[45] At the time, Max Weber was angry with his younger brother Arthur, an officer who treated money matters with the nonchalance customary in army circles, and who again needed money to buy a horse that befitted his rank (MWG II/8, 294ff.); he received it in the end but then spent it on something else – an act of impudence that made Max incandescent with rage. He wrote so many angry letters on the subject that Arthur felt 'mistreated'.[46] Even when war loomed larger on the horizon, Max Weber showed not the slightest respect for the officer in the family.

On 18 August 1914 Marianne complained to Helene that the 'Oerlinghauseners' had written to say that 'we should not count on any money but, if necessary, would have to get an overdraft!! A year ago they said that a war wouldn't do them any harm!'[47] For the income on their own capital, too, the war did not turn out badly in the end. 'Tinkle, tinkle, here it comes (*Tak tak tak da kommen sie*, quoted from Wilhelm Busch) – Mama's interest, and soon hopefully ours as well', Max wrote to Marianne in March 1916.[48] So, he was also getting some of the return on Helene's capital. When the promised victory failed to materialize, however, he developed major and perfectly justified fears about the threat of inflation. He warned that any victories would be in vain if, owing to runaway war costs

and 'paper (money) economy', confidence in the Germany currency collapsed for the foreseeable future and the dollar acquired global
supremacy.[49] Despite the advances in the east, he thought in the summer of
1917 that 'our financial ruin' was 'certain'.[50] Many German professors
embraced an illusory certainty that the state would always remain financially stable and, in particular, look after its professors well;[51] Weber had
long since lost this faith in the state typical of German civil servants.

On 21 October 1918, he wrote to Karl Loewenstein that the main priority was for the 'new people' in government to know how to prevent 'financial bankruptcy (through inflation)'.[52] He was aware that it would be very
difficult. The economist Georg Friedrich Knapp (1842–1926), one of the
founders of the Verein für Sozialpolitik and Theodor Heuss's father-in-law,
had impressively argued in his *Staatliche Theorie des Geldes* (1905) that
money was not merely a commodity subject to market laws but derived its
acceptance from the state. But, although he held Kapp in high esteem,
Weber was not so sure that his theory was the *whole* truth about money
(MWG II/5, 115ff.). The question of the validity of money was in some
ways analogous to that of the validity of law: in both cases, Weber had a
well-grounded dislike of any notion of the state as *prima causa*. Knapp –
whose disciple Karl Helfferich, permanent secretary at the Treasury, advocated funding the war through loans rather than taxation – continued to
perfect his theory of money until 1921, but then he personally suffered from
its inadequacies when the great inflation plunged him into poverty.
Melchior Palyi, the young temporary lecturer at Göttingen who later
worked with Marianne Weber on an edition of Weber's works, was shaping
up at the time as a currency and inflation expert at odds with the views of
Knapp.[53]

The inflation spelled the definitive defeat for the Historical School of
political economy, as the collapse of the currency gave the lie to its
unbounded confidence in the state.[54] For Max Weber, the inflation was not
the surprise it was for other people. Just as he took account of 'natural'
origins in explaining the authority of the law, he assumed that the value of
money was subject to laws of its own and could be only partly guaranteed
by the state. Indeed, he realized early on how great a temptation it was for
the state to discharge its astronomical war debts through inflation. On 20
April 1917 Weber complained in a letter (to Ludo Moritz Hartmann) that
because of money problems he was simply unable to travel to Vienna; for
'at the moment we have everything invested in war loans'. In those years
everyone with even a little money testified to their 'national idealism' by
purchasing war bonds, with the result that many lost their fortune in the
ensuing inflation. Max Weber the economist and the pessimist appears to
have been more cautious, however, and his complaint referred only to the
liquid part of their assets. Marianne's Oerlinghausen legacy remained in
the firm, where it was not threatened by inflation. War bonds seem to have
been purchased mainly out of Helene's money, which was evidently
managed by the war enthusiast Alfred. But, one way or the other, Max

Weber's financial worries grew more serious and were certainly one reason for his return to academic service.

In Vienna he met Ludwig von Mises, one of the pioneers of neoclassical economics, and thought his 'material theory of money' more convincing than Knapp's 'state theory' (E&S 185). In 1919, when he returned to academic employment and was put on the payroll, inflation became one of his greatest worries (MWG I/16, 478ff.); a sharp rise in income tax to pay for the lost war therefore seemed preferable to the printing of more money by the state (MWG I/16, 366ff.). In February 1920 he complained to his sister Klara about the 'foreign currency disgrace' (*Valutaschweinerei*) (R 551). Already in 1916, when he still thought a German victory possible, he wrote to Marianne that taxes on interest after the war would have to be as high as 50 per cent – and at the time the Webers were living on interest on their capital.

Heidelberg circles

Let us return from money to the social gatherings for which the Webers' premises were not unimportant, but which ultimately lived off the spirit that filled the space. This spirit was in the circle that Weber now joined, a spirit of unconventional, distinctly unorthodox curiosity about religion and, in particular, religious experiences in faraway times and places, deliberately ranging beyond the traditions of Christian doctrine. The discussions in the Eranos circle took it for granted that Christianity had no world-historical monopoly over revelation, but that a natural religious propensity was common to all human beings. The history of religion in various parts of the world was therefore full of analogies, whether at the level of asceticism or ecstatic tendencies, organization or contemplation. This would also be the starting point for Weber's sociology of religion.

Later, when the social gatherings centred on Weber, they became more informal and no longer had a pre-given thematic or organizational structure. A special atmosphere was created by the participation of women, who conveyed something of the tension between the influences of feminism and the 'erotic movement'; this was in competition with the concerns of people around Stefan George to draw closer to reality, reinforced by younger participants from the newly developing left-wing German-Jewish intelligentsia. All these networks of communication would be important for the worldwide impact that Weber's writings later had. The future justice minister, Gustav Radbruch, then a young and 'incurably shy' member of the circle around Max Weber (in which he lost his wife to the philosopher Emil Lask), was probably thinking of it when he reminisced with fascination, but also deep unease, about the 'Heidelberg spirit':

I do not think that in those days there was such a degree of thinking together at any other German university. One would have to go back to the Jena of the classical period: there too the ceaseless discussion, the never-ending conversation . . . there too the active participation of clever and cultured women in the intellectual world. But the darker side was the gossip, elevated by the intellect and psychological insights but all the more dangerous for that, and the many vagaries of an eroticism no longer under the control of principles. . . . The unsophisticated, respectable, normal and undemanding were sometimes given short shrift or even subjected to ridicule. The basic mood was an all-understanding relativism that never rejected anything, strengthening in their dangerous attitude those who could not resolve to sacrifice the wealth of possibilities for the unambiguity of a decision.[55]

Radbruch excluded Max Weber by name from this mood of relativism, but others saw him as the very prophet of a 'polytheism of values'. These contrasting images of Weber are still with us today.

Religious curiosity as a social bond: the Eranos circle

On 28 February 1904, Max Weber participated for the first time in a meeting of the newly founded Eranos circle, at which Troeltsch, the constitutional theorist Georg Jellinek, the historian Erich Marcks and the philosopher Wilhelm Windelband were also present. It was an illustrious circle, which Marianne described as the 'religious-philosophical coffee klatch', anyway a club of male professors, not a *salon des refusés*, not a gathering of eternally untenured lecturers. The only one who disturbed Weber was the neo-Kantian Wilhelm Windelbrand, since, according to Weber, he needed 'two rooms just for himself and the atmosphere around him' (WzG 176). Marianne thought it 'a real joy' that her husband had this new company that inspired him and broadened his mind, especially as his life was otherwise so 'monotonous'.[56]

On that 28 February the religious historian Albrecht Dieterich (1866–1908), one of the founders of the circle and since the previous year a full professor in Heidelberg, gave a report on the cult of Mother Earth. There followed a 'very lively discussion', in which everyone took part. The minutes make it sound quite secretive: 'The cult of Mother Earth recedes more and more into a mysterious obscurity, and the religiously profound idea of "Mother of us all", one of the roots of religious thinking in general, lays siege in the shadows of secret cult celebrations to the religious image of "Our Father" pushing ever more strongly into the light.' The following year, Dieterich published a book, *Mutter Erde: Ein Versuch über Volksreligion* (Mother Earth: An Essay on Popular Religion), which, although its author died in 1908, came to exercise a global influence and, from America to the Far East, led to the discovery of more and more 'Mother Earth' religions – so many, in fact, that it takes some effort today to return to a more nuanced view of this rather uniformly conceived primitive religion.[57] There is a lot of evidence that Max Weber's conspicuous interest in American Indian cultures during his trip to the United States (which, as we have seen, even took him to Oklahoma) was inspired by Dieterich's Mother Earth thesis, which met with a powerful response among students of America's indigenous peoples.[58] Dieterich himself drew most of his material from classical antiquity, but he also quoted the famous admission of the Shawnee chief Tecumseh to General Harrison: 'The earth is my mother; I want to rest in her bosom.'[59] In 1909, after Dieterich's death, Max Weber mentioned him as a 'magnificent specimen' of a strictly 'irreligious scholar of religion' (MWG II/6, 70).

On 5 February 1905 Weber's turn came to give a report at the Eranos circle, and he chose to speak on 'Protestant Asceticism and Modern Business Life'; the second part of *The Protestant Ethic* must have been as good as ready by then, so Weber would have had solid ground to stand on. His points met with general agreement, although the discussion was not as lively as it had been on 'Mother Earth'. On this occasion he was capable of speaking ad lib for two full hours. There was a time when he shied away from public speaking but felt no inhibition at the Eranos circle: he was surrounded by colleagues such as Gothein, Jellinek and Troeltsch, who were kindly disposed towards him. He was still taking many soporifics and tranquillizers every day, and Marianne was overjoyed that he got through the evening of 5 February and said he was feeling better for it; but he retorted that 'it's just a nice show produced by the drugs'.[60]

Eranos in ancient Greek means 'shared meal', but also 'act of loving kindness': it is related to the word *eros*. The Heidelberg 'Eranos' took place in an orderly setting: it had statutes, people wore formal dress, and minutes were taken of the proceedings. This private gathering of men often became really boisterous and 'all too male'; Dieterich dwelt with such relish on the ancient cult of the phallus – whose 'original significance' could scarcely be overestimated – that he admitted it would be 'easy to arrive in this way at an unpredictable pan-phallism'.[61] At the Heidelberg 'klatch', Eranos evidently had something to do with Eros,[62] even if most of the participants were no longer so young; the average age of the founder members was around forty-five.[63] Max Weber, at forty, was thus younger than most; he seems to have felt youthful here for the first time since the onset of his depression and to have learned how to laugh again.

'Light from the East' and religious naturalism

The initiative for the founding of the Eranos circle came from the New Testament scholar Adolf Deissmann (1866–1937), who since 1897 had been a full professor in Heidelberg. Strictly speaking, he was the only theologian in this religious discussion group – Troeltsch by now thought of himself as a scholar of religion – but his interests went beyond Christianity. Much as other scholars of the time were causing a stir by situating the Old

Testament within the newly discovered cultures of the Near East – the provocative book *Bibel und Babel* (1902)[64] by the Assyrian scholar Friedrich Delitzsch was *the* topic of conversation at the imperial court, especially as it fitted well with fantasies about a Berlin to Baghdad railway – Deissmann made it his speciality to place the New Testament within its Oriental–Hellenistic–Roman surroundings, filling it with new life in a manner at once evocative and pleasurable. In 1908 he published *Licht vom Osten*,[65] in which he quite uninhibitedly toyed with the voluptuous symbolism of the 'Orient', rather in the manner of the Orientalist magazine *Sonnen-Aufgang*. 'In the "Eranos" he would bring overly complicated thought processes down to earth by remarking that he alone "didn't get it".'[66]

The Eranos circle stimulated Weber to broaden his scholarly horizon to take in the Oriental religions.[67] For those who adhered to the Christian religion of their upbringing but wished to shake off its oppressive rigour, there was something liberating in an approach that submerged the world of the Bible in the ancient East and transformed the old Christian conception of a rift between Jehovah and Baal, the Bible and Babel, into something more like a continuum.[68] This procedure involved, so to speak, a symbolic synthesis of the familiar world of childhood with the world of eroticism. Weber, however, the man of harsh antinomies, did not find it so easy. Unlike Deissmann, he again situated Jewish–Christian religion in sharp contrast to the cults of the ancient Near East, although he recognized a structural affinity between the autonomous cities of ancient Palestine and the Greek polis.

Women were not permitted to attend the Eranos circle. The role of the wives was limited to preparing a lavish meal for the illustrious guests, who, according to Marianne, used to work up a 'huge appetite' during their sublime discussions.[69] 'Max is taking care of "Protestant asceticism". I am in charge of "ham in burgundy"' (WB 356). This barbed remark of Marianne's – she was far from passionate about cooking – deserves to become a familiar quotation. The exclusion of women from the circle, just as it was setting sail for new shores, takes us aback today. But that was not exactly how it looked in those days. Some women attended the traditional professorial societies in Heidelberg, but this meant that discussions there might switch abruptly to human issues instead of remaining limited to professional topics. Professors' wives who could take part in scholarly debate were still the exception, although, if an anonymous pamphlet on 'Academic Careers in the Present Day' is to be believed, spouses exerted considerable influence at a time when academic appointments were discussed more at social occasions than in the relevant committees. However, the thought that this was so led many to be suspicious of the female element in academic life.[70]

Nature, culture and the Gotheins

Marie Luise Gothein (1863–1931) confessed, precisely in relation to the 'Eranos gatherings', that she had 'often painfully regretted not being a

Figure 11.1 Marie Luise Gothein

man'. 'But I quite understood and accepted that women were excluded from this common scholarly life.' It was simply that – whether the blame lay with women or men – a female presence would have 'lowered the whole intellectual level of the conversation'.[71]

The wife of economic and cultural historian Eberhard Gothein, a highly educated, attractive and robust woman, caused general astonishment among the spouses of Heidelberg professors:[72] she brought four boys into the world, was active at sport, had a lover with her husband's agreement (alongside a happy marriage), worked on the 'seven deadly sins' in art, and in 1913, without having once attended a Gymnasium, published her still famous *History of Garden Art*, which widened out into a cultural history of the relationship between man and nature and was probably more read than most books by Heidelberg professors.[73] But she scorned the company of women, with all their gossip and children's talk and 'social' activities so popular in Marianne's circle. 'There's never a dull moment with her', wrote Mina Tobler.[74] Max Weber must have thought so too, he who in 1914 set himself up as judge on Marie Luise Gothein's behalf when he saw her being cheated by her publisher. She had translated a book of verse by Tagore for a modest fee, although the publisher knew that the Indian poet was in line for the Nobel prize and meant good business for them (MWG II/8, 497, 751ff.).

As she had no problems with patriarchy,[75] she was indifferent to the women's movement. She seemed cold to Marianne ('just an intellect and aesthete, with no trace of a general human warmth of feeling'), but really inspired envy in her.[76] In her biography, Marianne is silent about Marie Luise Gothein, even though she was one of the most striking women in their milieu and her marriage appeared a model intellectual–sexual partnership based on equal rights. Marianne once wrote to Helene that it would be perfect if Gothein and Rickert swapped wives for a year, so that poor Frau Rickert, talked to death by her husband, could catch her breath again.[77] Much later, when Marie Luise Gothein spoke of her trip to the earthly paradise of Bali, she captivated the circle around Marianne Weber (LE 209f.).

In comparison with Weber, Eberhard Gothein (1853–1923) strikes one as a kindred though more fortunate soul. Clearly envious, Weber told him more than once that, if he had 'such ideas' as Gothein had, he would 'forget about everything else'.[78] To others he said: 'If my memory was like that big idiot Gothein's, for example, what wouldn't I be able to do!'[79] Like Weber, Gothein had read an enormous amount and was bubbling with ideas, in a field stretching from economic to religious history. In 1892 he published the extensive first volume of an 'Economic History of the Black Forest', which put Weber on an important trail leading to *The Protestant Ethic*, and in 1895 he followed this with a book on Ignatius of Loyola, a real trove on questions to do with asceticism and meditative exercises. In 1910, at the founding congress of the Gesellschaft für Soziologie in Frankfurt, he even gave a lecture on the historical significance of panic and found Troeltsch a congenial partner with whom to discuss the idea that Christianity arose out of the disciples' panic after the Crucifixion.[80] He especially liked to get scholarly inspiration on long hikes; not for nothing did he focus on the economic and cultural history of the Black Forest. His wife, the historian of gardens with whom he conversed even on solitary walks, wrote that, 'with a bee's instinct', his mind 'drew the appropriate food from every flower'.[81] Max Weber, with his much lazier feet, found Gothein's treks 'barbaric' (MWG II/6, 544).

In the biographical *Lebensbild* published by his wife in 1931, Gothein appears as a cheerful and well-balanced personality; and we readily believe her when we see her husband pondering on Spinoza as he queued in the postwar crush for food.[82] To Marianne, however, he seemed like a 'pure intellectual machine, with endless amounts of knowledge but otherwise totally bloodless'.[83] Nor did the quiet man turn into a lion in the lecture hall: it might happen that, even on such an exciting subject as the Renaissance, only four students would be there to hear him.[84] In Heidelberg it was later said that Gothein sacrificed himself so that his wife could travel to India and study the gardens of the maharajah; that he saved money by eating poorly in the canteen during the hard postwar years and died of influenza as a result.[85]

The Sunday *jours* in the Fallenstein villa

From 1908 the Webers' drawing-room saw more and more visitors and social occasions, so that Max and Marianne no longer had to look for company outside their circle. Anyway Max 'very seldom let himself be lured out of the house' (WB 368). He was the main centre of attention at gatherings there, could talk for as long as he liked, took up topics of interest to himself, and withdrew whenever he became tired. In comparison with other, more formally constituted circles, this informal kind of gathering – which from spring 1911 had a *jour fixe* set apart for it – allowed the Webers to exercise 'skilful control' and to ensure the presence of an exciting range of people.[86]

Informal does not necessarily mean natural and egalitarian: indeed, more conventional forms can ensure that everyone is able to speak and a single individual does not monopolize the discussion. The gatherings in the Webers' home should not be thought of as an ideal type of communication free of domination. Many found them usually strained and stilted. One outsider recalled a female student who could scarcely utter a word when Marianne asked her a 'banal' question about whether she was happy with her accommodation.[87] Marianne admitted that she and her husband had not mastered the 'art of social discourse', which was so highly appreciated among the educated middle classes (WB 467). But there were quite a few others who also felt awkward with the usual conversation: the 'witty' exchange of pleasantries, the jumping from one subject to another and the talking for its own sake, without any intellectual return.

With their new prosperity from the Oerlinghausen legacy, the Webers became more generous in their lifestyle and hospitality. 'This summer we live differently from before', Marianne wrote to Helene in June 1908, 'as we have a lot of different people around us and their fates preoccupy us more than our own, even more than our work.' Apart from their old friends Troeltsch, Jellinek and Gothein, there were also the young philosophers Lask, Edgar and Else Jaffé, the Radbruchs, Alfred Weber and (the most recent of their acquaintances) Hans Gruhle. Mina Tobler also appeared on the scene with Lask. Max spoke 'an enormous amount', Marianne wrote to Helene, and 'of course, we both slept badly after these "excesses". . . . The intense involvement in other people's lives, about which we should not speak, uses up a lot of nervous energy.' Obviously there were some intimate subjects of conversation that affected Marianne deeply; the encounter with the 'erotic movement' was beginning. But it did the Webers no harm to be distracted from their own problems and to become caught up in other people's troubles.[88]

Marianne tells us that Max found 'worthwhile' only 'significant intellectual exchange or intimate conversations about personal matters' (WB 467): that too! Having been exposed to so much therapy himself, he now often saw himself in the role of psychotherapist (MWG II/7–2, 761); this brought him back to life and set things flowing again. 'He is inexhaustible in the telling of stories as in the distribution of more substantial intellectual fare . . . and the whole family always sits around him as though he were a sage, a saint and a *Pojaz* in one.' ('*Pojaz*', an East European Jewish corruption of 'Bajazzo', signifying 'clown', was the title of a novel published in 1905 by a Galician Jew, Karl Emil Franzos.) According to Marianne, these occasions aroused 'Homeric' laughter: 'all the old military and student lore' was revived and Max felt young again; his 'narrative skill pours forth like a dammed-up stream'; he does need 'a lot of drugs', but they do not seem to weigh on him as much as they used to.[89]

Previously Marianne had slowed the torrent of words, as too much 'chatter' was bad for Max's health,[90] but now she played along with his stage productions. It must be said that Max Weber was not the kind of solo performer who always talks about his own hobby-horses: he could also listen and, thanks to his enormous reading, had an unusual capacity to tackle many and varied themes: at least as much from 'life' as from the world of science. The social gatherings did not take place only on the *jour fixe*: the Webers made time for their friends and acquaintances. Let us quote here from Marianne's private recollections, in which Max is like the rock from which Moses struck water with his stick:

> Until the war, one friend or another would come round almost every day at five o'clock, then some more tea would usually be drunk, and then came the hour of the day when, if the guest had a Moses stick, things would start pouring out of Max. But not a lot of art was needed to draw him into exchanges – he was like a completely soaked sponge! His vast knowledge and unlimited interests enabled him to follow almost anyone in their field – a legal expert with legal experts, a historian with historians, a theologian with theologians, a philosopher with philosophers. What discussions there were on all scientific problems and, more intense still, on every kind of problem in life! And, whether he was speaking of Tolstoy and Russia, of Egyptian and Babylonian state forms and regents, of forward operations on the stock exchange, of Prussian agrarian policy, of value-judgements in science or the *Deus absconditus*, misguided imperial policy or Plato and Sophocles – all events and persons were always brought to life . . . with graphic force.[91]

Official scholarly gatherings paled in comparison. In 1908 Windelband presided over what was supposed to be a top-ranking event, the International Congress of Philosophers in Heidelberg. But scholars were by no means as keen on congress tourism as they are today; Marianne noted disdainfully that it was mostly 'lesser lights' who showed up, and in her view – which presumably reflected her husband's – the whole occasion was 'a terrible herring salad'.[92] 'Why, almost all of these scholars fought with one another! And each had his own language. . . . They usually talked past one another fruitlessly in the discussions; basically no one wanted to learn from anyone else' (WB 393). Today a regular visitor to such spectacles would scarcely expect anything else, but in those days they were still a novel gift bestowed by modern international transport.

Close personal communication was decisive for Weber's intellectual development. The Fallenstein villa on the Neckar, with its large (today shrunken) garden and its south-facing terrace with a view over the castle ruins, offered a piece of scenery whose likes would have been hard to imagine. In early May 1911, the Webers initiated the Sunday *jours* that would later become legendary. We should keep as close as possible to the testimony of contemporaries, so as not to be carried away by the myth of Weber and old Heidelberg. In the beginning the *jours* were rather a disappointment. After the first one, Marianne wrote to Helene: 'Roughly sixteen people turned up: far too many to form a "unit". . . . We invited a definite, rather homogeneous circle of younger married couples and "singles". . . . We found both very stressful this first time and were a little depressed.'[93] But the tone was different half a year later: 'The Sundays are blossoming and nearly always make us happy – we just have to be a little "hard" and take care that the circle does not become too large and heterogeneous. People who are complete strangers to us try to find all ways of having the door opened to them.'[94]

The Sunday *jours* were not completely closed, and participants seem to have been free to introduce someone new. But newcomers could sometimes get a distinct feeling that they did not fit in. This happened even to such a personality as Ernst Robert Curtius, who wrote to Lukács in 1912: 'My appearance at the Webers' *jour* was not a success.'[95] And it is true that this later famous novelist did not go down well at the Webers; nor did they welcome old hands from the Eranos circle at these new gatherings, as their preference was for young people. Marianne now spoke of 'the Eranos' as the 'klatch with old gentlemen'.[96] On 16 December 1911, according to Marianne, fifteen people came to the *jour*: 'nearly all young people; various single women also managed to force an entry – as well as older women, such as Frau Gothein, whom we would prefer not to have, because we cannot possibly have here the Troeltsches, Frau Jellinek and other old friends.'[97] As we can see, the Webers were quite deliberately trying to build a new human field around them.

The origin of the Weber myth

In this circle, a kind of cult following could take shape around Weber for the first time, something inconceivable among colleagues from the same generation. Consciously or unconsciously, Weber developed an ability to get younger intellectuals to engage with him in their thinking. To be sure, much in his power of attraction was not rational. A major reason why a new generation came to identify with Weber – a generation repelled by the smug smiles of Wilhelmine professors – was probably his sombre aspect that only a grim humour brightened up, and his aura of illness heroically coped with. One young admirer, the political scientist Karl Loewenstein (1891–1973), recalled after Weber's death that even people who had never seen him, and for whom he was all the more a *deus absconditus*, used to refer to him 'in jocular reverence' as 'the myth of Heidelberg'.

He, whom no one had seen at a university lectern or anywhere else face
to face, had the reputation of being a dark magician of science. It was
whispered that somewhere on the Ziegelhäuser Landstraße was a man
with legendary powers of thought, who was intimately acquainted
with the Roman agrimensors mentioned only in passing in our lectures, and who knew his way around medieval Florentine accounts as
our sort did a newspaper. So, anyone who had the fortune to be guided
by a friendly hand to the house on the banks of the Neckar . . . and to
spend a while under its roof, where Max Weber and Ernst Troeltsch
stretched the huge arc of the sociology of religion from the earliest
beginnings of human culture in India and China to the roots of the
modern vision of God, found the revelation that had too often been
wanting in the lecture hall and seminar room: the intellectual leader
who combined the deepest humanity with truly cosmic knowledge.
(WzG 48f.)

More than forty years later, no one was more violent than Karl
Loewenstein in attacking Wolfgang Mommsen's thesis that, in his justification of the Nazi dictatorship, Carl Schmitt had proved to be a quick-to-
learn disciple of Max Weber.[98] Gustav Radbruch (1878–1949) could still
recall decades later Weber's 'restrained, self-lowering lion's voice': 'I always
experienced Max Weber's shape and voice as if they would burst all space
if he did not keep himself firmly in hand: larger than life-size.'[99] And the
archaeologist Ludwig Curtius, whom Marianne regarded highly in later
years, even called Weber the 'dictator of an intellectual realm that encompassed all the problems of modern life'.[100]

An air of eroticism hung over the Weber circle: the talk was not only
scholarly but also turned to life's problems; those present were overwhelmingly young and unmarried and emphatically free of prejudices; the two
sexes were almost equally represented. Later, in the *Zwischenbetrachtung*,
Weber argued that the 'intellectualism of salon culture' had brought about
a 'further enhancement of the specifically sensationalist character of eroticism'. For 'salon culture rested upon the conviction that inter-sexual conversation is valuable as a creative power', so that 'the latent or overt erotic
sensation' became 'an indispensable means of stimulating this conversation'. Precisely because such intellectualism grew so remote from the
organic cycle of life, only 'sexual life' remained as a link to 'the natural
fountain of all life' (FMW 346).

Heidelberg polytheism: the Weber and George circles

If the Weber cult developed subliminally and in contradiction to the
master's theory – at least in so far as this was communicated verbally –
another circle that took shape around the same time in Heidelberg made
reverence of the master its distinctive style. This was the circle around

Stefan George (1868–1933). Untroubled by the rampant suspicions of homosexuality, it cultivated a more or less sublimated male eroticism in the ancient style and promised redemption through artistic sophistication and esoteric communion. What did Weber and George have to do with each other? Although George had friends in academia, he was strongly opposed to academic scholarship and considered it a waste of time; he even broke on the issue with his favourite disciple, Friedrich Gundolf, when he started out on a university career.[101] On the other hand, Weber did not take very seriously George's ambition to re-enchant the world and gave him the nickname 'Weihen-Stefan', which, apart from being a brand of Bavarian beer, humorously evoked the solemnity of a religious order.[102]

Yet the two men felt a certain esteem for each other. We know little of what George thought of Weber, but we do know that in 1910–11, when Weber was beginning to put together his own circle, he interested himself in George with an intensity that is difficult to understand if we imagine Weber as the guiding intellectual force of rationalization. Weber's respect for sects is well known, and with history in mind he had good reason to try to make an impact through a small group with deep psychological bonds. From this point of view, George must have felt that Weber understood him. In August 1915, when there was no one to look after them at home, both men put up at Pension Betzner on the Gaisbergstraße in Heidelberg and used the opportunity for discussion with each other.[103]

Distant as the two circles were from each other in spirit, there were personal overlaps – most notably, in the cases of Edgar Salin and Arthur Salz. Salz became Mina Tobler's 'second favourite person in Heidelberg', after Weber;[104] and in 1914 Weber defended him against a not altogether fanciful critique by the Prague economic historian Paul Sander, doing so with an extreme fury that did not stop at denigrating the entire faculty of philosophy in Prague (MWG II/8, 527ff.). Salz later returned the favour with an apology for *Science as a Vocation* – signs of group loyalty were distinguishable in and around Weber.

Gundolf, too, belonged for a time to the inner circle of Weber's acquaintances. At first, in the spring of 1911, Marianne was spellbound by this uncommonly handsome and enthusiastic literary theorist, and probably also a little envious of him: 'What a sunny boy he is! It's as if anything terrestrial whatsoever could be only material for his enthusiasm. . . . He is blissfully happy in himself. Always living with his idols.'[105] But her mood changed once she had established that the aesthete did not think much at all of the women's movement; she then spoke ironically of 'little Gundi' as she did of 'Troletschie': 'Ah, how utterly our "perfect" little Gundi has rejected "modern woman"! He has condemned our movement as the "primal outrage" blocking the production of heroes.'[106] Probably Marianne felt personally hurt – as if she herself and her commitment to women's rights were to blame for her childlessness.

Marianne, undoubtedly bolstered by conversations with Max, reduced George's majestic-sounding message to a more mundane core: rejection of the ideal of individual autonomy, 'subordination to the authority of the hero, and, for a woman, subordination to a man' (WB 461). Yet in December 1911 the Webers were still 'deeply affected' by George. He conceived of his poetic profession as a 'prophet's office' – a role 'to which he is perhaps not equal, although his will is certainly great'.[107] A curious argument developed between Marianne and George. She expressed some annoyance at the enthusiasm for war that she had detected in him when he lamented 'our enervation through the increasing pacification of the world'. Marianne objected that in the modern world intellectual struggles were becoming more important in comparison with physical wars. George then wrongly accused the childless woman of a general deprecation of the body: 'Miscreant, miscreant! You want to keep turning everything into spirit and thereby you destroy the body.'[108] For her part, Marianne heard in this only a fascination for brute force, which suited the sensitive George just as little as it had the frail Nietzsche. But, although George alluded to the biological function of the female sex, Georg Simmel, who knew his theories inside out, referred to them as 'the acme of anti-naturalism'.[109] Sabine Lepsius shuddered at how George wandered in the full bloom of nature without being in the least stirred by it.[110]

For Weber, the George circle was above all a fascinating experiment in how far, and under what conditions, it was possible to revive old gods in the modern age and to foster a charismatic cult of a prophet and leader. Weber's most detailed remarks about George are contained in a letter of 9 June 1910 to Dora Jellinek, the daughter of the constitutional theorist (MWG II/6, 559ff.); it is doubtful whether this was his last word, though, since he would have further personal encounters with George. Weber's reservations about the poet and his circle had nothing to do with scientific rationality, but centred on whether their displays of quasi-religious emotion and release were the real thing or just an artistically staged performance. But how was this to be determined? Weber thought he had one lead at least. When George cast himself as a Dante, Weber did not think it altogether grotesque: 'I have no doubt that a little spark of that huge fire lives in him.' But only 'a little spark', no more. The George circle struck Weber as a mere simulacrum of a redemptionist religion, without any inner substance; George gave the impression of conveying a message, but it was a grand gesture without content.

Weber knew from his own experience what a longing for redemption felt like, but he could not see any genuine feeling of that kind among members of the George circle. If we recall what Marianne wrote about the ever radiant Gundolf, we will understand what Max Weber meant. 'These people, it seems, are already only too "redeemed" – and so their only possible remaining goal is to strive for self-*deification*, by directly absorbing the divine into their own souls.' The circle was thus seeking both ecstasy and mysticism: that was 'its undoing'. Weber thought he knew, from the history of religion as well as his own intuition, that there was an Either–Or between them, and that the George circle, having attained neither, would produce no more than the 'tone of a wild harp'. Shortly afterwards, however, he sturdily defended the circle in public when the poet Rudolf Borchardt attacked it in the *Süddeutsche Monatsheften* as a disaster for German culture.[111] He was particularly furious that Borchardt had cast aspersions on the virility of George and his disciples; he even admitted later that he had not calmly read Borchardt's whole tirade but had pounced on expressions such as 'castratedness' and 'impotence' (MWG II/6, 700). It made his blood boil that references to sexual abnormality should be used to defame somebody.

Early in 1912 Weber got the impression that George was interested in the subject of communal households, which he had approached himself in the context of *Economy and Society*. He even gave Arthur Salz a kind of sociological explanation of the George circle. 'Our modern techniques of living have put an end to the "productive" tasks of the family household.' In these circumstances, a community bound together by strong feelings comes into being not through the family but, if at all, 'as a free union of *particular* people with *particular* desires remote from everyday existence'. A mere 'community of consumers' has 'no distinctive internal life'. Only someone with 'personal charisma' is capable of founding this new kind of community (MWG II/8, 429).

Ten years after Weber's death, Gundolf published a poem called *Max Weber*, a celebratory apotheosis with the style and mysterious vocabulary of George's lyrical verse: a homage to Weber as a fearless guide to truth through the fog of illusions.

WAHRHEIT nach dem untergang der sonnen / Abgerungen den erwürgten wähnen, / Ungelohnt vom Drüben, und mit tränen / Die der mann verbergen muß dem nächsten . . . / . . . Wahrheit als die blöße noch der würde, / Auf dem nacken wuchtend jede bürde / Der gestürzten götzen und die völle / des gehöhlten firmaments als hölle, / Trugst du aus dem Grund durch tausend türen, / Führer, frei vom lug wohin sie führen.[112]

It looks as if the Weber myth originated as a counterpoint to the George myth. Edgar Salin, who belonged to both circles, thought that 'everyone' must have felt that, 'among German figures', no one apart from George stood taller than Weber in 'the force of his personality'.[113]

Female networks in the Webers' world

If, in earlier periods of his life, Weber often sounded like a male club type, and if he also paid special attention to brotherhoods in the history of human socialization, female networks acquired growing significance for him after the Eranos years and even made a decisive contribution to his new social environment. The principal force behind this was undoubtedly Marianne and her involvement in the women's movement. Already before the onset of his illness, Max Weber – in complete agreement with his mother, who was an independent, emancipated woman by the bourgeois standards of the time – encouraged her to engage in such activities outside the home. Aware that people need a purpose in life, he had no illusions that marriage alone could adequately fulfil this need.

Marianne's entry into the women's movement was part of a more general educational idealism. Soon after the Webers moved to Heidelberg in 1897, she brought to life a branch of the 'Frauenstudium – Frauenbildung' association and called it an 'Association to Disseminate the Ideal of Modern Women'.[114] To open up every path into the world of the intellect was a goal that fired her with enthusiasm, and behind it lay a whole middle-class ideology of education. Her husband, as she put it, 'was soon more of a feminist than she was. He eagerly followed the pros and cons of public opinion, helped wherever he could, and stood by with his sword drawn when it was a matter of fighting off hostile acts of the old guard.' Nor did the 'old guard' consist only of men. At one public debate on women's rights, at which Max drew everyone's attention to himself, he hit out at 'old-fashioned women', who he said were 'much more vehement opponents of the entire movement than men'. 'He compared them to hens that mercilessly peck away with their beaks at a strange hen that has strayed into their barnyard'; Marianne and her friends, far from being irritated by the metaphor, found the scene 'wonderful' (WB 229).

In the early years of their marriage, Marianne made a move to slip into the role of her husband's academic assistant, when she undertook some petty statistical work for a continuation of Max's study of agricultural workers; but then he lost interest in the project. He did not think it a good idea in the long term that she should work in his field. When he advised her in 1898 to study the physiocrats for her work on Fichte, he added: 'Unfortunately I'm quite well up on them myself.'[115] But by then he was already at the Konstanzer Hof clinic. His illness was certainly a trying time for Marianne too, but the ending of her everyday routine opened up new space and sometimes gave her a sense of euphoria. She had 'big ideas' (*Rosinen im Kopf*), she noted joyfully on 17 November 1898 in a letter to Helene. Around that time her handwriting lost all schoolgirl touches and became faster and more spidery; the letters slanted towards the right. It must have been soon thereafter that she began work on her history of women and the law. For some years her capacity for reading and writing exceeded her husband's, and even afterwards she had a much greater tolerance for public speaking. Sometimes Max was presented as 'the husband of Marianne Weber'. At first her public involvement developed entirely within the framework of the National-Socials, who were receptive to women's issues even at a time when the exclusively male suffrage meant that they had little to gain from it electorally. Gertrud Bäumer (1873–1954), chairperson from 1910 of the Bund Deutscher Frauenvereine (BDF –

League of German Women's Associations), was a close friend of Friedrich Naumann, for whom Marie Baum (1874–1964) was also full of enthusiasm. Both women were on close terms with the Webers: we see how a network of relations was coming together.

Marianne's rise to become a scholarly authority of the women's movement

At a National-Social meeting in December 1903, Marianne found herself for the first time having to 'chirp a bit for a crowd of men', as she put it to Helene. 'It later struck me as an irony of fate that I, poor little Snouty [*ich armseliges Schnäuzchen*],[116] was at a political meeting until one in the morning, whereas our big boy had to be in bed by ten.'[117] We should not take this self-belittlement too seriously, by the way; Marianne could play with her own shyness because, in reality, her confidence was growing by leaps and bounds as she learned how to speak in public, to engage in political tactics and to write polished prose.

Not being a legal expert herself, she took advice from her husband for much of the historical material that she worked on in her *Ehefrau und Mutter in der Rechtsentwicklung*. But it was unquestionably her book, and anyway during those years Max Weber would have been incapable of drafting an outline, let alone a detailed plan, for a work on that scale. Nowhere in the chronology of his life is there a gap into which such activity could be inserted. When Marianne complained in 1906 that Max was so 'dreadfully demanding' in relation to the book, and that she was sometimes 'quite livid' about it (MWG II/5, 89), we obviously cannot infer that he more or less wrote it for her. Even the word 'development' (*Entwicklung*) in the title of the book did not go well with the struggle that Weber was then waging against 'naturalism'. Moreover, her geography of the history of women's rights looked different from his political geography: it was precisely in English common law that a woman was 'not regarded as a subject in her own right', whereas Russia of all places was more advanced in the division of matrimonial property and 'Prussian women were granted a legal claim to their spouse's fidelity approximately one hundred years before their English and French counterparts'. 'As we see', she concluded, 'the political freedom of Western Europe was freedom for men.'[118] When the proofs arrived, 'my clever little Max' smuggled in a few of his ideas; but then his wife started to 'scream'.[119] Evidently the couple did not always handle each other with the kid gloves we see in their surviving letters.

The spur to engage in this work came from feminist disappointment over the place of the family in the Civil Code (BGB).[120] As Marianne's friend Marie Bernays put it: 'Despite the energetic protests, women achieved neither the legal division of matrimonial property, nor the necessity for the wife to approve parental force, nor changes in the legal position of children born out of wedlock.'[121] Here Marianne came up against the hard core of patriarchy, which often remained hidden in social gatherings. Not in every respect was she one of the moderate feminists who avoided the conflict-ridden issues.[122] Through the discussions with Max, her confrontation with the Civil Code acquired a world-historical dimension. Even if she (probably rightly) did not believe in a happy bygone age of matriarchy, the development of civilization was for her bound up not only with progress but also with many retrograde steps in the legal position of women. To be sure, her approach to the women's question was very bourgeois and typical of a wealthy heiress; poorer women had different priorities. We sense the pain of her own marriage when she complains that the husband's control over all the money creates a 'harrowing situation' for any wife 'with a sensitive nature', since she 'has to keep asking him for small sums' for the housekeeping, while he keeps being unpleasantly surprised that the sum he has 'only just' given her has 'already been used up'.[123] Something like that used to happen in the Weber household.

When Marianne admitted in 1906 that scholarly work had 'really turned (her) into a slave in recent years', but that the slavery had been joyful and the work burden 'infinitely exhilarating',[124] we are reminded of Max Weber's earlier craving to 'succumb to the burden of work'. With her *magnum opus* Marianne became a scholarly authority of the women's movement, much as Lily Braun had been with her *Die Frauenfrage* (1901), an equally extensive work that had also traced its subject back to antiquity. Lily Braun was friendly with Sombart and could fall back on his knowledge of world history, but she was ignored by Marianne Weber. In the last few years before the war, Marianne repeatedly came under consideration for the national presidency of the League of German Women's Associations (BDF), but she felt that such a top position would be too much for her. However, she could see a day when she would no longer be able to say 'no'; 'then heaven help me!'[125] And in 1919 the day did indeed come.

If Marianne had pursued a university career, her work on Fichte and her legal history of women would have added up to a considerable qualification. But, for all her historical knowledge, she lacked a training in the law, and she does not seem to have thought herself capable of giving practical legal advice to women. For decades that was the job of Camilla Jellinek (1860–1940), the wife of the constitutional theorist Georg Jellinek. In this case, there was no equivalent on the wives' side to the friendship between the two husbands; a rivalry soon developed between them, although their skills were such that they could have complemented each other nicely. In 1902 Marianne complained that a 'conflict with the very, very ambitious and unidealistic Frau Jellinek' was causing her sleepless nights.[126]

Shortly afterwards, the two formed what now seems a rather curious action group against the Heidelberg brothel.[127] Marianne called for 'unrelenting struggle against male licentiousness' and, drawing a parallel with slavery, described their campaign as 'abolitionist' in line with international feminist usage. The campaign against officially supervised and therefore legitimated prostitution – her first public campaign, in which she drew on the whole register of moral revulsion – was for her also a struggle against a certain doctrine of natural law: 'Above all, we must drop the scientifically obsolete theory derived from the doctrine of natural law, according to which a distinction between "crime" and "vice"' means that prostitution, corresponding as it does to male nature, is a vice but not a crime.[128] Camilla Jellinek waged a campaign over many years against the employment of women as waitresses, on the grounds that it was often a cover for prostitution.[129] In a town such as Heidelberg, where waitresses were often very popular among students, this must have seemed to many an odd idea; and, much to Camilla Jellinek's disappointment, waitresses themselves were not at all in favour of it.[130] This would hardly have surprised Max Weber, who noted in *Economy and Society* that 'professional prostitution of both the heterosexual and homosexual types (note the training of *tribades*) is found even at the most primitive levels of culture' (E&S 607); it was thus something 'natural', not a product of certain social conditions. When the writer Anna Pappritz, chairwoman of the German section of the International Abolitionist Federation, resumed the campaign against brothels in the middle of the war and looked to Marianne Weber for support, Max Weber flared up: 'The devil take this Pappritz woman! What does she think she's playing at?'[131]

Abstract respect and practical ambivalence: the Webers and the women's movement

Commitment to the emancipated woman of the future did not necessarily go together with strong sympathy for actually existing women – nor did it in reality in the case of Max Weber. As Ingrid Gilcher-Holtey has written: 'Without a sensual-erotic component, the relationship to woman becomes for Max Weber the abstract women's question.'[132] In fact, Max Weber felt a degree of distaste for the female world characteristic of the upper classes of his time: the lavish spending on toiletries, the typical female conversation and the dances. In France and Spain in 1897, the female elegance does not seem to have had the slightest attraction for him, so that he could write of the women out for a stroll in San Sebastian: 'Their hats are a metre high, and although their faces rise above the horrifying emptiness of French women they too are on the whole chattering silk and flower stalls . . . a creature that can make you feel quite sick.'[133] But many feminists shared his abhorrence of this female type, who preferred to look in the mirror rather than at serious books.

Max Weber had a higher regard for the feminist movement at an abstract level than he did for most of the feminist women. 'Furies' (*Megären*) became his standard term for feminists, even if he sometimes put it between inverted commas. 'My wife is with other "furies" in Berlin visiting the

culture minister', he wrote in 1907 to Rickert, when a delegation from a
congress on higher education for women was invited to the ministry (MWG
II/5, 418). In 1910, speaking to Sophie Rickert, he referred to a BDF
meeting in Heidelberg as a 'furies' congress'; and, at the thought of the
women congregating there, he wanted to 'put his tail between his legs and
take it as far away as possible'. Marianne 'quite often openly conceded' that
'male feminists' – which included him – 'were not basically seen by women
as altogether of the male sex' (MWG II/6, 629).

But, however highly she thought of feminists, Marianne did not feel
comfortable at large women's congresses; more often than not, they were
a test of nerves rather than a source of strength. Women who attended
them, she wrote to Helene in 1894, were 'rather poorly endowed *in
corpore*'; they had not been 'brought up to feel solidarity with one another'
or to discuss 'in a logical and parliamentary manner'.[134] In July 1900 she
spoke dismissively of a 'long-winded women's meeting'; in 1905 she
described a meeting of the BDF presidency, to which she had allowed
herself to be elected, as an 'awful sacrifice' that caused her several days of
migraine; and early in 1911 she noted in her diary that a 'low-grade public'
had assembled in Karlsruhe for the founding conference of the Baden
Women's League.[135]

Sometimes she endured women's meetings with better humour and
treated them as a necessary stage for hitherto non-political women, where
they 'rabbit on about the purest nonsense'.[136] Occasionally – and, one
might say, forgivably for a woman living by the side of Max Weber – she felt
the intellectual superiority of men. 'I covet the wisdom of men', she wrote
in 1908 to Helene.[137] Such slips are probably one of the reasons why, despite
the many books by women about women, Marianne has still not found a
thorough female biographer. But we should bear in mind that she was not
alone in experiencing large women's meetings as a chore rather than a joy.
Even Gertrud Bäumer, who was elected BDF chairperson in 1910 and
appeared to be an archetypal political woman, confessed to her in early
1909 'that the world of objectivity' – that is, of politics and supra-individual
interests – was 'a pretty feeble affair', although she wanted this 'female'
admission to remain confidential, as otherwise 'men will look down on
us'.[138] Even for her, then, the women's movement was not a tightly fitting
reality. Her friend Ika Freudenberg wrote to her around that time: 'Let's
forget about the whole women's movement and find a nest for ourselves
somewhere in the bosom of nature.'[139]

When Alice Salomon was elected to the BDF presidency in 1900,
she found herself on a committee where the youngest person until
then had been 'not much less than sixty'; she quoted without comment a
male writer who described the women at BDF meetings as 'black
shadows'.[140] Marianne Weber's first impressions of the women's movement were similar.[141] Evidently, man-hating and pleasure-hating old spinsters were not a bogey invented by anti-feminists. Marie Stritt,
chairperson of the BDF from 1899 to 1910, placed a pointed remark at

the front of a book on contraception (1908): 'The women's question is not the spinsters' question.'

The generation change in the women's movement after the turn of the century brought new tensions, in which personal rivalries were combined with disputes on substantive issues such as the extent to which common cause should be made with social democratic women. In a letter to Max, who was then at the establishment in Urach, Marianne raged against the 'radicals' who spent two whole days 'scribbling' at a women's congress and 'talking everyone else half-dead' in order to make a 'declaration of love to the social democratesses (*Sozialdemokrateusen!*)'. 'Your little Snouty shot her mouth off a few times. Against the declaration of love, of course.'[142] Other controversies touched on more intimate issues. Should marriage – or celibacy in the unmarried – remain the ideal for women, or should the movement make unmarried mothers and contraception one of its special concerns? Should it demand equal rights in every respect or, basing itself on women's special nature, call for certain special measures to protect them? Marianne held the latter view, and Max Weber too, in arguing with his mother, condemned doctrinaire notions of equality that refused to recognize any particularities: 'Of course, this whole opposition on the part of some women is out of touch with the reality of life and is a source of amusement for factory-owners who profit by it' (MWG II/6, 78). As far as women were concerned, *life* does seem to have been a fount of law.

Weber's fury with the 'motherhood protection mob'

The seemingly innocuous question of the employment rights of expectant and nursing mothers was a delicate matter in those days, for it applied mainly to unmarried women; even Alice Salomon, who remained single all her life, thought that it 'threatened to leave married women out of consideration'.[143] In 1905 a League for the Protection of Motherhood was founded; its leading light was Helene Stöcker (1869–1943), publisher since 1903 of the *Frauen-Rundschau*, who had done a doctorate in philosophy, admired Nietzsche and actively promoted not only women's rights but also pacifism, greater sexual freedom and eugenics. The league expanded rapidly in its first few years: two-thirds of its members were women, but the proportion of doctors was also conspicuously high.

Both Max Weber and Werner Sombart signed the founding appeal,[144] but Weber withdrew before the end of the first year. For, under the aegis of Helene Stöcker, the league went in a direction he had not expected: to demand equal rights for unmarried mothers, the legalization of abortion and free distribution of contraceptives.[145] Early in 1907 Weber fumed to Michels that the 'motherhood protection mob' was a 'completely confused rabble': 'Crude hedonism & an ethics only to men's benefit, presented as a goal for women: that is simply twaddle.' He spoke of 'petty bourgeois run amok' (MWG II/5, 211).

Figure 11.2 Gertrud Bäumer (left) and Helene Lange, 1907

Weber's outburst may be seen as reflecting his sexual inhibition at the time, but a century later his view that free love is often at the woman's expense and that an intact family is the best protection of motherhood does not appear completely unrealistic, even if it is not theoretically conclusive either. Weber's lashing out at the 'motherhood protection mob' reminds one of his attack ten years earlier on the 'demon of matriarchy'; the theory of primeval matriarchy was then also part of the ideology of free love. Seven years later, however, the same Max Weber was using all his legal skills to fight for the mother's right to her child.

Although the women's movement may at first have had a somewhat spinsterly aspect, the League for the Protection of Motherhood introduced a new element that caused a great deal of tension and excitement. One part of the women's movement met up here with the 'erotic movement', the gospel of free love combined with free contraception; we may even say that it was under the banner of the protection of motherhood that sexual reformers formed themselves into a regular movement. Unfettered eroticism lay concealed beneath a slogan that seemed to speak of welfare and social protection.

Charity work by good middle-class women on behalf of 'fallen girls' had previously had a certain voyeuristic appeal. As Marianne wrote in 1895 of a visit to the Verein für Frauenschutz, 'hot and cold flushes came over' her as she saw how 'young women could speak of the most intimate aspects . . .

of their confinement'.[146] It was always entertaining to discuss the 'social question' as a sexual question, whether in relation to 'night lodgers' in large apartment blocks or to the defencelessness of female factory-workers. In the autumn of 1902, when Max was away travelling, various female visitors began to debate with Marianne 'so loudly and heatedly about issues of morality' that someone said it was fortunate that 'there was not a man in the house' – then Max suddenly appeared in the room and the discussion broke off. In 1903, at the time of her campaign against the Heidelberg brothel, Marianne wrote that 'the issue of morality', which then 'passionately occupied' her, was leading to tensions within the women's movement.[147] Questions of love, marriage and morality helped her gain a wider audience than Max ever had in his lifetime. Her book on women and love, *Die Frauen und die Liebe* (1935), was a late reply to Helene Stöcker's *Die Liebe und die Frauen* (1906).[148]

For all her criticism of patriarchal structures, Marianne always regarded monogamy as an ethical achievement for women in particular, whereas the BDF chairwoman and actress Marie Stritt (1855–1928), the wife of an opera singer, took a different line. In 1903 Marianne complained of her: 'She is attached with all her heart to the economic independence of women . . . and, to make this possible, she would happily send family and marriage to the devil and call upon all women to limit the number of their children.'[149] The BDF leader was 'quite beside herself' over Marianne's essay on professional life and marriage, *Beruf und Ehe* (1905), which on the one hand had energetically pleaded, in the spirit of *The Protestant Ethic*, for women to be instructed in 'methodical planning of their lives', but on the other hand had insisted on motherhood as woman's special vocation and rejected attempts to lift the burden on women through collective childcare.[150] Marie Stritt would never forgive her for this piece, and from now on Marianne worked to have her removed from her leadership position.[151] And in fact – as a result of 'intrigues behind the scenes',[152] according to Richard Evans – Marie Stritt was replaced in 1910 by Marianne's friend Gertrud Bäumer.

This was preceded by a sharp dispute over whether the League for the Protection of Motherhood should be accepted into the BDF – which at the same time was a dispute over marriage and sexual morality. Marie Stritt argued in favour of its acceptance, but the contrary position upheld by Gertrud Bäumer and Marianne Weber won in the end.[153] The whole controversy left an unpleasant aftertaste for Alice Salomon, who felt that Marianne Weber, Helene Lange and Gertrud Bäumer had conducted a 'smear campaign' against Marie Stritt. Her characterization of 'the Webers' casts light on how they were seen at the time outside their circle of friends, and shows once again that they were not naturally inclined to make critical use of knowledge:

But Marianne has for some time . . . been fighting hard, as the Webers often do, because they believe in the *unconditional truth* and *correctness* of their conviction. And this leads them to pass sentence on their

opponent, to sneer at other people who are aware of human errors &
find shades of grey between black & white.[154]

In 1907 Marianne dreaded the thought of a lecture that Helene Stöcker was
due to give in Heidelberg, although she was used to arguing with her about
the legal history of women.

On the other hand, of course, male and female students do not have
to be told twice that 'free relations' are much nobler than monogamy.
It is quite certain that H. St. is seriously harming our movement and,
even if it is not at all her intention, encouraging the libertinism of
youth. . . . You can imagine that the whole business is preying on my
mind. . . . And then this terrible effect on young people. It would seem
that in Munich they are all amusing themselves with free relationships
and trading in condoms.[155]

'Torn by revulsion' at the splendour of 'blood-warm life'

Between the lines Marianne assumed, like Max Weber, that human beings –
including girls – had a naturally polygamous sex drive, which immediately
broke through once it gained an appearance of legitimacy. In her biography, Marianne described with remarkable candour the inner turmoil that
the challenge of the 'erotic movement' aroused in herself and Max.
Arguments about it in their circle with 'highly principled, cultured people'
'shocked the Webers and perturbed them far more than the impersonal
public fight'; their world was indeed filled with lively people, essentially
from their personal circle. As they watched the gospel of free love take its
toll, mainly through the breakdown of marriages, they were 'torn by horror
and revulsion at the theory and by a profound sympathy for the unhappy
lives that prepared the ground for such misleading teachings' (WB 374).
   To be sure, there were no taboo subjects for Max and Marianne, and they
pondered whether each of them might not find sexual happiness in other
relationships; they therefore felt quite personally affected by the debates
about eroticism. Both Max and Marianne often travelled alone, not worrying too much about conventional bourgeois norms, and in 1907 she even
went to Pontresina and Sils Maria with the highly regarded young philosopher Emil Lask, with whom she was connected by a common interest in
Fichte. Already in 1915, 'we met up when Max was ill in Rome', she wrote
to Helene without any inhibition.[156] It was through Lask that Mina Tobler
entered the Weber circle; and, when Lask – who supported the idea of free
love – started a relationship with Lina Radbruch that led to the break-up
of the Radbruchs' marriage, the circle found itself devastated not for the
last time by the erotic movement.
   In today's history books, the ten years before 1914 were a time of growing
international tensions. But Marianne, with the Weber world before her eyes,

wrote in 1907: 'There seems no doubt that we are living in a period of sharp sexual tension.'[157] She must have felt this tension inside herself too. Admittedly she was indignant in 1902 when the Saxon crown princess scandalized Europe by running off to Switzerland with her private tutor:[158] 'Can that be considered from a general point of view?' she asked. 'It's really just an appalling act by one individual.'[159] A few years later, however, she came to see this kind of female autonomy more and more from a 'general point of view': 'What was the value of norms that so often stifled the magnificence of vibrant life, repressed natural drives, and, above all, denied fulfilment to so many women? Law, duty, asceticism – were not all these ideas derived from the demonization of sex by an outgrown Christianity? To shape one's future entirely on the basis of one's own nature, to let the currents of life flow through one and then to bear the consequences, was better than to sneak along on the sterile paths of caution hemmed in by morality' (WB 370f.). She was playing the devil's advocate here, but doing it so brilliantly that one feels something of herself in the words. For Marianne, too, nature was the origin of the human condition. Anyway, over the years she developed a certain understanding for the erotic movement, especially as a result of the turbulent relations with Else Jaffé.

'Snouty' and 'Sparrow': the first act of the Else drama

It is now high time to introduce the legendary woman who would keep Weber busy for the rest of his life: Else von Richthofen (1874–1973), after 1902 Else Jaffé by marriage. Since Eduard Baumgarten lured Weber researchers in the 1960s with allusions to the previously well-concealed love story, it has gripped the imagination of everyone also interested in Weber as a man; and it is not easy to reconstruct the reality behind the legend. Curiously enough, it has been little noticed that the great Else drama began with *Marianne's* falling in love with this captivating woman. The story of the relationship between them, its tensions and its ups and downs, is at least as exciting as the love story that later developed between Max and Else. In the first, most intimate phase of the women's friendship, Marianne became 'Snouty' [160] for Else as well as for Max, while Else was called 'Sparrow' by Marianne. At the very time of Max's breakdown, when Marianne must often have felt alone with her need for love, her friendship with Else took a passionate turn. Whereas Max always used the formal *Sie* pronoun even with colleagues who had long been his friends, the two women used *du* even though Else was still a student and Marianne a professor's wife. Unlike Marianne, however, Else was continuing her studies for a doctorate: only someone who has longed for one in vain can empathize with the envious admiration that Marianne must have felt for her. At Christmas 1899 Else wrote to 'dearest little Snouty' what Marianne must have experienced as a love letter. But Else loved only men and avoided any physical tenderness.[161]

Else von Richthofen came from a noble family that had fallen on hard times and needed to find a material basis of support. Through the examinations to qualify as a teacher, she became one of the first women in Germany to gain access to higher education,[162] studying political economy in Freiburg, Berlin and Heidelberg. The Webers first got to know this exceptional student during their time in Freiburg and met her again in Heidelberg. She was not a 'cute girl' type but an adult woman, who, not surprisingly, soon captivated Weber. 'Her quick repartee, sense of irony and fondness for mocking remarks were a challenge to him, while her grace and beauty attracted her to him.'[163] He already thought her competent to have a say in a professorial appointment, even a critical say. Thus in 1899 he told Alfred Weber that, 'according to reports from Fräulein von Richthofen', a candidate being considered for a professorship in Heidelberg was 'a stupid fool'.[164]

Naturally, Max Weber was not the only one who fell under her spell. Alice Salomon, who knew her well, reported how at the sight of her all male prejudices about female students melted like snow in the sun: 'The university was so proud of her, and there was scarcely a single academic dignitary who would not have asked for her hand if he had had the courage.'[165] No one else at Heidelberg university was better equipped to dispel the prejudice that female students were 'blue stockings'.

In 1898 Else again crossed Alfred's path in Berlin. Her sister Lili burst into tears of jealousy when she felt that Alfred and Helene were more interested in Else than herself,[166] and according to one report it almost reached the point where they became engaged to marry.[167] According to Else's memoirs, which she wrote sixty years later, Alfred was of all the men in the Charlottenburg household 'the most interesting by far, though completely wrapped up in his home-industry problems'. Else too began to occupy herself with homework, which had been a fashionable theme for social criticism since the first production of Gerhart Hauptmann's *The Weavers* [*Die Weber*] in 1892; around the year 1900 the Weber firm in Oerlinghausen still obtained most of its products from outwork. Else found that young women gladly took on work that allowed them to stay at home, and so she could not agree with the recriminating tone that was usual when the subject was being discussed.[168] We can imagine how she presented these findings to Alfred with her slightly amused smile. He, however, who would later remain faithful to her for fifty years, did not yet feel positively attracted to her, or anyway not for long.

In 1900, Else Jaffé obtained her doctorate in Heidelberg *summa cum laude*[169] with the already ailing Max Weber, who – although dissertations were then few and far between – looked through it with the utmost difficulty after months of pressure from Marianne and again reached the limits of his nervous energy.[170] In the same year, with Weber's help, she got a job in Karlsruhe at the Baden factory inspectorate, with particular responsibility for female workers. In those days labour protection extended to outwork, for which Else had a special competence. She was the first woman anywhere in Germany to hold such a post, which was strategically important both for the women's movement and for social policy in general. It was up to the inspectorates whether labour protection laws were actually implemented on the ground.

Under the direction of Friedrich Woerishoffer, the Baden factory inspectorate became a model for the whole Reich; the state authorities in Karlsruhe were already working closely with the trade unions, in a way that would have been unthinkable in Berlin. Woerishoffer was not immune to Else's charm – whereas a personal animosity developed between his successor, Bittmann, and her successor, Marie Baum – and even the union representatives, who initially ran down the genteel young lady at the factory inspectorate,[171] lost all ill-will as soon as they met her. Apart from her charm, she was highly competent and neither reactionary nor squeamish, and she went down well with the workers.[172] Such experiences may have contributed to Max Weber's more favourable view of the unions than of the Social Democratic Party, and to his belief that that it was possible to work with them constructively.

'It was part of the women's programme to obtain such occupations', Marianne wrote. 'They were convinced that they would be fulfilling a necessary social mission as advocates of the female workers' (WB 230). Years earlier, Marianne had 'jumped for joy' when women's factory inspectorates were introduced, and Max, to her 'anger and embarrassment', had teased her that 'of all possible people' she was a 'factory inspector in the making', and even seriously claimed that that was her secret wish.[173] If Weber was right, then Else stood in for Marianne's own secret wish. Marianne was filled with enthusiasm: the 'little sparrow' had become a 'big fish', or anyway an 'important high-born little sparrow'; it was just the right activity for Else and would not overtax her.[174]

Did Marianne think Else more robust than she was in reality? Certainly the factory inspectorate was one of the hardest jobs in the whole state administration. Without a large 'apparatus' of its own or real instruments of power, it was supposed to take on company managers and foremen and to find the balance between intervention and cooperation, without which little could be achieved. Early in 1902 Else complained in a letter to Marianne: 'You can't imagine how depressing it is to encounter so much resistance even to minor changes. . . . And unfortunately I am so inclined to give up and say: "All right, forget about it", when people scream blue murder if they are asked to instal a few spittoons.'[175] Sometimes there were even quarrels with management about the need for doors on lavatory cubicles.

It was already clear to Else that she would really like to quit the profession and get married and have children. At first she did not dare to tell Marianne of her planned 'desertion'. When this eventually came out, Marianne thought it 'a terrible shame',[176] confirming as it did the prejudice that the best education was of no avail since women would give it all up and marry at the first opportunity. And then, to much shaking of people's heads, Else married the economist Edgar Jaffé (1866–1921), by no means a good-looker but heir of a German–English firm of textile exporters, who built a magnificent villa for Else and himself at a prime hillside location in Heidelberg. He would actually have preferred it if Else had continued with her profession – it was an interesting field, which also interested him as a co-founder of the *Archiv für Sozialpolitik* – but she had had enough of inspecting factories and wanted to have a child.

For Marianne this experience was probably an indication of the strength of female nature, in which she – though childless – from now on always believed. Else later once described herself to Alfred as 'a lazy devil'[177] – and Marianne would probably not have disagreed during the times when she was angry with her. But, whereas in 1898 she had still felt a horror of children ('it's really terrible if the little worms also become the *intellectual* centre of one's whole existence'),[178] she probably understood Else's desire better now that, in her own marriage, any hope of having children had been dashed. 'Besides, the two are *very* happy with each other', she wrote of Else and Edgar in 1903;[179] and the stress on 'very' probably meant that their marriage was, sexually too, as she would have liked her own to be. It was not long before Else had two children by Edgar, and a third, 'little Peter', arrived in 1909, whose father – as the Webers knew – was Otto Gross. One can imagine Marianne's bewilderment as she watched these natural events unfold in a friend right next door to her. In the early years of her marriage, Else was 'very active in the cause of legal protection' and also served as a secretary at the Heidelberg Verein für Frauenbildung founded by Marianne.[180] But then her interests shifted from the women's and erotic movements to her children, although she frankly admitted that she sometimes felt no trace of maternal love within herself.[181] Marianne was resentful that she would now have to do all the work herself, since 'my dear secretary Else Jaffé' – no more talk of 'the sparrow' – was completely taken up 'with her little toy'.[182]

Edgar's looks do not seem to have mattered much to Else – anyway less than his Jewish origins – but she was disappointed that he did not become a great scholar.[183] Apparently Else had wanted to become the muse of a great man, and when Edgar failed to meet her expectations she lost interest in him sexually too. In male fantasies she continued to embody pure sensuality,[184] whereas in reality she was a highly intellectual woman,[185] who seemed to herself 'the only sensible one in her clan'[186] and who sought the proximity of great minds. Only such considerations – and scarcely sexual attraction alone – can explain her later relations with Alfred and Max Weber, two bookish men well past their youth. This is not to say that she could not really have loved them: sense and sensibility may be at odds with each other in romantic fantasies, but in the real world they are interlinked through the nerves, and for Else they were certainly associated at a conscious level.[187]

Even Else's affair with Freud's disciple Otto Gross, which led to the birth of a son, was probably the result of mental-intellectual as much as sexual attraction to a man who, before he destroyed himself through drugs, was a rising star of psychoanalysis. When, shortly afterwards, she came to feel sexually dependent on a surgeon, it was a source of 'shame and torment' for her.[188] Nor was her relationship to her libido as feline and free of brooding as men like to imagine. The fact that Otto Gross also started a sexual relationship with her sister Frieda – the historian now has to think in terms of two different Friedas – was not able to shake her, but she was not cut out to play the role of a faithful disciple; she soon got fed up with Otto's guru posture and was not content to listen in admiration to his monologues. She hit the mark with her analysis of his extreme ego-centrism and inability to communicate with others (which the Otto Gross cult seems unwilling to perceive): 'Now, as it were, the prophet has burned in his fire the last remnants of Otto the man, taking away the ability to love individually any individual person suited to his nature.'[189] Else did not need a charismatic leader; she had her own charisma. Later she was convinced that she herself, not her sister Frieda, D. H. Lawrence's wife, had served as the model for Lady Chatterley. Else's daughter Marianne, who as a 'half-Jew' was prevented from studying medicine in the Nazi period, turned to psychoanalysis and married a cousin of Adenauer's press chief Felix von Eckardt; she hated her mother, by whom she felt driven from pillar to post, yet acquired maternal impulses of her own in the 1950s when she translated the Kinsey report into German. A granddaughter of Else's, who lived in a commune in 1968, once tried to shock the 95-year-old with reports about group sex. But Else answered with a smile on her face: 'What of it?'

Otto Gross's wife Frieda, née Schloffer (1876–1950), niece of the philosopher Alois Riehl whom Marianne heard speak about Nietzsche, was a friend of Else's from their youth, and the triangle seems to have made their friendship even closer. On the other hand, Otto Gross was irritated by Else's affair with the surgeon, since, according to Else, 'he did not belong to the caste' – the word 'scene' did not yet have the colloquial meaning that it does today. For Gross, free love was applicable only within an elite of special people; he despised even Alfred and Max Weber as 'democrats'. As we have seen, Max Weber's simmering anger at Otto Gross and Else's relationship with this prophet of free love was vented in his famous letter to Else of 13 September 1907, though in the guise of an attack on value-freedom. Later he described how, in the development of human culture, eroticism and intellectualism drove each other on to ever bolder heights, intimately interrelated yet in a constant and painful tension. In Else he found both in the same person: a highly developed erotic sense together with intellectual powers. But were they necessarily such a torment to each other? Was there something inevitable about the tension? Else embodied a synthesis of Eros and intellect, but not at all a harmony free of all tension.

Marianne was pleased to see Else again in August 1906. 'Just Jaffé is always a rather boring accompaniment.'[190] Edgar Jaffé struck her as a 'somewhat capricious and unstable, as well as very nervous, element'. His collaboration on the *Archiv für Sozialwissenschaft* was a constant irritation to Max Weber, and Marianne added fuel to the flames, especially as she thought that all the energy he spent on the journal was 'only a surrogate'.[191] But for Max Weber, after his withdrawal from the university, the *Archiv* was for many years his only way of remaining a focus of scholarly attention – and therefore his relationship with Edgar Jaffé was existentially important. Else was not only the most attractive woman in his circle but also, next to Marianne, the one in whom there was the greatest overlap between the female and male worlds around him, and in whom the various networks were at their densest. She was a mediator between the circles of Max and Alfred Weber, but also between the Weber and George circles – as Gundolf too had a soft spot for her. This made her a key figure indeed in the world of the Webers. Max thought that Else had successive sexual relationships with Arthur Salz and Gundolf. Although he got worked up about this 'explosion of the flesh' (MWG II/6, 373), an erotic relationship with Else seems to have been an entrance ticket to the Weber circle. As Salin put it, her charm did a lot to ensure that 'intellectual antagonisms' among the people around Weber 'did not lead to human estrangement, or anyway never for long'.[192]

Poor Edgar cut a sorry figure beside his beautiful wife, and he suffered greatly because of her escapades. But there is much to be said for seeing him as the true hero of Else's drama. When Else's fling with Alfred turned into a lasting relationship, Max wrote to Marianne that in Jaffé's place he 'would hardly leave alive' a wife who not only deserted him but exposed him to ridicule; it would be best for Edgar too 'if someone were to kill him', and 'I would be prepared to do it right now, in *his* interest, if the police did not unfortunately forbid it' (MWG II/6, 482). In 1913 he repeated to Frieda Gross that 'to kill [Edgar Jaffé] is not morally reprehensible but the only decent thing to do – only unfortunately our crazy laws prohibit it & I cannot do anything else for Else's sake' (MWG II/8, 160). Probably he often brooded over what he would do if Marianne was unfaithful to him. But, of course, his lust to kill remained purely verbal.

In the end, however, Edgar Jaffé alone publicly broke away from all bourgeois convention, in a highly risky manner that led to his own destruction. In November 1918 he took office as finance minister in Kurt Eisner's revolutionary socialist government in Bavaria – surely one of the hardest and most thankless tasks one can imagine in politics, even though Jaffé, as a wealthy heir, did not have the slightest interest in a revolution. He brought his economic skills to bear as best he could, so that even the anarchist Erich Mühsam thought him 'by far the ablest mind in the Eisner cabinet', while Rilke considered him the best speaker in revolutionary Munich.[193] It would be quite misleading to see him only as a pitiful supernumerary in the Weber–Else drama.

But let us return to the opening act. Else had all the qualities to throw Marianne's emotions and world-view into complete confusion, and Marianne herself did not pretend otherwise. In 1910 she wrote to Sophie Rickert:

No one 'goes without', but each takes as many flowers, sunshine as the other allows him – and, ah well, that is so understandable. Anyway, I have lost all strength and all courage to demand of others anything else that I do not know for sure I could do in the same situation – I fear that all my 'ethic' has gone down the drain because of what has happened in the last few years – and I don't know if I have gained any humanity as a result.[194]

Looking back later in life, she was again remarkably honest with herself: 'My witnessing of their erotic fates and my immersion in this new "zest for life" certainly carried a danger for me. . . . My zeal for the old ideals – sexual purity, spiritualization of women and their settling into the realm of the supra-personal – all this was covered with ashes by Else's development.'[195]

Plagued by 'nerves' and insomnia, Marianne saw this friend as the very embodiment of unshakable calm; Else kept the ability in any crisis to lie down and go straight to sleep. On 30 July 1900, as one of the very first women in Germany to defend a doctoral thesis, she was unruffled while a male fellow student's teeth were chattering: 'fabulously blasé', Marianne commented in amazement.[196] Even when her affair with Alfred took a more serious turn, she managed to keep her marriage with Edgar more or less intact. 'She has an enviable nervous system altogether', Marianne sighed at this art of making the best of things.[197] Else, a distant cousin of the famous fighter pilot Manfred von Richthofen, was an archetypal 'cool' woman, as we would say today, who had no time for all the fuss about the nerves and looked ahead to the end of the 'nervous age' – rather like the young female pilot from the days of the first flying machines who got up from a crash landing, quickly felt herself and said dismissively: 'Just a broken collar-bone – the easiest thing to break after your marriage vows.'[198]

Else confounded all of Marianne's moral ideas, and she did it with charm and elegance. Sometimes Marianne tried to come to terms with it by developing a metaphysics of Else's 'real essence', in which her 'being' had 'an indestructible goodness and nobility', even if her external behaviour was not free of 'brutalities' and was 'often neither kind nor noble'.[199] 'Yesterday Else was here', she wrote in her diary early in 1911. 'It's the same as always: when I don't see her a feeling of protest weighs against her actions, but as soon as I am with her, I can't help feeling so positive about what she is that all criticism gets lost in a sense of the "purity" and nobility of her soul. The magic of her being is irresistible.'[200]

It made Marianne angry that Else never allowed herself to be pinned down, but then she interpreted this as an expression of the fluidity of life itself. 'Else's whole way of being exuded strong intellectual excitement (correction: strongly excited me) precisely because, to my frequent sadness, she did not hold on really firmly to any opinion. Everything about her was always in flux.' When Marianne sometimes pointed out that she had recently held a different view, Else reacted 'a little tetchily': 'But you know,

Marianne, I do say things that I don't mean.' This disarmed Marianne once more: 'She was like an instrument from which each finger elicits new tones, and there was usually a delightful melody to which everyone was eager to listen; the delightful way in which she knew how to express her inner emotion was probably what somehow made me, too, fertile during the time we were together – we always had so much to talk and gently argue about; with her I restrained my energetic inclination to express my own opinions . . ., because then the access to her soul was blocked.'

Marianne confided to her diary, before crossing it out, that she felt an 'urge for new passion' – but she did not cross out 'for some kind of experi- ence and adventure, for a full and varied life, for enjoyment of the beauty of the moment'.[201] She even confessed to Helene, when she allowed Else to take her to a 'lecturers' masked ball', that 'a bit of unspent childish joy still burns so inside me'.[202] On another occasion, they went together to a fancy- dress festival where the female students put on 'a really funny show' set in the year 3000 about 'men's individual talent for study'[203] – evidently a parody of contemporary male concoctions about women's talents.

Else constantly provided fresh material for intellectual discussion. For, despite the volatility that Marianne remarked upon, she did not jump ran- domly and thoughtlessly from one opinion to another: 'She also searches more than ever for theoretical clarity.'[204] Discussions about the nature of beauty were part of a tradition in cultured society; Max and Marianne Weber, too, occupied themselves with this problem inherited from classical antiquity. The question kept arising as to how aesthetic beauty was related to moral goodness and to sensuous excitement. In 1898 Marianne declared her belief that 'the function of our aesthetic perception of the world' was 'to free us from sensual needs'.[205] Else had a different view of things: for her, the aesthetic and erotic senses went hand in hand, and human values were also contained in the beautiful. In 1908 a colourful scene is supposed to have taken place between her and Max Weber against the backdrop of the Heidelberg castle ruins. Max Weber asked (in a threatening voice, we should imagine): 'But you wouldn't say that any *value* could be embodied in eroticism?' To which she replied, 'But certainly – beauty!' At which Weber fell silent and thoughtful. It was a new idea to him.[206]

Weber's musings on Eros and sexuality also pushed their way into his scholarly work, though at first in a half-disguised manner. In 1908 he pub- lished in the *Archiv*, signing it simply 'W.', a quite unusually detailed review of *Sexualethik* by the psychologist Christian von Ehrenfels, a colleague of Alfred Weber's from Prague, whom he (Alfred) later described as having been a kind of 'youthful sweetheart'.[207] Ehrenfels advocated polygamy for racially superior men as a way of serving the elevation of humanity, and branded monogamy as the ruin of European civilization. Since men were by nature polygamous, 'is' and 'ought' were here theoretically in harmony with each other.[208] Weber patiently presented in great detail this eugenic rationalization of polygamy, as if it were a highly significant book, but refrained from any explicit assessment of its worth. If he nevertheless

remarked that Ehrenfels conducted his attack on bourgeois sexual morality with a degree of moral feeling, we can detect a note of derision,[209] much
as he had earlier derided Michels for his theoretical praise of polygamy.

At Christmas 1911 Marianne had a dream in which Else said to her: 'I
almost never think about you – a sign of how alien you always were to me.'
In the dream Marianne began to cry and became really 'angry'; she
reproached Else that this alienness was purely imaginary. Else also felt a
sense of guilt; 'and then, out of pride, I no longer wanted to have anything
to do with her.'[210] For many years, however, her main problem with Else was
that her husband – who still called Else *Sie* until 1909 – felt uneasy about
his wife's close relationship with this enchanting creature. At times Max
behaved even more than Marianne as a guardian of the old morality.
Unsuspecting, Marianne felt a 'need to bring Else and Max closer to each
other'. In the spring of 1909, buoyed up by the waves during a boat trip on
Lake Maggiore, she asked him 'whether a sexual ethic was correct if its
ideals and standards were set so high that most people could achieve them
only at the cost of valuable life-energies'. But Max just growled 'angrily':
'No doubt you're thinking again of how Else can have her fun.'[211] Even at
a time when Max Weber hated Else out of disappointed love, Marianne
made an effort 'to break the evil spell between her and Max'.[212] But this
takes us right into the next act of the drama.

12

Max Weber's Love–Hate for the Germans

Germanophobia and self-hatred

One of Weber's most curious admissions, often quoted but never plausibly interpreted, comes in a letter of 5 February 1906 to Adolf von Harnack, in which he thanks the theologian for sending him the second edition of his *magnum opus Die Mission und Ausbreitung des Christentums*[1] (which by the fourth edition would swell to a thousand pages). Harnack's gift was in return for a copy of the much shorter *The Protestant Ethic* that Weber had sent him a year before, to which he had responded with a (non-extant) letter, 'very kind' in tone but so irritating in content that Weber had at first felt unable to reply to it.

To be sure, Harnack saw Puritan asceticism as an aberration from Christianity; in his *Wesen des Christentums* he had written that 'the greatest fact' about Jesus and the mark of 'his inner freedom' was that he 'did not speak like a heroic penitent' nor 'like an ecstatic prophet'. 'His eye rests kindly upon the flowers and the children, on the . . . birds in the air and the sparrows on the house-top.' Harnack detects in Jesus a joy in nature, quite unlike prophetic fanaticism. 'No one who reads the Gospels with an unprejudiced mind . . . can fail to acknowledge that this free and active spirit does not appear to be bent under the yoke of asceticism', and that any words of Jesus which suggest otherwise should not be taken as the kernel of his doctrine.[2] Asceticism as a 'yoke', not a source of strength, disciplined living and individual self-awareness. How much he must have disliked the basic tendency of *The Protestant Ethic*! He seems to have tried to give Weber a better understanding of Lutheranism. But Weber had replied:

> I have the feeling that different value-judgements are at the bottom of this. Luther towers so much above everyone else; Lutheran*ism* is for me – I do not deny it – the most horrifying of all horrors in its *historical* manifestations. . . . It is an internally difficult and tragic situation: *neither* of us could himself be a 'sect person', a Quaker, Baptist, etc.; *each* of us sees at once the superiority of the (essentially) institutional church, in terms of *non*-ethical and *non*-religious values. Above all, the

time for 'sects' or anything similar in nature is historically over. But that our nation never went through the school of harsh asceticism, in *any* form, is . . . the source of everything I find hateful in it (as well as in myself). (MWG II/5, 32f.)

Here Weber, the fighter against value-judgements in science, admits that value-judgements are at the foundation of *The Protestant Ethic*: he does not openly declare it, but only 'has the feeling'. When he called Lutheranism 'the most horrifying of all horrors', it was a provocation that must have been hurtful to Harnack, however much he himself was at odds with Lutheran orthodoxy. Relations between him and Weber broke down as a result; not a single letter was sent over the next seven years. Marianne, who 'at Harnack's urging' gave a lecture at Pentecost 1907 on her pet theme, 'Basic Questions of Sexual Ethics', at the Evangelical-Social Congress in Strasbourg (WB 373), always found the break 'painful' and was happy when the two met by chance in 1913 in Perugia and, having turned pale for a moment, shook hands and were soon talking with each other on the old familiar terms.[3]

The Weber of 1913 was no longer the same as the Weber of 1906; 'charisma', grace, the kernel of Lutheran doctrine, became his most successful new concept in the sociology of rule. He was in agreement with Harnack that strict asceticism was quite alien to Lutheranism, yet in 1913 this Lutheran composure was no longer as hateful to him as before. Like Troeltsch and many others, he assumed that Lutheranism had left its mark on the German mind. In 1906, to be sure, he had found nothing familiar in this German particularity and had pushed it away. He admitted that he was unable to connect with a Puritan sect of the Anglo-American type, but at the time he experienced this inability as 'tragic'. Between the lines – and not only here – one senses a longing for religion on the part of this man in such need of salvation.

Today it is not easy to understand this kind of hatred of one's own nation. Contemporary German self-hatred tends to be directed more against a (supposed) mania for work and a lack of the casual art of living; and it is usually assumed that German society was even harsher and more repressive in the imperial period. Weber's image of the Germans was quite different. The 'great industrious nations of the world', he stressed more than once (WB 427; MWG I/15, 351), were the British and the Americans, whereas they had long regarded the Germans, for all their apparent sluggishness, as outstanding performers.[4] In Weber, anyway, one finds scarcely any pride in 'German efficiency'. Nor did he, for years a restless traveller in southern Europe, think there was anything of substance in German *Gemütlichkeit*. In the second part of *The Protestant Ethic*, he takes a clear distance from the *Gemütlichkeit* or *Natürlichkeit* that is often seen as the German kind of freedom:

The typical German quality often called 'good nature' or 'naturalness' contrasts strongly, even in the facial expressions of people, with the effects of that thorough destruction of the spontaneity of the *status naturalis* in the Anglo-American atmosphere, which Germans are accustomed to judge unfavourably as a narrowness, unfreeness, and inner constraint. But the differences of conduct, which are very striking, have clearly originated in the lesser degree of ascetic penetration of life in Lutheranism as distinguished from Calvinism. (PE 127)

Similarly, in the article on American churches and sects that he wrote in 1906 for the *Frankfurter Zeitung*, we read that the American type of association derived from Puritanism lacks the 'boorish-vegetative *Gemütlichkeit* without which the German thinks no community can be maintained'.[5] 'Boorish-vegetative'! Here the Germans, with their Lutheran kind of *Gemütlichkeit*, still seem relatively close to the farmer's old 'organic cycle of life'. But in those days Weber did not know how to appreciate it. We are reminded of Nietzsche's disparagement of the Germans: 'We thought we were retreating into naturalness, but what we were really doing was letting ourselves go and electing for ease and comfort and the smallest possible degree of self-discipline.'[6] In the same way Weber complained in 1917 that, just as there was not a genuine aristocracy in Germany, 'no distinguished (*vornehme*) German social form exists' (PW 119).

At that time Germany did not strike anyone as especially Puritanical. This was true not only of people from the Anglo-American world, but also of the *Figaro* editor Jules Huret, who travelled in Germany in 1905 with an eye that was not necessarily friendly towards it. When walking in Berlin, he was astonished by the 'quest for pleasure' all around him – among mothers and half-grown children as well as adult males. Whereas Parisians celebrated major festivals only two or three times a year, people here seemed to be constantly feasting and bar-hopping. And at Wannsee the two sexes were jumbled together as they bathed 'almost naked'[7] – an unbelievable sight for a Frenchman, then and for a long time to come.

The 'fun society' did not make its first appearance in the present day: the Webers, and not only they, already felt they were living in one. D. H. Lawrence, the husband of Else's sister Frieda, who knew from experience the sexual niches of Wilhelmine Germany, depicted the country in *Lady Chatterley's Lover* as an eldorado of sexual freedom in comparison with Victorian England. Even Ivan Bloch, a founder of sexology and not exactly a Puritan, felt able to assert that, as 'we' overdo all the pleasures of the senses, 'we therefore make love three times too much'.[8] We need to be aware of this contemporary view in order to understand Weber.

Strangest of all, however, is the never explained outburst of self-hatred at the end of Weber's letter; there is nothing comparable to it anywhere else in the first-hand material available to us. How could he, the son of a mother marked by Calvinist traditions, claim that he was typically German in never having been through the school of religious asceticism, and how could he find himself repugnant because of this lack? What did he mean exactly by his lack of asceticism? One possible answer is that he was thinking of his marked penchant for alcohol, which began in his student days and continued through military service to his years as a professor.[9] This would fit into the alcoholism which, according to Weber, was widespread at the Lutheran courts. In his high-spirited periods, Weber was proud of being able to hold his drink; but later he regretted the alcoholic high spirits.

If, however, Weber really felt a victim of the 'iron cage' that went back to the ascetic morality of Calvinism, then his reference to Lutheranism as 'the most horrifying of all horrors' is more ambiguous than it appears at first sight. For in Weber's eyes the 'terrible' thing about Lutheran indolence was that it made him deeply insecure and raised the harrowing question of whether an unsuccessful upbringing had not condemned him to unhappiness. We should consider how he later spoke of Lutheranism in *Economy and Society*, in connection with the mystical-contemplative path to salvation:

> The mystic component in Lutheranism, for which the highest bliss available in this world is the ultimate *unio mystica*, was responsible . . . for the indifference of the Lutheran church towards the external organization of the preaching of the gospel, and also for that church's anti-ascetic and traditionalistic character. In any case, the typical mystic is never a man of conspicuous social activity, nor is he at all prone to accomplish any rational transformation of the mundane order on the basis of a methodical pattern of life directed toward external success. Wherever genuine mysticism did give rise to communal action, such action was characterized by the acosmism of the mystical feeling of love. (E&S 550)

Weber had gained new access to mysticism through Lutheranism. Lutheran indifference to the secular world and the anti-ascetic posture no longer had anything contemptible but derived – at least as an ideal type – from a 'mystical feeling of love'. Weber may also have experienced within himself that salvation came not as a result of concentrated effort but as undeserved grace. The changed attitude to Lutheranism must also have influenced Weber's feelings towards the Germans. Later he must often have wished that a little more German-Lutheran composure had rubbed off on his own person.

It may seem surprising how naturally Weber's letter to Harnack associates his experience of himself with his relationship to Lutheranism and the Germans. Here and there he shows himself to be well aware of the link between experience of the self and of the world; nor was he alone in this at the time. Treitschke, in the solitude of his deafness, complained that the 'inwardness of our nature' had 'intensified almost to the point of illness', and that in this respect he was 'a true German'. In the 'nervous age', it was popular to see reflections of one's own psychological weakness in the 'zigzag policies' of the German Reich. Thomas Mann admitted in retrospect that the bitter defiance of his *Reflections of an Unpolitical Man* was an expression of his 'sexual introversion', and that the 'German problem' described in it had really been his own problem.[10]

Weber's feelings were, however, as ambivalent towards his country as they were towards nature. The emotional basis of the chauvinism that had drawn attention to his Freiburg inaugural address in 1895 was shattered in the years of his depression, when he constantly yearned for the southern sun and felt a pressing desire 'to leave Germany forever' (WB 266). A social-Darwinist posture of national machismo no longer suited his condition, and his subsequent work on *The Protestant Ethic* took him in directions even more distant from those of his fellow Germans. There was also the fact that German 'world power' imperialism, still new and audacious in 1895, sounded rather banal just a few years later, when the Kaiser and his new chancellor, Bernhard von Bülow, spoke the same language, when even Schmoller, a former pioneer of social policy, reviled opponents of naval expansion as blinkered 'routinists' and 'beer-swigging philistines',[11] and when countless others engaged in bar talk along the same lines. Weber could no longer make a name for himself with such declarations, nor did it take the slightest courage to pronounce them.

Weber and *Modell Deutschland*: the social state

What still tied him to Germany, and what had he to contribute to the strengthening of the German nation? One of Weber's central themes in the following period was that any lasting system of rule required a particular kind of legitimacy; and precisely during the world war, for all the talk of 'the ideas of 1914', he could not find in German imperialism the authoritative principle that might be pitted against the power of the Western idea of liberty. For a social scientist linked to the Verein für Sozialpolitik, the German social state that had been under construction since the 1880s – together with the comparatively efficient and uncorrupted officialdom of Prussia-Germany – would have suggested itself as the kernel of a national identity and legitimacy offering excellent publicity for a greater Germany. Lujo Brentano, for example, argued that the Reich had an opportunity to win over workers in Alsace with German laws on trade and industry, instead of showing consideration for the (anyway anti-German) notables and manufacturers in the region.[12]

In the 1968 tradition of social history, it is customary to speak rather disparagingly of imperial German social policy as the paltry carrot accompanying the stick of anti-socialist legislation[13] and as a wretched substitute for the equality denied to the workers.[14] In this sense, Weber spoke sarcastically of 'so-called social policy' (WB 411). By contrast, the previously mentioned Jules Huret could not get over the German achievements: the 'splendid', indeed 'luxurious' sanatoria at Beelitz near Potsdam, where socially insured workers were admitted without payment; the public baths; and the fact that courts 'nearly always' found in favour of the workers in disputes with employers.[15]

We see the publicity potential contained in this 'German road' – except that, as today, many Germans did not know how to appreciate it. For many liberals, who held that the social contributions demanded of employers put them at a competitive disadvantage vis-à-vis Britain and the United States, the developing social state was as suspect as it was for radical socialists, who regarded it as a manoeuvre of social appeasement. It was not yet clearly apparent that in the long term welfare benefits and the beginnings of workers' participation built up a store of trust between workers and employers – indeed, even today this has not entered very deep into the collective consciousness in Germany. Neither liberals nor socialists had much time for this 'German road'.

Max Weber, too, did not think of building a new German self-consciousness on this foundation. In his father's professional world, he had the best example of the efficiency of German local administration, while the Baden factory inspectorate illustrated what could be done to protect the labour force in cooperation with the trade unions. But he did not have a conceptual framework in which these experiences could acquire a meaning. Rather, he developed an aversion to the 'welfare state', which he saw as the product of a patriarchal-authoritarian statism: 'The "welfare state" is the legend of patrimonialism, deriving not from the free camaraderie of solemnly promised fealty, but from the authoritarian relationship of father and children' (E&S 1107). His own ideal was a set of circumstances in which all population groups capable of solidarity and political struggle would fight for their existence, so that no one would need to be given anything by the state.

But had he himself not been ill for long enough to realize that large sections of the population – the elderly and infirm, the unemployed and other marginal groups – were in no position to wage such a struggle? And would not the war greatly increase the number of invalids? But Weber thought it a mistake to turn the fate of these groups into a major issue of social policy. In 1917 he wrote of Bismarck's social insurance:

> We were given pensions for the sick, the injured, the war-disabled and the old. That was certainly admirable. But we were *not* given the guarantees which are necessary above all else to *maintain* physical and mental strength and to make it possible for the *strong* and *healthy* to *represent their interests* in an objective and confident way, the interests, in other words, of precisely those people who mattered most in purely political terms. (PW 143)[16]

A synthesis of democratic and social-Darwinist attitudes! In Weber's favour it should be considered that retirement pensions began at an age which many workers never reached, and that at first the social state was more a lure than a reality.

Weber and *Modell Deutschland*: the bureaucracy as scapegoat

In the positions that Weber took in public, dissatisfaction with the welfare state is combined with a horror of bureaucracy. This too is not the matter of course that many admirers of Weber the great liberal think it to be. In his writings there is very little of the solemn liberal emotionalism with regard to freedom; his later thought, in particular, revolved far more around political rule or domination. He had no reason to come away from childhood feeling particularly angry with officialdom, and in fact the nineteenth century had shown that Prussian-German officials had a considerable potential for liberal and social reforms. The Prussian reform era was even legendary for its tales of heroism in the upper reaches of the state. 'The will to renewal', according to Heinrich Heffter, was alive 'only in an educated elite, essentially in liberal officialdom, which virtually alone embodied political progress and . . . political resolve.'[17] This innovative spirit was especially impressive in the university reforms of the early nineteenth century. In Weber's own day, Otto Hintze gave a still classical appreciation of the achievements of the Prussian civil service. And today, when worldwide comparisons are made, the merits of a correct, competent and efficient administration are recognized more than ever.

In those days many Germans – including Max Weber – took these qualities so much for granted that they were scarcely able to evaluate them. It is true that Weber was prepared to recognize the special efficiency and rationality of German officials, but he did not think that such merits were very important for the strength of the nation. Instead, he took over the concept of bureaucracy, which had started life in the opposition to late absolutism, more as a rallying cry than a value-free designation;[18] it conjured up images of bloodless pen-pushers, the raw material for many a cartoonist.

In Weber's day it was not only the liberal opposition that railed against bureaucrats; there had long been a conservative anti-bureaucratism as well. Even Treitschke, the herald of the Prussian-German state, denounced the 'refined stupidity of our mandarinate', whose 'examination torture' seemed designed to 'suppress any healthy energy in the "state youth"'.[19] In 1850 none other than the 35-year-old Bismarck, who soon afterwards abandoned a civil service career out of frustration, directed one of his first rhetorical fireworks against the Prussian bureaucracy, then still permeated by the liberal reform spirit. Comparing it to a boa constrictor, he wrote: 'A state that cannot shake off a bureaucracy like ours by means of a salutary thunderstorm is and will remain doomed. The bureaucracy is cancerous in its skin and members; only its stomach is healthy, and the laws that it excretes are the simplest muck anywhere in the world.'[20] Today, when we are used to bureaucratism of quite different dimensions, we are struck by the *lack* of bureaucracy at the apex of the Bismarckian state. The civil service remained essentially an affair of the individual states, the central bureaucracy never employing more than a couple of thousand people until 1914.[21] Bismarck worked with a tiny apparatus which, by today's standards, seems inconceivable for the head of government of a major power; he fought against any tendency for it to become autonomous, and studiously ensured that the reins were firmly in his hands.

Neither empirically nor theoretically, then, did Weber have any reason to feel a horror of bureaucracy, nor does it appear that his aversion to it was rooted in his own experience. It is not clear if or when Weber suffered personally from bureaucratic harassment. As we shall see, he was repeatedly incensed at the way in which Friedrich Althoff, the Prussian official in charge of university matters, treated scholars. But this highly unconventional, not at all bureaucratic, man was anything but a pedantic enforcer of the rules; he got his way more through charisma than through office regulations. And the state enforcement of labour regulations that Weber had observed in Baden, in the impressive person of Friedrich Woerishoffer (who recruited Else von Richthofen to his department), was by contemporary and even present-day standards a commendable institution, which took many initiatives and was far from seriously hindering the development of industry.

So, once again, how did the civil service become Max Weber's scapegoat 'bureaucracy'? Jürgen Kocka suggests that his main target of attack was civil servants who rose to positions in government and brought with them a 'bureaucratic incapacity for power politics'. 'He became a critic of domestic policy for reasons that had mainly to do with foreign policy' (WuZ 411). This would fit the fact that Weber's main assault on the bureaucracy dates from the period after the first Morocco crisis (1905–6), when the central government – in the view of impatient imperialists and their mouthpiece, Harden's *Zukunft* – had lost a unique opportunity (with Russia's defeat by Japan and ensuing revolution) to achieve a decisive victory over France through the cold-blooded use of war threats. Although the term 'bureaucracy' emphasized the element of rule in the civil service apparatus, Weber's main criticism was that it did not know how to rule effectively, did not really understand the game of power. However, Weber attacked not only the pedantic professionalism of the bureaucracy but also the highly unprofessional 'dilettantism' of the Kaiser, who repeatedly alarmed the world with his verbal sabre-rattling.

Another answer to the question of the origins of Weber's anti-bureaucratic passion is quite simple: *Alfred Weber*. For he had preceded his elder brother in polemicizing against the bureaucracy; he outlined a terrible vision of it in Prague to none other than the young Franz Kafka, whose friend, Max Brod, was a student of his.[22] Unlike Max, Alfred Weber had suffered a lot from school in his youth, and this must have laid the emotional basis for his hatred of bureaucracy. His vitalist world-view then helped this affect to develop intellectually: the bureaucracy became a cold, soulless apparatus, whose mechanical application of the law threatened to stifle life brimming with laws of its own. This chimed with Max Weber's painful experience of the 'iron cage', which seems to appear out of the blue at the end of *The Protestant Ethic*.

In 1909, at the Vienna congress of the Verein für Sozialpolitik, Alfred Weber gave a widely noticed speech attacking the tradition of the Historical School of political economy, in which the state and its officials were treated as bearers of the common good. He recognized that the bureaucracy had the virtue of technical efficiency, but its transmission to the whole polity was making 'our entire society petty-bourgeois and philistine' and – in an allusion to a recent cartoon by Olaf Gulbrannson in the weekly *Simplicissimus* – bringing into being a 'new human type': 'German, loyal and entitled to a pension'. 'There is a terrible danger that these little daddy and mummy existences will trickle down and poison or spoil the only great and viable elements for the future, from which we might accede to new and great cultural possibilities.'[23]

Alfred Weber's outburst has something of the late adolescent about it: he seems to be belatedly giving vent to a grudge that built up in his youth. A Prussian ministry official replied drily and to the point that the state offered greater freedom than a private entrepreneur, since the latter would have shown Weber the door after such an attack.[24] Max Weber, however, found his brother's polemical wit infectious and took the same line himself. He even tried to out-trump Alfred:

> My brother is assuredly . . . as convinced as I am that the advance of bureaucratic mechanization is irresistible. Indeed, there is nothing in the world, no machinery in the world, which works with such precision as these human machines do – nor so cheaply either! . . . The technical superiority of the bureaucratic mechanism is unassailable, as is the technical superiority of human-operated machinery over handicraft. . . . We are happy to acknowledge that there are honourable and talented people at the top of our civil service. . . . And even though the idea that some day the world might be full of nothing but professors is frightening, . . . the idea that the world would be filled with nothing but those little cogs is even more frightening, that is, with people who cling to a small position and strive for a bigger one. . . . This passion for bureaucratization . . . is enough to make a man despair! It is as though in politics a charwoman, with whose mental horizon a German can get along best anyway, were permitted to run things all by herself, as if we intentionally were to become people who need order and nothing but order, who get nervous and cowardly when this order becomes shaky for a moment, who become helpless when they are torn out of their exclusive adjustment to this order. (GASS 413f.; WB 416)

Today's reader, looking back at the experience of totalitarian bureaucracies, is at first amazed by the effectiveness – and even cheapness – that Weber here attributes to bureaucracy. There is no mention of the inertia, the squandering of taxpayers' money or the failure to make cost–benefit calculations; Weber's civil servants are truly well-oiled cogs in the great machinery of state.[25] In this he fully shared Schmoller's point of view. And it is true that, in the German Reich at the time, there was a comparatively well-functioning 'apparatus' of officials.

While Alfred Weber openly proclaimed a vitalist world-view, his brother's attacks on bureaucracy also contained subterranean elements of vitalist thinking. In so far as bureaucracy creates a separation between office and people, turns individuals into interchangeable bearers of a function, fixes them to a special area of competence and subjects their activity to firm rules, the resulting human self-estrangement is similar to what Marx ascribes to capital. In *Economy and Society*, Weber says of bureaucracy: '(It) develops the more perfectly, the more it is "dehumanized", the more completely it succeeds in eliminating from official business love, hatred and all purely personal, irrational and emotional elements which escape calculation. This is appraised as its special virtue by capitalism' (E&S 975). This 'dehumanization' takes its toll in a lack of vitality, so that, if bureaucracy gets mixed up with big industry, things happen as they did with King Gunther in the Nibelungen epic, who was chained by Brünnhilde to the marriage bed – a story that Weber found piquant enough to repeat more than once (MWG I/10, 412n.; GASS 415).

Precisely in the revolutionary period after 1918, however, when the unbroken continuity of the imperial bureaucracy became a real political danger, Max Weber did an about-face. Now the main peril for him was the administrative dilettantism of the political newcomers, which was further weakening Germany vis-à-vis the victorious powers and destroying the reputation of German industry (MWG I/16, 140, 438, 481). Even earlier he had talked of the 'sterile complaints about the Blessed Saint Bureaucracy' (PW 180). Yet his critique of bureaucracy had an impact as great as that of any of his other work, not least in the United States.[26] Weber later became famous for having anticipated 'Parkinson's Law' of the irresistible growth of bureaucracy, at a time when bureaucratism by today's standards seemed quite harmless, and for having foreseen that socialism would bitterly disappoint its dream of freedom by stumbling into the bureaucratic trap as soon as it came to power.

Official respect, secret loathing: Weber and Schmoller

Around the year 1909, the opposite position to Weber's on the question of bureaucracy was most clearly represented by the seventy-year-old Gustav Schmoller, the head of the Historical School of political economy and the Verein für Sozialpolitik, and the person in the Verein who, together with Althoff, decided on appointments to chairs in the social sciences, at least in Prussia. An archetypal insider, he liked to hint at his relations of trust with leading figures in the ministerial bureaucracy and conceived of the state as the champion of the public good in economic life.[27] 'His social vivacity and sense of well-being were linked to this circle of educated and intelligent statesmen and privy councillors; he liked to attend their dinners and valued their confidences and anecdotes' (Meinecke).[28] He thus epitomized the behaviour of the imperial German elites, and not least a slow and wily Lutheran deference to authority that Weber had learned to despise. This Prussianized Swabian, who all his life loved 'the mask of a Swabian Biedermann',[29] embodied an ancient German *Gemütlichkeit* at the same time as a modern orientation to efficiency – the synthesis that Weber never achieved. Especially in old age, he radiated a smug self-satisfaction along with trust in the superior wisdom of the Prussian-German civil service. With his air of jovial condescension, he had something disarming against which temporary adversaries such as the Webers found it hard to defend themselves.

As a young man, Weber held Schmoller in high regard and had a lot to thank him for. At the time he also shared Schmoller's sceptical attitude to classical liberalism and believed that the 'strongly bureaucratic streak' in the *Kathedersozialisten* would 'become milder' (JB 299). In March 1893 Schmoller recommended Weber, who was then not even twenty-nine, to the powerful Althoff, on the grounds that he was 'free of any Anglomania' and without socialist 'overtones'.[30] This shows that Schmoller did not try to run a clique, as Weber was by no means his disciple.[31] As Weber heard, Schmoller even 'expressed himself more kindly' about him than he 'thought he was entitled to expect, despite his considerably above-average vanity'.[32] In 1909 Weber still 'proudly' declared his belief in Schmoller's *Kathedersozialismus*, all the more since it appeared to be 'out of fashion at court and in the education ministry'.[33]

Nevertheless, after the years of his illness, he was working himself up into a real revulsion for the economist – a feeling that reveals at least as much about Weber as it does about Schmoller. Things came to a head in September 1905 at the Mannheim congress of the Verein für Sozialpolitik, when the discussion turned to the relationship between cartels (previously the subject of a Verein investigation) and the state. Cartels – that is, branch associations to keep prices high and to limit production – had been a characteristic feature of German industry since the 1890s; and Lujo Brentano, for one, thought that 'the power of the cartels over economic life' was 'overwhelming'.[34] This raised the question of how to judge them and how the state should behave in relation to them. Their champions defended their role in 'protecting national labour':[35] they were said to prevent sudden price slumps due to company failures and mass redundancies; and, in contrast to the American trusts, they corresponded to a German cooperative tradition. The cartels called for protective tariffs, since the cartellization agreements might otherwise be undermined by foreign competition. In the Verein für Sozialpolitik, the view prevailed that cartels should be seen as a stabilizing element in the ups and downs of the economic conjuncture; the age of neoliberalism, when Ludwig Erhard sounded the charge against cartels, was a long way off.

Even in those days, however, it was recognized that price-fixing might damage the whole economy. Schmoller's characteristic solution was to propose placing qualified civil servants on the boards of limited

companies – which would, of course, have offered lucrative career opportunities to some of Schmoller's disciples. This combination of state
bureaucracy and big industry, reminiscent of the neo-Marxist model of
'state monopoly capitalism', was a horrifying prospect for Weber, as it
would bring together the two giant monsters that threatened human
freedom; it would give almost official sanction to the process and add the
seal of social science. He thought it absurd to imagine that state officials
would bring into the boardrooms of industry a higher morality and a guarantee of the public good; experience told him that state enterprises had no
greater sense of social responsibility than their private counterparts. It
would be disastrous if the state no longer played a supervisory role in the
economy but allowed itself to be drawn into a monopoly function. Not
without reason did he assume that, within such an alliance, the quest for
private profit would be a stronger force than the civil service ethos. 'I will
say quite frankly that I am taking things to an extreme; I cannot do otherwise (*Ich kann nicht anders*)' (GASS 400). Weber in Mannheim posing as
Luther at Worms![36]

It was quite unnecessary to pull out all the stops, as Schmoller was
anyway relatively isolated; the end of the Schmoller era was in the offing.
Friedrich Naumann, on the other hand, trumped Weber's speech against
the proposal with the fire of his own rhetoric. Without mentioning
Schmoller by name, he ridiculed his project as the fruit of antiquated,
authoritarian thinking, which had no grasp of the power of big industry or
of the fact that the great countervailing power lay not with a few state-
appointed officials but with the labour movement. State intervention in the
manner envisaged by Schmoller was 'nonsense, both technically and from
the point of view of the national economy'. Naumann, a non-economist,
described as a dilettante the then head of economics in his own field.

When Naumann had expressed wide-ranging dissatisfaction with
Schmoller, the applause in the hall had risen to prolonged ovations.
Schmoller was seriously offended and reacted more angrily than was his
wont, even threatening to withdraw from the leadership of the Verein. He
called Naumann (who had already left) a 'demagogue' who, 'without real
knowledge of the subject', had supported 'the old Marxist phrases . . . with
very meagre evidence'. Then Max Weber and Lujo Brentano pitched in and
accused Schmoller of insulting Naumann and abusing his position to
censure a speaker he did not like. They demanded that he make a statement withdrawing his aspersions; Schmoller eventually did this, but in
what Weber called a 'deeply disloyal' form, and the whole affair left a bitter
aftertaste.[37]

In this situation Weber developed a psycho-physical repulsion for
Schmoller, which stands out even in his wide spectrum of irritability. After
the Naumann incident, Weber at first announced his own withdrawal, but
Schmoller persuaded him to stay on – he could scarcely afford not to in his
isolation from academia – and even praised him as a 'genius'. But Weber
found Schmoller's compliments 'the most repulsive flattery', as he wrote to

his brother Alfred, and described Schmoller's late retraction in connection with Naumann as a 'breech birth'.[38] When he further got the impression that Schmoller was blocking Sombart's career he called him – again in a letter to Alfred – 'a dubious person', whose behaviour was 'too disgusting' (MWG II/5, 121).[39]

Dark looks and shining eyes: Weber and Naumann

The stable friendship between Weber and Naumann is an amazing phenomenon, since on the face of it Naumann gave him much greater cause for anger than Schmoller ever did. With his shining eyes and his sometimes rather indiscriminate, analytically shallow enthusiasms, he was actually the antithesis of Weber, the man of science with a dark look and a burrowing intellect. His speeches and writings wildly mixed together support for war and peace, freedom and leadership, rule by the Kaiser and democracy, always with the same enthusiasm and obliviousness to contradiction. 'The face must shine' even in danger and adversity, he once declared.[40] He wanted as his followers 'people whose souls shine'.[41] There was nothing of Weber's *Lasciate ogni speranza*. Weber was not wrong to hear in Naumann's manner of speech an 'infinite yearning for human happiness' (WB 136).

'Religion consists not only in speaking but often just as much in remaining silent', Naumann once declared (WuZ 424). If only he had taken this to heart more often! A man such as Max Weber had every reason to despise Naumann as an unbearable phrase-monger, already manifest in the sentimental-charitable title of his periodical, *Die Hilfe*, which until 1902 carried the subtitle 'divine help, self-help, state help, brotherly help'.[42] Did not his basic principle of a *coincidentia oppositorum* – of the national and social, imperial and democratic ideas – seek to combine two fundamentally different passions, in a way that failed to appreciate the driving forces that motivate human beings? But Weber directed his anger more at Naumann's theological comrades-in-arms than at the man himself. At the Evangelical-Social Congress in 1893, he and his mother enjoyed 'listening to the somewhat naive, but mostly original pastors fighting it out around' them (R 495). But in 1896 he publicly described Naumann's supporters as 'political jumping jacks' (WB 221) and inwardly complained that the 'jabbering of the Holy Joes' was 'utterly pathetic'.[43]

Being childless themselves, the Webers were also irritated by Naumann's uninhibited celebration of large families as an expression of a nation's vitality and future. Weber's discussion of a collection of Naumann's essays culminated in a critique of his naive views on population growth, which were quite in keeping with a general confidence in the future that he held without any further justification:

He also approaches the population problem with this naive optimism. This oldest and most serious of problems in the history of society – one would not wish to discuss, at least scientifically, with anyone who disputes its importance – does not exist for Naumann's view of things. He is completely wrong historically when he characterizes the idea that economic distress is the result of large families as a distinctively 'heartless' idea of *modern* economics. . . . The fact that the problem does not exist for Naumann is also a consequence of his belief in the limitless future of technological progress. We do not share that belief either. When the present age of technological evolution nears its end, humanity will again be in a position to endow itself with economic organizations calculated to last. (MWG I/4-1, 359f.)

This quotation shows that, for Weber too, the dynamic of world history was ultimately rooted in the scarcity of natural resources, and that man would be forced to return to sustainable ways of handling resources – although, when it came to the consequences of this insight, he stood fast on the view that the essence of history is *struggle*. From a scientific point of view, Weber thought it simply impossible to discuss Naumann's writing. He could accept Naumann only because he believed that politics was subject to laws different from those of science.

Most irritating of all, however, was probably Naumann's sympathy for Wilhelm II, in whom he detected a kindred spirit capable of being won to his side. The Kaiser, according to Naumann, was 'an embodiment of the truly electric tendencies inside us all',[44] and there was indeed something very Wilhelmine about Naumann's joy in speaking and travelling, his erratic nature and his fantasies of empire. Schmoller thought there was a simple explanation for Naumann's hopes in the Kaiser: as soon as social democracy 'blossomed' into imperialism, 'Kaiser Wilhelm II, who in his heart of hearts was a friend of the workers and disliked the conservatives, would be willing to form an alliance with democracy.' Schmoller, who knew Wilhelm II better, could see that Naumann's image of him was no more than a projection of his own wishes.[45]

In *Demokratie und Kaisertum*, Naumann declared in bold type: 'Our hopes in progress are based more on the Kaiser than on the Reichstag as it is presently composed.'[46] His enthusiasm was especially strong for the imperial naval project: 'Since the Kaiser came up with his plans for an enlarged navy, his power of spiritual leadership has visibly increased over German popular thinking.' In 1899, during the trip to Palestine that destroyed his illusions about the 'Holy Land', he felt the Kaiser as a redeemer in the Church of the Redemption in the Jerusalem hills; he even worried that Wilhelm II's religiosity might impair his 'political effectiveness'.[47] Naumann deployed all the magic of his rhetoric to make the emperor 'almost attractive' to a Munich public that was not exactly well disposed towards him.[48]

For years Weber tried in vain to stop Naumann projecting his ideal for the future on to the Kaiser. In 1908, however, soon after Wilhelm II had driven Weber wild by currying favour with the British in an interview with the *Daily Telegraph*, Naumann was prompted to admit that he, Weber, had 'unfortunately been right in (his) judgement of the Kaiser'.[49] From then on, Naumann took his distance from Wilhelm II and turned without imperial reservations to the parliamentary principle; the main bone of contention between Weber and himself disappeared. Nevertheless, he let it be known that he would happily put up with a true 'Caesar' who had 'nerves of platinum'.[50] He was drawing close to Weber's 'charismatic leader' idea, but Wilhelm II was most certainly not that.

After the 1907 Reichstag elections – the 'Hottentot elections', through which Bülow managed to strengthen the right with colonialist slogans – Weber wrote to Brentano: 'The only bright spot: Naumann' (MWG II/5, 254). At the time, following the failure of his National-Social Association to make an impression at the 1903 elections, Naumann stood as a candidate for the liberal Freisinnige Vereinigung. He continued to be Weber's main bridge to politics, and for a time Weber must have toyed with the idea that Naumann could offer him a springboard into that world. His letters to Naumann are the most important testimony concerning his positions on contemporary politics during the years when he did not appear in public (MWG II/5, 7f.). Naumann's *Hilfe* and his trips abroad were supported financially by the Weber family.[51] During the Reichstag election campaign in 1907, although Max Weber did not yet have the Oerlinghausen legacy at his disposal, he was even prepared, if necessary, to forgo his summer holiday so that Naumann would have sufficient funds (MWG II/5, 301). Weber was selflessly matching Naumann's own material selflessness.

Weber was aware that, however much Naumann liked to fly into raptures, he actually tended to remain sober and rational in political matters;[52] in this respect Weber was a perfectly suited mentor. Naumann's letters to Weber are mostly quite objective and lack the pastoral rhetoric into which he repeatedly lapsed in his published writings. In October 1918 Naumann had a more sober view than Weber of how the war was going. Whereas Weber still looked to a continuation of the war and fumed that those in Berlin who were calling for an immediate ceasefire had lost their nerve, Naumann calmly replied that there was no talk in the government of a 'nervous breakdown', but that the 'daily casualty figures' at the front were averaging around ten thousand.[53]

Naumann's charisma and women

Another explanation of why Weber stuck to Naumann for the rest of his life is simply *women*. At first Max Weber showed no great inclination to support the Naumann movement journalistically or financially, but Helene stood behind Naumann, and Marianne triumphantly reported to her in 1895 that she had 'pestered' Max 'every day' until, 'with all manner of curses', he had finally written a piece for the Christian-Socials.[54] In 1897 Helene threatened to give Naumann money from her own pocket if Max

Figure 12.1 August Bebel, Werner Sombart and Friedrich Naumann (left to right) on their way to an SPD party congress in Breslau in 1895

and Alfred did not agree that he should be given 20,000 marks from the family assets; Naumann's wife had complained it would make her husband ill if he had to go begging.[55] As Theodor Heuss put it, Helene Weber enveloped this religiously inspired politician 'with maternal solicitude and loving advice'; her sister Ida provided for Naumann in her will so that he could travel around the world.[56] Else too joined the flock of admirers – although the corpulent Naumann, even in the eyes of an admirer, was 'as wide as he was tall'[57] – and showed in her wartime letters to Alfred a frequent vexation that Naumann did not have regular access to the Kaiser. Although Naumann never stopped being the pastor, he cultivated around him in the good years an aura of juvenile vivacity. The young Elly Knapp, future wife of Theodor Heuss, was delighted by the way in which young people danced around Naumann when he had finished speaking at a National-Social carnival.[58]

Max Weber once urged Naumann to keep politics and religion strictly separate, and in response Naumann entered politics under the label National-Social rather than Evangelical-Social. Yet his charisma – the word fits here – still had a lot to do with his clerical origin; he always retained something of a salvationist or revivalist preacher,[59] even if he piled on the realism to compensate for it. He liked to lapse into the language of the Bible: for example, he used the word 'publicans' to refer to those who advocated protective tariffs.[60] He became a focus of soteriological expecta-tions, as we can see from the words of one follower: 'We consider you a man called by God to overcome the sad inner turmoil of our nation.'[61] Weber's cousin Otto Baumgarten, the theologian, later spoke in raptures about Naumann, with whom he too had been on close terms: 'He shrouded his innermost depths so modestly, spoke so purely about the affairs of the world, yet revealed the enchanting pathos of his love of the nation to every congenial listener – a nation consisting for him of children of the everlast-ing Good. The guiding idea of his life was to carry them to the beams of the Holy Light.' Naumann was 'a gift from God to Germany's youth', who 'until the end was unable to resist his spell'.[62]

Max Weber could not fail to notice the secret of this spell. In a way, it is true, Naumann was living proof that charisma alone does not produce any-thing in politics. But did his radiance not have an indirect effect, by influenc-ing the minds of the public, and would the effect not have been even greater in a parliamentary democracy? He must have strengthened Weber's con-viction that, in the mechanism of politics, something great and new cannot arise only out of material interests and routine pragmatism, but must involve exceptional charisma, enthusiasm and selfless dedication. This also explains why the theme of religion – the history not of ecclesiastical insti-tutions but of religious passions and striving for salvation – did not let go of him until the end of his life. For his part, he became in Naumann's eyes the 'greatest human phenomenon' among the Germans 'since Goethe'.[63] One of the origins of the Weber myth should be sought in Naumann and his circle.

Freedom through free space: liberal imperialism

Weber and Naumann shared a belief in the ecology of freedom: the oppor-tunity for freedom increases with free space, hence an advance into new spaces contains a promise of freedom. The 'genesis of modern freedom' in England involved first of all 'expansion overseas', Weber believed (PW 69); and it was evident to him, as to many others, that there was a structural link between American freedom and America's wide open spaces. Like so many 'navy professors', he also valued the naval arms drive as a means to enthuse opposition liberals and parts of the working class for Germany's great power policies. Already in 1897, before the naval craze began, he thought it beyond doubt that sea power was absolutely necessary for 'civ-ilized peoples organized on civic principles'. It did not occur to him that this position required some cognitive check. Instead he hurled abuse at the sceptics:

Only complete political distortion and naive optimism can blind anyone to the fact that, after an interlude of extremely peaceful com-petition, the indispensable pursuit of commercial expansion among all civilized peoples organized on civic principles is now most certainly approaching the point where *only power* will decide each nation's share in the economic control of the planet and therefore the earnings of its population. (MWG I/4-2, 671)

It remains strange, however, that it was precisely Max Weber – who had no time at all for the increasingly popular Anglophobia – who did not see that a naval arms drive would push the German Reich on to a misguided anti-British course, in a Europe where France and Russia were already its adversaries. The above quotation reveals that at that time Weber was as little capable of rational calculation as Wilhelm II; naval imperialism was associated with deep passions, as it was for so many of his contemporaries. Even in 1916, when it had become clear that the German navy could not break out into the oceans against British resistance, the question: 'What do we need our navy for?' still seemed to him 'nonsensical' (MWG I/15, 166).

Murderous impulses: Weber and Wilhelm II

But the deepest discord between Weber and Naumann concerned none other than the Kaiser. A feeling of unease came over Weber shortly after Wilhelm II's coronation in 1888 – but it was more a conservative anxiety about the hasty, impulsive and populist manner of the youthful emperor. 'You feel as though you are seated in a high-speed railway train, but with doubts about whether the next points will be set correctly' (JB 323f.: the metaphor is repeated at JB 330). We should remember that the witnessing of a railway accident had been a traumatic experience for him as a child. At the same time, he was passing on rumours that the Kaiser had 'ruined' his 'mental powers' – the same kind of rumours that would later circulate about Weber himself. They were part of the flood of complaints about 'nerve trouble' that characterized the age. Soon afterwards, in fact, Wilhelm II was being thought of as the Reich's leading neurasthenic, in relation to whom 'nerves' sometimes functioned as a codeword for a more serious mental illness;[64] and, according to Weber, 'everyone [knew] what a "nervous" regimental commander means for the spirit of an officer corps' (MWG I/15, 379). Indeed, it was to be feared that an imperial neurasthenic would weaken the nerves of the whole nation. In 1904, in one of the first pieces he wrote after his breakdown, Weber observed that 'nervousness' (the inverted commas are his own) had acquired 'epidemic' proportions 'since 1888' (MWG I/8, 181) – that is, since the year of Wilhelm II's coronation. If his aversion for the Kaiser subsequently grew into hatred, one suspects a highly personal motive somewhere beneath the surface: a feeling that the Kaiser was partly to blame for Weber's own misery. In favour of a psychological explanation is the fact that for Weber – and not only for him – the Kaiser became a projection of an unloved aspect of the self, which it thereby became possible to separate from the self.[65] The imperial braggadocio, with no real energy behind it, reminds one of the equally ineffectual chauvinism of Weber's inaugural address in Freiburg.

Weber's first known attack of rage against Wilhelm II occurred in December 1900, when the Kaiser refused to receive Paul Kruger, the Boer president defeated by the British. The Boer War had led to a first powerful wave of Anglophobia in Germany, to which the British had responded in kind. The Kaiser's restraint on the issue, which had been very unpopular in Germany, was a sign of prudence on his part and for a while seemed to clear the way for an understanding between the two countries. The already sick Weber, however, showed no more circumspection than many a bar-room strategist: 'Max got terribly worked up about Siegmund Mayer's action against Kruger', Marianne reported from Ajaccio to Helene (in whose eyes Kruger seemed like an old Indian chief); 'sometimes he really itches to get stuck in himself.'[66] 'Siegmund Mayer' was an ironical codename for S. M., *Seine Majestät* [His Majesty]. Only later, during the war, when Weber recognized how disastrous it had been to make an enemy of Britain, would he condemn the 'foolish emotional policy on the Boer question' and observe, quite correctly, that it was not diplomacy but the nation that had been to blame (MWG I/15, 164). He said nothing about himself, though.

The most violent outburst came in Weber's letter of 14 December 1906 to Naumann. The date is important, because it was the day after Bülow had dissolved the Reichstag on the Kaiser's secret instructions, when it had looked as though a majority of the centre, the left liberals and the social democrats would withhold supplementary funding for the colonial troops involved in the Hottentot war. The dissolution, calculated in advance, was a masterstroke of power politics, for in the ensuing 'Hottentot elections' the government parties won a great victory with their colonial slogans and inflicted a major disaster on the SPD. Naumann, for his part, managed to get elected to the Reichstag. Bülow proceeded with tactical cunning, but in the manner of a head of government concerned about his majority in parliament. He and not Wilhelm II was the protagonist. Yet Weber's main worry was that Naumann might enter the election fray with a pro-Kaiser slogan; he was still bitter that Wilhelm II had not taken a tougher line in the earlier Morocco crisis and achieved more for Germany. Later he admitted that the government could never have dragged the nation into a major war over Morocco (MWG I/15, 63 and 78), but in 1906 he was furious:

> Abroad (Italy, America, everywhere!) the degree of positive contempt that is shown to us as a nation – rightly! that is crucial – *because* we 'put up with' *this* regime of *this* man has become a factor of absolutely first-rate 'world-political' significance for us. No man or party that cultivates ideals in any sense 'democratic' *and* 'national-political' should take responsibility for this regime, whose continuation threatens our whole position in the world more than do all manner of colonial problems. (MWG I/5, 202)

In a note to this passage, Weber claims that anyone who reads the foreign press for a few months must notice this. 'We are "isolated" *because* this man governs us in this way and *we tolerate it and gloss it over.*' It was a violent attack on Naumann and the hopes he placed in the person of the Kaiser, in a situation that nevertheless contained an opportunity for him to become a key figure in the government coalition. No circumstances were less politically unsuitable for him to turn publicly against the Kaiser, especially as he had little to reproach him with at that time.

For many years Weber vented his fury with the Kaiser only in private circles. In late 1908, however, amid the general outrage in 'national' circles following the *Daily Telegraph* interview, he aired his bitterness for the first time at a public meeting (WB 406). There he repeatedly stressed that what was at issue was not the person but the system (MWG II/5, 695, 697). Really? Was he at that time a convinced supporter of parliamentary rule? On the same occasion, he criticized the fact that the Kaiser was content with 'the *appearance* of power' (MWG II/5, 695). Later historians have liked to cite Weber as a key witness against Wilhelm II's 'personal regiment', but what so angered him about the Kaiser was not his striving for power but his failure to be a *real* man of power. A charismatic leader in Weber's sense did not need to give a running account of all his actions to a parliamentary body; the constant irritation to Weber was doubtless Wilhelm II's ham-actor imitation of a charismatic ruler, without any genuine charisma. His hunger for publicity, unusually strong in a monarch, constantly stimulated a yearning for charismatic leadership without being able to satisfy it. For a man such as Weber, this meant permanent frustration of his political libido.

Precisely because he had reason, as a social scientist, to focus his critique on social structures and the political system, his simmering hatred of the Kaiser's person seems all the more curious. Troeltsch wrote to Honigsheim in 1917 that Weber's life was 'basically an ongoing duel . . . above all with the person of the Kaiser, whom he holds responsible for most things' (B 489). Similarly, in Theodor Heuss's view during the war: 'Weber feels under pressure, intellectually and as a matter of conscience, to be *the* opponent of this man Wilhelm II' (B 499). In the imaginary duel that so excited him, he grew to the dimensions of a counter-Kaiser. 'I won't stand for people who always look on the dark side of things [*Schwarzseher*]', the Kaiser had threatened. 'Anyone who is not fit for work should drop out and look for a better country' (WB 398). It was easy for Weber to relate this kind of attack to himself. Incapable of work in his profession, he had long been the epitome of the man who looks on the dark side of things.

On 21 June 1911 he wrote a letter of many pages to Count Keyserling, with whom he disagreed on a number of points concerning the link between religion and national character. Weber stressed that the difference between the English and the Germans was based on religion, not on a national character preceding religion. Lutherans – 'and that means: the mass of Germans' – supposedly had 'the passive religiosity of resignation to the world (and, in particular, to their "calling" and to the historical powers)'. Then Weber found fault with the count's disdainful treatment of the French Revolution. One might laugh at its 'childishness', but one owed to it 'things without which life would be unbearable'.

> And a people which (like we Germans) has never had the nerve to behead the powers-that-be will never gain the proud self-assurance that makes the Anglo-Saxons and Romans so superior to us in the world, despite all our 'victories' (won through *discipline*) in war and technology. (MWG II/7-1, 236ff.)

A few lines further on, he describes the command 'to obey God rather than men' as 'the truly creative element in the development of Western civilization': an indication that Weber was not at all irreligious, that a certain kind of belief in God was for him the root of individual autonomy. What the quotation reveals above all, however, is Weber's fantasy of putting Wilhelm II on the guillotine as a sign of regained nervous health. He indulged in such murderous fantasies with other people too (WzG 172).

It is questionable whether British or French self-confidence is really based on the beheading of Charles I or Louis XVI. In retrospect, they look more like judicial murders than laudable historic deeds, and the monarchs in question seem positively mild and decent in comparison with Cromwell or Napoleon. But Weber did not reproach the Kaiser for his displays of brutality and verbal sabre-rattling, as in the famous 'Huns speech', but rather for his lack of real energy and martial resolve behind the warlike words. His loathing therefore came to a head when Wilhelm II seemed to be currying favour with the British in his *Daily Telegraph* interview. After Germany attempted another colonial breakthrough, in the Morocco crisis of 1911, Weber sent a circular letter to colleagues insulting pacifists as a band of 'eunuchs':

> I too desire . . . a stronger level of armament, together with a sober and ruthless foreign policy. But it is my view that, even with the strongest armament, we cannot conscientiously risk a European war so long as we have to expect that a crown-wearing dilettante will interfere in the leadership of our army – a man who would make a mess of everything on the field of honour, as he has already done many times in our diplomacy. (MWG II/7, 341)[67]

'Leading military men' had, it is true, assured him 'privately and confidentially' that he need not fear such interference 'in an emergency', for 'S. M. (His Majesty) can't stand the smell of gunpowder and leaves things to us' (WB 4120). The war would show that they were absolutely right about this. Weber was not convinced, and anyway this view of military men was apt to increase his contempt for the Kaiser. It should be noted, however, that his accusation of dilettantism was beside the point: it was not the business of the head of state to be an expert, since, as Weber himself later taught, modern conditions always require experts to wear the corresponding blinkers.

Weber's worries now seem absurd, for the real disaster was that imperial sabre-rattling proved *not* to be an idle threat; Wilhelm II was quite capable of a great war. Yet many contemporaries – especially those who knew the Kaiser at close quarters – thought otherwise: they believed that the main problem, on which Germany's enemies could reckon, was his inner 'cowardice' and unwillingness to go on the offensive at the decisive moment.[68] Before 1914 the sharpest attacks on the Kaiser came at least as much from the ranks of the chauvinists as from the left – themes from both sides were mixed together in Weber's rage. The pacifist Ludwig Quidde, by contrast – whose *Caligula* (1910) was by far the most successful satire on Wilhelm II, even if it ruined his career as a historian – became more and more conciliatory; he eventually believed that the Kaiser had been 'far from eager to draw the sword', and that he could 'claim with much greater justice' to be 'a prince of peace'.[69]

Even with today's knowledge, this view is not without a kernel of truth: even Fritz Fischer thinks, against the main thrust of his thesis, that the Kaiser recoiled from the consequences of a German offensive war.[70] Moreover, as far as Wilhelm II's person is concerned, it still seems that the military debacle was due not so much to a longstanding eagerness for war on his part as to a fatal interplay of factors: he wavered in his resolve to go to war, but he came to feel that influential circles at home and abroad thought of him as 'nervous' and 'cowardly'; this was why, during the July crisis of 1914, he felt under pressure not to back down at any cost. Had Germany's enemies realized long in advance that the Reich was capable of fighting a terrible war for a number of years, they would probably have accepted the Germans as an equal partner in the division of the world. But until 1914 Wilhelm II and his paladins did not exude such an air of resolve, and so from Weber's point of view his rage was not as absurd as it seems today. It is curious, however, that it continued unabated during the war years, when the Kaiser scarcely played any role on the ground.

When Mina Tobler was uplifted in June 1912 by the thought that Max Weber might become chancellor of the Reich, he commented 'at once in a soft tone': 'Of course the Kaiser would first have to be killed.'[71] Of course! Ernst Toller reported how in 1917, at one of the conferences held that year at Burg Lauenstein, Weber still named the Kaiser as 'the greatest evil' and a 'conceited dilettante': again the accusation of dilettantism. 'When the war was over he would publicly insult (the Kaiser) until he was forced to take action against him.' He presumably thought his young listeners would be impressed by such threats, but instead, according to Toller, they felt more strongly than before what separated them from him.[72] For the new social-ist and anarchist youth, marked by the years of war, the issue was no longer Wilhelm II but the whole of the existing order.

Deep down, Weber also knew that the age of the 'personal regiment' was long since over. 'I suffer less now than throughout the twenty-five years when I saw this monarch's hysterical vanity spoil everything I held sacred and dear', he wrote in February 1917 to Karl Loewenstein.[73] So much did he endure under the Kaiser that he felt even the war, with its terrible toll of suffering, to be a relief because Wilhelm II's theatrical role was all over. At the same time, this statement shows that in what he held 'sacred and dear' – and he knew values with such dignity! – he did not feel remote from the ideals that the Kaiser tried to embody; the Kaiser had spoiled those ideals by caricaturing them. Loewenstein heard Weber say more than once: 'If they would only let me at him, I would personally twist the bungling fool's neck.'[74]

Nature, nation, race

Schmoller, Naumann and Wilhelm II were all typical representatives of the German scientific and political elites, and in Weber's relationship to them is mirrored his relationship to the Germany of his time and what he felt to be characteristically German. But how did he define the nation and what bound him to his own? He had a passionate sense of national identity, but he found it more and more difficult to justify this theoretically. It was probably not least under the pressure of this dilemma that he developed a philosophical position which strictly excluded value-judgements from science.

The primary experience that brought some confusion into Weber's concept of the nation was his encounter with Alsatians during his period of military service. In discussing the question of the nation, he turned more than once to this example.[75] It was a sore point for all nationally conscious Germans, for when Alsace was forcibly integrated into the new German Reich in 1871 it was clear that its inhabitants, though of an ancestry that included stars in the firmament of German poetry such as Gottfried von Straßburg and Reinmar von Hagenau, felt proud to belong to the French nation, albeit with their own regional identity. Unlike today, moreover, everyone spoke the local German dialect, so that the region offered an illustration of the fact that language and ancestry as such do not generate a sense of national identity. But then what does constitute a nation? Which characteristic is decisive? Weber himself did not find a clear answer that took him beyond the almost tautological definition: a nation arises from the fact that a human group *wishes* to be a nation. For a social scientist, such a wish is not an adequate final explanation.

The Berlin congress of sociologists in 1912 revolved around the issue of nation and nationality. An opening report by Paul Barth attempted to dissolve the association of national identity and power ambitions by working towards a 'reconciliation of nationality and internationality'. But scarcely had he steered towards this goal when Max Weber – then treasurer of the Gesellschaft für Soziologie – rudely interrupted him and insisted that his introduction of value-judgements violated the statutes of the society.[76] Another reporter later attacked 'the naive fumbling and intrigues' of

German foreign policy,[77] without causing Weber to intervene; evidently he thought it a statement of fact rather than a value-judgement.

Apart from that, in the discussion he repeatedly made fun of the link that Robert Michels had tried to establish between the nation and eroticism. *Weber*: The love poem turned the nation into a cultural community at an especially early date; 'erotic verse aimed at women cannot very well be written in a foreign language.' *Michels*: 'In opposition to Max Weber, however, I would warn against overestimating the connection between nationality and eroticism'; Petrarch intended his Italian sonnets for the Provençale Laura. *Weber*: But 'Goethe's Roman elegies were chanted to the back of [Christine] Vulpius'; he was not aware that Michels 'values the favour of ladies less highly than I do'; but, seriously, the sense of national identity can already be detected in the Middle Ages, long before the national state.[78]

If the nation cannot be defined, this does not mean that there is no such thing at all – on the contrary, the definition dilemma may reflect the *reality* of the nation. In Weber's eyes, one major feature of the nation is that many people are willing to die for it: an unmistakeable sign that it is not a trifling matter. The 'very extraordinary quality of brotherliness of war, and of death in war' can, for Weber, be compared only to 'sacred charisma and the experience of the communion with God' (FMW 336). Naumann formulated it more boldly and straightforwardly: 'The national community is never greater and more moving than when people must die together.'[79] For Weber, the nation is the bearer of honour and therefore one of the highest human values, which in the knightly tradition is enveloped in the aura of eroticism (FMW 345f.).[80]

Especially famous today are Weber's attacks on race theory at the sociological congresses of 1910 and 1912, at a time when it was still conceivable that the racial paradigm would shape the future development of sociology. These attacks contributed not a little to Weber's growing international reputation after 1945, although – as Hans-Walter Schmuhl has shown[81] – their rejection of racism is not as fundamental as the sharp tone at first appears to signal. Weber thought it quite probable that people inherited certain tribal and racial properties, not least in pathological respects, but already in the *Psychophysik* he maintained that the 'importance of purely social conditions' had proved stronger than expected, offering a more plausible explanation in many cases where heredity had previously been thought to operate (GASS 247). By way of an example he mentioned 'that inmates of mental institutions were more strongly inclined to violence in Bavaria, to commotions in the Palatinate, and to suicide in Saxony – whereas the special tendency of the Romans and Slavs to hysteria . . . certainly, judging from the history of religion, should be identified more as a genuinely inherited "tribal quality".' Where religion was ruled out as an explanation for pathological phenomena, heredity acquired greater plausibility.

For a time Weber probably hoped that race research would break new ground in the explanation of human behaviour. The advances never materialized, yet many race theorists, encouraged by the trend of the times, behaved with a presumption that had no warrant in the results of their research. It was not clear how sociology, still so insecure in its foundations, would here find solid ground in the foreseeable future. This was an exasperating situation for Weber. At the Frankfurt sociologists' congress in 1910 he loudly denounced Alfred Ploetz (1860–1940), the founder of *Rassehygienische Gesellschaft* and the *Archiv für Rassen- und Gesellschaftsbiologie* – though only after a thick serving of compliments:

> Gentlemen, some extremely clever and interesting theories have emerged. The journal run by Herr Dr Ploetz is truly an arsenal of inestimable hypotheses (some enviable in their abundant intelligence) about the breeding effect of all possible institutions and processes, and no one can be more grateful than I for these stimulating ideas. But that we have today a single fact relevant to sociology, one clear and precise fact that plausibly and impeccably, exactly and conclusively traces a certain kind of sociological process to innate and inherited qualities which one race possesses and another definitively – please note: definitively! – does not possess: I dispute this quite categorically and will continue to dispute it until one such fact is precisely described to me. (GASS 459)

It might be asked whether any causality has ever been 'exactly' and 'conclusively' demonstrated within *non*-racist sociology. Weber would counter this by saying that his own constructions of causality should always be understood as ideal-typical, whereas the race theorists claim that their causality is real. Weber's struggle against them was mainly a struggle against epistemological naivety and presumptuousness. Racist theories were thus for him a 'crime against science',[82] not yet in the sense in which we have associated them with criminality since the Nazi period. At the Berlin sociologists' congress in 1912 Weber spoke his mind even more sharply about the 'race fanatics' (GASS 485). Race theories could be used 'to prove and disprove anything one wishes'. 'Race hypotheses' were fakes competing with the genuine article of sociological analysis (GASS 489).

From his experiences in the United States, Weber knew well enough how ideologically charged racism was and how absurd was its claim that whites had an innate physical aversion for blacks; after all, slave-owners had always taken special pleasure in sexual relations with female black slaves. To be sure, in Germany at that time, race theories were not generally associated with far-right political movements or with projects to discriminate against, let alone wipe out, whole sections of the population. Alfred Ploetz, though a manufacturer's son, came from a socialist background and had worked on a rural commune in America.[83] An inhuman tendency already made itself felt in 1910, however, when he combined racist with eugenic ideas and suggested that Christianity, with its institutionalized brotherly love and its solicitude for beggars and cripples, had contributed to the reproduction of inferior human types and the degeneration of the race. Weber, who had not done too well for himself by eugenic criteria and who was also on the point of discovering sexual love, spoke sarcastically about this defamation of Christian charity and the idea that an excess of it could actually be a danger for the modern world (GASS 456f.).

Weber thought it a self-evident piece of ideological mischief to turn the Germans into a race, and a superior one at that; nor was his diagnosis hard to arrive at. One of the favourite targets of satirical magazines was the boozy member of a student duelling society, or the beer-swilling ordinary citizen, who spoke in his cups of the superior German race; Weber knew that he too had once fallen prey to the vulgar attraction of this male milieu. In his circular letter of 15 November 1911 to Freiburg colleagues, he declared that a 'quintessentially hollow and empty nationalism' of the 'purely zoological' kind that was spreading in the student fraternities would inevitably lead 'to an unprincipled attitude to all the great problems of civilization' (MWG II/7-1, 356). One of the most repugnant aspects of racist theories was their tendency to highlight the purely animal side of human beings. He had no doubt that the nation could not be grounded upon *that* nature.

A German nation for which it was worth living could not be based on some Teutonic race, but only on German culture. This had reached its high points in various small states; it was also flourishing in Switzerland. Did it have any need of a powerful empire? However we look at it, the nation as a power-oriented state did not occupy a very convincing place in Weber's conceptual world; nor was it a primeval community or a brotherhood that could be animated by the 'communism of love'. Already before 1914, however, the nation was for Weber the expression of a 'powerful sense of community'.[84] And not least through war it acquired some of the emotional qualities of a natural community.

Eduard Baumgarten, Weber's nephew and later executor, reported in his memoirs that at Easter 1916, when he had got his *Abitur* and, being eighteen, could now be sent to the front, he had paid a visit to Max Weber in Heidelberg. He mentioned there that he intended to enlist in an infantry regiment, but Weber 'most vigorously and unexpectedly' contradicted him by saying that he should at all costs join a cavalry regiment. He would not be trapped for so long in the barracks and on the parade-ground. 'I know a colonel here', Weber told him. 'In three months at the latest you will be at the front.' 'He rolled his glaring eyes in a threatening circle around their huge sockets', while his nephew could take 'no inspiration at all . . . from his enthusiasm for horses'. For 'to wish myself on the back of a horse would increase my chances of dying fivefold *anno* 1916. Shrapnel at head height. Snipers all around.' Besides, it turned out that Weber was already 'firmly' convinced that Germany would lose the war. In 1916 Eduard made himself ridiculous to other soldiers by volunteering, but he stuck by his decision to join the infantry.[85] In later years he often recounted this odd little scene with 'Uncle Max'.

In a footnote to the *Psychophysik* Max Weber already stated: 'The more mechanical warfare becomes, the more it has to employ specialists with years of training' (GASS 254). Volunteers with a short training period were mere cannon fodder. Why was he so adamant about sending his nephew to an almost certain and pointless death? Where was the Weberian rationality in this? One cannot help thinking that Hellpach had been right to see a personality split in Weber: not unconscious, as in schizophrenics, but well and truly conscious. His nephew was supposed to fulfil Max Weber's own dream of galloping off to war like a knight on his trusty steed. In 1915 he wrote to Frieda Gross that he hated 'this war, which should have come twenty years earlier and found me on a horse' (B 491).

In one part of himself, the nation was indeed a higher entity, a kind of larger organism of which the individual was but a single member. The nation underwent a rebirth through war, and to feel completely alive the individual too had to experience war as strongly as possible, even if it was lost in the end. In this way, we are able to reconstruct the logic of Weber's behaviour towards his nephew.[86] Baumgarten later emphasized that for Weber the nation was a 'value', which 'his own nature affirmed with elemental impulses and feelings' (B 419). And yet he also spoke of Weber's 'national self-hatred'.[87] Again a Weberian self-hatred – also internally connected to his love–hate for nature. For, precisely because the nation was so hard to grasp rationally, it had something of the indefinability of a natural phenomenon.

In 1916 Weber wrote disparagingly in Naumann's *Hilfe* that Germans believe even in phrases 'with all the fervour of, might I say, feminine emotion' (MWG I/15, 181). As Weber saw it, then, the German embodied the 'female', emotional side of human nature, which he had for long been unable to accept in himself, but which he was gradually learning to affirm; this too is a possible reason why he felt something like a reluctant love for his nation. More than once he even showed warm feelings for the kind of German culture that had developed in Switzerland without any elements of a power-centred state, and which he considered at least as authentically German as most of the culture in the German Reich (MWG I/15, 95 and 191). In any event, he was not at all happy that the war had, as he put it, 'violently enhanced the reputation of *the state*'. 'The state, not the nation' seemed to be watchword of the day – and Weber regarded it as fundamentally wrong. We sense his aversion for the apparatus, the bureaucracy, breaking through. The war had shown that 'the state is capable of many things, but that it does not have the power to compel the free devotion of the individual' (MWG I/15, 181). Shortly before the war broke out, in answer to the Swiss legal expert Fritz Fleiner's assertion that people should love the state, he had written: 'What! Do we even have to love the monster!'[88] But to love the nation: that was different; it had the capacity to generate a collective Eros, to mobilize elemental passions. And yet, in the middle of war too, the nature of the nation was like his own nature: a power far too opaque for him to achieve conceptual clarity and consistency in relation to it.

Part III

Salvation and Illumination

Although the whole world agrees that increased erotic tension not only subjectively fosters an affirmative, active and courageous approach to life but also objectively improves performance in numerous areas, it is not usual in a biography to devote a chapter to these erotic-sexual details and their personal foundations. . . . There is no reason to suppress the erotic sphere in our description of an individual. Every historian is able, without losing his composure, to discuss the importance of his hero's attitudes to sexuality. Often this throws a clear light on the hero's character and conduct of life.

Hans W. Gruhle, *Geschichtsschreibung und Psychologie* (1953), pp. 147, 149

No doubt it is true that Christianity is the religion of redemption; but the conception is a delicate one, and must never be taken out of the sphere of personal experience and inner reformation.

Adolf Harnack, *What Is Christianity?* (1901), p. 197

Quests for salvation which arise among privileged classes are generally characterized by a disposition towards an 'illumination' mysticism . . . which is associated with a distinctively intellectual qualification for salvation. . . . The salvation sought by the intellectual is always based on inner need. . . . The intellectual seeks in various ways, the casuistry of which extends into infinity, to endow his life with a pervasive meaning, and thus to find unity with himself, with his fellow men, and with the cosmos. It is the intellectual who conceives of the 'world' as a problem of meaning.

Max Weber, *Economy and Society*, p. 506

In 1909 Max Weber again felt capable of long-term commitments and took on the editing of a multi-volume handbook, the Grundriß der Sozialökonomik. *At the December congress of the Verein für Sozialpolitik in Vienna, he pugnaciously argued against the idea of state direction of the economy. And in the following years he made a mark both in the Verein and in the Deutsche*

*Gesellschaft für Soziologie (which he had helped to found) through his cam-
paign against value-judgements in science. In the autumn of 1909 he fell in love
with Else Jaffé, but by January 1910, when Else began an affair with Alfred
Weber, their relationship was giving way to seven years of animosity. In the
summer of 1912 Max Weber started a relationship with the pianist Mina
Tobler, whom he had known since 1909. The relapses in his illness now ceased.
In the springs of 1913 and 1914, he holidayed at Ascona and came into contact
with lifestyle reformers who were living 'close to nature'. There he often met
Frieda Gross, the ex-wife of Else's former lover Otto Gross, and gave her legal
support in her battle for custody of her son. The years before 1914 witnessed
other violent controversies, but also periods of unusual scientific productivity.
Shortly before the war Weber began a study of Oriental religions: his book on
Confucianism and Taoism was published in 1915, and an even more detailed
work on Hinduism and Buddhism followed in 1916–17. When trusted colleagues at the* Grundriß der Sozialökonomik *deserted him, he began work on
the voluminous manuscript that has often been considered his* magnum opus;
it would eventually appear as a posthumous fragment under the title Economy
and Society. *After the outbreak of war in 1914, he worked in Heidelberg on
the organization of military hospitals and had special responsibility for disciplinary matters. But he quit this job in September 1915 and tried in vain to find
a position in the government service. In March 1916 he wrote an internal memorandum vigorously opposing the intensification of submarine warfare, which
led in April 1917 to America's entry into the world war. In the same year he
became active in political journalism and fought for a parliamentarization of
the Reich. He also risked a return to his profession, by accepting the chair in
economics at Vienna on a trial basis. In 1919 he was offered a professorship in
Munich, and when he moved there he began an erotic relationship with Else
Jaffé, who was also living in the vicinity. At the same time he joined the campaign against the idea of Germany's war guilt, travelling in May 1919 with the
German peace delegation to Versailles. On 14 June 1920 he died of a lung
infection.*

13

Value-Free Science, Love and Music

Value-freedom and eroticism

When Weber became increasingly worked up after 1909 over value-judgements in science, the issue for him was not just the purity of scholarship but at least as much the rescuing of life's supreme values from formal rationality. In a manuscript he wrote in 1912, he hinted that in the campaign against value-judgements (which was then nearing its peak) sex and marriage were not the least of his concerns:

> The attempt to handle material value conflicts with purely formal means reveals its intolerable consequences in relation to sexual problems. To achieve anything at all here, the problem must be located . . . in the sphere of formal legality: . . . belief in the value of eternity and the associated paradox of the hope that love will endure have to be flattened out into a contractual promise of permanence; and the responsibility of lover and beloved for the other's soul has to be converted into a kind of 'legal liability for damages'. There can scarcely be a more devastating criticism of ethical formalism than these unavoidable platitudes. (B 401)

As a legal theorist and sociologist, Weber could have argued along quite different lines: that, since love is all too often transitory, the state and society need marriage all the more as a legally sanctioned institution; that love alone is not a stable foundation for marriage. However, Weber's starting point here was not any needs of the social system, but rather the experience of love's magic. Love too does not create a space free of all responsibility, but the responsibility in question does not have the formal character without which scientific method is at a loss. These ideas reflect Weber's new experiences since 1909.

At first it was mainly a new proximity to his brother Alfred which set Max's life in motion. When Alfred Weber, formerly an even more hopeless bundle of nerves than his elder brother, took up a professorship in Heidelberg in 1908, he became for Max and Marianne a living example of the combination of scientific naturalism, free love and nervous recovery. Like Sombart and Michels, he cultivated an image of the erotic male and openly declared his belief in 'amoralism',[1] although he too was mainly a bookworm who, according to Else, took his brother's 'work mania' as a model.[2] In 1912, when the mother had long known about his relationship with Else, the son tried to spare her (or did he inwardly snort with laughter?) by telling her that sex was a necessary part of life for him: 'I know you find it painful – you *must* often find it painful – that the way my life has shaped up, the compulsion to get as much out of it as possible on the narrow and difficult path to another person seems to have been taking me away from you.'[3] But Alfred, with his candour and spontaneity, was one of those people with whom neither Helene nor Marianne could be seriously angry, although Marianne probably had exaggerated ideas about his loose living.[4] She had been joyfully looking forward to Alfred's move to Heidelberg, although she foresaw that the brothers' different attitudes to life contained 'a lot of explosive material' and that any discussion of them would be a strain on the nerves.[5]

At the time Marianne was less rigid than Max on questions of sexual ethics,[6] and she would have liked to regain the natural relations of their youth with Alfred.[7] She tried to pacify the mother: 'You shouldn't get too worried about his naturalist theories, and so on – in the end, the most important thing is how he *behaves*.'[8] But Alfred did not make it easy for her to be 'nice' to him. She got wind that he had once laughingly said that he needed people 'less given to moral indignation than his sister-in-law'. In 1908 it seemed that, on their return journeys to a 'social-political meeting' in Eisenach, Max and Alfred would talk 'for seven hours at a time': not at all about topical issues in social policy, but – as Marianne put it – 'naturally about – sexual ethics, etc.'. Alfred, again according to Marianne, had put forward 'peculiar' views in Prague about sexuality and German women. The brothers discussed these 'very intensely', but did not end up quarrelling.[9] Evidently things had not previously turned out like that. It is not only in the *Psychophysik* that we can see how much Max Weber was influenced by Alfred at that time.

The second act of the Else drama

With all this in the background, what a provocation it must have been when Alfred and Else got together in 1910! It joined together two people who already, *chacun pour soi*, had been muddling up Max's and Marianne's view of the world. And, to heighten the drama, Max had just previously fallen in love with Else – to the confusion and dismay of Marianne, whose main concern had previously been to urge her husband to be more lenient towards the loose-living Else. Out of a 'wish to see Max and Else get along more naturally with each other', she had even had the 'happy thought' that Max should become the godfather of Else's little

Peterle, whose father – as the Webers knew – was Otto Gross. 'And so Else asked him and he did it, not without joking a lot with me about my crazy idea.'[10] From then on, Else was Max Weber's kin in the broader sense, and he could have decently called her *du* rather than the 'Dear Frau Doktor' he had used in his angry letter of 13 September 1907 (ironically, because she had addressed him as 'Dear Herr Professor') (MWG II/5, 393n.). But he stuck to 'Else' and '*Sie*' in the only letter he sent to her in 1910 (MWG II/6, 567ff.).

As far as we know, the new period in Max Weber's life began not with an experience of love but with an intellectual upswing, which was accompanied by a new sense of physical well-being. In late September 1909 Weber was in fine form at the general meeting of the Verein für Sozialpolitik in Vienna. Whereas, as a young man, he had once enjoyed playing the old bear, he now entered the arena as the representative of 'young people' against the Verein's old guard. With a malicious wit, he joined Alfred in attacking the bureaucratism of the Schmoller school and launched his first offensive against value-judgements in science. Unlike his earlier critique of 'naturalism' in *Roscher and Knies*, the campaign against value-judgements was conducted in excellent spirits rather than a state of inner torment. Dolf Sternberger later thought that Weber's strict separation of science from value-judgements was a case of 'wilful, indeed furious asceticism', rather like 'a chronic state of convulsion'.[11] But this psychopathological interpretation of Weber's attacks on value-judgements rests upon a misunderstanding.

Venus and Mars

In Marianne's biography, 'Controversies' and 'The Good Life' come in the headings of two successive chapters, giving the impression that there was a similar sequence in Weber's life and that he discovered the good life after the struggles were over and his rage had subsided. In reality, however, a lot of things happened at the same time and in parallel. The struggle against value-judgements in science peaked in the years 1909 and 1913–14,[12] that is, in periods of love and euphoria. It did not involve irritability born of frustration, but rather a lust for battle that sprang from a new sense of energy. From being together with Else in Venice on 10 October 1909, Weber went straight to Leipzig for the congress of German university teachers, where he announced to shouts of 'Oho!': 'Value-judgements have no place in the lecture hall.'[13] For him the battle was not a continuation of the methodological dispute of previous years; in fact, his attack on value-judgements in 1913 ended with a hefty swipe at the 'methodological pestilence' under which political economy was labouring.[14] His formidable paper war against Arnold Ruge, Adolf Koch and Bernhard Harms, which he claimed to be waging for his own and others' honour, but which already struck his contemporaries as an expression of abnormal sensitivity, dragged on through the years from 1910 to 1913, a period of recovery such as he had not had before. If an element of aggression towards oneself is contained in depression, an outwardly directed attack may lead out of the depths; it looks as though Weber experienced that in himself. For the battles were followed by an explosion of creativity, in the sociology of music, religion and politics.

In 1909, when the value-judgement controversy flared up, Schmoller had just published a survey of the financial history of major countries since 1500; his declared aim was to arouse public opinion in favour of the central government finance reforms, in which the main question in debate was an increase in inheritance taxes (opposed by the conservatives). Under the banner of financial reform a broad front was taking shape among German political economists; work on the reform became a model for Wilhelmine *Gelehrtenpolitik*, the involvement of academics in politics.[15] The question is how far the initiative really lay with the academics. For the government treasury department, using a veritable 'propaganda apparatus' (Peter-Christian Witt), promoted publications that helped to tap new sources of finance for the Reich. Weber must have been aware of this affinity of Schmoller and his followers with the state bureaucracy.[16] It must have signified corruption in his eyes, although for him too it must have been an honourable objective to strengthen the Reich by increasing taxes (MWG II/6, 97). Of course, higher tax rates would have considerably affected him because of the Oerlinghausen legacy that was the basis of his new prosperity. Weber's name is missing from the phalanx of German economists who supported the financial reform. He wrote Schmoller an appreciative letter about his treatise, but spoke to another colleague of 'the unavoidable Schmollerian bowel movement' (MWG II/6, 141). Presumably he thought it scientific humbug to review four hundred years of history to justify a current policy measure.

Mixing up the fronts: 'terrorism' alarm against the Schmoller school

It is not easy to explain the violence of Weber's attack simply by the goings-on in academic politics around the year 1910. His fear must have been that he was forcing an open door and collecting applause in quarters that were not at all to his liking. At the time, the social-political orientation of the Schmoller school was coming under heavier fire from economists close to business circles: for example, Richard Ehrenberg's pamphlet of 1910, *Terrorismus in der Wirtschafts-Wissenschaft* [Terrorism in economic science], with its banner title 'Gegen den Katheder-Sozialismus' [Against academic socialism], left no doubt as to what was meant by terrorism, as it trained its sights on both Schmoller and Weber. The allusions to Weber's illness and the rumour-mongering about his state of mind – 'well known as an unpredictable, highly nervous man, to be disregarded in much of what he said' – must have made his blood boil.

The situation in 1909 would have been a reason for Weber to stick together with Schmoller. Instead, with his attacks on the unscientific value-dependence of the Schmoller school, he encouraged the rollback operation against social policy in general. Later neoliberal economists used to joke from the heights of theory and value-freedom about Schmoller and his people: 'They measure one worker's dwelling after another and then say: "The dwelling is too small."' In 1913, at the final peak of the controversy, the value-freedom position found impressive support from the manufacturer Jacob Epstein, who spoke on his own admission as an employer and, referring to Ehrenberg, 'most urgently' recommended the 'introduction of private economics as a special discipline' alongside political economy; this was the formative period for economic management theory, which until then had been considered an inferior subject to be taught at business colleges. Max Weber's embarrassment at the acclaim he received from such circles can be sensed in the position he took in 1913.[17]

Weber's struggle against value-judgements is more understandable if we relate it to other areas of his life and work during those years. When he spoke contemptuously of 'professorial prophecy' that risked nothing, because no student in the lecture hall would contradict it (WL 492), we should bear in mind that he was then engrossed in the prophets of ancient Israel, who drew no official salary for their thunderous words and indeed risked being stoned for them. Moreover, Weber's postulate of value-freedom, together with the method of ideal types, was nothing other than a transfer from the natural to the social sciences.[18] For the natural scientist also makes simplified models of reality, with which it is possible to conduct physical or conceptual experiments – and it went without saying for Weber, at least as an idea, that that meant observing rather than judging. Later he wrote in the preface to the sociology of religion:

> The question of the relative value of the cultures which are compared here will not receive a single word. It is true that the path of human destiny cannot but appal him who surveys a section of it. But he will do well to keep his small personal commentaries to himself, as one does at the sight of the sea or of majestic mountains, unless he knows himself to be called and gifted to give them expression in artistic or prophetic form. (PE 29)

'At the sight of the sea or of majestic mountains': human science in the mode of natural science, though admittedly one which has to do with a nature that does not leave the observer cold.

Marianne, who later thought she could detect a secret mystic in her husband, saw value-freedom as the basis for an ideal of science akin to mystical contemplation: 'Just as a mystic who wishes to "have" God first curbs every stirring of the will, a thinker must, if he is to be the mouthpiece of truth, first divest himself of practical self-interest in what happens' (WB 317). In fact Weber, who of necessity gave up all political ambitions, discovered during those years the attraction of contemplative science – and there was scarcely any better way of experiencing this than through immersion in the Oriental religions. The struggle against value-judgements was also a struggle for a special pleasure of thought; it marked a period of Weber's life in which he discovered pleasure.

A turning point in his life

'The great experience of the last few weeks was – Max and again Max', Marianne wrote joyfully to Helene in October 1909 from Vienna. 'It was as if he had shaken off his chains and were now stretching like an intellectual Titan up to the heavens – he was wonderful.'[19] Weber's new creativity seemed like a natural event to his wife: 'He was like a dammed-up stream of intellect, which cannot stop rushing forward and carrying everything with it.' At the same time, she worried that he would pay for the euphoria with a subsequent breakdown; the 67-year-old Knapp, who fifteen years earlier had experienced Weber's study of agricultural labour as a revelation, whispered to Marianne: 'How good he looks! We take delight in his fire, but it is consuming him!' (WB 414). The notes that follow this are not published in Marianne's biography: 'No, it did not consume him in those days but burned ever brighter. . . . I *loved* him, (more) delightedly than for a long time, and admiration of his genius and strength gave to love an awe that overcame desire.'[20] It was from then, above all, that Marianne saw genius in Weber – and indicated how she used the cult of genius to repress sexual desire.

A breakdown did not ensue; the vicious circle was broken. This time intellectual overactivity was not followed by sleeplessness: Weber slept 'almost without assistance'. Almost! 'It was a real exhilaration at being alive, *the miracle* of energy sources in long-buried hopes. . .', Marianne recalled later. 'Those ten days in Vienna became a truly great time, an incomparable festival of the mind and the heart. . . . Max's vigour and productivity rose up in all their splendour. For the first time since his illness (in eleven years, then) he was living beyond all constraints, he had the same intensity and vivacity from morning until late evening – he could do *everything* in those days . . . his gift of speech burst forth as a long dammed-up force, which almost overwhelmed the poor speakers.' 'The fact that all his intellectual productivity was still there cast a new light on his condition'[21] – we learn in passing that Marianne had been afraid that her husband's mind was irreversibly damaged. Now she thought she understood 'that on such days all personal demands, including of the most intimate kind, are superseded, and one has to give him the freedom to forget the other playmate.'[22] The Webers were by now living a very modern marriage, in which both felt it their duty to allow the other to be free. And it was not in his wife that Max Weber's new lust for life found an end goal, a body.

Some time before the Vienna congress Else suggested that Max Weber might like to go from there to Ragusa with her and Edgar; there was no talk of Marianne in this connection. Weber was 'very happy' to accept the invitation, but acted towards Marianne as if he were undecided, 'even though the beautiful sinner asked him so seductively'. He sensed that a sexual challenge lay concealed in the offer, as we can tell from the insinuation in the question he asked Else in reply: 'Are you sure you don't really mean Alfred?' So, he must have noticed that something was going on between his brother and Else, but that then as later she was wavering between the two brothers. Max Weber's question made her 'quite red and angry', and she assured him that she really meant him.[23] And so, Weber travelled to Vienna in the knowledge that he was sexually attractive to Else. One does not have to be a Freudian to make the association with his euphoria in Vienna.

Else and Edgar Jaffé waited for the Webers in Graz. Apparently there was no longer any mention of a trip to Ragusa, today's Dubrovnik, but Else had thought of something different that would not be quite so irritating to Marianne: she invited them both to accompany Edgar and herself to the Adriatic. Max spoke disparagingly of Else to Marianne: 'She's gone pretty badly wrong' (MWG II/6, 285), but his wife had a 'sneaking feeling' that 'he would really prefer to spend some time alone with Else than with the couple'; she displaced this foreboding into an 'almost feverish coming and going'. She felt it was her 'duty' to leave Max alone with Else, although she wanted so much to stay on; in the Kantian struggle between duty and 'inclination', she decided for the latter with a not altogether clear conscience. The two couples travelled to Trieste and stayed for a week at Grignano, a sea resort on the Adriatic.

Max had 'definitely calculated' that he would end up alone with Else, but neither Edgar nor Marianne thought of leaving. Max was enraged by this 'tackiness'; he even felt angry with Else that she did not take it upon herself to send her husband packing, but he took his bad mood out on Marianne instead. Meanwhile the two wives joined forces and laughed at their men. In Trieste, quite uncharacteristically, Max got up very early for several mornings to be alone with Else after she rose; this was a sign to Marianne that a deep change was taking place in her husband – a change that both enchanted and unsettled her. Looking back in later years, she recorded that Max found 'a wonderful image' on the Adriatic – an image of what? First she noted that 'a drop of erotic feeling is mixed in with the relationship between man and woman', but she crossed this out and wrote instead that 'the nobility of human beings is shown when sexuality remains unconscious and under control'. Then came Max Weber's image, which could have been modelled on a painting by Max Klinger:

Man and woman stand in the dawning valley of life and look together at the eternal stars, and neither sees the other's nakedness – until the large sun of their one and only love rises above them? He spoke like a god-filled poet and visionary, to replenish Else's senses with reverence for the old ideals.

But Else did not play this awe-inspiring scene so correctly. She even asked the pert little question: 'So, do we have to become virtuous again?'[24] She had something quite different on her mind. Marianne was going back to Heidelberg alone. Max would spend another three days with the Jaffés in Venice – which Marianne allowed him to do, though, as she put it to Helene, 'with a heavy heart for *Else's* sake'.[25]

10 October 1909: 'revolution' in Venice

In Venice, honeymoon city and legendary metropolis of pleasure, Max and Else were finally alone with each other for a few hours – even if the return journey was just two days away. Their bodies came closer and their souls opened up to each other. In a later autobiographical sketch, which unfortunately consists only of brief notes, Else remarked of this Venetian interlude: 'He sees my life as not yet sealed, speaks of the possibility and admissibility of occasional "adventures" – but: "Only one thing is not on: my brother." I think: "It's all very well for you to talk!" '[26] Max Weber was talking as Else's partner, who can set conditions for their relationship but is also aware that something is in the air between her and Alfred. The younger brother, unlike Max, is sexually experienced; and Else, who has only with difficulty shaken off her sexual dependence on the surgeon, is not a woman for mere comradeship or a love affair that is content with tender gestures. Shortly afterwards, Max Weber had to recognize that there really was a physical relationship between Else and his brother; and he felt it as a deep wound and breach of trust. This indicates that for him there had been something binding about the closeness with Else in Venice.

Eduard Baumgarten was aware of Max Weber's later love letters to Else when he wrote: 'In Venice . . . a revolution occurred in him which was comparable in scale to Albrecht Dürer's: "But the most important thing that Dürer took home from Venice was a belief that art is firmly rooted in nature: in truth, he later wrote, art is planted in nature. He who can pull it up is the one who has it" ' (B 667). Significantly, he remarked that the 'earliest origin' of Weber's *Zwischenbetrachtung*, the famous 'intervening reflection' on eroticism and salvation and the tension between brotherly and sexual love, was the experience in Venice on 10 October 1909.[27]

How must all this have looked from Else's point of view? Her years of close friendship with Marianne would certainly have put her in the picture about many an intimate aspect of the Webers' marriage. Bold psychological speculations are not required to imagine that the situation seemed much more straightforward to a woman like Else: Max Weber needed sexual satisfaction to be cured of his depression; and there was no longer any prospect that he would find this in his marriage. Spiritual and physical love do not always go hand in hand; sometimes life can be lived to the full only within a triangular relationship. All this must have been the most obvious thing in the world to Else. Just as Marianne felt it her 'duty' to leave Max alone with Else, so must Else have had the impression that Marianne was giving her complete freedom with regard to Max and considered physical contact to be in the best interests of his recovery. Since Else had no thought of separating Max from Marianne, there was no reason for her to feel guilty towards Marianne. At the same time, to be sure, she did not see why she should feel pangs of conscience towards Max if she were to start a relationship with Alfred; for she did not find with Max the sexual satisfaction that she needed and demanded. He seems to have soon slipped into the language of 'brotherly love' with her – to which she reacted coolly by saying that 'brotherliness' was a 'faraway land' for her (MWG II/6, 367).

On 28 November 1909 Marianne mentioned in passing in a letter to Helene that Else was 'now on close terms with Max'. A month later she was more explicit: 'Since Vienna he has been so expansive and says that he can take more in the way of "worldly pleasures" – as if he knew that he can actually *go* when he feels like it. For example, he has visited Else Jaffé several times up in her mountain house.' Once he even stayed there until midnight. 'Of course, he had to pay for it later with Trional', a not exactly harmless sleep-inducing drug. It seemed to her that he was working only a little and staying 'in bed until late in the morning'. And then the patronizing conclusion: 'But he must be allowed the rather more colourful side of life, until he can get away with anything.'[28]

Really, anything? If truth be told, Marianne was in despair that Else might bewitch her husband in a way that she was incapable of doing. Before her eyes, he was turning into the charming lover she had yearned for during their engagement – only not for her. He arrived in Trieste with his arms full of flowers: 'some mixed bunch or other' for Marianne, a 'carefully selected little bunch of roses and unusual lily-coloured vetches for Else, which, as he said, matched her clothes'. He went up to greet her 'with the new grace of knightly service'. Marianne asked herself: 'Did he ever, at any time, act like that when he brought me flowers? Ah, he never needed to "court" me in that way.' This thought 'flashed' through her mind 'for the first time, like a sharp pain'.[29]

The next year, when Marianne thought her husband went quite over the top in offering her 'knightly service' after a press article had wounded her female honour, this may have been an attempt on his part to make up for earlier scenes with Else. Still today, however, we can see from the surviving parts of Marianne's diaries – those not ripped out or crossed through and corrected – that the new situation threw her into complete confusion, all the more as she had only just begun to feel a renewed love for her husband. Seemingly trivial details began to ruffle her: that Max was breaking with old habits because of Else, getting up early and overcoming his distaste for walks. Already in Trieste a 'great feeling of sadness' came over her when she thought: 'He's in love with her!' 'He loves her not only with the soul of friendship, but differently . . . (She crossed out: 'passionately. The word eroticism and even another') would have been much too crude for his feelings. They were so beautiful, so ungreedy, so unselfish, and I understood only too well that Else must be unleashing in him this strong new emotion (as I for long have not known how to do).'[30] She did not kid herself that she too felt something more than mere friendship for Else.

Perhaps some mere 'fooling around' between Max and Else would have been more bearable to her, in the knowledge that it was helping him to recover his health. Instead, what was unfolding before her eyes was a passionate spiritual love, and she had no ethical position from which she might have judged it. On the contrary, she 'could only approve of it ethically' – yet was unable to bear it. A year later, when the crisis was over, she confessed: 'At the time I lost all pleasure in myself, and it became dreadfully clear to me that a lot of weeds were growing among the wheat in the garden of my soul.'[31] Or, in plain language: perfectly ordinary jealousy and a wish to have her husband to herself. For there was no mention now that Else, who was also sticking to her marriage, might want to take Max away. Marianne found particularly unsettling the sense that, inside her, a primitive, vapid nature was wearing down all her ethical ideals:

> O terrible inner turmoil, that is impossible to master! Trembling, loneliness, self-contempt – spiritual humiliation through the shame of not being able to do otherwise. Taking leave of one's reason and moral freedom. Impossible to think of a more painful and humiliating condition. Sadness about the objective cause . . . but still greater sadness and shame about my own feeling. And left its helpless victim because of how the most elemental force of nature breaks through all civilization as a thin husk.[32]

When she subsequently read *Madame Bovary* – a tale of adultery not likely to bring her any comfort – what shook her most in the end was not the wife's suicide but the death of the cheated husband: the unhappy man who broke down after her death when he learned of her unfaithfulness, because 'the last thing that remained of what had made his life worth living, the memory of it, was now poisoned. The writer makes it horrifyingly clear that one cannot be sure of anything until the end of one's days: if my lover or friend betrays me today, it changes everything we had together, every still-remembered gift of love, from gold into mud.'[33] She felt the danger that her whole life could be devalued in this way. When Max died ten years later, Marianne knew – though much was also hidden from her – that her husband had experienced with Else a joy that she had been incapable of giving him; this explains the sadness that hung over her life, even if she far exceeded Madame Bovary's husband in her zest for life.

When Marianne, in *Die Frauen und die Liebe*, sympathetically described the pain of Minna Planer, the first wife of Richard Wagner (who was unfaithful to her 'at the high point of life'), she again gave evidence of her own suffering. 'But, for the excitable artist, such break-outs from a marital routine begun too early in life were an inescapable destiny. . . . He was a strongly sensual man, and his muse obtained her creative ecstasies precisely from the sphere of the erotic.' In the years after 1910 Marianne had to recognize that Max Weber's nature was not so different. Minna Planer, childless and more and more frustrated sexually, 'did not recognize, like Cosima Wagner later, that it "is always a favour to be touched by the rays of a genius".' Such was Marianne's balance-sheet.[34] There can be no doubt that she too, who for a time was threatened with the fate of Minna Planer, wanted to acquit herself better. And, in fact, her 'remembrance policy' was still more effective than the one Cosima pursued with Richard Wagner; it is more difficult for researchers to pass over her testimony than it is for them to disregard Wagner's widow.

Else and always Else again

By early 1910 it was clear that a passionate relationship had developed not between Else and Max but between Else and Alfred. For Marianne this was an infinite relief, and unlike Max she could not bear the unmarried couple any malice. For years their liaison was a frequent topic of conversation for Max and Marianne, even helping to create a new element of togetherness in their marriage. In May 1910 Marianne wrote to Helene:

> Even now we are inwardly preoccupied with these matters, which display a different aspect . . . almost every day. I hope the time will now gradually come when we again have interest and strength for something else. It's been going on for four months. For Max, too, I would like there soon to be a little inner 'distance' from it, because with his temperament he is so colossally intense and 'obsessional' about everything.[35]

Of course, Marianne knew that Max had very special reasons to be so obsessively preoccupied with the love story. Her declared hope, whether real or not, that she and Max would soon turn their minds to other things would not be fulfilled for a long time to come. In August 1911, though otherwise usually forbearing towards her friend, Marianne said something reproachful that caused Alfred to fly into a rage and Else to react with an epistolary 'scream'. When Max read Else's letter, 'the terrible torment of not being understood in his will and thoughts' came back; 'for days it churned him up inside'. Presumably what pained him was the idea that Else simply thought he was jealous – and the realization that she was basically right! 'How often when the expression on his face becomes tense and sad do we think of the same thing: Else', Marianne confided to her diary.[36]

The failed triangle: the beginning of seven years of love–hate

Now it was again sometimes the frustrated Max who proclaimed the 'old ideals' in a thunderous voice and became angry if Else gently mocked his 'moralizing', while he at the same time was raging against value-judgements in science. In May 1910, once more a solid married man who 'embraces' his wife 'a thousand times', he wrote to Marianne running down the sinful Else as a 'silly little thing':

> So, has she once again managed to get safely through our 'moralizing'? She may imagine we are gone from H(eidel)b(er)g and ask herself whether things will then 'work out' here (without a divorce NB!). We could – as Alfred says – 'keep our shield over it', if it is a question of an infatuation that remains hidden – but no one here, whether he wants to or not, can cover up a lasting 'Cicisbeo' relationship that is disgraceful for all sides, in which the female partner plays 'Mother' at the same time. But we will not make any 'difficulties' inside or out. What right has the silly little thing to believe that we would? (MWG II/6, 544f.)

The 'Cicisbeo', or male friend of a married woman, refers to a delightful tradition in Italy going back to the Renaissance. The relationship between Alfred and Else, which would last forty-eight years until Alfred's death, became more stable than many marriages; but this solidity far beyond any infatuation was precisely the scandal for Max. Did he recognize that Else was a maternal mistress to whom Alfred submitted sexually: a domina type, for whom Max too secretly longed, an embodiment of the erotic charisma of domination? Around the same time, Alfred was writing to Else: 'My darling noble abbess, forgive me always my sins . . .'[37]

One can only wonder at the matter-of-fact way in which Max repeatedly interfered in Alfred's private affairs, as if the older brother had responsibility for the younger brother's love life even when they were well past maturity. Marianne actually saw this as a duty in relation to Else, a 'mission' indeed, in which the aim was nevertheless to ensure that Else was completely free.[38] And, stranger still, Alfred and Else were to some extent prepared to discuss their relationship with Max and Marianne, instead of – as one would expect nowadays – curtly rejecting any interference once and for all. Certainly it was clear to Alfred that his elder brother was basically jealous of him, but he also knew that Max would be mortally offended and break off all relations if he, Alfred, reminded him of the fable of the fox and the sour grapes.[39] We should not forget that Alfred and Else would have had to rely on Max and Marianne's covering for them in Heidelberg society; a demonstrative breakdown in relations between the brothers would probably have made it difficult for Alfred and Else to appear in society, even in the liberally minded city on the Neckar. Only much later, when the empire collapsed and Edgar was dead, could they afford to live together openly (or, to be more precise, wall to wall).

In the following period Alfred, Edgar and Else came to an arrangement: the marriage continued to exist on the outside, but Else had the freedom to be together with her lover. Max then wrote her an enigmatic letter, which was probably meant as a farewell: it anyway appears to have been the last he sent her for seven years. This letter of 20 June 1910 was scarcely less upsetting than the one of 13 September 1907, but because of its puzzling words it seems not to have been noticed for a long time. It concludes as follows:

> And now, dear Else, since you are very close to your wishes, a few frank words to end with. Naturally I had to dispel Marianne's illusion that we (or I) were *not* able to do certain things. No, you will *always* be allowed to say: 'Didn't you yourself help me?' and I will *never* be so cowardly as to give any other answer than: 'Yes', without my being, like you, under the pressure of *passion* – and, if you command it: 'da capo!'. . . . I have naturally known from the beginning that I, my existence here, and particularly my interference in these matters, would now become *very* irksome for you both – soon for the three of you . . . It's in the nature of things and doesn't disturb my humour. . . . I have known since November of last year that for you this is turning into an 'inability to understand one another' (for I 'understand' you well enough!) – but, much as I 'understand' it, little does it please me. For, as it is now over, your soul is looking for a reason that will give you the 'right' to detest me – and that is an alien body in your generous nature . . . Just as you always need a 'right' – though you don't see it is only a formal *pseudo-right* – in order to be 'allowed' to do what mighty forces irresistibly demand from you. (MWG II/6, 569f.)

In his imaginary dialogue, Else continues to address him as *du*, whereas he reverts to *Sie*. Max Weber often had conversations with an imaginary partner. When Else reproaches him: 'Did you yourself not help me?', this probably means: Did you not then – in Trieste, Venice and subsequently – help to break the taboo that the Weber family had previously placed on my need for physical love? As to Marianne's 'illusion', this must be the idea that Max was psychologically and physically incapable of such an escape from their marriage. But he hints that he would behave in the same way again – not out of inner passion, but as soon as Else commands it. What did he have to reproach Else with? Above all, one supposes, the hypocrisy of outwardly maintaining her marriage with Edgar, instead of building clear and honest relations.

It may seem curious how Weber introduces his theory of science into all this and plays the scholar committed to objectivity free of illusions and self-interest. Empathetic 'understanding', a key concept in Weber's *Verstehende Soziologie*, here becomes a ball to be tossed backwards and forwards in an imaginary game of communication. And then there is the argument about 'right'! 'Mighty forces' in face of which human beings are defenceless do not establish a right – in this sense, Max Weber is not a legal positivist. The source of law lies outside force or power. But was Else not simply following the natural law of love? It seems as if deep down Max Weber was convinced that Else belonged to him by nature rather than to Alfred, and that, precisely in order to suppress this natural destiny, she had to construct a right to detest Max. Probably he was not entirely wrong in believing this. Not only was he incapable of inwardly breaking from Else; her thoughts too continued to revolve around him.

In March 1911 Max Weber made oral reproaches to Else for the last time, but she spurned his interference. Marianne noted in her diary: 'For Max this experience has been unusually meaningful – there must be a feeling that something very pure and beautiful, which he wanted and thought to be possible, has failed to happen! No tender love was sufficient to make his leadership acceptable to E(lse) and A(lfred).'[40] In 1919 Max still remembered the 'terribly angry look' that Else cast at him when they parted.[41] He had wanted to play the leader, but she had rejected his offer. She knew that she had a ruler-like charisma of her own.

In 1910 seven years of love–hate began for Max and Else. It was a condition which, as he later admitted to her, held a certain appeal, even if, like Else at that time, he tried to talk himself into feeling nothing but hate. In the spring of 1919, however, he gave the beloved an assurance: 'Seven years of being an outcast did not manage to erase you from my life or to make you fade in importance. To tell the truth, if you had said just one kind word – "come here, be good" – there would have been no holding back and no standing on ceremony.'[42] But Else too had her pride and her reasons for being angry with Max. She did not open her arms to him again so quickly, but made some concessions to his self-opinionatedness that wound him up even more: yes, he was right, she had shown consideration for her own spiritual 'comfort' and for Alfred's feelings. Marianne thought that peace had finally been made between her husband and Else. No, he corrected her, 'it's not quite like that'. He detected some 'ugly things' in Else's and Alfred's behaviour towards him (MWG II/7–1, 145); he was no longer willing to allow Else a superior right to beauty.

In the spring of 1913, Else and Edgar Jaffé were expected to pass through Ascona – where Max had been advising Else's good friend Frieda Gross in her fight for custody of her son – but they decided to choose a different route, and Max Weber went on a two-day trip to Lake Orta to avoid the possibility of their meeting (MWG II/8, 186). The situation repeated itself the following year, but this time Else really did stop at Ascona – 'after she had been in Naples . . . with Jaffé and his mistress' (Edgar's affairs were by now relaxing the marital tension). Max hid himself in his room until her departure and got Frieda to deny any knowledge of his whereabouts. With Marianne he became indignant about Else's and Alfred's 'ugly and cowardly lack of chivalry', and as in the past he was obsessed with invoking noble values to justify his own conduct (MWG II/8, 594, 597). The pair of lovers made no secret of the fact that they had a quite different explanation for Max's rage, and he became even more furious when they informed him of it.

'I couldn't get drawn into seeing Else', he wrote to Marianne. 'It is not seemly. Basic reasons of chivalry have required her for years to come to me and say: "Is (or *was*) that not so?" As she did not do this, "for the comfort" of her soul, may she now enjoy that comfort. I won't disturb her any more in it, but nor will I pay her attention' (MWG II/8, 608). Not only did he like to play the knight himself, he also expected 'chivalrous' behaviour from her; it made his blood boil that Else avoided conflict with her lover and just wanted to enjoy her 'comfort'. From his later letters to Else, however, we know that he longed for the same thing himself. As he admitted to Frieda Gross in May 1914, he had always known deep down that the 'sensual' Else could do nothing other than act in accordance with her nature and regard his declarations of love as sexual challenges, so that, when she made no further headway with him, she turned in disappointment to his more daring brother. The author of this letter is already the Weber of the *Zwischenbetrachtung*, preoccupied with the tense proximity of brotherly and sexual love to each other. His theoretical reflections would by now have given him the basis for a reconciliation with Else.

Max's later letters to the 'beloved mistress' show how little we should take at face value his disparaging remarks about Else during those years. He knew he could never possess her, but she possessed him. He even found it natural that she would never be able to tell him: 'I am yours' – although

> once again, beloved mistress, you can say to me and of me, 'You are mine', in the most daring senses . . . Because I know from the dark years – ah, yes! – that you and you alone have the power to condemn me to humiliation and torment if you so wish it . . . Therefore, even if you were not so infinitely superior to me in each and every respect, I would still be in your thrall. . . . Believe me, I *know* that even everything that plunged me into uncertain darkness came from the best of you, which is holy to me – from a sense of responsibility and from the chivalrousness of your love, you wondrous child of the gods.[43]

A declaration in the style of a Wagnerian aria. Now Weber finds it a mark of grandeur or 'chivalry' that, in the winter of 1909–10, she did not play along with 'brotherly love' and did not join in Weber's self-deception.

And Else? For her, Max's 'seven years of being an outcast' appeared as 'the period of estrangement, when I often really, really hated him, yet knew that in a world where there was no Max I would not wish to live.' Yet that was just what she had to do when she wrote those lines three weeks after Weber's death – and Alfred recognized that at a deep level of her soul she had always loved Max more than himself (or anyway thought so in her mourning).[44] Now it was the shared memory of Max that tied her especially closely to Alfred, whereas he wanted to step out of his brother's shadow. Already earlier, nine days after Max Weber's death, Else had pondered in a letter to Alfred 'whether the worst wrong I did you was not ten years ago, when I strengthened and stirred up your rejection of Max. If we had found the right way of being completely fair to him, who knows if we would not all have been spared a lot of bitterness? And now you have this feeling of being torn that I understand so well – this wish to mourn the dead in a pure way, which you are now scarcely able to do.'[45] Else's dream was evidently a triangular relationship with the two brothers, in which spiritual and physical love could freely mingle and the intellectual superiority of the one could harmoniously complement the sexual superiority of the other: the dream that Thomas Mann depicted in *The Transposed Heads*. She sensed that Alfred too suffered from the disturbance to their brotherly relations, and that brotherly hatred cast a cloud over his humanity.

Music and love – salvation from the demons

Amazingly, Max appears to have coped perfectly well with Else's hostility in 1910; as far we can make out, the depressive relapses stopped in the autumn of 1909, even if a period of deep disappointment and irritation followed the euphoria of the weeks in Vienna and the Adriatic.[46] Anyway, the irritation did not grow into desperation. For Weber, a man already well into his forties, it must have been an overwhelming feeling that, after he had long given up all hope, the world of sensual pleasure was not closed and his own nature was not utterly ruined. From then on he was like a changed person, no longer experiencing his sexuality as a power detached from spiritual longing. We can imagine how Else, with her experience, had encouraged him to put fewer constraints on his fantasy, even if his new zest for life was still insecure.

Max Weber's more daring sexuality was now looking for a new object. His friendship with the pianist Mina Tobler, who had been introduced to the Weber circle by Emil Lask on 13 June 1909, assumed an intimate character in the summer of 1912. In April 1919, when he ended things with Mina after temporarily playing a double or treble game, he gave Else the impression that Mina had simply been a substitute for her, as Isolde Weisshand was for the real Isolde in Gottfried von Strassburg's *Tristan*.[47] It may have felt a little like that for him; the thought of Else's anger also had something arousing that inwardly bound him to her. Lepsius thinks that the love affair with Mina Tobler, however powerful it may have been, did not have 'an existentially binding character' for Weber; 'the spontaneous force of her love was not capable of knocking him sideways.'[48] Mina, who never permanently tied a man she loved to her, and probably often did not wish to, was not the type of woman to dominate and absorb Weber. But the non-binding lightness of their affair, unburdened by quarrels with an Alfred or Edgar, must have given Weber the kind of carefree pleasure he had never known before.

And Marianne? As far as we know, she did not undergo a crisis this time, although it hardly remained unknown to her that more than a simple friendship was developing between Max and Mina. But *Tobelchen*, as Mina was called in the Weber household, was not an Else-style mistress for Weber – rather a devotee and child-like woman,[49] even if she was already thirty-two in 1912 and was feted by the local press, not as a great artiste but

Figure 13.1 Mina Tobler

as a 'brilliant accompanist' (a role similar to the one she played for Weber).[50] Marianne must have sensed that such a woman was not a danger to her marriage and even relieved some of the tension in it; nor did her female instincts let her down. Only Bertha Schandau, the Webers' prudish and temperamental housekeeper, who got to hear about everything, treated Mina in such a way that Weber threatened to hound her out of the house if she did not stop being 'stupid' and show 'exemplary friendship' towards her (MWG II/7-2, 665; II/8, 224f.).

At first Marianne seems to have been a little sharp at times with Mina – for example, when she referred to her lover at that time, the philosopher Emil Lask (whom Marianne also liked), by punning on *Beziehung* [relationship], *Bezüge* [connections] and *Bettbezügen* [duvet covers, but literally 'bed connections'], so that 'the whole thing crystallized in the idea that bed and relationship usually went together', and *Tobelchen* was even 'proud' of this insinuation.[51] On 21 January 1911, however, Marianne wrote in her diary that Mina Tobler came 'really close' to her 'for the first time' when she poured her heart out and painfully admitted that Lask's love for her had 'waned'. Marianne felt 'profoundly shaken to the core' that she was unable to help as Mina told of her 'deep yearning for a higher love'. 'The erotic again became so hugely important that for me too any other possession seemed to pall by comparison.' Once more we see Marianne stirred by the erotic movement around her.

The deserted Mina was a different case from Else, who gave her men their marching orders. For Mina, *Tristan* symbolized the 'tragedy of the finitude of love'. In the summer of 1912, the Wagnerian opera gave Mina and Max a framework in which to legitimate their love aesthetically and to raise it to the level of myth, after the two had gone with Marianne to a performance in Munich on 13 August. As Marianne wrote beforehand to Helene, Mina had been 'wild' with joy at the prospect during the previous year; 'she made us familiar with the music from *Tristan*'. Early in 1911, in fact, Marianne noted that the pianist 'always leads a pure dream-life alongside her real life'.

The disenchanter and the 'sorcerer': Max Weber and Richard Wagner

On the day after the performance, Marianne tells us, all three were 'still reeling from the impact of *Tristan* – probably the loftiest and most powerful transfiguration there can ever be of the "earthly" = *erotic* . . . an intoxicating liquor. Fräulein Tobler, who was hearing it for the twelfth time and knew every word and note, was so worked up before that one could really fear she would die Isolde's *Liebestod* herself.' On the other hand, she had been rather critical of the production of *Parsifal* they had seen immediately before in Bayreuth;[52] Wagner's late 'festival piece', which mystically exalts the renunciation of sensual love, did not fit the mood of Mina and Max, and 'not for a moment did they (including Marianne) have the sensation of religious devotion' (WB 502). With the chaste Parsifal in mind, but in a conscious misunderstanding of Wagner, Weber more than once repeated the shallow sexual naturalism of the botanist Georg Albrecht Klebs: 'If someone comes into the world as a eunuch, it is no wonder that nothing happens to him' (WzG 246). At the same time, he told Gundolf and Honigsheim that he wanted to write something one day against 'Wagnerian pan-eroticism' (which he never did) (WzG 247).

The pompous Wagner cult in the Heidelberg circle around art historian Henry Thode (to whom Wagner was related by marriage) was in Weber's eyes an intellectual emetic. When, two thousand years after the 'mystery of Bethlehem', the heavens again took pity on wretched humanity and the snow-white dove of the Holy Spirit once more settled on the dark earth – so begins Thode's lecture on Wagner – the 'mystery of Bayreuth' was born (WzG 246). Weber recognized that he had a 'very ambivalent relationship' to Wagner, the 'great wizard' (MWG II/7-2, 638) – no wonder! Tristan and Parsifal: he observed in Wagner and in himself a sense of being pulled hither and thither in relation to erotic love. His love–hate for Wagner corresponded to his love–hate for Nature and Eros – and for himself.

In any event, Weber's relationship to Wagner does not seem to have been that of a scholar, even if he would have liked to pour out his flow of thoughts on humanity as simultaneously as Wagner did with his huge orchestra (B 482f.);[53] in Weber's musicology Wagner does not even make an appearance. On this issue a regular dispute broke out in 1969 between Hideharu Ando (a Japanese scholar who wished to study this aspect of Weber 'very scientifically') and the 95-year-old Else Jaffé. 'No, no', she protested, 'I would not call it scientific, you know. . .'[54] And indeed she knew better, as did Mina Tobler. Certainly the values conveyed by Wagner's operas were Weber's values without the scholarly analysis: love, honour, noble-mindedness, salvation, willingness to die . . . and tension maintained *ad infinitum*, unresolved dissonance.

In the beginning was *Tristan*: no, the idea is probably much too romantic. Months before, on 1 June 1912, Mina wrote with four exclamation marks to her mother: 'I content myself as in the past with other women's husbands!!!!'[55] To be sure, Marianne did not buy this philosophy of the single life: she thought that Mina concealed her longing for marriage 'behind the theory that she was too good' for it. 'So, a lot remains unredeemed in her'; 'it's terrible that there's no man for her – she is as if made for love and making people happy, and everyone likes her!'[56]

At that time Marianne was no longer capable of energetically resisting the natural power of love, or of seriously blaming her husband if, after so many years of torment, he once more gave free rein to his need for love. After the *Tristan* experience she herself felt 'really on edge', in such a 'state of turmoil' or spiritual intoxication that she was incapable of artistic enjoyment.[57] Curiously, the sadistic eroticism of *Salome* had a great effect on her in Paris in 1911; it was 'a stirring of all the senses to an exhilaration more artistic than sensual! The shape of naked shameless elemental desire. . . . Salome was . . . a little vulgar, yet her well-formed desires were like the screaming of wild animals in the forest . . . and this in contrast to the prophet!!'[58] Marianne did not experience natural animal desire as either perverse or disgusting. We see how little the deeply resigned Marianne of 1950, who lives on in the memory as a caricature of pleasure-denying prudishness, can be equated with the Marianne of that period before the First World War. One also suspects that the scenography of *Salome* was a backdrop to Weber's *Zwischenbetrachtung*: the confrontation, rising to deadly tension, between the prophet's baritone and the erotic soprano voice of Salome, whose longing for love degenerates into bloodlust at the sight of the uncompromising ascetic. Max Weber saw *Salome* again in Berlin: 'The audience left silently, in a state of shock, as if caught at some evil deed. Six people and myself turned up the applause' (MWG II/7-1, 60).

Marianne noted in amazement how, in the days following the performance of *Tristan* in Munich, her husband's customary reluctance to go for a walk seemed to have vanished, as in the early days of his love for Else: 'He runs like a hunting-dog and looks around and cannot get enough . . . *Tobelchen* is naturally "in raptures" for him . . .' Max and Marianne spoke 'nearly all the time about her and her various experiences': Mina drove away the eternal topic of Else and gave Marianne some much-needed relief. It is true that Mina's 'sparkle' reminded her of Else, but she was 'not so lively and articulate'. Marianne seemed to have no problems with her husband's new friendship: 'I am glad that in her Max has again found a friend to refresh him';[59] 'again', after his break with Else. But, when she wrote at the end of the year that Mina again seemed 'to be in a calmer state (*qui* [sic] *lo sa?*)' towards Max, and that this made their 'life together more uninhibited again',[60] we feel that Marianne's relationship with Mina – who would be surprised? – had meanwhile become inhibited.

Eros routinized and regularized

Nevertheless, with Marianne's approval, *Tobelchen* obtained and took advantage of her status as a 'legitimate' concubine, on the clear understanding that she did not wish to be more than Number Two. Saturday now became *Tobelchen*'s day. In *Economy and Society* Weber refers to the 'much-discussed phenomenon . . . that certain formalities were sometimes required for the marriage with secondary wives while the marriage with the chief wife might be entered into without any formalities' (E&S 673). The period about which we are talking was probably the one in his life when he had the greatest euphoria for work. Marianne had to get rid of many visitors, and once again it was 'difficult to reconcile work and life'. 'But *Tobelchen* gets her regular share, with nothing subtracted; she even makes sure of it with a priceless self-assurance.'[61] Occasionally Marianne developed her own philosophy of triangular living, modelled on Else's. When *Tobelchen* played the piano, Max and Marianne would sit holding hands on the sofa.[62] On the subject of an academic ball, Mina wrote to her mother: 'I chose the better part – to stay on the sofa next to Max from 7 to 10 – while Marianne was dancing.'[63]

Whereas Else later remained silent about her relations with Max Weber, Mina proudly declared: 'Max Weber loved me.' She had the sense of a fulfilled love and felt like a widow after Max's death. When he entered – she recalled later – it was as if 'a mountain were coming through the door'. In her eyes, Marianne was a 'blue stocking'; Max clearly needed love, and he got it from her, Mina: it was the most natural thing in the world; there was no moral problem involved.[64] '*I had a good time of it again*', she wrote in February 1914 with quite significant underlining; 'that is, a couple of extra little bits of togetherness' – which presupposed a regular cycle of togetherness. Sometimes Max does not come 'for an astonishingly long time, but then he always stays longer than one hopes for in one's wildest dreams! He is able to cope better every week in the world he has trod so little, and it is wonderfully moving to see how he now masters it with all the power and depth of his being.'[65]

Mina could feel herself to be the redemptress of a great man, for whom Eros had hitherto been an alien world. On reading *The Protestant Ethic*, she had a clear sense that, although the author made himself 'invisible', 'everything inside it inadvertently pulsates with the heart-beat of a great all-round personality'.[66] Once Weber read to her Rilke's *Requiem*, which he had read once before to Else; then the two of them spent 'a long time more' beside Mina's 'red lamp':[67] not appropriate lighting when one is *reading* together. Unlike the last time, Rilke's *Requiem* evidently did not spread an aura of renunciatory, celestial love. But, when Mina showed Max a picture of a baby, she must have 'confessed, without wishing to, that he had not proved worthy of the privilege by claiming that all little children looked alike and that human beings only began for him when they reached seven! Did I give him a piece of my mind!'[68]

The zeal with which Max fought in Ascona for Frieda Gross-Schloffer's custody rights over her son made Mina suspicious and not a little jealous. Did Max fall in love with this seductive woman, who, as Mina knew, had as few sexual inhibitions as she had herself? In May 1913 Max reported to her how he had met in Ascona a female supporter of free love with whom he had been acquainted before, and how, in referring to Freud, she had used a 'fine sentence' that must have reminded him of Otto Gross: 'Every unfulfilled relationship between man and woman is filth.' Of a professor's wife who had many 'intense' but only literary relations with young men, she said: 'a hog might dread that kind of relationship'. This confirmed Weber in his view that erotomaniacs cultivate their own kind of intolerant moralism. He 'drily replied: that may be so, but a hog is no authority.'[69]

For her thirty-fourth birthday on 24 June 1914 Weber gave Mina a copy of Gottfried Keller's autobiographical novel *Der grüne Heinrich*, on the title page of which he had written the notes of the St John's Day motif from *Die Meistersinger von Nürnberg*, Wagner's only love theme free of tragedy: in fact, the 24th of June is St John's Day! Writing to Lili Schäfer, he was in raptures over the 'humanly very beautiful *Johannisnacht* (St John's Night) and *Johannistrieb* ('lammas shoot') scenes'[70] – where *Johannisnacht* is a Freudian slip for *Johannistag*, and the lamma shoot stands for the joys of love reawakening at an advanced age. Even the outbreak of war did not interrupt the relationship. As a Swiss citizen, Mina belonged to a neutral foreign country; but she remained in Heidelberg, her heart on the German side, and felt indignant at the shrill Germanophobia abroad that had been spreading to Switzerland. Max, now an officer at the military hospital, seemed to her even more attractive than before. 'You should see him in uniform! . . . One would never like to see him dressed differently. Everyone turns to look at him in the street. The best are the boots, or the real knee-height gaiters. His magnificent stature then reveals itself . . .'[71] (The young Hans Staudinger, on the other hand, began to laugh when he saw Weber in uniform, causing him to get angry.)[72] The fact that no grenade splinters would threaten the new soldierly-masculine splendour meant that the woman's pleasure could remain unsullied.

When Mina's brother died in June 1915, she had a good cry on Weber's shoulder – and this too made him 'happy'.[73] There is no mention of any tears over Emil Lask, who passed away on the same day. In November 1915 Weber gave her a copy of Goethe's *Werther*, with a dedication drawn from the poet's *Pandora*: '*Ach ihr Götter, warum ist alles unendlich Alles, Alles – endlich unser*

Glück nur!' [Ah, ye gods, why is all infinite, absolutely all – only our happiness finite!] Was he hinting that sooner or later he would want to end their relationship? But a formal separation from Mina came only at the height of his new love for Else, on 15 March 1919; and even then he idolized her again as a child-woman, looking back at 'that strong sparkling magnificent bath of beauty and love which you ran for me, incomparable child', something 'never experienced before'.[74] Nor was the separation definitive.[75] Mina even made friends with Else, but she could not live with the knowledge that Else had in a sense been Weber's first.

Weber's view of the world and life, which had already taken a jolt from Else, became totally muddled as a result of Mina. When the Radbruchs' marriage broke up in spring 1913 because of Lina Radbruch's relationship with Emil Lask, Weber refused to go along with the young Karl Jaspers's moral condemnation of the couple and his ending of relations with Lask. Weber depicted Eros as a force of nature that turned even an otherwise fine and kindly man into a 'beast', who knew neither honour nor fraternity when anyone stood in the way of his instincts. Lask's conduct was 'unfortunately almost a child's game in comparison with other things I have experienced' (MWG II/8, 239f.). He knew that Lask had brought Mina to him, that it was Lask's inconstancy which had left her open to an erotic relationship with the professor sixteen years older than herself; how then could he be seriously angry with him?

In many respects Mina was more suited than Else to be Weber's muse. Else was not a child-woman but a mistress, who tempted him into pleasurable submission rather than autonomous activity. She, the erstwhile factory inspector, did not, as far we know, inspire any of Weber's ideas in the study of labour, nor did she probably want to, whereas Mina, the pianist, did inspire him in his sociology of music and help him to bring out the musical sense lying inside him. It is true that in 1878 Fritz Baumgarten reported of a hike with the fourteen-year-old Max Weber and the ten-year-old Alfred: 'Max simply won't sing, but Alfred is an enthusiastic singer. You won't soon find two brothers as fundamentally different as these two' (WB 49); and Marianne did not add anything to correct this assertion. But Else found Max 'very musical': 'When he went for a walk, he might be singing some little song'; and he could even 'sing well'.[76] Even his favourite sister Klara reported that, in her days as a schoolgirl, when the two of them played at being lovers, he 'whistled all the themes from the operas of Richard Wagner' (B 482). There was something liberating about song; Max evidently needed a touch of eroticism to overcome his inhibitions also in the sphere of music.[77]

Else was later either unable or unwilling to consider that Mina had had something to offer in 'music theory'; all she had done was play for him, mostly Chopin.[78] Mina always found it 'a waste of time' when she spoke in Weber's presence, because she wanted to listen to him as much as possible, but the roles became different as soon as she sat at the piano. In the hard years Weber had sold his piano to Robert Michels, apparently without pining for it too much afterwards; but in 1911 he acquired a 'very fine Steinway piano' – a birthday present for Marianne, by the way! – which became a kind of symbol for the change in his life that he eagerly set about using (MWG II/7-1, 253). A visitor around that time reported that, when Weber invited people to a lecture on the 'sociology of music' (or perhaps it was really 'sociology of muses'?), he 'greatly surprised us' by sitting at the piano and 'demonstrating points from the theory of harmony'; and 'from then on there were the most unexpected things'. 'He's never done anything more phenomenal, we said afterwards' (B 483n.).

Discovery of the power of rationalization in music

The rationalization of modern Western music under the influence of the piano – a new variation on the close link between technology and culture – became a central theme in Weber's sociology of music. In 'Der Sinn der Wertfreiheit' he wrote: 'The discovery of the piano, one of the most important technical bearers of modern development and its propagation in the bourgeoisie, was rooted in the distinctive indoor character of North European culture' (WL 522). This was not necessarily an advantage for a lover of the sunny South – here too Weber remained deliberately value-free. To be sure, there is technological progress in music as there is in art generally (WL 519f.), but this is not identical with progress in human perception – on the contrary. The piano's enforced tonal conformity deadens the much finer sense of hearing given to man by nature. This idea, derived from Hermann von Helmholtz,[79] was so important to Weber that he repeated and strengthened it in the introduction to his sociology of religion (PE 14).

On 5 August 1912, in a letter to his sister Lili that is the most important testimony on his writings on music, Max Weber announced:

> I shall probably write something on the history of music. That is, only on certain social conditions which explain why only we have 'harmonic music', although other cultures display a much sharper sense of hearing and a much more intense musical culture. Strange! – this is the work of monasticism, as will become clear. (MWG II/7-2, 639)

This is one of the earliest records of Weber's concern with the special Western path in world history; we can see the path-breaking importance of the study of music, which at first seems to be such an isolated part of his work. He thought he knew in advance what he would find: medieval monasticism as the origin of modern Western culture. It was no longer Puritanism that had brought the great change. But Weber never discussed in detail the significance of monasticism for music, despite the fact that his trips to Italy would have afforded him the best insight into it.

On 12 May 1912, several months before the *Tristan* experience with Mina, Marianne reported to Helene that at the previous Sunday's meeting of the Eranos circle Max had spoken for a full two and a half hours 'like a waterfall about the most difficult questions of musical theory and their connection with economic and sociological questions'. 'People nearly drowned in the flood, and in the end I had to save them and the waiting asparagus by making a grab for power.'[80] The sequence of events leads one to suspect that Weber's experience of love was not the origin of his preoccupation with music; rather, that his excursion into the history of music helped to open him up for the relationship with Mina Tobler and to create a scholarly justification for their being together. 'Like a waterfall', Marianne wrote: a lot of water had indeed been rushing forward, ready to pour over the top. Even more than before, his bursts of productivity appeared as natural events, and in his written output ideas came thick and fast, often without paragraphs or other aids to the reader.

Weber wrote his essay on music without a commission and without any expectation that it would soon be published in the *Archiv*; he evidently felt it as an inner need, and the resulting manuscript, hard to decipher even for his lady-friends, was not in his view ready for publication. It appeared only after his death and for a time became an appendix to *Economy and Society*; but until recently it received scant attention from Weber scholars, if they understood it at all. When he submitted a resumé of his interpretation of music history to the committee of the Verein für Sozialpolitik – as evidence that it was possible 'to operate in a completely value-free manner' with the concept of progress – he met with incomprehension and a shaking of heads (B 482f.). But in the 1920s the Soviet commissar of culture Anatoly Lunacharsky hailed the text as a model of an (at least rudimentary) 'materialist' conception of art, which interpreted the development of music on the basis of the immanent dialectic of the musical material.[81]

This work is anyway quite different from what is today understood as 'sociology of music'.[82] It is true that its original title was 'Die soziologischen Bedingungen der Musik',[83] but what interests Weber is not all the social aspects of the music business – sponsors, producers, audiences – or even the context in the history of ideas, but rather the music itself, its substance. And the question that he thinks is worth the trouble of asking in relation to music is not how far it reflects social relations, but how it leads to something new in history – a process that cannot be explained by any logic of developmental laws.

In *Economy and Society* Weber notes that 'every sort of intoxication . . . inevitably culminates in physical collapse'; whereas the 'perpetual equitableness' of Greek *sophrosyne*, prudence, tolerated 'only the purely musical, rhythmically engendered forms of *ekstasis*' (E&S 539). Music reconciles ecstasy with spirit and lends it duration. It is for Weber one of the greatest primal life-forces, originally wedded both to eroticism (as an element of orgiastic dance) and to religion. Through the increasing rationalization of human existence – today we would say: its differentiation into sectors – 'the religiosity of brotherliness' enters into 'the deepest inner tensions' with art and sexuality, 'the strongest irrational power of personal life'. 'Religion and art are intimately related in the beginning. That religion has been an inexhaustible spring for artistic expressions is evident from the existence of idols and icons of every variety, and from the existence of music as a device for arousing ecstasy or for accompanying exorcism, . . . [from] the artistic activities of . . . sacred bards, as well as the creation of temples and churches (the greatest of artistic productions).' But, with these expressions, art develops laws of its own and eventually comes to face religious-ethical values as a counter-world (E&S 607f.). In fact, in the *fin de siècle* through which Weber had been passing, this was the case to a greater extent than ever before in the history of the West.

Tension does not mean total opposition, however – on the contrary. 'Subjectively, there is an easy way back to art . . . (and) most readily to song and music' from 'every mystic religion of love that culminates in a transcendence of individuality' (E&S 609). The nexus joining art, religion and Eros did not exist only in times of old, but is also there today, at least as an opportunity, rooted indeed in a trans-temporal human psyche. Weber, being in need of an aesthetic legitimation of Else-style sexuality, thought of art and especially music as one of the dimensions of existence with which he wished to be spiritually imbued; his little treatise on music was meant to be the prelude to something larger, a 'sociology embracing all the arts' (WB 500) – but he would not have the time for it.

The text of the sociology of music, overloaded as it is with highly detailed points, indicates that Weber must have spent a long time collecting material and pondering over it. Once again, the lesser academic cannot get over his astonishment that Weber seems to know everything about the historical hierarchy of instruments: that the lute-player in Queen Elizabeth's orchestra was paid three times more than the violinist, and five times more than the bagpipe-player (M 69). It was from music that Weber now took the concept of *virtuoso* and transferred it to religion: he began to examine every expression of religiosity, to see whether it was assignable to the laity or to 'virtuosi'. The conceptual crossing of disciplinary boundaries is one of Weber's specialities.

It may seem paradoxical that, under the impact of his experience of love, Weber committed to paper what Eduard Baumgarten called one of his most 'refractory' pieces of work (B 482). Is this conclusive proof that in Weber life and work were not coherently joined together after all? Often, however, the connection between the two was not as direct as in Goethe, for example, for whom the love poem followed the experience of love; the link in Weber is typically more hidden, more tense and dialectical, but therefore also more exciting. It is unthinkable that love would have sent him into public raptures: his scholarly work was based on the cold shower principle; he was at his most sober precisely on subjects most heavily charged with emotion – in this he took a demonstrative distance from someone like Lamprecht.

On the CD-ROM edition of Weber's works, the term *Rationalisierung* appears no fewer than 455 times: most frequently (forty-six times) – one will be amazed – in his study of music. Here he developed, earlier and more consistently than elsewhere, the concept that he further deployed in the *Wirtschaftsethik der Weltreligionen*: rationalization combined with technology as the kernel of the West's special path in world history.[84] In Weber 'rationalization' means a methodical striving for rule-bound order; it has little to do with 'rationality' in the sense of reason; rather, it is 'highly ambiguous' (*höchst vieldeutig*).[85] Only this made it possible for Weber to arrive at the concept of rationalization through music of all things; it was here, in this unexpected context, rather than much earlier in his study of the stock exchange, for example, that he discovered the ubiquitousness of rationalization.[86] Unlike Kant, Weber did not think that natural reason was inborn in man: he mocked, in a letter to Mina Tobler, the 'utterly naive and childish belief in the power of the rational'.[87] On the other hand, he held the view that man strives by nature to bring order into his affairs, routine into his conduct; Weber found some form of rationalization everywhere, even in the magical rites of supposedly 'primitive peoples'. There is also something instinctual in rationalization. Weber's concept is related to the idea of rationalization in psychoanalysis, which Ernest Jones introduced in 1908:[88] that is, a procedure which gives a (visually, logically or morally) acceptable form to inherently irrational conduct.

From today's viewpoint, too, it seems that Weber – who knew from antiquity the close relationship between music and mathematics – was on the right track in underlining the rational element in the evolution of music. It is only for lay persons, not virtuosi, that music consists entirely of mood and feeling; a Richard Wagner had a masterful understanding of how to calculate his musical effects. Already in the Carolingian age, the Frankish monk Hucbald taught that consonance was 'the calculated and harmonious mixture of two notes'; and from then on *organizatio* became the accepted term for musical composition.[89] When Max Weber connected harmony and rationalization with each other, he was following ancient sources: knowledge was of fundamental importance; rationality and emotion were not opposites. For the musically minded Karl Löwenstein, the ideas about music that Weber aired on 'one of those glorious Heidelberg June evenings' were 'a wonderful and . . . decisive revelation'; when he went home from the Webers' villa he was 'literally drunk'. 'It was a turning point in my life', he recalled. 'From that moment on, I had taken the oath of fealty to him; I had become his vassal.'[90] Visitors who understood nothing of musical theory, however, were 'completely dazed and perplexed' by Weber's latest sally (B 483n.).

Music history and the natural human predisposition for music: Weber and Helmholtz

Weber developed his ideas about music chiefly through an encounter with the work of Hermann von Helmholtz, who in 1863, during his Heidelberg period, published an extensive *Lehre von den Tonempfindungen, als physiologische Grundlage für die Theorie der Musik*,[91] which he had conceived as a 'bold and adventurous attempt to push scientific method into the domain of aesthetics'.[92] Already in 1857, in Beethoven's city of Bonn, he had given a popular lecture on the physiological causes of musical harmony,[93] but the *Tonlehre* of 1863 was truly a *magnum opus* of the distinguished scientist, who – with a background in medicine – had made the physiological-psychological foundations of human sense-perception a lifelong focus of his work. He worked for seven years on his theory of music, conducted experiments with the support of the Steinway piano manufacturer and came up with 'ever more surprises', but 'scientific analysis (caused him) to lose any capacity to enjoy music'.[94]

Helmholtz proved that a melody, resulting from the vibrations of resonant bodies in the air, consists of a keynote and a series of harmonic tones.[95] Harmony is thus already structured into acoustic perception, so that the development of music consists in the unfolding of a human physiological predisposition. The subject was a hot potato at that time, when there was so much controversy surrounding materialism and naturalism. Wagner's Siegfried imitated bird song, while Wagner's opponent Eduard Hanslick spiritedly argued against the notion that harmony and melody were already part of the animal world: 'It is not the voices of beasts but their entrails which are important to us, and the animal to which music owes the most is not the nightingale but the sheep.'[96]

Helmholtz's physiological reductionism aroused Weber's opposition. As we have seen in other instances, however, Weber was the kind of thinker who takes a lot especially from those with whom he most finds fault. Between the lines of the score we can detect a fascination for Helmholtz, who had the greatest reputation as a scientist in Weber's day and had at one time taught in Heidelberg (even if, as Weber knew, he had been 'an appalling lecturer' (MWG I/17, 78)). Weber himself argued against Helmholtz 'on a strictly naturalistic basis'; he referred to 'the analysis of Patagonian phonogrammes' – then truly exotic material for a German humanities scholar – in order to register his doubts about the 'panharmonic' assumption that 'any melodics, even a primitive one, ultimately consists of dissected chords'. After all, how could someone like Max Weber believe in an all-embracing natural harmony?

On the other hand, harmonization and rationalization did go together for him; and he perceived a tendency to rules and order everywhere in the world. He did not think the issue closed in principle: on the contrary, he remarked that in the present state of knowledge there was no general answer to the 'most interesting question in the end', namely, 'to what extent "natural" tonal affinity as such has operated as an element in dynamic development' (M 22).[97] Natural human hearing, tonal vibrations, striving for 'rationalization': for Weber, all this does not add up by itself to form harmony; on the contrary, the dynamic of music springs from the tensions that arise out of the striving for harmony. The 'chord rationalization of music' lives 'in constant tension with the melodic realities . . ., which it is never capable of totally devouring' (M 9).

The ear of modern Western man has been aligned and deadened by the organ and piano, machine-like instruments with major chords; it cannot be equated with natural human hearing, any more than the history of Western music under the influence of instrumental technique can be interpreted as an unfolding of man's natural predisposition to harmony. The progress of instrumental technique does not bring about a higher development of human sense-perception – quite the contrary. But it does expand tonal possibilities. On the 'crutch' of musical instruments, tone formation initially takes 'great steps' that the human voice would not have achieved by itself; yodelling 'probably came into being through the influence of a horn instrument' (M 25) and is by no means a primal or natural sound. In the beginning, then, was technical innovation! In the *Zwischenbetrachtung*, Weber calls instrumental music the 'purest form', which is capable of becoming an 'irresponsible *Ersatz* for primary religious experience' (FMW 342f.).

This does not mean, however, that there is no natural human predisposition at all for tonal perception, or that it does not still operate in the modern musical sensibility. Weber warns against 'thinking of primitive music as a chaos of arbitrary irregularity' (WzG 452). He notes more than once 'that even peoples whose music completely lacks our kind of tonality . . . usually accept at least the major key triad as "beautiful" ', although they do not enjoy it in quite the same way as Westerners (M 42). The spread of Western harmonies around the world, which was not yet foreseeable in Weber's time, does indeed indicate that they contain something appealing to the human ear.

If Weber rejected a purely physiological explanation for the emergence of harmony in music, and if instead, basing himself on new ethnological findings from the Wedda of Sri Lanka to the Wanjamwesi of former German East Africa, he emphasized the West's special development of harmony, this does not mean that he replaced a naturalist with an idealist account, but that he focused on the significance of musical notation and mechanical instruments for the rationalization process in Western music, together with the methodical conduct of life that first took shape in the monasteries (M 52ff.). Nor did Weber forget to mention the 'creation of resonant bodies' as the condition for harmony. He seems to have thought, with some reason, that this was a 'purely Western invention': 'Working with wooden board and all the finer crafts of carpentry and veneering are more common among Northern peoples than in the East' (M 66). The argument is not conclusive, as it is not unusual for a fine art of woodwork to develop precisely where wood is expensive and in short supply.

It seems strange today that Weber continually equated 'modern' with 'harmonic' music; his modernity evidently began with the Renaissance. He did not address the fact that European music in his own age, since Wagner's *Tristan und Isolde*, was beginning to leave the ground of harmony; this would have been rather inconvenient for his concept of Western rationalization. Only occasionally did he touch on 'tone-destroying phenomena in our musical development';[98] and he saw them not as a musical revolution underpinning a new modernity, but as the 'product of affectedly baroque, mannered aestheticism and intellectualistic gourmandise' (M 58). He may even have been right from a sociological point of view!

Art: also a road to salvation

Richard Wagner announced a gospel of salvation through art and love. Such dreams were in the air in the age of Jugendstil and lifestyle reform: we can still discern them today in the art of that time. In the final years before the First World War, Max Weber's thoughts were also moving in that direction – which is one reason why his conversations with Georg Lukács (1885–1971) had a 'special magic' for him.[99] For Lukács's thinking revolved around binding obligations and the redemptive power of art,[100] before he completed the turn to communism under the impact of the world war and renounced his previous work as an expression of bourgeois decadence.

Lukács, who would become notorious in his Stalinist period for fighting the bugbear of 'formalism' (to be specific, the literary modernists), was reflecting in 1910 on the form of beauty. Later sociologists would be ready with the answer: beauty is a social convention. Not so the early Lukács: for him, beauty existed *before* the art connoisseur's judgement.[101] His seemingly banal question: 'There are works of art – how are they possible?' fascinated Max Weber, who was trying to find bases for the autonomy of beauty. Lukács spoke of the 'Luciferianism of art':[102] if not divine in origin, then demonic. 'When I have been talking with Lukács', Weber admitted, 'I have things to think about for days' (WzG 187). There was scarcely anyone else he said that about. Nor does Lukács seem to have paid him similar compliments in return; his main interest in Weber was probably as a way of approaching Windelband, for the purposes of his *Habilitation* diploma.[103] In fact, he was more enthusiastic about Georg Simmel;[104] but Simmel was not a full professor and was unwilling to read the young Hungarian's manuscript.

Weber was especially impressed by one of the young Lukács's essays, in which – to quote Marianne Weber – 'the creative power of love that brings about salvation is conceded the right to break through the ethical norm' (WB 466). In his *Heidelberger Ästhetik* Lukács taught that a form is already contained in experience;[105] the experience of love is capable of art and possesses a potential of its own. We can often assume that, in the time of peace before the First World War, 'experience' was thought of mainly as amatory experience; only after the outbreak of war was there a radical change in its associations. This alone allows us to understand the conclusion of the letter that Weber wrote to Lukács in March 1913:

I am eager to see how it will be when your concept of *form* emerges. After all, 'formed life' is not *only* the *value*-containing (*das Werthafte*)

Figure 13.2 Georg Lukács, 1911

element that rises 'above' the experiential, but also the *erotic* element that dips into the deep and outermost corners of the 'dungeon' in 'formed life' as well. It shares the fate of the guilt-laden with all formed life; and in the quality of its opposition to everything that belongs to the sphere of the 'form alien' [*formfremd*] God it is close to the aesthetic attitude. Its topographical position has yet to be determined, and I am quite curious to see *where* it is going to be located in your work.[106]

'Curious' twice over! Lukács had spoken of the 'dungeon of individuality', from which he tried to break free by surrendering first to love and later to the communist movement. Max Weber must also have thought of the 'iron cage' in which the Puritan-capitalist ethic locked souls doomed to solitary work. In the form of beauty, however, the 'erotic' seeped into the dungeon. When Weber reflects on the power of form, what he has in mind is Eros.

Body history: from corpulence to a trimmer sense of self

The redeeming turn in Weber's life brought with it a new era in his body history. As we have seen, Marianne Weber was aware of the significance of bodily phases for her husband's mental development. After his death she

wrote about 'Max's shape and his way of moving', which in wistful retrospect appeared better than in his lifetime:

> Already in his younger years he defended his girth, against which I
> waged a constant battle, as the form that God had intended for him.
> But as a result of the wartime diet, he became as slim and elastic as a
> boy and began to feel glad about it. . . . His gestures when talking
> (were) wonderfully graceful and expressive, sculptural. . . . Even more
> striking was the delicateness of his ankles and feet: they seemed almost
> too small to bear his large body, and he sometimes blamed on their
> tender condition his clumsiness in all physical exercise and his suscep-
> tibility to fatigue when out for a walk. But his gait was springy and
> graceful, and he sometimes boasted that in his army days, despite
> weighing more than 100 kilos (against 83 in recent years), he found
> marches easier to bear than did his slimmer and better-trained com-
> rades. Later, long walks were not his thing – he became terribly weary
> if he went for a walk during his illness, and as a convalescent he would
> ride for years to the library. On trips . . . he would always use a car –
> otherwise he got no pleasure out of it.

She crossed out a sentence she had begun after that: 'I was often worried
by this completely sedentary . . .'[107] It is not difficult to imagine a continuation, or to understand his wife's concern. The fact that for years Weber
avoided the short walk through the old town to the Heidelberg library
testifies to a near-pathological immobility. He had gone hiking in his youth,
but by the summer of 1899 he was warning the equally exhausted Alfred
not only against any intellectual activity but also against 'any forced physical movement'. 'I now know the incredible harm it did to me.'[108] Really?
His later erotic relationships got him back on his feet, much to Marianne's
surprise, but he never became a great walker, not to speak of a real hiker.
Unlike his brother Alfred, who in 1913 sent a message to the 'Free German
Youth' assembled in the Hoher Meissner massif in northern Hesse,[109] he
remained untouched by the new zest for life of the Wandervogel movement.

Marianne records that her husband finally grew slimmer only during the
war years: she sees them as purely beneficial, without mentioning that a
poor diet left people more susceptible to disease, including the kind of lung
infection from which he died. By contrast, Max's earlier time in the army
had seen him reach a peak of corpulence; he then identified with his portly
shape, although Marianne never liked it. But then his illness changed how
he related to his corporeal being; he no longer thought that a benevolent
God had intended his natural shape to be as it was.

Max Weber's life crisis was not least a lifestyle crisis, and he experienced
it as such. This is apparent from his later side-swipes at the alcoholism of
student fraternities, as well as from his frequent experiments with vegetarianism. When he became enslaved to sleep-inducing drugs, though he had no
illusions about the damage they caused, he probably cut down drastically on

his alcohol consumption, especially as the merriment of the old Heidelberg wine culture became alien to him during the years of depression. When people drink less with meals, they usually eat less as well: so it was with Weber, who grew 'thin and pale' (WB 239). Only on the ocean steamer, when he slept 'without assistance' and tucked in alongside the opulent diners, did he put on weight again and, no doubt to Marianne's regret, cease to look handsome. Other periods of weight loss followed, however, even before the war.

Vegetarianism and lifestyle reform

As a student, serviceman and young professor, Weber was proud of being able to hold his drink and felt that uninhibited high-living was a mark of ancient German manhood. In keeping with a common perception of the time, he observed that the relatively low ratio of potatoes to meat in the diet of East Elban agricultural workers was an important indicator of their improved lifestyle. Whether it was healthy to eat so much meat was not yet a question that many people asked; excessive meat consumption was anyway the least of the problems facing those workers. After Weber fell ill, however, he began his experiments with vegetarianism, partly to aid digestion. 'We live here very poetically on strawberries and vegetables and therefore have a healthy digestion', Marianne wrote in 1901 to Helene from Rome.[110] In March 1902, at their lodgings in Florence, the Webers were at first served a lot of meat and few vegetables, and Marianne thought that, unlike in Rome, the 'high meat consumption' was not good for her husband; 'but, after a few hints with the tulip stem, vast amounts of vegetables were dished up and we again noticed that the whole of humanity eats only half as much as we.'[111] So, the increased vegetarian element in their diet did not at first mean a reduction in quantity – though, as we shall see, it certainly did later.

   In the summer of 1903, by now studiously intent on economies, Weber grew angry at the high restaurant prices in Scheveningen and went instead to an 'excellent' and good-value vegetarian eatery in The Hague, 'of the kind established in all cities by the local vegetarian association': no pressure to drink wine, 'no tips – for 50–60 cents one lives on asparagus, rhubarb and *sinasappels* (oranges), and thus bilks the gang out of its exorbitant prices' (WB 269). Weber did not seem to miss meat – at least not when there were special vegetarian menus. Whereas he otherwise almost never reported what he ate, we learn that at the Pomona in The Hague he dined on 'sorrel with raisins or leeks or baked white beans or endives or apricot risotto or onion puree'.[112] Elsewhere too he kept to vegetarian restaurants for reasons of cost. And in the following years he sometimes made 'physiological experiments: he fasted or went hungry for prolonged periods in order to observe the effect on himself and possibly also to assure himself that he was independent of material requirements and everyday habits' (WB 480).

The theme of vegetarianism comes up fairly often in Weber's treatise on Indian religions. He observes quite rightly that it originated not in health concerns but in religious motives: it had an 'anti-orgiastic' element and appeared in combination with abstinence from alcohol and sexual continence.[113] This does not rule out that vegetarianism may give rise to a special sense of well-being. The relationship between lifestyle reform and the 'erotic movement' was full of contradictions. Robert Michels, an increasingly enthusiastic 'southerner' who was contemptuous of northern neuroses, jeered at chaste young men, who 'consist mainly of that great army of sexual cripples who are always thinking about their health; in part because they are really ill, or at least sickly; and in part from sheer fear and cowardice in face of the dangers of the extra-conjugal erotic life. They are rabbits, not men . . . they are reduced to mortify the flesh by living on vegetables and seltzer water, in order to keep their lusts from overheating.'[114]

On Monte Verità, however, Weber encountered vegetarianism in combination with free love and nudist culture. Already in 1906, when the Webers moved to the banks of the Neckar and no longer had anyone living opposite them, Weber began to wear his 'birthday suit' when he was 'sunbathing' (a term recently introduced by the lifestyle reform movement). The mark that such movements left on Max Weber is clearly visible, even if he also retained certain reservations: for example, when he sunbathed with 'a huge new pipe in his mouth', he may have looked 'a fine specimen for the gods or (the satirical weekly) *Simplicissimus*' (as Marianne reported),[115] but not for the lifestyle reformers, who were opposed to smoking.

Of course, it had been known since ancient times that well-being was strongly dependent on diet and lifestyle, but the period around 1900 marked a historical high point of the gospels of natural healing and lifestyle reform. The stresses of the industrial age, accompanied with factory-produced foodstuffs and city pollution – but also with the new ideal of natural living and the new (real or supposed) discoveries of science – generated a widespread sense of crisis, so that therapies often presented themselves as religions of salvation.[116] They opened a new gateway to the history of religion, and Max Weber was one of those who responded to the new impulse with the support of his own experience.

Before his illness he had owned a bicycle, at a time when cycling was an elite sport. Still in 1898 Marianne wrote to him at the clinic on Lake Constance that Alfred had strongly advised that he take up cycling: 'it seems to have done him a power of good, as I gather from his hints that he no longer has any sexual difficulties.'[117] At that time, when cycling was still an object of fantasy projections, it was often considered to be sexually arousing; a French novella of 1898, *Voici des ailes*, relates a cycling trip by two married couples, during which one wife gradually sheds more and more of her clothes until the whole thing ends in an orgy of partner-swapping.[118] Max Weber, however, was convinced that the last thing he needed was more excitement. Marianne wanted to sell her bicycle, then an object of considerable value, to

Helene, so that she could then pass it on as a gift to Arthur; Alfred was supposed to assess how much it was worth.[119] In its time it had cost her 450
marks, but prices had since fallen dramatically as a result of American mass
production. From now on there would be no more talk of cycling. Besides,
lifestyle reformers had divided views about the bicycle: there was indeed
some reason to regard the sport of cycling, with its pursuit of speed, as an
epitome of the hectic modern way of life.

It would never have entered Max Weber's head to become a sportsman,
and a gulf also separated him from the new cult of youth and the body. Yet
he began to display a more friendly and careful attitude to his own body –
especially after 1909, when he rehearsed a rebellion of 'the young' against
'the old' in the Verein für Sozialpolitik, and developed some confidence that
he was not hermetically sealed off from the realm of the senses. Early in
1910, to Helene's amazement, Marianne reported that 'Max has for some
time been eating less and feels really quite sprightly as a result.'[120] Formerly
he may have thought that a full belly promoted not only tiredness but also
a good night's sleep, but by April 1911 he attributed his 'difficulties in
getting to sleep' to the wretched 'evening guzzling' (MWG II/7-1, 167). For
people who have often eaten to excess, it comes as a revelation that a certain
asceticism has a pleasurable side to it.

Already in 1908 Ernst von Düring, the leading doctor at the large
Lahmann natural-healing clinic near Dresden,[121] made it clear to the
Webers that, like most of their affluent contemporaries, they ate too much
and courted nervous disorders by putting too heavy a burden on their
organism. He, Max, was 'much too thick'; he should rather give up sleep-
inducing drugs and eat far less. 'So, now I have support in my fight against
the eating instinct', Marianne triumphantly wrote to Helene,[122] with a tacit
dig at her for thwarting her efforts with a maternal instinct to feed her 'big
boy'.[123] In early 1911, on the only occasion when Marianne really let fly in
a letter to her mother-in-law, the reason was that her eternal spoiling of him
had again ruined his figure just when, in Marianne's eyes, he had become
more handsome than ever before. Marianne could not get over her rage that
this style of mothering had turned an erotic into an unerotic man – or,
worse still, a noble into a vulgar figure:

> Come, come: during the weeks of Mother's meat pots . . . a 'nobleman'
> has taken on the appearance of a 'fattened burgher'! I'm a little dis-
> gusted by his *dehors* and not only for aesthetic reasons; this bloated
> face does not even look healthier than the slim one did before. No, you
> should not *deliberately* make him fatter for me and seduce him into
> eating too much. I have to say it again, dearest Mama: since he gets
> absolutely no physical exercise, a premature fatty heart, gout and
> silting up of the small blood vessels in the brain (Note: plus early
> mental ageing, as with Papa) (capillaries) are to be expected. . . . Max
> has a definite tendency to eat too much for the sake of eating . . . in
> Oerlinghausen his excessive fondness of eating . . . really disturbed me

psychologically; it should not have been like that in a person of such nobility of mind, it was a blemish on him.

She was teaching Helene what she had learned from Düring: that the accumulation of unnecessary matter irritated the nervous system. And she added that it 'reduced the brain's capacity for work'. She also mentioned that at times (this was 1910) Max went to the opposite extreme of 'immoderate' fasting[124] – a physical side to the crisis in his relations with Else.

In March 1911 Max Weber himself tried to teach Marianne, who was plagued with migraine on a lecture trip, that the main point was to gain confidence in one's own body (MWG II/7-1, 145). In 1917 he recommended to the ailing Naumann – who before the war had been greatly overweight and was then, like Marianne, still consulting Düring – the Heidelberg internist Albert Fraenkel (1864–1938), an exceptional doctor whom Diego Rivera later honoured as one of the all-time greats in a mural at the University of Mexico. Fraenkel, according to Weber, was 'not a doctor in the usual sense' and was 'ostracized by many of his peers'. 'He does not cure people, but regulates your life in such a way that you can look forward to (or win back) decades of being fresh for work.'[125]

It had once enraged Weber that Bismarck, out of gratitude to his physician Schweninger for a dramatic lifestyle change that made him capable of work again, had forced through his appointment as a professor at Berlin university; now, after years of illness, Weber was declaring his faith in the same philosophy of regeneration. Like Schweninger, Fraenkel taught that the goal was to treat ill people rather than illnesses. Unlike Schweninger, however, he was an internationally noted authority in the field of pharmaceutical medicine, hence in established science, even if he was becoming increasingly sceptical about it. 'I know no one I could trust in the same way', Weber wrote to Naumann about Fraenkel, as he had never written before about anyone, least of all a doctor. Jaspers had already picked up Weber's 'limitless confidence' in him; he thought it was through him, Fraenkel, that he had first acquired confidence in his own capacity to produce results.[126]

Fraenkel's way of impartially taking in 'the essence of the patient', without judging and without projecting anything into the patient, became a model for Viktor von Weizsäcker:[127] it was, so to speak, the Weberian theory of science applied to the practice of medicine. Hermann Hesse, who was close to Fraenkel, wrote: 'He does not wish to force and violate people's natures, to make the delicate robust or the gaunt portly, but simply to make it possible or easier for everyone to remain in their own skin and personality, however ill they may be.' He was helped in this by 'an open-minded, noble respect for all the phenomena of living nature, a weighing of all situations, passions and aberrations . . . in a way that was virtually devoid of self-righteousness'.[128] We can imagine how this doctor must have helped Weber to affirm and live with his own corporeal being. After the experience with Fraenkel, he spoke only disparagingly of 'good Düring'.[129]

Among 'back-to-nature people' and 'enchantresses': Ascona beneath Monte Verità

In the spring of 1914, disappointed that 'vegetarian food' (MWG II/8, 159) had not been having the rapid effect for which he had hoped, Weber returned to his old belief that God had intended him to be corpulent – probably with a subliminal gibe at Marianne's sermons about fasting. After three days of fasting, he wrote from Ascona, all he had was a gnawing in the stomach: 'I cannot feel the slightest impact on my embonpoint and good looks; I am unchanged, as I was intended to be in the plan for creation' (MWG II/8, 580). And, after living on oranges for a couple of days: 'But the padding and the fatted burgher[130] are not giving an inch. This is how the creation plan wants me to be. Otherwise I look very "good" . . .' (MWG II/8, 585). Probably he had received a compliment from one of the women there.

When Weber stopped taking his 'aids' at Ascona in the spring of 1913, the expected 'catastrophe' failed to happen (MWG II/8, 155). The previous year in Avignon, in the Provençal spring, he had still needed 'a lot of bromide' – 'otherwise sleep did not come' (MWG II/7-2, 503). Lifestyle reform did not automatically bring a new life. This came only in combination with love – an experience that Weber must have found impressive and elemental. From then on, it was reflected in his sociology of religion, whose original power was said to derive not from an ascetic conduct of life as such but only when it was an expression of religious enthusiasm and the 'communism of love', spiritual-erotic and ecstatic religiosity.

At Ascona on Monte Verità (Lake Maggiore), where he spent the springs of 1913 and 1914 and would happily have returned even during the war,[131] he found vegetarian asceticism in non-ascetic society. All the lifestyle reform movements of his time were displayed there as in a kaleidoscope; almost nowhere else did the often disparate groups come together as closely as they did on that 'mountain of truth' sacred to the devotees of 'Mother Earth'.[132] Vegetarianism, nudism, free love, ecstatic dance, Oriental esotericism: all were jumbled together, partly in intimate association, but also partly in painful tension with one another. Among the 'back-to-nature people' of Ascona, Weber, who in his youth had once thought of himself as an 'old bear', felt a 'strangely youthful' fifty-year-old (WB 486, 489). When he saw the new savages at close quarters, he realized that many of them were not at all show-offs with regard to their strength or their nerves, rather ultra-sensitive types who had often, like himself, had to contend with illness. Part of him could identify with such people. In his way he too was a 'drop-out', and he was increasingly fascinated by others who had withdrawn from the world of everyday routine. 'The non-everyday' became an emotive word for Weber.

The erotic movement, which the Webers had found so disturbing from a distance, proved on closer acquaintance to reflect a relationship to sexuality which, far from being fundamentally animal-instinctual, often carried a high intellectual charge. This insight entered into the *Zwischenbetrachtung*, which he wrote around this time. Erotomania and erotophobia were sometimes strangely close to each other. The bohemian anarchist Erich Mühsam, who enjoyed occasional stays at Monte Verità but also made fun of the scene there, never tired of mocking the vegetarians and their horror of 'eating corpses'; he also thought their childless marriages significant and wondered 'whether the pressure towards vegetabilism arose mainly among individuals with low potency' – a category to which he himself belonged.[133] For Max Weber, it is true, the bohemian anarchists around Erich Mühsam were 'pitiful creatures' (MWG II/8, 440). 'Who can name them all?' wrote another; 'the noble anarchists, apostles of hunger, neo-moralists, neo-mystics, sexual ascetics, mumblers and stammerers, little men and little women who manage to glorify their crimes, making a virtue and a gospel out of their necessity'.[134] The Swiss labour doctor and anarchist Fritz Brupbacher portrayed Monte Verità, as he knew it in 1907, as the 'capital of the psychopathological International'.[135]

The mountain is a true laboratory for what happens when the non-everyday world of enthusiasm and world-denial tries to form itself into a movement. An ever more frequent visitor was Countess Franziska zu Reventlow, a woman shrouded in scandal, who was sometimes willing to perform courtesan's services for money or even for free. Having recently been the uncrowned queen of Schwabing, Munich's bohemian quarter, she was to those who knew her closely an often lonely and unhappy woman, constantly tormented by 'nerves'. Unlike in the case of Else, her 'virtuoso' eroticism – to use one of Weber's favourite terms – was no longer (or had never been) an expression of natural vitality, but rather appeared to Weber as a phenomenon of over-sophistication, a living example for the erotology of the *Zwischenbetrachtung*. Franziska was a 'spiritual beauty', her friend Hans Gruhle assured Marianne Weber (who later depicted her as a tragic-repulsive case of 'pan-erotic compulsion' doomed to disaster).[136] Gruhle about his friend: 'None of the filth through which she had passed had been able to harm her; it was a great and beautiful thing that a person lived for once entirely in accordance with her will; and it was a matter of indifference whether she went under sooner than others – she lived in one year more than the likes of us do in ten.'[137] The cult of personal autonomy and experience was the gateway to erotic activity in the world of the educated bourgeoisie. Weber too discovered that, if Reventlow lived entirely for 'the experience', she was 'not the cool detached "technician of the amorous"' that she outwardly pretended to be, but a disillusioned woman who felt the nullity of her existence – 'that makes up for quite a lot' (MWG II/8, 161).

How did Weber twice spend a whole month at Ascona without Marianne? Was it really just for relaxation? Ascona was not exactly a typical holiday resort in those days. He knew that he would meet there Frieda Gross, the seductively charming ex-wife of Otto Gross, and that Otto himself, who had caused Weber so much trouble in the past, had also been a lot in Ascona. Had he really been looking for peace and nothing else, he would hardly have settled for such a place. Before he went, he must at least have known about the subcultures and countercultures on Monte Verità, and about the presence there of 'Fanny' zu Reventlow; he was probably also aware that she had had affairs with Edgar Jaffé and Hans Gruhle. Frieda Gross, for her part, was linked to the Weber circle not only through Else Jaffé but also through a love affair with Emil Lask, who was funding her lawsuit at the time; the whole story reminds one of Schnitzler's play *La Ronde*, and it is scarcely imaginable that, in the euphoric period he was going through, Weber would not have been curious to see whether he would be drawn into the same round dance on Monte Verità.

'Wild Fanny'[138] crops up more than once in Max's letters from Ascona; he, like so many other men she encounters, is not unmoved by her, even if he assures his wife that such women do not think of him as their type, and that 'the countess' is 'simply faithless and cynical' (MWG II/8, 194). In May 1913, at Max's request, Marianne transferred to the ever impecunious countess the (for her and Max) considerable sum of 300 marks: how did she appear on the scene? how did it come about that Max felt some financial responsibility for the chaotic woman? (MWG II/8, 234f.). In a similar situation with Edgar Jaffé, she had given him 'sexual services' in return – though crying 'with horror'.[139] Max Weber liked to act chivalrously with such women, but the countess, extremely sensitive in her autonomy, could not stand the chivalrous type.[140] In any event, Mina Tobler was jealous at the 'seductive arts' of the countess (MWG II/8, 597). Evidently it gave Max Weber a certain pleasure to afford Marianne and Mina a glimpse of what went on at the foot of Monte Verità, which Marianne later passed on to readers of her biography.[141]

Max Weber, who seems to have liked women to take the sexual initiative, may have been secretly hoping that one of the Ascona 'enchantresses' would entice him, as the flower maidens in Klingsor's magic garden billed and cooed around Parsifal – whom Weber now inferred from his chastity to have been impotent. When he travelled back to Ascona in April 1914, having met Mina Tobler at her mother's house in Zurich, he admitted to Marianne that he experienced the journey to that 'world filled with enchantresses, grace, guile and desire for happiness' as a kind of homecoming (MWG II/8, 605). The concept of 'disenchantment', which now became part of Weber's vocabulary, often has for him an undertone of sadness that many readers fail to perceive. The great disenchanter yearns, if somewhat shamefaced, for a re-enchantment of the world; and the measure of enchantment is love. At the same time, the disenchanter in him get his money's worth on Monte Verità: for it swarms with tales that reduce anarcho-eroticism to an absurdity as a view of the world. Countess Reventlow herself, who then had her wildest years behind her, was by now – as Marianne Weber later noted with satisfaction – 'deeply ironical about the Schwabing-style blowing up of free love into a theory of salvation'.[142] In 'wild Fanny's' *roman à clef, Herrn Dames Aufzeichnungen*, Schwabing appears as 'Wahnmoching', a madhouse, and in her diary she noted: 'I can't take this Schwabing lifestyle any more.'[143]

Struggle for the rights of mothers: Max Weber as knight and saviour of women

The scene around Frieda Gross strengthened Weber's new self-esteem. The main reason for this was probably the fate of the man to whom she was still legally married: Otto Gross – that prophet of free love whose swankiness about his 'nerves' (i.e., his sex life) so nauseated Weber years before – had turned out to be a bundle of nerves, indeed a mentally ill drug addict, who in 1912 found himself on the wanted posters and in late 1913, at the instigation of his father (the prominent criminologist Hans Gross), was confined to a closed institution. Weber enthusiastically set himself up as the wife's saviour, her husband being meanwhile condemned to impotence.[144] Early in 1914 the Gross case received a lot of publicity in the German-speaking world: on 28 February Harden published in *Die Zukunft* a letter that had been smuggled out from Gross's mental institution, which showed that he still had a brilliant mind. First, he strongly urged that 'no one should interfere with [Frieda's] rights as a mother'; the cause taken up by Max Weber was becoming popular all over the country. In that high age of youth movements, when intergenerational conflicts were in fashion, the father–son drama in the Gross family fascinated the public: those who felt young and anti-bourgeois identified almost automatically with Otto, even though the father, on any sober analysis, was not the archetypal evil patriarch[145] and could point to his son's self-destructive behaviour – and the harm he might do to others: he had already helped two former girlfriends to commit suicide by poison and shown not a trace of responsibility for either them or their children – as a valid reason for his detention. Nor does the 'left-wing' slant of the Otto Gross cult fit the hero very well: he was, after all, so elitist in his guru self-image that he even despised Max Weber as a democrat.

The Paris-based writer Ludwig Rubiner, who had recently attacked Gross and psychoanalysis, tried to mobilize the elitism of the intelligentsia in support of the man forcibly detained in Germany, arguing that 'two kids still smelling from their contact with police dogs' should not have been allowed to grab a 'scholar' and consign him to an 'infernal, revolting mollusc's fate' in a madhouse.[146] Max Weber too recognized that, although he continued to dislike him as a person, Otto Gross had a creative mind and was in a sense a noble character. Presumably he learned from Frieda Gross a lot of private details that corrected his image of the 'nerve swank': Otto had originally had a horror of sexual intercourse, even of taking his clothes off, and after the divorce he still went to bed fully dressed.[147] His erotic gospel came out of a struggle with his own neuroses.

Max Weber must have felt a certain affinity with the man, who had also indirectly rendered outstanding services to Max's own sexual emancipation.

He did not seriously blame him for assisting the suicide of his two former partners, but probably assumed that Gross had acted from honourable motives and that, for all his egocentricity, he had not been subliminally glad to be rid of them.[148] Suicide was for him anyway a supreme expression of freedom, its criminalization a disgrace. To the outside world, Weber emphasized that Gross's writings up to the letter published in *Die Zukunft* 'in every respect give the impression of someone fully in possession of his mental faculties' (MWG II/8, 492); but he remarked to Marianne, already before the divorce from Frieda, that *dementia praecox* had been diagnosed in Otto, and that he had no doubts about the diagnosis (MWG II/8, 182, 160). Nor did it occur to him to join the campaign for Otto's release; he thought Frieda was basically 'very glad that her husband was locked up' (MWG II/8, 595) and showed understanding for the father's course of action.[149] He warned Frieda against treating the father as an 'enemy', with whom any lie was permissible (MWG II/8, 621f.): that would be unwise, since the father had until then paid for the upkeep of Frieda's and Otto's son, Peter, and for the maintenance of Frieda 'on a very modest scale' (MWG II/8, 504); true, he still had to be persuaded to leave Peter with her, but he should continue to think of himself as his grandfather and pay the costs of his upbringing – otherwise Frieda could simply refer to her changing relations with men and claim that Peter was not Otto's son after all. But the main danger was precisely that Hans Gross would dispute the legitimacy of Peter's birth (MWG II/8, 550, 602, 647, 671). After Frieda won the custody case over Peter in May 1915, she would have liked to assert the inheritance claims of her daughter Eva, whose father was Ernst Frick. But Weber would not play along with that little trick.[150]

The most recent volume of Weber's correspondence reveals the awesome scale of the paper war that he waged for this mother's right to her child, the most natural of all natural rights. And this was the Weber who had once raged against the 'demon of matriarchy' and the 'motherhood protection mob'! The expenditure of time and energy coincided with one of the most creative periods of his life, when according to today's Weber researchers he would have done better to focus all his powers on *Economy and Society*. Sometimes the initiative for the battle over women's rights came more from Weber than from Frieda Gross; he had to press her: 'Let me have some news, any news!' (MWG II/8, 536). Was he secretly in love with Frieda? He certainly felt close to her; he had known her longer than Else and had once even made contact with Else through her.[151] Frieda also treated him as someone close and received him in her dressing-gown with dishevelled hair. 'Her loose blond hair covering her whole back is . . . awfully "seductive" for men', he wrote to Marianne (MWG II/8, 629). In 1916 he told Frieda he regretted that she had given up her previous home, 'as it was so easy going from room to room – the way to the *panettone* was so close! And for other things also – especially chatting'.[152] So, not only for chatting.

Marianne had to agree that Frieda had '*great* charm in her way of thinking and being', and that, even if one could not morally approve of her conduct, she was 'generous and unselfish'.[153] Else, for her part, thought that in comparison with Frieda 'all other women (were) like withered leaves'. At the time when Max was keeping silent about Else, he and his wife would address the problem by speaking of Frieda; Marianne later confessed that 'when we said "Frieda" it really meant "Else"!'[154] Since Frieda suffered far more than Else from the consequences of her free love life, and was therefore in greater need of help, the 'Frieda' topic was more edifying for the Webers than the subject of 'Else'.[155] As Marianne saw it, Weber contented himself with the role of knight in shining armour in relation to Frieda.[156] But, to be sure, it was not unattractive for him to think that Else was also the recipient of his knightly service to Frieda.[157] And this was also, morally or sexually, a triumph over Otto Gross.

The new vision of a civilization close to nature

In March 1913, shortly after arriving in Ascona, Weber described it as a 'really filthy little Italians' nest' (MWG II/8, 150). Yet on 11 April 1914 he wrote to Marianne from Ascona, where 'divine weather' had put him in an elated mood after he had been with Mina in Zurich:

> Everything so completely different from Lake Zurich. There 'culture', the little houses in the green meadow stretching up to the mountains, nestling in every tiny fold, holding everywhere the human heart with its troubles and its joys . . . Here the villages stuck up there like a piece of nature, people as open as they are, implying nothing more than themselves – *also* beautiful, only less 'human', without intimacy, like a nude painting – like Frieda's life too, lacking a background, but not without pride and form. (MWG II/8, 612f.)

So, a contrast between nature and 'culture', in inverted commas; but not an absolute opposition. The 'culture' of the overdeveloped landscape above Lake Zurich is tied to nature in its way, 'nestling in all the tiniest folds' of the mountains. But Weber feels at least as strongly the attraction of the village culture in the Italian Alps, which has become 'a piece of nature'. It is this nature-culture that he compares to a naked woman – a harmonious beauty pointing to no higher meaning outside itself – and he sees this embodied in Frieda. Her kind of being is 'not without pride and form'. It is a kind of nature that holds cultural values within it.

The theme of *nature* had been preoccupying Weber for years. Already in the spring of 1911, at Vevey on Lake Geneva, he had 'for the first time in a long time' read Rousseau's *Julie, or The New Heloise* and found it excitingly topical: 'much of it admirable still today!' (MWG II/7-1, 170). We see how in Max Weber, who often experienced his own nature as inimical and fought against 'naturalism' in science, a new idea of nature was beginning to take shape: the idea of a nature stretching into human beings, which had long been there for Marianne. At the same time, he was developing a conception of culture as natural. The word *Kultur* and its compounds occur no fewer than 1,394 times in the electronic edition of Weber's work, yet he never thought it necessary to define this term that was then on everyone's lips. Lawrence A. Scaff considers that the most remarkable aspect of Weber's concept of culture is that it refers to 'a sphere of disunity, value conflict and struggle among competing world-views'.[158] So, culture contains a natural element; if its essence were spiritual-intellectual, one would have expected it to attain full harmony with the higher development of reason. During the war Weber spoke disparagingly about the 'operation of that loveless and unpitying economic struggle for existence which bourgeois phraseology designates as "peaceful cultural work"' (MWG II/15, 97), the point being that this economic warfare is far more meaningless and soulless than war itself (PW 78). For Weber, physical struggle is part of human nature, although it is bound up with a sense of leading life to the full.

In the way Marianne Weber wrote two decades later about the long-deceased Franziska zu Reventlow, there is still a reverberation of those last prewar springs which at times seemed to open up an enchanted world. As we read the pages in which she describes 'wild Fanny' as a prodigy of vital energy, we sense the fascination of a woman who gave full and uninhibited expression to everything that Marianne had renounced. Only towards the end does she point out that there was something 'increasingly empty and self-destructive' about her constant swapping of partners – which the countess herself would probably not have denied – and then comes the harsh judgement: 'crime against humanity'. Before the First World War, the Munich district of Schwabing, 'still magically embedded in forest and meadow', was the 'well-spring for all the anti-Christian and anti-bourgeois currents that had been seeping into the values and life of civil society', above all the 'devaluation of asceticism' through an 'appeal to the rights of natural instincts'. Scarcely anyone who participated in the bustling world of Schwabing depicted it in such alluring colours as did the reputedly prudish Marianne, who was excluded from this 'frenzy of sensuality'. The 'pan-erotic gospel of Schwabing' based itself on a cult of Mother Earth inspired by the Swiss anthropologist Johann Bachofen:

> People want to believe again in the primeval, blindly creative power of Mother Earth, in the possibilities of mothers' groups and matriarchy. 'Concubinism' became the most highly valued form of communion between the sexes, and it was taken to mean the woman's giving herself to the man she currently fancied – to any number of men – and therefore her forgoing any ties. . . . Sexuality was supposed to be subject only to the law of ebb and flow.[159]

If the paternal bond is a matter of choice, the maternal bond becomes all the more powerful. And, in the end, this was the strongest element in Franziska zu Reventlow's love life: in this, Marianne followed the notes in the countess's diary.[160] For her too there was something genuine in the cult of nature and motherhood, something based on the reality of life. But, in the countess's case, the cult did not prove its worth as a religion of salvation.

'*Zwischenbetrachtung* euphoria'

That period before the First World War also saw the composition of the *Zwischenbetrachtung*, the 'intermediate reflection' for the *Wirtschaftsethik der Weltreligionen*, which has became a sacred text for the modern Weber cult as *The Protestant Ethic* was for the earlier one. What one only suspects in the correspondence from those years becomes clear from his later remarks to Else about the *Zwischenbetrachtung* euphoria or, in the actual words, '*Zwischenbemerkung* (intermediate note or comment) euphoria': namely, that despite all the complaints and quarrels Weber then felt in a euphoric state of mind. The euphoria was carried by eroticism, and salvation was combined with illumination, with intellectual clarification.

The parts of Weber's *Sociology of Religion* that deal with 'Religious Ethics and the World' (E&S, ch. VI, §§xii-xiv, pp. 576–610; *Wirtschaft und Gesellschaft* ch. 5, §11) are close in content to the *Zwischenbetrachtung*, and indeed long sections sound like a preliminary draft for it.[161] On both occasions, Weber seems to be playing with the reader: the German subheadings focus on the tension between soteriological religion and 'the world', on 'stages and directions in the religious rejection of the world'. 'World' here means specifically the everyday world. Weber's thinking circles not so much around complete denial of the world in favour of the hereafter as around the non-everyday (*Außeralltägliche*), salvation from the everyday. After a few detours, the second part of each text addresses the relationship between salvation and sexuality, at times in the tones of a grand crescendo.

Eduard Baumgarten considered the *Zwischenbetrachtung* 'one of the most classical, probably immortal, chapters that Max Weber wrote' (B 473). It is indeed a rich document of illumination that compresses a multiplicity of ideas – a text that cannot be fully understood in one reading, and still offers new discoveries after half a dozen. Virtually nowhere else can we see just how difficult Weber found it to put order into the ideas rushing in on him, instead of pouring everything over the audience, as Wagner was able to do with his huge orchestra.

In the chapter on 'the sociology of religion', salvation appears to be still unreconciled with sexual pleasure. The hostility to sex among religions that strive to rise above the world sounds like a law of nature: 'Despite the widespread belief that hostility toward sexuality is an idiosyncracy of Christianity, it must be emphasized that no authentic religion of salvation had in principle any other point of view' (E&S 606). But the violence of the animosity betrayed a certain proximity: 'The relationship of religion to sexuality is extraordinarily intimate' (E&S 602). This intimacy is explained at greater length in the *Zwischenbetrachtung*, where the premise is that, in the realm of the 'other-worldly' and the 'non-everyday', the transitions are fluid for both psychological and physiological reasons, especially in the case of mysticism:

> The highest eroticism stands psychologically and physiologically in a mutually substitutive relation with certain sublimated forms of heroic piety. In opposition to the rational, active asceticism which rejects the sexual as irrational, and which is felt by eroticism to be a powerful and deadly enemy, this substitutive relationship is oriented especially to the mystic's union with God. From this relation there follows the constant threat of a deadly sophisticated revenge of animality . . . This psychological affinity naturally increases the antagonism of inner meanings between eroticism and religion. From the point of view of any religious ethic of brotherliness, the erotic relation must remain attached, in a certain sophisticated measure, to brutality. . . . The erotic frenzy stands in unison only with the orgiastic and charismatic form of religiosity. This form is, however, in a special sense, inner-worldly. . . . Eroticism enters easily into an unconscious and unstable relation of surrogateship or fusion with other-worldly and extraordinary mysticism. This occurs with very sharp inner tension between eroticism and mysticism. It occurs because they are psychologically substitutive. Out of this fusion the collapse into orgiasticism follows very readily. (FMW 348-9)

'Revenge of animality', 'collapse into orgiasticism', 'surrogateship or fusion': these explanatory terms, which astound the reader with their eccentricity, acquire their meaning only from the conviction that man forms a natural unit. At the level of ideas, redemption in the other-worldly religious sense may be sharply opposed to a thoroughly this-worldly eroticism; but in human nature the two are connected with each other. And mysticism, which gives free rein to man's inner life, makes it easy for the one to fuse with the other.[162] Between the 'orgiasticism' of religious ecstasy and the sexual orgasm, there is a fluid transition. 'Ecstasy' occurs no fewer than 261 times in Weber's works, mostly in association with the ancient Israelite prophets. In many places Weber plays at being an expert in ecstasy and orgiastic phenomena: for example, he knows how to distinguish between fertility orgies and intoxication orgies.[163] Studies by the philologist Erwin Rohde of the Eleusinian mysteries and the Thracian cult of Dionysus – studies which already inspired the young Nietzsche, a friend of his – seem to have led Weber to the significance of the ecstatic element in the history of religion. From then on, writes the religious historian Hans G. Kippenberg, 'the power of intoxication and orgy runs like a red thread' through Weber's 'construction of religious history'. Kippenberg also points out that Weber's dependence on Rohde is especially marked 'when he writes that the idea of the soul as an entity distinct from the body emerged in association with "orgies", that is, with mystery cults'; and that he found in Rohde the concept of 'charisma' as a special power of 'prophets, ascetics and exorcists'.[164]

Nevertheless, the starting idea is that the removal of modern civilized man from the 'organic cycle' of natural existence introduces a tension into the whole of life, precisely because the detachment is never complete and man always remains a natural creature in his physical being. The religious striving for salvation attempts to deny the creaturely side of humanity, yet it originates in the suffering caused by the loss of a natural existence. Beneath the surface, nature is at work throughout the rationalization and intellectualization of human existence – above all, man's sexual nature. But this in turn undergoes a kind of rationalization and systematic intensification, especially among people who make eroticism the meaning of their life (those with whom the Webers constantly argued for many years). Weber's thinking is marked by conceptions of a sometimes paradoxical dynamic of this kind, rather than by cleanly delineated sketches of a system. Simple souls believe in a clear-cut separation between Eros and intellect; Weber discovered that eroticism and spirituality intensify each other.

The *Zwischenbetrachtung* repeatedly reaches a climax in emphatic formulations that Weber researchers with an interest in logical systems find hard to digest: for example, 'the flowing out into an objectless acosmism of love' in the state of religious ecstasy, or the 'profound and quiet bliss of all heroes of acosmic benevolence', or, on the other hand, the 'world dominion of unbrotherliness' (FMW 331, 357). In effusive style, Weber writes that the lover 'knows himself to be freed from the cold skeleton hands of rational orders, just as completely as from the banality of everyday routine' (FMW 347). Who would doubt that such phrases contain a kernel of what was going on in Weber, and that they sprang not from logical argument but from a gladdening experience? However, harmony does not prevail even here, as erotic love comes into conflict with brotherly love: this major theme of the *Zwischenbetrachtung* mirrors the period in which Max Weber's reinvigorated brotherly relationship with Alfred broke down under the power of eroticism. Salvation through love was not a stable long-term condition, either in Weber's love or in his theory.

14

Charisma

Salvation as grace: sociology of religion and experience of self

Max Weber's most attractive concept, 'charisma', which he transferred from religion to other spheres – the literal meaning of 'grace-giving' has been almost forgotten – reflects a highly personal experience of unhoped-for grace and draws much of its suggestive force from that experience. In a *Kopfmensch* such as Weber, however, the primary element is not the experience but the intellectual development, which opens the spirit to the experience of grace. Whereas in *The Protestant Ethic* he understood the core of religion to be the overcoming of corrupt human nature, in later years he developed a view that its meaning and soul consist in a bodily–spiritual process of *salvation*. This was especially applicable to the 'higher' religions, which, unlike the 'natural religions', reflected the needs of civilized people who had detached themselves from the organic cycle of natural existence. Of the 482 occurrences of 'salvation' (*Erlösung*) in Weber's work, all of four are in *The Protestant Ethic*.

Only with these insights did Weber's depression come to terms with itself, as it were; so long as he had elevated asceticism into a source of strength, he had denied part of his experience of himself. Someone who falls into a despondent state has a boundless need for relief-salvation (*Erlösung*): he just has to acknowledge this, instead of making the depression part of his own self. This is what Weber managed to do over the years. Salvation, still far off at the time of *The Protestant Ethic*, now became an inexhaustible theme, not only in his writings on the sociology of religion, but also in *Economy and Society*.[1] Edith Hanke has pointed out that, 'contrary to his striving elsewhere for conceptual clarity', Weber does not here stick to 'a definite concept of salvation';[2] he starts not from the concept but from his own experience and its verification of the efficacy of the phenomenon. Towards the end of 1913, Weber presented his newly gestating sociology of religion to the publisher Siebeck as a 'sociology of doctrines of salvation and religious ethics' (MWG II/8, 449f.); it is first and foremost the striving for salvation which brings about a religious community. Weber had himself experienced how isolation goes hand in hand with desolation.

Logically speaking, there would have to be a number of different salvations corresponding to the variety of things from which one wished to be saved. For Weber, too, the negative side of salvation is the most important: distress is at the origin of all striving for salvation. But from what do they wish to be saved, all those people who flock into religious communities? 'Apparently everywhere from one and the same thing', Weber wrote to Keyserling in late 1912; yet there are also 'little nuances' that have a big effect (MWG II/7–2, 802). If this were not the case, there would not be different religions fighting against one another. In the introduction to the *Wirtschaftsethik der Weltreligionen*, Weber presents a long list of possible evils from which people might wish to be saved: from bondage, from 'being defiled by ritual impurity [or] incarcerated in an impure body', the list goes on. It ends with a longing peculiar to Weber: 'to be saved from senseless brooding and events' and to achieve 'dreamless sleep' (FMW 280f.).

Yet Weber thinks he can see a positive common denominator: the longing for meaning [*Sinn*] and the basic theme of a 'religious rationalism' that is 'borne by intellectuals'. 'The intellectual seeks in various ways, the casuistry of which extends into infinity, to endow his life with a pervasive meaning, and thus to find unity with himself, with his fellow men, and with the cosmos' (E&S 506). In the end, salvation is not a negative but a positive and all-encompassing process of reconciliation with the self and the world, an act of regeneration, sometimes even 'a sudden rebirth' (E&S 528) – hence not a liberation from nature, but a process with natural characteristics.

Salvation cannot be forced simply through a methodical conduct of life. In the 'Sociology of Religion' chapter of *Economy and Society*, Weber devotes a long section (§10 in the German edition, ix-xi in the English) to 'paths to salvation' – yet even there it is clear that the overwhelming force of salvation lies in a sphere removed from planned action. Weber sets out a number of quasi-natural laws of salvation, his main interest being to distinguish between temporary and lasting salvation. Salvation brought about through 'purely ritual activities and ceremonies of cults' is 'essentially ephemeral' (E&S 530). 'Acute ecstasies' too are 'transitory in their nature and apt to leave but few positive traces on everyday behaviour. Moreover, they lack meaningful content . . . [On the other hand,] it would appear that a much more enduring possession of the charismatic condition is promised by those milder forms of euphoria which may be experienced as either a dreamlike mystical illumination or a more active and ethical conversion.' These 'produce a meaningful relationship to the world' (E&S 535). Here salvation, illumination and charisma are combined. It would probably not be wrong to assume that Weber is designating his own ideal.

By now Weber was a long way from *The Protestant Ethic*. He never took back what he had written there, but he did emphasize that the lovelessness of Puritanism and its condemnation of natural creation meant that, whatever it claimed, it was not a religion of salvation:

First, the paradox of the Puritan ethic of 'vocation'. [It] renounced the universalism of love, and rationally routinized all work in this world into serving God's will and testing one's state of grace. . . . In this respect, Puritanism accepted the routinization of the economic cosmos, which, with the whole world, it devalued as creatural and depraved. This state of affairs appeared as God-willed, and as material given for fulfilling one's duty. In the last resort, this meant in principle to renounce salvation as a goal attainable by man, that is, by everybody. It meant to renounce salvation in favour of the groundless and always only particularized grace. In truth, this standpoint of unbrotherliness was no longer a genuine 'religion of salvation'. (FMW 332f.)

We detect an aversion to the period of his life when he had at least attempted to identify with Puritanism and found neither love nor salvation. His turning away from the ascetic ideal is even plainer in the opposition he draws between Confucianism and Puritanism. Evidently admiring the imperturbability of East Asians, he notes their 'striking lack of "nerves" in the specifically modern European meaning of the word; the unlimited patience and controlled politeness', so unlike 'hysteria-producing asceticist religious practices' (RC 231f.). The link between asceticism and hysteria is mentioned as if it were a well-known fact – so distant was he now from his angry outburst to Harnack concerning the lack of German asceticism. When he describes the 'soteriological orgies of the Methodist type, such as are engaged in by the Salvation Army' as 'substitutes for the magical-orgiastic supervention of grace', we can hear the distaste in his voice (E&S 486). The true homeland of the religions of salvation lies in the East. Indeed, '*Licht vom Osten*', the title of Adolf Deissmann's book first published in 1908,[3] acquired a deeper meaning for Weber. The change of focus to Oriental religions brought him a new peace of mind; the viewpoint of *The Protestant Ethic* was part of the bad old days.

When Weber expounded his theory of music to the small circle of people around him, he argued: 'Christianity is the only religion based on sacred texts which has never known cult dancing. It rejected the body with horror. This made possible a bodyless music, geared mainly not to rhythm but to melody, in a degree like virtually nowhere else' (WzG 248). But this is at most only half the truth, as a number of non-Western musical cultures also do not put the stress on rhythm. Weber's turn to the Oriental religions seems to be associated with a quest for religiosity that is more friendly to the body. This, above all, is what now promises Weber salvation.

Weber writes in the *Zwischenbetrachtung* – as so often, his argument is understandable only in the light of incidental remarks – that, in a large number of cases 'especially important for the historical development', 'prophetic and redemptory religions have lived not only in an acute but in a permanent state of tension in relation to the world and its orders', all the greater the more they have been 'true religions of salvation'. For the rationalized striving for means of salvation has typically led, on the one hand, to the accumulation of earthly goods and, on the other hand, to contempt for such goods; hence the religious and worldly spheres have drifted into mutual tensions 'which remain hidden to the originally naive relation with the external world' (FMW 328). And the religions of salvation carried this tension into the domain of love and sexuality. 'The brotherly ethic of salvation religion is in profound tension with the greatest irrational force of life: sexual love. The more sublimated sexuality is, and the more principled and relentlessly consistent the salvation ethic of brotherliness is, the sharper is the tension between sex and religion. Originally the relation of sex and religion was very intimate' (FMW 343).

'Brotherly' and sexual love can never be totally separated from each other once and for all, as they are joined together in man's physical nature: Weber speaks of the 'physiologically substitutive relation' (FMW 348) among various ecstatic states. The religions of salvation can never totally escape the earth's gravity and soar into sublime heights. 'The relationship of religion to sexuality is extraordinarily intimate, though it is partly conscious and partly unconscious, and though it may be indirect as well as direct', Weber emphasizes in *Economy and Society* (E&S 602): note: he says '*is*' not '*was*' (in ancient times, in the 'natural religions' of primitive peoples or the Baal orgies of ancient Israel). The soaring flight of an all-assertive spiritual love means that sexual needs become more violent, for man does not consist of spirit alone. By 1910 at the latest there is no complete salvation from the world of the senses – indeed, it is questionable whether Weber even thought it worth striving for. He was then drawing closer to the theme of *salvation* not only through his study of religion but also through his own experience of life and love; and we can see how the two inspired each other, keeping him away from a completely supra-sensory idea of salvation.

Charisma: the nodal point of the sociology of religion and domination

In the last few years before the war, when Weber felt a new strength in himself and began to exert intellectual power over other people in his Heidelberg circle, his thought turned not only to religions of salvation but also to power and domination. Studies of Weber's sociology usually treat the two conceptual worlds as completely separate, but we need to bear in mind that they actually developed at the same time, associated with each other through his transfer of the concept of 'charisma' from religion to politics. Whereas, in the first decade of the new century, the themes of his illness and tormented brooding – asceticism, psychophysics of industrial labour, limits of knowledge – occupied centre stage in his thought, they were now supplanted by themes of pleasure and a new feeling of elation. For the subject of rule or domination (*Herrschaft*) was in his mind associated with pleasure, as was the subject of salvation.

As Edith Hanke has pointed out, charisma is 'the birthplace of the true sociology of political rule'. Although in *Economy and Society* charismatic rule is superficially ranked behind rational and traditional rule, it is really both the starting point and the end point in Weber's thinking about systems of rule. His sociological studies of religion and political rule, according to Hanke, 'may thus be traced back to a common core'.[4] Since *The Protestant Ethic*, boundary-crossing between the religious and social sciences had been something of a Weberian speciality. His first use of the concept of charisma, in reference to Stefan George, came in a letter of 9 June 1910 to Dora Jellinek (MWG II/6, 560f.).[5] It is true that Weber had known since the 1890s, from the Evangelical-Social Congress, the expert in ecclesiastical law Rudolf Sohm, whom he names as his theological source for the concept of charisma (E&S 216); but, as Edith Hanke shows, there is much evidence 'that Weber recognized the true scope of Sohm's concept of charisma only in 1909–10', when Sohm analysed the charismatically grounded cohesion of the early Christian community and defended it against Harnack's thesis – a typically German-Lutheran notion, repugnant to Weber – that a legally structured corporate identity was already the decisive element for the early Christians.[6]

In *The Protestant Ethic*, as Tenbruck noted, Weber had 'no idea' at all of the 'revolutionary power of charisma', or indeed of the simple existence of charismatic phenomena (WuZ 362) – he did not know what to make of Zinzendorf and the ecstatic Moravians. Weber's 'theory of charisma', Tenbruck continued, was unusual in that it appeared 'suddenly', 'with no recognizable preliminaries', around the year 1913 (WuZ 360).[7] From then on Weber was very fond of the term, and in the last decade of his life the words 'charisma' and 'charismatic' occur well over a thousand times. It was his most attractive conceptual innovation: first for himself, later for others. After some decades,[8] the concept developed its own charisma, its own promise of salvation.

'Force of personality' is a typical secret of practical life and a favourite theme in popular biographical literature, although social scientists usually find it an irritating blind spot; but Weber's concept of charisma offered a fascinating and non-trivial entry to this whole dimension. In everyday language it is often equated with an indefinable 'personal radiance', which does not mean much to sociological analysts, but in Weber it acquires sharper contours: it becomes a promise for people who find themselves in distress, from a leader who has himself been through the depths and burst the confines of the everyday. With charisma the non-everyday and the ecstatic – whose natural force breaks down the natural barriers between eroticism and mysticism even at the ideal level – become a key category not only for the sociology of religion but also for the sociology of rule, with 'sociology' no more than a makeshift term for what Weber is actually pursuing.

The association of charisma with enthusiasm, ecstasy and the communion of love was already present in the church historians Rudolf Sohm (1841–1917) and Karl Holl (1866–1926), to whom Weber makes reference

(E&S 216, 1112);[9] they were the source of heat for this concept. Weber had listened to Sohm as a student in Strasbourg and found him a 'peculiar phenomenon': 'Until you hear him speak, his whole appearance gives the impression of a religious apostle, and sometimes, when he does speak, that of a fanatic preoccupied with a single, one-sided idea' (JB 85). For Sohm, too, charisma was evidently not a theme totally separate from his own self. But it served as part of an argument that emphasized the fundamental difference between religion and politics. Within the National-Social Association he was the fiercest spokesman of the right wing and one of Göhre's principal opponents.[10] There was no direct path from Weber's earlier experiences with Sohm to his idea of charismatic rule; rather, Sohm's way of thinking blocked any transfer of charisma into politics.

Are there models in history for the charismatic type of rule?

The ideal type of charismatic leader came from the history of religion and, as Wolfgang Mommsen notes, never lost all traces of this origin.[11] The charismatics *par excellence* were the builders of religions, the apostles and prophets. But was there an equivalent in modern political history that Weber had in mind? No one would have suggested himself more than Bismarck, a 'Caesarist figure' for Weber too (E&S 1452), as the prototype of a divinely gifted statesman. But, if Weber's inspiration had really been the founder of the Reich, he would have drawn quite a different picture of the charismatic leader and his entourage: 'communism of love' (E&S 153), 'withdrawal from the world' (E&S 829) and rejection of all rational economic activity (E&S 1113) were not associations that anyone could have made with Bismarck, even with the best will in the world. Nor does Weber ever give the chancellor as an example of charismatic leadership; he mentions him only in the context of bureaucratic rule (E&S 993, 997). Gladstone, whom Bismarck despised, was more in the way of a charismatic figure (E&S 1132). The socialist Carlo Mierendorff, presumably with *Politics as a Vocation* in mind, wrote after Weber's death that he 'made frequent use' of Gladstone's name.

Wilhelm II, who strove so desperately and vainly to revive the old divine right of kings, put on more of a performance as a charismatic ruler, but he unwittingly offered a perfect demonstration that charisma cannot succeed as a mere show. Once, at a swearing-in ceremony for new army recruits, he shouted to them: 'If your emperor orders it, you must fire on your father and mother!'[12] – and one is reminded of Jesus's saying (which for Weber marked the charismatic's radical break with traditional ties) that he who does not leave his father and mother, indeed hate his father and mother, cannot be one of Jesus's disciples (E&S 579, 580). The young Kaiser took this challenge to an extreme, but his conduct was anything but genuine; in reality, his rule depended on the power of tradition and collapsed in revolutionary times. Friedrich Naumann, on the other hand, did possess charisma, which was communicated to his followers, especially the female ones. Yet his political fate is also proof that charisma alone cannot ground a system of rule. The same goes for Stefan George and his circle, in relation to which Weber first used the concept of charisma. It had the 'special charisma' of a sect (MWG II/6, 560f.), but its Maximin cult seemed to Weber more like a pale imitation of the old religions of salvation.

Does the concept of charisma have any logic that can be derived from Weber's general ideas on the course of history and the processes of social-ization? At first sight, it sharply conflicts with Weber's analysis of the ubiq-uitous processes of rationalization and bureaucratization. But, for Weber, there is also something in human nature that rebels against disenchantment and routinization, against the straitjacket imposed on the individual. And it is this non-everyday element, passionate, ecstatic and bound by no fearful circumspection, which breaks the force of habit in history and creates something new. Here is the link to Weber's fundamental insights. He does not understand rationalization and bureaucratization as evolutionary processes advancing with law-like constancy. The individual always remains the basic reality, never a mere function of structures, and this is why the power of individuality is able to break through structural con-straints. It has something natural about it, and so too does charismatic leadership. Wolfgang Mommsen speaks of 'charismatic eruptions'.[13]

Nevertheless, one cannot arrive at charisma purely through a conceptual logic; it has always been a stumbling-block for those who would like to con-struct a logical system out of Weber's teachings.[14] Not by chance did this concept appear at a time when Weber suddenly had a personal experience of grace and caught a glimpse of salvation. He learned then that there are moments in human existence at which the inertia of the everyday breaks down. And now, more clearly than in the past, his whole thought was carried along by the realization that man lives not only on everyday routine but on moments of ecstasy, of 'standing outside oneself'.

Again and again Weber underlines that charismatic rule breaks from the everyday, although 'non-everydayness' is a term that hardly meets the requirements of scientific precision. Weber liked to use it at a time in his life when he felt capable of non-everyday intellectual fireworks: his own self-esteem was based on this talent for the non-everyday.[15] By ridding oneself of the everyday cares of petty egoism, one gains the opportunity for a special kind of strength; then many things become possible which previ-ously seemed impossible. Marianne too seems to have assumed that Weber, in a coded manner, was speaking of himself when he talked of charisma (WB 266).[16]

This background in Weber's personal experience does not make it easier to operationalize the charisma concept in research; the inflated use of the term, which can now be monitored on the internet in book titles such as *Charisma Training in Thirty Minutes*, leaves one in doubt whether authors who lack Weber's experiential background and meticulous approach are capable of applying it in an intellectually productive manner. At one point Weber himself points to the difficulty of empirically demonstrating charisma by any external indicators: 'It is not directly visible whether the companionage of a war leader with his followers has a patrimonial or a charismatic character; this depends upon the spirit which imbues the community' (E&S 1122). The social scientist thus needs to have a feel for this spirit in order to identify charisma as such; and such a feel is best developed through a charismatic experience of one's own.

The 'heroic ecstasy' of drunken elephants: charisma as an animal phenomenon

Charisma can be traced historically only as a connecting link of a community. But is it *rooted* in the community, or does it arise through, and depend for its effectiveness on, the radiant power of a charismatic? Whether charisma is essentially the gift of a leadership personality or arises only in the heads of his followers: this remains a controversial issue that provides the material for a ping-pong game of quotations from Weber. By the nature of things, it is mainly sociologists who sociologize charisma by making it a phenomenon of the led masses, and therefore of society. The section entitled 'Charismatic Authority' in chapter 3 of *Economy and Society*, which is part of a more general typology, begins with a certain ambiguity:

> The term 'charisma' will be applied to a certain quality of an individual personality by virtue of which he is considered extraordinary and treated as endowed with supernatural, superhuman, or at least specifically exceptional powers or qualities. These are such as are not accessible to the ordinary person, but are regarded as of divine origin or as exemplary, and on the basis of them the individual concerned is treated as a 'leader'. . . . How the quality in question would be judged from any ethical, aesthetic or other such point of view is naturally entirely indifferent for purposes of definition. What is alone important is how the individual is actually regarded by those subject to charismatic authority, by his 'followers' or 'disciples'. (E&S 242f.)

At the beginning of the 'Sociology of Religion' chapter, however, where he again introduces charisma, the emphasis falls elsewhere. Now the ideal-typical charismatic is a man capable of ecstasy. But:

> (Not) every person (has) the capacity to achieve the ecstatic states . . . We shall henceforth employ the term 'charisma' for such extraordinary powers. Charisma may be either of two types. Where this appellation is fully merited, charisma is a gift that inheres in an object or person simply by virtue of natural endowment. Such primary charisma cannot be acquired by any means. But charisma of the other type may be produced artificially in an object or person through some

extraordinary means. Even then, it is assumed that charismatic powers can be developed only in people or objects in which the germ already existed but would have remained dormant unless evoked by some ascetic or other regimen. Thus, even at the earliest stage of religious evolution there are already present *in nuce* all forms of the doctrine of religious grace. . . . Th(is) strongly naturalistic orientation . . . is still a feature of folk religion. (E&S 400f.)

The concept of 'charisma' or 'grace' already contains the idea that this capacity involves a gift of God or nature. Weber thus falls into organological language: charisma is not produced by social groups but arises through the development of a kernel (*'in nuce'*). We should note that Weber here presents this 'strict naturalism' as ultimately a belief of folk religion, but later he hints that it involves not simply an idea but also a regularly occurring experience: 'That people differ widely in their religious capacities was found to be true in every religion based on a systematic procedure of sanctification . . . As it had been recognized that not everyone possesses the charisma by which he might evoke in himself the experiences leading to rebirth as a magician, so it was also recognized that not everyone possesses the charisma that makes possible the continuous maintenance in everyday life of the distinctive religious mood which assures the lasting certainty of grace' (E&S 539). In the *Zwischenbetrachtung* Weber speaks of 'naïve, primitive heroism' (FMW 334) – a kind of naturalness that appeals to him.

In his sociology of law, Weber again asks the question that so preoccupies him: '(W)e must ask how anything new can ever arise in this world, oriented as it is toward the regular . . . The evidence of ethnology seems to show . . . that the most important source of innovation has been the influence of individuals who have experienced certain "abnormal" states (which are frequently . . . regarded by present-day psychiatry as pathological) and hence have been capable of exercising a special influence on others' (E&S 321). From the standpoint of 'present-day psychiatry', Weber too belonged among the 'abnormal'. With the concept of charisma he created an opportunity out of his pathological disposition.

Weber's 'charisma' has come in for criticism, on both the left and the right. At the Weber Congress in 1964, when all the PR in connection with J. F. Kennedy was still fresh in people's minds, Herbert Marcuse argued that the power apparatus needed and generated a 'charismatic apex', and that 'charisma', understood as a personal quality, was 'perhaps the most questionable' of all of Weber's concepts.[17] On the other side, the conservative theorist Leo Strauss – who fastens on Weber's statement that charisma is simply what adherents take it to be – accuses him of condemning the social scientist to take any swindle at face value.[18] At times it does indeed seem so. But, if charisma is to last any length of time, it must prove itself by results; more than traditional authority, more even than bureaucratic authority, charismatic leadership is subject to the performance principle. Even Hitler, after the collapse of his empire, had few followers who declared their faith in him. And the noisy divine right of Wilhelm II brought it home that one must *have* charisma, and that all the methods of modern publicity are unable to force it to appear.

The problem of which comes first, the charismatic figure or his disciples' belief in charisma, is a little reminiscent of the chicken and the egg; it is not necessary to choose between them. One way or another, the special charismatic gift of the leader is in Weber's eyes indispensable for charismatic authority; there can be no doubt about that. Weber does not recognize the people, the masses, as an historical agent; only the individual has a will, and it is to the individual that his interest is especially directed.[19]

The early Christians constituted the original type of charismatic community, but its natural characteristics continue to exist in modern forms. Also for 'plebiscitary *Führerdemokratie*', it is characteristic 'that there should in general be a highly emotional type of devotion to and trust in the leader'; 'this is a natural basis for the utopian component which is found in all revolutions' (E&S 269). There are not so many other instances where Weber uses the word 'natural' in such an uninhibited way, without quotation marks. The charismatic community has an aura similar to Eros. Let us listen to the opening passages of the original version of the essay on charisma, which comes at a later point in the existing edition of *Economy and Society*. Here Weber assures the reader straight away – which he needs to do more than on any other of his pet themes – that he is using the concept of charisma 'in a completely value-free sense':

> The heroic ecstasy of the Nordic berserk, the legendary Irish folk hero Cuchulain or the Homeric Achilles was a manic seizure. The berserk, for example, bit into his shield and all about himself, like a mad dog, before rushing off in bloodthirsty frenzy; for a long time his seizure was said to have been artificially induced through drugs. In Byzantium, a number of such 'blond beasts' were kept just like war elephants in ancient times. (E&S 1112)

Again the fondness for hair-raising examples, the fruit of excessive curiosity in his reading! Max Weber, who – if we are to believe the rumour spread by Rickert[20] – had 'sweet dreams' of elephants with long trunks and plentiful women, was fond of elephant examples in other contexts too; we find them sixteen times in his work, even when proboscideans are scarcely necessary for the purposes of his argument. Among the warrior tribe of the Mahratta, the most dangerous adversaries of the Moghul emperor in India, Weber detected 'a residue of heroic ecstasy' in 'the intoxicatory incitement of men and elephants before the battle' (RI 73). And twice he relates the old Indian legend that, after a victorious battle, a king once honoured the Buddha by releasing his elephants, which then ' "with tears in their eyes" hurried to join their companions in the woods' (RI 356n, and again 213). Nowhere is the wild, animal side of charisma plainer than it is here.

The ideal type of the charismatic was drawn from ancient models: founders of religions, prophets of ancient Israel. The ideal charismatic community rests upon the 'communism of love', on direct human solidarity, and is as remote from economics as it is unbureaucratic. At first sight, then, an extremely unmodern phenomenon. Indeed, Salin considers that Weber, unlike Stefan George, was convinced 'that the gift and strength of prophethood' was 'possible only under very special circumstances . . . two and a half thousand years ago'.[21] But, if Weber took his models from ancient times, it was not least because he believed that the *origin* leads to the *essence* of things; an ancestry stretching far into the past is no argument against topicality in the present. For Weber, moreover, charisma springs from natural human dispositions, on the side of the charismatic leader as well as that of his following.

Weber's view of charismatic authority as a primal phenomenon in both politics and religion is all the more remarkable because, at least until the First World War, he found no models for it in the world around him. More than in any other case he had to leave his own time in thought, although even his imagination was far from sufficient to envisage what the twentieth century would give humanity by way of quasi-charismatic leadership. Seven times in *Economy and Society* he mentions the Mahdi who in 1885 conquered the Sudan and installed his followers in power there, until he was defeated by the British in 1898; these had been dazzling events for the European imagination. As Weber saw it, the Mahdi conceived of himself as a prophet, not simply – as it was often claimed then and later – as a despot who represented the interests of slave traders. From today's point of view, Mahdi rule may sound like the beginning of modern islamic fundamentalism;[22] but, for the young war reporter Winston Churchill, the desert horsemen who rode with swords and lances against British machine-guns were picturesque relics of a bygone age. Be this as it may, Weber's own experience of grace was incomparably more important than any contemporary political-religious phenomena for the inspiration that led to his concept of charisma in the last few years before the war.

Charismatic charge of the concept of leader

In Weber's political writings during the world war, the influence of the charisma concept is visible especially in the central importance he attaches to 'leader selection' for the strength of a polity. *Führer* and its compounds appear 385 times in the electronic edition of his works – and they come mostly from this period. Again and again he tries to get across his pet idea that a parliamentary regime is necessary for Germany, so that powerful natural leaders steeled in political struggle can reach the top instead of colourless bureaucrats. This was one of Weber's most distinctive ideas, for in the advancing right–left polarization of the time it was more typical to combine calls for a strong leader with contempt for parliament. Weber saw eloquent popular tribunes such as Clemenceau and Lloyd George at the helm in enemy countries, while Bismarck's place had been taken by men of the ilk of Michaelis and Hertling, who were little known to the public and owed their jobs to obscure machinations in the corridors of power. For Weber, any nationally minded German had to feel disgusted by this wretched state of affairs. The anti-parliamentarians of the right were not capable of drawing any conclusions from this, but Weber now rose to the heights of his national political rhetoric.

In 1917 he found 'born, natural leaders' with 'a strong instinct for power' not so much in the Reichstag as – and here he became more specific – in 'the present leader of the Krupp works, formerly a politician from the Eastern Territories' (PW 172). He does not name names, and today's Weberologists pass over this passage in silence.[23] But the man he had in mind was none other than Alfred Hugenberg, future press baron and leader of the German National People's Party, who paved the way for Hitler. Even Else Jaffé was keen on him in the autumn of 1917: 'If we found an all-German dictator who understood how to govern and really led us towards a good objective, I would not fret about it. Why not Hugenberg? A thousand times better than Bülow.'[24] Later, Hugenberg's circle of friends around Leo Wegener – one of the most enthusiastic supporters of the early Weber – cultivated the memory especially of Weber's writings on agricultural workers and his hostility to Polish-Russian immigrants.[25]

Führer was not a concept that belonged to the classical political vocabulary of the eighteenth and nineteenth centuries;[26] its rise to prominence began in Weber's day, and he himself would contribute something to it in connection with his wartime experiences. 'Until 1914', according to Hans-Ulrich Wehler, '*Führer* was an innocent term.'[27] It did not have a tone of command: one followed the Führer through unfamiliar territory – only there was one necessary – voluntarily and in one's own interests. The new Führer concept, which the Nazis took up but did not invent, had military, parliamentarian and Platonic origins. Since Clausewitz and the anti-Napoleonic wars of liberation, it had become a customary idea that in the thick of battle a commander must not only issue orders but radiate the energy that keeps up spirits in desperate situations. The Führer concept created a bridge to the world of the intellect. But an origin can be found for it also in nineteenth-century parliamentarianism, borrowed from the Anglo-American 'leader'.[28] Weber, who had a high regard for war heroes and popular tribunes, was the man to tie together these disparate threads of tradition – though, to be sure, he was not the only one. Thus Arnold Zweig, later an honoured writer in the GDR, wrote on 16 January 1919 in *Die Weltbühne* that the nation knew, 'with its deepest instincts, that it now has to gather around certain figures, that only people larger than life are capable of offering a way out'. 'Only magicians can help against magic, only souls against souls. A unique man with a great nature, a single true Führer must rise up . . . and the crisis would be given a meaning and the fear of death associated with it would be lost.' Only in the light of such testimony can we gain some idea of where Weber's ideas on charismatic leadership become distinctively Weberian.

Charismatic authority: a value-free concept?

The most delicate question remains whether the charismatic was a 'value-free' type for Weber, or whether the ideal type was really his *ideal*. When Weber began his section on 'charismatic authority' in a tone suggestive of enthusiasm, he immediately (and characteristically) rapped himself across the knuckles and emphasized the value-free character of the concept; even the charisma of 'the type of *littérateurs*, such as Kurt Eisner, who is overwhelmed by his own demagogic success' is treated by 'value-free sociological analysis' on the same level as 'the charisma of men who are the "greatest" heroes, prophets and saviours according to conventional judgements' (E&S 242). But for Weber the Munich Republic of Workers' Councils, presided over by Kurt Eisner, was a political carnival and anything but a model of charismatic rule.

When Weber emphasizes elsewhere that charisma was in a 'purely empirical and value-free sense . . . the specifically creative revolutionary force of history' (E&S 1117), it is not so easy to swallow his claim of value-freedom. Again and again there is an underlying tone of enthusiasm in what he says about the topic, and virtually nowhere do we find so much as a hint that charismatic leadership may have terrible consequences.[29] Friedrich Meinecke appositely remarked: 'The only position in the state where, according to Max Weber's construction, there are still a truly inner vivacity and high levels of moral and intellectual performance – one might say: where it is worth being human – is the Caesarist leadership. Weber, who was otherwise so stinting with ethical and sociable accents, speaks of it in lofty and powerful tones.'[30]

After 1945, the searching question was inevitably asked as to whether Weber had prophesied Hitler with his ideal type of the charismatic leader, *and* whether he – not so prophetically – had wished for a leader in the mould of Adolf Hitler.[31] Naturally the answers can never be definitive. Hopes for a strong leader were widespread before the rise of Hitler, not only on the right; they were not necessarily directed towards someone of Hitler's ilk. In his biographical study, Ian Kershaw has shown how the Nazi leader slotted into a pre-given role and indeed only gradually came to don the Führer mantle with all the expectations invested in it. But he must have had an exceptional talent for the role: he was not merely a product of 'society'. The hopes in a Führer entertained by someone like Weber show precisely that different types, more rationally driven than Hitler, were imaginable on the basis of German expectations at the time.

Nevertheless, Weber strikingly illustrates the extent to which even highly intelligent, excellently informed and by no means extreme right-wing people shared the hope that a Führer would cleverly leap over existing conditions.

There is no reason to play down this fact for reasons of mass pedagogy. What history teachers often forget is that the Nazi experience can be understood only if it is made clear that Hitler did not triumph because a half of Germans had gone mad by 1933, but because it was to some degree possible on rational grounds to wish for a Nazi victory. Even Raymond Aron, who discovered Weber as a young teaching assistant in pre-1933 Germany and intensively followed events there as a press correspondent, admitted in retrospect that, if he was not swept along by the Nazi movement despite his French nationality and Jewish origins, it was due more to his 'temperament' than his powers of reason.[32] The present as a totality is unclear, the future is unpredictable and rationality is ambiguous: this banal point is all too often ignored in relation to the history of National Socialism. Weber's fantasies about charisma remind us of this. Someone who clearly perceived certain tendencies of his age may nevertheless have been very wide of the mark with particular prognoses – even if they knew as much as Max Weber and had put as much effort as he into epistemological critique. This is rather a depressing thought, and it is not easy to extract from it a more heartening quintessence.

This element of insecurity is a strong reason why basic principles of the constitutional state should never be sacrificed to political theories. Would Weber himself have been prepared to do this? It may be that much about Hitler and his paladins would have impressed him; they did not have the 'slow and ponderous innkeeper's countenance' that he had despised on SPD podiums. Doubtless the Nazi leaders possessed a 'Catilinian energy of the deed', willing to take risks regardless of the consequences. Weber could not have fundamentally blamed Hitler for his blatant disregard for the traditional rules; that, after all, was the mark of a charismatic leader. Even Hitler's pathological traits were in keeping with his charismatic authority; the prophets of ancient Israel, as they appear in Weber's account, also had something psychologically abnormal – as did Weber himself. When one reads in the Bible how Elias slaughtered the 450 priests of Baal, it is easy to think that a charismatic figure who has attained rulership will be capable of mass murder. In the logic of Weber's thought, however, there was more reason to worry that everyday normality would too quickly smother the charismatic élan.[33] Weber was writing at a time when, like so many others in Germany, he saw an excess of pedantic correctness and could not imagine the development of a cynical and systematic contempt for the constitutional order.

Weber was convinced that, in evaluating a political movement, close attention should be paid to its human types, especially its leadership elite, that one had to look these people in the face. Indeed, some observers became aware of the National Socialist danger precisely by looking into Nazi faces. Before 1933 Otto Hintze said to Meinecke of Hitler: 'This man really doesn't belong to our race. There is something quite alien about him, something of an extinct primeval race that is completely amoral.'[34] What would Weber have seen in that face: murderous fanaticism or perhaps, closer to his own feelings, a heroic faith in destiny? In any event, from what we know of him, he would have exploded with rage at the abominable treatment of the Jews. In his *being*, he embodied values that were not explicit in his 'value-free' science, which is one of the main reasons for studying his life as well as his work. Even Georg Lukács – who in *The Destruction of Reason* disavowed his earlier period as a follower of Weber and included him among the forerunners of National Socialism – gave a decisive answer in 1971, shortly before his death, to an interviewer's question: 'Do you think that Weber, had he lived, might have become reconciled to National Socialism?' 'No, never', Lukács replied. 'You must understand that Weber was an absolutely honest person.'[35]

Christoph Steding, an admirer of Weber and future Nazi ideologue, wrote in 1932 that the Weberian 'charismatic' should demonstrate a 'pneumatic capacity for ecstasy'; 'it follows that one is a leader only according to circumstances, since no one can be permanently in a state of ecstatic excitement.'[36] Weber himself noted that 'acute ecstasies are transitory in their nature' (E&S 535): the Nazi leaders were well aware of this, with or without Weber's help – hence the passion for organization, the intense effort to gain support from big business, and the 'icy' gesture in contrast to folksy sentimentality. The Nazi dictatorship should be analysed not only as an example for the Weberian ideal type, but also as a reaction to definite weak points in that type of authority. And this gives us a paradigm for dealing with Weberian ideal types in general.

15

The Naturalness of Community –
The Disguised Naturalism in
Economy and Society

Rediscovery of the universally human: in the world and in his own self

Thucydides saw the usefulness of his history in the fact that people would be able to see the future in it, 'as it will repeat itself in this or similar ways in accordance with human nature' (Book I: 22): it is a famous quotation, which Franz Eulenburg took as the motto for his contribution to the Weber memorial volume ('Are "historical laws" possible?').[1] Such insights, a foundation for all philosophy since antiquity, are sometimes encountered in Weber's day in the form of 'aha' experiences. Hjalmar Schacht, the 'finance wizard', reported in his memoirs how in 1906, at the age of twenty-nine, he went hiking with his father in the mountains of the northwest Balkans. His father was struck mainly by the strangeness of life in the mountain villages. Were the people there not completely different from in Germany? But the son replied that they only appeared to be so; they were 'at bottom human beings like you and me'. They too behaved in an economically rational manner, in accordance with their particular conditions. The fundamental problems of human existence and economic life were the same everywhere. 'They are more in evidence here because they are simpler.'[2] In the Balkan mountains, too, the economy was set in motion because people had to buy what they were unable to produce themselves. But, since they did not turn over as many goods as the Germans, it was rational for them to leave their roads in a poor state of repair. Travellers generally like to speak of how different foreigners are; Schlacht's observations make it clear how, precisely in the age of historicism and nationalism, imperialism and racism, the realization that the same basic human phenomena recur everywhere, albeit in exotic dress, could become a key to the understanding of economics – even for a man who would be Hitler's finance minister.

The Austrian marginalist school based itself on a rediscovery of the universal foundations of economic life, although its formula for economic progress led to heights of abstraction that did not appeal to Weber. His speciality was virtuoso zig-zagging between conceptual models and an abundance of colourful reality. For him, too, the idea of one basic human nature unleashed a flow of insights, indeed an explosion of creativity,[3] and enabled him to revel in world history without falling into globetrotter dilettantism. One idea after another came to him about new concepts to be created and related to one another: a common way of leaving one's mark in science. Karl Polanyi even asserted:

> Max Weber was the first among modern economic historians to protest against the brushing aside of primitive economics as irrelevant to the question of the motives and mechanisms of civilized societies. The subsequent work of social anthropology proved him emphatically right. For, if one conclusion stands out more clearly than another from the recent study of early societies, it is the changelessness of man as a social being.[4]

Experiences of love, a new feeling of strength and the new social milieu that formed around him must have meant a new experience of his own nature: whereas he had previously felt doomed to loneliness and sexual asceticism, and written in *The Protestant Ethic* as if the genesis of this special nature had been a world-historical event, he now felt he was part of a *universal* human nature that included sexuality and companionability, while not ruling out the existence also of historically shaped individual elements.[5] If until then Weber had been tormented by the gulf between vegetative nature and the world of the mind, he now became more and more aware of a continuum between mind and nature. He had long since felt that his own nature was subject to inexorable laws, but now he increasingly experienced the opportunities and freedoms contained in his nature – not least as a result of intense interaction between nature and mind.

From that time on Weber also began to recognize law-like aspects of mind–nature in human history: not necessarily *iron* laws, but *opportunities* that regularly arose under certain conditions. Theodor Heuss later thought that Weber had 'imported probability calculations into the sociological perspective', thereby making it 'more lively, colourful and exciting'.[6] It is true that what he discovered were not new laws of economics but law-like phenomena governing mysticism, asceticism, ecstasy and the relationship between religion and eroticism. Beginning with archaic magical-religious rituals, a rudimentary rationalization – a striving to bring order or system into one's own conduct – operates for Weber as a kind of basic law resting upon a disposition in human nature, quite independently of the rationality peculiar to the modern West. He could write this, for example:

> Asceticism becomes the object of methodical practices as soon as the ecstatic or contemplative union with God is transformed, from a state that only some individuals can achieve through their charismatic endowments, into a goal that many can reach through identifiable ascetic means . . . Everywhere the method was at first basically the

same as that developed by the most ancient monasticism, the Indian, with the greatest consistency and variety. (E&S 1169)

Sometimes we find an exaggerated faith in the 'nature of things', even in the case of bureaucracy, as if its principle had been everywhere the same from ancient Egypt to modern Prussia. But for Weber this was only one side of history: his world was characterized not only by uniformity but also by infinite diversity. In human nature itself, a plurality of opportunities existed because of various differentiations and degrees of autonomy. Since human beings are individuals and are increasingly aware of themselves as individuals, they are alike in their need to demarcate themselves from one another. In this way 'small differences' become large differences; the 'universal force of imitation' (E&S 388) runs counter to the need for demarcation.

Not without reason did Meinecke think that Weber had wanted to define 'iron laws for science and life', but had 'lived' them in his own life more than he had 'studied' them in his writings (WzG 145). Meinecke noted this with a sense of distance: knowledge of the individual was for him the quintessential revelation. For Weber, however – in the view of Eduard Baumgarten – mere historians were 'relatively uninteresting' precisely because they 'neither knew nor wanted to know anything about natural science' – by which he meant above all behavioural psychology. Baumgarten, who was concerned to bridge the gap between philosophy and behavioural research, thought that the task of Weber's successors was 'to take further his researches into natural science, with precision and circumspection' (B 589).

A great plan and the 'goddamn treadmill': the *Grundriß der Sozialökonomik*

The project through which Weber developed his new capacity for intellectual appropriation of the world was already in existence by the beginning of 1909, but only years later did he initiate the four-volume *Grundriß der Sozialökonomik*; the Tübingen publisher Siebeck had originally conceived it as a new edition of Gustav Schönberg's *Handbuch der Politischen Ökonomie*, though it became something quite different under Weber's direction. Already in 1905 Paul Siebeck had sounded Weber out, but it was only after Schönberg's death, in the autumn of 1908, that Weber took on editorial responsibility for the whole project.[7] In those years, when Weber felt incapable of lecturing or of publishing major works, he sought a new role as independent adviser, stimulator and organizer and saw his forte as the critical reading of other people's texts. But, presumably to spare the vanity of other contributors, he did not wish to appear officially as the editor of the whole Siebeck project (MWG I/22-1, 17): the title page of the *Grundriß* mentions him only as one of forty-five 'collaborators'. He was keen to play a central role in scholarship, but not in a publicly visible manner.

The handbook project, which repeatedly placed Weber under pressure until the end of his life, turned into a frustrating and demoralizing torture. For a long time it looked as if it would share the fate of the planned work on 'psychophysics' or the investigation into the press. To some extent it was a question of the editor's usual irksome tasks, but in addition he came to feel that he had no power to impose a minimum of discipline on the other authors, so that for years the project threatened to become a complete fiasco.[8] In contrast to his position at the *Archiv*, he felt that the editing job cast him in the role of a beggar rather than a ruler; he felt called upon to 'play the fool', as one tardy author appealing to others equally unforthcoming (MWG II/8, 47). A reader of the correspondence gets a sense of how terrible it all was: one letter after another, half-pleading, half-pestering, to designated authors who continually fob him off with talk of medical problems, wearing down an editor who has himself so often invoked his frail health – yet are able to continue writing other things (MWG II/8, 371); embarrassment in the face of authors who have delivered their manuscript on time and threaten to withdraw it unless it goes into print before it becomes outdated (MWG II/8, 397); embarrassment in dealing with the publisher, when one deadline after another falls far short of being met; and, probably worst of all, the guilty conscience that he is unable to keep his promises concerning his own contribution.

From this point of view, it was actually a relief for Weber that other authors did not come up with their contributions. Still in February 1912 – when a schedule was agreed that would again be far from met – he candidly wrote to Oskar Siebeck, the son of the company head: 'Things are really bad this winter as far as my capacity for work is concerned, and so the postponement of the deadline comes as a release for me too' (MWG II/7-1, 425). In January 1913 Weber gave vent to his feelings in a letter to the economist Johann Plenge (who had already delivered large chunks of his contribution and 'ascetically' vowed to abstain from other work (MWG II/8, 57), but who repeatedly maintained that 'working to a deadline' was bad for his delicate 'nerves').[9] The handbook project, Weber complained, was a 'goddamn treadmill', which had 'cost years of [his] life just in letters' and would 'cover him with shame' if he, Plenge, let him down again (MWG II/8, 50) – a foreboding that proved well founded when Plenge too dropped out. In November 1913 he groaned that the handbook had already cost him 'several friendships',[10] 'thanks to the quite indescribable thoughtlessness and idling of various colleagues', and that in the end everything would have been in vain: 'The handbook will drown in a jumble of proceedings' (MWG II/8, 382, 379). Instead of placing him in a key position, the large-scale project had landed him in a dilemma. This whole mood did not fit very well with Mina Tobler and the 'enchantresses' of Ascona, but perhaps it was precisely now, when other worlds had opened up for him, that he was able to confess with fewer inhibitions than in the past that the management of scholarly research was a pestilential nuisance and that he longed for quite a different kind of life.

Weber's knightly service for the honour of his publisher

And then, to make matters still worse, came the insulting dispute with Professor Bernhard Harms (1876–1939) in Kiel. This disciple of Schönberg's, a founder of the theory of world economy opposed to the nationally oriented political economy then dominant in Germany, made the accusation that the handbook project was ignoring the rights of Schönberg's legacy. Siebeck countered that it was an altogether new project, not a revamping of the Schönberg handbook. Actually the dispute was more the concern of the publishing house than of Weber, but Siebeck had to promise him not to get more closely involved. Weber believed that Harms was attacking his own honour, and he went into battle boiling with rage. He broke off his friendship with Tönnies, whom he had long esteemed but now saw as a supporter of his opponent, and vented to him all his anger not only with Harms but with the whole editing business:

> [G]iven the contemptible disloyalty, idling, indifference and thought-lessness of various colleagues, at whose repeated request I took on this wretched (wretched for me) business, I now face the danger of losing more than just my 'scholarly name' (which never meant a lot to me), and the honour of the publishing house is *one and the same with my own honour*. . . . This miserable handbook, which I agreed to edit at the insistence of scholars who then despicably and shamelessly betrayed me, . . . will probably take away not only my scholarly name (which never meant so terribly much to me), but . . . also my unblemished reputation. (MWG II/8, 126ff.)

Weber, already an outsider in academia, ran the risk of becoming a complete nonentity – and this he revealed to a man of whom it must be supposed that he would pass it on to Weber's opponent. In relation to the handbook it sometimes seems as if Weber had taken leave of his senses. For, if the other collaborators had got wind of his outbursts of rage against them, the project could easily have collapsed and even the best-intentioned ones might have pulled out.[11]

Weber complained to Plenge that Harms was an 'unchivalrous scoundrel',[12] who spread the slander that he, Weber, had betrayed Schönberg's legacy. Harms had also said 'with scorn and derision' that, 'if my illness prevented me from proper forward planning, I should not have assumed this function (as editor)' (MWG II/8, 49). This completed the embarrassment: Harms, who as founder and director of the Kiel Archive of World Economics had shown himself to have excellent managerial qualities, and who had probably hoped to take on himself the new edition of Schönberg's handbook, had been kept out of this position by Weber and in 1912–13 was able to point to the latter's failings in his task. In much the same way that Weber liked to think of himself as a knight fighting various battles, Harms acted the loyal warrior defending the rights of his dead teacher's family, especially as his daughters were not provided for financially;[13] it was a situation that cried out for a saviour. The protection of widows and orphans was the classical duty of the noble knight.

The role that fell to Weber was not exactly attractive. But he too felt himself in the right, as the planned collective work (which from now on traded under the name *Grundriß der Sozialökonomik*) really was supposed to be quite different from Schönberg's *Handbuch der politischen Ökonomie*. He challenged Harms to a duel by sabre, but when Harms accepted only after some time he lost interest. 'I won't fight a duel months later in cold blood, without passion, because a "code of conduct" or "code of honour" requires it. That's simply disgusting!' (MWG II/8, 81). Harms too then ceased to pursue the matter (II/8, 20). 'Simply disgusting!' was also how he responded to Weber's behaviour over the legacy of Schönberg, which he described as 'shameless vilification' (II/8, 35). In Harms, then, Weber had an adversary of similar calibre to himself. Marianne, however, laughed at him because of his challenge to a duel.[14]

The story has features of a grotesque comedy: precisely because Weber was incapable of keeping even half his editorial undertakings to Siebeck, he may have thought it a kind of compensation when he declared his willingness to fight for the publisher's honour, as if he had been a courtly lady. Weber's relationship to Siebeck, together with his many sighs and threats to call the whole thing off, is among the most energetic and best-documented of his life.[15] It is doubtful whether Siebeck found this knightly service agreeable. The honour for which Weber acted so militantly was not really *social* honour, but rather a product of very personal needs. From now on he would feel more than ever the compulsion to act and the pressure to succeed involved in the *Grundriß* project. As a result of Harms's challenge, it became a matter of honour for him to give proof of his abilities, and to demonstrate that the planned collective work really was something completely new.

Born of necessity: *Economy and Society*

Despite his complaints Weber experienced a new rush of creativity after 1912, and instead of grappling with new authors he began to form the plan of making his own contribution much more extensive than he had originally intended. In 1913 he got down to serious writing. Inevitably his work entered the maelstrom of the 'sociology of religion' – or, rather, the anthropology of religions of salvation, which would occupy him most intensely for the rest of his life. The bundle of texts that appeared after his death under the title *Economy and Society* contains far more exciting ideas about the relationship between eroticism and religions of salvation than about that between economy and society – indeed, connoisseurs of Weber are so used to this peculiarity that their attention is no longer drawn to it. In *Economy and Society*, even status groups and classes – the standard theme of any social theory – are discussed in detail only in the context of religion. Tenbruck has convincingly argued that Weber's true *magnum opus* and final word is not *Economy and Society* but the *Wirtschaftsethik der Weltreligionen*,[16] which widens out into an anthropology of religion.

Largely as a result of Tenbruck's provocative research, we know today that *Economy and Society* is a collage of texts undertaken under Marianne Weber's direction, in which it can no longer be precisely established what he did and did not intend to be part of the *Grundriß der Sozialökonomik*, what the overall structure should look like and – an unimportant question for him – what the title should be. 'Any title is fine by me', he wrote to Siebeck in April 1914. And even on the general structure of the *Grundriß*, 'anything is fine by me' (MWG II/8, 610f.). Many issues regarding the origins of this mass of material are still in dispute, but at least one thing is clear: the sequence in the posthumous edition of *Economy and Society* partly reverses the sequence in which it developed, creating the misleading impression that Weber conceived the sections on 'basic terms' and 'sociological categories'[17] as the basis for the whole work.[18] In reality his starting point had been *primitive communities* – an area for which he could fall back on Marianne's history of marriage and matriarchy. The edition of Max Weber's collected works has restored this formative sequence.

If what had originally been conceived as a contribution to the *Grundriß* took on such monumental dimensions, one of the main forces driving this was Marianne Weber. Since 1909 she had come to believe more and more strongly that her husband would be basically healthy if he led a regular life, and that what he now needed was a major task to give him a feeling of strength. In April 1911 she wrote to Helene: 'I'm really longing for him to create something "great" again, but for that he needs a steadier life.'[19] 'At last he concentrated on a uniformly great task', she wrote triumphantly of the time when, after all the disappointments with other contributors, he 'began to pour the stream of his knowledge into this vessel' of his own work (WB 419), instead of wasting it on mere rivulets.

After Weber's death, when Marianne began to create the *Economy and Society* package out of the texts and fragments he had left behind, she endeavoured to make the work appear as monumental and orderly as possible, rather as, to her husband's annoyance, she had from time to time tidied up the heap of papers on his desk. When there was more than one manuscript on the same theme – the sociology of domination, for instance – she was not content to publish the later version but also included the earlier draft, as if it had been the general as opposed to the more specialized exposition. Only after more than half a century did Weber researchers understand the arbitrary aspect of this collage.[20]

There is no doubt that, when Weber switched from editor to author, indeed principal author, he finally came into his own. With his sense of honour at stake, he set about rescuing the *Grundriß* project from disgrace and put on paper a flow of ideas that must have been building up inside him for years. The change of mood is discernible in his correspondence. On

8 February 1913, when he assured Paul Siebeck that the 'Harms affair' had 'not in the least' worked him up, he also held out the prospect that 'the major article on "economy, society, law and the state" will be *systematically* the best I have written up to now', precisely because he had to make up for the non-delivery by prominent economist Karl Bücher, which he mentioned at every opportunity (MWG II/8, 86f.). At the end of the year, he proudly wrote to the publisher as a highly regarded sociologist[21] – the letter is his most revealing testimony about the genesis of *Economy and Society*:

> As Bücher – stages of development – is completely inadequate, I have worked out a closed sociological theory and account that relates all major forms of community to the economy: from the family and the household community to the "business operation", the kinship group, the ethnic community, religion (*all* major religions in the world: sociology of salvation doctrines and religious ethics – what Troeltsch did, now for *all* religions, only much more succinct), and finally a comprehensive sociological theory of the state and domination. I may claim that there has not yet been *anything* like it, not even a 'model'. (MWG II/8, 449f.)

This was indeed the most effective riposte to Harms: a work that no longer had anything in common with Schönberg's handbook. A 'closed sociological theory': probably a lot more things were closed inside his head than he would be capable of putting on paper by the time he died – a constant stimulus for theorists to make a complete system out of the torso left in the shape of *Economy and Society*. In long sections one feels the traces of the *Wirtschaftsethik der Weltreligionen*; the Oriental religions are already discernible. Rather as, in the case of religion, his main concern was with small communities animated by charisma, 'sociology' in *Economy and Society* is the theory not of 'society' but of 'forms of community'. These stand in a relationship to the economy, but they are by no means just a function of it.

War as a release from onerous duties of his own creation

Weber did not always display such pride in the developing work. On 10 July 1914 he wrote to Georg von Below, perhaps to anticipate the criticism of a historian who anyway had little time for sociology: 'No one can be happy with my presentation that will appear next spring. . . . Today one cannot try to be a "maid of all work", but that is what I had to do after others had left me in the lurch' (MWG II/8, 750). Three weeks later war broke out: Weber became a medical officer, more absorbed in practical matters than at any time since his military service, and could no longer think of publishing *Economy and Society* to schedule. 'The poor GdS (*Grundriß der Sozialökonomik*)!' Siebeck wrote to him on 4 August. 'The demand for it was already building up so well.'[22] And at the end of the year: The 'fate of the GdS' is well and truly sealed; 'that's hard.'[23] But it would anyway have been impossible for Weber to deliver on time: in this and other respects the war brought him freedom from pressing obligations; nor was he the only German of whom this was the case. The extent of Weber's relief may be gauged from the fact that, a couple of days earlier, he had warned his publisher not to put too much pressure on him:

> I am a 'maid of all work'. For three years now I have worked only on this account and only for this, putting my health at risk (that is not saying too much). If, apart from my health and zest for life, I also lose my good name in this business – and that can happen! These are the trickiest and most controversial issues in our discipline and in sociology! – then I would surely never forgive you for it. That will start to happen if I am pushed. (MWG II/8, 776)

Again the old horror of deadline pressure. Nevertheless, the first volumes of the *Grundriß* did appear before the end of the war – including the one on the 'natural and technical relations of the economy'. First of all came the natural 'geographical conditions of the human economy', written by the geographer Alfred Hettner, a colleague of Weber's in Heidelberg, who had been 'forced to become a deskbound scholar' because of a disability.[24] Weber was disappointed with the contribution (MWG II/8, 575); he had had higher expectations of how the subject would be treated.

'*Gemeinschaft*': a term with overtones: Othmar Spann and Ferdinand Tönnies

When Weber began work on *Economy and Society*, the title had already been used for a basic work on the 'system of social theory' by the political economist Othmar Spann (1878–1950), whom Weber had wanted to write a contribution on 'conjunctures and crises' (MWG II/8, 385), and who after the war made a name for himself as the theorist of a new corporatist system of social estates. Not long before the outbreak of war he had declared it to be a profound sociological truth that was indispensable for a 'warm living community', and that 'the blood of fallen warriors' was 'fiery medicine for the circulating juices of the state organism' – sentiments which make us appreciate the (today no longer so unusual) stone-cold sobriety of Max Weber's writings, especially as the emotions fuelling such a glorification of war were by no means alien to him. He had understood that they were emotions, not lofty insights.

In Weber's day, the theme of 'community' had long been associated with a fundamental work of German sociology: *Gemeinschaft und Gesellschaft*, by Ferdinand Tönnies (1855–1936), which bore the subtitle 'Basic Concepts of Pure Sociology'.[25] Although it later came to be seen as a pioneering work, it had originally been 'hard to grasp': even for Max Weber, who, as he admitted to Tönnies in 1910, had had to 'struggle good and proper' with it (MWG II/6, 703f.). The second edition came out only in 1912, to be followed by six more until 1935. It was a genre that had not existed before: too abstract for the prevailing Historical School, but too concrete for philosophy. Tönnies contrasted the natural, warm-blooded primeval community with the cold, modern society governed by monetary relations. Both, of course, were not real historical phenomena but ideal types; Tönnies, however, did not yet understand as well as Weber how to conceptualize his methodological premises. In comparison with Weberian ideal types, his *Gemeinschaft* and *Gesellschaft* were much too uncomplicated: they gave no idea of the unruliness of historical reality and provided no impulse for a research programme. Later, when sociology became more sober and more international, Tönnies's *Gemeinschaft*, with its Romantic-nostalgic characteristics, was seen as epitomizing Germany's special path in sociology, which had led it into a dead end. By contrast, Weber's concept of *Vergemeinschaftung* had elements of cool rationality and connotations of conflict; it therefore sounds more modern today.

When Weber began work on *Economy and Society* – and, as we now know, he began with 'communities' – the word *Gemeinschaft* already had for social scientists Tönnies's overtones of organic harmony and warmth. Yet Weber made *Gemeinschaft* rather than *Gesellschaft* the central concept of *Economy and Society*. Following on from Tönnies, but with a dynamization of his conceptual polarity, Weber introduced *Vergemeinschaftung* and *Vergesellschaftung* (that is, respectively, the development of communal and associative social relationships) as 'basic sociological terms' (E&S 40ff.). From time to time – especially in his essay of 1913 'Über einige Kategorien der verstehenden Soziologie'[26] – the terminology of *Gemeinschaft* receded a little in favour of something more sober, but on the whole it still remained central. Curiously, Weber even speaks of *Marktgemeinschaft*; the fragment referring to this in the title (E&S 635-40) is his only text on the market, the constitutive phenomenon of the modern economy.

Unlike Tönnies, Weber does not consistently set up *Gemeinschaft* as an ideal type in contrast to *Gesellschaft*. It is true that at first he defines *Vergemeinschaftung* as a type of social action that 'is based on a subjective feeling of the parties . . . that they belong together' (E&S 40). But he then assumes, realistically enough, that actually existing communities support themselves not only on emotional but also on purposive relationships, and in some cases entirely on the latter (MWG I/22, 40).[27] Since human beings possess certain violent traits by nature, it is by no means the case that love and harmony alone govern the natural [*urwüchsig*] community; there is also a lot of hatred and violence; even rape is not uncommon, but belongs among the 'normal' factors of selection. One finds a brutal social Darwinism again and again in the late Weber.[28]

One of the most attractive aspects of Weber's writings is their ambiguity. A cursory reading of *The Protestant Ethic* and Weber's analysis of the bases of legitimate rule may lead one to think of him as an authority for political morality, but insiders who have read him more closely are familiar with an undercurrent of irony, supported on a stone-cold sober view of human nature. At times Weber even identifies a completely external, situation-dependent type of 'communal action' devoid of any coming together of minds. Take, for example, two cyclists who come to blows after colliding with each other:

> We shall speak of 'social action' (*Gemeinschaftshandeln*) wherever human action is subjectively related in meaning to the behaviour of others. An unintended collision of two cyclists, for example, shall not be called social action. But we will define as such their possible prior attempts to dodge one another or, after the accident, their possible altercation or negotiation about an amicable settlement.[29]

At such points Weber seems to be making fun of Tönnies's or Spann's concept of *Gemeinschaft*, charged with an excess of emotion and raw nature. Weber's community seems closer to reality precisely because it contains much of the unattractive banality of everyday life. But this is not all. Later, in 'Science as a Vocation', Weber declared that 'today only within the smallest and intimate circles, in personal human situations, in *pianissimo*, . . . something is pulsating that corresponds to the prophetic *pneuma*, which in former times swept through the great communities like a firebrand, welding them together' (FMW 155).

A new creative phase achieved by falling back on primary experiences of his own

Guided by the idea of a human nature that is everywhere fundamentally the same, Weber made his own primary experiences of family, household community and brotherly relations the key to his knowledge of the world, in a quite realistic spirit without any harmonizing romanticism. This recourse to early experiences of life allowed his creativity to blossom anew. Already when he was studying for his doctorate, Weber had discovered the importance of family ties in the medieval trading organizations of northern Italy. Later he thought that the soul of the consciously autonomous city republics of the Middle Ages was the blood brotherhood of the *coniuratio*, the sworn confraternity; and at the end of his life he saw this civic freedom, which existed only in the West, as the origin of the special Occidental path in world history (E&S 1248ff.), the worldly asceticism of the Puritans having become secondary in importance. Novelty repeatedly sprang from small communities, where social relations had a dimension palpable to the senses: in the history of religious sects among the disciples of prophets; and in politics among charismatic leaders, who, together with their followers, bore a resemblance to the prophets. 'Democracy in America is not a heap of sand but a maze of exclusive sects, associations and clubs', Weber told the sociologists' congress in Frankfurt (GASS 443); sociological knowledge in his view had something of 'insider knowledge'. In *Economy and Society*, it is true, the 'types of rule or domination' are placed *before* the 'primitive' forms of community; but Johannes Winckelmann, who took over this structure for traditional reasons, later distanced himself from it. According to Weber's 'final rigorous systematization', he wrote, 'rule could under no circumstances be treated *before* the development of political communities.'[30]

One dispute among historians at that time concerned, in Rudolf Stammler's words, 'whether the family should be considered the oldest form of common existence from which the state grew only later on, or whether the state must necessarily be assumed to have existed alongside the family.'[31] Stammler, the anti-naturalist, believed with a jurist's logic that the regulation of relations within the micro-group necessarily involved a wider legal order. Max Weber thought otherwise: he recognized no elemental compulsion towards macro-structure. At the sociologists' congress in Frankfurt in 1910 he spoke of the 'naturally grown community of the family' (in contrast to 'politically organized authorities'), as if it was a familiar concept that identified the province of sociology in the space between the organic and the organized (GASS 441f.).

One of Weber's very few handwritten drafts that have survived the years is a long-unnoticed outline entitled 'Household Unit, Kinship Group and Neighbourhood', which probably dates from the autumn of 1906 (MWG I/22-1, 36) and represents a kind of missing link between Marianne Weber's *Ehefrau und Mutter in der Rechtsentwicklung* and *Economy and Society* (I/22-1, 290ff.).[32] The first term in the title was originally 'household *community*', but Weber then replaced this with 'unit'. At the top left of the title page is a note: 'sexual relations prostitution'. It begins with a rejection of pure biologism: 'Sexual relations do not by themselves found communities. . . . Originally: community of *mother* & children . . . Decisive: *care* community. Never *only* "maternal groupings". Always alongside: male communities.' The male association is also *urwüchsig*, 'original', 'natural' or 'elemental': this was a discovery of the ethnology of the time. Under the heading 'household communities' in *Economy and Society*, we find the elaborated version corresponding to these keywords:

> Of all the relationships arising from sexual intercourse, only the mother–child relationship is 'natural', because it is a biologically based household unit that lasts until the child is able to search for means of subsistence on his own. Next comes the sibling group, which the Greeks called *homogalaktes* [literally: persons suckled with the same milk]. Here, too, the decisive point is not the fact of the common mother but that of common maintenance. Manifold groups emerge, in addition to sexual and physiological relationships, as soon as the family emerges as a specific social institution. (E&S 357)

'Natural' (*urwüchsig*) is between inverted commas – but these are dropped shortly afterwards when Weber calls the household community 'the fundamental (*urwüchsig*) basis of loyalty and authority, which in turn is the basis of many other groups' (E&S 359). That the family is not simply a natural phenomenon had long been one of the fundamental tenets of sociology; no more original was the idea that the sex drive as such cannot found a stable community. Not only was this common theoretical property among sociologists; a considerable part of literature and theatre dealt with how Eros thwarts the order of society. At that time Max Weber had conspicuous evidence of this in his own circle.

Although marriage has sexuality as its natural precondition, it also involves a domestication of the sex drive: this insight, too, was anything but novel. Yet the sexual dimension is far from incidental in *Economy and Society*. It is true that the German index contains only two entries under *Sexualität*, but the electronic edition turns up more than ninety references to *Sexualität/sexuell* in the text. The contrast is striking with Spann and Tönnies, in whose otherwise intimate communities the sexual aspect makes only sporadic appearances; their organological vision distracts us from the simple organic foundations. For Weber, too, sexuality as such does not found a stable community – of course not! – yet the sexual union of living bodies is more real than the organologically derived unity of collective corporations. The *homogalaktes*, suckled at the same breast, are for Weber an archetype of the community grounded upon elemental needs of subsistence.

The word *urwüchsig* appears 130 times in Weber's work – mostly in *Economy and Society*. Karl Marx preferred the term *naturwüchsig*, using it in the deprecating sense of 'primitive'; the path of progress led for him, as for many of his contemporaries, to the overcoming of man's dependence on nature and the creation of a distinctively human world. Weber's avoidance of this term in favour of *urwüchsig* actually appears to be deliberate, since it denotes not only human biological tendencies but also age-old patterns of behaviour. In the Freiburg inaugural lecture of 1895, Weber characterized the urge for freedom as 'one of the most elemental [*urwüchsigsten*] drives in the human breast' (PW 8), but also derived the nation state from 'deeply rooted [*urwüchsigen*] psychological foundations' (PW 21) that reappeared especially in time of war. Also *urwüchsig* is for him physical combat, which is already documented in the most ancient historical sources. The historically primeval here takes the place of nature; Weber would have shared the view of many historians that one gets to the heart of phenomena by tracing their origins but, let us be clear, not only their origins. Weber would not be the great disenchanter and unveiler if he had not also constantly destroyed myths of origin and exposed 'naturalness' as a fiction (B 428). His naturalism is always of the 'yes, but' variety.

Weber had experiences of his own to show that 'natural' community is not the only tendency in man. When he had married his cousin he doubtless hoped that family and sexuality would be compatible with each other; but this proved to be an illusion, and the failure must have been the great trauma of his life. Marianne tried to see her marriage partner as a 'comrade', but Else, in reply to Max's longing for brotherly community, said that 'brotherliness' was a faraway land for her. Whereas Tönnies contrasted non-natural 'society' with natural 'community', Weber knew that forces destructive of community are also part of the human make-up: the erotic drive, but also the drive for scientific knowledge, whose uncompromising quest for truth breaks up the communal consensus.

Large social units grew out of small communities: the city from the fraternity and the large state from the city-state; the princely economy from the household economy of the *oikos*; religion from sects and groups of disciples. All these were accompanied by processes of rationalization, bureaucratization and hierarchy formation. In Weber's view, struggle also leads to processes of evolutionary selection in a Darwinian sense, though without an inner law of higher development (E&S 39). He too, who once polemicized against the 'stages of development' so beloved of the Historical School, quite often lapsed into the language of evolutionism, whether in *Economy and Society* or in his sociology of religion. As if he had forgotten what he said in *Roscher and Knies*, he even wrote of 'stages in the formation of political association' (or, in another version, of 'communal relationships') (E&S 904ff.). Again with a penchant for shocking examples, he characterized the transition from archaic 'naturalism' to sublimated symbolism – in a sense, one of the first stages of rationalization, which had 'immeasurable consequences for the development of civilization' – as a regularly occurring process of development:

> When the primitive tears out the heart of a slain foe, or wrenches the sexual organs from the body of his victim, or extracts the brain from the skull and then mounts the skull in his home or esteems it as the most precious of bridal presents, or eats parts of the bodies of slain foes, . . . he really believes that he is coming into possession, in a naturalistic fashion, of the various powers attributed to these physical organs. The war dance is in the first instance the product of a mixture of fury and fear before the battle, and it directly produces the heroic frenzy; to this extent it too is naturalistic rather than symbolic. [But] the transition to symbolism is at hand insofar as the war dance . . . mimetically anticipates victory and thereby endeavours to ensure it by magical means. (E&S 406)

From such processes of sublimation, rationalization, institutionalization, bureaucratization, anonymization, disenchantment of the world and removal from the 'organic cycle' of natural existence, it is possible to construct a grand process of development: the one we today call 'modernization'.[33] But we need to be cautious: this takes us away from Max Weber himself. The last thing he wanted to do was to plane down and interlink the whole of history in this way. To be sure, he was quite familiar with long-term, more or less irreversible processes, unplanned and without a leading actor – and so, in that sense, 'developments'; but they did not add up to one great evolutionary totality advancing to become the subject of history. In Weber, organological notions never entirely displace real organisms, real human bodies; individuals and the small groups in which they are physically present remain the ultimate actors, and so there always remains a chance of breaking through the long-term trends, at least in certain 'non-everyday' situations.

He considers especially unscientific the teleological thinking often concealed in evolutionism: the equation of development with progress. In 1907 he told Rickert that he wanted some day to make a critique of the biologists' only seemingly value-free concept of development, which equated 'higher' with 'more complex and differentiated' – 'as if the embryo and a fortiori the "germ plasm" etc. with all its "predispositions" were not the most complex of all the things known to biology' (MWG II/5, 415). As we see, he kept up to date in genetic theory. He was able to deploy rigorous natural science against popular biology.

Animality in feudalism

Weber's classical example of a form of rule that had its source in the intimate two-way emotional relations within a small community was *feudalism*. The early modern theorists who invented 'feudalism' as a legal system tried to make it as objective as possible. Weber, however, thought of it as an essentially personal, *non*-objective relationship; the concept involved intuitive understanding of the living reality behind the historical documents. His most detailed and colourful account of feudalism comes in the 'sociology of domination' in part II of *Economy and Society*, which, unlike that in part I, was written before the war, when feudalism was still present in the German Reich (at least for those who polemicized against 'Junkerdom'). Weber writes:

> The feudal consociation [*Vergesellschaftung*] . . . permeated the most important relationships with very personal bonds; their peculiarity also had the effect of centring the feeling of knightly dignity upon the cult of the personal. This contrasts violently with all impersonal and commercial relationships, which are bound to appear undignified and vulgar to the feudal ethic. . . . The typical feudal army is an army of knights, and that means that individual heroic combat, not the discipline of a mass army, is decisive. . . . Therefore, one element finds a permanent place in training and general conduct, which . . . belongs to the original energy household of men and animals, but is increasingly eliminated by every rationalization of life – the *game*. Under feudal conditions it is just as little a 'pastime' as in organic life, rather it is the natural form in which the psycho-physical capacities of the organism are kept alive and supple; the game is a form of 'training', which in its spontaneous and unbroken animal instinctiveness as yet

transcends any split between the 'spiritual' and the 'material', 'body' and 'soul', no matter how conventionally it is sublimated. (E&S 1105)

This scarcely noticed passage deserves to be included in all the readers. Those who persist in worshipping Weber as the pope of rationalization who loathed feudal 'anti-modernism' do not know their man well and have no sensorium for his language. It is true that, in reality, feudalism was often associated with unfeeling exploitation, but Weber's ideal type has an element of idealization and is not exactly a model of value-freedom. During the final period before the war he liked to play the knight, in the service of women[34] as well as in the struggle for honour, and after the outbreak of war, with his emotions still in the age of the horse, he would have loved to ride off on his steed to face the enemy; he felt unmistakably at home in the world of feudalism as he described it. The elemental and 'undiminished animal impulses' of that world embodied health and happiness – that which he had long lacked but now at least glimpsed during the birth pangs of *Economy and Society*. When he quoted 'the famous herald's call of the French knighthood to their opponents before the battle of Fontenoy (in 1745): *Messieurs les Anglais, tirez les premiers!'* (RI 146) – a favourite anecdote of military historians – one senses his pleasure at the idea that the knights remained gallant even under attack. In reality, however, there was probably more irony than 'courtesy' in the call; what followed was not a knightly battle but a bloodbath under cannon fire.

Weber took great care not to confuse feudalism with the 'patrimonialism' associated with family patriarchy, which demands obedience and loyalty from dependants. Although in history the two cannot be sharply distinguished from each other, Weber drew his ideal type of feudalism precisely in contrast to patrimonialism, not, as one might expect, to capitalism.[35] He stressed that feudalism did not generate the kind of mental dependence characteristic of absolute patriarchy but, on the contrary, cultivated a brave, free spirit conscious of its own honour and dignity:

> The structure of domination affected the general habits of the peoples more by virtue of the *ethos* which it established . . . In this respect feudalism and patriarchal patrimonialism differ greatly. Both shaped strongly divergent political and social ideologies and through them a different style of life. . . . The specific element that determines the vassal's behaviour under fully developed feudalism is the appeal not only to his obligations of fealty, but to his sense of high status which derives from an exalted conception of honour. The warrior's sense of honour and the servant's faithfulness are both inseparably connected with the dignity and conventions of a ruling stratum . . . Thus, the peculiarity of the Occidental, fully developed feudalism was largely determined by the fact that it constituted the basis of a cavalry . . . We will frequently encounter the ramifications of this factor. (E&S 1104, 1077f.)

The *horse*: a by no means insignificant animal basis of feudalism[36] (or at least of its ideal type) and therefore of the Western path in general. For only in Europe did feudalism attain its supreme completion – at least for Weber, whose discussion of 'feudalism' continually takes in Asia, from Turkey to Japan. Fully developed feudalism is by no means an obstacle to capitalism in every respect. Rather, 'feudalism, with its closely delineated rights and duties, does not only have a stabilizing effect upon the economy as a whole, but also upon the distribution of individual wealth', through 'a synthesis of purely concrete rights and duties' that amount to a 'constitutional state' (*Rechtsstaat*) (E&S 1099). From today's viewpoint, Weber saw here more clearly than all those who – in accordance with the conventional liberal or Marxist model – constructed an opposition between 'feudalism' and 'capitalism'.[37] Trade, on the other hand – contrary to the faith of liberal free-traders – promoted 'the development of strong, centralized patrimonial bureaucracies' at least as much as decentralized non-bureaucratic feudalism (E&S 1092).

The triad of types of rule

Weber's thoughts on feudalism, in sharp contrast to those on 'charismatic rule', have also received less attention than they deserve.[38] Weber's 'feudalism' does not fit so well into the famous 'three pure types of legitimate rule: rational, traditional and charismatic'; it has traditional but also charismatic elements. The chapter on feudalism in *Economy and Society* is inserted between the ones on charisma. We should not think that Weber's ideas on rulership always and completely operated on the tracks of the well-known triad; the city republics that grew out of *coniurationes* did not fit into it either, and were incorporated into the work as forms of 'non-legitimate rule' (E&S 1121-64, 1368). But it would be a complete misunderstanding of Weber to conclude that he regarded such polities, in which he still saw something of the spirit of fraternity, as inferior in value: on the contrary, they were for him the origin of Western liberties and individual rights, as was feudalism.

Since Aristotle, political theory has traditionally identified three types of constitution: monarchical, aristocratic and democratic. Weber too preserved this 'mysterious dependence on the number three' (Henry J. Merry),[39] but democracy of all things does not feature in his typology of rule – at a time when democratization was the order of the day in Germany! There could be no genuine 'rule by the people', only rule by leaders and small elites – not an entirely unrealistic view with today's experience. After all, democracy occurs in a context of charismatic rule – which was no bad thing as far as Weber was concerned. Parliamentary rule, he hammered away to readers during the world war, proved its effectiveness mainly through the selection of leaders that occurred in the political struggle. 'For it is not the many-headed assembly of parliament as such that can "govern" and "make" policy. . . . The "principle of the small number" (that is, the superior political manoeuvrability of *small* leading groups) always rules political action' (PW 174). Michels made of this the 'iron law of oligarchy'. It follows that micro-communities are always to be found at the core of the macro-formations of 'society'. Seen in this light, the old triad of monarchical, aristocratic and democratic rule has only a superficially descriptive value, since on closer examination *any* rule is a form of oligarchy. When Nietzsche pleaded for sociology to be replaced by a 'theory of command structures',[40] Weber operated entirely in this spirit.

In *Economy and Society*, charismatic rule comes last among the three types of legitimate rule, yet it would appear to have been Weber's *way in* to the whole sociology of rule. Charisma too originally derives from a small community: the circle of disciples around the charismatic leader. To be sure, the victory of the charismatic makes his followers more and more anonymous, and the routinization of charisma exposes even this type of rule to bureaucratization; all that remains is the charismatic *legitimation*. But this is just the point: Weber's originality is his differentiation of forms of rule by their type of legitimacy, rather than by their institutions and instruments. With this latter method one might construct almost any number of forms of rule, based on the army, the police, terrorist organizations, bureaucracy, hierarchies, notables, parties, parliaments, press empires, capital ownership – the list could be continued. Weber, however, enquires into the preconditions of sustainable rule, on the assumption that sheer power and force offer no guarantee in the long run.

Now, as a matter of fact, 'legitimacy' was the watchword of royalists in the nineteenth century, while revolutionary governments claimed that their mode of legitimation had right on its side against systems of rule based on tradition and custom. This was the historical basis on which Weber developed his sociology of rule. However, the triad at which he arrived via the question of legitimacy is not just a mirror of (actually highly complex) historical conditions but also reflects, in its simplicity, an anthropological concept: *Homo Weberiensis*, we might say, lives off a trinity of custom, reason and enthusiasm.

The natural need for legitimation

To base a typology of rule on modes of legitimation has a meaning only if rule cannot create its legitimacy at random: that is, if there is a consciousness of law prior to the form of rule. If this were not the case, Weber's sociology of rule would run the risk of falling for the propaganda of various rulers and being uplifted by their chimeras – something that Weber hated more than anything else. For all that, we should remember that an urge to self-justification – not without a certain self-irony – runs through Weber's whole life, from his courtship letter to Marianne to his love letters to Else, and that his sociology of law comes precisely from a period when he was indulging in an orgy of self-opinionatedness. It is not surprising, then, that the need for legitimation seemed to him a natural drive, or that the mode of gaining legitimacy appeared to be the basic source of rule. His own dogmatic attitude presupposed that right was not at all something that any ruler could define as he wished; no one would get passionately heated over that kind of right.

The ideal types in which forms of rule are based on right, not on naked force, are an *idealization* of rule – and one may wonder whether, in this conceptual approach, Weber studiously adhered to his precept of freedom from value judgements. He remarked that 'belief in legitimacy' is a 'normal' component of rule, not only in the ideal case. 'Experience shows that in no instance does domination (or rule) voluntarily limit itself to the appeal to material or affectual or ideal motives as a basis for its continuance. In addition every such system attempts to establish and to cultivate the belief in its legitimacy' (E&S 213). This was not a completely new idea; despite his dictum that 'force is always the primary factor', Jacob Burckhardt – a man greatly admired by Weber – had written better and more succinctly: 'The State founded on sheer crime is compelled in the course of time to develop a kind of justice and morality, since those of its citizens who are just and moral gradually get the upper hand.'[41] The quest to legitimize a form of rule is therefore the norm, not only in the sense of what ought to be but also in that of the 'normal run of things' – one reason, in fact, to doubt any sharp hiatus between Is and Ought. In any event, one is left with the impression that Weber did not struggle too much with problems of value-freedom when he was working on *Economy and Society*.

Weber felt a special need to analyse forms of rule at a time when, having been powerless, he was again gradually becoming a powerful force in the academic world, through his advisory and editorial activity, his founding role in sociology and his success in drawing a younger generation of scholars around him. For a powerful professor, the ruler's authority is not a personal problem; people around him seem to do what he wants quite automatically. Weber's situation meant, however, that he had a personal impetus to reflect on the conditions of rule, especially as he tested (with varying degrees of success) a number of institutional and charismatic ways of regaining academic influence. During the world war he found more and more practical applications for his insight that military victories cannot be the only basis for rule, that a convincing legal foundation has to be part of any sustainable system of rule. German troops pushed deep into France and Ukraine, yet it was clear to anyone in the know that the military fronts did not mark the frontiers of a stable German empire. Charismatic rule, the primal form of power, has certain analogies in the realm of sexuality, and it suggests that the willingness of subordinates to follow, indeed their pleasure in being commanded, is part of the secret of success. Only through this insight did a theory of rulership become the *sociology* of rule.

On the natural sources of law

All the indications are that the sociology of law also belongs among the early parts of *Economy and Society* that Weber composed before the outbreak of war.[42] Now, for the first time in twenty years, Weber was able to return extensively to the legal studies of his youth. As everywhere else in his work, there is a tendency to make his ideas about social orders more fluid and dynamic and to think of these as opportunities for individual action. Again he begins with the natural or primeval [*urwüchsig*] conditions, this time without quotation marks:

> The primeval form of 'administration' is represented by patriarchal power, i.e., the rule of the household. In its primitive form, the authority of the master of the household is unlimited. Those subordinated to his power have no rights as against him, and norms regulating his behaviour toward them exist only as indirect effects of heteronomous religious checks on his conduct. . . . The authority of magi and prophets and, under certain conditions, the powers of the priesthood, can, to the extent that they have their source in concrete revelation, be as unrestrained by rights and norms as the primitive power of the master of a household. Belief in magic is also one of the original sources of criminal law, as distinguished from 'private law'. (E&S 645, 647)

The lack of inhibition with which the strongest exercise their power and sex drives is 'primeval'; the master of the household originally claims all its women for himself. The thesis of an original matriarchy is countered with the thesis of 'patriarchal polygamy' [E&S 688]. But the law, or at least criminal law, has 'original (*urwüchsige*) sources'. Most of the 'primitive [*urwüchsigen*] contracts' were 'fraternization contracts' (E&S 672): we see how the sociology of law is internally connected with the section on 'primitive communities'. For Weber it is not the state which underlies the development of law: he is not a deeply rooted legal positivist. 'The fusion of all those organizations which had respectively engendered their own bodies of law into the *one* compulsory association of the state, now claiming to be the sole source of all "legitimate" law', is for Weber a historically secondary process (E&S 666). Instead of the usual division into public and private law, he begins with the 'forms of creation of rights'; only later is this followed with a section on 'the emergence and creation of legal norms', at less than half the length. *Natural law* does not stand at the beginning, but is introduced only towards the end as 'the specific form of legitimacy of a revolutionarily created order' (E&S 867). Although 'an essentially Stoic creation', it is regarded by Weber not as a relic from ancient times but as a distinctively Western source of law pregnant with the future. 'Nature' is not only the primitive original condition: for Weber there is not only a return to nature but also a movement forward to nature, even if his horror of 'naturalism' keeps him from saying as much in a nutshell.

Organic versus organological thinking

The essay that Weber published in 1913 'on some categories of interpretive [*verstehenden*] sociology' reads as a rough outline for *Economy and Society*. To quote: 'The object of the discussion, "*Verstehen*", is ultimately also the reason why interpretive [*verstehende*] sociology (as we have defined it) treats the single individual and his action as its basic unit, as its "atom".'[43] 'Interpretive sociology' means first of all taking seriously the meaning intended by the actor – for example, understanding Pope Urban's call for a crusade in 1095 as the opening of *opportunities*, not as the opening of a safety-valve for overpopulated knightly castles (E&S 911) (which is what Malthusians argued, even in Weber's day). Individual action does take its bearings from social orders, but it is not determined by 'society', especially as a number of different social meanings often intersect with one another. Weber explained this by an example that was then highly topical for him: the duel.

> The commonly prevailing view of the 'meaning' of our system of law . . . absolutely forbids duelling. Certain widespread ideas of the 'meaning' of social conventions assumed to be valid require duelling. In engaging in a duel, the individual orients his action towards these conventional rules. But in concealing his action, he orients it toward the rules of law.[44]

Had Weber at that time made full public use of his own conduct, he might have gone even further in demonstrating the scope for individual action. As we have seen, he first challenged Harms to a duel but then – without fearing social sanctions as a result – withdrew the challenge because his rage subsided as the months went by and he no longer felt like pursuing the matter. He thereby revealed that, in the observance or non-observance of certain social conventions, people may be guided by their own pleasure principle without much happening to them. Weber himself emphasized the importance of 'being able to demand satisfaction' for a certain kind of social acceptability in the Germany of his time. But it was enough to demand satisfaction; the actual 'satisfaction' did not have to ensue in the form of bloodshed. Weber thought of it as an objective opportunity, not as a compulsion. And that is just how he proceeded in relation to social orders, over long sections of *Economy and Society*. Since the real world consists of individuals, not collectives, social relations for Weber contained in principle – certainly not always and everywhere – opportunities for freedom.[45] Even in 'an economic system organized on a socialist basis', individuals would be the element providing movement.

> What is decisive is that in socialism, too, the individual will under these conditions ask first whether to him, personally, the rations allotted and the work assigned, as compared with other possibilities, appear to

conform with his own interests. This is the criterion by which he would orient his behaviour, and violent power struggles would be the normal result: struggles over the alteration or maintenance of rations once allotted. (E&S 202f.)

Prophetic words. Today, after the collapse of the Soviet Union, we see that even seventy years of communist education could do nothing to drive egoism out of human existence.

Weber would have been no social scientist and no realist, however, if he had portrayed society as an El Dorado of individual autonomy. If individuals are not determined by social orders but simply endowed with *opportunities*, this does not mean that they have the strength and freedom really to take advantage of the scope offered in those opportunities. And, if Weber developed his theory of society more in the language of opportunities than of systemic constraints, we must add a large 'But', as so often in his writings. For it must always be taken into account that an option which was once a free choice for people becomes an 'iron cage' for those who come after. In particular, an increasing compulsion follows from the process of bureaucratization – if not by an inner logic, then in keeping with our experience of world history. As Weber put it:

> Bureaucracy is, however, distinguished from other historical bearers of the modern, rational way of ordering life by the fact of its far greater *inescapability*. History records no instance of its having disappeared again once it had achieved complete and sole dominance – in China, Egypt, or in a less consistent form in the later Roman Empire and Byzantium, except when the whole culture supporting it also disappeared completely. Relatively speaking, however, these were still highly irrational forms of bureaucracy; they were 'patrimonial bureaucracies'. Compared with all these older forms, modern bureaucracy is distinguished by a characteristic which makes its inescapability much more absolute than theirs, namely, *rational, technical specialization and training*. (PW 156)

With the alliance of bureaucratization and rationalization, history finally flows in an all-encompassing compulsory evolution. This differs from Darwinian evolution in that it does not signify higher development – rather the opposite. In a sense, Weber is more naturalistic than the Darwinians, who are fond of smuggling ideas about desirable cultural progress into their conception of evolution. Weber's truth is something that one resists.

16

From Deborah's Song of Triumph to the 'Titans of the Holy Curse': Pacifist Herdsmen, Prophets and Pariahs – the Israelites

The Jews as an emotive issue

Max Weber and the Jews: researchers can easily find evidence that Weber was an opponent of anti-Semitism or even a philo-Semite, but, if one wishes, a lot can be adduced that points in the other direction.[1] Today it has become difficult in considering the issue of Jews to think back to the time before Auschwitz, when Jews and non-Jews alike handled it with incomparably fewer inhibitions. What used to sound more or less 'harmless' no longer appears so; expressions now have an anti-Semitic ring that few detected in those days.

Nevertheless, the 'Jewish question' was not completely unproblematic in Weber's time; it churned up emotional depths precisely because it aroused in many such contradictory feelings. Weber's own attitude to Jews is one of his great ambiguities, and there is much to suggest that it preyed on his mind throughout his life and strengthened his basic feeling that one could reach the heart of things through religion. Then, as today, it was 'politically correct' in large parts of respectable society to reject anti-Semitism in any narrow sense as an expression of vulgar narrow-mindedness. But, for that very reason, attacks on Jews could serve as a token of courage and sincerity – of a virile German spirit which, not caring to mince its words, openly said what others only thought. This was already the drift of Richard Wagner's essay 'Jews in Music', which first appeared anonymously in 1850: it was all very well to have fought as a liberal for the emancipation of the Jews, but to be frank he thought it had been more a struggle for an 'abstract principle' than for 'a concrete case'; in his heart of hearts he felt 'instinctively repelled' by any actual contact with them.[2] The mayor of Vienna, Karl Lueger – who, in words if not in deeds, counted as the most prominent political anti-Semite around the turn of the century – represented even for the influential journalist Maximilian Harden (Jewish by origin and later the victim of an anti-Semitic attack) the epitome of a completely happy man, 'who was allowed to live out his dream'.[3]

People brought up as Christians learned in their Bible classes that the Jews were to blame for Christ's crucifixion, but also that Christ in his human form was himself a Jew. They grew up with Schnorr von Carolsfeld's illustrated Bible, and his childhood fantasies were populated by the heroes of ancient Israel: Samson, who strangled a lion with his bare hands; Gideon, who at night put the Midianites to flight with his trumpets; or the young David, who slew the giant Goliath with his sling. And then there were the great women: Deborah, Esther, Judith! To judge by Weber's writings, the figures of the Old Testament were at least as much at the centre of his fantasy landscapes as were the Homeric heroes; he evidently felt good in the world of ancient Israel and, at the age of fifteen or sixteen, 'of his own accord learned Hebrew in order to study the Old Testament in the original language' (WB 57).

But did modern Jewry still have anything in common with ancient Israel? Walter Rathenau, despite being the author of *Tales from the Talmud*, answered with a resounding 'No' in 1896, in an anonymous article entitled 'Höre, Israel!' ['Hear, O Israel!']. Yahweh would not want to have anything to do with modern Jews. 'The Lord of Wrath took delight in a nation of warriors; he is not interested in a nation of grocers and brokers.'[4] According to prevailing Christian doctrine, Christianity was the true inheritor of the divine spirit that filled those heroes of old; the Jews themselves had betrayed their tradition. The old orthodoxy was now at everyone's disposal in the era of liberalism and critical historiography. Today it is often recalled that Jesus's teachings were even more firmly situated within Jewish traditions than they appear to be from the Gospels. In Weber's time, however, liberal theologians in particular emphasized the opposition between Christian liberty and Jewish devoutness in observing the Law.

Mixed feelings

An ambivalent attitude to the Jewish tradition and modern Jewry was widespread among the liberal middle classes to which Weber belonged. In many cases it is even misleading to distinguish between anti-Semites and philo-Semites; mixed and changing attitudes were quite typical, not least for many German Jews, including their most prominent representative, Walter Rathenau, heir to the AEG corporation, critic of contemporary civilization and head of raw materials provision during the war, whose assassination in 1922 plunged his friend Troeltsch into a deep depression. Rathenau drew the wrath of anti-Semites, yet showed understanding for many of their opinions. Thus, in 'Höre, Israel!' he lamented the 'tragedy' that the Germans, a nation used to 'the air of forest and mountains', could be dominated by an 'Asiatic horde' whose power rested upon capital and superior knowledge.[5] This whole panorama has to be borne in mind if we are to situate Weber's position in his age.

The family tradition already contained elements of ambivalence. Fallenstein, Weber's grandfather, sometimes indulged in cheap anti-Jewish outbursts (R 447f.), which according to taste may be regarded as an expression of Teutonic honesty or of pathological irritability. The same was true of many anti-Jewish attitudes in Weber's milieu. Eduard Souchay, on the other hand, Fallenstein's brother-in-law and Max Weber's great-uncle, moved in the circle of the Berlin Mendelssohns and, as the Frankfurt 'Jews' commissar' from 1839 to 1848, did what he could 'to enlarge the rights of Jews' – although he was put off when, during the 1848 revolution, Jewish notables joined the Democrats and reached out for 'complete equality' (R 450ff.).

The 'Jewish question' was also an emotive issue in Weber's parental home (R 467). Theodor Mommsen, who castigated anti-Semitism as a 'national monstrosity', was the main authority opposing Treitschke in the Berlin anti-Semitism controversy; and, among Weber's professor uncles, Hermann Baumgarten resolutely sided with Mommsen, while Adolf Hausrath supported Treitschke no less forcefully. But even Mommsen had very mixed feelings on the Question and doubted that anyone seriously conscious of himself as a Jew could be a loyal German. When he identified Jews from antiquity to the present as an 'element of decomposition' in non-Jewish communities,[6] he coined a formula that would later be taken up by Goebbels. Adolf Hausrath, to the irritation of many of his colleagues, was one of the first theologians to use Talmudic sources as an approach to Church history, but he saw red when speaking of the influence of Judaism in the modern world.

It was a confusing picture for the young Max Weber. As a precocious fifteen-year-old, who still spun yarns about 'laws of national development', he claimed to know that 'the Semitic and the Indo-European' peoples had been 'divided by insurmountable antipathy' (WB 47). Among his 'strange fellow students' at university, however, he found 'many blasé types who are anti-Semitic for the sake of appearances and actually nothing else' (JB 173, 298): this was anti-Semitism as a substitute for non-existent political awareness and as an expression of primitivism. In 1885 Weber, who valued Treitschke in his way, told his adversary Hermann Baumgarten that he was nauseated by the 'frenzied cheering that broke out among Treitschke's students when he made some anti-Semitic innuendo'. 'Apart from that, many walls and most of the tables, etc., are daubed with anti-Semitic rallying cries of varying degrees of coarseness' (JB 174). A crude anti-Semitism was rife among students in those days.

In 1884 Ida Baumgarten wrote to Helene about Weber (who was alien to her at the religious level): 'What I like about him is that, in relation to anti-Semitism, for example, he always takes the side of the weak and oppressed, and that he can step outside himself and forget his assumed air of equanimity' (R 468f.). The Jews, however, did not always appear as 'the weak and oppressed'. The pseudonymously published *La Société de Berlin*, which Weber lapped up in his student days, depicted the Jews as Germany's new masters and Adolf Stoecker, the court chaplain and prophet of anti-Semitism, as a brave spokesman for the silent majority of Germans.[7] Weber did his doctorate with Levin Goldschmidt, the expert in commercial law and one of the first religious Jews to obtain a professorship (thanks to state intervention and against the vote of the law faculty), who was connected to several of Weber's relatives. Weber began his lecturing career as a deputy for Goldschmidt. But that does not tell us much about his attitude to Jews, since even Treitschke held Goldschmidt in high regard.[8]

A sense of well-being at Wellhausen's

When the sick Weber went to take a cure at the Konstanzer Hof in August 1898, he realized that it was not good for him to read Flaubert's *Madame Bovary*. 'Instead I am now reading Wellhausen's splendid *Israelitische Geschichte*.'[9] This seems to be the first evidence of a *scholarly* concern with ancient Israel. But already as a boy Weber was more at home with the Bible than many a theologian.[10] It is psychologically revealing that such material had a beneficial effect during his worst period, and that it constantly appealed to him. Julius Wellhausen (1844–1918) revolutionized our view of the history of ancient Israel by showing that the oldest parts of the Old Testament were not the Mosaic 'Books of the Law' but the writings of the prophets. Theodor Mommsen thought that his reading of Wellhausen had to some extent afforded him an insight into the 'enigma of Judaism'.[11]

In the beginning was not the Law or the patriarchs but the prophets: this too would become Weber's approach to ancient Israel when, spurred on by his concept of charisma, he actually went beyond Wellhausen and made the prophets the creators of Old Testament Israel.[12] Wellhausen had shown that, contrary to the traditional view, the beginnings were not a forty-year trek through the desert; the ancient Israelites were not fundamentally a desert people, nor was theirs a religion of the desert; the Mosaic Law was designed for a nation of farmers, although for the Israelites themselves the ideal figure was not the farmer but the free herdsman capable of defending himself.[13]

Like most Christian theologians, however, Wellhausen did not extend his high regard for ancient Israel to later Jewish history; the synagogue was not for him a living continuator of the old power of belief. Jesus shook himself free from the Jews; he 'did not suffocate in the odour of their old clothes'.[14] In 1882 Wellhausen had given up his chair of theology in Greifswald because he had not considered himself able to strengthen budding pastors in their faith,[15] but in his way he continued to think of himself as a Christian. Such a belief in Christ is not present in Weber, however, and still less is the accompanying deprecation of Judaism.

We have seen how angry Weber was that Jews were regularly passed over for academic appointments. Eduard Baumgarten tells us 'that Weber never forgave Dilthey, Rickert and Windelband for together blocking the path to a professorship for the man he regarded as the most important contemporary German philosopher: Georg Simmel' (B 611). This is not the whole truth; for, although Weber had great respect for Simmel's productivity ('infinite intelligence'), he considered him to be 'unsolid' and in 1912 once again tried to foil Simmel's prospective appointment in Heidelberg (MWG II/7, 734f.). However, his motive in doing this was certainly not of an anti-Semitic character. Weber even gave Lujo Brentano a proper dressing-down for ridiculing Franz Eulenburg, another Jewish man he admired: 'today is *not* the time to be telling anti-Semitic jokes, in which we again and again see the stupidest "Aryan" impotence preferred over the most competent Jews' (MWG II/5, 644). To Paul Honigsheim, himself of Jewish origin, Weber is supposed to have talked sarcastically of the subterranean academic anti-Semitism: 'When approached about appointment lists, I usually submit: a) a Jewish list and b) a non-Jewish list. The last one in a) is usually better than the first in b). But it is sure that they will select from the b) list' (B 611n.)

The Jewish intellectual: a worry for the educated middle classes – a chance for Weber

In Weber's day the Jewish intellectual, and to an increasing extent also the left-wing intellectual, became a new and disturbing figure for many members of the educated middle classes, in Eastern Europe as well as Germany; it was a spectre that had first appeared in the German intellectual world in the period between 1815 and the 1848 revolution, represented by Heinrich Heine, Ludwig Börne and Karl Marx. Weber could see in his own milieu how many Jews excelled in the pursuit not only of money but even more of intellectual values. It was even fairly common for heirs of Jewish businesses to reach out from the economy into the world of the mind. 'But Jews are keener on education than any other people', wrote Robert Michels, even in his fascist period.[16] As such intellectuals did not pursue an academic career out of financial necessity, and could not expect very much from one anyway, they did not need to exercise great caution, but could throw in their lot with socialism or the 'erotic movement' and write lively articles for the press. (This was also true of Werner Sombart, who, despite his anti-Semitic allusions, aroused the same kind of associations as Jewish intellectuals among his critics.)

Michels wrote that social democracy 'undeniably owed special thanks' to intellectuals of Jewish origin;[17] and so too did the newly advancing discipline of sociology. Friedrich Gundolf, himself of Jewish origin, mockingly described sociology in 1924 as a 'Jewish sect'.[18] Intellectual Jews became a characteristic element in the younger generation of academics that Weber grouped around him. He liked the human type, and they courted him. In these circles a 'vow that Weber had hardly meant seriously' was enthusiastically spread around: 'When I am healthy again, I shall only allow Russians, Poles and Jews in my seminars – no Germans' (B 610, WzG 172).

After Weber's death – according to Marianne (LE 129) – the 'cleverest and most devoted' of those who kept his work alive were 'the young Jews'.

At Weber's *jours* there were often 'unconstrained discussions' of Judaism and Zionism (WB 469). In November 1912 he wrote to Sophie Rickert that he was appearing more and more as a psychotherapist, who practised individual treatment during the week and 'the promotion of collective well-being' on Sundays, when patients raised the battle-cry 'Israel is on our side!' 'Recently', he said, there had even appeared the type of the 'conspicuous Jew' [*Knalljuden*] (MWG II/7-2, 761f.); this term, which he certainly did not mean nastily (he had already coined it for Rembrandt's *David*), probably referred to Ernst Bloch – in any case, not to someone like Emil Lask. For Weber this was an ideal milieu in which to float unconventional ideas about ancient Israel. Marianne called Bloch and Lukács the 'messiah kids, because they hope for a future Messiah and want to create the philosophical atmosphere for his coming'.[19] A *bon mot* was doing the rounds: 'Who are the four evangelists?' Answer: 'Matthew, Mark, Lukács and Bloch' (WzG 31).

At first Marianne felt slightly confused by this new intellectual type: 'Now another new Jewish prophet has been showing up on Sundays', she reported in 1912 to Helene about the young Bloch, 'a most peculiar fellow, very clever, with a metaphysical and religious-philosophical system in his head . . ., but with extremely uncivil manners, importunate and arrogant, and definitely a little mad', as well as easily offended. Tobelchen, that is, Mina Tobler, had already complained about him, and Marianne feared that 'he is driving some delicately constituted people away from us'. This gave her the opportunity for a semi-humorous sigh of a general kind, which suggests that the *jours* increasingly centred on 'Oriental' themes, but also that the term 'Aryan', without scare quotes, had already broken out beyond racist circles.

> In general the *Aryan* friends who come to us . . . find themselves being pushed into the background – and are desirous of special audiences – it is truly laughable! . . . We ourselves also laugh every Sunday about the Oriental contents of the big bourgeois room – but why are these people in particular so animated and talkative?[20]

Like many of their contemporaries, Max and Marianne Weber assumed that – whether for racial reasons or because of cultural traditions – there was a characteristic spectrum of Jewish human types. This included a type with ancient intellectual culture, who had a special attraction for Weber – for example, his friend Georg Jellinek, the constitutional theorist, from whom he had learned that the idea of innate human rights had its origins not only in revolutionary political thought but also in religion and the Reformation.[21] Weber's speech at his daughter's wedding on 21 March 1911, soon after Jellinek's death, is the humanly most beautiful of his surviving addresses. He says there of the bride's deceased father: 'His descent and the traditions of his family had given him something of that delicate fragrance which comes to us from the gentle and pure emotional world of the Orient.' He was thinking especially 'of that peculiarly sovereign attitude of the spirit toward the world which always returned to its equilibrium and remained in it after all mutations of passing moods, an attitude we may call "worldly wisdom" in the sense of the ancient Orient' (WB 477). We see how Weber was still inwardly living among the religions of the ancient East and toying with the idea that Judaism, in the sense of 'pan-Babylonianism', could be assimilated to them: an idea he would subsequently reject.[22]

But there were other human types that Weber also regarded as characteristically Jewish and found repugnant – especially if they seemed like pushy *parvenus* lacking in decency and solidity. It is striking that, in the quarrels in the years before the First World War, Weber's strongest aversion was for two scholars of Jewish origin who aroused 'typically Jewish' associations: Adolf Koch and Rudolf Goldscheid. Also of Jewish descent, and protagonists of a pro-business liberalism, were the two political economists against whom Weber fought at times with special bitterness, although they might have appealed to him as non-conformists in comparison with the dominant Schmoller school: Ludwig Bernhard and Richard Ehrenberg. In 1915 Weber raged against 'Jewish press scoundrels and other such riff-raff'.[23] In 1916, when he had switched from being anti-Polish to pro-Polish, he thought it 'out of the question' that eastern Jews should be allowed to emigrate to the German Reich (WB 556), much as he had lamented their 'dreadful immigration' into the United States when it had been at its height. Presumably he would have understood Treitschke's horror at the mass of 'youths assiduously peddling trousers' who flowed into Germany 'year after year from the inexhaustible Polish cradle'.[24]

In 1917, in his address on *Science as a Vocation*, Weber remarked: 'If the young scholar asks for my advice with regard to habilitation, the responsibility of encouraging him can hardly be borne. If he is a Jew, one of course says *lasciate ogni speranza*' (FMW 134): abandon all hope! These words above the gates of Dante's Inferno were a favourite quotation of Weber's. But why 'of course'? An academic career was harder for Jewish than non-Jewish scholars, but it was not impossible – sometimes as a result of state intervention. Weber had the best examples of this in his own circle. Were not Goldschmidt, Gothein and Jellinek of Jewish origin? Even Simmel and Eulenburg eventually obtained a full professorship; and Lask had had good prospects until he was killed in action in 1915. So, there is much to suggest that in 1917 Weber wanted to dissuade Jewish scholars from embarking upon a university career, precisely because he felt inwardly pressurized by Jewish members of his circle to do something for them. At the end of his address he spoke of being 'shaken when we realize the fate' of the Jewish people, and warned that the point was not to wait for a saviour but 'to meet the demands of the day' (FMW 156). Whereas anti-Semites excoriated the vile business acumen of the Jews, Weber saw the roots of the Jews' misfortune in their disturbed relationship with contemporary reality. But the language of these closing sentences also reveals how fascinated he was by those Jews who did not become completely absorbed in ordinary existence but waited for the extraordinary to happen: the messianic dawn after the well-nigh endless night.

In 1920, in the last political statement of his life, Weber said he thought it ill-considered that more than a third of the committee appointed by the National Assembly to investigate the question of war guilt was of Jewish origin. Marianne Weber, worried that it might hurt Jewish friends, later destroyed this memorandum. It would seem that Weber had two reasons for saying what he did: a fear that a target was being offered for the rapidly growing anti-Semitism but also, according to Eduard Baumgarten, a wish 'to prevent anti-militarist resentment on the part of Jewish committee members (since in the Wilhelmine period Jews had normally been denied officer rank) from exerting an influence on the examination of German officers' (B 611f.); or, in plain language, that such determined civilians might lack understanding for soldiers' honour and soldiers' conduct. 'Nearly everyone in my circle of friends is Jewish – I do not think I am suspected of being an "anti-Semite" ', Weber wrote in this connection. 'There I too am regarded as a Jew (officers' letters to me!)' (R 472).

In the empire, the informal closure of the officer corps to Jewish candidates had been a standard theme in the liberal critique of the armed forces. Weber, however, who criticized discrimination against Jews in the universities, found nothing wrong with similar practices in the officer corps. According to his own sociology of religion, Jews had a pacifist tradition stretching right back to the Babylonian exile, and so the officer corps was only being consistent when it refused to admit Jews. The professoriate, on the other hand, had no rational grounds for sealing itself off in this way, as there was no denying the high intellectual capacities of many Jews or their roots in a tradition going back thousands of years.

In 1919, although she did not feel equal to the task, Marianne allowed herself to be made first president of the Association of German Women's Leagues (BDF) instead of Alice Salomon, since there was a reluctance to appoint a Jewish woman in the face of the rising tide of public anti-Semitism.[25] Like Max Weber and many of her contemporaries, Marianne had mixed feelings towards Jews. Her father was given to outbursts of 'extreme Judeophobia',[26] but in his case it was part of a pathological persecution mania. Moreover, she detested her father, and that was the first reason why anti-Semitic rants seemed suspect to her. We have already noted her fondness for Emil Lask, the young philosopher of Jewish origin. And she followed with suspicion Martha Troeltsch's aggressive refrain that 'it was Jewish to be enthusiastically in favour of peace and against militarism' – until Max finally became 'very rude with her':[27] Judeophobia as a hysterical tic.

Yet Marianne had a violent antipathy to the *nouveau riche* Jewish milieu in Berlin. In 1901 she wrote from Sorrento that everything there was wonderful – 'Only I could do without the Berlin Jews and other fools, whose bare unaesthetic existence is disturbingly conspicuous here in Italy.' And again in 1915, from Hohenschwangau: 'The hotel is posh, expensive and packed; one sits among a lot of Berlin Orientals, a lot of overfed, high-bosomed little women and their bald-headed husbands.'[28] Many cultivated Jews would have been equally repelled by this milieu. By the standards of the time, neither Marianne nor Max Weber was an anti-Semite. They may have sometimes got annoyed with Edgar Jaffé, but there are no allusions to his Jewish origin even in their private correspondence. Certain anti-Jewish feelings are rather to be found in Else Jaffé, who married her not exactly good-looking husband more for money than for love.

The relevance of the remote past: Zionism

Jewish intellectuals in Weber's milieu confronted him with the issue of Zionism, although none of his inner circle was a firm supporter of it. In the summer of 1913, the doctor and physiologist Ernst J. Lesser had a discussion with Max Weber about Zionism. Lesser, who was the brother-in-law of Theodor Heuss, was active at the time in the local Zionist group in Mannheim. To his 'great amazement' Weber did not think that the main problem would be to acquire some territory in Palestine, since in his view the division of the Ottoman empire was in the offing. Did he not know that there was already a long-settled non-Jewish population in Palestine? He was certainly familiar with the travel reports of his friend Naumann, who gave the impression that the people living in the 'Holy Land' were mainly impoverished riff-raff; there was not yet any thought of a militant Arab nationalism, at least not in that region.

Weber continued to hold forth, finding 'natural' a number of statements that by no means went without saying: 'It is naturally quite possible that you can establish some settlements in Palestine, and that these will be able to flourish . . . but you will naturally not have achieved your goal of a rebirth of the Jewish people' (MWG II/8, 312). Shortly afterwards, Weber clarified his position in a long letter, which revealed how he was pondering even then over Jewish history: 'What is the main thing missing, then? *The temple and the high priests.* If those were in Jerusalem, everything else would be a minor matter' (MWG II/8, 315). Scarcely anywhere else did Weber make it so clear that for him religion was not one factor among many but the decisive issue, at least in the case of the Jews; and part of their religion was the unbroken tradition of the holy place. There was also the question of a 'primal community': it could not, in his opinion, be re-created, even by 'literati', which is what the founding fathers of Zionism essentially were.[29] What remained of the cohesion of the Jews had its roots in antiquity – and that was where his own interest lay.

Gender relations and agrarian relations: two approaches to ancient Israel

As we have seen, ancient Israel already had a special attraction for the young Weber. Later, some of this interest was transferred to the Puritans, who in their way possessed an Old Testament kind of severity. But then it must initially have been his collaboration on Marianne's legal history of women which took him back to ancient times. The passages she wrote about ancient Israel deal with an ambiguous relationship to sexuality: on the one hand, the prophets' 'abhorrence of the idolization of anything created', which anticipated Puritanism (EM 118); on the other hand, typical for the 'powerful sensuality of Oriental peoples', the rule of giving young men 'a female slave as a "companion" immediately after the onset of puberty', in order to keep them away from whoring (EM 130, 119). It is hard to imagine that Weber did not reflect on the neuroses that men were spared in this way; it was the ideal male combination of self-discipline and sexual uninhibitedness, which only a very thorough reader of the Bible could have discovered.

In comparison with Wellhausen, Weber in *Ancient Judaism* devotes considerable attention to the sexual prohibitions of Jewish law, although this is not necessary for a particular thesis and its significance is often unclear. He discusses in detail the Mosaic curses (Deuteronomy 27: 14–26), 'usually termed the "sexual Decalogue"' (AJ 236) – in fact, a theological insider's concept, not even to be found in major textbooks. The main objects of the curses are any forms of incest and sodomy: certainly a preoccupation for Weber, whose own marriage with Marianne had something incestuous, and who probably sometimes brooded over whether this was connected with his misfortune.

More important than marriage and sex in Weber's new approach to the Old Testament was his study of agrarian history, and especially his article of 1909 for the *Handwörterbuch der Staatswissenschaften*, which deals with Israel in some detail (AS 134-46).[30] If *Ancient Judaism* is read as a direct continuation of *The Protestant Ethic*, without any consideration of *The Agrarian History of the Major Centres of Ancient Civilization*, the focus will be too narrowly on the asceticism of the prophets and will miss the references to agrarian history that run through the whole work. Already in 1909 Weber held up the Song of Deborah, later his favourite source, as proof that the ancient Israelites should be seen in a similar way to the Swiss confederates[31] who defeated a cavalry army on foot: that is, as a 'free community' of infantrymen with a peasant background (AS 139).

Ancient Judaism is one of the rare cases in which we have a handwritten draft prior to the published version: the so-called *Deponatsmanuskript* in the Max Weber Deposit in the Bavarian State Library, which was probably written in 1911–12.[32] This shows that Weber's preoccupation with ancient Israel began in the years before the war, immediately after the appearance of Sombart's *Die Juden und das Wirtschaftsleben* (1911) and during that surge of creativity in which the major works of his final decade took shape. Around 1916, when Weber assumed the public role of a German Jeremiah, he returned to the prophets from a study of Chinese and Indian religions (WB 331); the first version of *Ancient Judaism* appeared in 1917–18, in the *Archiv für Sozialwissenschaft*. Here and there he lards the text with contemporary allusions, as when he comments with biting sarcasm on the fact that, according to the latest research, many Jewish tales of war and heroes were embellished at a time of 'decreasing power' and capacity for self-defence: 'The utopian phantasies of their champions were saturated the more with bloody images of Yahwe's heroic feats the more un-military they had become in fact. Just as today, in all countries, we find the highest measure of war thirst among those strata of literati who are farthest from the trenches and by nature least military' (AJ 112). The concept of 'pariah' – which Weber used merely in a marginal note in the *Deponatsmanuskript*[33] but later, in a public discussion with Martin Buber on 27 November 1913, promoted to the key for an understanding of Judaism (MWG II/8, 414n.) – became a leitmotif in his interpretation of the Jews' position in (and towards) the world, at the time when he began to look at Judaism in a perspective defined by his study of Hinduism. Thus, the published version of *Ancient Judaism* – it too only a fragment – contains several overlapping approaches and interpretive models from different periods of his life.

Sombart's provocation

An important initial challenge was the publication in 1911 of Werner Sombart's *Die Juden und das Wirtschaftsleben*,[34] which was meant as a response to *The Protestant Ethic*.[35] Sombart's basic thesis involves both an expansion and a refutation of the 'Weber thesis': the religiously grounded asceticism of work, which is so essential for capital accumulation and whose proprietary rights Weber assigned to Puritanism, may be found among the Jews from much earlier times and in a more complete form; hence the Jews and no one else were the real creators of capitalism. For pious Jews, unlike for pious Catholics, it was thought pleasing to God to grow rich by lending at interest, so long as this was done at the expense of non-Jews. Here Sombart points up a provocative contrast:

> Now think of the position in which the pious Jew and the pious Christian respectively found themselves in the period in which money-lending first became a need in Europe, and which eventually gave birth to capitalism. The good Christian who had been addicted to usury was full of remorse as he lay a-dying, ready at the eleventh hour to cast from him the ill-gotten gains which scorched his soul. And the good Jew? In the evening of his days he gazed with a broad smile upon his well-filled caskets and coffers, overflowing with sequins of which he had relieved the miserable Christians or Mohammedans.[36]

Lujo Brentano – for whom Sombart was by now a frivolous charlatan, 'who with sovereign contempt blows his whimsical soap bubbles in the face of readers stunned by his witticisms' – regarded Sombart's thesis as complete humbug. If it were true, he argued, then England (which expelled the Jews in the thirteenth century) should have come last in capitalist development, while Poland, which received Jews in especially large numbers, should have been in first place.[37]

In reality, Sombart was much too well educated to attribute capitalist development so monocausally to the Jews. His thesis, like so much of what he wrote, was a kind of sounding balloon – and elsewhere he traced modern capitalism to Thomas Aquinas or papal mistresses, to war or the shortage of wood. He could reply to critics that of course the Jews set a capitalist dynamic in motion only under certain external conditions, and that anyway he had been talking not of 'the Jews' but of a certain characteristic of the Jewish spirit. Weber probably understood the ideal-typical nature of Sombart's argument, and many of the attacks on Sombart's 'Jewish thesis' must have reminded him of wide-of-the-mark criticisms of his own Protestantism thesis. Nowhere in *Ancient Judaism* does he take issue with Sombart – indeed, curiously he makes not a single mention of him there.

Only later, in his lectures on economic history, does Weber turn his mind to Sombart's thesis. He rejects it, to be sure, but without any polemics, with reference to ideal types rather than actual history. Jewish capitalism was not 'rational capitalism' but simply 'pariah capitalism' – by which he means an economically parasitic form, a capitalism of coin and tax farmers incapable of generating modern industrial capitalism. On closer examination, many passages in Weber would have been at least as useful as Sombart's 'Jewish book' for anti-Semites who distinguished between creative and predatory capital (*schaffendem und raffendem Kapital*), the latter embodied in the figure of the Jew. It is in Weber's line of argument more than Sombart's that modern industrial society could have done without the Jews.

In the spring of 1911, when Weber received Sombart's book as a gift from the author, he bubbled over with compliments that strike today's reader as quite amazing, especially as they cannot be regarded as mere politeness. The book was 'literarily brilliant (ranks with the best you have written – an elegant yet lively scholarly, yes, *scholarly* style): these are things that seldom go together. As to the content, fabulously interesting in the mass of new things it presents. Many a disagreement stirred – then again most categorical agreement. . . . The most brilliant chapter is the one on religion' (MWG II/7–1, 154). The chapter on religion of all things! Evidently Weber did not yet have a firm position on the Jewish religion and was still looking for one. In late 1913, however, he said to someone that Sombart's book was 'splendidly written' but 'completely mistaken' in terms of content (MWG II/8, 412). He even told Sombart to his face that he thought 'nearly every word' in it was 'wrong'. At the time Sombart had just repeated his main thesis in his new book *Der Bourgeois*.[38] Weber commented: 'What you say about religion and how it fits together with the economy – things that ill become you! – are more than ever poor, second-hand goods' (MWG II/8, 414f.). Between the lines he seems to say that Sombart, an irreligious hedonist, is indiscriminately lumping all asceticism together. For Weber by now, however, it is clear that the asceticism associated with the prophets of ancient Israel was fundamentally different from that of the Puritans: it was an ecstatic asceticism, which opposed a different force of nature to the fertility orgies of the priests of Baal.

As far as we can tell, anti-Semitism was not one of the many things for which Weber reproached the author of the 'Jewish book', although it was not for nothing that it fell into disrepute as a source of ammunition for anti-Semites. But, whereas anti-Semites – Hitler in *Mein Kampf*, for one – attributed to Jews a demonic lasciviousness, Sombart's position was that the Jewish religion enjoined on them strict repression of (essentially evil) natural urges, and in particular a rigid discipline in sexual matters. This precisely was the ultimate reason why Jews became pioneers of capitalism. It is a cruder form of the argument in Weber's *The Protestant Ethic*, only transferred from Puritanism to Judaism.

Struggle against nature: a Jewish legacy?

According to Sombart, the 'terrible dualism which is part and parcel of our constitution' derives from Judaism: the division of man into sinful nature and a soul capable of being saved. 'The whole of human life is one great warfare against the inimical forces of Nature: that is the guiding principle of Jewish moral theology.' The effects of this are still present in the daily lives of Jews: they make long journeys without noticing the landscape; no wonder 'that there are far fewer Jewish painters than literary men'. Hegel already contrasted the Greek closeness to nature with the Jewish evacuation of meaning from nature, and Nietzsche once interpreted the history of Israel as 'a typical history of the denaturalizing of natural values':[39] – a view that is still today propagated by Eugen Drewermann.[40] For Sombart, the Jewish hostility to nature has especially profound effects on sexuality. 'We see this phenomenon – that a people with strong sexual inclinations (Tacitus speaks of it as *projectissima ad libidinem gens*) is forced by its religion to hold them in complete restraint. . . . The result of all this is obvious. Enormous funds of energy were prevented from finding an outlet in one direction and they turned to others.' (As we see, Freud's theory of sublimation was beating at open doors.) So, 'a good deal of the capitalistic capacity which the Jews possessed was due in large measure to the sexual restraint put on them by their religious teachers.' Then comes the key sentence: 'Before capitalism could develop, natural instinctual man had to have every bone in his body broken.'[41]

How was Weber to react to this mixture of imitation and provocation? Sombart's model was unmistakably *The Protestant Ethic*, but he replaced Weber's theological argument with a theory of psychic energy. To someone like Sombart it might well have seemed plausible that a period of abstinence was required to complete a thick book, but Weber had not at all experienced sexual asceticism as a source of energy. Indeed, the Jewish mode of 'rationalizing' sexual life could appear to him healthy and natural. Eckart Otto, who has been through Weber's revealing marginal notes to Sombart's *The Jews and Modern Capitalism*, points out that he wrote alongside the passages which depict Judaism as hostile to the instincts: 'Nonsense!'[42] Weber knew there were other elemental passions apart from the sex drive, and in his view they were embodied to the highest degree in the Jewish prophets. In contrast to Sombart, who described the Israelites as a nomadic people and detected a nomadic spirit even in modern Judaism, Weber emphasized the peasant element in ancient Israel. Part of this were the Baal orgies that the prophets so violently combated: for pious Christians the epitome of Satanic horror, but for modern ethnology nothing more than fertility cults typical of a peasant culture. The 'homeopathic sexual orgy', Weber wrote, 'was ritualistically strange to the Bedouins in contrast to the tillers' (AJ 191). 'Homeopathic' suggests an analogy between the fertilization of women and of the ploughed fields.

Here as elsewhere, Weber avoids an open clash with Sombart, and for his part he was far from finished with the subject. In *Ancient Judaism* we see him continually ponder the natural and sexual side of the Jewish religion, without ever solving the contradictions or arriving at a definitive view – any more than he did in relation to his own nature. Again and again he returns to the theme of circumcision, a particular interest of his uncle Adolf Hausrath, who in his first work had described with visible enjoyment the struggle between Paul and his opponents over the foreskin.[43] But what was the significance of circumcision? Evidently it goes back to archaic times, before the age of the prophets. 'As known, its origin is controversial', Weber notes (AJ 92), but in any event it is not unambiguously anti-sexual. Weber, who felt persecuted by 'demons' in his sexual life, thought that circumcision 'was believed to ward off demonic influence in sexual intercourse' (AJ 92); possibly it even had something to do with 'phallic orgiasticism' (AJ 93), since by making the glans insensitive it may increase potency, while also reducing sexual excitability. 'By far most probable', however, was that it was 'originally somehow related to warrior asceticism'; 'in any case hygienic, rationalistic interpretations, such as still appear, are improbable here' (AJ 93). Thus, a rationalization of sexuality was not at the origin of Judaism. Nor did Weber consider the sexual ethic of ancient Israel to have been particularly austere. 'All specifically Israelite regulations of sexual processes . . . are not ethical but ritualistic in nature' (AJ 191); there was 'an outspoken naturalism in the conception of natural processes', something 'in no way peculiar to Israel' (AJ 190).

An eternal people of the desert?

Although, in biblical criticism at that time, it was the unanimous view that the Books of Moses and their tales of desert wandering came from a much later period, Sombart assumed that the Jews really had come from the desert and were still marked by those origins. The Jewish Diaspora, with its restless wandering, was ultimately explicable not by external pressures but by the Jewish nature itself. Exile revived 'the nomadic instincts'; 'the Jew's inherent "nomadism" or "saharism" . . . was always kept alive through selection or adaptation.' The voice of the prophets rings out like a 'desert choir'.[44]

But how does the spirit of the desert fit into the urban spirit of capitalism? Sombart's answer was simple: there was a common penchant for abstraction, due to a defective sense of the blossoming diversity of nature; the wilderness produced this in the Jews and hence prepared them for the capitalist money-economy. In reality, however, this perception of the desert and steppe is more characteristic of the tourist than of the nomad, who has to have a keen eye for the sparse vegetation in order to ensure the survival of his animals. Brentano already described Sombart's idea of 'the desert as the locus of abstract thought' as sheer nonsense, and he quoted against it the figurative poetry of the popular Bedouin leader Abd el Kader (Abd al-Qadir, 1808–1883), who had fought in Algeria against the French colonial power.[45]

But what of Max Weber? On this point too his position was not diametrically opposed to Sombart's. In general, he does not paint a perfectly straightforward picture of the ancient Israelites; they display, rather, a profound inner tension – like Weber himself. He begins by discussing in detail the land of Palestine – an approach not in itself so special, as historical accounts of distant lands usually began with an introduction about natural conditions, as did Wellhausen's history of the Israelites. Weber's remarks on nature in Israel, however, are analytically much stronger than others of the same genre: they are not merely descriptive, nor are they simple overtures, but they contain reflections on how nature marked the destiny of Israel. We can see the origins of what he says in his work on agrarian history.

Not least because of these opening discussions, *Ancient Judaism* is paradigmatic of the way in which Weber conceived of a sociology and anthropology of religion. As Eckart Otto emphasizes,[46] Weber worked more extensively on the religion of ancient Israel than on any other: not only in its spiritual and political-economic but also its material and mental aspects. He could handle this task better for little Palestine (in which he had felt inwardly at home since childhood) than for such great distant countries as China and India, where a regionally differentiated analysis of the interaction between man and nature was not yet possible in the existing state of knowledge.

Ecology as a chance

Taking Palestine as his example, Weber developed the idea that natural conditions do not determine forms of human life but contain several different opportunities: instead of ecological determinism, then, a possibilism that corresponds to our present state of knowledge (AJ 5ff.). Perhaps it was an advantage that, unlike Naumann, Weber had never travelled to Palestine. In those days, visitors from the rainy North were usually taken aback by the dusty, sun-scorched wilderness of the 'Holy Land' and, finding nothing of the biblical land of milk and honey (a sign for Weber of a settled pastoral economy), soon arrived at the belief that its only salvation lay in artificial irrigation.[47] Weber, however, stressed that at least in ancient times agriculture and the resulting bureaucracies had been possible without irrigation in parts of Palestine (unlike in Egypt and Mesopotamia). The nature of the country allowed for agriculture, arboriculture, settled animal husbandry, pastoralism and even independent city-states like those of ancient Hellas. Long passages underline the affinity of Israel with the West rather than its 'Oriental' features; Weber even exaggerates the similarity between the cities of Palestine and the Greek polis. Yahweh sounds like a precursor of Wittfogel on hydraulic despotism in his warning to the Israelites 'that in Israel, unlike in Egypt, the harvest yield is not dependent upon irrigation. It is not a product of bureaucratic administration, of the king on earth and the work of the peasant, but it is the result of the rain given by Yahwe according to his free grace' (AJ 129).

It is true that, according to tradition, the Bedouin 'were the deadly enemies of Israel' (AJ 13f.), but curiously at a material rather than an ideological level; for Weber mentions again and again the 'nomadic ideal' of ancient Israel (AJ 114, 224, 285), a concept he had taken from an article in the *Preußische Jahrbücher* (1896) by Karl Budde, an Old Testament scholar from the Wellhausen school.[48] According to Weber, the prophets who fought against the Baal cult and led to victory the religion of a single God of the Heavens typically came from a nomadic or semi-nomadic background; parts of *Ancient Judaism* even come close to ecological determinism, although this is never spelled out and the weight of the ecological dimension is on the whole left open. The fight against the orgiasticism of the fertility cults was waged 'predominantly by stockbreeders'. 'The typical individual prophet, Elijah, the deadly enemy of Baal ecstasy, hails from Gilead and is a typical migratory nomad' (AJ 193).

As agriculture predominated in the north of Palestine and a pastoral economy in the south, orgiasticism, magic and 'mass ecstasy' sprang mainly from the north, whereas 'the rational Levitical Torah and the rational ethical emissary prophecy [came] from the south. To the latter this shamelessness is an abomination of Yahwe. . . . The dualism thus ran covertly throughout Israelite history since the beginning of the invasion' (AJ 193).[49] Weber was no longer so far apart from Sombart when he associated the religion founded by the prophets with pastoral economy, rationality and the struggle against orgiasticism.

In fact, the contrast between peasant and nomad religiosity provided perfect material for ideal types. For Weber, however, neither peasants nor nomads were typical of Israel – rather, small stockbreeders, who, while cultivating old heroic ideals in their memory, were increasingly 'boxed in' by their loss of power and restrictions on their living space (AJ 56), and who of necessity became as peaceful as their sheep. This cross between peasant and shepherd was the solution to the contradiction between nomadic ideal and sedentary or half-sedentary existence. Transhumance within a limited radius was for Weber a key to the sociology of religion in ancient Israel (AJ 37). Originally armed, these herdsmen underwent 'demilitarization' as a result of the rise of the cities and a settled peasantry (AJ 46). The terrible experience of warfare with militarily superior neighbours filled the Israelites with 'mad terror' (AJ 267), which was the ground on which the prophets had the effect that they did.[50]

Sometimes their storytellers revel in memories of heroic warfare, but then they make their patriarchs out to be as 'pacifistic', indeed as cowardly, as themselves. We detect Weber's contempt between the lines: 'The narrators expect their audiences to take for granted that the patriarchs would sooner pass off their beautiful wives as desirable sisters and surrender them to their respective protectors, leaving it to God to liberate them from the protector's harem by visiting plagues upon him, rather than defending the honour of their wives' (AJ 50). According to Weber, Genesis tells this shameful story no fewer than three times (12:13, 20:2, 26:7), in verses which the pious Christian prefers to skip, but which were a real gift for Nazi ideologue Alfred Rosenberg and led a spokesman for German Christians in 1933 to provoke a scandal by denouncing the Old Testament as a bundle of 'stockbreeders' and pimps' tales'.[51]

Nevertheless, in comparison with Sombart's 'Jewish book', large sections of which keep the reader in suspense with their alternation of anti-Semitic and philo-Semitic undertones, Weber's *Ancient Judaism* is a model of value-free scholarship; it was not just an idea to which he paid lip service. In any event, he refrains from developing his social ecology of the Jewish religion into a sharply focused thesis:[52] the essay remains a fragment; Weber never brought his ruminations to an end. Of what consequence, for example, are Mosaic prescriptions 'like the one protecting the mother bird' (Deuteronomy 22: 6–7), which are today being ecologically reinterpreted to defend the ancient Israelites against the accusation that they were hostile to nature?[53] Weber mentions them in some detail, but he does not know how to interpret them (AJ 261f.). Or what of the fallow year, the 'Sabbatical year' for the soil? (AJ 48f.)? Today this would be explained by the fact that the fragile soil of Palestine needed time to regenerate, but Weber, who spent a conspicuously long time on the subject,[54] mentions various hypotheses without taking a stand. Probably mindful of the polemics that modern agrarian reformers had directed at fallow periods, he tended towards religious and social-political explanations for the ban and did not think that rational reasons were involved. Rather, it told him how alien the priests of Baal were to the farming economy.

A god of natural catastrophes

But how rational was the Israelite conception of God? The Yahweh of the Old Testament was certainly not a 'nice' god: for Weber as for Freud[55] he was originally a 'god of nature', a 'god of certain natural catastrophes' (AJ 227). He was the god who sent the Great Flood, who rained down fire and brimstone on Sodom and Gomorrah, who sowed panic among the Egyptians with a series of nine natural catastrophes. The text of the Bible did not make this emphasis inevitable; Jacob Burckhardt, for example, maintained that Yahweh was *not* a 'god of nature'.[56] Wellhausen recalled that God came to the prophets with a 'still, soft sound'.[57] In Weber that is the god of farmers: the camel nomads could better endure a god of thunderstorms (AJ 10). The prophets fought against the worship of vegetation, but in the end they had their own kind of natural religion: one which had in common with modern science a decisive rejection of all natural magic. It was possible to accomplish something not by invoking this god but only by obeying his laws: a god similar to the nature studied by scientists. Thus Yahweh, originally an embodiment of the wildness of nature, became the court for good and evil.

As he spelled out most clearly in a late lecture on economic history, what ultimately counted for Weber was the overcoming of the belief in magic (WG 307f.), which in his view was a violent feat of strength. The prophets, though fundamentally so irrational, thereby unintentionally paved the way for universal rationalization. This is not so far from Sombart's position. Eckart Otto even thinks that in the end there was a sea-change in Weber's view of the role of Judaism in world history: it was interpreted 'as the religious-historical origin of modern Western rationalism', no longer as its opposite that led to the dead end of pariah capitalism.[58] But Weber did not consistently pursue this new approach. Even in his final lectures he remarks that, for the Puritans, 'the Jew was the epitome of everything repulsive', because 'he engaged in irrational and illegal business such as war profiteering, tax farming, the hiring out of office, etc.' (WG 313). This is still the 'pariah capitalism' model.

The 'chosen people': a 'pariah people'

In the *Wirtschaftsethik der Weltreligionen*, *Ancient Judaism* follows the essay on Indian religions and, although he justifies the claim only in part II, starts by establishing a direct link with India through the concept of *pariah*.

> Sociologically speaking the Jews were a pariah people, which means, as we know from India, that they were a guest people who were ritually separated, formally or *de facto*, from their social surroundings. All the essential traits of Jewry's attitude toward the environment can be

deduced from this pariah existence – especially its voluntary ghetto, long anteceding compulsory internment, and the dualistic nature of its in-group and out-group morality. (AJ 3)

Weber's definition of Jewish existence is strikingly apodictic and sweeping, although otherwise he often remained cautious about his interpretation.

The idea of applying the India-based concept of pariah to the Jews had been around for quite some time,[59] but it was used with a critical emphasis on the way in which Christian society reduced Jews to pariah status. In Weber's account, the Jews had originally made pariahs of themselves, through their special kind of hope in messianic salvation. Although he presented 'pariah' as a value-free concept, its derogatory overtones could never be entirely eliminated; it therefore became the 'most objectionable' term in Weber's account of Judaism,[60] especially as the associated line of argument is by no means historically compelling.[61] The pariah concept essentially implies that the Jews bear much of the blame for anti-Semitism. In short, Weber's reasoning is this: any 'chosen' people that isolates itself from others will in turn be excluded by them; anyone who spurns the company of others at table will be considered by them as socially unacceptable.

The distinction between 'in-group' and 'out-group' morality is for Weber not inherently objectionable but actually characteristic of primitive communities. 'You don't haggle with your brothers' – but you do all the more with strangers. Seen in this way, the Jewish pariah existence is nothing other than a continuation of the social life typical of archaic times. Sometimes, though, the brotherliness among Jews does not go very far: 'For years an amusing play goes on between Jacob and his father-in-law as they haggle for the desired wives as well as for cattle which the son-in-law has earned as a servant' (AJ 50). These are features of 'the ethic of a pariah people', Weber comments, 'undoubtedly' a reflection of the lives of 'defence-less small stockbreeders' living 'among military burghers' (AJ 51). The deprecatory tone is unmistakable. The turning point in world history, however – 'the hour of conception for the occidental citizenry' (RI 38), when Christianity changed from a Jewish sect into a potential world religion – was that day in Antioch when Jewish Christians for the first time accepted 'commensalism' (the Lord's Supper) with uncircumcised followers of their saviour. Here it is not Judaism but its overcoming which appears as the origin of Western civilization.

Although Weber thinks more in terms of opportunities than structures, he seems to regard pariah status as a Jewish destiny still continuing in his own day – probably not least because the hopes of salvation associated with that condition are so seductive. Weber put *Ancient Judaism* down on paper at a time when the integration of Jews into German society was increasingly showing itself to be an illusion. Based on her experience of this, Hannah Arendt took over the pariah concept from Max Weber and argued that, so long as Jews admitted its validity, it could be an opportunity rather than a stigma.[62] Of course, Weber did not wish to offer any encouragement to the still seething tide of anti-Semitism; rather, *Ancient Judaism* is linked with his emergence as a prophet of doom among the Germans. They too threatened to become a pariah people in the world: they had puffed themselves up too much on the 'ideas of 1914', on the dream of a greater German community, and had arrogantly cut themselves off from the mainstream of Western thought. Now this arrogance was rebounding on them and threatened to leave them in disastrous isolation.

Weber's favourite text: the Song of Deborah

The Bible criticism of the Wellhausen school had created doubts about the reality of the age of heroes and kings in ancient Israel, so that only the age of Jewish defencelessness remained historically tangible. Yet, according to Weber's account, the Jews had some reason to consider themselves a special people, as charismatic gifts had been present in them since early times, in a wide range of external circumstances. Before the 'scriptural prophets', after whom books of the Old Testament are named, there were many other prophets, including the most celebrated of the female ones, the judge Deborah, who under her palm tree delivered legal and oracular pronouncements and, together with the hero Barak, defeated the Canaanites and liberated the people of Israel from slavery. The victory was complete when Jael (a precursor of Judith) gave the enemy captain Sisera refuge in her bed and killed him in his sleep by driving a tent peg through his temple. Then Deborah sang her famous Song of Triumph (Judges 5), which has stood up to source criticism as one of the oldest parts of the Bible and offers an almost unique window on the early history of Israel.

Already in the view of Eduard Meyer, who had no liking for the Jews of later times,[63] this song was a magnificent national literary monument, comparable to those of Homer for the Greeks.[64] Weber must have been completely enraptured by this powerful, triumphant female charisma: he quotes the Song of Deborah no fewer than seventy times in his works, although in *Ancient Judaism* it rather distracts from his true theme of the rise of prophetic religion. Curiously, Weber researchers have paid little attention to Deborah's charisma in comparison with that of the prophets of doom. But there can be no doubt that Deborah's triumph was his favourite scene in the history of ancient Israel. This was not yet the mournful prophecy of the 'pacifistic small stockbreeders', but the 'war prophecy' of the 'good old times' (AJ 112): Weber used both terms without quotation marks. Moreover, the Song of Deborah is the source *par excellence* for the old 'Israelite confederacy',[65] the warrior community of free farmers and herdsmen which, despite the paucity of sources, Weber examined in greater detail and with greater pleasure than the subsequent 'development of the Jewish pariah people'. The martial community of free men bound together by an oath and a common passion – which did not exclude a charismatic role of special women – was for Weber the primeval type of community, for which life was worth living. Up to a point he could well understand the Zionists who wanted to regenerate Jewish existence through communities of well-armed farmers.

Without worrying too much about the truth content of the legend, Weber saw particularly clear signs of 'warrior ecstasy' in the hero Samson, who defeated whole armies single-handed (AJ 94): once again the combination of asceticism and ecstasy! Nowhere else in Weber's entire work is there as much talk of 'heroes' and 'heroism' as in the case of the 'Israelite confederacy', when the existential threat awakened a sense of charismatic religiosity even in farmers otherwise unreceptive to things supernatural. In *Economy and Society*, too, Weber quotes the Song of Deborah in this connection (E&S 468).

The 'prophets of doom': Weber in a distant mirror

What a contrast to the triumphant Deborah are the scriptural prophets and the prophets of doom! Marianne Weber felt there was a touch of identification when Max read to her about Jeremiah, who 'especially moved' him (WB 593). Jeremiah prophesied and then witnessed the destruction of the Temple in Jerusalem – but Weber would never have gone so far as to foretell in public the downfall of Germany. We have to compare him with Eduard Meyer[66] or Wellhausen to appreciate what was so unusual in his depiction of the prophets: namely, his capacity to reconstruct – actually or ostensibly – a religious passion that wildly intensifies in certain extreme situations.

Weber, who had escaped mental illness in his own person, revelled in the pathological features of the prophets. In the final analysis, their struggle against magic did advance the rationalization of the world, but they themselves, the 'titans of the holy curse' (AJ 273), showed few signs of rationality: their ecstatic states had an element of natural catastrophe and self-destructiveness, even if it was an 'important characteristic' that 'the prophets interpreted the meaning of their own extraordinary states, visions, compulsive speeches and acts', and that 'their interpretations always took the same direction' (AJ 288f.). In any event, they were not exactly consistent in their theology. Weber's Jeremiah rages even against Yahweh when he fails to follow through on the threats that Jeremiah has hurled in his name against his people. 'Often he appears actually to revel in the representation of the frightful doom of his own people which he prophesied as certain' (AJ 272).

Ezekiel (6:11, 21:14) smote with his hands, beat his loins, stamped the ground. Jeremiah was 'like a drunken man', and all his bones shook (23:9). When the spirit overcame them, the prophets experienced facial contortions, their breath failed them, and occasionally they fell to the ground unconscious, for a time deprived of vision and speech, writhing in cramps (Is. 21). . . . Jeremiah publicly smashed a jug,

. . . went around with a yoke around his neck, other prophets went around with iron horns, or like Isaiah for a long time, naked. . . . Jeremiah felt split into a dual ego. He implored his God to absolve him from speaking. . . . Unless he spoke he suffered terrible pains, burning heat seized him and he could not stand up under the heavy pressure without relieving himself by speaking. He did not consider a man to be a prophet unless he knew this state. (AJ 286-7)

Although Weber was supposed to be a sociologist of religion, he showed little interest in offering a sociological interpretation of these archetypal charismatics. He portrayed them mainly as solitary individuals, whose very solitariness differentiated them from the 'orgiastic mass ecstasy' typical of the prophets of the peasant fertility cults (AJ 192). Even when they later had disciples, their charisma did not derive from their community.[67] It will be recalled how Weber thought the Puritan preachers were more solitary than they actually were; he proceeded in the same way with the prophets.[68] One thing above all was clear to him: the prophets never found support among the farmers (AJ 279).

A yearning note at the end

In the long view, the prophets were essentially the undoing of the Jews: 'Prophecy and the after-effects of exile turned the indigenous population of Jews into a guest people, and from now on ritual excluded any fixed roots' (WG 175). The prophets, who helped pave the way for the religion of salvation, retained something that was not amenable to salvation. In one of the very few places in *Ancient Judaism* where Weber refers back to Indian religion, he says with a touch of wistful nostalgia:

Nowhere do we find the prophets mystically emptying their mind of all thought and perception of sense matter and structured objects, a process which initiates apathetic ecstasy in India. Nowhere do we find the tranquil, blissful euphoria of the god-possessed, rarely the expression of a devotional communion with God and nowhere the merciful pitying sentiment of brotherhood with all creatures typical of the mystic. . . . Moreover the prophet never felt himself deified by his experience, united with the godhead, removed from the torment and meaninglessness of existence, as happened to the redeemed in India, and for him represented the true meaning of his religious experience. . . . There was no room for . . . the inner oceanic tranquillity of the Buddhistic *arhat*. (AJ 313f.)

'Inner oceanic tranquillity'! There can be no doubt: Weber's unsatisfied yearning breaks through in the end, together with a sense of the disaster of the Western religiosity founded by the prophets.

When Weber gave a lecture on ancient Israel in January 1917, it was also attended by Else, who had done some preparatory reading of Wellhausen and the Old Testament. It was the first close encounter between the two in seven years. A year earlier, Else had cautiously ventured an approach – a first attempt to get beyond mere 'brotherliness', which sounded to her like 'internal missionary work'[69] – but Weber appears to have remained cold. Now, however, something happened inside him. On his death-bed he would dedicate his *Ancient Judaism* to Else.

Did she sense a yearning when Weber spoke of the old Israelite prophets of doom and their ecstatic despair? Did she, like Marianne, feel that he had himself in mind when he spoke of them? For in this situation she began to feel sorry for the man she passionately hated – and suddenly the old fascination was back. She wrote to Alfred that for two hours Max had presented 'a mass of knowledge in a wonderfully lively way. What a scholar Max truly is! And how terrible and senseless is the fate that no longer allows him to be a teacher!' 'I have also spoken with him' – it was an event after the long silence – 'and precisely in the reserve that conceals his fissures one understands the effect he has on people.' For his part, it no longer occurred to him to play the sickly moral apostle; that was over. Else, evidently deep in thought, got lost on her way to the station and missed her train.[70]

17

World War and Flight from the World

Embarrassing pleasure at the outbreak of war

Many subjective aspects of history are curiously remote from what actually happens: devastated cities become adventure playgrounds for young children. And not only for children. As we have seen, the outbreak of war initially brought personal relief for Weber, in more senses than one. The eternal pressure of the *Grundriß der Sozialökonomik* was lifted for the time being, as he now had an excuse for any delays and could turn his attention to other areas in which he felt more comfortable. But August 1914 also ended all the tiresome wrangles that had been pulling him down; he could now throw himself into the struggle for greater and worthier goals.

Furthermore, the Great War settled a number of little marital wars between the Webers, which for all their absurdity had been weighing on their everyday mood. For example, when Max on a sleepless night wolfed down cheese, blancmange 'and especially the little cakes meant to last several days', Marianne locked the door to the pantry, Max got angry over her distrust and promised to do better, but then went back to his old ways: 'How often has this game repeated itself!' Marianne humorously complained – a scrapping over the wife's power over keys that has been so significant in the history of law. Only during the war, 'when there was nothing anyway, sleep came despite everything far more regularly than before', as the night-time eating compulsion was also completely stilled'.[1] Whereas until then Weber had only temporarily subjected himself to a starvation diet, with disappointing results, the years of meagre fare caused a long-term slimming that probably did him no harm. Nor should it be forgotten that as a medical officer he was drawing a regular salary for the first time in eleven years – 7,600 marks per annum – which the Webers much appreciated, now that the income from their assets had plummeted because of the war.[2]

The beginning of hostilities also put an end to the erotic movement, which until then had been a constant source of unease in the Weber household. More generally, the fun-loving Wilhelmine society represented by Bülow and his overbearing smile suddenly collapsed around them. After the euphoria of early August, a deadly seriousness soon set in as the daily casualty reports started to appear. Weber, who had so often felt alone in his pessimism, was better equipped than others to handle the new situation; he felt like never before a part of his nation – indeed, a spokesman for an as yet unarticulated national mood. He saw the whole German people, as he had previously seen himself, in an extreme situation where its existence was at stake. Already before the war, though, he had had countless fellow sufferers from 'neurasthenia': it was a common view that one was living in 'nervous times'. He had been not only an outsider but also, in his neurotic characteristics, a typical person of his age. His development before and after 1914 therefore helps to explain why a large part of the educated middle classes, who, from a distance at least, seemed to be doing very well, appreciated their good fortune so little that they were prepared to put everything at stake.

Prophetic warnings even before the war?

One would search in vain through Weber's letters of July 1914 for the slightest reference to the impending war: there is absolutely nothing. All his thoughts seemed to revolve around personal problems. Have other letters been lost, in which he perhaps warned of what was to come? But the danger of war did not suddenly appear in July 1914: it had been visible on the horizon for a number of years. The term 'world war' was increasingly part of the list of fashionable compounds containing the term 'world'. Already at the turn of the century, at the time of the Boer War, Naumann had written: 'If one thing is certain in world history, it is the "world war" that lies ahead' – a war, it is true, that he had imagined between Britain and all the countries threatened by British imperialism.[3] By 1914 Weber, who was anyway given to gloomy scenarios for the future, must have long been accustomed to the idea of a coming great war.

But did he actually *worry* about it?[4] His thinking in general would suggest a very different concern: that the unenterprising bureaucrats at the head of the Reich, led by a vacillating dilettante of an emperor, were incapable of the determination to fight a war that might give an emphatic edge to German foreign policy. In May 1915 he wrote to Marianne: 'All the statesmanship of the past twenty-five years' is collapsing, and he himself had the 'very poor satisfaction of having "always said as much."'[5] He had certainly never once, publicly or privately, warned that German policies were creating a danger of war. The main threat to Germany, in his eyes, came from the domination of pedantic officials and phlegmatic Lutherans, who were equally incapable of astute and vigorous policies.

Theobald von Bethmann Hollweg, the German chancellor in 1914, was a far better example than his predecessor Bülow of the correct Prussian civil servant, and, judging by Weber's view of such bureaucrats, he could anyway not have been expected to get involved in a risky venture. In her biography, Marianne does not report any prophetic clear-sightedness on her husband's part during the crisis of July 1914 – which she would surely have done if he had said anything definite. Weber was not alone in this lack of foresight: according to one report, a fortnight before the outbreak of war Lujo Brentano 'triumphantly' demonstrated 'with his quite irresistible logic' that 'the interlinking and rationality of the modern world economy made any war, or at least a long war, completely impossible'.[6]

Well, Weber did believe in the ubiquity of rationalization processes in the modern world, but not at all in the omnipotence of reason. When Austria issued its ultimatum to Serbia on 23 July 1914, it must have been clear to him that any nation with a shred of honour would be unable to accept all of the demands. Karl Loewenstein recalls that, at the Sunday *jour* on 26 July, the last meeting of the Weber circle before the outbreak of war, Weber 'spoke of the Polish and the Alsatian question as the crucial issues in the coming events, with a forcefulness of political understanding that struck everyone there as in the deepest sense prophetic' (WzG 50).[7] It is not hard to imagine roughly what he said: France, looking at Alsace from the point of view of its national honour, can do nothing other than join a military front against Germany (see MWG I/15, 55), and the Reich, in order to strengthen its eastern defences, must win Poland as an ally.

Community in the face of death – for women too?

In the period immediately following the outbreak of war, Weber more than once wrote in private correspondence that it was 'great and wonderful', even 'incredibly great and wonderful': the stereotyped repetition sounds like an incantation. He does not seem to have been carried away by the enthusiasm of this early period, and he was not one of those who made a legend out of 'the ideas of 1914' and the national euphoria of the August days. The charismatic spirit of that time must have been rather irritating to him, since the Reich lacked a charismatic leader: Wilhelm II could be that only in the fantasies of his most loyal supporters, and even then only for a short time. But Weber too did think for a while that community – which otherwise existed only in smaller, tangible contexts – encompassed the whole nation, or at least the whole fighting army, in a war where existence was at stake.

Even in the *Zwischenbetrachtung*, where the war seems so remote, we read this passage: 'The community of the army standing in the field today feels itself – as in the times of the war lord's "following" – to be a community unto death, and the greatest of its kind.' War 'makes for an unconditionally devoted and sacrificial community among the combatants and releases an active mass compassion and love for those who are in need. And, as a mass phenomenon, these feelings break down all the naturally given barriers of association. In general, religions can show comparable achievements only in heroic communities professing an ethic of brotherliness' (FMW 335). Those

Figure 17.1 Max Weber (second from the right) as director of a military hospital, 1914 or 1915

who are enchanted by the erotic visions in the *Zwischenbetrachtung* prefer to overlook these sentences, since they reveal how deeply rooted the fascination for war was in Weber's thinking and feeling, and how intimately it was bound up with love. Weber, who was so fond of playing the anti-Romantic, here gives his own version of Novalis's aphorism: 'Death is the romanticizing principle in life.' In September 1915, after his brother Karl had been killed in action, he wrote to their mother that the front was 'at the moment' the only place 'where it is worthy for a human being to stand'.[8]

And Marianne? She initially revelled in the sense of a great community of brothers and sisters, and in 1915, in an anonymous article for *Die Frau*, she confessed that 'warm love' rose within her at the thought that the troops were fighting and dying for her too. 'I would like to obliterate myself in this community.' She described what she felt as breaking through 'the limits of our ego', an experience of 'mystical union', a selfless love serving 'everyone in need of it'. This is 'a-cosmic love' in Weber's sense of the term, a love with no possessiveness and no aggression.[9] In the early period of the war, she made every effort to direct her yearning for love towards the battling nation, even though, from the beginning, a shudder 'before the horror of what is to come' was mixed in with the dream of happiness.[10]

Yet by March 1915, when nine children and grandchildren of Heidelberg professors had already fallen in battle, she groaned: 'It is appalling to think that this killing might continue for an incalculable number of months!' She repeatedly used the pacifist language of 'killing' and 'butchery' to describe the war: 'Now, when the earth is awakening to new life, the killing seems twice as futile to me.'[11] Marianne's love of nature had none of the Darwinian glorification of struggle.[12] By late 1914 she found it 'almost eerie' how she had become dulled to 'everything terrible out there', and she wanted to work to overcome this loss of reality. In February 1915, when Max was serving as a medical officer, she wrote to Helene: 'I am able – this is my great pride – to see really major wounds without feeling ill. I always dreaded the thought of it so much.'[13]

She may have suppressed thoughts of what the growing number of war widows had to suffer, but she got some idea of it when Emil Lask, to whom she was very close, fell in Galicia on 26 May 1915, at the age of barely forty. Unlike Max Weber, she no longer forced herself to give death a meaning: 'Ah, he was as little made for war as any pure scholar; he couldn't shoot because of his poor eyesight . . . This sacrifice is so terribly pointless!'[14] She was even more affected than Mina Tobler, who had had a love affair with Lask. By November 1917 Else was furious with Marianne, 'who spoke again so "pacifistically" in Heidelberg, under the influence of her Jewish intellectual circles'.[15] At that time, when Else was in love with Max, she got so worked up over Marianne's 'pacifism' that she needed a while to 'abreact' her rancour. In 1920, at the end of the lament for the dead, Marianne burst into a rage against the war that she had never dared to show in her publications. It was no wonder, she wrote, that young people today no longer recognize any authorities or higher values; for her too the only value that remained was the elemental one of human feelings.

Not the Christian religion, whose lying servants said yes to the killing. Nor the state or the nation or the fatherland, in whose name people are for years subjected to unnatural atrocities and turned into robbers and liars. Nor science, which failed hopelessly to avert the disaster. Nothing is definite and beyond doubt except to breathe in the sunlight, nothing except one's home region, love, beauty and joy – the simple joy in life in order to gain new strength.

A dilettante against the 'dilettante sisters': Weber as medical and disciplinary officer

The chapter in Marianne's biography entitled 'Service', which covers the fourteen months during which Weber had to direct the establishment and disciplinary supervision of military hospitals, opens on a positive note. Weber's productive power was now 'so steady' that 'sometimes only the dark memories of his grave illness still kept him from being in good health. Those who were close to him frequently thought, "Oh, if only some great wave came and carried him into the mainstream of life!" ' (WB 517). Marianne's secret wish was being fulfilled, but the war was coming like a force of nature from outside. 'So the war had to come to outwit his inhibitions', Marianne triumphantly reported when Weber not only worked on the organization of military hospitals but also, without suffering any harm, held educational classes for the wounded, as if he had not for sixteen years refused any teaching duties on grounds of ill health (WB 527).[16] Max Weber became healthy as a result of the war: this was Marianne's private as well as official conviction, as she assured Jaspers after the Second World War.[17] She did not care to admit that erotic experiences had played a part in his recovery.

For Marianne it was like a miracle how, from one day to the next, her husband became capable of an exhausting and completely uncustomary work routine. A suspicion pops up: 'Had Weber's frequent feeling of sickness over the last few years been imaginary?' Weber a malingerer, even unwittingly? 'No', she answers, 'because even the most intensive activity of a (health) official is not nearly so much of a nervous strain as *creative* mental activity.' This does not sound very convincing, as Weber had already for a long time been mentally creative. Marianne, who probably really believed that her husband's illness had for some time involved compulsive auto-suggestion, continued: 'The only pathological emotional residue was Weber's fear of any task with a deadline' (WB 525f.). But, of course, the construction of a military hospital took place under extreme time pressure, and in comparison an academic deadline, on which no one's life depended, seemed a trifling matter.

Marianne had to accept, however, that Max did not believe his recovery was as obvious as she did; as soon as she spoke to him about it, 'he felt the still present residue of his illness'. He still felt 'on the other shore', separated by a dark stream from the world of the healthy, especially as he had to consume sleeping potions for his work as a medical officer, up to the limits of what his stomach could endure.[18] In wartime, however, such 'aids' are not a big issue; what used to remind him of the threat from 'demons' had become a trifling matter.

As far as his own person was concerned, Weber seems to have totally suppressed any idea that his illness might have involved unconscious malingering over the years. But, as disciplinary officer in the medical corps, he developed what civilians would consider a terrifying eagerness to prevent wounded soldiers (who would soon be sent back to the front) from feeling too well during their treatment. He fought the tendency of their loved ones at home to 'pamper' them and thereby undermine military discipline (WB 546ff.). In the first few months of the war, he was already imposing so many punishments for 'minor violations of discipline' that 'the whole prison' became 'overcrowded' and the 'poor sinners' often had to wait a week before they could serve their sentence.[19] Quite a few 'offences' were evidently of a sexual nature; the frequency of punishments increased during the spring, and Weber put this down, among other things, to the 'increased sexual excitement' (WB 550). One is reminded of his own dependence on the seasons, and the fact that spring was always the critical time for him.

Weber, who on his own admission was called to this post 'as an amateur' (WB 539) and resigned from it as the medical corps became more professional, spent a long time on the details of problems caused by typical 'amateur nurses', bourgeois girls driven by idealism and personal enthusiasm who, though relatively well brought up and educated, often brought with them too much 'sentimentality' and an 'unconscious hunger for sensation' (WB 544). One can well imagine how Weber's disciplinary measures frustrated such girls, filled as they were with sympathy and love for the wounded heroes. His final report to his superiors revolves around the problems of 'amateur administration' – which, if one thinks of his tirades against bureaucracy, he might have found more congenial – and creates the impression that sentimental 'amateur nurses' were the number one problem.

Weber speaks often indeed about the power of 'brotherliness' in history, but he did not have same sense for the potential contained in sisterliness. To be sure, he would have had in mind the charitable zeal of his mother and her assistants in the poor relief in Berlin, who got on his nerves with their sentimentality. There is virtually no sign that he was shocked by the wounds that he had to face every day, but growing signs that he was fed up with the constant office routine. 'More and more paper, fewer and fewer people.'[20] After a time, however, a number of peacetime comforts reappeared: 'Yesterday I went to see T(obelchen), today comes the "*jour*" ', he wrote in May 1915 to Marianne.[21]

The tiresome lobbying

Weber's life as medical officer was never to be more than an interlude; on 1 October 1915 he was again free of all external obligations. Since May he had been looking around for a political position – a search he would keep up for roughly a year. Those who think Weber was a born politician take this period very seriously and regard its lack of results as a major setback for him, but one has only to compare his efforts with those of his brother Alfred to realize that Max was neither very methodical nor exactly overzealous in pursuing an entrance into politics;[22] this was probably one of the reasons for his failure. The story of Weber the politician is in parts more comedy than tragedy.

It looks as if Marianne was more insistent than Max that he should assume a practical political role. Already in October 1912, under the impression of Weber's fulminating appearance in court against Adolf Koch (by whom he felt himself to have been slandered), she had 'emptied her heart' to Mina Tobler; Max had shown once again 'how his whole talent as well as his happiness lay not at the desk but at the speaker's rostrum – and more generally in an active life – and perhaps all that was necessary was for him to overcome a few inhibitions.'[23] Marianne saw his experiences in the medical corps as confirmation that the best thing for her husband would be to work among other people, forced to discharge specific duties that distracted him from his own illness. She would most have liked him to remain in the medical corps until the end of the war: 'I am sad and unhappy', she wrote to Helene on 1 October 1915, 'that before the war is over Max must give up a job into which he has grown so well and in which, despite its trying "monotony", he has been touchingly conscientious.'[24] And on 21 May 1915, when he returned to Heidelberg after vain efforts to find a position in Brussels and Berlin, she may not have been so happy at their reunion: 'Now I have Maxie (*Maxel*) back again, although I don't really allow myself to have him.'[25]

To her mind, he should not have sat at his desk at home but gone off to serve his fatherland in Berlin or another place where things were happening. But it would seem that Max once more felt himself to be above all an individual, not so much a member of the nation.[26] For a long time he had found the belief in collective organisms intellectually unattractive; he had come to realize that his nationalism was mainly a question of feelings. In November 1918 Marianne herself strictly opposed his going to Berlin 'without an official task': 'there's no point in chattering away there without real influence on the shape of things.'[27] By then she had had examples of such pseudo-activity.

For many frontline soldiers, the First World War came to be a war of technology: no other conflict in history had shown through such apocalyptic scenes the extent to which technological rationality can be cultivated without any link to human reason (an experience completely consistent with Weber's concept of rationalization). However, in the eyes of many *Bildungsbürger* at the rear – those who believed in 'the ideas of 1914' – the world war was a *Krieg der Geister*,[28] a 'war of minds', at least in the early period when the reality of war was still a long way from home. The first years of the war witnessed the inglorious climax of Wilhelmine academic policy: never since the founding of the Reich had so many professors developed such an enthusiasm for politics, travelling in swarms to political lectures and writing article after article about the war. For a time it seemed as if a professor had to be politically active, since there was such a powerful need to give the war a meaning.

In the end, however, a meaning could not be produced by academics at will – a fact that can hardly have surprised Weber. In April 1917 Else asked Alfred to consider 'whether Max was not right in thinking that intellectuals were generally not political people', since politics required 'strong instincts, a strong will and joy in action'. It was 'characteristic' that 'political professors are such relatively simple people as Sering and Schulze-Gävernitz'; and she asked Alfred to take a hard look at 'these threadbare thinkers'.[29] Else, now reconciled with Max, had already learned from him that the scientific intellect obeys laws that conflict with the political instinct. Inside herself she probably thought that, in comparison with Max, the over-zealous and politically vacillating Alfred was one of those 'relatively simple people' – and Max now stimulated her more.

A new political determination

Whereas Max Weber the scholar often expressed himself in over-complicated ways, he soon managed during the war to achieve a clear and simple conception, with a few basic ideas to which he stuck and which still seem plausible in hindsight. The war with the Anglo-American world was for him a great misfortune and the construction of an ideological front around 'God punish England!' turned things upside down; for he believed that if the Germans were to become a powerful nation they had rather to learn from the Puritan-formed British and Americans, instead of romantically glorifying non-Western German traditions. Unlike for Sombart in his war pamphlet *Händler und Helden* (Traders and Heroes), the British were not only traders for Weber; their economic success rested upon a 'record of piety' (PE 45), a religiously grounded work ethic.

Weber was completely free of the typical *Bildungsbürger* arrogance toward Anglo-American pragmatism, and also of the disastrous underestimation of US military potential that led even such a well-known expert on the country as Eduard Meyer to claim that it was 'completely unimportant' whether America entered 'the war more openly' in response to intensified U-boat operations.[30] For Weber America's entry into the war was a nightmare scenario, to be avoided at all costs. If the United States, lacking compulsory military service, did not yet have large, professionally trained armed forces, it was in his view a mistake, typical of Germany's overestimation of formal education, to conclude that they would remain militarily insignificant in the future. Weber knew the sporting spirit of Americans, and it was that spirit which counted for him in Britain too; Berlin therefore had to make it all the clearer – in order to keep the door open for an understanding with London – that it had no intention of annexing Belgium.

In essence, Weber thought that the war with France was also politically absurd and damaging, since Germany had nothing to gain in the west and the abiding hostility of its western neighbours would fatally restrict its room for manoeuvre in foreign policy. In his view it would even have been best to sacrifice Alsace-Lorraine, if that was necessary to reach an understanding with France, which considered it a matter of honour to regain its lost territories at the earliest opportunity. But Weber did not dare say that aloud, since, as he put it, the German chancellor who put Alsace-Lorraine on the negotiating table would not 'make it home alive' (MWG I/15, 674). This was the dilemma of his war articles: he could not speak openly and therefore could not argue consistently. Otherwise he would have had more to say. In his eyes, there was nothing inevitable about Franco-German enmity; he himself was proud to have Huguenot ancestors, and he thought it laughable to construct a deep-seated contradiction between the French and the Germans. It seemed obvious that the greatest threat to Germany's existence came from the east not the west – from a Russian expansionism supposedly driven by land hunger.

Since August 1915, the victorious advances of the German armies in the east had told Weber that there lay not only the greatest danger but also the greatest opportunities. But these could not be grasped through a policy of annexation followed by Germanization; that lesson he had learned from his agrarian studies on the provinces of East Prussia. Rather, the German Reich should establish a belt of small countries in the formerly Russian territories on its eastern frontier, autonomous in their internal affairs but dependent on Germany in foreign policy. Although Weber despised any splitting up of his own country into smaller entities, Germans were supposed to project themselves in the world as champions of the rights of small states.[31]

Weber tried to become an expert on Belgium, then on Poland. In both cases there were tricky problems that did indeed require experts for a solution. In Belgium, he thought the task was to ensure that it did not become a future invasion route into Germany, yet to restore Belgian independence in a manner credible to Britain; and so long as the Belgians had German occupiers this would be like trying to square the circle. The problem was no less delicate in Poland: to build a new Polish state as a bulwark against Russia, even though Polish industry in the former Russian territories relied on Russia as a market for its products; to win the Poles as allies and to maintain their independence, but to do this in agreement with the Habsburg empire, which encompassed Polish territories. Some of Weber's basic ideas on these questions were so obvious that they were already in the air, so to speak. Even Adolf Hitler thought it would be a huge mistake to take on the British empire and the United States, instead of concentrating all of Germany's strength on the conquest of *Lebensraum* in the east – only he did not manage to act consistently in accordance with this principle. Weber, on the other hand, who knew there was no future in settling large numbers of German farmers in the east, wanted to replace direct annexation with methods of indirect imperial rule.

Weber found himself isolated at Heidelberg University during the war; he was not invited to the inter-faculty club of professors that took shape there, and 'the exclusion hurt'. 'They called him a carping critic, claimed that he tried to monopolize discussion, were scared of his intemperateness' (Karl Jaspers).[32] Yet he was not alone in the positions he held. In the summer of 1915 two former colleagues of his at Heidelberg, the theologian Reinhold Seeberg and the historian Dietrich Schäfer, organized a petition to the Reich government, signed by 1,347 representatives of cultural life (including 352 professors), which set highly ambitious annexationist war aims in both the west and the east. A counter-group then sprang up on the initiative of Hans Delbrück and issued a declaration of its own rejecting the 'incorporation or annexation of nations which were politically independent or that were accustomed to political independence' – in support of the ostensibly more moderate policy of Reich Chancellor Bethmann Hollweg. Both Max and Alfred Weber were among the 141 who put their names to this declaration: only slightly more than a tenth of the number who signed the 'intellectuals' petition'.[33] On closer scrutiny, however, many of the public anti-annexationists, not least Alfred Weber, were not so distant in their imperial ambitions from their pan-German opponents; they just thought it a dictate of good sense to strive after these goals with more sophisticated, less provocative methods, or regarded it as a tactic for public consumption to reject annexations so long as victory had not been achieved.

'Anyone with an academic formation is opposed to annexation [of Belgium]', wrote Max Weber from Brussels in August 1915.[34] Anti-annexationism as a question of intellectual formation, despite the 1,347 signatories of the 'intellectuals' petition'! More specifically, 'formation' here meant knowledge of the history that made it impossible for Belgians to identify affectively with the German nation and ensured that Belgian neutrality was a *casus belli* for the British. In Brussels Weber saw for himself the 'ghostliness of German rule in this beautiful, essentially French city'.[35] A man of culture, who was able to speak French, did not see such a city only from the point of view of a German officers' mess; he realized that the Belgian metropolis could never be a German city. 'Anti-annexationism' became for Weber a certificate of like-mindedness. 'Ernst Mommsen is now anti-annexationist, we were in complete agreement' – in agreement 'that this bragging is a stylistic lapse on the part of people who sit at home'.[36] Ironically, Marianne reminded Helene in September 1915 that at the previous family meeting Alfred – who by now had joined the anti-annexationsts – 'wanted to swallow up Belgium or large parts of it' and had quarrelled with Max over the issue.[37] It is paradoxical that, precisely because Max Weber regarded struggle as a basic part of life, he did not need to have ambitious war aims; war, as long as it was not self-destructive, served a purpose by reviving the national community and did not necessarily require any further legitimation. Yet he too, as Marianne assured his mother, 'had nothing against a revision of our eastern frontiers'; 'he just doesn't want to know about any annexation of Belgium.'[38]

The difference between Max Weber and the pan-Germans (of whom he had been one until 1899) was partly a question of style. What they declared with ungainly candour, in the style of the loud-mouthed imperial dilettante that Weber found so abhorrent, he, the disciple of Machiavelli, wanted to pursue more quietly and therefore more effectively, in the British manner. But he was and never would be a politician: he could not get used to acting silently; speaking and writing were his forte. Thus, as a mere 'wannabe politician', he landed up with the dilemma that many of Machiavelli's maxims work only if they are kept secret. As soon as one said publicly that the aim was to restore the external independence of Belgium and Poland, while surreptitiously keeping them tied to Germany, one helped to ensure that this very stratagem misfired. It could not be said openly that concessions might eventually be made to one's opponent, nor that the prospect of such concessions was only a show.

Weber's temperament and whole way of thinking were such that he must soon have realized that a major war, in which the belligerents were driven to a wild frenzy, could not be steered by a professorial intelligence and could end only with the collapse of one side or the other. Most of the professors involved in politics were not taken seriously by the government, or even kept in the picture about topical matters on which they offered their expert services. For example, the plans for a great unified Central Europe [*Mitteleuropa*] put forward by Friedrich Naumann, with which Weber went along for a while because of their long-standing friendship (though without inner conviction),[39] were left hanging in the air.[40] Weber soon realized that there was a lot of self-important spurious activity among the numerous intellectuals who tried to curry favour with the government; in Brussels, in the autumn of 1915, he found 'countless acquaintances lolling around', 'far too many'.[41] He was offered the chance to write a report on the likely effects of applying German labour legislation in Belgium – potentially a not unattractive subject. (Lujo Brentano thought that a similar move in Alsace would have won over the workers there to the Reich.) But Weber considered the task 'deadly boring' – 'if only they were political questions!'[42] The maintenance of industrial health and safety standards was for him evidently more a matter of administration than politics.

After he returned from Brussels empty-handed, he hung around for months at his mother's while looking for a position in Berlin. In late May 1916 Naumann's committee, the Arbeitsauschuss für Mitteleuropa, which was examining the prerequisites for an economic community with Austria-Hungary, commissioned him to make a trip on its behalf to Vienna and Budapest. But what sounded at first like a political mission turned out to be nothing more than political tourism. Real politics was being conducted elsewhere.

Weber also became aware of this with regard to Poland. Now that he saw the main danger in Russia and enjoyed the company of Eastern Jewish intellectuals, he underwent a radical change from being an enemy to a friend of Poland. The war filled him with the idea that a new Polish nation, unobtrusively dependent on the Reich, had to be built as a bulwark against the vast Russian empire. From late 1915 the whole of Russian Poland was occupied by German troops, so that Germany was in a position to act on the Polish question. 'Only Polish matters are of interest to me', Weber wrote in May 1916 from Berlin; and in late 1915 he already had plans to learn Polish.[43] His idea of a Polish satellite state was no longer original – Ludendorff too had similar plans, and at his urging a kingdom of Poland was proclaimed on 5 November 1916. But this construct existing by the grace of the German occupying power, without political institutions that might draw in Polish forces to work with it, was a farce that rendered futile any efforts that Weber might make in relation to Poland.[44] The political objective that most enthused him in those days – perhaps also because his turn towards Poland symbolized a turn in his attitude to life – had been ruined. If, nevertheless, Berlin did not become unbearable to him, this was because for some time he had been immersed in Oriental religions in the university library.

Another factor seems to have been crucial in his decision to leave Berlin for good. Alfred had been living there since 10 May 1916, and thanks to his connections with the influential Helfferich, permanent secretary in the Reich treasury department, he achieved what Max never managed to do: he obtained a political position, a potentially key one at that, as a kind of personal adviser to the permanent secretary on the scientific and political preparation of the planned reform of government finances.[45] The key task – in Max Weber's view, the most delicate of the war – was to fund the sky-rocketing military budget.

After the outbreak of war, Alfred had volunteered for the front despite being a 46-year-old professor. For a time, the once so nervous man with depressive tendencies seems to have had no complaints, to have been good-humoured even, and in 1915 he published the political passages from his wartime love letters to Else as *Gedanken zur deutschen Sendung* (Thoughts on the German Mission); Thomas Mann paid him the high compliment that 'since the beginning of the war nothing I have read . . . has done me so much good or expressed so fully my own political thoughts and feel-ings'.[46] This little volume, in which Alfred's pleasure in war breaks all bounds, may be seen as an expression of the charismatic 'hero ecstasy' analysed by his brother, though certainly not as proof of scientific insight. Like Max, he sees Russia as the main danger, but at the same time he derides Belgium as a 'country of parasites', grouses about the 'revolting business instinct of the Anglo-Americans' and shows off in a way that his elder brother finds unbelievably stupid: 'How outwardly wretched and inwardly pitiful is that huge clod of the United States standing there without an army!'[47] After all, 'hatred of the British is brotherly hatred, no doubt abut that.'[48]

But brotherly hatred can be a powerful thing, as Alfred must have known. In Berlin the rivalry between the brothers, who had been avoiding each other for six years, again erupted in all its bitterness – or anyway that is what Max felt. Puffed up with his experience of the front and his new political function, Alfred struck him as unbearably theatrical. He could no longer stand to be in Berlin,[49] even though Marianne and Helene took it amiss that he wanted to turn his back on politics because of Alfred.[50] Again he hid behind his illness: 'Also, after repeated switches to other things, my brain's capacity to adjust is noticeably crippled for the time being.'[51]

An outsider sees little sign of a crippled brain at that time. But the 'other things' were now the 'Oriental religions', and by immersing himself in them Weber lost a sense for the murky routine of politics in the capital. In fact, with his new freedom, the time had come for him to remember the *Grundriß der Sozialökonomik*. As in the past, he fumed at the idle excuses of dilatory contributors, some of whom had in reality decided to publish elsewhere. But now a war was on, and Weber the organizer had the kind of sense of freedom that one has on holiday. He could simply do what he felt like doing![52]

A thwarted politician?

Or was he smarting from his lack of success in lobbying for a government job? Were the Oriental religions just a poor substitute for politics? The idea of Weber as a thwarted statesman has become a familiar trope in the literature. Already before the war, on a Saturday reserved for Tobelchen (14 June 1912), after she had played a Beethoven sonata for him, and after they had nibbled some wild strawberries together, Mina Tobler flattered him by saying that it had been one of the greatest 'misprints' in life – a term she probably took from him – 'that he had not become German chancellor'. And 'he thought that if that were so it was Germany's bad luck more than his.'[53] Mina was delighted by her lover's casual arrogance – yet the real meaning of the comparison was probably that it would have been 'bad luck' for him if he had become chancellor.

When Weber announced his withdrawal from the leadership of the German Democratic Party in April 1920, he gave the following reason: 'The politician should and *must* make compromises. But I am a *scholar* by profession. . . . The scholar does not need to make compromises or to cover folly. . . . Those who have other views . . . abdicate their responsibilities. I would act as an offender toward my profession.'[54] Shortly afterwards, however, following Weber's death, it was a common theme in the obituaries to suggest that the greatest tragedy of his life was that he had not been given the political leadership for which he had a vocation. As Gertrud Bäumer put it, Weber's whole scientific work was 'in a sense a makeshift, a substitute for the action that was denied him' (WzG 47).[55] Late in life Jaspers saw it differently: 'as a statesman' Weber 'would have failed, and probably quickly'.[56] It is curious how tenaciously people adhere to this image of Weber, especially as the extremely demanding picture he draws in *Politics as a Vocation* suggests that he did not relate so easily to the world of everyday politics. On a sober analysis, few of his statements that have survived from the early period of the war suggest great political understanding, and his tiresome tendency to get bogged down in unnecessary and unproductive controversies is not exactly evidence of a born politician. He himself seems to have had far fewer illusions on this score than many of his admirers. In May 1916 he reacted tetchily to Marianne's constant harping that he should do something in Berlin politics: 'I can't bring myself to pester the poor tormented people in the offices, just so that I can "do something".'[57] That would have been a mere substitute satisfaction for him: to join the army of desk strategists instead of fighting at the front.

Flight from the world: fun among the Chinese and Indians

But the Oriental religions were something quite different. Weber had begun his study of Hinduism in October 1915, immediately after finishing his military hospital service – not at all only after the disappointments in Berlin.

And soon he was also deeply immersed in ancient China; he was 'driven by a fury for work' on the Chinese (Hennis).[58] In the course of 1916 Weber assured people so often of his 'great pleasure' in going among 'his' Chinese and Indians, and how good it felt to be among Asians,[59] that we have no reason at all not to believe these admissions on the part of a man who rarely spoke of his emotions in science – especially as Marianne would rather have heard him say something else. From now on, one senses his new love even outside his writings on Oriental religions, in his tendency to draw on the most exotic examples from ancient Asian civilizations.

When his practical political prospects crumbled, he had a new surge of scholarly activity; his gift for political journalism was also released once he no longer needed to worry about how it might affect his chances of an appointment. It was only in the second half of the war that he became a political pamphleteer, but it is phenomenal how little this commitment caught the scholar up in its wake. Although he seemed to many others the epitome of a 'personality' closed in on himself, he was contemptuous of personality cults; he must have had a special aptitude for dividing his ego. He knew better and better how to use this talent, although sometimes it bordered on the pathological. His condemnation of value-judgements in science offered the theoretical basis for adopting a positive attitude to this split in himself.

An eerily productive writer such as Sombart lost the appetite for writing long books during the war; a great historian of the calibre of Eduard Meyer ran out of steam and could no longer write on early Christianity once he began giving bellicose lectures and contributing to victory fanfares; even such a gaily contemplative historian as Friedrich Meinecke lost all pleasure in his craft as the reality of the war came home to him.[60] Weber, however, previously incapable of taking on major projects, now built up a huge head of steam and developed a capacity for ecstatic contemplation he had never had before. As he wrote in 1917 to Tobelchen, he enjoyed this kind of flight from the world: 'I rejoice only when I am again among faraway things that take you out of the present day. For everything connected with it is somehow grimmer and tugs on the iron ring that you feel placed around your chest, head and neck.'[61] This flight from the world had nothing ascetic about it (whereas the 'worldly asceticism' of the Puritans, Weber now realized, was the most pleasureless of all), since the German world of that time was in no way gratifying. For Weber, flight from the world meant a liberating self-discovery and a coming to rest within himself. The 'stages and directions of the religious rejection of the world' – the secondary title of the *Zwischenbetrachtung* – have erotic fantasies hidden within them.

During the First World War, although he was the only one of Helene's four sons not to fight, Weber liked to think that he had 'the strongest *innate* warrior-instincts', with the word 'innate' each time underlined.[62] His knowledge that this was a natural instinct, not the result of a process of reasoning, even put him one up on the professors who wrote war pamphlets. But it may also be concluded from his behaviour that his survival instinct was even stronger than his warrior instinct. Significantly, in the *Zwischenbetrachtung* he points out that the words of Jesus: 'I came not to send peace, but a sword' (Matthew 10: 24) – which had been flogged to death by the war theologians – were said in connection ('and, it should be noted, only in connection') with his teaching that those who cannot be hostile to their father and mother cannot be his disciples (FMW 329). Moreover, the endless duration and routinization of the war had robbed it of the charismatic force that generates 'hero ecstasy'. By the end of the first year Weber was of the opinion that 'the war, which was magnificent as an extraordinary exertion of all heroic forces and loving readiness for sacrifice, would become satanical in every respect if it lasted for years' (WB 552). This too was a practical application of his idea of charisma.

In May 1916 in Berlin, Weber found it 'almost inconceivable and saddening' that fully forty performances of Strindberg's *Dream Play* had been sold out: a play he could not stand, in which the daughter of Indra, the Indian sky god, comes down to earth and experiences all the suffering of humanity.[63] He rightly sensed the creeping defeatism in the almost magical appeal that this display of compassion had for audiences. But in a way his turn to the Oriental religions was part of the same trend, which Carl Neumann, an admirer of the 'Nordic Rembrandt', lamented after the war: 'India, East Asia, primitivism', he wrote, were something 'that so many of today's quacks and so many who are genuinely diffident of an opiate-dependent public (Tagore) extol.'[64] The financial side of Weber's essays on the Oriental religions, which he hoped would boost the sales of the *Archiv*, was not unimportant to him; he needed the money to pay for repairs to the plaster figure ('Jack Johnson') by Hermann Haller, a sculptor friend of the Toblers, which, to everyone's amusement, he had accidentally knocked from its pedestal on 1 March 1916 at the Sezession exhibition in Berlin while deep in conversation with Franz Eulenburg about the Polish question.[65] Publicity for theologian Wilhelm Caspari's *Die israelitischen Propheten* began with the words: 'The keen interest of the present day in creative religious personalities finds satisfaction in the Israelite prophets.' There can be no doubt that, at the latest by the second year of the war, Weber's kind of flight from the world was 'all the rage'.

One deeply satisfying aspect of Weber's work on Oriental religions was that his *Protestant Ethic*, though itself only a fragment, now acquired a larger framework than had originally been conceived for it: it became the preliminary to a huge investigation into world history and the origins of the West's exceptional path. The high civilizations of the East were a kind of check on whether the religious factor had been decisive for the genesis of modern capitalism – a check that crossed boundaries in a way that none of his opponents, whether Rachfahl or Brentano or even Sombart, could match as soon as he moved eastwards from Israel. A circle closed with the Oriental religions, rather as Weber's period of despair now acquired retrospective meaning as a stage prior to erotic illumination. It is a fascinating picture. In the middle of the world war, Weber developed a vision of how the West fitted into the history of the world, in a way that made extra-European cultures appear extremely enticing. It was there if anywhere that an unbroken unity of mind and nature could be found.

Encounter with a future guru

Although Weber had previously announced that he would do further work on the Protestant ethic, we learn from Marianne that around the year 1911 he felt an urge to resume his studies of religion 'in the East'; and 'the East' meant above all China and India. Today's experts on India are irritated by Weber's view of sex as a key to Indian religiosity (again and again, talk of 'sexual orgiasticism'); moreover, even in his own day, research did not confirm the relevance of such an approach, and it was the fakirs, the most fanatical ascetics in the world, who thrilled Western travellers with their extreme control of the body.[66] From where did Weber derive his image of India? Was it mainly a projection of his own erotic experiences and fantasies? Probably it was, but it was not only that; such a lack of critical awareness should not be attributed to a man such as Weber. It is likely, however, that he did not reveal all his sources in the notes – especially not those which were scientifically questionable.[67] Chief among these must have been Hermann Graf Keyserling (1870–1946), an amateur philosopher who failed to get his *Habilitation* qualification, and who made a trip round the world in 1911. In 1918 he published his travel journal, which became a cult book and established its author as a guru in possession of Oriental wisdom; soon after his return, in autumn 1911, he had made the acquaintance of Alfred Weber, who was so captivated that he wrote after Keyserling's death in 1946 that he had been closer to him than any other human being.[68] Keyserling was a conversation partner with global horizons, in whose presence people could float odd and objectionable ideas in a way that never became vulgar. 'Chivalry is the only ethos I recognize as fully adequate', he wrote in 1917 to Alfred Weber[69] – an avowal one could also imagine in the mouth of Max Weber.

Keyserling first made contact by letter with Max Weber in 1911, before there was any talk of the Orient, and Weber responded with great interest and striking candour. Early in October 1912 Keyserling stayed with Max and Marianne for four whole days – an unusual display of hospitality for the Webers. He took it in turns to visit the two brothers. Max was by then avoiding private contact with Alfred, but in a long letter he described Keyserling as a 'very gifted, personally very attractive and, in my eyes, agreeable person, but with a completely dilettantish mind – he understands nothing at all of logic'. The reference to his dilettantism was certainly on the mark, yet he regretted that Keyserling did not want to obtain his *Habilitation*. For Weber thought there was more in him than met the eye, and that he would develop greater intellectual discipline (MWG II/7-2, 740).

Keyserling published some lectures on the philosophy of nature and battled it out with neo-Kantian epistemology in an effort to save the reality of reality. He taught that the body has much higher capacities than reason, even more imagination than the average intellect[70] – theses that must have given food for thought to Weber, who had seen how his own body could rebel. Apparently he would have much liked to keep him around as a disciple from whom he too could learn. A letter from Marianne to Else tells us more of Keyserling's fireworks and the impression he left after his visit. He was 'one of the strangest creatures' she had ever met.

> A spiritual nomad and wanderer, who channels all the religions and civilizations and possibilities through his mind. . . . The man speaks so fast that at first I can't understand him at all, still less follow what he says – it was altogether *exciting*, this cyclone that beat you about the ears with China, Confucius, Japan, India, Buddha, Brahmann (sic!), theosophy and God knows what else. He was here for three hours a day, speaking incessantly, laughing and clapping whenever Max said something he liked. . . . In short, he struck me as even a little foolish – but very likeable in a childlike sort of way . . . It is incredible that with this oddly voracious and talkative nature he really lives alone for nine months of the year – and *keeps silent*. But somehow this metamorphosing into a thousand shapes, from Indian holy man to Manchu prince and then a Japanese and an American, seemed to me a little terrifying.[71]

It is astonishing that Max Weber, who was used to holding his own monologues, put up with this bubbly and undisciplined character for hours and days on end – and would even have liked to expose him to the discipline of a *Habilitation* process. At that time, however, when Weber was looking for a way into the civilizations of the East, Keyserling must have seemed just the man he needed, who showed him how one could be transformed into a Confucian or a Brahman and, even more, how one could penetrate the mentality of Oriental high cultures through deep layers of the psyche, through magic and eroticism.

The travel journal that Keyserling published later gives a good idea of what the cascade of words must have been like at the Fallenstein villa in Heidelberg. 'The further south man lives', he writes, 'the more sensuous, in the animal meaning of the word, does he become and the less active in imagination . . .' Sexuality fulfilled makes love unromantic; it is unfulfilled drives which raise the imagination to a higher intensity. The traces of this reasoning are to be found in the *Zwischenbetrachtung*. In the tropics, according to Keyserling, all that grows is *longing*: 'the longing to escape from all abundance' to the great void, to Nirvana. This inspiration is especially strong in hot parts of the world. The same ideas underlie Weber's essay on religions in India, even if a straightforward climatic determinism is not his style. Keyserling, the husband of Bismarck's granddaughter, who later, as a herald of wisdom, made no secret even in the prudish American Midwest of his penchant for hetaeras,[72] was able to philosophize without any embarrassment in a Japanese brothel. Utterly delighted by its sexual uninhibitedness and the 'atmosphere of harmless cheerfulness', such as one finds 'among children round the Christmas tree', he discovers 'indiscriminate love of one's neighbour' in the prostitutes and considers their natural relationship to sexuality to be one of the roots of the difference between East and West. Many pages on the Indian hetaera's art of love culminate in the complaint:

> It is madness, almost a crime against the Holy Ghost, to ban eroticism from life, as the Puritanism of all countries and all times has done: it signifies in reality the fulcrum of human nature. Through the Eros every string of his being can be set in motion, and the deepest reverberations have generally emanated from it.[73]

For Keyserling, the kernel of Indian wisdom is that man achieves inner peace, which makes 'spiritual progress' possible, not by repressing his instincts but by satisfying them. He goes into veritable raptures about India:

> With what wonderful wisdom has this people solved the sexual question, how wisely, especially from the point of view of spiritual progress, with which it is concerned so much more than sanctimonious Christianity! There they never attempt to violate nature because they have known for centuries, what Freud has only discovered recently, that repressed desires are more corrupting in their effects than the most evil which are confessed freely.[74]

This view of the world and life was tailor-made for Weber in the autumn of 1912, at the beginning of his love affair with Mina. In *The Religion of India* he writes that 'all Indian authors agree' (can he really be so sure?) that 'each matron secretly envies the sophisticated hetaera' (RI 151). How could he not have been thinking of Marianne and Else?

For Weber the sociology of religion means seeing behind religious doctrines and rituals the spiritual elites who are the bearers of religion. He observes not only their material and legal position, but also their mentality, their nervous make-up and the ways in which they handle emotions. Although Weber so often attacked organological metaphors of society, he recognizes here the idea originating in antiquity that the whole people is like a single body, with its leaders as the head and its lower classes as the abdomen; the orgiastic elements of religion rise up from the latter. This conception, highly questionable for us today, was for Weber like a law of nature. Intellectual leaderships, with their 'ancient, cultivated, intellectual soteriology' (RI 295), are by nature alien to and mistrustful of alcoholic and sexual orgiasticism, but not as fanatically hostile to it in the civilizations of the East as the Anglo-American Puritans and Israelite prophets in the West. The 'sublimated type of intellectualist ecstasy', a new concept for Weber (E&S 537), is probably his own ideal!

Discovery of the art of ecstasy: a precursor of hippie Hinduism

At one point in *Economy and Society*, Weber seems to extract a formula from the Oriental religions through which one can reach – without alcoholic or sexual orgy – a lasting charisma, a euphoria that creates meaning and illuminates the spirit:

> It should go without saying that a methodical approach to sanctification was not the means used to produce the acute state of ecstasy. Rather, the various methods for breaking down organic inhibitions were of primary importance in producing ecstasy. Organic inhibitions were broken down by the production of acute toxic states induced by alcohol, tobacco or other drugs which have intoxicating effects; by music and dance; by sexuality; or by a combination of all three – in short by orgy. Ecstasy was also produced by the provocation of hysterical or epileptoid seizures among those with predispositions toward such paroxysms, which in turn produced orgiastic states in others. However, these acute ecstasies are transitory in their nature and apt to leave but few positive traces on everyday behaviour. Moreover, they lack the meaningful content revealed by prophetic religion. It would appear that a much more enduring possession of the charismatic condition is promised by those milder forms of euphoria which may be experienced as either a dreamlike mystical illumination or a more active and ethical conversion. Furthermore, they produce a meaningful relation to the world. (E&S 535)

One does not have to be a psychologist to notice that Weber is describing a state for which he himself longed, and for the attainment of which he now felt a certain competence. But was it really only milder but more permanent forms of euphoria that aroused this man who was given to extremes and fascinated by 'the extraordinary'? He pays striking attention to *tantrism* in India, to that 'heterodox' current, as he calls it, in both Buddhism and Hinduism, which revelled in magical-orgiastic rituals and held sway especially in Tibet. Strange though it may seem, Weber was in a sense the precursor of those hippies of the 1960s and 1970s who trekked to India and Nepal in search of the Tibet-style sexual orgiasticism of tantrism. In his own day it was not so easy to discover tantrism in that direct way, nor was there the popular tantra literature that we have today, richly illustrated with erotic diagrams. It is true that the beginnings of today's Western myth of Tibet go back to Weber's day,[75] but the literature on Buddhism – including most of what Weber consulted[76] – then treated tantrism and lamaism mainly as a grotesque deformation of an originally quite different doctrine.

For Weber, on the other hand, it was precisely the sexual orgies that were original and genuine; he made fun of the 'usual, puritanically prudish manner' in which British authors perorated about 'abominable practices' (RI 381). Here he evidently believed that he had understood the original essence of Indian religiosity better than had contemporary Indologists, who offered a purified and disinfected picture of it in order to gain the respect of Western readers. It should not be ruled out that, with his intuitive perception and his belief in passion as the driving force of the world, Weber identified a correct feature of Tibetan Buddhism despite his insecure research base. But this remains a controversial question.[77] The young Mircea Eliade (1907–1986), later to become the most comprehensive scholar of religion in his time, had to travel to the edge of the Himalayas to gain the similar insights that showed him a way forward.[78] The question of whether Weber's 'orgiastic' interpretation of Indian religion was misconceived led to 'lively discussion' at a conference in Bad Homburg in 1981. This inspired Wendy Flaherty to compose the following limerick.

> What Weber called orgiastic
> were cults that he thought were fantastic.
> To him, Hindu sects
> mistranslated as sex,
> and their mudras were crazy and spastic.[79]

The elites of the East: models of how to handle natural instincts

In a sense, Weber's essays on Oriental religions are studies of how intellectual elites with an ancient tradition of worldly wisdom were able to handle the wild instinctual life rising from below. They are like a symbolic representation of his own problems in life, at a time when he was becoming increasingly able to handle them. Yet we should be wary of reducing these works to an over-simple denominator. The picture he draws of the driving forces of Oriental religions is generally not at all simplistic, but on the contrary highly complex and fascinating.

Some of what Weber writes about China juxtaposes positive and negative images of the 'Middle Kingdom'. Among educated people in Europe, there was already a tradition in which it was seen either as the model of a country ruled by scholars (the mandarins) or as a terrible example of ossification stretching back thousands of years.[80] And yet, if we look not only at the content but also at the language, we notice unmistakable signs of sympathy, even identification, in his account of China's and India's intellectual elites. Evidently he saw the noble educated Confucian as a model for himself, one whose mentality and emotional economy he could comprehend especially well[81] – although admittedly a modern sinologist such as Weber's own great-nephew, Peter Weber-Schäfer, criticizes Weber's failure to define precisely who these 'Confucians' were.[82] Here is how Weber described the ideal type of a Chinese brought up in Confucianism, he who suffered so much from his own 'nerves' and irritability:

> the striking lack of 'nerves' in the specifically modern European meaning of the word; the unlimited patience and controlled politeness;

the strong attachment to the habitual; the absolute insensitivity to monotony; the capacity of uninterrupted work and the slowness in reacting to unusual stimuli, especially in the intellectual sphere. All this seems to constitute a coherent and plausible unit. (RC 231)

In the geography of nerves Asia was the El Dorado: one statistic that appeared in 1910 claimed that the proportion of mentally ill people in Prussia was 182 times higher than in India,[83] and one could also read in the press that no one in East Asia suffered from nerves. Typically, however, Weber presented other character traits that spoiled the pleasure of identification with this Chinese, such as 'an unlimited and good-natured credulity in any magical swindle, no matter how fantastic' or, worse, 'what is repeatedly maintained as the incomparable dishonesty of the Chinese' (RC 231f.). Shortly afterwards he notes the 'specifically cool temper of Chinese humanity' (RC 233): a trait he must have found not unsympathetic, if we remember how much the sentimentality of the 'amateur nurses' in the military hospital got on his nerves. 'The absence of hysteria-producing, asceticist religious practices and the rather thorough elimination of toxic cults could not fail to influence the nervous and psychic constitution of a human group' (RC 232). The sociologist of religion here becomes a nerve specialist of religion.

The following sentence does not sound entirely free of value-judgements: 'Always the proud, masculine, rational and sober spirit of Confucianism, similar to the mentality of the Romans, struggled against interference in the guidance of the state when such interference was based upon the hysterical excitation of women given to superstition and miracles' (RC 203). Weber detected 'manly beauty' in the memorandum written by the Confucian Tao Mo in 1901, in which he warned the empress of magic and eunuchs (RC 140). 'The Confucian desired "salvation" only from the barbaric lack of education' (RC 228): the idea reminds us that the seeds of unhappiness lie in the quest for salvation in anything external, and the secret of happiness in inner harmony and the absence of any need for salvation.

'Like for truly Hellenic man', Weber says in a choice comparison, the Confucian lacked 'all transcendental anchorage of ethics, all tension between the imperatives of a supra-mundane God and a creatural world' (RC 228). An ethic anchored entirely in the 'creatural world' thus led to being at one with yourself: where does this leave any sharp distinction between Is and Ought? Weber invokes some 'very good remarks in Ludwig Klages's writings', when he claims that 'alien to the Confucian was the peculiar confinement (sic!) and repression of natural impulse which was brought about by strictly volitional and ethical rationalization and ingrained in the Puritan' (RC 297n, 244). This calm attitude to one's own creaturely nature appears to be the secret of the Confucian's unshakable tranquillity.

For the highly nervous and salvation-seeking Weber, this Confucian remained an ideal type to which he drew a little closer in those years, but which was not unquestionably suited to him. His attitude to India's religious elites was different: they had a way to redemptive illumination that fitted into both scholarship and religion; and one need not be a depth psychologist to see how inwardly present it is in *The Religion of India*. Those who think of him only as a cool man of the intellect would suspect he had a special affinity with Confucianism, but the essay on Indian religions is written with more warmth and far greater detail. 'The specific soteriological methods and procedures for achieving sanctification are, in their most highly developed forms, practically all of Indian provenience', he argues (E&S 537), as is 'sophisticated Indian eroticism, in contrast to China' (RI 151f.). One should read how he writes about 'illumination' in the sense of 'ancient Buddhism'; if taken out of context, it might suggest that he had become a Buddhist himself. This salvation is a long way from the unyielding predestination of the Puritan God; it is a victory for which human beings can methodically work by immersing themselves in the truth and refusing illusions, in order to become Arhat, the Enlightened One, and to be sure that the 'state of grace' will last:

> The illumination, however, is not a free, divine gift of grace, but the wages of incessant meditative absorption by the truth for the sake of giving up the great illusions from which spring the thirst for life. Whoever achieves that illumination enjoys – note this – bliss here and now. The tone to which ancient Buddhism is attuned is triumphant joy. The Arhat who has reached the goal of the methodical, contemplative ecstasy . . . feels himself replete with a strong and delicate (objectless and desireless) experience of love, free from earthly pride and Philistine self-righteousness, but possessed by an unshakable self-confidence which guarantees a lasting state of grace, free from fear, sin and deception, free from yearning for the world and – above all – for a life in the hereafter. (RI 212f.)

Liberation from the world therefore has nothing to do with yearning for the hereafter: Weber emphasizes this-worldliness as a fundamental characteristic of Buddhism. And then – not at all a feminist as a result of his erotic experiences – he sets a Confucian-style value on the manly (or anyway decidedly non-feminine) character of the Arhat, perhaps also so as not to adapt his image of Buddhism too much to Western needs for Eastern wisdom:

> From the role that 'love experience' plays in this description of the condition of *arhat* one might conjecture a 'feminine' trait. That however would be false. The attainment of illumination is an act of the spirit and demands then power of pure, 'interest-free' contemplation on the basis of rational thought. The woman, however, at least in later Buddhistic doctrine, is not only an irrational being incapable of supreme spiritual power and the specific temptation for the aspirant to illumination – she is, above all, quite incapable of that 'objectless' mystic love mode which psychologically characterizes the state of *arhat*. (RI 212)

The 'power of pure, "interest-free" contemplation on the basis of rational thought': Weber's value-free science in Buddhist dress! When Weber wrote in January 1920 that 'contemplative existence' was 'once again' his 'form of life', and that he had no more to do with politics (and so '*basta*'),[84] he himself was establishing the relationship between his scholarship and contemplation. But was he altogether the man of suprasensual objectless love, and did he perceive only that among the religious elites of India? It was with pleasure that he lingered in the ancient Brahmanic world of the *Bhagavad Gita*, where the road to salvation lay through the warrior's life – an ethos that Weber felt to be 'organismic' in a sense 'hardly to be surpassed' (RI 189). The famous inscription of the Brahman Sivagana concerning the founding of a hermitage belongs to this world. What Weber wrote about this is one of the linguistic highpoints of *The Religion of India*:

> He had through his power of prayer helped his king to conquer innumerable enemies and to butcher them. In these verses, as usual, the earth is soaked with blood. Then, however, 'devoutly' he built this house and whoever in the world turns his eyes to it will be freed from the imperfections of the 'Kali Age'. . . . 'He built it', the following verses continue, 'in the season in which the wind bears the scent of the Acoka-blossoms and the mango shoots are sprouting. Swarms of bumble bees are everywhere and more than ever the gleam in the eyes of lovely women tells of their love. . . . (T)heir bodies shatter the bodice when they are stirred sitting on swings face to face with their lovers. Laughingly they hastily avert their half-closed eyes and only the quiver of their brows betrays the joy in their hearts.' . . . One sees that here everything in life receives its due: the wild battle fury of the hero, then the yearning for salvation, for the ever-new pains of separation composing life, the place of solitude for meditation, and, again, the radiant beauty of spring and the happiness of love. (RI 190f.)

This is the feeling for the world and life which, for Weber, 'in the last analysis also pervades the most characteristic parts of Indian literature'. And his comment reveals that the inscription quoted at such length reflects part of his own philosophy of life. After the heat of battle comes the blissful intoxication of blossoming nature and sensual love! Here is the intellectual resource on which Weber drew in his love letters to Else in the spring of 1919.

During those years, Weber discovered not only a friendlier relationship to his own nature but, after much charging around, a meditative type of science for himself; only through this did his struggle against value-judgements acquire vital significance. When he wrote on the Oriental religions, he no longer introduced any aggressive fantasies into his scholarly work. Here it is not precocity but great curiosity which drives him on; he shows no inclination to rush into well-barricaded positions that he can defend with self-opiniated fury. Not to be proved right all the time, but to be part of an intellectual current leading into the Infinite: this is his ideal of scholarship, which is in fact already discernible in the 'stream' metaphors of his 1904 essay on objectivity.

Literati and eunuchs: topical emotive issues in an exotic guise

Two themes of Weber's essays on China that were also emotive issues in his political writings of the time were *literati* and *bureaucracy*. Although, as he defined them, he too belonged to the literati, especially after the failure of his attempts to break into practical politics, they became his favourite whipping-boys in the writings he published on the war. Admittedly there were tactical reasons for this, as he was waging a campaign on two fronts: against megalomaniac agitators for annexation as well as revolutionary or pacifist intellectuals. As both categories overwhelmingly consisted of deskbound strategists – at least in the early stages of the war – the 'literati' label really did fit them. It packed a special punch against the new political right, since 'literati' was one of the insults it wielded against the rather cosmopolitan left-liberal intelligentsia. The best example is the '*littérateur* of civilization', alias Heinrich Mann, at whom his brother Thomas took aim in his *Reflections of a Non-Political Man*. It was thus not unintelligent of Weber to turn the word against the ever more combative right-wing intellectuals, implying as it did that these heroes sitting safely at their desks wanted soldiers at the front to go on bleeding indefinitely.

But, even if the literati are present everywhere in Weber's writings on the Oriental religions, he does not think for a moment of conducting his current German battles in the ancient Asian civilizations. In China the literati were largely identical with the Confucians; they made up the imperial bureaucracy, by a long way the oldest and largest in the world. Yet, when he painted bureaucratization as the spectre haunting Germany and looked around for historical precedents, his eyes fell more on Egypt and Byzantium than on China. 'The ancient Chinese mandarin was no specialist official; on the contrary, he was a "gentleman" with a literary-humanist education. The Egyptian, later Roman and Byzantine official was essentially much more of a bureaucrat in our sense of the word' (PW 156).

Of course, these ancient Chinese gentlemen-literati were not in every respect endearing for Weber. They could be humourless and domineering: 'Once when a prince's concubine laughed at one of the literati, all the prince's literati went on strike until she was executed.' They were also decidedly unwarlike (RC 281n.). That too could not fail to impress Weber, although it was the result of their general composure. They did combat the influence of eunuchs, concubines and magicians at the court, and their battle with the eunuchs in particular – who were often in league with magic and heterodox religions – was in Weber's view the leitmotif of Chinese history down the ages (RC 285f.). In this the literati were regularly victorious in the end, thanks to their superior administrative rationality (RC 139).

'In the most varied contexts Weber thought he could detect "charismatic" features in the Chinese literati-official';[85] his study of China reveals the truth of this observation of Arnold Zingerle's.

A tragic figure for Weber was the Confucian court historian Ssu-ma Ch'ien (later transliterated as Sima Qian *c*.145–90 BC), who was castrated for contradicting an imperial command;[86] Weber spends a strikingly long time clearing his name (RC 166ff.) and refers to him on many occasions. The efforts of this man to compensate for his loss of fertility through a different kind of virility evidently had something moving for Weber. He speaks of him as having been 'castrated', although he remained a Confucian and a court historian and was not at all one of the court eunuchs. Yet Weber assumed that castration changes the character even of an adult man with an established intellectual posture (RC 168). Gender was for him first of all a physical fact, and only then a quality of the mind.

In considering this struggle of the literati against the eunuchs, we should remember that not only 'literati' but also 'eunuchs' were among the most offensive terms used at that time in the political struggle in Germany. The accusation of unmanliness was the usual way of abusing pacifists before the era of 'Make love, not war'. In November 1911 this led to a major confrontation at Heidelberg University, when General Berthold von Deimling raged at a social occasion against supporters of the peace movement and accused them of wanting to 'castrate' Germans and turn them into 'political eunuchs'. Instead, he hoped that young German academics would again have the opportunity to live through times of war and victory (MWG II/7-1, 337) – a view with immediate relevance. The danger of war was looming as a result of the Morocco crisis, and with the German army still under-equipped for a war on two fronts even Max Weber temporarily supported the movement for peace.

The incident in Heidelberg led to fierce controversy in the press. Weber fumed with anger at the general and the student fraternity members who cheered him: a 'purely zoological nationalism, utterly hollow and empty', as he put it. He struck an equally manly and vigorously combative tone, hurling back at the general a reproach that has since become famous: so long as the military authorities 'try to brand' lower-ranking officers as 'eunuchs' by forbidding them to hold oppositional political views, he would 'not accept the right of any general to use that expression against other people' (MWG II/7-1, 355). Virility, both physical and mental, was a value for Weber too. When 'manly' Confucians combated the influence of court eunuchs, it was clear on whose side Weber stood.

China and India: contrast and unity

Whereas in the West today there is a tendency to view the whole of the 'third world' or 'developing countries' – apart from the East Asian 'tigers' – with a mixture of pity and condescension, perceptions were rather more nuanced in Weber's day. The old fascination with the high civilizations of the East did not fade even when imperialism was at its height. It was traditionally popular to set China off against India, contrasting mandarins to fakirs, wisdom to miracles, unfathomable tranquillity to tropical plenitude.

Hegel depicted China in his lectures on the philosophy of history as the country of perfect administration, which 'uniform and regular, like the course of nature', performs its duty, with an emperor at the top who, taught by philosophers, always speaks with 'paternal kindness and tenderness to the people', but whose rule means that it can never be self-reliant. India, though as immutable as China, 'has always been the land of imaginative aspiration and appears to us still as a fairy region, an enchanted world.' 'In contrast with the Chinese state, which presents only the most prosaic understanding, India is the region of phantasy and sensibility' – and, not least, 'a beauty of a peculiar kind in women', on which the philosopher dwells with obvious pleasure.[87]

The same basic perception is not difficult to recognize in Weber's essays, and it was by no means necessarily consistent with the sinological and Indological literature of his time. On the other hand, Weber emphasizes what is common to the high civilizations of Asia, in contrast to the West and its harsh schooling by prophets and Puritans. A modern specialized bureaucracy could not develop among the gentlemen officials of ancient China any more than it could in India; they too never completely rid themselves of magical ideas. In both cultures there was never a radical break between the mind and the reality of the senses, although in the history of Indian religions the tension between the alcoholic and sexual orgiasticism rising from the tropical temperament of the lower classes and the striving of the Buddhist elites towards the great Nirvana was more powerful than the tension between Confucianism and Taoism in China – and for that very reason India was more fascinating to Weber, beset as he was with tensions of his own. Both the Indian Buddhist elites and the Confucians, however, had a coolness of temper whose effect on Weber was equally beneficial; it was a long way from the sentimental Christian tradition, which commanded Weber's respect but often irritated him when he came across it in his mother's home. 'The concept of neighbourly love, at least in the sense of the great Christian virtuosi of brotherliness, is unknown', he remarks of original Buddhism – which sounds at first as if he is pointing out a fault. But then he quotes an enchanting sentence from the *Questions of King Milinda*: 'Like a mighty wind the blessed one blows over the world with the wind of his love, so cool and sweet, quiet and delicate.' And he comments:

> Only this cool temperance guarantees the internal detachment from all 'thirst' for the world and men. The mystic, acosmic love of Buddhism is psychologically conditioned through the euphoria of apathetic ecstasy. This love and 'unbounded feeling' for men and animals like that of a mother for her child gives the holy man a magical, soul-compelling

power over his enemies as well. His temper, however, remains cool and aloof in this. (RI 208)

Weber had often felt how hatred of his enemies made him inwardly dependent on them – and how Marianne's sentimental love awakened in him no love in return. It is 'cool' love (in which Else was a virtuoso) that bestows magical power. Later he mentions the always 'alert Asiatic self-control', which 'without exceptions' was basic to 'the life methodology of the educated intellectual strata and holy seekers' (RI 338): a self-control that has nothing in common with the Puritan asceticism produced through desperate struggle. If 'the striving of the typical Asiatic holy man' – for Weber there is such an ideal type – 'is centred in "emptying"' or Nirvana, this denotes Nothing in terms of the 'world' yet not actually something negative, rather the 'positive holy circumstance of ineffable, death-defying, this-worldly bliss' (RI 339 – translation modified). (We should remember that this was written in the middle of the First World War, when Weber's great longing was for 'death-defying bliss'!)

Not only India but also China was in its way a magical land, and for that very reason thoroughly different from the modern West. As we have said, the high civilizations of the East served Weber as checks for verification of *The Protestant Ethic*, and China was particularly suited to this purpose. For certain conditions that are regarded as prime causes of modern industrial capitalism were most probably also present in China: a world lead in technological innovation until early modern times, a hard-working mentality geared to practical solutions, a layer of moneyed merchants, and a rational state administration. Yet, despite all this, capitalism did not make headway. Weber saw one reason for this in irrational features of the most significant 'heterodox doctrine', Taoism. However, Confucianism was not an orthodox doctrine in a Western theological sense: it did not rigorously and indefinitely suppress all deviations,[88] but over time was prepared to accept at least a degree of coexistence with them (RC 213f.). The point for Weber is that in this way the 'enchanted garden' (reminiscent of the 'enchantresses' of Ascona!) was preserved, although he himself does something to dispel the magic:

> Finally, from our presentation it should be perfectly clear that in the magic garden of heterodox doctrine (Taoism) a rational economy and technology of modern occidental character was simply out of the question. For all natural scientific knowledge was lacking, partly as a cause and partly as an effect of these elemental forces: the power of chronomancers, geomancers, hydromancers, meteromancers; and a crude, abstruse, universist conception of the unity of the world. Furthermore, Taoism was interested in the income opportunities of prebendal office, the bulwark of magical tradition. The preservation of this magic garden, however, was one of the tendencies intimate to Confucian ethics. (RC 227)

For Weber, enforcement of the capitalist asceticism of work was a painful process involving the suppression of human nature, so it was really not so extraordinary that this revolution initially occurred in only one part of the world. It might have been pointed out to him that, precisely on the basis of his theory, there was no need to explain the *non*-enforcement of capitalism, only its enforcement; that the failure of capitalism to get beyond the initial stages was the norm in world history, since this corresponded to the pleasure-oriented inertia in human nature. Probably he would not even have disputed this. But, if his escapade into the great civilizations of the East excited him so much, there were surely other reasons than his wish to find more solid foundations for *The Protestant Ethic*.

Magic and hydraulics – anthropology and geography

Mark Elvin, the foremost expert on Chinese environmental history, is critical that, despite Weber's theoretically multicausal understanding of history, his 'interpretive sociology' means that he tends to 'overstress' conscious motives and to disregard silent determinants.[89] In the ecology of major construction projects, including the availability of timber and the suitability of watercourses for mill power, he might have found more clearly than in religion the decisive factors that held back capitalist development in China. The reference to nature that he traced in Eastern religions was above all, Elvin argues, a reference to nature in *man*.

Yet Weber knew that irrigation was of fundamental importance for Chinese agriculture and that it required the existence of a central bureaucracy; Wittfogel's theory of an 'Asiatic mode of production' or 'hydraulic society' has its origins in Max Weber at least as much as in Karl Marx. Weber thought 'the irrigation and construction bureaucracy' was 'undoubtedly ancient'; it had marked the whole mentality of the Chinese literati and 'repeatedly steered' their thinking 'to the tracks of administrative technology and bureaucratic utilitarianism' (RC 37). This point is indeed key to an understanding of China, even of its intellectual world, but Weber mentions it only sporadically and even more rarely in the case of India, although there too the political economy of irrigation was a rich field for investigation.

Weber understood better than Wittfogel that the concept of bureaucratic totalitarianism was quite misleading in relation to ancient China, as the smaller units of village, family and kinship group had a great deal of autonomy in the vast empire (RC 86ff.). But, even if the emperor was technically incapable of directing irrigation work throughout his sprawling realm, the constant fear of water shortages did mark his 'magical charisma'; the farmer needed help from above because of his dependence upon the great irrigation networks. Thus, the emperor was 'primarily' the 'old rainmaker of magical religion', though 'translated into ethics' (RC 31). Then, with a side-swipe at Wilhelm II:

Like all genuinely charismatic rulers, he (the Chinese emperor) was a monarch by divine right, and not in the comfortable manner of modern sovereigns who, by the grace of God, claim to be responsible to Him alone – that is, practically, not at all. . . . Thus, if rivers broke the dikes, or if rain did not fall despite the sacrifices made, it was evidence . . . that the emperor did not have the charismatic qualities demanded by Heaven. In such cases the emperor did public penitence for his sins, as happened even in recent times. (RC 31, translation corrected)

It is not altogether convincing to derive a 'hereditary charisma' from achievements in irrigation, for dams burst often enough in Chinese history without resulting in an emperor's abdication or overthrow. Indeed, the extensive use that Weber makes of his charisma concept in China and India may well strike the reader as questionable: here it appears in connection with the continuing importance of magic, of the enchanted world. Later, on the question of 'hydraulics', Wittfogel thought that Weber had got stuck at a point 'where he should have gone more deeply into the problem of nature'; it was a 'real shame' that 'lumpen Weberianism' then 'I will not say, castrated, the giant, but reduced him to a level' at which his incipient naturalism dropped completely out of sight.[90]

At the end of *The Religion of India*, Weber surprises us with a sweeping explanation in the style of geographical determinism, though it is more with a view to an unanswered residue: 'The lack of economic rationalism and traditional life methodology in Asia is, so far as other than psychological historical causes play a part, pre-eminently conditioned by the *continental* character of the social order as developed in terms of the geographic structure. Occidental culture was throughout established on the basis of the foreign or transient trade . . . It was different in Asia' (RI 340). This is the geographical-structural condition of the harmonious Asiatic mentality. But not everything in it is typically Asiatic: Weber believes that certain basic laws of the intellectual striving for perfection stand out particularly clearly in the development of the religions of the East, which have been 'far more ruthless than the West' in struggling to solve the emergent problems (RC 340, translation corrected). Weber even formulates a complicated 'if . . . then' law with universal applicability:

Wherever an intellectual stratum attempted to establish the meaning of the world and the character of life and – after the failure of this unmediated rationalistic effort – to comprehend experience in its own terms, indirect rationalist elements were taken into consideration. It was led in some manner in the style of the trans-wordly field of formless Indian mysticism. And where, on the other side, a status group of intellectuals rejected such world-fleeing efforts and, instead, consciously and intentionally pursued the charm and worth of the elegant gesture as the highest possible goal of inner-worldly consummation, it moved, in some manner, toward the Confucian ideal of cultivation. (RI 342)

This is another of those tangled Weberian thoughts, so hard for researchers to grapple with, which challenge us to establish a connection between the life and the work. We can imagine how, in the years of despair, Weber struggled in vain to give his life meaning in a purely rational way through thought alone – and how there were then experiences that lifted the spell from his affective as well as his intellectual life. But we do also see one side of Weber in the 'Confucian ideal of cultivation'. By now he has given up the ideal of the closed personality, and his affirmation of quite different aspects must have been a liberation for him.

The silence of Asiatics and the silence of nature

Right at the end comes an even stranger passage, where Weber laughs at how 'the reserved dignified countenance which seems so highly significant of the Asiatic intellectual tends to taunt the curiosity of the Occidental.' He draws a parallel between the silence of Asiatics and the silence of nature: 'Before the cosmos of nature we think: it must still . . . have some sort of "last word" to say as to its "significance." The unfortunate thing is . . . that "nature" either does not have such a "last word" or is in no position to reveal one. The situation is often the same with the belief that someone who tastefully remains silent probably has a lot to be silent about' (RI 340, translation modified). The silence of Asiatics – so Weber seems to think – is not silence *about* anything, any more than is the silence of nature; there is no secret to be looked for behind the silence. Asia, which, unlike Europe, has not been oriented to the ocean and distant trade, is at peace with itself and does not restlessly seek a meaning in a world outside it.

This idea, in its simple form, corresponds to a traditional Western cliché about the East. Sometimes, however, Weber is not so sure of his ground. Confucianism for him also has a distinctly rational side, which makes it akin to Western rationality. 'Confucian rationalism' – there was such a thing! – 'meant rational adjustment to the world', whereas 'Puritan rationalism meant rational mastery of the world' (RC 248). But in practice do the two often not amount to the same thing? Did not Francis Bacon teach that 'naturae non imperatur nisi parendo', that nature cannot be commanded except by obeying it? At the end of his essay on China, Weber rejects the then widespread assumption that the Chinese are 'by nature' not up to the demands of modern capitalism: 'The Chinese in all probability would be quite capable, probably more capable than the Japanese, of assimilating capitalism which has . . . been fully developed in the modern culture area' (RC 248).[91] Prophetic words from today's point of view!

18

Great Speeches, the Great Love and Death

Two or even three lives – masquerade and a quickening tempo

Sociology of Religion, Economy and Society, political speeches and writings under the impact of war, defeat and revolution, love and death: are these not quite different stories that belong in separate chapters, each with its prevailing mood of reflection, raging despair or blissful happiness? Yet it is one phenomenal aspect of Weber's life that these stories run in parallel or with only a brief gap between them. There is even more of an overlap in his relationships with Mina and Else than it was previously thought, or than one thought such a rigid man capable of enduring. There is no doubt that, from 1917 on, the pace of Weber's life quickened at every level: the political, the scholarly and the erotic.

After nearly two decades of silence, a kind of release now occurred in relation to public appearances as well as his long-denied love for Else: he must have had an ecstatic feeling that his time had finally come. He now conquered the public with the powerful eloquence that for years he had displayed only in the little household circle of the *jours*; for a while he seemed to be the man of the hour. Previously his name had scarcely been on everyone's lips, but his reputation as a public speaker must have spread fast and wide. Again and again he found himself speaking in packed halls. But, while he prophesied a long icy winter to the young students there, he himself, a man in his mid-fifties, was living an ecstatic springtime of love, such as he had never known in his youth.

In order to understand Max Weber, it is important to see the different stories together – otherwise there is a danger of taking his public pronouncements more seriously than he did himself, and of treating them far too much as if they were the whole Weber. Traditionally the presence of a single solid identity and authenticity in everything Weber said and wrote has been considerably overstated. In fact, it is not only for self-declared disciples that he has been the epitome of total honesty: even the first Soviet commissar of culture, Anatoly Lunacharsky, while keeping all his distance from this decidedly bourgeois sociologist, believed 'that Max Weber is deep down an honest man'.[1] 'Honesty is generally now the number one concern': this kind of statement, from a letter he wrote in November 1918, was considered the most genuine expression of his attitude of mind,[2] although Weber elsewhere put ironical inverted commas around the 'honesty' (*Ehrlichkeit*) so beloved of Germans.[3]

Did he really stand full square behind what he said in the much too often quoted addresses on 'Science as a Vocation' and 'Politics as a Vocation'? The sharp-sighted Ricarda Huch wrote in 1928 to her friend Marie Baum that, in reading Marianne's biography, she had again 'suddenly had the feeling that Max Weber had been play-acting'.[4] 'I had the same feeling quite spontaneously – I had been prepared for something quite different – when I once heard him give a lecture. I think it comes from the fact that the source of the instincts within him did not flow, and that he replaced that with his conscious mind, which I am simply not very prone to do' (MWG I/17, 123). The lecture in question was probably 'Politics as a Vocation' on 28 January 1919, where Ricarda Huch sat right at the front (MWG I/17, 122). In fact, the source of Weber's instincts was then flowing in quite a different direction. On 15 January, after one of his election speeches for the Democrats, at which he had received 'a storm of applause' plus some chair-throwing from the Spartacists, he wrote to Else that he had 'certainly spoken badly'. 'For what was I actually thinking about?' he asked her. 'About the "constitution" of this carnival "republic"? You know better. How you can express everything in language, and how wretched one is in comparison.'[5] It is doubtful whether he performed much better two weeks later, with 'Politics as a Vocation'. At the time Marianne was dreaming of him as future chancellor of Germany, and there was 'universal anger in our circles' when the Democrats did not even give him a good position on the election list for the National Assembly. He 'got over it completely', however; 'he does not get at all excited and laughs at my fury.'[6]

In Weber's love letters to Else, the Germany of war, defeat and deep demoralization lies far away. To his beloved he spoke of the 'masks' he has been wearing all the time. But it must at least be contemplated that there was a little play-acting not only in his political speeches but also in his love letters. In the *Zwischenbetrachtung* he noted with the voice of an authority that, while 'pretending to be the most humane devotion', the 'erotic relation' was 'a sophisticated enjoyment of oneself in the other' (FMW 348). At exactly the same time, he was learning the art of how to stage-manage oneself – as someone who is only apparently oneself – and to play various roles in a number of spheres; he was no longer much attached to the value of consistency as far as his own person was concerned. Indeed, while mocking the political 'carnival', in his way he took part in its masquerade. His nephew Eduard Baumgarten, who in those days had many an opportunity to observe Weber, later recalled how, when Weber described the political situation (probably more to an imaginary public than to his nephew), his thinking and speaking involved considerable physical activity:

> He roamed the large carpet in the middle of the room, walking round a somewhat darker rim woven into the rest. . . . He balanced on this

edge as if it were a tightrope. He seemed . . . to swing his leg high in the air like an ice dancer; his upper body bent so far forward that the tip of his elegant, Napoleon III-style grey beard appeared to rest almost on the ground. To this colourful, graciously elastic form of bodily accompaniment, he meditated aloud before me. . . . He meditated with no set purpose . . . and steered the excess of ideas into soothing, restraining dance-like movements on a rope.[7]

More clearly than ever, it became part of Weber's experience of life that scholarship, politics, marriage and sex were each separate spheres. In private company he spoke less often about politics than at many times in the past; and Marianne had the impression that he 'would much rather' not think about the future of Germany,[8] although he spoke about it a lot in public and wrote more than ever before in his life. During these final years we must be especially attentive to the sphere of life from which a particular quotation is taken, even if it is not possible in the end to split the man into different parts. Whereas in the 1890s the transitions between science and politics had been for him still partly fluid, both in content and in language, he now adopted for his political speeches and press articles a tone quite different from the one he used in his scholarly writings. Germany's defeat, which cast many nationally minded Germans into deep depression, did not arouse self-pity in him and did not affect in the least the intensity of his work and life. By now he was living inwardly in worlds that the German disaster could not damage.

The 'parliament of ghosts' in the Hall of Knights at Lauenstein Castle

Max Weber needed the right opponents to grow into a great public speaker; he had not had them in the dispute over value-judgements, and his irritability had too often drawn him into unpleasant quarrels. But at the conferences at Burg Lauenstein, in late May and late October 1917, he found a number of suitable adversaries: political irrationalists who behaved in a boy-scoutish manner yet avoided the harsh realities of the contemporary world. At the same time, he was spurred on by hopes in a new German youth, one that would understand his sharp sense of reality and not allow itself to be captivated by the fine-sounding verbiage of assorted seducers. In a letter to his mother at Christmas 1915 Weber had spoken of the 'many attractive types of young people who grew up in Germany and to whom the Great War, if it does not devour them, will give a firm, serious commitment and inner security alongside a joy in life: relief from the eternal "searching" for themselves, which is just another expression for "regarding themselves as important", as one does when one is not inwardly attached to any serious objective human problems.'[9] This was also how he saw the problem of the young people he now wanted to forearm against seducers and to help pass

Figure 18.1 The Lauenstein conference, July 1917: Eugen Diederichs is third from the left, then Theodor Heuss; Max Weber is standing second from the right, behind Ernst Toller seated on the ground

from fruitless egocentricity to a strictly objective attitude to the world. In student circles marked by war and impoverishment, those who set the tone were no longer foppish, beer-sodden members of duelling societies but more serious and emaciated, thoroughly sober types; someone like Weber could take to these much more easily.

Lauenstein Castle, which lies far from the city high up a steep mountainside in the south-east Thuringian forest, offered a perfect backdrop for medieval and knightly romanticism. This was the effect intended by the man behind the conference, Eugen Diederichs from Jena, who at that time was probably the most successful German publisher[10] and one of the commercial sponsors of Jugendstil; he had already helped to organize the meeting of the Free German Youth at the Meissner Heights in 1913.[11] In a situation in which German politicians were at their wits' end, Diederichs wanted to gather at the Lauenstein (where meetings were held in the Hall of Knights or in the castle yard (WB 597)) some of the leading minds of the older and younger generations, under the banner of a new spirit for

Figure 18.2 Audience listening to Max Weber in the grounds of Lauenstein Castle, 1917

Germany inspired by the religiosity and chivalry of the Middle Ages: a project strangely remote from the realities of the third year of war, but which may have seemed good for the publisher's profile (a man in whom Theodor Heuss detected a mixture of 'masked romanticism and energetic entrepreneurship').[12]

With politically committed young people more and more polarized to the left and the right, Diederichs was making another attempt to revive the unity of the youth movement. The first meeting took place at Whitsun, the feast of the Descent of the Holy Ghost. Friedrich Meinecke, one of those who attended, later recalled the peculiar 'parliament of ghosts', where 'probably all the Zwickau Prophets at Germany's disposal put in an appearance and fought it out with serious scholars' (WzG 146). According to Theodor Heuss, who was also there, Max Weber ridiculed it as a 'department store for world-views'.[13] Amazing though it may seem, the original invitation had been to Marianne rather than Max Weber[14] – one indication that her involvement in the women's movement had until then made her more of a public figure than her husband. As she reveals in the biography, she was also more susceptible than he to the romanticism of Lauenstein. And indeed, with his sharp anti-romanticism, he did dispel some of the atmosphere that Diederichs had wanted to create. When one of the young people there blurted out that a character like Diederichs deserved to be 'slapped long and hard', he was telling Weber just what he himself was thinking (WzG 269).

The array of intellectuals at the conference included Werner Sombart, who until then had far surpassed Weber in his impact on the public. But Weber soon pulled ahead, particularly impressing young people for whom the big words of the pre-war period had turned completely sour. Opinions were divided: 'To some he appeared as Satan, to others as their conscience' (WB 600). But in the end even Diederichs was content and described Weber as the 'most valuable acquisition' (MWG I/15, 704); after all, he did guarantee publicity and attract more young people. Weber therefore became involved in organizing a second conference in October, when – as Diederichs frankly confessed – the circle would need a 'violator' to ensure that it did not become a confused 'debating club'.[15] What a challenge for Weber!

Diederichs's first preference as chief performer had been Max Maurenbrecher (1874–1930), a former theologian whom Weber had once known well as a close colleague of Friedrich Naumann. Theodor Heuss thought that of all his disciples Naumann had liked Maurenbrecher best.[16] Like Göhre, who was similar to him in temperament and rhetoric,[17] he became part of the left wing of the National-Social Party, and after it split he joined the Social Democrats – which Marianne Weber found 'terribly sad'.[18] During the war – like another of Naumann's former left-wing collaborators, Gottfried Traub, who was dismissed from the pastorate because of his rebellion against the Church regime – Maurenbrecher mutated with a renegade's zeal to become a hypernationalist, an enemy of democracy and a pioneer of nationalist religiosity. In 1912 he had published with Diederichs a critique of religion (*Das Leid*) that asserted the superiority of Indian over Christian religiosity, dedicating it to 'the confluence of Karl Marx and Friedrich Nietzsche'. He was almost blind, and his celebration of struggle may have partly stemmed from a constant battle with his own disability. 'Where there was a truly religious experience', he wrote, 'groaning was turned into joyful energy.'[19] Salvation became the central focus in his philosophy of religion, as it did in Weber's – only in a different combination with politics.

For Weber, Maurenbrecher now came to epitomize a nebulous political romanticism, so extreme as to be intolerable, together with an inability to perceive the realities of the contemporary world – the malady of the political literati in its worst form. Here was the perfect opponent at whom Weber could direct his rhetorical fireworks: pitiless realism against woolly visions; the needs of the day against intellectual escapism! 'Max talked for days and half the night, chasing away with his criticism the swathes of romantic mist that gathered there', Marianne reported.[20] There was no thought of 'nervous' considerations, even if Max, as he put it to Mina Tobler, did not get through 'one night without strong doses of sleeping potion' during those 'inflammatory days';[21] but that no longer mattered, and so they were not followed by depression. Weber was in his element. Psychologically he understood the Maurenbrecher type all too well, as he himself had turned to the Oriental religions in the midst of the war. But he knew it was fundamentally wrong to mix politics with fantasies alien to it, and his polemic was all the sharper because he was struggling against a part of himself.

The natural vocation of scholarship and the 'hazard' of a scholarly career

On 7 November 1917, a week after the second Lauenstein conference, Weber gave his address on 'Science as a Vocation' in Munich.[22] His reluctance or inability as a scholar to play the role of prophet, together with his anger that others expected this of him, helped to raise his rhetoric to a peak that gave it precisely something of the prophetic. Karl Löwith later remembered being shaken by Weber's appearance: 'His face, with a shaggy beard growing all around it, recalled the mournful glow of the Bamberg prophets.'[23] Immanuel Birnbaum – who, on the instructions of the Freie Studentenschaft of Munich, talked Weber into giving both this and the lecture on 'Politics as a Vocation' – made a similar point: 'Outwardly the gaunt, bearded man looked now like a prophet tormented by visions of disaster, now like a medieval warrior before leaving for battle' (WzG 19). The prophet metaphor was commonly applied to Weber, who, for Marianne too, had occupied himself with the prophets of ancient Israel from anything but a position of cool and critical detachment. Can it be said that he actually aimed to make this impression on people? After all, he no longer experienced himself as a gloomy man of troubles; one of the happiest periods of his life was just beginning. Nor did he have any new faith to proclaim to the students. His main prophecy, as a man who had travelled to North America, was an Americanization of academic and all other areas of life (MWG I/17, 73f.), and in this respect he proved to be a good prophet, at a time when the German Reich was at war with the United States.

Birnbaum further recalled – again using a common trope – how the 'Science as a Vocation' lecture became a 'confession' that 'burst from the speaker's breast in jerky explosions' (WzG 20); so, Weber gave his audience the impression of labouring hard to give birth to new ideas. As usual, he spoke with only a few keyword notes and must have improvised as he went along, but the sharp rebuff that he administered to *ex cathedra* prophecy was in fact a rhetorical figure from the prewar dispute over value-judgements. Now, in the wartime situation, he mainly targeted the pan-German nationalist professors who still publicly dreamed of world power. The correct dating of the address has made this basic tendency clearer than before.[24]

In November 1917 Weber was still outside the academic hierarchy, even though he had been discussing an appointment with Vienna since October. If he made such an impact on his audience – only part of which (a disappointingly small part, in Weber's eyes (MWG I/17, 60)) consisted of students – this was probably due mainly to the blunt and sharp, indeed brutal, manner in which he addressed unpleasant aspects of academic life, and especially of academic careers. He did not make scholarship sound very inviting to most people, nor was it his intention to enlist recruits for a life of study – on the contrary. His main drift was to put off those who did not feel called to such a life. Early in 1919 he wrote: 'We have approximately fifty per cent too many students – therefore, more difficult exams, selection of gifted individuals!' (MWG I/16, 466). To appreciate the clarity and dramatic sobriety of the November 1917 address, we have only to read the contrary position of Erich von Kahler ('Der Beruf der Wissenschaft', 'The Vocation of Science', 1920), with its verbal bombast and its euphoria so completely out of tune with the academic requirements of the time, as if the previous daily routine was over and a day had dawned 'such as has not appeared for many hundreds of years'.[25]

Weber took it as given that an inner calling, and therefore also an inner gift, was part of the vocation of science, as was a stoical resignation to fate when the great scientific breakthrough failed to happen and there was no success in career terms. For he stressed more than once that an academic career is a game of chance: whether it carries you to a full professorship is 'simply a hazard. Certainly, chance does not rule alone, but it rules to an unusually high degree. I know of hardly any career on earth where chance plays such a role' (FMW 132). Or again: 'Hence academic life is a mad hazard' (FMW 134). He describes his own career as an example, without mentioning how family connections smoothed the way for him at the start. Fundamentally, he regards the whole business of German academic careers as a scandal: scarcely anywhere else is there so little confidence that good results will be rewarded. Scholarship should embody the highest rationality, but an academic career is the most irrational in the world. (The geneticist Erwin Chargaff, who studied in Vienna in the 1920s, later recalled a student proverb that was doing the rounds: 'There are only two routes to a university career: *per anum* and *per vaginam*. You had to try to become Professor's darling or to marry his daughter.'[26] The results were by no means worse, however, actually rather better, than in the modern career path through commissions.) The creative process itself contains an element of 'hazard': many toil honestly all their life, but absolutely nothing comes to their mind. And Weber rightly adds that it is not only in academia but also in business that success often hangs on a stroke of luck (FMW 136).

Running through the whole lecture is the idea that only a special type of person has a vocation for science. Scientific theory can do nothing about this unpredictable factor but must orient itself to an element more susceptible to planning: methodical work. And this is what Weber then does most emphatically: the demand for a self-denying work discipline is at the core of his lecture, which is thus in a sense the pedagogical pendant to *The Protestant Ethic*. Like the modern economy, modern academic life calls for strict asceticism. The time for gleefully soaring flights of intellect is over; the true scholar of today and tomorrow is a specialist. In his brusque manner, Weber impresses it upon students – he, who has long made it his speciality to jump across the boundaries of special disciplines – that his scientific horizon stretches from stock exchange law to the *Bhagavad Gita*. Then he spells out what he means by the injunction to asceticism: 'No sociologist, for example, should think himself too good, even in his old age, to make tens of thousands of quite trivial computations in his head and perhaps for months at a time.' One cannot 'with impunity' try to transfer this quantitative labour to assistants (FMW 135). He himself did precisely that.

'Science as a Vocation' contains an element of camouflage. Is he not speaking here in favour of just those 'specialists without spirit' whom at the end of *The Protestant Ethic* he condemned as nullities? But for Weber the evolution on this point had something inexorable; individuals could only endeavour to keep the spirit alive in the world of specialists. Not without reason did he detect, precisely among the sociologists of his day, a danger that lack of specialization would leave them stuck in an eternal amateurism. Weber's words were, and are, perfectly suited to keep this danger at bay – which is probably not the least of the reasons for his lasting fame in seminar rooms. In his usual way, he worked himself into the theme with great intensity; he even demanded that modern specialists wear 'blinkers', not only with regard to their career – he is not discussing that here – but for the sake of their own well-being, their 'experience' of science:

> Only by strict specialization can the scientific worker become fully conscious, for once and perhaps never again in his lifetime, that he has achieved something that will endure. A really definitive and good accomplishment is today always a specialized accomplishment. And whoever lacks the capacity to put on blinkers, so to speak, and to come up with the idea that the fate of his soul depends upon whether or not he makes the correct conjecture at this passage of this manuscript may as well stay away from science. For nothing is worthy of man as man unless he can pursue it with passionate devotion. (FMW 135)

Weber, whose work initially gives the impression of a learned legal scholar, always had a marked tendency towards shop talk, which did not care about lay readers and even demonstratively scorned concessions to what was readily intelligible to all[27] – and this at a time when many scholars in the humanities were writing for a broad middle-class readership rather than merely specialists, and when the boundaries between sociology and literature were to some extent still fluid.[28] Weber was exceptional for his day in being an interdisciplinary generalist, and when he wanted he could speak in a popular, even demagogic manner. But, as a scientist, he embodied the new trend to specialist language more markedly than many colleagues in the humanities, and quite accurately depicted this as the main current in the science of the twentieth century. He no longer cherished an ambition to unite the two sides of his personality, and sometimes even thought it fundamentally wrong to mix research with attempts to make a public impact. The one prohibited value-judgements, while the other demanded them. By openly conceding that the specialist should wear 'blinkers', he implicitly recognized that science could never replace everyday experience: something that many 'experts' like to deny. Weber himself knew how to appreciate the many-sidedness of our experience of life. 'He felt that all of science and learning was totally incapable of providing fulfilment in life.'[29]

It would have occurred to Weber to look in the world of Puritanism for the origins not only of modern capitalism but also of modern science.[30] But he did not pursue that kind of historical relativization in the case of science, leaving its origins rather in the Renaissance. He looks back with some nostalgia to the new science of that era, which was inspired by art and music, did not spring from minds stunted by specialization, and was experienced as the 'path to nature'. Weber, for whom the history of music was one key to the Western rationalization process, held the original view that experimentation in the natural sciences migrated from 'the sixteenth-century experimenters in music with their experimental pianos'. And he continued:

> What did science mean to these men who stood at the threshold of modern times? To artistic experimenters of the type of Leonardo and the musical innovators, science meant the path to *true* art, and that meant for them the path to true *nature*. . . . And today? 'Science as the way to nature' would sound like blasphemy to youth. Today, youth proclaims the opposite: redemption from the intellectualism of science in order to return to one's own nature and therewith to nature in general. (FMW 141f.)

Belief in the unity of art and nature, including the nature in man, was in Weber's account the great productive force in the history of European art and the European mind; here were the ultimate roots of the modern scientific impulse, the passion that cannot be given up. And a strong passion that culminates in ecstatic states actually needs science – or anyway a science that blazes new trails; this Weber believed from experience and conviction. 'For nothing is worthy of man as man unless he can pursue it with passionate devotion' (FMW 135). It is in this sense that science has an educational power and a vital significance for those who pursue it. Twice he speaks of the 'intoxication' or 'frenzy' [*Rausch*] that comes over the scientist who finally discovers the solution to a puzzle (FMW 135, 136). No wonder that science turns people into addicts. Inspiration cannot be 'forced', however methodical one's training; it is related to charisma. It is precisely by putting on blinkers that one lays the basis for this 'intoxication', and anyone who is not prepared to do that should steer clear of science. When Weber wrote in a letter about Sabine Lepsius that she was 'not my type', because she did not have a 'nature capable of giving itself to a cause or another person',[31] he evoked an inner affinity between science and erotic abandon. In the *Zwischenbetrachtung* he ascribed the same autonomous force to science as to sexuality.[32]

The intoxication of science cannot be rationally explained in terms of the tiny things which are all the modern specialist usually discovers. It is not possible to derive the passion for modern science from any great objective, any higher meaning. Weber was silent when asked whether science gave a meaning to life,[33] and many of his admirers saw this silence as the weak point in his thinking. Weber's remarks yield a meaning only if the scientific urge is thought of as a natural instinct, which in former times, in antiquity and the Renaissance, was based on the higher meaning of a faith, but which has become so much second nature to the scientific worker that he follows it without an identifiable objective.

The Viennese experiment of a return to his profession

Weber delivered his 'Science as a Vocation' at a time when he was again thinking of making science his regular profession, for the first time in eighteen years. In October 1917 he had travelled to Vienna, where he was being considered for the vacant chair in political economy. He had the best memories of his time there in 1909 and of its association with a new sense of health. In April 1918 he moved to Vienna and took the summer semester as acting professor on a trial basis; in the summer of 1919 he took up an appointment in Munich.

Weber witnessed Germany's military collapse far from the scene of action, although the fragility of the Central Powers became evident in Vienna earlier than in Berlin. There on the Danube he remained dependent on soporifics and fell into a panic when they once ran out (WB 606f.). His life continued to have a substratum of anxiety: he never achieved the inner security of having finally overcome his illness. The sensitive man felt 'terribly worn out' by all the visits he had to make to colleagues and by the 'walking and standing in electric streetcars' to get there (WB 604).

Nevertheless, Weber experienced the time in Vienna as a nice 'adventure' – although Marianne always wanted it to remain temporary, since he 'definitely belonged in Germany' (WB 605). Personally he would not have minded staying there, if Else had not lured him to Munich. The fact that, even in the last months of the war, someone with money could eat better in Vienna than in Heidelberg was one element in his new sense of well-being. Besides, as Marianne put it: 'In comparison with the breathless haste of ugly industrious Berlin, life in this city seemed charmingly casual, like the gait of a beautiful woman who does not strain under the yoke of labour and finds the meaning of her existence in being beautiful.'[34] One senses how the imago of Vienna merged with Else in the Webers' imagination.

Weber got off to a good start with his lectures in Vienna, although as always he faced the problem of making his charisma persist at a day-to-day level. He seems to have gone down especially well with women.[35] 'It is as if all the best people in academia would like to snatch this star from the skies, so that everything spiritual and good should find its crystallization point in it', Marianne wrote triumphantly to Helene a month after the beginning of the semester.[36] The elation of being married to a genius grew even stronger within her, though soon accompanied with a fear of losing him. In his first Viennese lecture, based on his work on the sociology of religion, Weber took a constructively critical look at 'the materialist conception of history', in a situation in which – for the time being only secretly – socialism was advancing on all sides among intellectuals, especially among the Eastern Jews strongly represented in Vienna.

Educating imperial army officers about socialism

Of the testimony we have from Weber's time in Vienna, the best documented is a report on socialism lasting several hours that he gave on 13 June 1918 to approximately three hundred Austrian officers, in the framework of a training course organized by the 'Department to Counter Enemy Propaganda'. As far as we know, it was the only time Weber spoke to army officers – which held a special attraction for him – and also the only time he dealt at length in public with the subject of 'socialism' (he usually mentioned Marx only in passing), which for many Viennese intellectuals was *the* topic of the day.

In retrospect, as well as in comparison with others of his speeches at the time, one is struck by the degree of Viennese *Gemütlichkeit* with which he addressed the controversial question of socialism. In June 1918, he seems not to have foreseen that revolution and nationalization would in a few months be no longer simply academic but fiercely topical issues, which would place him too under high tension. In May he predicted that, unless 'very great acts of folly' were committed, 'the position of the German dynasties' would 'still be intact at the end of the war' (PW 162). There was no unstoppable trend towards a republic, nor did his sociology of rule lay the foundation for one.

Not inappropriately for an audience of army officers at that time, Weber took great pains in his lecture to avoid knee-jerk reactions and to preserve calm discriminating reflection in the face of the challenge of socialism. In his view, the socialists were chasing after illusions; there could be no question of an unstoppable evolution to socialism, and so its opponents had no reason either for gloomy fatalism or for desperate action to combat it. Drawing on his old anti-evolutionary arsenal, he repeatedly defined socialism as a form of evolutionism and, as such, out of date. On a previous occasion he had described socialists as 'grumpy old men' (*greisenhafte Nörgler*) (MWG I/4–1, 340).

Weber showed understanding for socialism within the framework of world history. The present degree of domination by the rationality of private business was historically unique (PW 283f.), and so radical reactions against it were scarcely surprising. But quite different conceptions and contradictory interests were gathered under the banner of socialism, and it would be fundamentally wrong to lump them all together (PW 275). The main body of workers was not looking for a revolution and would be quite happy with an improvement in living conditions; it was possible to talk and work with many trade unionists who represented this side of the labour movement, as people had learned during the war in Germany (PW 274f.). In similar vein, Weber had welcomed in November 1918 the Stinnes–Legien agreement that provided for joint action in the emergency by leaders of industry and the trade unions (MWG I/16, 396).

To be sure, socialism contained elements of 'solemn prophecy' (PW 288), of a religion of salvation, and so all experience suggested that it would never be possible to convince genuine socialists (PW 302). (This realistic view reflects his belief in an insuperable 'polytheism of values'.) Even if the socialists were victorious, socialism (or at least the one for which they had fought) would not come to pass; socialists would simply advance 'inescapable universal bureaucratization' (PW 279) – an evolutionist kind of argument against socialist evolutionism![37] Since officials were usually inferior to business people, a fusion of economy and state would not lead to state control of the economy but have the opposite effect (PW 286f.). All in all, there was no reason to feel pleased, but also no reason for panic. In the summer of 1918 Weber still underestimated the susceptibility to crisis of an economy governed by private interests, and he believed, quite in the style of Schmoller, that cartels were a reliable safeguard against catastrophic market slumps (PW 291f.). He seems not to have considered that, although this might be true of an ideal type, it did not necessarily hold for the real economy. Of course, he was not alone among economists in failing to foresee the scale of future crises.

Brest-Litovsk: a victorious peace in the east

Before his audience of Austrian officers Weber vigorously defended the Brest-Litovsk treaty of March 1918: the German peace dictated to Russia, which later provided Germany's enemies with moral legitimacy for the peace treaty they dictated at Versailles. 'The discussions in Brest-Litovsk were conducted in the most loyal fashion on the German side', he assured them – by which he probably meant loyal to Germany's Austrian ally – 'in the hope of achieving real peace with these people' (PW 299, translation modified). And a little further on: 'One cannot make peace with people who are fighting for their faith. One can only render them harmless, and that was the meaning of the ultimatum and the enforced peace at Brest' (PW 300).

When Wolfgang Mommsen gives the impression that Weber was a sharp and clear-sighted critic of the Brest dictate,[38] a distinction must be drawn between private and public utterances. In letters to Marianne and Mina, Weber did sound very pessimistic about the prospect that Brest-Litovsk would lead to a lasting peace between Germany and Russia. He had long had a high, even exaggerated idea of the excitable national feelings of the Russians, including liberals and revolutionaries, and from this angle it seemed that Russia would never get over the territorial losses inflicted on it at Brest-Litovsk. Yet, already before the peace negotiations, Weber sensed a 'universal Russian hatred of Germany';[39] he therefore saw no chance of reconciliation between the peoples and thought it logically consistent for the German Reich to weaken Russia as much as possible. In May 1917, after the fall of the tsarist regime, Weber saw no reason to hurry any peace negotiations in the east – on the contrary. 'For it is only as long as the war continues that we shall be in possession of the Romanian corn-growing land and can dispose of these crops as we choose' (RR 264). Weber the agrarian economist was displacing Weber the politician.

He could have concluded instead that the land hunger of the Russian peasantry – in his view, the motive force in Russia's troubles since time immemorial (MWG I/15, 96f.) – was now directed against the large estates and was no longer the driving force of Russian imperialism. Weber himself reaffirmed after the February revolution that the peasant question was decisive in Russia, and that the peasants in particular – who 'represent the overwhelming majority of the Russian people' – 'have a real interest in peace' (RR 248). So, was there not a chance of a lasting peace? But Weber, in the style of later 'stab-in-the-back' theorists, fumed against all the spasms that led German socialists to seek out fellow thinkers in Russia, when in reality these were speculating that:

> with an army of negroes, gurkhas and all the barbarian rabble in the world standing at our borders, half crazed with rage, lust for vengeance, and the craving to devastate our country, . . . the German Social Democracy will still be a party to the fraudulence of the present Russian Duma plutocracy and, morally speaking, stab the army which is protecting our country from savage nations in the back. (RR 255)

And again, in an article in the *Frankfurter Zeitung* in September 1917: 'The enemy armies are increasingly made up of barbarians. Today on the Western frontier there also stands a dross of African and Asiatic savages and all the world's rabble of thieves and lumpens' (MWG I/15, 318).

War with the USA – 'lunacy' and 'hysteria' in Berlin

When Weber wrote those lines, however, the world's 'barbarian rabble' were not the only ones mobilized against Germany; the United States had also declared war on the Reich. Weber's greatest fear over the previous year had thus become a reality. Nothing angered him more at the time than the incredible levity with which Germany had risked, indeed provoked, America's entry into the war through its unlimited submarine warfare. In the spring of 1916 he wrote to Marianne: 'It is as if we were governed by madmen'; or again, 'as if a horde of lunatics were governing us'.[40] Else was in agreement with him: anyone who keeps acting like that, 'as if America means *nothing*', is 'sinfully irresponsible'; 'these pan-Germans are crazy'.

She got worked up about them all day long. Weber's anger reached a peak when it turned out that the navy did not have enough submarines to cordon off Britain.[41] The 'intensified submarine warfare' could therefore not be waged intensely, contrary to what the propaganda machine had been broadcasting to the world. It was one more example of impotent bragging, which merely played into the hands of American warmongers.

Weber was quite in his element, as a man who knew the United States and the intellectual and material sources of strength of the Anglo-American world. Narrow-minded Prussians might find relief in the fact that America did not have a large standing army drilled for years on the parade-ground, but Weber knew they had other trumps that more than compensated for it: a severe work discipline, sporting ambitions, plentiful capital, cutting-edge technology and inexhaustible natural resources. In February 1916 he wrote to his sister Lili:

> The main issue is whether these accursed fanatics from the navy are going to land us in a war with America. They are completely miscalculating. Their first success would be that 25 per cent of *our* trading ships in American ports would be confiscated and add to the enemy merchant navy. Plus 40 billion in gold – part of it earned during the war! – and half a million sporting types who want to join in a war. May the heavens send us reason![42]

When Berlin announced that it was resuming 'intensified submarine warfare' (which had been interrupted under US pressure), Weber tried for the first and last time in his life to influence the central government with a direct memorandum. He was supported in this by the 35-year-old economist Felix Somary,[43] a banker with connections in high places, whom Weber knew from the Mitteleuropa committee and who all his life had cultivated the art of exercising influence on grand policy. According to Somary's memoirs, he immediately passed the memorandum on to the great shipowner Albert Ballin, who had direct access to Wilhelm II and indeed handed it to him the next day. The Kaiser shouted 'What impudence!' several times as he read it, but became more thoughtful at the end. Immediately afterwards, on 4 March 1916, the decision was taken to sack Tirpitz and shelve resumption of the intensified submarine warfare.[44] Weber himself, who sent the memorandum to the Foreign Office only on 10 March (MWG I/15, 103), does not seem to have known anything about these behind-the-scenes moves. For, if he had, we would have to wonder why he did not make similar attempts after this speedy success.

It is strange, however, that instead of rejoicing over the demise of Tirpitz – who, through his pursuit of naval rivalry, was mainly responsible for the hostility between Germany and Britain – Weber also flew into a rage, branded the capitulation to the Americans as 'hysterical economics'[45] and presented the fallen head of the navy as a tragic hero 'callously' forced to resign. 'On the same day the herculean man stood in front of the Foreign

Office on Wilhelmstrasse and yelled at Privy Councillor Kiliani, who had asked him a question, in a voice loud enough for everyone to hear: "Did I *request* my dismissal? I was ordered to go – *ordered*!! – (in a thunderous voice) ordered!!! to leave." That arouses an awful lot of ill will and is bound to have a depressing effect on our friends and to encourage our enemies' (WB 565f.). Instead of feeling disgusted with Tirpitz for making this scene – the accusation of hysteria surely applied here, if anywhere – Weber was once again furious with the Kaiser. Wilhelm II could do what he liked: he was always wrong in Weber's eyes, if not in substance then in method. 'Hysteria'– which Weber himself had long been suspected of – was his standard reproach in this story: against the Kaiser, against the submarine agitators, but also against those who buckled too soon under American pressure. After Tirpitz's dismissal, Weber wrote to Marianne from Berlin: 'Like a hysterical fit from this hero-emperor: "Find me some way of putting an end to it" created the crisis, then an anxiety attack over war with America . . . another turnaround.'[46]

Since his own illness Weber had felt competent in anything to do with the nerves. It became a favourite idea of his: the supposed hardliners who had been pushing for ruthless submarine warfare were in reality people with weak nerves who, unable to face the war any longer, surrendered to the illusion that some miraculous means could bring it to an end. 'It was not people with a powerful spirit and strong nerves who ran behind the U-boat demagogues, but hysterically weak spirits who could no longer endure the burden of war', he declared on 27 October 1916 at a public meeting of the Progressive People's Party in Munich (MWG I/15, 693). He probably had a point, although 'hunger' was a more relevant factor that 'hysteria'. 'The masses are called for submarine warfare because of hunger and cold', Somary wrote.[47] Weber knew that the 'rabble-rousers' would class him among the 'wets' for his strong objection to unlimited submarine warfare and the public annexation plans. In their eyes he was now 'an arch-wimp' – he wrote, probably exaggerating, in March 1916 to Marianne.[48] This made him stress all the more that the real wimps were those who played at being rabble-rousers. As always, he was very concerned not to appear weak, even when he was pleading for caution. In his memorandum he called it 'moral cowardice' to support intensified submarine warfare out of fear, while otherwise being regarded as a 'wet' (MWG I/15, 122). He was right to think that, even among German professors, prudence required greater courage than did warlike shrieking.

The 'primal solidarity' on the enemy side

But Weber also had a feel for the ideological element in politics. Already in 1915, in an internal report that was published only posthumously, he warned that Germany's invasion of Belgium made things all too easy for its enemies, as not only the French and British would be outraged, 'but all those spiritual forces everywhere in the world which are stirred simply by the spectacle of the lasting violation and subjugation of a nation with a (formally) top-class civilization.' 'The primal feeling of solidarity among the world's Latin or Anglo-Saxon population is more significant for the positions of Italy and America than we have allowed' (MWG I/15, 55f.).

The 'primal (*urwüchsige*) feeling'! At the time, many Germans felt it was rank hypocrisy that the Western powers should pull out the moral stops and call on the world to mobilize against the Reich under the banner of 'freedom against militarism'. Did not the British and French brutally exploit their colonies? Did not capital run the show in America? Were the Germans not ahead of the world with their constitutional order and social welfare state? Yet Weber knew that, despite all the cant, the emotive use of the language of freedom against Germany was not mere phrase-mongering but expressed something 'primal' – and that it was so dangerous for that very reason.

A few months after America's entry into the war, when Russia's military collapse was looming and German armies were advancing from the Baltic to Bukovina, there was another abrupt change of mood in Germany from dejection to euphoria; even Weber, generally not unaffected by manic-depressive cycles among the population,[49] seemed for a while to forget the grievous prospects that resulted from US involvement in the conflict. The army supreme command, he noted jubilantly in the autumn of 1917, had brilliantly demonstrated 'that a military defeat of Germany (was) completely ruled out and that ultimate success (was) just a matter of time' (MWG I/15, 316). With the fall of tsarism, the most refined system of 'people's emasculation' anywhere in the world (MWG I/16, 184), the German war had despite everything found its meaning: this was how he tried to console his audiences after the defeat, even though he had previously sometimes pointed out that the reforms of the Stolypin era had not been a mere farce (MWG I/15, 242n.) and that the Russian revolutionaries were even more anti-German than Russian conservatives.

The Russian defeat offered the German Reich a splendid opportunity to appear before the world as the champion of the right of small nations to self-determination. Today, after the collapse of the Soviet empire, it is even clearer than it was then (when exaggerated ideas about the pan-Slavist threat were circulating in Germany) how little the various nationalities living there had grown into a single nation. But the German government was already trying to act the champion of the smaller peoples, even if this was never credible because it was the army command that set the tone in the occupied areas. Probably in the end Germany would have profited most if, instead of installing puppet regimes in the areas under its control, it had given free rein to the right of national self-determination, including in Ukraine. Weber for one saw that an opportunity had been squandered in the east.[50] Admittedly the Western powers now lost their Russian allies, but they also shook off the ideological embarrassment due to their alliance with the tsarist regime. The West's slogan of 'freedom against militarism', geared especially to American public opinion, became more convincing than before.

Ambivalent attitude to democratization

When Weber, from spring 1917 on, came out strongly in public for parliamentary rule and equal and universal suffrage, he did not use solemn appeals to democracy, natural equality and civic involvement, since he knew that political control everywhere rested with elites. Democracy was for him 'never an end in itself' but only a means to an end (MWG I/15, 234). His favourite argument was that the parliamentary contest for power improves the selection of political leaders (MWG I/15, 396), and in italics: '*Only master nations have a calling to intervene in the radius of global development*' (MWG I/15, 394). He also liked to use that kind of strong language to lament the fact that the Germans had become a subject people as a result of their history. The last quotation continues: 'If nations without that quality attempt to achieve this, then not only will the instinct for security in other nations rebel against them, but they themselves will inwardly fail at the attempt.'

Logically this meant that it was a natural necessity that the Germans would lose the war, since in Weber's view they were not a 'master nation' but a 'plebeian people' (PW 121). Like Naumann, he liked to fight for left-liberal objectives with power gestures of the kind that the new right used to assert itself, although they were weapons that could easily backfire. It would appear, however, that America's entry into the war brought Weber a certain peace of mind. 'What was previously the fault of human stupidity has now become a destiny, and it is possible to cope with a destiny'[51] – by which he probably meant cope inwardly; it is not possible to overcome destiny. With the United States in the enemy camp, Germany's defeat became a destiny, a process dictated by nature, so that there was no longer any point in becoming incensed over who was responsible for it.

For Weber, the most effective weapon in the struggle for equal suffrage was the argument that it would be a national disgrace if returning warriors had fewer political rights than those who had stayed at home (PW 106ff.). His particular scorn was reserved for the idea, so beloved of 'all species of literati', that people with education – or, more specifically, 'social layers with a patented diploma' – should have some kind of 'voting privilege'. He who knew about such things might say it 'most forcefully': '*No other social layer in Germany* is on average as little qualified for politics as this one. As is well known, the lack of political proportion shown by university teachers, especially during the war, exceeds all precedent' (MWG I/15, 229f.). Back in 1908 his brother Alfred had sneeringly remarked to his colleague in Prague, the future Czechoslovak president Tomáš Masaryk: 'Politically, you can never exaggerate how stupid professors are.'[52] He would provide a fine example of this himself during the war.

The *Frankfurter Zeitung* became Max Weber's regular political mouthpiece;[53] his open criticisms of the Kaiser caused problems with the military censorship and alienated readers of this leading liberal paper (MWG II/15, 424ff.),[54] but at the same time he developed a journalistic talent that one would never have suspected from many of his scholarly essays. For the economist Johann Plenge – a man once much admired by Max Weber who, though otherwise rather an outsider, became an influential figure after the outbreak of war by contrasting 'the spirit of 1914 with the ideas of 1789' (Theodor Heuss)[55] – the *Frankfurter Zeitung* in those days was the number one adversary. In August 1917 he wrote a furious letter to Weber, in which he even revived the dispute over value-judgements:

> Labouring under the delusion that you represent the demands of the present day, your articles in the *F. Z.* have contributed to the disastrously confused tactical policies of short-sighted and ambitious professional politicians . . . You, the representative of value-free science, have unquestioningly fallen prey to an obsolete value of youth . . . It is just not acceptable to sweep values to one side and to get on with value-free science. Rather, a method must be constructed out of the deep common experience of values.[56]

In fact, Weber and Plenge were not so far from each other in their judgement of leading German parliamentarians; Weber too had a low opinion of such politicians as Erzberger and Stresemann, the great political climbers of the time. In his struggle for parliamentary rule in Germany, it must have been a dilemma for him that he did not hold its likely beneficiaries in high regard.

Germany's defeat in sight

On 6 October 1918, when the German government asked Wilson for an armistice, Naumann honestly confessed with a sigh to his friend Gertrud Bäumer that 'the pacifists and shallow internationalists had been right';[57] such a disavowal of his own past would never have occurred to Max Weber. Long considered a 'leftie' by the right, he was anxious to demonstrate as strongly as possible that he was not linked to any group, even if that meant he never had the support of a party behind him. His defiantly individualist nature always triumphed over any political calculation. In any event, the fact that he could not easily be pigeon-holed was good for the public impact of his writings on current politics, as it was thought all the more that his whole personality stood behind everything he said and wrote.

The great historian Marc Bloch, who witnessed as a soldier both the Allied victory of 1918 and the French defeat of 1940, maintained that not even a well-read historian could know what victory and defeat meant unless he or she had been through such experiences of elation and 'terrible' impotence.[58] In the course of 1918 the Germans lived through the one experience shortly after the other: less than half a year lay between the Brest-Litovsk peace treaty of 3 March, which made the Reich master of the whole of Eastern Europe, and 8 August, the 'black day' when the Western front collapsed and the crushing superiority of the Americans asserted itself with full force.[59] This manic-depressive cycle of ups and downs severely affected everyone who had believed the final victory to be within reach; the *idée fixe* could thus take hold that there was something 'fishy' about Germany's defeat, that the revolutionaries had stabbed the army in the back.

Many German nationalists felt the territorial losses as an amputation of part of their own body. As we have seen, even a historian such as Meinecke, normally of a cheerful disposition, lost all pleasure in history for a time.[60] But what of Max Weber, who with his dark look and furrowed brow had appeared to many as a prophet of doom? In *Stille und Sturm*, a *roman à clef* set in this period, Berta Lask has Professor Wormann (Max Weber) say even before the outbreak of the war: 'Life for me has no meaning if Germany does not blossom anew and rise to greatness.'[61] Now Germany had not only not arisen, but had plunged into hitherto unimaginable depths. Yet Weber, despite his earlier tendencies, did not at all give the impression of being a depressive – on the contrary, these final years were a time of supreme creative euphoria and witnessed the great love of his life. Just as the higher purpose created by the nation was vanishing, he gave free rein to his senses and found a new meaning in life in the physical and mental here and now. As the imagined collective body of the nation was, so to speak, being castrated at Versailles, he was overwhelmed by the experience of his own corporeality.

The great emotive issue: war guilt

During the war, each side raised the question of who bore the guilt for it and published documents that were supposed to demonstrate the other's responsibility; it was thus agreed that the war required legitimation and should not be seen as if it were an act of God. As the fighting dragged on and turned into mass slaughter, there was a growing belief that wars were essentially crimes. Even Weber sometimes spoke in this vein, especially to Marianne and Mina Tobler, and angrily looked for guilty parties not only in the enemy camp. In May 1917, one month after the declaration of war by the United States, he fumed to Mina: 'The whole world has had enough, and a stubborn band of people crouched over their desks are forcing everyone to go on. *That* is truly appalling.'[62] But it would never have occurred to him to speak like that in public: it would have seemed the worst defeatism, indeed treason. Besides, he always regarded the war as inevitable, owing to Germany's rise as a world power and its geographical position in the centre boxed in by other imperialist powers, and he used this as the basis for a clear account of German history.

Figure 18.3 Portrait of Max Weber, 1917–18

Such lessons from history, typical of German nationalist thinking, sounded rational in the historical memory of the time. In particular, both the Thirty Years' War and the Napoleonic wars seemed to have shown that, when Germany is not united and strong, it becomes a battlefield for foreign armies and their German collaborators. 'Politics is struggle', Weber taught; there was no hope of perpetual peace; those who did not struggle were in danger of becoming a football for those who did. War comes suddenly, like a 'natural phenomenon', is how a Russian interlocutor put it to him shortly before the outbreak of the First World War (MWG I/16, 183). It had become a natural necessity mainly because of Russian expansionism.

But, if war was a more or less natural phenomenon, in which it was pointless to ask who was guilty, then it would have been logical to accept Germany's defeat with a Stoic resignation to fate: moreover, not to feel surprised that the enemy used his victory just as he pleased, imposing his terms on the other side instead of negotiating a new peacetime order. Did not Weber teach, with characteristic brutality, that power manifests itself in the opportunity 'to carry out (one's) own will despite resistance' (E&S 53)? Did he have reason to feel indignant that the victorious powers did precisely that at Versailles in May 1919 – where he was one of the German advisers, again a pure bystander – and involved themselves in scant discussion with the German side? Did all these events not have a natural logic?

What is more, Weber's own *Protestant Ethic* implied that the United States would enter a war against Germany on Britain's side, and that the Germans – not steeled by asceticism as a 'master nation' – would lose to such a coalition. Around the end of the war, Weber must in part of his being have found that tranquillity, if not grim satisfaction, which gave him the vitality for the great love of his life, in a situation that plunged others into crippling depression. But he did then feel an elemental sense of belonging to his nation, and a need to side with it openly and energetically. Things being as they were, he must also have refused to accept the victors' doctrine that the Central Powers had been responsible for the war.

With his heartfelt loathing for the 'literati' at the head of the Munich soviet republic, Weber fumed at the 'nauseating exhibitionism' and 'masochism' (B 537) of such pacifists as Kurt Eisner,[63] who conceded the Allied thesis of German war guilt. When Eisner, as Bavarian prime minister, gained access to the records, one of his first and most provocative actions was to publish extracts from the reports of the Bavarian representative in Berlin during the crisis of July 1914, which revealed that the central government did bear a heavy responsibility for the escalation of events.[64] Eisner was undoubtedly honest in his attempts to uncover the truth about the origins of the war, and as a Kantian he was convinced that it was always best to speak the truth openly. Weber did not accuse him of falsifying the documents, nor did he brand him in far-right style as a traitor, but he did despise his type of political literati as both undignified and unrealistic in believing that an admission of German guilt would secure better terms from the victors (MWG I/16, 179ff.). In the Foreign Office's committee of experts that prepared for the peace negotiations, Weber reported on 29 March 1919 that requests had been made to him 'from American circles' 'to counter at last these admissions of guilt', probably so as not to give ammunition to those on the Allied side who were advocating stiff peace terms. And indeed early in 1919 two American government representatives did seek out Weber (MWG I/16, 261) – a sign that his name was becoming an asset for Germany on the international stage.

As experiences after the Second World War demonstrate, it may help to disarm former enemies morally, at least in the long term, if a country admits its own responsibility for a war. If Germany had not done this after 1945, the reconciliation with its Western neighbours would have been unthinkable. Eisner's political calculation was thus not altogether naive.[65] But German responsibility for the outbreak of war in 1914 was not as evident as it was in 1939. To the outside world, the main player had appeared to be Austria-Hungary rather than the German Reich, while Russia had exacerbated the situation by mobilizing its army. It was anyway convenient to shift the main blame on to those two powers, which no longer existed as such by the end of the war.

What did Max Weber know about the causes of the war by the time it was over? Certainly he could not have understood the extent to which Russia had egged Serbia on in July 1914 to reject the Vienna ultimatum, or what role London and Paris had played in all this. But a man of his per-spicacity could not possibly have believed that the German government was as free from blame as it had claimed to be during the war. It became the official version in Berlin that Vienna, relying on a German 'blank cheque', had delivered an unacceptable ultimatum to Serbia on its own authority, but it defies all logic that Austria-Hungary would have proceeded on such a key issue without German backing.[66] And it was always clear that the Reich thereby risked a declaration of war by Russia and, consequently, France; it was not necessary to wait half a century for the source analysis of Fritz Fischer and his school to recognize this. A man such as Max Weber, so sensitive to questions of national honour, must have thought it crystal-clear that Serbia would find it completely impossible to accept the Austrian ultimatum, that Russia would not stand idly by if Austria-Hungary invaded Serbia, and that France would not pass up the golden opportunity to recon-quer Alsace-Lorraine. All this would have been even more obvious to him than it was fifty years later to West German historians who had grown up in a climate of peace.

At the time, however, there would have been no issue less amenable to unbiased study, nor any more in need of it. Weber could not get it out of his mind for most of 1919. From time to time he roared that the moralis-tic question of 'guilt' was something for 'old women' or 'old maids' (MWG I/17, 231; I/16, 261), but in fact it posed itself here with particular force for an ethic of responsibility. It also put to the test what Weber's reflections on historical causality could show for themselves in a specific case, since no one doubted that the assassination in Sarajevo was scarcely an 'adequate cause' for a war that cost ten million lives. What could have been foreseen in July 1914 as the likely consequences of an Austrian inva-sion of Serbia?

In 1919, Weber was no more able than most of his contemporaries to consider these questions with the necessary detachment. He joined the 'Heidelberg Alliance', which, with the support of Hanseatic bankers, was supposed to counter scientifically the Allied thesis of German war guilt.[67] His signature was appended to the so-called professors' memorandum on the causes of the war, which was handed to the Allies in Versailles in May 1919. But its line of argument had been laid down in advance by the Foreign Office; Weber was one of those who had wanted to sharpen the tone in a way that appeared 'not objective enough' to the head of the German delegation, Brockdorff-Rantzau (MWG I/16, 309). Once again it was made clear how little of a born diplomat Weber was. The Foreign Office showed little interest in further collaboration with him (MWG I/16, 316); his experience during the brief period of proximity to high-level politics was in the end rather an embarrassment. And, on top of it all, the more that leaked out about Berlin's policy during the crisis of July 1914, the more uncomfortable he came to feel. 'There is something about *our* actions that makes me shudder', he confessed on 8 October 1919 to Hans Delbrück (MWG I/16, 31n.), who probably felt no better about them.

Powerless in Versailles, close to the stab-in-the-back legend

Max Weber thought that the German peace delegation was too yielding in Versailles, and not only on the question of war guilt. In a formal note of protest to the delegation, he argued with reference to other experts that an 'absolute precondition' of a peace treaty had to be not only 'the absence of *any* shackling of the economy and the restoration of *all* private property' – probably not least in respect of all German patents, one of the Allies' most valuable war prizes – but also 'the return of the crucial colonies'. Did he really believe in the economic value of the former German possessions in Africa? And did he seriously think that German soldiers would go on fighting for such aims? Also unacceptable, in Weber's eyes, was the demand at Versailles for an army of no more than 100,000 men, since in future Germany would need a 'real army' (MWG I/16, 565).

All his protests fell on deaf ears, however. For he knew no better than anyone else how the German negotiators at Versailles, placed behind barbed-wire fences, could defend themselves against the victors' categorical demands. A short time ago German armies had been deep inside enemy lands; now Weber could feel – and, of course, it came as no surprise to him as a political thinker – how humiliating it was in international politics to have no possibility of using force. Otto Hintze thought that Versailles was the crucial factor in Weber's decision to withdraw from politics and to devote himself again entirely to scholarship.[68] To Mina Tobler, Weber wrote that politics was his 'secret love': 'But also, when a rope lies around the neck and someone slowly, slowly twists it, for three years, tighter and tighter, then one cannot say and write what is, no matter how one feels.'[69] He probably also meant that then one could not openly analyse the German policies that ultimately led to Versailles.

In the immediate postwar period, Weber sometimes expressed a conviction that, if the whole future of their nation was at stake, German troops at the front would be ready and willing to resume the struggle; and that it was the revolutionaries back home who robbed the Reich of any backbone in the face of the enemy. On 3 January 1919, at a Social Democrat election rally in Heidelberg, the new justice minister of Baden, Ludwig Marum, spoke about 'the new Germany and its future'. Weber then spoke first in the discussion, in a way that gave rise to tumultuous scenes. In the interests of a coalition of the moderate centre, it would actually have been more astute to adopt a conciliatory attitude to Marum, but instead Weber declared that 'because of the disgraceful mishandling of the economy in Berlin' it was 'not possible to campaign together with Social Democracy'. The revolution was 'condemning Germany to impotence'. 'Troops are withdrawn battle-ready to Berlin, and after three days of life in the barracks they have become worthless troops thanks to the socialists' (MWG I/16, 431f.). 'The revolution has made us defenceless and handed us over to enemy rule', he had already maintained on 1 December 1918, at a founding meeting of the future German Democratic Party (DDP) (I/16, 384). As he put it to Mina,

'7,000 people showed up' and there was thunderous applause at the end of his speech, whereas the opposition expressed itself 'only timidly' (MWG I/16, 377).

Did Weber forget at such moments that for years he had thought Germany's fate to have been sealed by America's entry into the war? Admittedly he did not blame the revolutionaries for the defeat, but he probably did consider them guilty of turning the armistice into a more or less unconditional surrender. In this respect he stood quite close to the legend that there had been a stab in the back.[70] The assumption was not totally absurd – even from today's point of view.[71] And yet, if the fighting spirit of the troops was so easily shattered, could it have held up much longer anyway? What could have been expected from the front after those four terrible years?

From the beginning Marianne was more sceptical than her husband. On 20 October 1918, even before the mutiny in the German deep-sea fleet, she wrote to Helene: 'Of course we intellectuals feel it's better to fight to the last drop of blood than to bear the shame of unconditional surrender! But we must tell ourselves that it's simply not on for us to sit at our comfortable desks and expect further *pointless* sacrifices . . . from the masses.' Max too had by then learned to love life. Should he not have understood those soldiers who, with the war lost, no longer wished to lay down their lives? On 1 March 1919, at a Heidelberg University protest rally against France's claims to the Palatinate and Saarland, he said it was 'certain' that 'Germany could not wage war for the next two generations even if it wanted to' (MWG I/16, 241). As we know today, Germany would be capable of another great war in less than one generation. Weber's remark shows that he was not unaffected by the general war weariness – as his life at the time shows much more clearly than his writing on current politics.

Guerrilla thinking and fury at the revolution

At the universities that had displayed the greatest enthusiasm for war in 1914, people liked to console themselves after the defeat with memories of the period under Napoleonic rule, when German intellectuals had had their great moment and students were in the vanguard of the wars of liberation. Could they not assume this mission once again, especially where mainly German territories were being severed from the Reich? The students burst into 'thunderous applause' when Weber prophesied in his speech of 1 March 1919:

Against the political rape of German brothers in the east or west, the world would see a German irredentist movement whose revolutionary methods differed from those in Italy, Serbia and Ireland only by having behind it the will of seventy million and – I suspect and say it openly and expect it – of young people at university. (MWG I/16, 241)

At another student rally in Heidelberg he was even more plain-speaking:

> You know what it means to stand up to an invading enemy who can
> no longer be resisted with an army. . . . It means to place all your faith
> in the future, to abandon all hope for yourself. The only things granted
> to the living are incarceration and a drumhead court martial. When
> the time comes, when you are determined not to give fine speeches but
> to quietly ensure that a bullet meets the first Polish official who dares
> to set foot in Danzig – then I shall be with you, then come to me! (WzG
> 140)[72]

The final words were spoken 'with a movement of his outstretched arm, as
if he wanted to pull his comrades to him'. Weber as guerrilla leader: the idea
sounds absurd. Yet at that time he justified terrorism as a weapon of the
defenceless, at least when it was a question of a people's self-determination
against foreign rule (MWG I/16, 110). In *Economy and Society* he made it
clear that 'the monopoly of legitimate violence by the political-territorial
association' (E&S 904) – his 'monopoly of violence' became famous as the
hallmark of the modern state – was by no means a matter of course but only
a phenomenon of modern times; besides, he had a weakness for duelling, in
breach of that monopoly. Weber's logic was not without its dangers, for the
assassination in Sarajevo could also have been justified in that way.

To his disappointment, the students this time responded with 'icy silence'
(WzG 140): probably their will to live asserted itself in the face of demands
for death-defying heroism, whereas Weber was more familiar with the
longing for death. His demand made sense only on the assumption that
individuals were not just individuals but integral parts of a national body
and were fully aware of life only as such parts. Weber, who as a scholar had
repeatedly castigated organological images of the people or nation, was not
so far from them in his emotions.

In view of the student nationalism of the subsequent period, we might
think that Weber's strong language in 1919 was beating on an open door.
He did not feel this at the time, but appeared to be promoting courage and
a clear head in a situation of general paralysis and despair. In November
1918 he complained that 'people all wanted to be told pacifist lies'.[73] The
chauvinists were silent during that period immediately after the defeat.
Such a perspicacious and independent-minded witness as Ricarda Huch
complained to Marie Baum in November 1919 of the Germans' lack of a
'sense of national honour'. That was the only explanation of why they put
up with Versailles. 'If everyone were filled with a common indignation and
avenging wrath, how much easier it would be to endure everything.'[74] Like
Weber, she had a feeling that the Germans coped best with their fate
through national fury and revolt, and she too had hopes in the anger of
young men in the occupied territories.

In another speech at Heidelberg, on 17 January 1919, Max Weber predicted: 'If, as it is to be feared, the peace breaks down – and this would be

due to the untimely outbreak of revolution – then a few years after the war a chauvinism would emerge in Germany such as there has never been before.' And it would have every right. For, if 'foreign rule' comes, 'we shall see a huge awakening of national feeling, unless we have only a dog's sense of honour within us' (MWG I/16, 463). A 'Germany, awaken!' rhetoric from the mouth of Max Weber in January 1919, when Adolf Hitler had not yet found his language.[75] Weber felt the national rage in his own breast and was convinced that he was anticipating a collective German mood; the future would prove him right.

Although Weber often hated the Kaiser and his henchmen from the bottom of his heart, and should therefore have been able to understand the hatred felt by the revolutionaries, he now heaped one insult after another on the revolution, as if it were nothing but a repulsive 'carnival' (MWG I/16, 441) put on by muddle-headed literati, at a time when it was a matter of life and death for Germans to hold together against the external enemy. In public he fumed over the 'parasites feeding at the manger of the revolution'[76] and the 'huge costs of the current administration, with its horde of blabbering drones' (MWG I/16, 105, 380), in a situation where the governing Social Democrats could much rather have been accused of leaving the old bureaucracy virtually intact and displaying too little of a power instinct. But could someone like Weber really have been surprised that a revolution was being made by careerists as well as idealists, or that the revolutionaries in power did not from the first moment run the administration in a professional manner? And was not Eisner more reminiscent of the ancient Israelite prophets than of the literati?[77] Moreover, one of the members of the Eisner government was Edgar Jaffé, undoubtedly a courageous, competent and selfless man in this role, who alone 'warmly' supported the proposal to offer Weber an appointment in Munich.[78] It may be, however, that this very fact raised Weber's excitement level: namely, that such a nondescript man, repeatedly deceived by his wife and cast in the distressing role of King Mark in a Tristan drama, should seem to end up playing the hero, whereas Weber, then passionately in love with Else Jaffé, should fail to make a breakthrough into politics.[79]

'In addition to breaking up our economy, the revolution also has it on its conscience that it has broken up our army', Weber thundered on 4 January 1919 in an election speech at Karlsruhe for the Democratic Party, although the party needed an alliance with the Social Democrats to enter government, and although in reality the structures of the German economy remained unchanged. He continued: 'We have this revolution to thank for the fact that we cannot send a single division against the Poles. All we see is dirt, muck, dung and horse-play – nothing else. Liebknecht belongs in the madhouse and Rosa Luxemburg in the zoological gardens' (MWG I/16, 441) – such fuming, eleven days before she was murdered; and the newspapers were delighted to hawk it around. Of course, he could not have predicted how soon these revolutionary leaders would themselves become victims, and it goes without saying that he publicly condemned their murders.[80] But, for today's admirers of Weber, his crude outburst against Rosa Luxemburg was his most embarrassing public appearance after the end of the war. As we see, he made a contribution of his own to the brutalization of political demagogy. His horror of Rosa Luxemburg actually went back to the days before the war. He once made a fuss when he noticed an intellectual fascination for her in Robert Michels: 'She is a phonograph. Show me one idea of hers that is her own' (MWG II/5, 618). Why was he incapable of seeing in her the charismatic revolutionary, later widely revered as such, particularly after her murder? But the charisma of charismatics is not apparent to all their contemporaries: they seem to many like mad people. The same was true of the prophets of ancient Israel.

Was it essentially the propertied *Bildungsbürger* who broke through in Weber's hatred of the revolution, suppressing memories of how often he had loathed aspects of the old system? To a considerable extent the answer is probably 'yes'. But his firm belief that a socialist planned economy would lead to suffocating bureaucratization and wasted resources, or that it was impossible for the German economy to prosper without the initiative of private entrepreneurs – a view by no means universally shared by economists in his day – rested on rational foundations and seems justified from today's point of view. Nor, in many cases, was he wrong to detect not only rational consideration and honest conviction but also a craving for power and sensation, even a cynical play-acting, in intellectuals who flirted with the revolution. Felix Somary reports one clash in Vienna between Weber and Joseph Schumpeter, who otherwise held each other in high regard, at the Café Landmann opposite the university:

> The conversation turned to the Russian revolution, and Schumpeter expressed his satisfaction that socialism was no longer a paper discussion but had to demonstrate its viability. Weber grew rather excited and declared that communism at Russia's stage of development was quite simply a crime . . .; the road would pass through untold human suffering and end in a terrible catastrophe. 'That may be so', Schumpeter said, 'but it will be a nice little experiment for us.' 'A laboratory with heaps of human corpses', Weber specified. 'All anatomy is like that', Schumpeter came back. . . . Weber flared up and spoke more loudly, Schumpeter more softly and sarcastically, while all around them the coffee-house customers interrupted their card game and listened to them with curiosity, until Weber jumped up and hurried out to the Ringstrasse with the words: 'That's more than anyone can take . . .'[81]

The scene later enchanted Jaspers and proved to him that there was a sensitive conscience behind Weber's 'value-freedom'.[82] In fact, Weber had once had Schumpeter's help in his battle against value-judgements, but now he flinched when Schumpeter callously spoke of bloody reality as a laboratory for value-free science. Although Schumpeter believed in socialism as little as Weber, he became in March 1919 the finance minister of the new

Austrian government headed by the Social Democrats; he took up residence in a sumptuous Viennese baroque palace, but soon his affected style of a soldier of fortune lost him both political credibility and his ministerial position.[83] Not unjustifiably Weber felt outraged at the lack of political seriousness of Schumpeter, who subsequently fell into states of depression.

In 1920 Marianne Weber wrote in *Die Frau* that 'the original nature of man blows apart communist ways of living as soon as they are no longer required for the preservation of life.'[84] Max Weber also believed, on the basis of his historical knowledge as well as personal experience, that man was individualistic by nature and that his egoism permanently undermined all collective efforts. In the logic of Weber's thought, communism was a doomed attempt to transfer egalitarian forms of coexistence, which are possible only in intimate and 'primal' communities, to large anonymous associations.

The case of Eisner's assassin: 'they should have shot him'

On 21 February 1919 the 22-year-old Bavarian officer Count Arco-Valley gunned down Kurt Eisner, on the very day he had been intending to resign as prime minister. The assassin was condemned to death on 16 January 1920, but the next day this was commuted to life imprisonment and in 1927 he was pardoned. Weber, who spoke of the verdict at the beginning of his lecture at the Munich Audimax on 19 January, made no secret of his respect for the count: 'His deed sprang from a conviction that Eisner had inflicted one disgrace after another on Germany. This is my view too' (MWG I/16, 270). And for someone who held that conviction, and whose scruples about killing had disappeared at the front, such a deed was perfectly logical. Weber also recognized that Arco's conduct 'before the court had been chivalrous and in every respect gentlemanly'. 'Nevertheless! However courageously Arco behaved, they should have shot him' (MWG I/16, 270): not because it was the only punishment available under the existing legal system – Weber did not even mention this point – but because otherwise Eisner rather than Arco would be remembered as a martyr, while Arco (who had been willing to die) would be reduced to a 'coffee-house curiosity' (MWG I/16, 270).

So, Weber demanded Arco's execution for his own sake and the sake of his cause. Yet those students who honoured Arco as a hero were impervious to his reasoning, and when he entered the lecture hall the next day 'it was completely impossible for him to make himself heard above the deafening chorus of whistles'. So shaky was his popularity among a section of students at the time. Having a greater feel for martyrdom than the protesting students, however, he felt visibly comfortable in the unfamiliar role and confident that he was the only man of honour in the situation. The often so gloomy-looking Weber put on an act and tried to laugh it off. 'He crossed his arms and looked with mocking humour at the unruly mass', one eye-witness reported, 'but it did not escape us that, in this grotesque situation, the laughing mask that he wore for nearly an hour inevitably created a somewhat strained impression' (WzG 23f.). For the rest of the semester it was necessary to show an identity card to attend Weber's lectures; the tumult had been organized not by his regular students but by members of the duelling society, 'the great majority of them from the veterinary faculty' (B 556n.).

But it did not go down well with duelling society members in his regular class when he said that anyone who really grieved the fate of the nation should show it by casting aside the multi-coloured caps and breast-bands of their society. There was a general scraping of feet in the auditorium, and – according to Ernst Niekisch – 'some students went so far as to throw their notebooks at Weber, who was standing at the lectern.' He silently assembled his notes and walked out of the room. Nor did things end with this one disturbance.[85] Weber was not able to maintain the fascination he had aroused with his first major speeches; he must have felt that his charisma was fading into everyday routine. He tried to keep his defiant independence amid the right–left polarization of the academic world, but he ran the risk of falling between all the stools.

The way in which Weber exposed himself over the Count Arco affair aroused the disapproval of some of his colleagues, and he was summoned to appear before the university senate. Once again there was a memorable scene. Before Weber entered the room, Karl Alexander von Müller remarked to the art historian Heinrich Wölfflin (who was seated next to him): 'Now, my dear colleague, the most nervous person on earth will come dashing in.' But, in fact, Weber was the embodiment of a superior calm. One of the things he said was: 'I hope you don't think you can impress me in the slightest with this performance. I like it best when chair legs start to fly' (B 625n.). What a triumph! The man who for two decades had been thought a bundle of nerves now successfully played the part of one who kept calm amid the turmoil and left others to work themselves up. And in this situation he also had reason to feel proud of representing a higher right – and honour too.

The scene was a model of how a nervous individual could shoot back the ball of 'nervousness' (a combative concept in Germany at that time).[86] Karl Alexander von Müller – who, then aligned with the extreme right, was discovering the rhetorical gifts of Lance-Corporal Adolf Hitler (who after 1933 would appoint him editor of the *Historische Zeitschrift*) – had himself once been through a psychosomatic life-crisis and often suffered on account of his 'softness' and weak will; when he served in a sanatorium during the war, he could not bear the sight of the wounded and took refuge in the office. Yet he compensated for these weaknesses with a wooden militancy.[87] He was the epitome of those 'war literati' whom Weber hated so much; and in his mouth the reproach of 'nervousness' – here as in many other cases – contained an element of projection (as it did for Weber, of course!).

Preliminary discussions on the Weimar constitution: counterweights to 'parliamentary corruption'

In December 1918 Weber was drawn into the discussions to prepare a new constitution, in the framework of the committee set up by the Reich Office for Internal Affairs (MWG I/16, 49ff.). He and Hugo Preuss had a high opinion of each other; the social democrat Max Quarck, who had often crossed Weber's path and sometimes been closer to him, also took part in these meetings. Weber was most strongly attached to the election of the Reich president by popular vote and to the right of parliament to order enquiries: both objectives linked up with core ideas in his political thought. The first was then in vogue, so much so that the *Königsberger Hartungsche Zeitung* wrote that Weber was knocking at an open door (MWG I/16, 218); it corresponded to a widespread belief that, with the Kaiser now gone, the Reich needed a head of state who represented the whole people. The underlying philosophy was that the nation was more than the sum of its parts, and that there was a popular will which should be directly expressed through the election of a president, since political parties and the individual German states represented in the Bundesrat reflected only particular interests.

Weber himself was no stranger to these ideas. 'Parliamentarianism with its party squabbles is avoidable if the unitary executive for the Reich is in the hands of a president elected by the whole people', Weber was quoted in the press as having said in Wiesbaden on 5 December 1918 (MWG I/16, 393). For a while he was undecided: 'Because of our long period of internal impotence, the outstanding political leaders who can have an impact on the masses . . . are lacking for the popular election of the president' (MWG I/16, 128f.). In his view, then, such a system would be meaningful only with a charismatic leadership. And was not the new president of the Reich, Friedrich Ebert, the epitome of that stolid 'innkeeper' type in the SPD leadership which Weber had once mocked so bitterly? In the confusion following the end of the war, however, he learned to value this thoughtful politician of integrity: 'a quite splendid man', he wrote in late 1918, who must be strengthened against his revolutionary opponents.[88]

An article of Weber's, 'Der Reichspräsident', which appeared in the *Berliner Börsenzeitung* on 25 February 1919, began with a categorical demand in italics: '*In future the president of the Reich absolutely must be elected directly by the people.*' And again: 'It is *essential* for us to create a *head of state* resting *unquestionably on the will of the whole people*' (PW 304). Was there such a thing for Weber: a 'whole people' that had a single 'will'? He starts by arguing that only a president directly elected by the people will have the authority 'to initiate the process of socialization'. But then comes the genuinely Weberian idea that only such an election 'will provide an opportunity and occasion to select leaders' (MWG I/16, 221). In 'Politics as a Vocation' he said: 'Only the president of the Reich could become the safety-valve of the demand for leadership if he were elected in a plebiscitarian way and not by parliament' (FMW 114). The natural demand for leadership as the basis of the constitution!

Believing as he did that the main task of politics was to select leaders, Weber considered proportional representation to be a disaster – since it handed power to party apparatuses and their lists of candidates (a system of which he himself had been a victim) (MWG I/16, 449; PW 306). He sullenly noted that 'the old professional politicians have succeeded everywhere, in defiance of the mood of the mass of voters, in excluding the men who enjoy the trust of the masses in favour of political "shopminders"' (PW 306). In the situation of the time, however, a struggle against proportional representation had no chance of success, and Weber did not pursue the matter for long. It later became a widespread feeling in Germany that the Weimar Republic did not allow strong political figures to rise to the top, and in this sense Weber may be said to have identified right from the beginning a particularly sore point in the new order. But, of course, voting systems are not everything; charismatic leaders need supporters to help with the development of charisma. And for Weber charisma was ultimately a natural gift and favour; it could not be generated simply by an electoral law.

Weber attached huge importance to an English-style parliamentary right of enquiry, and in Mommsen's view he 'probably contributed' to the 'exaggerated hopes' that were then being placed in this.[89] From his own experience as a young man he knew the importance of insider knowledge in politics, and so he considered it crucial to give the people's representatives a powerful weapon against the secrecy of the ministerial bureaucracy. Adapting Bacon's 'Knowledge is power', he even wrote that 'secret information' was 'officialdom's most important instrument of power' (PW 179); this was the decisive issue for him, not – as one might think today – a belief that investigations help to ensure the 'scientific' character of politics. The parliamentary committees of enquiry became an institution in which academics advised parliamentarians and strengthened their hand against the bureaucracy.

Already in 1917 Weber had underlined the importance of including a parliamentary right of enquiry in a future constitution; he even wrote a draft along these lines, in a burst of 'breathless labour' (MWG I/15, 263). This initiative was subsequently written into the Weimar constitution. Weber successfully insisted that parliamentary minorities should also enjoy this right – a key issue here being whether 'parliamentary corruption could thereby be tackled or not' (MWG I/16, 81) – and that deputies should have no right to refuse to appear before an investigative committee. All this testifies to Weber's characteristic optimism that the truth, or sufficient truth to provide political orientation, can be ascertained through dogged persistence and the blocking of all escape routes. Despite his polemics against value-judgements in science, Weber's ideal remained a close association of knowledge and action, so that in his sociology he energetically insisted that society should be conceived not as system but as an opportunity for action.

Weber as election speaker

Weber must have thought the enquiry all the more important as a forum for science in politics because his own direct leap into politics had failed. Thus, after the end of the war he made every move to give himself the image of a public speaker: he recognized by now, not without pride, that he had the stuff of a demagogue. Recent research has revealed the fervour with which he threw himself in January 1919 into the election campaign of the left-liberal German Democratic Party (DDP), for a time the strongest of the bourgeois parties, in which he once again campaigned side by side with Naumann. He gave one speech after another in packed halls, receiving thunderous applause as he dealt mighty blows without any regard for 'value-freedom'.

For a while he undoubtedly enjoyed such occasions and felt in his element there, at least in one part of his being. Marianne was thrilled that her husband spoke 'in a National Assembly tone and with the right kind of vivid gestures': 'I'm awfully glad he can speak and hold people in the palm of his hand!'[90] The effect of his speeches had a lot to do with his being a lateral thinker who never fitted people's preconceptions; he had an unusual capacity to work himself up into a rage against both the right and the left. He even seems to have been proud of this talent to fight on several fronts: he found it satisfying that he could not be easily pigeon-holed. That might have been a strength if he had become a political leader, but he knew very well that in the modern world one needs a party to rise high in politics. He must therefore have felt more and more that any zeal he aroused was only short-lived. On 2 February 1919 he wrote to Else that he was 'fed up with so much speaking and campaigning' (MWG I/16, 18). It is indeed questionable whether his rhetorical successes were ever likely to mobilize a potential for action. The left liberals were then in an alliance with the MSPD, the Majority Social-Democratic Party of Germany (from which the USPD, the Independent Social-Democratic Party, had split in 1917). But Weber still tried in many situations to make it impossible for social democrats of any hue to accept him as an ally.

In April 1920 he got a chance to serve as DDP representative on the first Socialization Commission (MWG I/16, 37),[91] and even Kautsky, the SPD's leading theoretician, urged him to take it. But what was he to do there? It was evident to him – and he repeated it at every opportunity – that only entrepreneurs, not bureaucrats or trade union leaders, were capable of standing at the helm of industry and making it creditworthy again; state ownership and control would cripple industry and deliver it to the clutches of the victorious powers (MWG I/16, 450ff.). After his refusal to sit on the commission, he resigned from the DDP on the grounds that he was unwilling to pay lip service to the goal of socialization: 'Politicians *have to* compromise – a scholar cannot justify this.' And by January 1920, as he wrote to Mina, he had clearly made up his mind to be only a scholar: the 'contemplative existence' was 'once again' his 'form of life'.[92] The accuracy of this admission can be seen in the context of his whole life. Whereas, after his first successes as a public speaker, he had counted on being given a place near the top of the DDP slate for the Hesse-Nassau constituency, he now found himself pushed so far down the list that he no longer had any prospect of being elected. Yet with a shrug of the shoulders he went on giving election speeches for the party. Marianne, on the other hand, served as a DDP delegate to the Baden 'National Assembly', which discussed the drafting of a new constitution for Baden, and on 1 October 1919 was 'ordered' by Gertrud Bäumer to become her successor as chair of the BDF, the League of German Women's Associations – after which Bäumer, 'as deputy chairperson and *eminence grise*, continued to determine its course' (Angelika Schaser).[93]

Politics as a natural vocation

On 28 January 1919 Weber gave a lecture in Munich on 'Politics as a Vocation', which left a powerful but rather unclear impression on his audience (MWG I/17, 123),[94] although the printed version has since become one of Weber's most oft-quoted texts. It is a concentration of Weberian strong language and flashes of inspiration from wide areas of his work, including the essays on Oriental religions. Like 'Science as a Vocation', the lecture was given at the invitation of the Free Student Youth – but, although they are often regarded as a pair, it has recently become clear again that two years lie between them, including the end of the war. The lecture on science came more from the heart than the one on politics, which dates from a time when Weber, though still giving campaign speeches for the DDP, had buried his hopes of a parliamentary career. 'Politics as a vocation' was no longer for him.

When the student organization approached him, his first reaction was to quote himself: 'No one has less of a vocation than I to speak about the vocation of a politician.' Only the threat to invite in his place the hated Kurt Eisner, then head of the Bavarian government, elicited his prompt agreement (WzG 21). This time, however, his heart was only half in it – his mind kept wandering to Else, and when he repeatedly spoke of 'passion' he was not thinking only of politics. On his sheet of notes – one of the few to have survived – he had jotted down that politics requires 'real *passion* – not sterile excitement', and 'a *mature* man's love different from a young man's (imbued with *knowledge*)' (MWG I/17, 153ff.). When he said that a moralist by conviction is often dishonest, because he tends to construct a moral justification for everything, he illustrated the point with a revealing analogy from private life: 'You will rarely find a man whose love has turned from one woman to another who does not feel the need to legitimate this fact to himself by saying, "She did not deserve my love"' (PW 355). This natural need for legitimation – perhaps involving reference to a higher meaning – Weber felt as strongly as anyone else in his love affairs, but, as far as we know, he was fair enough never to run down Marianne.

'Politics as a Vocation' [*Politik als Beruf*]: it is a misleading title, since Weber did not have a high opinion of professional politicians [*Berufspolitiker*], who made a living out of politics and therefore, once in a lucrative position, stayed put in their chair. Quoting Bismarck with the arrogance of someone who has some capital behind him, he more than once called this type a 'miserable clinger to office' (e.g., PW 161). But in fact his lecture deals more with the conviction politician, who, at least ideally, is a man of independent means; he belongs rather in the world of the old political notables, which Weber vividly experienced way back in his father's drawing-room and drew on for his characteristic type, but which he himself knew to be a thing of the past. In his rage against imperial dilettantism, Weber had stressed that the type of politician was much more important than the constitution: 'The form of state is all the same to me, so long as the country is governed by politicians, not by amateurish nitwits like Wilhelm II and his ilk' (WzG 138). But the need for consistent professionalism is not the main message of the lecture: its whole thrust, in fact, is that what counts in a politician are qualities of character rather than formal qualifications. The key is not so much acquired competence as natural talent.

One of Weber's most famous political maxims is that 'three qualities' above all make a politician: 'passion, a sense of responsibility, judgement' (PW 352). This triad, with its inbuilt tension, is the leitmotif of the central part of the lecture. *Augenmaß* ('judgement' or 'sense of proportion'): a Bismarckian term and an exquisite German word for 'realism'; as Weber puts it, 'the ability to maintain one's inner composure and calm while being receptive to realities' (PW 352). During the war Weber repeatedly accused pan-German propagandists with megalomaniac war aims of a lack of *Augenmaß*, but he also wrote, in the *Zwischenbetrachtung*, that erotic love is accompanied by 'illusionist shifts of a just sense of proportion' (FMW 355): the love object appears as the highest, indeed the only value, beside which all other values pale. The opposite of *Augenmaß* is 'lack of distance', which 'in and of itself' is 'one of the deadly sins for any politician'. And yet passion too is one of his necessary qualities of character. This precisely is the problem: 'how are hot passion and cool judgement to be forced together in a single soul?' (PW 353). Weber is here describing his own problem: as scholar, as political thinker and as lover. It is doubtful whether it is a typical politician's problem, but Weber's main aim in this section is to outline his ideal type of the politician.

Weber's lecture culminates in his often-quoted opposition between ethic of conviction (*Gesinnungsethik*) and ethic of responsibility (*Verantwortungsethik*) (PW 364ff.). Their respective adherents justify themselves in different ways: the former by the purity of their motives and ideals, the latter by the likely consequences of what they do. In fact, the two do not necessarily exclude each other – they form a false alternative if posed in that way. In the ideal case they will both be present in a statesman – although Weber's ideal types do not here correspond to the ideal case. Occasionally, it is true, he too says that ethic of conviction and ethic of responsibility are 'not absolute opposites'; rather, 'they are complementary to one another and only in combination do they produce the true human being who is *capable* of having a "vocation for politics" ' (PW 368). Again he was speaking from his own experience: he carried both ethics inside himself and was able to summon up either.

The whole tenor of his lecture is quite different, however. He emphasizes that the 'two fundamentally different, irreconcilably opposed maxims' are separated from each other by an abyss (PW 359). Although there is no logical contradiction between them, Weber associates the two ethics with quite different and opposite human types, in whom totally different passions are at work. That was indeed how things looked in Germany after the end of the war: there was no possible bridge of understanding between the passionate pacifists and those whom the defeat had filled with a dark spirit of vengeance; and when Weber spoke of the ethic of conviction he was thinking first and foremost of the pacifists.

But did this conceptualization fit? Did the world war not show that, given the nature of modern weapons technology, it was precisely the pacifists who embodied an ethic of responsibility, whereas the 'national idealism' of the war party had ultimately turned the youth of Germany into cannon-fodder? When Weber returned to the *Bhagavad Gita* to demonstrate 'how war is fitted into the totality of the orders of life' (PW 363), this affirmation of warrior values smacked more of an ethic of conviction and, in the context of 1919, did not necessarily point to a 'sense of proportion' or presence of mind. Sober realism, mindful of the actual consequences, was far more on the side of the pacifists than of their opponents.

Yet Weber's chief aim was to reduce the ethic of conviction *ad absurdum*. Once, in connection with Tolstoy, he had attributed spiritual grandeur to it; now he said nothing of Tolstoy as he explained that, for all its high-sounding words, the ethic of conviction was mostly hollow. 'It is my impression', he wrote, 'that, in nine cases out of ten, I am dealing with windbags, people who are intoxicated with romantic sensations but who do not truly feel what they are taking upon themselves' (PW 367). This is a new tone. He had not conceived of the ethic of conviction as *a priori* opposite to the ethic of responsibility, and had for a long time dealt (respectfully) only with it; the 'ethic of responsibility' was a newly minted concept. Weber made an essential contribution to the twentieth-century career of the concept of responsibility, up to and including the 'responsibility principle' of the ecological philosopher Hans Jonas;[95] it was later thought that it should actually be credited to him.[96] In the ecological era, 'responsibility' acquired a new resonance: it no longer had the echoes of artillery fire behind it, as it did in 1919. Erhard Eppler, leader of the green wing of German social democracy, who feels himself to be a 'responsibility moralist' through and through, was mortally offended when Helmut Schmidt, then federal chancellor, dismissed him as a 'conviction moralist'.[97]

It is important to bear in mind that during and after the First World War – for the first time in world history – a professor was the most powerful man in the world: Woodrow Wilson, president of the United States. At least on the surface, he was the epitome of the *ethically* driven type of politician, and it seems that it was not least the intellectual struggle with Wilson that was preoccupying Weber. He had shown that it was possible after all for a professor to become president in a democracy. After Versailles a large number of Germans saw him as a hypocrite, who proclaimed the right of national self-determination yet refused it to the Germans and practised it only to their disadvantage. Few seem to have realized that Wilson prevented the imposition of even harsher terms, which would have kept Germany bankrupt for the foreseeable future.[98] Weber had a prejudice against professorial presidents: 'Oh, yes, when professors start doing politics!' he said to Mina early in 1917. 'The unfortunate man used to be professor in international law and has remained a theoretician and a fanatic.'[99] But a hypocrite was not how he thought of Wilson; he took him seriously as a conviction politician, not out of place in *The Protestant Ethic*.

The full-blooded politician is not, in Max Weber's eyes, a pure pragmatist. To be sure, power is his main concern, but 'the *nature* of the cause the politician seeks to serve by striving for and using power is a question of faith.' Whichever one he subscribes to, 'some kind of belief must always be present; otherwise . . . even political achievements which, outwardly, are supremely successful will be cursed with the nullity of all mortal undertakings' (PW 355). 'Nullity': this was a reflection of the old Puritanical condemnation of 'all mortal undertakings'. It was not only in the charismatic that Weber recognized a fluid transition between religion and politics; religion for him, unlike for many modern philosophers of religion, was not the same as ethics. The finale of his lecture is a bizarre hybrid of the everyday and the visionary:

> Politics means slow, strong drilling through hard boards, with a combination of passion and a sense of judgement. It is of course entirely correct . . . that what is possible would never have been achieved if, in this world, people had not repeatedly reached for the impossible. But the person who can do this must be a leader; not only that, he must, in a very simple sense of the word, be a hero. (PW 369)

Whereas Sombart, for example, had long since haughtily turned away from politics, Weber's lecture was in a sense an exercise in timely political pedagogy, in which he used all his powerful eloquence to oppose the traditional German notion that politics is 'a dirty business'. True, politics in his eyes was not at all a moral matter; but nor was it either base or trivial. Yet he did indirectly help to confirm the German idea of 'political song, a nasty song',[100] by drawing such a demanding picture of the genuine politician that most real-life politicians appeared mean and petty by comparison. As with his ideal type of charismatic leader, he sketched an 'imaginary image of the politician' (Stefan Breuer),[101] a man who rose high above the triviality of everyday politics and conveyed no sense that, in most situations, it is preferable for a politician to be an everyday sort of person. Theodor Heuss, in his time as German president, recommended cabinet members to read Weber's 'Politics as a Vocation' once a year – for the purpose of self-criticism.[102] But Thomas Dehler, leader of the FDP liberals in the 1950s, thought he was probably the only one who took the advice;[103] and no party colleague annoyed Heuss as much as Dehler did with his nationalist rhetoric! Dehler too, who claimed to have induced Weber to give his 'Politics as a Vocation' lecture in 1919,[104] probably thought his later actions were in the spirit of Weber.

Weber only sporadically – perhaps this is his greatest weakness – recognized that everyday politics often involves an art of keeping options open, of keeping several balls in the air; this is not the least of the things that differentiate it from science and its fixed use of certain concepts and methods. Hellmuth Plessner had his sights trained on Weber too when he wrote: 'Germans are not light of heart when they engage in politics, because they do not trust themselves to play.' For Plessner, part of being a politician was not only to present oneself but to play a role in public, to be an actor.[105] When Weber describes the ideal-typical politician as a passionate driller through thick board, who tackles the demands of the hour yet is also a hero able to cope with exceptional situations, he is probably also describing an ideal image of himself. Indirectly he appears to imply that he is a born politician – and at the same time reveals how little of one he is.[106] The exemplary in Weber is often sought where it is least to be found: in his political theories. In fact, Else had a better grasp of much of politics when she wrote to Alfred in the wartime spring of 1917, with sapling rather than drill-board metaphors, to suggest that a future 'understanding with France' would require infinite patience and renunciation:

> When I yesterday . . . hacked at the little fruit trees and wished I could plant a beautiful orchard, I thought how much renunciation and foresight is required by the best of human labours. Whoever plants and sows does it for the future; who knows if *he* will see the crop? And so it is with politics: it has true value only when it is done in this frame of mind.[107]

Refuge in the Teutoburg Forest: the dream of nature and love

Even those with expert knowledge of Weber used to think that it was only after years of asceticism, and long after he had broken off relations with Mina, that he threw himself wholeheartedly into the affair with Else. In reality, however, he kept in close touch with Mina during and after the war; the great love with Else flourished in a euphoric phase of his relationship with the pianist, a summertime of ecstasy when, mentally far away from the horrors of war, he revelled in a dream of the oneness of nature and love. Evidently it was this elation that helped him to lose his inhibitions with Else, after years in which he had nursed a hostility for that bewildering seductress. The 'St John's Day' theme from Wagner's *Meistersinger*, with its musical scent of lilac that became the leitmotif of his love for Mina, rang out also in a love letter to Else, in which Weber made a St John's Night out of Wagner's St John's Day.[108] In so far as its chronology can be reconstructed today, this love story gives the impression that Weber's bourgeois morality fell apart together with the empire – and he was not the only German of whom this was true. Admittedly the demise of the old world caused Troeltsch and many others to sink into depression, but Weber belonged at least in part among those for whom the national collapse brought something vitally liberating.

In July 1917 Weber took a holiday in the little mountain town of Oerlinghausen, where he was 'stuffed' with plentiful good food – he especially appreciated it at the time – and 'was possessed like a savage with the idea of "eating"'.[109] He spoke of nature in a (for him) unusually rapturous way: there 'everything' called out '*Heimat! Heimat!*' he wrote to Marianne, and in similar vein to Mina: he who had not felt fully at home anywhere for years.[110] 'This landscape is unbelievably beautiful . . ., probably the most German there is and not without grandeur.' Weber, who had once described the reclamation of Campagna as a necessity for the Italian economy, now saw with regret how the Senne, the pastureland south of Oerlinghausen, was losing 'its ocean-like solitude' as a result of cultivation, at the very time when its magical attraction was being discovered.[111] As he gave more and more scope to his inner wildness, he also found pleasure in the wildness of external nature. The man whose laziness about walking had worried Marianne for years now strode through the Teutoburg Forest whistling the songs he had learned from Mina – which were surely not the war songs of the day.[112]

It would seem that Weber's only surviving love letters to Mina, in which he used the familiar *du*, come from this period; earlier ones may have been destroyed by Else, who spent the last years of her life in the same Heidelberg old people's home as Mina and in whose arms Mina died. By 1917 Tobelchen was no longer the child-woman, and indeed Max Weber signed one letter to her as 'Your vassal'. In the end, though, he was her knight rather than her slave. Things were otherwise with Else.

Through the Bruchsal tunnel to the Venusberg

Max Weber's *rapprochement* with Else Jaffé took place in the course of 1917, although, even after his lecture on ancient Israel in January brought a new familiarity between them, it remained timid and hesitant for a while. In January she wrote to Alfred that 'she longed for (him) most terribly', and 'no Max helps me with that'[113] – but the very idea that he *might* help was already in the air. They still addressed each other in letters as *Sie*, and even sometimes used it later in 'public' correspondence. Else now began to follow his publications more closely, though not in uncritical admiration, especially as she sensed behind them the man prone to illness. She told Alfred she had been disappointed by an article of Max's in *Die Hilfe* (probably 'Deutschland unter den europäischen Weltmächten', November 1916): 'it has that undertone of petulance which does not convince; he makes things too sharp from the start in relation to the Kaiser and our present conditions.'[114] She could clearly see that Weber's obsession with Wilhelm II was irrational and no longer corresponded to the real state of things.

Just three days later, however, Else was 'thrilled' by Max's article on the Prussian franchise, 'Das preußische Wahlrecht', which had just been published in the *Europäische Staats- und Wirtschafts-Zeitung* (of which her husband Edgar was one of the editors). 'I find him magnificent in the strength of his conviction, intellectual perspective and expression. It is a real shame that this power stands like that in the corner. . . . I took especially to heart what he wrote in the article against "exams" as proof of an aptitude for politics; as you know, I am always so much for the "educated".'[115] Else Jaffé, being of noble birth and one of the first German women to be awarded a doctorate, was not at all free of an arrogance associated with class and education. Evidently she felt it to be also a personal dressing-down when Weber ridiculed the idea of academic privilege in the franchise; and, like the quarrelsome Max, she liked it when people were not too tender with each other.

The new love for Max Weber came over her at a time when she was plagued by moods of sadness. On 15 October 1915 Peterle, her son by Otto Gross, had died before he reached the age of eight; there seemed no end to the war and the separation from Alfred; and this woman in her forties, whose self-esteem was so strongly based on her beauty, felt her youth ebbing away, while Alfred's thoughts were always on politics and his activity in Berlin. 'You men really are a heartless breed!' she complained, in a challenging outburst. 'Or at least an "impersonal" one!' And even on a beautiful spring day: 'But think: I can't find a way out of the terrible sadness in which I have been living for so many weeks: I am almost overcome by the feeling that life is passing and so very much remains unfulfilled – by thoughts of the beginning, hope, wasted energy.'[116]

When Max Weber travelled to Vienna in October 1917 to negotiate his professorial appointment, he called in on Else in the outskirts of Munich. Her report to Alfred hints that she had expected it to be an agitated reunion. Perhaps she was not entirely honest when she wrote that Max's visit went 'amazingly – well, how shall I say? – not agitatedly'. 'I was tired . . . and he probably was too. He looked so old and weary to me, and he too was taken up with thoughts about everything he can no longer do.'[117] For Max, however, the 43-year-old woman was still the picture of beauty, the child of the gods.[118] Only now – if her letter to Marianne is to be believed – did she feel that her relationship with Max was again 'normal'.[119]

Figure 18.4 Else Jaffé-Richthofen, around 1919

Soon afterwards he began a letter to her, still using the formal *Sie*: 'Don't be afraid.' Afraid of what? Of reproaches, over-hasty advances, a tense coolness? 'Above all', he added mysteriously, 'from now on I would like my life to be free of all mistaken ideas about what is possible that others might have in relation to me.' Perhaps he was asking the woman not to put too many demands on him, not to think she could awaken in him sexual powers that he did not have. A closeness seems to have developed between them mainly around thoughts of death, on the way to the grave of Little Peter, Weber's godson. 'I think of the room up there; I shall see again the not easily forgotten setting of the village cemetery and its walled perimeter and then the wide landscape.'[120] Else made a return visit to the Webers in Heidelberg and noted that they had learned to live with the lack of erotic enchantment in their life together: 'They get along so well with the veil of resignation that transfigures them both.'[121]

The course of the relationship between Max and Else cannot be clearly followed in 1918. As far as we can tell, all inhibitions ended only in January 1919,[122] when the bourgeois world seemed to be crumbling all around them and Max was shaking off all inhibitions as a political speaker. Allusions in their subsequent correspondence suggest that, when Weber went to Munich to give his 'Politics as a Vocation' lecture, he accompanied Else to a performance of *Tannhäuser* and spent the night with her, and that love-play developed between them on a journey together to Karlsruhe, 'in the tunnel near Bruchsal'[123] – here a future Weber cult would have its holy place! From now on Weber happily played the part of Tannhäuser to his beloved; a meeting with her was a trip to the 'Hörselberg',[124] the mountain near Eisenach identified with the Venusberg in Wagner's opera.

In the love letters to Else from that period, we find a new and long unknown Weber, indeed an almost unbelievable Weber: a rapturous romantic, exhibitionist in his feelings, drunk on the presentiments of spring, sensual in his submission, dismissive of his whole previous existence. In comparison, his epistolary displays of love to Marianne over the years sound conventional and formulaic.

Do we at last have here the *true* Weber? But who would seriously claim that he had not been truly himself for the longest part of his life? There was probably an element of self-stylization not only in the popular orator but also in Weber the lover. In 1913 he had written to Lukács: 'After all, "formed life" is not *only* the *value*-containing element that rises "above" the experiential, but also the *erotic* element that dips into the deep and outermost corners of the "dungeon" in "formed life" as well.'[125] The final allusion was to Lukács's talk of the 'dungeon of individuality', while 'formed life' unquestionably included Weber's declarations of love to Else, which were not without refinement. He played the part of the knight in shining armour, prepared to do anything in the service of his beloved lady; and he also played the erotic soul from the *Zwischenbetrachtung* (written before these declarations of love), whose sexual tension stemmed from a highly cultivated intellect. His development as a scholar helped to equip him for this role as lover. Now 'a talk on the *Zwischenbetrachtung* at Else von Richthofen's' became the code for an amorous tryst.[126]

Max Weber conveyed to Else the sense that she and she alone, the child of the gods with 'demonic'[127] energy, was the saviour of this demon-tormented man, and in doing this he gave her a happiness she had never known before;[128] he kept silent about Mina. And Else played along: although she was in reality a highly intellectual woman, cerebral also in many aspects of love, she was for Weber the wild cat-like creature and earth goddess he liked to have.[129] It increased their pleasure that both acted a little with each other. Yet what went on was much more than a game; something elemental breaks through all Weber's Jugendstil imagery and mythological allusions, something too long suppressed which one would have to be blind not to notice in these letters.

Else's letters to Max from that period have not been preserved. Probably she did not match his effusive style any more than she had the *Sturm und Drang* flourishes that Alfred retained even in his later years. But she excited Max all the more because of her 'plain' 'unsentimental' manner and the fact that she contradicted him more sharply than Marianne did.[130] 'But look how good your unsentimental manner is for me . . . precisely that plain, hard manner – oh, and how enchantingly it suits you!'[131] 'Your enchanting anger', he cried in delight, 'oh, let your "devil" really torment me, I love it so!'[132] 'But how you are when you're angry and how you were today – I love you indescribably like that!' 'Torment me, it does me and my love so much good!'[133] 'You hopelessly smug and spoilt witch, you!' he addressed her.[134] '*That* is the Else I serve': the Else who is 'herself and "sovereign"', for 'she also created that power which once and never again put such a thing on earth.'[135] There is a higher power which makes that love become destiny – 'the mighty power of magic – and the arousal of all the spirits and demons in me born out of torment and longing.'[136]

And repeatedly there is Else as wild cat, who subjugates the professor with animal instinct and brutish tricks – as well as with a higher power! That 'the wild cat *enjoys* mastering the "distinguished scholar" *like that*: ah, I can see it from the enchanting smile in the corner of your mouth and I get myself to feel it again. When my pride bristles – if you have just broken it, one is exceedingly lucky if you just laugh at it: "you see, it could be worse" – yes, indeed! Oh, you'll still have a lot of fighting to do with me, as I'm simply not cut out for humility. . . . You have a huge sense of mastery and power.' And he feels 'deeply satisfied by immeasurable beauty, striding past as in a dance across fields of flowers'.[137] Else, both divine and feline, embodies the seamless unity and self-identical Being that Weber always sought in vain for himself: 'So, this is also and above all else deafeningly true: "But I strove after beauty, after the beauty that she, you, were and can be and always, in every detail, are, that you "are", irrespective of whether at present the captivatingly beautiful "wild cat", who conquers the male in the perpetual, enchanting battle of the sexes, speaks from you in the whole defiant and supple splendour of your limbs – or the fineness of your soul marked by the goddess of love – or the deep goodness and responsibility of your heart. *That* is the Else I serve.'[138]

The sensual pleasure of being dominated: the missing link in the sociology of domination

At the same time that Max Weber, without knowing them well, berated people such as Eisner for national 'masochism' because they publicly acknowledged Germany's war guilt, he revelled with Else in the sensuality of total surrender and subjugation; more than once he enjoyed the thought that she, the 'beautiful despotic mistress' and 'slave-owner',[139] would come up to him from behind and put her hand over his eyes, then place a ring around his neck and deprive him of all his rights. 'You get angry and – well: you beat one, torture one, make one plead and feel a fool; that has such a powerful effect and such a strong fragrance of healthy earth – and it helps.'[140] It is a beam of light on the emotional subsoil of Weber's lifelong interest in the agrarian subsoil of history: it went together with a sensual yearning for ties to the soil, in keeping with the model of the giant Antaeus, 'who drew new strength from Mother Earth each time he rested on her bosom' (AS 410). On another occasion, the Weber who imagined history as a great current felt he had 'become the wave' caressing Else's knee, and saw in his beloved the 'daughter of the ocean', a naiad, though, with scorching ice: 'And you "burn" even "into his blood", quite without mercy, you proud daughter of the ocean – it suits him just right.'[141]

Once at a lecture, when he was again attacking the revolutionaries and chairs were flying across the room, he relished the situation by thinking of the 'dark gleaming eyes' of Else,[142] whose assaults he also allowed to wash over him. It was bliss when she hurt him and thereby entangled his life with hers: a bliss 'which you have given and will give me, proudly and severely keeping from me what it costs you. And I told myself again and again: "You naughty boy" – and again and again everything is deafened by the intoxication and beauty you arouse in me, and the knowledge that you were, are and will be my destiny.'[143] It would seem that it was mostly this belief in fate which drove out Weber's moral inhibitions. Now he felt the superior force he had looked for in vain when he married Marianne. He enjoyed the eroticism of power from the position of one overwhelmed: 'Let me just feel your power, limitless as it is – on every occasion your beauty quite simply makes me happy.'[144]

And this power, the power of beauty, proved its strength precisely by scorning all morality: 'In each crime, each outrage, I shall go with you, Else von Richthofen, whenever you call me – *any one, without exception*.'[145] Of course, he knew that the most Else would ever order would be not murder but separation from Marianne – and probably he was hoping for just that order to come! But it did not come. In the surviving letters to Else – others must have been destroyed – we find scarcely one bad word about Marianne; but he does once speak of feeling in an 'icebox' beside his wife.[146] The 'icebox' presumably refers not to Marianne but to his own brain: marriage with her kept him trapped in a cerebral existence. Marianne is evidently also intended when, playing the part of Tannhäuser, he remarks that he must devote himself for one or two days 'entirely to Saint Elisabeth'.[147] As to Else, she naturally embodies Venus for him. In Wagner's opera, it is the exalted Elisabeth who saves the errant knight even in death, but probably everyone has once felt how strongly Wagner was under the spell of Venus. Weber, who was wavering between Marianne and Else, gave the situation quite a twist by elevating it to the level of myth.

The element in Weber's account of charismatic rule that only appears between the lines now became for him a deeply moving experience: namely, the fact that not only the sensual pleasure of domination, but also the pleasure of obeying and being dominated is part of the magic of power. Only in this light does power become a sociological phenomenon.[148] It was only now that Weber, who liked to appear outwardly so commanding, was willing fully to recognize that the other pleasure was at least as strongly implanted in him as the pleasure of domination. One of the major causes of his sexual inhibitions may have been that he was long incapable of accepting the nature of his libido and integrating it into his self-image. Else, on the other hand, encouraged him to act out his sexual inclinations, whether or not they were 'normal'. When the educational reformer Gustav

Wyneken was charged in 1920 with sexually abusing his boarding pupils and defended himself by saying that, although while naked he had embraced two boys, he had not had sexual contact with them, Else scoffed that his self-justification was 'intolerable' and 'insensitive': 'people will just think: so he was homosexual then! Anything would be better than this "culture of nudity" plus Eros and theory.'[149]

As we have seen, Weber traced his inclinations back to the fact that a maidservant had sexually aroused him as a young boy, but there is some evidence that it was really his mother who spanked him and that, despite the exhibition fight with his father, it was really the bond with her that caused his lifelong troubles. No one can be sure today what went on in the depths of Weber's psyche, but a lot of what we know indicates that a mother-story formed the background to his life. Weber once raged against the 'monster of matriarchy', but he fought with great tenacity for Frieda Gross's maternal rights and held up the mother–child bond as the most natural of all human relationships. In Else he seems to have at last found the woman with whom he could associate his wish-dream of an erotic mother-goddess close to the earth, and to have overcome the power of his own prudish mother. When Helene died on 14 October 1919, no strong expression of feeling was recorded on Max Weber's part.

As Else later reported to Jaspers, Weber wrote to her in April 1920 with a verse from Wagner: 'Es ist das dunkle Reich der Nacht, woraus die Mutter mich gebracht' ['It is the dark realm of night from which my mother brought me'][150] – the realm of Tristan, the realm of love and death, of the primeval cycle of nature into which Else had carried him back.[151] 'You proud cosy little thing, strong sweet and unruly child of the gods, you from the source of Mother Earth', he wrote rapturously to her; 'I lie in chains of roses before you with the ring around my neck.'[152] And he, who signed the letter 'Your little grey tabby', called her his 'beloved brown joy';[153] it gave him pleasure to give Else the colour of earth in his fantasies. 'You most beloved brown joy . . ., treat me really bad, as you know how (I remain all the more in your power).'[154] When he raved that being with her was 'like being in Heaven', he immediately came up with something better: 'That's crazy – it's *far* nicer: like on the blossoming earth in May.'[155]

But Marianne? From time to time, Max shows some sign of feeling guilty towards her, and if he drives the pangs of conscience from his thoughts they become visible in his corporeal being. 'The bad days last week taught me that I must not become unscrupulous (towards Marianne) and must set some boundaries.'[156] As he hints in a revealing passage in 'Politics as a Vocation', which is probably addressed to Else, he is too clever to construct a cheap justification of his love along the lines that his wife is not worthy of him. For him it would be intellectually dishonest, or worse: a sign of weakness, to give a forced moral legitimacy to Eros, that power of nature; indeed, such false labelling would threaten to deprave this favour granted by a higher power, this charisma. 'For these last and highest powers of all our lives beckon with a smile, offering and approving; yes, you are right, but *only* if we are strong enough not to invoke them for our "legitimation" as if they provided a basis in law, not to want to have – beyond the magnificence and grandeur that they bestow on us in an act of grace – an "ethical" legitimacy that says to the other: I am in the right *against you*.'[157]

Fusion of Is and Ought – fate as legitimation

Had Else tried to legitimate her relationship with Max by referring to the lack of sensual pleasure in his marriage? Max reminded her that Marianne had loved her 'immeasurably': probably a hint that it would be shabby to say anything bad about Marianne. From everything we know, he never blamed his wife for his impotence but regarded it as a dismal fate; and that was what united him with Else. 'I don't have you – "one doesn't have the stars" – but you do have me, as the star has the man whose fate it is.'[158] But for Weber charisma too is a kind of legitimation; there is a natural right that rests upon neither law nor morality, and to it belongs the right of beauty and passion.

'So, has the "ethical" professor now become an "aesthetic" professor?' Of course not: 'the supposed "aesthete"' – is that what Else had claimed he was? – has 'come to grief in the garden of the great goddess', so that he, 'quite unlike an aesthete, followed *completely blind* the wonderful scent of roses, violets and carnations'.[159] By now Max Weber finds it ridiculous to enhance Eros through aesthetics; he would simply like to follow his natural instincts, just as an insect is attracted by them to a flower blossom. Yet he does not become a bee; his letters from that time still betray an urge to exalt his love mythologically and to charge it with deep meaning. A man like Weber cannot live without meaning: to belong to her, he tells his beloved, is not only 'nice' but in the ultimate sense that which 'ought to be'.[160] Having often insisted so furiously on a strict separation between Is and Ought, he enjoyed at the end of his life the blessed state in which they are one.

Already in the *Zwischenbetrachtung* he assured the reader with the air of a connoisseur: 'No consummated erotic communion will know itself to be founded in any way other than through a mysterious *destination* for one another: *fate*, in this highest sense of the word. Thereby, it will know itself to be "legitimated" (in an entirely amoral sense)' (FMW 348). He speaks of this belief in fate and this sense of right as if they were a natural law of eroticism. Else, who for herself probably never set much store by the distinction between Is and Ought, did not feel the same need for a higher meaning and right. 'What good fortune it is' – she wrote to Alfred, who was continuing to send her one letter after another that spoke of his love for her – 'that Mother Nature gave me this casualness, which tolerates a state of uncertainty better than does your character with its orientation to the clearly defined.'[161] She was referring here both to the unfathomability of Germany's future and to her own future financial circumstances – but these were not the only uncertainties that Else faced in the summer of 1919.

Returning as a demon: 'bludgeoned life'

In a period when life was becoming a magic word in philosophy, so too was it for Max Weber. It was associated with his perpetual craving for sun and warmth: 'This life, this corporeality, as it is now, expressing your being and nature, is what I wish to see and feel in the light of the sun as in the darkness of night – feel especially in your warmth and solar power.'[162] In retrospect his brain seemed to him an 'ice box' and his previous life a failure, as it did to the repentant sinner in pious devotional literature – except that in his case he was now awakening from asceticism. 'Yes, yes: "vocation", Puritanism, etc. were the things I used to brood over, and you were displaced on that road paved with such intentions.'[163] So evident was it to him that his fixation on Puritan asceticism came from his own joyless compulsiveness.[164] He even sent Else formal apologies – what an effort that must have been! – for his eternal reproaches against Alfred's bohemianism: 'I stand with utterly changed convictions towards him, feeling thoroughly in the wrong – but I could not and cannot do otherwise.'[165]

Had he not yet completely changed his spots? He spoke of a 'devil' who 'draws a hood over my head',[166] as a hangman does over a man on the gallows, but he knew that it was still part of his nature to torture himself with work and that he could not live without it: 'No human being . . . feels the measureless *torture* of work, which I cannot give up without ruining myself. But it is a technique that *constantly* tunes too high one's own incredible states; it takes all one's breath away and – since that thorough "uncorking" – lives in constant hostility with one's body of all things. There is always that "tension" that turns gushing life into a wily and mortal enemy of the intellect.' 'Gushing life': this is the new and emphatic conception of life to be found in *Lebensphilosophie*.

Weber now thinks that, behind the 'demons' that tortured him, nothing else was lurking than the life he had violated with his own lifestyle: 'the life which must now – with a thousand drugs and poisons, from opium to cocaine – be bludgeoned in the shape in which it stirs there'. He has realized that for him spiritual happiness lies in contemplation: this is what unites the scholar and the mystic. Of course, even Else cannot release him from the torment of writing: 'If I . . . let the thoughts come through inward contemplation, everything flows . . . it flows in abundance – and then begins the struggle to grasp it for the paper. This is the (for me) almost intolerable "torment" that people can probably detect in my "style".'[167] But Else, who 'joins together into a unity this oddly split or sundered, in many ways ruined life',[168] turns this torment into a purgatory, within a story that will grant release in the end, if only for a brief time. Weber's life acquired epic form shortly before his death – it is just that, unlike in *Tannhäuser*, the Venusberg lies at the end, not the beginning. Anyway, what else was there to come except death?

In Wagner's 'musical dramas' love and death are close to each other; love itself is a form of dying, a spirituality of self-dissolution. In the *Zwischenbetrachtung*, with his mind on 'the deadly earnestness of this eroticism of intellectualism', Weber speaks of the 'knowing love of the mature man' (FMW 347). In 1915 his brother Karl, the architect, was killed in action near Brest-Litovsk, and it later emerged that his fiancée, Martha Riegel, thought she was pregnant by him. Max Weber, who for a long time had thought this younger brother to be a hopeless wreck, was delighted to think that he had experienced the joy of physical love shortly before his death, and in a long letter to Martha, switching from *Sie* to *du*, he sees in his fallen brother a mirror of himself: 'After long years of self-imposed abstinence, he was greeted by the warm splendour of the living; he became young again and at one with himself, before he went to his death. . . . In many ways we were more alike than he may perhaps have been able to feel.'[169]

'Laughter at death and life' – and a secret fear

When Max Weber shook off his inhibitions towards Else, in the midst of his electioneering in January 1919, he felt a new energy for the round dance of life, a dance of love and death: 'Once again: life and death are the theme of every such "round dance" in the infinite space far from the world of events – and precisely that imparts its eternal beauty, this joyful laughter at human turmoil and misunderstanding, at the tangled obligations and all that there is – a laughter at death and life.'[170]

Yet there is also fear, indeed 'mortal fear', in his love for Else. 'You know about my many "masks"', he wrote to her, apparently after they had spoken of his 'masks', 'and my mortal fear is . . . always: She must think that, if he has them against others, why not also one against me?'[171] Ricarda Huch saw clearly that not everything in Weber's rhetoric came from the core of his being, that a lot of it was theatre; Else also surely realized what was genuine in him and what was play-acting – and he knew that he could conceal nothing from her. When he played the romantic lover, prepared to devote himself completely to her, was he really that? Or was that also theatre? And did Else not sense this and feel disappointed? He wavered between fear of losing her because she thought him not devoted enough and because she thought him too possessive. She must not believe that he imagined he could possess a child of the gods.

> But all that was by no means as uninhibited as it may have seemed to you: 'fear' and shyness . . . were always there in every rejoicing of the heart and the senses. You understand: a reverential fear of you, of touching the magnificence beyond belief that streamed from each of your gestures. . . . Your laughter at the 'knight' who is neither irreproachable nor fearless will perhaps give him more heart and make him dare to put his arms more tightly around you.[172]

He mentions 'occasional physical difficulties', which he probably did best to keep to himself ('No, no!' Else wrote in the margin). 'No one believes and knows, not even Marianne, . . . that in terms of health (purely physical!) I live beneath the point of a sword.'[173] As he saw it, his illness had a physical basis that was still there, even though his mental depression had long been overcome. And he knew that sexually Else was 'always the giver'; he the sheep, she the shepherdess.[174] In this Arcadia the lover was not the shepherd boy but the sheep. Alfred had already acted that part with Else.[175] Half a century later, Eduard Baumgarten reported to the aged Jaspers that he had learned from Else that 'it is difficult to give it (pleasure) to a man like that – obviously not in an ordinary sense, but orgasm and satisfaction.'[176] And Else herself, at the age of nearly one hundred, said to Martin Green of Max Weber: 'Nature did not intend him to be married.'[177] She had previously said much the same to Baumgarten: that Max Weber could not have become a 'real progenitor of a large family'; 'in that too he was relegated to the land of dreams'[178] – in that too, so also in other areas! Else thought that Max would have liked to be one of the hugely fertile patriarchs who lived on in their seed. Instead, the idea that he could not satisfy Else sexually must have made him secretly fearful. Probably one of the reasons why he so happily made her the dominator was that he could only satisfy her lust for power.

Could this happiness have lasted? Weber at least tried to ensure that it would, by taking up the appointment in 1919 to Lujo Brentano's old chair in Munich (close to where Else had moved), although he had also received a lucrative offer from Bonn, on a higher salary and with fewer teaching duties – a 'sinecure', according to Jaspers. The psychiatrist-philosopher, who worried about Weber, had been annoyed that the move to Munich would 'typically mess up his material destiny',[179] as if he had suspected that Weber's life would not last much longer there. 'Else Jaffé is mad keen to have us there', Marianne wrote in February 1919 to Helene, 'and she is certainly a strong magnet for us both.'[180] Afterwards, however, it probably dawned on her that this time Else wanted only *him*, and that he too would have preferred to go to Munich alone.

Erotic discussions of religion

Max Weber's discussions with Else around that time centred not only on love but also, with scarcely less intensity, on religion. On 24 May 1920, seven weeks before his death, he wrote to his beloved some puzzling words that the late Jaspers, sunk in thought about the true Weber, copied out forty years later.

Actually one cannot live 'against God' in the day; one can only seek out that realm of Tristan – and then die 'against him' when it is time and he requires it; in there he will become as Shylock, we can be sure he will choose the time himself. And those structures on which even Tristan's realm must not encroach (let he who is willing and able call it

'Luciferian') have ensured that we notice them there at every moment. Above all, I can live against a person only in the truth, and that I can and am allowed to do so is the ultimate necessity that is decisive for my life, higher and stronger than any God.[181]

Weber knows a God, even a quite definite one, almighty or anyway *almost* all-controlling; not a kind God, however, but a merciless avenging God who, like Shakespeare's Shylock, would cut a pound of flesh from the debtor's body, or like the Yahweh of the Old Testament. During the day one cannot live against him, but one probably can during the night, in the dark realm of Tristan; then, however, one must pay with one's life for the offence against God. But the *truth*, Weber's highest value, is something for the relationship with other people – or certain people – not for the relationship with God; Weber's God is not a source of values. He appears more as a power of nature standing outside all spheres of value. Unquestionably, though, a demonic power, whether divine or Luciferian,[182] also operates in erotic love.

In an undated letter to Alfred, Else writes that she is 'exhausted from orgies of discussion with Max about what you are writing on Max's "polytheism"'. And, in the same letter: she of all people is 'so in need of the *one* Max'.[183] In Alfred she did not find an interlocutor on religious questions: not surprisingly, since, as Marianne wrote to Helene as early as 1908, 'everything theological is now rat poison for him'.[184] In gloomy times, Else probably found Alfred's worldly vitalism a shallow philosophy fit only for periods of fine weather; and it probably annoyed her more and more when he played the life-affirming man of the here and now, in contrast to the supposedly ascetic Max. Her letters to Alfred tell us a lot about the long unsolved puzzle of Max Weber's religiosity.[185] Already in 1910, after her experience with Max in Venice and what followed, she wrote about him in a challenging way to Alfred: 'He has more true love for me than you do! Yes. For you are mainly in love with life, and with me because I love it together with you.' Max, on the other hand, was 'like the embodiment of divine love, who says: "Go, my child, live, suffer and be happy – it will be hard for me to let you go, but I know you belong to your Mother Earth and to those who are your brothers".'[186] Unlike Max, Alfred was probably for a lot of the time too possessive towards her; nor could she speak about death or share sorrow with him. That this was possible with Max appears to have been what first brought them close to each other again in the autumn of 1917.

The discussions with Max about religion had an exciting effect on Else. Religion for him was not simply a cultural phenomenon,[187] as it was for the 'cultural Protestantism' of his time, or a mere superstructure of society or an instrument for the stabilization of a social system, as it was for Durkheim[188] – on the contrary, religion was often an eternal reproach against everyday structures. It came from the depths of the human being and had a similar power to erotic love:[189] partly akin to, partly in struggle with it. In his writings on the sociology of religion, was he speaking simply of a phenomenon he had observed from a distance, or of a power that he felt inside himself? Weber's own religiosity is the greatest puzzle in the whole area of Weber studies,[190] up to now even more obscure than his sexuality. Here he was even shyer about revealing his inner being than he was in relation to his sexual life; perhaps he was also loath to focus on substrata of his thought and feelings, lest it interfere with his creative powers. After all, for many years he had to endure the torture of a watchfulness that prevented him from sleeping.

The puzzle of puzzles: Weber's religiosity

To one young participant in the discussions at Lauenstein Castle, who had evidently heard intimate confessions from him, Weber wrote: 'To me the limit of "confessing" is where things are involved that are "sacred"'; they should be spoken of only in a 'good hour' and in a circle of close friends (WB 599). This implied that there really were areas of 'the sacred' within his inner being. If Weber took up the cudgels against value-judgements in science, he did so not because there were no values in his eyes, but because his values were too 'sacred' to be mixed up with science. As Marianne wrote of the lectures on science and politics as vocations, 'final judgements sparkle . . . here and there, as lodestars through "open secrets" – more in indirect than direct communication, it is true – and for that very reason stimulate those who hear or read them to ask and search' (LE 123).

He (Weber) 'is suspected of being such an extremely "moral" person', Weber wrote with exclamation marks in 1912 to Sombart (MWG II/7-2, 606), who was suspected of being the opposite. Asked what was so 'mysterious' about Weber, the art historian Carl Neumann replied that in conversation with him one sensed a 'limitless moral energy', 'although he only gave out scraps about himself'[191] – by which was probably meant 'about the origin of his morality'. But the question is whether there actually was *one* origin. Weber was not the closed personality he seemed to be to others; his 'polytheism of values' corresponded to fissures within himself. The values that gave life a meaning for him[192] did not all originate in the same spirit. But the fact that they were sacred to him, and that he timidly kept them hidden, indicated that they came from religious roots that were removed from discussion.

Be this as it may, a lifelong fascination for religious phenomena is scarcely conceivable without some religious experience of one's own, and not at all in a man who pursued science out of passion. At the age of eighteen, he was already 'quite deeply immersed in theology' (JB 48), although it was distracting him from his studies. No other of his major research focuses came so entirely from within himself. And, as Hennis has written: 'There could in the history of the social sciences have been very few Germans who retained such a fine sense of the meaning of religion.'[193] His detailed knowledge of religious issues and his capacity to empathize with religious states of mind became his main trump cards in comparison with other economists and political theorists. His thesis that the power of religion unleashed capitalism made him famous around the world. He thought he understood better than most modern intellectuals what fear of hellfire and hopes of salvation meant for people in earlier times, and what effect they had on lifestyles and the general zest for life; he thought he could differentiate more precisely than others between various forms of asceticism and ecstasy, between genuine and feigned mysticism and charismatics – distinctions that are hard to derive from the sources alone unless one has also had personal experience of them.

The question of Weber's religiosity is usually much too hastily dismissed with a reference to his claim, made to Ferdinand Tönnies, that he was 'absolutely "unmusical" in religious matters'. Even there, however, one has only to read the whole sentence and the ones following it to recognize the ambiguity of the statement, which was addressed to a man notoriously contemptuous of all theology.

> For I am absolutely 'unmusical' in religious matters and have neither the need nor the ability to erect any spiritual structures of a religious kind within me – that is simply not on, or I decline to do it. But, on closer examination, I am neither anti-religious *nor irreligious*. In this respect too I feel a cripple, a mutilated person, whose inner destiny it is to have to admit this honestly. (MWG II/6, 65)

'Unmusical in religious matters' was an allusion to Schleiermacher, who had spoken of music as his 'religion'. But this kind of religion was not Weber's 'thing'; what he felt as divine was not associated with the sonorous harmony of intoxicating organ music. Nor would it ever have occurred to him to construct an edifying theological system. The quotation does clearly reveal, though, how in both religion and eroticism he felt himself to be a 'cripple', who would have liked to do something of which he was actually incapable. A complete person had the capacity for religion as well as love; religious potency appeared as a natural disposition akin to sexual potency, with none of the bigotry that anti-clericalists used to ascribe to the devout.

So, when Weber became an erotic man, did he not also feel a new energy for religious experience? Two weeks after the quoted letter to Tönnies, on 2 March 1909, he returned to the 'unmusical in religious matters' and remarked, from the point of view of an outsider, that the 'problems of the historical significance of mysticism' were unfathomable. And Weber, who otherwise used to react allergically to the cult of 'experience', acknowledged: 'There, only there, do I have the impression . . . that I must *experience* these mental states to understand their consequences. I have to confess this, although I myself am "unmusical" in religion' (MWG II/6, 70). Later he wrote about mysticism and felt competent to analyse the states of mind associated with it; he must have experienced them, if we take him at his word. And in that domain, as well as in erotic love, he no longer felt a 'cripple'.

In 'Science as a Vocation', Weber speaks of the 'religious organ' of 'a truly religiously "musical" man' (FMW 153). Already in many letters from his youth, there is a conviction that human beings have a natural predisposition to religion; and the same premise is discernible between the lines of his sociology of religion – where he mentions quite in passing the 'ineradicable demand for a theodicy' (FMW 275) as if it were a well-known fact. Even in the economic context of the satisfaction of needs, he points to the 'religious need' that can be met in diverse ways (GASS 472f.): *one* basic need, therefore, behind the various phenomena of religion.

The young Weber thought that the demythologization programme of liberal Bible critics was rather silly (JB 206f.); their know-all attitude to the stories of Jesus diverted attention from the sources of religious energy. He taught Alfred that religion made a mark even on people who wanted to have nothing to do with it; that we all behave 'involuntarily' in accordance with Christian doctrines (JB 107). The starting point of his sociology of religion is the idea that religion impacts on the world where we least suspect it: in the genesis of modern capitalism. In sharp contrast to notions prevalent at the time, he always worked on the assumption that religion and rationality are not necessarily opposites, and that the history of religion – especially of Judaism and Christianity – is shot through with processes of rationalization and spell-breaking (*Entzauberung*). As Hartmann Tyrell notes, Weber became 'magnetically attracted to issues of religious-ethical rationality';[194] the modern disenchantment of the world therefore does not necessarily entail secularization. At times Weber does give the impression that the power of religion is a thing of the past, but on the whole he gives reasons to expect that religious-like beliefs will in future continue to cast their spell on many people, since modern man in particular hankers after salvation.[195] Today it looks as if Weber's vision in this respect was clearer than that of many other pioneering theorists of modernization.

Weber's demonology

When Weber complained during his illness that 'demons' were tormenting him, this was more than a metaphor. And when he later, in the *Zwischenbetrachtung*, remarked that 'sexuality was readily considered to be specifically dominated by demons' (FMW 344), he was referring to an idea often encountered in the history of religion, which also corresponded to a hunch of his. According to Marianne, in the winter of 1898–9, the first of his illness, he was 'very unhappy with the Almighty and tormented us by pretty well rebuking the Good Lord'; it was the time when he despaired of ever being 'sexually normal'.[196] Twenty years later, in the winter of 1918–19, Marianne told Eduard Baumgarten that Max Weber could be heard talking aloud in his study: 'I fear he is again quarrelling with God and taking it too far by telling Him off.'[197] On 20 April 1920 she confessed to her husband that she could 'never hear him without shuddering' when he 'so often scolded, indeed blasphemed against, the Almighty' (B 633). For herself she noted: 'When the fortunes of war turned against us, Max quarrelled with God' and complained that God was not very keen on the 'strange character' (that is, himself).[198]

It is not surprising, then, that Weber did not wish to speak about his innermost religious convictions, within his close circle and scarcely even with Marianne. These beliefs were a far cry from his scholarly work – and, as we see, he even thought in the early period of the war that God should help the Germans to victory and concern himself quite particularly with Max Weber! Again and again he fell into a rage when he was bitterly disappointed. This was when his vision of an evil God, of Shylock, took shape, and so too of a Luciferian counter-realm that promised salvation for many nights, even if a high price had to be paid for such happy imaginings. 'But he kept talking of God', Jaspers recalled late in life; 'not praying, not trusting . . . "Shylock" – no humility – sheer rebellion . . . The good and the bad demon.'[199] It was the same crypto-religion that he detected in Goethe.[200]

When Weber lived in a presentiment of salvation, he probably liked to think that fate had singled him out for special torment because it intended something special for him. Guenther Roth detects in many letters from the period around 1908 that the idea of 'suffering more than most people' gave Weber a 'perverse satisfaction'.[201] Weber as the new Job? But, unlike the biblical Job, he never felt that he had regained lasting happiness and the security of a good God. He found it 'in the highest degree significant that, when God appeared to Job in a storm after being asked by him to explain the unjust order of human existence, he did not say a word to show the wisdom of how he had ordered human relations – which would have gone without saying for a Confucian, for example – but did nothing other than defend his sovereign power and grandeur in the phenomena of nature' (JB 142f.). Weber's God too had something of a force of nature: not in an idyllic sense but in the reality that recognizes no human law. Weber's insistence on value-freedom here appears in a new light: it implies that it was only the abandonment of value-judgements that enabled science to understand something about the power operating in the events of the world. After the Good Lord of childhood, after the evil God of his period of illness – at last a value-free God!

The Weber of the final years did not experience only tormenting demons. Here is the concluding sentence of 'Science as a Vocation': The 'demands of the day' are 'plain and simple, if each finds and obeys the demon who holds the fibres of his very life' (FMW 156). Weber was calling not only for freedom of scientific research but also for obedience to one's own demon. This smacks of the Socratic *daimonion*, the inner voice, but it is also a demon who imposes a destiny on the individual from outside that it is best not to resist. (In the philosophy of the nineteenth century, the fearsome demon of old seemed to be replaced for a time by the Socratic *daimonion*, although Kierkegaard brought the terrifying demon back into the picture.)

So, everyone has their personal destiny. Weber had grounds for imagining that a great but also tragic fate had been decided for him. The belief in *Schicksal* (fate or destiny), together with a heroic willingness to assume a tragic fate, is probably the kernel of Weber's own religion, especially as the power of fate also legitimates erotic love.[202] Eduard Baumgarten rightly finds it significant how often, and with what pathos and 'personal emphasis', Weber used the word *Schicksal* (B 658), little though it fits the terminology of Weber studies. *Schicksal* for Weber is associated with love and death; 'fate and death together form a single vision' (B 659).

Weber was probably speaking not least of himself when he wrote that 'all purely human heroism which has always proudly refused to believe in a benevolent providence' is characterized by faith in a 'specific concept of predestination, . . . an irrational, impersonal and fateful power' (RC 207). In a sense this faith unites the heroes of antiquity with the 'hard as steel' Puritans, for whom predestination elicits not passive fatalism but heroic self-mastery. To be sure, there is also grace, charisma, predestination for salvation and loving abandon; we need only think of the 28-year-old Weber's letter of courtship and its condition – whose import and consequences Marianne probably did not understand at the time – that 'only if (he is) under the divine compulsion of complete, unconditional devotion (does he) have a right to demand and accept it for' himself' (WB 177). There is that demon too, which also exerts a compulsion. However, as Weber only came to recognize in the course of his life, that power commanded him to love not Marianne but Else – and in so doing legitimated this love.

It would, of course, be a much too forced rationalization to cobble together a perfect theological system out of the fragments of Weber's religiosity. Probably he had his reasons for finding any personal admission of faith deeply repugnant. After all, his religion had no rational logic that could be clearly set out; it all fits together best if one assumes a half-conscious religion of nature. His higher power lies not in a Beyond but in the real world below; it makes human beings capable of erotic love, but also torments and destroys them and ultimately avenges any violation of its laws. Such a nature religion was already instilled in him by his mother's Unitarianism, and the extent to which it suited him even in youth is clear from the impression that the Alsatian pastor Riff made at Whitsun 1882, with a sermon that depicted the 'awakening of the Holy Spirit in the hearts of the disciples' as an awakening of nature, and a thoroughly sensuous nature at that (JB 53f.).

Paul Honigsheim thought he could see the jumping-off point for Weber's religiosity in his 'religiously grounded autonomism' (WzG 270): that is, in the fact that Weber had a highly personal relationship with his divinity, even if he often did not cultivate a very friendly relationship. The description does indeed fit Weber, and he had this characteristic in common with mystics who also sought a direct relationship with God. A Max Weber likes to be sovereign in relations with his God. In the end, however, one has to obey one's god or demon: that is the only way of achieving a kind of freedom. This recalls Bacon's well-known saying: '*Naturae non imperatur nisi parendo*', 'One can command nature only by obeying it.' Nature imparts general but also individual laws; it is the model of a power that is all-controlling yet creates the basis of individuality. And, when mysticism seeks oneness with a naturally understood godhead, it has an inner affinity with science and its quest for knowledge of nature. The mysticism which longs to be united with the totality of nature is close to the science which – albeit in a humble awareness of its limits – wishes to encompass the whole world. This striving permeated Weber's scholarly work in the last decade of his life.

The worldly mystic

After 1900, and especially after the First World War, mysticism came into fashion in Germany, with or without God. Troeltsch deliberately played a role in making it a distinctive type of religiosity; he admitted to his student Gertrud von le Fort, who worshipped him, that he was himself a secret mystic.[203] Eduard Baumgarten reports a conversation between Max and Marianne during the final period of Weber's life, in the dusk at the window of the Heidelberg villa:

> (Max Weber) 'Tell me, can you imagine being a mystic?' – 'That's certainly the last thing I could imagine of myself. Can you imagine it of yourself, then?' – 'It could be that I already am one. As I've "dreamed" more in my life than one ought to allow oneself, I'm not completely reliably at home anywhere. It's as if I could (and would) just as well withdraw entirely from everything".' (B 677)

It was not for Marianne's sake that he confessed to being a virtual mystic; she would have preferred him to be a man of action with a national impact, and indeed she omits from her biography this scene reported by her nephew Eduard. Perhaps she still had a narrow conception of mysticism and associated it with devout churchgoers, whereas Max had long seen it as a wider phenomenon corresponding to a basic need of civilized men and women. By late 1919 at the latest he had recognized that his path was not the *vita activa* but the *vita contemplativa*. Contemplation is not at all 'a passive abandonment to dreams', he emphasizes in *Economy and Society*. Rather, it is attained through 'very energetic concentration upon certain truths' (E&S 546).

Truth arrived at through mental concentration: this is the link between science and mysticism. 'He had a feel for mysticism', Honigsheim stressed above all when he came to Weber's religiosity; and Weber thought he could tell when mysticism was genuine and when it was mannered. In the latter case, it sent him into a rage: a sign that something he valued highly was at stake. 'Weber could be unrelenting if mysticism did not fulfil two conditions: it must not interfere in the domain of the particular sciences, and it must be the genuine article, not a sham; he could get really angry if he thought it was a put-up job' (WzG 268).[204] If he kept science and mysticism strictly separate, it was probably to save not only science from mysticism but also mysticism from science. Yet, precisely when he was battling against value-judgements in science, he thought that science and religiously inspired contemplation were closely related to each other. In his polemic against Ostwald, he recalled that the sciences advanced not so much through the striving for 'practical mastery of the external world' as through the quest for 'divine wisdom in the anatomy of a louse': 'in those days the Lord God did not function so badly as a heuristic principle' (WL 423).

The German equivalent of 'mysticism' or 'mystical' occurs no fewer than 510 times in the electronic edition of Weber's works: not only in the sociology of religion, but also in *Economy and Society*. 'But the disposition to mysticism is an individual charisma', he writes there (E&S 531). How would he think he knew that if he had not experienced it in himself? In typically Weberian manner, he then immediately pours some cold water: 'Hence, it is no accident that the great mystical prophecies of salvation . . . have tended to fall into pure ritualism as they have become routinized.' The spirituality of oneness with world-encompassing nature does not last; Weber also had enough experience to know that, in everyday life, contemplation becomes a compulsive ritual. Routinized science, with its methodological discipline and its laborious mental efforts to penetrate a slice of reality, has something of contemplation banalized into ritualism. Value-judgements destroy contemplation, especially in a man as liable to attacks of rage as Weber was; this explains his horror of value-judgements, which is scarcely understandable on purely rational grounds.

Value-judgements are also destructive of erotic love, and indeed for seven years moral hypocrisy blocked Max Weber's capacity to love Else. As he remarks in one of the most exciting passages of the *Zwischenbetrachtung*, 'the mystic's union with God' is closer than other forms of religiosity to the 'highest eroticism', psychologically and physiologically, if not theologically. In the 'unmediated slipping from the mystic realm of God into the realm of the All-Too-Human', Weber detects the 'deadly sophisticated revenge of animality' (FMW 348). Here Weber's mysticism links up with his belief in fate and demons. The Weber of that period not only feared this revenge of nature but secretly *longed* for it.

'Ecstasy of death'

Erwin Rohde, the friend of Nietzsche and co-discoverer of the Dionysiac element in Greek religiosity – and a man whom Weber held in high regard – pointed to the fact that in ecstasy 'ordinary everyday existence' in the 'circumscribed being' of the body was often felt as such a 'hindrance' that the ecstatic cheerfully, indeed avidly, faced death – especially death in battle.[205] Max and Marianne Weber too knew the 'ecstasy of death' and witnessed it in Otto Baumgarten, when the young widower spoke at the open grave to his dead wife (WB 80). Marianne and Else, who both sat at Max Weber's death bed, worked themselves up into an 'ecstasy' for a short time after his agony was over, feeling 'that this man was, is and will be, and that we must serve him'.[206] Religions are not least a way of coming to terms with the horror of death, and the secret attraction of a pessimistic view of the world is that it is easier to die with it. Fearlessness in the face of death was for Weber always the sign of a noble character; it marked his excitable sense of honour, his penchant for duelling, his nationalism, his heroic male ideal – and also the masochistic aspects of his libido. Constans Seyfarth and Gert Schmidt even argue that one way of reading Weber's typology of rule is that the 'theme of death' is 'systematically incorporated' into it, insofar as charisma is always associated with dangerous living in the proximity of death.[207] Michels recalled in his fascist period that one of the most important qualities of the charismatic in Weber's sense was a 'preparedness to die'.[208] In the *Zwischenbetrachtung* Weber even holds that the giving of meaning to death 'ultimately lies at the base of all endeavours to support the autonomous dignity of the polity resting on force' (FMW 335).

What is death? Weber mused in the spring of 1920, when a cardiac spasm filled him with thoughts of mortality. Is it – as in the quote from *Tristan* – 'the dark realm of night from which my mother brought me'? (WB 690). Is it a return to the maternal womb, of which his love for Else gave him a sensual foreboding? Death is part of nature: Weber had no problem with this fact (which many nature-worshippers prefer to drive away) – or at least he thought he had none, so long as he was not directly confronted with it himself. In *Roscher and Knies* he mocked the circumlocutions that the psychologist Wundt employed to avoid the short and simple word 'death'.[209]

Max Weber's grandfather Fallenstein, whose psychologically borderline states when 'the black beast came over him'[210] later seemed to have prefigured much of Weber's illness, had a favourite saying: '*Wen Gott lieb hat, den läßt er jung sterben*' (Those whom God loves He lets die young)[211] – where 'young' meant 'with their physical and mental powers intact'.[212] This ideal of death, originating in classical antiquity, had by then also been emphatically proclaimed by Max and Marianne Weber. A long life was, it is true, the goal of a certain type of hermit, who accordingly raised 'abstention from passionate desires' into 'the cardinal virtue' (RC 191), but Weber was most certainly not the embodiment of that type. 'Such a death without old age, illness, regression and loneliness, at the height of success, is wonderful for those to whom it is given', he wrote in 1913 to his Oerlinghausen cousin Wina (Alwine Müller), whose husband, the head of the Weber company, had suddenly died at the age of sixty-five (MWG II/8, 109). And those were not merely words of condolence on his part.

In 1898, following the death of an acquaintance, the philosopher Paul Hensel wrote to Rickert: 'Was not Plato actually right when he chided doctors for using their art to give human beings sixty years of dying?'[213] Probably Plato greatly exaggerated the art of ancient doctors, but modern intensive medicine can be reproached for making only the process of dying longer in many cases. In Weber's day doctors could not yet do so much in this respect, but in 'Science as a Vocation' Weber himself – whose trust in science may well have led him to overestimate the powers of medicine – was critical of attempts to prolong life at any cost (this in the midst of world war!), even when the terminally ill patient 'implores us to relieve him of life' and 'the costs of maintaining his worthless life grow unbearable' for his relatives (FMW 144). He did not think much of the Bismarckian type of state-run social insurance, which mainly handled the care of the old and sick. In 1909 he declared in a wine bar: 'I don't set any great store by our social policy. What help is it for workers to have a little contentment in their old age, if they have to go on obeying as long as their bones still hold together?' (WzG). He liked to speak of the '*pianissimo* of old age', but since his illness he had assumed that he would not reach an advanced age; and it is questionable whether he regretted that.

In 1879, at the age of fifteen, Weber wrote a Christmas letter to his cousin Fritz Baumgarten in which there is an almost ecological awareness of the North–South contrast in attitudes to death: people in the South know 'nothing higher than life, than the pleasant light of the sun'; 'whereas for those in the North death seems not to have held either terror or suffering. It has often seemed desirable to them.' Even for the 'Italic' (that is, the Roman), 'death did not appear so terrible at least. In contrast to the stock-farming Hellenes, he was used to receiving all that is good from the earth' (JB 32). That was the basis of Roman idleness.

'But speak not to me / Of Valhalla's brittle delights'

The ageing Weber felt a great longing for the sun, but in the end also for the earth (WB 686). One of his favourite quotations came from Wagner's *Die Walküre*, when the doomed Siegmund, having just made love with his sister, faces Brünhilde, who has come at Wotan's behest to take him to Valhalla to be among the heroes fallen in battle: '*Nur von Walhalls spröden Wonnen / sprich du wahrlich mir nicht*' [But speak not to me / Of Valhalla's brittle delights].[214] (On the day before his sister Lili committed suicide, on 7 April 1920, Weber went again with Else and Marianne to a performance of *Die Walküre*.) He sneaked these lines without motivation into the new edition of *The Protestant Ethic* (PE 107) and even jotted them down on his sheet of notes for the final crescendo in 'Politics as a Vocation' (MWG I/17, 151), although he did not in the end use the Wagnerian chord. Probably he found it magical how Siegmund showed no fear before the powerful emissary of death, and no longing for death either, but held with all his passion to his incestuous sensual love.

After the supreme delights of love, in which a new hero is produced, death in battle: there is something archaically grandiose about it, especially when the hero loves life and is not seeking death. Together with Tolstoy, Weber complains that death can have no meaning for modern man. 'It has none because the individual life of civilized man, placed into an infinite "progress", according to its own immanent meaning should never come to an end.' In olden times a peasant might grow 'satiated with life' when he had completed the 'organic cycle'; modern man can become only 'tired of life' (FMW 139f.). But Weber did not believe in progress towards a higher fullness of life, and he did not like to think of himself as a thoroughly modern man. He would gladly have fallen as a hero in battle once he had fulfilled his yearning for love – at least that is what he *thought*, a long way from the front. Did he secretly hope to die 'satiated with life'? Such a hope probably was one major part of the happiness that his love for Else gave him.

Marianne too, without any feminine weakness, generally expressed similar views about death, in the spirit of Nietzsche's teaching in *Thus Spake Zarathustra* that our goal should not be to live as long as possible but to die at the right time, and that many actually died too late. Although she otherwise had a tendency to be sentimental, her only worry in the case of her father – who, in her eyes, was mentally ill and personally detestable – was that he might live too long. And as to Emmy Baumgarten, Max's semi-fiancée of old, who suffered from a nervous disorder and constantly gloomy thoughts (but would still live another fifty years), Marianne wrote in 1895 that death would be 'a thousand times better for her'.[215] When the even more disturbed Otto Benecke became a burden on the Webers in 1903 in Corsica, Marianne 'waited trembling' at the thought that, already late from a walk, 'he would try to end it all himself'.[216] His eventual suicide actually was celebrated by Marianne as a triumph of the will; and she knew that Max shared her feeling that the poor Otto 'broke from his prison by a supreme effort of the will' (WB 247).

One thought in her mind may have been that women were expected to make a charitable self-sacrifice by enduring the long illness of those who were unwilling to die. She herself was chained to a sick husband for years, during many of which she did not see him as a future genius but despaired at the burden on her own life. At least subconsciously she may have sometimes felt a death-wish towards him. In the case of healthy men, she was fascinated by their fearless attitude to death after the outbreak of war: 'This great willingness of the men to die is a wonderful thing!'[217] This was at a time, however, when no one she knew had yet fallen in action; it did not take long for her mood to change. But, again in the Second World War, albeit a little apprehensively, she thought that young men 'experience upswings and fulfilment that are unattainable for the rest of us, and for which death at the front is not too high a price to pay'.[218] We sense the tragedy of a woman whose need for devotion had not been satisfied by life.

Suicide as the philosopher's death

The 83-year-old Jaspers wrote to Hannah Arendt that a man such as Max Weber 'may well reach amazing heights, but only momentarily' – the passion of thinking is subject to a natural law like that of sexual orgasm. Jaspers concludes: 'And so his lifelong penchant for death, his inclination to thoughts of suicide.'[219] For Max and Marianne Weber, it was self-evident that suicide can be a thoroughly honourable act, an expression of inner freedom and strength of will, whose condemnation by the church testifies to its narrowness of mind. In 1897, in his *Suicide*, a founding work of purely sociological sociology, Emile Durkheim had spent a colossal effort to demonstrate that an increase in suicide is explicable only by a crisis of society. That would have been unthinkable for Weber, who, despite his frequent reflections on suicide, took no notice of Durkheim's work. Why should he have? Any admirer of antiquity kept in mind the example of Socrates, who could have fled from his prison to escape death, and the suicide of Seneca; when life could no longer be lived in dignity, suicide was the death chosen by the wise. Shortly before his own death, Weber taught that 'only philosophers in the most genuine sense' are capable, 'out of disgust at the world', of 'carrying out the Stoic decision to disappear from life' (WG 309). In 1905 he had told Willy Hellpach that it was 'barbarism to prevent sick people from taking their life under any circumstances' and to lock people up in an institution after a failed suicide attempt.[220] In late 1910 he declared to Friedrich Gundolf, whose father had taken his life, that he emphatically believed in the 'standpoint of antiquity' on the right to suicide; and, on the tricky question of whether someone who is weary of life should inflict this step on their 'nearest and dearest', he referred to his own (admittedly ambivalent) experience:

> I think that one must *oneself* have been in a situation of difficult and theoretically hopeless illness, and have once seriously posed such a question to *oneself*, in order really to believe that these infinitely understandable and human feelings do *not* give someone a complete right to depart this life – even if he is not completely master of himself at the moment of decision. There are nervous states that make the sick person feel his existence to be so utterly pointless that he may take the justified view that he should bid his relatives farewell through this decision, however infinitely painful it may be to them. (MWG II/6, 741f.)

As we have seen, although he otherwise despised Otto Gross, he did not think at all ill of him when he gave two women friends the poison to take their lives (MWG II/8, 518). Nor, in his view, was severe illness or a threatened loss of honour the only justification for throwing one's life away. When his once so beloved sister Lili (whose husband was killed in the war) took her life three months before his own death, Max Weber became quite 'euphoric' about her deed (B 677), praised the willingness to commit suicide as a sign of genuine humanity, and declared that it was 'undignified' to want to go on living in any circumstances. He must have known the real reason for her action: she had been in love with Paul Geheeb – director of the educationally progressive Odenwald School, where she taught and where her three children were brought up – and had been abandoned by him.[221] For Weber this love of death was 'beautiful':

> I feel more and more sure that Lili's action was the only justified one. And: beautiful. She did not think of her capabilities as a mother but considered herself a 'misfortune' for the children. Rightly or, to be sure, wrongly. Who will speak then of 'duties' – and, besides, who has lived through that? It is undignified . . . to take life *thus*, as a 'value in itself'. If only our officers – like the Chinese and Japanese – had had the dignity, instead of writing 'war memoirs', to draw the consequences that an honest person draws when life has condemned them to lose a great game. The impression would be different. (B 676)

Weber, who at the time thought he could detect in the Confucian elites that Stoic resignation which he considered a sign of nobility of character, was fascinated at the end of the war by the idea that Germany's military leaders might save the nation's honour by taking their lives.[222] And he polemicized against Spengler, in whose eyes China had reached the senile stage in his cycle of civilizations:

> Although in your account China stands at a late, weary stage of civilization, Chinese generals still commit suicide in a lost war, whereas, in the youthful stage of Germany's civilization, the corresponding gentlemen guard their lives and write war memoirs. Anyway personally, whether from senility or youthfulness, my preference is for the Chinese attitude, which in my eyes is humanly superior. (B 554)

A vain appeal for martyrdom: Weber's verbal exchange with Ludendorff

Weber was disappointed that the Bavarian right, which wanted to keep Eisner's assassin alive at all costs, was so lacking in religiosity that it had no feel for the martyr's aura and left it to the likes of Kurt Eisner. He was also 'deeply disappointed' that Ludendorff, having sent hundreds of thousands to their death, should show so little preparedness for martyrdom. Shortly before Weber went to Versailles with the German peace delegation on 13 May 1919, he managed to reach Ludendorff 'through the good offices of some German National Party deputies' and tried for several hours to talk him into handing himself over to the Allies. If Marianne's biography is to be believed (WB 651f.) – no report of the argument is available from Ludendorff's side[223] – there were some exchanges worthy of the stage.

A curious mixture of closeness and aversion developed between the two men. Weber ascribed some blame for the German fiasco to the army high command, whereas Ludendorff regarded Weber as a 'democrat' partly responsible for the revolution. Weber tried to disabuse him of this (and, if we think of his public speeches around that time, the report seems credible):

Weber: Do you think that I regard the unholy mess (*Schweinerei*) that we now have as democracy?
Ludendorff: What is your idea of democracy, then?
Weber: In a democracy the people choose a leader whom they trust. Then the chosen man says, 'Now shut your mouths and obey me.' The people and the parties are no longer free to interfere in the leader's business.
Ludendorff: I could like such a 'democracy'.

Indeed he could! In 1933 Eduard Baumgarten would invoke Weber's words to justify to Marianne his turn to National Socialism and to identify the hand of God in Adolf Hitler;[224] and Michels would cite them as proof that Weber's concept of democracy had 'fascistic overtones'.[225]

Weber continued, however: 'Later the people can sit in judgement. If the leader has made mistakes – to the gallows with him!' Genuinely charismatic leadership involves a willingness to die. Ludendorff had been a leader and had made mistakes with appalling consequences. But he did not want to become a martyr; he was unwilling even to lose his freedom – he was scarcely at risk of being executed by the victorious powers – but just wanted to live in peace and enjoy his fat pension. Weber must have thought that he lacked any sense of the attractions of self-sacrifice, or of the embarrassment this would have caused among the victors. When the chips were down, he proved to be a commonplace sort of person – no trace of charisma.

Weber, for so long the pathological one, presumably enjoyed the part of urging heroic manhood on this army commander – a man whose crisis of nerves had, in his view, turned into a national catastrophe. Not long before, he had still praised Ludendorff as an 'outstanding strategic genius' (MWG I/16, 417), but also publicly called him a 'bloody dictator' who had 'carried on a criminal game with our nation' and belonged 'behind bars with all his accomplices' (I/16, 455). Now he could feel nothing but contempt for him. Ludendorff, for his part, wrote to Eduard Baumgarten in 1921 that Weber had 'several times been reported to him as a traitor to the fatherland' and that he wanted to have nothing to do with him (I/16, 546n.). To the nephew who met Ludendorff in January 1922 to discover his version of the conversation with Weber, the defeated commander sounded 'as nice and gentle as a . . . wounded animal carrying death within itself'. He thought Weber could have got through to him if he had been less brusque and treated him with greater sensitivity.[226] What Weber failed to achieve, Hitler won in 1923 with his march on the army commanders' hall in Munich: that Ludendorff should assume the risk of martyrdom.

Longing for death and fear of death

If Weber had been in Ludendorff's place, he would probably have found it very attractive to hand himself over to the victors and to pass into the nation's memory as a martyr. The aged dignity of the patriarch, who dies surrounded by his children and grandchildren, was anyway denied to him. In 1915 he wrote to Mina Tobler's sister-in-law, whose husband had died at the age of thirty-eight: 'When I was young, I longed for nothing more than to die at the height of my manly powers, before frailty and disease had marred my image of life.'[227] In his years of depression, the longing for death must often have been intense. His letter of condolences on the death of Otto Benecke (WB 247) – one of the most tender that have come down to us – shows between the lines how much his own thoughts must sometimes have circled around suicide, even if they never seem to have settled on a definite plan.

In 1915 he pondered quite soberly why he had not taken his life during the years of torment. He does not suggest that it was consideration for Marianne and Helene that held him back. 'What was decisive, I think, was that inwardly I was still so incoherent and unprepared, so much a seeker at odds with himself, who had not yet reached completion.'[228] In 1920, however, he may have felt that he had closed the circle of his life and arrived at a kind of completion: he had come to terms with his period of illness, which now had a higher meaning as a purgatory followed by a major phase of creativity; *The Protestant Ethic* had acquired a framework that took in the whole world; the 'spiritualist' approach to interpretations of the world had been buried; and he, Max Weber, had experienced the great love of his life, after which there could be no further intensification.

Having read Weber's last letters, Jaspers later noted: 'In the years of severe illness he had never pressed towards death, but now a longing for death entered his thoughts.'[229] In the summer of 1919, after the peace settlement at Versailles seemed to have realized Weber's worst forebodings of a 'polar night of icy darkness and hardness' (FMW 128), he dreamed of 'going further and further out into a southern blue sea'. 'But I would never do that to Marianne', he added.[230] A pleasurable vision of self-dissolution, which recalls the end of *Tristan und Isolde*: '*In dem wogenden Schwall, in dem tönenden Schall . . . ertrinken, versinken – unbewußt – höchste Lust!*' (In the heaving swell, in the resounding echoes, in the universal stream of the world-breath – to drown, to founder – unconscious – utmost rapture!).[231]

Marianne Weber suggests at the end of her biography that, at many moments in the last period of his life, Weber had a longing for death and felt that his time had come. 'Wonderful if one experiences a rise once more and then goes on', he said 'mysteriously' after his sister's suicide (WB 687); once he had the feeling that 'a cold hand had touched' him (WB 690). When his illness grew worse, he tried to keep his humour. 'He did not resist the dark force' (WB 698).

Weber had always been in his element when writing letters of condolence. Although he usually spurned the still thriving art of fine letter-writing, he showed on such occasions that he could be a virtuoso at it when he wanted. Perhaps the most enchanting speech we know of his is the one he gave at the graveside of constitutional theorist Georg Jellinek, who died in 1911 at the age of sixty. For Weber it was 'a quick, beautiful and dignified death', which came 'at the proper time, before sickness or old age could cloud his wife's image of the sweetheart of her youth' (WB 478). As ever he was ready to find meaning in an early death. When his brother Karl fell in action at the age of forty-five, even before he had married his fiancée, he consoled their mother by saying that doctors thought Karl anyway 'had not had a long period of mental vigour left'; that 'he would have been afflicted with premature ageing' and found it unbearable[232] – as if Weber believed in a wise Fate.

When Else asked him after Lili's suicide 'if he had ever lived through a death', he replied: 'No, oddly enough, not yet.' For a 56-year-old man who had served in a military hospital for a year during the world war, the only explanation is that he deliberately avoided witnessing the moment of death. Beneath the surface there must have been a fear of death inside him; he did not really have the warrior nature he would have liked. Else came back with a quick-witted repartee: 'Not death, nor birth, nor the War, nor power – as if Fate had drawn a veil between him and the reality of things – was that perhaps his star?' And Weber whispered: 'Yes, that's the way it is.'[233] He could play the role of great revealer with such energy because he also knew how to place a veil between himself and reality and to consider it as his fate.

When the anthropologist Margaret Mead lay dying, it is said, and the nurse tried to comfort her: 'There, there, dear, we all have to die sometime', she snapped back in a last show of vigour: 'Yes! But this is different!'[234] Countless people must have had the same experience: to speak of someone else's death or even of death *in abstracto* is quite different from being on the point of death oneself. Max Weber was not spared this either: dying was harder than he had imagined, harder too than he had thought at the beginning of his illness, when he had occasionally been 'in a euphoric state' (WB 697) and had displayed a Stoic resignation to those who still wanted to do something: 'Oh, children, do not bother any more; it won't do any good anyway' (WB 698). Then came the torments, with a 'terrible agitation of the body and the mind' (LE 169). Karl Loewenstein, probably the last person to see him alive, described his death as a 'titanic struggle'.[235] It seems that the demons were still there. 'They're really torturing you!' his wife called out. 'Yes, a crime, a crime', he groaned. 'What horror! Horror! Horror!'[236] Had he for a time believed in a higher justice that was favourably inclined towards him? Did he feel it had shamefully let him down?

On 4 June 1920, the day after the feast of Corpus Christi, students learned from a notice that Weber had had to cancel his lecture because of a cold (B 677, WB 697). Ten days later he was dead: the cold turned into flu and then into a lung infection; his heart gave out. At that time influenza was much

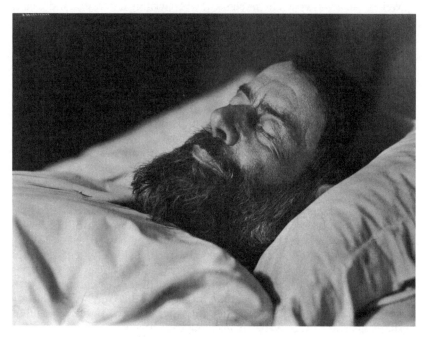

Figure 18.5 Max Weber on his death bed

more of an alarm signal than it is today, as there were no antibiotics and in 1918–19 'Spanish flu' had claimed more than 25 million lives around the world; if the great epidemic has not gone down in history, it is only because it raged in the shadow of the world war, although more people died of it than at all the war fronts together. Karl Loewenstein and Robert Michels thought that Max Weber too was a victim of it;[237] perhaps they were right.[238]

A man such as Weber would have had access to the best medical expertise, although it is curious that there is no mention of this. Marianne was oddly unperturbed during the first few days of his illness; only Else became agitated and, as Alfred put it, repeatedly 'set' a doctor on to the Webers, but at first he diagnosed only a mild and unimportant depression of the lungs.[239] After Max Weber's death, she made no secret to Alfred of her belief that Max would have survived if he had received better treatment. Her son's 'over-cautious' doctor told her that 'no one had ever died of flu under him and that a flu with lung infection could also be dealt with'.[240] The medical faculty in Munich also thought an explanation was required for his death,[241] and the resulting autopsy found: 'The spleen is 1½ times enlarged, soft, affected by inflammation. Bleeding is visible in its upper pole. . . . The liver is slightly enlarged. . . . The stomach displays major self-digestion of its mucous membrane.'[242]

In 1920 death at fifty-six was by no means as uncommon as it is today, even in a man who had dealings with the eminent medical authorities of his day. Lamprecht, Naumann, Simmel and Troeltsch did not live any longer. Many were worn out before their time by poor nourishment and psychological upheavals during the war, and it would appear that in Germany post-defeat depression often triggered an ageing process. Was that also true of Max Weber? Yet this was the springtime of his love and of a euphoria he had never experienced before.

Towards the end, Max Weber must have felt that the euphoria – in his intellectual work as well as his love life – would not last but give way to steep decline and crisis. Some time before he fell ill, he already reported a nervous 'cardiac spasm': 'The machine wouldn't work any more.' For a time a depression came over him (WB 687). And, soon after he began his teaching activity in Munich, he felt weary and lost his appetite for work (WB 664); it is hard to believe when we think of the veritable explosion of intellectual productivity. Probably he was deeply disheartened that his charisma did not support everyday life in the university; as always, routinization spelled the death of charisma. His strengths were in intellectual fireworks, volcanic eruptions, not in weekly lectures systematically making their way through the material. Max Horkheimer later recalled a lecture by Weber on the soviet system: 'The auditorium was full to bursting-point, and there came a complete disappointment.' No message, no political pointers, only ideal types and definitions – 'so that we went home feeling quite gloomy'.[243]

In Vienna, it is true, Weber had been 'the sensation of the university': 'everyone had to have seen and heard him at least once'. But for many a brief impression was enough, so that there was a constant coming and going in the great lecture hall – a 'cruel game' (Theodor Heuss) that tormented him and gave him a sense of futility ('you cannot bellow the word asceticism in a room like that').[244] As a scholar, Weber could project himself best in a small circle. At first his lectures were overcrowded, but the hall soon became emptier (WzG 34). He complained that 'this lecture gossip . . . is never intellectually satisfying'. He used to start in good spirits, but then – as Marianne wrote to Jaspers – there followed 'again and again an onset of despair; it seemed horrible to have to keep chattering, moreover about things that one no longer really mastered and found immeasurably boring!' He complained so much that Marianne could scarcely 'endure' these 'fits' any more.[245]

After Lili's suicide, the Webers decided to take into their home her four orphaned children, aged between nine and seventeen; Marianne would eventually adopt them in 1928. It seemed to Weber 'as though Marianne's becoming a mother was the crowning of her woman's life, its real fulfilment, a fulfilment hitherto denied her'; but 'of course' Marianne 'would not hear of that' (WB 687). Max, who had never really been able to get on with children, did not feel a match for the unfamiliar paternal role, especially as Lili's offspring had developed into 'little pests'.[246] He would have preferred it if

Marianne had stayed with them in Heidelberg or moved closer to the progressive Odenwald School on the Bergstrasse and sent them there.[247] Then he would have had both wife and children at a distance and been alone with Else in Munich. But he did not want to order it; Marianne had to decide herself, and she rejected the suggestion, probably all too well aware of why her husband liked the idea of a spatial separation. Outwardly she reacted with a sense of humour to the 'rum idea' and passed the buck back to Max for a decision. 'You silly boy. Only you can part me from you – and then only if I feel that the grace still to make you happy in some way has deserted me. Then (perhaps!) I would find the pride and strength to part with you' (B 635).

Max Weber would probably have liked to be entirely together with Else, but he knew that she was not a woman to be pushed into anything and that such a decision had to be left up to her; it looks as if she did not think of moving in with him – after all, she kept a spatial distance from Alfred for more than fifty years and decided when he should visit her. She called Max the 'man of beautiful moments', giving to understand that he was not the man 'for keeps', the man for day-to-day life. In her eyes, he was the man who 'wants to clasp all dreams to his breast'. But did he also want the real Else, this often very sober woman, who liked it best when love too went via the mind? True, she teasingly called Alfred a 'stubborn bear' when he made things 'complicated' because of her relationship with Max,[248] but the correspondence between the two remained intense during this period and does not give the impression that she wanted to separate from him – why should she have? In late February 1920 she complained to Alfred that being with Max had been 'stifling'. Max Weber had probably known for a long time that Else, unlike the patiently admiring Mina (and even unlike Marianne), really had no wish to hold out with him through his dark and irritable states.[249] And since the spring of 1920 he must have reckoned that another dark period lay ahead. In 1967 Karl Jaspers, then eighty-four years of age, wrote to the 93-year-old Else that he thought he could detect a 'biologically' determined manic-depressive predisposition in Weber, although he was not quite certain of his diagnosis:

> When I saw him for the last time, in the March before he died, he was in an almost ecstatic state, with an incredible energy for work. It must have been something like that before his illness . . . Then came the breakdown. Probably there would soon have been another one (psychiatrists speak of phases of hypomania and depression or suchlike generalizations; they certainly hit on something, a biological process that is inescapable).[250]

Weber dying, with Else and Marianne at his bedside: a scene which, against this background, has something uncanny! At least subconsciously all three feel that the death solves at a stroke all the tormenting problems; a silent agreement among all three may have prevailed beneath the surface. Most likely Else is still angry at the deficient medical care, but she holds herself back. On the day before Weber's death, it would seem, she wrote that there was still 'hope' at certain moments. 'But something inside me simply says: so, go forth in beauty, you great soul.'[251]

By now Else thought she was at least as much inside Weber's work as Marianne;[252] she was also ahead of Weber's wife by virtue of her academic formation and doctoral qualification. Perhaps in many respects she would not have been averse to becoming his literary executor. To Marianne it must have seemed that Max's death was coming at the last moment when she still appeared in the eyes of the world as his uncontested life's companion and sole executor. This is one factor that would explain the euphoria that initially came over her when he died; and the thought of what had gone unfulfilled in their marriage may have made the leaden grief that subsequently seized her all the more bitter. Yet Marianne stuck with Else for the rest of her life and even died in her arms, in 1954 – a love between women in many respects more curious and affecting than Max's affairs, and perhaps especially close because of the undercurrents of bitterness that it had to overcome.

Through the fire back to the cycle of nature

The urn containing Weber's ashes was placed in the hillside cemetery in Heidelberg, where the gravestones still today remind strollers of the academic world of his time.[253] Cremation was not yet a common practice, accounting for only 1 per cent of funerals in Germany around 1920;[254] it met with stern disapproval in ecclesiastical circles and was actually forbidden by the Catholic church. The whole issue had stirred people's spirits for decades: a bibliography that appeared in 1913, for example, contained 1,200 titles on cremation.[255] Many of its advocates argued pseudo-scientifically that cremation served to enrich the carbon dioxide content in the atmosphere and thereby promote the growth of vegetation – a curious idea if we bear in mind the frequent complaints about smoke levels in the cities.

With its precedents in antiquity and old Germanic customs, the incineration of corpses had a noble aspect for those who cultivated a historical awareness and wished to demonstrate their lack of prejudices. On 5 June 1904 the Eranos circle held a discussion on 'cremation and burial among ancient peoples'. For Oswald Spengler cremation actually marked the beginning of classical antiquity. Above all, however, the practice typically signalled a belief in free-thinking and philosophical monism, in the oneness of man and nature. Ludwig Büchner, in his new bible of materialism *Kraft und Stoff*, made fun of his many contemporaries who preferred to let their 'wretched corpses slowly rot underground in pathetic wooden caskets', rather than 'copy the beautiful and sublime example of antiquity and, with the help of purifying fire, directly return to the whole of nature that which it (humanity) received from it and cannot keep from it for long'.[256] Through fire, the body returns more quickly to the cosmos of nature than it would with the help of worms. There is no confirmation that Max Weber actually expressed a wish to be cremated; the matter is not mentioned in the will drawn up by Max and Marianne on 26 March 1918. In June 1915, however, he said to Mina Tobler that 'old people should be buried, young people cremated'. Mina herself favoured cremation.[257] Presumably Marianne had also heard such views from her husband. In keeping with the ancient ideal, he died not in old age but in the prime of life, so like Marianne we have reason to believe that he would have approved of that manner of self-dissolution.

19

Epilogue: Powerplay and the Wrangling over Max Weber's Spirit

'Should I fit the image that you once had of me?'

Weber's worldwide impact, which began only decades after his death, is not the subject of this book: it is a never-ending story, which includes scenes everywhere from New York to Tokyo and has new chapters added every decade. But it has little to do with Weber's life, and much more with the rise of the social sciences in the twentieth century and the general course of world history – with the Cold War, the new left and the global triumph of Western civilization, but also with the revival of religious fundamentalism.

The last act in this book, however, takes place in the small circle of people who knew that Weber's creative process sprang not only from the development of a theoretical system but at least as much from his experience of life – his experience of the world and of himself. Within the vast reception history, the subplot most concerned with Weber himself is the wrangling over his spirit between his two main direct successors: Karl Jaspers and Eduard Baumgarten. On 17 July 1920, a month after Weber's death, Jaspers gave a speech at a memorial meeting organized by Heidelberg students, which became a trailblazer for the Weber cult; it was then that a relationship of trust began to develop between him and Marianne. It is likely that he advised Marianne on the parts of her *Lebensbild* relating to Weber's scholarly work.[1] For many years after Weber's death, Marianne supported her distant cousin Eduard Baumgarten as an adopted son, until he finally rebelled against her mothering and heaped bitter reproaches on her. He had appeared to her as 'exceptionally mature' so long as he 'swore to and "corroborated" every word of Max Weber's', but once he stopped playing along with this worship of the dead she applied to him only 'mistrustful categories' such as 'Romantic', 'dreamer' or 'subjectivist'. Heidelberg thus became the 'most hateful city' for him. He even thought that he understood 'Uncle Max' better than she did in her 'Philistine' way.[2]

Baumgarten's relationship with Max Weber had elements of love–hate. From the beginning he had a burning curiosity about him, especially about his sexuality: when he sat a whole night at the wake, he could not stop

Figure 19.1 Marianne Weber in the mid-1920s

himself uncovering the body to see him naked.[3] In the long run love and fascination prevailed over other feelings, and he and Marianne became reconciled; he even inherited most of Weber's literary estate, and Marianne probably intended that he should write the great biography of Max Weber – a task with which he struggled in vain for the rest of his life. Both Baumgarten and Jaspers had intimate knowledge of the connection between Weber's life and work, and both never stopped thinking about it, even if the results were diverse and changing.

From 1920 until the early 1960s, Karl Jaspers was the main herald in Germany of Weber's approaching international fame.[4] After 1945 he was highly regarded abroad as an opponent of the Nazi regime, and a common admiration for Weber linked him early on to the new president of the Federal Republic, Theodor Heuss. Later he became West Germany's 'angry old man', including for readers of *Der Spiegel*, and also made a name for himself among the generation of '68. For a long time, until Baumgarten shocked him with the love letters to Else, he probably thought of Weber as a kindred soul, although he confessed to lacking 'the heroic trait, the grandeur in excess, that [he] liked in Max Weber'.[5]

Jaspers presented Weber as an existentialist philosopher who had only inadvertently been caught up with the neo-Kantians – a man such as he was himself, or would have liked to become after Weber's death. In the 1920s in Heidelberg (where he held a professorship from 1921 on), Jaspers had to compete for Weber's philosophical legacy with Heinrich Rickert, head of the neo-Kantians and reputedly Weber's mentor in philosophy, who found it ridiculous that Jaspers should want to make of Weber a philosopher and cult figure;[6] all the greater pleasure did it give him to undermine the developing myth with spicy anecdotes. Like Baumgarten, Rickert conjured up the living Weber against Jaspers's cult of the dead.[7] Rickert detected a kind of 'naturalistic biologism' in Jaspers, who for his part felt slighted by Rickert's attitude to him as a philosopher and interpreter of Weber. The two eventually fell out over the issue of whether Weber had actually been a philosopher or not.[8]

For Jaspers, a declared enemy of Sigmund Freud,[9] sexuality was a power that threatened human values. Ludwig Binswanger, also a psychiatrist and philosopher, thought that Jaspers was 'almost blind to things sexual', and, although Jaspers liked to emphasize Weber's 'manliness', his image of it was indeed for a very long time a-sexual. In old age, however, when he showed a picture of Freud to his biographer Hans Saner, he asked: 'Do you know who he resembles? Max Weber! He is a person, and therefore an enemy, you have to get involved with.'[10]

Jaspers was convinced that the source of Weber's thought was not Kant's critique of knowledge but, on the one hand, belief in the existence of a truth that could be, if not known, then experienced, and, on the other hand, an existential experience that opened his eyes to the abyss: to a life on the brink of despair. Jaspers himself suffered from 'nerves' and often felt on the verge of a breakdown, and from what we know today he was on to something when he partly recognized the interaction between Weber's creativity and his experience of life. In his *Psychologie der Weltanschauungen* (1919), written under Weber's influence, he describes 'three types of human existence': the 'chaotic', the 'consistent' and the 'demonic'. He spends ten times longer on the third of these than on the other two together, and although he never mentions Weber by name there can scarcely be any doubt that he had him in mind. In the 'demonic individual', 'the life process burns most intensely'; antinomies in this way found a synthesis that appeared outwardly mysterious. 'Wherever the demonic spirit appears in the world, it becomes actual in *fragments*. . . . This fragmentariness grows more intense through a tempestuous rushing from one experiment to another, from each work to the next: scarcely has one been worked out than another becomes important.'[11]

Eduard Baumgarten, fifteen years younger than Jaspers, knew Weber even more closely. In a letter to Karl Mannheim on 30 December 1932, he exploded at the celebratory tone in which Jaspers had spoken in his recently published book on Weber:

[T]here are a lot of recollections and accurate descriptions that are all fine and good, but in general the image of the man himself, who loved reality in a pagan and, if necessary, grumbling sort of way, comes under disruptive pressure from a piously apologetic-metaphysical

Figure 19.2 Eduard Baumgarten

interpretation, which does not shrink from exploiting impatience and 'mistakes' rooted in Weber's hopelessly irritable nature and turning them into so many symptoms of an unhappy *age*. . . . As I knew him, he would, with a friendly laugh on his huge face, have passed back the wistfully indirect idealizations of today's philosopher, all the more as he had had a liking for Jaspers the psychiatrist and psychologist.[12]

For many who knew Weber from afar, he had the reputation of being completely without humour – an image that continues to stick to him. The sociologist Stanislav Andreski is amazed by this, because he thinks there is a link between 'a sense of humour' and 'the ability to appraise social situations realistically'.[13] But in reality Weber did have a sense of humour, though not in every period of his life. He showed a strong sense for the irony of history when he described how the sharpest rejection of worldly goods leads to their most successful accumulation. When Eduard Baumgarten reminded Marianne of the laugh on Weber's face,[14] he was taking the words out of her mouth: she had already spoken of Weber's 'inexhaustible humour' in her obituary notice.[15] And in 1932 he was pulling his aunt's leg when he said: 'I did see Uncle Max laugh for a moment, when you said in public that you didn't care two hoots about Goethe.'[16] Of course he knew that in the Weber household 'Goethe' – especially in connection with a value-judgement – had been a codeword for free love.

Eduard Baumgarten, thirty-four years younger than Max Weber, hesitated for a long time whether he wanted to build his own identity for or against him, but after 1945, when Weber's popularity suddenly shot up,[17] there was everything to be said for going *with* him. He had a grudge that in 1916 his uncle had wanted to send him galloping off to the front to present an ideal target for the enemy ('Uncle Max wanted to get me shot'), but he used this same militant Weber when he sought to justify his conversion to National Socialism. In his book on Benjamin Franklin he laughed at how Max Weber had tried to present this hedonistic free spirit as an ascetic Puritan, but then he made it his greatest ambition to show that, rightly understood, Max Weber was in many respects close to the Franklin tradition of life-affirming pragmatism.

Eduard Baumgarten's career in the 1930s was not without dramatic interludes and sheds light on contradictory aspects of academic life in the Nazi period. In 1933, when he was in line for an appointment as lecturer in Göttingen, he applied to join the Nazi association of university teachers. But none other than Heidegger, the Third Reich's new philosophical star who had earlier been friendly with Baumgarten, put a spanner in the works by describing him in a letter to the association as a 'phoney'; he was 'everything but a National Socialist' and had 'become closely tied with a Jew'; he came 'from that liberal-democratic circle of intellectuals gathered around Max Weber'.[18] This base denunciation was a major reason for Heidegger's removal from academic service after 1945. It also helped to rehabilitate Baumgarten, although, notwithstanding his overt sympathy for American pragmatism, he blithely cultivated his own network of Nazi contacts, especially the cultural philosopher Alfred Baeumler. (Baeumler, though an enthusiastic supporter of Bachofen's theory of matriarchy, was commissioned by Alfred Rosenberg to provide a philosophy for National Socialism, and it was through his intervention that Baumgarten made it to Kant's chair of philosophy in Königsberg, despite being regarded with hostility by the leader of the Nazi university teachers' association.)

Baumgarten's subsequent history remained full of suspense and introduced a number of naturalistic elements into the construction of Weber's thinking. As professor of philosophy in Königsberg, he became the patron and friend of biologist Konrad Lorenz (1903–1989), the best-known behavioural scientist of the postwar period, who explained human behaviour by analogy with that of animals and in the same way made animal behaviour 'humanly' understandable. For admirers of this researcher, who liked to live among his grey geese, he was the 'Einstein of the animal soul'. In 1940, after years in which Lorenz had struggled even to obtain food for his research with animals, Baumgarten managed to get him a professorial appointment in Königsberg, with the aim of establishing a link between philosophy and behavioural psychology. A lively intellectual exchange developed between the two men and led to a lifelong friendship.[19] One of Lorenz's theories – that 'man's so-called spinal shiver of excitement' derives from the threatening display of the chimpanzee with ruffled fur[20] – opened Baumgarten's eyes to the animal basis of 'charismatic enthusiasm'; the lead wolf became for him the ideal type of charismatic leader.[21]

However, this sociobiology could not make any headway with Weber. Lorenz, who believed he was discovering a whole host of animal-human instincts, tried to make thought itself a mere extension of instinctual behaviour. But how could Baumgarten interpret Weber's thought along such lines? For Lorenz, both man and his animal relatives were gregarious creatures, whose instincts served the survival of the species rather than the individual – a concept of evolution which, though able to impose itself in the era of world wars, fascism and communism, was dropped (to Lorenz's annoyance) by a later generation of sociobiologists, on the grounds that it was incompatible with much of the evidence.[22] If, as Löwith established, only the individual was 'truly real' for Weber,[23] this meant that there was a gulf between his approach and the evolutionary biology of his day, whereas from today's point of view Weber's way of thinking was more 'naturalistic' than that of contemporaries who saw individuals merely as members of imaginary social organisms. In Weber's day, and still in Baumgarten's, there was not yet a sociobiology that could provide a bridge to an anthropology compatible with Weber.

After the end of the Second World War, Alfred Weber treated Baumgarten as a 'Nazi criminal' and closed the door on him when he tried to take refuge in his native Heidelberg and (as once before with Marianne) to use his association with Max Weber to justify his membership of the Nazi party. Like Alfred Weber, Jaspers was then one of the few prominent anti-Nazis in Heidelberg, and his voice carried weight in the de-Nazification procedures applied to the academic world. In 1946 Jaspers attracted considerable attention with a text on Germany's guilt for the crimes of National Socialism. This brought back to Baumgarten the rage that Weber had felt over admisssions of German guilt after 1918. It was true, he wrote to Marianne Weber, that Jaspers wrote 'as if he were guided by the scientific ethos and the political ethos of Max Weber', yet his text had not at all been written in the spirit of Weber. And he ridiculed Jaspers's 'hangers-on', who had formerly paid homage to Hitler and now mechanically recited 'the rosary of "Max Weber – Karl Jaspers, Karl Jaspers – Max Weber" in a loud and weepy voice'. Probably his remarks were indirectly aimed at Marianne too, whose 'heroic and moral image of Weber' he had never been able to stomach.[24]

In Baumgarten's notes for lectures during this period, we come across a heading 'Theory of "human nature"'. He begins with Hegel ('Man is spirit'); then come Feuerbach, Marx and Nietzsche; but at the centre stands Max Weber, who brought 'human nature back down to size'. His 'nature of man' remains 'at the level of what Feuerbach introduced into anthropology'. 'However, it is not a psychology of the senses but the dual (?) phenomenology of *homo faber*: man's social casing and structures, *reflected* in the actual conduct of subjects who *are active* within and through those structures.' At another point he notes:

In relation to the achievements of science . . ., Max Weber had the attitude of a scientific experimenter who, in the passionate zeal of discovery, marvels at it all and describes with pleasure what appears in the course of analysis. However, he does not apprehend this within a system of truths that he posits as absolute, but allows to that which appears its open and fluid character as a phenomenon. . . . Max Weber's passion for experiment was remote from any absolutist or cynical dogmatism in methodology . . . (When by nature he nevertheless felt drawn to it, he kept it remote.) But those who saw him in his mature years had the impression that the spirit of Laplace was walking the earth, since it seemed that those imperious and authoritative eyes knew *everything* and surveyed *everything*.[25]

As an experimenter, Weber was for Baumgarten the epitome of natural man: 'From a biological point of view, we may regard man as the creature who lives essentially by experimentation', beginning already as a little child.[26]

If Baumgarten identified with Weber, he liked to think that he was as full of *joie de vivre* as himself, just as Jaspers liked to think that Weber shared his own ascetic nature. Yet the nephew knew Weber's darker side only too well. In his lectures on Weber in 1948–9 he appears to have paid scant attention to the *Zwischenbetrachtung*. But in 1957, when he again vainly sought a reconciliation with Alfred Weber in Heidelberg and then started to leave in rage, Else appeared from the flat next door having probably overheard everything. 'But what is there really between us? Why didn't you write any more for such a long time?' – (Baumgarten) 'Because I thought you were partly to blame for Max Weber's death.' From what he had observed of Weber 'when he was ill and dying', it seemed that the feeling of being pulled between marriage and love had 'added a hidden wish for death' to the lung infection. Until then, presumably, he had thought of Weber as so rigid in his personal morals that his love for Else must have caused him more torment than pleasure. And he may well have believed that Else did more to increase the torment than to relieve it.

In reply, Else gave him Weber's last letter to her and then gradually other love letters; she continued to tell him of this final love right up to her own death.[27] At this point Baumgarten's draft memoirs come to an end: a sign that the revelation of a new Weber also meant the beginning of a new phase in his life. Six years later, in February 1963, 'the sly and mischievous Eduard Baumgarten' (Manfred Schön)[28] could not stop himself shocking the eighty-year-old Jaspers with a selection from these letters, probably in the knowledge that it would cause a whole world to crumble for him.[29] And indeed he did not know (or had not wanted to know, even with his psychiatrically trained eye) the Weber that he encountered in these love letters, revelling in dreams of spring amid Germany's agony, heedlessly confusing Ought and Is, feigning blindness over the need to choose between marriage and eroticism – and, on top of everything, not a commanding mind but one

that wallowed in the sensuality of submission. 'Betrayal!' was his spontaneous reaction. 'Max Weber committed a betrayal – of Marianne, of
himself, of all of us who saw how he appeared.'[30] As Marianne seems never
to have spoken to him of the affair, he wrongly thought that she had been
in the dark about it.

Subsequently, whether through Else Jaffé or Eduard Baumgarten,
Jaspers learned something else. In 1966 he wrote to Hannah Arendt, again
half-reconciled with Weber: 'He was truly serious about unlimited
honesty. . . . [He didn't] allow himself any secret cheating but live[d] passionately, struggle[d] with himself, and [had] no goal.'[31] And yet Weber's
love letters to Else haunted him for the rest of his life, even in his dreams.
He recognized that what they contained was not just a brief adventure but
something that made it necessary to form a new picture of the man. 'It was
not an ill-starred moment', the shaken Jaspers groaned, 'but a long period
of time – a confusing self-betrayal, a spectacular dance into nihilism under
the spell of magic.' All this was possible because in Else he encountered 'not
a common harlot' but 'a hetaera of the highest, mind-lulling art – beyond
good and evil – yet still a hetaera in her uninhibited nature: kindly when it
pleases her . . . tough deep down and permitting any disaster', experienced
in anything 'from the quite simple performance of intercourse' to the 'artful
beauty of mature erotic play'.[32] Jaspers too felt Else's magic, and on her seventieth birthday in 1944, with the war still on, he admitted in an unusually
effusive tone that she embodied for him the 'glamour of a Heidelberg that
has vanished for ever'; 'its wide-open understanding, its spiritually vibrant
heart' lived on in her, 'to the joy of us all'.[33]

It is not surprising that he could not get Weber's love letters to this woman
out of his mind. He copied long extracts for himself, tried to take Weber at
his word even in his love-drunk reverie, and analysed the philosophy contained in many of the letters. And again he worked himself up into a rage,
issuing mental reprimands to Weber in the familiar *du* form (which would
have been unthinkable during his lifetime). The reproaches come in points,
'first, second, third'. It was intellectually dishonest of him to play 'Abelard
and Heloise' in a letter to Else: when Abelard wrote his famous letters, he
was already castrated and had dedicated himself to celestial love. In his
'ecstasy' Weber adorned himself 'with false feathers': he 'spoke with clichés
in his passion. The botched solemnity, the painfully embarrassing emotionalism': Jaspers is angry with Weber for precisely the things that Baumgarten
could not stand in himself. He knew that, if Weber had been alive, he would
not have put up with such rebukes. 'Why should I conform to the image you
have made of me? he might have replied. I am free and do what I wish, draw
the consequences and endure them. I don't lie.' But that did not wash for
Jaspers: 'You forgot that lying . . . is associated with this kind of eroticism.
You couldn't rescue the truth by stepping into "the realm of Tristan".'[34]
Still, he feels that Weber has punished him for saying this. He keeps appearing to him in a dream: he either won't speak to Jaspers or never invites him
over to his house. Jaspers wakes filled with sadness and 'greatly agitated'.[35]

A long time before, apparently under the influence of his lectures on Weber in autumn 1928, Else had expressed doubts to Jaspers about his image of Weber, adding some gentle hints that he had not wished to understand: 'So, is the Max who recognized a "daytime God" and sought out what he called the Luciferian realm of the night, is this divided Max really the Max Weber that Jaspers sees? The Max who speaks of the fact that people serve various gods, who even had different, *completely* separate spheres in his own life!' To be sure, she gave the impression that the 'Luciferian realm of the night' was only the realm of the dead, not that of Eros; 'oh, how many, many times' had she reproached Max for going into the 'shadowy kingdom' and leaving her life behind in pieces.[36] In the end Jaspers had to revoke the image he had had of Weber nearly all his life: '[Weber's] rational figure displays general honesty, inner turmoil, struggles, but not unity . . . For a long time I supposed as a matter of course that (it) was effectively present. That supposition is clearly not correct.'[37]

In May 1967 the 84-year-old Jaspers wrote once again to Else, then aged ninety-three. This time it was a long and calm letter. He even liked Baumgarten's occasionally indiscreet, dreadfully unstructured documentation on Weber: 'His enthusiasm for the unique great man has something touching.' And he continues:

When I think of Max Weber, there is no end to the characterizing of him. I ask, for example, what happens with a man for whom truth stands above everything. Max Weber faced the realities without reservation, in the same uncompromising way as Kierkegaard and Nietzsche; not like those eternal adolescents, however, but as a man who allowed himself to be torn apart. The science in which he performed such exceptional service was basically unimportant to him. He was not able to say why he devoted himself to it, what meaning it had for him. . . . He introduced the *Zwischenbetrachtung*, the 'intermediate reflection' on possible conflicts of meaning, as merely one way among others of looking at things. It is, I think, much more: a key piece in his philosophical thinking. It was uncanny how his answer failed to materialize at decisive points. The more I read his work and keep noting that I do not know it well enough, and everything that lies behind it, the more I think of it as a titanic effort reaching into the void.[38]

At the end of his life, Jaspers had to recognize that he had lost his Weberian superego and that Weber had been identical neither with himself nor with his wishful imaginings. 'Max Weber was too great and too terrifying in the force of his intellect for me to have been able to love him', he wrote in 1967 to the woman who, he knew, had loved Weber. And to Hannah Arendt he wrote of his conviction that 'the abyss of his despair was of a kind that made me sense he was charged with something I was not charged with; there was an explosive force in him that I lack.'[39] What the philosopher does not say is that Weber had not only a despair but also a pleasure that remained alien to him. To Else, however, he wrote: 'When self-deceptions appear in me, Max Weber stands there and tells me to keep away from them. He is a salutary companion in our life.'

Really only salutary? In one of Jaspers's imaginary dialogues, the dead Weber – without reciprocating his use of the *du* form – replies to the philosopher's new diagnosis that the profound inner turmoil following his illness was the basic factor:

> 'Your judgement is correct. It is my own. You cannot tell me anything that I have not said even more sharply to myself. But I would ask you to keep silent. If it became known, it would have disastrous public consequences in the world as it is, as well as for people who are infinitely precious to me. Such consequences are completely unnecessary.' He would further say: 'There are things that cannot be resolved. They must be taken up and lived through. I am becoming a criminal and cannot change it without surrendering something that has been given to me for the fulfilment of my existence. . . . If you . . . expose me when I ask for silence, and if we do not come to an understanding . . ., we shall become mortal enemies. . . . If you speak out, I shall challenge you to a duel with heavy sabres.' And he would further say: 'Only one person has the right to speak for me – the one with whom I have broken trust in a sense, but not in total. That you should be quiet until this single person learns of it, is a human demand – for time – which you will fulfil. This time is limited. For I shall reach with her the place where we belong together. Then the time will come when you have the freedom to speak.'[40]

Jaspers remained silent – and he died four years before Else, who was nine years older than he. Today everyone who was 'infinitely precious' to Max Weber has long been dead: there is no longer any reason for silence. And the truth about Weber has a certain quality of release: it destroys none of the magic of the great anti-magician.

A Chronology of Max Weber's Life

1864	21 April	Max (Maximilian) Weber born in Erfurt, the first of eight children; father: Max (Maximilian) Weber (1836–97); mother: Helene Weber, *née* Fallenstein (1844–1919).
1866		Max Weber falls ill with meningitis.
1868	30 July	Birth of Alfred Weber, Max's brother (d. 1958).
1868		The Berlin city council appoints Max Weber senior for twelve years as a paid councillor; at the same time he is elected to the Prussian parliament as a candidate of the National Liberal Party.
1869		The Weber family moves to Berlin. An academic commission set up by the Berlin council begins discussing the sewerage question.
1870	2 August	Marianne Schnitger, Weber's future wife, born in Oerlinghausen (d. 1954); her grandfather, the textile manufacturer Carl David Weber (1824–1907), is a brother of Max Weber's father.
1870		Max Weber attends the Döbbelin private school in Charlottenburg, Berlin.
1872		Max Weber senior is elected as National Liberal deputy to the Reichstag for the Coburg constituency; the Webers obtain a villa of their own in Charlottenburg, where Max attends the Empress Augusta Gymnasium. The Verein für Sozialpolitik is founded by the so-called academic socialists (*Kathedersozializten*), Gustav Schmoller, Adolf Wagner, Lujo Brentano, et al.
1873		Max Weber, senior takes charge of the Berlin building commission; the city council orders the construction of a multi-purpose sewerage system.

1874	8 October	Else von Richthofen born at Château-Salins (d. 1973).
1875		Max Weber's favourite sister, Klara, is born (d. 1953; married in 1896 Ernst Mommsen, son of the ancient historian Theodor Mommsen).
1878		Max Weber travels with his father and brother Alfred through Thuringia and on the Rhine. Bismarck's 'Anti-Socialist Law' and turn to tariff protection.
1879		The fifteen-year-old Max Weber writes an essay on 'the character, development and history of the Indo-Germanic nations'.
1880		Max's sister Lili born (suicide in 1920).
1882		Max Weber passes his *Abitur* and begins to study law (plus history, economics and philosophy) at Heidelberg; he joins the 'Alemannia' student fraternity as an associate member. Friendship with his cousin Otto Baumgarten, who is completing his last semester in theology; also becomes on close terms with Otto's father, Hermann Baumgarten (1825–93), professor of historical sciences at Strasbourg, who is married to Ida Fallenstein (1837–99), a sister of Weber's mother.
1883–4		Weber begins his one-year military service in Strasbourg, in the 2nd Infantry Regiment of Lower Saxony; relations grow deeper with the Baumgarten family.
1884		Weber continues his studies in Berlin, attending lectures by Theodor Mommsen, Heinrich von Treitschke, Otto von Gierke, Rudolf von Gneist, and others.
1885		Promoted corporal, Weber performs military practice in Strasbourg. Prepares for civil-service exam in law at Göttingen University.
1886		Completes the exam in law and continues studying in Berlin, particularly with Levin Goldschmidt and August Meitzen. Lives from now until 1893 in his parents' home in Charlottenburg. The *Ostmarkenvorlage* – a law strengthening German settlements in the provinces of Posen and West Prussia – is passed.
1887		Weber's second period of military practice in Strasbourg; promoted first lieutenant. Close relations at the time with Hermann Baumgarten's daughter Emmy (1865–1946).

1888	Third period of military practice, in Posen, where he gains an insight into the new settlement policies. Joins the Verein für Sozialpolitik.
1889	Receives doctorate *magna cum laude* for dissertation under Goldschmidt and Gneist on 'the development of the solidarity principle and the special assets of the trading companies out of the household and business communities in the Italian cities'. Works it up into a major study, 'History of the Trading Companies in the Middle Ages. Based on Southern European Sources'.
1890	Bismarck is dismissed from office; end of the 'Anti-Socialist Law'. Weber, for first time on the Reichstag electoral register (the age qualification then being twenty-five), votes conservative. Takes part in the first Evangelical Social Congress and makes contact with Paul Göhre and Friedrich Naumann. Commissioned by the Verein für Sozialpolitik to analyse and evaluate material on the eastern provinces for its planned study of agricultural workers. Also active (from 18 October) as court assessor.
1891	Weber takes part in further military exercises in Posen. Editorial work for the *Evangelische-soziale Fragen* paper founded by Otto Baumgarten. Applies without success for a post as legal adviser to the city of Bremen; finishes his *Habilitationsschrift* under Meitzen on Roman land use systems, *Die römische Agrargeschichte in ihrer Bedeutung für das Staats- und Privatrecht*.
1892	Spring: Marianne Schnitger spends a long period at the Webers' house in Charlottenburg, where her relationship with Max (until then only a relative) grows deeper. From the summer semester, in addition to his court work and his analysis of agrarian surveys for the Verein für Sozialpolitik, Weber substitutes for the ailing Goldschmidt with lectures and seminars at Berlin University. Autumn: Weber visits Emmy Baumgarten, who is being treated for nerves in a south German clinic; she still thinks of herself as his fiancée. Then a visit to her parents in Strasbourg.

| 1893 | 11 January | Marianne rejects a marriage proposal from Paul Göhre, causing an intense conflict with Helene Weber. Shortly afterwards she becomes engaged to Max Weber and on 20 September marries him in Oerlinghausen. |

On 6 July Weber is appointed regular professor in economics and finance studies at the University of Freiburg. Ministerial Director Althoff tries to reverse this in order to make Weber an extraordinary professor in commercial law at Berlin University.

Weber reports to a Verein für Sozialpolitik congress on the survey of agricultural workers, and together with Göhre is commissioned by the Evangelical Social Congress to conduct a survey of rural pastors.

Weber joins the Pan-German League (ADV) founded in 1891 and lectures on the Polish question.

1894   Further military exercises in Posen. Moves to Freiburg in the autumn. Reports on the agricultural workers' survey to the Evangelical Social Congress in Frankfurt; his opposition to large estates leads to a break with the conservatives around Adolf Stöcker.

Friedrich Naumann founds the weekly *Die Hilfe*.

| 1895 | 13 May | Weber gives his inaugural lecture in Freiburg, 'The Nation State and Economic Policy'. |
| | August–October | Max and Marianne Weber travel in England, Scotland and Ireland. |

1896   Weber succeeds Karl Knies in the chair of economics and finance studies at the University of Heidelberg. Having sharply criticized the new stock-exchange legislation, he is asked to report on it by the Bundesrat and is appointed to the commission on the grain trade.

November   Attends the conference of the National Socials in Erfurt and joins the Nationalsozialer Verein that is founded there. Takes part in the Evangelical Social Congress on 7 November. Participates in the provisional committee on the stock exchange set up by the Bundesrat.

1897   Weber is not included in the final committee on the stock exchange. He rejects an offer to stand as a parliamentary candidate in Saarbrücken,

		the stronghold of the industrialist 'King Stumm'. In the summer the Webers move to Heidelberg.
	10-11 July	At the eighth Evangelical Social Congress, Weber takes sharp issue with Karl Oldenburg's warnings of a looming industrial state.
	14 July	A fierce argument with his father, who dies on 10 August. Shortly afterwards the Webers make a trip to Spain.
1898		The Reichstag passes the first Navy Law.
	30 July	Death of Bismarck. Weber participates in a meeting for striking dockworkers organized by Naumann and Otto Baumgarten. Spring: first signs of Weber's illness; he seeks a cure at Lake Geneva. Summer: starts to become incapable of work; spends several months at a clinic near Konstanz. Another breakdown towards the end of the year.
1899		Weber is excused teaching duties and unsuccessfully requests to be discharged from academic service.
	22 April	Leaves the Pan-German League. Early summer trip across the Alps to Venice.
1900	2 July to 17 November	Treatment at a nerve clinic in Urach. The house in Heidelberg is no longer maintained.
	November	A period in Ajaccio.
	to March	Bernhard von Bülow becomes German chancellor. Georg Simmel, *Philosophy of Money*. Friedrich Naumann, *Demokratie und Kaisertum*. Sigmund Freud, *The Interpretation of Dreams*.
1901		Max Weber travels to Rome, in April–May to Naples and Sorrento, then back to Rome; spends July–September in Grindelwald and Zermatt and in March 1902 returns to Rome.
1902		Weber spends part of March and April in Florence, then returns on 20 April to Heidelberg for his thirty-eighth birthday. Slowly regains his capacity for work. Busy with problems of methodology and scientific theory; begins the 'essay of sighs' on Röscher and Knies (published in 1903–6). In December travels to the Italian Riviera (Nervi).

1903	March	Weber once more travels to Rome. In summer to Netherlands and Belgium, and in October again to Netherlands. Begins work on *The Protestant Ethic*.
	1 October	Finally released from academic service and appointed honorary professor, with a lectureship but no right to confer doctoral degrees. Naumann's National-Soziale Partei fuses with the Freisinnige Vereinigung (Liberal Union).
1904	28 February	Weber attends Eranos circle for first time; Albrecht Dieterich speaks about 'Mother Earth'.
	August	At the invitation of philosopher-psychologist Hugo Münsterberg, Weber travels to the World Academic Congress, part of the World Exhibition in St Louis, and reports on 'German agrarian problems in the past and present'. Returns to Germany in December after a trip through the USA. Assumes with Edgar Jaffé and Werner Sombart the editorship of the *Archiv für Sozialwissenschaft und Sozialpolitik*, formerly the *Archiv für soziale Gesetzgebung und Statistik*.
1905	January	Large miners' strike in the Ruhr.
	23 February	Weber reports to the Eranos circle on 'the Protestant ethic'. Part II of 'Die protestantische Ethik und der "Geist" des Kapitalismus' appears in the *Archiv für Sozialwissenschaft und Sozialpolitik*. The first Russian revolution begins with 'Bloody Sunday' in St Petersburg on 9 January. Max Weber learns Russian in order to follow events in the press.
	27 September	At the congress of the Verein für Sozialpolitik in Mannheim, Weber defends the right to strike.
	October	The tsar issues the 'Manifesto on Liberties' and grants Russia a constitution; Weber sees this as no more than 'sham constitutionalism'.
1906		Weber writes detailed analyses of developments in Russia. He attends the Mannheim congress of the SPD and notes the petty-bourgeois character of the party. The Morocco conference in Algeciras strikes many supporters of German 'world power' – not only Weber – as evidence that the

		Wilhelmine leadership of the Reich is incapable of expansive imperialism.
	November	Weber travels to Sicily and visits Robert Michels in Turin.
1907		The 'Hottentot elections': Naumann is elected to the Reichstag for the Heilbronn constituency, with SPD support in the second ballot.
		At the congress of the Verein für Sozialpolitik, Weber criticizes the Kaiser and the SPD's petty-bourgeois narrowness of vision. At the Webers' home in Heidelberg, a discussion group is formed with Emil Lask, Karl Löwenstein, Paul Honigsheim, Karl Jaspers, Werner Sombart, Robert Michels, Georg Simmel, Gertrud Bäumer, and others.
		The Webers travel to Lake Como in the spring and to the Netherlands in the summer.
		Marianne Weber publishes her major work on women in legal history, *Ehefrau und Mutter in der Rechtsentwicklung*. At the Evangelical Social Congress she gives a talk on 'questions of principle in sexual ethics'.
1908		Marianne's inheritance from the head of the Oerlinghausen firm relieves the Webers of financial worries and makes them full members of the property-owning bourgeoisie. Alfred Weber takes up an appointment in Heidelberg.
		In the spring Weber travels to Provence and Florence. In the autumn he spends a long period with relations in Oerlinghausen to carry out studies in the factory there for his *Psychophysik der industriellen Arbeit*.
	20 September	In the *Frankfurter Zeitung* Weber attacks German faculties for refusing to give a *Habilitation* qualification to social democrats.
	28 October	The bitterness of Weber and others over Kaiser Wilhelm II's incompetence comes to a head after his interview with the *Daily Telegraph*.
1909		Weber takes on the editorship of the *Grundriß der Sozialökonomik*; embarks on the work posthumously published as *Economy and Society*.
	13 June	Weber meets Mina Tobler (1880-1967) for the first time. Attends the conference in Vienna of the Verein für Sozialpolitik. Takes a stand against the state patronage of working people advocated by Schmoller.

		Alfred Weber, *Über den Standort der Industrie: Reine Theorie des Standorts.*
1910	April	Moves to the house of the Fallenstein grandparents at Ziegelhäuser Landstraße 17, Heidelberg. A more intense social life. Gets to know Stefan George, Georg Lukács and, from November 1911, Ernst Bloch.
	October	Plays a considerable role in organizing the first Congress of Sociologists in Frankfurt, and outlines its first programme of work. Founding of the Soziologische Gesellschaft.
	December	Beginning of the controversy with Arnold Ruge. Furious attacks on critics of *The Protestant Ethic.* Travels to Italy (Lerici) in spring and England in summer.
1911		Spring trip to Italy (Alassio), another visit to Michels in Turin, a trip to Paris in September.
	12–13 October	At the fourth conference of German university teachers, Weber sharply criticizes the 'Althoff system' (the training and personnel policy of the deceased ministerial director at the Prussian Ministry of Education) and the introduction of business colleges. His criticisms cause a major stir in the press. Founding of the Althoff-inspired Kaiser Wilhelm Society for the Advancement of Science (later renamed the Max Planck Society).
1912		Spring trip to Provence. Visits the Bayreuth festivities with Mina Tobler in summer.
	October	Adolf Koch's lawsuit against Weber. At the Congress of Sociologists in Berlin Weber gives the report on the preceding two years. Ernst Troeltsch, *The Social Teaching of the Christian Churches.*
1913		Spends some time in spring at Monte Verità in Ascona. Travels with Marianne in autumn to central Italy (Assisi, Siena, Perugia, Rome). Karl Jaspers, *Allgemeine Psychopathologie.*
1914		Spring in Ascona, and also Zurich. Debate on value-judgements in a committee of the Verein für Sozialpolitik in Berlin. After the outbreak of war, Weber takes the post of disciplinary officer in the reserve medical commission in Heidelberg, where he equips and has charge of several military hospitals.

Hermann Schäffer, the husband of Weber's youngest sister, Lili, is killed on the eastern front.

1915 Emil Lask is killed in action, as is Weber's younger brother, Karl.

Weber signs the Seeberg Address, submitted to the Kaiser by 1,347 representatives of cultural life (mostly university professors), which contains a set of wide-ranging demands relating to war aims.

Greater professionalization of the military hospital service leads to Weber's release from duties on 30 September.

Through Edgar Jaffé, Weber has a chance of doing consultative work on economic policy for the German military administration in Belgium. He travels to Brussels but is not taken on. In Berlin his efforts to obtain an advisory post, especially on the Polish question, are equally fruitless. After the failure of his political ambitions, he becomes engrossed in the study of Eastern religions.

1916 March Weber writes a memorandum (unpublished at the time) against the intensification of submarine warfare; it is sent to the Reich Chancellery, the Foreign Office and the various party leaders. Joins Naumann's Arbeitschuss für Mitteleuropa, which considers the prerequisites for a customs union and economic community of Central European countries. It sends him on a mission to Vienna and Budapest in late May.

1917 Weber's critical articles in the *Frankfurter Zeitung* on government policy and Prussian-German relations bring him into conflict with the military censors.

6 April The United States declares war on Germany.

May & October Takes part in the 'Lauenstein conferences' of socialist and pacifist students. There he meets Ernst Toller and Erich Mühsam, who visit him several times in the winter.

20 September Weber publishes a sharp polemic against the German Fatherland Party in the *Münchner Neueste Nachrichten*.

October Travels to Vienna, where his appointment to the chair in economics is under consideration.

7 November Lecture on 'Science as a Vocation' in Munich.

1918		Weber takes the Vienna chair in economics on a trial basis. Lectures on his studies in the sociology of religion, under the title 'Positive critique of the materialist conception of history'.
	13 June	Lectures on socialism to Austrian army officers.
	4 November	At a meeting of the Progressive People's Party in Munich, Weber warns against 'peace at any price'. But he is unable to finish his speech because of tumult in the hall.
	21 November	Weber becomes a freelance contributor to the *Frankfurter Zeitung*.
		Under pressure from Alfred Weber and Friedrich Naumann, Weber joins the German Democratic Party (DDP). He is given a place with few prospects on the party's list of candidates for the Reichstag. But, in an unofficial capacity, he takes part in advisory discussions on the future constitution of the Weimar Republic.
		Edgar Jaffé becomes finance minister in the Bavarian revolutionary government under Kurt Eisner.
1919	January	Active in the DDP's election campaign.
	28 January	Lecture on 'Politics as a Vocation' in Munich.
		In early February, on the proposal of former German chancellor Prince Max von Baden, the Heidelberger Vereinigung für eine Politik des Rechts is founded in Weber's home, its main activity being to combat the thesis of Germany's war guilt.
	11 March	At a protest meeting of Heidelberg lecturers and students against the Allied peace terms, Weber calls for a national revolution.
	13 May	Weber travels with the German peace delegation to Versailles and helps to formulate the response to the Allied thesis of Germany's war guilt. He then visits Ludendorff in Berlin, to persuade him to hand himself over to an Allied court.
	late June (?)	Moves to Munich, where he takes over Lujo Brentano's chair in social science, economic history and political economy.
	24 August	Death of Friedrich Naumann.
	14 October	Death of Max's mother, Helene Weber.
		Marianne Weber becomes the first chairwoman of the BDF, the League of German Women's Associations (until 1924).

1920	mid-January	Weber in conflict with rightist students after he argues for the execution of Kurt Eisner's assassin, Count Arco.
	7 April	Suicide of Max's sister Lili. Max and Marianne Weber plan to adopt her four children. Weber works on an edition of his writings on religion and the first part of *Economy and Society*.
	4 June	Falls ill with a lung infection. Dies on 14 June in Munich.

Notes

At the Den of the Sick Lion

1 Marianne Weber, *Max Weber: A Biography*, trans. and ed. Harry Zohn, New York, 1975 (hereafter WB), p. 355. Berta Lask, *Stille und Sturm*, Halle, 1974, pp. 162f.
2 Max Weber, 'Some Categories of Interpretive Sociology', *Sociological Quarterly*, 22 (spring 1981), p. 158; WL 439.
3 'What a guy! But also a poor sod!' – Wilhelm Hennis to the author, 7 July 2003.
4 Horst Gravenkamp, *Geschichte eines elenden Körpers: Lichtenberg als Patient*, Göttingen, 1989, p. 62.

Chapter 1 Great Mother and Harsh Nature

1 Friedrich Lenger, *Werner Sombart 1863–1941: Eine Biographie*, Munich, 1994, p. 30.
2 Not only French sociology, but also social policy theorists; see Franz-Xaver Kaufmann (*Varianten des Wohlfahrtsstaats: Der deutsche Sozialstaat im internationalen Vergleich*, Frankfurt, 2003, pp. 221ff.) on 'the crisis of the family and population as the central problem in French social policy'.
3 Sammlung Grathoff (hereafter SG). Marianne to Helene Weber, n.d. (1893; Ana 446) on Klara: 'We must finally get to know each other a little better, as she is really, as I always say, Max's first woman.' See Weber's letters to Klara: JB 350ff. Concerning the kiss on the mouth, see the Jaspers Nachlaß No. 13.
4 Ana 446 Sch. 20 V.
5 Otto Döhner, *Das Hugenottengeschlecht Souchay de la Duboissière und seine Nachkommen*, Neustadt an der Aisch, 1961.
6 GStA I Rep. 92, NL M. Weber Nr. 30 Bd. 4, 15 April 1894.
7 Hermann Oppenheim, *Lehrbuch der Nervenkrankheiten*, 7th edn, 2 vols, Berlin, 1923, p. 1209.
8 Hannes Isenberg, *Meningitis im Kindesalter und Neugeborenensepsis*, 2nd edn, Berlin, 1990, pp. 1ff., 42ff., 47.
9 Hannes Isenberg to the author, 12 January 2004.
10 Ana 446 Sch. 20 VI Bl. 119f.
11 Marianne gives a somewhat different impression: 'In the spring of 1882, Max Weber took his final examinations (*Abitur*) at the Gymnasium and he also

helped his friends to cheat their way through. His teachers certified his outstanding knowledge, though it had unfortunately not been acquired through traditional academic industriousness. But they expressed doubts about the *moral* maturity of the troublesome, inwardly disrespectful youth' (WB 64).

12 Max Weber to Else Jaffé, 4 March 1919.

13 Ernst Nolte, *The Three Faces of Fascism*, London, 1965, p. 446.

14 Eduard Baumgarten, 'Spielräume unter Hitlers Herrschaft', privately owned manuscript, p. 249.

15 GStA Nl M. Weber Nr. 30 Bd. 1, Brügge, 20 August 1903; see WB 32.

16 On the first of the 1060 closely printed pages of *The Works of William D. Channing* (Boston, 1899), we read: 'The following writings will be found to be distinguished by nothing more than the high estimate which they express of human nature.' On page 392: 'Unitarism is peculiarly favourable to piety, because it accords with nature, with the world around and the world within us; and through this accordance it gives aid to nature, and receives aid from it, in impressing the mind with God.' In the end 'Nature' is written like 'God' with a capital letter. On page 940: 'Until thus we see the Infinite in Nature, we have not learned the lesson that wisdom is everywhere teaching.'

17 Karl Lamprecht, *Americana*, Freiburg, 1906, p. 111.

18 Marianne to Helene Weber, 1 April 1904 [SG], where she evidently shared the same feeling: 'A cold and rainy Good Friday. This morning, after a long break, I once again went to church, but, as nearly always, I came home feeling so crushed by the priest – the dogma of our immeasurable trespasses and the sacrificial lamb required by God for them – the passion of Christ on our behalf – is so disagreeable that I find it impossible to accept; terrible to think that God required a scapegoat for us all!'

19 Marianne to Helene Weber, 17 March 1912. Similar but more restrained is Max Weber: MWG II/7-2, 506.

20 MWG II/9, Max to Marianne Weber, 28 March 1916.

21 MWG II/9, Max to Marianne Weber, 25 November 1915.

22 GStA Nl M. Weber Nr. 30 Bd. 2, 9 December 1915 to Marianne Weber.

23 Theodor Heuss, *Friedrich Naumann*, 2nd edn, Stuttgart, 1949, p. 206.

24 Erich Fromm, *Sigmund Freud's Mission: An Analysis of his Personality and Influence*, London, 1959, p. 14.

25 Quoted without a source in Hans Norbert Fügen, *Max Weber*, Reinbek, 1985, p. 14.

26 Ana 446 Sch. 14, 28 December 1894. On 20 December she had written to Helene: 'I am now so used to regarding your house as my late-found parental home.'

27 MWG II/9, Max Weber to Lili Schäfer, 28 February 1916; he insinuated this calculation to his brother Arthur. [The 'little ducat man' of Goslar is a humorous medieval statue of a defecating male figure that was erected on the market square in response to attempts by a nearby ruler to acquire its coin-minting rights. The reference relies upon an association of faeces and money, or more precisely of defecation and minting. *Trans. note*]

28 Christa Krüger, *Max und Marianne Weber*, Zurich, 2001, p. 62.

29 From Rome, Marianne wrote to Helene on 11 April 1903 [SG] about Alice Salomon: 'Judging by her hints, she has already experienced the "great passion" that you wish for her; such a warm and loving person as she is, so in need of human contact, cannot get through life without an experience like that. How much I hope that fortune will once again smile on her.'

30 Joachim Köhler, *Zarathustras Geheimnis: Friedrich Nietzsche und seine verschlüsselte Botschaft*, Nördlingen, 1989, pp. 311, 365.
31 [A group of professors at the University of Göttingen who were dismissed by Ernst August, king of Hanover, after they had protested against his alleged violations of the constitution. *Trans. note*]
32 Walter Boehlich (ed.), *Der Hochverratsprozeß gegen Gervinus*, Frankfurt-am-Main, 1967. On the intolerance of the martyr cult driven by the Göttingen Seven, see Klaus von See, *Die Göttinger Sieben: Kritik einer Legende*, 2nd edn, Heidelberg, 1997.
33 See also the letter to Else Baumgarten, 1 March 1913 (MWG II/8, 103f.).
34 The author, Princess Catherine Radziwill (R 332, 443), came from an aristocratic family which, though Frenchified, was friendly with the family of future Reich Chancellor Bernhard von Bülow.
35 Count Paul Vasili, in *La Société de Berlin*, 2nd edn, Paris, 1884, pp. 66ff., 172f., 190ff., 18.
36 MWG II/9, Max to Marianne Weber, 20 November 1915.
37 Max Weber, 'Remarks on Technology and Culture' (1911), *Theory, Culture and Society*, 22/4 (2005), pp. 23–38; Werner Sombart, 'Technik und Kultur', *Archiv für Sozialwissenschaft und Sozialpolitik*, 33/2 (1911), pp. 305–47.
38 Friedrich Lenger, *Werner Sombart*, Munich, 1994, pp. 162f.
39 Max Weber, 'Remarks on Technology and Culture', p. 29.

Chapter 2 Max and Minimax

1 Hans Heinrich Muchow, *Jugend und Zeitgeist: Morphologie der Kulturpubertät*, Reinbek, 1962.
2 Ana 446 Sch. 20 V.
3 Eberhard Demm, 'Alfred Weber und sein Bruder Max', in Demm, *Geist und Politik im 20. Jahrhundert*, Frankfurt am Main, 2000, p. 61.
4 Eberhard Demm, *Ein Liberaler in Kaiserreich und Republik: Der politische Weg Alfred Webers bis 1920*, Boppard, 1990, p. 7.
5 Alfred to Max Weber, 14 November 1899, from a spa near Merano [SG].
6 Else Jaffé, 'Biographische Daten Alfred Webers', in Eberhard Demm, ed., *Alfred Weber als Politiker und Gelehrter*, Stuttgart, 1986, pp. 184f.
7 Alfred to Max Weber, 18 February 1899 [SG].
8 Alfred to Max Weber, 2 November 1899.
9 Marianne to Helene Weber, 10 December 1902 [SG].
10 Marianne to Helene Weber, 30 August 1901.
11 Demm, *Ein Liberaler*, p. 10.
12 Jaffé, 'Biographische Daten', p. 188.
13 Eberhard Demm, personal communication to the author, 20 December 2003.
14 Alfred to Max Weber, 2 August 1887, in Alfred Weber, *Ausgewählter Briefwechsel*, ed. Eberhard Demm and Hartmut Soell, Marburg, 2003 (= *Alfred-Weber-Gesamtausgabe*, vol. 10), vol. 1, pp. 45f.
15 Marianne to Helene Weber, 26 June 1908.
16 Hans Staudinger, *Wirtschaftspolitik im Weimarer Staat: Lebenserinnerungen eines politischen Beamten im Reich und in Preußen 1889 bis 1934*, ed. Hagen Schulze, Bonn, 1982, pp. 8f.
17 Alfred Weber, *Gedanken zur deutschen Sendung*, Berlin, 1915, pp. 13, 24.

18 GStA Nl M. Weber No. 30 vol. 2, letters to Marianne Weber dated 23 November 1915, 14 May 1916 and 17 May 1916.

19 Eberhard Demm, *Von der Weimarer Republik zur Bundesrepublik: Der politische Weg Alfred Webers 1920–1958,* Düsseldorf, 1999, pp. 4ff.; Demm to the author, 20 December 2003.

20 Eberhard Demm in conversation with the author, 8 February 2003, revising the picture of Alfred Weber that he himself had earlier drawn.

21 Deutsches Literaturarchiv Marbach, A: Jaspers 75.12072, 30 May 1958.

22 Wilfried Nippel, 'Max Weber zwischen Althistorie und Universalgeschichte: Synoikismus und Verbrüderung', in Christian Meier (ed.), *Die okzidentale Stadt nach Max Weber,* Munich, 1994, p. 49; George Thomson, *Studies in Ancient Greek Society: The Prehistoric Aegean,* London, 1949.

23 Moses I. Finley, 'Max Weber and the Greek City-State', in Finley, *Ancient History: Evidence and Models,* New York, 1986, pp. 91ff.

24 In Johannes Winckelmann, ed., *Die Protestantische Ethik* II (*Kritiken und Antikritiken*), 3rd edn, Gütersloh, 1978, p. 294.

25 Adolf von Harnack, *The Expansion of Christianity in the First Three Centuries,* London, 1905, vol. 2, p. 31.

26 Christian Meier, 'Bemerkungen zum Problem der "Verbrüderung" in Athen und Rom', in Meier (ed.), *Die okzidentale Stadt,* p. 8.

27 Klaus Schreiner, communication to the author, 30 December 2003. 'In developing the concept of an "oath fraternity", Weber was not following the language of the sources. The oath taken by burghers in the communes of northern Italy established not a community of brethren but a legal and social association of rich and poor, ruling families and citizens, with a duty to obey. Brotherhood (*fraternitas*) does not appear in the sources as a term for the legal and social association of the commune; nor is there any mention there of *confraternity* in the sense of socialization or the formation of cooperative relations.' I am grateful to Klaus Schreiner for valuable suggestions on this topic.

28 Klaus Schreiner, 'Legitimität, Autonomie, Rationalisierung: Drei Kategorien Max Webers zur Analyse mittelalterlicher Stadtgesellschaften – wissenschaftsgeschichtlicher Ballast oder unabgegoltene Herausforderung?' in Christian Meier (ed.), *Die okzidentale Stadt,* p. 193, also pp. 182ff. 'The securing of legitimacy through consent does not feature in Weber's concept of legitimacy; he criminally neglected and greatly underestimated civil association as . . . a criterion of legitimacy.' Ibid., p. 166.

29 Joachim Radkau, *Das Zeitalter der Nervosität,* Munich, 1998, pp. 166ff.

30 Adolf Wagner, 'Meine Duellangelegenheit mit dem Freiherrn von Stumm', *Die Zukunft,* 10 (1895), pp. 408–27. He further argued that the duel was often in reality mere 'shadow boxing', a 'comedy' in which 'blank shots were fired in the air'.

31 Dieter Lindenlaub, *Richtungskämpfe im Verein für Sozialpolitik,* part I, Wiesbaden, 1967, p. 59. See MWG II/8, 71.

32 Heinrich von Treitschke, *Deutsche Geschichte,* Leipzig, 1879–94, vol. 2, pp. 56f.

33 Dietmar Klenke, *Der singende 'deutsche Mann': Gesangvereine und deutsches Nationalbewußtsein von Napoleon bis Hitler,* Münster, 1998, pp. 145ff.

34 Raymond Descat, 'Der Historiker, die griechische Polis und Webers "Stadt"', in Hinnerk Bruhns and Wilfried Nippel (eds), *Max Weber und die Stadt im Kulturvergleich,* Göttingen, 2000, esp. pp. 85ff.

35 Joachim Radkau, 'Der Mann Weber und die erotische Emergenz der Soziologie', in Karin Tebben (ed.), *Abschied vom Mythos Mann*, Göttingen, 2002, pp. 26f. Norbert Elias paid too little attention to these limits of the duel; see his *The Germans*, New York, 1998 ('Duelling and Membership of the German Imperial Class: Demanding and Giving Satisfaction', pp. 44–120).

36 *Faust*, part I, scene V, in *Selected Works*, Everyman edn, London, 1999, p. 803.

37 WzG 661, 862.

38 Jürgen Reulecke, 'Das Jahr 1902 und der Ursprung der Männerbund-Ideologie in Deutschland', in Gisela Völger and Karin von Welck (eds), *Männerbande, Männerbünde*, Cologne, 1990, vol. 1, p. 5.

39 Heinrich Schurtz, *Altersklassen und Männerbünde: Eine Darstellung der Grundformen der Gesellschaft*, Berlin, 1902, pp. ivf., 174f.

Chapter 3 From Father's Boy to Mother's Boy

1 GStA Nl M. Weber Nr. 30 Bd. 1, Max to Marianne Weber, mid-January 1893. Marianne was to remain in the house in Charlottenburg. 'Therefore I think it right that I should leave it. I shall move to Berlin and see you on Sundays, for a shorter time than hitherto. . . . I must *not* look *too often* into your eyes.'

2 Ana 446, Marianne to Helene Weber, 4 September 1893, on Max: 'His mental qualities of a bachelor will still sometimes weigh on him.' And that was a discreet formulation!

3 Ana 446 Sch. 14, Marianne to Helene Weber, n.d.

4 M. Rainer Lepsius ('Mina Tobler, die Freundin Max Webers', in Bärbel Meurer (ed.), *Marianne Weber*, Tübingen, 2004, p. 87) pertinently remarks: 'Marianne had wooed Max Weber before their marriage, and her wooing lasted until his death.'

5 Or, as Marianne put it: 'She had an idea of the weight that was upon him and why he was burying himself in his work' (WB 170).

6 I have been able to convince myself that, except for a few inconsequential points, the text there precisely corresponds to the original.

7 Ingrid Gilcher-Holtey ('Max Weber und die Frauen', in Christian Gneuss and Jürgen Kocka, (eds), *Max Weber: Ein Symposion*, Munich, 1988, p. 144) reads in this passage a 'sharp downgrading of the natural, the sensual, the physical'. That may be so, but stronger still is the impression it gives of the *superior power* of nature.

8 (The German word *Kamerad* can have the force of the English 'comrade', derived from a military context, but in relation to spouses its main connotation is similar to that of the English 'companion'. *Trans. note*)

9 MWG II/9, Max to Marianne Weber, 6 May 1916.

10 Deutsches Literaturarchiv Marbach, A: Jaspers, Marianne Weber to Jaspers, 8 September 1926.

11 Siegfried A. Kaehler, *Wilhelm von Humboldt und der Staat*, Munich, 1927, pp. 59–107; see also Hans-Ulrich Wehler, *Die Herausforderung der Kulturgeschichte*, Munich, 1998, pp. 89f.

12 Bruno Müller (Carl Weber & Co.) to Max Weber, 8 February 1894.

13 Ana 446 Sch. 20 IV Bl. 22.

14 Ana 446 Sch. 20 IV Bl. 13.

15 GStA, Nl M. Weber Nr. 30 Bd. 4, Max to Helene Weber from Paris, 29 September 1893.

16 Deutsches Literaturarchiv Marbach, A: Jaspers Nr. 113 V.

17 Ana 446 Sch. 14, Marianne to Helene Weber, 9 March and 7 July 1895. Eaedem, 29 January 1902 (?), SG: 'It is horrifying to think that you still have to spend so much time and energy on the household machine that you would otherwise urgently need for more important tasks.'

18 Marianne to Helene Weber, 5 November 1918.

19 Hermann Glockner, *Heidelberger Bilderbuch*, Bonn, 1969, p. 101.

20 Jürgen Kuczynski (*Memoiren: Die Erziehung des J. K. zum Kommunisten und Wissenschaftler*, 2nd edn, Berlin, 1975, p. 61) refers to Glockner as Rickert's 'brilliant disciple'.

21 The relationship between Rickert and Weber was close at times but also tense. Weber described Rickert's theory of value as his 'sentimental nonsense' (Wilhelm Hennis, *Max Weber's Science of Man*, trans. Keith Tribe, Newbury, 2000, p. 183).

22 Ana 446 Sch. 20 VII.

23 Ana 446 Sch. 20 VI Bl. 50, 11 August 1911.

24 Ana 446 Sch. 20 VI Bl. 50, 23 February 1911.

25 Ana 446 Sch. 20 IV Bl. 10.

26 Marianne to Helene Weber, 29 June 1909.

27 Ana 446, Marianne to Helene Weber, 9 July 1893.

28 GStA Nl M. Weber Nr. 30 Bd. 4, Max to Helene Weber, 29 July 1893; Marianne's remark is on one of Weber's postcards from Paris, ibid., Nr. 3.

29 Eberhard Demm, *Von der Weimarer Republik zur Bundesrepublik: Der politische Weg Alfred Webers 1920–1958*, Düsseldorf, 1999, p. 8. On Rickert, see George W. F. Hallgarten, *Als die Schatten fielen*, Berlin, 1969, p. 108.

30 Marianne to Helene Weber, 12 April 1912.

31 Ana 446 Sch. 20 VI, 12 April 1911. On 24 April 1916 Max Weber wrote to Mina Tobler (MWG II/9) about Sophie Rickert: 'She is closer to us than he is and in herself a person of exceptionally high intellect, with a phenomenally difficult life full of sacrifice and an artistic soul condemned never to blossom forth.'

32 Meinecke thought that Marianne Weber's biography had been conspicuously sparing of detail about Weber's important friendship with Troeltsch (WzG 146). In the memoirs of Gertrud von le Fort (*Hälfte des Lebens*, Munich, 1965, pp. 87ff.), who studied under Troeltsch and whose 'best friend' she became, the theologian is presented as a sensitive and tolerant man with a private tendency to mysticism – a sign that one should take Marianne's horror reports to Helene with a pinch of salt.

33 Marianne to Helene Weber, 8 March 1900 (SG). Previously 'our Troeltschie' had 'conceded' to her that 'he did not want a wife who was not independent'. He 'has often wondered whether he should marry at all and is very afraid that the woman by his side would always lack something; I then told him it did no harm at all if he felt no *passion*, that would come later, but he must be all the more attentive to common intellectual interests.' One is continually struck by the way in which Marianne observes Troeltsch's difficulties with women through the prism of her own marital experiences.

34 Hans-Georg Drescher, *Ernst Troeltsch: Leben und Werk*, Göttingen, 1991, p. 106. As one might have expected, Hausrath and Troeltsch also pulled each other to pieces.

35 Marianne to Helene Weber, July 1900: 'Anyway, he wants a woman at all costs. I feel terribly sorry for the poor fellow.' Troeltsch had homosexual inclinations that caused him a lot of trouble in his student fraternity. See Friedrich Wilhelm Graf, 'Polymorphes Gedächtnis: Zur Einführung in die Troeltsch-Nekrologie', in Graf (ed.), *Ernst Troeltsch in Nachrufen*, Gütersloh, 2002 (*Troeltsch-Studien* 12), p. 168.

36 Drescher, *Troeltsch*, pp. 110f.

37 'His glorious laughter is still reverberating in those mountains', wrote Harnack in 1899, after a trip with Troeltsch to Transylvania and the Carpathians. Agnes von Zahn-Harnack, *Adolf von Harnack*, Berlin 1936, p. 437.

38 Marianne to Helene Weber, 11 July 1901 [SG]. More generally, see Graf, 'Polymorphes Gedächtnis', pp. 119ff.

39 Ibid., p. 171n.

40 Marianne to Helene Weber, 9 June 1903.

41 Eaedem, 10 May 1903 and 6 March 1904 (SG). The last remark refers to the historian Erich Marcks, who, according to Marianne, was 'afraid' that his wife would be 'infected' by 'wild women'.

42 Ana 446 Sch. 20 VI, 11 January 1911.

43 Ana 446 Sch. 14, Marianne to Helene Weber, 9 March 1895; Wilhelm Hennis, *Weber und Thukydides*, Göttingen, 2003, p. 44.

44 Ana 446 Sch. 14, Marianne to Helene Weber, n.d. (1893, after the wedding).

45 Ana 446 Sch. 14, Marianne to Helene Weber, n.d. (autumn 1894).

46 Eaedem, 7 July 1895.

47 Joachim Radkau, 'Der Mann Weber und die erotische Emergenz der Soziologie', in Karin Tebben (ed.), *Abschied vom Mythos Mann*, Göttingen, 2002, pp. 23f. Similarly, Troeltsch closed his obituary of Weber with the lines from the end of Shakespeare's *Julius Caesar*: '. . . and the elements / So mixed in him that Nature might stand up / And say to all the world, "This was a man!"' (WzG 46).

48 A: Jaspers Nr. 113 V.

49 Friedrich Wilhelm Möller to Theodor Möller, 21 April 1858, in *65. Jahresbericht des Historischen Vereins für die Grafschaft Ravensberg* (1966–7), p. 177.

50 Hedwig Wachenheim, *Die deutsche Arbeiterbewegung 1844–1914*, Cologne, 1967, p. 219.

51 See Manfred Rauh, *Die Parlamentisierung des Deutschen Reiches*, Bonn, 1977.

52 Between 1986 and 1998 historians at Bielefeld University conducted a long-term research project on the social history of the modern German *Bürgertum*. After the first eight years Wolfgang Mager concluded that 'a central assumption has proved to be unsustainable: namely, the thesis of Germany's special path or *Sonderweg*. Studies on the development of the *Bildungsbürgertum* in the eighteenth and nineteenth centuries lead to the clear conclusion that, with their performative knowledge both as functional elites and in their domination of culture, German experts trained in higher educational establishments appear comparable to corresponding middle-class groups in the West. There can be no talk of a "civic deficit". It would not be going too far to speak of a definite success story in the case of the German bourgeoisie.' Peter Lundgreen (ed.), *Reformuniversität Bielefeld 1969–1994*, Bielefeld, 1994, p. 327.

53 Ibid., p. 537.

54 On the technical and general historical significance of the sewerage system and other major urban projects, see Joachim Radkau, *Technik in Deutschland: Vom*

18. Jahrhundert bis zur Gegenwart, Frankfurt am Main, 1989, pp. 204ff.; and Radkau, 'Zum ewigen Wachstum verdammt? Jugend und Alter großer technischer Systeme', in Ingo Braun and Bernward Joerges (eds), *Technik ohne Grenzen*, Frankfurt am Main, 1994, pp. 76ff.

55 James Hobrecht, *Die Canalisation von Berlin*, Berlin, 1884 (reissued Berlin, 1993).

56 See Hans Boldt, ' "Den Staat ergänzen oder sich mit ihm versöhnen?" Aspekte der Selbstverwaltungsdiskussion im 19. Jahrhundert', in Edith Hanke and Wolfgang J. Mommsen (eds), *Max Webers Herrschaftssoziologie*, Tübingen, 2001, pp. 139 and 163ff.

57 Heinrich Heffter's great work *Die deutsche Selbstverwaltung im 19. Jahrhundert* (Stuttgart, 1950) begins by stating that 'the idea of local self-government' has always 'sounded good in recent German history', but above all as an 'idea' into which many things can be inserted. 'This conspicuous appeal of the idea certainly does not derive from the sober routine of administration through which it is put into practice.' It is precisely this routine of administration which Max Weber had before his eyes.

58 Hugo Preuß, 'Die kommunale Selbstverwaltung in Deutschland', in Paul Laband et al. (eds), *Handbuch der Politik*, vol. 1, Berlin, 1912, p. 207.

59 Dirk Käsler, 'Der retuschierte Klassiker: Zum gegenwärtigen Forschungsstand der Biographie Max Webers', in Johannes Weiß (ed.), *Max Weber heute: Erträge und Probleme der Forschung*, Frankfurt am Main, 1989, p. 41.

60 For greater detail, see Arthur Mitzman, *The Iron Cage: An Historical Interpretation of Max Weber*, New York, 1969, pp. 109ff.

61 See Theodor Spitta, *Aus meinem Leben: Bürger und Bürgermeister in Bremen*, Munich, 1969, p. 151, on Weber's lectures in Berlin: 'He was the most dazzling and witty lecturer I had in my student years.'

62 Max to Arthur Weber, December 1910 (MWG II/6, 763): For the father, 'religion *fundamentally* = hypocrisy, theologians hypocrites. The bad correspondence which developed out of that also completely alienated me from Papa for the first time.'

63 [Steel baron Karl Ferdinand Stumm, ennobled by Kaiser Wilhelm II, was popularly known as 'König Stumm'. *Trans. note*]

64 EM 480f. See Lutz Graf Schwerin von Krosigk, *Die große Zeit des Feuers*, vol. 2, Tübingen, 1958, p. 174; Fritz Hellwig, *Carl Ferdinand Freiherr von Stumm-Halberg*, Heidelberg, 1936, esp. p. 560.

65 When Max Weber had first met Emily Fallenstein, a year and a half before, he had found her most charming: 'Emily has something incredibly attractive and loveable about her' (JB 62).

66 Jan Goldstein, 'The Hysteria Diagnosis and the Politics of Anticlericalism in Late 19th-Century France', *Journal of Modern History*, 54 (1982), pp. 209–39.

67 Ana 446 Sch. 14, Marianne to Helene Weber, 28 January 1895.

68 Max to Marianne Weber from Posen, 17 March 1894 and 5 April 1894 (GStA Nl. M. Weber Nr. 30 Bd. 1). The mother was currently feeling 'the effects of long years of exceedingly pathological nervous tension'. Max described as 'nonsense' his mother's belief that he had 'somehow been a support for her' and that she now lacked that support; the father should be made to feel his 'responsibility' for her poor condition. Thus, while Max Weber made his father the target, he also parried his mother's indirect blaming of himself.

69 Alfred to Max Weber, n.d. (marked: early 1897) (SG).

70 Marianne Weber, *Die Frauen und die Liebe*, Königstein-im-Taunus, 1950, p. 14.
71 Marianne to Helene Weber, 25 May 1901 [SG].
72 WB 231. A letter that Max wrote the next day to Alfred Weber (GStA Nl. M. Weber Nr. 30 Bd. 4, 15 June 1897) contains his own detailed account of the family scene: 'The confrontation then took place here in the evening. Very stormy and with no agreement – i.e., I stopped it when there was no longer any point. Papa revealed such a sea of insincerity and big fat lies that Mama was at first quite flabbergasted; she then reinforced each one of the things for which I had reproached him. He claimed "some of my brothers and sisters share his view about our demands" [meaning that the father was evidently in the right!], upon which I remarked that I would . . . break with them. He demanded that he alone should decide . . . when Mama comes here; that is in keeping with his position as paterfamilias, etc. . . . You can imagine for yourself how I responded to these grotesque pieces of impertinence. . . . He is in the extreme paroxysm of jealousy and the most childish spite.' From a distance we may wonder whether the closing diagnosis was not at least equally applicable to the son.
73 See a number of letters in GStA Nl. M. Weber Nr. 30 Bd. 4.
74 Mitzman refers to this in *The Iron Cage*, pp. 151f.
75 Max to Alfred Weber, 15 June 1897.
76 Eidem.
77 Marianne to Helene Weber, 27 February 1906 [SG].
78 Ana 446 Sch. 14, Marianne to Alfred Weber, 28 July 1896.
79 D. H. Lawrence, *Mister Noon* (1934), London, 1985, p. 157.
80 Hideharu Ando, 'Die Interviews mit Else Jaffé, Edgar Salin und Helmuth Plessner über Max Weber 1969/70', *Kölner Zeitschrift für Soziologie und Sozialpsychologie*, 55 (2003), p. 599.
81 GStA Nl. M. Weber Nr. 30 Bd. 4, Max to Helene Weber, 8 March 1894.
82 Ibid. Max to Alfred Weber, 8 March 1905: 'It is monstrous . . . that Mama's extremely modest lifestyle still swallows up 14–15,000 marks a month. The reason must be systematic theft on someone's part or beneficence that cannot possibly continue like this.'
83 Alfred Weber, *Ausgewählter Briefwechsel*, ed. Eberhard Demm and Hartmut Soell, Marburg, 2003, vol. 1, pp. 62ff.

Chapter 4 Antaeus, Antiquity and Agrarians

1 Translation modified to accord with the imagery in the original German.
2 Alfred Weber, *Ausgewählter Briefwechsel*, ed. Eberhard Demm and Hartmut Soell, Marburg, 2003, vol. 1, p. 57.
3 Joachim Radkau, *Das Zeitalter der Nervosität*, Munich, 1998, p. 319; Max Weber, Review of Franz Eulenburg's *Die Entwicklung der Universität Leipzig in den letzten hundert Jahren*, in *Literatur-Anzeiger*, 1909, p. 673; Alfred Giesecke-Teubner (ed.), *Das Gymnasium und die neue Zeit*, Leipzig, 1919, pp. 133f.
4 Wilhelm Hennis, *Weber und Thukydides*, Göttingen, 2003, p. 16.
5 Friedrich Meinecke, *Straßburg – Freiburg – Berlin 1901–1919*, Stuttgart, 1949, pp. 246f.
6 Helmuth Schneider (ed.), *Sozial- und Wirtschaftsgeschichte der römischen Kaiserzeit*, Darmstadt, 1981, pp. 4ff., 12.

7 GStA Nl. M. Weber Nr. 30 Bd. 4. See Hennis, *Weber und Thukydides*, p. 40.

8 Jürgen Deininger (ed.), *Max Weber: Die römische Agrargeschichte in ihrer Bedeutung für das Staats- und Privatrecht*, Tübingen, 1986, pp. 6, 182; Dieter Flach, *Römische Agrargeschichte*, Munich, 1990, pp. 1ff.

9 Aloys Winterling, ' "Mit dem Antrag Kanitz also säßen die Cäsaren noch heute auf ihrem Throne": Max Webers Analysen der römischen Agrargeschichte', *Archiv für Kulturgeschichte*, 83 (2001), p. 422.

10 Theodor Mommsen, *Historische Schriften*, 2 vols, Berlin, 1965, p. 93 n.117; Deininger, *Max Weber: Die römische Agrargeschichte*, p. 185.

11 A pioneer of ecological agriculture even praised this as Mommsen's wise insight: see Sir Albert Howard, *An Agricultural Testament*, Oxford, 1940, chapter 1.

12 Stefan Rebenich (*Theodor Mommsen: Eine Biographie*, Munich, 2002, p. 164) thinks that Mommsen was then 'proclaiming' Weber to be 'his legitimate successor', but that Weber 'did not want to stand in his shadow'. Though politically a liberal, Mommsen was highly impatient and authoritarian in his own special area. Karl Julius Beloch, who had to seek salvation in Italy because Mommsen consistently blocked his appointment to a German professorship, spoke bitterly of the fact that Mommsen had bred a 'race of parrots'. Weber, who voted conservative in those days, mocked the 'truly childish hatred of Bismarck' on the part of old liberals like Mommsen (JB 346). Clearly he wanted to be outside that political and intellectual milieu.

13 In 'Mit dem Antrag Kanitz . . .' (p. 428), Winterling alludes to the problematic character of this premise, to which Weber himself did not subsequently adhere.

14 Deininger, *Max Weber: Die römische Agrargeschichte*, p. 168.

15 Santo Mazzarino, *The End of the Ancient World*, London, 1966, p. 137. Michael Rostovtzeff – who was well known to Weber – put forward the contrasting idea that the economic foundation of Rome was destroyed when 'scientific cultivation disappeared utterly' (*A History of the Ancient World*, vol. 2: *Rome*, London, 1945, p. 352), but this is less plausible and sounds as if it is based on the ideas of modern Russian agrarian reformers.

16 MWG I/4-1, 525ff.; and again in a letter to Georg von Below, 23 August 1905, GStA Nl Weber Nr. 30 Bd. 4.

17 Lynn White, *Medieval Technology and Social Change*, London, 1964, pp. 41ff.

18 Lujo Brentano, *Mein Leben im Kampf um die sociale Entwicklung Deutschlands*, Marburg, 2004, pp. 125ff.

19 Max to Marianne Weber, 1 March 1894, GStA Nl Weber Nr. 30 Bd. 1.

20 Heinrich Herkner, *Die Arbeiterfrage*, 3rd edn, Berlin, 1902, p. 72n.

21 Kenneth D. Barkin, *The Controversy over German Industrialization 1890–1902*, Chicago, 1970, p. 4.

22 Lujo Brentano, *Die Schrecken des überwiegenden Industriestaats*, Berlin, 1901.

23 In a long footnote to his work on Roman agrarian history (MWG I/2, 160), Weber even formulated a general rule that, both in Rome and in Germany, 'undivided possession' could be lastingly maintained 'only on dependent land'; as soon as farmers were at liberty to do so, they divided the estate among their children. The agricultural economist Max Sering, who had been in contact with Max Weber and was later cold-shouldered by the Nazis in the time of their 'law on farm estate' [*Erbhofgesetz*], pointed out that the 'custom of division' had 'originally developed' in the Rhineland and 'in no way conflicted with ancient Germanic legal conceptions'. Max Sering, *Deutsche Agrarpolitik auf geschichtlicher und landeskundlicher Grundlage*, Leipzig, 1934, p. 50.

24 Arthur Mitzman, *The Iron Cage*, New York, 1969, pp. 84f.
25 Moritz Julius Bonn, *So macht man Geschichte*, Munich, 1953, pp. 73f.
26 Dieter Lindenlaub, *Richtungskämpfe im Verein für Sozialpolitik*, Wiesbaden, 1967, p. 34.
27 Ana 446 Sch. 14.
28 Gustav Schmoller, *Charakterbilder*, Munich, 1913, p. 287.
29 Wolfgang J. Mommsen, *Max Weber and German Politics 1890–1920*, Chicago 1990, p. 22.
30 Ludwig Bernhard, *Das polnische Gemeinwesen im preußischen Staat: Die Polenfrage*, Leipzig, 1907, p. 623.
31 Ludwig Bernhard, *Der 'Hugenberg-Konzern': Psychologie und Technik einer Großorganisation der Presse*, Berlin, 1928, pp. 10f.
32 See, for example, in the final report on East Prussia (MWG, I/3-1, 260): 'As the loss of village pasture through subdivision was in its time the heaviest blow that could have hit landowning workers, the keeping of cattle, and secondarily of livestock in general, is still today the first prerequisite for a healthy household.'
33 Only occasionally do the responses contain some relatively direct confirmation, as in the complaint (MWG I/3-2, 741) that military service leads prospective landowners to treat their 'people' as if they were conscripts. 'I must say, with complete conviction, that many people are driven out of agriculture by foolish treatment.'
34 Werner Hegemann, *Das steinerne Berlin* (1930), Berlin, 1963, p. 280.
35 GStA Nl M. Weber Nr. 3 Bd. 4, Marianne to Helene Weber, 2 May 1896.
36 Ana 446 Sch. 14, Marianne to Helene Weber, 9 March 1895.
37 Ana 446 Sch. 14, Marianne to Helene Weber, 2 September 1896.
38 MWG II/9, Max Weber to Mina Tobler, 22 April 1916.
39 Wilhelm Hennis, *Max Weber's Central Question*, 2nd edn, Newbury, 2000, p. 55.
40 L 493; MWG II/7-1, 252; II/7-2, 502.
41 Marie-Louise Plessen (*Die Wirksamkeit des Vereins für Sozialpolitik von 1872–1890: Studien zum Katheder- und Staatssozialismus*, Berlin, 1975, p. 46) argues that, in the decisive years between 1880 and 1890, the Verein influenced social policy not directly but through the formation of public opinion. Weber's critic of the time, Max Quarck, later paid the Verein a compliment from a social-democratic perspective, by recalling 'how valuable [its] surveys were to us in the economic struggle' (ibid., p. 28).
42 Mommsen, *Max Weber and German Politics*, p. 28.
43 In a letter to Helene Weber dated 26 July 1900 [SG], therefore in the worst period of Weber's illness, Marianne called Leo Wegener 'Max's most devoted disciple, who simply adores him'.
44 Ludwig Bernhard, *Der 'Hugenberg-Konzern'*, p. 3.
45 MWG I/4-1, 462: 'It is only a silly fear of ideas of "expropriation" which prevents broad circles of people from saying what each one silently thinks: that a large part of the big estates in the east cannot be kept in private hands.' And he wished that the state would buy up these lands, convert them into demesnes and hand them over to tenants with ample means.
46 See Veronika Bennholdt-Thomsen and Maria Mies, *The Subsistence Perspective: Beyond the Globalized Economy*, London, 1999.
47 Melita Maschmann, *Account Rendered: A Dossier on my Former Self*, London, 1964, p. 66.

48 Theodor Fontane, *The Stechlin* (1899), trans. William L. Zwiebel, Columbia, SC, 1995, p. 60.
49 In the 1971 edition of Weber's *Gesammelte politische Schriften* (p. 28), the words '*von Tieren*' are omitted!
50 [A quotation from Wilhelm Gerhard's poem '*Der Edelacker*', alluding to a famous incident in the twelfth century when a soft ruler was admonished by a blacksmith with whom he happened to be spending the night. *Trans. note*]
51 Cornelius Torp, *Max Weber und die preußischen Junker*, Tübingen, 1998, p. 82. On this point, Torp's otherwise successful study seems in need of correction. See also the review by Eberhard Demm in *Zeitschrift für Geschichtswissenschaft*, 47 (1999), p. 845.
52 Rebenich, *Theodor Mommsen*, p. 207.
53 Mommsen, *Max Weber and German Politics*, p. 17n.
54 GStA, Nl Weber Nr. 30 Bd. 4, 18 January 1895.
55 Weber was not alone in thinking that nobles had a more 'natural' relation to sex than the bourgeoisie. Ludwig Gurlitt, an eloquent supporter of pedagogic reforms, happily spread it around that an Austrian nobleman had celebrated with friends the birth of his hundredth child out of wedlock. Ludwig Gurlitt, *Erziehungslehre*, Berlin, 1909, p. 331.
56 Hans-Ulrich Wehler (ed.), *Friedrich Kapp*, Frankfurt am Main, 1969, pp. 37, 128.
57 [The German 'Michel', a variant of Michael, is the personification of the German nation, rather like Uncle Sam is of the United States. *Trans. note*]
58 Wehler (ed.), *Friedrich Kapp*, pp. 12f., 29f.
59 Otto Baumgarten, *Bismarcks Glaube* (1900), Tübingen 1915; Baumgarten, *Meine Lebensgeschichte*, Tübingen, 1929, p. 280.
60 See B 352.
61 Marie Baum, *Leuchtende Spur: Das Leben Ricarda Huchs*, Tübingen, 1950, p. 34.
62 GStA Nl Weber Nr. 30 Bd. 1, Max to Marianne Weber, 3 August 1898.
63 Ana 446 Sch. 14, Marianne to Helene Weber, 5 November 1895.
64 Eberhard Demm, 'Alfred Weber und sein Bruder Max', in Demm, *Geist und Politik im 20. Jahrhundert: Gesammelte Aufsätze zu Alfred Weber*, Frankfurt am Main, 2000, p. 47n.
65 Georg Schwarz, *Ernst Schweninger: Bismarcks Leibarzt*, Leipzig, 1941, pp. 5, 74, 80, 86.
66 Richard Koch, 'Schweninger's Seminar', *Journal of Contemporary History*, 20 (1985), p. 759.
67 Universitätsarchiv Heidelberg H IV-102/130, Bl. 274 (15 June 1899): dissertation by Adolf Tienken: *Die wirtschaftlichen und gewerblichen Verhältnisse in Marsch und Geest der Provinz Hannover*.
68 GStA Nl Weber Nr. 30 Bd. 12, Max to Helene Weber, 14 August 1895 (Loch Lomond): 'In England . . . one does not see a single farming village on the entire journey from London to Edinburgh, but only an occasional castle in a park, with leaseholders' dwellings and individual farm buildings at some distance. From time to time one also sees churches from the thirteenth and fourteenth centuries which stand among a dozen workmen's huts instead of among fifty to sixty farmhouses, as they once did. These churches have become too big for their congregations, like a consumptive's suit. And in England one gets the feeling that there would be room for hundreds of thousands of farmers, while

Scotland was made to be a cattle pasture and, even more, a sheep walk' (WB 208). Clearly Weber did not know that the solitude of the Scottish highlands was also due in part to the 'clearances' of the eighteenth century.

69 GStA Nl Weber Nr. 30 Bd. 12, Max to Helene Weber, 14 August 1895.

70 Eidem, 29 August 1897.

71 Eidem, 18 September 1897 (Las Arenas).

72 Karl Jaspers, *On Max Weber*, New York, 1989, p. 126.

73 Paul Honigsheim, 'Max Weber as Rural Sociologist', *Rural Sociology*, 11 (1946), pp. 207–18; Honigsheim, 'Max Weber as Historian of Agricultural and Rural Life' (1949), in *The Unknown Max Weber*, ed. Alan Sica, New Brunswick, NJ, 2000, pp. 33–97.

74 Alfred Heuss, 'Max Webers Bedeutung für die Geschichte des griechisch-römischen Altertums', *Historische Zeitschrift*, 201 (1965), p. 538.

75 In a rather unusual distancing of himself from his earlier views, Weber confesses that his *Die römische Agrargeschichte* 'has many of the errors young scholars make' (AS 384).

76 See G. L. Ulmen, *The Science of Society: Toward an Understanding of the Life and Work of Karl August Wittfogel*, The Hague, 1978, especially the numerous references to Weber in the index, pp. 745f.

77 Joachim Radkau, *Natur und Macht: Eine Weltgeschichte der Umwelt*, 2nd edn, 2002, pp. 115f. See, in general, Stefan Breuer, 'Stromuferkultur und Küstenkultur: Geographische und ökologische Faktoren in Max Webers "ökonomischer Theorie der antiken Staatenwelt"', in Wolfgang Schluchter (ed.), *Max Webers Theorie des antiken Christentums*, Frankfurt am Main,1985, pp. 111–50; and on this point, esp. p. 122.

Chapter 5 Eruptions from the Ice

1 Even an admirer such as Hennis can groan that Weber's expectations of his readers border on 'impudence'. 'From time to time', he writes, 'Weber really strains our patience.' Wilhelm Hennis, *Max Weber's Central Question*, 2nd edn, Newbury, 2000, pp. 20 and 17.

2 Already at the age of twenty, Weber concluded an interminable letter to Hermann Baumgarten with an apology: 'I have never managed to express myself with particular brevity; everything just keeps growing and growing.'

3 There is already a literature on this too: see the entry 'Quote marks and italics in Weber's texts', in Richard Swedberg, *The Max Weber Dictionary: Key Words and Central Concepts*, Stanford, CA, 2005, pp. 219f.

4 Review of Adolf Weber's *Die Aufgaben der Volkswirtschaftslehre als Wissenschaft*, *Archiv für Sozialwissenschaft*, 29 (1909), pp. 615ff.

5 Wilhelm Hennis, *Max Weber's Science of Man*, Newbury, 2000, p. 64n. During the 1919–20 winter semester in Munich, Weber noted: 'Method is the most sterile thing imaginable. . . . Nothing has ever been created with method *alone.*'

6 Ana 446 Sch. 14, Marianne to Helene Weber, 28 October 1895: Max Weber had given a speech in Giessen. 'Just think: *unfortunately* he is not writing it up – "one shouldn't write down everything one says" – so *we* will know of it only from the newspaper reports. He has promised to tell me today what it contained, but I scarcely believe that he'll get round to it.' So, Weber did not feel

that all his thoughts and ideas were so precious that he should carefully preserve them – perhaps because, in his good periods, he always had so many and suffered from the superabundance. One notes, by the way, how closely Marianne and Helene followed his work – or at least his public appearances.

7 N.d., but according to information from Birgit Rudhard it should be dated to 17 August 1910.

8 Ana 446 Sch. 20 VI.

9 See Weber to Willy Hellpach, 18 April 1906: 'Forgive my bad handwriting! Spring always considerably increases my nervous tension' (MWG II/5, 83).

10 Marianne to Helene Weber, 29 December 1902 [SG].

11 In 1911, after seeing the huge scores of *Tristan* at Mina Tobler's house for the first time, Weber said that he was 'deeply affected'. 'Such a writing technique should be available to me, as then I would finally be able to say many separate things side by side yet simultaneously' (B 482n.). When listening to Wagner, even the supposedly unmusical Max Weber felt that his own wishful dreams were being fulfilled!

12 Eduard Baumgarten's emphasis is different: he employs the topos that Weber was a would-be statesman. The 'secret of his special mode of teaching and scholarship' lay in the fact 'that he was a researcher with the instincts and vision of a politician. This was why everything in his research "made sense" to him so rapidly and pertinently; it was "probably" the "point" from which his element of genius derived' (Max Weber, *Soziologie, weltgeschichtliche Analysen, Politik*, ed. Johannes Winckelmann, Stuttgart, 1956, XIII).

13 Marianne to Helene Weber, 10 December 1905 [SG].

14 Joachim Radkau and Orlinde Radkau, *Praxis der Geschichtswissenschaft: Die Desorientiertheit des historischen Interesses*, Düsseldorf, 1972, p. 62.

15 Judith Marcus and Zoltán Tar (eds), *Georg Lukács: Selected Correspondence 1902–1920*, New York, 1986, p. 93.

16 Gregor Schöllgen, *Max Weber*, Munich, 1998, p. 21.

17 A detailed analysis of Weber's procedure in his studies of ancient Judaism, which is easier to conduct on the basis of source material than in the case of most of his writings, led Eckart Otto to reject as clearly wrong the view that 'Weber thought he knew the essence of biblical Judaism before he had examined the texts'. Eckart Otto, *Max Webers Studien des Antiken Judentums*, Tübingen, 2002, p. 277n.

18 Robert Michels, *Masse, Führer, Intellektuelle*, Frankfurt am Main, 1987, p. 263.

19 Elly Heuss-Knapp, *Ausblick vom Münsterturm: Erinnerungen*, Tübingen, 1952, p. 101.

20 Karl Loewenstein, 'Personal Recollections of Max Weber', in Loewenstein, *Max Weber's Political Ideas in the Perspective of our Time*, Amherst, MA, 1966, p. 101.

21 Friedrich Meinecke, 'Drei Generationen deutscher Gelehrtenpolitik' (1922), in *Staat und Persönlichkeit*, Berlin, 1933, pp. 155f.

22 Friedrich Meinecke, 'Kausalitäten und Werte in der Geschichte', in Fritz Stern (ed.), *Geschichte und Geschichtsschreibung*, Munich, 1966, pp. 280f.

23 Moritz Julius Bonn, *So macht man Geschichte*, Munich, 1953, pp. 61 and 71. He had reason to feel resentful, since in 1919 he had headed the Munich faculty shortlist for the professorship that the Bavarian government subsequently offered to Weber (MWG I/17, 77n.).

24 Friedrich Meinecke, *Straßburg – Freiburg – Berlin 1901–1919*, Stuttgart, 1949, p. 74.

25 Hermann Glockner, *Heidelberger Bilderbuch*, Bonn, 1969, pp. 111, 101.

26 After a meeting with Naumann in Rome, during which Weber overstrained himself by talking a lot and getting worked up, Marianne wrote to Helene (10 February 1902; SG) 'that for the time being contact with books is much less wearing for Max than contact with real life and the political problems that occupy him so intensively'.

27 Glockner, *Heidelberger Bilderbuch*, pp. 56 and 106, on both occasions recorded by Jaspers, who found this carefree attitude quite proper in Weber's case: 'Anyone who has only two or three ideas likes to nurse and pamper them and dress them up prettily. But where things keep bubbling and new ideas keep flowing forth, they simply have to escape on to paper. In such cases, it is not possible to bother about style.'

28 Marianne to Max Weber, 30 December 1902, referring to the essay *Roscher and Knies*: 'I just think it's a pity that you pack into the footnotes so many pearls of wisdom that should be up there in the text; they look much better there.' Today's reader will agree with her. Incidentally, we should note that Marianne – who, in the view of present-day Weber experts, was incapable of understanding Max Weber – closely followed his work even on *Roscher and Knies*, the so-called essay of sighs, which still wrings many a sigh from today's experts.

29 Even Friedrich Tenbruck, a great admirer and a pioneer of Weber studies, felt 'weighed down' by the reading of *Economy and Society*. 'This oppressive feeling . . . also arises from the inner organization of the text, which often rolls pitilessly over several pages without paragraph breaks or sub-headings and provokes a sense of the futility of all efforts.' Friedrich Tenbruck, *Das Werk Max Webers*, Tübingen, 1999, p. 110.

30 BA Koblenz, Nl 197/85, Else Jaffé to Alfred Weber, May 1919.

31 Georg Lukács, *The Destruction of Reason*, London, 1980, pp. 610ff.

32 What the twenty-year-old Weber admired in the National-Liberal leader Friedrich Kapp was evidently the same goal that he had set for himself in life: 'effortlessly to bring the most diverse things into connection with one another, and unobtrusively to open up perspectives that take in the whole world' (JB 140).

33 See Alfred Heuss, 'Max Webers Bedeutung für die Geschichte des griechisch-romischen Altertums', *Histörische Zeitschrift*, 201 (1965), p. 534. In answer to my question about what was so distinctive about Weber, Hans-Ulrich Wehler also replied that it was his ability to generate surprising associations, to illuminate phenomena from unfamiliar angles, and consistently to think through this multiple perspective. Of course, there is also another kind of 'multiperspectivality', which is obtained through flights of intellect.

34 Ana 446 Sch. 20 V.

35 Adolf von Harnack later remarked to Theodor Heuss that he had enough of a perspective to say that, 'internationally speaking, between 1880 and 1920 Max Weber had undoubtedly been the man with the greatest powers of intellectual consumption. He did not simply take from others, however, but made his own sense of everything he received' (Max Weber, Soziologie, weltgeschichtliche Analysen, Politik, XIf.). It must mean something if even Harnack, who had a huge capacity for intellectual consumption, recognized Weber's superiority in this respect, especially as his admiration for Weber was otherwise by no means unqualified.

36 See Hermann Kantorowicz, *Gutachten zur Kriegsschuldfrage 1914* (1927), ed. Imanuel Geiss, Frankfurt am Main, 1967.

37 Karl Jaspers, *The Great Philosophers* (vol. 1 of the Nachlaß), ed. and trans. Michael Ermarth and Leonard H. Ehrlich, New York, 1995, pp. 334, 330.

38 Wilhelm Hennis, *Weber und Thukydides*, Göttingen, 2003, p. 7.

39 Quoted in Peter Gay, *Weimar Culture: The Outsider as Insider*, London, 1974, p. 39.

40 Karl Jaspers, *Psychologie der Weltanschauungen*, 3rd edn, Berlin, 1925, p. 14.

41 BA Koblenz, Nl 197/97, Else to Alfred Weber, 4 April 1920.

42 Radkau and Radkau, *Praxis der Geschichtswissenschaft*, p. 222.

43 'The "Objectivity" of Knowledge in Social Science and Social Policy', trans. Keith Tribe, in *The Essential Weber: A Reader*, ed. Sam Whimster, London, 2004, p. 403.

44 Roger Chickering, *Karl Lamprecht: A German Academic Life*, Atlantic Highlands, NJ, 1993, p. 322.

45 Pierre Bourdieu, 'Mit Weber gegen Weber', interview, in Bourdieu, *Das religiöse Feld*, Konstanz, 2000, pp. 115, 111, 119.

46 A vivid example of this is Gottfried Christian Bohn, *Wohlerfahrener Kaufmann*, 5th edn, Hamburg, 1789 (repr. Wiesbaden 1977), pp. 579ff., which makes the point that, although scholars 'particularly need a spirit of observation' in their travels, merchants need it even more.

47 Ana 446 Sch. 14, Marianne to Helene Weber, 13 October 1895 (after she and Max had returned from Scotland).

48 This passage is already included in Marianne's letter of 16 June 1903 to Helene Weber (SG), with the comment next to 'discursively': 'Alfred must wonder what this is'!

49 'The priestly physiognomies are also constantly interesting: along with fat old Falstaffs oozing contentment and straightforwardly coarse and ugly faces, there are young pale wide-eyed fanatics whose severe mouths speak of struggles to mortify the flesh, or others who have won the struggle, or others still who have abandoned it and either sunk dull-witted into materiality or developed in the direction of a witty scepticism.' 'Sunk dull-witted into materiality': how anti-materialistic Weber could sometimes sound, at least in writing to his religiously idealist mother!

50 GStA Nl Weber Nr. 30 Bd. 12, Max to Helene Weber, 29 August 1897.

51 Eduard Meyer, *Urgeschichte des Christentums*, vol. 1, Tübingen, 1923, pp. 77–81.

52 Radkau and Radkau, *Praxis der Geschichtswissenschaft*, p. 110.

53 Johann Gustav Droysen, *Historik: Vorlesungen über Enzyklopädie und Methodologie der Geschichte*, ed. Rudolf Hübner, 3rd edn, Munich, 1967, pp. 361, 287, 26; see Radkau and Radkau, *Praxis der Geschichtswissenschaft*, pp. 66ff.

54 Radkau and Radkau, *Praxis der Geschichtswissenschaft*, pp. 68f.

55 On the CD-ROM of Weber's works, '*Erlebnis*' occurs most frequently in the *Roscher und Knies* essay (*Roscher and Knies: The Logical Problems of Historical Economics*, New York, 1975), and precisely there often between quotation marks.

56 In *Roscher and Knies*, Weber tackles at length the notion that 'our own immediate experience is the most certain piece of knowledge that we have' (ibid., p. 160), which he attributes to the highly reputed economist Gottl-Ottilienfeld and sweepingly dismisses as unscientific.

57 Manfred Hettling, 'Das Unbehagen in der Erkenntnis: Max Weber und das "Erlebnis"' (original of his postdoctoral *Habilitation* lecture at the University of Bielefeld), *Simmel Newsletter*, 71 (1997), pp. 49–65.

58 Hideharu Ando, 'Die Interviews mit Else Jaffé, Edgar Salin und Helmuth Plessner über Max Weber 1969/70', *Kölner Zeitschrift für Soziologie*, 55 (2003), p. 605.

59 Hennis, *Max Weber's Central Question*, p. 152.

60 Karl Jaspers, *On Max Weber*, New York, 1989, p. 129.

61 Hennis, *Max Weber's Science of Man*, pp. 48f.

62 GStA Nl Weber Nr. 30 Bd. 4, 14 March 1898.

63 Hennis, *Max Weber's Science of Man*, p. 169.

64 See Michael Sukale, *Max Weber: Leidenschaft und Disziplin*, Tübingen, 2002, pp. 57ff.

65 Heino Heinrich Nau, *Der Werturteilsstreit*, Marburg, 1996, p. 155.

66 Dieter Lindenlaub, *Richtungskämpfe im Verein für Sozialpolitik*, Cologne, 1967, p. 306.

67 Harry Breßlau, in Sigfried Steinberg (ed.), *Die Geschichtswissenschaft der Gegenwart in Selbstdarstellungen*, vol. 1, Leipzig, 1925, pp. 5f.

68 Of course, this applied to his listeners as well as himself. 'But we felt as if under a cold shower', a former student recalled of a time when Weber said that, if he had been minister, he would have ordered Kurt Eisner's assassin, Count Arco, to be shot (WzG 26).

69 Paul Feyerabend, 'Consolations for the Specialist', in Imre Lakatos and Alan Musgrave (eds), *Criticism and the Growth of Knowledge*, Cambridge, 1970, p. 229.

70 Eduard Baumgarten, 'Über Max Weber: Brief an Nicolaus Sombart', *Merkur*, 344–55 (1977), p. 298.

Chapter 6 A 'Gospel of Struggle' and Old German Corpulence

1 Hermann Glockner, *Heidelberger Bilderbuch*, Bonn, 1969, p. 102.

2 AWG 10, p. 81, Alfred Weber to Max Weber senior, 16 February 1889.

3 GStA Nl Weber Nr. 30 Bd. 1, Max to Marianne Weber, 1 March 1894.

4 In 1910 Weber wrote to Karl Bücher, as if it were a well-known fact, that things had gone 'undeservedly well' for him early in his academic career (MWG II/6, 522).

5 Ana 446 Sch. 14, Marianne to Helene Weber, 17 February 1896; July 1896 (?): 'Yes, you were right again: the suffering and hardship in the world feel more remote here than in Berlin. That's precisely why it is necessary to rein yourself in, so as not to become shallow.' To be sure, Marianne was partly expressing her regrets because she knew how they would sound to the addressee.

6 Klaus Kempter, *Die Jellineks 1820–1955*, Düsseldorf, 1998, pp. 270f.

7 Ana 446 Sch. 14, Marianne to Helene Weber, 25 February 1895.

8 Ibid., Marianne to Helene Weber, 17 February 1896.

9 GStA Nl Weber Nr. 30 Bd. 12, Max to Helene Weber, 14 August 1895 (Loch Lomond).

10 Emil Kraepelin, *Lebenserinnerungen*, ed. H. Hippius, Berlin, 1983, pp. 79ff.; Joachim Radkau, *Zeitalter der Nervosität*, Munich, 1998, p. 167.

11 GStA, Nl Weber Nr. 30 Bd. 1, Max to Marianne Weber, 29 July 1894.

12 Ana 446 Sch. 14, Marianne to Helene Weber, n.d. (July 1896 ?).

13 GStA Nl Weber Nr. 30 Bd. 4, 9 May 1897.

14 WB 201, 203f.; David Chalcraft, 'Love and Death: Weber, Wagner and Max Klinger', in Sam Whimster (ed.), *Max Weber and the Culture of Anarchy*, London, 1999, pp. 196–213.

15 Joachim Radkau, 'Nationalismus und Nervosität', in Wolfgang Hardtwig and Hans-Ulrich Wehler (eds), *Kulturgeschichte heute*, Göttingen, 1996, p. 308.

16 Ana 446 Sch. 20 VI.

17 Ana 446 Sch. 14, Marianne to Helene Weber, n.d.

18 Eaedem, 23 March 1896.

19 Ana 446 Sch. 20 IV Bl. 9.

20 Marianne to Helene Weber, 13 September 1900 (SG).

21 Eadem, 28 December 1903 (SG). See eaedem, 20 December 1903: 'Public activity and scientific work, with all the personal duties on top, are very awkward to combine – especially for someone like me whose nerves are not so solid.' In 1895 Marianne still felt more nervous than Max: a mouse nibbling at a door robbed her of sleep for several nights. Max, she wrote, 'sleeps like a bear, while I tremble every evening at the nibbling monster'. Ana 446 Sch. 14, Marianne to Helene Weber, 10 February 1895.

22 Marianne to Helene Weber, 21 December 1904 (SG).

23 Ana 446 Sch. 14, Marianne to Helene Weber, 26 July 1985.

24 GStA Nl Weber Nr. 30 Bd. 1, Max to Marianne Weber, 20 July 1894; WB 196.

25 Radkau, *Zeitalter der Nervosität*, pp. 38ff.

26 Ana 446 Sch. 14, Marianne to Helene Weber, n.d. (before the inaugural lecture): 'Max is at present very contented; he claims not to have felt so fresh and productive for a long time, as he always notices the extent to which his flow of speech at the university is under his control.' Eaedem, 9 March 1895: 'Max walks up and down in his room thinking about tomorrow's lecture; he complained that he wants to say absolutely nothing in the next few years, as this little bit of speaking costs him a disproportionate amount of time.'

27 See Radkau, *Zeitalter der Nervosität*.

28 See the international overview in Marijke Gijswijt-Hofstra (ed.), *Cultures of Neurasthenia: From Beard to the First World War*, Amsterdam, 2000 (= Clio Medica 63).

29 See Igor S. Kon, *Die Geschichtsphilosophie des 20. Jahrhunderts*, vol. 1, Berlin, 1964, pp. 152f.

30 Eduard Baumgarten, *Benjamin Franklin, der Lehrmeister der amerikanischen Revolution*, Frankfurt, 1936, esp. pp. 93ff., 111ff., 117ff. and 138ff.

31 Gerd Fesser, *Der Traum vom Platz an der Sonne: Deutsche 'Weltpolitik' 1897–1914*, Bremen, 1996, p. 29.

32 Fritz Fischer, *War of Illusions: German Policies from 1911 to 1914*, London, 1975, pp. 33f. (which suggests that Weber, with his *Weltmacht* fanfares, was actually in advance of Delbrück); Gerhard Ritter, 'Eine neue Kriegsschuldthese?' (1962), in Ernst W. Graf Lynar (ed.), *Deutsche Kriegsziele 1914–1918*, Frankfurt am Main,1964, p. 124. Hans-Ulrich Wehler (*Deutsche Gesellschaftsgeschichte*, vol. 3, Munich, 1995, p. 1140) calls Weber's Freiburg address a 'trumpet blast' which, 'having become widely known because of its passionate emotionalism', was followed by 'a long chain reaction of concurring statements'. According to Wehler (oral communication to author), Treitschke was a chauvinist, though not an imperialist.

33 Hans Delbrück, 'Die gute alte Zeit', in Delbrück, *Erinnerungen, Aufsätze und Reden*, Berlin, 1907, pp. 179–212.

34 Ibid., p. 578.

35 Bernhard von Bülow, *Denkwürdigkeiten*, vol. 1, Berlin, 1930, p. 112.

36 Peter Winzen, *Bülows Weltmachtkonzept: Untersuchungen zur Frühphase seiner Außenpolitik 1897–1901*, Boppard, 1977, pp. 62, 66. In Volker Ullrich's view (*Die nervöse Großmacht 1871–1918*, Frankfurt am Main, 1997, pp. 194f.), the *Weltmacht* conception that Winzen attributes to Bülow is too sharply defined even for his time as foreign minister; this would, of course, make Weber's pioneering role even more striking.

37 Wolfgang J. Mommsen, *Max Weber and German Politics 1890–1920*, Chicago, 1990, p. 37. In Mommsen's view (ibid., p. 49), 'Weber shared his strong nationalist feelings with his entire epoch.' But in that case how could his speech have aroused 'general consternation'?

38 I found this garishly handwritten letter in the German State Archives in Berlin, among letters from Max Weber to his sister Klara. At first I suspected that 'Klärchen' had composed it herself in altered handwriting, as yet another of her practical jokes. Wolfgang Mommsen was not able to give me any information about it. But, since Weber himself mentioned the letter after he had gone over to a pro-Polish position (MWG I/15, 187), my suspicion was doubtless not well founded. (See the footnote in MWG I/15, to the effect that the editors were not the ones who found the letter concealed in the correspondence with Klärchen!) When I was in Berlin-Dahlem in February 2000, to get a first impression of Weber's unpublished writings – undecided though I still was about whether to accept a publisher's contract for a Weber biography – the letter from Lemberg was almost the first thing I came across. As I was staying at the *Wilder Eber* hotel and had even once absent-mindedly signed something there 'W.Eber', I took the coincidence as a sign that fate was nodding me on to sign the contract.

39 Ana 446 Sch. 14, Marianne to Helene Weber, 19 May 1895.

40 Elsewhere, in a lecture given in Mannheim on 10 September 1897 at the invitation of the local commercial association, Weber defended the very position he had corrected on the previously mentioned occasion, and again he maligned as 'philistines' those who did not share his position: 'We are moving with disturbing speed towards the point when the expansion of supplies from Asian half-educated nations will have ceased. Then what will be decisive on the external market will be nothing other than power, naked force. Only petty-bourgeois philistines can doubt that' (MWG I/4–2, 851).

41 Friedhelm Biesenbach, *Die Entwicklung der Nationalökonomie an der Universität Freiburg i. Br. 1768–1896*, Freiburg im Breisgau, 1969, pp. 190f.

42 Wilhelm Hennis, *Weber und Thukydides*, Göttingen, 2003, p. 56.

43 Hans-Ulrich Wehler, 'Die Zukunft Max Webers hat erst begonnen', *Frankfurter Allgemeine Zeitung*, 31 December 2001.

44 Arnold Bergstraesser, 'Max Webers Antrittsvorlesung in zeitgeschichtlicher Perspektive', *Vierteljahreshefte für Zeitgeschichte*, 5 (1957), p. 217.

45 Friedrich Wilhelm Foerster, *Erlebte Weltgeschichte*, Nuremberg, 1953, pp. 134ff. ('Schweizer Segen für Europa').

46 Theodor Heuss, *Friedrich Naumann*, 2nd edn, Stuttgart, 1949, p. 101.

47 See Dieter Düding, *Der nationalsoziale Verein*, Munich, 1972, pp. 36ff.

48 Alfred Weber, *Ausgewählter Briefwechsel*, ed. Eberhard Demm and Hartmut Soell, Marburg, 2003, vol. 1, p. 293.

49 Heuss, *Friedrich Naumann*, p. 101.
50 Peter Theiner, *Sozialer Liberalismus und deutsche Weltpolitik: Friedrich Naumann im Wilhelminischen Deutschland (1860–1919)*, Baden-Baden, 1983, p. 48.
51 Heuss, *Friedrich Naumann*, p. 102.
52 A: Jaspers Nr. 113 IV, Winckelmann to Engisch, 24 January 1963.
53 Marianne to Helene Weber, 10 December 1901 (SG).
54 GStA Nl Weber Nr. 30 Bd. 3, Weber to Adolf Wagner, 14 March 1895.
55 Charles Gide and Charles Rist, *A History of Economic Doctrines from the Time of the Physiocrats to the Present Day*, London, 1915, p. 518. 'The new school had one distinctive characteristic. In its search for a basis upon which to build the new theory it hit upon the general principle that man always seeks pleasure and avoids pain. . . . Today we speak of it as Hedonism.'
56 Ibid., p. 523n. Even the French economists Gide and Rist, who were rather sceptical towards the Vienna School, expressed their agreement: 'There is something very impressive about this deductive process that irresistibly reminds one of the genie of the *Thousand and One Nights*, who grew gradually bigger and bigger until he finally reached the heavens.' 'But', they continue, 'the genie was nothing but the flame. It still remains to be seen whether this is equally true of the Hedonist theories.' Ibid., p. 528.
57 Knut Borchardt, *Max Webers Börsenschriften: Rätsel um ein übersehenes Werk*, Munich, 2000 (Sitzungsberichte der Bayerischen Akademie der Wissenschaften, Philosophisch-Historische Klasse, 2000/4), p. 41.
58 Manfred Schön, 'Gustav Schmoller and Max Weber', in W. J. Mommsen and J. Osterhammel (eds), *Max Weber and his Contemporaries*, London, 1987; Max Weber, *Grundriß zu den Vorlesungen über Allgemeine ('theoretische') Nationalökonomie*, repr. Tübingen, 1990.
59 Quoted from Christian Köhnke, *Der junge Simmel*, Frankfurt am Main, 1996, pp. 452f.
60 Universitätsarchiv Heidelberg, Akademische Quästur Rep. 27, 1409; Volker Hentschel, 'Die Wirtschaftswissenschaften als akademische Disziplin an der Universität Heidelberg (1822–1924)', in Norbert Waszek (ed.), *Die Institutionalisierung der Nationalökonomie an deutschen Universitäten*, St. Katharinen, 1988, p. 228.
61 Biesenbach, *Entwicklung der Nationalökonomie an der Universität Freiburg*, p. 213.
62 Hentschel, 'Wirtschaftswissenschaften . . . an der Universität Heidelberg', p. 205.
63 Correspondence with the author.
64 On the connection between the two, see Radkau, *Zeitalter der Nervosität*, pp. 12f.

Chapter 7 The Demons

1 In a letter of 18 February 1892 to Emmy Baumgarten, Weber mentioned 'the awful modern disease' that had befallen her, and 'whose enormous pressure on one's whole mood I have also unpleasantly sampled in one brief, quite fleeting attack' (JB 338). Curiously, he does not name the disease but assumes that Emmy knows what he is referring to. Wilhelm Hennis (*Max Weber's Science*

of Man, Newbury, 2000, p. 164n.) thinks with good reason that Weber was speaking of 'neurasthenia', which was then considered the modern illness *par excellence*, even a certificate of modernity (Joachim Radkau, *Zeitalter der Nervosität*, Munich, 1998, pp. 49ff., 173ff.).

2 Ana 446 Sch. 14, Marianne to Helene Weber, 26 December 1895: 'Max is better again. I'm glad he is not going to Berlin so overwrought.' Max Weber had been 'terribly agitated' because of disputes over Rickert's appointment in Freiburg (ibid., 21 December 1895) – a state that is hard to explain on the basis of what the philosopher meant to Weber at the time.

3 A year later, when Weber's illness had become acute, Marianne reminded him (SG, 19 August 1898): 'Do you know how hungry you were there for ever new impressions – it was probably also some nervous tension – and how your little nose seemed annoyingly heavy to you?'

4 GStA Nl Weber Nr. 30 Bd. 12, Max to Helene Weber, 18 September 1897.

5 Marianne to Helene Weber, 19 March 1898 (SG).

6 August Cramer, *Die Nervosität: Ihre Ursachen, Erscheinungen und Behandlung*, Jena, 1906, p. 121; Leopold Löwenfeld, *Pathologie und Therapie der Neurasthenie und Hysterie*, Wiesbaden, 1894, pp. 296f.

7 GStA Nl Weber Nr. 30 Bd. 4, Max to Helene Weber, 14 April 1898.

8 Oral communication from Hans-Ulrich Wehler to the author.

9 GLA Karlsruhe Abt. 235 Nr. 2643 (application for leave on 16 July 1898).

10 Marianne to Helene Weber, 6 December 1901 (Rome) (SG); in the biography (WB 252) 'a silly goose' is replaced with 'foolish'.

11 GStA Nl Weber, Nr. 30 Bd. 4, Max to Alfred Weber, 5 May 1903.

12 Georg Fischer, *Heilanstalt für Nervenkranke im Konstanzer Hof zu Konstanz*, brochure in the Konstanz university library.

13 Radkau, *Zeitalter der Nervosität*, pp. 109f.

14 GStA Nl Weber Nr. 30 Bd. 1, Max to Marianne Weber, 1, 3 and 4 August 1898.

15 Eidem, 4 September 1898.

16 Eidem, 26 August 1898.

17 Eidem, 21 August 1898.

18 Ana 446 Sch. 14, Marianne Weber to Emilie Benecke, 15 May (1900).

19 Marianne to Helene Weber, 10 July 1900 (Urach) (SG).

20 Deutsches Literaturarchiv Marbach, A: Jaspers Nr. 113 V.

21 In a letter dated 4 August 1898 from the Konstanzer Hof, Weber speaks of 'my abnormalities' (GStA Nl Weber Nr. 30 Bd. 1), which Marianne changed to 'my sickly disposition' (WB 236).

22 GStA Nl Weber Nr. 30 Bd. 4, Max to Helene Weber, 23 July 1899.

23 Marianne Weber to Emilie Benecke from Urach, 19 October 1900 (Ana 446 Sch. 14): 'We generally have to think in terms of very long periods of time.'

24 GLA Abt. 235 Nr. 2643.

25 GLA Abt. 235 Nr. 2643.

26 GStA Nl Weber Nr. 25, Weber to Rickert, 14 June 1904.

27 Marianne to Helene Weber, 28 January 1900 (SG).

28 Eaedem, n.d. (1900).

29 Marianne to Emilie Benecke, 19 October 1900 (Ana 446) on Klöpfel: 'Apart from Fischer he is so far the only doctor who has not got on my nerves with his views about Max's condition.' Georg Fischer was the director of the Konstanzer Hof. The doctors who 'got on Marianne's nerves' were mainly those who located the kernel of Max's illness in sexual problems.

30 Marianne to Helene Weber, 10 and 26 July 1900 [SG].
31 Marianne to Max Weber, July 1900 [SG]: 'Won't you do *me* a favour and stop being timid.'
32 Marianne to Helene Weber, August 1900 [SG].
33 *Illustrierter Führer durch Bäder, Heilanstalten und Sommerfrischen*, 4th edn, Leipzig, n.d. (approx. 1906), p. 180.
34 Willy Hellpach, *Wirken in Wirren*, vol. 1, Hamburg, 1948, p. 495.
35 See Joachim Radkau, 'Nationalismus und Nervosität', in Wolfgang Hardtwig and Hans-Ulrich Wehler (eds), *Kulturgeschichte heute*, Göttingen, 1996, pp. 314n.
36 GStA Nl Weber Nr. 30 Bd. 1, Max to Marianne Weber, 9 August 1898.
37 GStA Nl Weber Nr. 30 Bd. 4, Max to Helene Weber, 2 May 1896: 'Work is going better than for years. Maybe it's partly because twice a week I race up the castle hill in ten minutes, so that up there I always think my chest is bursting – it keeps the blood flowing and is thoroughly good for me.'
38 Marianne to Helene Weber, 23 June 1901 (SG).
39 Eaedem, 23 April 1907.
40 GStA Nl Weber Nr. 30 Bd. 1, Max to Marianne Weber, 19 and 21 August 1898.
41 Marianne to Helene Weber, 24 March 1903 (SG).
42 GStA Nl Weber Nr. 30 Bd. 1, Max to Marianne Weber from Scheveningen, 14 October 1903 (?).
43 What 'this' refers to is not clear from the immediate context. But, since on the next page Weber again lets fly at Gross's talk of 'the filthiness of unsatisfied eroticism' (WB 381), the passage must refer to the letter to Else.
44 Weber to Lukács, 14 August 1916, in Judith Marcus and Zoltán Tar (eds), *Georg Lukács: Selected Correspondence 1902–1920*, New York, 1986, p. 263.
45 Radkau, *Zeitalter der Nervosität*, p. 88.
46 Marianne to Helene Weber, 4 September 1913 [SG].
47 GStA Nl Weber Nr. 30 Bd. 1, Max to Marianne Weber, 14 October 1903 (?).
48 Edvard Poulsson, *Lehrbuch der Pharmakologie*, Leipzig, 1930, pp. 36f.; Otfried K. Linde, 'Chemie und Schlaf – Hoffnung und Hilfe für die Psychiatrie', in Linde (ed.), *Pharmakopsychiatrie im Wandel der Zeit*, Klingenmünster, 1988, p. 69.
49 Poulsson, *Lehrbuch der Pharmakologie*, pp. 38 ff. According to this manual, veronal was first marketed in 1903 – yet Weber was already taking it in 1902!
50 GStA Nl Weber Nr. 30 Bd. 1, Max to Marianne Weber from Verchelli, 18 April 1902.
51 Marianne to Helene Weber, 7 August 1903 [SG].
52 Marianne to Helene Weber, 8 June 1906 [SG]: 'I get along fine with the help of veronal.'
53 Alfred W. McCoy, 'Heroin aus Südostasien: Zur Wirtschaftsgeschichte eines ungewöhnlichen Handelsartikels', in Gisela Völger (ed.), *Rausch und Realität: Drogen im Kulturvergleich*, vol. 2, Cologne, 1981, p. 622. Cf. Alfred W. McCoy, *The Politics of Heroin in Southeast Asia*, New York, 1972.
54 Matthias Seefelder, *Opium: Eine Kulturgeschichte*, Munich, 1990, p. 210.
55 BA Koblenz, NL 197/87, 24 June 1920.
56 Georg Schwarz, *Ernst Schweninger*, Leipzig, 1941, pp. 64f.
57 Marianne to Helene Weber, 2 June 1901 [SG].
58 Eaedem, 17 July 1901.
59 Max to Marianne Weber, 26 March 1913 (MWG II/8, 147): 'Last night I slept brilliantly for twelve hours, normally, without any assistance.' On 30 March he

wrote (MWG II/8, 158): 'Sleep indifferent, but the great disquiet of the last year not present. Naturally the worst time still lies ahead.'

60 See Adolf Bach, *Geschichte der deutschen Sprache*, 8th edn, Heidelberg, 1965, pp. 202f., on the mystical origin of many German abstract nouns ending in -*heit* or -*keit*. In 1906, R. Rattke presented a dissertation in Jena on abstract word-formation ending in -*heit* in the work of Meister Eckhart.

61 Marianne to Max Weber, 10 July 1898 [SG].

62 Eidem, 19 August 1898.

63 Marianne to Helene Weber, 25 February 1899, Ana 446 Sch. 15.

64 Eaedem, 18 September 1898, Ana 446 Sch. 14.

65 What Gruhle wrote about nocturnal emissions in his manual (*Psychiatrie für Ärzte*, Berlin, 1918, p. 112) had a novel tone and sounded as if he had the highly regarded Weber in mind: Emissions 'not only occur with abnormal frequency in neurotics, hysterics and psychasthenics but often remain a subject of their thoughts long after the event. If a psychopath continually ponders whether an emission will occur the following night, and if he becomes intensely worried that it will make him incurably ill, shatter his nerves, and so on, the illness naturally becomes more and more firmly entrenched.'

66 Goethe, 'Das Tagebuch' (1814). 'But now the maestro is down in the dumps / Will not take orders or be awoken / Suddenly he is there and in complete silence / Raises himself to his full splendour.'

67 Marianne to Helene Weber, 10 December 1902; the same quotation may be found in WB 261, but *without* the emissions.

68 Eaedem, 23 June 1901. In the winter, however, things were worse even in Rome. Marianne wrote on 6 December 1901: 'He had two ejaculations last night, after an interval of six weeks, and is today calm; I'm dying to see how quickly he will get over the after-effects.' It is clear from this how Marianne made the clinical perspective her own.

69 Radkau, *Zeitalter der Nervosität*, p. 361.

70 Ibid., p. 147.

71 Marianne to Max Weber, 19 August 1898 [SG].

72 Ana 446 Sch. 20 IV Bl. 46: where we also learn that she 'never thought she had the strength to master everything connected with it'. Around the year 1890 a woman would most likely have had to go abroad to train as a doctor.

73 Marianne to Helene Weber, 4 September 1898.

74 Eaedem, 9 September 1898 [SG].

75 Eaedem, 28 March 1900 [SG].

76 The eponymous hero of Ibsen's play (1896). The influence of the founder of 'naturalist' drama can be repeatedly observed in the Webers.

77 Copy of the original in GStA, Nl Weber, Nr. 30 Bd. 1, Max to Marianne Weber, 4 August 1898.

78 Charles-Louis de Montesquieu, *Mes Pensées*, in *Oeuvres complètes de Montesquieu*, vol. 1, Pléiade edn, Paris, 1949, p. 1065.

79 Marianne to Helene Weber, 20 October 1902 [SG].

80 Eaedem, 26 August 1903. She continues: 'But I know that, the last time you were here, you must have had the impression that it is better for *me* to be alone with him; I was so terribly tired and miserable in February.'

81 Eaedem, 26 November 1901.

82 See eaedem, 15 February 1904 and even 19 October 1910 and 31 January 1911: '. . . the detoxification trip he needs to make early in the year'.

83 Eaedem, 29 January 1902 [SG].
84 Eaedem, 10 February 1902.
85 Eaedem, 28 March 1902. And on 8 November 1902, when Weber had wanted to hold a seminar but then dropped the idea: 'But each time there is again something desperate for both of us. One always thinks that one should be entitled to a certain regularity of performance, or that one should be able to force it out of the heavens.'
86 Eaedem, 16 June 1903 [SG]: 'It is very good for me psychologically to be with other people, but it puts an undue strain on the nerves.' She added that she usually slept badly and often had anxiety dreams – a sign, one would think, that her 'psyche' was also involved!
87 Willy Hellpach, *Heilkraft und Schöpfung*, Dresden, 1934, p. 85; Radkau, *Zeitalter der Nervosität*, p. 88.
88 Gertrud Bäumer, *Des Lebens wie der Liebe Band: Briefe*, ed. Emmy Beckmann, Tübingen, 1956, p. 20.
89 Marianne to Helene Weber, 11 April 1903 [SG].
90 Radkau, *Zeitalter der Nervosität*, p. 137.
91 Ana 446 Sch. 14, Marianne to Helene Weber, 13 October 1895.
92 Marianne to Helene Weber, 5 March 1900 [SG].
93 Marianne to Helene Weber, 21 September 1902 [SG].
94 Ana 446, Marianne Weber to Emilie Benecke, 18 December 1901.
95 Eaedem, 15 June 1903.
96 Eaedem, 9 June 1910.
97 This was pointed out by Bärbel Meurer, who is working on a biography of Marianne Weber.
98 MWG II/6, 798; Gotthard Schettler, 'Ludolf Krehl 1861–1936', in *Semper apertus*, Berlin, 1985, pp. 114 ff. I owe this reference to Birgit Rudhard.
99 Marianne to Helene Weber, 12 January, 14 June and 29 June 1909.
100 Dmitrii Chitzevskii, for example, makes no mention of it in his *Russische Geistesgeschichte*, 2nd edn, Munich, 1974. But see Laura Engelstein, *Castration and the Heavenly Kingdom: A Russian Folktale*, Ithaca, NY, 1999.
101 Radkau, *Zeitalter der Nervosität*, p. 85; Conrad Rieger, *Die Castration in rechtlicher, sozialer und vitaler Hinsicht*, Jena, 1900; Paul Julius Möbius, *Über die Wirkung der Castration*, Halle, 1903.
102 Cesare Lombroso, *The Man of Genius*, London, 1891.
103 See Steven E. Aschheim, *The Nietzsche Legacy in Germany: 1890–1990*, Berkeley, CA, 1992.
104 Ibid. This is also true in the United States: see Horst Baier, 'Friedrich Nietzsche und Max Weber in Amerika', *Nietzsche-Studien*, 16 (1987), pp. 430–6, on Robert Eden, *Political Leadership and Nihilism: A Study of Weber and Nietzsche*, Tampa, FL, 1984.
105 Marianne to Helene Weber, 7 January 1908.
106 WB 262f. Weber himself said that it was not his resignation as such which bothered him but rather his wife's lack of understanding, since 'no doctor was candid enough to convince Marianne' of its necessity.
107 Marianne to Helene Weber, 11 June 1900; 26 November 1901: '. . . how you were again and again tormented by doubts that perhaps Max could get over it through an *act of will*, and I was worried that he would feel this and find it painful.'
108 Radkau, *Zeitalter der Nervosität*, pp. 359ff.

109 Peter Bieri, *Das Handwerk der Freiheit: Über die Entdeckung des eigenen Willens*, Munich, 2001.
110 GStA Nl Weber Nr. 30 Bd. 1, Max to Marianne Weber, 19 August 1898.
111 GStA Nl Weber Nr. 30 Bd. 4, Max to Helene Weber, 23 July 1899.
112 Ana 446 Sch. 15, n.d.
113 Marianne to Helene Weber, 13 April 1906 [SG].
114 Eaedem, 10 March 1907.
115 Eaedem, 29 November 1907: 'Our big boy is working, but he keeps taking a lot of stuff from the pharmacy, since the functional excitability is as strong as ever. But it's okay as long as he isn't downhearted as well.'
116 Max Weber to Else Jaffé, 3 April 1919.
117 Radkau, *Zeitalter der Nervosität*, p. 79.
118 See Martin Green, *The von Richthofen Sisters: The Triumphant and the Tragic Modes of Love*, London, 1974, p. 291.
119 Deutsches Literaturarchiv Marbach, A: Jaspers, Nr. 113.
120 Jaspers considered these tendencies an established fact, as did Eduard Baumgarten. See Michael Sukale, *Max Weber: Leidenschaft und Disziplin*, Tübingen, 2002, p. 196. Hannah Arendt thought that Weber suffered from *ejaculatio praecox*, but Baumgarten denied this and maintained that 'Weber was a masochist and Else Jaffé satisfied his desires'.
121 The same is true of Marianne. She wrote later – as if it was a well-established fact – that 'the modern sciences of the mind and of youth and childhood have discovered that early sexual experiences with which we fail to come to terms are the most frequent cause of neurotic disorders' (*Die Frauen und die Liebe*, Königstein, 1936, p. 18). Evidently she was thinking of her husband.
122 Letter to Leo Popper, 9 October 1910, in *Georg Lukács: Briefwechsel 1902–1917*, Stuttgart, 1982, p. 150.
123 Klaus Lichtblau, *Kulturkrise und Soziologie um die Jahrhundertwende*, Frankfurt am Main, 1996, p. 334n.
124 This, with some qualifications, is also the position taken in J. Frommer and S. Frommer, 'Max Webers Krankheit: Soziologische Aspekte der depressiven Struktur', *Fortschritte der Neurologie und Psychiatrie*, 61 (1993), p. 168: the 'demons' are supposed to denote 'unintended manifestations of sexual excitement'.
125 Marianne to Helene Weber, 10 May 1905 [SG]. The metaphors of illness are not always the same; on 23 July 1905 she speaks of the 'chains that fate winds around him'.
126 Eaedem, 21 December 1905.
127 Augustinus, *Bekenntnisse*, ed. Joseph Bernhart, Frankfurt am Main, 1987, p. 69.
128 Peter Brown, *The Body and Society: Men, Women, and Sexual Renunciation in Early Christianity*, New York, 1988, p. 422; cf. Brown, *Augustine of Hippo: A Biography*, Berkeley, CA, 1967, p. 179.
129 B. Legewie, *Augustin: Eine Psychographie*, Bonn, 1925.
130 AJ 190.
131 'Marianne, however, did what her own conscience (*daimon*) prompted her to do . . .' (WB 188). Yet according to her memoirs (LE 45), the young Marianne saw her egoistic self-assertiveness as a 'demon': 'Ah, now I began to master the demon that had been in control of me.'
132 Deutsches Literaturarchiv Marbach, A: Jaspers Nr. 113 V.

133 Richard Willstätter, *Aus meinem Leben*, 2nd edn, Weinheim, 1958, p. 243.
134 Deutsches Literaturarchiv Marbach, A: Jaspers Nr. 113 V.
135 Karl Jaspers, *The Great Philosophers*, vol. 4 (Nachlaß 1) , New York, 1995, pp. 335–6.
136 'The Social Psychology of the World Religions', FMW 271.
137 MWG II/9, Max Weber to Lisa von Ubisch, 1 January 1917.
138 Helmut Fogt, 'Max Weber und die deutsche Soziologie der Weimarer Republik', in M. Rainer Lepsius (ed.), *Soziologie in Deutschland und Österreich 1918–1945*, Opladen, 1981, p. 255.
139 Guenther Roth, who went to the United States in the 1950s, repeatedly emphasized to me the role of émigrés as the crack troops in the veneration of Weber. The philosopher Dieter Henrich, who succumbed to Weber's magic in the postwar years, became especially 'fascinated' by the 'experiential seriousness' of Weber's texts, 'which can scarcely be separated from Weber's illness' (letter to the author, 15 January 2005).

Chapter 8 'A Sort of Spiritualistic Construction of the Modern Economy'

1 GStA Nr. 30 Bd. 4.
2 See, for example, 'Weber's First Reply to Rachfahl' (1910), in *The Protestant Ethic Debate: Max Weber's Replies to his Critics, 1907–1910*, ed. David J. Chalcraft and Austin Harrington, Liverpool, 2001, p. 83.
3 Ibid., p. 121.
4 Recently Wilhelm Hennis, in particular, has taken this Weberian theme literally. See Hennis, 'The Spiritual Foundation of Max Weber's "Interpretive Sociology": Ernst Troeltsch, Max Weber and William James's *Varieties of Religious Experience*', in *Max Weber's Science of Man*, Newbury, 2000, pp. 50ff.
5 Walther Köhler, *Ernst Troeltsch*, Tübingen, 1941, pp. 270, 287f.
6 Volkhard Krech, 'Mystik', in Hans G. Kippenberg and Martin Riesebrodt (eds), *Max Webers 'Religionssystematik'*, Tübingen, 2001, p. 251n.
7 Hartmann Tyrell, 'Katholizismus und katholische Kirche', in Hartmut Lehmann and Jean Martin Ouédrago (eds), *Max Webers Religionssoziologie in vergleichender Perspektive*, Göttingen, 2003, pp. 193–228; Gottfried Eisermann, 'Max Weber und der Katholizismus', in Eisermann, *Max Weber und die Nationalökonomie*, Marburg, 1993, pp. 159–215.
8 GStA Nl Weber Nr. 30 Bd. 12, Max to Helene Weber, 29 August 1897.
9 GStA Nl Weber Nr. 30 Bd. 1, Max to Marianne Weber, 30 July 1898.
10 A week later, the Webers waited patiently for five hours at St Peter's for the pope to appear. Max's patience was even greater than Marianne's: 'I was shattered afterwards, but he wasn't. It was as if an old idol were being taken from the grave and carried around' (Marianne to Helene Weber, 10 March 1902). Nevertheless, Marianne developed a greater sympathy than Max for Catholicism.
11 Robert Michels, *Masse, Führer, Intellektuelle*, Frankfurt am Main, 1987, p. 260.
12 Friedrich Wilhelm Graf, 'Fachmenschenfreundschaft: Bemerkungen zu "Max Weber und Ernst Troeltsch" ', in WuZ 328.
13 Friedrich Lenger, *Werner Sombart 1863–1941*, Munich, 1994, p. 131.
14 Hennis, *Max Weber's Science of Man*, pp. 46–65.

15 Joachim Radkau, *Zeitalter der Nervosität*, Munich, 1998, pp. 367f.
16 William James, *The Varieties of Religious Experience: A Study in Human Nature*, London, Fontana, 1960, p. 469.
17 See Robert D. Richardson, *William James: In the Maelstrom of American Modernism*, New York, 2006.
18 See Max Weber, *Die protestantische Ethik und der "Geist" des Kapitalismus*, ed. Klaus Lichtblau and Johannes Weiss, Bodenheim, 1993, p. xxxi; and Klaus Lichtblau, *Kulturkrise und Soziologie um die Jahrhundertwende: Zur Genealogie der Kultursoziologie in Deutschland*, Frankfurt am Main, 1996, p. 328.
19 In Johannes Wincklemann (ed.), *Die Protestantische Ethik* II *(Kritiken und Antikritiken)*, 3rd edn, Gütersloh, 1978, p. 11.
20 Karl Barth, *Protestant Theology in the Nineteenth Century*, 3rd edn, Berlin, 1961, pp. 412, 424f.
21 Ernst Fraenkel (ed.), *Amerika im Spiegel des deutschen politischen Denkens*, Cologne, 1959, pp. 130f.
22 Paul Münch, 'The Thesis before Weber: An Archaeology', in Hartmut Lehmann and Guenther Roth (eds), *Weber's Protestant Ethic: Origins, Evidence, Contexts*, Cambridge, 1993, pp. 66ff.
23 In Winckelmann (ed.), *Die Protestantische Ethik* II, p. 119.
24 Ibid., p. 159.
25 Joachim Radkau, *Technik in Deutschland*, Frankfurt am Main, 1989, p. 89.
26 Richard van Dülmen, 'Protestantismus und Kapitalismus: Max Webers These im Licht der neueren Sozialgeschichte', in Christian Gneuss and Jürgen Kocka (eds), *Max Weber: Ein Symposion*, Munich, 1988, p. 90.
27 Weber puts this last sentence in quotation marks, but its provenance has not been determined. It recalls 'Zarathustra's foreword' in *Thus Spake Zarathustra*, also referred to in Weber's 'Science as a Vocation' (FMW 143), where Nietzsche pokes fun at the 'last men'.
28 Ulrich Langer, *Heinrich von Treitschke*, Düsseldorf, 1998, p. 276.
29 Only Richard H. Tawney, who in the interwar years was a leading figure in Britain's comparatively sparse reception of Weber (in comparison with the USA), approvingly understood this conclusion to be a criticism of capitalism, although his judgement of *The Protestant Ethic* was otherwise rather negative. Communication from Sam Whimster.
30 As Klaus Lichtblau and Johannes Weiss have shown, Weber first introduced the concept of 'disenchantment' into *The Protestant Ethic* when he had fallen under the spell of the Oriental religions (*Die protestantische Ethik . . .*, p. xxiii). In the later footnotes, Weber repeatedly referred to the struggle that Puritanism had waged against 'merrie old England' (PE 217, 236ff.).
31 At another point (PE 75) Weber approvingly refers to Sombart's depiction of 'economic rationalism' as 'the salient feature of modern economic life as a whole'.
32 Hartmann Tyrell, 'Max Webers Soziologie – eine Soziologie ohne "Gesellschaft"', in Gerhard Wagner and Heinz Zipprian (eds), *Max Webers Wissenschaftslehre*, Frankfurt am Main, 1994, pp. 390–414. At that time the macro-concept of society was already enticing sociologists; there was 'method' in Weber's deliberate avoidance of the term (p. 391).
33 'Weber's First Reply to Rachfahl' (1910), in *The Protestant Ethic Debate: Max Weber's Replies to his Critics, 1907–1910*, p. 83.

34 Karl Jaspers, *On Max Weber*, New York, 1989, p. 81.

35 Particularly impressive and competent is Herbert Lüthy, 'Variationen über ein Thema von Max Weber', in Constans Seyfarth and Walter M. Sprondel (eds), *Seminar: Religion und gesellschaftliche Entwicklung: Studien zur Protestantismus-Kapitalismus-These Max Webers*, Frankfurt am Main, 1973, pp. 104ff.

36 Johannes Winckelmann (ed.), *Die Protestantische Ethik* II, Gütersloh,1978, p. 76.

37 Lujo Brentano, 'Puritanismus und Kapitalismus', in Brentano, *Der wirtschaftende Mensch in der Geschichte*, Leipzig, 1923, p. 424. In the same context (p. 411) Brentano accused Weber of 'seriously misusing Franklin' when he invoked him as the main authority for an ascetic Puritanism-capitalism.

38 Anonymous [Georg Gottfried Gervinus], *Georg Friedrich Fallenstein: Erinnerungs-Blätter für Verwandte und Freunde*, Heidelberg, 1854, p. 6.

39 Julius Wolf, *Der Geburtenrückgang: Die Rationalisierung des Sexuallebens in unserer Zeit*, Jena, 1912. 'Rationalization' appears there as a mere headword, however, without any theoretical conceptualization or further development of the idea.

40 Radkau, *Technik in Deutschland*, p. 270.

41 Already in the original edition (PE 78): 'We are here particularly interested in the origin of precisely that irrational element which lies in this, as in every conception of a calling.'

42 In 1967 the economic historian Werner Lüthy, in a sociology of religion inspired precisely by *The Protestant Ethic*, 'wreaked veritable havoc on the "idealtypical" method'. Quoted from Richard van Dülmen, *Protestantismus und Kapitalismus*, p. 100.

43 Winckelmann (ed.), *Die Protestantische Ethik* II, pp. 266ff.

44 When Weber speaks of an 'elective affinity' [*Wahlverwandtschaft*] between capitalism and Puritanism, the term should be understood – as Goethe understood it in his novel with that title – within the framework of the *chemical* theory of Goethe's day; the word 'elective' does not therefore imply any element of human choice. Weber, who knew Goethe well, must have been acquainted with the chemical meaning of *Wahlverwandtschaft* – further evidence for the naturalist element in his thinking.

45 GStA Nr. 30 Bd. 4. Similarly, on 24 November 1918 he wrote to Friedrich Crusius that 'authoritarianism . . . is now a complete failure, except in the form of the church'. Max Weber, *Gesammelte politische Schriften*, Munich, 1921, p. 483.

46 Hartmut Lehmann, 'Max Webers Pietismusinterpretation', in Lehmann, *Max Webers 'Protestantische Ethik'*, Göttingen, 1996, p. 57.

47 Albrecht Ritschl, *Geschichte des Pietismus*, vol. 1, Berlin, 1966, pp. 254 f.

48 Karl Barth, *Protestant Theology in the Nineteenth Century: Its Background & History*, London, 2001, pp. 642, 598ff.

49 'Weber's First Reply to Fischer' (1907), in *The Protestant Ethic Debate: Max Weber's Replies to his Critics, 1907–1910*, p. 36.

50 Francis Fukuyama, *Trust: The Social Virtues and the Creation of Prosperity*, New York, 1995, pp. 44f.

51 Cf. the long footnote on sexuality and marriage (PE 263): 'We may here neglect the Herrnhut theory and practice of marriage.' He touches here on a once highly popular subterranean theme in Protestantism: the practice of sexual intercourse in certain positions, which for a time was current among the Moravians.

52 Hans-Christoph Schröder ('Max Weber und der Puritanismus', *Geschichte und Gesellschaft*, 21 (1995), p. 464) also comes to the conclusion that Weber misinterpreted in a secular-economic sense the Puritans' high appreciation of the value of time, and that in fact time was precious to the Puritans above all for the purposes of prayer. Weber would doubtless have retorted that he had been speaking of unintended, not conscious and deliberate, contexts of interdependence.

53 Ferdinand Kürnberger, *Der Amerikamüde*, Berlin, 1985, p. 27, where Franklin's saying comes from the mouth of the repugnant Dr Mockingbird, who occasionally earns money as a teacher and trains his pupils entirely for the pursuit of profit. Weber writes in a footnote (PE 192) that this book is 'incomparable as a document of the (now long since blurred-over) differences between the German and the American outlook'. But for that reason it is not an authentic testimony of the American outlook in the eighteenth century.

54 Eduard Baumgarten (*Benjamin Franklin: Der Lehrmeister der amerikanischen Revolution*, Frankfurt am Main, 1936, pp. 176ff.) rightly subsumes Franklin's natural researches under his 'doctrine of happiness'.

55 Mark Stoll, *Protestantism, Capitalism, and Nature in America*, Albuquerque, NM, 1997, p. 86. Stoll calls Franklin 'one of the most secular Americans of the 18th century' (p. 85).

56 Baumgarten, *Benjamin Franklin*, pp. 94f.

57 Ibid., p. 112.

58 Ibid., p. 117.

59 Edgar Salin, *Geschichte der Volkswirtschaftslehre*, 2nd edn, Berlin, 1929, p. 98.

60 Similarly, in distancing himself from Weber's ban on value-judgements in science, Schmoller wrote in 1911: 'Weber would not have been able to write his fine essays on the Protestant ethic if he had not himself deeply felt the link between the economic and the ethical' (Manfred Schön, 'Gustav Schmoller und Max Weber', WuZ 97). This was really playing Weber off against Weber.

61 Wilhelm Hennis (*Max Weber's Central Question*, Newbury, 2000, p. 20) considers that much of Rachfahl's critique is justified and even that 'one can only admire Rachfahl's patience'.

62 Cf. *The Protestant Ethic Debate*, p. 94 ('that admixture of hair-splitting pedanticism and petty superiority that describes the essence of the "professorial" ') or p. 120 ('professor with such self-confidence'). On Rachfahl's angry response, see Michael Sukale, *Max Weber: Leidenschaft und Disziplin*, Tübingen, 2002, pp. 256f.

63 Lichtblau and Weiss in Max Weber, *Die protestantische Ethik und der 'Geist' des Kapitalismus*, p. x; and Wilhelm Hennis, *Max Weber und Thukydides*, Göttingen, 2003, p. 117.

64 Hartmut Lehmann, 'Max Webers "Protestantische Ethik" als Selbstzeugnis', in Lehmann, *Max Webers 'Protestantische Ethik'*, pp. 109–14, 118.

65 Benjamin Franklin, (*Autobiography*, http://www.ushistory.org/franklin/autobiography, p. 38) gives as the twelfth and longest of his thirteen precepts of virtue: 'Rarely use venery but for health or offspring, never to dullness, weakness, or the injury of your own or another's peace or reputation.' And earlier he reports in a perfectly natural way that 'that hard-to-be-governed passion of youth hurried me frequently into intrigues with low women', which 'were attended with some expense' and 'a continual risk to my health' (p. 34). In those days, the well-founded fear of syphilis was by no means necessarily a sign of prudishness.

66 Weber himself later praised Schulze-Gaevernitz's work (PE 198), but he wrote *The Protestant Ethic* with at most marginal attention to British imperialism.

67 Gerhart von Schulze-Gaevernitz, *Britischer Imperialismus und englischer Freihandel zu Beginn des 20. Jahrhunderts* (1906), 2nd edn, Leipzig, 1915, pp. 49, 376.

68 Ibid., p. 387.

69 Hennis, *Max Weber's Central Question*, p. 18.

70 Wolfgang Schluchter has repeatedly emphasized this point. See, for example, his *Unversöhnte Moderne*, Frankfurt am Main, 1996, p. 212: 'The psychological lever for Max Weber is the need for release.'

71 In direct opposition to Weber, Hans-Christoph Schröder ('Max Weber und der Puritanismus', p. 471) even maintains that the Puritans were 'filled with a positive "hunger for community"'.

72 Weber's article on the Protestant sects hints that his attitude to them changed as a result of his trip to the United States. Guenther Roth (communication to the author, 25 March 2004) even considers, on the basis of his decades-long experience of the USA and Weber's writings, that Weber later *over*estimated the ability of the sects to exercise control.

73 Friedrich Wolters, *Stefan George und die Blätter für die Kunst*, Berlin, 1929, pp. 471ff. I am most grateful to Thomas Karlauf for this reference.

74 *The Protestant Ethic Debate*, p. 61; Johannes Winckelmann (ed.), *Die protestantsche Ethik II*, pp. 28, 149. Weber always remained on formal '*Sie*' terms with Sombart; we should bear in mind that it was unusual in those days to use '*du*' among adult scholars who were not related to one another. My question as to whether Weber called Troeltsch '*du*' was left unanswered at the Heidelberg symposium in March 2004, since not one of the many letters that must have passed between the two men has survived. Apparently their widows agreed to destroy the entire correspondence. Friedrich Wilhelm Graf thinks that they would have called each other '*du*', as they were on very familiar terms with each other for a time.

75 He even occasionally called Simmel or Schulze-Gaevernitz 'friend': MWG I/17, Max Weber, *Gesammelte politische Schriften*, ed. Johannes Winckelmann, 5th edn, Tübingen, 1988, p. 227; 463; 'Politics as a Vocation' in FMW, p. 115.

76 Graf, 'Fachmenschenfreundschaft', pp. 325f.

77 Ernst Troeltsch, *The Social Teaching of the Christian Churches*, vol. 1, London, 1931, e.g. pp. 150ff. Curiously, at the Frankfurt Sociologists' Congress in 1910 Weber did not focus on this in a contribution to the discussion on Troeltsch's lecture 'The Stoic-Christian Law of Nature'; he simply alluded to the 'conflicts among church, sects and mystical currents and their relationship to the world, to natural law, etc'. (GASS 467).

78 Troeltsch, *The Social Teaching*, vol. 1, p. 306.

79 Karl Barth, *Protestant Theology in the Nineteenth Century*, preface and p. 417. Troeltsch's biographer Walter Köhler later spoke more favourably of 'the uncommon receptiveness of his mind'. See Friedrich Wilhelm Graf (ed.), *Ernst Troeltsch in Nachrufen*, Gütersloh, 2002 (*Troeltsch-Studien*, vol. 12), p. 261.

80 Troeltsch, *The Social Teaching*, vol. 1, p. 106.

81 Ibid., p. 643.

82 B 624; Hans-Georg Drescher, *Ernst Troeltsch*, Göttingen, 1991, p. 214; Friedrich Wilhelm Graf in *Süddeutsche Zeitung*, 1–2 February 2003; Graf, 'Max Weber

und Ernst Troeltsch', in Wolfgang J. Mommsen and Wolfgang Schwentker (eds), *Max Weber und das moderne Japan*, Göttingen, 1999, pp. 473ff.

83	See Ernst Troeltsch, *Spektator-Briefe: Aufsätze über die deutsche Revolution und die Weltpolitik 1918/22*, ed. Hans Baron, with a foreword by Friedrich Meinecke, Tübingen, 1924; and Ernst Troeltsch, *Die Fehlgeburt einer Republik: Spektator in Berlin 1918 bis 1922*, with an afterword by Johann Hinrich Claussen, Frankfurt am Main, 1994.

84	Lenger, *Werner Sombart*, p. 235.

85	Ibid., pp. 180f.

86	In 1937 the economist Götz Briefs, who in 1919 had been one of the originators of the idea of factory councils, could still write from his American exile hailing Sombart on his seventy-fourth birthday as an eternally youthful Jupiter of science (GStA Nl Sombart Nr. 10b, Götz to Sombart, 8 January 1937). In Raymond Aron, however (*German Sociology*, London, 1957), Sombart's memory is damned and Weber becomes the supreme leading mind.

87	Jürgen Kuczynski, *Memoiren: Die Erziehung des J. K. zum Kommunisten und Wissenschaftler*, 2nd edn, Berlin, 1975, pp. 70f. The 'soap bubbles' appear again in Lujo Brentano, 'Judentum und Kapitalismus', in Brentano, *Der wirtschaftende Mensch in der Geschichte*, Leipzig, 1923, p. 429, along with a torrent of invective. In later years Brentano's dislike for Sombart was reinforced by a feeling that he was an unprincipled renegade on social and political issues, who stabbed his former comrades in the back: see Brentano, *Mein Leben im Kampf um die sociale Entwicklung Deutschlands*, Marburg, 2004, p. 411.

88	Otto Hintze, *Soziologie und Geschichte*, ed. Gerhard Oestreich, Göttingen, 1964, p. 387.

89	At least this is how it appeared to Edgar Jaffé, who knew the two men extremely well: see Hartmut Lehmann, 'Die Entstehung des modernen Kapitalismus: Weber contra Sombart', in Lehmann, *Max Webers 'Protestantische Ethik'*, p. 98.

90	*The Jews and Modern Capitalism* [translated extracts from *Die Juden und das Wirtschaftsleben*], London, 1918; *Luxury and Capitalism*, Ann Arbor, MI, 1967; *The Quintessence of Capitalism: A Study of the History and Psychology of the Modern Businessman*, London, 1915.

91	Michael Sukale, *Max Weber*, Tübingen, 2002, p. 251.

92	Lenger, Werner *Sombart*, pp. 237f. *Der Bourgeois* contains an explicit critique of *The Protestant Ethic* that deploys almost ecological metaphors: 'In my view, the reproach of having done things *too well* (in the theological sense) applies to Max Weber's celebrated study of the significance of Puritanism for the development of the capitalist spirit. . . . Deep ploughing is not always what a rational approach to the soil indicates!' We glimpse here a connoisseur of Mediterranean agrarian relations. The criticism that Weber had become obsessionally fixated on theological details, without looking to his left or right, was not unjustified.

93	Lehmann, 'Die Entstehung des modernen Kapitalismus', p. 106.

94	Marianne to Helene Weber, 22 April 1906. Characteristically, in his letter of 13 September 1907 to Else Jaffé, Weber advised that Otto Gross might try out his essay on Sombart, who would certainly 'serve it up as a special treat'.

95	Emil Ludwig, *Geschenke des Lebens: Ein Rückblick*, Berlin, 1931, p. 125; Sombart went out with 'the most beautiful female singers'.

96 Nicolaus Sombart, who valued this epicurean side in his father, emphasized it to the author. Edgar Salin (*Lynkeus*, Tübingen, 1963, p. 45) recalled that Sombart, 'in the core of his being', was 'shy, in need of affection and very vulnerable', 'the very type of the old-style scholar'.

97 GStA, Nl Sombart, Nr. 4c, Else Jaffé to Sombart, 5 January 1907.

98 Lenger, *Werner Sombart*, pp. 181f.; Julie Braun-Vogelstein, *Ein Menschenleben: Heinrich Braun und sein Schicksal*, Tübingen, 1932, pp. 102ff., 120, 259f. et al.

99 Marianne to Helene Weber, 29 February 1904. Similarly, in an undated letter probably written in Autumn 1903: 'Sombart is an unbearably vain person!' She had heard from the 'little sparrow', Else Jaffé, that he wanted his name to appear before Weber's on the title page of the *Archiv*, even though Weber did the main editorial work. 'I wished you didn't have him around. Your rebellious little Snouty (see chapter 11, note 116, below).'

100 Willy Hellpach, *Wirken in Wirren*, vol. 1, Hamburg, 1948, p. 380.

101 GStA Nl Weber Nr. 30 Bd. 1, 19 September 1903.

102 For a criticism of this thesis, see Joachim Radkau, 'Holzverknappung und Krisenbewußtsein im 18. Jahrhundert', *Geschichte und Gesellschaft* (1983), pp. 513–43. The debate continues to this day.

Chapter 9 South – North – West – East

1 Joachim Radkau, 'Aloha – Vom Abheben deutscher Eliten: Die verborgenen Inseln der Insider und die Demokratisierung der Nervosität', in *Die neuen Eliten*, Berlin, 2000 (= *Kursbuch* 139), pp. 45–58.

2 Joachim Radkau, *Zeitalter der Nervosität*, Munich, 1998, pp. 248ff.

3 Marianne to Helene Weber, 10 July 1900.

4 Dieter Düding, *Der nationalsoziale Verein 1896–1903*, Munich, 1972, pp. 73f.

5 Hans-Georg Drescher, *Ernst Troeltsch*, Göttingen, 1991, p. 212n., 213; Hermann Glockner, *Heidelberger Bilderbuch*, Bonn, 1969, p. 68.

6 Marianne to Helene Weber, 8 June 1900.

7 Ana 446, Marianne Weber to Emilie Benecke, 12 June 1901.

8 Ibid., Sch. 20 VI, 29 April 1911, Marianne to Helene Weber.

9 Marianne to Helene Weber, 12 April 1901.

10 Eaedem, early May 1901. And on 17 May 1901: 'For a time, though, I was in really terrible spirits, as if this life of travelling without any regular activity would be impossible for me to stand physically and mentally for another year.'

11 Eaedem, 26 July 1900: 'But the state of idleness into which one falls when travelling makes me so dissatisfied that I have to work hard to stay on an even keel.' And on 14 March 1902 from Florence: 'This life of idling simply won't work any more . . .'; she absolutely wanted to be back home in the next five (!) years. Already on 14 September 1893 (?) she wrote to Helene (Ana 446): 'You soon get tired of just lazy scudding (!), and I hope I'll always manage to establish a life with some degree of regularity.'

12 Marianne to Helene Weber, 26 August 1903.

13 Eaedem, 13 December 1902.

14 Eaedem, 4 October 1913.

15 Friedrich Naumann, *Asia*, 7th edn, Berlin, 1913, p. 6.

16 Ana 446 Sch. 20 VI.

17 Willy Hellpach, *Heilkraft und Schöpfung*, Dresden 1934, p. 228.
18 Willy Hellpach, *Universitas Litterarum: Gesammelte Aufsätze* (1944), ed. Gerhard Hess and Wilhelm Witte, Stuttgart, 1948, pp. 309, 311.
19 Marianne to Helene Weber, 21 April 1903.
20 Eaedem, 25 May 1900.
21 Eaedem, 28 July 1910.
22 Eaedem, 3 February 1901.
23 Eaedem, 25 May 1901: 'You can live here more peacefully and contentedly than elsewhere, if you don't go off hunting for tourist sights – and that we *don't* do.'
24 Ana 446, Marianne to Elisabeth Benecke, 18 December 1901.
25 Eaedem, 8 January 1902.
26 GStA Nl Weber Nr. 30 Bd. 4, 14 April 1902.
27 Marianne to Helene Weber, 10 February 1902; cf. WB 254.
28 Eaedem, 17 December 1900.
29 Marianne to Helene Weber, 31 March 1903.
30 Marianne to Helene Weber from Rome, 19 October 1913; cf. WB 504.
31 Joachim Radkau and Orlinde Radkau, *Praxis der Geschichtswissenschaft*, Düsseldorf, 1972, pp. 110, 176; Friedrich Meinecke, *Erlebtes 1862–1901*, Leipzig, 1941, pp. 218f.
32 Wilfried Röhrich, *Robert Michels: Vom sozialistisch-syndikalistischen zum faschistischen Credo*, Berlin, 1972, p. 119.
33 A basic text on this is Francesco Tuccari, *I dilemmi della democrazia moderna: Max Weber e Robert Michels*, Rome, 1993; Tuccari, 'Der politische Führer und der charismatische Heros: Charisma und Demokratie im politischen und soziologischen Werk von Max Weber und Robert Michels', *Annali di Sociologia/Soziologisches Jahrbuch* (Trento), 9/2 (1993), pp. 100–25.
34 Curiously, in his otherwise most knowledgeable essay 'Robert Michels und Max Weber' (in WuZ), Mommsen does not look in any detail at the erotic side of their communication with each other or at Michels's erotic writings. Even odder is the fact that Arthur Mitzman, the author of both a psychoanalytic biography of Weber, *The Iron Cage*, and a biography of Michels (*Sociology and Estrangement: Three Sociologists of Imperialist Germany*, New York, 1973, pp. 267–344), completely ignores this aspect of relations between the two men.
35 Wilhelm Hennis, *Weber und Thukydides*, Göttingen, 2003, p. 91.
36 Things were not like that at the beginning, when the picture of health that Michels offered was irritating to Weber and spoiled any visit to him. See his letter of 20 April 1907 (MWG II/5, 281): 'I am a little afraid of Turin. It is charged with unfortunate associations: the great unbridgeable gulf between the sick and the healthy . . . again struck me so forcefully and put a psychological strain on me, even though neither of you – thank God – noticed it!'
37 Wolfgang Mommsen (WuZ 198). Weber recommended Michels to Achille Loria, who like himself had been a disciple of Meitzenitzenschüler: see MWG II/5, 185, 221.
38 Wolfgang J. Mommsen, *Max Weber and German Politics 1890–1920*, Chicago, 1990, pp. 112–13.
39 In the Weimar committee, Quarck was especially resolute in supporting the view that gender equality should be written into the constitution. See Heide-Marie Lauterer, *Parlamentarierinnen in Deutschland 1918/19–1949*, Königstein, 2002, pp. 142ff.
40 Mommsen, *Max Weber and German Politics*, pp. 112f.

41 Robert Michels, *Soziologie des Parteiwesens*, 4th edn, Stuttgart, 1989, p. liv.

42 Sandro Segre ('Notes and Queries: On Weber's Reception of Michels', *Weber Studies*, 2 (2001), pp. 103–13) tries to explain Weber's silence by the fact that he did not agree with Michels theoretically. But, as Tuccari's work has shown (*I dilemmi della democrazia moderna*), one can find a lot in common if one so wishes. Once again the desire to find rational motives for Weber's behaviour at any price leads one into error.

43 Marianne to Helene Weber, 28 November 1906.

44 *Sexual Ethics: A Study of Borderland Questions*, London, 1914.

45 Robert Michels, *Die Grenzen der Geschlechtsmoral: Prolegomena, Gedanken und Untersuchungen*, 2nd edn, Munich (Frauenverlag), 1911, p. 20.

46 Michels, *Sexual Ethics*, pp. 139f.

47 Ibid., p. 227.

48 Robert Michels, 'Erotische Streifzüge', *Mutterschutz*, 9 (1906), p. 362.

49 Michels, *Sexual Ethics*, pp. 9ff., 64f.

50 Marianne to Helene Weber, 2 July 1905: 'Max could stand only one week in Z (Zopot); he again claimed that such trips no longer have any meaning for him, and that he is now at a stage where he does better to keep trying to work. . . . Well, I don't fully trust that theory.' And on 23 July 1905: 'I wanted Max to decide to go to the North Sea again at least, as Zopot was recently too weak for him, but for the moment he won't hear of it.'

51 Carl Neumann, *Rembrandt*, 2 vols, 4th edn, Munich, 1924, esp. vol. 1, pp. 115f., 132f.

52 Ibid., pp. 30–8; vol. 2, p. 461.

53 For a later impression of Rembrandt, see MWG II/6, 674f.

54 Marianne Weber, *Erfülltes Leben*, Heidelberg, 1946, pp. 223ff., 213ff.

55 Marianne to Helene Weber, 6 August 1904.

56 Eaedem, 22 July 1904.

57 The chemist Wilhelm Ostwald later gave a detailed account of the world congress (*Lebenslinien: Eine Selbstbiographie*, Berlin, 1933, vol. 2, pp. 390–430); he found it unsatisfactory because of the lack of a 'general and all-embracing viewpoint'. 'Sociology seemed especially bitty' (p. 395). He did enjoy Tönnies, but made no mention at all of Weber. On Weber's failure to make an impact, see Guenther Roth, *Politische Herrschaft und persönliche Freiheit*, Frankfurt am Main, 1987, p. 182; and Hans Rollmann, 'Meet Me in St. Louis', in Hartmut Lehmann and Guenther Roth (eds), *Weber's Protestant Ethic*, Cambridge, 1993, pp. 357, 361ff.

58 Roth, *Politische Herrschaft*, p. 182.

59 Hugo Münsterberg, *The Americans*, New York, 1904, p. 32.

60 Roth, *Politische Herrschaft*, p. 184.

61 Hans-Ulrich Wehler (ed.), *Friedrich Kapp: Vom radikalen Frühsozialisten des Vormärz zum liberalen Parteipolitiker des Bismarckreichs: Briefe 1843–1884*, Frankfurt am Main, 1969, pp. 21f.

62 Marianne to Helene Weber, 30 October 1903.

63 Wolfgang Mommsen, 'Die Vereinigten Staaten von Amerika', in Mommsen, *Max Weber: Gesellschaft, Politik und Geschichte*, Frankfurt am Main, 1982, pp. 77f.

64 Marianne to Helene Weber, 19 November 1904 (GStA Nl Weber Nr. 6) and 21 December 1904.

65 Joachim Radkau, *Technik in Deutschland*, Frankfurt am Main, 1989, pp. 34ff.

66 Eduard Meyer, *Nordamerika und Deutschland* (1915), quoted from Ernst Fraenkel (ed.), *Amerika im Spiegel des deutschen politischen Denkens*, Cologne, 1959, p. 218.

67 Wilhelm Hennis, *Max Webers Wissenschaft vom Menschen*, Tübingen, 2003, p. 58n.

68 Ostwald, *Lebenslinien*, vol. 2, p. 422; vol. 3, pp. 47f.

69 GStA Nl Weber Nr. 6, Marianne Weber, 2 September 1904.

70 Rollmann, 'Meet Me in St. Louis', p. 372.

71 Lawrence A. Scaff, 'The "cool objectivity of sociation"': Max Weber and Marianne Weber in America', *History of the Human Sciences* 11/2 (1998), pp. 61–82.

72 Adolf von Harnack, *What Is Christianity? Sixteen Lectures Delivered in the University of Berlin in the Winter Term 1899–1900*, London, 1901.

73 Karl Lamprecht, *Americana*, Freiburg, 1906, p. 89.

74 Roger Chickering, *Karl Lamprecht*, Atlantic Highlands, NJ, 1993, p. 344.

75 See Rollmann, 'Meet Me in St. Louis', p. 370.

76 In Winckelmann (ed.), *Die Protestantische Ethik* I, pp. 284f.

77 As Hans-Ulrich Wehler has pointed out to the author, both impressions of Weber's were quite wrong.

78 Winckelmann (ed.), *Die Protestantische Ethik* II, p. 312.

79 Ibid., I, pp. 279f.

80 According to Guenther Roth (oral communication), the relative was Jefferson Miller: see R 355.

81 Winckelmann (ed.), *Die Protestantische Ethik* I, p. 282.

82 Ibid., p. 299.

83 The trade union leader Karl Legien, for example, was most disappointed: see Fraenkel, *Amerika im Spiegel des deutschen politischen Denkens*, p. 226.

84 Friedrich Naumann, *Briefe über Religion*, Berlin, 1913, p. 15.

85 Richard White, *'It's your Misfortune and None of my own': A New History of the American West*, Norman, OK, 1991, pp. 309f.

86 Christopher C. Sellers, *Hazards of the Job: From Industrial Disease to Environmental Health Science*, Chapel Hill, NC, 1997, pp. 78f.

87 *Verhandlungen des 2. Deutschen Soziologentages*, Tübingen, 1913, p. 191.

88 Oral communication with Guenther Roth, 25 March 2004.

89 Maldwyn Allen Jones, *American Immigration*, Chicago, 1960, pp. 202, 207. In 1902 rabbis originating in Eastern Europe founded their own Union of Orthodox Rabbis (Nathan Glazer, *American Judaism*, Chicago, 1957, p. 78). Polenz's book on America was an extreme reflection of the growing American hostility to immigration, which was said to involve 'all kinds of used-up, impure and incapable persons from the lowest dregs of European population' (Wilhelm von Polenz, *The Land of the Future*, New York, 1904, p. 109; *Das Land der Zukunft*, Berlin 1904, p. 144) and 'fewer and fewer representatives of superior, pure, healthy races and nationalities' (*Land der Zukunft*, p. 144).

90 E. Schultze, 'Die Verschwendung von Menschenleben in den Vereinigten Staaten', *Zeitschrift für Sozialwissenschaft*, 4 (1913), p. 835.

91 Karl Lamprecht, whose public pronouncements on German Americans aroused a wave of indignation, wrote in his *Americana* (p. 25): 'One sees only the typical role of Germans in American comedies and comic literature: the man who always comes too late, always wants a lot or obtains little, is despised by others silently or vocally, even if he has certain traits of *Gemütlichkeit* in full measure.'

92 Hugo Münsterberg, *Die Amerikaner*, 4th edn, Berlin, 1912, vol. 1, p. 43.
93 GStA Nl Weber, Nr. 6, Marianne Weber, 12 October 1904; and, in a somewhat milder form, WB 297f.
94 See William E. B. Du Bois, *Die Seelen der Schwarzen*, Freiburg (Orange Press), 2003, pp. 8f. and 267ff.
95 Scaff, 'The "cool objectivity of sociation"': Max Weber and Marianne Weber in America', pp. 70ff., 80.
96 At a symposium in Heidelberg in March 2004, M. Rainer Lepsius referred to the fact that ethnic differences were the 'general theme' of Weber's trip to America.
97 Weber to Du Bois, 17 November 1904, quoted in Scaff: The 'cool objectivity of sociation', pp. 72f.
98 William E. B. Du Bois, 'Die Negerfrage in den Vereinigten Staaten', *Archiv für Sozialwissenschaft* (1906), p. 37; cf. 'The Souls of Black Folk', in Eric J. Sundqvist (ed.), *The Oxford W. E. B. Du Bois Reader*, Oxford, 1996, p. 103.
99 'The Souls of Black Folk', pp. 199–200.
100 Fraenkel, *Amerika im Spiegel des deutschen politischen Denkens*, p. 112.
101 Ibid., p. 160.
102 FMW 385 – adapted from the translation 'The Relations of the Rural Communities to Other Branches of the Social Sciences', *Congress of Arts and Science, Universal Exposition, St. Louis*, vol. 7, Boston, 1906, pp. 725–46.
103 Lamprecht, *Americana*, p. 29.
104 Ibid., pp. 41f.
105 Helene to Marianne Weber, 2 October 1904.
106 Rollmann, 'Meet Me in St. Louis', p. 380n.
107 Fraenkel, *Amerika im Spiegel des deutschen politischen Denkens*, p. 268.
108 Marianne to Helene Weber, 20 January 1905.
109 Eaedem, 12 January 1909.
110 Weber to Naumann, 7 February 1916, in Max Weber, *Gesammelte politische Schriften*, Munich, 1921, p. 461.
111 Marianne to Helene Weber, 13 July 1906.
112 Eaedem, 3 April 1905.
113 Robert Michels, *Masse, Führer, Intellektuelle*, Frankfurt am Main, 1987, p. 260.
114 The Russia expert Otto Hoetzsch (*Rußland: Eine Einführung auf Grund seiner Geschichte von 1904 bis 1912*, Berlin, 1913, p. 183) later criticized Weber's thesis that, despite the 1905 constitution (which was only partly in force), Russia was simply on the road to 'pseudo-constitutionalism'. Between 1907 and 1912, Hoetzsch noted, 'the government brought before the Duma a total of 2567 draft laws'; the Duma 'proved itself capable of existing and working', with the result that 'a constitutional life is possible in Russia too'. Writing seventy years later, Heinz-Dietrich Löwe also thought the 'pseudo-constitutionalism' thesis was misguided (*Die Lage der Bauern in Rußland 1880–1905*, St Katharinen, 1987, p. 359). Today it is applied to the Putin government!
115 Marianne to Helene Weber, 11 August 1906: 'The terrible thing is that these two Russian volumes are being paid for out of his own pocket – he will be charged a total of 1800 marks for them'; this meant that for a year he received neither royalties nor an editor's income from the *Archiv*.
116 Eaedem, 10 March 1907.
117 Richard Pipes, *Russia under the Old Regime*, London, 1974, esp. chapter 2.

118 In 1914 he defended it against Below: MWG II/8, 725.
119 Paul Honigsheim ('Max Weber as Rural Sociologist', *Rural Sociology* 1/1–4 (1946), p. 214) emphasized this point on the basis of his intimate knowledge of Weber: '*The rural structure of Russia* had always attracted Max Weber's attention. Even more than that, he had always been affected by the collectivist feeling of the Russian peasant, by the Greek-Orthodox Saint and the passive sufferer in the fictions of Dostoevsky, and by Tolstoy's attempt to teach and to live a life conforming to the precepts of the Sermon of the Mount.'
120 See the conclusion to his essay on Russia, where he refers to the 'horrifying poverty of "spirit"' in the tsarist regime and says that there are already 'far too many' who would tell it to its face: 'Conjurer! You will summon up no more spirits!' (PW 73f.).
121 Richard Pipes emphasizes this in 'Max Weber and Russia', *World Politics*, 7/3 (1955), pp. 399f.; as do Yuri Davidov and Pyama Gaidenko in *Rußland und der Westen*, Frankfurt am Main, 1995, pp. 9f.
122 Alexander Ular, *Die Russische Revolution*, Berlin, 1905, p. 105.
123 The terms *mir* and *obshchina* are often confused with each other in the literature. In fact, *mir* specifically designates the village as a commune with voting rights, while *obshchina* refers to the common ownership of land. Weber deals overwhelmingly with the latter.
124 As Weber rightly pointed out, the agricultural cooperative movement in Germany was 'saturated with the spirit of "calculation"', in such a way that it 'ultimately trained farmers to become "businessmen"'. Weber accordingly floated the idea that the same model might be used for the modernization of the *obshchina* (MWG I/10, 230n.).
125 Hoetzsch, *Rußland*, p. 192.
126 On 1 August 1916 Weber declared in a public speech in Nuremberg: 'When a Russian peasant has 10 hectares (from which a German peasant can live well) he thinks he will have to go hungry, because he is a savage who does not understand how to use modern agricultural tools; he has therefore always shouted for more land, and as he used to demand it from his grand dukes and large landowners he now demands it from Germany – a war aim with which we shall have to reckon for several generations to come' (MWG I/15, 664f.). Weber did not suspect that within a year the peasants' fury would turn against their own lords of the manor.
127 T. Wünsch in Thomas M. Bohn and Dietmar Neutatz (eds), *Studienhandbuch Östliches Europa*, vol. 2, Cologne, 2002, p. 26.
128 Paul Rohrbach, *Deutschland unter den Weltvölkern* (1903), Leipzig, 1912, pp. 103ff.
129 Joachim Radkau, *Natur und Macht: Eine Weltgeschichte der Umwelt*, 2nd edn, Munich, 2002, pp. 214f., 395. The latest and best regional study is David Keran, *Mind and Labor on the Farm in Black-Earth Russia, 1861–1914*, New York, 2001, esp. pp. 37–41, which argues that the kernel of the undoubted crisis was village overpopulation combined with the introduction of techniques (grazing on fallow land) which were suitable in the heavy forest soil of the north, but not in the southern steppe opened up since the eighteenth century.
130 [This passage and others are omitted from the two English translations of Weber's article 'Zur Lage der bürgerlichen Demokratie in Rußland': 'On the

Situation of Constitutional Democracy in Russia', in PW 29–74; and 'Bourgeois Democracy in Russia', in RR 41–147. *Trans. note*]

131 Stefan Breuer, *Sozialgeschichte des Naturrechts*, Opladen 1983, pp. 216ff. He argues (p. 506) that the modern Western bourgeois idea of 'natural law without nature' was the beginning of the end for natural law in general.

132 In *The Agrarian Sociology of Ancient Civilizations* he describes an ancient Egyptian 'tax levy' in accordance with a Russian and generally 'Oriental' model: 'The officials arrived unexpectedly, the women began to cry, and soon a general flight and hunt began; those liable for taxes were hunted down, beaten, and tortured into paying what was demanded by the officials' (AS 131). It would be hard to find such a canvas in other accounts of Egyptian history.

133 Also, 'Russia's Transition to Pseudo-Constitutionalism', in RR 230–1. See Felix Schnell, 'Ordnungshüter auf Abwegen? Herrschaft und illegitime polizeiliche Gewalt in Moskau, 1905–1914', dissertation, University of Bielefeld, 2004. Weber was able to use Russian press reports of the time. But these can be read in quite a different way, to suggest that the not exactly sophisticated lower ranks of the Russian police, for all their brutality, were very unprofessional and indeed rather awkward in their operations.

134 'Russia's Transition to Pseudo-Constitutionalism', RR 231.

135 Raymond Aron (*Memoirs: Fifty Years of Political Thought*, New York, 1990, p. 46) rightly claimed that Weber 'linked awareness of history with that of the present'.

136 In 1949 Eduard Baumgarten noted for a lecture on Weber (private archive) that, in all his political writings, Weber wanted 'to serve not some theories or ideologies but – quite practically – the present moment'. That was certainly true of what he wrote on Russia.

137 'Russia's Transition to Pseudo-Constitutionalism', RR 231.

138 Hoetzsch, *Rußland*, p. 516.

139 Fritz Fischer, *War of Illusions*, London, 1975, pp. 384f.

140 Ibid., pp. 81f.

141 Willy Birkenmaier, *Das russische Heidelberg*, Heidelberg, 1995, pp. 149f.

142 Max Weber, 'Zum Thema der "Kriegsschuld"' (*Frankfurter Zeitung*, 17 January 1919), in *Politische Schriften*, ed. Johannes Winckelmann, 3rd edn, Tübingen, 1958, p. 491.

143 It is clear today that, although Kistiakovsky familiarized Weber with Ukrainian strivings for autonomy, he never speculated about the break-up of the tsarist empire into its various nationalities, which would have offered glittering prospects to German imperialism in the east. Weber, who was himself an ardent nationalist, evidently overestimated the nationalism of many Russian revolutionaries.

144 Susan Heuman, *Kistiakovsky: The Struggle for National and Constitutional Rights in the Last Years of Tsarism*, Cambridge, MA, 1998, p. 21.

145 Hubert Treiber, 'Die Geburt der Weberschen Rationalismus-These: Webers Bekanntschaften mit der russischen Geschichtsphilosophie in Heidelberg', *Leviathan*, 19 (1991), pp. 435–43.

146 Karl Schlögel (ed.), *Vechi/Wegzeichen: Zur Krise der russischen Intelligenz*, Frankfurt am Main, 1990, pp. 213, 218.

147 Ibid., p. 217. Cf. Jurij N. Davydov, 'Max Weber und die *Vechi*: Zwei Auffassungen von der russischen Intelligencija', in Davydov and Piama P. Gaidenko, *Rußland und der Westen*, Frankfurt am Main, 1995, esp. pp. 107f.

148 Robert Service, *Lenin*, London, 2000, pp. 167, 172f., 328. Otto Hoetzsch, on the other hand (*Rußland*, pp. 112f.), mentions Gapon as a 'very dubious' and 'depraved' priest.

149 Communication to the author (20 April 2004) from Dittmar Dahlmann, editor of MWG I/10: It has symbolic importance whether two or three fingers are used: 'either the two natures of Christ or three including the Holy Spirit'.

150 Edith Hanke, *Prophet des Unmodernen*, Tübingen, 1993, p. 37.

151 Harnack, *What Is Christianity?*, pp. 86f.

152 Hanke, *Prophet des Unmodernen*, p. 171.

153 Hartmann Tyrell points to this in 'Die christliche Brüderlichkeit: Semantische Kontinuitäten und Diskontinuitäten', in Karl Gabriel et al. (eds), *Modernität und Solidarität (Festschrift für Franz-Xaver Kaufmann)*, Freiburg, 1997, pp. 207ff.

154 Romain Rolland, *Tolstoy*, London, 1911, p. 146.

155 Lawrence A. Scaff, *Fleeing the Iron Cage: Culture, Politics, and Modernity in the Thought of Max Weber*, Berkeley, CA, 1989, pp. 100f., 109.

156 Rolland, *Tolstoy*, p. 121.

157 Hubert Treiber, 'Max Weber und die russische Geschichtsphilosophie', in Volkhard Krech and Hartmann Tyrell (eds), *Religionssoziologie um 1900*, Würzburg, 1995, p. 275.

158 On Weber and Tolstoy in general, see Hanke, *Prophet des Unmodernen*; and on Tolstoy as a critic of contemporary civilization, within the context of the German discussions at the turn of the century, see Edith Hanke, 'Max Weber, Leo Tolstoy and the Mountain of Truth', in Sam Whimster (ed.), *Max Weber and the Culture of Anarchy*, London, 1999, pp. 144–61.

159 Hans G. Kippenberg, in *Max Weber: Wirtschaft und Gesellschaft: Religiöse Gemeinschaften, Studienausgabe*, Tübingen, 2005, p. 188.

160 This might be seen in a different light. Contradicting the usual view, Dmitrii Chizevskii (*Russische Geistesgeschichte*, 2nd edn, Munich, 1974, pp. 275f.) argues that Tolstoy was 'one of the most consistent rationalists in Russian intellectual history', and that his religious ideas were 'strongly influenced by the "liberal theology" of Protestantism'. Weber would have found something to discover in Tolstoy if he had been open to it!

161 Marianne Weber wrote (EM 360) that, although various ideologues tried to deny it, the 'terrible fate of women' in the Russian peasantry was confirmed by the fact that 'a husband's murder was often their last resort' and that the courts were aware of this when they mostly released them.

162 According to Edith Hanke (*Prophet des Unmodernen*, p. 36) the book had been a 'sensation'.

163 Christa Krüger, *Max und Marianne Weber*, Zurich, 2001, p. 62.

164 Marianne to Helene Weber, 17 February 1913.

165 See already the letter of 4 August 1908 to Robert Michels (MWG II/5, 615). In a letter to Heinrich Simon on 15 November 1911 (II/7-1, 348), he sternly reprimands the 'nothing-but-pacifists' who should be more consistent and enjoy Tolstoy 'not simply as a literary dessert': 'Anyone who regards war as the worst of all evils in foreign policy should on no account get enthusiastic about revolutionaries and, in their personal life too, should always resolutely turn the other cheek.' In 1914 he tried to convince Frieda Gross that her lover, the anarchist Ernst Frick, should adopt 'Tolstoyan asceticism' if he wished to be consistent; and she gave Weber the impression that she agreed with him (MWG

II/8, 582). Jurij Davydov ('Max Weber und Lev Tolstoj: Verantwortungs- und Gesinnungsethik', in Davydov and Gaidenko (eds), *Rußland und der Westen*, p. 69) notes that Tolstoy's 'ethic of love – unlike Max Weber's ethic of conviction – does not require turning a completely blind eye to the consequences of ethically oriented action and releasing people from responsibility for those consequences.'

Chapter 10 From the 'Essay of Sighs' to 'Psychophysics'

1 FriedrichTenbruck, *Das Werk Max Webers*, Tübingen, 1999, p. 55.
2 Marianne to Max Weber, 5 January 1903.
3 An external stimulus seems to have given birth to the work, but it is still not known what this was. Wilhelm Hennis, *Weber und Thukydides*, Göttingen, 2003, p. 38n.
4 Tenbruck, *Das Werk Max Webers*, p. 11: 'The text and language of the essay have . . . something studied about them', which suggests a 'long and forced preoccupation with an unrewarding object' that 'the author found uncongenial'. 'For it is evidently not the case that any new insight into the matter appears in the essay on Roscher.' Hennis, *Max Weber und Thukydides*, p. 41: Weber's critique of Roscher and Knies tells us 'next to nothing' about these two economists. 'The essay is the fruit of tormenting efforts by a still sick man, who troubles himself with Roscher only to display his own "critical faculties" to him.'
5 Wilhelm Hennis, *Max Weber's Central Question*, 2nd edn, Newbury, 2000, p. 142. Werner Gephart, on the other hand (*Handeln und Kultur: Vielfalt und Einheit der Kulturwissenschaften im Werk Max Webers*, Frankfurt am Main, 1998, p. 49n.), thinks that Hennis 'completely overinterprets' Knies's influence on Weber.
6 Tenbruck, *Das Werk Max Webers*, p. 26.
7 Max Weber, *Roscher and Knies: The Logical Problems of Historical Economics*, New York, 1975, p. 171.
8 Fritz Ringer, *Max Weber: An Intellectual Biography*, Chicago, 2004, pp. 80f.
9 Harald Propach, 'Ein Taufstein und vier Professoren: Die Evangelisten am Taufstein der Nicolaikirche zu Bielefeld', in Johannes Altenberend (ed.), *Kloster – Stadt – Region: Festschrift für Heinrich Rüthing*, Bielefeld, 2002, pp. 393–412. The font was destroyed during an air raid in 1944.
10 Richard Swedberg, *The Max Weber Dictionary: Key Words and Central Concepts*, Stanford, CA, 2005, p. 30. Weber's theory of causality, he argues, 'consequently differs from the way that causality is perceived in the natural sciences' (p. 28). In my view this is a misjudgement, however, which impedes a correct understanding of Weber.
11 Hanno Heinrich Nau (ed.), *Der Werturteilsstreit*, Marburg, 1996, p. 186.
12 Johannes Winckelmann, *Webers hinterlassenes Hauptwerk*, Tübingen, 1986, p. 166.
13 Nau, *Der Werturteilsstreit*, p. 186.
14 Max Weber, 'The "Objectivity" of Knowledge in Social Science and Social Policy', trans. Keith Tribe, in *The Essential Weber: A Reader*, ed. Sam Whimster, London, 2004, p. 383 (WL 184).
15 Ibid., p. 403.

16 Ibid., p. 398.
17 Ibid., p. 403 (WL 214).
18 Ibid., pp. 403–4. The quotation is from Goethe's *Faust*, Part I, Scene ii.
19 See Uta Gerhardt, *Idealtypus: Zur methodischen Begründung der modernen Soziologie*, Frankfurt am Main, 2001, which establishes a link to Simmel over nearly five hundred pages.
20 Weber, 'The "Objectivity" of Knowledge', p. 394.
21 Ibid., p. 389.
22 Ibid., p. 387.
23 Hennis, *Max Weber und Thukydides*, p. 65.
24 GStA Nl Weber Nr. 30 Bd. 4, 28 April 1905.
25 Quoted from Kurt Blaukopf, *Musik im Wandel der Gesellschaft*, Munich, 1982, p. 166.
26 Horst Baier, '*Von der Erkenntnistheorie zur Wirklichkeitswissenschaft: Eine Studie über die Begründung der Soziologie bei Max Weber*', dissertation, Munich, 1969, pp. 175f.
27 Hideharu Ando, 'Die Interviews mit Else Jaffé, Edgar Salin und Helmuth Plessner', *Kölner Zeitschrift für Soziologie*, 55 (2003), p. 605.
28 Max Weber, *Critique of Stammler*, New York, 1977.
29 Edith Hanke, 'Max Webers "Herrschaftssoziologie": Eine werkgeschichtliche Studie', in Hanke and Wolfgang J. Mommsen (eds), *Max Webers Herrschaftssoziologie*, Tübingen, 2001, p. 37.
30 Even such an astute Weber expert as Karl Löwith, one of the few to say anything at all detailed about Weber's critique of Stammler, twisted the point when he wrote that Weber's target was 'Stammler's adoption and modification of the materialist conception of history' (*Gesammelte Abhandlungen*, Stuttgart, 1960, pp. 62ff.). In reality, his target was Stammler's one-sided *anti*-materialism. But that does not fit into the current image of Weber.
31 Rudolf Stammler, *Wirtschaft und Recht nach der materialistischen Geschichtsauffassung: Eine sozialphilosophische Untersuchung*, 3rd edn, Leipzig, 1914, p. 670.
32 Ibid., pp. 165–73.
33 Leo Strauss, *Natural Right and History*, Chicago, 1953, pp. 35–80.
34 Significantly, the most voluminous modern German book on natural law from a Catholic point of view (950 pages!) contains scarcely any examples of how how people work with the concept in the practice of law: Johannes Messner, *Das Naturrecht*, Innsbruck, 1950. This work, which refers to Max Weber at various points, was written in exile in America during the Nazi period and sought to reconcile Catholic natural law with liberal economics.
35 *Historisches Wörterbuch der Philosophie*, vol. 6, p. 607.
36 See his contribution 'Zur Soziologie der mittelalterlichen Scholastik: Die soziologische Bedeutung der nominalistischen Philosophie', in Melchior Palyi (ed.), *Erinnerungsgabe für Max Weber*, 2 vols, Munich, 1923, esp. vol. 1, pp. 195ff. On p. 196 he emphasizes that the spirit of natural law was originally 'atomistic', in the sense that it recognized only natural persons, not states, as bearers of law.
37 Jellinek's position on natural law was also ambivalent and ambiguous: see Klaus Kempter, *Die Jellineks 1820–1955*, Düsseldorf, 1998, p. 310, where Jellinek is assigned to the ranks of positivism.
38 Wolfgang J. Mommsen, *Max Weber: Gesellschaft, Politik und Geschichte*, Frankfurt am Main, 1982, p. 116.

39 Theodor Heuss, *Deutsche Gestalten*, Munich, 1975, p. 249.

40 Franz Wiesacker, *Privatrechtsgeschichte der Neuzeit*, Göttingen, 1952, p. 173.

41 Eberhard Demm, 'Max und Alfred Weber im Verein für Sozialpolitik', in Demm, *Geist und Politik im 20. Jahrhundert: Gesammelte Aufsätze zu Alfred Weber*, Frankfurt am Main, 2000, p. 72; Wolfgang Schluchter, on the other hand ('Psychophysics and Culture', in Stephen Turner (ed.), *The Cambridge Companion to Weber*, Cambridge, 2000, pp. 59–80), rightly emphasizes the systemic significance of the psychophysics.

42 Demm, 'Max und Alfred Weber', pp. 69f.

43 AWG vol. 5, p. 438.

44 Ernst Haeckel, *Die Welträtsel*, Stuttgart, 1984, pp. 132f.

45 MWG I/11, 21f.; see Henri F. Ellenberger, *The Discovery of the Unconscious: History and Evolution of Dynamic Psychiatry*, New York, 1981. Worth reading is the congenial biography of Fechner by one of the earliest German science-fiction writers, Kurd Lasswitz: *Gustav Theodor Fechner*, Stuttgart, 1910.

46 Joachim Radkau, *Zeitalter der Nervosität*, Munich, 1998, pp. 315ff.

47 Communication from Horst Baier, 23 July 2006.

48 Marianne to Helene Weber, 11 May 1909.

49 Demm, 'Max und Alfred Weber', p. 72 agrees with this judgement of Alfred Weber's.

50 *Verhandlungen des Vereins für Sozialpolitik in Nürnberg 1911*, Leipzig, 1912 (= *Schriften des Vereins für Sozialpolitik*, 138 vols), p. 121.

51 Ibid., p. 190.

52 Ibid., p. 149. Cf. Herkner (ibid., p. 127): 'So, there comes a critical turning point, a kind of career crossroads in the life of the qualified worker. . . . If he has not managed to rise higher by the time he is forty, it will be hard for him to avoid a gradual decline.'

53 Richard Woldt, *Die Arbeitswelt der Technik*, Berlin, 1926, p. 187; Radkau, *Zeitalter der Nervosität*, p. 220.

54 *Verhandlungen des Vereins für Sozialpolitik in Nürnberg 1911*, p. 200.

55 Ibid., p. 152 = AWG vol. 5, p. 453.

56 Radkau, *Zeitalter der Nervosität*, pp. 243 ff.

57 Wilhelm Ostwald, 'Warum sind wir Monisten?' *Monistische Sonntagspredigten* No. 1 (2 April 1911), pamphlet in the author's possession.

58 Roger Chickering, *Karl Lamprecht*, Atlantic Highlands, NJ, 1993, p. 296.

59 Luise Schorn-Schütte, *Karl Lamprecht: Kulturgeschichtsschreibbung zwischen Wissenschaft und Politik*, Göttingen, 1984, p. 79.

60 Wilhelm Ostwald, 'Die internationale Hilfssprache und das Esperanto', in Ostwald, *Die Forderung des Tages*, 2nd edn, Leipzig, 1911, pp. 458–80; other articles in the same volume demonstrate the depth of his commitment to this cause.

Chapter 11 From the Eranos Circle to the 'Erotic Movement'

1 Eugen Rosenstock-Huessy, *Ja und Nein*, Heidelberg, 1968, pp. 40f.

2 Eduard Baumgarten, 'Spielräume unter Hitlers Herrschaft' (privately owned manuscript), p. 142.

3 Pierre Bourdieu, *Das religiöse Feld*, Konstanz, 2000, p. 13.

4 Marianne to Helene Weber, 18 September 1903.

5 Marianne to Helene Weber, 10 December 1901.
6 GStA Nl Weber Nr. 30 Bd. 4, 11 August 1905.
7 Agnes von Zahn-Harnack, *Adolf von Harnack*, Berlin 1936, pp. 549f. As Rudolf Stammler ironically remarked (*Wirtschaft und Recht nach der materialistischen Geschichtsauffassung*, 3rd edn, Leipzig, 1914, p. 86), 'coral sticks' enjoyed great popularity at the time among people who thought that the basic forms of society could be discovered in animal nature.
8 Jacob von Uexküll, *Niegeschaute Welten: Die Umwelten meiner Freunde*, Berlin, 1936, p. 174.
9 Marianne to Helene Weber, 23 February 1900, 26 July 1900 and 16 June 1903; to Max Weber, 16 June 1903.
10 Marianne to Helene Weber, 21 December 1905.
11 See, e.g., Richard Ehrenberg, *Terrorismus in der Wirtschafts-Wissenschaft*, Berlin, 1910, p. 39.
12 Wilhelm Ostwald, *Zur Geschichte der Wissenschaft*, Leipzig, 1985, p. 181.
13 See GStA Nl Weber Nr. 30 Bd. 4, Max to Alfred Weber, 5 May 1903, with the request for information about Karl Helfferich, a potential candidate for a Heidelberg professorship in political economy: 'Helfferich's special qualities, especially on the following points: is he, as people have said here, tubercular or otherwise health-impaired? . . . His reputation for enormous self-satisfaction and egoistic unlovability naturally stands in his way.'
14 Ana 446 Sch. 20 VI.
15 Marie Luise Gothein, *Eberhard Gothein*, Stuttgart, 1931, p. 141. Similarly Edgar Salin, *Um Stefan George*, Munich, 1954, p. 13: 'The city of joyful lanes amid sweet-smelling gardens'.
16 Marianne to Helene Weber, 13 April 1906.
17 Eaedem, 28 November 1909.
18 Eaedem, April 1910.
19 Eaedem, 28 November 1909.
20 Eaedem, 14 June 1912.
21 Eaedem, 28 July 1910; cf. WB 461.
22 Eaedem, 9 June 1910.
23 Eaedem, 17 December 1911.
24 GLA Karlsruhe Abt. 235 Nr. 2643.
25 Hermann Glockner, *Heidelberger Bilderbuch*, Bonn, 1969, pp. 101f.
26 Ana 446 Sch. 14, Marianne to Alfred Weber, 18 July 1896.
27 Ibid., Marianne Weber to E. Benecke (1901).
28 GLA Karlsruhe Abt. 235 Nr. 2643.
29 Ibid.
30 Marianne to Helene Weber, 8 January 1903.
31 Alwine ('Wina') Müller to Marianne Weber, 6 April 1897.
32 Marianne to Helene Weber, 30 December 1902 and 9 January 1903.
33 Eaedem, 28 December 1905; cf. 9 November 1905: 'But it is still reckless to use up so much money when we keep running shorter and shorter and the meat prices get higher and higher. A dreadful business!'
34 The size of the Oerlinghausen legacy may be calculated from the fact that Max and Marianne Weber, in their will dated 26 March 1918 [SG], bequeathed a sum of 160,000 marks, an annual income of 1,200 marks and other unspecified amounts. According to an undated letter from Alfred to Helene Weber (circa 1900), the maternal legacy consisted of approximately 530,000 marks in capital

and 240,000 marks in real estate, to be shared among six children. Cf. Eberhard Demm, *Ein Liberaler in Kaiserreich und Republik*, Boppard, 1990, p. 106.

35 Marianne to Max Weber, 31 December 1899.

36 Marianne to Helene Weber, 1 April 1901. Already on 10 November 1900 she wrote to her: 'You ask if we have any other wishes. Not for the present, dearest Mama; we don't want to fleece you completely.' So, she must already have 'fleeced' her quite a bit. The common view in Weber studies that the Webers lived on Marianne's money during those years underestimates the importance of the mother's gifts.

37 Marianne to Helene Weber, 11 August 1905, 10 December 1905.

38 Eaedem, 3 June 1900.

39 Marianne to Max Weber, n.d. (July 1900).

40 Weber wrote a critical essay on Simmel's *Philosophy of Money* and *Sociology*, but he did not publish it so as not to spoil Simmel's career chances; only fragments of the essay have survived. See Donald N. Levine, 'Ambivalente Begegnungen: "Negationen" Simmels durch Durkheim, Weber, Lukács, Park und Parsons', in: Heinz-Jürgen Dahme and Otthein Rammstedt (eds), *Georg Simmel und die Moderne*, Frankfurt am Main, 1984, pp. 329ff.; and David Frisby, 'The Ambiguity of Modernity: Georg Simmel and Max Weber', in Wolfgang J. Mommsen and Jürgen Osterhammel (eds), *Max Weber and his Contemporaries*, London, 1987, pp. 422–33.

41 Marianne to Helene Weber, 26 June 1908: 'We had scarcely taken such little joy in writing before.'

42 Eaedem, 15 July 1908; 12 May 1912.

43 Ana 446 Sch. 20 VI S. 64 (10 August 1911).

44 E.g., MWG II/6, 276 and 440.

45 Marianne to Helene Weber, 6 April 1913.

46 Eaedem, 22 December 1913.

47 Eaedem, 18 August 1914.

48 MWG II/9, Max to Marianne Weber, 19 March 1916.

49 See the memorandum 'Zur Frage des Friedensschließens', written in late 1915/early 1916 and first published posthumously (MWG I/15, 66), and the memorandum 'Der verschärfte U-Boot-Krieg', also from 1916 (MWG I/15, 117). Both of these texts mainly emphasize the fatal impact of 'paper economy' on the international position of the German economy, rather than on the living standards of people with a fixed income.

50 MWG II/9, Max Weber to Mina Tobler, 19 July 1917.

51 Even such an expert on money and credit as Johann Plenge, for whom Weber had a high regard, wrote amid the war euphoria of 1915: 'In the worst case people will make money. We have been doing that since the beginning of the war, and we have seen that it has been useful to us. Today we understand how to make secure paper money on the basis of a good banking system.' Hanns Linhardt (ed.), *Cogito ergo sumus: Eine Auswahl aus den Schriften von Johann Plenge*, Berlin, 1964, p. 39.

52 GStA Nl Weber Nr. 30 Bd. 10.

53 Melchior Palyi, *Der Streit um die Staatliche Theorie des Geldes*, Munich, 1922. In the *Erinnerungsgabe für Max Weber* (II, pp. 339ff.), he wrote on 'The Nature of Inflation'.

54 Even Edgar Salin, the Historical School's most prominent late recruit, recalled in *Lynkeus* (Tübingen, 1963, p. 12): 'Anyone who talked with Gothein, Knapp

or Brentano in those days . . . noted with surprise that these splendid connoisseurs of monetary history were quite unable to find their bearings . . . amid the inflation and monetary confusion of their own time. Gothein, who knew all there was to know about money and credit after the Thirty Years' War, seriously thought in late 1922 that he had never saved as much in his life as in the preceding year, even though his savings were in devalued marks.'

55 Gustav Radbruch, *Der innere Weg: Aufriß meines Lebens*, Stuttgart, 1951, pp. 65f.

56 Marianne to Helene Weber, 29 February 1904.

57 Sam D. Gill, *Mother 'Earth': An American Story*, Chicago, 1987, is one such examination of Dieterich's book, which tries to furnish proof that as a rule Indian 'Mother Earth' religions originated in quite modern times under European influence.

58 I owe this point to the international symposium on *The Protestant Ethic and the Spirit of Capitalism – A Hundred Years On*, held in Heidelberg from 24 to 26 March 2004.

59 Albrecht Dieterich, *Mutter Erde: Ein Versuch über Volksreligion*, Darmstadt, 1967, p. 13. At the Heidelberg symposium in March 2004, the view was expressed that such material stimulated Weber's trip to Oklahoma.

60 Marianne to Helene Weber, 27 February and 5 March 1905.

61 Dieterich, *Mutter Erde*, p. 93.

62 Glockner reported (*Heidelberger Bilderbuch*, p. 102) some remarks by the art historian Carl Neumann, who did not belong to the Eranos circle: 'Albrecht Dieterich and Windelband and Troeltsch and Weber, the whole Eranos society in fact, regularly went over the line and, in confidence, their behaviour was wilder than they actually were. Their eyes are bigger than their bellies – as one says of children. But God alone knows how far they took the male, all-too-male side of things and the vanity of the poor souls.'

63 I am grateful to Hubert Treiber's report at the 2004 Heidelberg symposium for this and other information on the Eranos circle.

64 Friedrich Delitzsch, *Bible and Babel: A Lecture on the Significance of Assyriological Research for Religion*, Chicago, 1902.

65 Adolf Deissmann, *Light from the Ancient East: The New Testament Illustrated by Recently Discovered Texts of the Graeco-Roman World*, London, 1910.

66 Communication from Hubert Treiber.

67 Including the religions of East Asia. On 29 July 1906 Arthur von Rosthorn gave a report to the Eranos circle on 'The Beginnings of Chinese Religion'.

68 Joachim Radkau and Orlinde Radkau, *Praxis der Geschichtswissenschaft*, Düsseldorf, 1972, pp. 144f.

69 Marianne to Helene Weber, 4 February 1905.

70 Anonymous (Johannes Flach), *Die akademische Carriere der Gegenwart*, Leipzig, 1885, pp. 16 and 20ff.: the 'female circles flourishing' in southern Germany, in particular, often decided the fate of lecturers; 'in recent years' female influence had become 'a real calamity' in many German universities; and 'in any case, lies, intrigues and gossip have entered academic life, or at least increased in it, as women have appeared on the horizon'.

71 Marie Luise Gothein, *Eberhard Gothein*, p. 151.

72 Marianne to Helene Weber n.d. (1907): 'Just think, Frau Gothein does virtually everything you can imagine: scholarly work, music, cycling, skiing, tennis, dancing, a lot of friends . . . as a result of which someone is at her place *daily*

(only men, as she finds women too boring) etc. etc. Plus a wonderful house and four children, who wash up "by themselves". A fairy-tale!'

73 Christine Göttler, 'Marie Luise Gothein (1863–1931): "Weibliche Provinzen" der Kultur', in Barbara Hahn (ed.), *Frauen in den Kulturwissenschaften*, Munich, 1994, pp. 44–62.

74 Mina Tobler to her mother, 12 January 1913, in Achim Tobler (ed.), 'Auszüge aus den Briefen von Mina Tobler', manuscript, Aalen, 1988.

75 Salin, *Um Stefan George*, p. 104: 'Not only did she give the orders in the Gothein house, she was also its main centre intellectually. Eberhard Gothein, old and wise and supercilious in his composure, went along with her and accepted a subordinate role.'

76 Marianne to Helene Weber, 4 February 1905.

77 Eaedem, n.d. (1907).

78 Marie Luise Gothein, *Eberhard Gothein*, p. 234.

79 Eduard Baumgarten, 'Spielräume unter Hitlers Herrschaft' (privately owned), p. 72.

80 Ibid., pp. 216ff.

81 Ibid., pp. 221, 68.

82 In Melchior Palyi (ed.), *Erinnerungsgabe für Max Weber*, Munich, 1923, vol. 1, p. 195.

83 Marianne to Helene Weber, 4 February 1905.

84 Hermann Uhde-Bernays, *Im Lichte der Freiheit*, Frankfurt am Main, 1947, p. 212.

85 Jürgen Kuczynski, *Memoiren: Die Erziehung des J. K. zum Kommunisten und Wissenschaftler*, 2nd edn, Berlin, 1975, p. 68.

86 Ulf Matthiesen, 'Im Schatten einer endlosen großen Zeit: Etappen der intellektuellen Biographie Albert Salomons', in Ilja Srubar (ed.), *Exil, Wissenschaft, Identität*, Frankfurt am Main, 1988, p. 308.

87 Ibid., p. 463.

88 Marianne to Helene Weber, 26 June 1908.

89 Eaedem, 21 September 1908; 17 November 1908; WB 395.

90 Marianne to Max Weber, 23 August 1907: '*Please* don't chatter so much and so vehemently – otherwise the little profit from your trip to the sea will go up in smoke.'

91 Ana 446 Sch. 20 VI.

92 Marianne to Helene Weber, 21 September 1908; the Webers were anyway prepared in advance for it to be a 'herring salad': Eaedem, 30 August 1908.

93 Eaedem, 10 May 1911.

94 Eaedem, 19 January 1912.

95 Georg Lukács, *Briefwechsel 1902–1917*, Stuttgart, 1982, p. 300 (6 November 1912).

96 Marianne to Helene Weber, 12 May 1912.

97 Eaedem, 17 December 1911.

98 Wolfgang J. Mommsen, *Max Weber and German Politics 1890–1920*, Chicago, 1990, pp. 382f. Carl Schmitt's relationship with Max Weber is a controversial issue. In 1964 Jürgen Habermas described Schmitt as 'Max Weber's legitimate disciple', but he later corrected this to 'natural son'. Schmitt does not appear to have seen himself in this way, however – or else he nurtured an Oedipal hatred of the father. Christian Meier, the biographer of Julius Caesar, who knew Schmitt well, reported to me on 13 January 2008 that Schmitt took great

issue with Theodor Heuss for making Weber the lodestar of political thinking in the postwar Federal Republic. Clearly Schmitt experienced Weber as a rival!

99 Radbruch, *Der innere Weg*, p. 62.
100 Ludwig Curtius, *Deutsche und antike Welt: Lebenserinnerungen*, Stuttgart, 1958, p. 259; on Curtius, see LE 195.
101 Salin, *Um Stefan George*, pp. 48f.
102 MWG II/9, Max Weber to Mina Tobler, 28 August 1915; to Marianne Weber, 29 August 1915.
103 MWG II/9, Max to Marianne Weber, 16 August 1915.
104 Mina Tobler to her mother, 21 June 1914 (private collection).
105 Ana 446 Sch. 20 VI, 4 April 1911.
106 Ibid., 11 December 1911.
107 Marianne to Helene Weber, 17 December 1911; WB 463.
108 The text at WB 463 corresponds almost word for word to her journal entry: Ana 446 Sch. 20 VI Bl. 102f.
109 Georg Simmel, 'Stefan George: Eine kunstphilosophische Betrachtung' (1898), in *Georg Simmel Gesamtausgabe*, vol. 5, p. 294.
110 Stefan Breuer, *Ästhetischer Fundamentalismus: Stefan George und der deutsche Antimodernismus*, Darmstadt, 1995, p. 25.
111 Ibid., pp. 148ff.
112 Wolf Lepenies, *Between Literature and Science: The Rise of Sociology*, Cambridge 1985, p. 296. ('TRUTH after the setting of the sun / Extracted from the strangled imagining, / Unrewarded from yonder, and with tears / That the man must conceal from his neighbour. . . . / . . . Truth as nakedness and dignity / of the hollowed firmament as hell, / You carried from the ground by a thousand doors, / Leaders, free from lies about whither they lead.')
113 Salin, *Um Stefan George*, p. 108.
114 Ingrid Gilcher-Holtey, 'Max Weber und die Frauen', in Christian Gneuss and Jürgen Kocka (eds), *Max Weber: Ein Symposion*, Munich, 1988, p. 147.
115 GStA Nl Weber Nr. 30 Bd. 1, 7 August 1898.
116 *Schnauzel* or the diminutive *Schnäuzchen*, current in the Lippe district, was used by the Webers as a pet name to refer to Marianne. It is translated here as 'Snouty'.
117 Marianne to Helene Weber, 20 December 1903.
118 Marianne Weber, *Frauenfragen und Frauengedanken: Gesammelte Aufsätze*, Tübingen, 1919, pp. 14–17.
119 Marianne to Helene Weber, n.d. (1907).
120 Klaus Lichtblau, 'Die Bedeutung von "Ehefrau und Mutter in der Rechtsentwicklung" für das Werk Max Webers', in Bärbel Meurer (ed.), *Marianne Weber*, Tübingen, 2004, p. 200, and R 566. See also Marianne Weber to Eduard Baumgarten, 4 July 1950, where it is her analysis of the place of women in the BGB which 'swung' her back into seven years of work on the past: 'It was a massive undertaking. Max Weber took a passionate interest in it, before he was able to work himself, and forced me on from one stage to the next. Naturally he kept an eye on the book. But I howled out if he tried to interfere.'
121 Marie Bernays, *Die deutsche Frauenbewegung*, Leipzig, 1920, p. 35.
122 See Ute Gerhard, *Unerhört: Die Geschichte der deutschen Frauenbewegung*, Reinbek, 1990, p. 225: 'To conceive of women's issues as above all else legal issues was the new element in the policy of the radicals.' Although she singles

out *Ehefrau und Mutter* as a 'still unsurpassed compendium on the legal history of women' (p. 348), she otherwise makes no mention of Marianne Weber. In Ute Gerhard's 960-page anthology of writings on women in the history of law (*Frauen in der Geschichte des Rechts*, Munich, 1997), where Marianne Weber should rightfully hold centre-stage, she appears on only five successive pages (pp. 677–82), in the contribution by Stephan Buchholz, 'Das Bürgerliche Gesetzbuch und die Frauen'; and in the anthologist's eyes even those five pages paid her too much honour (see Stephan Buchholz, 'Marianne Webers Bedeutung für die Rechtsgeschichte', in Meurer (ed.) *Marianne Weber*, p. 165).

The disdain for Marianne Weber in the mainstream of feminist studies, legal history and the Weber industry is certainly irritating. Émile Durkheim, who kept silent about Max Weber, wrote a very detailed and very critical review of Marianne's *magnum opus*, which culminates in the accusation that she was incapable of seeing the patriarchal family as 'the source of female grandeur': 'All her theory rests on the principle that the patriarchal family brought about a complete enslavement of women' (*Journal sociologique*, 11 (1906–9), pp. 363–9). However reactionary Marianne Weber may appear by the lights of today's feminist communes, this does not at all mean that she was seen in the same way in the spectrum of her time! In 1913, in her essay 'Die Frauen und die objektive Kultur', she took issue with the attitude to women in the work of Simmel (a man she knew well personally). She thought his theory of the sexes implied that women must 'surrender to the male principle' the task of 'moulding the supra-individual world'. Otthein Rammstedt, the editor of Simmel's collected works, considers it absurd to accuse Simmel of discrimination against women (communication to the author, 21 May 2004). But, although quite a few passages can be found in his work that have a feminist ring, they do so only when they are taken out of context. Simmel's 'Zur Philosophie der Geschlechter' (1911) should be read closely, and read to the end, as evidence in this respect. For it makes it clear that Marianne was quite right to detect discrimination beneath his charmingly sympathetic attitude to women. He really did believe in an eternal, unchangeable 'metaphysical essence of women' – and it was exclusively female, not generally human. Creative achievements in 'objective culture' conflicted with this alleged essence, as Marianne accurately perceived. Cf. Katja Eckhardt, *Die Auseinandersetzung zwischen Marianne Weber und Georg Simmel über die 'Frauenfrage'*, Stuttgart, 2000.

In a public debate at the sociologists' conference in Kassel on 12 October 2006, Uta Gerhardt, the Weber researcher and biographer of Talcott Parsons (not to be confused with Ute Gerhard!), accused me of greatly exaggerating Marianne's intellectual significance. 'Marianne was a stupid woman [*eine doofe Frau*]!' she insisted. Yet that 'stupid woman' discovered the young Talcott Parsons at a time when he was still completely unknown even in the United States. And, with meagre funds and in the most difficult circumstances, she brought out a usable edition of Weber's works (the *Weber-Gesamtausgabe*) in the space of just three years – something that the editors of the MWG were unable to complete in thirty years with a hundred times more resources. Another rumour that is hawked around alleges that Marianne Weber joined a Nazi organization after 1933. In reality, her correspondence with Eduard Baumgarten, who was a Nazi, shows as clearly as possible that she was and remained a bitter opponent of the Nazi dictatorship. But no one seems to have bothered to read those letters.

123 Stephan Buchholz, 'Das Bürgerliche Gesetzbuch und die Frauen: Zur Kritik des Ehegüterrechts', in Ute Gerhard (ed.), *Frauen in der Geschichte des Rechts*, Munich, 1997, pp. 679f.

124 Marianne to Helene Weber., 4 March 1906.

125 Eaedem, 13 January 1914.

126 Eaeden, n.d. (early 1902).

127 Fedor Stepun, *Vergangenes und Unvergängliches*, Munich, 1947, p. 131. In Stepun's account, Camilla Jellinek was the driving force behind the campaign, which caused something of a stir in Heidelberg. Asked to support the banning of the brothel, the philosopher Windelband banged the table and shouted that he was 'fed up with this *Camillentee* [camomile tea].'

128 Marianne Weber, *Zur Sittlichkeitsfrage*, and 'Die Aufgaben des Abolitionismus', in *Centralblatt des Bundes deutscher Frauenvereine*, 5/10 (15 August 1903) and 5/14 (15 October 1903).

129 Klaus Kempter, *Die Jellineks 1820–1955*, Düsseldorf, 1998, pp. 385–96.

130 Klaus Kempter, 'Camilla Jellinek und die Frauenbewegung in Heidelberg', in Meurer (ed.), *Marianne Weber*, p. 120.

131 MWG II/9, Max to Marianne Weber, 8 September 1916; Anna Pappritz addressed Marianne as 'dear little Weber' (*liebes Weberlein*): Margit Göttert, 'Gertrud Bäumer und Marianne Weber', in Meurer (ed.), *Marianne Weber*, p. 137n.

132 Gilcher-Holtey, 'Max Weber und die Frauen', p. 147.

133 GStA Nl Weber Nr. 30 Bd. 12, Max to Helene Weber, 7 September 1897.

134 Ana 446 Sch. 14, Marianne to Helene Weber, 24 April 1894.

135 Marianne to Max Weber, 21 July 1900; to Helene Weber, 7 March and 3 April 1905; Ana 446 Sch. 20 VI, 9 January 1911 (to continue: 'but the excitement of doing something always seizes one . . . although my mind is a long way from these apparatus things').

136 Marianne to Helene Weber, 20 December 1903.

137 Eaedem, 14 February 1908. In 1896 Marianne still held the view that the birth of a boy was a more joyful event than the birth of a girl: Ana 446 Sch. 14, to Helene, 29 January 1896.

138 Gertrud Bäumer, *Des Lebens wie der Liebe Band: Briefe*, ed. Emmy Beckmann, Tübingen, 1956, p. 19.

139 Angelika Schaser, *Helene Lange und Gertrud Bäumer: Eine politische Lebensgemeinschaft*, Cologne, 2000, p. 107.

140 Alice Salomon, *Charakter ist Schicksal: Lebenserinnerungen*, Weinheim, 1983, p. 52.

141 In her unpublished biography of Gertrud Bäumer, she wrote of her first women's congress in 1901: 'There were almost only older women there, most of them unmarried, working campaigners who were visibly having a hard time in life. Charm and elegance were not much in evidence; it was easy to get the impression that those present had had less than their fair share in life.' Göttert, 'Gertrud Bäumer und Marianne Weber', p. 129.

142 Marianne to Max Weber, n.d. (1900). However, on the issue of whether maidservants should have formal rights, especially to time off – a delicate problem for good middle-class feminists – Marianne sided with the left: 'It is strange that, when it comes to servants, even socially aware women are governed by such a strong class-consciousness and are quite unable to weigh impartially the rights and duties of masters and mistresses against those of maids.' Even she,

though, considered it self-evident that she had a right to meddle in her maids' personal lives.

143 Alice Salomon, *Charakter ist Schicksal*, pp. 127f.

144 Anna Bergmann, *Die verhütete Sexualität: Die Anfänge der modernen Geburtenkontrolle*, Hamburg, 1992, pp. 86ff.

145 Richard J. Evans, *Sozialdemokratie und Frauenemanzipation im deutschen Kaiserreich*, Berlin, 1984, p. 119.

146 Ana 446 Sch. 14, Marianne to Helene Weber, 28 October 1895.

147 Marianne to Helene Weber, 21 September 1902 and 18 September 1903.

148 Christl Wickert, *Helene Stöcker*, Bonn, 1991, p. 47.

149 Marianne to Helene Weber, 30 October 1903.

150 Marianne Weber, *Frauenfragen und Frauengedanken*, esp. pp. 25 and 35f.

151 Marianne to Helene Weber, 9 November and 21 December 1905; 10 September 1906: 'I am now also completely at odds with Frau Stritt and have had a lot more trouble with her. She will probably have to resign.' This suggests that by then Marianne had considerable influence over the BDF leadership.

152 Evans, *Sozialdemokratie und Frauenemanzipation im deutschen Kaiserreich*, p. 152. Cf. Schaser, *Helene Lange und Gertrud Bäumer*, p. 145. Bäumer's behaviour may also be seen as normal political tactics. According to Margrit Göttert ('Gertrud Bäumer und Marianne Weber', p. 137), Bäumer actually spoke of a 'plot' between herself and Anna Pappritz against Marie Stritt. But Stritt's refusal to publish Bäumer's review of Marianne Weber's *Ehefrau und Mutter* in the *Centralblatt* of the women's movement (of which she was editor) was a considerable affront, which makes the revolt against her leadership understandable.

153 Gertrud Bäumer, *Lebensweg durch die Zeitenwende*, Tübingen, 1933, pp. 230ff.

154 Göttert, 'Gertrud Bäumer und Marianne Weber', p. 137.

155 Marianne to Helene Weber, 29 October 1907.

156 Eaedem, 10 June 1915.

157 Marianne Weber, *Frauenfragen und Frauengedanken*, p. 45.

158 Joachim Radkau, 'Zwischen freier Liebe und Koitus interruptus: Sexualität in Psychiatrie und Patientenerfahrung um 1900', in Karin Tebben (ed.), *Frauen – Körper – Kunst*, Göttingen, 2000, pp. 55ff.

159 Marianne to Max Weber, 30 December 1902.

160 See note 116 above.

161 Marianne Weber noted in her diary (Ana 446 Sch. 20 VII): 'Our relationship was always very tender and chaste – she didn't like petting – and I never forced so much as a kiss on her.' It is not hard to imagine, then, how happily Marianne would have kissed her.

162 See Kempter, *Die Jellineks*, p. 367n., on how Else von Richthofen was permitted to attend Georg Jellinek's lectures with Jellinek's support, even though the faculty of law did not admit women at that time.

163 Gilcher-Holtey, *Max Weber und die Frauen*, p. 152.

164 GStA Nl Weber Nr. 30 Bd. 4, 2 August 1899.

165 Salomon, *Charakter ist Schicksal*, p. 63.

166 Marianne to Max Weber, December 1898.

167 Gilcher-Holtey, *Max Weber und die Frauen*, p. 152.

168 Else Jaffé, 'Biographische Daten Alfred Webers (1868–1919)', in Eberhard Demm (ed.), *Alfred Weber als Politiker und Gelehrter*, Stuttgart, 1986, p. 187.

169 Robert Lucas, *Frieda von Richthofen*, Munich, 1972, p. 51.

170 Marianne to Helene Weber, 13 April 1900.
171 See 'Fräulein Dr. von Richthofen', a long and ironic article on the front page of *Der Badische Landmann*, 3 August 1900.
172 Wolfgang Bocks, *Die badische Fabrikinspektion: Arbeiterschutz, Arbeiterverhältnisse und Arbeiterbewegung in Baden 1879 bis 1914*, Freiburg, 1977, p. 560 et al.; also oral communication from W. Bocks, 18 November 2003.
173 Ana 446 Sch. 14, Marianne to Helene Weber, 29 January 1896.
174 Marianne to Max Weber, n.d. (autumn 1900) and 25 July 1901.
175 Bocks, *Die badische Fabrikinspektion*, p. 164n.
176 Marianne to Helene Weber, n.d. (early 1902).
177 BA Koblenz, NL 197/77, Else Jaffé to Alfred Weber, 18 January 1917.
178 Marianne to Helene Weber, 15 August 1898.
179 Eaedem, 16 June 1903.
180 Eaedem, 3 April 1905.
181 BA Koblenz, Nl 197/54 (A. Weber), Else Jaffé to Alfred Weber, 12 May 1910. And, on meeting him again after a long time with her young son by Otto Gross: 'The voice of blood squeaks only softly. . . . A truthful book on maternal love – that could still be written.'
182 Ibid., 13 July 1906.
183 These points are based on the fragment of an autobiographical sketch written by Else Jaffé after 1925, which forms part of the materials deposited by Martin Green at the library of Tufts University (Medford, MA). 'Feeling of disappointment, thankfully hidden in the early period of marriage, over what Edgar was achieving. The first child was on the way. Problem of Jewishness. . . . Closer and closer relations with Webers. I was awakening.' This awakening is evidently meant in the erotic sense of Franz Wedekind's *The Awakening of Spring*.
184 The memoirs of Edgar Salin show that she could also be seen quite differently; he speaks of her as 'the woman with expressive features', in which 'so much kindness and so much suffering were engraved' (Salin, *Um Stefan George*, p. 111). According to another account, the war between her parents that she had experienced as a young girl cast a shadow on her life: Kirsten Jüngling and Brigitte Roßbeck, *Frieda von Richthofen*, Berlin, 1998, p. 26. Today we have to try to uncover the real Else behind the male fantasies.
185 Her granddaughter Bettina Henrich emphatically stressed this point to the author – no doubt with good reason.
186 Marianne to Helene Weber, 31 July 1898.
187 Martin Green (*The von Richthofen Sisters: The Triumphant and the Tragic Modes of Love*, New York, 1974, p. 129) argues that Else 'did not love Alfred in any passionate way'. Evidently he has not studied the 13,000 or so pages of the correspondence between Alfred and Else in the Bundesarchiv Koblenz.
188 See the autobiographical sketch cited in note 183.
189 Martin Green, *Else und Frieda*, Munich, 1996, p. 86; cf. the variant translation in Green, *The von Richthofen Sisters*, p. 57. Marianne to Max Weber (30 April 1908) on a get-together between Otto and Else: 'But the ecstatic was simply unable . . . to talk about anything other than' areas in which he felt himself to be a missionary; 'he sat rigid until the conversation slid on to such paths and he could let himself go.'
190 Marianne to Helene Weber, 1 August 1906.
191 Eaedem, 26 August 1903.
192 Salin, *Um Stefan George*, p. 111.

193 Gerhard Schmolze (ed.), *Die Revolution und Räterepublik in München 1918/19*, Munich, 1978, pp. 20, 76. For the rather conservative Moritz Julius Bonn, however (*So macht man Geschichte*, Munich, 1953, pp. 190f.), Jaffé's speeches were 'the most blood-curdling': 'Jaffés vanity ran away with him; he absolutely had to play a role.'

194 Ingrid Gilcher-Holtey, 'Modelle "moderner" Weiblichkeit', in Meurer (ed.), *Marianne Weber*, p. 53. Max Weber had earlier defended women who practised free love to the philosopher Heinrich Rickert, arguing that some people lived like that not out of animal thoughtlessness but out of 'deepest convictions of their own': MWG II/5, 530.

195 Ana 446 Sch. 20 VII.

196 Marianne to Max Weber, 28 July and 30 July 1900: '*pomadig*' (blasé), a trendy word in the late nineteenth century, denoted the leisurely, composed, perhaps cynical attitude that Bismarck had told his diplomats to maintain in all discussions with negotiating partners. Naturally Else did not manage to do this in every situation: during her first pregnancy she was sometimes 'rather nervy' and no longer 'as pretty as before' – as Marianne noted, probably to her relief (Marianne to Helene Weber, 2 July 1905).

197 Marianne to Helene Weber, 3 May 1910.

198 Joachim Radkau, *Zeitalter der Nervosität*, Munich, 1998, pp. 448f.; Ernst Heinkel, *Stürmisches Leben*, Stuttgart, 1953, p. 33.

199 Ana 446 Sch. 20 VII.

200 Ana 446 Sch. 20 VI, 12 February 1911.

201 Ana 446 Sch. 20 VII.

202 Marianne to Helene Weber, 27 February 1906.

203 Eaedem, 15 February 1904.

204 Marianne to Max Weber, 30 April 1908.

205 Marianne Weber to Knittel, n.d.

206 Green, *The von Richthofen Sisters*, p. 171.

207 Alfred Weber to Max Brod, 29 June 1938, AWG vol. 10, p. 449; Christian von Ehrenfels, *Sexualethik*, Wiesbaden, 1907.

208 Edward R. Dickinson, 'Sex, Masculinity, and the "Yellow Peril": Christian von Ehrenfels' Program for a Revision of the European Social Order, 1902–1910', *German Studies Review*, 25/2 (2002), pp. 255–84.

209 *Archiv für Sozialwissenschaft*, 27 (1908), pp. 613–17; I am grateful to Guenther Roth for having pointed this out to me.

210 Ana 446 Sch. 20 VI, p. 97.

211 Ana 446 Sch. 20 VII.

212 Ana 446 Sch. 20 VI, diary entry of 12 February 1911.

Chapter 12 Max Weber's Love–Hate for the Germans

1 Adolf von Harnack, *The Mission and Expansion of Christianity in the First Three Centuries*, London, 1908.

2 Adolf von Harnack, *What Is Christianity?*, London, 1901, pp. 39, 40, 89.

3 Marianne to Helene Weber, 4 October 1913.

4 Arthur Shadwell, *Industrial Efficiency*, 2nd edn, London, 1911, pp. 11f.: 'The Germans are slow, deliberate, careful, methodical and thorough. Some people use the word "plodding", which carries a touch of disdain; but Germany can

afford to smile at it. . . . They have an unequalled capacity for mapping it out in the right direction and following it steadily. Their dislike of hurry and their love of thoroughness are shown in innumerable little things.'

5 K 239.
6 Friedrich Nietzsche, 'On the Uses and Disadvantages of History for Life', in Nietzsche, *Untimely Meditations*, Cambridge, 1983, p. 80.
7 Jules Huret, *Berlin um Neunzehnhundert*, Berlin, 1979, pp. 62f., 40f.
8 Joachim Radkau, *Zeitalter der Nervosität*, Munich, 1998, p. 164.
9 Guenter Roth inclines towards this interpretation (communication to the author).
10 Joachim Radkau, 'Nationalismus und Nervosität', in Wolfgang Hardtwig and Hans-Ulrich Wehler (eds), *Kulturgeschichte Heute*, Göttingen, 1996, pp. 308, 313.
11 Gustav Schmoller, 'Die wirtschaftliche Zukunft Deutschlands und die Flottenvorlage' (speech in Berlin on 28 November 1899), in Schmoller, *Zwanzig Jahre Deutscher Politik*, Munich, 1920, pp. 2ff., 9.
12 Lujo Brentano, *Elsässer Erinnerungen*, 2nd edn, Berlin, 1917, pp. 88ff.
13 See, for example, Volker Hentschel, *Geschichte der deutschen Sozialpolitik 1880–1980*, Frankfurt am Main, 1983.
14 Werner Abelshauser argues that the development of a successful 'German production regime' began in the age of Bismarck, with a balancing of competition and cartellization and the first elements of workers' participation; Schmoller recognized more clearly than Max Weber the shape of things to come. See Werner Abelshauser, 'Umbruch und Persistenz: Das deutsche Produktionsregime in historischer Perspektive', *Geschichte und Gesellschaft*, 27 (2001), p. 512.
15 Huret, *Berlin um Neunzehnhundert*, pp. 41, 186, 241ff.; on this report: Cécile Chombard-Gaudin, 'Frankreich blickt auf Berlin 1900–1939', in Gerhard Brunn and Jürgen Reulecke (eds), *Metropolis Berlin*, Berlin, 1992, pp. 367ff.
16 See Horst Baier, 'Vater Sozialstaat: Max Webers Widerspruch zur Wohlfahrtspatronage', in Christian Gneuss and Jürgen Kocka (eds), *Max Weber: Ein Symposion*, Munich, 1988, pp. 47ff.
17 Heinrich Heffter, *Die deutsche Selbstverwaltung im 19. Jahrhundert*, Stuttgart, 1950, p. 84.
18 In Germany the first writer to use this term in its modern sense seems to have been the constitutional theorist Robert von Mohl, in his essay *Über Bürokratie* (1846), although he asks whether it may be just a short-lived 'buzzword'. See Heffter, *Die deutsche Selbstverwaltung im 19. Jahrhundert*, p. 257.
19 Radkau, *Zeitalter der Nervosität*, p. 320.
20 Quoted from Gottfried Eisermann, *Max Weber und die Nationalökonomie*, Marburg, 1993, p. 151.
21 Hans-Ulrich Wehler, *Deutsche Gesellschaftsgeschichte 1849–1914*, Munich, 1995, p. 861; Thomas Nipperdey, *Deutsche Geschichte 1866–1918*, vol. 2, Munich, 1992, p. 114. Wehler praises Weber's diagnosis, but deals with the issue of bureaucracy in a mere seven pages (or 0.5 per cent of the total book).
22 Eberhard Demm, *Ein Liberaler in Kaiserreich und Republik*, Boppard, 1990, pp. 47ff., 115f.; Reiner Stach, *Kafka: The Decisive Years*, London, 2005, p. 292.
23 Demm, *Ein Liberaler in Kaiserreich und Republik*, pp. 112f.
24 Ibid., p. 113.

25 Weber also exaggerated the rationality in the bureaucracies of the early modern period. As Stefan Breuer points out (*Bürokratie und Charisma*, Darmstadt, 1994, p. 44), the reality at the time looked very different: 'Princes lived from hand to mouth, constantly teetering on the verge of bankruptcy, and were again and again driven to desperate measures such as tax-farming, debasement of the coinage, and so on.'

26 Renate Mayntz, 'Max Webers Idealtypus der Bürokratie und die Organisationssoziologie', in Mayntz (ed.), *Bürokratische Organisation*, Cologne, 1968, pp. 27ff.

27 From Brentano's critical point of view (*Mein Leben, im Kampf um die sociale Entwicklung Deutschlands*, Marburg, 2004, p. 134), Schmoller made economic science a chorus of acclamation for the state leaders. In later life, to be sure, Schmoller was anxious not to jeopardize his relations with people in high places, but he managed to retain his inner autonomy vis-à-vis Bismarck. Despite his hostility to the bureaucracy, Alfred Weber remained on friendlier terms than Max with Schmoller: see AWG vol. 10, pp. 155ff.

28 Friedrich Meinecke, 'Drei Generationen deutscher Gelehrtenpolitik', in Meinecke, *Staat und Persönlichkeit*, Berlin, 1933, p. 152.

29 Moritz Julius Bonn, *So macht man Geschichte*, Munich, 1953, p. 53.

30 Manfred Schön, 'Gustav Schmoller und Max Weber', in WuZ 90.

31 Wilhelm Hennis, *Max Weber's Science of Man*, Newbury, 2000, pp. 112f.

32 GStA Nl Weber Nr. 30 Bd. 4, to Karl Oldenberg, 28 January 1895. Already then, however, he did not find Schmoller a likeable person, as he seemed too short-tempered and 'not diplomatic enough'.

33 In the review of Adolf Weber's *Die Aufgaben der Volkswirtschaftslehre als Wissenschaft*, in *Archiv für Sozialwissenschaft*, 29 (1909), pp. 615ff.

34 Brentano, *Mein Leben*, p. 234.

35 Otto Ballerstedt (legal adviser to the Central Association of German Industrialists), 'Schutz der nationalen Arbeit und Kartellwesen', in *Deutschland als Weltmacht*, Berlin, 1911, pp. 238ff.; p. 239: 'Cartels have developed in Germany as in scarcely any other country.'

36 (The allusion is to the famous words with which Luther was reputed to have concluded his address to the Diet of Worms in 1521: 'Here I take my stand, I cannot do otherwise.' *Trans. note*)

37 Theodor Heuss, *Friedrich Naumann*, 2nd edn, Stuttgart, 1949, pp. 239f.; Brentano, *Mein Leben*, pp. 254ff.; Schön, 'Gustav Schmoller und Max Weber', pp. 90ff.

38 Marianne to Helene Weber, 9 November 1905; GStA Nl Weber Nr. 30 Bd. 4, Max to Alfred Weber, n.d. (1905) and 2 November 1905.

39 Cf. II/5, 253, to Lujo Brentano, 6 February 1907: Schmoller got 'all huffy about *any* criticism of a disciple'. Alfred Weber, however, remained friendly towards Schmoller and even told him it was through him that he had first understood the cartel issue (AWG vol. 10, p. 159).

40 Heuss, *Friedrich Naumann*, p. 277.

41 Unpaginated, large-format declaration at the end of Friedrich Naumann, *Das Blaue Buch von Vaterland und Freiheit*, Königstein, 1913.

42 Heuss, *Friedrich Naumann*, p. 89.

43 Max to Marianne Weber, GStA Nl Weber Nr. 30 Bd. 1; in her biography (WB 221) Marianne changed 'jabbering of the Holy Joes' (*Gequatsch der Pfaffen*) into 'the speech-making of the pastors' (*Gerede der Pastoren*).

44 Friedrich Naumann, *Demokratie und Kaisertum*, Berlin, 1905, p. 172.
45 Gustav Schmoller, 'Friedrich Naumann', in Schmoller, *Charakterbilder*, Munich, 1913, pp. 295f.
46 Naumann, *Demokratie und Kaisertum*, p. 187.
47 Friedrich Naumann, *Asia*, 7th edn, Berlin, 1913, pp. 71f. Paul Göhre was nauseated by the 'empty enthusiasm' for Wilhelm II's trip to the East that prevailed 'among most of the National-Socials'. Paul Göhre, 'Meine Trennung von den Nationalsozialen', *Die Zukunft*, 22 (13 May 1899), p. 293.
48 Ludwig Curtius, *Deutsche und antike Welt*, Stuttgart, 1958, pp. 109f.
49 Naumann to Max Weber, 30 October 1908, Naumann Nachlaß; extracts in Heuss, *Friedrich Naumann*, p. 258.
50 Friedrich Naumann, *Das Blaue Buch von Vaterland und Freiheit*, p. 23.
51 Ibid.; Marianne to Helene Weber, 29 January 1896.
52 Theodor Heuss, *Erinnerungen 1905–1933*, Stuttgart, 1963, p. 231. In 1896 Marianne Weber expressed amazement at 'Naumann's tremendous objectivity, sobriety' (WB 221).
53 Naumann to Weber, 15 October 1918, Naumann Nachlaß.
54 Ana 446 Sch. 14, Marianne to Helene Weber, 19 May 1895.
55 Alfred to Max Weber, 18 November 1897.
56 Heuss, *Friedrich Naumann*, pp. 206, 160.
57 Ludwig Curtius, *Deutsche und antike Welt*, p. 106.
58 Ursula Krey, 'Der Naumann-Kreis: Charisma und politische Emanzipation', in Rüdiger von Bruch (ed.), *Friedrich Naumann in seiner Zeit*, Berlin, 2000, p. 140.
59 One senses the gentle irony in Bernhard von Bülow, *Denkwürdigkeiten*, vol. 1, Berlin, 1930, p. 202: 'The former preacher is always present in Naumann's speeches, but with a tone that is a little too pastoral, here and there not quite genuine.'
60 Friedrich Naumann, *Neudeutsche Wirtschaftspolitik*, Berlin, 1917, pp. 407, 430.
61 Peter Theiner, *Sozialer Liberalismus und deutsche Weltpolitik: Friedrich Naumann im wilhelminischen Deutschland (1860–1919)*, Baden-Baden, 1983, p. 54 (14 August 1896).
62 Otto Baumgarten, *Meine Lebensgeschichte*, Tübingen, 1929, pp. 399f. Similarly, Ludwig Curtius (*Deutsche und antike Welt*, p. 108): 'The radiant goodness of his nature, . . . a certain kind of transfiguring, poetic love with which he also beheld his opponents and enemies and did them justice . . .: all this sprang from the most profound piety safe in God, although he took the greatest care not to speak of it.'
63 Heuss, *Friedrich Naumann*, p. 102.
64 John C. G. Röhl, *Wilhelm II.*, vol. 2, Darmstadt, 2001, pp. 1162ff.
65 Nicolaus Sombart suggested in conversation with the author (15 July 2000) that Weber subliminally identified with Wilhelm II, and that his hatred of him was in reality self-hatred.
66 Marianne to Helene Weber, 17 December 1900; Helene to Marianne Weber, 31 December 1902.
67 Repeated almost word for word in a passage that Schmoller urged him to delete from a statement of his views on the value-judgement controversy: MWG II/8, 340f.
68 Radkau, *Zeitalter der Nervosität*, pp. 407ff., 416ff.

69 Ludwig Quidde, *Caligula: Schriften über Militarismus und Pazifismus*, ed. Hans-Ulrich Wehler, Frankfurt am Main, 1977, p. 56.
70 Fritz Fischer, *War of Illusions*, London, 1975, pp. 128f.
71 Mina Tobler to her mother, 15 June 1912 (privately owned).
72 Ernst Toller, *I Was a German*, London, 1934, p. 91.
73 Max Weber, *Gesammelte Politische Schriften*, Munich, 1921, p. 467.
74 Karl Löwenstein, 'Personal Recollections of Max Weber' (1964), in Löwenstein, *Max Weber's Political Ideas in the Perspective of our Time*, Amherst, MA, 1966, p. 98.
75 At the Berlin congress of sociologists (GASS 484) and in *Economy and Society* (pp. 395f.).
76 *Verhandlungen des 2. Deutschen Soziologentages*, Tübingen, 1913, pp. 48, 73.
77 Ibid., pp. 96f.
78 Ibid., pp. 51, 54, 75, 190.
79 Naumann, *Das Blaue Buch von Vaterland und Freiheit*, p. 103.
80 Karl-Ludwig Ay, 'The Meaning of Honour in Weber's Concept of the Nation', manuscript, Munich, 2004.
81 Hans-Walter Schmuhl, 'Max Weber und das Rassenproblem', in Manfred Hettling et al. (eds), *Was ist Gesellschaftsgeschichte? (Festschrift für Hans-Ulrich Wehler)*, Munich, 1991, p. 337. Weber's distance from race theory is even more strongly emphasized in Karl-Ludwig Ay, 'Max Weber und der Begriff der Rasse', *Aschkenas* 1 (1993), pp. 189–218.
82 *Verhandlungen des 2. Deutschen Soziologentages*, p. 188.
83 Alfons Labisch and Florian Tennstedt, *Der Weg zum 'Gesetz über die Vereinheitlichung des Gesundheitswesens' vom 3. Juli 1934*, Part 2, Düsseldorf, 1985, pp. 467ff.
84 Breuer, *Bürokratie und Charisma*, p. 134.
85 Eduard Baumgarten, 'Spielräume unter Hitlers Herrschaft' (privately owned manuscript), pp. 53ff.
86 M. Rainer Lepsius, with knowledge of Weber's still unpublished letters from the war years, stressed in conversation with the author (24 March 2004) a point that was extremely repugnant to him: that Weber, contrary to his own theory of science, ascribed an ontological substance to the nation at war.
87 In: *Max Weber und die Soziologie heute*, ed. Otto Stammer, Tübingen, 1965, p. 147.
88 Karl Jaspers, *Lebensfragen der deutschen Politik*, Munich, 1963, p. 205.

Chapter 13 Value-Free Science, Love and Music

1 Marianne to Helene Weber, 15 July 1908.
2 Else Jaffé, 'Biographische Daten Alfred Webers', in Eberhard Demm (ed.), *Alfred Weber als Politiker und Gelehrter*, Stuttgart, 1986, pp. 185, 179.
3 AWG 10, 144.
4 On 22 February 1909 she reported that Alfred's housekeeper had handed in her notice because she did not wish to recognize and serve his women friends 'as proper ladies'. Eberhard Demm, however, thinks it doubtful that Alfred ever had a passionate erotic relationship before he met Else.
5 Marianne to Helene Weber, 22 December 1907 and 7 January 1908: 'Well, your two big strange boys are here, and poor me will have to rack my

brains to get on with this pair, as I would like to be able to include Alfred in our love.'

6 On 13 April 1909 Marianne wrote to Helene that she had to 'worry all the time' lest Max 'take offence at Alfred's lady friends'. She added: 'Please tear up this letter' – which Helene did not do. The letter indicates that Marianne thought Helene would show more understanding than Max for a loose sex life. Sometimes she even showed a certain sympathy for Alfred's criticism of 'rigorist sexual morals', especially when they bound a woman to be faithful to a husband who was not faithful himself and became infected with a sexually transmitted disease. (See Marianne to Helene Weber, 22 February 1909.)

7 See Marianne to Helene Weber, 12 April 1908, on Alfred: 'Ah, how I would like him to be as naturally warm with us again and to feel that all we want is to love him.'

8 Marianne to Helene Weber, 7 January 1908.

9 Eaedem, 26 June 1908.

10 Ana 446 Sch. 20 VII.

11 Dolf Sternberger, 'Max Weber und die Demokratie' (1964), in Sternberger, *'Ich wünschte ein Bürger zu sein': Neun Versuche über den Staat*, Frankfurt, 1967, p. 99.

12 Heino Heinrich Nau (ed.), *Der Werturteilsstreit: Die Äußerungen zur Werturteilsdiskussion im Ausschuß des Vereins für Sozialpolitik (1913)*, Marburg 1996, pp. 11, 48. This collection of materials is also the basis for further analyses of the value-judgement controversy.

13 *Frankfurter Zeitung*, 14 October 1909.

14 Nau, *Der Werturteilsstreit*, p. 186.

15 Rüdiger vom Bruch, *Wissenschaft, Politik und öffentliche Meinung: Gelehrtenpolitik im Wilhelminischen Deutschland (1890–1914)*, Husum, 1980, pp. 133f. For the view from the opposite side, see Richard Ehrenberg, *Terrorismus in der Wirtschafts-Wissenschaft*, Berlin, 1910, p. 69: 'The leaders of the *Kathedersozialisten* not only prepared and inaugurated . . . the day-to-day political struggle over the financial reform, but led it with all the instruments of high-pressure journalism involving a whole lot of fellow experts in a mixture of politics and scholarship which, though in existence for a long time, had never been displayed so nakedly or on a greater scale. The *Kathedersozialisten* really did "make" public opinion.'

16 Peter-Christian Witt, *Die Finanzpolitik des Deutschen Reiches von 1903 bis 1913*, Lübeck, 1970, pp. 217f. In conversation with the author (7 October 2004) Witt thought it very likely that Weber's polemic should be understood against the background of this academic support for the financial reform.

17 Nau, *Der Werturteilsstreit*, pp. 68, 153f. (on Weber's distance from this 'pseudo-value-free', actually 'tendentious' position). A similar critique of the *Kathedersozialisten* was advanced by the economists Julius Wolf and Ludwig Bernhard, both of them close to business circles, of Jewish extraction and outsiders within their academic fraternity.

18 Christian von Ferber makes this point in *Die Gewalt in der Politik: Auseinandersetzung mit Max Weber*, Stuttgart, 1970, p. 43.

19 Marianne to Helene Weber, 15 October 1909; this follows the long quotation in WB 414.

20 Ana 446 Sch. 20 VII.

21 Ibid.

22 Ibid.
23 Ibid. In fact, Weber wrote to Helene shortly before the Vienna congress that he would probably travel afterwards to Ragusa (MWG II/6, 276).
24 Ana 446 Sch. 20 VII.
25 Marianne to Helene Weber, 15 October 1909.
26 Tufts University Archive, deposit on Else and Frieda von Richthofen.
27 Baumgarten mistakenly gives the year as 1910.
28 Marianne to Helene Weber, 22 December 1909.
29 Ana 446 Sch. 20 VII.
30 Ibid.
31 Ana 446 Sch. 20 VI, 11 January 1911.
32 Ibid., 6 January 1911.
33 Ibid., 9 January 1911.
34 Marianne Weber, *Die Frauen und die Liebe*, Königstein-im-Taunus, 1950, pp. 138ff.
35 Marianne to Helene Weber, 3 May 1910.
36 Ana 446 Sch. 20 VI Bl. 56f. (10 August 1911).
37 BA Koblenz, Nl A. Weber 197, 53, Alfred Weber to Else Jaffé, 20 June 1910.
38 Marianne to Helene Weber, 3 May 1910: 'For the time being, however, we must . . . in Else's interests do everything to achieve the revocation of her shared life (with Edgar) for years to come. . . . To be sure, Jaffé will create many difficulties with regard to the present arrangement: to let Else herself shape her life with the children, and that will always be *our* mission.'
39 According to a communication from Eberhard Demm, there is no such mockery in the correspondence between Alfred and Else. Probably Alfred knew that she would not listen to disparaging remarks about Max.
40 Ana 446 Sch. 20 VI, 23 March 1911.
41 Max Weber to Else Jaffé, 15 January 1919.
42 Max Weber to Else Jaffé, 25 March 1919.
43 Max Weber to Else Jaffé, 15 January 1919.
44 BA Koblenz, Nl A. Weber, 197/87, Else Jaffé to Alfred Weber, 8 July 1920.
45 Ibid., 23 June 1920.
46 M. Rainer Lepsius ('Mina Tobler, die Freundin Max Webers', in Bärbel Meurer (ed.), *Marianne Weber*, Tübingen, 2004, p. 84) maintains that 'Weber's complaints about psycho-physical breakdowns' ceased only in 1912, when the relationship with Mina Tobler became more intimate.
47 Max Weber to Else Jaffé, 22 April 1919: 'Only two years after your nasty letter of 1910 did I – . . . now you know roughly what ? did in 1912. But nothing changed, nothing at all. Isolde (not "the blonde", no, the "brunette" Isolde!) was still there, even when Isolde Weisshand took Tristan's hand; your anger kept breaking from afar against my heart.' It follows that Weber's relationship with Mina Tobler began in 1912, probably at the time when they went together to a performance of *Tristan* in Munich – although Wagner did not introduce an Isolde Weisshand to confuse Tristan's love for Isolde!
48 Lepsius, 'Mina Tobler', pp. 82, 80.
49 Marianne to Helene Weber, 19 August 1912 on Mina: 'She is a strange creature: in one way very mature, in another still like an eighteen-year-old at the age of thirty-three, so intensely preoccupied with *herself* and her destiny.' This impression is confirmed by a reading of Mina Tobler's letters from those years.

50 *Karlsruher Tagblatt*, 27 January 1912, in '*Auszügen von Briefen Mina Toblers*', collected by Achim Tobler, manuscript, Aalen, 1988, and sent to the author by Mina Tobler's grandnephew Tilman Evers (Kassel).

51 Marianne to Max Weber, n.d.

52 Marianne to Helene Weber, 3 August and 14 August 1912.

53 This seems to me to have been a fleeting idea. Wilhelm Hennis quotes an unpublished passage from Hans Staudinger's memoirs, which recalls an occasion on which he asked:

'Max Weber, what is your guiding supreme value?' Weber was astonished and replied that few had posed him this candid question. 'I have no supreme value', he answered. 'How can you live then?' cried Staudinger. Weber smiled and said: 'Imagine that hanging from the ceiling of my study there are violins, pipes and drums, clarinets and harps. Now this instrument plays, now that. The violin plays, that is my religious value. Then I hear harps and clarinets and I sense my artistic value. Then it is the turn of the trumpet and that is my value of freedom. With the sound of pipes and drums I feel the values of my fatherland. The trombone stirs the various values of community, solidarity. There are sometimes dissonances. Only inspired men are able to make a melody out of – prophets, statesmen, artists, who are more or less charismatic. . . . (not, like himself) a scholar whose . . . instruments are to be found in bookcases.' (*Max Weber's Central Question*, 2nd edn, Newbury, 2000, pp. 173f.)

Whether or not we buy this profession of modesty, we see how in his euphoric periods Weber was capable of the idea that not only struggle but also harmony – if not logical, then musical – was possible between divergent values.

54 Hideharu Ando, 'Die Interviews mit Else Jaffé', *Kölner Zeitschrift für Soziologie*, 55 (2003), p. 599.

55 Achim Tobler (ed.), '*Auszüge aus den Briefen von Mina Tobler*', part II, manuscript, Aalen, 1988, p. 83.

56 Marianne to Helene Weber, 19 January and 19 August 1912.

57 Eaedem, 19 August 1912.

58 Ana 446 Sch. 20 VI Bl. 75.

59 Marianne to Helene Weber, 19 August 1912.

60 Eaedem, 7 December 1912.

61 Eaedem, 1 June 1913. Similarly, on 6 June 1914: 'Max is working very intensively and is not to be distracted by worldly pleasures – only *Tobelchen* gets her now legitimate share.'

62 Ana 446 Sch. 20 VI.

63 21 January 1912; *Briefauszüge* II, p. 75.

64 Communication to the author from Tilman Evers, 11 March 2003.

65 12 December 1914, 'Auszüge aus den Briefen', II, p. 100.

66 6 October 1912, ibid., p. 85.

67 1 February 1913, ibid., p. 94.

68 15 December 1912, ibid., p. 90.

69 4 May 1913, ibid., p. 96.

70 MWG II/9, Max Weber to Lili Schäfer, 7 December 1915.

71 Mina Tobler to her mother, 19 September 1914, 'Auszüge aus den Briefen', II, p. 105.

72 Hans Staudinger, *Wirtschaftspolitik im Weimarer Staat*, Bonn, 1982, p. 15.

73 Mina Tobler to her mother, 17 June 1915, 'Auszüge aus den Briefen', II, p. 114.

74 Lepsius, 'Mina Tobler', p. 80.

75 Lepsius (ibid., p. 86) writes of Weber's intimate letter to Mina of September 1919, in which he said that he had used some old notes from his 'sociology of music' for a colloquium. 'I could hardly stop myself saying that the work on it had been done "under a lady-friend's guidance" – but then I thought it would be too indiscrete.' We learn from this, by the way, that Mina Tobler's significance for Weber's sociology of music could not have been quite as incidental as Else Jaffé suggests.

76 Hideharu Ando, 'Die Interviews mit Else Jaffé', p. 599.

77 All the stranger is the twenty-year-old Weber's remark in a letter to his father that he went 'very wearily to a Wagner concert at which Emmy sang' (JB 101). Emmy Baumgarten, with whom he was then unofficially semi-engaged! The fact that his weariness did not vanish when she sang Wagner seems, with hindsight, clearly to indicate that his feelings for her had little to do with erotic love.

78 Hideharu Ando, 'Die Interviews mit Else Jaffé', p. 599.

79 Leo Koenigsberger, *Hermann von Helmholtz*, Brunswick, 1911, p. 166. Helmholtz even added a number of musical-programmatic reflections, arguing that a return to the pure tones for which the (miseducated) human ear longed might generate a new enjoyment of music.

80 Marianne to Helene Weber, 12 May 1912.

81 Anatoli Lunatscharski, *Die Revolution und die Kunst*, Dresden, 1960, pp. 33ff. ('Über die soziologische Methode in der Musiktheorie und Musikgeschichte', 1925).

82 Even Kurt Blaukopf (*Musical Life in a Changing Society: Aspects of Music Sociology*, Portland, OR, 1992), who devotes a whole chapter to 'music in Max Weber's sociology', spends barely two pages on his 'music sociology fragment' and evidently does not consider it to be sociology.

83 Christoph Braun, *Max Webers 'Musiksoziologie'*, Laaber, 1992, p. 137.

84 Michael Sukale, *Max Weber, Leidenschaft und Disziplin: Leben, Werk, Zeitgenossen*, Tübingen, 2002, p. 300: 'I would even . . . claim that in this treatise Weber for the first time fully demonstrated the rationalization thesis in a single field.'

85 *Wirtschaft und Gesellschaft* I , p. 60; cf. E&S 85.

86 Marianne Weber already recognized this, or learned it from Max Weber. In her preface to the second edition of *Wirtschaft und Gesellschaft*, she wrote: 'What he found so gripping the first time he scrutinized the musical structures of the Orient and Occident, was the discovery that precisely in music – an art form which seemingly flowed directly from the emotions – reason played such an important role and that music's unique form in the Occident, like the unique form of its science and all its state and social institutions, was conditioned by a specifically-shaped rationalism.' Quoted from Wolfgang Schluchter, *Rationalism, Religion and Domination: A Weberian Perspective*, Berkeley, CA, 1989, p. 418.

87 MWG II/9, Max Weber to Mina Tobler, 24 August 1915.

88 See the article on 'Rationalization' in J. Laplanche and J.-B. Pontalis, *The Language of Psycho-analysis*, London, 1988.

89 Alec Robertson and Denis Stevens (eds), *The Pelican History of Music*, vol. 1: *Ancient Forms to Polyphony*, Harmondsworth, 1960, p. 212. This quotation does not stand alone; throughout the Middle Ages music was thought of as 'a science closely related to arithmetic' (ibid., p. 274).

90 Karl Loewenstein, 'Personal Recollections of Max Weber', in Loewenstein, *Max Weber's Political Ideas in the Perspective of our Time*, Amherst, MA, 1966, pp. 93f.

91 For an English translation, see Hermann von Helmholtz, *On the Sensations of Tone as a Physiological Basis for the Theory of Music*, Bristol, 1998.

92 Koenigsberger, *Hermann von Helmholtz*, p. 175.

93 Hermann von Helmholtz, 'On the Physiological Cause of Harmony in Music', in David Cahan (ed.), *Science and Culture: Popular and Philosophical Essays by Hermann von Helmholtz*, Chicago, 1995.

94 Koenigsberger, *Hermann von Helmholtz*, pp. 173, 183ff.; Friedrich Wilhelm Foerster, *Erlebte Weltgeschichte 1869–1953: Memoiren*, Nuremberg, 1953, pp. 68f.

95 Franz Werner, *Hermann Helmholtz' Heidelberger Jahre (1858–1871)*, Berlin, 1997, p. 106.

96 Werner Friedrich Kümmel, 'Musik und Musikgeschichte in biologistischer Interpretation', in Gunter Mann (ed.), *Biologismus im 19. Jahrhundert*, Stuttgart, 1973, p. 109.

97 Weber's 'most interesting question in the end' has up to now aroused scarcely any interest among Weber researchers: see Braun, *Max Webers 'Musiksoziologie'*, pp. 202ff.

98 Braun, *Max Webers 'Musiksoziologie'*, pp. 84ff.

99 Marianne Weber later recalled: 'The conversations between Max and Lukács had a special magic because Lukács, though so much younger than Max, was one of the few who were a match for him in argument' (Ana 446 Sch. 20 VI). Eva Karádi ('Ernst Bloch und Georg Lukács im Max Weber-Kreis', WuZ 695) thinks that for years Weber did not give up the 'struggle for Lukács', even though he sometimes told him to his face that he would 'hate it' if Lukács were to slip into essay-writing and drift away from serious, systematic scholarship (Weber to Lukács, 14 August 1916, in Georg Lukács, *Selected Correspondence 1902–1920*, New York, 1986, p. 265). Even in 'Science as a Vocation', when Weber raised the question 'whether or not the realm of art is perhaps a realm of diabolical grandeur' (FWM 144), this alluded almost word for word to 'Lukács's theory of the demonic nature of art'.

100 Elisabeth Weisser, *Georg Lukács' Heidelberger Kunstphilosophie*, Bonn, 1992, p. 10.

101 Kurt Beiersdörfer, *Max Weber und Georg Lukács*, Frankfurt am Main, 1986, p. 19.

102 Ulf Matthiesen, 'Im Schatten einer endlosen großen Zeit: Etappen der intellektuellen Biographie Albert Salomons', in Ilja Srubar (ed.), *Exil, Wissenschaft, Identität*, Frankfurt am Main, 1988, pp. 309ff.

103 Dirk Käsler, 'Max Weber und Georg Lukács: Episoden zum Verhältnis von "bürgerlicher" und "marxistischer" Soziologie"', in Käsler, *Soziologie als Berufung*, Opladen, 1997, pp. 44ff.

104 Éva Fekete and Éva Karádi, *Georg Lukács*, Stuttgart, 1981, p. 30.

105 Weisser, *Georg Lukács' Heidelberger Kunstphilosophie*, p. 67.

106 Lukács, *Selected Correspondence 1902–1920*, p. 222.

107 Ana 446 Sch. 20 VI.

108 GStA Nl. Weber Nr. 30 Bd. 4, to Alfred Weber, 2 August 1899.

109 Winfried Mogge and Jürgen Reulecke (eds), *Hoher Meißner 1913*, Cologne, 1988, p. 247.

110 Marianne to Helene Weber, 23 June 1901.
111 Eaedem, 14 March 1902.
112 Max to Marianne Weber, 15 June 1903.
113 RI 158, 199, et al.
114 Robert Michels, *Sexual Ethics*, London, 1914, p. 155.
115 WB 360; Marianne to Helene Weber, 13 April 1906.
116 In the last few decades, these themes have been revived in various ways by the health food and alternative medicine movements. See Cornelia Regin, *Selbsthilfe und Gesundheitspolitik: Die Naturheilbewegung im Kaiserreich (1889–1914)*, Stuttgart, 1995; Judith Baumgartner, *Ernährungsreform – Antwort auf Industrialisierung und Ernährungswandel*, Frankfurt am Main, 1992; Albert Wirz, *Die Moral auf dem Teller*, Zurich, 1993; Alexander Fenton (ed.), *Order and Disorder: The Health Implications of Eating and Drinking in the Nineteenth and Twentieth Centuries*, East Linton, East Lothian, 2000. The natural healing movement initially took shape in opposition to university medicine, but since the latter had much less to offer in treatment than in diagnosis – the pharmaceuticals industry was still in its infancy – doctors often relied on a combination of academic and natural medicine. Even a man of science such as Weber did not think that the theory of the healing powers of nature was not necessarily anti-scientific.
117 Marianne to Max Weber, n.d. On 18 February 1899 Alfred Weber suggested to Max that he needed to overcome the 'unpleasant side-effects' of cycling – pressure on the genitals, no doubt – 'by suitably adjusting the seat'. Otherwise he should follow Friedrich Naumann's example and give horse-riding a try.
118 Joachim Radkau, 'Das Fahrrad in den Technikvisionen der Jahrhundertwende oder: Das Erlebnis in der Technikgeschichte', in Volker Briese et al. (eds), *Wege zur Fahrradgeschichte*, Bielefeld, 1995, p. 21.
119 Marianne to Helene Weber, 29 January 1902.
120 Marianne to Helene Weber, February 1910.
121 On the founder, Heinrich Lahmann, see Alfred Brauchle, *Die Geschichte der Naturheilkunde in Lebensbildern*, Stuttgart 1951, pp. 228–39. Brauchle calls him the first *scientific* natural healer, who used his medical and organizational talents to 'promote the natural healing method in an absolutely marvellous way'. 'One of Lahmann's strokes of genius was to take specific gravity as the measure for a person's general state of health' (p. 233). No wonder that Max Weber's corpulence was the main thing that attracted the attention of the leading doctor at the clinic!
122 Marianne to Helene Weber, 29 March and 17 November 1908.
123 Eaedem, 4 October 1908: The 'fattening of another little belly' at the mother's house in Charlottenburg *pained* her.
124 Eaedem, 31 January 1911.
125 Max Weber to Friedrich Naumann, apparently on 11 May 1917; Naumann Nachlaß.
126 Jaspers to Fraenkel, 1 June 1934, quoted from *Albert Fraenkel, Arzt und Forscher*, ed. Georg Weiss, 2nd edn, Mannheim, 1964, p. 18.
127 Viktor von Weizsäcker, *Natur und Geist: Erinnerungen eines Arztes*, Göttingen, 1954, pp. 57f., 220.
128 Hermann Hesse, *Haus zum Frieden*, quoted from *Albert Fraenkel, Arzt und Forscher*, pp. 47f.
129 MWG II/9, Max to Marianne Weber, 30 April 1916.

130 The 'fatted burgher' (*Mastbürgertum*) was not a term coined by Weber but a popular insult for an affluent pot-bellied citizen.
131 Marianne to Helene Weber, 1 October 1915.
132 Joachim Radkau: 'Die Verheißungen der Morgenfrühe: Die Lebensreform in der neuen Moderne', in Kai Buchholz et al. (eds), *Die Lebensreform: Entwürfe zur Neugestaltung von Leben und Kunst um 1900*, vol. 1, Darmstadt, 2001, pp. 55–60; and Ulrich Linse, 'Der Rebell und die "Mutter Erde": Asconas "Heiliger Berg" in der Deutung des anarchistischen Bohemien Erich Mühsam', in *Monte Verità, Berg der Wahrheit*, Munich, 1980 (catalogue of the exhibition in the Villa Stuck museum), p. 30.
133 Ibid., p. 32; Erich Mühsam, *Ascona* (1905), Berlin, 1982, p. 46.
134 Robert Landmann, *Monte Verità: Die Geschichte eines Berges*, 3rd edn, Ascona, 1934, p. 99.
135 Ulrich Linse, 'Der Rebell und die "Mutter Erde" ' ', p. 36.
136 Marianne Weber, *Die Frauen und die Liebe*, pp. 180–95.
137 Ana 446 Sch. 20 VI Bl. 98.
138 Marianne Weber, *Die Frauen und die Liebe*, p. 180.
139 Franziska Gräfin zu Reventlow, *Tagebücher 1895–1910*, ed. Else Reventlow, Frankfurt am Main, 1976, p. 441 (9 August 1908).
140 Marianne Weber, *Die Frauen und die Liebe*, pp. 192f.
141 See the particularly enigmatic, apparently never explained passage on Weber's morning walk in the Ticino delta (WB 492): 'But behind me the nymph Calypso slipped out of the arched grotto of her *palazzo* in golden garments. To escape her – for she does not fit in there – I walked faster, went off to the right, then to the left. Finally she must have seen that Odysseus was not to be had, for she turned around; but now she angrily pelted me with a thunderstorm that did not leave a dry stitch on my body, . . . and chased me homeward at a gallop. But it *was* beautiful.' Who was meant by 'the nymph Calypso', who was transformed into a force of nature? Why did Marianne reproduce such mysterious words without comment? The editors of the *Max-Weber Gesamtausgabe* think it was most probably Countess Reventlow (MWG II/8, 628), but Weber himself did not want to give Marianne that impression. Shortly afterwards he wrote that he thought the countess 'simply dull and uninteresting', after Frieda had reported to him that the countess found him 'inhibiting' and 'crippling' – a signal between the lines that Franziska zu Reventlow would have liked to get closer to him. A little earlier (MWG II/8, 620) Weber had assured Marianne that the countess was 'completely uninteresting' to him: so there must have been some reason for him to keep underlining this lack of interest. If 'wild Fanny' is the nymph Calypso, then he is Odysseus, and Marianne/Penelope can be sure he will return home to her, even if he sleeps with the nymph!
142 Marianne Weber, *Die Frauen und die Liebe*, pp. 192f.
143 Franziska zu Reventlow, *Herrn Dames Aufzeichnungen*, Munich, 1969, p. 135 (with an afterword by Friedrich Podszus).
144 On this whole question, see Sam Whimster, 'Max Weber Counsels Frieda Gross', in: Raimund Dehmlow and Gottfried Heuer (eds), *Erster Internationaler Otto Gross Kongress*, Marburg, 2000, pp. 55–73.
145 This is apparent even in many passages of the book that rediscovered Otto Gross and presented him as a figure to be identified with: Emanuel Hurwitz, *Otto Gross: Paradies-Sucher zwischen Freud und Jung*, Zurich, 1979. The magazine *Revolution* devoted a special issue to the plea for Gross's release, yet it

appreciated the tragedy of the father, who had a high opinion of his son, although his 'genius . . . ground itself down on that of the son'; it also characterized Hans Gross the criminologist as a man who 'stood up for young people with admirable gentleness and helped everyone to assert themselves' (ibid., p. 25).

146 Ibid., pp. 20, 22.

147 Ibid., pp. 50, 139.

148 MWG II/8, 518,18 February 1914, to Frieda Gross: 'It would be an easy thing to prove that the provision of poison for suicide in both these cases (which now come under the statute of limitations) casts no shadows on his character and his mental powers.' See also ibid. pp. 489, 491, 503, 510: nowhere in this connection is there the slighest reproach against Otto Gross. One could, however, think that to help two young, not seriously ill people to kill themselves was the most evil thing this man did, especially as the honesty of his motives was not beyond all doubt.

149 MWG II/8, 182, 160, 5 April 1914: 'I now also understand why the old man has had him isolated in this way.' Some years before, Otto Gross had had the audacity to send his father a manuscript and to ask him to take care of its publication and funding – a manuscript in which 'the same father's sex life' was described 'in detail and with names' as the 'most important example of exceptionally disgusting behaviour'. If Weber had been the judge – he said as much to Frieda – he would have had 'such a blackguard locked up for that alone, without all the psychiatric reports'. On 14 April 1914, however, he wrote to Marianne (MWG II/8, 622): 'But only now am I beginning to get a reasonably secure picture of Gross senior's "principles" – and ugh, how disgusting! is all you can say.' Presumably Weber thought that the son's revelations about his father's sex life were accurate, if also outrageous.

150 MWG II/9, Max to Marianne Weber, 21 March 1916.

151 Autobiographical notes of Else Jaffé, deposited by Else and Frieda von Richthofen in the Tufts University Archives.

152 MWG II/9, Max Weber to Frieda Gross, 25 June 1916.

153 Marianne to Helene Weber, 30 April 1914.

154 Ana 446 Sch. 20 VII. She added: 'But Max held to the view that she was as she was not because of, but *despite*, her unfettered surrender to erotic adventures.' At that time, in discussions with Marianne, Max was stricter on moral issues than Marianne had meanwhile become.

155 MWG II/8, 182, Max to Marianne Weber, 14 April 1913, on Frieda: 'This life is in terrible ruins. . . . (Her marriage with Otto Gross put) such crazy psychological demands on her, totally "ate her up", without any mercy, and on top of that – as she admits – there is the polygamy that is so terribly wearing on the psyche. . . . (To Weber's question) whether here a cranky idea about love may not have driven a crazy *squandering of psychological energy*, the answer burst out: *yes*. It *is* terrible and completely hopeless. And she no longer has any strength, she can hardly cope any more. That's how it is. She is *very* neurasthenic.'

156 Marianne to Helene Weber, 11 March 1914: 'Max is really a rescuing angel for her.'

157 See Max to Marianne Weber, 21 April 1913 (MWG II/8, 1914): 'Please, if you write to Else, think that F(rieda) will hear every word that concerns her.'

158 Lawrence A. Scaff, 'Max Webers Begriff der Kultur', in Gerhard Wagner and Heinz Zipprian (eds), *Max Webers Wissenschaftslehre*, Frankfurt am Main, 1994, p. 688.

159 Marianne Weber, *Die Frauen und die Liebe*, pp. 180, 194f., 182f.

160 Else Reventlow (ed.), *Franziska zu Reventlow: Autobiographisches: Novellen, Schriften, Selbstzeugnisse*, Frankfurt am Main, 1986, p. 288.

161 Wolfgang Schluchter refers to this proximity in his 'Weltflüchtiges Erlösungsstreben und organische Sozialethik', in Schluchter (ed.), *Max Webers Studie über Hinduismus und Buddhismus*, Frankfurt am Main, 1984, p. 12; and Eduard Baumgarten (B 667) spoke earlier of the 'conversion of §11 into the corresponding section of the *Zwischenbetrachtung*'.

162 Section 11 of the *Sociology of Religion* contains similar ideas in Freudian-sounding formulations about sublimation and substitute satisfaction: 'The intoxication of the sexual orgy can . . . be sublimated explicitly or implicitly into erotic love for a god or saviour. . . . Yet there can be no doubt that a considerable portion of the specifically anti-erotic religiosity, both mystical and ascetic, represents substitute satisfactions of sexually conditioned physiological needs' (E&S 603). Note: 'there can be no doubt'!

163 Max Weber, *Das antike Judentum*, 5th edn, Tübingen, 1971, p. 420.

164 Erwin Rohde, *Psyche: The Cult of Souls and Belief in Immortality among the Greeks* (1893), London, 1925, p. 292; Hans G. Kippenberg, 'Religionsentwicklung', in Kippenberg and Martin Riesebrodt (eds), *Max Webers 'Religionssystematik'*, Tübingen, 2001, pp. 87f.; Bernhard Lang, 'Prophet, Priester, Virtuose', ibid., p. 173; Volkhard Krech, 'Mystik', ibid., p. 243.

Chapter 14 Charisma

1 In the electronic edition of Weber's works, 'salvation' (*Erlösung*) appears 482 times and 'soteriological' 130 times – almost exclusively in his later writings. In the only place in *The Protestant Ethic* where this keyword occurs, Weber hints at its huge importance but immediately sets the subject aside: 'We can likewise not enter into the tremendous change which the inner attitude toward the world underwent with the Christian form of the ideas of grace and salvation which contained in a peculiar way the seeds of new possibilities of development' (PE 271n.).

2 Edith Hanke, 'Erlösungsreligionen', in Hans G. Kippenberg and Martin Riesebrodt (eds), *Max Webers 'Religionssystematik'*, Tübingen, 2001, p. 211.

3 Adolf Deissmann, *Light from the Ancient East: The New Testament Illustrated by Recently Discovered Texts of the Graeco-Roman World*, London, 1910.

4 Edith Hanke, 'Max Webers "Herrschaftssoziologie": Eine werkgeschichtliche Studie', in Hanke and Wolfgang J. Mommsen (eds), *Max Webers Herrschaftssoziologie*, Tübingen, 2001, p. 32. Wolfgang Mommsen (*Max Weber: Gesellschaft, Politik und Geschichte*, Frankfurt am Main, 1974, p. 128) also thinks it 'a fact' that 'in Weber the type of charismatic rule is always conceived as logically prior'.

5 Admittedly in *Die protestantische Ethik* (p. 102) he spoke of 'the charisma of apostolic destitution' (see 'charisma of the disciples' in PE 179), but in that passing remark there was no recognizable idea of charisma as a source of power.

6 Hanke, 'Max Webers "Herrschaftssoziologie"', pp. 53ff.

7 Eckart Otto, *Max Webers Studien des Antiken Judentums*, Tübingen, 2002, p. 190.

8 Arnold Zingerle (*Max Webers historische Soziologie: Aspekte und Materialien zur Wirkungsgeschichte*, Darmstadt, 1981, p. 133) is struck by the 'late date' – the 1940s – at which the charisma concept began to have its 'widespread impact'.

9 Kurt E. Becker, *'Der römische Cäsar mit Christi Seele': Max Webers Charisma-Konzept: Eine systematisch kritische Analyse unter Einbeziehung biographischer Fakten*, Frankfurt am Main, 1988, p. 75; Karl Holl, *Enthusiasmus und Bußgewalt beim griechischen Mönchtum: Eine Studie zu Symeon dem neuen Theologen*, Leipzig, 1898, reissued Hildesheim, 1969.

10 Paul Göhre, 'Meine Trennung von den Nationalsozialen', *Die Zukunft*, 22 (1899), pp. 287ff. (13 May 1899). In 1897 Sohm issued the blunt slogan: 'Swing right!' To which Göhre replied no less bluntly: 'The effect of Sohm's proposal would be to turn the National-Social Association into a cohort of socialist-killers; and I do not wish to be a killer of socialists.' On Sohm's political role at that time, see Dieter Düding, *Der Nationalsoziale Verein 1896–1903*, Munich, 1972, esp. pp. 85ff. In opposing Göhre, he described the masses as a 'non-people' and as 'something dull, obtuse and incapable' (ibid., p. 93). A demagogic-revolutionary appeal to the masses, in the style of Weber's charismatic leadership, was thus repugnant to Sohm.

11 Wolfgang J. Mommsen, *Max Weber: Gesellschaft, Politik und Geschichte*, Frankfurt am Main, 1974, p. 120; cf. Mommsen, *Max Weber and German Politics, 1890–1920*, Chicago, 1990, p. 62.

12 Erich Eyck, *Das persönliche Regiment Wilhelms II.*, Zurich, 1948, p. 62: 'For years this was quoted in speeches at every rally of the Social Democratic Party.'

13 Mommsen, *Max Weber: Gesellschaft, Politik und Geschichte*, p. 129.

14 Guenther Roth noted in 1979: 'No other part of Max Weber's sociology of rule . . . has proved as difficult and provocative as the section on charisma.' Quoted from Rongfen Wang, *Cäsarismus und Machtpolitik: Eine historisch-biobibliographische Analyse von Max Webers Charismakonzept*, Berlin, 1997, p. 12.

15 After an effective lecture, Max Weber used to tell Marianne: 'I would have to read like that every day if I wanted to be a professor.' But Marianne always retorted 'that such achievements are not part of everyday routine, any more than Tristan's singing is possible every day' (Ana 446 Sch. 20 V).

16 The point is made especially sharply in Rongfen Wang, *Cäsarismus und Machtpolitik*, the most detailed investigation so far of the background in Weber's life to the concept of charisma.

17 Herbert Marcuse, 'Industrialization and Capitalism in the Work of Max Weber', in Marcuse, *Negations: Essays in Critical Theory*, London, 1988, pp. 217f.

18 Leo Strauss, *Natural Law and History*, Chicago, 1953, pp. 55f.

19 Wolfgang J. Mommsen, 'Politik im Vorfeld der "Hörigkeit der Zukunft"', in Mommsen and Edith Hanke (eds), *Max Webers Herrschaftssoziologie*, p. 316: 'The broad mass of a charismatic ruler's following in traditional regimes, as well as the citizenry in democratic states, does not feature prominently in his field of vision. The population is mostly, if not exclusively, allocated a passive role in the political process, even if its voice is essential for the founding of a legitimate order.'

20 Hermann Glockner, *Heidelberger Bilderbuch*, Bonn, 1969, p. 101.
21 Edgar Salin, *Um Stefan George*, Munich, 1954, p. 110.
22 Wilfried Westphal, *Sturm über dem Nil: Der Mahdi-Aufstand: Aus den Anfängen des islamischen Fundamentalismus*, Cologne, 2002.
23 Unlike Christoph Steding, the future Nazi ideologue, in *Politik und Wissenschaft bei Max Weber*, Breslau, 1932, pp. 16f.
24 BA Koblenz, Nl 197/77, Else Jaffé to Alfred Weber, 22 October 1917.
25 Ludwig Bernhard, *Der Hugenberg-Konzern: Psychologie und Technik einer Großorganisation der Presse*, Berlin, 1928, pp. 10f.
26 It is therefore absent from the great lexicon-handbook *Geschichtliche Grundbegriffe*, despite its huge importance for the twentieth century.
27 Oral communication to the author, 11 August 2004.
28 See C. F. L. Hoffmann, *Vollständiges politisches Taschenwörterbuch*, Leipzig, 1849, reissued Düsseldorf, 1972, p. 74: '*Führer* is how the most significant talent of a political fraction is called, who through expertise and prudence directs the course and regulations for its undertakings.'
29 Mommsen, *Max Weber and German Politics*, p. 408: 'Weber did not fear the transformation of a leadership democracy into a charismatic dictatorship.'
30 Friedrich Meinecke, *Staat und Persönlichkeit*, Berlin, 1933, p. 163.
31 Ian Kershaw (*The 'Hitler Myth': Image and Reality in the Third Reich*, Oxford, 1987, pp. 8–9) gives the impression that the application of the charisma model to the Nazi dictatorship was a new idea; he then, of course, used it as the basis for his own highly successful biography of Hitler. But already in 1959 Wolfgang J. Mommsen pointed to the links between Weber's concept of charisma and the Nazi Führer cult, although he aroused considerable opposition: see *Max Weber and German Politics*, esp. pp. 388, 408–10.
32 Raymond Aron, *Memoirs: Fifty Years of Political Thought*, New York, 1990, p. 49.
33 Grotesque though it seems today, this worry was expressed in 1932 in the conclusion to a history of the movement by Konrad Heiden, who later as an émigré wrote the first major biography of Hitler. In 1932 he already believed it possible to write an epilogue on National Socialism: 'Anyone who, for all their hostility to National Socialism, recognizes its great success, might prefer to wish it a more tragic and grander end. For at least the Hitler movement has shown the nation one thing – which is how one fights politically when one is filled with enthusiasm' (Konrad Heiden, *Geschichte des Nationalsozialismus*, Berlin, 1932, p. 295).
34 Gerhard Oestreich in the introduction to Otto Hintze, *Soziologie und Geschichte*, 2nd edn, Göttingen, 1964, p. 45.
35 Kurt Beiersdörfer, *Max Weber und Georg Lukács*, Frankfurt am Main, 1986, p. 19.
36 Steding, *Politik und Wissenschaft bei Max Weber*, p. 97.

Chapter 15 The Naturalness of Community

1 Melchior Palyi (ed.), *Erinnerungsgabe für Max Weber*, vol. 1, Munich, 1923, p. 23.
2 Hjalmar Schacht, *My First Seventy-Five Years*, London, 1955, p. 114.

3 M. Rainer Lepsius, 'Mina Tobler', in: Bärbel Meurer (ed.), *Marianne Weber*, Tübingen, 2004, p. 84: in the years from 1911–12 to 1914, Weber wrote 'roughly a thousand pages for *Economy and Society* and the "comparative sociology of religion".' To be sure, Weber felt that his capacity for work was 'for the moment not getting any greater' – as he complained to Johann Plenge on 11 August 1913 (MWG II/8, 305), with reference to his 'article' (still such a modest description) on 'economy and society'. 'I have only four working hours a day', he wrote to Friedrich Naumann on 30 June 1914 (MWG II/8, 745) – at a time when his work on *Economy and Society* must have been in full swing.

4 Karl Polanyi, *The Great Transformation*, Boston, 1957, pp. 45f.

5 On 8 September 1914 he wrote to his sister Lili Schäfer (whose husband had fallen at the battle of Tannenberg): 'Nature did not predispose him to be a really "fortunate" person. You brought him everything in the way of luck that he had been created to "have"' (MWG II/8, 791). As far as we know, Weber must have seen his own nature in a similar way. All the more important for him, therefore, was the realization that his unfortunate natural disposition still left him opportunities and spaces where he could be himself.

6 Theodor Heuss, *Deutsche Gestalten*, Munich, n.d., p. 248.

7 MWG II/5, 666ff.; II/6, 15ff. On 26 June 1908 Marianne wrote to Helene that Max 'had no major productive work in prospect'.

8 Johannes Winckelmann, *Max Webers hinterlassenes Hauptwerk*, Tübingen, 1986, p. 10.

9 Bielefeld University library, Plenge Nachlaß, Plenge to Max Weber, 16 January 1913: 'Had I properly appreciated the need to rest my nerves after the hard period of coming to terms with and mastering my fields of work, I would never have got involved in working to a deadline.' Weber, being himself in the 'glasshouse' of his nerves, at first responded so gently that Plenge flattered him on 24 January 1913: 'What a nice kind man Max Weber is, with his honourable temperament!'

10 Johann Plenge of all people, whom Weber courted so intensively and in whom he evidently detected a kindred spirit (an 'unusually chivalrous nature' (MWG II/8, 309), marked by courage, intellectual originality and sharpness of mind), subsequently became one of Weber's opponents. See Hanns Linhardt, *Cogito ergo sumus: Eine Auswahl aus den Schriften von Johann Plenge*, Berlin, 1964, pp. 11, 169, 182.

11 Even to the 'sociological coffee circle' in Kiel – which was quite likely to use such information to his disadvantage – Weber wrote with amazing candour that he had to accept Harms was 'right' on one score: 'it would have been more proper if I had not taken on the editing of the new work'. He had 'lost a huge amount of time' on it and had 'to an improper degree been taken away from the style of work that suits me, while my capacity for work during those years had once again unexpectedly deteriorated' (MWG II/8, 41).

12 To Tönnies he described Harms (a friend and colleague of Tönnies) as a 'pathetic fellow' and an 'unspeakably contemptible fellow' (MWG II/8, 82).

13 From Harms's point of view, it was more a question of moral than legal right (MWG II/8, 77n.). This explains why he argued especially in terms of morality – and thereby wounded Weber's honour. Even Plenge was on the opposite side in this conflict and challenged Weber: 'As I know from books the shameless contract that Schönberg was given, I am especially able to

appreciate Harms's nobility of mind.' Bielefeld University library, Plenge Nachlaß, Plenge to Weber, 24 January 1913.

14 Marianne to Helene Weber, 25 January 1913.

15 Wolfgang J. Mommsen, 'Die Siebecks und Max Weber', *Geschichte und Gesellschaft*, 22 (1996), pp. 19–30.

16 Friedrich Tenbruck, *Das Werk Max Webers*, Tübingen, 1999, pp. 59ff.

17 '. . . the peculiarly puzzling Basic Concepts', Wilhelm Hennis calls them (*Max Weber's Central Question*, 2nd edn, Newbury, 2000, p. 18n.). In his view the section on 'basic sociological terms' with which *Economy and Society* begins is itself in need of explanation – or of 'human understanding' – and by no means provides an ultimate foundation from which the whole work can be deduced.

18 Friedrich Tenbruck, *Das Werk Max Webers*, Tübingen, 1999, p. 146: 'How could it be believed that Max Weber had wanted to write a "theory of sociological categories", when that term does not appear once in the 180 pages of his supposed theory of categories and is equally absent from the German editor's index to the nearly 700 pages that follow?' The background was a fixed idea of Weber as a consistent Kantian, who thought on the basis of categories.

19 Marianne to Helene Weber, 13 April 1911.

20 Pioneering in this respect was the article first published by Friedrich Tenbruck in 1977: 'Abschied von *Wirtschaft und Gesellschaft*', in Tenbruck, *Das Werk Max Webers*, pp. 123–56. See also, based on this, Wolfgang Schluchter, '*Wirtschaft und Gesellschaft* – Ende eines Mythos', in Johannes Weiß (ed.), *Max Weber heute: Erträge und Probleme der Forschung*, Frankfurt am Main, 1989, pp. 55–89.

21 Already on 6 November 1913 he had written to Siebeck that his greatly expanded contribution would 'approximate' to a 'sociology' (the inverted commas are his), although, he added, 'I would *never* give it that name' (MWG II/8, 349). If Weber had offered a complete sociology, it might have seemed that further sociological contributions were superfluous.

22 Winckelmann, *Max Webers hinterlassenes Hauptwerk*, p. 41.

23 Mommsen, 'Die Siebecks und Max Weber', p. 28.

24 Alfred Philippson, *Wie ich zum Geographen wurde*, Bonn, 1996, p. 473; Ernst Plewe, 'Alfred Hettner', in Wilhelm Doerr (ed.), *Semper Apertus*, vol. 2, Berlin, 1985, pp. 516–34.

25 Ferdinand Tönnies, *Community and Society*, New Brunswick, NJ, 1988.

26 For an English translation, see 'Some Categories of Interpretive Sociology', *Sociological Quarterly*, 22 (1981), pp. 151–80.

27 In his introduction to Christian Meier (ed.), *Die okzidentale Stadt nach Max Weber*, Munich, 1994 (= *Historische Zeitschrift*, special issue no. 17), p. 13, the editor writes: 'Weber dissolved "aspectively" the opposition between *Gemeinschaft* and *Gesellschaft*: that is, he spoke of *Vergemeinschaftung* and *Vergesellschaftung*, and established that both the one and the other occur in most relationships.'

28 E&S 42: 'The communal type of relationship is, according to the usual interpretation of its subjective meaning, the most radical antithesis of conflict. This should not, however, be allowed to obscure the fact that coercion of all sorts is a very common thing in even the most intimate of such communal relationships if one party is weaker in character than the other. Furthermore, a process of the selection of types leading to differences in opportunity and survival, goes on within these relationships just the same as anywhere else.'

29 'Some Categories of Interpretive Sociology', p. 159.
30 Winckelmann, *Max Webers hinterlassenes Hauptwerk*, p. 87. 'Under Palyi's influence' Marianne 'decided, albeit with a heavy heart', to change the sequence of texts originally intended by Weber (ibid.). Melchior Palyi, 'neither an economist nor a historian nor even a sociologist', had no time for Weber's intentions and proved to be a 'failure' in the compilation of *Economy and Society* (ibid., p. 108). Marianne, who was anyway the only person who could read Weber's handwriting well, would have done better to take control herself. Palyi, who, though otherwise unknown in the circles of Weber researchers, later made a name for himself internationally in the theory of currency, was an advocate of economic productivity – the concept that Weber attacked so violently in 1909 – and a critic of backward-looking cultural pessimism. He certainly wanted to give Weber's 'life's work' a structure that would make it seem as modern as possible – and 'primitive communities' would not have been a fitting way to begin.
31 Rudolf Stammler, *Wirtschaft und Recht nach der materialistischen Geschichtsauffassung*, Leipzig, 1914, p. 102.
32 See Klaus Lichtblau, 'Die Bedeutung von "Ehefrau und Mutter in der Rechtsentwicklung" für das Werk Max Webers', in Meurer (ed.), *Marianne Weber*, esp. pp. 201 ff., 208.
33 Hans-Ulrich Wehler (in Christian Gneuss and Jürgen Kocka (eds), *Max Weber: Ein Symposium*, Munich, 1988, p. 124) detects a basic evolutionary structure in Weber's thought: 'As Weber specialists such as Schluchter rightly point out, Weber too, who in one respect is the father of modern theories of modernization, has a definite conception of evolution.' This can be seen in Wehler's summary of Klaus Lichtblau in his review of MWG I/22–1, *Gemeinschaften*: 'Until his death Weber constantly had a tendency to "lapse back" into development-historical figures of thought' (*Max Weber Studies*, 3/2 (2003), p. 237). But this does not have to be seen as 'lapsing back': evolutionism is neither a disease nor a primitive stage.
34 At the sociologists' congress in 1964 Eduard Baumgarten quoted a letter from Weber to Else Jaffé: 'You see, vassals in times of old often said to their gracious lord, "Lead us to hell if that's how it must be, and our hand and our heart will gladly belong to you. Just know, gracious lord, that you are in the wrong. Our head tells us that, and it's still on our shoulders!"' (*Max Weber und die Soziologie heute*, ed. Otto Stammer, Tübingen, 1965, p. 149). Feudalism as an ideal of loyal service but with a free spirit – in sexual matters, too!
35 Susan Reynolds (*Fiefs and Vassals: The Medieval Evidence Reinterpreted*, Oxford, 1994, p. 10) points to this striking feature of Weber's ideal type of feudalism. The whole thrust of this revisionist book is to demonstrate that the concept of feudalism prevailing from Weber to Marc Bloch, which focused on fiefs and the reciprocal loyalty of lord and vassal, was an imaginary construct of early modern legal theorists resting upon a romantic overestimation of the feoffment rituals that marked the popular images and schoolbook accounts of the 'knightly' Middle Ages.
36 For Weber the horse is one of the main factors in history: all over the world 'use of the horse . . . was instrumental in the ascendancy of individual hero combat' (RC 24).
37 See Paul Sweezy et al., *The Transition from Feudalism to Capitalism*, New York, 1976, where most of the contributions (in criticism of Sweezy) rather stress the affinity of feudalism and capitalism, which as in Weber became especially

apparent from a study of non-European cultures without a developed feudal system.

38 See Heide Wunder, in the editor's preface to *Feudalismus*, Munich, 1974, p. 8. In conversations with the author, Hans-Ulrich Wehler more than once recalled the surprise with which he once discovered that all the insights into feudalism that he had gained from the specialist literature were already present in Weber. It was above all this 'aha experience' that convinced him of Weber's genius.

39 Henry J. Merry, *Montesquieu's System of Government*, West Lafayette, IN, 1970, p. 349.

40 Wolf Lepenies, *Between Literature and Science: The Rise of Sociology*, Cambridge, 1988, p. 239.

41 Jacob Burckhardt, *Force and Freedom: Reflections on History*, New York, 1943, p. 117.

42 Winckelmann, *Max Webers hinterlassenes Hauptwerk*, p. 65.

43 Weber, 'Some Categories of Interpretive Sociology', p. 158.

44 Ibid., p. 162.

45 On 'Max Weber's individualism' and its various consequences, see Douglas Webster in WuZ 715ff.

Chapter 16 From Deborah's Song of Triumph to the 'Titans of the Holy Curse'

1 Eugène Fleischmann, 'Max Weber, die Juden und das Ressentiment', in Wolfgang Schluchter (ed.), *Max Webers Studie über das antike Judentum*, Frankfurt am Main, 1981, pp. 263–86; Gary A. Abraham, *Max Weber and the Jewish Question: A Study of the Social Outlook of his Sociology*, Urbana, IL, 1992.

2 Richard Wagner, 'Judaism in Music', in *The Theatre: Richard Wagner's Prose Works*, New York, 1894, p. 80.

3 Maximilian Harden, *Köpfe*, part II, 12th edn, Berlin, 1911, p. 445.

4 Walter Rathenau, 'Hear, O Israel!', at http://germanhistorydocs.ghi-dc.org/docpage.cfm?docpage_id=1175.

5 Ibid.

6 Theodor Mommsen, 'Auch ein Wort über unser Judenthum', in Walter Boehlich (ed.), *Der Berliner Antisemitismusstreit*, Frankfurt am Main, 1965, p. 219; see Hans Liebschütz, *Das Judentum im deutschen Geschichtsbild von Hegel bis Max Weber*, Tübingen, 1967, pp. 198, 252.

7 Comte Paul Vasili [pseud.], *La Société de Berlin*, 2nd edn, Paris, 1884, pp. 190ff.

8 R 459ff.; Reinhard Riese, *Die Hochschule auf dem Weg zum wissenschaftlichen Großbetrieb*, Stuttgart, 1977, pp. 99ff.

9 GStA Nl Weber Nr. 30 Bd. 1, 15 August 1898, to Marianne Weber.

10 At the symposium on the Weber–Troeltsch relationship held in Heidelberg in March 2004, it was even asserted without contradiction that Weber knew his Bible better than Troeltsch.

11 Liebeschütz, *Das Judentum im deutschen Geschichtsbild*, p. 245.

12 Ibid., pp. 246f.

13 Julius Wellhausen, *Israelitische und jüdische Geschichte*, 5th edn, Berlin, 1904, pp. 86f., 9.

14 Liebeschütz, *Das Judentum im deutschen Geschichtsbild*, p. 259; Wellhausen, *Israelitische und jüdische Geschichte*, p. 390.

15 Liebeschütz, *Das Judentum im deutschen Geschichtsbild*, p. 251.
16 Dirk Käsler, 'Das "Judentum" als zentrales Entstehungs-Milieu der frühen deutschen Soziologie', in Käsler, *Soziologie als Berufung*, Opladen, 1997, p. 210.
17 Robert Michels, *Soziologie des Parteiwesens*, 4th edn, Stuttgart, 1989, p. 255.
18 Käsler, 'Das "Judentum" als zentrales Entstehungs-Milieu der frühen deutschen Soziologie', p. 213.
19 Marianne to Helene Weber, 21 December 1912.
20 Eaedem, 7 December 1912.
21 Klaus Kempter, *Die Jellineks 1820–1955*, Düsseldorf, 1998, p. 313.
22 See AJ part I, chapter 1.
23 MWG II/9, 28 August 1915, to Mina Tobler.
24 Boehlich (ed.), *Der Berliner Antisemitismusstreit*, p. 9.
25 Alice Salomon, *Charakter ist Schicksal: Lebenserinnerungen*, Weinheim, 1983, pp. 186ff. It even looks as if Max Weber similarly profited from the rising tide of anti-Semitism when he secured the appointment in Munich instead of the man at the top of the list of candidates, Moritz Julius Bonn, who was undoubtedly more *au fait* with the latest state of the economic sciences. The MWG (I/17, 77n.) tells us laconically that the appointment was 'not free from political influences'. What were these? Bonn was not such a long way from Weber in his liberal political position – but he was of Jewish origin. In the Eisner cabinet, the proposal to give Weber the post came from Johannes Hoffmann, who belonged to the right wing of the majority SPD and subsequently became prime minister of the counter-government formed in opposition to the Munich government of councils. See *Die Regierung Eisner 1918/19: Ministerratsprotokole und Dokumente*, ed. Franz J. Bauer, Düsseldorf, 1987, p. 313.
26 Kurt Bohnsack, 'Oerlinghausen und die Weber-Familie', manuscript, Kirchlengern, 1998, p. 71.
27 Marianne to Helene Weber, 20 January 1907.
28 Eaedem, 12 April 1901 and 18 August 1915 (?).
29 See Guenther Roth, 'Max Weber's Views on Jewish Integration and Zionism: Some American, English and German Contexts', in *Max Weber Studies* 3/1 (2002), pp. 69ff. Roth, however, does not think that the reasons for Weber's attitude to Zionism are very clear (ibid., p. 73).
30 See Eckart Otto, *Max Webers Studien des Antiken Judentums: Historische Grundlegung einer Theorie der Moderne*, Tübingen, 2002, pp. 83ff., 148.
31 Wellhausen also speaks of 'confederates': *Israelitische und jüdische Geschichte*, p. 26.
32 Ibid., pp. 43ff.
33 Ibid., pp. 46f.
34 Ibid., p. 36.
35 Werner Sombart, *The Jews and Modern Capitalism*, New Brunswick, NJ, 1997, esp. pp. 3ff., 191f., 248f.
36 Ibid., pp. 243–4. Translation modified.
37 Lujo Brentano, 'Judentum und Kapitalismus', in Brentano, *Der wirtschaftende Mensch in der Geschichte: Gesammelte Reden und Aufsätze*, Leipzig, 1923, pp. 429, 435, 438.
38 Werner Sombart, *Der Bourgeois: Zur Geistesgeschichte des modernen Wirtschaftsmenschen*, Munich, 1913.

39 Friedrich Nietzsche, *The Anti-Christ*, trans. R. J. Hollingdale, Harmondsworth, 1968, p. 135.
40 Liebeschütz, *Das Judentum im deutschen Geschichtsbild*, p. 31; Jacob Taubes, 'Die Entstehung des jüdischen Pariavolkes', in Karl Engisch et al. (eds), *Max Weber*, Berlin, 1966, p. 190; Eugen Drewermann, *Der tödliche Fortschritt*, Freiburg, 1991, p. 73.
41 Sombart, *The Jews and Modern Capitalism*, pp. 226–7, 262, 236ff. [the English translation is considerably less vivid, and has been modified accordingly – *trans.*].
42 Otto, *Max Webers Studien des Antiken Judentums*, p. 23.
43 Adolf Hausrath, *Der Apostel Paulus*, Heidelberg, 1865, pp. 47f., 92.
44 Sombart, *The Jews and Modern Capitalism*, pp. 323ff., 328, 327.
45 Brentano, 'Judentum und Kapitalismus', pp. 486ff.
46 At the symposium on Weber held at Heidelberg in March 2004. See also Otto, *Max Webers Studien des Antiken Judentums*, p. viii: Weber's studies of ancient Judaism show 'more clearly than any other text' his 'style of work and the development of his *Wirtschaftsethik der Weltreligionen*'.
47 The travel reports of a leading US soil expert, Walter Clay Lowdermilk, were especially famous. See his *Palestine – Land of Promise*, New York, 1944, which became the bible of Zionist irrigation enthusiasts.
48 Karl Budde, 'Das nomadische Ideal im Alten Testament', *Preußische Jahrbücher*, 85 (1896), pp. 57–79.
49 See Otto, *Max Webers Studien des Antiken Judentums*, p. 208.
50 Hans-Ulrich Wehler (*Die Herausforderung der Kulturgeschichte*, Munich, 1998, p. 105) considers this the decisive point in Weber's argument.
51 At a rally of German Christians at the Berlin Sports Palace on 13 November 1933, which marked the beginning of their decline. See Günther van Norden, *Kirche in der Krise*, Düsseldorf, 1963, pp. 130f.
52 The philosopher Julius Guttmann (1880–1950), who in 1933 published a 'philosophy of Judaism' and in 1934 emigrated to Jerusalem, summarized the agrarian-sociological essence of Weber's *Ancient Judaism* in 1925 in an essay that is still worth reading today: 'Max Webers Soziologie des antiken Judentums', reprinted in Schluchter (ed.), *Max Webers Studie über das antike Judentum*, pp. 289–326. In 1913 he had subjected Sombart's 'Jewish book' to a formally subdued yet substantively withering critique in the *Archiv für Sozialwissenschaft*: see Hartmann Tyrell, 'Kapitalismus, Zins und Religion bei Werner Sombart und Max Weber', in Johannes Heil and Bernd Wacker (eds), *Shylock? Zinsverbot und Geldverleih in jüdischer und christlicher Tradition*, Munich, 1997, pp. 203ff.
53 Udo Krolzik, *Umweltkrise – Folge des Christentums?* Stuttgart, 1979; and, far more emphatic, Aloys Hüttemann, 'Umweltsensibilisierung in antiken Juden(und Christen)tum – warum hat sich nichts erhalten?', in Studenteninitiative Wirtschaft und Umwelt e. V. (ed.), *Umweltsensibilisierung – Gefahr erkannt, Gefahr gebannt?* Münster, 1998, pp. 9–30.
54 Otto, *Max Webers Studien des Antiken Judentums*, pp. 90f., 120f., 149f.
55 Sigmund Freud, *Moses and Monotheism: Complete Psychological Works of Sigmund Freud*, vol. 23, London, 1964, p. 45n.: 'Yahweh was undoubtedly a volcanic god.'
56 Liebeschütz, *Das Judentum im deutschen Geschichtsbild*, p. 222.
57 Wellhausen, *Israelitische und jüdische Geschichte*, p. 79n.

58 Otto, *Max Webers Studien des Antiken Judentums*, p. 78.
59 Ibid., pp. 51f.
60 Liebeschütz, *Das Judentum im deutschen Geschichtsbild*, p. 303.
61 For a detailed and sharply critical analysis, see Shmuel N. Eisenstadt, 'Max Webers antikes Judentum und der Charakter der jüdischen Zivilisation', in Wolfgang Schluchter (ed.), *Max Webers Studie über das antike Judentum*, Frankfurt am Main, 1981, pp. 134–84.
62 Friedrich Georg Friedmann, *Hannah Arendt*, Munich, 1985, pp. 27ff.
63 Liebeschütz, *Das Judentum im deutschen Geschichtsbild*, pp. 290f.
64 Ibid., pp. 272f.
65 The concept of a 'confederacy' [*Eidgenossenschaft*] may already be found in Wellhausen, *Israelitische und jüdische Geschichte*, p. 26. But for long stretches Wellhausen too seems to forget his own source criticism, taking as historical truth the epic tales in books of the Old Testament whose late date of composition he has already established. An impressive history of ancient Israel could not have been written in any other way, and many subsequent historians have also been unable to resist the colourful tales of heroes from Joshua to David. Only the latest historiography draws all the consequences from the unreliability of the sources: see Israel Finkelstein and Neil Asher Silberman, *The Bible Unearthed: Archaeology's New Vision of Ancient Israel and the Origin of its Sacred Texts*, New York, 2001.
66 Liebeschütz writes of Weber (*Das Judentum im deutschen Geschichtsbild*, p. 303): 'His language had greater scope than Eduard Meyer's to express an emotional relationship to the object.'
67 Otto, *Max Webers Studien des Antiken Judentums*, p. 215: For Weber 'the non-everyday states of the prophets were so important that he listed them, since they showed that their prophecies were individually-endogenously determined and not produced by any mass emotion at the time.'
68 Eisenstadt, 'Max Webers antikes Judentum. . .', p. 156: Weber 'left out of account' the 'insertion' of the prophets 'into the religious and political centres and their local population'.
69 Already on 10 January 1916 Else Jaffé had written Weber a letter in which she had made certain personal avowals, though addressing him with the distinctly formal 'Professor Weber'. A conversation ensued, but it evidently remained tense as Else later felt that both of them had been lost for words. 'We don't need to fathom now where this helplessness comes from (complexes?). . . . But you should know that I can't really get over you, for part of the homeland I want to put together for my vagabond soul is there with you . . . Isn't it true that the "brotherliness" is still there? But I shouldn't let slip this word that is so alien to me (it makes me think of . . . internal missionary work); I should tell you quite simply and humanly that you are one of the people I love – just so – without mentioning the admiration and deep gratitude on top of it.'
70 BA, Nl 197/77, 18 January 1917.

Chapter 17 World War and Flight from the World

1 Ana 446 Sch. 20 VI.
2 Marianne to Helene Weber, 6 March 1915.
3 Theodor Heuss, *Friedrich Naumann*, 2nd edn, Stuttgart, 1949, p. 160.

4 Wolfgang Mommsen claims (*Max Weber and German Politics 1890–1920*, Chicago, 1990, p. 157) that Weber 'was not taken by surprise' by the outbreak of war in 1914, on the grounds that he had long supported a 'powerful *Weltpolitik*' and 'differed from his contemporaries only insofar as he pursued this goal with rigorous consistency'; this can only mean that he was prepared to risk a major war, though surely not a war against the British empire and the United States.

5 MWG II/9, Max to Marianne Weber, 8 May 1915. The actual occasion was Italy's impending change of sides. In a letter of 15 October 1914 to Ferdinand Tönnies, he wrote that 'hundreds of thousands would have to bleed on account of the dreadful incompetence of our diplomacy', but neither there nor anywhere else did he explain what that incompetence had involved.

6 Karl Alexander von Müller, *Aus Gärten der Vergangenheit: Erinnerungen 1882–1914*, Stuttgart, 1951, p. 229.

7 In another account by the same author (Karl Löwenstein, 'Persönliche Erinnerungen an Max Weber', in Karl Engisch et al. (eds), *Max Weber*, Berlin, 1966, p. 31), Weber was 'deeply pessimistic' and 'literally' said: 'The war will last a very long time; Prussian militarism is extremely tenacious.' He saw 'Prussian militarism' as the driving force of the war and could imagine an end only if it was defeated.

8 MWG II/9, Max to Helene Weber, 4 September 1915.

9 'Erlebnisse der Seele', *Die Frau*, 22/5 (1915), pp. 258f.

10 There is no enthusiasm for war in a letter of 2 August 1914 from Marianne to Helene Weber: 'What terrible things may now lie ahead of us!' On 4 August, however: 'Who wouldn't somehow disappear into this great stream of our willingness to help! . . . All are so filled with an awareness that we are marching into war justly and with a clear conscience, that it is a *holy* war of defence, and this sense of community among the whole nation is a wonderful thing. In such times you feel you have become the nation.' But she does not report similar statements on her husband's part, as she presumably would have done if there had been any.

11 Marianne to Helene Weber, 6 and 23 March 1915; 10 July 1915: 'For every nation is so terribly sick of this butchery and everyone would like to return to peaceful work.'

12 See also her letter of 8 May 1917 to Helene Weber, in which she writes rapturously of the 'flower intoxication': 'Ah, you think that people out there should throw away their weapons and embrace one another!'

13 Eaedem, 10 December 1914 and 12 February 1915.

14 Marianne to Helene Weber, 10 June 1915.

15 BA Koblenz, Nl 197/77, Else Jaffé to Alfred Weber, 29 November 1917.

16 The passage in question comes from a letter of 2 January 1915 to Helene Weber, in which Marianne writes: 'I am now almost convinced that he can do what he thinks he can, and that it's just a question of continuing to outwit the psychological inhibitions.'

17 Deutsches Literaturarchiv Marbach, A: Jaspers, Marianne Weber to Jaspers, n.d., in the context of the dispute with Hellpach (1948).

18 Marianne to Helene Weber, 20 October 1915. See Max Weber to Robert Michels, 18 December 1914 (MWG II/8, 804): 'When this war is over, I myself shall be incapable of any work for a long time.' And to Lili Schäfer, 28 September 1915 (MWG II/9): It was time for him to finish his work as a medical

officer. 'My stomach gradually refused the sleeping potion in such quantities and I am no longer working in a precise way.' By then, however, the work no longer had the appeal of novelty but was boring him stiff.

19 Marianne to Helene Weber, 10 December 1914.

20 Max to Marianne Weber, 28 August 1915, MWG II/9.

21 9 May 1915, MWG II/9.

22 This is actually pointed out by Wolfgang Mommsen (*Max Weber and German Politics*, pp. 196, 200), who has done the most to underline the importance of Weber's political involvement.

23 Mina Tobler to her mother, 20 October 1912 (privately owned).

24 Marianne to Helene Weber, 1 October 1915.

25 Eaedem, 21 May 1916.

26 Mommsen (*Max Weber and German Politics*, p. 192) writes of Weber's state of mind during the war: 'It took an enormous effort to escape constant depression.' But there is only a little evidence for this in Weber's correspondence of the time: his love affair with Mina Tobler continued, and in comparison with earlier years it is rather the *absence* of severe depression that stands out. If one thinks of other professors who were involved in politics, one may well consider it extraordinary how little the gloomy political prospects affected his vitality.

27 Marianne to Helene Weber, 5 November 1918.

28 See Hermann Kellermann (ed.), *Krieg der Geister: Eine Auslese deutscher und ausländischer Stimmen zum Weltkriege 1914*, Dresden, 1915.

29 BA Koblenz, NL 197/77, 26 April 1917.

30 Eduard Meyer to Victor Ehrenberg, 3 October 1916, in Gert Audring et al. (eds), *Eduard Meyer–Victor Ehrenberg: Ein Briefwechsel 1914–1930*, Berlin, 1990, p. 78. In his pro-war book *Nordamerika und Deutschland* (Berlin, 1915) Meyer depicted the Americans as a 'nervously overwrought, physically and mentally unhealthy nation', which thought of itself as a 'degenerating race doomed to go under' (ibid., p. 37).

31 Mommsen, *Max Weber and German Politics*, pp. 206, 79.

32 Karl Jaspers, *Philosophische Autobiographie*, Munich, 1977, p. 70.

33 Fritz Fischer, *Germany's War Aims in the First World War*, London, 1967, pp. 329f.; Mommsen, *Max Weber and German Politics*, p. 197; Eberhard Demm, *Ein Liberaler in Kaiserreich und Republik: Der politische Weg Alfred Webers bis 1920*, Boppard, 1990, p. 169.

34 Mommsen, *Max Weber and German Politics*, p. 201.

35 Max Weber to Lili Schäfer, 28 September 1915.

36 GStA Nl Weber, Nr. 30, Bd. 2, 21 February and 22 March 1916.

37 Marianne to Helene Weber, 3 September 1915.

38 Ibid.

39 Mommsen, *Max Weber and German Politics*, p. 219. That a close union with Austria-Hungary was economically senseless for Germany – which conducted only 4 per cent of its foreign trade with the Habsburg empire – was not even the decisive point for Weber. Rather, 'the most important is this: "Mitteleuropa" means that *we* shall have to pay for *every* stupidity with our blood – and you know it – that will be committed by the thick-headed policies of the Magyars and the Vienna court' (ibid., p. 217). Apparently he assumed that in 1914 the German Reich had been drawn into the world war by the policies of Vienna.

40 Ibid., pp. 223ff.

41 Marianne to Helene Weber, 3 September 1915.
42 Eaedem, 18 August 1915 (?).
43 MWG II/9, Max to Marianne Weber, 7 December 1915 and 12 May 1916.
44 Mommsen, *Max Weber and German Politics*, p. 227.
45 Demm, *Ein Liberaler in Kaiserreich und Republik*, pp. 179f.
46 Ibid., p. 155.
47 Alfred Weber, *Gedanken zur deutschen Sendung*, Berlin, 1915, pp. 78, 29f.
48 Ibid., p. 37.
49 Max to Marianne Weber, 14 May 1916, MWG II/9: 'But I do not feel in the slightest like "collaborating" with him or even like remaining here now that he is here too.'
50 Eaedem, 17 May 1916.
51 Max to Helene Weber, 15 June 1916, MWG II/9. Two days earlier he had written to Helene: 'For a few weeks now my brain has again been working amazingly well: I can do good *scholarly* work. What got me down was all the fruitless running around and *talking* in Berlin.'
52 Wilhelm Hennis (*Max Weber und Thukydides*, Göttingen, 2003, p. 121n.) rightly notes: 'His reluctance to get to work on the part of the *Grundriß* he had taken on is almost comically apparent in his letters. While he is enthusiastically working on his "Chinese", the publisher who wants to push ahead with the *Grundriß* is put off with lame excuses.' See Weber's assurance to Siebeck on 20 February 1917 (MWG II/9), which sounds hypocritical in view of other testimony of his: 'If only the war would end, so that I could get down to *my* volume of the *Grundriß*! That is just not possible for me now psychologically, and so I prefer to press on with these articles on the sociology of religion. But the other is what I am longing to do.' War as a licence for his escapade in the East: here Weber is quite open about it!
53 Mina Tobler to her mother, 15 June 1912 (extract supplied by Achim Tobler).
54 Mommsen, *Max Weber and German Politics*, p. 310.
55 Lukács even thought during the war that Weber would be the ideal future leader of the socialist movement, while Honigsheim could imagine him more in the role of the last Mohican (WzG 186).
56 *Hannah Arendt/Karl Jaspers Correspondence, 1926–1969*, New York, 1992, p. 549 (24 March 1964).
57 Max to Marianne Weber, 17 May 1916, MWG II/9.
58 Hennis, *Max Weber und Thukydides*, p. 91.
59 Max to Marianne Weber, 17 February 1916, MWG II/9, before the inaugural meeting of Naumann's Mitteleuropa Committee, which offered Weber a possible route to practical political influence. 'After four months of "Hinduism", I am actually so remote from the problems that it will probably be a while before I really work on them – perhaps even a long while.' And again on 16 May 1916: 'I feel so well and so fit for work as soon as I have to deal with Chinese and Indian matters; I long for that a lot. . . . The thing is now finally under way and it will be interesting.' Similar assurances recur in other letters from those months. For example, on 7 August he wrote to Mina Tobler: 'I am again turning to my Chinese and Indians, with great pleasure. For I am suited to politics only when I can say quite openly what I think and what I want.' But it is in the nature of politics that one *cannot* say this in many situations.
60 Friedrich Meinecke, *Straßburg — Freiburg — Berlin, 1901–1919: Erinnerungen*, Stuttgart, 1949, p. 245.

61 Max Weber to Mina Tobler, 23 November 1917 (?), MWG II/9.
62 Max Weber to Frieda Gross, 16 November 1915; again to Helene Weber, 24 April 1916, MWG II/9.
63 Max to Marianne Weber, 3 May 1916, MWG II/9.
64 In his obituary of Troeltsch, in Friedrich Wilhelm Graf (ed.), *Ernst Troeltsch in Nachrufen*, Gütersloh, 2002 (= *Troeltsch-Studien* vol. 12), p. 470.
65 Max to Marianne Weber, 2 March and 11 March 1916, MWG II/9.
66 Hermann Kulke, 'Orthodoxe Restauration und hinduistische Sektenreligiosität im Werk Max Webers', in Wolfgang Schluchter (ed.), *Max Webers Studie über Hinduismus und Buddhismus: Interpretation und Kritik*, Frankfurt am Main, 1984, pp. 302ff. On the image of India at that time, see Erwin Rohde, *Psyche*, London, 1925, p. 185.
67 Karl-Heinz Golzio 'now and again' has a 'suspicion' that Weber deliberately tried to make his mode of work 'non-transparent': 'Zur Verwendung indologischer Literatur' in Schluchter (ed.), *Max Webers Studie über Hinduismus und Buddhismus*, p. 366.
68 Demm, *Ein Liberaler in Kaiserreich und Republik*, p. 62.
69 AWG vol. 10, p. 504.
70 Hermann Graf Keyserling, *Prolegomena zur Naturphilosophie*, Munich, 1910, p. 49.
71 Marianne Weber to Else Jaffé, 4 October 1912 [SG].
72 Eduard Baumgarten found the by now world-famous Keyserling hard to bear when he saw him at an event in Madison, Wisconsin. 'Clever, rather garrulous and arrogant. Personally he behaves in a very stupid manner. He gets fantastic money, but on top of that demands a contract from each of his hosts guaranteeing him wine, oysters, a certain kind of female company, and so on. Rather tasteless and impudent.' He 'acted the prophet, as if *blessing* everyone as he entered!' (to Marianne Weber, 22 March 1928 ?). It is all the more remarkable how impressed Weber was by this man, who, it is true, certainly behaved more modestly in 1912.
73 Count Hermann Keyserling, *The Travel Diary of a Philosopher*, London, 1925, vol. 1, pp. 44f., 178; vol. 2, p. 194.
74 Ibid., vol. 2, p. 199.
75 See Peter Bishop, *The Myth of Shangri-La: Tibet, Travel Writing and the Western Creation of Sacred Landscape*, Berkeley, CA, 1989, according to which the British military expedition of 1904 to Lhasa under Younghusband turned into a Western initiation into the myth of Tibet (pp. 152–63).
76 See especially Heinrich Hackmann, *Der Buddhismus*, Halle, 1906, pp. 47f.: 'The shallow and extreme superstition that [yoga practices, JR] brought to Buddhism is still shown by its form in Tibet. . . . From the heights of a philosophical religion, believers slipped down to the level of blind credulity and crude deception. The nadir was reached with the development of ideas that followed the yoga doctrine and may be termed tantrism. . . . In tantrism, belief in the Buddha absorbed a strong sexual-religious current . . . Buddhism gradually suffocated in a welter of superstitions, fantasy and sensuality.'
77 For a more detailed discussion, see Kulke, 'Orthodoxe Restauration und hinduistische Sektenreligiosität im Werk Max Webers', pp. 302ff. Weber's 'overemphasis on every imaginable orgiastic and especially erotic-sexual feature of Hinduism' poses a 'difficult problem'. 'His fundamental and (as his various points repeatedly show) fateful mistake was to see in tantrism an expression of

popular religiosity . . . and hence to present it at the beginning of his account of Hindu sects as, so to speak, the original source of medieval Hinduism. . . . Nothing could be more erroneous than to place popular religiosity and the development of tantrism in a causal relationship, or *a fortiori* to equate the two, as Weber repeatedly does in at least a rudimentary manner.' This 'highly esoteric quest for salvation' is precisely the path most common among 'intellectuals'. For Kulke, then, one sometimes 'cannot help suspecting' that Weber's own erotic experiences marked his image of Hinduism – and there is indeed some evidence of this. In his own life, however, Weber encountered the tendency to orgiasticism in two highly cultured aristocratic women: Else von Richthofen and Countess Franziska zu Reventlow. This might have led him to the idea that orgiasticism is not at all typical of the dully sensual lower classes!

78 Mircea Eliade, *Autobiography*, vol. 1: *1907–1937: Journey East, Journey West*, Chicago, 1990, p. 203.

79 Hermann Kulke, 'Orthodoxe Restauration', p. 329n.

80 Joachim Radkau, *Nature and Power: A Global History of the Environment*, New York, 2008, pp. 103ff. Mark Elvin ('Why China Failed to Create an Endogenous Capitalism: A Critique of Max Weber's Explanation', *Theory and Society*, 13/3 (1984), p. 381) argues that in *Economy and Society* Weber implies that the Chinese economic system was ultimately irrational, whereas in *The Religion of China* he 'attributes rationality' to it.

81 Nathan Sivin, 'Chinesische Wissenschaft: Ein Vergleich der Ansätze von Max Weber und Joseph Needham', in Wolfgang Schluchter (ed.), *Max Webers Studie über Konfuzianismus und Taoismus*, Frankfurt am Main, 1984, p. 356: 'As soon as Weber fixed his gaze on China, it rested on the elite and its literary legacy. . . . Occasionally his gaze wanders to other parts of society . . ., but it soon returns fascinated to the irrationalism and unrelieved traditionalism of the Centre.' [A revised version of this essay appeared as 'Max Weber, Joseph Needham, Benjamin Nelson: The Question of Chinese Science', in *Civilizations East and West: A Memorial Volume for Benjamin Nelson*, ed. E. Victor Walter et al., Atlantic Highlands, NJ, 1983, pp. 37–49.]

82 Peter Weber-Schäfer, 'Die konfuzianischen Literaten und die Grundwerte des Konfuzianismus', in Schluchter (ed.), *Max Webers Studie über Konfuzianismus und Taoismus*, pp. 202ff.

83 Joachim Radkau, *Zeitalter der Nervosität*, Munich, 1998, p. 26.

84 Mommsen, *Max Weber and German Politics*, p. 311.

85 Arnold Zingerle, *Max Weber und China*, Berlin, 1972, p. 90.

86 On Sz-ma Tsien and his complaint about the castration, see Wolfgang Bauer, *Das Antlitz Chinas: Die autobiographische Selbstdarstellung in der chinesischen Literatur von ihren Anfängen bis heute*, Munich, 1990, pp. 77–89.

87 Georg Wilhelm Friedrich Hegel, *The Philosophy of History*, New York, 1956, pp. 127, 138, 139f.

88 For a criticism of Weber's use of 'orthodoxy' and 'heterodoxy' in relation to India, see Kulke, 'Orthodoxe Restauration und hinduistische Sektenreligiosität im Werk Max Webers', p. 300.

89 Elvin, 'Why China Failed to Create an Endogenous Capitalism', p. 380.

90 Mathias Greffrath, *Die Zerstörung einer Zukunft: Gespräche mit emigrierten Sozialwissenschaftlern*, Frankfurt am Main, 1989, p. 310.

91 Michio Morishima (*Why Has Japan Succeeded? Western Technology and the Japanese Ethos*, Cambridge, 1982, p. 2) attributes this statement to Weber's

defective knowledge of Japan. For Japan too stands within the Confucian tradition and even developed a form of Confucianism that goes best with capitalism: 'The neglect of benevolence . . . and the emphasis placed on loyalty, must be regarded as characteristics peculiar to Japanese Confucianism' (p. 6). That too was a kind of disenchantment of the world! Morishima's argument has often been quoted since; he was, anyway, writing before China's post-Mao economic boom. But the theme of 'Confucianism' has remained marginal in the already long and wide-ranging reception of Weber in Japan: see Wolfgang J. Mommsen and Wolfgang Schwentker (eds), *Max Weber und das moderne Japan*, Göttingen, 1999. Weber himself mentioned Japan only sporadically, and he evidently had no satisfactory interpretation of Japan's already discernible rise.

Chapter 18 Great Speeches, the Great Love and Death

1 Anatoli Lunatscharski, *Die Revolution und die Kunst*, Dresden, 1960, p. 34.
2 Weber to Friedrich Crusius, 24 November 1918, quoted from Max Weber, *Gesammelte politische Schriften*, Munich, 1921, p. 484.
3 Weber to Friedrich Naumann, 8 May 1917, quoted ibid., p. 472.
4 Max Weber referred to this remark in 1966, without contesting the truth of it. *Hannah Arendt/Karl Jaspers Correspondence, 1926–1969*, New York, 1992, p. 636.
5 Weber to Else Jaffé, 15 January 1919.
6 Marianne to Helene Weber, 2 January 1919.
7 Eduard Baumgarten, 'Spielräume unter Hitlers Herrschaft' (privately owned manuscript), p. 141.
8 Marianne to Helene Weber, 19 August 1918.
9 MWG II/9, Max to Helene Weber, 25 December 1915.
10 Wilhelm Vershofen, in Hans Bott and Hermann Leins (eds), *Begegnungen mit Theodor Heuss*, Tübingen, 1954, p. 48.
11 Winfried Mogge and Jürgen Reulecke, *Hoher Meißner 1913*, Cologne, 1988, pp. 35, 63.
12 Theodor Heuss, *Erinnerungen 1905–1933*, Tübingen, 1963, p. 194.
13 Ibid.
14 Marianne to Helene Weber, 4 June 1917; she is curiously silent about this in the biography, although she otherwise describes the Lauenstein meeting at considerable length.
15 Deutsches Literaturarchiv Marbach, A: Diederichs to Max Weber, 5 October 1917.
16 Theodor Heuss, *Friedrich Naumann*, 2nd edn, Stuttgart, 1949, p. 152.
17 Ibid.
18 Marianne to Helene Weber, 4 July 1903.
19 Max Maurenbrecher, *Das Leid: Eine Auseinandersetzung mit der Religion*, Jena, 1912, p. 6.
20 Marianne to Helene Weber, 4 June 1917.
21 MWG II/9, Max Weber to Mina Tobler, 2 June 1917.
22 Only recent research has established that this address (which was first published in 1919) was given not in 1918 (the date featuring in Marianne Weber's biography) but on 7 November 1917 (MWG I/17, 43–6). It therefore originated

not amid the great disillusionment of the end of the war – as it often used to be assumed – but under the fresh impact of the second 'cultural conference' at Burg Lauenstein. On the long guessing game over the precise dates of both addresses, see Wolfgang Schluchter, *Rationalismus der Weltbeherrschung*, Frankfurt am Main, 1980, pp. 236ff.

23 Karl Löwith, *Mein Leben in Deutschland vor und nach 1933: Ein Bericht*, Stuttgart, 1986, p. 16. According to MWG I/17, 45, it may be assumed that this impression really did refer to *this* address and not to 'Politics as a Vocation'.

24 Karl Löwith (*Mein Leben in Deutschland*, p. 17) maintains that 'Weber's talk came as a relief after the countless revolutionary speeches by literary activists', but he wrongly (see above) dates it to the winter semester of 1919–20. In November 1917, when military censorship was in operation, there could scarcely have been 'countless revolutionary speeches'.

25 Erich von Kahler, *Der Beruf der Wissenschaft*, Berlin 1920, p. 100. This was thought at the time to be inspired by Stefan George, but George was actually disgusted by it, and it ascribed to science spiritual values which, in his eyes, it did not and could never have. Edgar Salin, *Um Stefan George*, Munich, 1954, p. 252. George also believed that, as far as science was concerned, Weber was at least honest.

26 Erwin Chargaff, *Das Feuer des Heraklit*, Stuttgart, 1981, p. 179.

27 See Weber's side-swipe at 'the question of style, which is today usually overestimated at the expense of the objective content of ideas' (WL 396n.).

28 The general separation of sociology from literature, first in France through the work of Comte, is the leitmotif of Wolf Lepenies's brilliant account in *Between Literature and Science: The Rise of Sociology*, Cambridge, 1988.

29 *Hannah Arendt/Karl Jaspers Correspondence, 1926–1969*, New York, 1992, p. 636.

30 Paul Feyerabend (*Against Method*, London, 1978, p. 46) points to 'the strong connections between Puritanism and modern science'.

31 MWG II/9, Max to Marianne Weber, 23 March 1916.

32 Hans G. Kippenberg points this out in his 'Religious Communities and the Path to Disenchantment', in Charles Camic et al. (eds), *Max Weber's 'Economy and Society'*, Stanford, CA, 2005, p. 177.

33 He was answering Jaspers and Salin. See Edgar Salin, *Um Stefan George*, p. 111.

34 Ana 446 Sch. 20 V.

35 Friedrich A. Hayek, who had experience of Weber in Vienna, later wrote in *The Fortunes of Liberalism* (London, 1992, p. 22): 'Our female contemporaries . . . were full of Max Weber.'

36 Marianne to Helene Weber, 23 May 1918.

37 In those days, the susceptibility of a socialist planned economy to bureaucratism was not common intellectual property; critics of socialism rather tended to associate it with chaos. One of the few scholars in Weber's circle or anywhere else to develop specific plans for a socialist economy was the Viennese sociologist and theoretician Otto Neurath, who later made a name for himself as a philosopher of science, but not before he had energetically thrown himself into practical economic planning in the revolutionary Bavaria of 1919 (Ernst Niekisch, *Gewagtes Leben*, Cologne, 1958, pp. 53ff.). He proposed socialization on the base of a natural economy. Weber dealt with this conception in a detailed and strikingly non-polemical manner, absurd though it must have seemed to him in relation to a modern economy (E&S 104ff.).

Neurath's planned natural economy rested upon the premise that all human beings had certain basic natural needs for which it was possible to plan. This seemed respectable enough in Weber's eyes, though not realistic for the modern age at least; he rightly warned against taking the war economy as the model for a socialist planned economy (as Lenin did). The war economy was at bottom a 'bankrupts' economy', whereas peace required a 'sustainable economy' (note Weber's early appreciative use of this term, which he most often applied to land rents, although there sustainability depends on the maintenance of soil fertility and is therefore ecologically determined).

38 Wolfgang J. Mommsen, *Max Weber and German Politics 1890–1920*, Chicago, 1990, pp. 271f., 274f.

39 Ibid., p. 227 (letter to Eulenburg, 23 June 1917).

40 MWG II/9, Max to Marianne Weber, 27 February and 5 March 1916.

41 MWG II/9, Max to Marianne Weber, 14 January 1916; also WB 566.

42 MWG II/9, Max Weber to Lili Schäfer, *c.* 20 February 1916.

43 Felix Somary, *Erinnerungen eines politischen Meteorologen*, Munich, 1994, pp. 32f., 60f.

44 Ibid., p. 156.

45 MWG II/9, Max Weber to Lili Schäfer, 24 February 1916: 'It seems we are giving in to the Americans. It is ghastly to witness the hysterical economics here.'

46 MWG II/9, Max to Marianne Weber, 7 March 1916.

47 Somary, *Erinnerungen*, p. 159.

48 MWG II/9, Max to Marianne Weber, 11 March 1916. Things were probably not so bad, and many pan-Germans would have continued to have respect for Weber. On 28 March 1916 he wrote to Marianne: 'Yesterday evening at the "German Society". Usual squabbling with the pan-Germans, *otherwise all very friendly*' (emphasis added).

49 MWG II/9, Max Weber to Mina Tobler, 7 August 1916: 'The mood is good in relation to the war . . . apart from a few scaremongers . . . The war may – unfortunately – last a long time yet, but that's how it has to be.'

50 Mommsen, *Max Weber and German Politics*, pp. 275f.

51 Karl Jaspers, *On Max Weber*, New York, 1989, p. 50. Translation modified.

52 AWG vol. 10, p. 173 (to T. Masaryk, 17 April 1908).

53 From 21 November 1918 he even regularly assisted in the editing of the paper (MWG I/16, 92). According to Jaspers (letter to Arendt, 16 September 1961), however, it soon 'stopped printing Max Weber because he, so grossly out of step with the times, derided the revolution.' *Hannah Arendt/Karl Jaspers Correspondence, 1926–1969*, p. 453.

54 Eduard Baumgarten, in *Max Weber und die Soziologie heute*, Tübingen, 1965, p. 167.

55 Heuss, *Erinnerungen 1905–1933*, p. 230.

56 Bielefeld University library, Plenge Nachlaß, 30 August 1917.

57 Gertrud Bäumer, *Lebensweg durch eine Zeitenwende*, Tübingen, 1933, p. 320.

58 Marc Bloch, *The Historian's Craft*, Manchester, 1984, p. 44.

59 As late as March 1918, Alfred Weber suggested to the future chancellor Prince Max von Baden that an 'ethically grounded imperialism' was 'today a secret religion', and that to embrace it was 'the great opportunity for the Kaiser to get back the power he has lost'. Golo Mann (ed), *Prinz Max von Baden: Erinnerungen und Dokumente*, Stuttgart, 1968, p. 269.

60 Friedrich Meinecke, *Straßburg — Freiburg — Berlin, 1901–1919: Erinnerungen*, Stuttgart, 1949, p. 245.

61 Berta Lask, *Stille und Sturm*, Halle, 1974, p. 163.

62 MWG II/9, 7 May 1917, Max Weber to Mina Tobler.

63 Max Weber to Friedrich Crusius, 24 November 1918, in Weber, *Gesammelte politische Schriften*, Munich, 1921, pp. 483, 484. The *Frankfurter Zeitung* quoted from a speech by Weber in Frankfurt on 1 December 1918: 'No real democracy can be created with such servile spirits, who wallow like political masochists in revelations of guilt.' Similarly, the *Wiesbadener Zeitung* on his speech of 5 December 1918 in Wiesbaden: 'Peace among nations is not achievable through the disgraceful behaviour of someone like Eisner, who is conducting a repugnant quest for the guilty ones.'

64 Ulrich Heinemann, *Die verdrängte Niederlage: Politische Öffentlichkeit und Kriegsschuldfrage in der Weimarer Republik*, Göttingen 1983, p. 25.

65 Heinemann (*Die verdrängte Niederlage*, p. 31) suspects that concessions on the question of war guilt would have made it easier to re-establish international relations, especially as a refusal to accept any German guilt sounded completely untrustworthy abroad (where it was only much later that revisionist historians argued a contrary case). According to several reports, Eisner ably represented the German cause at the International Socialist Conference in Berne: see Gerhard Schmolze (ed.), *Revolution und Räterepublik in München 1918/19 in Augenzeugenberichten*, Munich, 1978, pp. 204f.

66 This was already acknowledged at the time by Hans Delbrück (MWG I/16, 308), with whom Weber signed the 'professors' memorandum' on the causes of the war.

67 Heinemann, *Die verdrängte Niederlage*, pp. 33f., 55f.

68 Otto Hintze, *Soziologie und Geschichte*, Göttingen, 1964 (= *Gesammelte Abhandlungen*, vol. 2), p. 154.

69 Mommsen, *Max Weber and German Politics*, p. 311n.; see MWG I/16, 19n.

70 See ibid., p. 296.

71 See Militärgeschichtliches Forschungsamt (ed.), *Deutsche Militärgeschichte 1648–1939*, vol. 5, Munich, 1983, p. 134. After explaining that the stab-in-the-back legend in its usual form was undoubtedly a bare-faced lie, Wiegand Schmidt-Richberg here argues that after the armistice 'the revolutionaries' created a 'chaos' that 'robbed the German negotiators of any support and took away from them the theoretical possibility of negotiating better terms'.

72 Similarly in a letter from November 1918; see Mommsen, *Max Weber and German Politics*, p. 312, and WB 631.

73 Marianne to Helene Weber, 29 November 1918.

74 Ricarda Huch, *Briefe an die Freunde*, selected by Marie Baum, Tübingen, 1955, p. 61.

75 'Deutschland, erwache!' (Germany, awaken) was one of the favourite combat songs of the Nazi movement.

76 This complaint was, to be sure, not without any referent. Ernst Niekisch, himself one of the leaders of the revolution, noted in his memoirs (*Gewagtes Leben*, p. 65): 'The characters I liked to call "revolution bugs" came crawling out of every hole.' However, a sweeping dismissal of the Eisner government in Munich as a carnival of the literati soon became a common and funny-sounding trope, which the rival Social Democrats eagerly took up for reasons of their own; it should not be taken at face value. See Freya Eisner (ed.), *Kurt*

Eisner – Zwischen Kapitalismus und Kommunismus, Frankfurt am Main, 1996, pp. 277, 281, 290.

77 With his full beard and remarkable bearing, Eisner was already being compared – without irony – to one of the Apostles: Freya Eisner (ed.), *Kurt Eisner*, p. 121. Even the historian Karl Alexander von Müller, who in those days had been linked to the extreme right and saw Eisner at close quarters, displayed respect, even sympathy, for the revolutionary leader in his memoirs: see Karl Alexander von Müller, *Mars und Venus*, Stuttgart, 1954, pp. 338f.

78 Bayerisches Haupt- und Staatsarchiv, Munich, Arbeiter- und Soldatenrat 4, Aktions-Ausschuß-Sitzung vom 26. 3. 1919.

79 A letter from Else Jaffé to Alfred Weber (5 September 1919) hints that he was jealous of Edgar at the time, perhaps all the more as he was about to become a martyr who aroused people's pity.

80 On the quiet, however, the Webers must have felt a certain relief at the demise of these revolutionaries. On 29 November 1918 Marianne had written to Helene: 'If only we could be rid of Liebknecht and Rosa! They are a terrible menace.'

81 Felix Somary, *Erinnerungen eines politischen Meteorologen*, pp. 179f. On the high opinion that Weber and Schumpeter otherwise had of each other, see Richard Swedberg, *Joseph A. Schumpeter: His Life and Work*, Cambridge, 1991, pp. 45f., 90f.

82 Karl Jaspers, *Lebensfragen der deutschen Politik*, Munich, 1963, p. 287.

83 Swedberg, *Joseph A. Schumpeter*, pp. 15ff.

84 Marianne Weber, 'Untergang oder Anfang?', *Die Frau*, 27/9 (1920), p. 260.

85 Niekisch, *Gewagtes Leben*, pp. 59f. Niekisch, who later became an admirer of Weber, spoke in 1919 at the Munich Workers' and Soldiers' Council *against* his appointment in Munich: 'Brentano has poisoned our students, and Max Weber too operates within bourgeois-capitalist trains of thought. He is hostile to the idea of the councils and was still standing up for the monarchy shortly before the revolution.' Bayerisches Haupt- und Staatsarchiv, Munich, Arbeiter- und Soldatenrat 4, Aktions-Ausschuß-Sitzung vom 26. 3. 1919.

86 Joachim Radkau, *Zeitalter der Nervosität*, Munich, 1998, pp. 384ff.

87 Ibid., p. 512n.

88 Max Weber, *Gesammelte politische Schriften*, Munich, 1921, p. 485 (to Friedrich Crusius, 26 December 1918).

89 Mommsen, *Max Weber and German Politics*, p. 364.

90 Marianne to Helene Weber, 29 December 1918.

91 Mommsen, *Max Weber and German Politics*, p. 308f.

92 Ibid., pp. 309, 311.

93 LE 83, 85ff., 112; Angelika Schaser, *Helene Lange und Gertrud Bäumer*, Böhlau, 2000, pp. 148f.

94 Karl Löwith (*Mein Leben in Deutschland vor und nach 1933*, p. 17) felt that this lecture 'did not have the same riveting sweep' as 'Science as a Vocation'.

95 See Kurt Bayertz, 'Eine kurze Geschichte der Herkunft der Verantwortung', in Bayertz (ed.), *Verantwortung – Prinzip oder Problem?* Darmstadt, 1995, pp. 3f.

96 See Edgar Alexander, *Adenauer and the New Germany*, New York, 1957, pp. 138ff.

97 Eppler: oral communication to the author, 24 February 2006.

98 Georges-Henri Soutou, 'Die Kriegsziele des deutschen Reiches, Frankreichs, Großbritanniens und der Vereinigten Staaten während des Ersten Weltkrieges:

Ein Vergleich', in Wolfgang Michalka (ed.), *Der Erste Weltkrieg*, Munich, 1994, pp. 43ff.

99 Mina Tobler, *Briefauszüge*, part II, p. 133.

100 ['Ein garstig Lied! Pfui, ein politisch Lied!': a line spoken by the student Brander in Auerbach's cellar, in part I of Goethe's *Faust*. *Trans. note*]

101 Stefan Breuer, *Bürokratie und Charisma: Zur politischen Soziologie Max Webers*, Darmstadt, 1994, p. 174.

102 Hildegard Hamm-Brücher and Hermann Rudolph, *Theodor Heuss*, Stuttgart, 1983, p. 185.

103 Friedrich Henning (ed.), *Theodor Heuss: Lieber Dehler! Briefwechsel mit Thomas Dehler*, Munich, 1983, p. 177.

104 Udo Wengst, *Thomas Dehler 1897–1967: Eine politische Biographie*, Munich, 1997, p. 31.

105 Hellmuth Plessner, 'Grenzen der Gemeinschaft' (1924), quoted in Kari Palonen, *Das 'Webersche Moment': Zur Kontingenz des Politischen*, Opladen, 1998, pp. 231, 232f.

106 Even Wolfgang Mommsen questions Weber's talent for politics, although he thereby casts doubt on the importance of his one great theme: see Mommsen, *Max Weber and German Politics*, pp. 308, 307n.

107 BA Koblenz, Nl 197/77, 26 April 1917.

108 Max Weber to Else Jaffé, 4 March 1919.

109 He reported this to Else, at the same time stressing how closely one's mental state was bound up with food. Else Jaffé to Alfred Weber: BA Koblenz, Nl 197/77, 22 October 1917.

110 Paul Honigsheim (WzG 257) reports that Max and Marianne Weber had fun imitating the Lippisch dialect, in which the teeth barely parted.

111 MWG II/9, Max to Marianne Weber, 10 and 19 July 1917; to Mina Tobler, 10 July 1917; to Lili Schäfer, 25 July 1917: 'Admittedly it has no longer been the old Senne since people started ploughing and digging there; the old picture of an endless ocean of pasture has been broken, just as that of the Roman Campagna has been since the *bonificamento*.' See Roland Siekmann, *Eigenartige Senne: Zur Kulturgeschichte der Wahrnehmung einer peripheren Landschaft*, Lemgo, 2004, esp. pp. 222ff.

112 MWG II/9, to Mina Tobler, 21 July 1917.

113 BA Koblenz, Nl 197/77, Else Jaffé to Alfred Weber, 12 January 1917.

114 Eidem, 21 April 1917.

115 Eidem, 24 April 1917.

116 Eidem, July 1917 and 2 May 1917.

117 Eidem, 22 October 1917.

118 MWG II/9, Max Weber to Else Jaffé, 28 November 1917, with metaphors indicative of his yearning for her: 'May fate give you the warmth and light you need to blossom in the beauty that the gods planted in you.'

119 MWG II/9, Else Jaffé to Marianne Weber, 2 November 1917.

120 MWG II/9, Max Weber to Else Jaffé, 28 November 1917.

121 BA Koblenz, Nl 197/77, Else Jaffé to Alfred Weber, 16 November 1917.

122 On 15 January 1919 Max could still write to Else: 'That "wall" is still immensely strong and high, I think so (or: I'll test it), and it will never be climbed over flippantly and without thinking; that is *impossible*.'

123 Max Weber to Else Jaffé, 7 March 1919: 'I admit it, *your* zoology is often worthy of the rating *summa c(um) l(aude)* (No. 66! Tunnel near Bruchsal!).'

And on 18 March 1919: 'The hours stand luminously pure before me, in every detail: the night when I became your guest, the radiant morning by the Isar, your hand in mine at *Tannhäuser*, the car journey . . .'

124 Max Weber to Else Jaffé, 6 March 1919.

125 *Georg Lukács: Selected Correspondence 1902–1920*, ed. Judith Marcus and Zoltás Tar, New York, 1986, p. 222.

126 Max Weber to Else Jaffé, 7 March 1919.

127 Eidem, 8 September 1919.

128 Else's granddaughter Bettina Henrich said of her that she often put on an act for others when it was expedient, but that there was nothing she liked more than to give others pleasure.

129 According to M. Rainer Lepsius (communication to the author), Else had the female cunning to pass herself off with men as less intellectual than she was in reality. Bettina Henrich too portrays her as a highly intellectual woman, who in her youth was always the most acute of the three Richthofen sisters; see Robert Lucas, *Frieda von Richthofen*, Munich, 1972, p. 32.

130 See Else Jaffé to Alfred Weber, 29 June 1917 (BA Koblenz, Nl 197/77): 'I had to laugh at how quickly the imagination "gets to work" in you Webers, and how striking it is that vague possibilities become realities, as it were.' (Apparently, no sooner had Alfred obtained an advisory post in the finance ministry than he dreamed of becoming head of the 'Reich Chancellor's office'!) 'Only Marianne is much nicer about it than I am: she does not immediately step in with callous scepticism but goes along with the fantasies.'

131 Max Weber to Else Jaffé, 30 April 1919.

132 Eidem, 18 March 1919.

133 Eidem, 22 April 1919.

134 Eidem, 4 March 1919.

135 Eidem, 15 January 1919.

136 Eidem, 1 February 1919.

137 Eidem, 15 January 1919.

138 Ibid.

139 Eidem, 26 February and 22 January 1919.

140 Eidem, 30 April 1919. For Else, 'earth' then held fewer pleasurable associations. In 1917 she dreaded the thought of the future after a bad end to the war: 'For nothing at all will one have more money and be chained terribly to the earth by pathetic worries.' To Alfred Weber, 31 January 1917, BA Koblenz, Nl 197/77.

141 Max Weber to Else Jaffé, 17. 9. and 1. 2. 1919.

142 Eidem, 15 January 1919.

143 Eidem, 18 March 1919.

144 Ibid.

145 Eidem, 15 January 1919.

146 Eidem, 17 September 1919.

147 Eidem, 22 April 1919.

148 In this connection it is interesting to note that Talcott Parsons had one 'very serious reproach' to make against Reinhard Bendix's otherwise celebrated portrait of Weber: namely, that he translated *Herrschaft* by 'dominion', whereas he, Parsons, preferred 'leadership' as the term for *Herrschaft* 'by his followers', not 'over his followers' (*American Sociological Review*, October 1960, p. 752). This is the difference with Weber's concept of 'power' (*Macht*), which denotes

an ability to force someone to do something he or she does not want to do. By now there is a whole series of alternatives to 'domination': see Swedberg, *Weber Dictionary*, pp. 65f. (In this book, the term 'rule' has generally been preferred as a less weighted rendering than 'domination' (the usual English term in *Economy and Society*) or other alternatives, which often do not seem appropriate in a sociological context. There are other contexts, however, especially interpersonal ones, where 'domination' or another term has been chosen. *Trans. note*)

149 BA Koblenz, Nl A. Weber, Else Jaffé to Alfred Weber, 28 November 1920. On the 'Wyneken affair', see Ulrich Geuter, *Homosexualität in der deutschen Jugendbewegung*, Frankfurt am Main, 1994, pp. 195ff.

150 Richard Wagner, *Tristan und Isolde*, Act II, scene 3: 'Es ist das dunkel nächt'ge Land, daraus die Mutter mich entsandt.' So, Weber adapted Wagner to make 'his own rhyme'.

151 Deutsches Literaturarchiv Marbach, A: Jaspers 75.12072, Else Jaffé to Jaspers, n.d.; the quotation in B 677 is evidently drawn from the same letter.

152 Max Weber to Else Jaffé, 7 September 1919.

153 Eidem, 18 March 1919.

154 Eidem, 30 April 1919.

155 Eidem, 4 March 1919.

156 Eidem, 22 April 1919.

157 Eidem, 7 September 1919.

158 Eidem, 22 April 1919.

159 Eidem, 7 March 1919 (?).

160 Eidem, 7 September 1919.

161 BA Koblenz, Nl 197/85, Else Jaffé to Alfred Weber, 20 June 1919.

162 Max Weber to Else Jaffé, 13/14 August 1919.

163 Eidem, 18 March 1919; similarly on 25 February 1919.

164 Jaspers, however, probably thinking of Weber, referred to the pleasurable-masochistic element in asceticism: Karl Jaspers, *Psychologie der Weltanschauungen*, 3rd edn, Berlin, 1925, p. 95. This would suggest that in a sense Weber always remained true.

165 Max Weber to Else Jaffé, 7 September 1919.

166 Eidem, 30 April 1919.

167 Ibid.

168 Ibid.

169 MWG II/9, Max Weber to Martha Riegel, 20 June 1917. In WB 532f. Marianne quotes the letter over two pages but omits this revealing passage!

170 Max Weber to Else Jaffé, 15 January 1919.

171 Eidem, 4 March 1919.

172 Eidem, 1 February 1919.

173 Eidem, 4 March 1919.

174 Ibid.

175 BA Koblenz, Nl 197/54, Else Jaffé to Alfred Weber, 7 January 1910. She was writing to him 'respectably, I'm afraid'. 'If I had followed my instinct – no, my intuition and my longing – I would have just written: Come, my sheep.'

176 Deutsches Literaturarchiv Marbach, A: Jaspers Nr. 13.

177 Oral communication from Martin Green to the author, 1 December 2000.

178 Eduard Baumgarten, 'Über Max Weber: Brief an Nicolaus Sombart', *Merkur*, 31 (1977), p. 298. Dieter Henrich, the husband of Else's granddaughter, thinks

that this alludes to an incapacity for sexual intercourse (oral communication to the author).

179 Deutsches Literaturarchiv Marbach, A: Jaspers, Nr. 113, IV, Jaspers to Radbruch, 20 April 1919.
180 Marianne to Helene Weber, 17 February 1919.
181 Deutsches Literaturarchiv Marbach, A: Jaspers Nr. 13; in B 677 it appears without the final sentence.
182 Marianne Weber notes (probably reproducing ideas that Max Weber took from Georg Lukács and pursued further): 'Art, the Luciferian realm, creates perfection in the world and thereby calms man's longing for salvation, and this was the last thing necessary to bring the eternal cycle of life to a conclusion.' This Luciferian realm of beauty, as Weber understood it, encompassed erotic love. In Marianne's account of Max Weber, the battle between the divine and the Luciferian comes at the end. 'Before then, of course, all Luciferian grandeur, strength and beauty should have been developed to the full.'
183 BA Koblenz, Nl 197/87.
184 Marianne to Helene Weber, 26 June 1908.
185 A month after Max Weber's death she wrote to Alfred, who wanted to resume their relationship as if nothing had happened: 'The thing with Max is not at all decisive, is it? Or it is only a symptom of something else: whether we still have the same "faith", no?' She then goes on to speak of faith or belief (*Glaube*) without inverted commas. Belief in 'transcendence', she puts it to Alfred, does not at all contradict an affirmation of this life. 'Max, for example, was in a certain sense much more this-worldly than you.' 'In a certain sense': she may have been referring to his affirmation of certain profound aspects of erotic love, but probably also to his marked sense for concrete phenomena that Alfred, in his academic way, preferred to rise above. 'But, look, it is . . . not a mistake when you say that *your* field has involved taking life *positively*, in contrast to Max. As a human being, Max was totally life-affirming (certainly in the last decade), and that is also how he shaped his own life.' And, against Alfred's strictly this-worldly, hedonistic view of life: 'But I demand from a faith that it allows life to be valuable to me *under all circumstances, whatever may happen.*' 'Look, nor do we two see love as also something other-worldly. That is precisely what makes it the Absolute. Look – *this* is the direction in which I would like to speak with you – I have changed *in that way* in the past ten years: I know it.' BA Koblenz, Nl 197/54, Else Jaffé to Alfred Weber, 13 July 1920. Without a doubt, 'in the past ten years' she had become convinced that Max Weber believed in transcendental values, and precisely on account of that her love for him had become a higher passion.
186 BA Koblenz, Nl 197/54, Else Jaffé to Alfred Weber, 7 January 1910.
187 See Hartmann Tyrell, 'Antagonismus der Werte – ethisch', in Hans G. Kippenberg and Martin Riesebrodt (eds), *Max Webers 'Religionssystematik'*, Tübingen, 2001, p. 318, on the distinction between Christian and 'cultural' values in Weber. Wolfgang Schluchter (*Rationalism, Religion and Domination*, Berkley, CA, 1989, p. 414) points out that in 1909, in *Economy and Society*, Weber still wanted to subsume religion under the concept of culture.
188 This is emphasized in Johannes Weiß, *Max Webers Grundlegung der Soziologie*, 2nd edn, Munich, 1992, p. 136. Steven Lukes, *Emile Durkheim*, London, 1973, p. 481: 'He was, indeed, quite obsessed by the vision of society as the unique and all-encompassing *fons et origo* of religion – as it was of morality and of

knowledge.' It is especially here that we see the striking difference between Weber and Durkheim; it is also apparent how certain 'naturalistic' basic convictions contributed to the fact that Weber left open the question of the 'first cause' and did not manoeuvre 'society' into that founding role in the manner of systems models.

189 Klaus Lichtblau, *Kulturkrise und Soziologie um die Jahrhundertwende*, Frankfurt am Main, 1996, p. 339.

190 Paul Honigsheim and Johannes Weiß have offered especially detailed and insightful analyses of Weber's relationship to religion. But they too treat it as a mainly external relationship, only hinting at any religiosity of his own. The main points on this are to be found in Honigsheim's observations on Weber's 'attitude to religion' (WzG 249-71). Weiß gives more attention to the matter in his *Max Webers Grundlegung der Soziologie*, pp. 105–57: 'Webers Verhältnis zur Religion in seiner Entwicklung' [Weber's relationship to religion in his development]. Here he takes it for granted that 'personal experiences . . . preceded' the working out of Weber's sociology of religion (p. 152), but he addresses almost exclusively Weber's contacts with religiously minded people in his milieu, beginning with his mother, rather than personal experiences of his own.

191 Hermann Glockner, *Heidelberger Bilderbuch*, Bonn, 1969, p. 105.

192 See 'The "Objectivity" of Knowledge in Social Science and Social Policy', in *The Essential Weber: A Reader*, ed. Sam Whimster, London, 2004, p. 403: 'the belief that we all possess in one form or another in the meta-empirical validity of the ultimate and highest evaluative ideas, with which we anchor the meaning of our being . . .'

193 Wilhelm Hennis, *Max Weber's Science of Man*, Newbury, 2000, p. 171.

194 Tyrell, 'Antagonismus der Werte – ethisch', p. 323.

195 In his commentary on the 'religious communities' section of *Economy and Society*, Hans G. Kippenberg notes: 'Not without reason Weber often uses the present tense in his account. The types of action he investigates are still applicable in the contemporary world. The reader is surprised and touched by Weber's perception that perfectly everyday action is closely and indissolubly bound up with a striving for salvation.' *Max Weber: Wirtschaft und Gesellschaft: Religiöse Gemeinschaften, Studienausgabe*, Tübingen, 2005, p. 159.

196 Ana 446, Marianne to Helene Weber, n.d. (winter 1898).

197 Eduard Baumgarten, 'Spielräume unter Hitlers Herrschaft', manuscript, p. 142.

198 Ana 446, Sch. 20 VI.

199 Deutsches Literaturarchiv Marbach, A: Jaspers Nr. 113 V.

200 Jaspers, *Psychologie der Weltanschauungen*, p. 197.

201 Guenther Roth, '*Sachlichkeit* and Self-Revelation: Max Weber's Letters', *Telos*, 88 (summer 1991), p. 201.

202 See Dieter Henrich (*Die Einheit der Wissenschaftslehre Max Webers*, Tübingen, 1952, p. 126): 'Max Weber tends to understand religious faith, too, in terms of a life's demon.'

203 Gertrud von le Fort, *Hälfte des Lebens: Erinnerungen*, Munich, 1965, p. 89.

204 Wilhelm Hennis too (*Max Weber's Science of Man*, pp. 63f.) speaks of Weber's 'profound conviction that the human significance of mysticism could not be overstated'.

205 Erwin Rohde, *Psyche* (1893), London, 1925, pp. 265, 264.

206 A note of Marianne Weber's [SG].

207 Constans Seyfarth and Gert Schmidt, 'Der Tod als Thema bei Max Weber', in Klaus Feldmann and Werner Fuchs-Heinritz (eds), *Der Tod ist ein Problem der Lebenden*, Frankfurt am Main, 1995, p. 110.

208 Francesco Tuccari, 'Der politische Führer und der charismatische Heros', *Annali di Sociologia*, 9/2 (1993), p. 121.

209 Max Weber, *Roscher and Knies*, New York, 1975, p. 109.

210 Anonymous (Georg Gottfried Gervinus), *Georg Friedrich Fallenstein: Erinnerungsblätter für Verwandte und Freunde*, Heidelberg, 1854, p. 6.

211 (A German version of the English 'Those whom the gods love die young'. – *Trans. note*)

212 Anonymous, *George Friedrich Fallenstein*, p. 85.

213 Paul Hensel, *Sein Leben in seinen Briefen*, Wolfenbüttel, 1947, p. 129.

214 According to Marianne, he 'loved this song and often quoted it' (Ana 446 Sch. 20 VI). (Translation by G. M. Holland and Peggie Cochrane)

215 Marianne to Helene Weber, 28 October 1995 (Ana 446 Sch. 14). Similarly, when the architecture teacher Karl Schäfer (1844–1908), Lili's father-in-law, declined mentally and physically, so that he often belched while eating and threatened to squander the inheritance with a new wife, Marianne expressed a wish to Helene (10 September 1906) 'that the old man will die soon'. And, when an already depressive aunt was diagnosed with 'cancer in her lower abdomen': 'My God, would that she died straightaway of a heart attack, instead of being slowly eaten up by cancer' (Marianne to Helene Weber, 15 July 1908).

216 Eaedem, 23 November 1903; and compare Max Weber's feelings (B 675).

217 Marianne to Helene Weber, 31 August 1914.

218 Marianne Weber, *Erfülltes Leben*, Heidelberg, 1946, p. 331.

219 *Hannah Arendt/Karl Jaspers Correspondence, 1926–1969*, p. 636.

220 GStA, Nl M. Weber, Nr. 30 Bd. 4, Max Weber to Willi Hellpach, 10 September 1905.

221 Golo Mann, *Reminiscences and Reflections: Growing Up in Germany*, London, 1990, p. 163.

222 He wrote almost the same words to Mina Tobler: see Mommsen, *Max Weber and German Politics*, p. 324.

223 MWG (I/16, 545f.) reproduces several reports of the conversation, but they all stem from Weber.

224 Eduard Baumgarten to Marianne Weber, 16 March 1933 (MWG-Forschungsstelle Heidelberg).

225 Francesco Tuccari, 'Der politische Führer und der charismatische Heros', pp. 119, 121.

226 Eduard Baumgarten to Marianne Weber, 24 January and 4 September 1922.

227 MWG II/9, Max Weber to Bertha Tobler, n.d. (June 1915).

228 Ibid.

229 Deutsches Literaturarchiv Marbach, A: Jaspers Nr. 113 V.

230 Ana 446 Sch. 20 VI.

231 Translation from http://www.rwagner.net/libretti/tristan/e-t-tristan.html.

232 MWG II/9, Max to Helene Weber, 4 September 1915.

233 Martin Green, *The von Richthofen Sisters*, New York, 1974, p. 164.

234 Niles Eldredge, *The Miner's Canary: Unravelling the Mysteries of Extinction*, London, 1992, p. 228.

235 Karl Loewenstein, 'Personal Recollections of Max Weber', in Loewenstein, *Max Weber's Political Ideas in the Perspective of our Time*, Amherst, MA, 1966, p. 102.

236 Marianne Weber, 'Der Tod', manuscript, SG, p. 1; and see B 678.

237 Loewenstein, 'Personal Recollections', p. 102; Robert Michels, 'Max Weber', in Michels, *Masse, Führer, Intellektuelle*, Frankfurt am Main, 1987, p. 256.

238 Alfred W. Crosby, *America's Forgotten Pandemic: The Influenza of 1918*, Cambridge, 1989. The main wave of Spanish flu had passed by the spring of 1919, causing it to drop out of the public eye, but the epidemic seems to have broken out again here and there in 1920. It is therefore not ruled out that Weber was one of its victims. The fatality rate was only 1 to 2 per cent, however, and so it would be strange if someone who had the best doctors still died of it.

239 BA Koblenz, Nl 197/87, Else Jaffé to Alfred Weber, 9 June 1920 (two letters!). Alfred tried to calm her (10 June 1920): 'We Webers don't get *that* ill so easily. Our nerves are our weak points – but the "physiological corpus" is rock-solid in all of us.' He was evidently right in his own case, as despite his nervous troubles he lived to the age of ninety.

240 Else Jaffé to Alfred Weber, 23 June 1920.

241 An inspection of the corpse was stipulated at a cremation (Ursula Staiger, 'Die Auseinandersetzungen um die Feuerbestattung in Deutschland im 19. Jahrhundert', diss., Mainz, 1981, p. 45), but that was not the same as an autopsy.

242 Autopsy report by Prof. Dr Oberndorfer, 16 June 1920 [SG].

243 In Otto Stammer (ed.), *Max Weber und die Soziologie heute*, Tübingen, 1965, pp. 65f.

244 Theodor Heuss, *Erinnerungen 1905–1933*, Stuttgart, 1963, p. 203.

245 Deutsches Literaturarchiv Marbach, A: Jaspers, extract from Marianne's letter to Max Weber of 24 April 1920; Marianne Weber to Jaspers, 6 November (1919).

246 MWG I/9, Max to Marianne Weber, 27 February 1916.

247 In fact, Marianne had been in touch since 1916 with Paul Geheeb, the founder and director of the school, with a view to placing Lili's children there. The Oswald School became 'a kind of attraction for the whole family', although Marianne was not keen on Geheeb's 'somewhat sissy, *unmanly* style'. Marianne to Helene Weber, 15 July and 12 October 1916.

248 BA Koblenz, Nl 197/85, Else Jaffé to Alfred Weber, n.d. (March/April 1919).

249 Max Weber to Else Jaffé, 22 April 1919, after he had shown her a letter from 'Judit' (Mina): 'Can *your* love get through such "unfathomable" inhibited states and hours together with me? Well, this time you simply couldn't. Will you be able to in future . . .? – because in times when the work is throttling me – no one knows what I am like then – that often happens!' To be sure, he received no assurance from Else that she would patiently allow all his irritabilities to wash over her.

250 Deutsches Literaturarchiv Marbach, A: Jaspers, Nr. 75.8444, to Else Jaffé, 5 May 1967. Similarly, in a letter to Hannah Arendt (29 April 1966), without being able to specify the 'biological' determinant: 'He did not suffer from paralysis or schizophrenia but from something as yet undiagnosed. He experienced in his life those elemental phases that are somehow grounded in biology: peaks of energy and productivity and then total collapse in which he couldn't read anymore. In the last year of his life . . . he was in a "manic" but completely disciplined state. He said that never had the sentences and concepts flowed

from his pen with such clarity, ceaseless continuity and force . . . He was constantly making political trips and giving speeches; he glowed and suffered at the same time; and that suffering seemed without limits. If he had remained alive, he would probably have had another collapse. And at the end, his conscious dying, completely calm . . .' *Hannah Arendt/Karl Jaspers Correspondence 1926–1969*, p. 637.

251 BA Koblenz, Nl 197/87, Else Jaffé to Alfred Weber, apparently 13 June 1920.

252 BA Koblenz, Nl 197/87, Else Jaffé to Alfred Weber, 24 June 1920: 'Also I know almost more than she [Marianne] about his professional affairs during the *last* year; after all, I have learned so much from *us* how to ask a man about his thoughts and intentions.'

253 See Leena Ruuskanen, *Der Heidelberger Bergfriedhof: Kulturgeschichte und Grabkultur*, Heidelberg 1992.

254 *Religion in Geschichte und Gegenwart*, vol. 2, 2nd edn, Tübingen, 1928, pp. 572ff.

255 Staiger, 'Die Auseinandersetzung um die Feuerbestattung in Deutschland im 19. Jahrhundert', p. 3. There was still something deeply shocking about cremation, even for intellectuals. See Karl Alexander von Müller, *Aus Gärten der Vergangenheit*, Stuttgart, 1951, p. 161 (on the last years before the war in Munich): 'The ground on which the intellectual and moral life of Europe had rested for one and a half thousand years began to shake around us. The first cremations in the big cities were taking over from old-style burials, and modern crematoria and ash urns announced for miles around the demolition of a whole life-cycle of humanity.'

256 Ludwig Büchner, *Kraft und Stoff*, 21st edn, Leipzig, 1904, p. 52; cf. the English translation of the 10th edn: Louis Büchner, *Force and Matter: Empirico-Philosophical Studies*, London, 1870, p. 31.

257 Achim Tobler (ed.), 'Auszüge aus den Briefen von Mina Tobler', manuscript, Aalen, 1988, part II, p. 15.

Chapter 19 Epilogue

1 There is a widespread view in Weber studies that Jaspers not only read but actually wrote the parts of the *Lebensbild* relating to Weber's work. But in neither Marianne's nor Jaspers's personal effects is there any indication that he co-authored sections of the biography.

2 Bayerische Staatsbibliothek, Nl M. Weber, Eduard Baumgarten to Marianne Weber, 20 June 1923 and n.d. (*c.* 1923). For Marianne's view of the crisis in her relations with Eduard Baumgarten: LE 128, 135f.

3 He then noticed that Weber wore a genital truss (oral communication from his son-in-law Wilhelm Schoeppe and from Nicolaus Sombart), which suggests that he had suffered a scrotal hernia. But there is no mention of this in the autopsy report. Eduard Baumgarten probably thought that what he saw confirmed that Weber's sexual inhibitions at least partly had a trivial external cause and did not derive from an ascetic antipathy to pleasure.

4 The great schism in Weber studies in Germany ultimately goes back to Jaspers. Wilhelm Hennis turned to him when he issued his provocative challenge to existing research, whereas M. Rainer Lepsius saw Jaspers as 'naturally quite horrifying' (Lepsius to the author, 11 January 2005).

5 Karl Jaspers, *Philosophische Autobiographie*, Munich, 1977, p. 69.

6 Christopher Adair-Toteff, 'Max Weber as Philosopher: The Jaspers–Rickert Confrontation', *Max Weber Studies*, 3/1 (2002), pp. 15–32.

7 Hermann Glockner, *Heidelberger Bilderbuch*, Bonn, 1969, pp. 101f., 113: ' "If only Weber were still alive!" Rickert shouted more than once in my presence, when an assiduous informer told him something vexing about Jaspers. "Weber would rebuke Jaspers and tell him that he hadn't been made professor of philosophy to put such nonsense in young people's heads!" Rickert used to make fun of the then fashionable *Lebensphilosophie* and its idea that "life" as such could be taken as the starting point for philosophical thought.'

8 Jaspers, *Philosophische Autobiographie*, p. 42; Rainer Wiehl, 'Die Heidelberger Tradition der Philosophie zwischen Kantianismus und Hegelianismus', in Wilhelm Doerr (ed.), *Semper apertus: 600 Jahre Ruprecht-Karls-Universität Heidelberg 1386–1986*, vol. 2, Berlin and Heidelberg, 1985, p. 417. Jaspers himself did not consider Weber philosophically competent in a professional sense, or anyway in the sense of Rickert's neo-Kantianism: 'Max Weber knew next to nothing about Kantian ideas and did not respond' (16 November 1966, *Hannah Arendt Karl/Jaspers Correspondence, 1926–1969*, New York, 1992, p. 660).

9 Jaspers to Theodor Heuss, 23 February 1956 (Deutsches Literaturarchiv Marbach, A: Jaspers Nr. 75.8351), when he refused to write a contribution on Freud for a 'Great Germans' collection: 'I think I know my Freud, and since my youth I have seen him as an enemy of serious science and philosophy or a serious attitude to life.'

10 Hans Saner, *Karl Jaspers in Selbstzeugnissen und Bilddokumenten*, Reinbek, 1970, pp. 136ff.

11 Karl Jaspers, *Psychologie der Weltanschauungen*, 3rd edn, Berlin, 1925, pp. 354ff.

12 The Eduard Baumgarten estate (privately owned).

13 Stanislav Andreski, *Social Sciences as Sorcery*, London, 1972, p. 88.

14 Eduard Baumgarten to Marianne Weber, 2 November 1936 (privately owned).

15 Ana 446 Sch. 20 V.

16 Eduard Baumgarten to Marianne Weber, 17 October 1932 (privately owned).

17 See the communication from the publisher Georg Siebeck, 25 September 1945: 'The demand for Max Weber's works is growing by the day, and I think that next year we should reckon on a considerably greater demand than in the last fifteen to twenty years. For the Americans, moreover, Max Weber is already a figure without whom American sociology would be unimaginable.' I am grateful to Edith Hanke for this quotation.

18 Rüdiger Safranski, *Martin Heidegger: Between Good and Evil*, Cambridge, MA, 1998, p. 273; Carsten Klingemann, *Soziologie im Dritten Reich*, Baden-Baden, 1996, p. 180 (also for the following details).

19 Klaus Taschwer and Benedikt Föger, *Konrad Lorenz*, Vienna, 2003, pp. 99ff. At first Baumgarten was interested in the scientific side rather than the person; he had had other preferences for the professorship in Königsberg, but passed them over in favour of Lorenz.

20 Ibid., p. 138.

21 Eduard Baumgarten, *Gewissen und Macht: Abhandlungen und Vorlesungen 1933–1963*, ed. Michael Sukale, Meisenheim 1971, pp. 292ff.

22 Taschwer and Föger, *Konrad Lorenz*, pp. 249ff.; Axel Meyer, 'Die Entstehung

der Arten: Neue Theorien und Methoden', in Ernst Peter Fischer and Klaus Wiegandt (eds), *Evolution: Geschichte und Zukunft des Lebens*, Frankfurt am Main, 2003, p. 77.

23 Karl Löwith, *Gesammelte Abhandlungen: Zur Kritik der geschichtlichen Existenz*, Stuttgart, 1960, p. 18.

24 Eduard Baumgarten, 'Spielräume unter Hitlers Herrschaft' (manuscript), p. 68.

25 Lecture script, 4. September 1948 (privately owned).

26 Lecture script summer semester 1949.

27 Baumgarten, 'Spielräume unter Hitlers Herrschaft', p. 349.

28 Manfred Schön to the author, 17 September 2003.

29 Dieter Henrich, in Karl Jaspers, *Max Weber*, Munich, 1988, p. 24.

30 Ibid., p. 26.

31 *Hannah Arendt/Karl Jaspers Correspondence 1926–1969*, p. 636.

32 A: Jaspers, Nr. 113.

33 A: Jaspers Nr. 75.8444, to Else Jaffé, 6 October 1944.

34 A: Jaspers, Nr. 113.

35 A: Jaspers Nr. 113 V, note dated 19 October 1966.

36 A: Jaspers Br. 75.12072, Else Jaffé to Jaspers, n.d. (with the note: '1920s').

37 Dieter Henrich, in Jaspers, *Max Weber*, p. 29.

38 A: Jaspers Nr. 75.8444, to Else Jaffé, 5 May 1967. See Jaspers to Hannah Arendt (29 April 1966): 'But back to Max Weber: Although he was no genius and inferior to both Nietzsche and Kierkegaard, he is nonetheless, in comparison with those eternal adolescents and dubious figures, plainly and simply a man. And that is physically the case, too.' *Hannah Arendt/Karl Jaspers Correspondence 1926–1969*, p. 637.

39 Ibid., p. 549.

40 A: Jaspers Nr. 113 V.

Index